S0-BOZ-827

MASTERPIECES OF CATHOLIC LITERATURE
IN SUMMARY FORM

Masterpieces of Catholic Literature

IN SUMMARY FORM

EDITED BY

Frank N. Magill

WITH
ASSOCIATE EDITORS

A. Robert Caponigri
Thomas P. Neill

Harper & Row, Publishers

New York, Evanston, and London

Imprimatur: ✠ Joseph Cardinal Ritter
Archbishop of St. Louis
November 25, 1964

C-P

LIBRARY OF CONGRESS CATALOG CARD NUMBER: 63–20740

Acknowledgments

The articles describing the following works were prepared in whole or in part by reference to the editions indicated. The editors and staff gratefully acknowledge the use of these editions.

The Didache. From *Ancient Christian Writers.* Translated by James A. Kleist, S.J. Published by The Newman Press.

The Epistles of Saint Ignatius of Antioch. Translated by James A. Kleist, S.J. Published by The Newman Bookshop.

The Shepherd by Hermas. From *The Apostolic Fathers.* Translated by Kirsopp Lake. Published by G. P. Putnam's Sons.

The Epistles and Martyrdom of Saint Polycarp. Translated by James A. Kleist, S.J. Published by The Newman Press.

Ecclesiastical History by Eusebius Pamphili. Translated by Roy J. Deferrari. Published by Fathers of the Church, Inc.

Epistle XXI: To the Most Clement Emperor and Most Blessed Augustus by Saint Ambrose. From *Saint Ambrose, Letters 1-91.* Translated by Sister Mary Melchior Aeyenka, O.P. Published by Fathers of the Church, Inc.

The Dialogues of Sulpicius Severus. From *The Western Fathers.* Edited by F. R. Hoare. Published by Sheed and Ward.

The First Catechetical Instruction by Saint Augustine. From *Ancient Christian Writers.* Translated by Joseph P. Christopher. Published by The Newman Press.

The Confessions by Saint Augustine. Translated by Vernon J. Bourke. Published by Fathers of the Church, Inc.

Seven Books of History Against the Pagans by Paulus Orosius. Translated by Irving Woodworth Raymond. Published by Columbia University Press.

Faith, Hope, and Charity by Saint Augustine. From *Ancient Christian Writers.* Translated by Louis A. Arand. Published by The Newman Press.

Enarrations on the Psalms by Saint Augustine. From *Ancient Christian Writers.* Translated by Dames Scholastica Hebgin and Felicitas Corrigan, O.S.B. Published by The Newman Press.

Tome by Saint Leo the Great. From *The Letters of Saint Leo the Great.* Translated by Brother Edmund Hunt, C.S.C. Published by Fathers of the Church, Inc. Also: *Peter Speaks Through Leo, the Council of Chalcedon, A.D. 451* by Francis X. Murphy, C.SS.R. Published by Catholic University of America Press.

The Writings of Saint Patrick. From *Ancient Christian Writers.* Translated by Ludwig Bieler. Published by The Newman Press.

The Call of All Nations by Prosper of Aquitaine. Translated by P. De Letter, S.J. Published by The Newman Press.

On the Divine Names and *The Mystical Theology* by Dionysius the Pseudo-Areopagite. Translated by C. E. Rolt. Published by The Society for Promoting Christian Knowledge.

The Contemplative Life by Julianus Pomerius. Translated by Sister Mary Josephine Suelzer. Published by The Newman Bookshop.

The Rule of Saint Benedict. From *Documents of the Christian Church.* Published by Oxford University Press. Also: as translated by Abbot Justin McCann, O.S.B. Published by The Newman Press.

Pastoral Care by Saint Gregory the Great. Translated by Henry Davis, S.J. Published by The Newman Press.

Dialogues by Saint Gregory the Great. Translated by Odo John Zimmerman, O.S.B. Published by Fathers of the Church, Inc.

History of the Franks by Saint Gregory of Tours. Translated by O. M. Dalton. Published by Oxford University Press.

The Etymologies by Saint Isidore of Seville. *Etymologiarum sive originum, Libri* XX. Edited by W. M. Lindsay. Published by Oxford University Press.

The Ascetic Life by Saint Maximus the Confessor. Translated by Polycarp Sherwood, O.S.B., S.T.D. Published by The Newman Press.

The Ladder of Divine Ascent by Saint John Climachus. Translated by Archimandrite Lazurus Moore. Published by Harper and Brothers.

Ecclesiastical History of the English People by Saint Bede. Translated by John Stevenson. Published by E. P. Dutton and Company.

Concerning Rhetoric and Virtue by Alcuin. From *The Rhetoric of Alcuin and Charlemagne*. Translated by Wilbur Samuel Howell. Published by Princeton University Press.

The Life of Charlemagne by Einhard. Translated by Samuel Eps Turner. Published by Ann Arbor Paperback, University of Michigan Press.

Book of Proverbs by Otloh of St. Emmeram. From *Othloni Libellus Proverbiorum*. Edited by Charles Korfmacher. Published by Chicago University Press.

Proslogion by Saint Anselm. From *Obras Completas de San Anselmo*. Published by Biblioteca de Autores Cristianos.

On the Steps of Humility and Pride by Saint Bernard. Translated by Barton R. V. Mills. Published by The Macmillan Company.

Noah's Ark by Hugh of St. Victor. From *Hugh of Saint Victor: Selected Spiritual Writings*. Translated by a Religious of C.S.M.V. Published by Faber and Faber.

Treatise Concerning the Pursuit of Learning by Hugh of St. Victor. From *Didascalicon: Concerning the Pursuit of Learning*. Translated by Jerome Taylor. Published by Columbia University Press.

On the Necessity of Loving God by Saint Bernard. From *The Wisdom of Catholicism*. Translated by Terence Connolly, S.J. Published by Random House.

The Two Cities by Otto of Freising. Translated by Charles Christopher Mierow. Published by Oxford University Press.

The Letters of Saint Bernard of Clairvaux. Translated by Bruno Scott James. Published by Burns Oates.

Policraticus and *Metalogicon* by John of Salisbury. From *The Statesman's Book*. Translated by John Dickinson. Published by Alfred A. Knopf, Inc. Also: *Frivolities of Courtiers and Footprints of Philosophers*. Translated by Joseph B. Pike. Published by The University of Minnesota Press. Also: *The Metalogicon*. Translated by Daniel D. McGarry. Published by University of California Press.

Benjamin Minor and *Benjamin Major* by Richard of St. Victor. From *Richard of St. Victor*. Translated by Clare Kirchberger. Published by Faber and Faber.

On Being and Essence by Saint Thomas Aquinas. Translated by Armand A. Maurer, C.S.B. Published by The Pontifical Institute of Mediaeval Studies.

On Kingship by Saint Thomas Aquinas. From *On the Governance of Rulers*. Translated by Gerald B. Phelan. Published by The Pontifical Institute of Mediaeval Studies.

On the Power of God by Saint Thomas Aquinas. Translated by Lawrence Shapcote, O.P. Published by The Newman Press.

Opus majus by Roger Bacon. Translated by Robert Belle Burke. Published by University of Pennsylvania Press.

On Spiritual Creatures by Saint Thomas Aquinas. Translated by Mary C. Fitzpatrick. Published by Marquette University Press.

On the Soul by Saint Thomas Aquinas. Translated by John P. Rowan. Published by B. Herder Book Company.

On the Virtues in General by Saint Thomas Aquinas. Translated by John P. Reid. Published by The Providence College Press.

Opus Oxoniense by John Duns Scotus. From *Philosophical Writings*. Translated by Allan Wolter. Published by Thomas Nelson and Sons, Ltd.

The Life of Saint Louis by Jean de Joinville. From *History of Saint Louis*. Translated by Joan Evans. Published by Oxford University Press.

De monarchia by Dante Aligheri. Translated by Aurelia Henry. Published by Houghton Mifflin Company.

The Divine Comedy by Dante Alighieri. Translated by Dorothy L. Sayers and Barbara Reynolds. Published by The Penguin Classics.

The Little Flowers of Saint Francis. Translated by W. Heywood. Published by Florence G. Fattorusso.

The Treatises and Sermons of Meister Eckhart by Johann Eckhart. From *Meister Eckhart: Selected Treatises and Sermons*. Translated by James M. Clark and John V. Skinner. Published by Faber and Faber.

Meditations on the Life of Christ attributed to Saint Bonaventure. Translated by Sister M. Emmanuel, O.S.B. Published by B. Herder Book Company.

The Little Book of Eternal Wisdom by Blessed Henry Suso, O.P. From *The Exemplar*. Translated by Sister M. Ann Edward, O.P. Published by The Priory Press.

The Cloud of Unknowing. Translated by Father Augustine Baker, O.S.B. Published by The Newman Press. Also: Edited by Phyllis Hodgson. Published by The Early English Text Society.

The Spiritual Espousals by Blessed Jan Van Ruysbroeck. Translated by Eric Colledge. Published by Harper and Brothers.

On His Own Ignorance by Francesco Petrarca. Translated by Hans Nachod. Published by University of Chicago Press.

The Dialogue of Saint Catherine of Siena. Translated by Algar Thorold. Published by The Newman Press.

Revelations of Divine Love by Julian of Norwich. Translated by Grace Warrack. Published by Methuen and Company.

On the Education of a Gentleman by Pier Paolo Vergerio. From *De Ingenuis Moribus: an English Version* in *Vittorino da Feltre and Other Humanist Educators*. Edited by William H. Woodward. Published by Cambridge University Press.

Of Learned Ignorance by Nicholas of Cusa. Translated by Father Germain Heron. Published by Rutledge and Kegan Paul.

Oration on the Dignity of Man by Giovanni Pico Della Mirandola. From *The Renaissance Philosophy of Man*. Translated by Elizabeth L. Forbes. Published by University of Chicago Press.

The Imitation of Christ by Thomas à Kempis. Translated by Monsignor Ronald Knox and Michael Oakley. Published by Sheed and Ward.

The Ladder of Perfection by Walter Hilton. Translated by Leo Sherley-Price. Published by Penguin Books.

Enchiridion militis Christiani by Desiderius Erasmus. Translated by John P. Dolan. Published by Notre Dame University Press.

The Praise of Folly by Desiderius Erasmus. From *The Essential Erasmus*. Translated by John P. Dolan. Published by New American Library.

The Paraclesis by Desiderius Erasmus. Translated by J. R. O'Donnell, C.S.B. Published by Random House, Inc.

The Prince by Niccolò Machiavelli. Translated by A. Robert Caponigri. Published by Henry Regnery Company.

The Dialogue Between the Soul and the Body by Saint Catherine of Genoa. Translated by Charlotte Balfour and Helen Douglas Irvine. Published by Sheed and Ward.

The Spiritual Exercises by Saint Ignatius of Loyola. Translated by W. H. Longridge. Published by A. R. Mowbray and Company.

Jerusalem Delivered by Torquato Tasso. Translated by Edward Fairfax. Published by Colonial Press.

The Way of Perfection by Saint Teresa of Ávila. From *The Complete Works of Saint Teresa of Jesus*. Translated by E. Allison Peers. Published by Sheed and Ward.

The Ascent of Mount Carmel and *The Dark Night of the Soul* by Saint John of the Cross. Translated by E. Allison Peers. Published by Image Books, Doubleday and Company.

The Interior Castle by Saint Teresa of Ávila. Translated by the Benedictines of Stanbrook; revised by Benedict Zimmerman, O.C.D. Published by Benziger Brothers.

An Introduction to the Devout Life by Saint Francis de Sales. From *Philothea, or An Introduction to the Devout Life*. Translated by John C. Reville, S.J. Published by The Peter Reilly Company.

The Autobiography of a Hunted Priest by John Gerard. Translated by Philip Caraman. Published by Image Books, Doubleday and Company.

Letter to the Grand Duchess Christina by Galileo Galilei. From *The Discoveries and Opinions of Galileo*. Translated by Stillman Drake. Published by Doubleday Anchor Books.

The Love of God by Saint Francis de Sales. Translated by Vincent Kerns, M.S.F.S. Published by Burns and Oates.

Dialogue Concerning the Two Chief World Systems by Galileo Galilei. Translated by Stillman Drake. Published by University of California Press.

The Hind and the Panther by John Dryden. From *The Best of Dryden*. Edited by Louis I. Bredvold. Published by The Ronald Press.

The Autobiography of Saint Margaret Mary Alacoque. Translated by the Sister of the Visitation, Roselands, Walmer, Kent. Published by Burleigh Press.

The New Science by Giovanni Battista Vico. Translated by Thomas Goddard Bergin and Max Harold Fisch. Published by Cornell University Press.

The Mysteries of Christianity by Matthias Joseph Scheeben. Translated by Cyril Vollert, S.J. Published by B. Herder Book Company.

L'Action by Maurice Blondel. Published by Presses Universitaires de France.

The Woman Who Was Poor by Léon Bloy. Translated by I. J. Collins. Publblished by Sheed and Ward.

The Story of a Soul by Saint Thérèse of Lisieux. From *The Little Flower of Jesus*. Translated by the Reverend Thomas N. Taylor. Published by P. J. Kenedy and Sons.

The Path to Rome by Hilaire Belloc. Published by Henry Regnery Company.

History of Freedom and Other Essays by John Emerich Edward Dalberg Acton. Published by Macmillan and Company.

Orthodoxy by Gilbert Keith Chesterton. Published by Dodd, Mead and Company.

The Mystical Element of Religion by Baron Friedrich John von Hugel. Published by E. P. Dutton and Company.

The Servile State by Hilaire Belloc. Published by Henry Holt and Company.

Saint Francis of Assisi by Johannes Jörgensen. Translated by T. O'Connor Sloane. Published by Image Books, Doubleday and Company.

The Poems of Gerard Manley Hopkins. Published by Oxford University Press.

Art and Scholasticism by Jacques Maritain. Translated by Joseph W. Evans. Published by Charles Scribner's Sons.

The Intellectual Life: Its Spirit, Conditions, Methods by Antonin Gilbert Sertillanges. Translated by Mary Ryan. Published by The Mercier Press.

The Poems of Alice Meynell. Published by Oxford University Press.

The Spirit of Catholicism by Karl Adam. Translated by Justin McCann, O.S.B. Published by Doubleday and Company.

Saint Francis of Assisi by Gilbert Keith Chesterton. Published by Image Books, Doubleday and Company.

The Everlasting Man by Gilbert Keith Chesterton. Published by Image Books, Doubleday and Company.

God and Intelligence in Modern Philosophy by Fulton J. Sheen. Published by Image Books, Doubleday and Company.

A Key to the Doctrine of the Eucharist by Dom Anscar Vonier, O.S.B. Published by The Newman Bookshop.

The History of the Popes from the Close of the Middle Ages by Ludwig von Pastor. Published by B. Herder Book Company.

Progress and Religion by Christopher Dawson. Published by Image Books, Doubleday and Company.

The Autobiography of Johannes Jörgensen. Translated by Ingeborg Lund. Published by Longmans, Green and Company.

The Christian Education of Youth by Pope Pius XI. Vatican translation. Published by National Catholic Welfare Conference.

Casti connubii by Pope Pius XI. Vatican translation. Published by Daughters of St. Paul Press.

Quadragesimo anno by Pope Pius XI. Vatican translation. Published by National Catholic Welfare Conference.

The Spirit of Mediaeval Philosophy by Étienne Gilson. Translated by A. H. C. Downes. Published by Charles Scribner's Sons.

The Making of Europe by Christopher Dawson. Published by Meridian Books.

Degrees of Knowledge by Jacques Maritain. Translated by Gerald B. Phelan. Published by Charles Scribner's Sons.

Liturgy and Personality by Dietrich von Hildebrand. Published by Longmans, Green and Company.

Edmund Campion by Evelyn Waugh. Published by Sheed and Ward.

The Good News Yesterday and Today by Josef Andreas Jungmann, S.J. Translated by William A. Huesman, S.J. Published by W. H. Sadlier.

The Unity of Philosophical Experience by Étienne Gilson. Published by Charles Scribner's Sons.

The Lord by Romano Guardini. Translated by Elinor Castendyk Briefs. Published by Longmans, Green and Company.

Catholicism by Henri de Lubac, S.J. Translated by Lancelot C. Sheppard. Published by Sheed and Ward.

Atheistic Communism by Pope Pius XI. Vatican translation. Published by National Catholic Welfare Conference.

Mit brennender Sorge by Pope Pius XI. Vatican translation. Published by National Catholic Welfare Conference.

Church and State by Luigi Sturzo. Translated by Barbara Barclay Carter. Published by Notre Dame University Press.

The Origin of the Jesuits by James Brodrick, S.J. Published by Longmans, Green and Company.

The Monastic Order in England by Dom David Knowles. Published by Cambridge University Press.

The Church of the Word Incarnate by Charles Journet. Translated by A. H. C. Downes. Published by Sheed and Ward.

Basic Verities by Charles Péguy. Translated by Anne and Julian Green. Published by Pantheon Books.

Divino afflante Spiritu by Pope Pius XII. Vatican translation. Published by National Catholic Welfare Conference.

The Mystical Body of Christ by Pope Pius XII. Vatican translation. Published by The Paulist Press.

The Heart of Man by Gerald Vann. Published by Longmans, Green and Company.

Homo Viator by Gabriel Marcel. Published by Harper and Brothers.

The State in Catholic Thought by Heinrich Rommen. Published by B. Herder Book Company.

The Character of Man by Emmanuel Mounier. Translated by Cynthia Rowland. Published by Harper and Brothers.

Theology and Sanity by Frank Joseph Sheed. Published by Sheed and Ward.

The Mind and Heart of Love by Martin Cyril D'Arcy, S.J. Published by Meridian Books.

Human Destiny by Pierre Lecomte du Noüy. Published by Longmans, Green and Company.

Mediator Dei by Pope Pius XII. Vatican translation. Published by The Paulist Press.

Growth or Decline? The Church Today by Emmanuel Cardinal Suhard. Translated by James A. Corbett. Published by Fides Publishers.

Essay on Human Love by Jean Guitton. Published by Aubier.

The Seven Storey Mountain by Thomas Merton. Published by Harcourt, Brace and Company.

The Meaning of Man by Jean Mouroux. Translated by A. H. C. Downes. Published by Sheed and Ward.

The World of Silence by Max Picard. Translated by Stanley Godman. Published by Henry Regnery Company.

Leisure the Basis of Culture by Joseph Pieper. Translated by Alexander Dru. Published by Pantheon Books.

Communism and the Conscience of the West by Fulton J. Sheen. Published by Bobbs-Merrill Company.

Transformation in Christ by Dietrich von Hildebrand. Published by Helicon Press.

The Mass of the Roman Rite by Josef Andreas Jungmann, S.J. Translated by the Reverend Francis A. Brunner, C.SS.R. Published by Benziger Brothers.

Seeds of Contemplation by Thomas Merton. Published by New Directions.

Peace of Soul by Fulton J. Sheen. Published by McGraw-Hill Book Company.

Enthusiasm by Ronald A. Knox. Published by Oxford University Press.

The End of Time by Josef Pieper. Translated by Michael Bullock. Published by Pantheon Books.

The Mystery of Being by Gabriel Marcel. Published by Henry Regnery Company.

Man and the State by Jacques Maritain. Published by University of Chicago Press.

Ascent to Truth by Thomas Merton. Published by Harcourt, Brace and Company.

Philosophy of Democratic Government by Yves René Marie Simon. Published by University of Chicago Press.

Traité du Libre Arbitre by Yves René Marie Simon. Published by Sciences et Lettres, Liège.

Saint Francis Xavier by James Brodrick, S.J. Published by The Wicklow Press, Pellegrini and Cudahy.

The Lord of History by Jean Daniélou, S.J. Translated by Nigel Abercrombie. Published by Henry Regnery Company.

The Christ of Faith by Karl Adam. Translated by Joyce Crick. Published by Pantheon Books.

Jesus and His Times by Henri Daniel-Rops. Translated by Ruby Millar. Published by Image Books, Doubleday and Company.

The Manner Is Ordinary by John LaFarge, S.J. Published by Harcourt, Brace and Company.

Liturgical Piety by Louis Bouyer. Published by University of Notre Dame Press.

The Phenomenon of Man by Pierre Teilhard de Chardin. Translated by Bernard Wall. Published by Harper and Brothers.

Science, Religion and Christianity by Hans Urs von Balthasar. Translated by Hilda Graef. Published by The Newman Press.

The Discovery of God by Henri de Lubac, S.J. Translated by Alexander Dru. Published by P. J. Kenedy and Sons.

The Two-Edged Sword by John L. McKenzie, S.J. Published by Bruce Publishing Company.

Act and Being by Michele Federico Sciacca. Published by Marzorati.

The Seat of Wisdom by Louis Bouyer. Published by Pantheon Books.

The Meeting of Love and Knowledge by Martin Cyril D'Arcy, S.J. Published by Harper and Brothers.

Insight by Bernard J. F. Lonergan, S.J. Published by Longmans, Green and Company.

On the Theology of Death by Karl Rahner. From *Modern Catholic Thinkers,* edited and translated by A. Robert Caponigri. Published by Harper and Brothers.

The Divine Milieu by Pierre Teilhard de Chardin. Published by Harper and Brothers.

Christian Humanism by Louis Bouyer. Translated by A. V. Littledale. Published by The Newman Press.

Contemporary European Thought and Christian Faith by Albert Dondeyne. Translated by Ernan McMullin and John Burnheim. Published by Duquesne University Press.

The Humanity of Christ by Romano Guardini. Translated by Ronald Walls. Published by Pantheon Books.

American Catholic Dilemma by Thomas F. O'Dea. Published by Sheed and Ward.

God in Modern Philosophy by James D. Collins. Published by Henry Regnery Company.

American Catholic Crossroads by Walter J. Ong, S. J. Published by The Macmillan Company.

Death and Immortality by Michele Federico Sciacca. Published by Marzorati.

The Hollow Universe by George De Koninck. Published by Oxford University Press.

The Philosopher and Theology by Étienne Gilson. Translated by Cécile Gilson. Published by Random House, Inc.

Nationalism: A Religion by Carlton J. H. Hayes. Published by The Macmillan Company.

Moral Philosophy by Jacques Maritain. Published by Geoffrey Bles.

We Hold These Truths by John Courtney Murray, S.J. Published by Sheed and Ward.

Come, Let Us Worship by Godfrey Diekmann, O.S.B. Published by Helicon Press.

Mater et magistra by Pope John XXIII. Vatican translation. Published by The Paulist Press.

The Council, Reform and Reunion by Hans Küng. Translated by Cecily Hastings. Published by Sheed and Ward.

Joseph: The Man Closest to Jesus by Francis L. Filas, S.J. Published by Daughters of St. Paul.

The Church by Giovanni Battista Cardinal Montini. Published by Helicon Press.

Belief and Faith by Josef Pieper. Translated by Richard and Clara Winston. Published by Pantheon Books.

Zen Catholicism by Dom Aelred Graham, O.S.B. Published by Harcourt, Brace and World.

The Millennium by Oscar Halecki. Published by Notre Dame University Press.

Pacem in terris by Pope John XXIII. Vatican translation. Published by The Paulist Press.

PREFACE

THE VIGOR with which the early Church leaders pressed forward the Christian message as it was made known to them—at the risk of liberty, and of life itself—has won for them the reverence and gratitude of Christians everywhere and in all ages. Their inspired leadership and their great spiritual insight in interpreting the *idea* of Christianity as Christ meant it to be interpreted enabled the new Faith to withstand the powerful and repeated onslaughts of the pagan world. With a dedication born of a serene and sure faith they lifted the great light of Christianity up through the dark shadows of ignorance and evil until it illuminated the entire face of the Western World.

No one man was most important and yet no Christian was unimportant, for each believer, low as well as high, helped to carry forward the growing idea that man was no longer alone and no longer lost. Nevertheless, it was given to certain hearts and minds to read more clearly than others God's intent and God's will and to interpret and set down in inspiring terms the truths that were revealed to them. It is the works of these and later Church leaders with which this book is concerned.

MASTERPIECES OF CATHOLIC LITERATURE IN SUMMARY FORM is a survey of Roman Catholic historical, philosophical, theological, spiritual, and devotional literature from earliest times to the present. Three hundred separate titles are examined by a highly qualified staff consisting of sixty-five members drawn from the faculties of two dozen of our foremost Catholic colleges and universities. Original essay-reviews of some two thousand words were prepared for each of the three hundred books under study and, for accuracy and balance, each review manuscript came under the scrutiny of at least four different staff members during the writing and editing.

Because of the vast number of books under consideration for inclusion in MASTERPIECES OF CATHOLIC LITERATURE, the co-operation of scores of professors of Christian literature at many leading Roman Catholic universities and colleges was sought in connection with the final selection of the three hundred titles to be reviewed. These scholars were asked to help select the three hundred books in the entire range of Roman Catholic literature which, in their opinion, had been most influential in the development of Christianity. I wish to acknowledge with thanks the generous response of these individuals, whose suggestions have helped to broaden the scope of our work and to fill the pages between the DIDACHE and Pope John XXIII's PACEM IN TERRIS with studies of many of the most important writings in the realm of Catholic thought.

The basic work of interpreting the three hundred books under consideration fell to the writing staff of sixty-five scholars and teachers, whose names and academic affiliations appear elsewhere in this volume. I am sure that Associate Editors A. Robert Caponigri of the University of Notre Dame, and Thomas P. Neill of Saint Louis University join me in expressing great appreciation for the dedicated way in which the staff turned to the task of making this book a highly useful reference for all Roman Catholics.

All the articles in MASTERPIECES OF CATHOLIC LITERATURE were written expressly for this book. While every effort was made to evaluate the original work in the light of the best current scholarship, each article is animated by the insight of the individual scholar who undertook to interpret the particular book under discussion. The main points to be elaborated upon are listed in italics at the beginning of the article under the heading PRINCIPAL IDEAS ADVANCED.

Arrangement of the articles is chronological rather than alphabetical by book title, so that the orderly development of Roman Catholic thought will be clearly evident. However, two indexes enable the user to locate any article promptly without regard to chronology: a title index at the front of the book, an author index at the end. Except in the case of articles worked on by several staff members, reviews are signed with the initials of the scholar responsible for the original article. A list of initials identifying these contributors appears in the front part of this volume.

I am sure that the entire staff shares my hope that MASTERPIECES OF CATHOLIC LITERATURE will serve a useful purpose for those who wish to examine, or review, the great expressions of Christian thought that have sprung from the hearts and minds of Catholicism's most revered leaders. Their towering faith and passionate dedication have helped to create an enduring message of hope that rests on divine love and carries upon it the eternal imprint of the Cross.

FRANK N. MAGILL

ALPHABETICAL LIST OF TITLES

Act and Being — *Michele Federico Sciacca* 1031
Action, L' — *Maurice Blondel* 706
Aeterni Patris — *Pope Leo XIII* 691
Against Eunomius — *Saint Basil* 98
Against the Heresies — *Saint Irenaeus* 37
American Catholic Crossroads — *Walter J. Ong, S.J.* 1076
American Catholic Dilemma — *Thomas O'Dea* 1066
American Republic, The — *Orestes Augustus Brownson* . . . 667
Anxiety and the Christian — *Hans Urs von Balthasar* . . . 969
Apologia pro vita sua — *John Henry Cardinal Newman* . . . 661
Apology of Aristides, The — *Aristides* 10
Apology of Tertullian, The — *Tertullian* 41
Ars logica — *John of St. Thomas* 589
Art and Scholasticism — *Jacques Maritain* 766
Ascent of Mount Carmel *and* The Dark Night of the Soul, The —
Saint John of the Cross 558
Ascent to Truth — *Thomas Merton* 979
Ascetic Life, The — *Saint Maximus the Confessor* 252
Atheistic Communism — *Pope Pius XI* 858
Autobiography of a Hunted Priest, The — *John Gerard* . . . 571
Autobiography of Johannes Jörgensen, The — *Johannes Jörgensen* . . 801
Autobiography of Saint Margaret Mary Alacoque, The —
Saint Margaret Mary 615

Basic Verities — *Charles Péguy* 879
Belief and Faith — *Josef Pieper* 1121
Benjamin minor *and* Benjamin major — *Richard of St. Victor* . . 339
Book of Proverbs — *Otloh of St. Emmeram* 276
Book of Sentences, The — *Peter Lombard* 328

Call of All Nations, The — *Saint Prosper of Aquitaine* . . . 204
Carmen Deo nostro — *Richard Crashaw* 600
Casti connubii — *Pope Pius XI* 808
Catechetical Lectures, The — *Saint Cyril of Jerusalem* . . . 90
Catholicism — *Henri de Lubac, S.J.* 856
Character of Man, The — *Emmanuel Mounier* 902
Christ of Faith, The — *Karl Adam* 1000
Christian Education of Youth, The — *Pope Pius XI* 801

Christian Humanism — *Louis Bouyer* 1058
Chronica majora — *Matthew Paris* 376
Church, The — *Giovanni Battista Cardinal Montini (Pope Paul VI)* . . 1118
Church and State — *Luigi Sturzo* 864
Church of the Word Incarnate, The — *Charles Journet* 875
City of God, The — *Saint Augustine* 188
Cloud of Unknowing, The — *Unknown* 466
Come, Let Us Worship — *Godfrey Diekmann, O.S.B.* 1103
Commentary on Aristotle's *De anima* — *Saint Albert the Great* . . . 360
Commentary on the Apostles' Creed, A — *Rufinus of Aquileia* . . . 169
Commentary on the *Summa theologica* of Saint Thomas — *Saint Cajetan* . 516
Commonitory, A — *Saint Vincent of Lérins* 198
Communism and the Conscience of the West — *Fulton J. Sheen* . . 944
Concerning Rhetoric and Virtue — *Alcuin* 261
Confessions, The — *Saint Augustine* 165
Consolation of Philosophy, The — *Saint Anicius Manlius Severinus Boethius* 229
Contemplative Life, The — *Julianus Pomerius* 220
Contemporary European Thought and Christian Faith — *Albert Dondeyne* 1061
Contra Celsum — *Origen* 71
Council, Reform and Reunion, The — *Hans Küng* 1110
Cur Deus Homo — *Saint Anselm of Canterbury* 286
Cursus theologicus — *John of St. Thomas* 605

De contemptu mundi — *Pope Innocent III* 342
De magistro — *Saint Augustine* 140
De monarchia — *Dante Alighieri* 438
De potestate regia et papali — *John of Paris* 432
De primo principio — *John Duns Scotus* 423
De sacro altaris mysterio — *Pope Innocent III* 345
De trinitate — *Saint Augustine* 173
De trinitate — *Saint Anicius Manlius Severinus Boethius* 223
De veritate — *Saint Thomas Aquinas* 379
De viris illustribus — *Saint Jerome* 148
Death and Immortality — *Michele Federico Sciacca* 1078
Decretum Gratiani — *Johannes Gratian* 324
Degrees of Knowledge — *Jacques Maritain* 828
Demonstration of Apostolic Teaching, The — *Saint Irenaeus* . . . 47
Dialogue Between the Soul and the Body, The — *Saint Catherine of Genoa* 530
Dialogue Concerning the Two Chief World Systems — *Galileo Galilei* . 593
Dialogue of Saint Catherine of Siena, The — *Saint Catherine of Siena* . 473
Dialogues — *Saint Gregory the Great* 241
Dialogues of Sulpicius Severus, The — *Sulpicius Severus* 157

Didache, The — *Unknown* 1
Discourse Against the Greeks, The — *Tatian* 23
Discourse on the Priesthood — *Saint John Chrysostom* 123
Discourse on Universita History — *Jacques Bénigne Bossuet* . . . 608
Discourses Against the Arians — *Saint Athanasius* 94
Discovery of God, The — *Henri de Lubac, S.J.* 1025
Divine Comedy, The — *Dante Alighieri* 443
Divine Institutes, The — *Lactantius* 81
Divine Milieu, The — *Pierre Teilhard de Chardin, S.J.* 1054
Divino afflante Spiritu — *Pope Pius XII* 883

Ecclesiastical History — *Eusebius Pamphili* 88
Ecclesiastical History of the English People, The — *Saint Bede* . . 258
Edmund Campion — *Evelyn Waugh* 838
En Route — *Joris-Karl Huysmans* 716
Enarrations on the Psalms — *Saint Augustine* 196
Enchiridion militis Christiani — *Desiderius Erasmus* 498
Enchiridion symbolorum et definitionum — *Heinrich Joseph Dominicus Denzinger* 658
End of Time, The — *Josef Pieper* 964
Enthusiasm — *Ronald Knox* 961
Epistle to Diognetus — *Unknown* 62
Epistle XXI: To the Most Clement Emperor and Most Blessed Augustus — *Saint Ambrose* 127
Epistles *and* The Martyrdom of Saint Polycarp, The — *Saint Polycarp* . 16
Epistles of Saint Ignatius of Antioch, The — *Saint Ignatius of Antioch* . 7
Essay on Catholicism, Liberalism, and Socialism — *Juan Francisco Maria de la Saludad Donoso Cortés* 650
Essay on Human Love — *Jean Guitton* 923
Essay on Indifference in Matters of Religion — *Félicité Robert de Lamennais* 632
Essay on the Development of Christian Doctrine, An — *John Henry Cardinal Newman* 644
Etymologies, The — *Saint Isidore of Seville* 248
Everlasting Man, The — *Gilbert Keith Chesterton* 785
Extant Writings of Saint Francis of Assisi, The — *Saint Francis of Assisi* . 349

Faith, Hope, and Charity — *Saint Augustine* 184
First Apology *and* The Second Apology, The — *Saint Justin Martyr* . . 19
First Catechetical Instruction, The — *Saint Augustine* 161
Five Theological Orations, The — *Saint Gregory Nazianzen* 116

Glories of Mary — *Saint Alphonsus Mary de' Liguori* 624

God and Intelligence in Modern Philosophy — *Fulton J. Sheen* 788
God in Modern Philosophy — *James D. Collins* 1071
Good News Yesterday and Today, The — *Josef Andreas Jungmann, S.J.* . . 843
Grammar of Assent, A — *John Henry Cardinal Newman* 678
Great Catechism, The — *Saint Gregory of Nyssa* 120
Growth or Decline?: The Church Today — *Emmanuel Cardinal Suhard* . 920

Heart of Man, The — *Gerald Vann, O.P.* 889
Hind and the Panther, The — *John Dryden* 611
Historia calamitatum — *Peter Abelard* 307
History of England, The — *John Lingard* 638
History of Freedom and Other Essays, The — *John Emerich Edward Dalberg Acton* 739
History of the Catholic Church in the United States, A — *John Dawson Gilmary Shea* 702
History of the Councils — *Karl Joseph von Hefele* 686
History of the Franks — *Saint Gregory of Tours* 244
History of the Popes from the Close of the Middle Ages, The — *Ludwig von Pastor* 796
Hollow Universe, The — *George De Koninck* 1084
Homilies — *Aelfric* 272
Homilies of Saint John Chrysostom — *Saint John Chrysostom* 154
Homo Viator — *Gabriel Marcel* 893
Hound of Heaven, The — *Francis Thompson* 709
Human Destiny — *Pierre Lecomte du Noüy* 913
Humanity of Christ, The — *Romano Guardini* 1064
Hymns of Saint Ambrose, The — *Saint Ambrose* 152
Hymns of Saint Thomas Aquinas, The — *Saint Thomas Aquinas* . . . 421

Idea of a University, The — *John Henry Cardinal Newman* 653
Imitation of Christ, The — *Thomas à Kempis* 491
Immortale Dei — *Pope Leo XIII* 695
Incarnation of the Word of God, The — *Saint Athanasius* 84
Insight — *Bernard J. F. Lonergan, S.J.* 1043
Institutes of the Monastic Life, The — *John Cassian* 193
Intellectual Life, The — *Antonin Gilbert Sertillanges* 771
Interior Castle, The — *Saint Teresa of Ávila* 561
Introduction to the Devout Life, An — *Saint Francis de Sales* . . . 568

Jerusalem Delivered — *Torquato Tasso* 548
Jesus and His Times — *Henri Daniel-Rops* 1006
Joseph: The Man Closest to Jesus — *Francis L. Filas, S. J.* 1115

Key to the Doctrine of the Eucharist, A — *Dom Anscar Vonier, O.S.B.* . 793

Ladder of Divine Ascent, The — *Saint John Climacus* 254
Ladder of Perfection, The — *Walter Hilton* 494
Lectures on the Philosophy of Life — *Friedrich von Schlegel* 635
Leisure the Basis of Culture — *Josef Pieper* 940
Letter of the Church of Rome to the Church of Corinth, The — *Saint Clement I* 4
Letter to the Grand Duchess Christina — *Galileo Galilei* 579
Letters and Sermons of Saint Leo the Great, The — *Saint Leo the Great* . 211
Letters of Saint Basil, The — *Saint Basil* 110
Letters of Saint Bernard of Clairvaux, The — *Saint Bernard* 332
Letters of Saint Jerome, The — *Saint Jerome* 180
Liber de Corpore et Sanguine Domini — *Lanfranc* 283
Life of Alfred — *John Asser* 268
Life of Charlemagne, The — *Einhard* 265
Life of Our Lord Jesus Christ, The — *Louis Veuillot* 665
Life of Saint Louis, The — *Jean de Joinville* 435
Little Book of Eternal Wisdom, The — *Blessed Henry Suso, O.P.* . . . 458
Little Flowers of Saint Francis, The — *Unknown* 448
Liturgical Piety — *Louis Bouyer* 1014
Liturgy and Personality — *Dietrich von Hildebrand* 835
Lord, The — *Romano Guardini* 849
Lord of History, The — *Jean Daniélou, S.J.* 997
Lord's Prayer, The — *Saint Gregory of Nyssa* 136
Love of God, The — *Saint Francis de Sales* 584
Lyfe of Sir Thomas More, Knighte — *William Roper* 543

Making of Europe, The — *Christopher Dawson* 824
Man and the State — *Jacques Maritain* 973
Manner Is Ordinary, The — *John LaFarge, S.J.* 1010
Mass of the Roman Rite, The — *Josef A. Jungmann, S.J.* 949
Mater et magistra — *Pope John XXIII* 1106
Meaning of Man, The — *Jean Mouroux* 933
Mediator Dei—*Pope Pius XII* 915
Meditations on the Life of Christ — *Unknown Franciscan Monk and Saint Bonaventure* 455
Meeting of Love and Knowledge, The — *Martin Cyril D'Arcy, S.J.* . . . 1040
Millennium of Europe, The — *Oscar Halecki* 1128
Mind and Heart of Love, The — *Martin Cyril D'Arcy, S.J.* 909
Mind's Road to God, The — *Saint Bonaventure* 371
Mit brennender Sorge — *Pope Pius XI* 860

Monastic Order in England, The — *Dom David Knowles, O.S.B.* . . . 870
Moral Philosophy — *Jacques Maritain* 1094
Mysteries of Christianity, The — *Matthias Joseph Scheeben* . . . 672
Mystery of Being, The — *Gabriel Marcel* 966
Mystical Body of Christ, The — *Pope Pius XII* 886
Mystical Element of Religion, The — *Baron Friedrich John von Hügel* . 749
Mystical Theology, The — *Dionysius the Pseudo-Areopagite* . . . 218

Nationalism: A Religion — *Carlton J. H. Hayes* 1091
New Science, The — *Giovanni Battista Vico* 618
Noah's Ark — *Hugh of St. Victor* 304

Octavius — *Minucius Felix* 50
Of Learned Ignorance — *Nicholas of Cusa* 482
On Being and Essence — *Saint Thomas Aquinas* 364
On Education — *Juan Luis Vives* 519
On First Principles — *Origen* 65
On Free Choice — *Saint Thomas Aquinas* 406
On His Own Ignorance — *Petrarch* 469
On Kingship — *Saint Thomas Aquinas* 391
On Spiritual Creatures — *Saint Thomas Aquinas* 402
On the Christian Faith — *Saint Ambrose* 112
On the Divine Names — *Dionysius the Pseudo-Areopagite* 215
On the Duties of the Clergy — *Saint Ambrose* 145
On the Education of a Gentleman — *Pier Paolo Vergerio* 479
On the Genesis of the Species — *St. George Jackson Mivart* . . . 682
On the Necessity of Loving God — *Saint Bernard* 311
On the Power of God — *Saint Thomas Aquinas* 394
On the Resurrection of the Dead — *Athenagoras* 30
On the Soul — *Saint Thomas Aquinas* 409
On the Steps of Humility and Pride — *Saint Bernard* 296
On the Theology of Death — *Karl Rahner* 1047
On the Unity of the Catholic Church — *Saint Cyprian* 75
On the Virtues in General — *Saint Thomas Aquinas* 413
Opus majus — *Roger Bacon* 398
Opus Oxoniense — *John Duns Scotus* 427
Oration and Panegyric Addressed to Origen, The — *Saint Gregory Thaumaturgus* 69
Oration on the Dignity of Man — *Giovanni Pico della Mirandola* . . 487
Origin of the Jesuits, The — *James Brodrick, S.J.* 868
Orthodoxy — *Gilbert Keith Chesterton* 744

Pacem in terris — *Pope John XXIII* 1131
Paraclesis, The — *Desiderius Erasmus* 505
Parish Life in Mediaeval England — *Francis Neil Aidan Cardinal Gasquet* . 736
Pastoral Care — *Saint Gregory the Great* 237
Path to Rome, The — *Hilaire Belloc* 734
Peace of Soul — *Fulton J. Sheen* 958
Phenomenon of Man, The — *Pierre Teilhard de Chardin, S.J.* . . 1017
Philosopher and Theology, The — *Étienne Gilson* 1088
Philosophy of Democratic Government — *Yves René Marie Simon* . . 982
Plea for the Christians, A — *Athenagoras* 27
Poems of Alice Meynell, The — *Alice Meynell* 775
Poems of Ernest Dowson, The — *Ernest Christopher Dowson* . . . 720
Poems of Gerard Manley Hopkins, The — *Gerard Manley Hopkins* . . 760
Policraticus *and* Metalogicon — *John of Salisbury* 335
Political Writings — *Saint Robert Cardinal Bellarmine* 564
Praise of Folly, The — *Desiderius Erasmas* 501
Prince, The — *Niccolò Machiavelli* 523
Progress and Religion — *Christopher Dawson* 798
Proslogion — *Saint Anselm* 280

Quadragesimo anno — *Pope Pius XI* 812

Refutation of All Heresies — *Saint Hippolytus* 58
Rerum novarum — *Pope Leo XIII* 699
Revelations of Divine Love — *Julian of Norwich* 476
Rule of Saint Benedict, The — *Saint Benedict* 234

St. Francis of Assisi — *Gilbert Keith Chesterton* 781
Saint Francis of Assisi — *Johannes Jörgensen* 756
Saint Francis Xavier — *James Brodrick, S.J.* 990
Science, Religion and Christianity — *Hans Urs von Balthasar* . . . 1021
Seat of Wisdom, The — *Louis Bouyer* 1037
Seeds of Contemplation — *Thomas Merton* 955
Sermo contra Auxentium — *Saint Ambrose* 132
Servile State, The — *Hilaire Belloc* 754
Seven Books of History Against the Pagans — *Paulus Orosius* . . . 178
Seven Storey Mountain, The — *Thomas Merton* 930
Shepherd, The — *Hermas* 12
Sic et non — *Peter Abelard* 291
Six Books of the Republic, The — *Jean Bodin* 552
Soirées de Saint-Pétersbourg, Les — *Joseph Marie de Maistre* . . . 630
Spirit of Catholicism, The — *Karl Adam* 778
Spirit of Mediaeval Philosophy, The — *Étienne Gilson* 816

Spirit of Saint Francis of Sales, The — *Jean Pierre Camus* 597
Spiritual Espousals, The — *Blessed John Ruysbroeck* 461
Spiritual Exercises — *Saint Ignatius Loyola* 534
Spiritual Friendship — *Saint Aelred* 319
State in Catholic Thought, The — *Heinrich Rommen* 897
Story of a Soul, The — *Saint Thérèse of Lisieux* 729
Stromateis — *Clement of Alexandria* 44
Summa contra Gentiles — *Saint Thomas Aquinas* 385
Summa de creaturis — *Saint Albert the Great* 352
Summa theologiae — *Saint Thomas Aquinas* 416
Summa universae theologiae — *Alexander of Hales* 382
Symbolism — *Johann Adam Möhler* 640

Theology and Sanity — *Francis Joseph Sheed* 906
Theophilus to Autolycus — *Saint Theophilus* 33
Three Ways, The — *Saint Bonaventure* 356
Tome — *Saint Leo the Great* 201
Traité du Libre Arbitre — *Yves René Marie Simon* 986
Transformation in Christ — *Dietrich von Hildebrand* 946
Treatise Concerning the Pursuit of Learning — *Hugh of St. Victor* . . 300
Treatise on Laws — *Francisco Suarez, S.J.* 575
Treatise on the Holy Spirit — *Saint Basil* 107
Treatise on the Laws and Customs of England — *Henry of Bracton* . . 367
Treatise on the Mysteries — *Saint Hilary of Poitiers* 103
Treatise on the Passion — *Saint Thomas More* 538
Treatise on the Promises — *Saint Dionysius of Alexandria* . . . 78
Treatises and Sermons of Meister Eckhart, The — *Johann Eckhart* . . 451
Treatises on Marriage — *Tertullian* 54
Two Cities, The — *Otto of Freising* 316
Two Discourses on Universal History — *Anne Robert Jacques Turgot* . . 628
Two-Edged Sword, The — *John L. McKenzie, S.J.* 1028

Unity of Philosophical Experience, The — *Étienne Gilson* . . . 845
Utopia — *Saint Thomas More* 509

Way of Perfection, The — *Saint Teresa of Ávila* 555
We Hold These Truths — *John Courtney Murray, S.J.* 1098
Woman Who Was Poor, The — *Léon Bloy* 726
World of Silence, The — *Max Picard* 936
Writings of Saint Patrick, The — *Saint Patrick* 207

Zen Catholicism — *Dom Aelred Graham, O.S.B.* 1124

PROJECT STAFF MEMBERS

	GRADUATE SCHOOL	PRESENT AFFILIATION
Ralph J. Bastian, S.J., S.T.D.	Gregorian University, Rome	Loyola University, Chicago
Vernon J. Bourke, Ph.D	University of Toronto	Saint Louis University
Edward L. Burke, Ph.D.	University of Louvain, Belgium	Loyola University, Los Angeles
Raymond S. Burns, Ph.D.	University of Pennsylvania	Saint John's University, Jamaica, N.Y.
A. Robert Caponigri, Ph.D.	University of Chicago	University of Notre Dame
Francis Paul Carpinelli, M.A.	University of Notre Dame	Saint Benedict's College, Atchison, Kansas
Francis J. Catania, Ph. D.	Saint Louis University	Loyola University, Chicago
George A. Cevasco, M.A.	Columbia University	Saint John's University, Jamaica, N.Y.
Joseph McDill Cozy, C.M., J.C.L.	Angelicum University, Rome	De Paul University
John Dennis Crowley, S.J., S.T.L.	Weston College	College of the Holy Cross
Robert L. Cunningham, Ph.D.	Laval University, Quebec	University of San Francisco
Gerard J. Dalcourt, Ph.D.	University of Montreal	Seton Hall University
James Phillip Degnan, M.A.	University of Notre Dame	University of Santa Clara
Howard Delaney, Ph.D.	Saint Louis University	University of Santa Clara
John J. Fauser, M.A., S.T.L.	Saint Louis University	Saint Louis University
Joseph E. Fee, M.A.	Saint John's University	Saint John's University, Jamaica, N.Y.

Francis L. Filas, S.J., S.T.D.	Bellarmine Pontifical University	Loyola University, Chicago
Desmond J. FitzGerald, Ph.D.	University of California, Berkeley	University of San Francisco
Edward S. Fody, M.A., L.L.B.	Columbia University	Caldwell College
Robert T. Francoeur, M.A., M.S.	University of Detroit, Johns Hopkins University	Fordham University
Jack P. Franzetti, Ph.D.	Saint John's University	Saint John's University, Jamaica, N.Y.
Angelus Gambatese, O.F.M., M.A.	Saint Bonaventure University	Saint Bonaventure University
Richard J. George, Ph.D.	University of Notre Dame	University of Santa Clara
John B. Gleason, Ph.D.	University of Chicago	University of San Francisco
Marc F. Griesbach, Ph.D.	University of Toronto	Marquette University
Sister Jane Marie Dempsey, V.H.M., M.A.	Saint Louis University	Academy of the Visitation
Donald H. Johnson, S.J., M.A.	Gonzaga University	Loyola University, Chicago
Edward A. Johnson, Ph.D.	Saint John's University	Saint John's University, Jamaica, N.Y.
Edward J. Kealey, Ph.D.	Johns Hopkins University	College of the Holy Cross
John F. Kiley, Ph.D.	University of Ottawa	College of the Holy Cross
William Charles Korfmacher, Ph.D.	University of Chicago	Saint Louis University
Nicholas Paul Kostra, M.A.	University of Notre Dame	Catherine Spalding College
Robert J. Kovarik, Ph.D.	Saint Louis University	Chicago Teachers College
Gerald Francis Kreyche, Ph.D.	University of Ottawa	De Paul University
Jerome Bowman Long, Ph.D.	Fordham University	University of Santa Clara
William L. Lucey, S.J., Ph.D.	Georgetown University	College of the Holy Cross
William A. McBrien, Ph.D.	Saint John's University	Saint John's University, Jamaica, N.Y.

Joseph A. McCallin, S.J.	Saint Louis University	Saint Louis University
Daniel D. McGarry, Ph.D.	University of California, Los Angeles	Saint Louis University
Ralph McInerny, Ph.D.	Laval University	University of Notre Dame
Sister Mary Evelyn, S. N.D. de N., A.B.	Saint Louis University	Saint Louis University
Sister Mary Lawrence, V.H.M., M.A.	Saint Louis University	Academy of the Visitation
Paul T. Mason, Ph.D.	Saint Louis University	Duquesne University
Vincent J. Moran, Ph.D.	University of Toronto	University of San Francisco
Elizabeth Muller, M. A.	Fordham University	Caldwell College
John J. Murphy, M.A.	Saint John's University	College of Saint Teresa
Thomas P. Neill, Ph.D.	Saint Louis University	Saint Louis University
Vincent C. Punzo, Ph.D.	Saint Louis University	Saint Louis University
Donald Quinn, B.S.	Rockhurst College	*St. Louis Review*
James Charles Rauner, M.A.	University of Notre Dame	University of Notre Dame
Melvin K. Reitzner, O.F.M. Cap., M.A.	Saint Louis University	Capuchin Seminary of Saint Mary
Sister M. Rita Margaret O.P., Ph.D.	Saint John's University	Caldwell College
James H. Robb, Ph.D., L.S.M.	University of Toronto, Pontifical Institute of Mediaeval Studies	Marquette University
Louis W. Roberts, S.J., M.A.	Saint Louis University	Saint Louis University
Barbara J. Rogers, M.A.	State University of Iowa	Seton Hall University
David M. Rogers, Ph.D.	Wayne State University	Seton Hall University
José M. Sánchez, Ph.D.	University of New Mexico	Saint Louis University
Kenneth L. Schmitz, Ph.D.	University of Toronto	Marquette University
Richard J. Schoeck, Ph.D.	Princeton University	Saint Michael's College, University of Toronto
Joan Schwartz, M.A.	Marquette University	Marquette University
Edward D. Simmons, Ph.D.	University of Notre Dame	Marquette University

Francis J. Thompson, Ph.D.	Saint John's University	Good Counsel College
Richard H. Trame, S.J., Ph.D.	Catholic University of America	Loyola University, Los Angeles
Jeanne K. Welcher, Ph.D.	Fordham University	Saint John's University
E. G. Weltin, Ph.D.	University of Illinois	Washington University
John P. Wickersham, A.B.	Saint Louis University	Saint Louis University, Maryville College
William J. Young, S.J., M.A.	Saint Louis University	Society of Jesus, Spiritual Director

INITIALS IDENTIFYING CONTRIBUTORS OF SIGNED ARTICLES

A.G.	Angelus Gambatese
A.R.C.	A. Robert Caponigri
B.J.R.	Barbara J. Rogers
D.D.M.	Daniel D. McGarry
D.H.J.	Donald H. Johnson
D.J.F.	Desmond J. FitzGerald
D.M.R.	David M. Rogers
D.Q.	Donald Quinn
E.A.J.	Edward A. Johnson
E.D.S.	Edward D. Simmons
E.G.W.	E. G. Weltin
E.J.K.	Edward J. Kealey
E.L.B.	Edward L. Burke
E.M.	Elizabeth Muller
E.S.F.	Edward S. Fody
F.J.C.	Francis J. Catania
F.J.T.	Francis J. Thompson
F.L.F.	Francis L. Filas
F.P.C.	Francis Paul Carpinelli
G.A.C.	George A. Cevasco
G.F.K.	Gerald Francis Kreyche
G.J.D.	Gerard J. Dalcourt
H.D.	Howard Delaney
J.A.M.	Joseph A. McCallin
J.B.G.	John B. Gleason
J.B.L.	Jerome Bowman Long
J.C.R.	James Charles Rauner
J.D.C.	John Dennis Crowley
J.E.F.	Joseph E. Fee
J.F.K.	John F. Kiley
J.H.R.	James H. Robb
J.J.F.	John J. Fauser
J.J.M.	John J. Murphy
J.K.W.	Jeanne K. Welcher
J.M.	Sister Jane Marie Dempsey
J.M.C.	Joseph McDill Cozy
J.M.S.	José M. Sánchez
J.P.D.	James Phillip Degnan
J.P.F.	Jack P. Franzetti
J.P.W.	John P. Wickersham
J.S.	Joan Schwartz
K.L.S.	Kenneth L. Schmitz
L.W.R.	Louis W. Roberts
M.E.	Sister Mary Evelyn
M.F.G.	Marc F. Griesbach
M.K.R.	Melvin K. Reitzner
M.L.	Sister Mary Lawrence
M.R.M.	Sister M. Rita Margaret
N.P.K.	Nicholas Paul Kostra
P.T.M.	Paul T. Mason
R.H.T.	Richard H. Trame
R.J.B.	Ralph J. Bastian
R.J.G.	Richard J. George
R.J.K.	Robert J. Kovarik
R.J.S.	Richard J. Schoeck
R.L.C.	Robert L. Cunningham
R.M.	Ralph McInerny
R.S.B.	Raymond S. Burns
R.T.F.	Robert T. Francoeur
T.P.N.	Thomas P. Neill
V.C.P.	Vincent C. Punzo
V.J.B.	Vernon J. Bourke
V.J.M.	Vincent J. Moran
W.A.M.	William A. McBrien
W.C.K.	William Charles Korfmacher
W.J.Y.	William J. Young
W.L.L.	William L. Lucey

THE DIDACHE

Author: Unknown
Type of work: Catechetical manual
First transcribed: c.60-90

Principal Ideas Advanced

Conversion must be marked by a moral and spiritual regeneration and by a loyal adherence to the universal belief and practice of all other Christians.

Revere and support those mystics and teachers whose message is sealed by holiness of life and orthodoxy of doctrine, but be alert for charlatans and false teachers.

The complete Christian life embraces the moral and spiritual perfection of the individual soul as well as the growth of the Christian community in sanctity through its common liturgy, alms, and fraternal love.

The exact date of the *Didache* or *The Teaching of the Twelve Apostles* has always been a matter of dispute, but the document reflects the very primitive organization of the first century Church, insofar as we know it. The place of composition is also uncertain, but it is likely to have been rural Egypt, Syria, or Palestine. Throughout its few concise, impersonal pages, there is little to suggest authorship by a single individual with his own unique attitudes and personality. Multiple authorship is probable, and the authors were evidently concerned only to record practical, basic material, not to be theologically daring or to promote organizational novelties. The *Didache* was planned as an adjunct to a written Gospel, referred to several times in the text, and they were both intended to serve in the education of pagan catechumens. Already the need seems to have been felt to supplement the historical narrative of Christ's life and teaching with a handbook interpreting common contemporary Church practice. In the young Church, threatened as it was on all sides, there developed a strong sense of Church identity, unity of doctrine and exclusiveness from all other religions. The *Didache,* like other early Christian records, reflects a commitment both to the inner life of the community as it was lived liturgically and morally and also to its outward existence as an institution.

The *Didache* opens with a metaphor common to the Greek world: a contrast between "The Way of Death" and "The Way of Life." The former is a general, brief enumeration of the sins that lead to destruction: self-indulgence, pride, greed, hypocrisy, and oppression of the poor. Christians are particularly enjoined to serve the poor, for "men that have no heart for the poor . . . do not know their Maker." The "Way of Life" is organized on the principle that the new, reborn man must oppose the natural man's bad impulses with supernatural good ones. Certain interior dispositions must be cultivated, among them those countering fanaticism, hot temper, lust, complaining, and self-will. Positive virtues must be substituted: patience, mercy, silence, and association with the humble rather than the powerful. A supernatural attitude toward suffering is basic to Christian fulfillment: "Accept as blessings the casualties that befall you, assured that nothing happens without God." Over all else, the Gospel injunctions to love God and neighbor must be the foundation of the spiritual life.

Interior dispositions in turn flower in active charity. There are three ways one can show love of men, depending on one's situation: direct correction of their faults, prayer for them, and a sacrifice of one's own life for their sake. Strong injunctions are given to material charity, and the practical advice against its abuse indicates a long-established custom of Christian sharing of resources. The moral obligation and spiritual benefits of charity are made clear: "Do not turn away from the needy; rather, share everything with your brother and do not say, 'It is private property'. . . . If you have means at your disposal, pay a ransom for your sins." Material charity is not the only outward duty of the Christian. A demanding and uncompromising code of moral conduct is to be adhered to. There must be no adultery, fornication, sodomy, abortion, infanticide, perjury, covetousness, or calumny. In all cases one's good deeds must match one's words; faith must be accompanied by good works. The inner man is expressed by his outward action, and his identity with other Christians in the Church confirms his own soul in its charity and fraternal responsibility.

The traditions of the Church and the unity of Christians are to be guarded at all costs: "My child, day and night remember him who preaches God's word to you, and honor him as the Lord. . . . Do not start a schism, but pacify contending parties. . . . Do not by any means neglect the commandments of the Lord, but hold fast to the traditions. . . . In church confess your sins, and do not come to your prayer with a guilty conscience." Thus, the relation of the Christian's inner life to the life of the whole united body of the Church is upheld. Whether confession was made publicly or in private is not historically certain, but it is evident that the primitive Church had achieved a highly effective and realistic co-existence among the contending elements of conscience, authority, and doctrine, fusing these with the unity of all Christians in sorrow for sin and communal sacrifice to God.

The ritual life of the Church, as new converts were introduced to it, centered around baptism and Holy Communion. The procedure for baptism, in particular, occupies a position of some importance in the *Didache*. Originally the ritual of baptism had required "living" or naturally flowing water as in a stream or river, but the *Didache* accepts the fact that such a source is not always available: "But if you have no running water, baptize in other water; and if you cannot in cold, then in warm. But if you have neither, pour water on the head three times in the name of the Father and of the Son and of the Holy Spirit." Already in the short history of the Church, the need had arisen for flexibility in the administration of the sacraments, and the Church clearly felt itself in possession of the authority to adapt these channels of grace to human needs.

The long section on the celebration of the Eucharist indicates an early date for the *Didache's* composition. The communal meal is still celebrated before the Sacrament and the cup offered before the bread, in imitation of the actual Last Supper. A series of liturgical prayers is given, each with the phrase "To Thee be the glory forever more" repeated at the end, and they culminate in a plea for the Second Coming of Christ. As the leader begins the rite with "We give Thee thanks," the note of participation in the sacrifice by all present is sounded, reaffirming the unity that a common moral, doctrinal, and spiritual life has previously established.

Such a unity was not the result of chance; the early Church had a lively institutional life and a strong sense of its own identity. There were two classes of leaders, according to the *Didache:* the elected regular authority, bishops and deacons, and the prophets and teachers. Both ministered to the same needs, though the mystical and charismatic gifts of the prophets evidently attracted greater popular interest and devotion than did the self-effacing and undramatic service of the elected officials, for the authors of the *Didache* find it necessary to remind Christians to give bishops and deacons the respect they deserve.

Christian communities were apparently experienced enough by this time to have learned how to guard themselves against false teachers and parasitical new members. The *Didache* is careful to give practical instructions on the control of abuses. If a traveling prophet should stay more than a day or ask for money or "teach a different doctrine," then the community should suspect him of fraud. Christians are instructed to support their own resident prophets and teachers and not give money to itinerants. If an itinerant asks for more than food or shelter, he is not a genuine preacher. It is necessary to observe the prophet's holiness of life and orthodoxy of doctrine before judging him truthful; his words must be united to his works.

With these reminders that the Church in this world is never free from the ills that universally beset all humanity, the *Didache's* final message is redoubled in strength. Christians are warned about the trials to come during the last days. The end of the world was very real to the authors of the *Didache,* and it was perhaps this consciousness that enabled them to maintain the pure and uncompromising standards of virtue necessary to set the primitive Church apart from the world around it. The longing for the ultimate reconciliation of Heaven and earth in the Parousia sums up the entire spirit of the Christian life as it is outlined in the manual: "Of no use will your lifelong faith be to you if you are not perfected at the end of time. . . . The Lord will come and all the saints with Him . . . the world will behold the Lord." The Christian is thus encouraged to see his own triumph over himself identified with the triumph of Christ and the whole Church over the world.

B.J.R.

THE LETTER OF THE CHURCH OF ROME TO THE CHURCH OF CORINTH

Author: Saint Clement I (died 97)
Type of work: Pastoral letter
First transcribed: c.96

Principal Ideas Advanced

The schism within the Church of Corinth should be healed, for rivalry and envy lead to fratricide, while repentance leads to salvation.

Men will be kind to one another if they turn their eyes and hearts to Christ.

The humility and obedience of those who submit to the Lord have benefited men; therefore, everyone should seek peace.

The Apostles received the Gospel from Christ, and the bishops and deacons continue the tradition; thus, to be obedient to God one must be obedient to his rulers and governors on earth.

Clement I of Rome became the fourth pope of the Church in 88, and his famous *First Epistle* or *Letter of the Church of Rome to the Church of Corinth* was written in the year 96, or soon thereafter, in the attempt to heal a serious schism which had developed within the Church of Corinth. The quarrel at Corinth was particularly serious in that it centered about a challenge to the rulers, the presbyters, within the Church. Clement realized that the perseverance of Christ's spirit depends upon sustaining that humility which allows the tradition to be maintained through the orderly succession of bishops and presbyters within the Church. In promptly exercising and thereby demonstrating his papal authority, Clement strengthened the Roman Church at a critical moment in its early history. The letter not only stresses the values of humility and obedience; it also establishes definitively the role of the Roman Church as the defender of the apostolic tradition which begins with Christ.

Clement begins his letter by calling attention to the persecution under Domitian which has kept the pope from dealing with the schism at Corinth. He refers to "a few impetuous and headstrong fellows" whose rash actions have caused the name of the Church of Corinth to fall into disrepute, and he suggests that the decline in reputation is especially to be regretted when one considers the spirit of piety and faith which has always characterized the Corinth Church. But despite Corinth's humility and Christian service, the pope adds, the Church there has shown that it is not immune from revolt; envious young men within the Church have turned against the ruling presbyters and bishops and have deposed them. Thus, in Corinth, as in the days of Jacob, Joseph, and Moses, "rivalry and envy are responsible for fratricide."

Clement cites a number of Biblical instances of corruption and defeat which have resulted from the unbridled exercise of power by envious men. The only solution, not only for Corinth but also for the world, Clement writes firmly, is to "turn to the glorious and holy rule of our tradition. . . . Let us fix our eyes on the blood of Christ and let us realize how precious it is to his Father. . . ." The opportunity for repentance remains for those who are ready to be washed and made clean. Enoch, Noah, and Abraham all proved faithful to the Lord, and they were rewarded with salvation. But Lot's wife, who because of her act of disobedience was turned to salt, makes it evident that those who challenge God will be condemned.

Clement thus urges that his brothers at Corinth attach themselves to the peacemakers and not to those who stir up rivalry. He reminds Corinth that the danger that will come to those who launch "strife and sedition" is "no ordinary harm. . . ." Christ belongs not to those who seek power and who, through pride, oppose their duly appointed superiors, but to those who are humble in their recognition of God's majesty. Christ Himself came in humility, and He suffered for man's sins and transgressions. Like the prophets Elijah, Elisha, and Ezekiel, and like Abraham, Job, Moses, and David, all men should seek to be imitators of Christ, who humbled Himself for all. The submissiveness of the heroes should encourage all men to be kind to one another and to be compassionate and tender, as Christ was.

When one considers how the entire universe exists and moves through God's creative power, writes Clement, it becomes clear that peace and harmony will come to men only if they seek the compassion of Christ. To reverence Christ involves respecting the rulers of the Church and honoring the elders.

Clement reminds those at Corinth that both through His sacrifice of Himself and through the changing of the seasons, the Lord promises men that there will be a resurrection of the dead. Even those who have erred in their obedience to God may rise again, like the phoenix of Arabia, provided only that they become humble in their submission to the Lord. But there is no use in merely pretending to be humble; the Lord knows everything, and He is quick to act against transgressors.

Man knows himself through the Word of God to be a holy portion of the divine; hence, everyone should seek holiness and flee from corrupt practices. Clement argues that since God created man in His own image, each man is obligated to work energetically in the service of the Lord: "He bids us, therefore, to believe on him with all our heart, and not to be slack or negligent in 'every good deed.' "

The rewards for those who rid themselves "of all wickedness, evil, avarice, contentiousness, malice, fraud, gossip, slander, hatred of God, arrogance, pretension, conceit, and inhospitality" are great, Clement insists, and he declares, "How blessed and amazing are God's gifts, dear friends! Life with immortality, splendor with righteousness, truth with confidence, faith with assurance, self-control with holiness!"

Through Jesus Christ, who is described by Clement as "the high priest of our offerings," men learn God's will; in Christ men "see mirrored God's pure and transcendent face."

Having reminded those at Corinth of God's demands for humility and obedience, and having emphasized both the great danger of giving way to pride and the lust for power and the great advantage of submitting to the Lord, Clement approaches the delicate problem of the revolt at Corinth by first of all using a military analogy. "Really in earnest, then, brothers," he writes, "we must march under his [the Lord's] irreproachable orders." Clement asks the Corinthians to note how those who serve under generals obey the orders of the generals readily and with a fine show of discipline. Not all men are generals, and hence some give orders and others obey; but the great depend on their subordinates, and those who are under orders depend on their superiors. Clement then draws the moral: "All are linked together; and this has an advantage. Take our body, for instance. The head cannot get along without the feet. Nor, similarly, can the feet get along without the head. . . . Following this out, we must preserve our Christian body too in its entirety."

The preservation of the Christian body depends upon performing the sacrifices and services which God has ordered. According to Clement, the Lord requires that the "sacrifices and services" be done at particular times and by particular persons whom He has designated: "The high priest is given his particular duties: the priests are assigned their special places, while on the Levites particular tasks are imposed. The layman is bound by the layman's code."

Having stressed the point that the priests are under orders from God Himself, Clement specifically calls attention to the apostolic succession: "The apostles received the gospel for us from the Lord Jesus Christ; Jesus, the Christ, was sent from God. Thus Christ is from God and the apostles from Christ. . . . And so the apostles, after receiving their orders . . . went out in the confidence of the Holy Spirit . . . and appointed their first converts, after testing them by the Spirit, to be the bishops and deacons of future believers."

Clement argues that anyone who deposes from the episcopate men who have properly been appointed through the apostolic succession, is guilty of a great sin, and he notes with dismay that Corinth has deposed some of its presbyters.

As he continues to discuss the revolt in the Church of Corinth Clement allows himself to show greater and greater displeasure. "Why do we reach such a pitch of insanity that we are oblivious of the fact that we are members of each other?" he asks, and he declares, "It is disgraceful, exceedingly disgraceful, and unworthy of your Christian upbringing, to have it reported that because of one or two individuals the solid and ancient Corinthian Church is in revolt against its presbyters."

Clement insists that there be an end to the revolt, that those responsible for challenging the presbyters beseech the Lord for forgiveness, and that the rebels submit to the presbyters. The pope prays for the peace which accompanies humility and repentance, and he asks God that all men "be obedient to your almighty and glorious name, and to our rulers and governors on earth."

Clement closes his letter with the news that he is sending delegates from the papacy as witnesses to insure that peace is quickly restored to the Church of Corinth. (The names of the pope's delegates are given: Claudius Ephebus, Valerius Bito, and Fortunatus; nothing further is known about these emissaries.)

Clement's *First Epistle* is of great importance as a clear and persuasive affirmation of the essential importance of the apostolical succession as insuring the integrity, unity, and authority of the Church. The pope, as Bishop of Rome, demonstrated his authority as the divinely appointed head of the Church, and in declaring that revolt against the priests and bishops was an act of disobedience and pride which placed the souls of the rebels in great danger, Clement gave decisive support to the growing and divinely ordained authority of the Roman Church.

THE EPISTLES OF SAINT IGNATIUS OF ANTIOCH

Author: Saint Ignatius of Antioch (died c.107)
Type of work: Dogmatic theology; ecclesiology
First transcribed: c.107

Principal Ideas Advanced

The Church has a hierarchical constitution, and authority in the Church is vested in the bishops.

Jesus Christ has a real human nature; His life, death, and resurrection are historically verifiable.

Faith and love are the distinctive virtues of the Christian; martyrdom is the ultimate proof of discipleship.

The unity of all Christians with one another and with their Head, Christ, is maintained and manifested in the celebration of the Eucharist.

Saint Ignatius of Antioch wrote seven epistles while he was being brought as a prisoner to Rome. The letters have a signal importance because they are the earliest independent witness outside the New Testament writings to historic Christianity and to Christian doctrine. In seven short letters a martyr and bishop reveals his concept of Christianity and draws a vivid picture of the early Church during a period of persecution in the reign of the emperor Trajan (98-117).

Knowledge of the life of Saint Ignatius must be gleaned almost entirely from the letters themselves and from short notices by such writers as the Church historian Eusebius and Saint Jerome, Father of the Church and Scripture scholar. As the third bishop of Antioch, Ignatius was the second successor of Saint Peter, who himself had resided at Antioch for some time before going to Rome. Captured during a local persecution, and guarded by ten Roman soldiers whom he described as "leopards," Ignatius was being transported in chains to Rome for execution. The prison ship put in at Smyrna, and during this delay Ignatius was visited by delegations of Christians from three churches of Asia Minor: the Ephesian, Magnesian, and Trallian. To each of these churches Ignatius wrote a general letter. Besides thanking them for their charity shown in their concern for him, he wanted to strengthen them in their faith, and to warn them against two rampant heresies, Judaism and Docetism. During the stopover at Smyrna, Ignatius also wrote to the Romans, but with a different end in view. He knew that in Rome there were some Christians in influential positions, and he feared that they might try to bring about his release. Ignatius begged them not to interfere with his execution, which he saw as the greatest of all graces, the opportunity to seal his witness to Christ by the shedding of his own blood.

Saint Ignatius intended his letters to be publicly read. He saw them as extensions of his personal witness to Christ. Their tone is one of friendly warmth, and there is no effort at literary style. What shines forth in these letters is the soul of a man whose life was completely absorbed by his single devotion to the God-Man. Saint Ignatius calls himself "Theophorus," or "God-bearer," pointing up the fact of his realization that all the significance of his life was in his relationship to God in the Person of Jesus Christ.

In the first three letters, Ignatius writes strongly against the Docetist heresy, which held that Christ did not have a true human nature and, therefore, that He did not truly live, suffer, and die in the flesh and rise again. Ignatius insists on the historical reality of the God-Man. He does not attempt to give a theological explanation of the mystery of the Incarnation; rather, he acts as witness to a historic fact. His goal is to maintain tradition, to guard the deposit of faith and hand it on exactly as he has received it. He tells the Trallians to refuse to listen to anyone who does not believe that Jesus Christ "was really born and ate and drank, really persecuted by Pontius Pilate, really crucified and died while heaven and earth and the underworld looked on; who also really rose from the dead, since His Father raised Him up—His Father, who will likewise raise us also who believe in Him through Jesus Christ, apart from whom we have no real life."

Scholars see in this emphatic antiheretical teaching an indication of the prevalence of heresy in the environment of the Church at this early date. Almost more emphatic than his teaching against Docetism is Saint Ignatius's repeated insistence on obedience to the bishops as an indispensable mark of orthodox Christianity. He draws an unmistakably clear picture of a hierarchical Church with an essential distinction between hierarchy and laity. The Magnesians are told not to take advantage of their bishop's youth, "because he embodies the authority of God the Father." It is the bishop who "is to preside in the place of God." In a later letter to the Smyrneans he is adamant about the consequences of this doctrine, insisting, "Let no one do anything touching the Church, apart from the bishop. Let that celebration of the Eucharist be considered valid which is held under the bishop or anyone to whom he has committed it. Where the bishop appears, there let the people be, just as where Jesus Christ is, there is the Catholic Church."

Another characteristic of the letters from Smyrna is an exultation in approaching martyrdom. The tense tone of Ignatius's remarks on this subject reveals his human apprehension of the approaching ordeal, but conquering this fear is joy at the thought of finally achieving true discipleship through martyrdom, which he sees as the closest possible identification with Christ. Saint Ignatius's attitude is a classic example of the early Christian mentality, which carried the conviction that only in the sacrifice of life was there achieved a perfect following of Christ. The epistle to the Romans contains the frequently quoted passage in which Ignatius vividly describes this ideal: "I am writing to all the Churches and state emphatically to all that I die willingly for God, provided you do not interfere. I beg you, do not show me unseasonable kindness. Suffer me to be the food of wild beasts, which are the means of my making my way to God. God's wheat I am, and by the teeth of wild beasts I am to be ground that I may prove Christ's pure bread. . . . Then only shall I be a genuine disciple of Jesus Christ when the world will not see even my body."

When the ship carrying Ignatius stopped at Troas, he wrote three more letters, two of which were general letters to the Philadelphians and Smyrneans, and the other a personal letter to Saint Polycarp, Bishop of Smyrna. Again there are the warnings against heresy, together with calls for obedience to the local bishop. The letter to the Philadelphians speaks of the central place of the Eucharist in the life of the Church. The Eucharist at once the means by which the life of the Church is nourished and the sign and seal of her unity. "Take care, then, to partake of one Eucharist," he urges, "for, one is the Flesh of Our Lord Jesus Christ, and one the cup to unite us with his blood. . . . Thus you will conform in all your actions to the will of God."

The reader of Saint Ignatius's seven brief letters cannot fail to catch the spirit of the early Church, a spirit showing itself in mutual interest in and concern for one another's trials and victories. Learning that peace has been restored to his own diocese, Ignatius asks the Philadelphians and the Smyrneans to send a delegation to Antioch bringing greetings and congratulations. To the Romans Ignatius writes pleading with them to do nothing to save him from the civil authorities. Polycarp is asked to take care of several pieces of unfinished business, remembering that "a Christian is not his own master; his time belongs to God. This is God's work; and it will be yours, too, once you have accomplished it."

The *Epistles of Saint Ignatius* was immediately popular. Another work of the same period, the *Epistles of Saint Polycarp,* tells us that Saint Polycarp forwarded Ignatius's letters to the Philippians who had requested copies. In the Middle Ages at least seventeen letters were attributed to Saint Ignatius. In the nineteenth century there was a prolonged controversy about their authenticity. Today the consensus of scholars, both Catholic and Protestant, is that seven, those to the Ephesians, Magnesians, Trallians, Romans, Philadelphians, Smyrneans, and to Saint Polycarp are genuine. Together they continue to be studied as one of the most valuable literary sources for the history of primitive Christianty.

Sister M.E.

THE APOLOGY OF ARISTIDES

Author: Aristides (died c.125)
Type of work: Apologetics
First transcribed: c.125

Principal Ideas Advanced

Of the four classes of men, Barbarians, Greeks, Jews, and Christians, only the Christians trace their religion to Jesus, the Son of God.

The Barbarians worshiped created things; the Jews approach the truth, for they believe in one God and worship Him, but they do not have the whole truth; the Greeks follow base practices and persecute the Christians.

The Christians alone have found the truth; they follow the Law of God and Christ; they do not worship false gods, they take in strangers, they defend one another, they praise God, and they know Jesus as the Messiah.

The *Apology of Aristides the Philosopher,* although referred to in early histories of the Church as one of the influential works written in defense of Christianity, was lost to scholars from about the fifth century until the late nineteenth century. A group of Armenian monks in Venice published in 1878 a Latin translation (with additions by the enthusiastic translator) of an Armenian version of the first two chapters of the work; eleven years later a Syriac version of the complete *Apology* was found in the Convent of Saint Catharine on Mount Sinai. Even later, much of the original Greek version was made available, indirectly, through an eighth century Christian romance, *The Life of Barlaam and Josaphat,* which apparently incorporates the defense written by Aristides. (Barlaam and Josaphat, fictional characters in a story of Buddhist origin, were regarded in the Middle Ages as saints and were given a feast day.)

The *Apology* was probably written about the year 125, when, it is reported by Eusebius, the work was given to Hadrian. Some scholars argue, however, that the defense was one presented to Antoninus Pius some twenty or thirty years later.

Unlike later apologies, which usually called attention to atrocities committed against the Christians and sought to counter false charges with theological distinctions and examples of Christian heroism, this early apology of Aristides is a fairly straightforward defense based on the practical difference that Christianity has made in the lives of those who embrace it. Basically, the argument is that those who are not Christians are in some way deficient in their worship and practice; Christians, on the other hand, show by their exemplary lives that the truth is known to them through Christ.

Aristides begins his plea in behalf of Christianity with a moving comment on the power of God: "I, O King, by the grace of God came into this world; and when I had considered the heaven and the earth and the sea, and had surveyed the sun and the rest of creation, I marvelled at the beauty of the world. And I perceived that the world and all that is therein are moved by the power of another; and I understood that he who moves them is God. . . ." But Aristides professes himself, like other men, too limited to comprehend the nature of God, and he declares that he will not attempt to engage in theological speculation. Simply but forcefully he says, "I say, however, concerning this mover of the world, that he is God of all, who made all things for the sake of mankind. And it seems to me that this is reasonable, that one should fear God and should not oppress man."

Despite his disclaimer, however, Aristides has something to say about the nature of God. He declares that God is without beginning or end, that He is perfect, without name or form, incapable of anger or indignation, all-knowing, and without any needs.

Aristides then states that he will examine the four classes of men in order to determine which is closest to the truth concerning God. He refers to the Barbarians, who trace their religion to Kronos and Rhea; the Greeks, whose religion springs from Zeus and Helenos; the Jews, who trace their race to Abraham, Isaac, and Jacob; and the Christians, who "trace the beginning of their religion from Jesus the Messiah; and he is named the Son of God Most High."

Reference is made by Aristides to "a Hebrew virgin" who gave birth to the Son of God. Jesus, then, was born of the Hebrews; He had twelve disciples; He died and was buried; on the third day He rose and ascended to Heaven. The twelve disciples then went throughout the known world, teaching of His greatness. The Christians, Aristides explains, are those who follow Him.

Aristides devotes more time to the Barbarians and the Greeks than to the other two classes of men. Undoubtedly he wished to emphasize the tendency of those who worship false gods to go astray as a result.

The Barbarians, according to Aristides, "went astray among the elements, and began to worship things created instead of their Creator. . . ." Aristides, who here shows himself to be a philosopher, argues that the elements could not be gods, for what is true of the earth, for example—that it can be trodden under the foot of man, that it can receive bloodstains and be dug open to receive corpses—cannot be true of God. The waters, also, admit of change and the reception of impurities. In short, the elements are created; they cannot be identified with the Creator. As Aristides says in a passage which prefaces his criticism of the Barbarians, ". . . the wind is obedient to God, and fire to the angels; the waters also to the demons and the earth to the sons of men." How, then, could the elements, themselves subservient, be the Lord Himself?

The Barbarian belief that the sun is a god or that certain men are gods is also in error, Aristides argues.

Aristides describes the Greeks as "more subtle" than the Barbarians, and he concludes that this accounts for the fact that the Greeks have gone further astray. The Greek gods, Aristides claims, have all the weaknesses of men; they have gross moral flaws; they are passionate and vengeful; they kill and are killed. Dionysos, for example, is described as carousing drunkenly and as carrying off women; he is said to have eaten serpents and to have been killed by Titanos. Surely such a drunken and vulnerable creature could not have been a god.

Aristides then makes passing reference to the gods of the Egyptians, and he declares that they are even more base than the Barbarians or the Greeks, for the Egyptians have invented gods from animals.

The Jews appear to come closer to the truth than do the Barbarians, Greeks, or Egyptians, says Aristides, for the Jews worship God Himself and not His creatures. Furthermore, they show compassion and do much that is in accordance with His Law. But the Jews also err, for they spend their days honoring the angels through feasts and rites of various sorts.

Thus, it is the Christians, who follow the Commandments, do good to their neighbors, call all men brethren, do not worship false gods, take in strangers, defend one another when persecuted, give thanks to God for their blessings, and acknowledge Christ as the Son of God, who have found the truth. Not only their loving-kindness and righteousness, inspired by Christ, but also their writings testify to the fact that they alone, of all men, have found the truth and know God.

Aristides concludes by declaring that "verily whatever is spoken in the mouths of Christians is of God; and their doctrine is the gateway of light." The Christians form "a new people, and there is something divine in the midst of them." Those who do not know the truth should listen to the Christians; there is then some hope that those who are now critical of the Christians will survive that Day of Judgment when the words of Jesus will be seen to have been incorruptible from all eternity.

THE SHEPHERD

Author: Hermas (second century)
Type of work: Apocalypse
First transcribed: c.120-c.150

Principal Ideas Advanced

Though everyone is to some degree guilty of sin, the devout as well as the lukewarm, the seriousness of sin may be mitigated by a consideration of the sinner's intention or by his previous commitment to a holy life.

Repentance is a constant Christian requirement, not imposed only upon conversion, and the Church must deal with it as the rule rather than as the exception.

The perfect unity of the Church is a fusion of the wide variety of human gifts, temperaments, and degrees of virtue.

Though visions and allegories form a large portion of *The Shepherd,* the solid core of the work is concerned with practical and ethical problems. Men are considered not as angels, but as creatures of flesh and spirit, varying according to their own unique combination of abilities and virtues. There cannot be one single standard of perfection for all, for the Church was meant to embrace all mankind. Throughout the early history of the Church there was a pronounced division of opinion, with the "exclusivists" on one side and the "universalists" on the other. The impulse toward exclusiveness was marked by a fervent otherworldliness or transcendentalism, and by the idea of an obligation binding on all Christians to lead a life of uncompromising perfection. The other trend, toward universalism, represented the "incarnational" idea with its concern to unite soul and body, spirit and matter, and to incorporate members of widely varying spiritual commitments within the Church. This conflict is reflected in the penitential doctrines preached by Hermas. The first of the work's three parts, the *Visions,* reveals the human need for repentance; the second, the *Commandments,* defines the life proper to the Christian penitent; and the third, the *Parables,* suggests a general theology of repentance.

Hermas's own conviction of personal sin establishes the tone and subject of the work at its inception. It is apparently his state of contrition that is the occasion for the first of his visions, in which he is told that his own purity of intention and previously innocent life lessen his guilt in God's sight. In his vision, Hermas is taught by an old woman who eventually proves to be the Church herself. The universal note is struck by the reference to the old woman's age: ". . . she was created first of all things . . . and for her sake was the world established." She tells him that interior disposition is taken into consideration in the judgment of sin. The implication is clear that sin is so complicated that it cannot be judged and punished by men on the basis of outward appearance alone. The old woman goes so far as to suggest that the sin of which Hermas was accusing himself (impurity) was not in fact his real failure. Instead, he is blamed for practical failures in his daily life, especially for failure to discipline his sinful family.

Hermas is given the commission to call both his family and the leaders of the Church to a new awareness of Christian repentance. Evidently the Church in Hermas's region had become so rigorous as to declare forever anathema all those who sinned seriously after Baptism, regardless of their inner condition. Hermas was to enlighten the Church leaders, telling them that sinners must be given a second opportunity to repent. Beyond this, his intention in writing down his visions was to edify his brethen, so that they who "hear these things may know the Lord in great joy."

Hermas begins by establishing a firm personal testimony to the truth of his communications. His spiritual instruction has been prefaced by a penitential fast and by the heavenly promise that he will ultimately be cleansed from those sins he confesses and sorrows over. When he reveals his inward contrite state, Hermas is shown the vision of the Tower (another symbol for the Church and one which is to reappear throughout the book). The Church, as the woman, speaks to her children warning them that once the Tower is completed, no one will be able to add to his earthly merits; his place within the Tower (as the completed Church) will be settled forever. Practical works of mercy are obviously what the woman has in mind, for she observes that while some members of the Church are ill from overeating, others are dying of starvation. A closer union in charity between all the members of the Church is clearly in order if the health of all is to be maintained. Thus, the other-worldly aspect of the allegorical white Tower is closely associated with life in this world as Christians experience it.

Hermas's own spiritual enlightenment parallels his moral advance, and this dynamic process of purification is personified in the progressively more youthful and fair appearance of the Woman in his visions of her. Despite the evidence of holiness in his life, Hermas is warned against the chief sin that tempts Christians: "double-mindedness." The double-minded man is not pure in his commitment to spiritual things; he tries to please himself and God too. Hermas is shown the Beast, which stands for the persecution awaiting the Church, a persecution from which only the pure will be saved. Those who remain double-minded to the end will be devoured by the Beast. Having been shown the horror from which he has been saved, Hermas is confirmed in a life of repentance.

The outward sign of Hermas's new commitment to perfection is the appearance to him of the Shepherd, the angel of repentance, who will remain with him for the rest of his life. Repentance is thus not a mere episode at the beginning of the Christian life, but a permanent condition of humility and dependence on God for all one's virtues. The angel tells Hermas of ten virtues which he is to pursue with true fidelity, unmarked by double-mindedness: belief in God, simplicity, love of truth, chastity or purity, patience, faith as expressed in good works, fear of God (obedience), temperance, single-mindedness, and conversion of sorrow for sins into amendment of life. In the commandment to seek the amendment of life, the Christian is again reminded of his perpetual vocation of repentance, which is itself "understanding."

Hermas thus proposes a consistent and all-sufficient point of view for the direction of the Christian life. True repentance depends on an accurate and realistic judgment of one's own nature and of God's, and such "understanding" is the entire basis for a proper relationship with God and with the Church.

The relationship between God and the Church is not a static one. There is a constant inward battle in every man in which good and evil seek to overcome each other, and these two forces are externalized in the person of a man's good angel and his bad angel. Hermas, by this time, is so overpowered by his sorrow for his sins that he wonders how God can ever forgive him. The angel declares to him that when the penitent relies upon the mercy of God, the gap between his own meanness and God's holiness is closed. The role of repentance is thus not ultimate in Christian experience, though it has a fundamental place in that experience. A sinner's grief over his faults and failures becomes almost insensibly an act of contrition and a desire for the Holy Spirit. Ultimately, then, therapeutic suffering and sorrow for sin meet the forgiveness of God and are blotted out in a new and divine relationship. Faith is necessary to this happy consummation, however, for the rigorous commands of the angel can be kept only by a man who truly resolves that they can and will be kept. Hermas, who is by no means perfect, expresses some doubt as to whether he can indeed keep the commandments, and the angel, to confirm him in holiness, gives him a sermon in parables which reveals to him clearly the ultimate basis and end of Christian truth.

In the parable of the Vineyard (the created world), the Incarnation establishes the first law in human life: that soul and body are one, and that the sins committed by the body can never be divorced from the condition of the soul. Against all Gnostics and dualists, Hermas says of the Incarnation: "The Holy Spirit which pre-exists, which created all creation, did God make to dwell in the flesh which he willed. Therefore this flesh, in which the Holy Spirit dwelled, served the Spirit well, walking in holiness and purity, and did not in any way defile the spirit." This ideal is held up before man, and in order to attain it, he must discipline the flesh and mortify his spirit, bringing both into a perfect union with each other. Since this union is not accomplished by a simple act of conversion, it must come through a lifetime of perpetual penance and interior growth. Mere form is not enough. Hermas is told that an outward fast is valuable only if accompanied by a penitential spirit within. Virtue and faith must thus be united in the Christian life, and repentance is the link between them.

Despite the universalist tone of clemency heard throughout *The Shepherd,* the parables section reveals a sternness and rigor toward sin that reflects the uncompromisingly pure attitude of the new faith. Hermas is shown a great plain where the Shepherd of Punishment is afflicting those who were previously under the sway of the Shepherd of Luxury. He finds it hard to believe that they are being punished so harshly although they have repented. The angel asks: "Do you then think that the sins of those who repent are immediately forgiven? By no means; but he who repents must torture his own soul, and be humble in all his deeds and be afflicted with many divers afflictions." These sufferings are intended to purify the soul, and all men experience them in some degree. The parable of the sticks which are in various stages of greenness or barrenness reinforces Hermas's conviction about the need for pardoning the weak; such pardon is not unjust, for, as the angel revealed, one always suffers the penalty naturally attached to one's sin, whether one is pardoned or not. The parables all tend to emphasize the variety of spiritual gifts among men, and the need for unity despite such differences. Those who are responsible for division in the perfect unity that should exist in the Church (perhaps those insistent on too unrealistic a degree of virtue for everyone) are to be severely punished: "If any of them turn again to schism he shall be cast out from the tower, and shall lose his life . . . among the schismatic and law-breakers there is death." Hermas continually stresses the unity of the Church, not as the unity of a single type or temperament, but as a diversity made one by grace, and symbolized by the white Tower, with its many stones but apparently seamless exterior.

In his final vision of the Tower, Hermas sees a great white rock in the plain, large enough to contain the world. Later he learns that the rock is Christ Himself, under the aspect of the pre-existent and eternal, while the door in the Tower which is being erected on the white rock is also Christ, under the aspect of his appearance in time, the Incarnation. From the twelve mountains, utterly different in character and appearance (just as mankind varies from place to place), a multitude gathers stones for the Tower. Though they are of different colors to begin with, all the rocks (except a few impure ones) become a uniform white and blend with the rest of the building: "For this reason you see that the tower has become one solid stone with the rock. So also those who believe on the Lord through his Son, and put on these spirits [Christian virtues] will become 'one spirit and one body.'" At this point, the Lord becomes identified with the Church in a mystical union, just as the Church itself is gathered from the ranks of every sort of man, including within itself the simple, the innocent, and the learned.

B.J.R.

THE EPISTLES OF SAINT POLYCARP and THE MARTYRDOM OF SAINT POLYCARP

Author: Saint Polycarp (died 156); Marcion (fl. 155)
Type of work: Dogmatic theology
First transcribed: Epistles, probably before 135; *Martyrdom,* c.155

Principal Ideas Advanced

The Christian's faith is in Jesus Christ, true God and true Man, whose life, death, and resurrection are historical facts.

Faith in Christ is manifest by a life in accord with His teachings, and the ultimate proof of living faith is seen in the martyrs who die for the sake of Christ.

Christians adore Christ as God; they venerate martyrs as heroes and exemplars of the Christian life.

The *Epistles of Saint Polycarp* and the *Martyrdom of Saint Polycarp,* a letter reporting an eyewitness account of Polycarp's martyrdom, are representative of the early effort to use literary works to advance Christianity. Christian communities in urban centers of Asia Minor corresponded with each other for mutual encouragement and in order to unite their efforts against the prevalent doctrinal errors and moral dangers of the day.

The occasion of the first epistle of Saint Polycarp, bishop of Smyrna, was a request from the Christians of Philippi, a commercial center on the southern coast of Macedonia. The Philippians asked Polycarp to send them the *Letters of Saint Ignatius of Antioch* (died c. 110). These were the letters which Ignatius had written while being taken to Rome as a captive destined for martyrdom. In complying with the Philippians' request, Saint Polycarp added a covering letter of his own.

This letter, which is a fragment of only six sentences, praises the epistles of Saint Ignatius as sources of great spiritual profit, "for they deal with faith, patient endurance, and, in general, with matters that bear upon spiritual growth in Our Lord." Saint Polycarp requests a reply about his fellow bishop, indicating that this letter was written before Saint Ignatius's martyrdom, or at least before news of it had reached Smyrna. Such concern shows the bond of sympathy that existed between the early Christian communities.

A second letter was written sometime later, again in reply to a request from the Philippian Church, this time for advice and encouragement at a time of crisis. The Docetist heresy was rampant in Macedonia. Docetist teaching denied the reality of the Incarnation of Christ and the redemptive value of His passion and death. To offset Docetist influence, Saint Polycarp's epistle stated clearly the traditional teaching of the Church about Christ, and it exhorted the Philippians to keep the true faith.

This second epistle shows that the Philippian Church enjoyed a reputation for fervor and orthodoxy, qualities which were expected of the first European church, founded by Saint Paul. Saint Polycarp congratulates the Philippians on their "firmly rooted faith." He insists on the historic reality of the Christian mystery and tells his readers that anyone who departs from the traditional faith of the apostles is "anti-Christ" and "the firstborn of Satan." The Philippians are reminded that their faith is in Jesus Christ who died for their sins and who conquered death by rising again: "You never saw Him, and yet believe in Him with sublime and inexpressible joy—a joy which many desire to experience." Saint Polycarp is writing to men only a generation removed from those who remembered the Apostles, and he shows his understanding that their faith is being put to a severe test. Faith in Christ, he tells them, is a free gift which in turn calls for a generous response from those who have received it.

This response consists in doing God's will, by making His commandments the rule of life, and loving what He loves. Specifically, the Christian worthy of the name must not give way to revenge when injured and must shun avarice, slander, false testimony, and love of money. Love of money is cited as the beginning of all evils.

The particular duties of certain classes within the Church are mentioned. Husbands and wives are exhorted to fidelity and reminded to educate their children in the fear of God; widows have a special obligation to pray for the Christian community; deacons must remember that "they are God's and Christ's servants, and not men's." The directives for presbyters show the high ideal proposed for the clergy in the second century. The presbyter must be kindhearted and merciful toward all, "trying to reclaim what has gone astray, visiting any that are sick, not neglecting widow, orphan, or the poor."

The Christian life is more than an external imitation of Christ; it is a participation in His life, which is continued in His Church. "For our sakes," Polycarp reminds the Philippians, "that we might live in Him—He endured everything." The Philippians should find courage in the realization that they glorify Him whenever they suffer for the sake of His name.

The epistle concludes with an exquisite summary of Saint Polycarp's entire theology: "May God and the Father of Our Lord Jesus Christ, and the eternal High Priest Himself, the Son of God, Jesus Christ, further your growth in faith and truth and in meekness that is perfect and without a vestige of resentment, as well as in patient endurance and long-suffering and perseverance and purity. May He also grant perfect fellowship with His saints to you . . . and indeed to all who are under heaven and destined to believe in Our Lord Jesus Christ and His Father, who has raised Him from the dead."

The *Martyrdom of Saint Polycarp* inaugurates a new genre of Christian literature, the acts of the martyrs, which were accounts written to inspire other Christians and to keep vivid the high ideal of the Christian life. Later accounts of the martyrs were not often written in letter form, as was the *Martyrdom of Saint Polycarp,* but their purpose and treatment were basically the same.

Saint Polycarp was an old man at the time he met his death in a Roman persecution, and he was widely known and revered by his fellow Christians of Asia Minor. At the request of the Church at Philomelium, a certain Marcion, of whom nothing is known except his name, wrote an account of Saint Polycarp's capture and subsequent death. The account is remarkably free of the legendary material so characteristic of stories written later, in the Middle Ages, about Christian heroes. In contrast to medieval writings, the *Martyrdom of Saint Polycarp* seems surprisingly modern in its eyewitness approach.

The author presents martyrdom as a glorious victory over the forces of evil, both human and diabolic, showing that through suffering and death Polycarp proved his discipleship and shared in the passion and death of Christ, as he will share in His resurrection. The martyr is depicted as a conquering hero, his victory made possible by Christ, whose invisible presence strengthened the sufferer during his torments.

Written in a vivid narrative style, the account of the martyrdom has the suspense of drama. Marcion tells how Polycarp was taken when his hiding place was betrayed by a slave under torture. On trial before a Roman magistrate, the aged bishop refused to perform the pagan ritual of swearing by the Roman goddess Fortuna. To do so would have been tantamount to denying Christ. Urged to conform, he replied in words revealing the quality of his personal devotion to Christ: "For six and eighty years I have been serving Him, and He has done no wrong to me; how, then, dare I blaspheme my King who has saved me!"

In relating the struggle to obtain Saint Polycarp's remains after his death, the author states clearly the ancient Christian attitude towards the veneration of the saints. Again, it is instructive to compare the clear concept with the superstitious attitude that had to be battled in a later barbarian age. The author of the *Martyrdom* explains, "Him [Christ] we worship as being the Son of God, the martyrs we love as being disciples and imitators of the Lord; and deservedly so, because of their unsurpassable devotion to their King and Teacher. May it be our good fortune, too, to be their companions and fellow disciples."

To keep alive the memory of the martyrs, the Christians enshrined their remains in places of honor where they gathered to celebrate the Eucharist, the central act of Christian worship. The *Martyrdom* breathes the spirit of exultation shared by the Christians who celebrated the martyr's anniversary as his "natalis" or birthday, and it is an important primitive witness to the Christian idea of death as a birth, an entrance to eternal life, rather than an exit from temporal existence.

Students of primitive Christianity find the *Martyrdom of Saint Polycarp* a valuable source of information about the Christian attitudes toward death, suffering, and the demands of the Christian way of life. The work also shows forms of prayer used in the early Church. Polycarp is described as praying for "all that had met him at any time—both small and great, both known and unknown to fame, and the whole world-wide Catholic Church." This is one of the earliest recorded uses of the term "Catholic Church."

The *Martyrdom of Saint Polycarp* enables the modern reader to see the Church's adjustment to a hostile environment. The picture is that of a body of believers unaccepted by society, but joyful in the victory of Christ over suffering, sin, and death, a victory which is shared by the Christian par excellence, the martyr who attains perfect discipleship by the sacrifice of his life. The acts of the martyrs, of which this work is the prototype, go far to explain why it became a commonplace that the blood of Christians is the seed of the Church, and why eventually Rome had to come to terms with the new religion from the East which only grew stronger when its members were destroyed.

Sister M.E.

THE FIRST APOLOGY and THE SECOND APOLOGY

Author: Saint Justin Martyr (c.110-c.165)
Type of work: Apologetics
First transcribed: c.150-c.161

Principal Ideas Advanced

Christians are unjustly persecuted for the Name; any accusations of atheism against them are equally undeserved.

In reality, Christianity is a rational dispensation, some of whose doctrines, such as that of the Logos, have been anticipated even by pagans.

The reform of morality which attends converts, and the simplicity of Christian rites attest Christianity's harmlessness and wholesomeness.

Disillusionment with pagan philosophy, disgust with anti-Christian slander, and admiration for the Christian contempt of death led Justin of Flavia Neapolis in Palestine to become a convert about 130. He spent much of his later life in Rome writing and conducting a Christian school and was martyred in the capital under Marcus Aurelius.

Saint Justin is best remembered for his two apologies, the products of an enlightened and earnest Christian anxious to neutralize as much as possible the emotional animosity and intellectual criticism which Christianity had already aroused against itself in the classical world. As a matter of fact, what are preserved in manuscript as two apologies are probably but one, since the Second, a short treatise of only fifteen chapters, is best considered an appendix to the First, a longer work of sixty-eight headings. The first is addressed to Antonius Pius (138-161), his son Marcus Aurelius, the Roman senate, and the Roman people; the second to Romans in general. However, it is very unlikely that Justin's plea ever came into the emperor's hands.

Unfortunately, Justin's compositions leave something to be desired. Besides being repetitious, disorganized, and wandering, they move on assumptions more credible to his age than to ours. Yet *The First Apology* and *The Second Apology,* as the only such Greek works to survive in full, are unparalleled in early Christian literature. They represent the first sustained record of the doctrines, liturgy, experiences, and attitudes of infant Christianity, and they were first in forging the arguments which characterized apologetic literature for centuries. But more important, Justin's apologies virtually initiated the process of synthesizing Christianity and Hellenism, and the fact that he continued to wear the pallium, or philosopher's cloak, betrayed his full consciousness of purpose. Disappointed by his progressive career as a Stoic, Peripatetic, and a Pythagorean, yet charmed by Platonism, Justin was eminently fitted to give this synthesis an intelligent perspective, one it was destined to wear until the movement culminated in the thirteen century with Saint Thomas Aquinas. Highly important is the fact that Justin's synthesis emphasized a Christianization of Hellenism rather than the reverse.

If a logical division of the *First Apology* can be made, it might be the following: Chapters 1-3, the introduction; Chapters 4-12, an attack on the official Roman attitude which punished Christians for the Name; Chapters 13-67, an endeavor to defend the Christian position by describing its beliefs and practices.

The first major art of the work begins with the observation that an indictment of Christians for atheism is equally as indefensible as their punishment for the Name. Pagan philosophers, observes Justin, taught atheism with impunity, and the Romans themselves, without penalty, ignored different gods in different localities. Far from being atheists, he insisted, Christians worshiped the true God of ineffable excellence; due regard for His just promise of reward and punishment makes them peaceful and useful citizens. But Justin's most unique and telling argument is his identification of the pagan gods with demons, creatures of the pagans' own making, which he identifies as illegitimate sons of transgressing angels.

The bulk of the *First Apology* attempts to justify Christian doctrine and practices as both reasonable and wholesome.

The emperor should know, in the first place, that the teachings and experiences of Jesus, as well as the activities of the Spirit, were all vouched for by the prophetic writings of such venerable seers as Moses, David, Isaiah, Ezekiel, Daniel, and Zacharias. These were records of unimpeachable historicity preserved in the pristine text of the Septuagint. The truth of these prophesies (though some of them, such as those of the Second Coming and the final Resurrection and Judgment, were yet to be fulfilled) was compelling in the face of the obvious and dramatic fall of Jerusalem. Moreover, much of pagan belief derived from them as is evidenced by the fact that pagan authors, such as Plato, had plagiarized from the prophets, chiefly from Moses, whose utterances were clearly more ancient than theirs. Whatever poets and philosophers knew in general about spiritual things came from the sacred Jewish writings. Thus, Plato recorded that God produced the world from shapeless matter; the Stoics predicted a destruction of the world by fire; and Menander insisted that idol worship was irrational. Much of this plagiarism, says Justin, had been, indeed, unintentionally contrived, as it were, by demons. These crafty creatures had learned surreptitiously from the prophets, but in a garbled fashion, about future divine dispensations. They had prematurely released these dispensations in order to confound God's plans. Thus, events later associated with Christ would appear as trifles stolen from pagan mythology. Since the demons had misunderstood, for example, the prophecy that it was the Christ who was to come, they had garbled it by substituting stories of Jupiter's sons. They had misrepresented many prophesies by applying them to Bacchus; Christ's riding upon an ass was presented as Bellerophon's ascent to Heaven on Pegasus; the Virgin Birth was associated with the birth of Perseus, and Christ's miraculous healings with the work of Aesculapius. The Cross, however, had escaped mishandling since it had been successfully disguised in such far-fetched symbols as sails, tools, and even the human form with arms outstretched. Only Plato had been permitted a prevision of the Cross, but his references to it in the *Timaeus* were hopelessly confused. In imitation of the waters of Baptism the demons had concocted misleading libations and ablutions, to confound the Eucharist they had introduced the Cup into the liturgy of Mithraism. These pagan similarities, however, even as misdirected prefigures of Christian truth, should cause pagans to consider Christian claims as reasonable.

Even though final and complete truth could be known only through the revelation of the prophets and the "memoirs of the apostles," Saint Justin insisted that Christianity was basically a religion of reason. Many of the Greek-Christian religious similarities were envisaged by pagans of virtuous life and represented, therefore, not the twisted revelations of demons but the promptings of a divine impulse. All races of men, concedes Justin, partook of the merits of the Word, of the Spermatikos Logos, of divine Reason. Men who lived long before the advent of Christ, philosophers such as Socrates, Heraclitus, and Musonius, were as much Christians in principle as were Abraham and Elias. The demons worked at cross purposes with men of such noble stamp.

Justin's enlightened proposition that

all peoples had some element of truth in their traditions, especially the Greeks who spoke so well in proportion as the Spermatic Word moved them, became probably the most ingenious and potent argument ever devised to bridge the gap between Christianity and Hellenism. It set in motion the entire intellectual synthesis which became "the West."

One of Justin's most profound contributions to Christian thought resulted from his pioneer efforts to Christianize further the pagan philosophic concept of the Logos. Heraclitus's Logos, as a permanent principle of order in the world, had been developed by late Stoics into God, the universal Mind, of which man had a part or sperm. Neoplatonists continued this identification of God with the Logos: as Reason, He was the center of all Platonic Ideas; as the Word, He was the instrument of Creation. This divine Word or Reason, Justin identified with the Incarnate Christ. An ideal approach, Saint Justin's account interpreted Christ to Greeks in terms of divine emanation, while it forestalled Jewish tendencies to see in Christ a compromise with polytheism.

The reasonableness of Christianity, Justin implies, should likewise be apparent from its devotion to the free will, a tenet quite amenable to Greek humanism. Men were not, argues Justin, as trees or animals, victims of fate experiencing no merit or blame. The prophesies, by foretelling events, did not force the events by foreordination. Men still remained responsible before God.

Besides being a rational arrangement, Christianity to Justin was a lofty, wholesome dispensation which validated its claims by its positive impact upon ethics. Conversion brought in its train a complete substitution of virtues for vices. The demons had deliberately blurred the truth by making Christ and His followers appear as magicians or trouble-makers by conjuring up men like Simon Magus or Marcion. These same demons misled the Romans unjustly to accuse and to persecute Christians, the very men by whom and for whom the world was being preserved.

Justin hoped that an exposé of Christian rites, the first on record, would vouch for the new religion's purity and sobriety. Not bloody orgies, but prayer, fasting, and repentance identified the Baptismal initiate sealed in the name of the Trinity. Introduced to the assembly, the neophyte learned only to pray in common, to receive the kiss of peace, and to partake of the Eucharist, a salubrious rite celebrated by the presiding officer in obedience to Jesus' injunction to commemorate Him by saying: "This is My Body; This is My Blood." The Eucharistic elements were unique, "for we have been taught that the food which is blessed by the prayer of His word . . . is the flesh and blood of that Jesus who was made flesh." Deacons carried reserved portions to those unable to attend. On Sundays the assembly gathered peacefully to read the Scriptures, hear homilies, pray, and partake of the same Eucharist. A modest collection served only to succor the orphan, the widow, the sick, and the captive.

The *First Apology* concludes that Christians did not deserve death, and it warns Romans to fear lest their injustice invite divine retribution. In a postscript the Romans were reminded of the enlightened regulations concerning Christians which Hadrian had issued in about the year 125 to Fundanus, his proconsul of Asia, in which he had ordered that only regular court procedure be employed in dealing with Christians, that they be punished only for an offense against the law, and that calumniators and informers be dealt with severely.

Spurred on by a special incident, Saint Justin, in his *Second Apology*, complained that Urbicus, the prefect of Rome, was highhandedly condemning Christians for the Name. It further indicted Crescens, a Cynic philosopher, for his calumnies. Justin felt it necessary in the *Apology* to reply negatively to pagan taunts that Christians ought to commit suicide if they wished to anticipate death; he boasts that persecution permitted Christians to demonstrate the superiority of their beliefs.

Justin's orthodoxy has been questioned in part. Since his ineffable God could communicate with the world only through His Logos, Jesus is correctly pictured as "Son of God" or "God" long before His Incarnation; the theophanies in the Old Testament were of Him. He became, however, an independent emanation only shortly before Creation and expressly for the purpose of bringing the world into existence. Thus, Justin is a subordinationist. In addition, Justin's pagan background made it difficult for him to envisage Creation as "ex nihilo." About the Holy Spirit he is vague despite his tripart formula for Baptism.

E.G.W.

THE DISCOURSE AGAINST THE GREEKS

Author: Tatian (c.110-c.172)
Type of work: Apologetics
First transcribed: Latter half of the second century

Principal Ideas Advanced

The Greek view of life, fashioned by its philosophy, religion, and arts and sciences, is trivial, arrogant, and immoral.

The Greek view, as well as evil itself, was effected by man, whose free will has been misled and warped by demons.

In contrast to the Greek, the barbaric teachings of Moses, who is older than Homer, are unpretentious, sane, and profound, worthy of the most serious Greek consideration.

Tatian seems to be as interesting personally as he is provocative literarily. An Assyrian, initiate of the mysteries, student of Greek philosophy, disciple of Justin in Rome, Tatian eventually terminated his Christian career in Antioch sometime after 172 as founder of the Encratites, an heretical Gnostic puritanical sect. He is known to have composed at least six works other than the *Discourse,* only one of which, the controversial *Diatessaron,* is extant.

The *Discourse Against the Greeks* is generally considered to be an apology, although its brevity, forty-two chapters, and other features encourage a few critics to label it as a speech. At any rate, as a biting diatribe against Greek culture, it stands almost unique in early Christian literature. Unlike his master, Justin, and other Christian writers in general, who encouraged the synthesis of Classicism and Christianity, Tatian considered the Greek way an aberration, an enormity, as silly and demoralizing as it was sinful. Entirely borrowed and plagiarized from other peoples, Greek culture was an inconsistent, arrogant, and absurd culture, appropriately supported, Tatian averred, by philosophers stupid enough to plaster themselves fatally with cow dung as a medicinal remedy or to fall into pits while studying the heavens. Tatian would, therefore, go further in his rejection of ancient learning than Tertullian, who was largely content to ask what Athens had to do with Jerusalem.

After a somewhat sarcastic introduction, Tatian proceeds in Chapters 4-7 to sketch the highlights of Christian cosmology. God, as eternal and self-sufficient Spirit, created the universe through His Logos. Just as the utterance of words did not detract from the wholeness of a speaker, so the emanation of the Logos from the Father did not lessen His Godhead. Man, created immortal, was endowed, as were angels, with free will subject to no foreknowledge of God or Fate. In choosing to follow fatuous deifications, however, man began to worship charlatans, planets, animals, and even secular ambition. Even so, from God's original perfect and good creation some vestiges of justice yet remain; the same pain and travail afflict the rich and poor, and the same length of life constrains them. Man was induced to forfeit his original ideal heritage through misuse of his free will by a host of demons who taught him not only how to manufacture wickedness but to invent Fate as an explanation for his fallen plight. Now promised resurrection in his lapsed state, man has to repent if he is to pass final judgment and enjoy immortality.

The second section of the *Discourse,* Chapters 8-20, deals largely with demonology. Throughout the material world, explains Tatian, a spiritual hierarchy of souls exists, based on the degrees of nobility animating different things. Baser objects have only a material soul; man as a distiguished and more beautiful creature incorporates, in addition to his soul, an image of God. The demons, as base creatures, naturally possess only a gross, material enlivening principle. Driven from their original heavenly abode, these maleficent beings, as not fleshy but airy and fire-like, can be sensed only by truly spiritual persons. The demons enter into a man's very sinews to cause sickness and work their evil designs, and they manifest their presence within the possessed through dreams. Emotionally disturbed, revengeful, and hateful persons easily enter into alliance with them.

Authors of much Greek science, the demons contrived the vaunted and erroneous field of medicine by leading men to believe that, rather than having recourse to God for health, men could in an arrogant way cure themselves, just as dogs eat grass to purge themselves. The demons also invented astrology, so highly prized by the Greeks.

As deceivers who cause man to abuse his free will, the demons can be defeated by man only when, striving for union with God, he causes his soul to enter into union with the Divine Spirit. Thus, realigning himself with his divine companion, man foils the demons who first led him to forsake the Spirit and thus to reduce himself to the status of a being distinguishable from animals only by speech. The Spirit serves as wings to the soul; when it is cast off, the soul falls to earth as a nestling from its perch. With the Spirit united to the soul, however, man soars in spiritual realms, pursuing the image of God and seeking out a superior world beyond the material heavens. Assured of resurrection and immortality, man triumphs over the demons, for the demons are unable to repent.

The indictment of the Greek way, which begins with Tatian's attribution of Greek medicine and astrology to demonic origins, goes on apace in Chapters 21-30 of the *Discourse*.

The Christian apologist first castigates philosophy as the product of a warped, confused, and deceitful clique. All philosophers: Aristippus, Diogenes, Plato, Aristotle with his presumptuous humanism, Heraclitus, Empedocles, and Zeno with his silly cycles, teach absurdities. They do little else than live abominable lives of vice, grow affected beards and long hair, sport an uncovered shoulder, nurse a fat wallet, and enjoy a bevy of servants while quarreling with one another and mouthing their plagiarized ideas. Tatian indicts Crescens, for example, for supposedly professing to be indifferent in regard to death while apparently, at the same time, considering it to be a great evil: has not Crescens inconsistently wished to inflict death both on Justin and Tatian himself as a punishment?

Greek religion, according to Tatian, is a complete farce and monstrosity. The Greek gods are so ridiculous, anthropomorphic, lewd, and fickle that any comparison of them with the true God is disgusting. By assigning their deities beginnings, the Greeks admit that the gods are mortal. Is not the immortal Olympian Zeus himself buried in Crete? The debased art of sculpture administers to the gods' tawdriness by appropriately commemorating them as prostitutes, courtesans, fratricides, and hermaphrodites. What sane man feels a need to worship a wandering star or a stupid swan? Equally ridiculous are the solemnities of the festivals with their silly gesticulating and indecent mimicry.

Greek sports, Tatian continues, glorify detestable boxers and impious gladiators; the raving Euripides contributes his share to the degradation of the theater. Ever busy with words but lax in deeds, the rhetoricians, Tatian declares, encourage the whole dubious art of idle talk and pedantically exhibit their inane and pseudo-sophisticated addiction to this or that dialect.

The *Discourse* shows no reverence even for secular law. The inconsistencies within Greek law, says Tatian, have contributed to the bankruptcy of the Greek way. Instead of encouraging a universal polity, the law adjusts itself to the diversified fancies of each individual state, so that in one place incest with one's mother is disgraceful and unlawful, while in another, it is honorable and highly esteemed.

To what avail, asks Tatian, is all this trivia: the Attic style, the foolish stories of Herodotus, the battles of philosophers with their syllogisms, the pronouncements of scientists with their earth measurements and astral calculations, in short, the whole nonsensical corpus of Greek thought?

In contrast, the last part of the *Discourse,* Chapters 31-41, praises the sanity, venerableness, and moral respectability of the "barbaric" Christian dispensation. Greeks, willing to listen to Chaldean soothsayers and even prophetic trees, would do well to hearken to the Christians and their wisdom rather than to punish them for their name.

In Chapter 35 Tatian relates the manner of his conversion. Learned in rhetoric, widely traveled, and alive to the arts, he learned the shabbiness of Greek culture at first hand. As a devotee of the mysteries he felt only disillusionment upon seeing the rites performed by the effeminate and the pathological. Searching for truth he encountered "barbaric" writings which he readily sensed were too ancient and sacred to be Greek. The unpretentious language, the profundity of the precepts, and the sanity of monotheism led him to follow Moses. Finally, his experience with Justin in Rome brought him to Christianity.

The Greeks, Tatian suggests, would do well not to ridicule and despise this barbaric treasure of wisdom. It is more ancient than the learning of the Greeks and older than the very invention of writing among them. To demonstrate his contention Tatian compares the sages representative of the two ways: Moses and Homer. The former he finds far more ancient. Calculation of authorities placed Homer from eighty to five hundred years after the Trojan War. Even if it were granted for the sake of argument that the Greek poet was contemporary with Agamemnon, records from the Phoenicians, Chaldeans, and Egyptians readily demonstrate that the Jewish seer is still more ancient. The Egyptians, in declaring Moses to have lived four-hundred years earlier than the fall of Troy, made him older than all the Greek heroes. Were not all Greek sages and events dated by Olympiads which started 407 years *after* the Trojan defeat?

Thus, Tatian announces, he was introduced to sanity, to the Christian fold, where all human opinion is rejected and where instruction awaits all, even the weak and ugly. Women too are welcome, women who glory in their estrangement from their pagan acquaintances who tend so readily to emulate the lewd and love-sick Sappho.

In the final chapter, Tatian professes himself, who was once a follower of the heathen way and is now a disciple of the "barbarian philosophy," to be ready for any examination of his doctrines, for he has been strengthened by the conviction that he is now firmly established in the mode of life which most pleases God.

E.G.W.

A PLEA FOR THE CHRISTIANS

Author: Athenagoras (Second century)
Type of work: Apologetics
First transcribed: c.177

Principal Ideas Advanced

Persecution meted out solely for the name "Christian" is incompatible with the enlightment which generally characterizes the government of Marcus Aurelius.

The Christians are innocent of the charges of atheism, sexual crimes, and cannibalism made against them by slanderers and the misinformed.

As loyal citizens, Christians should be allowed the same rights as other philosophical dissidents to live an unmolested life.

Athenagoras, a converted Athenian philosopher, is probably the most eloquent of second century apologists. He addressed *A Plea for the Christians* jointly to the emperor Marcus Aurelius and his son Lucius Aurelius Commodus. Since the imperial title was accorded the latter in 176, the work was probably written in 177.

The purpose of the composition is sharply pointed up in the introduction and the conclusion. The author wished to convince the great Stoic philosopher-prince that Christians were harassed unjustly, especially since they were virtuous and loyal subjects devoted to the emperor's house and prayerful for its prosperity. Athenagoras hoped his plea would cause the pious emperor to reciprocate this good feeling by allowing Christians to enjoy a peaceful, quiet life and the untrammeled practice of their religion.

The tone of the apology is respectful learned, and thoughtful. The emperors are addressed as enlightened, well-informed, and open-minded rulers. In a restrained way, the apology assumes that any injustice they perpetrated was due to misinformation rather than to perversity. As a learned man, Athenagoras sprinkles his treatise with facile excerpts from poets, specific references to historians, and honored tenets of philosophers. Thus Homer, Hesiod, Orpheus, Herodotus, Plato, Aristotle, the three tragedians, the Sibylline oracles, Callimachus, Hermes Trismegistus, and Apollodorus are all marshalled to support the truth of his allegations. Aware that he is addressing pagans, Athenagoras appropriately cites Scriptural passages only rarely. The organization of the apology is tighter and more orderly than that of most early Christian writings. It readily divides into three sections: the introduction and statement of purpose (Chapters 1-3); the body of the composition (Chapters 4-36) refuting principally three accusations against Christians; and the conclusion (Chapter 37) reminding the emperor again of the purpose of the plea.

The opening chapters express regret that the Antonine age of enlightenment which so happily promoted equal rights, urban autonomy, and universal peace, should permit subjects kindly disposed to the government to be harassed simply because they were Christians. Prejudiced by false information, they suffered trials offensive to all law and reason since they were indicted for a name alone rather than for a specific crime. The most cursory investigation, Athenagoras promised, would absolve Christians of the three crimes most generally imputed to them: atheism, sexual enormities, and cannibalism.

According to Athenagoras, belief in one God did not constitute atheism. Had not philosophers, such as Plato and Pythagoras, and poets, such as Euripides, spoken of monotheism with impunity? Did not the Stoics teach that God was a single spirit, a seminal force or generative fire, diffused through matter? Certainly Christians, believing in a triune God, who created all things through His Logos and maintained them through His Spirit, should be no less reasonably treated than these respected pagan thinkers.

Athenagoras charged that, while monotheism was revealed by prophets inspired by the Spirit, polytheism was concocted by men indulging in fantasy. Apply reason to the latter and its absurdity would become obvious. Since all uncreated things were indivisible and homogeneous, the multiplicity of the classical gods clearly evinced their created character. By contrast, the Christian God, as uncreated, was not a compound of parts but an invisible and eternal unity, intelligible to reason alone. Unlike the progeny of pagan gods, the Son was eternal, the Logos of the Father, the generative force of all things. In the same dignified manner, the Holy Spirit, Inspirer of prophets, flowed out, as it were, from the Godhead. The Christians were so well informed about the simultaneous unity and distinction of Persons in their triune God that only those with an ill will could accuse them of atheism.

Along with reason and knowledge, the elevated ethical teachings of Christians gave evidence of their piety toward God. All the learned prattling of logicians, grammarians, geometricians, and Sophistic rhetoricians had been unsuccessful in teaching men even to love their neighbors. The Christian message, successful despite the fact that it was promulgated by the uneducated, gave ample and concrete proof of faith in God through honorable deeds. What availed such an ethic of charity and love to an atheist?

Refusal to offer sacrifice, Athenagoras cautioned his readers, was not necessarily a hallmark of atheism, for the true God, as perfect fragrance Himself, required neither flowers nor incense. His resplendent creation, the vaulted heavens and the restless sea, offered Him all the glory He required. Nor should one be called an atheist simply because he rejected the gods of a local city. Since each city disagreed with the others over its divinities, Christian aloofness to any provincial deity was not a unique position. Nor could contempt for images and idols logically indict one for irreligion. The Christian had merely learnt correctly to distinguish matter from God, the product from its Artificer. If the magnificent universe could not be worshiped because it was mere matter subject to dissolution, then man-made products of earth, stone, and brass could not be accepted as divine. Images, like the names of the gods themselves, were of recent origin. Indeed, within historical times Homer and Hesiod had devised divine nomenclature, but the gods themselves apparently did not become bona-fide divinities until painting and sculpture were invented to enshrine them. Since names of such artists as Praxiteles and Phidias were of yesterday, the gods, like their creations, were still more recent.

Should one retort that the gods were independent beings existing apart from the images made only to honor them, he should be reminded that the pagan pantheon came into being in the process of time through Oceanus and his subsequent progenies. Greek philosophy, however, clearly taught that God must be eternal, uncreated, and imperishable. Plato had correctly stated that while the sensible was originated, only the intelligible was unoriginated. Deriving from tangible and temporal water, the gods obviously arose from matter, matter which was younger than its true Creator because the efficient Cause was prior to the product. One might assume with the Stoics, Athenagoras conceded, that the spirit of God pervaded matter as an independent force, sufficiently detached as to survive the periodic conflagrations, and that this spirit was called by different divine names depending upon its varied manifestations. But even a god of this kind was fatally allied with matter and its corruptible implications. If Kronos was associated with Time by his worshipers, he was patently considered changeable.

If idols seemed to perform miraculous deeds, forces other than divine were in operation. That other powers in fact did exist was attested by ancient philosophy and Christian thought alike. Such were the demons who had cohabitated with virgins to spawn giants. They habitually conspired to produce, in the normally rationally operating universe, enough of the disorderly and unusual to cause some thinkers to postulate a haphazard and unjust natural dispensation. It was they who acted under the name of the gods associated with images, hoping to revel thereby in sacrifical odors and the blood of victims. They, in the name of idols, gave out oracles and distorted the minds of worshipers by impressing upon them hallucinations which eclipsed the rational.

The gods as such not only violated rational tenets of Greek philosophy but offended as well a human sense of dignity. Often portrayed as brutes with impure and ridiculous loves and procreations, and with emotions of anger, grief, and pain, they were, thought Athenagoras, more akin to products of matter than to powers of divinity. Sometimes they were actually portrayed as hired servants of men.

Athenagoras concluded, as did Euhemerus earlier, that the gods were merely heroic men. He called upon the ancient authorities themselves, Herodotus, Egyptian priests, Apollodorus, Homer, Pindar, and Euripides, to corroborate his position. Hercules, he contended, became celebrated for his strength; Asclepius for his art. Other gods, such as the recent Antinous, were created by rulers. Fear, conservatism, and an uncritical attitude did the rest to fasten such deceptions upon history.

Having thus dealt with the charge of atheism, Athenagoras turned to the accusation that Christians were guilty of sexual abuses. After baldly stating that Christians enjoyed no impious revels, he reminded his critics that slander always pursued the worthy. Had not Pythagoras and Socrates been executed, Heraclitus and Democritus banished? Did not the adulterer himself, the homosexual, the pederast, and the white slaver generally impute similar crimes to others? Assuredly, if one indicted Christians for incest and adultery, he must necessarily include the gods as well. As the matter stood, however, Christians were guiltless. Restrained by fear of eternal retribution on the part of an omniscient God, and inspired by the same respect for others as they entertained toward themselves, Christians frowned upon even a lustful glance or a prolonged kiss. They indulged their sexual appetite only when it was necessary to produce children, and they avoided second marriages as a specious form of adultery.

Christians could never be cannibals. Unable to watch even executions for capital crimes, and intolerant of gladiatorial spectacles, they could under no circumstances kill. One, who out of respect for the rights of the fetus could not permit abortion, one who could not expose children, could scarcely devour them. Who, believing in the Resurrection could make his own body the tomb of another person destined to arise with him?

Chapter 37 brings the work to a close with the hope that the emperor, convinced of the libels against Christians, will permit them to live a peaceful, obedient, and prayerful existence.

E.G.W.

ON THE RESURRECTION OF THE DEAD

Author: Athenagoras (Second century)
Type of work: Eschatology
First transcribed: c.180

Principal Ideas Advanced

Resurrection of the dead is amenable to the nature of God as both possible to Him and agreeable to His will.

Because man has both body and soul, logic and equity make resurrection of the body practically mandatory upon God.

Thus, God's creative design and His teleological planning are both served by His judgment over man as a dual unit.

Since Athenagoras in *A Plea for the Christians* promised to write an essay *On the Resurrection of the Dead,* this latter work probably was composed shortly after 177, the probable date for the earlier treatise.

A short tract of twenty-five chapters, *On the Resurrection of the Dead* is a tightly logical, philosophical exposition worthy of Athenagoras's training as a classical philosopher prior to his conversion to Christianity. The organization of the composition is well planned and permits repetitions only to clarify the stage of the argumentation at strategic points. Chapters 1-10 attempt to demonstrate that resurrection of the dead is not incompatible with the power and will of God and is, therefore, possible. Chapters 11-25 try to prove that resurrection of bodies is so necessary that it actually commands God's sense of logic and equity. To demonstrate the latter stand, Athenagoras employs four arguments: (1) man is created for eternal survival, (2) "man", by definition, is a dual creature of body and soul, both of which must share eternal life, (3) body and soul must alike reap reward or punishment for their mutual actions, (4) man's final end cannot be fulfilled by his soul alone.

The doctrine of the Resurrection, Athenagoras concedes, is such a thorny one that some disbelieve it entirely, others doubt it, and still others are baffled by it. Skeptics, he contended, are forced, however, to agree that it is possible. Impossibility involves either lack of knowledge and direction, or lack of power. To impute ignorance to God concerning the body, its composition, and its dissolution is obviously theologically offensive. Likewise, to deny Him power is unthinkable. He who in the first place arranged matter into meaningful shapes and forms can obviously reorganize disarranged bodies, even though their dissolved parts have been dissipated as food for fishes and animals. Cases where human flesh has nourished men, either through intermediary hosts or direct cannibalism, require more serious attention to obviate the embarrassing conclusion that some parts of a man might arise in two or more different persons.

Athenagoras's physiological explanations directed to the solution of this problem turn out to be far more philosophic than scientific. Much food, he argues, remains undigested and is voided. Moreover, since metabolisms differ and only substances amenable to a particular metabolism are accepted to become integral parts of a body, it is difficult to say what foods actually turn into flesh. Even basic flesh, however, as Athenagoras saw it, is constantly changing, wasted away by toil or dislocated by an unbalanced condition of the humors which cause fevers, chills, and diseases. Philosophy assured Athenagoras that these metabolic vagaries and bodily mutations eventually discarded ingredients compounded of human flesh. Since eating human flesh is unnatural, a living body rejects such food as unnatural and refuses to permit it to combine with itself. Thus cast off, these parts are available for God to recollect and re-establish in their original structures preparatory to the resurrection. To argue that God is unable thus to repair His handiwork is foolishly to cite the human as a norm.

Certainly, says Athenagoras, resurrection of the flesh is agreeable to God's will, for only the unjust and unworthy are unbecoming to Him. To whom is resurrection unjust? No creatures other than man, whether spiritual, irrational, or inanimate, are adversely affected by it. Spiritual natures require no resurrection at all, and irrational ones, unlike God, have no claim upon it. Man's soul cannot rationally object to a resurrection which glorifies and immortalizes its companion vessel, the body. The body, in turn, surely approves of a boon which helps it discover a new affinity with the soul. Besides being a just measure, man's resurrection is also one quite worthy of God and one which He can readily will. For if creating a corruptible body was not unbecoming to Him originally, making it incorruptible could scarcely be so.

Chapters 11-25 set out to prove that the resurrection is a project which is not only possible and permissible to God, but is also one which is necessary to His sense of logic and equity.

In the first place, Athenagoras argues, man is destined for eternal existence. Since God's wisdom always presupposes a teleological purpose, man's creation entails an appointed end. Clearly man is not called into existence for God's benefit. Nor, as a rational creature, can he be subject to an irrational one. Indeed, dignified in a superlative degree by reason, he cannot be subservient even to another rational being. Those who bear the image of the Creator and thus enjoy understanding, reason, and judgment must bear their own excuse for being. Their task is perpetually to enjoy their own incomparable spiritual endowment to the fullest. Logically, anything thus created for the express purpose of living and of fulfilling its unique nature can admit no foreign cause which would annihilate it. This glorious prospect of man is not a vain hope, says Athenagoras, but an infallible truth guaranteed inherently by the purpose of the Creator. Gifted with consciousness, man must exist perpetually in order to exercise the intellectual effort required to contemplate his Creator's grandeur, an eternal end necessitating man's perpetual continuance.

Secondly, Athenagoras emphasizes repeatedly that man is a dual personality, a composite of both soul and body. This consideration, more than the fact of Final Judgment, argues for man's resurrection, especially in view of the fact that some persons, such as those who die in infancy, will not be judged at all. As a dual personality, then, man strives to his end. If his creation and his life concern both his natures as a unit, so does his fulfillment. As his experiences are common to both his sensible and reasonable components, so the end of these experiences, by necessity, involves both his constituent parts. To fulfill his final cause man's twin character has to be present, making his bodily resurrection a logical necessity. If there is no resurrection, argues Athenagoras, the soul has vainly been fitted to the body and its experiences, and the body has futilely been restrained by the soul. Without resurrection, the dual nature of man becomes, in short, pointless, bereft of a final cause, a prospect entirely incongruous with God's wisdom as the source of all reason. Man's dispensation requiring a resurrection after an interruptive bodily death and dissolution, not unlike sleep, puts him logically somewhat between the lot of immortal beings whose continuance is unbroken and that of irrational creatures whose life is terminated.

Not only logic but equity demands resurrection. Athenagoras's third argument stresses the contention that man has to be rewarded or punished according to his merits if his final purpose is to be realized. Man's body requires food and progeny, but his reason simultaneously demands judgment to determine whether these bodily requirements are legitimately met. Lacking judgment leading to a just recompense, man is, according to Athenagoras, less favored than the brutes which, at least, serve their passions with impunity. Without justice virtue is a mockery, and indulgence an obvious good. Justice, therefore, has to be meted out either in this life or after death. Experience conclusively demonstrates that justice is not exacted on earth; nor, indeed, can it be, since no mortal life is long enough to endure punishment commensurate with the heinous acts of great criminals. Nor is there reason to believe that justice is dispensed during any temporary period when man's body is separated from his soul. Consequently, resurrection of the body is a necessity.

Justice in the afterlife, however, is offensive if the being which practices virtue or wickedness no longer exists to reap reward or punishment. Both body and soul must survive. The body cannot fairly be cheated of reward for its good deeds. Nor should the soul suffer alone for its co-operation with the passions of the body. By the same token, the soul cannot justly be rewarded for courage and fortitude, for the soul does not fear death; nor can the soul be credited with self-control and temperance, for it requires no food; nor with chastity, for it hungers for no intercourse; nor with generosity, for it covets no money. How can laws be justified if the soul alone is credited with their observation or castigated for their infringement? Souls, as sexless, cannot commit adultery; as parentless, they cannot honor their fathers and mothers; as propertyless, they cannot restrain themselves from theft. How, indeed, can the soul be called just when it stands in no relationship with any fellow creature but exists only before God?

In conclusion, Athenagoras stresses man's final end. The same teleology postulated for the reasonable, the intelligent, and the immortal, cannot be assigned to the irrational, the sensible, and the temporal. Man's fulfillment cannot be realized in this life or, apparently, during any temporary period when body and soul are divorced by death. A reunion of the two component parts is thus essential. Since man's end concerns each person individually and not man in general, each body has to be reconstituted exactly in its original state to enjoy that final purpose decreed for an intelligent, rational, judging being: delight in the eternal contemplation of God.

E.G.W.

THEOPHILUS TO AUTOLYCUS

Author: Saint Theophilus (died 181)
Type of work: Apologetics
First transcribed: c. 180

Principal Ideas Advanced

The Christian dispensation is far more noble than classical polytheism with its falsehood and baseness.

The true God can be known only by His revelation through the Prophets and the Gospels and through an appreciation of His created works.

History, through the Old Testament writers as well as secular historians, attests the continuity of the Judeo-Christian system.

Biographical details concerning Saint Theophilus are lacking, but according to Eusebius, Theophilus, a convert, was the sixth Bishop of Antioch, Syria. In defending Christianity against the objections of his pagan friend, Autolycus, Theophilus evinces an easy and deep familiarity with the wide corpus of Greek literature as well as with Hebrew and Christian writings; hence, he must be taken as one of the most learned of the early Christian apologists.

Theophilus is, moreover, a pioneer in many ways. Profoundly knowledgeable about the past, indeed a self-confessed historian, he should probably be thought of as the original Christian chronologist. He was the first to use the term "Trinity" for the triad: God, the Word, and Wisdom; in addition he early speculated upon the Logos and was one of the earliest commentators upon the Gospels. In referring to the work of "the Prophets and the Gospels" as both inspired by the same God, he clearly foreshadowed the concept of the New and Old Testaments.

The *Autolycus* is divided into three books each representing a different interval of discussion between Theophilus and his partner Autolycus. There are some eighty chapters in all.

At the outset of Book I Theophilus warns his friend that the pagan must remove the film of sin from the eyes of his soul if he is to see God as a sun in all its brilliance. Uncreated, superlative in all qualities, unlimited in all capacities, God can only partly be sensed and appreciated through His works. As a ship demands the presence of a pilot, and laws an artificer, so the universe requires an Author and providential sustainer. Even though man breathes the very breath of God, an additional quality, faith, is required if he is to approach his creator. In contrast, the pagan gods can never be known because all of them, whether the classical and lewd Jupiter and Venus, the Egyptian Osiris, the Phrygian Attis, or the Alexandrian Serapis, are dead, nonexistent beings.

Secure in his knowledge, Theophilus assures Autolycus that he finds the epithet "Christian" by no means a term of reproach, for a Christian is truly an "anointed" person. Nor does Theophilus think that belief in man's resurrection is naïve. Have not the pagans themselves, he asks, conceded resurrection to some gods, and are not natural prototypes of resurrection plentiful: the returning seasons, germinating seeds, the waxing moon?

Theophilus ends Book I with an earnest plea that his friend believe; he himself, having encountered the Holy Scriptures with their prophesies and guarantees of reward or punishment, has learnt to do so. Eternal punishment, he admonishes, is the price of disbelief, since adultery, covetousness, and other evils inevitably accompany it. To the believer, in contrast, go promises of everlasting life, peace, and rest.

Book II in a very human way repeats many of the arguments of Book I, to which Autolycus apparently has failed to respond. In general, it attempts to discredit the entire pagan account of reality as against that of the Christian.

Again, Theophilus reminds his antagonist that the pagan gods are but brass, wood, and stone. The very attempt to fasten a geneology upon them makes them anthropomorphic; to link them with royal families serves to cheapen them. To localize them in shrines robs them of omnipresence, thus making the place of their confinement more important than the god himself. The very inactivity of the old gods should bring doubt. If they are immortal, why do they no longer generate? Why is Olympus deserted? Celebrating gods as drunkards, fornicators, and murderers so clearly debases them that writers such as Homer, Hesiod, the tragedians, and comedians must obviously be under the spell of demons. Have not some devils exorcised by Christians admitted that they once possessed these artists?

The philosophers, Theophilus adds, contribute greatly to the confusion over the gods. Some Stoics and Epicureans deny them entirely; others, teaching a naturalistic determinism, make God a mere figment of the conscience. Others, again, insist that He is an all-pervading spirit. By illogically holding that both God and matter are uncreated, Plato wrongly elevates matter to the rank of divinity and deprives God of the distinction of creating *ex nihilo*. Hesiod foolishly calls upon the muses to explain the origin of things, even though they were not present to witness it. Indeed, the entire explanation of the universe among pagans is filled in incongruities, anachronisms, contradictions, and unadulterated nonsense. Unfortunately, the poets' beauty of diction is wasted in their accounts of creation, since their factual falsehoods poison the entire story.

By comparison, says Theophilus, the Hebrew prophets were directly inspired by the Logos who spoke to Adam. The Sibyl corroborated much of what they said. God, His Word, and His Wisdom formed a "Trinity" before all things. To help in the creation *ex nihilo,* God emitted His Word indwelling within Him.

In explaining to Autolycus the six days of creation Theophilus finds much to allegorize and philosophize. Just as God devised fresh waters to replenish the sea and check its acrid saltiness, so He provided the law of God and the Prophets to keep man from ruin by welling up righteousness. As in the sea there are fertile islands of refuge, so in the storm-tossed world the Church is a place of safe anchorage. Heresies are barren islands wrecking those who approach too closely. The plants and seeds, according to Theophilus, were created before the sun solely to confound philosophers. The sun, as great, splendid, and stable, is an image of God; the moon, like men, wanes and dies to be born again. The bright stars are images of the prophets since the stars are fixed and firm; the planets suggest men because they wander in their courses. The animals rising from the water prefigure the baptized; carniverous ones symbolize robbers and murderers; wild ones foreshadow those who know not God. Since man is master of all, the animals subject to him shared in his Fall. Thus, originally created good, some animals became ferocious and venomous. They will remain so until man stops sinning.

Theophilus points out that God made man by His own hands, rather than only by oral fiat, in order to lend man a special dignity. Created neither mortal nor immortal, man enjoys the opportunity to shape his future as an entirely free agent. To Theophilus, Paradise is situated in the East; from it the Tigris and Euphrates eventually issue. Woman was created from Adam's body to cement the relationship between man and wife and to forestall later stories of separate creations by different gods. Man's desire to possess knowledge of good and evil did not cause his Fall, because knowledge is good when properly used. Man's disobedience is to blame for the Fall. After the Fall God chose to grant immortality to every man who keeps His commandments.

Greek sages, poets, historians, and gods, Theophilus explains, are not aware of the story of creation and man's early history down to Assyrian times because the Greeks were born too late. Only Christians can know the true account through the Prophets. Although the Prophets were mostly illiterate shepherds, they told a consistent story because they were directly inspired by the Creator Himself. Classical poets and philosophers sense only scattered and elementary truths: that, for instance, the wicked should be punished, that certain acts are right, that there is a Providence, and that there is an afterlife. Sometimes, as in the case of the Sibyl, they have an awareness of monotheism.

Book III glorifies both the moral and historical superiority of the Christian dispensation.

To what avail, asks Theophilus, are all the theogonies, science, tragedies, histories, and philosophies of the classical world when their authors were not eyewitnesses and did not deal with contemporary accounts? Inconsistency is bound to result, so that some philos ophers, such as Euhemerus, Epicurus, and Pythagoras, deny the very existence of gods, others declare that the gods are atoms, and still others, such as Protagoras, are skeptics.

The God of the Prophets and the Gospels—both accounts being inspired by the Spirit of the same God—is not only the providential Creator but also the moral Lawmaker. God's Ten Commandments demand charity, mercy, chastity, love, and humility. Consequently, Autolycus is in error in believing that Christians hold wives in common, practice incest, and eat human flesh. The Greek philosophers, however, were guilty of these sins; did not even Plato, the most respectable of all, propose common wives in his ideal republic?

The last part of the work displays Theophilus' amazing interest in history. In reply to Autolycus' objection that the Christian way is young, Theophilus sets out to demonstrate the antiquity of the Hebrews. Did not the Hebrews build the very cities of Egypt? According to Theophilus, Manetho claimed that Moses lived 900-1000 years before the Trojan war. The Jewish temple was built 143 years before the founding of Carthage; the last prophet, Zechariah, was contemporary with Darius and Solon. Before Lycurgus, Draco, and Minos, the sacred books of Moses were in existence.

Based on Old Testament calculations, and Josephus, Theophilus concludes that, give or take a few years, 4954 years have elapsed from Creation to the exile. From then to Marcus Aurelius, 744 years have passed. In all, the world has gone on 5698 years. Of all this the Greeks are ignorant, since even their knowledge of letters is recent. They are, besides, very much interested in pursuing evil, inanities, and blasphemy; yet they do not suffer. Apparently only the zealous in pursuit of virtue and truth are stoned and tortured.

Theophilus ends his work with the hope that Autolycus will study these matters and thus finally arrive at the truth.

E.G.W.

AGAINST THE HERESIES

Author: Saint Irenaeus (c.125-c.203)
Type of work: Theology
First transcribed: c.185

Principal Ideas Advanced

Gnosticism as a Christian heresy is a fanciful reinterpretation of pagan theogonies and Greek philosophy.

True doctrine holds against the Gnostics that the God of the Jews, the Creator, is the Father of Jesus who, in turn, is true God and true man.

Such orthodoxy is demonstrable not only by reason and the Scriptures but also by the universal teaching of Christendom based on the tradition of the churches, especially at Rome, which enjoyed Apostolic succession.

Through Saint Polycarp, whom he knew as a boy, Saint Irenaeus stood in indirect contact with Saint John and the Apostolic age of the Church. His mission to Bishop Eleutherus of Rome in 177-178 concerning the Montanist issue probably spared his life when persecution struck his adopted city of Lyons during his absence. Later, as bishop of that see, Irenaeus attracted attention as a peacemaker in the paschal controversy between Victor of Rome and the Asiatic bishops.

As a literary man, Irenaeus is best known for his work, *The Detection and Overthrow of False Gnosis,* usually called *Adversus haereses* (*Against the Heresies*). Its five books are preserved in a Latin translation estimated to have been made anywhere between 200-400. Although long and somewhat tedious, the work in general presents a well-reasoned and documented polemic against Gnosticism. This fantastic school of heresies arranged, on the pretext of esoteric knowledge, an extended hierarchy of divine emanations, or eons, to explain creation as an accidental, defective, or ignorant act of a semidivine sub-deity. As creator, this Demiurge, often identified with the God of the Jews, functioned outside the Pleroma, the celestial realm enveloping the abstract eons which served as archetypes for all material forms below. The system thus hoped to breach the classical hiatus between the finite and the infinite.

Besides preserving the outline of Gnostic theology, which today seems little more than provocative nonsense, Irenaeus's treatise mirrors, in an artless way, much of early Christian thought: its fledgling speculations on theology, its pristine comments upon ecclesiology, and its primitive interpretations of revelation.

Irenaeus's general line of argumentation is clear. His complaint is loud that the Gnostics exploited the Scriptures by mutilating and contorting them: the Ebionite sect, for example, used only Matthew; the Marcion truncated Luke and Paul. Further, the Gnostics shamefully misinterpreted passages, especially enigmatic ones, to discover types for their eons, and they audaciously perverted the written word by using apocryphal works such as Valentinus's supposed *Gospel of Truth.* To Irenaeus, the Gnostics, far from reflecting Scriptural truth, were clumsily reviving clichés from ancient pagan theogonies and classical philosophy. Doing little more than changing names, they virtually deified the Water of Thales, the Infinite of Anaximander, the Seeds of Anaxagoras, and the Ideas of Plato. From Empedocles and Plato, Irenaeus declared, they borrowed the view that the Demiurge created the universe out of existing matter. Even Hesiod's Pandora was a fair prototype of the Gnostic version of Jesus who, pictured as a mere creature, was generously endowed with gifts by beneficent eons. From Pythagoras the Gnostics learned to symbolize the universe in a bizarre cryptography of numbers, letters, and syllables.

Such sources, twisted Scriptures and undigested Greek philosophy, naturally spawned, according to Irenaeus, a blasphemous, sinful, and nonsensical message. Thus, Gnostics impiously taught the existence of an evil creator in addition to an impassive great God. Declaring that Creation arose out of a fault or apostasy, it made both the emanations "Christ" and "Holy Spirit" products of defective eons. It denied the Incarnation of the Word of God by asserting, in a somewhat adoptionist manner, that the eon "Christ" or "Savior" descended upon Jesus and then returned to the Pleroma. Further, it regarded the resurrection of the flesh as a glorification of sordid matter and quite often pronounced the Old Testament a covenant of the evil Demiurge. Spurning truth, Gnostics spoke in novel and fanciful terms of Bythus, Achamoth, Ialdabaoth, Proarche, Propater, Sige, Nous, Anthropos, Sophia, Dyads, and Ogdoads. Carpocrates injected the transmigration of souls. Basilides so stultified the matter with his 365 heavens that by his own admission only one follower in a thousand could understand his system. Irenaeus suspected that such meaningless jargon easily opened doors to a revolting and immoderate morality. According to him, some Gnostics, as Marcus, lived scandalously; Basilides not only espoused personal lust but taught promiscuity and polygamy. The Encratites rejected marriage, others the use of animal food.

Against those heresies Irenaeus proceeds with the concrete implements of reason, Scripture, and tradition. He admits that Scripture is at times a baffling tool whose meaning is not always clear to men who, by nature, are so imperfect as not to understand even their own immediate physical environment. Still, he assumes that readers would not look kindly upon heretics who dared tamper textually with the sacred Septuagint so miraculously prepared by God. Consequently, he everywhere buries his opponents under an avalanche of Scriptural references drawn from the Old Testament and the four Gospels. His firm appeal to Apostolic tradition, the universal teaching of the Church, the rule of faith handed down by episcopal succession, serves to make him today the recognized literary architect of the Catholic Church.

Book I generally describes the various Gnostic sects and their doctrines under a bewildering array of names, including Valentinus and Ptolemy, Saturninus, Basilides, Carpocrates, Cerinthus, Cerdo, Marcion, the Ebionites and Ophites, Marcosians and Barbeliotes. Much of this description is preserved in the later Greek works of Hippolytus and Epiphanius.

Books II-V are counterargumentative. More than the others, the first book emphasizes proof drawn from reason. Irenaeus argues that any postulation of a Pleroma automatically encouraged the concept that its eons were, in turn, mere images of still greater ones. The heavenly, once considered the type of something lesser, could readily be construed as an image of something greater making God the reflection of yet another Father and driving the process to infinity. The Gnostic assertion that the world was made by sub-powers solved nothing, Irenaeus writes, since, as God's creatures, they and their works remained in the last analysis products of His will. Such a thesis served only to detract from God's omnipotence. That the world was created through defect or accident by angels ignorant of God challenged divine omniscience. Besides, such a proposition was self-contradictory for, as impassible powers, these angels could not be of the same nature as their own father who was not all-knowing. Moreover, eons which were homogeneous, eternal, simple, incorruptible, and small in number could scarcely be archetypes of created things which possessed the opposite qualities.

In Book III Irenaeus counteracts novel Gnostic claims with the ancient authority of the Church, the common doctrinal tradition of Christendom based on the teaching of the Apostolic sees.

Any possible secret private instruction to the Apostles, Irenaeus assures the Gnostics, would be known to the great sees of Christendom where Apostolic succession guaranteed purity of tradition. Since the history of episcopal succession in every great Apostolic church would be too tedious to relate, Irenaeus singles out, as a sample of pristine orthodoxy, only the "very great, very ancient, and universally known church founded and organized at Rome by the two most glorious apostles, Peter and Paul." He adds: "To this church, because of its superior leadership, all churches must necessarily resort, that is to say, the faithful of all places, because in it the apostolic tradition has been always preserved by those [the faithful] from all places." This sentence, because of its crabbed Latin and its sententious import, remains one of the most controversial in all early patristic literature. Irenaeus thoughtfully appends a list, the most accurate in existence, of all Roman bishops after Peter down to Eleutherus of his own day, who was already twelfth from the Apostle. He further attests the renown of the Roman Church, and the novelty of Gnosticism, by recording that the upstart heretics themselves, Valentinus, Cerdo, and Marcion, flocked to the capital church. Neither Peter nor Paul, retorts Irenaeus, nor Polycarp, personally known to him, nor John, who lived at Ephesus till Trajan, knew doctrines resembling those advanced by the heresiarchs. All would do well, cautions Irenaeus, to heed the tradition of these ancient churches as did the barbarians, who possessed as yet no written scriptures; to obey the presbyters in Apostolic communion and to hold in suspicion any who depart from the primitive succession, for they assemble as heretics and schismatics unfit to celebrate the Eucharist, since they deny the divinity of Jesus. Christ had predicted that truth would be witnessed to by martyrdoms; thus, the fact that the heretics had suffered only light casualties further attested their false breed. Miracles, too, witnessed to the truth in orthodox places.

In defending the universal tradition that the Son, the Logos, the Christ, was actually Jesus, true God and true man, Irenaeus employs his famous recapitulation theory. Jesus, as the Redeemer, summarized and offset the work of Adam. As the sin of one man rendered all men sinners, so the virtue of one man restored all men. If the pride of one brought death, the humility of the other assured life. The dove stalemated the serpent. Just as the first Adam took form from virgin soil, so the second Adam issued from a virgin body. As the human race fell into bondage by the disobedience of one virgin, so it was rescued by the obedience of another. In terms anticipating later Mariological vocabulary, Irenaeus refers to Mary as the "advocate of Eve," and the "womb of Mankind." Christ, in short, was constrained to assume the role of second Adam if He would overcome the enemy of man. To be saved, man had to unite himself to incorruptibility and immortality; but divine qualities had first of all to associate themselves with man. The Son of God must become man if man would become a son of God.

Book IV, drawing heavily on the sayings of Jesus, demonstrates that the God of the Law and the Prophets was identical with the Father of Christ. It further maintains that the Creator's works were not evil. The destruction of Jerusalem, Irenaeus warns, was misinterpreted as a sign that its king was not the great God; the city had merely borne its fruit and had become as chaff. Jehovah's covenant was not evil. The Old Testament prophesies regarding the Son amply proved that it was inspired by the identical God who authored the new law. Jesus himself identified the message of the Law and the Prophets with the New Testament commandment to love of God and neighbor. The tone of the two testaments were quite similar; Irenaeus claims that Christians merely tended to overemphasize the newer note of mercy over justice. He suggests that sinful deeds recorded in the Old Testament were to be interpreted figuratively when they were not expressly condemned. All in all, the Mosaic arrangement was a legitimate interlude in the historical process between the covenant of Abraham, who was a true Christian patriarch, and the dispensation of Christ which was foretold by prophets sent by the Father to prepare the way.

Irenaeus assures his readers that the Jewish God, the reputed hardener of Pharaoh, was not the author of sin. As the Creator, He had from the beginning endowed men with free will both in works and in faith, repeatedly exempting them from any divine compulsion. Men are, indeed, not perfect by the very fact that they are created, for perfection can exist only in the uncreated. Everything which has a beginning has to undergo growth and experience opportunity to prove itself in order to be glorified.

The final book argues that the flesh is not necessarily evil, rather, as the handiwork of God, says Irenaeus, flesh is capable of incorruptibility. The Eucharist, the true body and blood of Christ, so restores man that even man's flesh is accorded the opportunity for salvation, resurrection, and immortality. Christ evinced the same concern for saving the flesh as did His Father when He translated the bodies of Elijah and Enoch. As Christ arose triumphant in the flesh, so would man arise.

The close of the book describes Irenaeus's curious notions of eschatology. The earth, he thought, would recapitulate in six thousand years the six days of its creation; the Antichrist's name Irenaeus symbolizes by the mystic number 666. The just would arise to enjoy a millennium of one thousand prosperous years of earthly utopia under Christ. A final judgment would dispatch the saints to Heaven. Since the world, however, would not be annihilated, the less perfect would be sent to Paradise, while the least blessed would be consigned to the new terrestrial Jerusalem.

E.G.W.

THE APOLOGY OF TERTULLIAN

Author: Tertullian (Quintus Septimius Florens Tertullianus, c.155-c.220)
Type of work: Apologetics
First transcribed: c.197

Principal Ideas Advanced

The persecution of the Christians is illegal and unjust since it is based solely on the name Christian rather than upon any specific crime, and is unsupported by any effort to learn the truth about Christian beliefs or actions.

The chief accusations made against Christians are false; Christians are not guilty of private enormities, impiety, or treason.

The Roman Empire has already been saturated by Christianity; illogical persecution only serves to establish Christian innocence and encourage its growth.

Tertullian's *Apology* was written soon after his conversion in 193 and early in his literary career; the work is commonly regarded as his masterpiece. Like his writings in general, the *Apology* is characterized by a legal and rational approach, clothed in a pithy rhetorical style rich in invective and paradox, and demonstrative of the author's confident and defiant attitude. This fifty-chapter work was written for the enlightenment not of the Roman emperors, as Eusebius alleged, but for the instruction of local provincial governors, especially those of Africa, Tertullian's homeland.

The composition is arranged in an orderly fashion and states its thesis at the outset (Chapters 1-6): that the persecution of Christians as carried on by the Roman government was both unlawful and unjust since it was based on faulty legal theory and ignorance. The bulk of the *Apology* demonstrates Christian innocence of secret crimes (Chapters 7-9); of impiety toward the state gods (Chapters 10-27); and of treason toward the government (Chapters 28-45). Chapters 46-50 make up a triumphant conclusion defiantly predicating failure for the anti-Christian policy of Rome.

As a trained lawyer Tertullian realized that any prosecution of Christians based only on the name "Christian" was dictated by ignorant bias and was, therefore, unlawful. He pronounces Trajan's "enlightened" policy entirely paradoxical; while it forbade Christians to be sought after as innocent, it yet commanded them to be punished as guilty! Contrary to all orthodox juridical procedure, Christians, Tertullian observes, were forced to deny their "crimes," while other criminals were obliged to confess. Such corrupt laws could not be from Heaven; such misguided contention over the mere name of Christian was not only illogical but also obviously perverse, for even in popular circles the name was associated with ethical reformation. Despite the illegality of prosecuting without naming a crime, Tertullian accused, the authorities made no effort to investigate alleged Christian misdemeanors.

Any fair inquiry would prove that Christians were innocent of such heinous private atrocities as infant killing and incest, Tertullian insisted. Was the Christian to be considered of such a different nature from the pagan that he could plunge a knife into a guiltless baby and saturate his bread with its blood? Ridiculous charges, Tertullian exclaims, and he adds that apparently one who had no mother to rape could not be a Christian! According to Tertullian, the Roman's own gory traditions and customs made such abominations plausible to him; even his gods were cruel and bloody. Was not Zeus a notorious expert at incest? Did not the pagans expose their children, countenance the drinking of gladiators' blood by epileptics, and gingerly eat the animals slain in the arena, even though human blood and flesh was still undigested in them?

Continuing with devastating logic, Tertullian suggests that, before accusing Christians of impiety, the persecutors investigate their assumption that their own gods were truly gods. Going beyond the thesis of Euhemerus, which stated that the gods of polytheism were but deified human beings, Tertullian pictures the Roman gods as being so essentially evil that any spark of goodness in a Roman would be regarded by the gods as an affront to them! Should Romans not deify their criminals if they wished to serve the gods? Any assumption by the pagans that their gods were truly gods implicated the Romans in a simultaneous indictment for impiety. Did they not treat the gods scandalously by slighting one in favor of another, by hawking their images, by bribing them, by applauding comics and philosophers who mocked them and indecent actors who impersonated them? Were not their temples haunted by procurers? The assertion that the prosperity of Rome was bound up with its worship of the gods was equally preposterous, for the gods could not protect even their own tiny bailiwicks. Else, why did Zeus permit Crete to fall to Rome? Or Juno, Carthage? Did not Caesar own the gods' temples? It is obviously truer to say, Tertullian wryly noted, that disaster overtook the gods than to maintain that the gods prevented disaster. According to Tertullian, the "sacrilege of the Romans were as numerous as their trophies." Apparently the classical world had mistaken demons for gods, an egregious blunder indeed, since the Christians had the latter completely under their power. Any public exhibition would demonstrate how readily Christians could handle these crafty winged fallen angels, purveyors of blight, sickness, passion, and error.

In contrast to these false pagan claims, the Christians possess the only true deity, Tertullian insisted. Research would disclose that the Christian religion is an elevated monotheistic concept. It believes in and worships an incomprehensible God whose works and dispensation were revealed through prophets more ancient and venerable than any classical philosopher, legislator, or historian. Christ, born of a Virgin rather than, as is the case with some pagan gods, of a snake, was the Logos of the philosophers, the very God of God, an extension of divine substance, not a division. In these last days of the world He had come to choose more faithful worshipers for the Father than the perfidious Jews and, in general, to renovate and illuminate. His passion and death during the reign of Tiberius had been clearly signaled by darkness on the earth. The truth of these Christian beliefs, Tertullian claimed, was amply attested by the believers' own reformation and power of miracles. Since Roman gods were no gods at all—the only God being the Christian God—Tertullian concluded that there was no case of impiety against the Christians and he pronounced them innocent.

Equally unjust, in Tertullian's opinion, was the accusation that the followers of Christ were enemies of Caesar. He assures his readers that Christians respected in the emperor the ordinance of God who set rulers over nations. In truth it might even be claimed that the emperor belonged basically to the Christians since their God had established him. Consequently, they prayed for him, his life, his security, the organs of his administration, fully aware that Rome was a bulwark against the collapse of the civilized world. However, since the emperor was human, not divine, Christians would not carouse in his honor or swear by his genius. Tertullian avers that Christians, unlike others, did not assassinate emperors, nor cast hexes upon them, nor rebel against them. The empire could be thankful that Christians did not choose to show their displeasure by insurrection, considering that their numbers had grown so formidable. "We are but of yesterday," writes Tertullian, "but we have filled every place among you, your cities, islands, fortresses, towns, market-places, the camp itself, tribes, companies, palace, senate, and forum. We have left you nothing but the temples of your gods." Should Christians decide to emigrate, the empire would be left a solitary desert. Obviously, then, Christians formed no political faction. Rather, they were a well administered corporate community engaged in prayer, reading of the Scriptures, the inculcation of good habits, and the performance of charitable work. Since they lived daily among the pagans it was evident they were not an antisocial group, except when it came to spectacles, festivals, crowns, pimps, diviners, and assassins.

Chapters 46-50 conclude that the Christians alone were without crime, and Tertullian prophesied that their triumphant success was assured. As true philosophers, Christians should, along with other philosophers, be freed from the compulsion to sacrifice and reverence the pagan gods. Christians were, indeed, the original philosophers, for their pagan colleagues of old copied from Christian sources, largely through the agency of evil spirits who anticipated and revealed the future. Consequently, it was unwise for the Romans to deride Christian doctrines such as the Resurrection, for they themselves often held and supported similar beliefs.

If the Christians were fools, Tertullian pointed out, their harmless fancies at least served to improve people. They were destined to prevail because they were impervious to unjust attacks. True, they objected to the persecutions in principle, but once the conflict raged they acted like good soldiers in fighting with all their strength. The more they were mistreated, the more obvious became their innocence and the greater became the acceleration of their growth. Who would not join a Christian when he saw him triumph? "The blood of Christians is seed," Tertullian claimed.

The *Apology* had an immediate impact upon its age: Cyprian, Lactantius, and Jerome were devoted to it. Its continued popularity is attested by a great number of manuscripts, by its translation into Greek, and by the fact that textual criticism of the work has gone on steadily from the sixteenth century to the present time.

E.G.W.

STROMATEIS

Author: Clement of Alexandria (Titus Flavius Clemens, c.150-c.215)
Type of work: Moral exhortation
First transcribed: c.200

Principal Ideas Advanced

Classical philosophy is a partial revelation to the Greeks of divine Truth and, therefore, is a legitimate supplement to Christian Faith.

Both faith and knowledge implement each other to create the perfect Christian or Gnostic.

The Gnostic's perfection culminates in the love and contemplation of God.

As a student and headmaster at the Christian school of Alexandria for about twenty years prior to 203, Saint Clement labored to effect a judicious synthesis of the classical intellectual tradition and the vibrant faith of the new Christian dispensation. His chief work furthering this design was his *Stromateis* (Carpets), or Miscellanies. In choosing such a title, Clement effectively disarmed criticism of this work as poorly organized, repetitious, and loosely proportioned. Under such a heading he was free to discourse upon various learned topics as they came to mind, aware that the variegated subject matter would compose itself into a leisurely pattern delineating the character of the perfect Christian.

In general, Book I centers around the proposition that faith without knowledge is presumptuous. Clement's strong Platonic conviction that knowledge is virtue drove him to exhort the Christian, striving for comprehension of the things declared by faith and seeking the attainment of moral perfection, to resort to ancient philosophy. Secular philosophy, although only a partial revelation to the pagans of divine truth, was a legitimate corpus of knowledge nonetheless, for, according to Clement, God permitted the Greeks to plagiarize from the Jewish prophets.

An eclectic set of ideas and techniques conducive to righteousness and piety and opposed to sophistry was to be culled from all the great classical systems, Stoic, Platonic, Aristotelian, even Pythagorean and Epicurean. These systems would thus provide the tools of reasoning and of allegorizing needed not only to probe the truth behind the Scriptural faith but also to defend Christians against the thrusts of pagan sophists. Indeed, *all* branches of secular study—music, geometry, astronomy, dialects, semantics— should be employed for what they can contribute. Equipped with these disciplines and grounded in the Faith, the Christian or Gnostic would be prepared to reintegrate all the scattered fragments of the truth to be found in philosophy and secular learning into the full corpus of the truth. In short, philosophy would then provide a systematic approach to the wisdom which Clement defines as "the sure knowledge of things divine and human in the past, present and future."

Book II hastens to remind the reader that, for all its virtue, Greek philosophy is a childish fare intended for persons not yet brought to adulthood by Christ. The Greeks, deprived of the Faith and guided only by human pride, had, indeed, distorted the truth. Clement, in a semi-Stoic fashion, envisages faith as a voluntary assent to unseen propositions. Since it involves choice, faith is the beginning of all action. Consequently, it is the wellspring of all Christian virtues, especially love, virtues which, Clement claims, are closely interrelated among themselves in characteristic Platonic fashion. Influenced also by Aristotle, Clement argues further that faith is the base of knowledge because all first principles are undemonstrable. Surely, then, the First Cause of the universe can be apprehended by faith alone. Without preconceptions, in other words, there is no learning.

This combination of faith and knowledge in the Christian is more than a simple mixture of knowledge, learned in the Stoic way through sensation, concept, and judgment, and faith based on the Scriptures. Faith and knowledge together engender a mystic comprehension of Reality, of the greatest Platonic Idea, God Himself. The Gnostic knows the past through the Scriptures, the present through philosophy, and the future through his ability to solve all enigmas, and with allegory he has the key to unlock divine things wrapped up in figurative speech both in sacred and heathen writings. Intuitively secure in his convictions, the Gnostic possesses the talent to inspire his less well-favored Christian brothers who know only the comforts of faith.

Book III is an excursus on moderation in marriage directed against the extreme doctrines of heretics brought on by their unbalanced combination of faith and knowledge. Clement's classical and humanistic leanings caused him to regard, in a way unparalleled in Christian literature, the married state as superior to virginity.

The remaining books of the *Stromateis* (IV-VII) extoll the characteristics of the true Gnostic. In general, Clement expects the Gnostic to believe, to learn, to obey the commandments, and to influence others by his example. He is cautioned, however, not to make the spring of knowledge indiscriminately available to all; some, unable to tolerate the heady waters, would be dislodged from their simple faith, which at least prevents them from performing sinful actions. In classical Stoic phraseology, Clement advises the Gnostic to give evidence of the things which are "in his power" and which "pertain to him."

The way of the true Christian Gnostic was to Clement basically a Platonic one. He was to strive to reflect the ineffable virtues of a God who was above qualification. He was to seek an impassive and passionless character in imitation of a docetic Christ. This studied impassivity of the body would free the soul for contemplation and allow it to attach itself to the abstract Good, to attain God, to reach the Ultimate which Plato, "learning from Moses," spoke of as the realm of Reality where all things are contained universally. He who contemplated the unseen God would automatically live as a god among men, inspired by a vision of Deity, the epitome of all excellence. He would, as it were, be an intimate of God through the good graces of the High Priest, His Son.

Aristotle would equip the Christian Gnostic with a skill in dialectic and logic, teaching him to distinguish the general from the particular and the part from the whole. From the same philosopher, the Gnostic, while accepting the necessity of the body and of material things in his quest for the good life, would learn to value the use of moderation in all things, including marriage, and to temper his attitude toward martyrdom. In accordance with Aristotle's teaching, Clement would have his Gnostics practice virtues until they became hardened into habits.

Following the Stoic, the Gnostic was never to equate pleasure and pain with good and evil, nor permit ignominy, exile, confiscations, or persecution to wrench him from his innate freedom to practice virtue. If need be, he was to co-operate with any situation which required him to expedite his own martyrdom, the perfect work of love. In the Beatitudes, the Gnostic would find inspiring examples of the sublimation of poverty, pain, and deprivation. While the Gnostic knew that the presence or absence of knowledge automatically divided Christians into the perfect and the simple, he should accept the Stoic tenet that equal natural righteousness was common to all men, and that all beings had a graduated interdependence in the universe.

Clement apparently believed that

even the Pythagorean science of mystical numbers, mysterious ratios, and musical harmonies had some esoteric value which might help in the solution of hidden enigmas.

Clement served Christianity in several distinguished ways. He taught the difference between the true Christian Gnostic and the heretical one in whom an immoderate love of classical philosophy, through a perversion of the Scriptures, caused a contamination of the deposit of faith. He introduced into Christian ethics the Greek virtue of moderation, especially in regard to the material world and marriage. He insisted consistently on the necessity of free will, almost to the exclusion of grace, and then, by interjecting a strong note of classical humanitarianism, Clement helped to reinforce Christian dedication to the idea of the dignity of man. Finally, Clement of all the early Christian Fathers, most forcefully insisted that Christianity be an intellectual, cultural experience, that the Judeo-Christian and the Graeco-Roman views be synthesized. The perfect Christian must be both a saint and a scholar.

The *Stromateis* is not important in the development of theology, and its Christology from an orthodox point of view is faulty since it leans heavily toward Docetism. Nor has the work influenced ecclesiastical development. However, in his devotion to the universal Church and its unity, Clement repeatedly deplores the existence of heretical sects and warns that they can be detected by their tendency to call themselves after their founders, their place of origin, a peculiar custom, or a particular belief. Nor does the *Stromateis* emphasize sacramentalism. Clement's views on penance tend to follow those of *The Shepherd* of Hermas in seeming to recognize only one forgiveness after baptism.

E.G.W.

THE DEMONSTRATION OF APOSTOLIC TEACHING

Author: Saint Irenaeus (c.125-c.203)
Type of work: Apologetics
First transcribed: c.200

Principal Ideas Advanced

God's plan for man's salvation is a continuous and consistent one, extending from the day of Creation, through Old Testament times, to the present.

The truth of the Apostles' message and of contemporary preaching can be demonstrated from a study of the prophecies foretelling the Christian dispensation.

Any attempt by heretics, especially the Gnostics and Docetists, to distort the arrangement of the Trinitarian God must be abhorred if one would gain salvation.

From Eusebius's *Ecclesiastical History* it was long known that Irenaeus had written a book entitled *The Proof of the Apostolic Preaching,* or *The Demonstration of Apostolic Teaching.* But the length, plan, and contents of the composition were virtually unknown until an Armenian text of the entire work was discovered in 1904 and published in 1907. This Armenian version, whose provenance seems to be Byzantium, appears to have been made between 570 and 590. Harnack's arbitrary division of the treatise into one hundred chapters has become well established.

The essay is addressed to "Brother Marcianus," probably an ordained blood brother of the author. The twofold purpose of the work is clearly stated in the dedication. Marcianus, Irenaeus hopes, will find his efforts not only informative as a handbook of basic theology and helpful as a confirmation of his faith, but also instrumental as a weapon to confound dissenters, with their false views. On the one hand, then, the work is an exposition of revealed truth, an abbreviated summary of theology, the earliest systematic treatment of the divine economy in relation to man. On the other, it is an apology, an attempt to demonstrate that the Christian dispensation is true. It falls accordingly into two great divisions. Chapters 4-42 explain God's plan from Creation through the Incarnation and Resurrection, and Chapters 43-97 marshal a battery of Old Testament references to make this divine economy credible. That the treatise was not intended solely as an expository piece of writing seems clear from the consideration that the role of the Church in God's plan is not explained by Irenaeus. The omission was due not to any wish on Irenaeus's part to minimize the subject but to the fact that ecclesiological matters had already been treated quite heavily in his *Adversus haereses.* Moreover, Chapter 86 clearly suggests that the apologetic purpose of the composition was uppermost in Irenaeus's mind. The prophets, this chapter argues, not only predicted that the Son of God would appear on earth, but they also designated where, how, and under what circumstances He would appear. Since Christ fulfilled all these prophecies in detail, it is evident that the Christian faith is solidly grounded, the testimony of the Apostles firmly established, and the truth of contemporary preaching fully guaranteed.

Emphases throughout the essay demonstrate that the author keeps heresy constantly before him, especially the heresy of the Gnostics. These thinkers, finding God and matter completely incompatible, divorced the One ineffable Deity from the God of the Jewish law. The latter they equated with the Demiurge or evil creator of material things. To counteract such teachings, Irenaeus takes pains to show that a complete continuity operates from beginning to end in the divine plan arranged for the salvation of men. It is, incidentally, natural that Irenaeus should have been deeply impressed with the concept of continuousness. As a youthful listener of Saint Polycarp of Smyrna, who was himself an immediate disciple of Saint John, Irenaeus personally bridged the chronological gap between Apostolic days and the early third century. To confound the Gnostics he would prove that the Jewish and the Christian ways were but pages of one divine blueprint in which events of the Old Testament world were directly connected with those of the New. From the Creation of the world to the creation of the Church, the divine plan was consistently unfolded by the Father through the Son, and by the Son through the Holy Spirit. The Father created through the Son; the Son, eternal in existence and as the only medium of approach to the Father since the beginning of creation, dealt with man. By giving the Holy Spirit to the prophets, the Son made knowledge of Himself possible. Thus, the entire divine economy throughout the ages and in all of its manifestations was the work of the same triune God, not the product of a Gnostic demiurge.

A more detailed breakdown of the sections of the work reveals an orderly pattern of thoughts. In the introduction Irenaeus maintains that man owes a tribute to God for each of the components of his bipartite nature: the body's contribution must be both the performance of good works and abstinence from evil; the soul's offering must be an unadulterated faith in God. Through this dual program, the keeping of the commandments and the subscription to the rule of faith, man will achieve the end for which he was created.

It is to the content of this rule of faith that Irenaeus addresses himself in the first half of his work. One must, at the outset, believe that everything came from nothing by order of a rational Creator who is completely beyond understanding. This trinitarian Being is at once the invisible Father, God of Jew and Gentile alike; the Word, who became incarnate as man to bring life; and the Holy Spirit, who became the teacher of prophets. As everything originally proceeded to man from the Father through the Son and through Him to the Holy Spirit, so, conversely, fallen man will be brought back to incorruptibility by the Holy Spirit, who conducts man to the Word, who, in turn, will present man to the Father.

In Irenaeus's vast panorama of creation the reader meets Powers, Angels, and Archangels, and the seven heavens in order. Man, created in the image of God, enters the scene in due time as a free agent and master of all he surveys. His Fall from Paradise brought confusion and evil, so readily carried on by Sem and his children that wickedness became habitual. Even angels presumed to mate with human beings to produce a monstrous progeny of giants. After the purging by the Flood, Cham became the new transmitter of evil to his descendants the Chanaaites, Hittites, Amorrhites, Arabs, Egyptians, and Lydians. However, from Sem eventually descended Abraham and his race. In proper time followed the Exodus, the Mosaic law, and the prophets who foretold the coming of Jesus Christ, seed of David according to the flesh, but Son of God according to the spirit.

To explain the Incarnation Irenaeus draws heavily upon the recapitulation theory, an attractive thesis heavily dependent upon topology. God would, as it were, rehabilitate His entire original plan for man's salvation which had been subverted by Adam's Fall. In a vicarious way, He would re-enact the experience of Adam through the Person of His Son. Each evil, each mistake originated by the first man as representative of the human race, would be counterbalanced by the virtues and redeeming activities of the Son. As Adam was man, so Christ would be man. Reliving the situation in which the first Adam lost life, the Second Adam would restore it. The World would be made Flesh to destroy sin which initially had gained control through the flesh. Eve, as the virgin source of all evil, would be balanced by Mary, the virgin author of all good. Disobedience must be destroyed by obedience. As sin was wrought through a tree, it would be counteracted by the Tree. Finally, Christ would assure man's resurrection through the Resurrection. To this great experience of death and resurrection, the Gentiles were called when the Church was established.

The second half of the book (Chapters 43-97) promises to prove that the events already narrated were duly foretold by the Spirit of God through the prophets so that those who would serve God would believe them. Over a hundred prophecies are cited to demonstrate Christ's genuineness as God and Savior; they are drawn basically from Isaias but also from the Pentateuch, Psalms, Ezechiel, Osee, Amos, Micheas, Zacharias, and even apocryphal literature. Some are mistakenly attributed to Jeremias. These prophecies, in general, demonstrate that the Son is eternal; that even the theophanies of the Old Testament were of Him. Since He had spoken to Abraham and Moses it is clear that the Father caused the Son to be revealed to men long before His physical birth. All was foretold: the Virgin Birth, the miracles, Christ's arrest, the activities of Herod and Pilate, His death, Resurrection and Ascension, His descent into Hell, even the parting of His garments, and the giving of the thirty pieces of silver. Prophecies further foretold that the Jewish law would be supplanted by a new covenant, that the Gentiles would inherit the promises made to the Jews, that, in short, the Church would supersede the synagogue. Chapter 97 assures the reader that the same providence of God demonstrated in the past still holds; He stands ready to help anyone who believes in Him and obeys Him.

The conclusion reiterates the assurance that all the foregoing is true. Such is the way of salvation, a continuous economy through the prophets, Christ, the Apostles, and the Church down to the present time. The reader is advised to consult Irenaeus's *Adversus haereses* about those who would deny these truths, and he is cautioned that, if he hopes for salvation, he must be especially wary of those who would corrupt the Trinity, the seal of Christian Baptism.

E.G.W.

OCTAVIUS

Author: Minucius Felix (fl. c.200)
Type of work: Apologetics
First transcribed: c.200

Principal Ideas Advanced

Christianity, according to the pagan Caecilius, is foolish, unpatriotic, and incestuous.

Octavius, his Christian partner in discussion, demonstrates with an appeal to common sense, to philosophy, and to literature that such is not the case.

The discussion, moderated by the Christian Minucius Felix, ends in the pagan's determination to become a Christian himself.

Without doubt, the *Octavius* of Minucius Felix is one of the most charming and straightforward compositions in early Christian literature. The forty-one chapters of this apology record a dialogue between the pagan Caecilius and the Christian Octavius while the latter's fellow-convert friend, Minucius Felix, acts as moderator. The author shows a great familiarity with both pagan poetry and philosophy, but there is no reference to the Scriptures. As a lawyer, the author probably saw that such appeals were logically out of place in a discussion with a heathen. The work, unlike most early Christian literature, is marred by no digressions; it shows a significant indebtedness to Cicero for its form, possibly to Tertullian for its ideas and phraseology (or vice versa), and to Stoic philosophy for its arguments.

The discussion takes place during a pleasant walk along the beach to Ostia after Caecilius saluted a statue of Serapis. Octavius interpreted this action as quite inconsiderate of his and Minucius' Christian consciences. Caecilius, in return, in the first fifteen chapters of the work, launches into an attack on Christianity which turns essentially around three accusations: that the new religion is (1) presumptuous and sacrilegious, (2) stupid and naïve, and (3) barbarous and salacious.

According to Caecilius, Christians are, first of all, annoying because they presume to solve things divine, to pry into the heavenly when they do not understand the simplest civil matters. Confession of ignorance, he argues, is the height of wisdom, especially since reality is so doubtful. The mechanistically deterministic world has no place for Providence, presenting, as it does, only the prospect of an incomprehensible fate. Consequently, faced with the impenetrable mysteries of destiny it seems best to honor the traditional gods. To act otherwise is not only arrogant but also unpatriotically sacrilegious, for it has been Rome's dutifulness in honoring its own gods and in appeasing foreign ones that has made it great.

Next, Caecilius charges that the Christians are made up of loafers, unskilled workers, and women who stupidly but garrulously skulk in corners benightedly worrying about resurrection and eternal justice rather than about their present afflictions. Moreover, they blindly worship, without benefit of altar or temple, a God they cannot identify and one who unjustly punishes them for what fate made them do. Association of the Christian deity with the Jewish God is, to Caecilius, ridiculous indeed, considering that Jehovah is a conquered divinity. Furthermore, as omnipresent, the Christian God makes men uncomfortable. The very poverty of Christians belies either the providence or the power of their God. For this defeated God, now vanquished by the Romans, Christians stupidly give up fun and spectacle. Just as they do not live in the present, so they will not live in the hereafter.

According to Caecilius, Christian worship is both cannibalistic and lewd. Under the specious guise of a brother-and-sister relationship, incest is the accepted practice in darkened Christian conventicles. Here they worship not only the head of an ass but also the generative organs of their priests; here they butcher infants covered with meal and wait to devour the quivering raw flesh and drink the steaming blood.

Octavius argues in rejoinder that the discussion of divine things is not a presumptuous act, for intelligence is a native gift open to all, not a purchased or strictly inherited commodity. Nor does an incomprehensible fate make such discussion pointless. Obviously, the harmonious cosmological arrangements are made to serve man and his own complicated nature, and the finely correlated dispensations of nature which balance deficiencies in one place with assets in another, all present to view so well-arranged a house that only government by an intelligent Being, rather than fate, can explain it. This Being must be one, for many masters entail confusion; He is clearly eternal, and all-powerful beyond perception. To call Him simply God is best because the term nicely avoids anthropomorphisms. Besides, a specific name is superfluous, for, as absolutely unique, God requires no identification. Not only logic attests the superlative divine qualities, but also ancient authorities as well: Virgil, Thales, Anaximenes, Diogenes, Anaxagoras, Xenophanes, even Democritus and Aristotle, Zeno, Chrysippus, and Plato. Octavius explains the origin of the gods by asserting that rustic, untraveled peoples in time long past deified not only monsters but also local heroes. The fact that the gods had birthdays, physical disabilities, and even obsequies is proof of their human origin. Was not Vulcan crippled, and Jupiter a corpse in Crete? Since vices were imputed to the gods merely to justify man's evil desires, Plato quite appropriately banned poets and their corrupting divine nonsense from his ideal republic.

Naturally, to Octavius, Christianity can never be sacrilegious and unpatriotic. Rome's greatness, he argues, does not derive from the gods but from the city's own rapaciousness and audacity. Was not Romulus a fratricide, Rome even in its infancy an asylum for criminals, and its early citizens perpetrators of wholesale rape? Its spoils were irreverent confiscations of temples and blasphemous loot from religious funds. The Roman divinities are clearly of no service to the state, for in many cases they are actually borrowed gods of conquered peoples, gods unable to defend their original devotees. Their worship scarcely makes Rome virtuous when the temples are places notorious for violence, procuring, and pandering. Lastly, other states, such as Assyria, Greece, and Persia survive without Roman priesthoods, omens, and prophetic chickens. Besides, what had auguries availed a Regulus or a Paulus, or a Pythia, who sold out to Philip?

Clearly, says Octavius, the Romans mistake the operations of demons for divine manifestations. It is the demons who dwell in the idols, animate the entrails, and direct the oracles in much the same way as they, the demons, possess men, making them sick, insane, and spastic. These facts the demons themselves have revealed to the Christians who exorcised them.

Furthermore, Christians are not stupid. Nor are they necessarily the dregs of society simply because they refuse to chase honors and robes and to cultivate a mannered loquaciousness. To worship God without recourse to temples and altars is more a sign of enlightenment than of ignorance, for it recognizes, in a lofty way, that man himself is the image of God. Why search for God when one cannot look squarely even at His sun or see His zephyrs? God infuses Himself into man's being just as gently and surely as the sun bathes the land. As our intimate tenant, as it were, He logically knows our most intimate secrets. Such a providential God did not arbitrarily forsake the Jews; they first neglected Him.

Belief in the destruction of the world and in immortality is hardly childish, says Octavius, for such beliefs are accepted by Stoics and Epicureans, Pythagoreans and Platonists. Moreover, nature amply prefigures immortality or resurrection, and even the poets have some knowledge of a fiery punishment. And is not creation clearly more difficult than restoration? Man's decomposed parts never become lost to God their Creator, even though they became mixed with elements foreign to man. To eschew fate surely is not a sign of stupidity; it is merely another way of naming what God has determined for man by His foreknowledge.

Far from indicating an inane wretchedness, Octavius argues, poverty indicates a happy lack of cupidity. Riches are a burden; but labor is a boon, adversity a challenge, and persecution a fulfillment. The worldly powerful and rich are almost synonymous with the wicked; as such they are marked victims for inevitable retribution.

Christian abstinence from spectacles, idol worship, and meat sacrifices is not dictated by a naïveté which springs from a fear of magic but, rather, from the realization that these practices encourage adultery and blasphemy, assure intimacy with demons, and bring shame on the true religion.

Christians, in short, have a wisdom all their own. Let the sophisticated Carneades, Pyrrho, Simonides, and members of the Academy deliberate and procrastinate while knitting their brows in contemplation of corruption and vice. Christian wisdom resides not in the philosopher's cloak but in his mind; his merit is not in speech but in action.

The third charge, that Christians are cannibalistic and lewd, results, according to Octavius, from the lying propaganda of demons. Actually, tales of parricide, adoration of asses' heads, and monstrous sexual aberrations reflect pagan practices. No one would believe the infamous stories of Christian infanticide except those who were themselves familiar with abortions, exposures, human sacrifice, and cannibalistic gods such as Saturn, who ate his children. While Christians do not so much as use the blood of legitimate animals for food, pagans gladly eat the wild bear who has fed in the arena upon human flesh. The tragedies celebrate incest, the gods practice it, and so great is the number of illegitimate and abandoned children that anyone who makes a specialty of sexual affairs is bound eventually to traffic with his own kin. Christians, by contrast, are monogamous, often virginal, always modest.

Caecilius finally admits that he has been defeated by Octavius, and he announces his plans to pursue further instruction in Christianity. The work ends on a joyous note. All are happy: Caecilius because he has seen the light, Octavius because he has won the debate, and Minucius because the other two are happy.

E.G.W.

TREATISES ON MARRIAGE

Author: Tertullian (Quintus Septimius Florens Tertullianus, c.155-c.220)
Type of work: Philosophy of Christian marriage
First transcribed: 200-217

Principal Ideas Advanced

Virginity is the ideal; monogamy a necessary evil.
Digamists defy God's permissive will.
Christian marriage is indissoluble.
Remarriage after the death of a spouse is no more defensible than remarriage after divorce.
Christian marriage is of a sacramental nature and comes under the jurisdiction of the Church.

In Tertullian's three specific treatises on marriage, *Ad uxorem* (*To My Wife*). *De exhortatione castitatis* (*An Exhortation to Chastity*), and *De monogamia* (*On Monogamy*), the theme, the argumentation, and the presentation are very similar. The tracts, however, tend to grow progressively more narrow and sarcastic in attitude, more specious and causistic in argument, more vehement and blunt in expression as Tertullian moves away from orthodoxy, through semi-orthodoxy, to the excessive asceticism of Montanism. The first work, written between 200 and 216 and the most liberal of the three, presents remarriage after the death of a spouse as a permissible act but one subject to criticism and restriction. The second, drafted between 204 and 212, implies that remarriage, as a sort of fornication, is scarcely legitimate. The last, composed probably in 217, virtually brands remarriage as adulterous. The first composition describes Christian marriage as a happy event planned and blessed by God to procreate children; the last treatise castigates it as an unclean, unseasonable lust featuring "swollen breasts, nauseating wombs and whimpering infants." Yet even in the De *monogamia* Tertullian regards his Montanist views as quite moderate, standing between two extreme positions: that espoused by heretics or Marcionites who never married, and that recommended by "Sensualists" or Catholics who married repeatedly. Whatever Tertullian's views and however unnatural his cause, he shows himself in these works, if not always a logical pleader, a sincere, brilliant, and passionate one.

These three works, however extreme in part, are cardinal to an understanding of early Christian views of marriage. At the outset Tertullian clearly disallows a double marital standard for the sexes, and he regards marriage as absolutely indissoluble. He would, in an immoderate fashion, extend its indissolubility even beyond the grave. His *Ad uxorem* contains probably the most explicit and significant remark in centuries of Western Christian literature recognizing the sacramental character of the marriage rite: "How," asks Tertullian, "shall we ever be able adequately to describe the happiness of that Christian marriage which the Church arranges, the Sacrifice strengthens, upon which the blessing sets a seal, at which angels are present as witnesses, and to which the Father gives His consent?" Tertullian's exposition further corroborates other evidence that the Church, in establishing ecclesiastical jurisdiction over Christian marriage, chose to disregard state law forbidding interclass wedlock. Clearly, too, mixed marriages were already deplored and discouraged.

Tertullian in his own way regards remarriage after the death of a spouse to be as reprehensible as remarriage after divorce, a recourse he justifies solely on grounds of adultery. He reasons that marriage, as basically a bulwark against adultery, can be considered nullified once the crime it is designed to prevent is committed. But just as, in Tertullian's opinion, adultery itself can never be forgiven, so too the bonds of marriage can never be dissolved by either a divorced person or by a married party who survived the death of his partner. Virginity from birth represented to Tertullian the highest state of perfection; less meritorious was postbaptismal virginity resulting from a mutual agreement of husband and wife or from the refusal of a widow or widower to remarry. Monogamy enjoyed the lowest legitimate claim to praise. After the termination of the first marriage by divorce or death, Tertullian argued, the remaining member should eschew all further experience with sex. Tertullian finds it difficult to understand how the surviving party could keep his former spouse in his heart when he admitted another to his flesh, or how, under such circumstances, he could pray for his deceased partner and offer the Sacrifices for her. In these latter remarks, incidentally, some theologians discern an oblique reference to Purgatory.

Since Tertullian often repeats his arguments against remarriage, his *Ad uxorem* may fairly be used as a guide in discussing them. After urging his wife, strictly for her own sake and not because of any impossible postmortem jealousy on his part, to remain single after his death, Tertullian at once presents his favorite argument against remarriage. God decreed monogamy in Paradise when he created only one woman from the side of the first man, although Adam had many other ribs to spare. Consequently, it was obvious that there were to be two in one flesh, not three or four. *De exhortatione castitatis* explains that the Old Testament stories, relating the subsequent but transitory polygamous character of marriage among the patriarchs, were given as types and symbols of future events. If a Christian must emulate Abraham, let him copy Abraham's early monogamous life. Better, though, as *De monogamia* urges, is a return to the very beginning of things, back to Paradise itself, where neither divorce nor circumcision obtained. Or one may refer to Noah, who had only one wife; even the animals in the ark were evenly paired off.

Tertullian's second argument against remarriage exploits Saint Paul. The tone of the Apostle's remark (I Corinthians 7:9): "It is better to marry than to burn," made his preference for celibacy over marriage obvious to Tertullian. Adroitly twisting the term "better" by ignoring its obvious positive relationship to "good" and "best" and by emphasizing only its negative contrast to "worse," Tertullian argues that marriage can scarcely be a good, since it is preferred only to an evil. It is a lesser evil at best, as is the possession of one eye over none. In order to force Paul to enjoin monogamy, Tertullian's *De monogamia* balances I Corinthians 7:39, expressly permitting remarriage, with I Corinthians 7:1-11, picturing marriage as a permissible indult rather than a positive good. He attenuates the message of the former Corinthian verse by culling inconsistent Pauline excerpts out of context and finally by explaining limply that Paul allows remarriage only by way of concession. This permission Paul gave, Tertullian arbitrarily insists, only to Christians married before their conversion. While the newly initiated Christian could not put away his pagan partner, he was free to marry a Christian after his pagan spouse's demise. According to Tertullian, Paul sensed that neophyte Christians required a nurse. He had acted subjectively according to circumstances before. Had he not circumcised Timothy?

The widower, who hypothetically retorted that remarriage was necessary to supply him with provisions and care, was reminded by Tertullian that God provided everything except perseverance. *De exhortatione castitatis* assures the widower that he requires no wife as housekeeper and organizer because all Christians, as soldiers of Christ, are fully disciplined to order affairs. Besides, he could, with the blessing of charity, hire a whole bevy of old widows as housekeepers. Since the last days were upon the world, no clamor for heirs is rational, or legitimate either. Even apart from such a consideration, children in general are such trouble that no sane man would want them. *De monogamia* offers the objector, as a substitute for heirs, the many brethren in the Church. Surely no one thought that the pagan Julian laws, penalizing the childless, applied to Christians.

Another of Tertullian's arguments turns about his conviction that the Second Coming was imminent. The time was near when the predicted woe would come to those with child; those so soon to approach Judgment should not come with the "baggage of children in the womb." Would people incessantly pursue accursed nuptials right up to the last moment? Considering the approaching end, and taking into account the general overpopulation of the earth, Tertullian declares obsolete the Old Testament's injunction to increase and multiply.

Even pagans, Tertullian next suggests, occasionally cherished celibacy and monogamy. Many heathen women had guarded their monogamous state with their blood; Flamens and the Pontifex Maximus could be married but once. Vesta had her consecrated virgins as did Juno, Apollo, Minerva, and Diana. If the very priests of Hell were continent, it behooved Christians also to be continent, asserted Tertullian.

One of Tertullian's favorite dictums holds that the death of a marriage partner clearly signifies God's will that the survivor remain single. The fact that a single leaf cannot fall without His permission assures that the death of a spouse does not occur without purpose. Any attempt to repair the situation presumptuously aims to restore what God has meaningfully rent asunder. No one should exercise his free will to choose what God does not desire. At best, God's permission to remarry is an indulgence, and to choose something granted only conditionally is undignified. In fact, God's permission to do anything is granted by Him only as a test to weed out the robust from the imperfect. The perfect will do what God desires rather than despise what God prefers.

Tertullian's seventh argument recalls that no digamist could officiate as bishop and that no widow, twice-married, could serve the Church. Persons who sought a second marriage from ministers pledged to monogamy acted inconsistently. Moreover, since the clergy must be elected from the laity, lay remarriage restricted the clerical supply. Montanist influence encouraged Tertullian to strengthen his stand against clerical digamy. He declares that all laymen ought to be monogamous, since, as real priests, they should be ideally prepared at all times to administer sacraments, especially Baptism.

Lastly, Tertullian thinks the New Testament and the example of Christ should be persuasive. *De monogamia* maintains that the Virgin married but once after the birth of Jesus and that Christ Himself was entirely continent. His spiritual nuptials with a single spouse, the Church, should be, to those who require one, a superb example of monogamy. In support of marital restraint Christ enjoined persons to be like little children and to imitate the dove, a one-mate creature. Moreover, Christ symbolically attended only one marriage feast and associated only with monogamists and celibates. If the example of the first Adam is too remote, let that of the second compel.

It remains to comment upon Book II of *Ad uxorem,* which so colorfully indicts mixed marriage. Tertullian interprets I Corinthians 7:39 as ordaining that no second marriage is legitimate unless it involves two Christians. It followed, in Tertullian's view, that any Christian who married a pagan should be excommunicated as a fornicator. Such a bastard union forced the Christian party, in order to please his mate, to enjoy sex rather than to accept it as a necessary evil. Moreover, such a marriage hampered the Christian's observance of rites and practice of charity. Toleration by the pagan party was not only patronizing but dangerous as well, since it implied knowledge of Christian secrets which would be held over the head of the Christian partner as a reserve weapon. A Christian wife necessarily became involved in pagan family practices; soon she would be adorning the door posts and drinking libations. True, the Christian convert previously married to a pagan subjected himself to the same unpleasantries. In his case, however, his election by God for conversion fashioned him into a storehouse of grace which would serve to sanctify the pagan party so closely associated with him. Besides, the moral advancement of the new Christian convert would impress the pagan member.

Even slave masters restricted the liberty of their charges to marry outside the household. All should stay within the fold even if it involved marriage to a poor Christian brother rather than to a wealthy pagan foreigner. Such a blessed Christian union puts no obstacles in the way of proper worship and the performance of spiritual and corporal works of mercy. In this environment, the Christian, having no fear that his alien spouse might attribute magical powers to his sacramentals, could openly make the sign of the cross.

E.G.W.

REFUTATION OF ALL HERESIES

Author: Saint Hippolytus (c.170-235)
Type of work: Polemical apology
First transcribed: c.225

Principal Ideas Advanced

Heresies depend more upon different schools of Greek philosophy than upon Scripture.

The Gnostic heresies, especially, combined, in a bizarre way, ideas from Greek philosophy, mystery cults, and astrology.

Sabellianism, derived from Heraclitus, had the support of both Roman bishops, Zephyrinus and Callistus.

Although a voluminous writer, Hippolytus, both as a person and as an author, virtually lost his identity in the West. This eclipse occurred partly because his theological speculations were not highly prized in the static Roman intellectual environment and also because his schism with the Roman church, although, eventually healed, left unpleasant aftertones. Probably more significant, however, was the fact that, as the last Roman writer to employ Greek, he used a language soon destined to become unintelligible to most of the Latin world. Even after Books IV-X of his *Philosophumena,* or *Refutation of All Heresies,* were discovered in 1842 at Mt. Athos, the assembled work was edited in 1851 under Origen's name. The treatise itself, however, speedily became popular, perhaps because its unfavorable comments on third century papal history were welcome to those anxious to disparage the pronouncements of Vatican I.

As the introduction promises, the treatise attempts to deflate prominent heresies, mostly Gnostic, by demonstrating, in some thirty-five case studies, that these theologies were monstrous concoctions of Greek philosophy, mystery cultism, and astrological magic, rather than legitimate systems based on Scriptural authority. By implication, Hippolytus castigates Greek philosophy as a misguiding influence and fails to regard it as a legitimate vehicle of partial revelation worthy of assimilation into Christian thought.

As background material, Book I supplies short summaries of each principal Greek philosophical school. Books II-III, still missing, apparently treated mystery cults and mythology. Astrology and magic are the subjects of Book IV. Much of the remaining parts of the treatise, Books V-IX, are drawn from Irenaeus. They describe the principal Christian heresies and endeavor to relate each to its supposed roots in pagan thought, particularly Greek philosophy. While discussing Sabellianism in Book IX, Hippolytus takes the occasion to indict bishops Zephyrinus and Callistus of Rome for Monarchianism. The work concludes with a summary in Book X and a final brief statement of orthodoxy as Hippolytus saw it.

The compendium of Greek philosophy in the first book, while extensive in coverage from Thales to Aristotle and Epicurus, is so based on ancient handbook materials that it leaves much to be desired both in thoroughness and analytical power.

Book IV, as a wide panorama of ancient astrology and magic, affords an intriguing view of the hazy pagan intellectual scene. Hippolytus discounts astrology on the ground that an infant's horoscope could not be fixed accurately because of the uncertainty of the exact moment of conception or of the precise minute of actual birth. Even should a split-second casting of the horoscope be possible, its illogical predictions were necessarily fallible. The assumption, for instance, that persons born in Virgo would be fair of complexion ludicrously excluded Negroes from being born during certain times of the year. Along with much such astrological gibberish, Book IV records the fanciful systems of prophecy that hopeful diviners built upon esoteric meanings of names, numbers, and letters. Obviously the acceptance of an *a priori* theory of harmony in the universe produced on one hand an abortion of astrological computations and symbolism postulating sidereal influences over man, and led, on the other, to a logical naïveté in legitimate astronomical calculations.

Hippolytus shows that by assuming an unquestioned sympathy among all parts of the universe, magic held that a microcosm, such as the body or the brain, could unveil mysteries of the macrocosm and, conversely, that the latter, principally through the stars, could influence the microcosm. Also under the heading of magic, this book preserves a repertoire of simple parlor tricks performed through collusion, sleight-of-hand, or knowledge of basic chemical properties. The combination of astrology read into the Scriptures by allegory and of hocus-pocus injected into the Christian liturgy by a new Magi produced, according to Hippolytus's thinking, a weird and blasphemous combination of patent nonsense.

Besides describing Gnostic heresies, Books V-IX attempt to explain Montanism and Sabellianism. The Gnostic system, even though bewildering, extravagant, and esoteric, is set forth as a calculated effort to relieve the Absolute and Immovable of the onus of creating matter. It strives for this end by setting up a hierarchy of divine emanations, or eons, to bridge the gap, as ideal archetypes, between the Absolute and the phenomenal, and by ascribing the actual physical creation to an errant, ignorant, accidental, or apostate act of one of the eons.

Hippolytus opens Book V with a description of the Ophitic school of Gnosticism which worshiped the serpent, Naas, as a beneficent deceiver of Eve. The Naaseni, he reported, tried to justify their composite confusion of Phrygian Judaism, Egyptian mystery cultism, and Christian revelation by resorting to the Gospel of Thomas. Hippolytus's original material on the teachings of Justinus provides a glimpse into the very origins of Ophitic doctrines. Justinus is pictured as grafting Jewish sacred lore on to Herodotus's classical legend of Hercules in which the Greek demi-god's sexual intercourse with a snake-maiden produced three offsprings from which, as principles or roots, creation eventually emerged. After a time, Jesus, the son of Joseph and Mary, a prophet impervious to the wily Naas, was requested by superior eons to redirect the material world. The Naas, however, resented the interference and contrived Jesus' crucifixion.

After discussing the equally fantastic theories and activities of Simon Magus, Book VI devotes itself principally to the Valentinians, whom Hippolytus considered indebted mainly to Plato and Pythagoras. Stating it simply, this Gnostic school constructed a threefold plane of reality: the absolute realm of "Depth" and "Silence," the Ideal sphere of "Word" and "Life," and the actual world of "Man" and "Church." The emanation, "Christ," and the composite eon, "Jesus," respectively, reshaped and espoused the errant "Sophia" who broke the barrier of the Pleroma indirectly to engender the physical universe.

In Book VII occur the heresy of Basilides, which Hippolytus traces back to Aristotle, and the heresy of the strange Melchisedecians, who assigned to Melchisedec a priority over Christ. Hippolytus ascribes Marcion's dualism to the Greek philosopher Empedocles, who long before had emphasized two fundamental causes in the cosmos: Friendship and Discord. The latter, supposedly translated into the Demiurge by Marcion, served him as a ready-made artificer of plurality.

Hippolytus claims in Book VIII that the Docetae likened the creative God to the seed of a fig tree which produced three offspring: Stem, Leaf, and Fruit, as triple eons destined to germinate further hermaphroditic emanations whose eventual discord was composed by a joint eon, "Savior." The last, as a sum total of all eons, was equal, except in so far as he was begotten, to the original fig seed. Book VIII also lists the Quarto-decimans, who insisted on celebrating Easter on the fourteenth day of Nisan, and the Montanists, proscribed not so much for theological errancy as for their over-rigid system of ethics and for their presumptuous claims that their prophetesses were inspired by the Paraclete.

The controversial Book IX contains a large and important section on the Essenes and their tenets. But principally it is devoted to contemporary Christian heresies, especially Monarchianism, which tried to preserve the unity of the Godhead by denying the individuality of the three Persons. Hippolytus maintains that these unorthodox ideas were derived from Heraclitus, who taught that the universe was one: that unity came from plurality and it, conversely, from unity. As promulgated in Rome, with different accents by Epigonus, Cleomenes, and Sabellius, this heresy professed a modalism asserting that God merely changed His name as He manifested Himself under different guises and circumstances. At this point the *Philosophumena* accuses two Bishops of Rome, the "stupid" Zephyrinus (died c. 217) and the "knavish" Callistus (died c. 222) of espousing and spreading this new Sabellian message. According to Hippolytus, Zephyrinus was goaded by the scheming Callistus into making public statements that the Father and the Son were one and the same. Callistus, in turn, claimed that his assailant was a "ditheist," apparently implying that Hippolytus, in his Sabellian phobia, overemphasized the distinctions of the Persons. In the dispute, Hippolytus chose to dub Callistus's church as a mere faction or "school" of thought, and Hippolytus thereby set himself up as a rival schismatic bishop. History reveals that Hippolytus maintained this position as antipope throughout the reigns of the next two pontiffs, Urban and Pontian, until eventually he was exiled, along with the latter, to Sardinia. Here both died together, reconciled. In the *Philosophumena,* Hippolytus defensively explains Callistus's popularity by declaring that the pope used a message of moral laxity as bait to attract followers, then goes on to indict him on several new counts: that, excessively lenient in forgiving sins, he was the "first" to remit sensual offenses; that he retained sinful bishops and relaxed restrictions on clerical continency; and that by recognizing as ecclesiastically valid marriages between matrons and slaves, he abetted abortions and murders. Callistus, Hippolytus further accuses, also permitted rebaptism.

Hippolytus's tone throughout is vehement and personal; his characterization of Callistus's marriage regulation is distorted. His sketch of the pope as a roguish ex-slave, embezzler, and drifter, although colorful and humorous, betrays more pathetic vindictiveness than scrupulous accuracy. The heretical statements imputed to Zephyrinus and Callistus are at best ambiguous, isolated, and out of context. Even Callistus's eventual excommunication of Sabellius, Hippolytus smugly attributes to his own intimidation of the pope. The debatable charge that Callistus "first" forgave sins of the flesh, possibly supported by a remark of Tertullian, serves still to encourage critics of Rome to cite Callistus as a serious innovator rather than as a bishop who merely implemented the full power of the keys. Undoubtedly, unlike the sterner Hippolytus, the pope chose not to interpret the Church as an aristocracy of the virtuous.

Book X begins with a summary of the entire work. A Jewish chronology, now somewhat mutilated, was injected to demonstrate the antiquity of the Hebrew dispensation over that of the pagan. Finally, Hippolytus states what he considers to be the true nature of God, and especially of the Father and the Logos.

E.G.W.

EPISTLE TO DIOGNETUS

Author: Unknown
Type of work: Christian apologetics
First transcribed: c.130-c.230

Principal Ideas Advanced

The gods of the Gentiles are lifeless idols made of stone and earthenware; the God worshiped by the "new race" of Christians is the Creator who sent His beloved Child, as God, to save man by persuasion.

Although the Jews worship God, they show that they do not understand Him, for they offer Him sacrifices; in this respect the Jews are like those who worship idols.

Christians dwell in the world, but they do not belong to the world; nevertheless, as citizens of Heaven, they provide the world with unity, through their incorruptible spirit.

Christians love their enemies, and they assume the burdens of their neighbors; in so acting, Christians imitate the love which God has for the world and which He proved through sending His Son, by whom the Church is made rich in the benefits of grace.

The anonymous Christian apology which comes to us under the title *Epistula ad Diognetum,* or *Letter to Diognetus,* was probably composed by more than one early apologist, for historical and stylistic evidence suggests that the early part of the letter was written by one man in the second century, while the latter part was composed by another in the third. The survival power of the epistle may be attributed to the distinctive spiritual forthrightness which illuminates it and to the clear and authoritative manner with which the letter argues that the Church is the historical body which the Incarnation made possible and through which God proves His love for man.

The "Diognetus" to whom the letter is addressed can be identified with no particular historical personage, but since the importance of the letter resides in its spirited defense of the early Christian Church, it is enough to realize that here we have a powerful and undoubtedly influential statement composed by a confident Christian and addressed to a secular ruler who has shown some curiosity about the new religion.

The author of the letter begins by calling attention to the interest which Diognetus has expressed in undertaking a thorough investigation of Christianity. Diognetus, it appears, would like to know more about the God whom Christians worship; he would like to understand the unique Christian attitude toward the world and death; and he wishes to learn the reasons for the Christian rejection of the religious beliefs and practices of both the Greeks and the Jews.

Two specific questions which the author undertakes to answer become central in the epistle. The writer states, "You would also like to know the source of the loving affection that they [the Christians] have for each other. You wonder, too, why this new race or way of life has appeared on earth now and not earlier." The answer, of course, is that God came to man and through exhibiting His love inspired the Christians with a world-transforming love for one another; the new race appears when it does because it could not have come into being prior to Christ's life in the world. The answers to all the questions which Diognetus presumably has asked are developments of the central claim that the Church is the creation which the Incarnation inspired and which God strengthens through His grace.

Even to understand the epistle, its author tells Diognetus, it is necessary for Diognetus to clear himself of old ideas and to become "like a new man. . . ." If one looks anew at the practices of the Greeks and the Jews, one discovers the superstitious basis of the old religions. The gods which the Gentiles worship turn out, upon critical examination, to be nothing more than lifeless idols made of wood, silver, stone, and earthenware. The Jews are superior to the Gentiles in that the Jews worship the one God who is the Creator, but they show their gross misunderstanding of the divine nature when they attempt to offer blood, fat, and burnt offerings as sacrifices to God. The Gentiles err in making offerings to lifeless idols; the Jews err in making offerings to God, who needs nothing.

The secret of Christianity is not to be found in the customs of the Christians, the author explains; Christians have no distinctive language, manner of life, or place of residence. Christians follow the customs of the country in which they live, but they are nevertheless aliens and foreigners wherever they live, for "their citizenship is in heaven." Christians love all men, even though men persecute them; Christians meet suffering and death with confidence, for through suffering and death they are brought to life.

The writer of the epistle emphasizes the spiritual unity of the Christian body by arguing that just as the soul, which is invisible, lives in a mortal and corruptible body of which it is not a part but to which it is indispensable, so Christians live in the world but are not of it. The world is held together by the Christians who are imprisoned in it. The task of informing the world with love is one which God has prescribed for the Christians, and even though they are persecuted, they will persist in their duty to God.

The author insists that the Christian is inspired by "the holy, incomprehensible word" which comes from God Himself. The revelation of the word was through no earthly administrator, nor did it come even from an angel. God sent "the Designer and Maker of the universe himself"; God sent the one whose purposes order the world, and He sent Him "out of kindness and gentleness, like a king sending his son who is himself a king." The climactic, paradoxical, yet revealing claim follows: "He sent him as God; he sent him as man to men."

How else, the apologist asks, is one to account for the unvanquished spirit of those Christians who, though thrown to wild animals, do not deny the Lord, than by supposing that God's power does indeed support those who find themselves new persons through His Child? The knowledge of God strengthens all Christians, the writer of the epistle insists; God brought the knowledge of Himself to man by showing Himself as a man. While in the world, God showed Himself to be a compassionate friend of man, and He freely suffered for the salvation of man. Although God did not approve of man's sins, He allowed men to prove through sinful acts that they were unworthy when left to their own powers. Then God gave His own Son, the righteous and incorruptible Child, as a ransom for guilty and corruptible man. Thus men came to learn and wonder at the power of God's love, and they rejoiced in the new life which the sacrifice of the Son made possible.

The writer of the epistle then advises Diognetus that the first requirement for those who would share the joyous Christian faith is to seek knowledge of God. God has given man the power to reason and to learn, through Christ, of God's love. Once God is known, God is loved, for He alone is good. And once God is loved, the author continues, those who love Him then seek to imitate Him, for God wills that they do so.

The imitation of God consists in taking one's neighbor's burden on oneself; it involves helping the weak and providing for the needy. In such a life a man knows true happiness.

The remainder of the letter, a part attributed by some scholars to a writer of the early third century, is written in praise of Christ as the Logos. This concluding section is only a few paragraphs long, but it is in accord with the ideas and sentiments of the preceding part of the letter, and it has a persuasive fervor of its own.

The writer establishes his authority as one who has been a disciple of the Apostles. He argues that the Logos was sent in order that men might learn the mysteries of the Father, and he describes the Logos as "he who was from the beginning, who appeared new and was found to be old, and is ever born young in the hearts of the saints. This is the eternal one, who today is accounted a Son, by whom the Church is made rich and grace is multiplied as it unfolds among the saints. . . ."

The importance of knowing God is stressed by the author as he compares the Church to a Paradise in which may be found both the Tree of Life and the Tree of Knowledge. Not knowledge but disobedience is destructive; to know God's love and to act with reverence is to insure one's place in Paradise. To pick the fruit of the tree of knowledge when one lives according to the love of God is to emulate the Virgin, not Eve. Thus, the writer concludes, "salvation is displayed, and the apostles are interpreted, and the Lord's Passover goes forward, and the seasons are brought together and set in order, and the Logos rejoices as he teaches the saints—the Logos through whom the Father is glorified. To him be glory forevermore. Amen."

ON FIRST PRINCIPLES

Author: Origen (Origenes Adamantius, c.185-c.254)
Type of work: Dogmatic theology
First transcribed: 220-230

PRINCIPAL IDEAS ADVANCED

The defection of celestial spirits originally created pure by God has resulted in a hierarchy of different spiritual beings each burdened with a body dense in proportion to its sinfulness.

Man, like the other fallen spirits, is sufficiently equipped to purge himself and regain his pristine position through his untrammeled free will and God's help.

Knowledge of the divine economy is gleaned by theologians from the Scriptures and tradition; the former, to be intelligible, must be allegorically interpreted to augment its literal meaning.

The four books of the *De principiis* (*On First Principles*) were written rather early in Origen's career during the time he still directed the catechetical school in Alexandria. This work represents one of the earliest serious efforts to synthesize basic tenets of Christian thought into an organized corpus. Unfortunately for students, the book is preserved in a loosely edited Latin translation by Origen's admirer, Rufinus, who labored too zealously at times in attempting to chasten the original Greek text of dubious and heterodox passages.

The first Christian writing to recognize the validity of the theologian as a professional man, the *De principiis* encouraged the development of a new class of thought purveyors destined to dominate the Western intellectual scene for over fifteen hundred years. The preface expresses Origen's conviction that a definition of some basic theological premises was imperative since Christians differed so widely not only in doctrinal details but even in fundamentals such as the doctrine of the Trinity. While the Apostles had made the credal essentials sufficiently clear to warrant such a formulation, Origen believed that the Apostles deliberately left peripheral matters obscure. In so doing, the Apostles intended to open up a legitimate field of investigation in which men, favored by a charism of wisdom and knowledge, could exercise their talents by fathoming origins and reasons, supplying details, and synthesizing conclusions.

As an imaginative and speculative work, unrestricted by any official doctrinal definition, the *De principiis* involved Origen in theological controversy; his views were denounced by some, but the Church has never condemned him. He was certainly one of the most influential of early theologians.

The Alexandrian announces that his tools of investigation in this grand attempt to give meaning to God's entire economy will be the Scriptures and the Apostolic tradition of the Church; however, he calls liberally upon pagan demonology with its quasi-magical overtones, Greek rationalism with its logical and allegorical ramifications, and Hellenistic philosophy with its rarefied and mystical implications. If Origen Christianizes Plato, Plato Hellenizes Origen. While he tempers Plato's dictum that wisdom is virtue and sufficiently modifies the philosopher's basic dualism to stay within Christian boundaries, the Greek thinker fatally convinces the Christian theologian that all punishment is educative and persuades him to such a degree that pre-existence of souls is a necessary explanation for reality that Origen virtually accepts a limited form of the Pythagorean doctrine of transmigration of souls. The Porch further diluted Origen's orthodoxy by contributing the thesis that the world would be restored periodically. Origen seeks even to accommodate Aristotle's psychological speculations on the nature of the soul to his analysis of the Christian free will.

Despite some digressions, the *De principiis* proceeds in quite an orderly fashion. Book I opens with a consideration of the apex of Reality, the supernatural world with all its constituents. Its Alpha and Omega is the incomprehensible Trinitarian God. The Father, as Master of the entire creation, bestowed all existence. The Son, as the Word, was the agent through which the Father exercised His power; as Reason, the Son conferred rationality upon man. The Holy Spirit, unknowable except through Revelation, as Sanctifier dealt with the regenerate. Besides the uniquely incorporeal Trinity, an enigmatic host of rational creatures, both good and evil, exists in this spiritual world: the Devil, "Princes of this World," Angels, Thrones, Principalities, Powers, Dominions, souls of men, and even stars. Created in time, and endowed with absolute free will, without any foreordained flaw in their constitution, these beings are subject to change. Originally all identical as celestial rational natures, these creatures, made by God out of sheer goodness, began, either through slothfulness or perversity, to defect from their lofty ethereal estate. Commensurate with the degree of their desertion and their remaining spiritual vigor, in short, according to their conduct, these rational creatures were saddled with bodies of more or less density. Men, as fallen angels, whose souls were, it might be said, chilled condensations of divine love, stand somewhat midway in the supernatural order, struggling, like all other fallen beings, to recapture the fervor of their pristine ghostly state. This defection and purging, this fall and rise of spiritual bodies through the different stages of the heavenly hierarchy, began in a state which antedated their bodily careers. It will continue through ages of time and through a series of worlds until all will have compensated for their shortcomings and will finally stand in rarefied form before the incorporeal Trinity. Thus, the consummation of things will revert to the beginning.

About the stars, Origen was more imaginative than definite. He classes them as rational creatures with souls implanted from without, tenuous in nature, yet still burdened with corporeal bodies.

Book II deals with the role of the material world in God's economy. This world, Origen wrote, comprises the irrational creation, the heavens, and all animate and inanimate things consisting of created matter upon which, in a Platonic way, qualities have been impressed to give them form. The great diversity of objects in this world, as well as the different future worlds themselves were designed to accommodate the rational creatures in their various stages of perfection who require an environment of time and place to complete their required cleansing. The world itself Origen envisages, in a quasi-Stoic manner, as a huge animal animated by something suggestive of the Neoplatonic World Soul.

To discredit Gnostics, Origen securely identifies the Jewish God, the Creator of the material world, with the Father of Christ. The Son, required as a mediator between created things and God, became incarnate to restore order, moderation, and regulation in the world. That the spiritual and material spheres were truly joined in the Person of Christ is guaranteed by His miracles, the Old Testament prophesies, and the effectiveness of His message. Christ's human soul provided the intermediate link to join these two diverse natures in a union so thorough that it could be likened to a piece of molten iron impregnated with the brightness of fire. The Holy Spirit contributed to the overall divine plan by revealing to man the mysteries of God's divine economy.

In Origen's opinion, just as man's general position in the spiritual hierarchy of rational souls depends upon the extent of his defection from God and also upon his regeneration, so each individual's diversified position on earth reflects his conduct in a previous life. All human vessels, according to their purity or impurity, receive a definite office to discharge on earth in order that they might mutually assist one another in the task of working out their salvation. At the end of each world-era, all bodies will arise, but with different qualities according to the degree to which each man has been purged. Some, Origen argues, might be resurrected with bright bodies, others with dark. Each contaminated soul kindles his own temporary hell-fire with his sins as fuel. This fire serves to weld together again, as it were, the soul still disarranged and racked by centrifugal feelings, affections, passions, and pangs caused by the dislocation from God's purpose. Thus, restoration can proceed and remedial work continue in a subsequent world. The same resurrection will usher the blessed into an afterlife of education. Their first classroom, in an earthly location, probably Paradise, will instruct them in the causes, meaning, and operation of physical nature. Their progress will determine their promotion to a higher school for more intensive coaching in the intricacies of the stars and of creation as a whole. Finally, in the highest realms, insight into the heavenly mysteries will be imparted through the contemplation of God Himself.

Book III is a treatise on moral theology dealing with man's struggle for salvation. Nothing, according to Origen, limits man's power of volition. God permits even evil to go unpunished temporarily, not only in order that the truly good might stand out but also to insure that the sinner will become ill enough to desire the Physician. Free choice, not foreordination, determines whether one is a vessel of honor or dishonor in this world and whether he will reverse his position tomorrow in another world.

Man was never a hopeless victim of evil invisible spirits, Origen claimed. These demons control a person only after he, through an initial intemperate use of his natural instincts and emotions, has given access to the evil one and permitted him to inflate indiscretions into full-fledged sins. Moreover, God especially aids men in their unequal fight with bad angels. Prolonged subjection to evil spirits and to the worldly wisdom they exploit means not that a man is divinely foreordained to evil but that he is suffering from guilt inherited from a prior existence.

Nor do bodily instincts and emotions cancel out free will, Origen believed. Defeat results primarily from man's own slothfulness, which attenuates his resistance. Nor does any fatal flaw in the soul permit temptations to overpower men. The will of the spirit is superior to any possible irrational part in man's soul or to his animal soul, which was transmitted in his blood by traducianism. Certainly no mechanical world negates free will. All things in the universe are purposely ordered to assist men. All ranks in the rational creation, planets and angels included, form something of a communion of spirits to assist souls, especially those of men who, on account of their excessive defects, stand in need of grosser bodies and require more training. Thus, the entire material world is, in the last analysis, the result of God's intention to create the necessary diversified environment which each man's free defection requires as an aid to his regeneration. This material world, even the final enemy death itself, ends when all souls, after countless ages and worlds, completely terminate the state of enmity with God.

Book IV deals with the Scriptures, man's principal tool in trying to appraise the economy of God intelligently. According to Origen, the unattractive phraseology and hackneyed presentation of the sacred books were purposely intended lest, if well written, they be taken for mere polished literary exercises of men. The Scriptures not only contain apparent mistakes and specious assertions about God but often, in the historical sections, record impossible or fictitious events such as Jesus' reported viewing of all the kingdoms of the world from one mountain. Again, the legislative parts, Origen argues, often command inappropriate, unreasonable, or impossible actions, such as the injunction not to eat griffins and the order to cast away one's right eye if one has looked at a woman lustfully. So obscure, to Origen, was the mystical economy of the sacred writings that he writes that no one, even though enlightened by the grace of God and gifted with an informed mind, can ever hope entirely to fathom it. No student, certainly, can make an intelligent effort to do so if he resorts only to a literal interpretation, since all the Scriptures have a basic spiritual meaning. The Scriptures are like a field filled with plants of all kinds in which hidden treasures lie around buried under the stalks. These treasures of wisdom can be uncovered by the allegorical method, assuming that, besides the literal and historical meaning, a mystical and a moral signification is intended. These three interpretations, Origen contends in conclusion, correspond to the three parts of man: flesh, soul, and spirit and are intelligible respectively to the simple-minded, the partly instructed, and the wise.

E.G.W.

THE ORATION AND PANEGYRIC ADDRESSED TO ORIGEN

Author: Saint Gregory Thaumaturgus (c.213-c.268)
Type of work: Philosophy of Christian education
First transcribed: c.238

Principal Ideas Advanced

In rendering thanks to anyone, especially to one's spiritual teacher, one should thank God the Father, who is the fount of all blessings, through Christ, who is the Word and the Truth.

Through divine providence Origen became Gregory's teacher; from Origen, Gregory learned to value philosophy as the foundation of piety, to understand the virtues through practicing them, and to appreciate the importance of knowing oneself.

Origen also taught that piety is the beginning and end of all the virtues.

Saint Gregory Thaumaturgus, called "Thaumaturgus" or "Wonder-worker" because of the miraculous wonders attributed to him—including such legendary deeds as the moving of stones by a word, the casting out of demons, and the drying up of lakes—was Bishop of Neo-Caesarea, in Pontus, from about 238 until his death. The last thirty years of his life were distinguished by his preaching, which he continued despite the Decian persecution and the harassment of the Northern barbarians. But his place in the history of Catholic thought is secured through his tribute to his renowned spiritual teacher, Origen, who converted both Gregory and his brother Athenodorus to the Christian faith. A few Scriptural commentaries from the hand of Gregory remain, together with his brief but influential *Declaration of Faith,* but it is *The Oration and Panegyric Addressed to Origen* which continues to be of interest, both because of the charm and simplicity of Gregory's expression of gratitude to his teacher and because of the Christianized Socratic image of Origen which emerges from Gregory's oration.

Gregory begins his oration with the traditional disclaimer that other occupations have impaired his meager skill in oratory. He declares that it has been eight years since he has addressed the public, for he has been preoccupied with the study of Latin and the law, and he has not had the opportunity to learn the art of using language eloquently. Yet he must make his rude language speak in praise of a man, a teacher, whose virtue exceeds any descriptive power of language; namely, Origen, with whom Gregory and his brother Athenodorus have studied for several years.

Gregory describes Origen as a man of great intellectual caliber, endowed with noble and "well-nigh divine" powers. The task of paying homage to such a teacher is made more difficult by the decision which Gregory has made to deal with that which is godlike in Origen, with "that in him which has most affinity with God. . . ."

The orator, who is about to leave for his native town, wants to spend his last moments in Caesarea (of Palestine, where he has studied with Origen), attempting to express his gratitude for all that he has learned from Origen. Gregory declares that thanksgiving to the Father is made possible through the Son; thus, it is through Christ, who is the Word, the Truth, the Wisdom, and the Power of the Father, that Gregory will thank God for having providentially arranged to have Origen introduce Gregory to the Christian faith and the virtuous life.

Gregory explains that he was born of heathen parents, that when he was fourteen he lost his father, and only his mother remained to supervise his education. He began the study of public speaking. His teacher encouraged him to undertake the study of the law, for the law would be useful whatever profession Gregory finally settled upon. Gregory had planned to study in Berytus, but through a series of accidents, which Gregory interprets as providential, he and his brother came to Caesarea and thus to Origen. At first Gregory was inclined to leave the town and go to Berytus, as he had originally planned, but Origen, with great persuasive powers, convinced Gregory that philosophy, as the pursuit of wisdom, the knowledge of good and evil, was the only study by which a reasonable man could hope to attain to the virtuous life. According to Origen, no man could be truly pious who did not philosophize.

Origen's defense of philosophy was supplemented, according to Gregory's account, by the persuasive powers of the teacher's affectionate disposition. In knowing Origen, Gregory knew the power of that love which God inspires, and in response to that love Gregory was willing to abandon everything, even his fatherland and his friends, in order to study that philosophy by which one could acquire the virtues which divine love both inspires and strengthens.

Athenodorus and Gregory were then instructed in logic, physics, geometry, and astronomy. But these studies were secondary in importance to the study of ethics, the philosophy of morality. Origen endeavored to impart to his students "a well-disciplined and stedfast and religious spirit," and thus he taught not only by words but also by deeds. The virtues of prudence, temperance, righteousness, and fortitude were developed in their souls by the manner and deeds of Origen, who taught more through action than through discourse.

Origen stressed the importance of the study of Greek philosophy, and he commended to Gregory the Socratic dictum, "Know thyself." True prudence consists in the acquisition of self-knowledge, and it is in knowing oneself, Origen claimed, that one shares a virtue with God.

With humility Gregory declares that, through no fault of the teacher, Gregory has not yet acquired the virtues which, through the teacher, he has learned to understand and love. But he has learned that philosophy is the foundation of piety and that piety is the beginning and end of all the virtues. What Origen has accomplished is to fire Gregory with the ambition to make himself like God, to draw near to God by pursuing the virtues.

Gregory explains that Origen taught philosophy by urging his students to become familiar with various writings, both theological and philosophical, having to do with the nature of God as "the Cause of all things." Origen urged Gregory and his brother to read everything that had been written about the Divinity, but he suggested that they avoid premature critical judgments and that they abstain from the reading of atheistical works.

Origen discussed the works of those who had fallen into error, in order that his students might acquire the ability to discriminate between truth and error. The teacher insisted that authoritative teachings in divine matters were to be found in the Scriptures, not in the views of human teachers who had not been inspired by the Prophets and the Word.

In closing, Gregory compares his having to leave Caesarea with Adam's having to leave Paradise. He suggests that he has not devoted himself to silence and the practice of the virtues and that he must, like Adam, "eat of the soil all the days of my life. . . ." Like the prodigal son and the deported Jews, Gregory must leave the place where he has had access to the mysteries of God, and he must begin a new life in a strange land.

The only consolation, Gregory declares, is that there is a Keeper of all men, a Savior, Protector, and Physician, who will watch over him. Gregory addresses Origen with the request that Origen pray for him in order that, when Gregory is no longer in the presence of Origen, God will send a guardian, "some angel to be our comrade on the way."

Ahead of Gregory lay the demanding task of leading the people of Neo-Caesarea as their bishop; the love of virtue which Origen had encouraged in him would give him the strength to persist for thirty years in preaching of divine matters. But already, in his *Oration and Panegyric,* delivered in praise of his teacher, Gregory had shown the eloquence which the love of Christian piety, and of the Word which is its source, made possible.

CONTRA CELSUM

Author: Origen (Origenes Adamantius, c.185-c.254)
Type of work: Apologetics
First transcribed: c.245-250

Principal Ideas Advanced

Christianity is not barbarous, childish, novel, low-class, or treasonable, as Celsus asserts in his True Discourse.

Rather, the wholesomeness of Christianity is guaranteed by sacred Revelation and by the effectiveness of its ethical message.

Christianity is compatible with much of classical thought and Christians are loyal to the Roman government; however, to be a completely legitimate ruling body, the Roman government must conform its administration to the natural law.

The *Contra Celsum* (*Against Celsus*) remains the most trenchant apology in early Christian literature. Convinced that Christianity was invulnerable because of its intrinsic merits, Origen undertook this work somewhat reluctantly and at the prodding of his friend Ambrose. Less robust than Origen, Ambrose feared that Celsus' learned *True Discourse,* if left unchallenged, might prove an embarrassing assault upon Christian faith. Even though Celsus had written his four-book treatise as early as 178, establishing himself in the eyes of posterity as the most resourceful critic of Christianity before Porphyry, Origen had never heard of him. He finally identifies the pagan author simply as an Epicurean parading under various philosophical disguises in order to render his assault less parochial.

Origen's reply, in eight books, comprising over 620 chapters, probably preserves as much as three-quarters of Celsus' text. On the whole, the apology records an engaging battle of wits between two cultured and sincere men representing antithetical intellectual worlds. The work's repetitiousness is probably the fault both of Celsus and of Origen. On the one hand, Origen in the *Contra Celsum* followed the arrangement of Celsus' *True Discourse* point by point. On the other, as his *De principiis* shows, he had a natural tendency toward discursiveness.

In Books I and II, a hypothetical Jew poses objections to Christ's pretensions. Book III emphasizes Celsus' classical charge that Christianity was not intellectually respectable. Discussion of the prophesies occupies much of Book IV, while V, VI, and VII gather up sundry accusations. Especially instructive is Book VIII, in which Celsus dwells for some thirty chapters on pagan objections to the Christian attitude toward the state.

In this somewhat disorganized composition, five or six indictments against the new religion seem to crystallize. Origen is called upon immediately to face the charge that Christianity was of barbarous origin. To Celsus, the Jews were a groveling Mediterranean race, artless and unproductive fugitives from Egypt, whose teacher, Moses, had to acquire wisdom from foreign nations. In Celsus' mind, the rude Jewish prophets spoke as jugglers of words, relating childish anthropomorphic tales about a God who, after fabricating an unsophisticated cosmology in which spirit and matter were mixed, occupied Himself with ribs, serpents, and arks. Jehovah, to his way of thinking, was not only a weak disciplinarian but also an inhuman ogre who demanded the bloody sacrifice of his Son.

The cultivated Epicurean consequently branded Christianity a new Jewish offshoot, a foolish, irrational, and stupid superstition which encouraged its devotees to creep behind blind faith. Christian instructors, knowing that no wise man could possibly accept the Gospel, bypassed the educated and prudent and bade only the dull-witted and uninstructed to approach with confidence. Self-deluded, these presumptuous tutors acted as drunken men or victims of ophthalmia when they dared to teach others. More specifically, Celsus reproached Christian thought for blissfully disregarding weighty intellectual problems posed by Greek philosophy, especially the dichotomy between being and becoming. The Incarnation, he complained, outraged the Eternal since it necessarily involved change from good to evil, assumed that God is passible, immersed divinity in pollution, and stained the spirit with contact of the body. The

Jewish account of Creation violated the philosophical dictum that nothing corruptible could be the handiwork of God. Classical cosmology taught, according to Celsus, that matter was eternal and formless, and that any qualities it assumed were derived from a source other than divine. No product of matter could be immortal, for evil was an inherent constant in matter. As a true Epicurean, Celsus held that man, animals, and all their works, as well as all operations of nature, were but part of an irrational mechanism running in fatalistic circles. Consequently, a belief in Providence was unscientific.

The third onslaught against Christianity revolves about the accusation that it attracted only the riffraff and the wicked. Even Jesus' immediate disciples, Celsus writes, denied Him perfidiously and then shamefully abandoned Him rather than face death. He points out that Christ could gather to Himself at best only ten sailors and tax collectors of the most disreputable and shiftless character. Unlike the holy pagan mysteries which excluded the unclean, Christians put a premium upon sinfulness for admission to theirs by opening doors to thieves, poisoners, plunderers, and blasphemers.

Celsus' fourth charge labels Christianity's founder a human sophist who brought crucifixion upon Himself by His arrogance. Jesus' doubtful parentage was clearly reflected in the suspiciously confused geneologies of the Gospels. According to Celsus, Jesus was born of an adulterous relationship between Mary and a soldier, Panthera. Rejected at home, His family fled to Egypt where He was raised as an illegitimate child and where He learned simple tricks of magic. Later on, something of a brigand chief, He reneged on His promises, hid when accosted, and hawked about a message quite contradictory to that of His acknowledged Father. Thus, His claims as a teacher, a model, and a divinity were arrogant in the extreme. His unheroic actions belied His claim to deity. Nowhere did He shame His enemies, revenge Himself on evil doers, requite insult and ridicule, nor did He conquer final adversity by coming down from the cross. His puny and ignoble body was no worthy receptacle for a god. Christians, thought Celsus, would do better to worship the more versatile Jonah than this Jesus who was on the level of a demon.

The fifth indictment Celsus brings against Christianity is that it offers nothing new. It appropriated Jewish books and then proceeded to quarrel over their interpretation. Many Jewish ideas stolen by the Christians, Celsus points out, were not themselves indigenous to the Hebrews. Jehovah Himself could properly be addressed under names of many other divinities. Christianity's ethics duplicated those of much classical philosophical teaching, especially that of Plato. The latter's concept of the Deity, his ideas of the human soul, and even his dialectical method, all were repeated in Christian teaching. Doctrines of the new faith, with superficial differences, often suggested to Celsus the mythology of the Egyptians; Christian Scriptures related many events familiar to Greek and barbarian alike. Even Mithraism arranged, as did Christianity, for the soul's ascent to God. In agreement with Stoicism, the young religion taught that God should be regarded as a spirit. If Christianity required someone's death as a feature of its doctrinal system,

Celsus suggests that it could have found many apt heroic examples to choose from among pagan characters.

Finally, Celsus taunts Christians with treason in forming secret and illegal associations. Originating as a rebellion against the Jews, the Christian movement remained throughout an esoteric forbidden society which shunned official altar and temple. Now that the fruit of Christian impiety was ripening in the form of barbarian threats to the state, Christians blithely disclaimed any obligation to serve in the Roman army. By denying that state law was the final arbiter of good and evil, Christianity constituted an internal separatist movement. Its devotees, a group of frogs holding council in a marsh, a ball of worms crawling together in a dungheap, presumptuously asserted that they had a monopoly upon God and that everything existed for their sake and under their dominion. After making such accusations, Celsus ends Book VIII with an impassioned and sincere appeal to the Christians to lay aside their nonsense and perversity and make common cause for the public welfare.

Origen responds to Celsus' onslaught with admirable erudition, acuteness, and decorum, drawing imaginatively and with telling effect both on his own wit and on stock answers in earlier Christian apologies. Only on a few points does he accuse Celsus of irreverence, ignorance, or illogicalness of such magnitude that a rebuttal would be unworthy of Origen's talents.

Depending upon the situation, the Christian doctor relies upon one or more lines of argumentation. He often counters by preying upon the weaknesscs of classical religion and philosophy, especially the stupidity of idol worship and the enervating effect of ideological dissension. Sometimes to disarm criticism, Origen takes advantage of similarities between pagan and Christian thought. Only rarely does he have the opportunity to capitalize upon misinformation, for Celsus is an accurate and careful scholar although he sometimes does confound heretical and orthodox views. Seldom, too, can Origen find reason to turn a faulty logical argument against his adversary. If possible, he counterbalances Celsus' examples by marshaling an impressive array of his own. In general, he relies upon the trustworthy and venerable background of Christianity to guarantee his premises; to him, statements of sacred Scripture vouched for by God through the agency of wise Jewish sages and institutions was unassailable materials, if tempered properly by allegory. Origen believed that to any open-minded pagan the moral regeneration that accompanied conversion should be conclusive evidence of the new faith's supernatural power and legitimacy. In the end Origen forcefully appeals, in a cosmopolitan way, to natural law, maintaining its superiority over the narrow claims of Roman positive law. Counterattacking Celsus' last objection, Origen holds that the legitimacy of the state depended upon the extent to which it implemented the natural law, which is synonymous with the law of the Gospel. Origen agrees, for practical purposes, to advocate payment of taxes, but he insists that Christians substitute prayer for military service. Eventually he envisages a peaceful, universal, spiritual anarchy where the restraint of law and state compulsion would disappear in the face of the Gospel's regenerative powers, and where every world citizen ultimately would be transformed into a model of Christian virtue.

Eusebius judged the *Contra Celsum* so compelling and conclusive that he considered it virtually a final vindication of Christianity against all pagans and heretics. The popularity of the work increased greatly during the Enlightenment when a premium was put on any materials critical of any *a priori* system of thought.

E.G.W.

ON THE UNITY OF THE CATHOLIC CHURCH

Author: Saint Cyprian (Thascius Caecilius Cyprianus, c.200-258)
Type of work: Ecclesiology
First transcribed: c.251

Principal Ideas Advanced

Disunity in the Church is an intolerable condition inspired by the Devil and resulting, at least in part, from ignorance of the origins and sources of ecclesiastical authority.

Authority in the universal Church came through one man, Peter, into the hands of the general episcopacy; each bishop exercises the fullness of this episcopal power in his own area.

Membership in the one Church, institutionalized under the episcopacy, is essential; otherwise, no one secures reward for his faith and works even if they include martyrdom.

On the Unity of the Catholic Church, an ardent plea for Church solidarity in the face of schism, is the first extant work on Christian ecclesiology. Although this treatise is but a small pastoral letter of twenty-seven chapters, it came to be one of the most controversial writings of the early Church. It seems to have been composed in 251 partly in reaction to the rise of factionalism in the African church led by the deacon Felicissimus, who favored lenient treatment of the Lapsi after the Decian persecution. But, more pertinently, it was issued in response to the schism of Novatian in Rome. The work underwent revision in or about the year 255 at the hands of Cyprian himself.

The controversial character of the work stems specifically from the fact that one crucial chapter, namely, the fourth, exists in two recensions. One version supports essentially a collegial, or episcopal, attitude toward Church government and has been cited as a significant witness against acceptance of papal government in the early Church. The other supports a primatial view, which readily lent itself to Roman pretensions. The style of the work compounds the dilemma because it reflects such a studied attempt at rhetorical flair and artistic effect that ascertainment of the exact meanings of phrases and words, even in context, is quite difficult. Even though the general tone of Cyprian's many letters helps to reveal his true basic attitude regarding Church government and therefore serves to clarify the viewpoint of *On the Unity of the Catholic Church,* the precise message of this work still continues to be a matter of disagreement although no longer on strictly Catholic-Protestant party lines.

In Chapters 1-4, Cyprian warns that the world should be on guard against the deceits of Satan. The Devil's awareness of Christianity's success in robbing idols of their efficacy to mislead worshipers emboldened him to recoup his loss by plaguing Christianity with confounding disunity. Converts to Christianity, as a result, were being dragged unwittingly into novel paths of deception; even tried members of the Church, confessors included, were being seduced into heresy and schism. Clement warns that a serious effort must be made to adhere more closely to the teaching of the Master by reinvestigating the origins of ecclesiastical authority in order to reinculcate an understanding and reverence of the Church's fundamentally indivisible character.

Chapter 4 opens with the thesis that any such a study would necessarily center around Matthew 16:18f: "I say to thee, that thou art Peter and upon this rock I will build my Church, and the gates of hell shall not prevail against it. I will give to thee the keys of the kingdom of heaven and what thou shalt bind upon earth shall be bound also in heaven, and whatever thou shalt loose on earth shall be loosed also in heaven."

It is at this point that Chapter 4 opens itself to debate. Convincing scholarship tends to demonstrate that the primatial version is the older form, being written originally in rebuttal to the Novatian schism. It states that "a primacy is given Peter," that there was but "one church and one chair," and that he who did not hold fast to the "oneness of Peter" and who deserted the "chair of Peter" could scarcely comfort himself with the belief that he was adhering to the Faith as a bona-fide member of the Church.

Later, about 255, when Cyprian's quarrel with Pope Stephen over the validity of baptism administered by heretics grew bitter, strong papal protagonists supposedly read more into the text of Chapter 4 than the author had intended. Consequently he revised it, toning down his emphasis upon the primatial aspect of Church government and emphasizing the collegial outlook. In this new account, the Church is said to have been built upon "one man" rather than upon Peter in particular. Very pointedly this second rendering carefully reiterates the first version's statements insisting that Christ "assigns a like power to all the Apostles," and that "the others were all that Peter was." Moreover, it reinforces this idea of equality with a new Biblical quotation (John 20:21-23). These statements, then, obviously say what Cyprian intended to imply in the first place. The term "chair" is carefully omitted in the second recension, as well as the all-important clause "a primacy is given Peter." Cyprian's letters make it evident that the new revision of Chapter 4 does not represent a basic change in his convictions about ecclesiastical authority, but merely a softening of some passages in the original edition susceptible to misinterpretation in the heated light of the baptismal controversy. It seems logical, then, that the meaning of the debated items in the first version must be seen in the light of Cyprian's revised edition. Consequently, the alterations make it imperative to define the term "primacy" of the first version as meaning some sort of "seniority," and the phrase "oneness of Peter" as signifying "oneness originating in Peter." The introduction of a Pauline verse (Ephesians 4:4-16) in the second version further demonstrates Cyprian's intention to counterbalance the Petrine emphasis.

In a new transitional paragraph to Chapter 5 in the second version Cyprian makes his message quite obvious: that authority in the Church was vested in the general episcopal power. This episcopalism, a force one and indivisible, Cyprian understood in a somewhat Platonic way as an aggregate of all living bishops. The totality of this episcopal power each individual bishop exercised in his own sovereign jurisdictional area.

Only by returning to such episcopal origins can error and division be overcome, Cyprian argues, for death surely comes to any branch severed from the tree. Some critics, with a degree of justification, interpret the difficult and variegated imagery of Chapter 5 as evidence that Cyprian is, after all, referring all along narrowly to the see of Rome rather than to the Church at large. But since Chapters 6 and 7 continue uninterruptedly with such references to the general Church as: "You cannot have God as your Father if you have not the Church for your mother," or again, "man cannot possess the garment of Christ who rends and divides the Church of Christ," the interpretation favoring reference to the Roman church is very unlikely.

The rest of the work, Chapters 7-27, causes no difficulty. The chapters constitute a simple, eloquent plea for unity by a man passionately devoted to ecclesiastical unity. Cyprian assures his audience that heresy and schism were necessary evils, not only because they were predicted heralds of the coming end of the world but also because they brought about cleansing processes within the Church. Without such purges of heresy how could the views approved by God stand out? But even though there had to be those who would set themselves up illegitimately as clergy to infect and poison their followers, Cyprian adds, such clergy were, nonetheless, thoroughly despicable characters, desecrators of sacraments, architects of rival altars, inventors of unauthorized liturgies, and enemies of the lawful hierarchy. They were, indeed, more blameworthy than the Lapsi who had sinned but once and were penitent. These schismatic deserters could function neither meritoriously as individuals nor efficaciously as Church officials. Let no one, says Cyprian, attempt to justify schismatic action by misinterpreting out of context: "Wherever two or three are gathered together in My name, I am with them." The two or three had first to be in the Church. Even martyrdom could not benefit deserters. Their ministrations were at best pseudo-services, and since they had themselves abandoned the fountain of life, they could not validly baptize. Consequently, those washed by them, being born of a lie, could inherit no truth. This harsh view, discrediting any *ex-opere-operato* efficacy of the sacraments, and viciously attacked by Pope Stephen, came to be discredited in the long run.

The author exhorts his public not to be scandalized by dissension. Disunity was a test; since it had been predicted, it should actively serve to strengthen faith. Even confessors could become contentious and develop into quarrelsome schismatics. Their former faithfulness under fire did not guarantee permanent steadfastness; only those who persevered to the end would be saved. There would ever be a Judas.

Cyprian closes his treatise by urging all those who have been misled by dissenters, whether through their own simplicity or by conviction, to hasten their return to Mother Church so that the ideal days of Apostolic peace and unity might be recaptured. He observes, somewhat tangentially, that unity in the Church apparently had declined in proportion to its charity. In Apostolic days Christians had sold their estates for the benefit of the poor; at the present not only did they refuse to tithe but actually devoted themselves to an accumulation of wealth. Without charitable zeal, faith, good works, and fear of God all but vanished. Let all arise, Cyprian suggests, obey the commandments, and alertly await the coming of the Lord so that the Devil will be cheated out of his ambition to overcome his victims in their sleep.

E.G.W.

TREATISE ON THE PROMISES

Author: Saint Dionysius of Alexandria (c.195-c.265)
Type of work: Theology
First transcribed: c.250-264

Principal Ideas Advanced

Epicurean materialistic determinism is irrational and unscientific, for both logic and observation demand that objects have a maker and sustainer.

High criticism shows that the Apocalypse of John cannot have been written by the same man, John the Apostle, who wrote the fourth Gospel.

The Roman bishop is assured by the author that he subscribes completely to the proposition that the Son is coeternal with the Father.

Saint Dionysius of Alexandria, after his conversion, entered upon an illustrious career first as a student of Origen, then as head of the Christian catechetical school of Alexandria in 232, and finally as bishop of that patriarchy from 248. Dionysius' episcopacy, however, was a troubled one. Only flight saved his life during the Decian persecution; under Valerian he suffered exile to Libya and Mareotis. Even after returning to his see, probably in 262, he witnessed little but physical calamity, civil war, and heretical dissension. His learned writings, however, which contributed much to the development of Christianity's intellectual integrity and respectability, had, by the fourth century, already earned for him the epithet, "Great."

Fortunately for posterity, Eusebius entertained such a high regard for Dionysius' scholarship that he devoted to his praises almost the entire seventh book of his *Ecclesiastical History* in addition to some space in his *Preparation for the Gospel.* Thus were preserved most of the few extant fragments of Dionysius' work, a corpus, happily for us, large enough to vindicate antiquity's great respect for the Alexandrian's talents.

Dionysius' extant letters reveal an extensive academic fund of secular learning in the fields of philosophy, science, and history as well as an active interest in the practical ecclesiastical concerns of his day: theology, heresy, and Church discipline. Throughout these letters he appears as a man of strong opinion and conviction; as contexts demand, he subscribes in one place to rebaptism of persons washed by heretics, advocates in another mild penitential discipline toward the lapsed, and ascribes in yet another miraculous efficaciousness to the Eucharist. One letter, addressed to Basilides of Pentapolis, became so revered that its instructions were assembled as four canons in the Eastern church. An epistle to Bishop Fabius of Antioch graphically sketches the horrors of persecution in Alexandria. In another, Dionysius urges Novation to abandon his schism and to resume communition with the rightful Roman bishop, Cornelius. Yet another letter warns Pope Xystus II of Sabellian successes.

The one short fragment of Dionysius' provocative book, *Against the Sabellians,* adequately displays his talent for subtle philosophical speculation. If one, it argues, accepts the proposition that matter is ungenerated and is merely shaped by God, he has made matter and God, as both eternal, basically alike. Yet, simultaneously, the contender, while following this reasoning, is actually saying that likeness and unlikeness are synonymous. For if matter could be shaped by God, it must of necessity be pliable, mutable, and tractable to God's alterations. But He, as premised, is by nature impassible, immutable, and imperturbable.

Three fragments of Dionysius' work are of special interest: *On Nature, On Promises,* and *The Refutation and Apology.*

The first, *On Nature,* demonstrates Dionysius' easy familiarity with Greek philosophy, whether Platonic, Pythagorean, Stoic, or Epicurean, and his anxiety to make, in general, a proper adjustment between that corpus of classical learning and Christianity. *On Nature* aims to show that the materialistic determinism of Democritus and Epicurus was entirely incompatible with Christian thought. That nature is divisible into an infinite number of atoms of spontaneous origin, and that these particles operate fortuitously, clashing aimlessly in a void, combining and separating at random, to form material objects in the world, appeared to Dionysius an illogical and unscientific assumption. He argues impassionately that all human observation discredits belief in chance or coincidence; rather it demonstrates consistently the existence not only of design and teleology but also of beauty and grace. Even the spider's instinct for pattern evinces more wisdom than that possessed by determinists. Armies, ships, houses, everything, far from emerging by spontaneous generation, require artificers and sustainers. Disintegration in objects does not set in at the dictate of a fortuitous dislocation of atoms but at the will of the planner as he withdraws his supervision after the objects lose their serviceability. The macrocosm of the universe, with its harmonious combination of eternal celestial bodies and everlasting spiritual beings, displays evidence only of purpose and providence. The complex task of differentiating the many kinds of objects in the world obviously demands that a rational force direct the unique synthesis of atoms required in each case unless one wishes to postulate the doubtful axiom that atoms of a kind are automatically attracted to one another. Also, in the microcosm of the human body the teleological performance of the cells of the embryo, as well as the intellective, rational operation of the mind, preclude any possibility that irresponsible particles of matter work without direction.

Dionysius' two-book work, *On Promises,* was written to refute Bishop Nepos of Arsinoe, who taught Christians to interpret certain Scriptural passages as promises guaranteeing a millennium featuring bodily delights and indulgences. The excerpts from this composition, as preserved by Eusebius, record two significant items of interest. The first, Dionysius' description of a meeting he called in Arsinoe to combat the local version of Nepos' teaching, remains a rare record of primitive Christian synods in session. The presbyters and teachers assembled at this three-day gathering are pictured as open-mindedly, and with brotherly love, moderation, and decorum, searching out truth through a study of the Scriptures. Although the section implies that to reach decisions some disorderly discussion, concession, and change of opinion on both sides were necessary, the artlessness of the assembly disarms criticism.

But more important is the excerpt analyzing the authenticity of the Apocalypse of Saint John. Since Nepos had appealed to the Book of Revelation in support of his chiliastic interpretations, Dionysius felt that some critical observations on the Apocalypse were germane; the more so, because the Apocalypse was already under fire in some quarters as an illogical and unintelligible forgery foisted off on Saint John. Some critics, Dionysius states, ascribed the book to the heretical millenarianist, Cerinthus. Dionysius, however, rejects the thesis and declares his unwillingness to brand the Apocalypse uncanonical. He claims that it clearly contains wonderful and inspired information, intelligence so lofty as to surpass his powers of comprehension. His humility induces him to surrender his reason in the face of tradition and awe.

That the Apocalypse was the work of a John and that he was inspired, Dionysius does not doubt. But as a worthy pupil of Origen, trained in Biblical scholarship with all its tools of textual criticism, he admittedly finds it difficult to accept John the Apostle, the son of Zebedee, the brother of James, as its author. There were, as he points out, many Johns: John Mark, John the Elder, John the Apostle. Certainly the last, who wrote the Gospel and the Epistle, could not rightly be identified with the author of Revelation.

That the two Johns were different men, Dionysius deduces from two observations. In the first place, the two authors identified themselves differently. The composer of the Apocalypse mentioned himself repeatedly as John, but never as the Apostle, or as the brother of James, or as the beloved Disciple who rested on the Lord's bosom. The writer of the Gospel, however, never identified himself by name at all. In the second place, Dionysius draws his conclusion from a comparison of language and ideas. The Gospel and the Epistle supported each other in phraseology and their Greek was elegant and pure, free from barbarisms and idiomatic blunders. By comparison, Revelation is stylistically quite inferior.

Both Eusebius and Athanasius preserved fragments of Dionysius' third work, *The Refutation and Apology*. After his return from exile, Dionysius began to write actively against the Sabellian heresy. In his anxiety to denounce this modalist teaching, he apparently swung past center and seemed to emphasize excessively the differences between the three divine Persons. Consequently, he was denounced by critics to his namesake, Pope Dionysius (reigned 259-268), who speedily invited his Alexandrian colleague to demonstrate his orthodoxy. The four books of *The Refutation and Apology* contain Dionysius' reply. The patriarch freely admits that many of his illustrations in *Against the Sabellians* were badly chosen and that he inadequately expressed his belief in the consubstantiality of the Son and the Father. He categorically assures the Roman bishop, in the *Refutation,* that the Son is eternal, along with the Father, just as surely as brightness exists with light. There was complete coexistence of the two Persons from the very beginning, Dionysius writes. Since there never was a time when God was not the Father, there could never be a time when the Son was not God because the two terms are meaningful only in conjunction. Just as the mind and the word are inseparable, so the almighty Father and universal Mind had the Son or Word as an inseparable associate in every way from the very beginning.

This incident between Dionysius of Alexander and Pope Dionysius became important in the development of papal history when later popes tended to expand it into a full *ad-cathedram* appeal. Julius, c. 340, considered it a precedent requiring that Alexandrian matters be referred to the Roman see. Even Cyril of Jerusalem alluded to the affair as sanctioning the custom of communicating problems to Rome.

E.G.W.

THE DIVINE INSTITUTES

Author: Lactantius (Lucius Caecilius Firmianus Lactantius, died c.325)
Type of work: Apologetics
First transcribed: c.310

Principal Ideas Advanced

The gods of the Romans, Greeks, and Barbarians are false gods; poets, philosophers, and prophets have agreed that there is but one God.

Stoics and other philosophers who have mistaken conceptions of God have misused their reason.

True wisdom and religion cannot be separated; through the Incarnation of God, Christians have learned that Jesus is one with the Father.

Immortality is the reward of the pious and virtuous, who find in the love of God the true end of man.

The *Divine Institutes* (*Divinarum institutionum*) of Lactantius is an ambitious attempt, in seven volumes, to show the superiority of Christianity by contrasting it with false religion and philosophy. The work was an attempt on the author's part to supplement the apologetic writings of Minucius Felix, Tertullian, and Cyprian. The occasion was one which called for a fervent champion of the faith, for the Emperor Constantine, although himself still a pagan, was coming more and more to respect the Christians as loyal subjects and men of integrity. If Lactantius, through his *Institutes,* begun perhaps as early as 304, a year after his conversion, could win the sympathy of the emperor and perhaps contribute to the emperor's growing realization that Christianity holds the truth, the Church would gain a new and powerful champion. (Victory in battle at Milvian Bridge, near Rome, in 312, led Constantine, who had fought under a sign of the Cross, to issue the Edict of Milan, by which Christianity was tolerated in the Empire. About 317 Lactantius was made Latin tutor for Constantine's son. Then, in 337, shortly before his death, Constantine was baptized.)

Lactantius declares at the outset of the *Institutes* that his intention is to direct the learned to true wisdom, and the unlearned to true religion. There is no true wisdom without religion, Constantine is told in Lactantius' dedication, and there is no true religion without wisdom.

Lactantius begins his formal explanation of Christianity by asking whether there is a providence which governs all affairs, and he answers that although he is not prepared to give an elaborate defense of an affirmative answer, anyone who considers the order and beauty of the universe and its laws realizes that some being orders the visible universe. As to whether the universe is governed by one God or many, the answer is that surely there is but one all-powerful, eternal Mind, for if several gods were needed, none would be without weakness. Prophets, poets, and philosophers have all come to the conclusion that there is but one God; and if one then turns to divine testimonies, one finds that the Sibylline prophetesses spoke repeatedly of a single God.

If there is but one God and He is alone worthy of being worshiped as divine, then those who claim that there are many gods of various temperaments, who marry, quarrel, and die, are mistaken. Lactantius contends that none of the pagan gods is powerful enough and morally elevated enough to be anything other than a fictional deity. Apollo, Mars, Bacchus, and even Jupiter engaged in licentious activity, committed adultery, debauched virgins, and in general behaved like the most sinful of men. The Romans, and the Barbarians too, have invented gods of such disreputable character that no responsible person could regard such beings as in any way divine.

Lactantius then turns to those who worship the heavens, the sun, and the moon. Not only the ignorant but also the presumably learned Stoic philosophers have regarded heavenly bodies as gods. That such persons were in error is evident from the fact that the heavenly bodies do not move themselves voluntarily but are controlled by immutable laws, the signs of the workmanship of a supreme Creator.

The Genesis story of the Creation is then recounted by Lactantius, who argues that the fallen angels, the demons, have led men to believe in false gods. But, Lactantius argues, those who have the truth through faith are safe from the lies which the demons tell; piety is the defense against falsehood.

Turning to the philosophers, Lactantius claims that error arises either from false religion or false wisdom. (Throughout the *Institutes* the emphasis is on the identity of true wisdom and true religion; consequently, philosophers who fail to commit themselves to Christianity, when they have the opportunity, must be false philosophers.) Philosophers rely on knowledge and conjecture, but since the philosophers are mortal beings, they cannot attain that knowledge which God alone possesses; and when philosophers conjecture, the results are fanciful and conflicting.

When one turns to the question of the chief good of man, says Lactantius, one finds that the philosophers were far from being wise. Some, the Cyrenaics, have taken pleasure to be man's chief end; others have argued that the chief good is to live in accordance with nature; still others have made worldly knowledge that at which man aims. But these are ends which are either shared with animals or are not truly ends, but instruments.

The chief good of man, Lactantius argues, is the knowledge and worship of God. The wise man desires virtue as the means to immortality, and he desires immortality in order that he might know God. The philosophers have on occasion come close to recognizing this truth—Plato in particular—but they have failed to grasp the whole truth because they have not known God or worshiped Him. True wisdom, which consists in the knowledge of God, is possible only to those who find Him through religion. There are, of course, many false religions which turn men's worship to idols and other false gods; but there is one true religion, a religion which springs from the birth and ministry of Jesus. Jesus, the Word of God, was sent to teach men righteousness. The Passion, Death, and Resurrection of Jesus were also foretold by the prophets; it was through the Incarnation that God made men aware of the true wisdom. Thus, it is in the knowledge of Jesus and through the practice of the virtue which He taught that men are able to come to true religion and wisdom.

Some critics, Lactantius writes, charge that Christians believe in two Gods, God the Father, and God the Son. But Father and Son are of one substance; there is but one God.

Those who would avoid heresy and know the truth should go to the temple of God, the Catholic Church, for "the true Catholic Church is that in which there is confession and repentance, which treats in a wholesome manner the sins and wounds to which the weakness of the flesh is liable."

Lactantius explains that his work differs from the *Apology* written by Tertullian in that the latter was concerned to answer particular charges made against Christianity, while Lactantius sets out to instruct men regarding the Christian religion and to show that Christianity differs from other religions in that Christianity alone possesses the knowledge of what is necessary to true wisdom. Justice is possible, Lactantius insists, only when men relate the laws to the true God.

There are two principal virtues which are essential to true justice: piety and equity. It is piety to know and worship God; it is equity to regard all men as of equal concern to God. Those who punish the Christians are rebelling against God, for the Christians relate virtue to God's will, and they aim at knowledge in order that they might come to a better understanding of the divine will.

The passions make the virtuous life difficult, Lactantius admits, but those who know Christ understand that through repentance the sinner may receive forgiveness. Repentance involves a recognition of the wisdom of God's justice, and those who resolve to do what is just according to God will be strengthened in their struggles with passion.

"For this reason He has given us this present life," Lactantius writes, "that we may either lose that true and eternal life by our vices, or win it by virtue." Since virtue consists in doing what God wills, and since what God wills is revealed only to those who know God, man must use his reason to discover, through Christ, what can be known of God. If man worships God and lives virtuously, God will reward his piety by granting man immortality so that man will "be blessed to all eternity, and . . . be for ever in the presence of God and in the society of God."

THE INCARNATION OF THE WORD OF GOD

Author: Saint Athanasius (c.295-373)
Type of work: Apologetics; dogmatic theology
First transcribed: c.320

Principal Ideas Advanced

The Incarnation and Resurrection were necessary to restore the image of God, which was fading in man because of his transgressions.

Moreover, after the failure of other media, the Father could restore man's recognition of God only through an agent familiar to man, a fellow human being who was at the same time divine.

The Jew should consult the Scriptures and the Greek should reflect upon the obvious fruits of the Redemption to be appraised of the Truth.

Although Saint Athanasius, as Bishop of Alexandria from 328 until his death in 373, became so involved in the maelstrom of church politics that it cost him some fifteen years of exile, he found time to earn a reputation as a prolific and influential writer of apologetic, dogmatic, historical, and exegetical treatises. Since his *De incarnatione verbi Dei* (*The Incarnation of the Word of God*) reflects no traces of the Nicene settlement, it may have been written before 320 when Athanasius had not yet assumed the episcopal office. Some critics, however, place its composition as late as 336.

De incarnatione verbi Dei is properly a sequel to an earlier tract, *Oratio contra gentes* (*Against the Heathen*), which indicts both the worship of polytheistic gods and the profession of philosophical pantheism. It concludes with praise of the rational soul which perceives in creation evidence for the unity of God.

The Incarnation of the Word of God is a readable, popular work of some fifty-seven chapters and is readily divisible into two large sections. The first, emphasizing the moral necessity of the Incarnation, avoids the popular Christological and Trinitarian theological speculations and polemics of the day. Instead, it explains in a strikingly simple but effective way the reasons for the Incarnation, the Passion, and the Resurrection, and the manner of their fulfillment. The second section of the treatise attempts to defend these mysteries against the disbelief of the Jew and the cynicism of the Greek. The composition as a whole is quite impressive as a result of the deep personal feeling of the work, the straightforward reasoned presentation, and the choice of apt analogies which effectively reduce God's unfathomable arrangements to the level of human experience and understanding.

At the outset, Athanasius postulates man's exalted position in the universe as an image of the Creator, endowed with a portion of His divinity or rationality. Man's transgression, however, demonstrated conclusively that he lacked the perseverance to remain in this blissful state. His insatiable hankering after adultery, thievery, murder, plunder, and homosexuality served progressively to dull his divine image and, through death, to return him to the nothingness from which he had emerged. The dreary prospect of death threatened to erase the very image of God and thus to nullify, or at least to stultify, the Creator's design and handiwork. Such a waste of his creative act God could not tolerate, since the degeneration of man reflected upon His unchangeableness, omnipotence, and goodness.

Correction of this trend, Athanasius argued, was clearly outside the province of any creature. Man's repentance was by nature powerless to modify the execution of God's inexorable law that man as a sinner must die. Logically, a creature could not himself redeem a nature which he had received as an incomprehensible gift from outside himself. Since to honor the claims of God the reconstruction of man must start anew from the beginning, only the Word was equipped to rescue His original work from dissolution. Thus, of necessity, Christ assumed a body, itself subject to death, so that He could nullify the law of death decreed against sinful man and satisfy man's debt by surrendering His own Temple to destruction. The Resurrection, by guaranteeing a new beginning to a life now clothed in corruption, gloriously revealed the success of the Creator's efforts to free His handiwork from disintegration and to restore it to its pristine condition.

Saint Athanasius offers a second, and quite similar, reason for the Incarnation. The Word became incarnate not only to redeem man from the law of extinction but also to acquaint him with the Father. Equipped with rationality and created in the image of the Word, man originally was capable of recognizing God. But man hastened to becloud His image by idol worship, magic, and astrology, and thus the knowledge of the Divine became more and more perverted and obscured. When other incentives in turn, such as the majesty of the created universe, the utterings of the Prophets, or the directives of the Law, were unsuccessful in recalling man to knowledge of the Deity, God provides still another aid to his weak and blind creatures by providing another and more striking teacher of divine knowledge. Since man had succumbed completely to things of sense, the Word logically united Himself with a body which, in a miraculous way, entailed no circumscription of His omnipresence or contamination of His perfection. To no avail, He had formerly supplied miracles in abundance to encourage man to recover his sight. Only by yielding Himself, as a last resort, to suffering and death was He finally able to cancel out the power of death, ignorance, and the Devil.

In order that the Word could effectively lead men to recognition of the Father, the Savior's death had to be dramatic and drastic. The Lord's dying naturally by growing sick and weak would have done Him, as the source of all strength and healing, an injustice. Death by public execution would best forestall denial of His death. Christ's form of death could not be a pleasant, self-chosen one, Athanasius argues, for Christ had to show that he permitted no challenger, even death, to go unconquered. Decapitation was providentially avoided, for Christ's severed body would then, according to Athanasius, be cited by later schismatics as a legitimate basis for division within the Church. Crucifixion provided the ideal means, for only by accepting the Cross, the form of death prescribed as a curse, could the Word properly bear the curse laid upon man. Athanasius felt, too, that the symbolism of the Cross was particularly significant: the outstretched arms were a sign that the Word beckoned all Jews and Gentiles; His suspension above ground was a token that He had defeated the prince of the powers of the air.

Just as the manner of Christ's death was important, so also was the manner of His Resurrection, Athanasius writes. The Resurrection, for instance, had to be accurately timed, for if the Resurrection had followed Christ's death too closely, the appearance of Christ's body would not have been regarded as miraculous. Since a three-day interval normally produces visible signs of bodily decay, the Resurrection, without any doubt, demonstrates Christ's incorruptibility. A long period of putrefaction, though, normally makes physical disintegration complete and thus, if Christ had risen later, critics might have suggested that Christ arose with a different body.

To Athanasius, the fact of the Resurrection, as a great token of man's restoration, is demonstrable from several angles. Christ's victory so sweetened death, so deprived it of its sting, that Christians actually practiced to embrace it. Moreover, the virile grace of conversion nourishing so many different races could logically flow only from a living source. Athanasius argued, too, that only as a living agent could

Christ so effectively foil the false gods of the pagans.

The second part of the treatise attempts to provide Jews and Gentiles with convincing proofs of the Incarnation and Resurrection. For the former, Athanasius thought the prophecies of the Scriptures should suffice. All events had been duly predicted, the flight into Egypt, the time of the Advent as announced by Daniel, and the Cross. How could the Jews persist in looking for another Messiah? Moreover, Christ's recorded miracles were unprecedented in Jewish history. Very convincingly Athanasius confronted Jews with a startling reminder that prophecies had ceased with John the Baptist and that the kingdom of Jerusalem as well as the temple had been destroyed. Such final events, obviously providential, conclusively demonstrated that the Jewish dispensation had run its course with the Advent of Christ. Now even the Gentiles were being converted to the very God of Moses. What more could the Jews wish a persuasive Christ to do?

In addressing himself to the Greek objections, Athanasius assumes a Neoplatonic and Stoic stand which conveniently accepted the Logos as the active agent of creation and governance in the universe. Much of his argumentation is *ad hominem*. If, as the Greeks maintained, the Word of God was united with the great body of the universe, it was clearly illogical to sneer at the possibility of the Word's uniting Himself to a man, for it would be absurd to claim that divinity was in the whole but not in the part. It appeared puzzling to the Greeks that the Logos, who had obviously chosen to manifest Himself in only one part of creation, namely, man, had not identified himself with some nobler part of the universe, such as the sun or moon. Such a criticism Athanasius condemned as both irrelevant and harmful. He pronounced it irrelevant because man had already demonstrated his failure to recognize God through His works of creation. Man's limited capacity apparently demanded a more familiar agent to recall him to divine knowledge. God as man must deal with man. Moreover, it was man who had dimmed his image through transgression and therefore required reconstruction. A dramatic display such as a solar theophany would actually have been harmful to God's purpose, for the Healer must approach His patient in a manner the sick man can bear, lest He overpower and overstimulate him.

Athanasius next responded to a possible Greek query: Why did not the Logos cure man's sickness through a fiat, since He had originally created him through one? Athanasius answered by asserting that man's plight was a matter of repair or correction within an existing framework. Christ was constrained, in a manner of speaking, to put on a human body in order to defeat death in its own lair. Athanasius compared a situation in which death would be removed from man by a simple decree to one in which fire would be restrained from straw or stubble by an asbestos wall. Man, like the straw, would, under such circumstances remain vulnerable; fire and death themselves must be extinguished.

The truth of the Incarnation, thought Athanasius, should be patent to the Greeks because of its fruits. The whole creation resounded with the glory of God; Zeus, Chronos, and Apollo had been reduced to mere men; idols had been abandoned, the oracles of Delphi and Dodona were struck mute, the springs and rivers were deserted by god and demon. Greek wisdom, although copiously recorded, artistically expressed, and logically well reasoned, had been unable to convince even a few neighboring souls of virtue and immortality. Christ, by contrast, made His message prevail universally even though he used ordinary language and simple examples.

Everywhere the world sang Christ's triumph, Athanasius writes. Virgins led a new vanguard of virtue, the sign of the Cross vanguished demons, greater miracles than those of Asclepius and Heracles were in evidence, everywhere Christ's doctrines prevailed. Just as the dead had never before arisen, nor the sun darkened its face, so neither had savage and superstitious tribes, such as the Scythians, Ethiopians, Persians, Armenians, Goths, and others, become docile and pacifistic. Truly, the achievements of the Word were as numerous as the waves of the sea.

Finally, Athanasius recommends that all study the Scriptures and await the Second Coming while inspired by true knowledge and virtue, animated by a pure soul and mind, and encouraged by the salubrious examples of saints and martyrs.

E.G.W.

ECCLESIASTICAL HISTORY

Author: Eusebius Pamphili (c.260-c.340)
Type of work: Church history
First transcribed: c.311-323

Principal Ideas Advanced

Many early Christians passionately sought martyrdom.

Some early Christians defected under threat of persecution, and others defected intellectually, becoming heretics.

God sustained the early Church, sometimes by helping Christians gain the crown of martyrdom, sometimes by preserving them to teach others.

With the victory of Constantine the Church achieved victory, through the providence of God, the blood of the martyrs, and the sword of the emperor.

Eusebius was Bishop of Caesarea from shortly after 313 until his death late in 339 or early in 340. He was widely recognized during his lifetime as the most learned and prolific Christian writer of the day. Apparently this was the principal reason he was given first place of honor, sitting at Constantine's right hand, at the Council of Nicaea in 325. He was also personally friendly with Constantine, delivered the council's opening address to him, and later wrote his life. Besides historical writings, many exegetical, apologetic, and dogmatic works were written by Eusebius. He played a mediating role during the Arian controversy, and though he wrote extensively against the anti-Arians, he never went contrary to the Nicene Creed, which he apparently helped formulate.

Since his death Eusebius has been best known for his *Ecclesiastical History,* which is an expansion of his previously composed *Chronicle.* This was, as its full title reveals, *Chronological Tables, to Which Is Prefixed an Epitome of Universal History Drawn from Various Sources.* Eusebius was a diligent collector of materials, but he failed to synthesize them into a coherent, flowing narrative. His *Ecclesiastical History* reads more like a scissors-and-paste work than a true history. But it remains invaluable as the sole source of information about much Church history from the time of Christ until the end of the persecutions under Constantine.

Eusebius lived during the last and most severe of the Roman persecutions under Diocletian and Galerius. We do not know whether he was imprisoned or personally witnessed the persecutions, but his work is filled with graphic accounts of apparently reliable witnesses. He lived in an age of transition from the persecuted Church to a quasi-established one, an age of intellectual transition in which Christological doctrine came to be clearly defined. His greatness lies in his sensing this change and preserving for later ages the detailed history of the Church from its beginning till Constantine became sole emperor in 323.

In the opening words of Book I Eusebius accurately describes what his work will include: "It is my purpose to hand down a written account of the successions of the holy Apostles as well as of the times extending from our Saviour to ourselves; the number and nature of the events which are said to have been treated in ecclesiastical history; the number of those who were her illustrious guides and leaders in especially prominent dioceses; the number of those who in each generation by word of mouth or by writings served as ambassadors of the word of God; the names, the number, and the times of those who out of a desire for innovation launched into an extremity of error and proclaimed themselves the introducers of knowledge falsely so called, mercilessly ravaging the flock of Christ like ravening wolves; and besides this what straightway befell the entire Jewish race as the result of its plot against our Saviour; furthermore, the number, and times of the war waged by the Gentiles against the divine Word; and the character of those who on various occasions have passed through the contest of blood and tortures in His behalf; and, in addition to this, the martyrdoms of our own times and with them all the gracious and kindly succor of our Saviour."

The ten books of Eusebius's *Ecclesiastical History* contain short biographies of such important early Church figures as Polycarp, Clement of Alexandria, Irenaeus, Dionysius, and Origen, as well as many lesser and otherwise unknown bishops, martyrs, and apologists. Thus Eusebius became the chief source of factual information used by later Church historians. Fortunately, Eusebius used his materials critically, and he is usually proven accurate. He tends, however, to exaggerate the numbers of martyrs, and perhaps to minimize the number of those who defected under torture or the threat of death.

The *Ecclesiastical History* is an apologetic in that Eusebius sees the history of the Church as its vindication and proof that it is indeed a divine institution. Its ultimate earthly victory, from his point of view, was achieved during his own lifetime under the emperorship of Constantine. This was a victory sealed with the blood of the martyrs, a victory of pure doctrine achieved by heroic battle of the Truth against heresy, but a victory made possible only by divine support. The last sentence of this long work is typical of Eusebius's style, and it indicates how he believed that the last stage of history had arrived: "And when they [Constantine and his sons], as the first of all their actions, cleansed the world of hatred for God, mindful of the blessings bestowed on them by God, they manifested their love of virtue and love of God and their piety and gratitude with respect to the Deity by the deeds which they performed openly in the sight of all men."

T.P.N.

THE CATECHETICAL LECTURES

Author: Saint Cyril of Jerusalem (c.315-386)
Type of work: Instructions for catechumens
First transcribed: 348

Principal Ideas Advanced

Catechumens should know that two things are necessary: faith in a pious doctrine and the performance of good works, which includes the keeping of the commandments.

Without Baptism or martyrdom, both of which imply confessional aspects, there is no salvation.

The sacraments of the church: Baptism, Unction, the Eucharist, and even the liturgy in general, have an ex-opere-operato *efficacy through invocation, although improper dispositions may nullify the grace imparted.*

It is hardly surprising that Saint Cyril's ecclesiastical career was turbulent and his orthodoxy suspect, for he lived in the early Post-Nicene period when Christianity spent its new freedom in dissension. Three expulsions from his see of Jerusalem as a defender of the Athanasian faith, honorable participation in the ecumenical Council of 381, and the theology of his *Catechetical Lectures,* however, all go far to vindicate his Nicene orthodoxy even though he studiously avoided the term "homoousious" as being non-Scriptural and pro-Sabellian.

Cyril's *Catechetical Lectures,* comprising some 150 octavo pages, remains one of the most attractive writings of primitive Christendom. Twenty-four in number, the lectures divide readily into two groups. The Introduction, or Procatechesis, and the eighteen lectures following were given during Lent to candidates preparing for Baptism on

Easter, 348. The remaining five, the so-called Mystagogical Catecheses, are post-Baptismal discourses and are taken by a few critics to be later fourth century compositions by John of Jerusalem.

This first complete set of instructions for converts in the early Church retains an authentic air of urgency and convincingly reflects the aura of mystery, secrecy, and suspense which accompanied the thrill of conversion in these times. Casual references to the wintry weather, to the sacred sites of Jerusalem, and to the ennui of the audience lend to these discourses an atmosphere of engaging informality. Injunctions against heathen meat offerings, idol worship, amulets, divination, theaters and spectacles, horse racing, hunting, and tavern slumming clearly reveal the pagan background of the convert class. The discourses are colorful with nature imagery, studded with abrupt questions, and enlivened generally with an oratory skilled at making the sublime personal.

In the Catecheses, Cyril appeals liberally to the Scriptures, often to the vagaries of the classical Pantheon, and in a lesser degree to the teachings of Greek philosophy. Occasionally, time-worn myths, such as those of the phoenix, Simon Magus' statue in Rome, and the miraculous translation of the Septuagint, are marshaled innocently to astound the sincere neophyte with prospects of new light and security.

The Procatechesis describes the temper of mind proper to Baptism. Cyril reminds the assembled novitiates at the outset that, since the fragrance of the Holy Spirit had breathed upon them and the torch of faith had been lighted, there was no longer place for sin, distraction with worldly news, and slothfulness in attendance at instructions.

The first five lectures present basic background material. They request, first, that the catechumen confess his sins with the assurance that no crime, even lust or murder, would stay the mercy of God; no ailment could foil the Physician. Two things were fundamental: a pious doctrine and good works. Faith, they should know, was of two kinds: subscription to a credal formula which had to be committed to memory, and trust in the power and grace of God. The former by necessity stressed belief in the Trinity and always rested on Revelation. Since not even a casual remark could go unsupported Scripturally, the novices were ordered to study the books of the canon and avoid apocrypha. Good works, they were given to understand, issued from free will, not from the pressure of environment, hereditary, chance, or the conjunction of stars; nor did good works indict the *moderate* use of wealth, the body, sex, marriage, dress, wine, and food; destined for resurrection, the body was so beautiful and wholesome as to merit tender treatment.

Catecheses VI-XVIII successively acquaint the candidate with the esoteric articles of the Christian creed as preserved in Alexandria. Belief in "One God, the Father almighty, Creator of heaven and earth and all things visible," as Cyril explains in Catecheses VI-IX, demanded humility in the face of divine incomprehensibility and perfection. Cyril bids the presumptuous, who would dissect God, first to count the stars and raindrops. Even though divinity was completely intelligible to God alone, enough can be known to make one realize that aberrations such as polytheism with its divine unions and anthropomorphisms, Gnosticism with its hermaphroditic Christ, and Manichaeism with its duality and pollution were patently intolerable. The Father, even though the God of Abraham, Isaac, and Jacob, adopted all without reservation and predestination. His omnipotence, Cyril assures his hearers, was not inhibited by His toleration of evil, the Devil, heretics, and sinners. His power as Creator could be appreciated the better as one grasped the grandeur of His works: His watery heavens with their luminous orbs, His seasons and clouds, His crimson rose, the whale and the eagle, as well as human metabolism and embryonic development.

Catecheses X-XI deal with the credal article: "One Lord, Jesus Christ, the only-begotten Son of God, begotten of the Father, true God before all ages, by whom all things were made." After explaining all terminology to his understudies, Cyril explains that the Son became incarnate so that man might approach him for instruction, not as formerly in Old Testament theophanies but more intimately. Christ readily adjusted His imagery to men; if one required gladness, He responded as the Vine; if entrance, as the Door. Everything eloquently witnessed to His genuineness: Peter, Gabriel, Mary the mother of God, Symeon, the Jordan, splinters of the Cross, miracles, even barbarians; Golgatha was beneath foot, the palm tree still stood, the house of Caiaphas and the Praetorium of Pilate lay in ruins, the environs of the rock grave and the lid itself were at hand to testify to His death and Resurrection. The Son's actual begetting, however, was a mystery unknown to the sun and angels alike; even the Holy Spirit gave little explanation. Christ was, nevertheless, of one substance with the Father, yet separate from Him, the agent of Creation which His Father designed.

Explanation of the credal statements regarding Christ's Incarnation, crucifixion, burial, Resurrection, Ascension, and His repose at the right hand of the Father occupies Catecheses XII-XIV. Born of the Virgin and the Holy Spirit, Christ became man, according to Cyril, to heal the wound left in human nature by the transgression in Paradise, and to rededicate the flesh so misused by the Devil. The Virgin Mary, by bearing Jesus parthenogenetically, finally repaid Eve's debt to Adam for her birth from his rib. Since sexual members are honorable in themselves, Christ suffered no indignity in His earthly birth, the time of which had been accurately predicted by Daniel. Since death, which came through man's eating from a tree, had been conquered on the Tree, Christians should glory in the Cross as the foundation of all faith. They should sign themselves with it at all times and employ the sign to vanquish demons and drugs. Cyril exhorts his class to take heart from the experience of the penitent thief who found the crucified King anxious to lavish on him unmerited favors. He reminds his hearers that the very church edifice in which they stand, encrusted as it is with gold, silver, and precious gems, attest the Ascension along with the moonlight, Christ's gravestone, His clothes, and the Apostles. The Scriptures recorded it; nature prefigured it; God's omnipotence guaranteed it.

The section of the creed speaking of Christ's return in glory to judge the living and the dead, and of the permanence of His kingdom, allows Cyril, in Catechesis XV, to discuss the end of the world. If heretics were potential antichrists, and if the confusion in the Church were the predicted desolation, the end was imminent, particularly in view of the fact that all nations had already been evangelized. The Roman empire was patently nearing its end as the last of the scheduled four kingdoms. Ten kingly ursurpers, possibly dominating Rome simultaneously, would quickly be followed by the eleventh, the Antichrist, Satan incarnate, who would rule harshly for three and a half years. Christ's coming would then herald the Last Judgment, at which everyone, rich and poor, educated and simple, would appear clothed only in his sins and virtues. Since every prayer, psalm, fast, and alm, as well as every covetous deed, fornication, and theft would be recorded, Cyril urges his listeners to be good stewards of their individual mental and physical talents.

Confession of the "Holy Ghost, the Comforter, Who spoke through the prophets," is the subject of Catecheses XVI-XVII, and in some respects the discussion is the most impressive of all. Cyril cautions his understudies that the Holy Spirit had revealed as much about Himself as He was pleased to have discussed. So let all arrogant heretics speculating on the Spirit be silenced. The Spirit's names were manifold: He was the divine Sanctifier, Healer, Teacher, Exhorter, Comforter, Illuminator, and Vivifier. He revealed the Testaments, converted Paul, descended as the Dove, moved the Apostles, and inspired glossalia at Pentecost to confound Babel by effectively clothing an intelligible message in many languages. As versatile as the uniform rain which becomes white in the lily and purple in the hyacinth, and which nourishes palm and vine alike, the Holy Spirit grants to each His grace and gifts, causing even the soul withered by sin to put forth clusters of righteousness. Cyril reminds his charges that as the Holy Spirit had touched Romans, Indians, Goths, Moors, Ethiopians and other far-flung peoples, He was now prepared to seal them in turn and to enter their deepest hearts as fire permeates iron to burn out the dross. Cyril admonishes the candidates, then, to approach Baptism with their attention on the Holy Spirit, not on the minister. The Paraclete, knowing their innermost dispositions, would accordingly withhold His graces or grant gifts beyond their wildest expectations.

Discussion of "And in one Baptism unto remission of Sins, the Holy Catholic Church, Resurrection of the Flesh, and Life Everlasting" brings to a close the examination of the creed. To uphold the Resurrection, Cyril employs arguments from the phenomena of nature, its seeds, the phoenix, the periodic restoration of the moon; from natural instincts of man, including even his automatic abhorrence of grave-robbing; from the spiritual conviction that earthly justice is a myth, and, of course, from the Scriptures. To him, the Church's universality signifies that it exists everywhere, teaches a complete message, and serves all classes. Life eternal, he sums up, is gained through faith and obedience to the commandments, involving either Baptism or martyrdom, with their confessional implications, without which there is no salvation.

The five mystagogical lectures, XIX-XXIII, are shorter and intended for post-Baptismal instruction.

Catecheses XIX-XX discuss Baptism. The ritual involved facing West, renouncing Satan and his works and pomps, anointment with exorcised oil, confession of the Trinity, and descent naked into the water. The imitative features of the Baptismal liturgy especially interested Cyril. He recalls repeatedly that, as images of Christ, the candidates in their triple descent to and immersion in the water and their emergence therefrom re-enacted imitatively the three-day burial and Resurrection of Christ. Thus, by sharing His sufferings vicariously, by experiencing a counterpart of His Passion and Resurrection, the baptized arose triumphantly with Him. The water, according to Cyril, received through invocation a power of holiness to impress an indelible seal unto salvation and to impart grace for the remission of sins.

Catechesis XXI concerns chrism, an unction with sacred oils. These oils, in Cyril's mind, were capable, after a blessing, of imparting the divine nature of Christ. Whether this anointing on the forehead, ears, nostrils, and breast immediately after Baptism can be regarded as a primitive form of the later independent sacrament of Confirmation has been much disputed.

The Eucharist is the theme of Lecture XXII. Cyril insists that in this rite there takes place a complete change in the elements. When Christ said, "This is My Body; this is My Blood," could doubt remain? Just as He turned water into wine, He changed wine into blood. Cyril strongly enjoins his new Christian converts not to regard the taste nor to trust the palate, for the bread is no longer bread. He claims that the partaking of the Body and Blood of Christ causes its recipients to be of the same Body and Blood with Him as the sacred species courses through their members.

The final discourse, XXIII, remains one of the earliest accounts of the liturgy of a primitive "mass," or the offering-up of Christ-Sacrificed-for-sin. Here already appears the Washing of Hands with the invocation: "I will wash my hands among the innocent," the Kiss of Peace, the Sursum Corda, the Preface, the Sanctus, and the Consecration. Subsequent prayers for peace, rulers, and the sick are followed by intercessions for the dead and the martyrs. The Pater Noster and the Sancta Sanctis precede the Communion, at which the congregation sang, "O taste and see that the Lord is good." At the actual Communion the body of Christ was taken carefully by each recipient into the palm of his hand. After drinking of the cup, the communicant's hands touched his moist lips so that he could hallow his body.

E.G.W.

DISCOURSES AGAINST THE ARIANS

Author: Saint Athanasius (c.295-373)
Type of work: Apologetic theology
First transcribed: c.360

Principal Ideas Advanced

The Arian heresy must be exposed as the seductive product of madness; the followers of Arius believe that God existed before the Son, that the Son is not eternal but is merely a creature.

The correct Catholic belief is that the Son is very God, one in substance with the Father; the Son, like the Father, is eternal and everlasting; the Son is begotten of the Father; the Son is the Only-begotten; He is the Word of the Father, the true Son, God from God.

Scriptural evidence, which supports the view that the Son is eternal and begotten, is in opposition to the Arian opinion.

Saint Athanasius's celebrated defense of the Catholic faith, his *Discourses Against the Arians,* is a scathing critical attack on the heretical view propounded by Arius (c. 256-336) and his followers; namely, the view that God existed before His Son, that the Son is not eternal, that He is not of the same substance as the Father, and that He is, in fact, merely a creature.

The condemnation of Arianism at the Council of Nicaea in 325 was a victory of the minority, a victory largely due to the persuasive power of Athanasius.

A letter from Arius, written in or about 321 to Eusebius, Bishop of Nicomedia, contains a statement of Arius's position: ". . . what we say and think we both have taught and continue to teach; that the Son is not unbegotten, nor part of the unbegotten in any way, nor is he derived from any substance; but that by his own will and counsel he existed before times and ages fully God, only-begotten, unchangeable.

"And before he was begotten or created or appointed or established, he did not exist; for he was not unbegotten."

Apparently Arius resisted claiming that there was a *time* when the Son did not exist; Arius wanted to agree with those who maintained that the Son was begotten *before* time. But he could not rid himself of the notion that if the Son is begotten, He did not exist prior to His being begotten. Hence, Arius reached the paradoxical and heretical conclusion that the Son, although "fully God" is not part of God or of one substance with God. "We are persecuted," Arius writes in his letter to Eusebius, "because we say that the Son has a beginning, but God is without beginning. For that reason we are persecuted, and because we say that he is from what is not. And this we say because he is neither part of God nor derived from any substance."

Athanasius begins the First Discourse with the comment that Arianism is more to be feared than those heresies which have already been recognized as expressions of madness; Arianism cloaks itself in Scriptural language and thereby seduces the foolish. It is not proper for the Arians to be called Christians, Athanasius insists, for Arius held such views as that "God was not always a Father," and "once God was alone, and not yet a Father, but afterwards He became a Father." According to Arius in the *Thalia,* Athanasius reports, the Son, the Word of God, was "made out of nothing," and "once He was not. . . ." The Arian belief, then, is that the Son is a creature, for He was created by God.

Arius has also written, Athanasius writes, that "the Word is not the very God . . . though He is called God, yet He is not very God," and Arius concludes that it is only by God's grace that the Word is God, and the Word is God in name only. Arius holds also that the Son is different from the Father in substance and essence, that the Son is limited in His knowledge of the Father, and that, in fact, the Son has only incomplete knowledge of His own nature.

Having set forth the views of Arius and having expressed his horror that such ideas have ever been tolerated, Athanasius contrasts the opinions of Arius with those which constitute Catholic doctrine. Once again Athanasius reminds the reader that the Devil, "the author of heresies," is very adept at using Scriptural language to support seductive errors. Those who attend closely to Scripture, however, will find that the Son of God is Himself God: "Very Son of the Father, natural and genuine, proper to His essence, Wisdom Only-begotten, and Very and Only Word of God is He; not a creature or work, but an offspring proper to the Father's essence. Wherefore He is very God, existing one in essence with the very Father. . . ."

Athanasius takes note of the Arian reluctance to speak of "a time" when the Son was not; the Arians seek to avoid the obvious heresy of claiming that the Son was created *in time* by using the expression, "Once the Son was not." But however the Arians attempt to avoid blasphemy they fall into it, for Scripture clearly states, "In the beginning was the Word, and the Word was with God, and the Word was God." God's "Power," Athanasius claims, "is the Word of God, by whom all things have been made." The Son, like the Father, is eternal and uncreated; the Son is begotten, but He is the only begotten Son, and He is begotten from all eternity. Furthermore, Athanasius insists, the Son is begotten not from nothing, but from God the Father. The Arian view that the Son could not have come from the Father but must have come from nothing is another instance of blasphemy.

The Arians also suggest that if the Word is co-eternal with the Father, it would be more appropriate to call the Word the "brother" of God. But Athanasius objects strenuously. If the Word is begotten of the Father, then the Word is the Son of the Father, even though both Father and Son are without beginning.

Furthermore, Athanasius continues, to deny that the Word is co-eternal with God is to deny that God is the Creator, the Maker of all things, for it is through the Word, which is God's Wisdom, that all things which are have come to be. To deny the eternal being of the Son is to deny the eternal being of God's power and wisdom.

The Son is the image of the Father, Athanasius reminds the reader; consequently, the Son shares the attributes of the Father: "The Father is eternal, immortal, powerful, light, King, Sovereign, God, Lord, Creator, and Maker. These attributes must be in the Image, to make it true that he 'that hath seen' the Son 'hath seen the Father.' "

The arguments advanced by Athanasius are clearly and subtly constructed. They rest on Scripture and the Catholic faith, but they are valuable as bringing into clear light the implications of the passages and beliefs he cites. To deny his conclusions is to deny the beliefs on which Christianity rests, and to deny those beliefs is tantamount to denying God. As the argument proceeds it becomes more and more evident that this ancient quarrel was not simply a theologian's squabble brought on by some trifling difference in definition or logical inference. Arius may have found it difficult to reconcile the Son's eternity with His status as the only begotten Son of the Father, but in seeking to avoid paradox Arius fell into the fatal error of denying the central faith. The arguments of Athanasius make that error clear, and it is not surprising that the Athanasian position prevailed.

A great deal of the argument is devoted to citations from Scripture, and Athanasius shows both the diligence of the scholar and the insight of the saint in finding passages that will illuminate the faith and, by contrast, reveal the falsity of the Arian position. But evidence from Scripture would not be as forceful as it is were it not arranged to support arguments that underscore the insupportable consequences of claiming that the Son, before He was begotten, was not. Athanasius throughout develops the theme, which is central to the faith, that the Son is God; the Son is God who became man; He was not a man who became God.

The Second Discourse begins with an expression of Athanasius's disappointment that he has to return to the attack on Arianism; he had hoped that he had said enough: "They, however, for whatever reason, still do not succumb; but, as swine and dogs wallow in their own vomit and their own mire, rather invent new expedients for their irreligion." Once again Athanasius insists that to describe the Son as a "creature" and "work" is to speak of Him as one is justified in speaking only of things generated out of nothing by the power of God. But the Word was not generated or created; He is the Only-begotten.

Athanasius attempts to distinguish between the ordinary use of the word "son," a use which makes sense when one talks about mortal fathers and sons, and the unique use of "Son," a use which has its justification only in the Christian context. He points out the dangers of drawing analogies on the basis of a presumed parallelism of language; Christ was not a son; He is *the* Son. To fail to understand the difference is to lose the faith completely. If it is sometimes proper to talk about our Lord's having been "made," it is only because reference is being made to His having become man; God made the Son man, but the Son was not made Son; He was begotten. Reasons may be given for the Son's having become man, but it would be inappropriate to give reasons for His divine nature, for the Son was not made for a purpose; He was not made at all; He is begotten.

The Third Discourse continues Athanasius's careful explication of Scriptural texts. The Christian belief that the Father and Son are distinguishable Persons but nevertheless one God, each Himself whole and perfect, is carefully analyzed and defended. To say that God is one is not to deny that the Son is God; it is to distinguish God from false idols and to emphasize the essential unity of Father and Son. God the Father is first as the origin of all things through the Word, but the Son is also first, in that He is the image of the Father.

The Arians ask whether the Son is

begotten of the Father's will; they ask this, Athanasius writes, because they want to draw the conclusion that the Son was created. But the Son is not an offspring produced by the will and pleasure of God; the Son is Son by His nature as being one with God.

In the Fourth Discourse, which is somewhat more fragmentary than the first three, and which deals more with Monarchianism than with Arianism, Athanasius emphasizes the claim that the Son and the Word are identical; the Son, co-eternal with the Father, is the Word. This claim is supported not only by Scripture but also by arguments based upon theological demands for consistency and full honor to the Son; if the Son is to be perfect like the Father, He must be the Word through whom the power of the Lord became manifest.

Athanasius's *Discourses Against the Arians* serves, even now, as a reminder of the unity of the Trinity. It may be that the vigor of Christian theology is in part attributable to the strength of the heretical challenges which early theologians had to meet, but one must remember that the inspiration which fired such champions of the faith as Athanasius existed before the exercise of the apologetic arts. Athanasius was able to defend Christ as being one with God precisely because God as man made no other theology tenable.

AGAINST EUNOMIUS

Author: Saint Basil (c.329-379)
Type of work: Patristic theology
First transcribed: c.364

Principal Ideas Advanced

There exists no name which embraces the whole nature of God and is sufficient to declare it; rather, many and various names, each with its proper meaning, give us an understanding which, though quite obscure and limited when compared with the whole, is sufficient for us.

In speaking of the Divine Nature, it is preferable to use terms from Scripture rather than philosophical ones not found in Scripture, however correct these latter may be.

All our statements about God are made by analogy and cannot be urged unduly, but this limitation of our predication is no reason for abandoning our faith.

Saint Basil's *Against Eunomius* is an excellent example of the theological controversy of the turbulent but decisive fourth century. It is polemic, at times sarcastic and even angry, vigorous yet subtle. These "disputes over words" may strike the modern reader as empty and pointless, but the formulations of the Catholic faith to which we subscribe today, at times so casually, were achieved only after the refining controversies of generations of these early Church Fathers. They were not always able to keep personal motives out of the controversies, but there is no doubt that their prevailing motivation was a burning concern for maintaining the purity of the deposit of faith which they had received.

The controversies of the fourth century were not idle controversies; they were concerned with the very central mysteries of the Catholic faith. A more familiar acquaintance with them leads to a deeper appreciation of what the faith means and how much it cost the early Fathers to preserve it.

Saint Basil, called "the Great" was one of the giants of the early Church. Together with Saint Gregory of Nyssa, his brother, and Saint Gregory Nazianzen, his dearest friend, he is grouped under the title "The Three Cappodocians." These were a new breed of Christians; they were part of a Church which had emerged from the catacombs, and they educated themselves at the great centers of pagan learning. Basil studied at first in Caesarea. Later he studied in Constantinople and finally at Athens, where he met Gregory Nazianzen.

Basil had been brilliant and distinguished as a student, and at the completion of his studies several cultural centers were bidding for his services as a teacher. He decided to return to Caesarea. There he came under the influence of the Bishop Dianius, who apparently baptized him. It was not unusual in those days for Christians to delay their baptism until their adult years.

In terms of secular learning Basil was well equipped for life, but now he had his attention drawn toward the Gospel, and he began to think of reforming his life on the model of evangelical perfection. In order to study the ways of perfection he visited the monasteries of Egypt, Palestine, and Mesopotamia. He returned full of admiration for their austerity and piety and founded a monastery himself in Pontus. The way of life of a hermit already existed in Asia Minor, but Basil added the distinctive contribution of the cenobitic or community form.

In 360 Basil was called out of his monastic solitude by raging theological controversy. Almost the whole rest of his life would be spent fighting the Arian heresy.

Basil's *Against Eunomius* was one of his earliest works, written in 363 or 364. It assails the equivalent Arianism of Eunomius and defends the divinity of the Second and Third Persons of the Blessed Trinity. It comprises five "books." The first three of these are generally accepted as forming part of the original work. The last two are sometimes regarded as doubtful both because of differences in style and format and because of their omission in some early manuscripts. It has been suggested that they may possibly be notes on the controversy in general and not immediately directed against Eunomius. Be that as it may, their content is so in harmony with Basil's work that later authors have been inclined to attribute them to him.

Eunomius was also a Cappadocian. He went to Alexandria in about 356 and resided there for two years as the admiring pupil and secretary of Aetius the Anomoean. He accompanied Aetius to Antioch in 358 and took a prominent part in the formulation of extreme Arian positions, which offended the generally moderate semi-Arians. He became a sort of champion and spokesman for the extremists. This made him obnoxious to the Emperor Constantius and resulted in his banishment to Phyrigia. He was soon restored, however, and, as a result of the influence of Eudoxius, Bishop of Constantinople, he was appointed Bishop of Cyzicus. For a while he remained silent, but soon he became even more vocal than before. He was once more summoned by Constantius, and, upon his refusal to appear, was condemned and deposed, *in absentia.* He now became more prominent than ever in his assertion of the most open Arianism, and adherents to the extreme party were henceforth known as Eunomians. The accession of Julian the Apostate to the imperial throne permitted the return of Eunomius to Constantinople, and this city became the center for the spreading of his views.

About this time Eunomius wrote a relatively brief work entitled *Apologeticus.* In giving the work this title, Eunomius gave the appearance of imitating previous apologies written by various defenders of the Faith. He also created the impression that the work was not a spontaneous exposition of doctrine on his part but a reply forced upon him by previous attack.

The work professes to be a defense of what Eunomius called "the simpler creed which is common to all Christians." This creed is summarized by him as follows: "We believe in one God, Father Almighty, from whom are all things: and in one only-begotten Son of God, God the Word, Our Lord Jesus Christ, through whom are all things: and in one Holy Spirit, the Comforter."

Certainly this creed is in itself orthodox and unobjectionable. What it *means,* of course, depends upon the explanations one gives of the terms involved. In the case of Eunomius, these explanations ran distinctly counter to the traditional faith of the Church.

In the creed of Eunomius, as we have seen, the Son is called "God," but in his doctrinal system there is a practical denial of His divinity. Whatever words may be used, the Son, as described by Eunomius, is a creature and therefore, in the strict sense, not God at all. For the Arians, the Father, "unbegotten," was alone and supreme. The Son was the "only begotten" of the Father, but the very idea of "begotten," for the Arians, implied posteriority, inferiority, and unlikeness. Basil protests against this position. Eunomius' position, says Basil, is really equivalent to what was, apparently, an Arian formula; namely, that "ingenerateness is the essence of God," that "the Only-begotten is essentially unlike the Father."

But, asks Basil, what is the real value of this word, "unbegotten," of which Eunomius and his supporters make so much? Certainly it agrees well with the orthodox doctrine of the Trinity, but "it is nowhere used in Scripture, it is one of the main elements of their (the Arians') blasphemy; I judged it had better be left alone." The scriptural term "Father" implies all that is meant by "Unbegotten" and has moreover the advantage of suggesting at the same time the idea of the Son. The title "Unbegotten" will not be preferred by us, says Basil, unless we wish to make ourselves wiser than the Savior, "who said, 'Go and baptize in the name' not of the unbegotten, but of the Father."

The Eunomians contended that the word "unbegotten" was not simply an honorary title, but one required of strictest necessity in that it makes a confession of *what God is;* the word, they claimed, expresses the divine nature or essence. Basil answers that, on the contrary, it is only one of many negative terms applied to God, none of which completely expresses the divine essence. In a succinct passage Basil expresses what has become the classic Catholic position on man's attempts to express God's nature: "There exists no name which embraces the whole nature of God and is sufficient to declare it; rather many and various ones, each with its own proper meaning, give us an understanding which, though quite obscure and limited when compared with the whole, is sufficient for us."

The word "unbegotten" like such words as "incorruptible" and "invisible," formally express only negation: *not* corruptible, *not* visible. They indicate things which are *not* characteristic of the divine nature. "Yet substance or essence is not one of those things which are absent in God, but signifies the very being of God: to count this among those qualities which are non-existent is folly." Basil is quite ready to admit that the essence of the nature of God is unbegotten, but he objects to the statement (made by the Arians) that the essence and the unbegotten are identical.

Basil then chides Eunomius for his pride in presuming to have discovered the divine essence itself, when so many witnesses in Scripture protest its incomprehensibility. He cites David, Isaias, and Saint Paul, all of them exponents of the divine transcendence, and then he turns upon Eunomius to demand his credentials.

Just as Eunomius had made ingenerateness the essence of the Divine, so, with the object of establishing the contrast between Father and Son, he represented the *being begotten* as the essence of the Son. God, said Eunomius, being ingenerate, could never admit of generation. Now, as Basil points out, this statement may be understood in two ways. It may mean that ingenerate nature cannot be subject to generation. It may also mean that ingenerate nature cannot generate. The former formulation is quite reconcilable with Catholic doctrine, and Eunomius makes converts on the basis of such an interpretation. The second formulation, however, is what Eunomius really means, for he adds to the words "could never admit of generation," the words, "so as to impart His own proper nature to the begotten."

Basil now makes the same objections against the term "begotten," as applied to the Son, that he previously made against "unbegotten" as applied to the Father. Nowhere is it found in Scripture. If this word indicated the essence of the Son, no other word would have been revealed by the Spirit. Things are not made for names, but names for things. Eunomius has been led by distinction of name into distinction of being.

If the Son is begotten in the sense in which Eunomius uses the word, Basil continues, He is neither begotten of the essence of God (with the same nature), nor begotten from eternity. Eunomius represents the Son as not of the essence of the Father, because begetting is only thought of, by him, as a sensual act and idea, and therefore is entirely unthinkable in connection with the being of God. Here are the words of Eunomius: "The essence of God does not admit of begetting; no other essence exists for the Son's begetting; therefore we say that the Son was begotten when nonexistent."

Basil's reply is that no analogy can hold between divine generation or begetting and human generation or begetting. Living beings which are subject to death generate through the operation of the senses, but we must not on this account conceive of God in the same manner: "Nay, rather we should be hence guided to the truth that, because corruptible beings operate in this manner, the Incorruptible will operate in an opposite manner." We must, then, try to conceive "a generation worthy of God, without passion, partition, division or time." We must try to conceive of the image of the invisible God not after the analogy of images which are elaborated in imitation of a model, but as of one nature and subsistence with the originating archetype; namely, the divine essence. This image is not produced by imitation, for the whole nature of the Father is expressed in the Son.

Basil was well aware of the limitations of our knowledge of such realities, and he shows little patience with those who pose conundrums about the precise manner in which generation takes place: "Don't ask me what is this generation? Of what kind is it? How could it be brought about? The manner is ineffable and wholly beyond our understanding, but we shall not on this account throw away our firm and unshakable faith in the Father and the Son. For if we wish to measure everything by our understanding and to declare nonexistent what our mind cannot grasp, then farewell the reward of faith, farewell the reward of hope!"

If the Son is not of the essence of God, He could not be held to be eternal. Eunomius had put the dilemma: When God begot the Son, the Son either was or was not. If He was not, then the Arian position is true and He is a creature. If He was, then he needed no begetting. Basil answers by making a distinction between being eternal and being unbegotten. The Eunomians maintained that these two were identical and that consequently they belonged to the Father alone. Basil shows that the term "unbegotten" means that which has origin of itself, while "eternal" refers to that which is in being beyond all time and age. These two are not formally the same. The Son can exist eternally, but eternally *as* Son, begotten of the Father.

The main point of Basil's opposition to Eunomius, then, is that the word "unbegotten" is not a name which is indicative of the divine nature, but only a condition of existence. The divine nature has other predicates. If every particular mode of existence causes a distinction in essence also, then the Son cannot be of the same essence or nature as the Father, because the Son has a peculiar mode of existence and the Father another. Quantitative differences are not reckoned in relation to essence; the question is only of being or non-being. Regarding Father and Son, then, the dignity of both is equal. The essence of Begetter and Begotten is identical.

The fourth book of this work, as we noted above, differs considerably in presentation from the preceding three, which took the form of a sort of dialogue, alternating excerpts from Eunomius' work with Basil's replies. In the fourth book we find what appears to be a series of notes which successively propose and interpret Scriptural texts urged by the Arians against the divinity of the Son. The answer to almost all the texts is the same; namely, that such texts refer to Christ's human nature, which was in truth created and subject and inferior to the Father. Failure to distinguish the dual nature of Christ, "true God and true man," but possessed by the one person, the Son, Second Person of the Blessed Trinity, is the source of most heretical interpretations in this regard.

In the third book Basil turns to Eunomius' doctrine on the Holy Spirit, which is simply a logical extension of his previous attitudes. For Eunomius, the Holy Spirit is third in order and dignity and is therefore also third by nature. Basil concedes that there is a sense in which the Son can be considered second in order and dignity to the Father, but not second in nature since they share the one divine nature. Similarly, though the Holy Spirit may be considered second to the Son in order and dignity, it does not follow that the Holy Spirit is of a different nature from the Son.

The fifth book continues this discussion regarding the Holy Spirit, showing that the Holy Spirit is not a creature, that His power is the same as that of the Father and the Son. Basil also comments at length on those divine operations which are generally attributed to the Holy Spirit; namely, the remission of sins, prophecy, and the participation of creatures in the divine image.

Thus ends Basil's work, *Against Eunomius*. It was not the end, but rather the beginning of his labors as a controversialist. In 370 he became Bishop of Caesarea in Cappadocia. Basil's diocese, like his monasteries, became an active center for the defense and spread of the orthodox Nicene doctrine of the Trinity against Arian opposition and misconstructions.

E.L.B.

TREATISE ON THE MYSTERIES

Author: Saint Hilary of Poitiers (c.315-c.368)
Type of work: Scriptural exegesis
First transcribed: c.364

Principal Ideas Advanced

The essential message of God's revelation to mankind is already present in the Old Testament, both in regard to salient points and to a knowledge of the divine plan for salvation.

An examination of the Old Testament as a whole as well as of its individual episodes shows that it prefigures events in the life of Jesus Christ and of the Church founded by Him.

The figurative meaning of the Old Testament does not deny the historical genuineness of the individual events, but rather builds upon and expands it in the light of later events in the history of salvation.

Thus, the events of the New Testament are the consummation of the prophetic happenings of the Old Law.

Saint Hilary of Poitiers is most widely known for his speculative anti-Arian works, whence he derived the title, "Athanasius of the West." But he also wrote a number of exegetical works, the most extensive being his commentaries on Matthew and on the Psalms, lengthy explanations in the prevalent style of the day, which was to dissect the sacred texts almost word by word. In contrast to these exegeses, Hilary's *Tractatus mysteriorium* is brief and concise. The only extant manuscript, dating from the eleventh century, and not discovered until 1887, displays several lacunae which add to its already difficult text. Despite these defects, the work is rightly considered as an important stage in the development of exegesis and especially in the understanding of the typical or spiritual relation of the Old to the New Testament.

Exegetical work had already appeared in the West in the writings of Tertullian and Saint Cyprian, Bishop of Carthage, but they showed little inclination or aptitude for the speculative efforts that the school of Alexandria, particularly Saint Clement of Alexandria and the learned scholar Origen, displayed in the East. It was Hilary, anticipating the great exegetical works of Saint Ambrose and Saint Augustine, who helped extend the swelling current of Christian speculation on the Scriptures from the East to the West. In contrast to the rudimentary and sketchy exegesis of the Scriptures given by some of his forebears in the West, Hilary's commentaries on Matthew and the Psalms display the richness of interpretation which make him a true successor to Origen and the school of Alexandria. Contributing to his development was a period of six years which he spent in exile in Phrygia, during which he obtained firsthand acquaintance with Oriental thought.

The *Treatise on the Mysteries* is not a work which explicitly sets forth the principles behind this type of exegesis, nor is it strictly an example which demonstrates these principles by their use, although the cases which Hilary treats do tend in that direction. The chief merit of this treatise is that it explicitly attempts to justify a spiritual or typical interpretation of the Old Testament, for Hilary's main contention is that one cannot fully understand the events of the Old Testament without a knowledge of their fulfillment in the New Covenant. It is in the events of the New Testament, understood now in the full revelation of Jesus Christ, that the whole Old Testament is illuminated and takes on new meaning as a preparation for and prophecy of the coming of Christ.

Hilary states this purpose clearly at the very outset of this treatise. He wishes to demonstrate that in every person, era, and event in the Old Testament, the totality of the prophecies projects, as if in a mirror, an image of the coming, preaching, Passion, and Resurrection of Our Lord Jesus Christ and of our aggregation into His Church, for, the author insists, every happening contained in these sacred books announces by words, reveals by facts, and establishes by examples the coming of Our Lord Jesus Christ. Hilary's purpose, so clearly stated, is then illustrated in a single sentence as he shows a prefigurement of the generation of the Church in the sleep of Adam, of its purification through Baptism in the deluge, of its sanctification in the blessing of Melchisedech, of its election in the justification of Abraham, of its separation from the wicked in the birth of Isaac, and of its redemption in the servitude of Jacob. From this first paragraph of the work the main characteristics of Hilary's thought can already be traced. First, he sees the Old Testament as a collection of symbols or types; second, he sees these types as representatives, in the spiritual order, of historical realities pertaining to the life of Jesus Christ in his mortal, glorious, or mystical body.

The Old Testament is more than a collection of diverse images, Saint Hilary maintains, for if one views it as a whole, one sees the work as a single and imposing figure with an easily perceptible principle of unity. Adam, Abel, Cain, Noah, and the other Old Testament figures are not independent figures, but so many facets, explanations, and refinements of a single image, the outlines of which begin with the origins of humanity and continue to grow sharper until the coming of Christ. Thus, although considering the events of the Old Testament in their historical sequence, Hilary really introduces an underlying order and sees in it a progressive image of the foreordained life of Christ and His Church.

All this is not to say that Saint Hilary commits the error of rejecting or even overlooking the literal meaning of individual passages, a fault often encountered in writers who are swept away by flights of fancy into a world far removed from the words before them. He does, it is true, disagree with an exegesis which would take account of the literal sense alone and accept no other meaning. In cases where the literal sense may seem impossible or erroneous, the wider view given by the other interpretations will enable the exegete to comprehend the correct literal sense also. Nor does Hilary extend the use of the spiritual sense indiscriminately, for the exegete must exercise great pains to distinguish passages in which the historical account is to be taken in its literal simplicity from those wherein the typical sense is also present. To confuse these refinements is to run the risk of falsifying the literal meaning or of missing the spiritual meaning of those passages.

The work itself is divided into two books of unequal size, the first taking up individual accounts of Adam and Eve, Cain and Abel, Lamech, Noah, Abraham, Isaac, Jacob, and Moses. The second book treats Osea and Joshua, concluding with some further thoughts on the relation between the two Testaments. Some of the typology which Hilary brings out is Adam and Eve as a figure of Christ and the Church, and the creation of Eve as a type of the resurrection of the body. In the episode of Cain and Abel he sees foreshadowings of the Passion of Our Lord and of the calling of the Gentiles to the Church. Noah he sees as, in many ways, a type of Christ—one who saves from universal destruction as a sanctifier, even as a figure of the Passion in his drunkenness, which is caused by the fruit of a vine which had been transplanted and cared for just as God had transplanted and cared for His people. Esau's right of inheritance is seen as a sign of the election of the people of Israel, but Jacob's succession to it points to the call of the Christian people to take part in the kingdom. In connection with Jacob, it is interesting to study Hilary's care for the literal meaning of this passage. Isaac's blessing promised an abundance of the fruits of the earth and dominion over his brethren and all the nations. But it seems that none of these promises was fulfilled during Jacob's life, for he suffered from hunger, was delivered to the power of Pharaoh, and underwent a long enslavement to Laban. Hilary, however, to find a meaning which will verify this blessing, shows how the words of Isaac, although addressed to Jacob, find their full meaning and fulfillment in the people whom they foreshadow, for all these things are reserved to the faithful, to those who will judge the world and partake in the heavenly Kingdom.

For Saint Hilary, Joshua, like Moses, is a figure of Christ. Joshua was chief of the synagogue; Christ, of the Church; Joshua was the guide toward the Promised Land; Christ is the guide towards the land where we will possess our inheritance. Joshua comes after Moses; Christ, after the Law. Joshua received an order to renew circumcision with flint knives, while the Savior, who is the piercing Word which penetrates to the division of the soul, and is also the cornerstone set up by God, inaugurated circumcision of the heart in the spiritual order. As one divided the waters of the Jordan; the Other divides the peoples.

Hilary has not merely left us a collection of occasional sermons on a Scriptural theme or book; the *Treatise on the Mysteries* was written as a whole and was intended to furnish an exegetical explanation of the typology of the Old Testament. Hilary does not limit this typology to a particular figure or genre of Old Testament writing, but, limited though his examples are, he attempts to show that the Old Testament as a whole announces the coming of Christ, no matter how diverse the historical events and persons are through which this is accomplished. Joined to what was said about the history of exegesis before him, one can see that Hilary wanted to write a handbook for the spiritual interpretation of Scripture and did so by grouping and systematizing the essential data which could guide the reader in such a reading of the Bible. One could go a step further and speculate that the intended readers of this treatise in typological exegesis were the priests of Poitiers commissioned to explain the *lectiones divinae* (readings in Sacred Scripture) to the faithful. The originality displayed by Saint Hilary here is the union effected between the traditional exegesis, which was concerned largely with the letter of Holy Writ, and the learned disquisitions found largely in the East. Hilary enriched the first with the substance of the second in the measure in which he felt his flock would benefit from it. Thus, the *Treatise on the Mysteries,* more than Hilary's anti-Arian writings, which stemmed from his desire to ward off heresy, are an authentic expression of his fatherly and pastoral care for the faithful of his diocese.

R.J.B.

TREATISE ON THE HOLY SPIRIT

Author: Saint Basil (c.329-379)
Type of work: Dogmatic theology
First transcribed: 375

Principal Ideas Advanced

Semantic arguments based on the doxology and designed to support anti-Trinitarian positions, such as those of the Arians, Sabellians, and Macedonians, are unjustified.

The Son and the Holy Spirit are "consubstantial" with the Father and deserving of equal honor with Him.

The form of the doxology which ascribes equality to the three Persons is guaranteed by the Scriptures as well as by the usage of many illustrious churchmen.

Basil of Caesarea wrote *Treatise on the Holy Spirit* at the request of his friend Amphilochius, a relative of Gregory of Nazianzus and Bishop of Iconium in Asia Minor. It is a sincere treatise which reflects the personality of the author and his deep involvement in the heated theological disputes of his day. At the outset of the composition, Basil commends his friend's inquisitiveness concerning things divine and welcomes the opportunity to enlighten him; yet, at the close of the essay, Basil expresses doubts that any effort can prove effective in curbing the overwhelming confusion and acrimonious discord in the Church. He adds, however, that love and duty command him to speak.

In the fourth century the question of the Holy Spirit was, indeed, a hotly contested one. While the Nicene settlement had determined the consubstantiality of the Son with the Father, it had done virtually nothing to define the nature of the Holy Spirit. Sabellians became louder in their overemphasis of the Unity of God at the expense of the individuality of both the Son and the Holy Spirit. Arians grew more articulate over the subordinationism of the Son, and they indirectly challenged the integrity of the Holy Spirit as a member of the Trinity. While the many Arian creeds of the fourth century did not basically concern themselves with the Holy Spirit, the Pneumatomachians, or Macedonians, those who openly opposed the divinity of the Spirit, came more and more to feel an affinity with the Arian Homoiousians.

Basil's work was prompted not only by the general theological contention but also by a personal attack. Critics accused him of doctrinal innovation for using as his form of the doxology: "Glory be to the Father 'with' [amid] the Son, 'together with' [at the same time] the Holy Ghost." The more usual form was " 'through the Son' [through the instrumentality of], 'in the Holy Spirit' [by means of]." Consequently, Basil saw, as he quickly pointed out to Amphilochius, that much depended upon theological terminology even to the point of syllables or prepositions. If the nod of a head, he remarked, served to bring death at times during persecution, how much more significant were words.

Both forms of the doxology were legitimate, Basil declares, and he interprets the attack upon his own formula as basically a concealed excuse to assault the Person of the Holy Ghost. He maintains that his critics were sophists intoxicated with overadmiration for pagan learning. They argued unfairly that in the common doxology the different prepositions used before the references to the "hypostases" of the Godhead are deliberately introduced to convey the impression that different relationships existed between the three Persons. Only an illegitimate, hybrid Aristotelian-Christian argument could contend that the preposition "of," implying the essential or formal cause, should be specifically predicated of the Father; that the words "by" and "through," indicating agency or means and referring to the efficient cause, should be associated exclusively with the Son; that the term "in," normally suggesting location, should pertain rightfully to the Holy Spirit. Such suppositions naturally encouraged Basil's critics to insist that the normal doxology, which employed the dissimilar expressions "through" the Son and "in" the Holy Ghost, taught an orthodox subordinationism. Basil, by choosing another form of the doxology, was heretical, the critics claimed.

Such rigidity in word meanings, Basil argued, might well characterize secular philosophy but did not apply to the Scriptures. The Sacred Writings varied the use of prepositions depending upon the sense they intended to convey. "Of" was not always employed in connection with the Father, or "through" with the Son, or "in" with the Holy Ghost. "Through Whom" was, for example, at times associated with the Father, and "of Whom" with both the Son and the Holy Spirit.

Basil's positive arguments for the equality of the Holy Ghost with the Father and the Son are drawn almost entirely from the Scriptures, although tradition is invoked to cite usages in baptismal confessions. To Basil the term "Spirit" itself, as used in the expression, "Holy Spirit," predicates incorporeality, incomprehensibility, indivisibility, and infinity, an intelligent essence which cannot be circumscribed. From this essence derives, according to the Scriptures, all understanding, all knowledge, and, indeed, all spiritual gifts. A Being of such dimensions and potential could be nothing other than divine. Furthermore, the Scriptures definitely demand that the Father, Son, and Holy Spirit be associated equally in the baptismal formula. Would the heretics be so persistent in their blind prejudice against the Holy Ghost as to omit the invocation to Him and thereby render the sacrament ineffective? At the baptismal services catechumens publicly professed belief in the three Persons when they recited the creed. The entire disputation seemed irrational and contentious: Christians profess belief in the Spirit and then quarrel over their confessions; after they are baptized in the Spirit they fight over Him; while they call upon Him with lofty epithets they consider Him a slave; after they accept His ministrations along with those of the Father and Son they dishonor Him with the status of a creature.

Scriptural evidence that the Spirit's particular function is that of Sanctifier,

Revealer of mysteries, and Donor of charismatic gifts precludes any possibility that He is a creature. From the first, as Revelation attests, He has operated in conjunction with the Father and the Son. In the Creation the Father was the original cause, the Son the creative cause, the Holy Spirit the perfecting cause. The Sacred Writings reveal, too, that the Holy Spirit was inseparably associated with the Son at all important events of His earthly life: at His Baptism and on the occasions of His miracles, whether he exorcised or healed. Even after Christ's resurrection the Holy Ghost was deeply involved in the Son's acts, especially when the latter said: "Receive yet the Holy Ghost; whosoever's sins ye remit they are remitted unto them and whosoever's ye retain they are retained." As co-worker in the entire dispensation arranged for man, the Spirit took from the beginning a fundamental part in the ordering of the Church. Finally, He would appear with the Son on the day of judgment. How, indeed, were the angels in Heaven to cry out "Glory to God in the Highest" without being empowered by the Spirit, since "no man can say that Jesus is Lord but by the Holy Spirit?"

Scriptural remarks, such as those recording Baptism "unto Moses" or "into water" to the seeming neglect of the Holy Ghost must be understood as types. Similarly, terms attached to the Spirit suggesting inferiority must be understood in full context. He is indeed called intercessor, but, then, so is the Son. Nor is the assumption valid that the Persons of the Trinity should be numbered as one, two, and three, as indicative of some sort of inequality, for Scripture nowhere uses numbers in relation to the Trinity. Moreover, enumeration does not affect the nature of articles nor introduce any essential inferiority into their being, because, after being numbered, they remain what they were. Besides, numbers primarily refer to quantity, not to quality. But by their very insistence that the Persons can be numbered, the enemies of the Holy Ghost confound their own position, since a series of numbers can logically be assigned only to things which have a common denominator.

Not only Scripture proclaims the lofty position and equality of the Holy Spirit and therefore enjoins that equal honor be paid Father, Son, and Holy Ghost. The tradition of the Apostles preserved in the confessions of the Church also demands the same. Basil maintains that his formula "with" the Holy Spirit had the support of some of the most illustrious men of the Church: Irenaeus, Clement of Rome, Dionysius of Rome, Dionysius of Alexandria, Origen, Africanus, Gregory Thaumaturgus, Firmilian, and Meletius. Such a tradition guaranteed that he was no innovator.

Basil's work is considered orthodox with the exception that he, like all his contemporaries, holds that the Holy Ghost proceeds from the Father through the Son rather than from both. The Spirit issues, as it were, as a breath from the mouth of the Father, not through generation as does the Son. Basil's treatise on the Holy Spirit was used a few years later by Ambrose as a source for his own *De Spiritu Sancto*. The fact that Basil never distinctly calls the Holy Ghost "God" in this essay and never uses the term "consubstantial with the Father" led some later fathers to accuse him of semi-Arianism. Athanasius defended Basil's orthodoxy, however, declaring that to be of assistance to the weak, Basil had to be somewhat reserved in his statements.

E.G.W.

THE LETTERS OF SAINT BASIL

Author: Saint Basil (c.329-379)
Type of work: Moral, ascetic, and doctrinal letters
First transcribed: c.357-c.379

Principal Ideas Advanced

The Arian view that the Father, Son, and Holy Ghost are not one in substance is mistaken; neither the Son nor the Holy Ghost is a creature.

The monastic life provides that solitude wherein a man may, through contemplation and deeds, make his life worthy of Christ's Gospel.

The study and practice of virtue will make a man worthy of the good things promised by the Lord.

The *Letters of Saint Basil* is a source of inspiration and delight. The insights and advice of the great monastic Doctor of the Church are for the most part as pertinent now as when they were written in the latter half of the fourth century.

Basil was born in Caesarea; he studied with Saint Gregory Nazianzen as a classmate at Constantinople. In 355 he was baptized and entered upon the monastic life. Basil became Archbishop of Caesarea in 370, when he succeeded Eusebius. He dealt successfully with hostile bishops and critics; he enlisted himself in the struggle against Arianism; he preached daily; he cared for the poor and infirm, and through his writings he contributed to the expression of the thought and spirit of the Church. His *Rule* became the foundation upon which Saint Benedict built his own regulations for the monastic life, and his *Treatise on the Holy Spirit* and *Adversus Eunomium* are landmarks in the history of theology.

One of the earliest extant letters is one written by Saint Basil to Gregory Nazianzen, shortly after Basil's retirement to a monastic retreat at Pontus in 357. Basil begins ingenuously by saying, "I recognized your letter, as one recognizes one's friends' children from their obvious likeness to their parents." He declares that one must strive after a quiet mind, that the obligations of a practical life, especially if one is married, make the preparation of the heart difficult. One must learn in solitude, through contemplation and study of the Scriptures, and also through prayer and attending to the conversation of others.

A very important letter is one written in the year 360, when Basil left Caesarea after discovering that Bishop Dianius, who had baptized him, had subscribed to an Arian creed; Basil withdrew to Nazianzus, where he joined his friend Gregory. The letter is addressed to the monks of Caesarea. Basil declares that he is not "embracing a city life"; he has chosen to be near Gregory, "Christ's mouth." Basil refers to the Arians as "shepherds of the Philistines," and he warns the brothers that the view that God became a Father and that the Holy Ghost is not eternal is opposed to the Faith. Basil argues that God is one in nature; Father, Son, and Holy Ghost are of the same nature and substance; neither the Son nor the Holy Ghost is a creature. Further claims concerning the Trinity are made to refute the charge that Basil is a Tritheist, one who believes in three Gods. His arguments are a point-by-point refutation of the Arian propositions. Finally, in conclusion, Basil contends that the "inner man consists of nothing but contemplation," and he maintains that only those who have "heeded the right faith" will see God.

A letter written during the same period to a widow illustrates the breadth of spirit which enabled Basil to be at once a man of humor and a man of God: "The art of snaring pigeons is as follows. When the men who devote themselves to this craft have caught one, they tame it, and make it feed with them. Then they smear its wings with sweet oil, and let it go and join the rest outside. Then the scent of that sweet oil makes the free flock the possession of the owner of the tame bird, for all the rest are attracted by the fragrance, and settle in the house. But why do I begin my letter thus? Because I have taken your son Dionysius, once Diomedes, and anointed the wings of his soul with the sweet oil of God, and sent him to you that you may take flight with him, and make for the nest which he has built under my roof. If I live to see this, and you, my honoured friend, translated to our lofty life, I shall require many persons worthy of God to pay Him all the honour that is His due."

In a letter written about the year 364, Basil writes of the perfection of the solitary life. He begins by reviewing the obligations of every Christian: the life and conversation of the Christian should be worthy of Christ's Gospel; the Christian should not be of doubtful mind; he ought not to swear or lie, to speak evil, fight, or be angry; he ought to be patient, avoid slander, be moderate, and regard himself as subject to God's will. The Christian brother should work without complaining; he should not offend another either by glances, words, or deeds; he ought not to be envious or hold grudges; he ought not to seek the riches of the world but rejoice in his poverty. Every injunction is supported by an implicit Scriptural reference.

Many of Basil's letters were written to Amphilochius, Bishop of Iconium; Eusebius, Bishop of Samosata; Athanasius, Bishop of Alexandria; and to various churches. Letters to Gregory Nazianzen are frequently concerned with theological matters. A number of the letters are addressed to those in need of spiritual counsel: lapsed monks, a fallen virgin, widows, and others in distress. Several letters are canonical, making more explicit the laws concerning second marriages, adultery, sorcery, perjury, and other violations.

In a letter to "the learned Maximus," written near the end of Saint Basil's active life, Basil writes that "the only thing that deserves our exertions and praises is our everlasting welfare; and this is the honour that comes from God." He then adds: "Human affairs are fainter than a shadow, more deceitful than a dream. Youth fades more quickly than the flowers of spring; our beauty wastes with age or sickness. Riches are uncertain; glory is fickle. The pursuit of arts and sciences is bounded by the present life; the charm of eloquence, which all covet, reaches but the ear: whereas the practice of virtue is a precious possession for its owner, a delightful spectacle for all who witness it. Make this your study; so will you be worthy of the good things promised by the Lord."

The struggles against Arianism were over; the challenges to the Emperor Valens were forgotten; the quarrel with Gregory of Nazianzen was seen to have been an unfortunate consequence of Church politics; Athanasius had died in 373, and in 374 Eusebius of Samosata had been banished to Thrace. But Basil could remember the major victories of his public life: the establishment of orthodoxy, the regulation of Eastern monasticism. It is not surprising, then, that one of his last letters is a reflection of the satisfaction he felt in the possession of that virtue which the love of God makes possible. It is also characteristic that on his deathbed, when those about him were sure that he had gone, he roused himself to give some final words of advice, and then said with finality, "Into thy hands I commend my spirit."

ON THE CHRISTIAN FAITH

Author: Saint Ambrose (c.339-397)
Type of work: Dogmatic theology
First transcribed: 379-380

Principal Ideas Advanced

The Scriptures, as well as the Nicene definition, assert that the Father and the Son are distinct Persons, yet without a plurality of substance.

The Son is described with the same epithets as the Father; their wills are in harmony and there is unity in their action.

The Son acts and speaks as God; all Scriptural passages suggesting inferiority of the Son must refer only to His manhood.

Before the emperor Gratian departed for the East in 378 to aid his uncle, Valens, against the invading Goths, he requested from Ambrose of Milan a statement of orthodox Christology as a bulwark against the wiles of Eastern Arianism. Thus were written two of the five books of *De fide*, or *An Exposition of the Christian Faith*. Both in the prologue and in the conclusion of Book II, Ambrose assured Gratian of victory. Now that the labarum with Christ's monogram had supplanted the eagles at the head of the legions, Ambrose wrote, the success against the Goths prophesied by Ezechiel was at hand.

During the period 379-380 three additional books were appended to the *De fide*. Here Ambrose, in an unabashed manner, resourcefully attributes the tragic rout and death of Valens at Adrianople to an adverse divine judgment against the Arians. It seems proper to him that defeat should occur on the spot where Christ was vanquished by those heretics, that belief in the Roman empire should be overthrown where faith in God had given way.

The subject matter in *De fide* is not progressively unfolded, book by book; the last three units are merely extensive explanations of the earlier two. The purpose of the treatise is to demonstrate, against Arianism, the consubstantiality of the Son with the Father. The Arian heresy was still flourishing not only in the East, thanks to Valens' earlier support, but even in the vicinity of Milan, where the influence of Ambrose's predecessor, Auxentius, still lingered and where Justina, the mother of Valentinian II, yet worked to promote the Arian cause. In his own words, Ambrose labored to demonstrate a "distinction, not the confusion of Father, Son, and Holy Spirit: a distinction without separation, a distinction without plurality" of substance.

The famed Milanese bishop entered upon his task with trepidation. The generation of the Son, he confesses, involves incomprehensible mysteries of which no one dare speak without purification, grace, good conscience, and love. Without faith, the proper wedding garment, no one can come to the banquet table. Ambrose entertains fear lest, in unworthily measuring the Son of God, he will insolently impinge upon the boundlessness, immeasurableness, ineffability, and incomprehensibility of the Father.

Underlying this tone of humility, there is a sarcastic note of abuse reserved for the hypothetical Arian protagonist whom Ambrose occasionally addresses in the work. In rather a scurrilous vein, Ambrose advises his readers to trust John, whose head rested on the bosom of Christ, rather than Arius, whose mouth was besmirched when he wallowed in filth at the time of his disgusting death. Ambrose reproaches Arius for arrogating to himself greater knowledge than that claimed by Moses, Aaron, or Paul. Arius and his followers have to be repulsed as men of monstrous wickedness who, having no control over their own procreation, yet usurp the power to inquire into the divine generation. Indeed, says Ambrose, they are veritable antichrists. Arian internal dissension, spawned by leaders such as Eunomius, Aetius, and Auxentius, make the system a multiple-headed Hydra or Scylla.

Since Scripture is a medium common to both orthodoxy and Arianism, Ambrose naturally relies first and foremost on the Sacred Writings for evidence. The Scriptures are the gates that open Heaven; without them, worldly wisdom, imagination, even angelic knowledge and the insight of John the Baptist, stand bewildered before the heavenly mysteries. Throughout the Old and New Testaments, Ambrose claims, passages or combinations of passages distinctly uphold the divinity of Christ. He shows that the Prophets and Paul all maintain that the Son is like the Father, and that John teaches His eternity with the words, "In the beginning was the

Word." Terms implying divinity are applied to Christ consistently throughout the Scriptures: He is the Son, the Begotten One, the Expression, Mirror, and Image of the Father. Much of the *De fide* is naturally devoted to refuting interpretations of many favorite Arian Scriptural passages, such as, "Why dost thou call me good? No one but God is good," (Mark: 10:19), or "The Father is greater than I" (John, 14:28). Ambrose declares that when Arians quote such verses they act like the Jews, who fear to associate the weakness of mankind with the dignity of divinity.

In explaining both his own Scriptural references and those of his antagonists, Ambrose chooses to minimize the use of analogy. He not only exercises wariness in employing comparisons but actually apologizes when he does resort to them. His favorite analogy likens Christ's eternal Sonship with the Father to the complete coexistence of brightness with light. Nor is Ambrose anxious to use allegory copiously although he does consent at times to gloss over the literal text to pry into hidden meanings. One example of a forced and circuitous interpretation is his association of Jesus' sandal with the mystic concept of Jesus as the true Bridegroom.

Ambrose feels, too, that dialectic had best hold her peace, for the Arians had used argumentation so effectively that it led to their own destruction. They had, as it were, too freely dyed their impiety in the vats of philosophy. The entire *De fide* is a panoramic indictment of Arians for their reliance upon subtle objections, blasphemous paradoxes, empty babblings, and semantic juggling of the type which caused them to equate "created" with "begotten." Even so, Ambrose himself relies quite heavily upon dialectic. He operates on premises hallowed by Greek philosophy: the Eleatic and Platonic suggestion that the Ultimate is immovable, unchangeable, timeless, and omnipotent; the assumption that the end is greater than the agent; the Aristotelian tenet that the whole is greater than the part; and the Platonic doctrine of dual worlds.

Ambrose also resorts to tradition as a support of his position. He emphatically tells Gratian that he regards the Nicene settlement as a basic guide. In his mind the Nicene symbol pointedly foils Arian teachings by its deliberately repetitious statement: "God of God, Light of Light, Very God of Very God, begotten of the Father not made, of one substance with the Father." Its canonical decrees go straight to the point by promulgating that those affirming "there was a time when the Son of God was not" or that He is "of another substance or ousia" are duly accursed by the Catholic and Apostolic communion. The number 318, mysteriously designating the number of delegates at Nicaea and at the same time representing in Greek letters the Cross and the first two letters of the name "Jesus," constitutes for Ambrose a mystic, secret sign that God obviously sanctions the council and its work. He argues, therefore, that both the symbols bequeathed to the Church and the precepts of the Fathers must be faithfully preserved. They have wisely ordained the term "homoousios," since it so adequately declares simultaneously a distinction of the two Persons and the unity of the divine Being. If Sabellians find this word difficult to accept because they misinterpret it to mean "identical with," they should reflect that "of the same substance" in itself demands a distinction of two things since clearly no one thing could be "of the same substance" with itself.

Relying, then, upon Scripture and tradition, and employing devices such as allegory, analogy, and dialectic, Ambrose points up several lines of argument. First, the Son's speech and acts are those of God. It is relatively easy for Ambrose to shore up his thesis with certain Scriptural references to Christ: the Son opened the Red Sea; He dispatched manna; He is the Good Shepherd, as well as the Lamb who took away the sins of the world; He is the sacrificed High Priest whose blood is the propitiation for sin. At the same time, Ambrose had to contend with many Scriptural passages implying the inequality of the Son. Such verses as "My God, my God why hast Thou forsaken Me?" or "Father, if it be possible let this chalice pass from Me," and all remarks stating that the Son was "made," or that He was "obedient," or that He "worshiped" the Father, had to be discounted as evidence against His divinity since they arose from Jesus' role as man. As God, He "commanded" the sea to be quiet or the dead to arise; only as man did he "pray." Solely in regard to His body was He a "servant" of the Father. The Son suffered no inferiority because He had a Father but no son. Even childless human beings do not suffer loss of esteem. Moreover, the Son has uncountable adopted heirs. Ambrose assures the Arians that the divine Father-Son relationship involves no temporal precedence, for time and space are entirely human measurements. To postulate that the Son was begotten in time makes the Father's act appear to have been transitory, as though He spent time in conception as does a woman in travail. Nor does the Son's sitting at the right hand of the Father entail dishonor.

Ambrose asserts that the Son's Incarnation, far from being a degrading episode, was actually a glorious event required to demonstrate that flesh could be subject to spirit. As conqueror over human nature, the Son gave men eloquent examples of contempt for riches, ambition, and intemperance. Even if, as man, He feigned ignorance of the hour and day of retribution, He did so lest He encourage sin. He wept that we might weep; He consoled that we might be consoled; He forgave that we might forgive. His human actions foreshadowed triumphs: He roused the sea that it might be calmed; He became weary that we might be refreshed; He drank that we might have spiritual drink; He died yet lived again; He was buried yet rose again.

Ambrose points out that everywhere the Son's and the Father's wills are identical; there is complete unity in their actions. In the very beginning God indicated this eternal co-operativeness by saying: "Let Us make man to Our image and likeness"; the Son without any reservation felt free to give away the keys of His Father's Kingdom and to invite the penitent thief into His Paradise. This same unity of purpose and love is apparent in the Passion; the Father willed it, the Son accepted it, saying: "Not as I will but as Thou wilt." Since Father and Son together sent the Spirit, the unity of action clearly extends to the Third Person as well.

Finally, Ambrose asserts that the Scriptures assign the same attributes to the Son as to the Father. Christ is spoken of as good, eternal, immortal, almighty, blessed; He is Brightness, Power, Truth, and Life. As Creator, could He be a creature? As Law-giver, could He include Himself as a subject among those to whom He ordered His Gospel preached? As supreme and final Judge, could He be judged as an inferior? The Arians claim that the Son is of "another substance," but, says Ambrose, Christ, as the Son of God, can be of no substance other than that of the Father.

E.G.W.

THE FIVE THEOLOGICAL ORATIONS

Author: Saint Gregory Nazianzen (c.329-c.390)
Type of work: Dogmatic theology
First transcribed: c.380

Principal Ideas Advanced

Since divine matters are most grave and holy, the qualities requisite for theological discussion are purity and integrity.

The Eunomians and Macedonians, if they relinquished their pride and pseudo-sophistication, would see that Holy Scripture and reasonable thinking confound their position.

Both Scripture and reason support the idea of one incomprehensible Godhead in a distinct Trinity of Persons, all fully divine, co-eternal and consubstantial.

The *Five Theological Orations,* composed of orations preached by Saint Gregory Nazianzen in his Bishopric of Constantinople about 380, won him the title of "The Theologian." The sermons, composed in a straightforward, serious, and earnest manner, are filled with brilliant barbs against his heretical opponents and are pervaded by an adroit sense of humor and a wise sophistication. Gregory's language, often lofty and moving, is generously studded with imagery and with Scriptural phrases.

The first oration, "A Preliminary Discourse Against the Eunomians," berates these proud Arian dialecticians, their systems, and their thinking; the Eunomians thrive, Gregory avers, on absurd babbling, sophistry, and semantics, rather than on common sense and action. Their idle, destructive gossiping shows them to be totally unaware of the great mystery of God. Not every one, Gregory writes, is sufficiently lofty and purified to be worthy of philosophizing about God; nor is every audience suited for such a grave undertaking, nor is every occasion proper. The unworthy cannot behold the glare of divine things; the proud cannot understand them. One's discourse on Deity must always avoid unbridled speculation and vain dialectics, which better befitted the pomp, trivia, and absurdities of Greek philosophy. Even proper discussion of divine matters is out of place before a heckling, disputatious, and unsympathetic audience.

The second oration deals with God the Father. Gregory calls upon the Son for help and upon the Holy Ghost for inspiration to equip him to deal with God's mysterious, incomprehensible nature as revealed in Scripture. Gregory is content to see the "back parts of God," His glory and majesty, which, says Gregory, fell like shadows behind Him as divine manifestation. To men in the flesh, God's essence is indescribable; His infinity and limitlessness incircumscribable. While His presence is attested by His orderly creation, He defies all qualification as the motionless Prime Mover, the Efficient and Maintaining Cause of all things, entirely incorporeal, unchanging, unoriginate and incorruptible. Men can only say what God is *not;* they cannot comprehend what He *is,* nor can they adequately depict His glory. God does not, in an immature fashion, attempt to safeguard His awe and mystery by making it difficult for man to know Him; comprehension of God, the Limitless, is simply impossible to man, the limited. Man's inadequacy has a purpose, possibly to prevent man from neglecting wisdom were it too easily achieved, or to forestall rash deeds, like Lucifer's, if man discovers wisdom prematurely, or to reward justly those in Heaven who have patiently striven for wisdom.

Gregory reminds his readers that even man's abstract ideas are inadequate to describe God because earthly conceptions of "spirit," "fire," "light," "love," "wisdom," "righteousness," "mind," "reason," and "justice" are always impure, always associated with their opposites and with man's own experiences. Satan took advantage of men's inability to envision God and caused men in an idolatrous way to transform visible things into gods. Thus, men deified heavenly bodies and such human qualities as beauty and strength. They worshiped with beastly rites even base passions and barbaric monstrosities. Reason, however, relentlessly drove men to long for God; looking beyond the orderly created earth and heavens they logically demanded the conscious Author of motion in the universe. But in this quest for God even favored heroes, such as Noah, Abraham, Jacob, Elias, Peter, and Paul, were not able to disrobe Him of His mystery.

Gregory ends this discourse on God the Father with a beautiful sweep across creation. He beholds man completely in all his wonder, then the various stages of crawling things, next the "fishy tribe," the variety of birds with their melodies and habits, the complex architecture of the simplest animals, the plants and fruits of the earth, the vast seas and underground waters, the earth supported only by the will of God, the skies and vapors, the moon together with the sun, stars, heavens, angels, and arch-angels. All were shadows of God's greatness but, even so, shadows defying comprehension.

The third and fourth orations discuss the Trinity, but particularly they confute the Eunomians with the doctrine of the consubstantiality of the Son.

The Unity of the Godhead, having from all eternity arrived by motion, or self-consciousness, at duality, finds its rest in Trinity, according to Gregory. God the Father is the timeless and unoriginate Begetter of the Son, the Emitter of the Holy Spirit. All are mutually co-eternal from the beginning, since a cause is not necessarily prior to its effect, as is evident in the case of the sun and its light. Besides, as the Source of time, the Trinity is not subject to time.

Any argument over the term "begetting" must, Gregory suggests, involve the consideration that the Son was begotten without passion as the issue of an incorporeal Father and the Virgin Mother. Since God as Father had no beginning, so neither had the Son as Son. The many variations and interchanges of tenses used in connection with the word "begotten" by the Scriptures in no way disprove that the Son "was begotten from the beginning."

Gregory considers the quibble whether the Son was begotten voluntarily or involuntarily entirely ridiculous as trying, in the one case, to put the Father under some sort of outside compulsion and, in the other, to give the Son a new sort of mother, the will. It was obvious to Gregory that he who wills or begets is not identical with his act of willing or begetting. One might as well ask, Gregory remarks, whether God was the Father willingly or unwillingly! Since even the shrewdest dialectician understands little of his own birth, he acts presumptuously indeed when he pretends to dissect the divine generation.

To argue that, since the essence of God is to be unbegotten, the Son as begotten must be of unlike essence with the Father is similar, Gregory writes, to claiming that a human son cannot partake of his father's essence unless he is in turn a father to his sire. As in human relationships, the role of the Father and the Son are not interchangeable, even though the Persons are of the same substance. The supposition that God the Father stopped begetting after having begotten the perfect Son, and that this cessation necessitated a beginning of begetting, is the kind of semantic babbling and tricky logic which, Gregory maintains, does much to weaken the Arian position.

The divinity of the Son is amply attested by the Scriptures, writes Gregory. The Arians unthinkingly adhere to "the stumbling-block of the letter" when they refer to Biblical passages to support their case. Verses suggesting inequality between the Father and the Son are interpreted by Gregory as referring to Christ's human nature, not His Godhead.

In the fourth oration, Gregory, confident of the meaning of the Scriptures, attempts to point out the orthodox meaning of the passages distorted by the Arians. He insists that it was by stripping figurative language of its poetic import, by haggling over prepositions, and by restricting the meaning of verbs that the Arians came to reject the consubstantial incarnate Son, failed to see the Father and Son as acting with equal authority, and passed over Christ's human will. They tried through language to subjugate the Son to the Father by making the latter appear as some demonic tyrant, and they failed to emphasize Christ's actions as fulfillments of the Father's will. The Arians, thus, are "sacrilegious robbers of the Bible and thieves of the sense of its contents." All this controversy over language naturally results from man's inability to express the Deity, Gregory suggests; the Hebrews understood the difficulty and consequently were silent about His name. The only way to treat of God is through His attributes: the Father is the timeless Being, the Son the only begotten Word, the Holy Spirit the Distributor of righteousness. Thus, in short, Gregory attempts in the third and fourth orations to substantiate the divinity of the Son and to refute the Eunomians with both logic and revelation.

The fifth oration deals with the Holy Spirit. In opposition to the Macedonians, or Pneumatomachi, who asked, "From whence . . . this strange God of Whom Scripture is silent?" Gregory upholds the full divinity of the Holy Ghost, maintaining that this was no novel Deity, but an integral completion of the Trinity.

Strictly speaking, Gregory writes, the Holy Spirit is either self-existent or the product of another's contemplation. The former, by definition, would be substance; the latter, accident. As accident, the Holy Spirit would be the product of an activity of God which ceased after its completion. Scripture, however, clearly recorded the Spirit's sayings and emotional qualities as characteristic of "one that moves and not of movement" itself. Obviously, then, the Holy Spirit is clearly substance; yet He is not a creature, for one does not believe "about" him but "in" Him, and one is made perfect in Him. He "proceeded" from the Father, yet not as His Son nor as His grandson. His unique position is, again, not interchangeable with the Father and the Son, even though he is consubstantial with Them. The unity of the Trinity is not Sabellian but distinctive. An analogy might be Adam, Eve, and Seth: here there was one begotten son, one father, and Eve who was neither. As a fragment of Adam her position was somewhat similar to the Spirit's procession from the Father.

Just as there was one substance of humanity with individual human beings, so the Godhead is Unity with three Persons. To argue that the Persons of the Trinity are unequal by referring to their number is to forget that numbers are quantitative and not relative to quality. It is equally faulty to deduce inequality from the order in which the Scriptures cite the Persons. Gregory preferred to refer to God with the prepositions "of Whom," "by Whom," and "in Whom," by which he professed to distinguish Father, Son, and Holy Spirit respectively.

Holy Scripture, Gregory admits, is quite silent about the Spirit. Revelation, however, does not speak of everything; one must infer many things by logic. This is especially true of the divine economy. In the Old Testament God the Father is proclaimed with only obscure hints of the advent of Christ. In the New Testament, the Son is announced with suggestions of the immanent indwelling of the Spirit: "Now the Spirit Himself dwells among us and supplies us with a clearer demonstration of Himself." The light of the Trinity came thus to shine upon men gradually so as never to overburden his eyes, Gregory writes.

Gregory closes his last oration by citing the inadequacy of analogy to represent faithfully the Godhead and the three Persons. He takes leave of his reader with the reverent injunction to adore "Father, Son, and Holy Spirit, the one Godhead and Power," for to Him belong all glory and honor and might for ever and ever.

E.G.W.

THE GREAT CATECHISM

Author: Saint Gregory of Nyssa (c.330-394)
Type of work: Dogmatic theology
First transcribed: 385

Principal Ideas Advanced

In catechetical work it is necessary to have a systematized approach befitting the different experience of the Jew and the Greek and based, therefore, on both Scriptures and reason.

The doctrine of the Trinity, a unique Christian doctrine, defies analysis as a blend of Jewish monotheism and Hellenic polytheism, while the doctrines of the Incarnation and of Redemption can be understood partially through analogy.

The sacraments of Baptism and the Eucharist, as nonmagical but yet ex-opere-operato *operations, dispense the grace of the Redemption to man.*

Saint Gregory of Nyssa is generally regarded as the most profound of the three Cappadocian Fathers who included, in addition to himself, his brother Basil, and his friend, Gregory of Nazianzus. As Bishop of Nyssa, Gregory's record leaves much to be desired. He did, however, take part in the Council of Constantinople in 381. His fame rests upon his talents as a speaker and writer who interpreted Christianity in a fresh way, as a consuming mystical experience.

The most significant of Gregory's dogmatic works is his *Great Catechism,* purposely composed as a systematic guide for Christian teachers proselytizing among Jews, Greeks, and heretics. Actually, it is a brief *summa theologiae,* the last such written in the East until Saint John of Damascus in the seventh century.

The Great Catechism, expressing the convictions of a devoted Christian Hellenist, ardently encourages its readers to speed the synthesis of sacred revelation and secular philosophy. Gregory's own indebtedness to Plato is far reaching. Much of his Christian thought was affected by the Platonic doctrine that evil was not a real Idea, but merely a negation of Good. Origen's Christian Platonism led Gregory to hold that punishment was solely medicinal or educative; he therefore regarded the ultimate salvation of all men—as well as of the Devil—as axiomatic. His Platonic position, that all individual traditional virtues are inseparably interrelated in virtue as a whole, influenced his analysis of the Redemption. His mysticism, clearly of the Neoplatonist stamp, made him deeply aware of God's image in man, of man's intuition of God, and of man's natural yearning to ascend to the divine. But for effective catechesis, Gregory considered Aristotle's tools indispensable as well. Conversion of the Hellenist and of the Jew demanded, in his view, the combined resources of both Greek metaphysics and of the Jewish Scriptures. Sound teaching rested upon premises and propositions cogently argued so that the prospective Greek convert could proceed logically in a familiar way from the known to the unknown.

Gregory's complete awareness that eternal things could never be judged adequately in terms of human experience did not deter him from constantly employing daring analogies to help illuminate divine mysteries.

Gregory's ardent devotion to the idea of free will, to man's ability to choose, helps reinforce Christian ethics with the best of Greek humanism. Absence of freedom of choice was an intolerable prospect to the great Cappadocian, a prospect tantamount to the loss of the intellect and demotion to the realm of the brute world. Without free will, virtue, merit, praise, dignity, and even sin, would all surrender to a hopeless and colorless fatalism.

In general, *The Great Catechism* falls into three distinct units: Chapters 1-4 comprise the introduction; Chapters 5-32 deal basically with problems of the Incarnation and Redemption; Chapters 33-40 treat of the methods designed to apply to man the graces of the Redemption.

Very logically, the Introduction begins with a discussion of the Trinity. Gregory realizes that this mystery is not only the basic unique Christian doctrine, but is also an excellent premise with common denominators familiar to both Jew and Greek. Viewed in terms of a unity, the Trinity is amenable to the Jewish tradition of monotheism; seen as three individual Hypostases it is suggestive of the Hellenic experience with polytheism. Even though orthodox Christianity envisaged the Trinity as a mysterious blending of the two positions well beyond the reach of rational illumination, Gregory believed that reason and analogy could readily convince the Greek that God's Word or Logos, and His Breath or Spirit, were, in consideration of their source, substantial entities, eternal and providential. But reason, too, had to defeat the conclusion that the three Persons, as cosubstantial with the Father, were, in a polytheistic way, three gods. In the case of the Jew, the Scriptures would suffice to convince him that the Father did not exist alone.

The section of the work centering about the mission of Christ proceeds in cogent and ponderous fashion. The entire divine economy of the Incarnation and Redemption is made to depend upon the basic premise that man's creation in the image of God automatically conferred free will upon him. To Gregory, the assumption that no one under a yoke or in bondage could rationally be considered an image of the Master Being appears completely logical. God was absolved from all authorship of evil by the proposition that evil was not a true subsistence and that God did not create anything as nonexistent. Nor could God logically deprive Himself of good and thereby experience its absence as evil. Reason demanded the solution that man, by choosing to shut his eyes to the sunlight of virtue, had himself brought evil into existence by default.

With logic and analogy, Gregory obviates the conclusion that God's generous plan to restore fallen man necessarily involved His Son in disgrace when He partook of human nature. Virtue, he submits, has only one opposite: vice. Since vice, in turn, is in no way synonymous with human nature, God's assumption of an earthly body did not associate Him with evil or weakness. Gregory blocks further vain speculations about God's economy for men by observing that the physician's judgment as to the opportune time for treatment, the purpose of his motivation, and the propriety of his methodology are all his own concerns.

While Gregory claims that such glaring historical facts as the disappearance of demon worship, the number of Christian martyrdoms, and the fall of Jerusalem sufficiently attest the truth of the Incarnation's claims, he considers it more cultivated, in this case, to resort also to logic. Assuming, with Plato, that all virtues are inseparably related as one, Gregory maintains that any divine activity, to be authentic, has to display a full complement of virtues. The Incarnation abundantly meets this requirement. God's Goodness is evidenced in His decision to save all men; His Justice displays itself in His plan to make redemption of captive man a matter of honorable exchange with the Devil; even the Devil has a right to his fee. God's wisdom revealed itself in His overall intelligent plan to clothe His divinity in flesh in order to allow the Devil to approach and gulp down the concealed hook of Deity and thus impale himself. God's power was obvious in His invulnerability to the humiliation of humanity and in His capacity to perform miracles. Even the instrument of Redemption, the Cross, Gregory considered a sublime device. Symbolically, its form indicated that the redemptive force was efficacious in all directions, upward, downward, and even laterally, as the crossarms suggest.

The last section of the work, Chapters 33-40, discusses the channels devised for the dispensation of the grace released through the redemptive process. Basically it discusses two sacraments; namely, Baptism and the Eucharist. Even though elsewhere Gregory subscribes to the rebaptism of persons washed by heretics, *The Great Catechism* supports an *ex-opere-operato* view of the sacramental outward signs in so far as they operate infallibly by virtue of a covenant with God. Gregory clearly wished these efficacious signs distinguished from mere magical rites. The water of baptism is but water; its efficacy depends upon the promise of God that He will be present as often as He is invoked for the sanctification of the baptismal process. The outward sign should, though, be symbolical and imitative in detail of Christ's activities. Two persons who wish to reach the same goal are forced to travel the same path. In the baptismal ceremony the candidate has to re-enact Christ's death, His three-day burial in the earth, and His triumphant Resurrection. The neophyte is required, therefore, to die mystically and to be buried, as it were, by the triple immersion beneath the water, then to imitate the Resurrection by emerging from his watery grave. As the separation of the soul and the body in true death breaks the bond of sin, so Baptism, as symbolical death, allows sin to flow out; just as Christ had the power to rise triumphant out of the earth, so the candidate has the power to rise refreshed from the water.

However, the effect and proof of sacramental power, Gregory warns, depend upon the recipient's faith and disposition. The outward sign avails little toward regeneration if the proper attitude and subsequent reform do not accompany it. Acceptance of the Trinity as an eternal Agent makes the results of Baptism all pervading and eternal; acceptance of the Son and the Spirit as mere creatures, however, makes hope for any effective change vain. In short, the heart determines the degree to which the efficacy of the sacrament exhibits its power. No amount of babbling about regeneration will assure it if passions are not broken, evil affections not discarded, in short, if sinning is not abandoned.

Man, who has eaten the poisonous apple, requires, according to Gregory, a direct antidote, the Eucharist. The bread consecrated by the Word of God is changed into the Body of God, the Word, in the same thorough manner as the bread which Christ ate during His lifetime became His body. The analogy limps, however, in that in the case of the Eucharist the change of the bread into the Word's Body is not a gradual one developed through the process of eating; rather, it is an instantaneous transformation by indult of the Word: "This is My Body," again the result of a divine covenant. While this explanation lacks the Aristotelian sophistication of the doctrine of Transubstantiation, it does, by envisaging a basic change in the element, anticipate it. Only through eating can this Body be effectively diffused to blend with our own flesh and thus assure us of Christ's incorruptibility, the fruit of the Redemption.

The work closes with the sober advice that it is wise to live piously and thus avoid the long afterlife of the fire and the worm.

E.G.W.

DISCOURSE ON THE PRIESTHOOD

Author: Saint John Chrysostom (c.347-407)
Type of work: Spiritual instruction
First transcribed: c.381-386

Principal Ideas Advanced

The priesthood is the most glorious calling to which a human being can aspire.

Those who accept the honor of the priesthood when they are unworthy of it or are compelled to take it are in grave danger.

The principal obligation of the priest is to preach Christ crucified; to do so well the priest must be immune to flattery, and he must actively seek the salvation of the souls of those under his care.

Since Basil is more suited to the active priesthood than John is, John must refuse the honor of assuming the priesthood.

Saint John Chrysostom was born in Antioch between 344 and 354, and he died in Comana, Pontus, in 407. He was surnamed Chrysostom, or "Golden-mouthed," which term first appears in the "Constitution" of Pope Vigilius in 553 in acknowledgment of John's status as one of the finest orators in the Christian Church and one of the noblest bishops in the Greek Church.

Saint John's vast writings fall into

three categories, (1) "Opuscula," containing both monastical and ascetical subjects, (2) "Homilies," including the present work "On the Priesthood," and (3) the "Letters" (about 238 of them) written during his exile.

The homily "On the Priesthood" is the best known and best loved of all Saint John's works. In the introduction to this treatise Saint John Chrysostom tells of his close friendship with Basil and, in an apparent dialogue with Basil, he continues with the reasons he could not (at the time, while he was a monk) take upon himself the glories of the priesthood. Rumors arose in 375 that Chrysostom and Basil were to be elevated as either priests or bishops. In those days the selection of priests and bishops came by election; sometimes even by force. That is, if a person were considered competent enough, he might well be physically carried to the consecrating bishop to be ordained or consecrated. This fact partially explains why Chrysostom took so many pains to explain why he "deceived" Basil into thinking that John himself would accept the ecclesiastical honors offered to him. Basil was worthy and could bear the office with dignity. He, John, would fall deeper into sin through pride and ambition.

Saint John's deception has been the subject of much comment. "Did Chrysostom lie to insure the consecration of Basil?" "Was such a deception an example of the end justifying the means?" For when Basil had been informed of the stratagem that John had perpetrated on him, he sought out his friend with hurt in his heart for the deception and fear in his soul for John's fate. However, the entire episode of Basil's misgivings may be a literary fiction, for Basil has never been identified as having been involved, nor was he ever mentioned afterwards in the many literary works of Chrysostom. Chrysostom does try to make a distinction between "apatn" (deceit) and "oikonomia" (stratagem). The two earliest biographers of Saint John, Palladius and Socrates, never mentioned this "stratagem" as deception, leading us to conclude that this episode was Chrysostom's method of introducing the readers to the topic, "The Grandeur and the Glory of the Priesthood." It would seem also that John was writing particularly on the episcopacy or the bishopric. At any rate, he produced a document that has excelled all John's other works in style, thought, and diction—in the very qualities for which the saint was called "Golden-mouthed."

The essay is the most widely read of all John's works; it is a sublime commentary on the sacerdotal dignity; it is a charge and a challenge to all who might aspire to the priesthood; and it is a glorious apology for any who have undertaken its burdens and its benefits. The homily explains the vocation to the priesthood, the responsibility of the priesthood, the stupidity of accepting the priesthood without valid motives, and the futility of accepting it with ambition as the only motive. This classic on the priesthood, not excelled even today, is one of the treasures of patristic literature.

Since Saint Jerome mentioned in *De viris illustribus* (392) that he had read but one work by Chrysostom, namely, "On The Priesthood," we can reasonably assume that the homily was published prior to 392, probably in 386 the year of John's diaconate.

The first book is, in effect, an invitation to the priesthood. Family, friends, and future fame all enter into this vocation. Chrysostom would sacrifice even his dearest friend in order that the vocation be accepted by Basil. John's mother, Anthusa, though never named by her son in the treatise, makes a great plea that Chrysostom stay with her in her widowhood. She had an intuition that her son intended to leave the world and spend his days as a monk with Basil. To her poignant entreaties John was happy to accede. And in his *De compunctione* he contritely explained how the life of a monk in the desert with its fastings and penances, its hard, sweaty, and dusty labors and its lack of sociability, once appealed to him, then terrified him, the lover of the college life, the theater, the circus, and the banquets. However, immediately after his mother's pleas John tells of the stratagem he had devised to make sure the Church did not lose Basil: "Perceiving then his eagerness, and considering that I should inflict a loss upon the whole body of the Church if, owing to my own weakness I were to deprive the flock of Christ of a young man who was so good and so well qualified for the supervision of large numbers, I abstained from disclosing to him the purpose which I had formed although I had never before allowed any of my plans to be concealed from him."

Consequently, Basil was seized and ordained to the priesthood. It was customary in those days for the elders (who selected the bishops) to settle on their choice and then go out and escort him to the Church to be consecrated by the bishop. Even at that time there was legislation against this practice but it was widespread nonetheless. Surely the high dignity of the priesthood and the obligations it demanded would justify anyone's trying to escape so high an office, Chrysostom thought.

In Book Two, Chrysostom continues his explanation of the deceit he practiced, but now he calls it "good management" worthy of all admiration. He explains how the office of priest demands so many qualities for tending the flock of Christ, for understanding their corporeal and spiritual difficulties, and for treating them with appropriate remedies, that only solid spiritual men should apply.

Even though Basil said he was just as unworthy as his friend, Chrysostom denied it by recounting the various perfections found adequately in Basil; namely, love of Christ, love of his neighbor, and practical wisdom.

Here Chrysostom had to defend himself from the charge of insulting the electors who selected him for the office of priest. But he would not offend God even if it meant offending his electors. Far from insulting them, he writes, he paid them a great honor in refusing, for he prevented them from being charged with favoritism in electing a young man of wealth but of no true spiritual strength for the office. Thus, Chrysostom, who had spent his whole life in secular learning, deemed himself unworthy to be a priest and argued that others who had slaved and toiled for the Church many years deserved the honor.

Saint John makes it clear that his motives for rejecting the priesthood were neither vainglory nor arrogance. Anyone who would so construe his intentions, he declares, does not understand the glories of the priesthood: "For the priestly office is indeed discharged on earth, but it ranks amongst heavenly ordinances; and very naturally so; for neither man, nor angel, nor archangel, nor any other created power, but the Paraclete Himself, instituted this vocation, and persuaded men while still abiding in this flesh, to represent the ministry of angels." John explains the majesty of this office and the tremendous burdens one called to the priestly vocation must bear. Invoking the example of Saint Paul, who trembled at the government of souls, Chrysostom shows how the grandeur of this office would expose his "feeble and puny soul" to "more stormy billows."

The saint inveighs somewhat against women having any position of power in the Church: "The divine law indeed has excluded women from the ministry, but they endeavor to thrust themselves into it; and since they can effect nothing of themselves, they do all through the agency of others; and they have become invested with so much power that they can appoint or eject priests at their will. . . ."

But, John continues, there are many men who are so superior as priests that they can use the powers of the priesthood properly and thereby gain merit from God. One who has the right motive wants this office not for the worldly glory attached but for the possible salvation of souls, the purpose of the office. Thus, free from desiring the trappings of earthly glory, the priest is not concerned about the things of the world but only about the heavenly things that will result from his labor for souls. A priest, then, must be wise, forbearing, self-controlled, strong enough to resist the wild beasts of "wrath, despondency, envy, strife, slanders," and the unmerciful buffetings of public life.

If he were bishop, John writes, political intrigues and base flattery would beset him continually; thus, Chrysostom cannot accept the honor. A bishop must be ready not only to withstand those who importune him to advance unworthy members to the priesthood out of family friendship or the like, but also he must be willing to wear himself out for the benefit of those entrusted to his care, such as widows, virgins, the sick. In concluding this book Chrysostom asks Basil to believe that he refused the office only because of fear for his own salvation and awe at the dignity of such an office.

It must not be thought, John writes, that if one is forced to take the sacerdotal honor upon himself, he is inculpable for his transgressions, for the goodness of God in giving the honor is not to be accounted to him for righteousness. Rather, the special favors of God should encourage him to improve himself.

Bishops themselves must be on guard that they do not ordain unworthy men to the priestly office, for they surely will be punished as much as the culprits.

Even in the days of Christ, when miracles abounded, the preaching of the Word was necessary; thus, the priest must develop his talent to preach, and try to persuade the Greeks without falling into the hands of the Jews or the Manicheans. Indeed, Saint Paul, who was a cause of much wonder because of his miracles, made great use of the preaching of the Gospel. Thus, the priest should foster this quality and develop it in order to assist in the sanctification of his flock.

Continuing the discussion on preaching, Chrysostom lays down several rules for a good preacher. Surely the preacher must realize that his hearers are not like ordinary pupils; rather, they are like spectators at an entertainment. If the speaker charms them they will applaud; if not, they will be silent and curt. But the true priest will take no notice of flattery if he feels he is successful, nor will indifference on the part of the hearers fill him with sadness. In concluding this book Chrysostom warns the preacher that this "beast" of "many heads" which is "public fame" must be destroyed lest he be drawn into maelstroms of too great depth.

In the final book John discusses the tremendous responsibilities of the priesthood, especially those regarding the souls of the priest's own flock. The priest is the trumpet for the people; if anyone fall because of the laxness of the priest ". . . his blood I will require at the watchman's hands."

And while the monk in the desert has his own problems (as John knows through experience) still, in contrasting the active and the contemplative life, Chrysostom shows that it is easier for a monk to save his own soul than for the active priest to save his and those of his flock. For this reason the priest needs fortitude and great magnanimity of soul. Then once again Saint John denies he has the qualities requisite for the priesthood. Still he wants Basil to know that John will come to his aid at any time and will do whatever he can for his friend. This last book is a truly moving one in which the saint paints an analogy of the priest and the general of an army. In it he contrasts the loss of a limb and the loss of a soul, the carnage of physical injuries and the desolation of spiritual damnation. Finally, he shows how one who is unprepared to lead the soldiers of Christ, is, in effect, a general for Satan, doing his work; and this is what Chrysostom must avoid.

But the Divine Truth had the last word, for Saint John, son of Secundus and Anthusa, later took upon himself the mantle of the priesthood in 386 at the hands of Bishop Flavian.

J.D.C.

EPISTLE XXI: TO THE MOST CLEMENT EMPEROR AND MOST BLESSED AUGUSTUS

Author: Saint Ambrose (c.339-397)
Type of work: Patristic moral theology
First transcribed: 386

Principal Ideas Advanced

In a matter of faith or of any Church regulation, the decision should be given by those competent to judge; priests should be judged by priests, bishops by bishops.

An emperor passes laws which he first of all keeps.

The Arians are not really different from Jews or pagans, since they too deny the divinity of Christ.

Few documents can better give the modern reader the peculiar flavor of the life of the Church in the fourth century than this letter of St. Ambrose, together with his *Sermo contra Auxentium.*

One is often tempted to think of these early centuries after the great persecutions as a sort of idyllic period, filled with saintly fathers of the Church, stiffly posturing, like their statues in our churches, or busy at their desks, as the medieval and early Renaissance artists depict them.

An examination of these short works of Ambrose will quickly disabuse the reader. It is true that in the fourth century the Church had moved out of the catacombs and was no longer officially persecuted. But this new situation brought with it new problems, problems equally as threatening to the life of the Church. The resolution of those problems has profoundly affected the basic character of Roman Catholicism.

Two problems were of particular gravity: that of heresy and that of relations with the imperial court; unfortunately, these two problems were not always separate. They were often almost inextricably intertwined.

The heresies of this period were centered around the doctrine of the Holy Trinity. It is almost impossible for a modern man to imagine the heat and the antagonisms which these controversies generated. The controversies were followed with passion by the general public.

The principal Trinitarian heresy was Arianism. For the Arians, the Son, the Logos or Word of God, of whom Saint John speaks in the prologue of his gospel, and who became flesh in Jesus Christ, was the first and most perfect of God's creatures, but nevertheless a creature, created, made by Almighty God. The consequences of this position are evident. It makes Christ the Redeemer, the most perfect of men, indeed the most perfect of creatures, exalted above the angels—but it denies His divinity.

However attractive and simple such a doctrine might be to some persons, this was not the faith which had been handed down from the beginning, and the assembled fathers in the Council of Nicaea expressed that faith in the Credo. Speaking of the Son, they say, ". . . born of the Father before time began; God from God, light from light, true God from True God; begotten, not made, one in essence with the Father; and through whom all things were made."

The controversy did not end with Nicaea and its condemnation of Arius. What was worse, it became inextricably complicated with politics and palace intrigues. There were two empires at this time, East and West, and these in turn were further subdivided. Thus, there was a multiplication of emperors, with a corresponding multiplication of palace plots, usurpations, and the like. Some of these emperors or would-be emperors were Catholics, others intended more or less to become Catholics, others were frankly Arian, others secretly so, others pagan. One can easily imagine how such a situation would complicate the doctrinal controversies cited above, for each faction sought to gain adherents or to favor its own party once in power.

It is against this background of controversy and strife that Ambrose's letter is to be read. It is one of the earliest declarations of the Church's independence of the state in doctrinal matters, a declaration all the more necessary because of the penchant of some of the emperors of that time for indulging in theological controversy and for enforcing their preferences by an appeal to arms.

A fearless declaration of this type called for a great deal of courage, in a day when an emperor's whim might easily put an end to one's life. We must bear in mind that in this work, and in the sermon against Auxentius which follows it, Ambrose's statements about being ready for death are not mere flights of oratory. He was in deadly danger, and he knew it.

Ambrose was well prepared for dealing with the great ones of this world. He came of an old noble Roman family. His father had been prefect of Gaul, a province which at that time included modern France, Britain, Spain, and part of Africa. It was one of the four great prefectures of the Empire. Ambrose himself studied to become a lawyer and eventually rose to become the consular governor of the province of Liguria and Aemilia, with his official residence in Milan. The emperors of the West had also moved their capital from Rome to Milan, so that Ambrose was living at the center of the Empire.

In the year 374, the Bishop of Milan died, and a serious dispute arose between the Catholics and the Arians about the appointment of his successor. Election of the bishop by popular vote had been the custom, but the other bishops of the province feared that such an election in the present circumstances might lead to a riot. They petitioned the emperor, Valentinian I, to appoint a successor by imperial edict. Valentinian, however, refused to interfere in Church matters and ordered the election to take place in the usual way. Ambrose's task as civil governor of the province was to see that order was maintained in the city during this difficult and potentially explosive time.

The election took place in the basilica, which was full of clergy and people in violent disagreement. Ambrose entered the basilica and began a discourse to the assembled crowd, advising both sides to use restraint and moderation in their deliberations. Suddenly he was interrupted by a cry, "Ambrose, bishop!" The cry was taken up by the assembly, and Ambrose, to his consternation, found himself the unanimous choice. The emperor gladly approved the choice of a man he himself admired so greatly.

Although Ambrose came from a family which had been Catholic for generations and which had even given martyrs to the Church, at the age of thirty-five he had not yet received baptism. Perhaps his status as a catechumen had helped make him acceptable to the Arian faction in the election. This delay of baptism, however, was a common practice in those days. Thus, after his election Ambrose received the sacraments of baptism and holy orders and was consecrated bishop of Milan.

Valentinian I died suddenly the next year, 375, and, after a certain amount of skirmishing among rivals, the rule of Italy, Illyrium, and Africa went to his son, Valentinian II, a boy of four. The boy's mother, the Empress Justina, was an Arian, and she now sought to use her new position of power to restore Arianism in the West. This brought her into frequent conflict with Ambrose. Arianism had never been popular in Milan among the people. It was principally a court heresy, fostered by courtiers and by court clergy seeking preferment.

The battle between Ambrose and the Empress Justina reached its peak in the year 386. In 385 the empress demanded one of the Catholic basilicas as a place of public worship for the Arians. Ambrose refused to hand it over. The struggle continued for more than a year.

In Holy Week of 386, Ambrose received a summons from the Emperor Valentinian II to appear in an imperial consistory, there to dispute the matter in the presence of the emperor with Auxentius the Younger, an Arian bishop and protegé of the empress. Auxentius had chosen his judges for the dispute, and Ambrose was invited to name those whom he wished to be his choice among the judges.

It is at this point that Ambrose writes the letter which we are discussing. Ambrose refuses the emperor's summons to the consistory. The letter is a classic of boldness on the one hand and tact on the other. He explains to the emperor his reasons for his refusal and, for all his outspokenness, Ambrose takes great pains to protest his loyalty and devotedness to the emperor.

Ambrose comes to the main point of his argument immediately. Appealing to the memory of Valentinian I, the father of Valentinian II and the man who had sanctioned Ambrose's election, Ambrose enunciates the principle which the former emperor had expressed by word of mouth and had incorporated into law: "In a matter of faith or of any Church regulation, the decision should be given by him who is neither unsuited to the task nor disqualified by law"; that is, priests were to be judged by priests, bishops by bishops.

In the proposed consistory, laymen would be sitting as judges in an ecclesiastical matter. Ambrose addresses himself directly to the young emperor: ". . . when have you heard the laity judge a bishop in a matter of faith? . . . in a matter . . . of faith, bishops usually judge Christian emperors; not emperors bishops."

Appealing again to the memory of Valentinian I, Ambrose sharply contrasts his competence and his conduct with those of Valentinian II: "By God's favor your father, a man of ripe old age, said: 'It does not belong to me to judge between bishops'; your Clemency now says: 'I must be the judge.' He, although baptized, thought he was unfit for the burden of such a judgment; your Clemency, who must still earn the sacrament of baptism, takes to yourself a judgment concerning faith, although you are unacquainted with the sacraments of that faith."

These are strong words, especially when addressed to an emperor not used to having his orders questioned or his desires thwarted. Ambrose anticipates the accusation: "Who, then, has given your Clemency an insolent answer? One who wishes you to be like your father, or one who wishes you to be unlike him?"

If Auxentius is so anxious to dispute, says Ambrose, let him come to the church and do so before the people. If, after hearing him, they wish to follow his faith, Ambrose will not be jealous. He reminds the emperor, however, that the people have already shown their preference. It was they who had demanded Ambrose as their bishop. Ambrose had been unwilling to accept that burden and had done so only after having been promised by Valentinian I that peace would be kept if he would consent. Ambrose has kept his part of the bargain. It is the Arians who are now causing trouble.

Valentinian II had passed a law which gave to the Arians also the right to assemble in the churches. It was an extremely severe law in that it not only inflicted a capital penalty on those who forcibly opposed it, but also it condemned even those who would offer to the emperor petitions for the law's abolition. Ambrose offers some comments on the nature of law, comments which could hardly have been palatable to an absolutist prince: "When you made such a provision for others, you also made it for yourself. An emperor passes laws which he first of all keeps."

By summoning this consistory to decide the matter, the emperor is rescinding his own law in part, Ambrose claims. Ambrose, with that freedom of expression characteristic of the saints, boldly urges the emperor further in the same direction: "See, O Emperor, you are rescinding your own law in part. Would that you did so, not in part, but entirely; for I would not want your law to be above the law of God."

But who will dare to oppose such a severe law? If even a priest is not allowed to stand against it, how will a layman dare to do so? Ambrose is invited to choose laymen as judges, but he refuses to do so. Such a choice would expose them to one of two evils; either to denial of the truth, if they support the law, or to punishment by the emperor, if they oppose it.

Similarly, the judges appointed by Auxentius, invoking the severity of the law in question, could not possibly render a decision against the desired surrender of the basilicas.

These are questions involving life and death. Ambrose has clearly weighed the seriousness of the situation and is ready for whatever sacrifice is required of him: "Ambrose is not worth so much that he would throw away his priestly office for his own sake. The life of one man is not worth the dignity of all the priests on whose advice I made these statements."

The fear is that Auxentius, perhaps under the guise of impartiality, will appoint some pagan or Jew as judge in the dispute between the Catholics and the Arians, and thus "betray the triumph of Christ." Any such apparent impartiality would be completely fallacious, however, for the pagans and the Jews share the Arians' denial of Christ's divinity. "What else can please them except that . . . Christ's divinity is being denied? Plainly, they agree with the Arians, who say that Christ is a creature, for heathens and Jews readily admit this."

Ambrose renews his appeal to history: "If there must be discussion, I have learned from my predecessor to have the discussion in church. If there has to be a conference about the faith, it should be a conference of bishops, as was done under Constantine. . . ." If Auxentius appeals to a synod to dispute the faith, ". . . when I shall hear that the synod is gathering I myself will not be missing."

Ambrose would have come to Valentinian's consistory to make these remarks in person, he says, but he was dissuaded from doing so by the bishops and the people, for if Ambrose were to leave the basilica now to go to the consistory, he suspects that his absence will be equivalent to handing it over to the Arians.

It is not for himself that he fears, he says, but for the churches: "Would that there were the assurance that no one would harm the churches! I choose that you pass on me whatever sentence you wish." One might imagine that he were reading Saint Paul.

Such was the reply of this fearless Father of the Church to this attempted interference in the life of the Church on the part of civil authorities. It took an uncommon amount of courage, and its results benefited not only the Church, which henceforth stood clearly free from improper secular influence, but also the young emperor himself. Writing to the Emperor Theodosius after the death of Valentinian II six years later, Ambrose said of him, ". . . he had become so devoted toward our God and clung to me with so much affection as to love now one whom he had formerly persecuted; he now esteemed as a father one whom he formerly repulsed as an enemy."

E.L.B.

SERMO CONTRA AUXENTIUM

Author: Saint Ambrose (c.339-397)
Type of work: Patristic theology
First transcribed: 386

Principal Ideas Advanced

"Rendering unto Caesar the things which are Caesar's" does not include handing over the churches of God to the control of the emperor.

The emperor is within the Church, not above it.

The good and faithful pastor must be willing to lay down his life, if necessary, in resisting usurpation.

Saint Ambrose's *Sermo contra Auxentium* was delivered in close association with Letter XXI ("To the Most Clement Emperor and Most Blessed Augustus") and is to be read against the same historical background. The Arian heresy, which denied the divinity of Christ, had been a cause of division within Christendom for many years. The situation was further complicated by the fact that the heresy affected a great deal of the political maneuvering within palace politics.

Milan at the time of Ambrose's sermon was the capital of the Empire of the West, and the strife there between the Arians and the Catholics had produced a state of religious chaos. The people generally were Catholic; the principal proponents of the Arian position were found in the imperial court and among members of the clergy seeking preferment there.

In the year 355 the Catholic bishop of Milan, Dionysius, had been sent into exile in chains, and an Arian, named Auxentius (the Elder), had been put in his place. Auxentius ruled the see of Milan for almost twenty years and proved to be a violent persecutor of his Catholic subjects.

It was the death of Auxentius in 374 which produced the crucial situation in which Ambrose was elected bishop. The Arians were determined to retain their position of strength, while the Catholics were equally determined not to have another man of Auxentius' stamp ruling the see of Milan.

One can easily imagine the tension generated, especially in view of the fact that at that time the customary way of choosing a bishop was by popular vote of the faithful. The bishops of the dioceses surrounding Milan had petitioned the emperor to intervene and to appoint a new bishop by imperial edict. When Valentinian I declined to interfere and ordered the election to proceed as usual, the stage was set for serious trouble. Each side was determined not to yield.

As provincial governor, Ambrose was responsible for keeping order in the city during this tense time. The story of his unexpected election at the moment that he was exhorting both sides to moderation and restraint is well known. Though not yet baptized, he came from an illustrious Catholic family and was preparing for baptism. This intention made him acceptable to the Catholics. Perhaps the fact that he was only a catechumen and had been a lawyer and a political figure rather than a professional churchman made him acceptable to the Arians. In any event, he was a candidate upon whom both sides could agree, at least for the moment. The situation eased considerably and the crisis abated.

In 375 Valentinian I died suddenly, and he was succeeded in Milan by his four-year-old son, Valentinian II. The boy was entirely dominated by his mother, the Empress Justina. She was an Arian and was determined to use her power to affect a re-establishment of the Arians in the West, beginning with Milan.

The tool chosen by Justina to bring about this restoration was a favorite of hers, a Scythian named Mercurinus, who changed his name to Auxentius (the Younger). Auxentius was set up by the Arians as an anti-bishop to Ambrose, who had been showing himself a fearless champion of orthodox Catholicism and an uncompromising opponent of Arianism.

The battle reached its peak in the year 386. In that year Auxentius challenged Ambrose to a public dispute, in which the judges were to be the court favorites of the Arian empress. He also demanded for the Arians the use of the new basilica which Ambrose had just built. Ambrose's refusal to surrender it, even when ordered to do so by an imperial edict, brought on a situation which can only be described as a state of siege. The crisis came during Holy Week of 386.

Ambrose had previously been summoned to appear at an imperial consistory and had declined. Now he received an imperial order to go "wherever he wished." This gave Ambrose the possibility of avoiding further troubles by going into a sort of voluntary exile. Ambrose refused, and he proceeded to conduct the customary Holy Week services in his newly constructed basilica. As the services progressed the basilica was surrounded by imperial troops, intent upon seizing both the bishop and the church. However, the people refused to allow this.

They slammed the great doors shut, and Ambrose and his congregation endured a siege of several days.

Ambrose composed several hymns on this occasion, and they were fervently sung by the congregation to keep up its morale, especially during the long nights of vigil. The experience gave great impetus and popularity to the form of the hymns, the plain chant. Even the soldiers outside, many of whom sympathized with the people, joined in the singing. Under the circumstances, the empress had no choice but to yield, and peace was restored.

It was while this siege was at its height that Ambrose rose to address his flock and delivered this celebrated *Sermon Against Auxentius.*

In his sermon Ambrose notes the uneasiness among his people. The rumor that he has received an imperial order to go wherever he wishes has made them fearful that he may be leaving them. He views such a course of action as a betrayal of Christ and a desertion of the Church. In particular he fears that his departure at this moment would amount to a surrender of the basilica to the Arians.

But such a decision would be impossible for him, he tells them, "because I fear the Lord of the universe more than the emperor of this world." For this reason Ambrose is ready to undergo physical torture, if necessary, as becomes a priest of God. He will never depart willingly. If forced, of course, he cannot resist. In the face of arms and soldiers, his only arms are his tears. Neither, however, can he leave the church of his own accord, lest his move be interpreted as motivated by fear of greater punishment.

This is not the first time, Ambrose reminds the congregation, that he has been brought into conflict with imperial power. He invites the people to recall his previous conduct in this regard: "You yourselves know that I am accustomed to show deference to emperors, but not to yield. . . ."

Ambrose had also been ordered to hand over the church's sacred vessels. He explains the response which he had sent to the emperor: ". . . if something of my own were demanded: land, or home, or gold or silver, something which were mine to dispose of, I would gladly offer them, but I can neither take nor surrender what I have received not to hand over but to preserve. . . ." Ambrose also expresses a concern for the emperor's salvation, for what Ambrose has no right to give, the emperor has no right to receive.

"Accipiat enim vocem liberi sacerdotis": "Let the emperor hear the voice of a free priest!" "A free priest": this is the way in which Ambrose characterizes himself more than once, and the description fits him well. He presents himself as neither seeking favor nor fearing threats, ready to lay down his life if necessary, loving the emperor well enough to tell him the truth to his face, not like the palace sycophants, who surround the emperor and who fear to oppose him on any point whatever, seeking only favors and preferment. If the emperor wants good advice, warns Ambrose, "let him desist from doing Christ an injustice."

"These words," says Ambrose, "are full of humility." How true, but they are strong words too, quite different from the timid, faltering, or uncertain attitudes with which popular piety has often erroneously associated humility.

Ambrose is ready for bodily wounds, "for the wounds which we receive for Christ are not wounds by which life is lost, but by which it is propagated." He presents himself as an athlete of Christ, and, with the supreme confidence that is the companion of his deep humility, he invites the people to be spectators of the approaching contest. In a manner reminiscent of Ignatius of Antioch's famous letter to the Romans, Ambrose appeals to the people not to try to interfere with his fulfilling Christ's will. He exhorts them to trust in God's protection, recalling miraculous deliveries recounted in the Scriptures; Eliseus from the king of Syria, Peter from Herod.

To these exhortations Ambrose adds the *Quo vadis?* tradition used by Christ's apparition to Saint Peter when Peter was fleeing Rome. To Peter's question as to whither He was going, Christ responded "to be crucified again." Ambrose gives a new interpretation of this traditional exchange. Most interpreters assume that Christ's reply means that since Peter is fleeing Rome, Jesus was returning to be crucified again in Peter's place. Ambrose rightly rejects this interpretation as inconsonant with Christ's glorified state, "for Christ was not able to be crucified again." "Peter, therefore, understood that Christ was to be crucified again in His servant. And hence he returned of his own accord . . . and, forthwith apprehended, he honored the Lord Jesus by his Cross." This is what Ambrose also is ready to do.

Referring to Jesus' escaping when His time had not yet come but His undergoing His passion when He Himself willed it, Ambrose concludes, ". . . that clearly shows that a person is found and taken when the Lord wills it." Ambrose compares his present situation to that of his Lord.

To reassure further his troubled flock, Ambrose protests that even if he were to consider going into exile, there is nowhere he could go where he would not find cause for tears, because throughout the empire Catholic priests are being thrown out and those who resist are struck with the sword.

Ambrose will not hand over the legacy of Christ, the legacy handed down to him by the holy fathers who have preceded him in the see of Milan. Ambrose has done what befits a priest. Let the emperor do what befits an emperor. But the emperor must also clearly understand that only by taking Ambrose's life can he take away Ambrose's faith.

Ambrose compares the Arians to the buyers and sellers whom Christ drove from the temple, and to the Jews who complained of the children's singing Christ's praises in the Temple. He attacks Auxentius for his bloody intentions and laws. Ambrose claims that Auxentius errs in trying to substitute laws for faith. Does the emperor think that the law can command men's faith?

Turning now to that faith which Auxentius has attacked, Ambrose briefly answers certain texts offered by the Arians as speaking against the divinity of Christ. Ambrose says that although he would gladly dispute further these questions with Auxentius before the whole people, Auxentius prefers to dispute before pagan judges of his own choosing. Knowing that the people are well acquainted with the Catholic faith, Auxentius fears their close examination of his own. Frustrated in his other attempts to bring about Anbrose's capitulation, Auxentius has finally appealed to the emperor's envy. But, asks Ambrose, what sort of a judge can an emperor be who is an adolescent, a catechumen, not yet baptized, and ignorant of the Scriptures?

Ambrose's final argument is an appeal to the classical confrontation of Christ and the Pharisees on the question of tribute. "Render to Caesar the things which are Caesar's and to God the things which are God's." Can the Arians allege the occupation of the Church's basilicas as a coin of Caesar? If it is tribute the emperor seeks, the Church pays its taxes. But the Church belongs to God, not to Caesar. The emperor is within the Church, not above it; and a good emperor seeks to help the Church, not to oppose it.

Such is Ambrose's attitude; simple, respectful, but uncompromising: "We say these things humbly, but we put them forward with constancy." For the rest, threats of fire, sword, or deportation do not frighten this servant of Christ.

E.L.B.

THE LORD'S PRAYER

Author: Saint Gregory of Nyssa (c.330-394)
Type of work: Hortatory homilies
First transcribed: c.380-390

Principal Ideas Advanced

Prayer is a necessity; unfortunately, prayer is universally neglected in the face of worldly diversions, even though it assures success in all undertakings except those which are frivolous or evil.

The Lord's Prayer should make man deeply aware of his awful presumption in addressing God as his Father and of his serious responsibility in setting himself up as an example for God to imitate in extending forgiveness.

Consequently, prayer becomes an indictment of oneself unless the petitioner vows his service to God, flees worldly vanities, and strives for complete virtue.

Although Saint Gregory of Nyssa was neither the first nor the last early Christian writer to comment upon the Lord's Prayer, his series of five homilies on the subject is unique. While he seemingly owes some ideas to prior expositors, especially Origen in *On Prayer* and Cyril of Jerusalem in *Catecheses,* the great Cappadocian stamps this composition with his own distinctive interpretations, themes, and literary devices.

These peculiar Nyssan traits are many. Since Gregory was active in attacking the heresies of his age, especially those of the Arians, who questioned the deity of the Son, and the Pneumatomachians, who denied the divinity of the Holy Spirit, he was especially careful in this treatise to vindicate the integrity of the Trinity. Gregory's *Lord's Prayer* reveals his unusually deep devotion to asceticism, with its contempt of the world and all its baubles and frivolities. The treatise shows, too, his natural inclination to lose himself in mysticism and allegory, fascinated as he was with the image of God in man and with man's yearning to ascend to his Maker. In these connections, Gregory brings in his colorful, often touching, references to the beauties of nature which invite man to contemplate the providence and majesty of the Creator and to dissolve himself in God's perfection. Neither does he neglect to emphasize his peculiar and passionate devotion to man's autonomy and free will. Nor does Gregory consider any discussion of God's economy rational without reference to Original Sin, that basic blight which man inherited through Adam's fatal choice. His attachment to Greek philosophy, his Platonic arguments, his delight in Neoplatonic concepts of the ineffability of the Godhead, and his attraction to Stoic Apatheis, or detachment from passion, are all present in the *Lord's Prayer*. Lastly, Gregory is sure to impress the reader here, as always, with his inimitable ability to clothe sublime truths in homely analogies drawn from science and nature, staccato metaphors and similies piled one upon another with crescendo effect.

The first homily is both a general exhortation to prayer and an exposition of its nature. Gregory defines the prayer of adoration as "intimacy with God and contemplation of the Invisible," and the prayer of petition as an "offering to God of a supplication for good things." At the outset of the sermon, Gregory notes with dismay that his contemporaries, sinfully drugged with the allurements of the shop, the bench, the farm, are commonly neglecting to pray. Everywhere they disregard the familiar truth that any work begun with prayer bears fruit in the form of crops, successful lawsuits, happy homes, military victories, and steadfast virtues.

Although the entire work is in itself a prayer of adoration, Gregory formally turns his attention chiefly to prayers of petition and thanksgiving. To him, seeking the intercession of God for any good thing is entirely valid provided that the thing desired is not suggested by childish fancy and silly daydreams or prompted by the viciousness of evil design in which the petitioner serves only to insult God, to drag Him down from His ineffable position, by requesting that He abet frivolity and foolishness, bitterness and malice. Gregory contends that Old Testament stories concerning the favorable answering of prayers for vengeance and other doubtful ends were allegories. Indeed, he argues, God occasionally answers requests for such heathenish tinsel as honors and wealth, but in doing so He does not put His stamp of approval on these trifles but grants them merely to convince the weak of the efficacy of prayer in general.

Prayers of thanksgiving should express man's gratefulness not only for his own creation and past sustenance, but also for his beautiful natural surroundings: the flame of the sun, the spring in the ravine, the animal in the field.

Sermon Two deals exclusively with the salutation: "Our Father, Who art in Heaven." According to Saint Gregory, God's noble condescension in inviting men to address Him gently as Father, so unlike the Jewish dispensation in which Moses alone was singled out for fearful and fiery interviews, puts upon men an awful obligation to make themselves worthy sons. If man would be a son of God, he must approach prayer with a sober disposition, a virtuous character, and a definite guarantee of service. The suppliant must rise from the world of flux and evil and ascend beyond the vaulted stars to God. If man chooses to remain disfigured by passions, tortured by vacillation, and distracted by worldly deceits, his prayer succeeds only in hailing God as the author of his instability and wickedness. In such a condition his prayer actually addresses and invokes the Devil. Unless man welcomes retribution, he must make himself perfect before he dares call God, "Father."

Homily Three takes up the petitions: "Hallowed be Thy name; Thy kingdom come." Gregory rejoices that under the new Law all men, as spiritual priests of Israel, are permitted to hallow God's name in the Holy of Holies of their own hearts. But such intimacy with God, such glorification of His name, necessarily requires virtue in the suppliant as evidence that God's kingly power is reigning in His shrine.

When Gregory bids his readers pray that God's Kingdom come, he seemingly has two Kingdoms in mind: God's spiritual Kingdom, and the Kingdom of the Holy Spirit. In the first case, he hopes for the establishment of God's overlordship as a curb to man's confusion and wickedness, a bulwark against the relentless dominion of man's passions and the tyrannous slavery of death. Man's misuse of freedom and his resultant Fall have caused him, so to speak, to elect himself as his own enemy. The advent of God's Kingdom, by assuming jurisdiction, will unleash the divine royal legions to war against the forces of evil and thereby restore man to peace.

While commenting upon this petition from the Our Father, Gregory takes the occasion to attack contemporary heresy and to plead for the recognition of the divine Kingship of the Holy Spirit. Much of Sermon Three is allocated to an important analysis of the nature of the Trinity, emphasizing both the community of nature and the personal distinctions among the three divine Persons. Chief of the peculiar properties of each of the three Hypostases, according to Gregory, is the unique manner of generation or progression. The section, in general, so supports the famous Filioque doctrine (which affirms the double procession of the Holy Spirit) that some critics tried, unwarrantedly, to brand it as a spurious interpolation.

The double prayer, "Thy will be done on earth as it is in heaven," and "Give us this day our daily bread," is the subject of Homily Four. Here Gregory interprets God's will as His divine intention that man's sick soul should be restored to health and that all the good things associated with spiritual health would result. In the imagery of contemporary Greek medicine, Gregory explains that man poisoned himself in Paradise and upset the normal balance of humors in the soul. The element of concupiscence thus gained control to produce the disease of sin. Gregory would call upon the Physician to restore the pristine balance so that the evil desires of man's free will would be frustrated. Gregory moves quickly to forestall any interpretation of his words as an attack on free will itself: prayer, he argues, is offered not so that God will dictate the choice of Good, but so that He will supply ample grace when man entertains any impulse to Good. Just as God's will is honored by Thrones, Principalities, Powers, and Dominions, that host of incorporeal intelligences in the upper realms of the universe where no evil exists, so might the Good, synonymous with the will of God, be honored by men on earth.

According to Gregory, the bread men pray for should be the material bread of everyday life. God designed this particular petition to teach His human creatures that they ought to long for *Apatheia* and seek the simplest bodily necessities, which are required so that man, after achieving the satisfaction of his demands, will be able to turn his attention to God and thereby be in competition with the angels, who are naturally free from patterns of created things, Augustine Gregory, must never beg for robes, gold, estates, commands, horses, slaves, cruises, or spices, but only for bread earned by just labor. Should bread require seasoning, he adds, let hunger provide it. All vanity must be banished lest covetousness slither into the soul to demand first couches, vessels, and candlesticks, then money, and finally the despoiling of a neighbor. Those enjoying material abundance can legitimately pray for bread from their Father only if their ownership of property does not impinge upon another's goods, thereby causing him tears or hunger.

The term "this day" inspires Gregory to dwell upon the uncertainties of time. The life of man is secure only a day at a time. Worrying about the morrow is presumptuous, for it assumes that He who provided the sky, the animals, and all necessities requires man's solicitude to be bounteous. Asking for daily physical transitory bread, Gregory advises, in no way precludes praying for the eternal spiritual kingdom to which the soul belongs.

The last sermon, Homily Five, concludes the exposition of the Our Father by considering the remaining petitions: "Forgive us our debts as we also forgive our debtors. And lead us not into temptation, but deliver us from evil."

Since forgiveness of debts is a special prerogative of God, Gregory says, the role of man as a forgiver of debtors is a divine one. Moreover, as the prayer stands, man virtually asks that God be his agent in ratifying what he decides to do; he actually sets himself up as an example for God, saying, in effect, "Imitate thy servant's charity, oh Lord." Clearly, such a role is a mockery if the petitioner is not virtuous. If man requests forgiveness he must first have forgiven. The debts spoken of by the prayer represent the price man owes for deserting God through sin, a desertion reoccurring daily as the inevitable result of man's share in Adam's exile and brought about through the agency of the senses, which provide practically uninterrupted opportunity for wrongdoing.

The treatise concludes with Gregory's observation that since the Lord's Prayer makes evil and temptation synonymous, only separation from the world can remove man from temptation; retreat offers the only effective cure for evil.

E.G.W.

DE MAGISTRO

Author: Saint Augustine (354-430)
Type of work: Christian epistemology
First transcribed: c.387-391

Principal Ideas Advanced

We may be said to speak in order to teach; and since speech involves signs, we must inquire into the way signs may be said to teach.

Signs signify either things or other signs.

Only signs which signify things should be honored in disputation; knowledge of what is signified is always superior to the sign itself.

Nothing at all can be learned through signs alone, since a sign can function only if we already know what it signifies.

If we learn, we learn from things themselves; and we do this by consulting the inner light of the soul, the interior Teacher, who is Christ.

The *De magistro* (*Concerning the Teacher*) is a dialogue between Augustine and his son, Adeodatus. The conversation took place and was recorded during the period after Augustine's baptism and before his ordination to the priesthood, probably after his return to Tagaste in Africa. This period in his career (387-391) is similar to that which he spent at Cassiciacum, near Milan, when he was preparing for baptism (386-387). During both periods Augustine lived a secluded life in the company of friends, and during both periods philosophical conversations or dialogues were recorded. The *De magistro* is of particular importance, since in it is given an essential statement of what might be called Augustinian Platonism.

It is generally agreed that Augustine's contact with the writings of Plato was slight at best; consequently, his assimilation of the thought of Plato into a Christian context is in no way a matter of commentary and exegesis. Rather, it consists of a concern with the central issue of Plato's thought and the employment of the same vocabulary to express what is actually a doctrine quite different from Plato's. The central issue is the ground of certain and true knowledge, and the vocabulary is that of the Ideas; the result is a distinctively Christian epistemology.

In the forty-sixth of the 83 *Diverse Questions,* Augustine turns his attention to the Ideas, and his discussion takes up four points: the word "Idea," its definition, the location of the Ideas, and the way in which we come to know the Ideas. Augustine says that while Plato was the first to use the term "Idea" in the sense that Augustine wishes to discuss it, that which the term signifies existed before Plato; these realities, the Ideas, were always known by men, "since unless these be known no one can be wise."

Augustine maintains that Plato's journeys to Southern Italy and Sicily brought him into contact with men who knew the Ideas, though they might have had other names for them. The Latin *species* and *forma* are etymologically close to the Greek ἰδέα, but the best translation is *ratio,* meaning notion, that which is known. Augustine then gives the following definition of the Ideas: "The Ideas are certain chief forms, the stable and unchangeable notions of things which have not themselves been formed but exist always and eternally in the same manner and are contained in the Divine Intelligence." The Ideas are the patterns of created things, Augustine insists, and he maintains that he who would deny them must say that God did not know what He was doing when He created the world. The Ideas, in other words, constitute the intelligible world after which God modeled the visible world. Augustine's answer to the question concerning the location of the Ideas is that they exist in the mind of God.

The fourth question, as to how the Ideas can be known by us, introduces us to the most difficult aspect of Augustine's doctrine, and the *De magistro* may be taken to be a contribution to his answer to this question. The Ideas, he says, provide stable patterns for the being of sensible reality, and they are also the guarantee of the certitude and truth of our knowledge. We are able to attain to truth through reference to the Ideas; their role in learning is to provide intellectual illumination.

The metaphor of light is one of the oldest employed in discussions of knowledge. Plato, in the *Republic,* spells out the analogy quite explicitly when he speaks of the sun's relation to the visible world and goes on to suggest that there must be some agent with a similar relation to the intelligible world. So, too, did Aristotle speak of the agent intellect as a kind of light. Plato, Aristotle, and Augustine may be said to have assumed the fact of certain, apodictic knowledge, and then to have explained their assumption by an appeal to light and illumination. But just as there are vast differences between the meanings assigned by Plato and Aristotle to "intellectual light," so Augustine differs from them both. In many places, Augustine speaks of illumination in terms of the theological virtue of charity, and here he seems to be speaking not of a knowledge possible for man in the ordinary or natural course of events, but of a gift given particularly to the Christian. The distinctiveness of Augustine's view is emphasized in the *De magistro,* in which the knowledge in us is attributed to Christ the Teacher, who instructs within the soul.

The dialogue begins with Augustine's asking his son what we are trying to do when we speak. Adeodatus replies that we are trying to teach or to learn. (We may note here in passing that in the *Retractationes* Augustine says that Adeodatus, who did not long survive this dialogue, really did say what is attributed to him in the *De magistro.*) The reply of Adeodatus sets the stage for the central problems of the dialogue: What is going on when we say we are learning, and what may be said to be the cause of this process?

By beginning with language, Augustine sets himself the problem of dealing with sensible signs, and in that which we are calling the first part of the dialogue he and his son develop an intricate and interesting doctrine of signs. This accomplishment is surprising both antecedently and consequently: antecedently, because the signs which make up language are sensible, and Augustine shares with Plato a lack of conviction concerning the efficaciousness of the sensible to play a direct and essential role in the genesis of knowledge; and consequently, because, at the turning point in the dialogue, when, having been prepared by the first part to see in signs an important element in the genesis of knowledge, we suddenly find Augustine brushing aside the implications of the preceding discussion and taking up an entirely new line of thought.

The purpose of speech is to teach, and this teaching takes place in a manner that can be called reminding. When we speak, we seem to be remembering, for our memory, stimulated by words, causes to come to mind the things of which the words are signs. Now a sign is that which signifies something, and words are signs. But as soon as this is agreed upon, the word "nothing" becomes a problem: How can the word "nothing" be the sign of something? When Augustine asks his son the meaning of the Latin preposition *de,* his reply is another word, *ex.* But if we sometimes show what a sign means by appealing to another sign, might it not be possible to bypass signs by pointing or pantomime? But such actions could also be called signs. However, if, when we are asked what walking is, we answer by getting up and walking, the action would be what "walking" signifies and yet is not itself a sign of walking. A distinction, therefore, is made between explanations by signs and explanations by demonstrations.

Augustine discusses the way in which signs can be shown by appeal to other signs. Words, being signs, are signs either of things or of other signs. The word "stone," for example, is a sign of a thing, whereas the words "gesture" and "letter" are signs of signs. Not only may one sign signify another, but that signified sign may signify yet a third sign. For example, "Romulus" is signified by "noun," and "noun" by "word." Moreover, some signs signify themselves as well as other signs, as, for example, "word." Further, there can be a reciprocity by which a sign is signified by the sign it signifies: "word" signifies "noun" and vice versa.

Augustine comes to the conclusion that there are signs which are fully reciprocal; that is, signs which signify one another, which signify themselves as well as other parts of speech, and differ from one another by sound alone.

It is important to remember that these abstract and rather formal points are made in the course of a spirited and lively, sometimes witty, exchange between Augustine and his son. In Chapter 8, Augustine turns from the discussion of signs which signify signs, to signs which signify things, the signifiables. The foregoing distinctions are now seen to have rather a negative role to play since Augustine suggests that in disputation we should give serious attention only to those questions which bear on *things.* Since the primary function of the sign, he explains, is to signify things, not other signs, the sign should not take precedence over that for which it exists. The signifiable is always more perfect than and preferable to its sign. But a difficulty arises when we consider such words as "filth," for it would seem obvious that in such cases the word or sign is preferable to the signifiable. This difficulty prompts Augustine to adopt a triadic theory of signification. There is the sign, the knowledge it stands for, and the thing of which we have knowledge. The sign is related to the thing by way of our knowledge of it, and it is this knowledge which is preferable to the sign taken as such.

Thus, Augustine is able to claim that he and his son have seen that some things can be shown without signs and have concluded that while some signs are preferable to the things they signify, it is the knowledge involved in signification which is most important and always preferable. He points out: "It is established therefore that nothing can be taught without signs and that knowledge itself ought to be dearer to us than the signs by which we know, although not every thing is better than its sign." With this summary in Chapter 10, what we have called the first part of the dialogue comes to an end, and the sequel proceeds in a somewhat different dircction.

Augustine now asks if what he and Adeodatus have arrived at is beyond doubt. Is it really true, for example, that nothing can be taught without signs? Earlier, when it was pointed out that one might perform an activity when the meaning of the word signifying that activity was inquired after, this was seemingly discounted as an appeal to a nonverbal sign. Now Augustine wants to insist that we do come to knowledge apart from the use of signs. Merely by observing a man fish or hunt, we can come to a knowledge of the nature of these activities. Thus, there would seem to be some things which are learned without signs. But it is not merely an exception to a rule that Augustine is after here; what he wants to call into question is the previous assumption that anything can be learned through signs. "If we should consider the matter more diligently we should discover perhaps that nothing is learned through its sign." This is the thesis Augustine now wants to defend.

His procedure is actually quite simple. If we do not already know what a sign means when we hear or observe it, would the sign alone be sufficient to cause us to know the signifiable? In short, in order for the sign to function as a sign, we must already know the signifiable, from which it follows that the sign does not confer knowledge of the signifiable but presupposes such knowledge. Words can only remind us of what we already know and, if it makes sense to say that we come to know, that we learn, this process cannot be traced to the agency of signs. What teaches is not signs, then, but the truth within ourselves. "With respect to anything that we understand, we do not consult the one speaking but the truth presiding within the mind itself though the words may be taken to admonish us to do this. He who is consulted teaches and it is Christ who is said to dwell in the interior man, the changeless power of God and the sempiternal wisdom whom every rational soul indeed consults and he reveals himself to each according to his capacity due to his good will or bad." The Scriptural verse *Magister vester unus est Christus* (You have but one teacher, Christ) is taken to be saying just this.

Signifiables are either sensible or intelligible things, and when words signify sensible things which are present, they direct us to these things; if we learn, it is from the things. If they signify absent sensible things, we turn to our memory for the relevant images and learn from them. If words signify intelligible things, these things are seen in the interior light of truth which illumines man within his soul. In no case, therefore, can the words themselves be said to teach. One learns not from others, not from signs, but from the things themselves. The things themselves come to be known by consulting the inner Teacher, Christ, so that knowledge depends upon illumination.

What precisely is the nature of the illumination of which Augustine speaks? We have already seen that, following Plato, Augustine regards Ideas as the objective guarantee of truth, but since Augustine has described these Ideas as being creative patterns in the mind of God, problems of great difficulty present themselves. Does Augustine wish to say that in order to know anything for certain we must in effect know God? Is illumination a special act of God given to believers and denied to unbelievers? There has been much discussion of these points. Later ontologists professed to find in Augustine a forerunner of their doctrine.

Concerning illumination, it must be said that what Augustine is trying to give is an explanation of how any man comes to knowledge of the truth; his discussion is not intended to provide a means of distinguishing Christian from pagan. Divine illumination, unlike mystical knowledge, is natural and continuing, common to all. Finally, the inner light in which we see the truth is said by Augustine not to be that light which is the Divine Word, the Second Person of the Trinity. No doubt it was such a denial that led Thomas Aquinas, in the thirteenth century, to see a similarity between Augustinian illumination and Aristotle's doctrine of the agent intellect, whose operation is also spoken of in terms of light.

The *De magistro* starts with the apparently innocent inquiry into what we are up to when we speak; it undertakes a sophisticated and complicated discussion of signs, types of signs, and relations between signs. Augustine presents a triadic theory of signification, and he argues that the knowledge of things is always superior to signs. Finally, he again denies that signs can in any way be the source of learning. What teach us are the things themselves, and they are able to do this because of an interior light of the soul, a light which is related to Christ the Teacher. Augustine does not intend to say that knowledge of anything presupposes that we already have knowledge of God, nor does he claim that illumination is a supernatural grace. Like Plato, Augustine sees that sensible, changeable things are inadequate to explain a knowledge which is neither sensible nor changeable. There must, then, be eternal patterns or Ideas, and while we cannot contemplate these directly in this life, the ontological similarity of the rational soul with God suggests the doctrine of participated light, a thesis which is somewhat obscured by saying that Christ teaches within the soul. Augustine's doctrine of illumination, variously understood, exercised a tremendous influence on subsequent thought and may be said to have reached its flower in the thirteenth century with Saint Bonaventure.

R.M.

ON THE DUTIES OF THE CLERGY

Author: Saint Ambrose (c.339-397)
Type of work: Moral theology
First transcribed: c.391

Principal Ideas Advanced

Man's end is eternal blessedness with God, to be achieved through a virtuous life here.

The pagans opposed the useful to the virtuous, but Christians do not, because they consider something useful only if it leads to God.

All good qualities and actions are reducible to the four cardinal virtues: wisdom, justice, temperance, and fortitude.

Since all men are parts of the human community, any evil action harms every member.

The fourth century was one of the most troubled and decisive periods of Church history. In it Constantine ended the great imperial persecutions and granted freedom and legal recognition to Christianity, which then became under Theodosius the established religion. Meanwhile, however, the Arian heresy, the most serious internal menace ever faced by the Church, had almost succeeded in taking over. To meet this threat the first two general councils, of Nicaea and Constantinople, were held. And just as the Church was learning how to organize itself to be able to handle the vast influx of converts, the barbarian invasions began. Such was the era in which Saint Ambrose was a major figure.

Elected Bishop of Milan while still a catechumen and only thirty-three years old, Ambrose soon made up his theological studies and became an exemplary prelate. A Father and Doctor of the Church, he was also noted as an orator, composer of hymns, and statesman.

Ambrose wrote *On the Duties of the Clergy* (*De officiis ministrorum*) primarily for the further instruction and guidance of his clergy, that they might themselves lead better lives and be able to teach the faithful to do likewise. However, he also wanted to show that the Christian code is not only superior to the pagan but that, deriving from the Old Testament, it is also much older. His model in writing this book is Cicero's Stoic treatise *On Duties,* to which he can be said to have written the Christian answer, even though he borrows from it many of his basic notions and doctrines. He manifests his pastoral concerns by the many exhortations and Biblical examples he introduces.

The importance of this work lies in the fact that it is the first extended and systematic (at least in intention) study of what Christian behavior should be. As such it was a big step in the development of a scientific moral theology, despite its obvious weaknesses. It was widely read throughout the Middle Ages, and by favoring the doctrine of the cardinal virtues it did much to cause the doctrine to be accepted by medieval thinkers.

On the Duties of the Clergy is divided into three books. According to the announced agenda, the first book deals with the virtuous; the second, with the useful; the third, with a comparison of the two. This plan, however, is followed only very loosely, and there are throughout numerous digressions and repetitions.

Ambrose begins the first book with a lengthy discussion of the need to be silent and to speak at the proper times. The meditation on such matters, he says, led him to write on duties. Both the philosophers and writers of Scripture have spoken of them. The former have distinguished among duties that which is virtuous and that which is useful, and they debate which should be chosen. Christians, however, care only for the virtuous and for that which is useful to gain eternal life. What the worldly consider useful, they look on as a burden. Following Scripture, they divide duties into the ordinary ones binding all men and those we must perform if we wish to achieve the heights of holiness. As Christ himself said, to enter into life, we should keep the commandments; if we would be perfect, we must sell all our goods, give the proceeds to the poor, and follow Him.

Many men are kept from doing their duty because they believe that God does not know or care about what we do. Ambrose therefore next refutes this view and shows that all men receive their proper punishments or rewards, either in this life or in the next. The wicked may prosper now, but they will pay for it through all eternity.

Ambrose then goes in varying detail into the duties we should practice from our youth up: "A good youth ought to have a fear of God, to be subject to his parents, to give honour to his elders, to preserve his purity; he ought not to despise humility, but should love forbearance and modesty." Modesty, Ambrose says, should characterize all we do; we should not talk or sing too loudly, speak out of place or of shameful things, uncover ourselves, copy the gestures of actors, or walk in unseemly haste. We must guard against anger and keep it in check. Our language should be mild, quiet, full of kindness and courtesy, and free of insult. Jesting is permissible for others but should ordinarily be avoided by clerics. In all this, he notes, there are three principles to follow: to control our passions by our reason, to proportion our efforts to the importance of the end, to maintain in our actions a right order and timing.

All duties are derived from the four cardinal virtues: wisdom, justice, fortitude, and temperance. Ambrose shows how these mutually depend on one another, how from each of them various lesser virtues flow. Wisdom is the source of all other virtues, for by it we seek out the Author of our being and learn how He rules and judges the world. Justice is to be exercised first in regard to God; then to one's country; next, to parents; and lastly, to all others. The practice of justice gives rise to kindness, and these two are the bonds which hold society together. Kindness itself consists of good will and liberality, and these nourish many other virtues. Fortitude, the loftiest of the virtues, is of two types, one shown at war and the other at home. By it we train the mind and reduce the flesh to subjection so that it readily listens to and obeys the commands of reason. It thus entails contempt of the world and love of the seemly. Temperance is the virtue "wherein, before all else, tranquillity of mind, the attainment of gentleness, the grace of moderation, regard for what is virtuous, and reflection on what is seemly are sought and looked for." Following the example of Ambrose and basing themselves on his quadruple scheme, many medieval writers worked out elaborate systems of classification for the virtues.

In Book Two Ambrose compares the philosophical views of happiness with that of the Christians. Even the Aristotelians, who hold that a happy life results from virtue, maintain that this happiness is made complete by bodily and external goods. The Scriptures tell us, however, that eternal life rests on a knowledge of God and on the fruits of good works, that riches are no help to living a holy life, and that "poverty, hunger and pain, which are considered to be evils, not only are not hindrances to a blessed life, but are actually so many helps toward it." The really useful, then, is not measured according to worldly standards but according to how close it brings us to God: "There is therefore not only a close relationship between what is virtuous and what is useful, but the same thing is both useful and virtuous."

Ambrose then elaborates on what are the useful goods. There is nothing so useful as to be loved; hence, there is the necessity to gain the good opinion and confidence of others by being kind, courteous, humble, and of service to them. Another means of gaining the affection of men is to give advice, as long as it is impartial and prudent. Of great weight also are uprightness of life, excellence in virtues, and the charm of good nature. Glorious, too, is it "to gain the love of the people by liberality which is neither too freely shown to those who are unsuitable, not too sparingly bestowed upon the needy." Though rare, especially useful is the liberality shown by those who redeem captives from the barbarians, take care of orphans and widows, and provide dowries for orphaned maidens. Our liberality, however, must be prudent, because never "was the greed of beggars greater than it is now. . . . In the clothes that cover them they seek a ground to urge their demands, and with lies about their lives they ask for further sums of money. If any one were to trust their tale too readily, he would quickly drain the fund which is meant to serve for the sustenance of the poor." But even those excommunicated from the Church must be given food if they are in want. Also very useful is the company of good and wise men. The defense of the weak and an open hospitality enhance one's reputation. "Moreover, due measure befits even our words and instructions, that it may not seem as though there was either too great mildness or too much harshness. Many prefer to be too mild, so as to appear to be good. But it is certain that nothing feigned or false can bear the form of true virtue." One should strive too to win preferment, but only by good actions and with a right aim. However, it is better to act when mercy requires it, even if it will bring down on you the displeasure of others, as when Ambrose suffered the odium of some when he melted the sacred vessels to redeem captives. For the Church's gold is not to be stored up but to be spent on those in need. Far better it is to preserve living vessels than gold ones.

In Book Three Ambrose again emphasizes the identity of the virtuous and the useful. He therefore, like Cicero, adopts the rule: "The upright man must never think of depriving another of anything, nor must he ever wish to increase his own advantage to the disadvantage of another." This is a law of nature. For we all make up the community of the human race. If any one member is injured, the whole is wounded, as is the Church, "which rises into one united body, bound together in oneness of faith and love. Christ the Lord also, who died for all, will grieve that the price of his blood was paid in vain." It is clear then, from this unity of mankind, that "the advantage of the individual is the same as that of all, and that nothing must be considered advantageous except what is for the common good." We should then never do evil, even if it could never be discovered. We must exclude from our hearts the love of money which leads one to use cunning shrewdness and adroit tricks to profit from the misfortune of others. We ought not in times of famine to refuse strangers a share of our supplies. We are obliged to avoid fraud, deceitful lies, and dishonorable promises. In all of this Ambrose adduces numerous examples of how the saints by seeking the virtuous have achieved the useful.

Saint Ambrose concludes with extended remarks on friendship. There is nothing in the world more beautiful than this, he says, and no one is more hateful than the person who violates it. For an enemy can be avoided, but not a friend who is plotting against you. Nevertheless, friendship must not be placed above religion, patriotism, or justice. We should then, without harshness, bitterness, or arrogance, rebuke an erring friend, but never forsake an innocent one. We ought, too, to open our hearts to our friends and even undergo hardships and revilings in defence of them. Most precious, however, is the friendship we have with God who has Himself told us that we are His friends if we do whatsoever He has commanded us.

G.J.D.

DE VIRIS ILLUSTRIBUS

Author: Saint Jerome (c.342-420)
Type of work: Biographical sketches of Christian writers
First transcribed: 392

Principal Ideas Advanced

Pagans can learn to appreciate the depth and extent of Christian culture by reviewing the impressive literary output of Christian scholars.

Up to the end of the fourth century some 135 writers on theology deserve mention.

Their contributions are diversified and include canonical Scriptural writings, exegetical commentaries, apologies, textual restorations, and histories.

By the time Saint Jerome began his serious literary career about 380, Christianity had become somewhat historically conscious. As hopes for the Second Coming receded and prospects of a long mundane career for the Church increased, ecclesiastical historians emerged to demonstrate, in an apologetic way, that Christianity, because of its respectable Jewish background, was a rich heir of the hoary wisdom of the past. Sextus Julius Africanus began the serious Christian historical tradition about 220; the scholarly work of Eusebius's *Chronicle* and *Ecclesiastical History* carried it farther. Jerome's *De viris illustribus* launched historical inquiry into the new field of Christian literature.

The preface of *De viris illustribus* (*On Illustrious Men*) records that Jerome undertook this work at the suggestion of a Flavius Lucius Dexter, whom Jerome identifies in Chapter 122 as the reported author of a *Universal History*. Jerome's announced intention to limit his record to persons who had written treatises on Holy Scripture was apparently revised, as time went on, to include all theologians in general. The composition features 135 short biographies ranging from a few words, such as chapter 50, to over 650 words in chapter 54, which treats of Origen. Each essay deals with one author, and the whole is arranged more or less in chronological order beginning with Peter and terminating with Jerome himself. The project covers an era, as Jerome describes it, from the Lord's passion to the fourteenth year of Theodosius (392). The list includes not only orthodox but also heterodox names such as the heretics Tatian, Novatian, Donatus, Photinus, Eunomius, and Priscillian. Among the Christian Greek and Roman authors, the pagan Seneca appears, as well as the Jews Philo and Josephus. (Jerome's quotation of the "testimonium Flavianum" from Josephus's *Antiquities* constitutes one of the rare cases in which he cites the words of his subject.) Included, too, are the Syriac writers Bardesanes and Ephraim of Edessa, whose books Jerome read in translation.

Jerome acknowledges that his models were, among others, Suetonius, Varro, and Cicero, who had composed classical biographies on lives of emperors, grammarians, rhetoricians, orators, and remarkable personages in general. He asks indulgence for errors and omissions, on the ground that a review of all manuscripts was difficult in his "isolated corner of the earth" in Bethlehem. Besides, the field of Christian literary history was a virgin one where no predecessor afforded ready research materials. Jerome readily acknowledges his obvious debt to Eusebius, from whose *Ecclesiastical History* he culls, more or less intact, biographical details for his first eighty biographies. The last half-hundred essays do most to make *De viris illustribus* significant, because they are the result of Jerome's own extensive independent reading and study and provide a contemporary account of the fourth century, the golden age of patristic literature. The treatise remains an impressive testimony to Jerome's industry in collecting and apparently reading some 450 works.

The purpose of the undertaking is

clearly stated: the book aims to demonstrate to pagans the cultural quality of Christianity. Men like Celsus, Porphyry, and Julian, rabid critics of the new faith, could learn here that the Church had produced its own philosophers, orators, and scholars; no longer could the Church be dismissed or ridiculed as a haven for the foolish and rustic.

De viris illustribus quickly became popular. Genadius of Marseilles saw fit in the fifth century to add some ninety literary names to Jerome's list, thus making the work more comprehensive and valuable as a historical handbook of ecclesiastical literature. Moreover, a Greek translation was made of Jerome's work, probably by the Sophronius mentioned in Chapter 134. This translation, in turn, was used by the learned Photius in the ninth century. The great number of editions which *De viris illustribus* enjoyed from the fifteenth to the nineteenth centuries attests its continued popularity.

The composition has recognized faults. In some cases it is incomplete. Jerome assumes that any restatement of works by well-known authors would be redundant. He mentions, for instance, only six tracts of Tertullian, written during his Montanist period. Cyprian's reputation he considers so eminent that he assumes a universal knowledge of the African's literary biography. Because he had treated of Origen's writings elsewhere, Jerome refers only to the *Hexapla,* dear to him, no doubt, because of his research on the Vulgate. Simply because Ambrose was an active contemporary, Jerome refuses to pass judgment on his production. Moreover, in most cases, the biographies are quite limited in that they contain very little personal information beyond the provenance and time of the subject. The work is, in addition, hurried and sometimes uncritical. For example, Jerome accepts as genuine the correspondence between Paul and Seneca and admits ignorance as to the episcopal position of the Roman Clement and the identification of the see of Hippolytus. On the whole, however, Jerome's natural critical instincts prompt him to exercise adequate restraint in accepting traditions of authorship; whenever in doubt he turns to internal criticism. He questions, for instance, the theory that Clement of Rome had written the Epistle to the Hebrews, a letter usually associated with Paul. Clement's work, he observes, was indeed similar to the disputed book in style but was very different in ideas and vocabulary.

In listing the sacred Scriptural writers of the New Testament, Jerome parades in full view the reservations of contemporaries about certain books of the canon. Although two epistles of Peter were generally accepted, there were doubts about the authenticity of the second since it differed so in style from the first. Jerome ascribes to Peter the contents of the Gospel of Mark, the latter being merely an interpreter eventually destined to become bishop of Alexandria. Since the original Gospel of Matthew was in Hebrew, Jerome tends to identify it with the Gospel according to the Hebrews, which had long been popular, particularly in Egypt. John he credits with the Gospel, the Apocalypse, and one epistle. The other two letters attributed to the beloved Apostle, Jerome attributes to John the Presbyter. He continues the tradition that the Apostle John died of old age at Ephesus and was buried there after he had evangelized all Asia Minor. Both Jude and James he pictures as disputed books which only age and use had clothed with authority. He excludes Hebrews from the Pauline corpus.

The *De viris illustribus* did much to make respectable certain traditions about Peter. It helped fix, for instance, the story that the Apostle enjoyed a twenty-five-year episcopacy in Rome after having labored as bishop of Antioch and as a proselytizer among the Jews of Pontus, Galatia, Cappadocia, Asia, and Bithynia. Jerome sends Peter to Rome in the second year of Claudius (42) in order to confound Simon Magus, and has him executed in the last year of Nero, or 67. Further, Jerome popularizes the colorful story, first mentioned by Origen and reiterated by Eusebius, that Peter was dramatically crucified head downward in Rome on the same day that Paul was beheaded there. The *Liberian Catalog* of 354 encouraged Jerome to relate that Peter was buried on the Vatican and Paul on the Ostian Way, a report puzzling in the light of modern archaeological research.

Jerome also provides some interesting sidelights on the intellectual character of the early Roman church. Although the Pastor of Hermas was of Roman provenance and was still used publicly in some Greek churches, it was, according to Jerome, virtually unknown to contemporary Latins. The nonliterary bent of the Roman Christian mind becomes clearly obvious from the pages of Jerome, which record only four Roman bishops as authors, and minor ones at that. The first was Clement, whom most Latins, influenced by the fanciful Clementine literature, listed as bishop immediately after Peter. Clement's epistle to the Corinthians was still popularly read in churches. Jerome dismisses Victor (c. 195) briefly as having written "*On the Pascal Controversy* and some other small works." He attributes to a Gaius, mistakenly described as a bishop of Rome "in the time of Zephyrinus," a work *Against Proculus,* which reportedly states that Paul's Epistle to the Hebrews was ignored as unauthentic in Rome. Jerome credits Pope Cornelius (c. 252) with four letters dealing in part with the Novatian heresy. The flashy Damasus, who had encouraged Jerome to undertake the task of revising the Scriptures, is commemorated briefly for his talent at writing verses in heroic meter. Jerome refers here to the epitaphs which the pope had composed to mark the graves of Christian heroes he had identified and embellished in the course of his career as a Christian archaeologist.

Many important fourth century writers appear in swift review. The volumes of Pamphilus on the *Commentaries of Origen* Jerome treasures "as the wealth of Croesus." Despite the fame of Eusebius, the historian, Jerome sees fit only to list his bibliography. Athanasius's various tracts, "too numerous to mention," are reported in full circulation. Hilary, violent anti-Arian, is reported already dead, as is Basil, composer of scholarly treatises. Both the controversial Cyril of Jerusalem, author of the *Catechetical Lectures,* and the eloquent Gregory of Nazianzus, Jerome's former instructor and the author of 30,000 lines, had died recently. Didymus of Alexandria, great scholar despite his blindness, was still active at the advanced age of eighty-three; still productive, too, was Epiphanius, bishop of Salamis in Cyprus, despite his extreme old age. Ambrose was in his prime. Among other important fourth century figures mentioned are: Lactantius, tutor to Crispus, the son murdered by Constantine; Arnobius, whose volumes were "everywhere"; Marcellus of Ancyra, suspect of heresy; and Optatus of Milevis, enemy of the Donatists.

Significantly, Jerome ends his work with a full identification of himself and a list, exclusive of his letters, of some thirty-five titles, many of them multivolumed.

E.G.W.

THE HYMNS OF SAINT AMBROSE

Author: Saint Ambrose (c.339-397)
Type of work: Devotional hymns
First transcribed: Latter half of the fourth century

Principal Ideas Advanced

[*The hymns of Saint Ambrose, "Father of Latin Hymnody," display doctrinal and devotional ideas in accord with the subject and occasion with which each is concerned.*]

An immediate distinction must be made between the hymns of Saint Ambrose and "Ambrosian hymns." Certain hymns may definitely be ascribed to Ambrose himself; others, even long after his day, are still called "Ambrosian" as being reproductive of his meter and form of composition.

It becomes clear, then, that Ambrose was a pioneer, though not the very first in point of time, in the composition of Latin hymns for the Western Church. The distinction of originating Latin hymns belongs to Saint Hilary, Bishop of Poitiers and Doctor of the Church. After his conversion Saint Hilary, who was born near the beginning of the fourth century, devoted his powers to combating the Arian heresy, and as a result he suffered a four-year exile in Asia Minor. During this time Hilary encountered the Greek hymns in vogue among Christians in the East, and on his return he initiated the composition of similar hymns in Latin. Little, however, of what he wrote survives.

Thus, for all practical purposes, Ambrose is truly the "Father of Latin hymnody." The descendant of a noble Roman family, Ambrose, who was born in Gaul, began his professional education with the study and practice of law. In 374, while Prefect of Liguria, but still a catechumen religiously, he was elected Bishop of Milan. Like Hilary, he was an energetic and tireless opponent of the Arian heresy. The fame of his ability as a preacher captivated the great Augustine when the latter had come to Milan, still unconverted, as state professor of rhetoric. But admiration on Augustine's part as to the *manner* of Ambrose's preaching led to appreciation of the *matter* as well and, ultimately, in 387, to Augustine's conversion and the initiation of the remarkable career which culminated in Augustine's becoming Bishop of Hippo in 396 and the greatest of the Doctors of the Western Church.

Ambrose, true to the vigor and zeal so characteristic of him, censured the Eastern Roman Emperor for his cruelty and Justina, Empress of the West, for her Arianism. The long feud between Justina and Ambrose reached a climax in 385, when the empress called upon him to surrender his basilica to the Arians and he refused. In Holy Week of the ensuing year, 386, she gave him orders to leave the city. Again he refused to comply with the imperial command and proceeded with services in the basilica. The empress retorted by besieging the bishop and his congregation for several days in the basilica during Easter Week. "Then it was," says Saint Augustine in the ninth book of his *Confessions,* "that the practice was begun of singing hymns and psalms according to the custom of the East, so that the people might not utterly pine away through tedium or grief." The outcome was that presently many of the besieging troops joined in the singing heard from within the basilica, and the empress was again defeated.

Something under twenty of the hymns ascribed to Ambrose have been considered as genuinely his. The rest are "Ambrosian hymns." As early as 529, in the *Rule* of Saint Benedict, the term "an Ambrosian" is found as synonymous with "a hymn."

The meter chosen by Ambrose himself was the four-line iambic dimeter, but "dimeter" or "two measures" is understood in the sense of "dipodies" or "double feet," so that there are really four *single* iambic feet to a line, as in the stately opening verse, "Aeterne Rerum Conditor," "Eternal Founder of the World."

In their metrical techniques, the early writers of hymns seem to have been torn between two principles—the *quantitative* technique, inherited from classical Latin poetry, and the *accentual* technique, far more acceptable and understandable for popular community singing. Quantitative verse depended upon a regular pattern of long and short syllables; it had been the principle of Greek verse and had early been adopted at Rome as one of the many cultural importations from Hellas. Accentual verse, as in modern English poetry, depended upon a regular pattern of stressed and unstressed syllables.

Writers of the Gospel epic—Juvencus, for example, Cyprian of Gaul, Sedulius, Avitus—employed the quantitative dactylic hexameter, just as Virgil and his classical successors had done. But those hymn writers who were sensitive to the dual call of tradition and present need hit upon a unique solution; they wrote verses that would scan *both* quantitatively and accentually. In time, of course, the claims of tradition progressively faded, and the accentual principle triumphed—thus recalling, incidentally, the interesting fact that the earliest remains of classical Latin verse seem to be involved in accentual ties; that accentual verse persisted in popular usage, as in the soldiers' songs; and that writers as distinguished as Plautus and Virgil, while writing quantitatively, manifested a conscious deference to accentual claims.

Hymns may be "liturgical," forming part of the Divine Office or the Missal, or "nonliturgical," not so appointed. Dom Matthew Britt, O.S.B., in his *Hymns of the Breviary and the Missal* (1948 edition), includes certain hymns of Saint Ambrose, or at least ascribed to Ambrose: "Nunc, Sancte, Nobis, Spiritus," hymn for Terce throughout the year; "Rector Potens, Verax Deus," hymn for Sext throughout the year; "Rerum, Deus, Tenax Vigor," hymn for None throughout the year; "Aesterne Rerum Conditor," hymn at Lauds on certain Sundays of the year; "Somno Refectis Artubus," Monday at Matins; "Spendor Paternae Gloriae," Monday at Lauds; "Consors Paterni Luminis," Tuesday at Matins; "Jam Sol Recedit Igneus," Saturday at Vespers and on Trinity Sunday; "O Lux Beata Trinitas," Vesper hymn on Trinity Sunday; "Aeterna Christi Menera," hymn at Matins out of Eastertide.

The schedule of "Canonical Hours," an understanding of which will make clearer certain allusions within the hymns, is as follows: Matins, at midnight; Lauds, at 3:00 A.M.; Prime, at 6:00 A.M.; Terce, at 9:00 A.M.; Sext, at noon; None, at 3:00 P.M.; Vespers, at 6:00 P.M.; Compline, at nightfall.

Of the quality of the hymns of Saint Ambrose, the following comments by Richard Chenevix Trench, in his *Sacred Latin Poetry* (1869), may be representative of informed critical opinion: "The great objects of faith in their simplest expression are felt by him so sufficient to stir all the deepest affections of the heart, that any attempt to dress them up . . . were merely superfluous. The passion is there, but it is latent and represt, a fire burning inwardly, the glow of an austere enthusiasm, which reveals itself indeed, but not to every careless beholder. . . ."

The "Ambrosian hymns" are, of course, exceedingly numerous. Some are quite early, such as the "Jam Lucis Orto Sidere"—assigned to the fifth or sixth century and used liturgically at Prime daily throughout the year; or the "En Clara Vox Redarguit"—of the sixth century and a hymn at Lauds on the Sundays and weekdays of Advent; or the seventh century "Te Lucis Ante Terminum"—used at Compline throughout the year.

The number and excellence of the "Ambrosian Hymns" indicate the wisdom of Saint Ambrose himself in his choice of meter and form and in the selection of a technique of composition that has survived the needs of the centuries.

W.C.K.

THE HOMILIES OF SAINT JOHN CHRYSOSTOM

Author: Saint John Chrysostom (c.347-407)
Type of work: Ascetic and pastoral homilies
First transcribed: c.381-398

Principal Ideas Advanced

Those who trust in Christ and thank God for their difficulties will become spiritually rich.

Evil is the consequence of the misuse of man's free will, but those who are not slothful in attempting to do God's will can defy demonic temptations.

Those who are humble and seek repentance for their sins will be forgiven; those who slander others, seek vengeance, and use oaths are in jeopardy.

Saint John Chrysostom, the "golden-mouthed" orator, Doctor of the Church was born at Antioch, Syria; his father was a soldier, and his mother, Anthusa, who was widowed at twenty, saw to the education of the youth. Since she was a devout Christian, his education encouraged the early interest which John showed in the religious life. John's facility in rhetoric was recognized by the classical rhetorician and Greek scholar, Libanius, who was largely responsible for the development of John's skill as an orator, a skill which was later to be dedicated to the expression of the values and injunctions of the Church. John was baptized in 369 or 370 by Bishop Meletius, who recognized in the young lawyer, who had come to be dissatisfied with the secular life, a future champion for the Church. John became a lector and then, in 374, after the death of his mother, who had opposed his becoming a monk while she was still alive, he joined an ascetic community in the mountains near Antioch. His health was undermined during his six years of study and self-mortification, and he returned to Antioch in 381 and was made deacon by the bishop; in 386 he became a presbyter, with Bishop Flavian as his superior. Until 398, when John became Patriarch of Constantinople, he led an active life in the priesthood at Antioch, and his reputation as an orator and churchman of integrity grew as he devoted his homilies, sermons on Scripture but having reference to the demands of the Christian life, to both an explication of the Gospels and critical comments on the morality of the times.

Saint John Chrysostom's uncompromising spirit brought him into conflict with Archbishop Theophilus of Alexandria when, in 401, John undertook the defense of some fifty monks who had fled to Constantinople as a result of the severe measures imposed by Theophilus, who had joined the movement against Origen's views and influence. Theophilus joined with the Empress Eudoxia, whose extravagant and luxurious mode of living had been criticized by John, and brought about John's conviction on charges of immorality and treason. John was deposed and banished, but an earthquake which damaged the capital led the empress to order John's return; he was welcomed with rejoicing, but he continued to criticize the empress and other segments of the nobility, with the result that in 404 he was once again banished to Cucusus, a mountain village in Armenia. For three years he continued his correspondence, of which about 240 letters remain. The empress ordered John transferred to the Caucasus, but the difficulty of the journey brought about his death on September 14, 407.

Among the homilies perhaps none are better known than the twenty-one homilies "On the Statues," delivered by Saint John in 387. The homilies were delivered during a time of great unrest in Antioch. A protest against excessive taxation became an occasion for violence; the statues of Emperor Theodosius and the Empress Flacilla were dragged through the streets of the city. Saint John, who would have delivered a series of Lenten sermons in any case, took the opportunity as one for recalling the people to their Christian sanity; he sought to pacify them and also to remind them that their own vices had something to do with their distress.

Speaking to the people about a week after the overthrowing of the statues, John declared, "The present season is one for tears, and not for words; for lamentation, not for discourse; for prayer, not for preaching." Saint John expresses his dismay that the reputation of the city had been smirched by violence. But the rioting in the streets is but an outward sign of the turmoil within. Nevertheless, he insists, it is time to shake off despondency; those who trust in the Lord cannot long remain in a state of melancholy. John reminds the people that a week before he had warned them of blasphemers, and he had suggested that they chastise those who resorted to violence; his words were little heeded, and the violence he foretold has now occurred. John uses as his text a passage from Timothy, in which Paul is quoted as saying, "Charge them that are rich in this world that they be not high-minded." Those who are rich in the other world are rich in spiritual gifts, but those who are rich in this world are rich in the sense that they put wealth before virtue, and they are "high-minded," full of pride because of their possessions. It is better to adorn one's soul than one's house, says Saint John; if one is spiritually wise, poverty is a blessing. Those who trust in Christ will survive the present difficulties.

In subsequent homilies John advised the people that slander is evil and not sweet. He urged them to pray and be patient, and on more than one occasion he warned them against the use of oaths. He attempted to allay their fears of the punishment which might come as a result of the emperor's anger, and he argued that those who suffer unjustly will profit spiritually, provided that they give thanks to God. In urging the people to bear their sorrows and to be calm in the face of adversity, he suggested that God did not furnish men with horns, tusks, and claws, but made them gentle animals. The body's function, John declared, is to minister to the rational soul. When those who had offended the emperor were pardoned, John gave thanks to God, and he then argued that one could deduce from the course of events that God has placed a natural law in man's conscience, in order that he might know how to act rationally and according to God's will.

Saint John Chrysostom delivered a great many exegetical sermons over the years. His teacher was Diodorus of Tarsus (died 392), who headed a monastery near Antioch. John's exegeses were not primarily of the dogmatic sort; he was more concerned with the immediate spiritual use of Scripture than with its clarification. Nevertheless, his homilies on Matthew, Paul, and Romans are particularly interesting and valuable. Saint Thomas Aquinas declared himself very much impressed by Chrysostom's homilies on Matthew. Nevertheless, Saint John was not a theologian, and the effectiveness of his exigetical homilies must be measured in the probable effect which they had on the consciences and practical commitments of the people John addressed. He was called "Golden-mouthed" not simply because he exhibited great skill as a rhetorician, but also because he moved others to a deeper understanding of their obligations as Christians.

Among other homilies of particular interest to modern readers, even in those cases when the emphasis is on matters that appear on the surface to have no connection with present concerns, are Saint John's homily "Concerning Lowliness of Mind," in which he shows the spiritual benefits of humility and prayer; "Against Those Who Say that Demons Govern Human Affairs," in which he argues that evil is the consequence of a misuse of the will, which is free even though men have a tendency to sin; "On the Power of Man to Resist the Devil" (two homilies), in which John maintains that those who are diligent and not slothful can overcome temptations and, to the degree that they have failed, seek repentance; "Against Marcionists and Manichaeans," in which Chrysostom declares with great vigor and enthusiasm that Christ instructed men in virtue by acting in accordance with His teachings; and "Against Publishing the Errors of the Brethren," in which he argues that those who err can be cured by the truth which the Church honors and there is thus no need to chastise publicly those who publish false doctrine; in any case, it is better to forgive than to condemn, and one should love one's enemies.

In reading the homilies of Saint John Chrysostom one is struck again with an awareness of the spiritual liveliness of the early Church. If men need a reminder that the welfare of the soul is of more importance than the welfare of the body and that the Church has as its first concern the spiritual dimension of everyday life, the homilies of Saint John Crysostom will satisfy that need.

THE DIALOGUES OF SULPICIUS SEVERUS

Author: Sulpicius Severus (c.363-c.420)
Type of work: Hagiography
First transcribed: c.399

Principal Ideas Advanced

Postumianus tells his friends Gallus and Sulpicius of his experiences with the Egyptian monks, who showed themselves to be dedicated ascetics and workers of miracles.

Sulpicius responds by telling something more of the inspiring life and miracles of Saint Martin of Tours, with whom Sulpicius was personally acquainted and about whom he had written.

Gallus, a disciple of Martin, then tells what he remembers of the miracles and saintly deeds of Martin; and Postumianus is instructed to carry the news of Martin's life and holiness to the East.

Sulpicius Severus is famous for his lively and personal biography of Saint Martin, Bishop of Tours, with whom Sulpicius was personally acquainted. Sulpicius is known, too, for his *Chronicles,* an account of the early persecutions and difficulties of the Christians. But in many respects the *Dialogues* is the most interesting and revealing of his works, for the dialogue form probably led Sulpicius to believe that he could, with immunity, extend himself in his description and endorsement of monasticism and in his criticism of those whose views did not coincide with his own. The result is that the book, composed of two dialogues, *Postumianus* and *Gallus,* is a fresh and to some extent unguarded account of what was happening in the Church during the late fourth and early fifth centuries. Much of what is learned is by extrapolation, of course, for the *Dialogues,* like the work on which Plato's fame rests, is a mixture of invention and actual experience; what one receives is not a dispassionate historical account but a personal creation in which one senses the presence of actual men, none of them perfect but some of them saintly.

It may be that the *Dialogues* represents an attempt on the part of Sulpicius to capitalize on his popular biography of Saint Martin, the *Life of Saint Martin,* for the *Dialogues* contains, in the latter half of the first dialogue and throughout much of the second, further accounts of the miracles wrought by Saint Martin; but the *Dialogues* is also an account of Egyptian monasticism, and as such it had some influence in the West, where the institution of monasticism was growing steadily.

The first part of the dialogue *Postumianus* was probably designed to serve as a critical rejoinder to the attacks made by Vigilantius, a former disciple of Sulpicius, on monasticism in general and Saint Jerome in particular. Jerome is known to have written a rejoinder himself: *Adversus Vigilantium.* In any case, *Postumianus* does offer evidence to counter the traditional charges of sexual immorality and hypocrisy brought against monastic communities.

Sulpicius Severus begins the dialogue *Postumianus* by telling of the return of his friend Postumianus from the coast of North Africa and Egypt. Sulpicius had been talking with Gallus, whose company was desired by Sulpicius because Gallus had been a disciple of Martin, the saintly monk whose life Sulpicius had recounted in his earlier biography. Postumianus greets Gallus and Sulpicius and then accepts the invitation to tell of his travels. Sulpicius is eager to know how Christianity is faring in the East, whether the Christians are allowed to worship in peace, how the monks are prospering, and whether miracles are being worked there.

Before he begins to answer these questions, Postumianus asks about the local bishops. The somewhat bitter reply which Sulpicius makes suggests that this is one expression of the author's resentment against those who did not join with him in the adulation of Martin of Tours: "I can't conceal the fact that those you are enquiring about are no better than when you knew them. . . ."

Postumianus tells of an ascetic community in Cyrenaica, "next to the desert which lies between Egypt and Africa" (meaning by "Africa" the countries to the west of Egypt and

Cyrenaica), where neither fraud nor theft is known, for the members of the community neither buy nor sell and have no use for money, either gold or silver. They seem to prosper spiritually in their isolation.

In Alexandria, Postumianus found that there was a feud between the bishops and monks, centering about some heretical passages ascribed to Origen. Origen's supporters claimed that the passages had been inserted by heretics attempting to undermine Origen's influence, but the bishops imposed a ban on Origen's writings. Postumianus decided to read the works for himself, and he reports that he found much of interest there; he agreed, however, that some passages were contrary to the Faith, particularly one in which it was claimed that Jesus would forgive even the Devil. (This reference is particularly interesting, because in his *Life of Saint Martin,* Sulpicius had reported Martin as saying that Christ would forgive even the Devil, were the Devil to repent of his rebellion. It may be that this passage in *Postumianus* is an indirect retraction of the earlier reference, which was somewhat favorable in its tone.)

Civil authorities were called in to maintain order in the Church when the rival parties began to riot. Postumianus reports that Jerome, who had been a follower of Origen, was among those who censured Origen; and Postumianus admits that he was "disturbed" to learn this. However, later acquaintance with Jerome led Postumianus to the conclusion that Jerome well deserved his reputation for virtue and learning.

Gallus, who represents the rustic Celts of Gaul, breaks into Postumianus's report to claim that Jerome once wrote a work attacking the Gallic monks and accusing them of gluttony, avarice, vanity, pride, and superstition. Jerome also, according to Gallus, accused the monks of intimacies with consecrated virgins.

F. R. Hoare, editor of *The Western Fathers,* a collection of lives of saints which includes the *Dialogues* of Sulpicius Severus, suggests that the reference here is to Jerome's letter *Ad Eustochium,* Epistle XXII, in which there is no reference, either explicit or implicit, to the monks of Gaul. Jerome's defense of virginity was no attack on monasticism. Perhaps this interjection was designed by Sulpicius in order to allow Gallus to be the spokesman, by hearsay, of those who criticized and found fault with monasticism. Postumianus's account which follows contains what is, in effect, a point-by-point refutation of the charges attributed to Jerome.

Postumianus contends that his six months' stay with Jerome has convinced him of Jerome's worth: "But most certainly all good men admire and love him . . . the man's learning is Catholic and his teaching sound." After leaving Jerome, Postumianus visited the desert solitudes of the Egyptian monks. From his many experiences, he selects a few which reveal the sanctity of these dedicated men.

Obedience and humility are the virtues which the Egyptian monasteries insist upon. A boy who boasted that the Lord would not allow an asp to bite him was beaten and scolded for being conceited about spiritual powers. A monk, undergoing a test for obedience, watered a stick for three years before the stick flowered and grew into a tree. Another monk, claiming that he would obey any order, was ordered to walk into a fire, which he did, whereupon the fire parted and the man was bathed with "a cooling dew."

The spiritual power of the monks was so great, Postumianus reports, that even wild beasts became domestic in the presence of their human companions. A she-wolf which had been living with a holy man took advantage of his absence and ate some food left in the hut; she was then so overcome with shame that she stayed away for several days, and she could not be comforted upon her return until the holy man forgave her. "And there is cause for us to sigh," comments Postumianus, "when the wild beasts recognize Thy majesty and men revere Thee not."

Other accounts by Postumianus support his assertion that the Egyptian monks excelled in virtue, ascetic discipline, and the power of miracles. Postumianus then asks Sulpicius to add to his earlier account of the life of Martin, and Sulpicius admits that he had been comparing the deeds of the Egyptian monks with those which Martin had performed, and he had come to the conclusion that "no one can be compared with Martin." Martin, also, had subdued wild beasts; he had ventured harmlessly into fire; he had cured the ill through nothing more than shreds of his clothing; he conversed with angels; he was humble despite his spiritual powers. Gallus and Postumianus concede that Martin exceeded even the monks of Egypt in his virtue and power; and Gallus, a disciple of Martin, is then prevailed upon to give his two friends some further instances of Martin's spiritual powers.

Significantly, Gallus begins with a story of Martin's giving his own tunic to a beggar when the senior deacon of a church was slow in providing the garment. Martin then took the rough rag which the deacon brought and secretly clothed himself with it. (This incident, a tribute to the selflessness of Martin, reminds one of the incident which, more than any other, is associated with Martin. The story is told in Severus's *Life of Saint Martin.* Martin gave half of his only garment to a beggar whom everyone else passed by. Later, Christ appeared to Martin in a dream and identified Himself as the beggar. Such stories enable one to appreciate the accounts of miracles as signs of Martin's extraordinary spiritual power and humility.)

Gallus reports that the news of Martin's arrival was enough to restore to health a man near death. When a boy was bitten by a deadly snake, Martin's fingers at the wound drew all the poison from the boy's body. A woman came to Martin with her dead son in her arms; he knelt down, prayed, and restored the living child to the mother.

Other miracles wrought by Martin are cited by Gallus as evidence both of Martin's holiness and humility; he never boasted about the wonders which were worked through him. Gallus also quotes some of Martin's "homely sayings, salty with spiritual wisdom." For example, upon seeing a shorn sheep, Martin said, "It has fulfilled the Gospel precept. It had two coats and has given one of them to someone who has none."

Martin's relationships with women could serve as models, Gallus claims. He allowed the empress, wife of Maximus, to draw near, but only to listen and to serve him. When a virgin refused to allow even Martin to visit her, he praised her and commended her to all persons.

Finally, Gallus reports Martin's belief that Nero and Antichrist had to come before the Second Coming would once again bring the world under God's rule. (This section was often omitted in early editions.)

The dialogue *Gallus,* which is the shorter of the two dialogues, is a continuation of the accounts of miracles wrought by Martin. Martin, Gallus reports, cured a young girl of her loss of the power of speech; by lying outside a tyrant's gate, Martin caused the man to be beaten by an angel for planning to torture and execute prisoners; Martin had the power to exorcise demons; he prayed that there be no hailstorms in a certain district, and the hailstorms ceased; through Martin's prayers an idolatrous temple was destroyed by a storm. These and other incidents, some of them of minor importance, testify to Martin's spiritual power, Gallus suggests.

Most of the remainder of the dialogue is taken up with an account of Martin's attempt to end the persecution of the Priscillianists, who had been accused of Manichaeism and whose leader, Priscillian, had been executed by civil court order at the instigation of Ithacius, Bishop of Ossanova. At one point in the negotiations, Martin consented to enter into communion with the bishops who opposed him, and he later blamed this concession for a weakening of his spiritual powers. However, Gallus reports, Martin regained his powers, and he banished many demons.

As the dialogue closes Postumianus is enjoined to return to the East with the accounts of Martin's miracles; Egypt will learn that "Europe will not take second place to her, nor to all Asia, for the sufficient reason that she possesses Martin."

THE FIRST CATECHETICAL INSTRUCTION

Author: Saint Augustine (354-430)
Type of work: Catechetical manual
First transcribed: c.400

Principal Ideas Advanced

A person who asks admission to the catechumenate is to be given an instruction which will encourage examination of his motives for approaching Christianity and serve as a basis for later development.

The instruction is to be adapted to the condition and needs of the individual to whom it is directed and is to cover the more important aspects of salvational history from the creation down to the present era of the Church.

A model catechesis is proposed which explains in some detail the elements which Augustine thought worthy of including in the first instruction to one who had asked to be a Christian.

Saint Augustine's *First Catechetical Instruction,* one of the early works of the fruitful period of his life which began with his consecration as bishop, shaped the course of instruction in the rudiments of the faith for centuries after his death. Intended as an answer to a request from the deacon Deogratias, who had written to Augustine from Carthage for some advice on how to make his task of instructing new converts more interesting for them and less tedious for himself, the work gives a wealth of information about Augustine's theory of catechizing, about adapting the instructions to the background of the neophyte, and about the catechist himself. It then goes on to give as an example two masterful instructions, one rather lengthy, the other quite brief but containing all the elements essential for the occasion.

The Latin title *De catechizandis rudibus* (literally, *On Catechizing the Unlearned*) indicates the strength of the word "first" in the English title given the work. This lesson was meant to represent the outsider's first contact with the Catholic faith; it was not, therefore, intended to serve as a complete course of instructions which would accompany the catechumen during his progress toward baptism nor to provide material for further lessons in the faith after the convert was baptized. It was, rather, the very minimal and very basic truths which were necessary to ascertain whether the person was interested in entering the catechumenate. As such, the instruction had to set forth the essential truths of Christianity while not going into such detail as to confuse or alienate the mind not yet accustomed to the teaching of the Gospels and the tenets of the Catholic Church. The Latin word *rudis* used in the title does not imply that the instruction is meant only for those who were ignorant, untaught, or rustic. It simply states that even candidates of polished and finished education are still beginners, lacking knowledge of matters pertaining to the Faith.

This short treatise is an invaluable means of learning about daily life in the Church of its period and about the manners and customs of north Africa in the fifth century. Its usefulness is not limited to the problems facing Deogratias in his job at Carthage, for Augustine's pedagogical and psychological hints were of such merit that subsequent works on catechetics in the monastic schools, and even later when printing made the widespread diffusion of catechisms possible, were all based on the model set down by the saintly doctor in this treatise. Short as it is, one sees the mature mind of Augustine at work, a mind which was one of the great formative influences of Western civilization. This contact with the thought of Augustine would suffice to render the work worth while, even if the advice imparted were no longer of use. But a short résumé of the contents will disclose that much of what Augustine found true in his day is still apposite for modern man.

The work can be divided into two parts. In the first of these Augustine encourages Deogratias in his somewhat tedious and seemingly unrewarding task as catechist by recounting some of his own experiences. Then he describes the component parts of the introductory talk, namely, the narration of the story of salvation, intended to enlighten the mind, and an exhortation, which must be directed to the will. He concludes this part with a list of some of the qualities a good catechist must possess and the means to acquire them. The second part of the work contains two sample talks which follow the principles he has outlined in the first part. In the following account Augustine's advice relating to pupil and instructor will be treated first, followed by some comments on the sample talks.

The first task is to determine what type of persons the catechumens are. Is there a group to whom a formal discourse must be delivered, or one person, with whom one can sit down and have a personal talk? Are they farmers or townspeople? Are they uneducated, learned, or perhaps intellectuals already possessing some acquaintance with the Christian faith? In the last case one should be brief and avoid all show, interrupting the talk with such expressions as, "Of course, you understand this already," which will enable the catechist to cover the essential points of his talk without at the same time appearing to set himself up as superior to the one he is instructing. If, on the other hand, the catechumens have had training only in grammar and rhetoric, they should be warned to be more careful in the future of faults of character than of shortcomings in diction. Augustine draws on personal experience from his own youth when he cautions the catechist to draw the attention of such people to the unpretentious but solid words of Holy Scripture, and to urge them not to despise it because of its simple literary form. They should be directed in particular to the spiritual or allegorical meaning of Scripture, "for it is most useful for these men to know that the meaning is to be regarded as superior to words, just as the spirit is to be preferred to the body. . . . Let them be assured, too, that there is no voice to reach the ears of God save the emotion of the heart." This procedure will discourage laughter at grammatical mistakes of the bishop during his sermon and will encourage the catechumens to judge its merit by the sincerity of its deliverance.

Most important of all, the catechist will ascertain the motives which draw his charges to the faith, for there are some who desire to became Christians merely to derive benefit from men or escape some injury. Such are mere pretenders, for faith is not a matter of outward observance alone but of inner believing. Should the person's motive appear less than praiseworthy, the lesson is not to be broken off on that account, Augustine advises, for the catechumen may experience a change of heart during the lesson and truly begin to seek what he came for in pretense.

As for the catechist himself, Augustine exhorts Deogratias not to fall victim to discouragement. After all, what to the catechist is commonplace and tedious is new to the catechumen, who often finds his teacher's set speech full of God's unction and blessing. The mere fact that one is called to give instruction shows that others think highly of his ability. Be sure, above all else, Augustine advises the catechist, not to allow weariness with the repetitious task to manifest itself by any lack of cheerfulness in countenance or bearing, for joyfulness is the secret of the catechist who succeeds in touching the soul of the catechumen.

Granted, Augustine continues, that there are various reasons why the teacher may be discouraged by recognition of his own failings, especially when, in his extemporization, he falls into some solecism or infelicitous way of expressing his thought. However, if no one notices the mistake, Augustine advises the teacher, resolve not to use the expression again, but do not try to change it at the time for, after all, reminds Augustine, it is the content of the message which counts, not its form.

Another cause of dissatisfaction is that language is not capable of expressing the profound Christian truths; winged concepts take on plodding shoes when transferred into words. The thing to remember, Augustine counsels the teacher, is that the pupil will regard with wonderment the newness of the truths, even though the teacher knows that they are clad in pedestrian language. This advice also helps when we think that our memorized discourse is so insipid and flat that it cannot possibly be of any use to the catechumen. For him it is vibrant with the warmth of Christ and cannot fail to arouse in him a desire to learn more about the Faith. Should the one listening not show much response to the instruction, it does not necessarily mean that he is not moved by it. Question him to see what he understands, or give a further explanation of some point to help him adopt a more relaxed attitude. If he should turn out to be very slow-witted, then "impress upon him in a way to inspire awe the truths that are most necessary concerning the unity of the Catholic Church, temptations, and the Christian manner of living in view of the future judgment; and we should rather say much on his behalf to God, than to say much to him about God."

In replying to Deogratias's question about the content of the narration to be given, Augustine writes that the narration is complete when the story of God's love for men has been told from the Creation down to the present period of Church history. This does not mean that the events of the Old Testament need to be recited verbatim, but that the more remarkable facts which constitute the cardinal points in this history should be presented so that the pupil can understand them; it serves no purpose merely to unroll the scroll to the various episodes without allowing time to bring them to life so that they may be examined and admired. Above all, Augustine reminds the teacher, this is the story of salvation, not a theory. One should show that the events of the Old Testament point forward to the coming of Christ, who is the center of the narration. It is in Christ that the pupil will see most clearly that God loved the world, and he will then be stirred to humility and love in return.

It is evident that Augustine does not expect the teacher to offer a systematic explanation of the Faith in this first instruction; a system is present, but the sweep of the story of God's love toward man is the main thing which should attract the catechumen to embrace the Faith. Only later will the pupil be entrusted with knowledge of the mysteries of the Trinity and the sacraments and the text of the creed; for the present it suffices if he be drawn by the account of God's love for man.

Following this narration, which should enkindle the love of God in the heart of the catechumen, there should be a short exhortation which will serve to make the will ready to obey. This is best done by recalling to mind the judgment, and the eternal punishments which await the wicked. It would also be well to warn the pupil against the scandals he will encounter in daily life, so that he will not be discouraged and give up all thought of aspiring to a life of perfection. The true Christian will place his trust in God and not be led astray by evils which he finds in the world around him.

The second half of the *First Catechetical Instruction* gives two examples of typical instructions, one about two hours in length and the other about thirty minutes. In these Augustine exemplifies the principles he has set forth in the first part of his work, showing how to adapt the matter and language to the particular audience Deogratias would have. It is interesting to note that these examples contain foreshadowings of later Augustinian themes; notably, that of the two cities of the wicked and the just. The theme was a common one from Plato's time and had already appeared in Christian literature. Indeed, Augustine himself made reference to the two rival communities in his work *On True Religion,* without, however, using the word *civitas.* It is in this catechetical work that he first refers to them as two *civitates,* a theme which he later developed at length in the *City of God.*

These two instructions to the catechumen form the best picture that we have of the popular catechism of the ancient world. In them we see Augustine using his tremendous talents to help an ordinary person become acquainted with the great fact of Christianity. The hints he gives relative to the different backgrounds of the prospective neophytes present an unparalleled picture of the life in the Church of the day, and his use of Scripture in the two exhortations shows how Augustine used exegesis to make Scripture pertinent to the purpose at hand. The treatise is, lastly, not only an interesting memorial to a past age, but also the basis from which the catecheses of subsequent centuries continued to be drawn. As such, it marks a high point in the age-old task of adapting the abstract truths of Christianity to succeeding times and ages.

R.J.B.

THE CONFESSIONS

Author: Saint Augustine (354-430)
Type of work: Religious autobiography
First transcribed: 397-401

Principal Ideas Advanced

God is praised for His mercy to Augustine as a sinner in the remembered past, for His presence in Augustine's soul at the time of writing, and for His greatness as Creator of the universe.

Memory is that function of the human soul in which one holds in consciousness the images of things sensed, affective and volitional experiences, the objects of mathematics and similar disciplines, the standards of true judgments, and even God Himself.

Time is a mental extension rather than a physical dimension.

All human wisdom is theocentric; all values are rooted in the divine.

The thirteen books of Saint Augustine's *Confessions* were written within a few years of his consecration as bishop for the Catholic diocese of Hippo (now Bône, Algeria), in North Africa. He was born at Tagast, in the same region, in 354. After grammatical and literary studies in his home town and in Madaura, Augustine studied and taught rhetoric in Carthage. The son of a Christian mother and a pagan father, Augustine was not baptized as a child and did not become an active Christian during his youth. Instead, for nine years at Carthage, he was interested in Manichaeism, a religion which claimed two supreme divinities, the god of good and the god of evil.

Dissatisfied with his life and teaching in Carthage, Augustine traveled to Rome in 383 in search of greater opportunities. In the following year he was appointed as municipal teacher of rhetoric for Milan, then the imperial city. There he contacted the great Bishop Ambrose and met a cultured group of scholars who introduced him to Platonic philosophy. After being converted to Christianity and baptized by Ambrose, Augustine returned to Africa to become a world-renowned ecclesiastical figure. The first nine books of the *Confessions* tell his story up to this point. Augustine was to live for thirty years after writing his autobiography and to compose many other literary masterpieces but, for most people, the *Confessions* remains his most human and appealing work.

The early books of the *Confessions* contain far more than autobiography; they introduce most of the insights which characterize the wisdom of Augustine. As a youth, he firmly believed in God but had the greatest difficulty in forming any exact notion of such a divine Being. As we are told in Book VII, Augustine was at first inclined to think of God as a vast physical substance, unbounded on all sides, stretching throughout and even beyond the universe. Actually, the young Augustine was unable to conceive of any substance that was not material until the reading of some philosophical treatises from the school of Neoplatonism enabled him to think of a reality that was not extended in space but was incorporeal and dynamic in character.

A key teaching in the first part of the *Confessions* centers on the explanation of sin and evil. In a famous passage, Augustine tells of the incident, in his sixteenth year, of his stealing some pears. He tries his best to discover what motivated him: it was not that he liked or needed the fruit or that he obtained any positive enjoyment from the act of stealing them. Finally, he concludes that this particular sin, like every sin, is a perversion of man's will, a turning from what is really good to some unreal objective which is not good. There is, then, no positive cause for moral evil; or better, its sole cause is the twisted will of the moral agent. Reacting against the Manichaeism to which he had briefly given his adherence, Augustine decided, as a mature thinker, that all evil is but the privation of what is good. He did not deny the occurrence, or the importance, of evil; he saw evil as a sort of wound in being or goodness. According to Augustine, evil is an important factor in man's life, but evil has no positive character; it is merely an absence of some perfection because of the subject in which the lack occurs. Both physical and moral evil are negative; the former in a privation of bodily integrity; the latter a defect in the ordering of the will.

The second part of the *Confessions* (Books X-XI) deals with Augustine's thoughts and dispositions at the time of writing. He is a bishop who frankly reveals even his moral failures. Above all, he writes as one who seeks to find God, both in nature and within his own consciousness. From a consideration of such perfections as physical beauty, Augustine concludes that the cosmos does proclaim God as its Maker, but he feels that he can find even more immediate traces of divinity within his own soul. In a tremendous effort of introspection, the contents of memory are now reviewed. By memory Augustine means not merely the remembrance of things past but also the grasp of all present experiences, and indeed the anticipation of future events. Thus, memory becomes coextensive with personal consciousness. Some objects are represented in memory by their images, but others are present in themselves. The truths of the various scholarly disciplines, for instance, are themselves present in consciousness. Augustine is especially emphatic concerning mathematical principles: such items as equality and unity are directly intuited in our conscious memory. The same is true of feelings of desire, joy, fear, and sorrow: they are experienced in present memory. Even oblivion is a privation of remembrance which occurs, in a way, within memory. It takes all of Augustine's dialectical skill to explain how forgetfulness may be remembered; yet this is not a trivial matter, and in working it out he developed one of the key methods of psychological and phenomenological research.

Augustine even finds *himself* within his memory. This introspective journey through the fields of consciousness eventually brings him to the consideration of the kind of power that is most distinctive of mind. He finds his soul revealed through its functions of remembering, knowing, and loving.

Then, in a final, almost ecstatic, moment, Augustine rises to make contact with God, who is also present within memory: "What shall I do, Thou true Life of mine, O my God? I shall pass over even this power of mine that is called memory; I shall pass over it to reach Thee, sweet Light. What dost Thou say to me? Behold, going up through my mind to Thee, who dwellest above me, I shall even pass over this power of mine which is called memory, desiring to attain Thee where Thou canst be attained, and to cleave to Thee where it is possible to be in contact with Thee." This is no ordinary demonstration of an abstractly apprehended Deity. Augustine is offering his description of a real experience and suggesting how others may work toward such an encounter with God.

The next book (XI) links the study of memory to Augustine's analysis of the Book of Genesis by examining the nature of time. In a very real sense, Augustine suggests, temporality is characteristic of creatureliness. Time is created by God and belongs in the account of God's creative activity that is suggested by Genesis. However, in another sense, time is a sort of protraction, or continuation, of memory. All experience occurs in the present, but until it occurs it is in the future and, as soon as it has happened, it is in the past. Like Henri Bergson, (1859-1941), the French philosopher, Augustine sees the present as the past eating into the future. The notion that time is merely the physical motion of celestial bodies is sharply criticized in the *Confessions.* Augustine claims that although motions of the sun and stars may be measured in terms of time, time itself must be superior to, and independent of, such corporeal events.

After much meditation, Augustine concludes that time is some sort of mental extension or duration. It has three periods, past, present, and future; or better, there is the present of things past, the present of things present, the present of things future. For the first there is remembrance; for the second, intuition; for the third, expectation. These three psychological factors also correspond to the three major divisions of the *Confessions.* We have seen how the first nine books detail Augustine's remembrance of God's mercy to him in his past, and how Augustine examines his present consciousness in Books X and XI. Now we have to observe his expectation, his looking forward, to the outcome of creation. This third part of the *Confessions* finds its eschatological development in the later *City of God.*

The last three books constitute one of Augustine's several efforts to explain what is taught in the opening verses of the Book of Genesis. At first reading it is difficult to see why such a commentary should have been appended to a highly personal work such as the *Confessions.* However, as we have suggested, these last books are actually instances of looking forward in memory (*exspectatio*) toward the ultimate climax of God's creative activity. God's power, grace, and mercy may thus be seen at work in the past, in the present, and in the future of creation.

Augustine's interpretation of the Biblical account of Creation, as found at the end of the *Confessions,* is partly literal and partly allegorical. Indeed, he makes quite a point of his view that Scripture may have a variety of meanings, each useful to some possible reader. He is quite sure that God made all things out of nothing: there was no previously existing matter (as Plato's *Timaeus* contends) on which the Creator worked. God creates both formless matter and the species, or forms, which determine the natures of various creatures. Already we see in these books some anticipation of the more thorough exposition which Augustine was to write in his *Literal Commentary on Genesis.* In effect, God is viewed as the divine Artist who planned creation within His divine mind. This ideal plan contains the eternal Ideas (*rationes aeternae*), the patterns in accord with which God fashions creatures in the making of the universe. Divine exemplarism thus becomes an important theory in Christian intellectualism; later thinkers who use the concept of exemplary Ideas owe much to the formulation given the theory by Augustine, in the *Confessions* and elsewhere.

Still another central theme in Augustinianism is broached in these final books. Starting with the phrase, "Let there be light," Augustine speculates on the meaning of light itself. What could physical light have been before the sun was made? Is there some sort of mental or spiritual light which acts upon minds in a manner parallel to the activity of physical light which makes bodies visible to our sense of sight? Meditating on the nature of physical light, Augustine understands it to be a principle of order which exerts a determining influence on the formlessness of physical matter. From these speculations, too, comes the magnificent theory of divine illumination. Briefly, Augustine suggests that men are enabled to make some absolutely true judgments (for example, "seven plus three equals ten") by means of a special assistance which God provides in the form of intellectual "light." This spiritual illumination provides the basis, the guarantee, the stability, for man's most certain knowledge. There are many points of dispute among Augustine scholars concerning the precise significance of this divine light. The foregoing suggests the main outline of the theory as hinted at toward the end of the *Confessions.*

As Augustine was finishing the writing of the *Confessions,* he was starting to write one of his greatest doctrinal studies, the fifteen books of *On the Trinity.* Its central theme (that there are many vestiges and images of the divine Trinity in all created things and particularly in the human soul) is not entirely new. Already in the last book of the *Confessions* we find that Augustine is thinking of possible "analogies" of the divine Trinity within man's soul. One such image is the triad of being, knowing, and writing. From one point of view, these are three different functions of a spirit; from another viewpoint, to be, to know, and to will is but one act for a spiritual entity. This is the sort of comparison which Augustine exploits more fully later—not to explain the Holy Trinity (for he insists that it is an incomprehensible mystery) but to show that there is nothing unreasonable in such a belief, even though it exceeds our powers of positive understanding.

At the very end of this masterpiece, Augustine prays for that peace which transcends mutable goods, insisting that the wisdom which he has long sought is to be gained from one source only: God. There is no other teacher who is able to convey this precious knowledge to us: "What man will give any man the actual understanding of this? What angel will give it to an angel? From Thee must it be asked; in Thee must it be sought; at Thy door must one knock. Thus, will it be received; thus, will it be found; thus, will Thy door be opened.

V.J.B.

A COMMENTARY ON THE APOSTLES' CREED

Author: Rufinus of Aquileia (Tyrannius Rufinus, c.345-410)
Type of work: Expository theology
First transcribed: c.404

Principal Ideas Advanced

The purpose of the study is to restore and expound the simple meaning of the creed originally composed by the Apostles after Pentecost.

This creed is most authentically preserved in Rome where no heresy originated to force non-Apostolic additions to the text.

Guided by this creed, Christians are delivered from confusion and are enabled so to direct their course that they can confidently await the crown of justice prepared for them.

At the outset of his work, Rufinus states that his purpose is to write, at the invitation of an unknown Bishop Laurence and especially for the benefit of catechumens, an essay expounding the contents and organization of the Apostles' Creed.

Rufinus believed, along with his contemporaries, that the Twelve Apostles, before they scattered after Pentecost on their mission to teach all nations, drew up a symbol of faith to assure the propagation of a unanimously approved message. The Roman Church, he believed, managed to preserve the original Apostles' formulation, for the Church was singularly free and it followed the practice of reciting the creed aloud publicly at baptismal ceremonies. However, since Rufinus reverenced the symbol of Aquileia under which he was raised, he chose to use it as the basis of his exposition, and he promised to point out the relatively small differences between this confession and that of the Church of Rome.

Since Bishop Ussher's study in 1647, scholars almost unanimously hold that a satisfactory text of the old Roman symbol can be gleaned from Rufinus. By identifying this version, in turn, with an old Greek edition recited in 340 by Marcellus of Ancyra before Pope Julius, the history of the Roman creed can be traced back readily to the mid-third century and beyond. Since the Roman formula became a model for creeds of churches in Italy, North Africa, Spain, and southern France generally, Rufinus's *Commentary* sheds invaluable light on the entire evolution of Western credal forms. Significant, too, is the fact that the old Roman symbol eventually developed, with later Gallic additions, into the modern Apostles' Creed.

Rufinus's progressive comments upon each article of the Aquileian confession reveal a sound orthodoxy on all cardinal points of doctrine: the Trinity, Christology, the Incarnation, and the Redemption. In order to make them respectable before learned critical pagans, he argues throughout the work that the great truths of revelation harmonize with natural reason. While his arguments at times are on a sophisticated level, his allegory is usually fancifully strained, and his imagery is of the stock variety readily found in early Christian apologetics. Since he was not the first to write on creeds, he was indebted to the work of others, especially to the confessional observations made by Saint Cyril of Jerusalem in his *Catechetical Lectures* and, in a lesser way, to the work of Saint Gregory of Nyssa.

The first article, "I believe in God, the Father almighty," leads Rufinus to describe God as a simple substance, incomprehensible and ineffable. How the Son was generated from this indivisible and divine substance, Rufinus cautions his readers not to try to comprehend, and he adds that one had better first understand his own generation of speech and natural mysteries before advancing to such a problem. Nevertheless, if "the spark, which is so unsubstantial and yet is fire, generates from itself a creature made out of nothingness, [since the original creation was *ex nihilo*] thereby preserving its original status, why should it be inconceivable for the substance of that Eternal Light, which has always existed because it contains nothing insubstantial in Itself, to produce from Itself a Brightness which is substantial?"

Jesus Christ was conceived in the Virgin Mary, Rufinus explains, as the result of joint action by both Father and Son. The inviolability of Mary he protects with a battery of exaggerated Scriptural allegories. Concerned about the venerable Greek philosophical dilemma of how Being and Becoming can be harmonized, Rufinus develops an ingenious explanation of the dual nature of Christ. This union between the spiritual substance and the corporeal substance was effected, Rufinus suggests, through a natural catalyst, the spiritual constitution of Jesus' human soul. The physical incarnation of the Son was accomplished without any pollution of Deity, just as the illumination of the murky pool is effected without contamination of the sunbeam.

Rufinus apparently believed that the sufferings and disgraces which Christ faced in the course of the redemptive process required heavy allegorized prophetic support from the Old Testament to become credible. The Redemption he interprets as essentially a triumph over the Devil. Having recourse to a common and somewhat crude simile, Rufinus explains that the Prince of the World, lured by the human flesh of Jesus as bait, was impaled on Christ's divinity which lay as a hidden hook or barb under the covering of His human flesh. To Rufinus, the shape and position of the Cross clearly symbolizes Christ's universal triumph. The upper portion signifies His conquest over the demons in the air; the arms, His open welcome to believers on the earth; and the buried butt, His subjection of the underworld. Rufinus spares no allegory in extending the recapitulation theory of Redemption. Since, he argues, the source of sin and death proceeded from the first woman, who was a rib of Adam, it was necessary for Christ to shed water and blood from His side to show that the source of redemption and life proceeded from the rib of the Second Adam. Christ's entrance into the realm of human passion and death did no violence to His divinity; His career of indignities resembled the experience of a king going down with impunity into a dungeon to open doors for captives.

With the "Descent into Hell," an article which he reports absent from the old Roman creed, Rufinus seems baffled. He interprets it to mean simply the equivalent of "Buried," a term which the Roman formula did carry.

In Rufinus's explanation, the "Holy Spirit" proceeds from the "mouth of God," rather than, as later versions would have it, from the Father and the Son. His assertion that the Holy Spirit is the source of inspiration leads him thoughtfully to append a complete list of all books of the Old and New

Testaments which he considers canonical and therefore legitimate vehicles of the Spirit's revelation. This valuable section shows that by the year 400 all twenty-seven books of the New Testament were recognized at Aquileia as inspired. His inclusion of the Epistle to the Hebrews and his relatively modern arrangement of the books of the New Testament reveal that he is quite independent of his great contemporary Scriptural experts. Rufinus lists as "ecclesiastical" such writings as Ecclesiasticus, Machabees, and Hermas. Rather liberally, he permits these to be read in church as exhortations but not as sources for faith. A third class, the "apocryphal" books, could not be read in official circles at all.

The "Holy Church" which the creed bade one to accept was to be identified by contrasting it with heretical conventicles such as those of Marcion, Mani, Paul of Samosata, Arius, and Donatus. Although specifically unnamed, the implication is clear that Pneumatomachians, Apollinarians, and Origenists also had no part in the orthodox fellowship. The true Church was that Church which, in summary, "proclaimed its faith in God the Father almighty, and His only Son Jesus Christ our Lord, and the Holy Spirit, as existing in one harmonious and indivisible substance, and believes that the Son of God was born from the Virgin, suffered for man's salvation, and rose again from the dead in the identical flesh with which He was born."

Of "The Resurrection of the Flesh" Rufinus is an ardent advocate. This final event is to be experienced by all persons, good and evil. Everyone's personal spirit of immortality will be, as it were, the agent or seed which will gather up and restructure the dispersed and dormant substance of his own flesh.

The work ends with a prayer, an intelligent summary, and the wish that the knowledge contained in the *Commentary* will be helpful.

Rufinus's *Commentary,* besides being a valuable witness to Rome's central position in Western credal history and a priceless record of a contemporary Western canon of Scriptures, is also important as Scriptural textual criticism. Rufinus's quotations are drawn exclusively from the old Roman Latin version based on the Septuagint, which was in vogue before Jerome's Vulgate set up a new *textus acceptus* based on the original Hebrew.

Although Rufinus as a translator and a humble scholar enjoyed the confidence and support of such great contemporaries as Saint Augustine, his influence was dampened for centuries by the insidious influence of his enemy, Saint Jerome, who became estranged from him over Origen. The fact that the *Commentary* exerted substantial influence in the Middle Ages was due to its being mistakenly ascribed to other authors, such as Cyprian and even to Jerome himself.

E.G.W.

DE TRINITATE

Author: Saint Augustine (354-430)
Type of work: Theology
First transcribed: c.400-c.416

Principal Ideas Advanced

The Scriptures, which address themselves to both simple and wise men, convey the teaching that there is one God and three divine Persons, Father, Son and Holy Spirit.

We can make use of the analogy of the human spiritual soul to explain the procession of Persons from the divine nature; the Son is the Word proceeding from the Father, and the Holy Spirit proceeds from Father and Son as the substantial term of their love.

There are myriad vestiges and images of the Trinity in creatures but principally in man who has been made in the image of God.

In his work on the Trinity, the *De trinitate,* Saint Augustine addresses himself to the central mystery of the Christian faith, and his efforts at clarifying the content of this mystery make full use of the heretical positions antecedent to and contemporary with his writing in order to warn the believer from interpretations which would undermine his faith. It is difficult to overestimate the impact of this work. Its influence on Boethius was almost total, of course, and in the subsequent theology of the Trinity the distinctions, the method, and the resolutions of Augustine were destined to occupy a prominent and well-nigh definitive position.

Of this work, which contains fifteen books, Augustine says that he began it as a young man, and completed it when old. It is thought that Augustine began the composition of the *De trinitate* in 400 and completed it in 416. Needless to say, during this same period, Augustine was producing other works, notably the *City of God* and his commentaries on *Genesis.* The span of time its composition involved, while it may have permitted the maturation of his ideas, also seems to have led to a proliferation of discussions, and the result is lacking in taut organization. Augustine was conscious of this, of course, and ends by apologizing for his prolixity.

It is possible to see the work as dividing itself in half, with the first seven books devoted to the Trinity itself and the remaining books devoted to the image of the Trinity in man. It is in terms of this bifurcation of the *De trinitate* that we shall attempt to give a presentation of it. In the *Retractationes,* after recalling the fate of the book, namely, its premature circulation by his friends, Augustine has only two corrections to make of the contents of the *De trinitate,* and these are relatively minor.

The opening chapters of Book One of the *De trinitate* are prefatory to the work as a whole, and in them Augustine, as could be expected, makes some points of great importance. He is prompted to write on this subject, he says, because there are current erroneous opinions on the doctrine of the Trinity and he feels compelled to counteract them. Augustine describes the attitude of his adversaries as that of men who would subject to human measures the truth that God has chosen to reveal, men who do not see the necessity of an appropriate subjective disposition if one is to approximate to an understanding of the mystery of the Trinity. Small wonder that their presumption has led them into the grossest errors. Augustine will first attend to Scripture to see what in fact is there revealed of the triune God. That being done, he will try to fashion supplementary arguments.

Scripture addresses itself to all men, the simple as well as the wise, Augustine writes, and consequently it employs words drawn from corporeal things in speaking of God. This use of ordinary imagery is Scripture's strength, but it is also the source of possible misinterpretation, for the reader may falsely think that God is just like corporeal things. Only rarely does Scripture speak of God in terms which apply only to Him. Thus, for the most part, Scripture demands a mode of interpretation of a spiritual kind, and one indisposed to give it will find himself cut off from its message. Augustine makes it clear that he writes for those whose minds and hearts have been made receptive by faith and charity; he asks his reader to inquire with him. If the reader finds obscurity, let him blame the author; if the book proves too troublesome, lay it aside. There can be little doubt that this diffidence is sincere, and one may wonder why Augustine undertakes to write of the Trinity. It is well, he says, that men speak in different styles, though with the same faith, of this great mystery.

What is the Catholic faith concerning the Trinity? "All those who have previously written on the trinity whom I have been able to read and who have treated as Catholics the divine books of the old and new [testaments] understand the Scriptures to teach that Father and Son and Holy Spirit constitute a divine unity of one and the same substance in inseparable equality, such that there are not three gods but one God although the Father generates the Son and the Son, consequently, is not that which the Father is; the Son is generated from the Father so the Father is not who the Son is; the Holy Spirit is neither the Father nor the Son but only the Spirit of the Father and the Son, He too coequal with the Father and Son and pertaining to the unity of the trinity." Immediately after this summary statement, Augustine notes that it was not the Trinity which was born of the Virgin Mary, suffered under Pontius Pilate, and died on the Cross. This is important to note, because a good deal of Augustine's discussion of the Trinity bears on the Incarnation and the modes whereby some things are attributed to Christ as God and as Man. While it cannot be said that the occasions for such discussions do not arise naturally enough in the course of his exposition, it must nevertheless be said that the resultant dual discussion leads to a diffusiveness which militates against the literary and, to a degree, the doctrinal unity of the work.

The Incarnation becomes fairly central to Augustine's discussion because he seeks to maintain the equality of the Persons of the Trinity, and yet he realizes that there are Scriptual passages where Christ says He is less than the Father. So, too, later Augustine will try to show that the fact that the Holy Spirit is sent to perfect the work of Christ does not make the Third Person of the Trinity unequal or inferior to the other two. The two natures in Christ are often the explanation of certain Scriptural passages; that is, Christ in his human nature is less than the Father. However, certain acts are attributed to one Person of the Trinity, and sometimes this is the explanation of passages which may seem to imply the inequality of the Persons. The introduction of the Incarnation also leads Augustine to discuss at some length those Scriptural passages which speak of theophanies, of God's appearing to holy men in some sensible image, as, for example, the burning bush. Augustine wants to make clear that these instances are not to be construed as a union of the divine nature with a created nature, as is the case with the hypostatic union in Christ. This in turn leads to a discussion of what is involved in the appearances of angels to men, and this, in turn, leads to a discussion of miracles and magic. One can see how Augustine allows the argument to lead him where it will, no matter what tangents present themselves. By the same token, there is always a return to the central question, but the impression is left that Augustine is here attempting to handle every conceivable difficulty that could occur and pose an impediment to the doctrine of the Trinity.

Book Four is almost exclusively concerned with the mission of Christ, and the reader finds an almost Pythagorean disquisition on the perfection of the number three, although towards the end of the book there is a warning against the arguments of philosophers. The following book is overtly polemical, and Augustine confronts the Arian heresy which refused to see the Son as the equal of the Father. Augustine summarizes the Arian position thus: "Whatever is said or understood of God must be taken substantially and not accidentally; therefore the Father is ungenerated according to His substance and the Son is generated according to His substance; therefore the substance of the Father differs from that of the Son." Augustine's solution, which Boethius develops in his *De trinitate* with explicit reference to the Aristotelian categories, admits that nothing is said of God accidentally, but he insists that some things are said relatively and substantially. Whatever is said of God substantially is said of each of the Persons taken singly, for in God there is one substance yet three Persons or hypostases. The term "person" must not be understood in its proper or creaturely sense as applied to God, of course. Augustine goes on to develop what he means by relative predication, which is the means of distinguishing the Persons without multiplying the divine substance or essence. This being done, he discusses those things which are said of God in a temporal sense and argues that these predications, too, are relative and not accidental. The first part of the *De trinitate* draws to a close with a variety of distinctions with respect to problems having to do with the attribution of certain terms. Why, for example, is the Son called the *Wisdom* of the Father? Throughout these chapters Augustine tries to account for such appropriations, while insisting on the equality of the Persons. When he mentions that it is in terms of the Trinity that we must understand the truth that man is made in the image of God, he strikes a note that is sounded again and again in the *De trinitate.*

At the end of Book Nine, Augustine speaks of an analogy or vestige of the Trinity in charity, for in charity there is the *lover,* the *beloved* and *love* itself. This is the first of a mounting number of such creaturely analogies to the Trinity, and Augustine obviously takes great pleasure in finding them. It is not always easy to know just what methodological role these analogies are intended to play, but it seems safe to say that Augustine is not suggesting that there is anything like a demonstrative move from created triads to the truth of the Trinity. Rather, in the vein of faith seeking understanding, *fides quaerens intellectum,* the Augustinian motif which defines the work of Saint Anselm of Canterbury, Augustine begins with faith in the Trinity, established on the basis of Scripture, and he then seeks in creatures some semblance, vestige, or analogy of the divine triune nature. And, of course, it is principally in man that he seeks such semblances, since of man it is said that he is made in the image of God. (We have here the distinction between vestige and image which figures so prominently in Saint Bonaventure's writing.)

The following is Augustine's charter for his search: "If one confirmed in faith inquires what is most difficult either to know or to express, no one can find this reprehensible." There is no infidelity involved in inquiring about things already firmly believed. Returning first to the image of the Trinity he has seen in charity, Augustine observes that the mind can love itself only if it knows itself. So we have: mind, knowledge, love. But there is also the triad: being, understanding, life. Again: memory, understanding, will; capacity, learning, use. All these are images of the Trinity in the spiritual soul, man's soul, and Augustine develops them with great attention and in much detail. These "trinities" are the most important semblances in creatures of the divine Trinity of Persons. But, with what has been called a rare inventive power, Augustine comes to see other analogies. In man's sensitive soul, for example, there is the object seen, external vision, and attention of mind; further, memory, internal vision, volition. In creatures generally Augustine finds more remote vestiges: Unity, form, order; existence, knowledge, love of both; being, knowing, willing; being, having form, following law; source of things, distinction, harmony; nature, education, practice; physics, logic, ethics. Simply stated in this way, these triads may seem more forced and artificial than they appear in the context in which Augustine is using whatever springboard presents itself to approximate to an understanding of the great Christian mystery of the Trinity of Persons in God.

The *De trinitate* was destined to exercise a deep and lasting influence on the Catholic theology of the Trinity, particularly as the Augustinian doctrine was incorporated by the scholastics. After Augustine, the question of the equality of the Persons, particularly of the Father and Son, is settled once and for all. Augustine summarizes the achievements of earlier Latin Fathers and adds clarifications of his own which provide the channels according to which subsequent discussions could run.

According to Augustine, the three divine Persons participate fully and equally in the one divine nature. The nature or essence is the source of the unity, equality, and sameness; the distinction of Persons is based on relative opposition. The absolute properties of the essence should be predicated in the singular; the same is true of what is predicated of the Person in Himself and not as related to the other Persons. Thus, the nature of God must be established and its properties articulated before we enter into a discussion of the Persons. Moreover, all divine actions which are *ad extra,* creation for example, must be attributed to the entire Trinity. Finally, the procession of Persons for the divine nature is explained in terms of psychological processes.

The merit of the first mark of Augustine's doctrine is that it obviates by anticipation difficulties with respect to the equality of the Persons. If one begins with God the Father and thinks of the essential attributes as pertaining first of all to Him, then one may begin to have trouble with respect to the Son's equality with the Father. As has been pointed out, this priority is reflected in the Scholastic procedure whereby the treatise on the One God came before the treatise on the Trinity as, for example, in the *Summa theologiae* of Thomas Aquinas.

The unity of operation of the Trinity in external operations like the Creation, which does not preclude the "appropriation" of such activity to a given Person, is perhaps not as striking a mark of Augustine's teaching on the Trinity as his appeal to psychological processes in his effort to show the distinction of Persons in the divine nature. This idea is brought to marvelous fruition in the Trinitarian doctrine of Aquinas, but the source of the explanation of the procession of the Persons is Augustine. Since the divine nature is possessed of intellect and will, the Son can be understood as generated from the Father in the way in which the *verbum,* the mental word or concept, is generated. The Holy Spirit proceeds from the Father and the Son as the substantial term of the divine love.

One begins to see the distinctive features of Saint Augustine's conception of the Trinity in his doctrine of the spiritual soul and his emphasis on the triads. A doctrine, basically a philosophical doctrine, of the psychology of human intellection is used to approximate to an understanding of the "genesis" of the Three Persons in God. Once more it should be noted that Augustine's account is not a proof in any strong sense of the term, for one must concede that it has *de facto* been revealed that there are three Persons in God. In contemplating this truth, in answering the invitation to bring it into conjunction with what he knows from sources other than revelation, an invitation implicit in the fact that the mystery is presented to a rational creature for acceptance, the man of faith will seek in his knowledge of creatures whatever aid he can find to articulate the mystery. The Scriptural remark that man is made in the image of God indicates the most profitable direction of research, and in reflecting on that part of man which is least unlike God, his spiritual soul, an understanding of understanding reveals that there is, in addition to mind, the object or concept of intellection, called the "word" because it is this that language expresses. The fact that the Son is called the

Word in the Gospel of John lends support to the interpretation. Knowledge is presupposed by love; we love things only when we know them. Thus, an analysis of human psychology reveals a triad which enables us, however imperfectly, to bridge the gap between what we can know and the ineffable mystery which God has chosen to propose for our belief.

R.M.

THE SEVEN BOOKS OF HISTORY AGAINST THE PAGANS

Author: Paulus Orosius (born c.385)
Type of work: Philosophy of history; apologetics
First transcribed: 417

Principal Ideas Advanced

History is a tale of trial and tribulation, of repeated disasters.
Evil and suffering result from man's sin and God's just punishment for sin.
Christians can be optimistic, because the future lies with a Christianized Roman Empire, and times are even now (417) less wretched than formerly.

Paulus Orosius was a younger contemporary of St. Augustine. He was born and educated in western Spain when barbarian invaders were ravaging the country. He became a priest, and at the age of thirty went to Hippo, where he met Saint Augustine. The latter described Orosius as one "who is in the bond of the Catholic peace a brother, in the point of age a son, and in honor a fellow presbyter—a man of quick understanding, ready speech, and burning zeal." Orosius studied with Augustine, who then sent him to Palestine to study with St. Jerome. He returned to Hippo in 416, when Augustine was beginning the second part of his *City of God*. Augustine asked Orosius to write a treatise against the pagans which would include examples from all over the world and which would substantiate Book III of the *City of God*. Orosius finished his substantial volume within a year. Then in 418, he disappeared from history.

Orosius's *History Against the Pagans* is basically a work of Christian apologetics, which involves a view of history very much like St. Augustine's. In the dedication to Saint Augustine, Orosius writes: "You bade me reply to the empty chatter and perversity of those who, aliens to the City of God, are called 'pagans' because they come from the countryside and the crossroads of the rural districts, or 'heathen' because of their wisdom in earthly matters. Although these people do not seek out the future and moreover either forget or know nothing of the past, nevertheless they charge that the present times are usually beset with calamities for the sole reason that men believe in Christ and worship God while idols are increasingly neglected. You bade me, therefore, discover from all the available data of histories and annals whatever instances past ages have afforded of the burdens of war, the ravages of disease, the horrors of famine, of terrible earthquakes, extraordinary floods, dreadful erruptions of fire, thunderbolts and hail storms, and also instances of the cruel miseries caused by parricides and disgusting crimes."

Underlying Orosius's *History* are the usual Christian assumptions, which he takes from Holy Scripture. God created all things. We do not know why, for His ways are unsearchable. All evil is the result of man's sin, as suffering is God's hidden punishment for sin. Suffering is universal because of the transmission of the effects of original sin to all mankind. This fact raises the problem of evil, which has been a stumbling block for many good minds. Orosius offers the simple solution of a man of faith. "If a man knows himself, his acts and thoughts, and the judgments of God, would he not admit that all his sufferings are just and even insignificant?"

Because of sin, men are inclined to be wicked, ambitious, lustful, greedy, intemperate, proud, and cruel. History thus becomes a story of disaster and suffering. The better side of man's nature grows stronger as his story unfolds and history approaches the time of Christ's coming. This progress is the result of God's chastising His children, causing them ever so slowly to mend their ways. "I have discovered," Orosius reports to Augustine, "that the days of the past were not only as oppressive as those of the present but that they were the more terribly wretched the further they were removed from the consolation of true religion."

Orosius describes history as a drama in which God, in His struggle against the Devil and sin, tries to win the soul of man. God is no mere spectator in this struggle. He is an actor, along with the Devil and all men. He frequently exercises His power to intervene providentially in history. Orosius adopts the classic Christian position on the need of government and law to regulate unruly man and to make possible a safe society out of sinful men who would otherwise annihilate one another.

The *History Against the Pagans* is divided into seven books. The first extends from the creation of the world to the founding of Rome, the second to the conquest of Rome by the Gauls, the third to the wars of Diadochi, the fourth to the destruction of Carthage, the fifth goes to the Slave Wars, the sixth to the reign of Augustus and the birth of Christ, and the seventh to Orosius's own time.

But the important divisions of history are by references to four great empires. The Babylonian, Macedonian, and Carthaginian empires each came to an end after performing its appointed historic tasks. The Roman Empire was given a definite historic mission in reference to the coming of Christ, for God desired a world unified and at peace when His Son should come. "The empire of Caesar" was prepared "for the future advent of Christ." "Neither is there any doubt," Orosius tells us, "that it was by the will of our Lord Jesus Christ that Rome was brought to such heights of power since to her, in preference to all others, He chose to belong when He came, thereby making it certain that He was entitled to be called a Roman citizen." The future, Orosius believed, lies with the Church in the Roman Empire.

Orosius's *History* is a classic example of the paradox of Christian optimism in the midst of disaster and suffering. He believed that the barbarians would become good Christian Romans and that under God's guidance, with Christ for a model and supernatural grace for an aid, mankind would continue to grow better. In the last pages of his work, Orosius concludes of his time: "My description, I think, has shown not more by words than by my guiding finger, that countless wars have been stilled, many usurpers destroyed, and most savage tribes checked, confined, incorporated, or annihilated with little bloodshed, with no real struggle, and almost without loss. It remains for our detractors to repent of their endeavors, to blush on seeing the truth, and to believe, to fear, to love, and to follow the one true God, Who can do all things. . . ."

The *History Against the Pagans* was written hurriedly from such existing histories as those of Livy, Suetonius, and Eusebius. As a result, the chronology is not always consistent and some dates are even contradictory. But this does not affect the book's apologetics or its avowed purpose of stating a Christian view of history.

Orosius' *History* was widely used and frequently cited throughout the Middle Ages. It served as a text in the schools for centuries. It was imitated by such scholars as Isidore of Seville and Otto of Freising. It influenced Dante, and it was translated from Latin by Alfred the Great. It was one of the principal works through which medieval scholars viewed the ancient world, and it continued to be printed and translated through the sixteenth century.

T.P.N.

THE LETTERS OF SAINT JEROME

Author: Saint Jerome (c.342-420)
Type of work: Christian moral philosophy
First transcribed: c.370-420

Principal Ideas Advanced

A life of celibacy is best for one who would serve the Lord, but the celibate must beware of the dangers of spiritual pride.

Virgins should keep the blessed Mary before them as the ideal example of chaste and virtuous woman.

It is difficult, in a world in which temptations constantly beset men, to discipline the self and to work for Christ, but faith makes the task easier, and all men can be encouraged by the knowledge that the reward will be great beyond all expectation.

In his letters Saint Jerome shows himself to have been not only a scholar, whose Latin translation of the Bible (the Vulgate version) has been so influential in the Roman Church, but also an intensely observant and passionate human being, a champion of monasticism, celibacy, and the hierarchy of the Church, and an enemy of pagan practices and of misbehavior by those who have vowed to serve the Church. Although the letters are especially interesting because of their lively narrative content, so revealing of the manners and attitudes of the Roman society of his time, they are useful also to one who would know more of the Church of the Middle Ages. Jerome's letters bring to life the paradoxical temper of the medieval Church: its dedication to asceticism while struggling to become a decisive influence in the world of commerce and public life; its concern for peace while exhibiting, through such champions as Jerome, a violent belligerency in defense of the faith; its commitment to the divine truths, while handicapped by the constraints of dark superstition.

Almost 120 letters by Jerome are extant and have been translated, and they provide an adequate sampling of the correspondence in which this busy churchman engaged. The letters range from simple expressions of thanks for gifts to the Church to spirited defenses of the ascetic life and scathing denunciations of immoral conduct by members of Roman society and even the priesthood. Many incidents from Jerome's personal history are reflected in his letters, and the letters also show the society of which Jerome was a part and with which, as with an enemy, he contended. A survey of the letters, then, is a survey of the medieval Church in action, and the final impression is of one who, though not wholly good, was enough of a devoted champion to have attained sainthood. His personal fortune was, in that respect, like the fortune of the Church he defended: though not without fault, for the medieval Church worked through imperfect men and was handicapped by passion and superstition, the Church was predominantly in the right spirit, and its influence has prevailed.

The first of Jerome's letters, written about 370 to Innocent, one of Jerome's followers at Aquileia, was in response to a request which Innocent had made that Jerome write a detailed account of the miraculous delivery from execution of a woman falsely charged with adultery. Jerome's account is exciting and vivid; every feature of the story is dramatically, even melodramatically, colorful: "Send help, Lord Jesus. For this one creature of Thine every species of torture is devised. She is bound by the hair to a stake, her whole body is fixed more firmly than ever on the rack; fire is brought and applied to her feet; her sides quiver beneath the executioner's probe; even her breasts do not escape." The story is one of an accused lover's false confession, of a woman's faith and courage and refusal to confess, of the executioner's inability to strike off her head with his sword, of her apparent death, recovery, and final pardon. The miraculous account is notable for the simplicity and perseverance of the faith which undergirds it, a faith held in common by the persecuted woman and the narrator of her harrowing adventure. Whatever the truth of the incident recounted, the power of trust in the Lord is made evident.

An early indication of Jerome's predilection for the ascetic life is found in a letter from Antioch, written to Theodosius the anchorite, in 374. "How I long to be a member of your company," Jerome writes, but he declares that he is burdened with sin, and he asks the anchorites to pray for him and thereby to deliver him from "the darkness of this world."

In the latter part of the same year, writing from the Syrian Desert to Florentius, a friend, Jerome indicates that he has taken the monastic vows and has retired to the desert for study and contemplation. He asks that certain books be sent to him, and he mentions a runaway slave whom Florentius is seeking and about whom Jerome has some information. The letter is interesting as an expression of Jerome's divided feelings: he is happy to have decided to retire to the desert; at the same time, he longs for Jerusalem and the company of his friends; in any case, he makes certain that his library is adequate, and he remarks, "Such books, you know, must be the food of the Christian soul if it is to meditate in the law of the Lord day and night."

After a number of letters in which Jerome makes the effort to encourage correspondence from those who have been neglecting him during his desert retreat, there is one to Heliodorus, a monk, who decided against the solitary life and returned to Aquileia and has become Bishop of Altinum. Jerome berates Heliodorus for having refused to discipline himself through retiring to the desert. The letter is blotted with his tears, Jerome writes, and he addresses Heliodorus as "effeminate soldier" and asks, "When have you spent a winter in the field?" Jerome tells Heliodorus plainly that covetousness is one form, the most pernicious form, of idolatry, and he suggests that there is a covetousness that can keep a bishop from being a Christian. "Does the boundless solitude of the desert terrify you?" Jerome asks Heliodorus; "In the spirit you may walk always in paradise. Do but turn your thoughts thither and you will be no more in the desert." Heliodorus is warned that the time of judgment will come, and Jerome writes, "You are too greedy of enjoyment, my brother, if you wish to rejoice with the world here, and to reign with Christ hereafter." Jerome was a man who would not compromise or temper his remarks; it is no wonder that his efforts at proselytizing provoked bitterness in those to whom he wrote such letters.

While in the desert Jerome found himself in bitter theological disputes. The defenders of the Sabellian and Arian views attacked him, but it was no crime to be an enemy to heretics; what disturbed Jerome was that he was accused of impiety for refusing to take an active part in the controversies. A letter to the presbyter Marcus (written c. 378) makes the point that Jerome may have to leave the desert if the demands for confessions of faith continue to interrupt his solitude.

A letter to Eustochium, written from Rome in 384, is perhaps the most famous of the letters. After leaving the desert in 379, Jerome had studied in Antioch under Apollinarius of Laeodicaea and then, in 380 and 381, in Constantinople under Gregory Nazianzen. In 382 he moved to Rome, where he worked closely with Pope Damasus, for whom he composed translations and exegetical treatises. Through his friend Epiphanius, Jerome made the acquaintance of a wealthy lady, Paula, and her children and friends. It is to Julia Eustochium, one of Paula's unmarried daughters, that Jerome's long and impassioned letter in defense of virginity was written.

Eustochium had taken vows to remain a virgin in the service of Christ, and Jerome writes, he tells her, not to praise virginity and to show the drawbacks of marriage, but to warn her of the difficulties that await her. "My purpose," he writes early in the letter, "is to show you that you are fleeing from Sodom and should take warning by Lot's wife." He tells her that there are evil virgins, virgins who by impure thoughts "are shut out by the Bridegroom." Jerome offers countless Biblical passages which argue against gluttony and the lust to which gluttony gives rise, but his strictures against yielding to the temptations of the flesh are only preparatory to more strenuous and subtle warnings against spiritual weakness. Idle women, whose frivolous thoughts turn to other than spiritual matters, soon find themselves fallen in spirit if not in body; such women follow the fashions of a worldly society, and they are easy prey to flattery and fashion. Eustochium is to follow the example set by the ascetics and monks, who know the discipline which is needed if one is to remain faithful to the Lord. Jerome advises the noble virgin to keep before her the image of "the blessed Mary." The way may seem difficult, he admits, but to those who love Christ, everything is easy and the vision of the eternal reward is a cause of great joy.

There are many letters to Paula, Eustochium, Marcella (one of Paula's friends), and to other friends in Rome who had come to admire Jerome's ascetic ideals and to seek spiritual counsel from him. Some of Jerome's letters were written to answer rumors concerning his relationships with these ladies and virgins, and others were designed to fend off the criticism that in praising virginity Jerome was condemning marriage. Jerome's position throughout is that a virtuous married woman is a good woman, but a virgin, provided she is also virtuous, is better.

Jerome sometimes found it necessary to discuss theological points, but his letters show no particular theological gift. He is more notable for his enthusiasm than for his creative intellect. He was a man of learning, and his arguments are bound to Scripture, point by point, but he had neither the genius nor the ambition to be an innovator in theology.

The saint is at his best when he labors to defend what he most cherishes: the ascetic life of pure devotion. In a letter to Rusticus, written in 411, Jerome advises the young monk to stay in the community of monks and not isolate himself. Jerome's advice concerning proper behavior for a monk shows that he has considered the matter thoroughly. The writer warns Rusticus that there are many monks who are not much better than persons who have made no vows at all; the true monk, Jerome notes, is one who is more careful of his soul than of his property: "Let your garments be squalid to shew that your mind is white; and your tunic coarse to prove that you despise the world. But give not way to pride lest your dress and language be found at variance. Baths stimulate the senses and must, therefore, be avoided; for to quench natural heat is the aim of chilling fasts. Yet even these must be moderate, for, if they are carried to excess, they weaken the stomach and by making more food necessary to it promote indigestion, that fruitful parent of unclean desires."

The argument against living in the desert as an anchorite is that when a man is alone he tends to take pride in his solitary state; he soon seeks the company of others in order that he might boast of his life in the cave and tell of his mortal struggles with demons. The monk who works with others in a community, on the other hand, must learn to get along with others, and he must keep himself busy with the tasks of community life; if he is tempted, he can count on his brother monks to remind him of his duties or to scourge him with criticism. After a man has strengthened himself through community living, he can set forth to face the challenges and rewards of the solitary life.

Jerome's advice is practical. He advises Rusticus to keep himself apart from women; he must not even look upon them, and whenever circumstances force him into their company, he must realize that they are "so many snares laid to entrap you. . . ." There are other dangers, also, not so easily foreseen: "Do not be carried away by some mad caprice and rush into authorship. Learn long and carefully what you propose to teach. Do not credit all that flatterers say to you. . . ."

Jerome's letters are testimonials to the constant struggle of a man who, having committed himself to a life of continence and virtuous action, found himself continually challenged by the pleasure-seeking world of Roman society. He had to explain and defend his ascetic position; he had to encourage his friends and followers in their efforts to enjoy the rewards of chastity; he had to fend off those who would draw him into trivial or esoteric discussions about Biblical or theological matters; and, one senses, he had to continue to explore his own motives, to warn himself against spiritual pride and ambition, and to strengthen himself by the very passages with which he sought to strengthen others. Not only the social world of his times comes alive in Jerome's letters; the interior world of a saint's soul, no easy place to penetrate, also emerges to do its cleansing work even now.

FAITH, HOPE, AND CHARITY

Author: Saint Augustine (354-430)
Type of work: Religious philosophy
First transcribed: c.421

Principal Ideas Advanced

Man's worship of God takes place by means of the virtues of faith, hope, and charity, for these are the summation of the Christian life.

These virtues are contained in the Lord's Prayer and the Creed in the sense that the former answers our need to call upon the name of the Lord and the latter tells us who He is on whom we call.

Saint Augustine's treatise, *Faith, Hope, and Charity,* demonstrates a trait common to many of his works: the extremely occasional nature of their origin. A certain Laurentius, who was thought to be a Roman layman, although details about him are lacking, requested of the great Bishop of Hippo a short treatise on Christian faith and practice. Augustine's response gave posterity his only complete account of the Christian life as a whole, and indeed, in many aspects, goes beyond what one would consider the essentials of the Faith. Being a work of Augustine's maturity, written at the height of his powers, and following most of the great controversies (Manichaeism, Donatism, Pelagianism) in which he engaged, it contains his final thought, much of which had been worked out with great effort and with no little pains to present clearly the truths of the Faith. This work is also an example of Augustine's manner of considering Christian dogmas not apart from life in a purely speculative order, but in their relations with the soul and the great duties of Christian life. That is the reason he reduces all Christian doctrine to the three theological virtues, considering the different activities of the soul in the mysteries by which it must live.

The very nature of the book explains its Latin title, *Enchiridion ad Laurentium de fide, spe, charitate.* The work is sometimes called the *Enchiridion* (Handbook) because of its avowed purpose to serve Laurentius as a *vade mecum* of the Christian life. But its basic structure, arranging as it does the exposition of the Faith around the three theological virtues, led Augustine to refer to it as "my book concerning faith, hope, and charity," the title by which it has been commonly known through the ages.

The major part of the work consists of a commentary on the Apostles' Creed, and this is also the section devoted to a discussion of the virtue of faith. The remarks on the virtue of hope are contained in a brief exposition of the Lord's Prayer; these are followed by the section on charity, which brings the work to completion. Actually, while the basic structure of the Creed with its threefold profession of faith in the Father, Son, and Holy Spirit provides an outline for the major section of the work, Augustine's many digressions to investigate special questions which occur—a trait characteristic of all his writing—somewhat obscure this fundamental plan. On the other hand, the habit of pursuing casual phrases and suggestions with detailed discussion enables Augustine to give the reader a summary of Christian virtues which is, at the same time, an expression of the themes which occupied his attention throughout his lifetime.

Augustine neglects, it is true, to devote proportionate space to topics such as the sacrifice of the Mass and Redemption through the God-Man (although these are mentioned), or to the Church, her liturgy and hierarchy; he fails to treat the virtue of charity with the same fullness and detail that he devotes to the virtue of faith. On the other hand, his mention of God the Creator leads him to a detailed exposition of the origin and problem of evil, the nature of error and deception, of sin and its penalties, and of God's purpose for mankind. Speaking of Christ the Mediator, he gives ample space to His virginal conception and birth, with a detailed analysis of the expression of Scripture that He was made to bear sin for us. This analysis leads him to consider Baptism and its power to cleanse from sin. The third article of the Creed, concerning the Holy Spirit, gives rise to the author's thoughts on the angels and their nature, and on the final restoration of all things in Christ. The long section on the remission of sins discusses the effect of penance on the remission of future punishment and the distinction between mortal and venial sins. The discussion of the resurrection of the body provides Augustine with the occasion to give his views, some of them distinctive, on Heaven, Hell, and Purgatory, and to present in capsule form his doctrine on predestination, the fruit of his long polemic (which was still continuing and would do so until his death) against Pelagianism.

Augustine had struggled for years with the problem of evil and its origin, plagued as he was by his early Manichaean ideas of a double principle of all things, and of evil as a substantial being. It was the Neoplatonist teaching of the subordinate degrees of good that finally enabled him to arrive at the doctrine so clearly presented in this work. God is the cause of all things, which are good because they were made by Him and because they contribute to the total beauty of the universe. Evil is not a being, but rather a corruption of something which is good. Insofar as the corruption deprives a being of some goodness it should have, there is evil; but there could be no evil at all if it did not exist in a being; that is, in a good. The cause of moral evil in the world is not God, but the free will of man which, since it is not immutable good, can turn from good and thus perform actions which upset the correct order of the universe. God permits this turning, for no evil is strong enough to prevent Him from drawing good from it; namely, the glory of the just in overcoming temptation, and the manifestation of His justice in punishing the wicked.

The result of sin has been to deprive man of his supernatural destiny and to make him prey to temptation because of the weakness resulting from ignorance and concupiscence. This theme of sinful mankind—a favorite one of the holy Doctor—is perhaps nowhere depicted so starkly as in this present work. Augustine paints in sharp strokes a picture of "the whole mass of condemned human nature," which "lay prone in evil, indeed, wallowed in it, and precipitated itself from one evil into another." But even here, where man is pictured as so depraved, there is the further thought: the goodness of the Creator is not to be outdone by the wickedness of His creatures, "for He deemed it better to bring good out of evil, than not to permit any evil to exist at all."

Christ, of course, is God's remedy for fallen mankind, the One who could act as Mediator between the sovereign majesty of the Creator and the abject nothingness of the creature, reduced by sin to the point where he could perform no act of supernatural worth without a further gracious act on the part of God. Augustine's grasp of Christ as true God and true man is so clear and penetrating and set forth so tellingly that the heresies of Nestorianism and Monophysitism, which were soon to sweep the East, never gained a foothold in the Latin Church. The phrases used by Augustine in this description have striking parallels in the Athanasian Creed, which probably had its origins in his writings. The paragraph on the need of the Mediator to restore fallen humanity to its original destiny after the sin of Adam, is a masterful recapitulation of the dogmas of the Incarnation and Redemption.

Some of Augustine's most distinctive contributions are in the area of eschatology, which, before his time, was a welter of bizarre opinions because of the strong and diverse influences of the opinions of Origen and the millenarian movement. Augustine is one of the first to establish with certainty the existence of Purgatory, although there is still some doubt about the nature of the punishments undergone there by the soul. In this work he presents as good a proof, apart from Scripture, as can be found anywhere: "But these things [the sacrifice of the Mass and alms] benefit those only who during their lives merited that these services should one day help them. For there is a manner of life neither so good as not to need such help after death, nor so bad that they cannot be of benefit." If he doubts "whether some of the faithful are saved by a sort of purgatorial fire," this is evidently a doubt concerning the means used in Purgatory, for he later states categorically that these souls do suffer. Augustine rigidly maintains the existence of an eternal Hell against the prevalent view of the Origenists that it would come to an end. But this work manifests a weakening of his earlier adamant stand against any diminution of the torture of the damned, for he conceded: "Let them believe, if they care to, that the torments of the damned are to some extent mitigated at certain intervals." Whatever this mitigation might entail, it would never include complete freedom from the torments of Hell. The lot of infants dying without Baptism is also mentioned. While Augustine tried to convince himself in his early work *On Free Will* that such infants did not undergo punishment, he could never free himself from the idea that some punishment was necessary, and here, as elsewhere, he mentions that the unbaptized infants will suffer "the mildest punishment of all." This opinion, of course, has not found acceptance and has been universally abandoned today.

The resurrection of the body is seen by Augustine as the first step toward the final consummation of the world. The problem of the identity of the risen body with that possessed during life is handled ably by the saintly bishop, who points out that the soul imparts individuality to the body and will continue to do so in the afterlife.

The long years of the Pelagian controversy are reflected again and again in *Faith, Hope, and Charity,* as Augustine reiterates his teaching on the Fall of Adam, the effects of Original and actual sin, and the redemption through Christ's grace. In particular, Augustine summarizes for the benefit of Laurentius his teaching on predestination. God's action in showering sinful mankind with graces which lead to salvation is entirely free on His part, and without respect to our good acts. Yet, even though the omniscient God knows from all eternity the results of His saving action and the extent of co-operation of each individual with the graces given him, man's salvation is free from his side also, for he freely earns salvation for himself by his co-operation with the divine initiative. Thus, God's mercy is unmerited by man, since He sets free those who were undeserving of it. But it does not remove from man the obligation of giving his free and full co-operation to God's calling; thus, the ultimate responsibility for salvation or damnation rests squarely on the shoulders of man, not in the inscrutable designs of the Almighty.

The Semipelagians, of course, admitted all the above with one exception: man himself provides the first inclination, the very first step, on the path to justification. Many have accused Augustine of harboring a lingering Semipelagianism throughout his attacks on Pelagianism itself. This charge is wholly misplaced, and the present work alone is enough to refute it. Augustine writes: "Again, in order that no one shall boast, not indeed of his works, but of the free choice of his will, as if any merit had its origin in himself and the very freedom to do good had been bestowed upon him as a just reward, let him listen to what the same herald of grace says: 'For it is God who worketh in you, both to will and to accomplish according to His good will [Philippians 2:13].'" Augustine here, as he always had since the year 397, places the whole initiative for salvation in God.

In closing his examination of the virtues, Augustine says to Laurentius: "But it is time that we should reach the end of this book. Judge for yourself whether you should call it a handbook, or should use it as such. As for myself, thinking as I did that your zeal in Christ should not be esteemed lightly, and believing and hoping good things of you in the help of the Redeemer, and loving you deeply as one of His members, I have to the best of my ability written this book for you on faith, hope, and charity. May its usefulness be equal to its length."

R.J.B.

THE CITY OF GOD

Author: Saint Augustine (354-430)
Type of work: Philosophy of history
First transcribed: 413-426

Principal Ideas Advanced

The pagan accusations that Christians are responsible for the sack of Rome in 410 are false.

God is the creator of all things, including time and history; and He is the Lord of History.

The City of God and the earthly city are commingled through history and they will be separated only in eternity.

The two cities are commingled in each person and are struggling to possess him.

The two cities are founded by two loves, the one of God, the other of self.

History does not move in meaningless cycles, but rather toward the ultimate consummation of God's design, to be realized at the end of time.

The *City of God* is one of the most important books ever written. It is the classic statement of the Christian philosophy of life and understanding of history. For this reason it has been called the "Charter of Christendom." There are more manuscript copies of the *De Civitate Dei* than of any book except the Bible. It dominated medieval thought and has been the point of departure for modern Christian philosophies of history. Charlemagne spent years listening to it; Saint Thomas More lectured on it for four years in London; it is included in almost every "great books" course in the Western world.

Saint Augustine may never have intended to write a single volume. He began to publish early sections of the book in 413, after the Roman world had been shocked by Alaric's sack of the "eternal city" in 410. Charges were widely made that Christians had weakened Roman power by condemning "manly" sports and attitudes that had made Rome strong and proud and instead, had cultivated the debilitating virtues of compassion and love. These had so weakened the Romans, the charge went on, that not even Rome itself could withstand the barbarians' assault.

It was to answer these charges that Saint Augustine began the *City of God.* But he was too profound a thinker to be content with merely answering a superficial accusation against the Christians. He soon involved himself in justifying the ways of God to man and in exploring the relationship of human history to eternity. Since the *City of God* was published in sections through fourteen years, it is naturally digressive, occasionally repetitive, and apparently without over-all plan or structure. But underlying the entire work, in the words of the historian Edward Gibbon (who is fundamentally opposed to Augustine's thesis), is "the merit of a magnificent design, vigorously, and not unskillfully executed."

Saint Augustine was a brilliant scholar of the Greek and Roman classics, who was converted to the religion of his mother, Saint Monica, and became bishop of Hippo in North Africa. He was well versed in Scripture and studied the early Fathers of the Church. Thus, he brought to focus a combination of classical and early Christian learning, combining especially the philosophy of Plato and the Christology of Saint Paul. He was apparently influenced by a certain Tyconius, who had written: "Behold two cities, the City of God and the City of the Devil. . . . One of them desires to serve the world, and the other to serve Christ; one seeks to reign in this world, the other to fly from this world."

The *City of God* consists of twenty-two books. The first ten are a critique of the political and philosophical institutions of antiquity, and the last twelve deal with the struggle between the City of God and the Earthly City. Book I is concerned with the sack of Rome, and with the causes of the city's weakness. In this and the following nine books, Saint Augustine examines Rome and its predecessors against the teaching of Christ and the conduct of His followers. Rome is seen to be the most powerful and glorious of empires, for the Romans had achieved great things and subdued their lusts for the sake of human glory. But the Romans were led by pride and demons into luxury, cruelty, and immorality.

Saint Augustine points out that some great souls of antiquity had risen above purely earthly desires. The greatest of these was Plato, whose philosophy "has come nearest to the Christian faith." But even Plato is not to be compared "with any of Christ's apostles or His martyrs, nor with any Christian man"—citizens of the City of God. After refuting pagan charges against the Christians and showing the shortcomings of pre-Christian and non-Christian societies, Saint Augustine concludes Book X by saying to the reader: "It remains now . . . to proceed in our discourse of the two cities that are confused together in this world and distinct in the other; whose origin, progress, and consummation I will now unfold."

The core of history, for Augustine, is found in the two cities, which have been running their course, mingling one with the other through all the changes of times from the beginning of the human race, and shall so move on together until the end of the world, when they are destined to be separated at the last judgment. The struggle between these two cities is the substance of history. Augustine puts the essence of his *De Civitate Dei* in a single sentence: "Two loves therefore have given origin to these two cities, self-love in contempt of God unto the earthly, love of God in contempt of one's self to the heavenly." Nowhere does Augustine define the two cities, but many times he describes them in contrast to each other. The earthly city is governed by expediency, pride, and ambition. It is a temporal city that desires to be absolute, eternal. It lives by natural generation, and it is consumed by vanity. The heavenly city, on the other hand, is governed by self-sacrifice, obedience, humility. It is an eternal city, transcendent and timeless, determined by the love of God, and living by supernatural generation.

The two cities are distinct from each other, but they are commingled through history, and separated only after death. Both are found in each person, and their struggle within every man is the essence of history. The City of God is a pilgrim sojourning on the earth. It is not to be identified with the Church, nor is the earthly city to be identified with the secular state, for citizenship in each city is a matter of love, either of God or of one's self.

The ancients had held that history has no ultimate meaning, for it moves in endless cycles, always repeating itself and making no progress. Augustine describes such a view as impious and abhorrent, for it fails to recognize the unique event which is the center of all history, Redemption through the Incarnation, a failure that robs history and life itself of meaning. "Christ is the straight way," he tells us, "by which the mind escapes from the circular maze of pagan thought." Therefore, "let us follow Christ, our right way, and leave this circular maze of the impious."

In contrast to the cyclical pattern of

history, Augustine proposes a linear pattern which Christians have consistently held since his time. For Augustine history has a beginning, a unique event, and an end. The beginning is in creation by God the Father. The unique event is God's personal intervention in history in the person of God the Son. The end is the Kingdom of God, brought about through the sanctifying work of the Holy Spirit. All history from the Fall leads to Redemption through the Incarnation, and all history after this unique event is a movement toward its consummation in the eventual triumph of the City of God over the earthly city.

The problem of progress in history is not a simple one with Augustine. The earthly city seems to go through endless successions of generations, much as the Greeks had described. But he sees man as inventive genius and lauds his achievements in medicine, navigation, astronomy, and mathematics, as he speaks of his becoming more enlightened in history. The only real progress, however, is the development of religious understanding and perfection, the enlargement and purification of the City of God and the diminution of the earthly city. In another place Augustine tells us that God, who is "the unchangeable Governor as He is the unchangeable Creator of mutable things, orders all events in His providence until the beauty of the completed course of time, of which the component parts are the dispensations adapted to each successive age, shall be finished, like the grand melody of some ineffably wise master of song."

Augustine distinguishes six epochs in the history of mankind, corresponding to the six days of creation. The first is from Adam to the great flood, the second from Noah to Abraham, the third from Abraham till the reign of David, the fourth from David till the Babylonian exile, the fifth from exile till the birth of Christ, and the last from Christ's birth till His second coming at the end of time. Augustine refrains from making any prognosis about the length of future time, and he disdains those who try to predict details of the future. It is enough to know that the City of God will triumph in the end, for this gives meaning and intelligibility to history.

To show that there is meaning in history is the underlying purpose of the *City of God*. Granted that man cannot puzzle out history's full meaning, it is there nonetheless. It is found partly and darkly, but not fully or clearly, in the Book of Revelation. Though history is full of puzzles and mysteries, "we know that God did not act without reason in these things which surpass the reason of mortal man." Augustine also rejects the pagan deities *Tyche* and *Fortuna* on the grounds that the appearance of Fate or Chance is due to our inability to see the reasons involved in the course of events. Meaning is found in history's moving toward its consummation, Saint Augustine assures us, and when it is viewed from the end of time all will be clear, for the meaning of history comes from the eventual triumph of the City of God.

As Augustine eliminates the pagan deities from history, so he gives the Christian God sovereign place as the Creator of all things, including history and time. All happenings are under the control of providence. "God can never be believed to have left the kingdoms of men, their dominations and servitudes, outside the laws of His providence." Unlike the God of Hegel, the God of Augustine remains distinct from history. He is the Lord of History; He controls it, and through providence He overrules the intentions of men. From history, as well as through revelation, we can discern some fragments of knowledge about God, those fragments which God pleases to manifest to us. Thus, history becomes a divinely appointed pedagogue.

Saint Augustine was less provincial than most Christians in facing the question of the destiny of those outside the Jewish and Christian households. Are the great masses of men condemned to the earthly city, governed by the Devil? Are only a relatively few to enjoy the fruits of Redemption? Although Augustine did not direct himself squarely to this question in any one place, he seems to answer it in his considerations on Adam and on Christ. We are all one in Adam, according to Augustine, and thus there is organic unity in the history of mankind. Moreover, he accepts the *logos* doctrine of Saint John's gospel and Saint Paul's epistles: "all things were created through Him and for Him." Thus, his Christology is universalist; Christ suffered and died to redeem all men. Augustine cites pagan as well as Old Testament prophecies of Christ's coming, and he seems to believe that good men, whose love is rightly directed, are all somehow in the City of God.

Scholars have long argued whether the *City of God,* as a loosely written, discursive work, should be considered a philosophical, theological, or historical essay. Certainly it cannot be called historical. Only two of the twenty-two books deal with temporal history. Saint Augustine did not consider historical events as intrinsically important, for his purpose was to show the working out of God's design from an examination of the historical process. Augustine uses Biblical revelation copiously, but his method of reasoning is philosophical, for his theory of history is deduced from his theory of human nature, which follows from his theology of creation and grace. Christopher Dawson has summed it up well: "In so far as it begins and ends in revealed dogma, it is not a rational theory, but it is rational in the strict logic of its procedure and it involves a definitely rational and philosophic theory of the nature of society and laws and of the relation of social life to ethics."

Into whatever genre of work the *City of God* is to be placed, it has dominated Christian thinking about the meaning of history until the present time. Even today Christian studies of the meaning and matter of history do little more than modify Saint Augustine's study in the light of additional information which has been discovered since his time.

T.P.N.

THE INSTITUTES OF THE MONASTIC LIFE

Author: John Cassian (c.360-c.435)
Type of work: Monastic instruction
First transcribed: c.419-426

Principal Ideas Advanced

The fear of the Lord is the beginning of wisdom, for from the fear of the Lord arise compunction of heart, renunciation of all possessions, humility, mortification of desires, extirpation of faults, budding of virtues, purity of heart, and apostolic love.

The eight principal faults, which all men, and especially monks, must resist, are gluttony, fornication, covetousness, anger, dejection, spiritual sloth, vainglory, and pride.

John Cassian's influential treatise on the monastic life, a work based upon his experiences as a monk in Egypt, is at once a practical guide to monastic discipline and a course in spiritual instruction. *The Institutes of the Monastic Life* (or *The Twelve Books of John Cassian on the Institutes of the Coenobia and the Remedies for the Eight Principal Faults*) was followed by another work based upon Cassian's Egyptian experience, *The Conferences on the Egyptian Monks,* in which John once again combined his knowledge of monastic customs with his convictions concerning the spiritual life. Both works call attention to the "eight principal faults" to which all men are prone, and advice is given concerning the means to the avoidance or elimination of gluttony, fornication, covetousness, anger, dejection, "accidie" (spiritual sloth), vainglory, and pride.

The *Institutes* was written by John Cassian in response to a request made by Bishop Castor of Apta Julia, near Marseilles, who needed a set of instructions which he could use in establishing monastic communities in his diocese. Cassian, born in Scytha or Provence, received a liberal education and then, with a friend, Germanus, entered a monastery in Bethlehem. While engaged in the monastic practices inherited from Egypt, Cassian and Germanus developed an interest in Eastern monasticism which could be satisfied only by an exploratory journey to the land which was monasticism's birthplace. Consequently, in the years between 380 and 400 Cassian and Germanus made two trips to Egypt, and there they were enlightened by a number of conferences with the famous ascetics of Egypt, monks whose words of spiritual guidance are recorded in Cassian's *Conferences.*

Cassian then settled in Constantinople, where he was ordained deacon by Saint John Chrysostom. When Chrysostom was deposed, Cassian and Germanus were sent to Rome with a letter of protest from the friends and supporters of Chrysostom, and while in Rome John Cassian was probably ordained as a priest by Pope Saint Innocent I. Finally, after a stay in Gaul, Cassian settled in Marseilles, in about the year 415. His famous works on Eastern monasticism were written there, and Cassian came to be regarded as an authority concerning monastic discipline. Near the end of his life Cassian became involved in the Semi-Pelagian controversy, but his reputation as one of the founders and organizers of Western monasticism has survived to win him great respect in the history of the Church; and in the Greek Church he is venerated as a saint.

Book One of the *Institutes* describes the dress of the monks. "A monk . . . as a soldier of Christ ever ready for battle," writes John, "ought always to walk with his loins girded." The monk's robe should cover the body and protect the monk from the cold; it should be free enough to enable him to move about easily as he works. But no attention should be paid to what is fashionable in the world, and every item of dress should be designed to remind the monk of his spiritual obligations.

Cassian then discusses the twelve Psalms and twelve prayers which, presumably from the teaching of an angel, became established as the canonical Psalms and prayers for the Eastern monks. John suggests that the monks not rush into their prayers but prepare themselves by prostrating themselves and then arise with "outspread hands," while composing their thoughts in reverence. The canonical system is explained in detail in Books Two and Three.

In Book Four the author presents the institutes of the renunciants. The procedure by which one who renounced the world is to be admitted to the monastery and trained for his vocation is carefully outlined. The renunciant is to be allowed inside the monastery only after having humiliated himself before the doors for over ten days, and he is then to enter without any possessions. The renunciant must begin his monastic life in the guest house of the monastery, and he must at first stay aloof from the others. He must discipline himself so that obedience becomes for him a rule of life. (Cassian gives several examples of unquestioning obedience.)

John summarizes the spiritual instruction which he has given the monks: "Hear then in few words how you can mount up to the heights of perfection without any effort or difficulty. 'The beginning' of our salvation and 'of wisdom' is, according to Scripture, 'the fear of the Lord.' From the fear of the Lord arises salutary compunction. From compunction of heart springs renunciation, i.e., nakedness and contempt of all possessions. From nakedness is begotten humility; from humility the mortification of desires. Through mortification of desires all faults are extirpated and decay. By driving out faults virtues shoot up and increase. By the budding of virtues purity of heart is gained. By purity of heart the perfection of apostolic love is acquired."

Book Five begins that section of the *Institutes* which deals with the eight principal faults. (Conference Five of Cassian's *Conferences,* the report of the conference with Abbot Serapion, attributes to Serapion the enumeration and analysis of the eight principal faults.)

Gluttony, the first of the faults to be discussed, is defined as "pleasures of the palate," and the remedy is self-control, with particular attention to the spiritual benefits of fasting. There are no set rules for determining how much one is to fast; that is a matter for the conscience to decide. And one must remember, John points out, that abstinence from food is not enough; the other virtues of the mind must be joined to abstinence, and even the desire for food and wine must be eliminated. Spiritual conflicts are won, John advises, only by those who have already triumphed over the demands of the flesh; in overcoming gluttony a monk prepares himself for more strenuous battles. The essential point to remember is that the enemy is internal, not external; the struggle is not against food or other matters which arouse desire, but against desire itself.

Self-discipline is best achieved, Cassian argues, if one can find an inspiring example of a person who has already mastered the spiritual discipline one seeks to acquire. To assist the monks who will use the *Institutes* as their spiritual handbook, Cassian offers numerous examples of exemplary abstinence as exhibited by the Egyptian monks.

Book Six deals with the fault of fornication, and Book Seven discusses the spirit of covetousness. Cassian argues that the impulses of the flesh, impulses which can lead to adultery and debaucheries or to harmful anger or other vices, are nevertheless useful to man and are planted in the human body by the Creator. Carnal impulses serve to perpetuate the race; anger at vice encourages abstinence. Thus, the problem for man is to discipline himself so that his impulses will strengthen his virtues. The monk is to desire only that he serve God; in conquering lust and covetousness, the monk frees himself for useful work in the community.

Dejection is a fault, says Cassian, for it leads to despair of salvation. Those who would love God and profit from the contemplation of divine things must have confidence in His power. Spiritual meditation will remedy the fault of dejection.

Cassian then discusses "accidie," which he describes as "weariness or distress of heart." Accidie is a kind of spiritual laziness, a reluctance to do what is demanded of one who would discipline himself according to God's will. Manual labor will do much to prevent this fault. A man who works with his hands will learn the spiritual value of activity, and those who do not work will not eat.

Vainglory and pride are the last of the eight faults to be discussed. Vainglory can attack a monk spiritually as well as carnally, Cassian warns, and the fault may be exhibited in a monk's dress, voice, work, or in anything he does ostensibly to honor God. A man cannot escape vainglory by going into the desert or other solitude; vainglory is a stubborn vice which, once crushed, can easily rise again. Cassian reminds his brothers that "The Lord hath scattered the bones of those who please men," and he suggests that they avoid all action undertaken for the sake of receiving the praise of others. The virtuous man seeks to win the favor of God, not the favor of men.

Pride, the subject of Book Twelve, is "an evil beast," says Cassian, an evil which "in the order of time is the first." Pride destroys all the virtues; it turned Lucifer from an archangel into the Devil. God Himself is the adversary of pride, Cassian states, and the only answer to pride, the only remedy, is humility, an awareness of one's need for God's support in the effort to win perfection. Only those who give up everything of their own in the attempt to attain spiritual perfection can hope to possess that humility by which pride can be vanquished.

Although John Cassian's *Institutes* is described by its author as a work devoted to the external requirements of the monastic life, the emphasis on the eight principal faults is in conformity with Cassian's own claim that the external life is but a reflection of the internal, and that it is the internal life which matters to God.

ENARRATIONS ON THE PSALMS

Author: Saint Augustine (354-430)
Type of work: Biblical commentary
First transcribed: 391-430

Principal Ideas Advanced

Between the Psalms of the Old Testament and the Christian teachings of the New Testament there is a remarkable parallelism, such that the latter is frequently but the explication of what is implicit in the former.

One such recurrent theme is that of the two cities: Jerusalem and Babylon in the Old Testament, the City of God and the Earthly City in the new dispensation.

God's grace and Christian faith are repeatedly presented as free gifts, unmerited by any works of men.

Another recurrent theme is simply an amplification of the basic reason for the Psalms: just as the Jews sang the praises of Jehovah, so must the Christian express his admiration, love, and joy at the majesty of his God, as manifested in all created things.

Saint Augustine's *Enarrations on the Psalms* forms the longest literary work produced by the Bishop of Hippo. From his earliest years as a priest and continuing through the whole period of his episcopacy, Augustine meditated daily on various parts of the Songs of David and he took care to jot down all these thoughts and to have the resultant sermons recorded by secretaries. Called *Enarrationes* by the famous Renaissance humanist Erasmus of Rotterdam, these personal meditations were originally entitled *Expositiones* (Explanations). Essentially, they were sermon notes. Some were actually expanded and orally delivered by Augustine, who often preached on each day of the week and more than once a day. Not a few of these sermons were preached outside Augustine's own diocese; he was in great demand as an orator, wherever he traveled. More than thirty of the sermons from the *Enarrations* were preached in Carthage, for instance. However, some of these commentaries (such as those on Psalms 67. 71, and 77) were never used as orally delivered sermons. As Augustine wrote, in his foreword to the sermons on Psalm 118, "with the help of God, I have expounded the Psalter, in part by preaching to the people, in part by dictating." At some time after the year 416, he reviewed these meditations and notes and discovered that he had somewhat neglected one of the psalms. As a result he went to work and prepared thirty-two sermons on Psalm 118; this is by far the largest commentary on any individual psalm.

These *Enarrations* are filled with homely but historically valuable details on life and society in fifth century North Africa and also on Augustine's personality and relations with his parishioners. At the end of one sermon (on Psalm 88) he tells his listeners that he realizes that he has kept them standing a very long time. Then Augustine advises his audience to go out and get something to eat, to refresh their bodies, but he tells them that he is not finished; they are to return that evening for the rest of the sermon. At the close of another talk (on Psalm 72), Augustine apologizes for the length of his discourse and then he comments unfavorably on the odor in the church after such a long session. Apparently, the listeners hung avidly on his words, frequently shouting out their appreciation of things that they liked in these sermons. Nothing better brings home the lively character of African Christianity, in Augustine's day, than a careful reading of these *Enarrations.* Quite apart from their religious message, they are a genuine social document.

One ever-present theme in these meditations is the continuity between the Jewish and the Christian religion. There is no question in Augustine's mind but that the God of the Old Testament is identical with the God of the New. The events of Jewish history are frequently explained as prefiguring key developments in Christian times. Both parts of the Bible are made important to Augustine's audience.

Certain points of Christian doctrine are especially stressed in the *Enarrations.* Much emphasis is placed on the teaching that divine grace is freely given to men by God, that no human deeds can merit this divine assistance, and that none of man's works is truly meritorious until after such grace has been received. As he tersely puts it, in the second sermon on Psalm 18, "grace is no grace, unless it is gratuitous." Much the same is said of the gift of faith, in many of these sermons. One of the commentaries (Psalm 36, II, 8) contains a beautiful allusion to the experience of the blessed in Heaven. They will have, Augustine says, some kind of blissful vision in which the radiant beauty of the happiness provided by God for these beatified souls will transcend all man's powers of expression.

One need but read a few of these sermons to discover the main source of many of the social, political, and historical views developed by Augustine in his famous treatise, the *City of God.* The germ of the main theme of this great work goes back to those three or four places in the Psalms where the City of God is mentioned. Both the terminology and the thought content of the distinction between a heavenly and an earthly "city" are obvious throughout these commentaries. Explaining Psalm 86, for instance, Augustine interprets "Jerusalem" as the city of the saints and "Babylon" as that of the wicked. More fundamental is his explanation of the manner in which the two kinds of citizens are distinguished. As he expounds Psalm 64: ". . . two loves make up these two cities: love of God maketh Jerusalem [the City of God], love of the world maketh Babylon [the Earthly City]; therefore, let each one question himself as to what he loveth: and he shall find of which he is a citizen." This differentiation through the respective objects of their loves is, of course, the key to the understanding of the two "cities" in the *City of God.*

It was Augustine's considered opinion (developed in his treatise, *On Catechizing the Uninstructed*) that a preacher could, and should, use any device available to hold the attention of his listeners. The *Enarrations on the Psalms* is enlivened by many puns and jokes; episcopal dignity rested lightly on Augustine's shoulders. For example, in patristic and medieval Christian writings religious teachers are frequently called "hills." The usage seems to derive from Psalm 103:13, where God is pictured as "watering the hills" with the rain of His wisdom which, in turn, flows down to the lower levels. In one of his meditations (Psalm 124, I, 5), Augustine quips: "Do not imagine that heresies are the product of little minds; it takes a big mind to make a heresy; but the bigger the mind the worse these 'hills'!" Again, he makes a joke that fits almost any century (On Psalm 83, I, 3): "There is nothing more unsatisfactory than a thing that rolls away; that's why money is made round, it won't stand still." And one of his sharp comments on pride is the sort of pun that depends on the nature of the Latin language but which is still meaningful in English (On Psalm 95, I, 9): "How can you be proud, unless you are empty? For, if you were not deflated, you could not be inflated."

The Psalms are Jewish hymns of praise to God. Augustine's *Enarrations* maintains this motif throughout, singing of the greatness, the majesty, the justice, the power, the wisdom, and the much-sought mercy of the God who sent the Redeemer to mankind. It was not by chance that Augustine's *Confessions* opened with two texts from these same Psalms (144:3 and 146:5): "Thou art great, O Lord, and greatly to be praised;" and "Thy power is great and of Thy wisdom there is no number." These two quotations sum up the message of the *Enarrations on the Psalms.*

V.J.B.

A COMMONITORY

Author: Saint Vincent of Lérins (died c.450)
Type of work: Guide to Christian doctrine
First transcribed: 434

PRINCIPAL IDEAS ADVANCED

True Catholic doctrine can be distinguished from heretical opinion by referring to Scripture and the Catholic tradition.

The opinion of the whole body of the Church is to be preferred to that of a dissenting part; the views of antiquity are to be given priority over novel views; the views of a Council are to prevail over the views of a few individuals.

Eminent men are permitted by God to advance heretical views in order that the faithful be tried.

The true Catholic loves God and the Church and esteems the Catholic faith above all.

In order to provide a "remembrance" or "memory aid" to which one could refer when in doubt as to how to distinguish Christian truth from heretical error, Saint Vincent of Lérins wrote *A Commonitory for the Antiquity and Universality of the Catholic Faith Against the Profane Novelties of All Heresies.* Saint Vincent, who wrote under the name Peregrinus, was a monk of Lérins, and he died there in or about the year 450. There is little more known about his life. Vincent has been charged with Semi-Pelagianism, but there is no conclusive evidence for the truth of the charge.

Vincent declares at the outset of his *Commonitory* that his intention is to commit to writing what his weak memory could not otherwise retain of the teachings of the holy Fathers of the Church. His objective, he writes, is not to create anything new but merely to record what the Fathers have had to say about the very difficult problem of determining, in cases where the matter is not clear, whether a particular view is true doctrine or false heresy.

What Vincent requires is a general rule for distinguishing "the truth of the Catholic faith from the falsehood of heretical pravity," and what he has been told is that there are two reliable avenues to the truth: "Divine Law . . . and . . . the Tradition of the Catholic Church."

It might be supposed, Vincent suggests, that Scripture alone would be sufficient for determining truth. And so it would be, but for one difficulty: interpretations differ. How is one to decide which of conflicting interpretations ought to prevail?

In the most famous sentence of his treatise, Vincent declares that, "in the Catholic Church itself, all possible care must be taken, that we hold that faith which has been believed everywhere, always, by all" (*Quod ubique, quod semper, quod ad omnibus*). Only that is truly "Catholic," Vincent insists, which is universal. Thus, the rule for determining Catholic Truth is the rule of "universality, antiquity, consent"; and Vincent makes the rule explicit: "We shall follow universality if we confess that one faith to be true, which the whole Church throughout the world confesses; antiquity, if we in no wise depart from those interpretations which it is manifest were notoriously held by our holy ancestors and fathers; consent, in like manner, if in antiquity itself we adhere to the consentient definitions and determinations of all, or at the least of almost all priests and doctors."

From the rule, then, it follows that if a small part of the Church dissents from the rest, the whole body of the Church must prevail over the few. If a novel view threatens the Church, an appeal to antiquity will show the fraudulence of the novelty. If within antiquity itself one finds a division of opinion, the rule again applies: the view of the whole body, as determined by a General Council or by acknowledged authorities, must stand as the truth.

To illustrate the usefulness of his rule, Saint Vincent refers to the Donatists and Arians. If the faith of the whole body of the Church had been preferred to the views of a single man and his few followers, Donatism would have perished soon after its inception; if the ancient doctrine had been given priority over "novel disbelief," Arianism would not have spread so rapidly throughout the Church.

Vincent quotes from the *De fide* of Saint Ambrose, in which Ambrose, having declared, "Let us observe the precepts of our predecessors," urges that the example set by the confessors and martyrs be followed. Vincent applauds the defense of universality and antiquity, and he describes the martyrs as men who, "adhering to the decrees and definitions of the universal priesthood of Holy Church . . . chose rather to deliver up themselves than to betray the faith of universality and antiquity."

In applying the rule one must be careful, Vincent warns, not to be persuaded by heretical arguments based upon ancient writings taken out of context or misinterpreted.

Vincent then considers the question, "How is it, then, that certain excellent persons, and of position in the Church, are often permitted by God to preach novel doctrines to Catholics?" The answer is that, as Moses said when warning his people not to hearken to a prophet, even though formerly respected, who urges them to follow new gods, ". . . the Lord, your God, trieth you, to know whether you love Him with all your heart and with all your soul." It is difficult to resist the claims made by an old master, Vincent adds, but the trial of faith is one designed by God to strengthen the true believer. Nestorius, Photinus, and Apollinaris were once admired and respected, but Nestorius, in holding that there were two Christs; Photinus, in denying the Trinity; and Apollinaris, in teaching that the nature of Word is mutable and in denying that there were two substances in Christ, placed themselves in opposition to the universal Faith of the Church.

Vincent reviews the Catholic view of the matters bearing upon the three heresies which he discusses, and he concludes, "Accursed be Photinus . . . Apollinaris . . . Nestorius. . . . But blessed be the Catholic Church, which worships one God in the completeness of the Trinity. . . ."

If one considers anew the cases of Origen and Tertullian, Vincent remarks, one realizes the truth of the claim that "the teacher's error is the people's trial, a trial by so much the greater in proportion to the greater learning of the erring teacher."

According to Vincent, "he is the true and genuine Catholic who loves the truth of God, who loves the Church, who loves the Body of Christ, who esteems divine religion and the Catholic Faith above every thing, above the authority, above the regard, above the genius, above the eloquence, above the philosophy, of every man whatsoever; who . . . continuing steadfast and established in the faith, resolves that he will believe that, and that only, which he is sure the Catholic Church has held universally and from ancient time. . . ."

Real progress within the Church, says Vincent, depends upon building on the universal and ancient truth to which the whole Church holds; the doctrine may grow, but it must grow like a living thing, not by unrelated and novel additions.

The Second Book of the *Commonitory* has been lost. But a recapitulation of the Second Book remains, in which it appears that in the Second Book Vincent developed the themes already stated in Book One. He concludes with some references to the Councils and with the injunction "to adhere henceforward to the holy faith of the holy Fathers, to be wedded to it, to die in it. . . ."

TOME

Author: Saint Leo the Great (c.390-461)
Type of work: Dogmatic theology
First transcribed: 449

Principal Ideas Advanced

Jesus Christ possesses two complete and distinct natures, the divine and the human, united in the eternal Person of the Word of God Incarnate; He possesses intact the distinct character of the divine and the human nature, and these two natures coalesce in one Person.

Consequently, it can be asserted truthfully that God was actually born with the entire and perfect nature of a man, complete in His own nature and complete in ours, each nature retaining its own properties without defect or confusion; therefore, the human nature was not absorbed into the divine after the Incarnation.

Each nature is united with the other in the Person of the Word made flesh, and each performs the actions which are proper to itself; the Word does not lose its equality in the glory of the Father, nor does the flesh depart from the nature of our race.

Pope Leo's *Tome,* actually his letter of June 13, 449, to Patriarch Flavian of Constantinople, propounds in definitive terms the Catholic doctrine concerning the distinction of the human and divine natures united in the person of Jesus Christ. Together with letters addressed to the Emperor Theodosius II, his sister Pulcheria, the archimandrites of Constantinople, and to the council about to convene at Ephesus, all carried east by papal legates, Leo sets forth for Flavian a complete exposition of his doctrinal position to counteract the heresy of Eutyches.

Ever since the Council of Ephesus had condemned Patriarch Nestorius of Constantinople in 431 and had defined against his teaching that in Jesus Christ there was but one indivisible Person, doctrinal unrest continued to disturb the bishops of the Catholic world, particularly in the eastern Roman Empire. This unrest had been engendered because of the theological explanations and the *Twelve Anathemas* of Saint Cyril, Patriarch of Alexandria, who in his anxiety to emphasize the oneness of Christ's person made statements which while in fact orthodox nevertheless tended to imply that the human nature of Christ had been absorbed into the divine nature. Dogmatic disputes became particularly acute when an aged and unlearned monk of Constantinople, Eutyches, whose reputation for asceticism and sanctity lent weight to his assertions, taught that after the Incarnation Christ was not really a man, since the human nature had been totally overshadowed by the divine. In this *Major Tome,* Leo stigmatized this assertion of Eutyches as absurd, perverse, foolish, and blasphemous.

Eutychianism or Monophysitism, however, quickly found enthusiastic adherents, particularly under the fanatical leadership of Cyril's successor, Dioscorus, Patriarch of Alexandria. Dioscorus's adhesion to this heresy gave expression not only to the opposition of the see of Alexandria to the growing importance of the imperial see of Constantinople, but also to the increasing sense of awakened Egyptian and Oriental nationalism against Roman imperial overlordship.

Theological uncertainty and agitation became rife among the Eastern bishops. Some, such as Bishops Ibas of Edessa and Theodoret of Cyrus, who had pointed out the errors of Eutyches and had attempted their refutation, found themselves sucked into a veritable maelstrom of violent ecclesiastical rivalries and politics. The Emperor Theodosius II favored Eutyches and the Dioscoran faction and decided to settle affairs through the convocation of an ecumenical council. This council, meeting at Ephesus in August, 449, was completely dominated by Dioscorus and the pro-Eutychian imperial commissioners. Eutyches was exonerated of any heresy. His opponent, the orthodox Flavian, was physically assailed and then imprisoned; he died after appealing to Pope Leo against the appalling treatment meted out to him and bishops opposed to the Eutychians. After having amply informed himself about the council's proceedings and after having received several appeals from its decisions by condemned or concerned bishops, the pope formally denounced this assembly as the "Robber Synod of Ephesus."

When Theodosius II died in 451, his sister Pulcheria and her husband Emperor Marcian determined to secure a clear statement of the Catholic faith concerning the natures of Christ, and in the same autumn they summoned a council to meet at Chalcedon. After the first session meeting on October 8 had clearly indicated the Fathers' desire to condemn Dioscorus, they proceeded on October 10 to secure a dogmatic statement against Monophysitism. Leo's *Tome* was now read as the clearest expression of the orthodox faith. At the conclusion of its recitation the assembled Fathers exclaimed that Peter had spoken through Leo and that Leo's teaching was that of Cyril and the true faith.

Subsequent to its acceptance by the Conciliar Fathers, Leo secured at one time or another the adherence of most bishops, who signed it as the official teaching of the Church. Indeed, numerous Catholic theologians today consider it to be an infallible papal pronouncement.

Speculation concerning the sources

of Leo's thought indicates that he does not teach a new doctrine but rather one gleaned from his study of the Fathers of the Church. Shortly after writing the *Tome* he provided his legates to the Council of Chalcedon, who carried it with them, a document containing excerpted testimonies from the writings of the Fathers in support of his teaching. The *Tome* does not define such philosophical concepts as nature, person, substance, and consubstantiality. Leo bases his teaching on a reasoned exegesis of passages from Holy Scripture and the Apostles' and Nicene Creeds. The pope's ideas received perhaps even more lucid expression in a letter called the *Minor Tome* sent on August 17, 458, to the Emperor Leo I. Both *Tomes,* consequently, are regarded as providing original explanations inasmuch as they do not contain excerpts from previous writers.

In his introductory remarks to Flavian, the pope makes it clear that he considers Eutyches a heretic since he has wilfully blinded himself to the light of Christian truth, whose guide is the Creed. He is not solidly grounded in this fundamental expression of the Church's faith, particularly the words concerning belief in "God the Father Almighty and in Jesus Christ His only son Our Lord who was born of the Holy Spirit and the Virgin Mary." If Eutyches had meditated on these words, Leo insists, they would have served to guide him in his inquiries into Holy Scripture.

Leo now presents several passages from the Old and New Testaments, such as Romans I: 1-4; Luke I: 35; John I: 14; Isaias 7: 14 and 9:6, which serve to highlight the dual nature of Christ, His divine origin as the Word of the Eternal Father, united with our human nature by conception through the power of the Holy Spirit in the womb of the Virgin Mary. According to Scripture, then, the distinctive character of both the divine and human nature is preserved intact and the two natures coalesce in the one Person. Each nature retains its own properties without defect. Consequently, Jesus Christ could, as one and the same Mediator between God His Father and men, whose nature He shared fully in all things except sin, carry out the divine plan of reconciliation. In fact, Leo argues, if the two natures do not remain distinct with their own operations, the redemption of men could not have been achieved.

The pope now elaborates with numerous illustrations from the Gospels how each nature in Christ performs actions which are proper to itself. The divine nature shines through the veil of Christ's humanity in its miracles; the human nature is manifested through hunger, weariness, sorrow, toil, and suffering. It is not the same nature which weeps before the tomb of the dead Lazarus and which at a word summons him back to life. It is not the same nature which hangs battered and broken on the cross and which is responsible for the Resurrection after the third day. Even after the Resurrection Christ retained His complete human nature, for He ate and drank and invited His Apostles to probe the wounds He had endured: "See my hands and my feet, that it is I myself. Feel me and see, for a spirit does not have flesh and bones as you see that I have" (Luke 24:39). Since both distinct natures find their unity in the Person of Christ, the Son of man is said to have descended from Heaven, while the Son of God is said to have been crucified and buried, although He endured these sufferings not in His divine nature but in the weakness of His human nature.

If, consequently, Eutyches holds that the human nature after the Incarnation was absorbed into the divine and that Christ had but one nature, Leo writes, then Eutyches must deny the reality of Christ's redemptive passion and death, or he must say that the divine nature endured these. If Eutyches holds to the Christian faith, Leo asserts further, let him realize the kind of nature it was that was pierced with nails and hanged upon the cross and let him understand how it came to be.

Leo concludes with the recommendation to Flavian that if Eutyches foreswears his errors and once again embraces the true faith, he is to be treated with clemency and mercy.

R.H.T.

THE CALL OF ALL NATIONS

Author: Saint Prosper of Aquitaine (c.390-465)
Type of work: Theology of grace
First transcribed: c.450

Principal Ideas Advanced

No one can merit grace, nor do God's graces wait on human initiative: grace is absolutely gratuitous.

God wishes all men to be saved, and gives all, including infidels and infants, at least a general grace; only some, however, are given the special graces required for salvation.

God's judgments are mysterious and impenetrable.

The Call of All Nations was written to answer the question: Why, since God wills all men to be saved, are all men not saved? It is a controversial work directed against those Prosper called "*pelagianae pravitatis reliquiae*" (remnants of the Pelagian wickedness), later known as "Semi-Pelagians," and is the first treatise in early Christian literature on the salvation of infidels.

The consensus of opinion is that its author was Prosper Tyro of Aquitaine, a layman connected with the monasteries of Southern Gaul and a follower and occasional correspondent of Augustine of Hippo. Prosper was the author of a number of poetical, theological, and historical works, including the *Liber sententiarum ex Augustino delibatarum* (about 451), parts of which were embodied in the decisions of the Council of Orange in 529, at which the fate of the Semi-Pelagians was finally sealed.

A brief outline of its historical setting will give some idea of what can and what cannot be expected from the *Call.* In 418 the Sixteenth Council of Carthage had confirmed Augustine's position against that of Pelagius and his followers, who had maintained that a man's good works should be attributed to his own free will and not to God's freely-given grace. But Augustine's position seemed to some monks in North Africa to leave too small a role to man's striving for virtue, and his answers to their objections (in *De gratia et libero arbitrio* and *De correptione et gratia*) raised still other objections in the minds of some monks in Southern Gaul, the most notable of whom were Cassian, abbot of the Marseilles monastery of St. Victor, and Saint Vincent of Lérins. Prosper wrote to inform Augustine of these new objections. Augustine answered with his *De praedestinatione sanctorum* and *De dono perseverantiae,* in which he insisted that unless one were to attribute to grace both the beginning of faith and final perseverance, he would have effectively done away with the gratuitousness of grace (grace is a free gift and in no way merited by human effort), and thus have gone over to the Pelagians. Augustine died in 430, and Prosper went to Rome in 432 to attempt to persuade Pope Saint Celestine to condemn the anti-Augustinian positions being taught; but he failed: Celestine wrote a letter in which he took no sides and demanded only silence and peace. So Prosper went back to Gaul, where he wrote three works against the Semi-Pelagians. About 435 Prosper returned to Rome and occupied a place in the Papal Court under Pope Saint Leo, continuing to defend the Augustinian position with his *Capitula* (440), in which he states the main points of Catholic doctrine involved in the controversy, and his *Call,* in which he reviews the whole dispute and argues for his own position, generally held to be consistent with Augustine's positions, but softening it in some ways.

The *Call* is a work written in two books, in the first of which Prosper asks: How is it that many do not receive the grace which saves if God wills the salvation of all? In Book II the inverse question is discussed: How can there be in God a really universal will for the salvation of all if many do not receive the grace which saves? Augustine himself had wanted to emphasize the fact that one cannot merit saving grace, and he had somewhat ambiguously taught a universalist doctrine about God's will of saving men; the Semi-Pelagians had wanted to stress man's initiative in the work of salvation so as to account for the damnation of some (those perish who do not wish to be saved: grace waits on human initiative), and so tended to give insufficient emphasis to the gratuitousness of grace. Prosper believed that God had called all men to salvation and so faced the problem of seeing how to make the "call of *all* nations" consistent with the gratuitousness of grace.

It is in Book II that Prosper states his own position—he does not mention Augustine's name, nor does he feel obliged to use all Augustine's terminology—most clearly. Three things are certain: "First, we must confess that God wills all men to be saved and to come to the knowledge of truth. Secondly, there can be no doubt that all who actually come to the knowledge of the truth and to salvation, do so not in virtue of their own merits but of the efficacious help of divine grace. Thirdly, we must admit that human understanding is unable to fathom the depths of God's judgement, and we ought not to inquire why He who wishes all men to be saved does not in fact save all." God's universal salvific will is expressed in a general grace he gives to all, even to infants and to infidels. Yet not all are actually saved, because not all receive the special graces which are necessary to salvation; God does not, however, predestine anyone to evil and damnation: He only foreknows the destiny of all. The general grace given to all has two components: an exterior help furnished by created things, which testify and reveal to men their Maker; and an interior help provided by the illumination of the heart by God. (The notion of a "general grace" given all men was first stated explicitly by Prosper.) Now anyone who co-operates with this general grace will receive special graces, either the grace to practice virtue—which, however, may be lost by a failure to co-operate—or the special grace of final perseverance. But anyone who does not co-operate with the first general grace will not receive the special graces necessary to salvation.

Children are given a general grace in their parents. But if the parents fail to co-operate with this grace, their children will not receive the special grace of Baptism and will not see Heaven; however, neither these children nor un-baptized infants can be said to have been treated unjustly, for no one can be said to deserve grace. All the Gentiles in Old Testament times received general grace, but only some co-operated and were given the special graces which lead to salvation. God freely chose to give the Israelites not only general grace but also certain special graces, the Law and the Prophets, which helped save those who co-operated and who were given the necessary special interior graces. Ever since Christ's coming the special grace of the Gospel has been available and will reach all the Gentiles, though it has not done so yet; those it has reached and who accept it will be saved if they are given the necessary interior graces. The good works and prayers of the elect are a factor in the work of their salvation.

Prosper's formulation of his "solution" was not found perfectly satisfactory by later theologians (but neither were the solutions found in the high Middle Ages: witness the Molinist-Thomist controversies over a thousand years after Augustine and Prosper). For the "general grace" is insufficient for salvation; no one can be saved without additional, special graces, and these are not available to all—and Prosper does not clearly say that the only reason why these special graces are not given to some is that they themselves refuse them. He hints at this, but he also emphasizes God's free election. Yet with Prosper's stress on God's universal salvific will, progress had been made; and though it waited for later theologians to speak of grace and free will more satisfactorily, the bringing of human freedom into relief without any abandoning of Augustine's thesis of the gratuitousness of grace pointed the way for the theologians of the Middle Ages, who were influenced by this work, to find a better way of saying how and why all men are given sufficient grace for salvation. Prosper ends his treatise with these words which summarize his position: "Let, then, Holy Church pray, let her give thanks for those who have received the faith, let her make entreaty for their progress and perseverance. Let her plead on behalf of infidels that they may believe.

And when her prayers are not heard for some of them, let her not desist from praying. For God who *wills all men to come to the knowledge of the truth,* cannot repel anyone without a just reason."

R.L.C.

THE WRITINGS OF SAINT PATRICK

Author: Saint Patrick (Magonus Sucatus Patricius, c.389-c.461)
Type of work: Spiritual autobiography
First transcribed: Middle of the fifth century

Principal Ideas Advanced

God often chooses weak mortals to accomplish His grand designs.

No matter how unprepared the subject, His divine assistance can make possible that which appears impossible; such "human success," then, even in the face of tremendous obstacles, is proof of God's power and unfailing mercy, and is, in fact, a "divine success."

There are but few extant, authenticated writings of Saint Patrick: two letters, two brief fragments of letters, and three equally brief "sayings." We also have a set of canons, issuing from an ecclesiastical council, convoked probably by Patrick; and the "Lorica" or "Breast-Plate" of Saint Patrick, an Old-Irish prayer for divine protection, commonly held to be inspired by him.

The longer of the two letters is known as Saint Patrick's "Confession." It is an "open letter" in Latin, of some sixty-two chapters, most of which are but a paragraph in length. A comparison of this work with the famous *Confessions* of Saint Augustine, published about the year 400, immediately comes to mind (internal evidence gives weight to the theory that Saint Patrick had read some of Augustine's works); and one might well say of it, what a modern critic said of Augustine's *Confessions,* that "the whole . . . is an outpouring of his soul to God—God is the immediate audience. . . ." The reader can be prepared, then, to find it an intensely personal, and in its tenor, a deeply spiritual work. Patrick's "Confession" is not primarily autobiographical, and so it is only of partial assistance in sketching an outline of his life. Oral and written tradition, together with reams of legendary material, supplements the little Patrick tells us of himself.

Saint Patrick intends his "Confession" to stand, in part, as a defense against his detractors, upholding his actions as part of a life spent, in its main design at least, according to God's will and not his own: "And He inspired me . . . before others, to be the man . . . who . . . should faithfully serve the people [the Irish] to whom the love of Christ conveyed me and gave me for the duration of my life. . . ." He continues, "On the other hand, I did not go to Ireland of my own accord . . . and He made me fit so that I might be now what was once far from me—that I should care and labour for the salvation of others. . . ." He wishes this fact to be known by all.

Patrick further intends the letter as a tribute of praise to God for His mercy and sustaining grace, and for favors in his behalf. This is certainly his more profound and explicit intention. Innumerable passages attest Patrick's recognition of indebtedness to God as the true Author of all his accomplishments. The flavor of his gratitude is carried in: "And therefore I ought to cry aloud and so also render something to the Lord for His great benefits here and in eternity—benefits which the mind of men is unable to appraise."

That the reader of the "Confession" also learns much of Patrick's human failings is not through any accident of self-revelation on his part; he, seeing these weaknesses in the clear light of God's strength, wishes to hide none of them from view. Thus, the opening lines of the letter: "I am Patrick, a sinner, most unlearned, the least of all the faithful, and utterly despised by many."

As the letter unfolds, it becomes apparent what type of person Patrick is: strong-willed, yet docile to God's commands; boundlessly enthusiastic, yet given to occasional discouragement; a strong personality who exerted a magnetic attraction on many, but one who was the target of much criticism from others; unscholarly by his own admission, yet well versed in Scripture (and showing himself especially fond of Saint Paul) and hardly, as some of his contemporaries thought of him, a "country-bumpkin"; an ascetic and a mystic, yet one through whose activities an entire people were converted.

Magonus Sucatus Patricius was born about 389 (he himself gives no dates) in northern Britain. He was immensely proud of being both a citizen of the Roman Empire and a member of the Catholic Church. He came of good family, and he had the usual education youths of good family received in those days. In a relatively detailed passage of the "Confession," Patrick describes how at sixteen he was captured, made a slave together with "many thousands of people" (perhaps by the great Irish king Niall Norgiallach, whose power would have made a raid of such proportions possible), and taken to northeastern Ireland, probably Antrim. (His captor's son Loigaire was High-King, with a seat at Tara, when Patrick many years later arrived to begin his missionary work.) While alone, tending sheep in the rough mountain country, he turned to God seriously and underwent a profound religious experience, which he describes laconically, ". . . the love of God and His fear came to me more and more, and my faith was strengthened." Hearing a voice in a dream (he was to hear other voices in other dreams) and taking this as a sign of divine intervention, he made his escape aboard an Irish ship bound for Gaul. He had been a slave of the Irish for six years. After a series of remarkable adventures, he managed to return to his family in Britain. But once more through his dreams, Patrick was called to action, this time to the fullness of dedicated life—as apostle to the pagan Irish peoples. "We ask thee, boy, come and walk among us once more," said the voices of the Irish in his dreams. He was perhaps 24 or 25 at the time.

Now education was needed for his future work, and Gaul was the logical place to acquire it. Tradition has it that he spent some fourteen years in Auxerre, in prayer and study, and that he was ordained to the diaconate, but Patrick makes only the briefest mention of this period in the "Confession." He continued to nurture in his heart a desire to go to Ireland, though this meant leaving the Roman world he loved so well.

When in 429 a delegation was organized with Pope Saint Celestine's blessing to go to Britain to fight a revival of the Pelagian heresy, it was suggested that Patrick be sent to Ireland as bishop at the same time, thus to ensure the healthy growth and life of the Church in the British Isles. However, a close friend betrayed an old trust and revealed to his superiors a sin Patrick had committed as a youth (what it was he does not tell us). This revelation of his sin, together with the fact that some of his superiors thought Patrick to be intellectually poorly equipped for so important a role, brought about the cancellation of his assignment. Nevertheless, by a turn of events which in the light of later happening appeared to him providential, Patrick in 432 returned as bishop to the land of his captivity.

The "Confession" records little of what was in fact thirty years of extraordinary missionary activity in Ireland. He himself realized how impossible such a recitation would be: "Now, it would be tedious to give a detailed account of all my labours or even a part of them." We know, however, that his particular talents and his unfailing zeal effected the conversion of thousands of the Irish, from kings to slaves; the establishment of parishes, with the metropolitan see (his own) at Armagh, and the building of churches and monasteries; the consecration of fifty or sixty bishops (some later accounts raise this number to three hundred and fifty); the organization of a training-program for the young as a countermeasure to the activity of the influential druids; and the laying of the foundations of a unique and rich "Irish spirituality," which is undiminished to the present. In general, he put the stamp of "Roman" upon the inchoate state of the Church in Ireland, binding her to the universal Church, an accretion for the Church of great value in later centuries. Countless trials were his along the way—he speaks of "twelve dangers in which my life was at stake"—but he minimizes these and others, "for I do not want to bore my readers." The closing chapters redound with praise and thanksgiving to God for the successes Patrick feels were his through Him—Patrick, the stone lying in the mud which God picked up and put on top of the wall, to use his own metaphor. It is obvious that he also considers these successes in his missionary work as ample justification for his "audacity" in undertaking his mission at all.

Saint Patrick's "Letter to the Soldiers of Coroticus" is but a few thousand words in length, written some years before the "Confession." Its occasion was a "horrible, unspeakable crime" committed by a Christian Roman prince of northern Ireland, Coroticus, and his band of marauding soldiers. They had raided the Irish coast, come upon a group of Patrick's own newly baptized Christians— ". . . the fragrance was still on their foreheads" (that is, the sweet scent of holy chrism used in Baptism)—murdered some, and kidnaped the rest as slaves. Deeply grieved over the death of his converts, thoroughly angered at this violence and at Coroticus's refusal to pay heed to Patrick's emissaries, Patrick writes to demand that Coroticus acknowledge his guilt, return Patrick's Christians and make retribution, or face excommunication. In this letter as well as in the "Confessions," paragraph after paragraph abounds in Scriptural quotations.

We possess two fragments from other letters of Saint Patrick. The first in its entirety runs: "I heard some [voices] singing psalms in me, and I do not know who they were." In the other fragment, Patrick reprimands two of his local ordinaries because they had ordained bishops without his knowledge and consent.

The extant "sayings" of Patrick are brief indeed: "The fear of God I had as my guide through Gaul and Italy and the islands in the Tyrrhene Sea" (perhaps Patrick, before his stay at Auxerre, had spent some short time in this Mediterranean area); "From the world you have gone to Paradise. Thanks be to God" (from the "Letter to the Soldiers of Coroticus"); "Church of the Irish, nay of the Romans . . ." (this, and the "Thanks be to God" above were perhaps favorite phrases of Patrick).

There are 34 canons, or ecclesiastical decrees, enacted by Bishops Patrick, Auxilius, and Iserninus, at a synod the date of which is now unknown. The canons are drawn up as rules for the government of the Church in Ireland, but they legislate with local problems in view. There are, for example, recommendations on the dress of clerics and bishops, regulations concerning their handling of money, prohibitions against and suggested penances for public sinners, and the like. Particularly choice among the canons are "Lectors should acquaint themselves with the Church in which each is to sing" and "Also a monk who goes wandering without consulting his abbot is to be punished."

To include the "Lorica" or "Breast-Plate" among Saint Patrick's writings is perhaps to stretch an already attenuated point. However, it most certainly is a very ancient Old-Irish prayer, recorded perhaps around 750, found in the *Irish Book of Hymns,* but with an oral tradition preceding its literary transcription. The "Breast-Plate," or shield, is an invisible one—a "corselet of faith"—protecting the wearer from evils of soul and body. Patrick composed this hymn, it is said, as a prayer against the machinations of Loigaire, High-King of Tara. It is in litany form, of nine stanzas. Its powerful opening and its moving conclusion still stir that Irish "spirit" that is Patrick's particular legacy:

I arise to-day
  through a mighty strength, the
    invocation of the Trinity,
  through a belief in the Threeness,
  through confession of the Oneness
  towards the Creator.
Christ to protect me to-day
  against poison, against burning,
  against drowning, against wounding,
  so that there may come abundance
    of reward.

Christ with me, Christ before me,
 Christ behind me,
Christ in me, Christ beneath me,
 Christ above me,
Christ on my right, Christ on my
 left,
Christ where I lie, Christ where I
 sit, Christ where I arise,
Christ in the heart of every man who
 thinks of me,
Christ in the mouth of every man
 who speaks of me,
Christ in every eye that sees me,
Christ in every ear that hears me.

R.L.C.

THE LETTERS AND SERMONS OF SAINT LEO THE GREAT

Author: Saint Leo the Great (c.390-461)
Type of work: Pastoral letters; sermons
First transcribed: 440-461

Principal Ideas Advanced

[*The letters stress matters of ecclesiastical administration and disciplinary action under the primacy of the Roman bishop. "The Tome," epistle 28, so authoritatively states the basic tenets of Christology that it became a key document at the Council of Chalcedon. The sermons, given generally on liturgical feasts, emphasize the need for moral regeneration, a rededication to Christian ethics, and a renewed appreciation of Christ's work.*]

Saint Leo, Bishop of Rome, left to posterity a literary corpus containing 173 letters, 143 in his own hand, and 96 sermons. In general, these writings graphically reflect the talents of this greatest pope of the ancient Church as a supreme administrator, sincere moralizer, and zealous defender of orthodoxy. Both his letters and his sermons deal artlessly with plain facts and situations embellished by no flourish of classical learning or speculative Biblical exegesis. Everywhere there is serious comment and ponderous exhortation, characteristic of a Roman mind linguistically unequipped to avail itself of the subtlety and depth of Greek *paideia.*

The letters demonstrate convincingly that, by Leo's time, the new spiritual unity forged in the West by the Christian Church under the leadership of the Roman bishop was sufficiently wide and mature to replace the political cohesion once provided by the Roman state but now in a state of dissolution. Leo's letters traveled world-wide; they were sent not only to the local churchmen of Italy and Sicily and to the papal vicar at Thessalonica, but also to the bishops of Spain, Gaul, Africa, Egypt, Asia Minor, and Palestine; many went directly to the patriarchs of Constantinople themselves. Besides addressing bishops, monks, and congregations, they also address the great political figures of the day such as Theodosius II and his sister Pulcheria; the emperor Marcian; Galla Placidia, the mother of Valentinian

III; the emperor Leo; Eudocia, the widow of Theodosius II; and Eudoxia, the wife of Valentinian III. The letters also went to Church Councils: to that of Ephesus in 446 and that of Chalcedon in 451.

In a typically Roman fashion, Leo's epistles demand a respect for order and uniformity, discipline and authority, conservatism and legitimacy. Consequently, all heretics: Pelagians, Manichaeans, Priscillianists, Nestorians, Macedonians, and especially the contemporary Eutychians, find themselves berated for spurning the standards of antiquity which, the pope declares, must be scrupulously maintained in the Christian rule of faith and in discipline. Heretical innovations, Leo writes, ignore the views of earlier Roman bishops such as Innocent, outrage the teachings of the Fathers, contort the eternal decrees of Nicaea, and deny the respect due Peter. Leo requests the secular arm, as well as his "brother" bishops, to proceed with vigor against the heretics. In a practical and merciful way, however, Leo argues that reconverted heretics should be reconciled and treated with cautious moderation.

All sorts of matters come up for review in Leo's communications. By his time, Roman claims of Petrine supremacy had already so long been promulgated that Leo could insist upon them as a matter of course. Christ, he submits, placed the principal charge on the blessed Peter as chief of the Apostles; from him, as head, the divine gifts flow to the entire mystical Body of Christ. Anyone who dares secede from Peter's solid rock enjoys no part of the divine mysteries. Through Peter, Rome derives power to maintain truth, and the Apostle, with wondrous concern, can be counted upon to sanction the judgments of his see. Watchfulness on the part of Rome is imperative if the Apostolic See is to be diligent and true to its Petrine commission. Because Rome abides by the traditions of Peter, Leo urges other bishops to accept the Roman liturgical and doctrinal views as standard. Thus Alexandria, he argues, cannot justify any deviation from the Petrine norm since Mark, as Peter's disciple, cannot have established any dispensation which jars with his master's arrangements. The bishops of Sicily and the West, in general, are enjoined reverently to observe the constitutions of apostolic Rome. In short, any sharer of the Roman communion has to be obedient to Rome; all are required to take their observances from the same source as that from which they derive their powers of episcopal consecration. As Peter is the author of priestly dignity, so also is he, by extension through Rome, the director of Church procedure.

Especially two letters, 6 and 167, addressed to the bishops of Illyricum and of southern Gaul, reveal the kind of administrative, liturgical, and disciplinary points which Leo thought worthy of propagation and emulation.

Ordinations, says Leo, are to be held on Sunday and with the approval of the laity. Careful screening of candidates is essential, since serfs, slaves, and digamists, among others, are ineligible. Deacons and higher clergy are denied cohabitation with their wives. Promotions have to honor the rules of seniority, and there are to be no episcopal translations from see to see. Ecclesiastical government has to be graduated; only larger cities are to have bishops. Questions insoluble on the local synodal level are to be referred to Rome; those who would approach the pope are required to do so through their metropolitans. Baptism is to be administered only at proper times. Those once baptized by heretics cannot be rewashed. However, abandoned infants and children captured by barbarians, as uncertain of their Baptism, are permitted rebaptism. Penance involves confession to priests, and those under penitential discipline, or after it, have to avoid the temptations of the business and legal world, as well as military service. The Eucharistic Sacrifice can be repeated on Sundays as often as necessary to serve different congregations. Final sacramental ministrations are to be denied to no one.

Obedience is imperative, Leo claims. Roman jurisdiction tolerates no insubordinations such as Hilary's in Gaul or Anastasius' in the papal vicariate of Illyricum. The latter is reminded that obedience to Rome in his area begins with him. Dumfounded and grieved over the inappropriateness of his vicar's actions, Leo pointedly urges him to practice more circumspection and respect. He does not hesitate to rebuke even Anatolius, the Bishop of Constantinople, for his self-seeking.

Probably Leo's letters are most valuable in reflecting the effectiveness of Roman influence on the East. Advancing on the successes of his predecessor, Coelestine, Leo saw papal relations with Constantinople reach a new high. The excuse for continued communication with Flavian, Bishop of Constantinople, and with Eastern emperors together with other court dignitaries, turns about the new heresy of Eutyches, the misguided synod of Ephesus, and the great Council of Chalcedon.

Leo writes Flavian, "We are the chief sharer of your worries . . . on the eastern church we have always spent much care." He reminds the synod of Chalcedon that, since no precedent permits papal presence at a council, it should reckon that the pope presides at the meeting in the persons of those deputed there by the Apostolic See. Letter 97, written by the council to Leo, commends the pope, as the mouthpiece of Peter in the chain of command from Christ, for imparting the orthodox faith. Christ, they write, supplied the council with an imperial spiritual banquet through Leo's letters. The pope is indeed the head of the convention's members. Charged by the Savior with the custody of the vine, Leo has most graciously extended the Apostolic prestige which pertains to him to the Church of Constantinople.

Despite the council's deference to him, Leo refused to honor its request to recognize Constantinople as second after Rome in ecclesiastical rank. In a letter he reminds the East that a royal city cannot make itself apostolic, and that the Nicene canons recognizing Alexandria and Antioch after Rome can never be gainsaid. Since no synod can undo this permanent and inviolate code, Leo assures the Bishop of Antioch that the bishop's ecclesiastical rank is secure against Eastern pretensions.

Probably the most famous letter in Leo's collection is epistle 28, the so-called "Tome," sent to Flavian of Constantinople explaining the dual nature of Christ as against the teaching of Eutyches. Even though relatively short, it remains the most significant explanation of dogma by a pope of the early Church. The gist of the exposition is that both natures of Christ retained their proper character without loss. Quite appropriately, Christ could be pierced with nails even as He opened the gates of Paradise to the robber's faith. Acclaimed, abbreviated, and explained at the Council of Chalcedon, Leo's Tome became the central document of the meeting.

Finally, Leo's letters reveal his attitude toward the state. He asks Valentinian III to deprive Manichaeans of their political rights, and he attributes to the emperor Leo a serious partnership with him in carrying out the divine economy. The Lord, the pope assures the ruler, has enriched the emperor with special insights into divine mysteries and has enabled him on his own virtue to distinguish right from wrong. He reminds the emperor that the kingly power conferred upon him relates not only to the governance of the world but also to the guardianship of the Church. Ordained to rule the whole earth, the emperor owes the Church aid, for example, against heretics; the state will benefit in proportion as its governor is thus solicitous for religion.

Leo's nearly one hundred homilies date from his early pontificate. Sermons 3, 82, and 83 deal quite extensively with Peter. Through him, Leo declares, the priesthood is transmitted. The Apostle's power still lives and prevails in his see; he was, in fact, present when Leo celebrated the anniversary of his consecration. The popes achieve what they do through Peter; when the Roman bishop exhorts, Peter speaks. Sermon 84 bewails the fact that the feast of Saints Peter and Paul, established to commemorate the liberation of Rome from Genseric, is already being neglected.

Some five sermons concern almsgiving, which is especially dear to Leo's heart, and other pious works, such as being merciful to the poor, and persevering in prayer, fasting, and self-denial. Prayer, Leo says, propitiates, fasting purifies, almsgiving redeems. All these works to be meaningful have to be accompanied, of course, by a serious purpose of amendment.

Most of the sermons celebrate the feasts of the liturgical year. Some ten, for instance, are devoted to Christmas, eight to the Epiphany, others to the Passion season, to Easter, Ascension, and Pentecost. Leo exploits all festivals as propitious occasions to exhort his hearers to strive for moral perfection through examinations of consciences, rejection of vice, devotion to prayer, the practice of charity, and the cultivation of kindness toward one's neighbors. Usury he considers entirely incompatible with the latter.

Leo's sermons do not fail to reveal his deep dedication to correct Christological formulations. Whenever opportunity arises he reminds his listeners of Christ's unique dual nature, asserting that He who was pierced with nails was simultaneously the same as He whom no wound could affect, that He who underwent death was the same as He who never ceased to be eternal. All heresy, Leo warns, stems basically from a denial or misunderstanding of Christ's twofold nature.

Sermon 75, delivered on the occasion of Epiphany, centers around the Trinity and is one of the few formal explanations of this topic in Leonine literature. Leo describes the Holy Spirit as consubstantial with Father and Son, distinguishable from Them by neither time, grade, nor any iota of difference in nature.

E.G.W.

ON THE DIVINE NAMES

Author: Dionysius the Pseudo-Areopagite (fl. c.490)
Type of work: Mystical theology
First transcribed: c.490

Principal Ideas Advanced

Whatever conception of the Godhead is possible through the Scriptures, it cannot be out of proportion to the powers of our spirits, for the Super-Essence surpasses all essences, the Super-Intellectual Unity surpasses all intelligences, the One which is beyond thought surpasses all conceptions, and the Good surpasses all names.

Although the Godhead is nameless, a relative understanding is granted through the Scriptures, and each of the names used to suggest the indescribable nature of the Godhead provides some light concerning the whole nature of Divinity.

"Unity" and "Differentiation" may at once be applied to the whole Godhead; "Goodness," "Being," "Eternal Life," "Wisdom," "Mind," "Truth," "Cause," "Beginning," "Reason," and "Power" are a few of the names by which, through Scripture, we seek some understanding of the Super-Essence.

On the Divine Names is a Neoplatonic attempt to explore the limited but nevertheless suggestive meanings of the various names by which the indefinable and indescribable Godhead is mentioned and praised in Scripture. The book is the work of an inspired and diligent intellectual and mystic, an unknown monk, probably of the latter half of the fifth century. He was, one surmises, a Syrian, and his work makes references which some scholars have interpreted as showing the influence of Proclus (c. 410-485). He called himself Dionysius, and he claimed in his work that he was the Athenian convert of Saint Paul, but internal evidence clearly supports the view that this name must not literally be applied to the author of the book; rather, in line with an old convention, the pseudonym was fashioned, in all probability, to suggest the spiritual intensity and aspirations of the author: it was *as if he were* the one whom Paul had converted.

Analogously, the names by which God is mentioned and praised in Scripture are names which cannot literally be applied to the Godhead, the Super-Essence which is eternally beyond the reach of all names and finite understanding; the names, such as "One," "Goodness," and "Being," are suggestive and relative, providing glimpses, however inadequate, of the Divinity. This theme—that the divine names are to some extent illuminating although never adequate—is the central theme of the work by the Syrian monk whose own place in the history of theological writings is marked by a name that cannot be taken literally.

The views of Dionysius have long been respected even by those who find it necessary to reject something of the method or substance of his work. Saint Maximus, John Scotus Erigena, and Saint Thomas Aquinas, among others, were acquainted with his work and found it to be a significant contribution to mystical theology. Dionysius has on occasion been charged with pantheism, and it is contended by some critics that his work is dangerous in that it encourages an extravagant and sometimes contradictory use of language; the fact is that Dionysius himself makes the effort to emphasize the claim that God is transcendent and in no way definable by the use of names, and his entire treatise is designed to illustrate the care with which one must undertake the attempt to utilize Scripture as a source of truth, however relative and inadequate, concerning the Godhead.

Dionysius begins his work by calling attention to the effort which men make, through the reading of Scripture, to grasp "in a manner surpassing speech and knowledge" the truths which are themselves surpassed by the Truth, and he declares, "We must not then dare to speak, or indeed to form any conception, of the hidden super-essential Godhead, except those things that are revealed to us from the Holy Scriptures."

But if the Godhead is "unutterable and nameless," how is a study of the divine names possible? We can say that Divinity is One, the Super-Essential Godhead, the Absolute Good, the Trinal Unity of Persons, but the Godhead is the Unknowable, beyond the range of all conceptions. Even those who, like the angels, enter into a state of union with the Godhead can say nothing of the Super-Essence other than that It surpasses all description. Thus, says Dionysius, "it is not lawful to any lover of that Truth which is above all truth to celebrate It as Reason or Power or Mind or Life or Being, but rather as most utterly surpassing all condition, movement, life, imagination, conjecture, name, discourse, thought, conception, being, rest, dwelling, union, limit, infinity, everything that exists."

Nevertheless, continues Dionysius, despite the fact that the Godhead is said to be the Nameless, the writers of Scripture, who were inspired men, "celebrate It by every Name. . . ." The Godhead is said by the writers of Scripture to have declared, "Why askest thou thus after My Name seeing it is secret?" and yet to have also declared, "I am that I am," and "I am the Life . . . the Light . . . God . . . the Truth. . . ." The names which have been used to denote the Super-Essence, then, cannot be regarded as in any way describing the Godhead; the attributes which the names connote do not, as such, belong to the Godhead which surpasses all attributes. But the names are useful as relative terms, as intelligible terms of discourse by which, in a kind of negative way, one realizes that the Godhead is Transcendent, Goodness beyond conception, Unity beyond comprehension.

Such names as "Absolute Goodness" should not be regarded as referring to some distinguishable aspect of the Supernal Godhead, Dionysius insists. Such a term refers to the whole Godhead, and to suppose otherwise is to divide the Supreme Unity. Whatever name is used to suggest the nature of God must be regarded as making reference to the whole Being.

A distinction is then made by Dionysius between "Undifferenced Names" and "Differentiated Names." One must be able to speak of God's unity and transcendence, and thus the undifferenced names are necessary; but one must also be able to speak of "the beneficent Differentiations of the Supreme Godhead," the Divine Persons which constitute an undivided Trinity, one with Unity, and thus the differentiated names are needed. Some names apply to the Godhead as undifferentiated and some apply to It as differentiated. Among the undifferenced names are such names as "Super-Essential," "Super-Divine," and "Supra-Sapient." The most important differentiated names are, of course, "Father," "Son," and "Spirit." Differentiated names are used in speaking of Jesus. One must remember, however, that there is but one Super-Essence which is the ground of all unity and differences.

It is by prayer, says Dionysius, that we are lifted to the Primal Goodness, the Trinity. "Goodness" is the highest name, and the Trinity, conjointly as the Source of goodness, "is nigh unto all things" which prepare themselves for union by drawing near to God in prayer.

According to Dionysius, who deliberately undertakes the resolution of the problem of evil, what we call evil is whatever is in some way deficient or inadequate, tending toward nonexistence. Anything which exists has being from the Cause, and since the Cause is also the Good, anything which has being partakes of the good to the extent that it has being as realized fully in the Godhead. Thus, evil is nonexistent in the sense that it is a feature of things just insofar as they fail to be what they would be were they realized as God would have them realized; "evil . . . is weakness, impotence, and deficiency. . . ."

God is the Cause of Life, the Beginning and End of all things; that is, God not only endows whatever exists with being but also determines the purpose of every existing being. Of course, the conception of God's creative activity cannot be made entirely intelligible, for He transcends both time and eternity in that, as the Godhead, He is absolutely undifferentiated.

God is Perfect and One, says Dionysius: "Thus Scripture speaks of . . . One God Who is the Father and One Lord Jesus Christ and One unchanging Spirit, through the transcendent indivisibility of the entire Divine Unity. . . ." The intelligible names by which the writers of Scripture have referred to God enable us only in part to begin to appreciate the mystery which lies beyond all human comprehension.

THE MYSTICAL THEOLOGY

Author: Dionysius the Pseudo-Areopagite (fl. c.490)
Type of work: Spiritual theology
First transcribed: c.500

Principal Ideas Advanced

Only through being plunged into the Darkness of Unknowing and rejecting all knowledge is it possible to be united to the Super-Essential, Super-Divine, Super-Excellent Unknowable.

The Super-Essential Darkness is known by the negative method of going beyond all sight and knowledge, beyond all qualities and objects of knowledge, to that which is beyond the light of all existent things.

The Universal Cause is not any sensible or intelligible thing, nor is the Cause any quality of any sensible or intelligible thing.

The *Mystical Theology* of Dionysius the Pseudo-Areopagite is the theological sequel to *On the Divine Names,* a work in which Dionysius tried the positive method of exploring the significance of those names ordinarily attributed to the ultimately unknowable and unnamable God. In the *Mystical Theology* the method is that of the *via negativa,* and Dionysius carefully explains why it is that the work *On the Divine Names* was longer and more copious: in *On the Divine Names* the course of speculation and clarification was downward, from the most general and abstract names to the more particular and concrete, while in the *Mystical Theology* one moves quickly from the particular matters, already discussed by the affirmative method, to the negative considerations, which are most general; finally, in the attempt to realize the "Super-Essential Darkness," which is the Godhead, one finds words completely inadequate. The theme of the *Mystical Theology,* then, is that nothing sensible or intelligible is of any assistance in the attempt to know God; one must acknowledge this fact and keep silent. If one abandons the knowledge of things, if one is willing to be completely in darkness, there is some possibility of a union with, a unitive knowledge of, the Divine Unknowable.

The theology of Dionysius, which is essentially spiritual or mystical, was very influential in the early Church. The most important popularizer of his ideas was John Scotus Erigena (or Eriugena, c.810-c.877), who translated the works of Dionysius from Greek into Latin. Erigena's own masterpiece *De divisione naturae* is a careful examination and elaboration of the theology which Dionysius espoused. However, Erigena so emphasized the absolute transcendence of the Godhead, while at the same time regarding the Divinity as the source and ground of all being, that which transcends being but without which nothing is, that he was accused of pantheism and his work was condemned at Vercelli in 1050 and at Paris in 1225. Furthermore, the work has frequently been the target of theological attacks, and it is listed in the *Index librorum prohibi-*

torum. Nevertheless, the work of Erigena stimulated theological speculation and encouraged more satisfying orthodox developments within theology.

The theology of Dionysius also shows its influence in the works of Saint John of Damascus, Hugh of St. Victor, and Saint Thomas Aquinas. Thomas wrote a commentary on *On the Divine Names,* and he was very much stimulated, although usually into opposition, by the challenging language of the Greek theologian. The consensus of later theologians is that although Dionysius' Neoplatonism embodies an objectionable form of pantheism, his emphasis on the glory and mystery of God provides an inspiring, if sometimes philosophically unacceptable, expression of the Catholic faith.

Dionysius (who was, of course, no disciple of Saint Paul: see article on *On the Divine Names*) begins his treatise on mystical theology with a prayer to the Trinity "which exceedeth all Being, Deity, and Goodness!" He asks that he be enlightened by Scripture and that he be enabled to take the mystical course of going beyond light and knowledge to "union with Him whom neither being nor understanding can contain."

The author argues that the "Super-Essential" is beyond all human understanding because He is "beyond all positive and negative distinctions." Even the highest and most divine of things known through perception or the use of the intellect are "but the symbolic language of things subordinate to Him. . . ." Only when one is plunged into "the Darkness of Unknowing" and has renounced all knowledge of things is it possible to know through mystical union the Unknowable Cause.

Dionysius maintains that vision is possible only through loss of vision and that one can know God only by losing all sight and knowledge. The Divine Unknowable is to be offered "the praises of a transcendent hymnody," and what is called for is the negative way of denying all positive statements in order that one might come to that ultimate Darkness which is the source of all Light. Dionysius says that in *On the Divine Names* he proceeded from the most universal statements or names and worked to the more particular names; now his interest is in ascending to the more general names in order that he might finally come to the point of abandoning names altogether, for that which Dionysius seeks to know, the Super-Essential Unknowable God, is the transcendent Cause which cannot be grasped by any particular perception or conception or combination of them.

In earlier works (*Outlines of Divinity* and *On the Divine Names*), Dionysius explains, he developed those distinctions by which men attempt to understand God. God is one, but He is also the Trinity; He is above essence, but Jesus became man. Now it is necessary to attempt preparations for a unitive knowledge of God by going beyond all distinctions. Naturally, then, the present work is briefer than the others, for there is soon nothing more to be said: one ascends to the most general terms, and one then abandons language altogether and thought as well.

The negative method is not, however, purely negative. Some negations are truer than others. It is truer, says Dionysius, to deny that God is drunkenness or fury than that the categories of human thought or sense apply to

Him. A positive statement which incorporates the conclusions of the negative way then becomes possible: "We therefore maintain that the universal Cause . . . is neither impersonal nor lifeless, nor irrational nor without understanding. . . ," and Dionysius adds that God is not a material body and thus does not possess any of the deficiencies of material bodies.

Dionysius denies that God is a material body, but he also denies that God is soul or mind. The point is that none of the terms used to refer to matters with which human beings are, through sense or thought, acquainted are terms which apply to God. Thus he writes, ". . . nor is It a Spirit, as we understand the term . . . nor is It any other thing such as we or any other being can have knowledge of. . . ." The conclusion, then, is that "It transcends all affirmation by being the perfect and unique Cause of all things, and transcends all negation by the pre-eminence of Its simple and absolute nature—free from every limitation and beyond them all."

THE CONTEMPLATIVE LIFE

Author: Julianus Pomerius (fl. c.497)
Type of work: Spiritual instruction; pastoral theology
First transcribed: c.500

Principal Ideas Advanced

The active life makes a man holy; the contemplative life makes him perfect.

Those who wish to be like Christ must walk spiritually; they must forego carnal pleasures; they must be temperate and beware of pride.

There are four principal virtues: temperance, prudence, justice, and fortitude; God, the source of all the virtues, confers these virtues on those who live by faith.

Julianus Pomerius was born in Mauretania in North Africa, but his life as a priest was spent in Gaul, at Arles, where his work included teaching and, probably, the direction of some sort of monastic community. Among his pupils was a youth who later became Bishop of Arles, Saint Caesarius (470-543). The dates of the birth and death of Julianus Pomerius are not known.

De vita contemplativa is the work for which Pomerius is now known and respected, although for centuries this charming essay of pastoral theology was attributed to Saint Prosper of Aquitaine, perhaps because the essay was written by one who confessed himself to be an admirer of the theology of Saint Augustine. In fact, the identification of *The Contemplative Life* as having come from the pen of Pomerius is not absolutely settled, although scholars generally concede that the style, the tone, and other internal evidence strongly support the claim that not Prosper but Pomerius wrote this study of the contemplative life, the active life, and the virtues. A careful discussion of this matter accompanies the graceful translation by Sister Mary Josephine Suelzer, Congregation of the Sisters of Providence, who edited *The Contemplative Life* for the *Ancient Christian Writers* series edited by Johannes Quasten, S.T.D., and Joseph C. Plumpe, Ph.D.

Julianus Pomerius addresses himself to a Bishop Julianus, perhaps the Julianus who was Bishop of Carpentras. Apparently the bishop had requested that Pomerius write on the contemplative life; it may be that Pomerius's talks on the subject, together with his reputation as a spiritual director, prompted the bishop to make the request. In any case, Pomerius mentions that the bishop has asked him to discuss the nature of the contemplative life and to explain the difference between the contemplative and the active life. Pomerius then refers to nine other questions which he has been asked to consider, and with appropriate modesty Pomerius states that he realizes that no man could ask ten such searching questions were he not already familiar with the answers. It is for the benefit of students, then, and for the discipline of Pomerius that the task of composing suitable replies has been assigned to him.

Julianus begins with the definition of the contemplative life. To contemplate God is to see him; consequently, "that life in which God can be seen is to be regarded as contemplative." But the present life is a time of trial and confusion; God will not be seen clearly until virtue is rewarded in the everlasting life which is to follow. That future life will be one of supreme happiness, for there is no greater joy to the spirit than that of contemplating God. Men are not to be discouraged, however, at the thought that in this life they cannot see God clearly, for some intimation of God's glory is possible even in this life for those who are willing to discipline themselves and turn their desire toward God.

The distinction between the contemplative life and the active life can be understood, says Pomerius, by comparing the two. "It pertains to the active life," he writes, "to advance in the midst of human affairs and to restrain the rebellious movements of the body by the rule of reason; to the contemplative, to ascend above things human by the desire of perfection and constantly to devote oneself to the increase of virtues." Both kinds of life are necessary to the exercise and training of the soul: "The active life is the journeying; the contemplative life is the summit. The former makes a man holy; the latter makes him perfect." The discussion which follows the statement of the basic distinction is one which develops a central theme: it is by the active practice of the virtues that one develops that disposition of soul whereby it becomes possible to understand others and to forgive them; by the practice of the virtues one develops the ability to discipline oneself and to free oneself from wordly desires, so that in the "blessed quiet" which follows, one can give oneself to the contemplation of God.

The bishop has asked whether those who rule within the Church can lead the contemplative life, and the answer is now apparent: if the active life is not incompatible with the contemplative but is preparatory to it, then the princes of the Church can hope to know the joys of the contemplative life. But the bishops may become so preoccupied with their wordly business that they think more of themselves and their reputations than they do of virtue and divine matters; they then run the risk of being denied the benefits of contemplation.

Pomerius cites many passages from Scripture which emphasize the importance of faith. Faith is necessary to understanding, but faith without good works is without justification: "For he who can use the choice of free will is justified neither by works without faith nor by faith alone without works." For a priest, to do good works involves correcting those who do not lead a virtuous life and making clear to those who are perplexed what the virtuous life is. This latter obligation entails resisting the temptation to impress others with the powers of oratory. It is by "holy living and preaching" that priests are active in the world, and it is by such action that they can hope to become sharers in the contemplative life.

Book One, says Pomerius, has been concerned with the contemplative life; Book Two treats of the active life.

In response to Bishop Julianus's question as to whether those who go against the divine commands are to be tolerated or reproved, Pomerius answers that there are various "disorders of the soul," and whether the sinner is to be tolerated or chastised depends upon the nature of the sin: ". . . who does not know that men sin in one way by unpremeditated thought, in another by determination; in one way by speech, in another by deed; in one way by necessity, in another of their own will?"

Pomerius discusses with some care the various kinds of spiritual faults and their remedies. He defends confession as a way of reconciling oneself with God and escaping the vice of deceit.

Several chapters, each a page or so in length, are devoted to the claim that priests should have no possessions, for the possessions of the Church are to be shared by all as common goods. Those who seek to profit from the Church or to deny the Church the goods that she needs to do her work in the world are sinners. Those who would know God must banish covetousness, but no one should confuse abstinence for the body with the whole requirement for man; "This virtue, then, which is called abstinence with regard to abstaining not merely from all dainty food but also from all evils" is especially to be sought by those who have renounced their earthly possessions and have entered upon the common life.

It was by his disregard of abstinence, Pomerius writes, that Adam lost the blessings of Paradise, but those who are able to discipline themselves in both body and soul may hope to regain the blessings which Adam lost. To know the happiness of Heaven, we must walk as Christ walked: "What is to walk as He walked except to contemn all prosperity which He despised; not to fear adversities which He bore; to do gladly what he did; to teach men to do what He commanded; to hope in what He promised; and to follow where He himself went before?"

In Book Three, Pomerius discusses the virtues and vices, and he begins by distinguishing between true virtues and their imitations. Simulated virtue is a lie; real virtue is truth. False virtue leads to death; true virtue leads to life. The pretenders to virtue are doubly guilty, for not only do they refuse to do what God demands, but they also practice deceit. Such hypocrisy is possible even for those who profess themselves to be believers, for the faithful, or those who claim to be faithful, may live according to the ways of men and not according to the way of God.

Pride, says Pomerius, is the cause of all sins. Sin is the contempt of God, and "that which prompts men to this contempt of God is pride alone." Both the Devil and Adam were ruined by pride, and all men are corrupted by it. Nevertheless, by the power of the will it is possible for men to resist pride and to seek virtue; the virtue of humility leads to the other virtues, and the virtues can combine to defeat the vices. Cupidity, envy, gluttony, lust, and other vices are all forms of pride; even when pride is hidden, it can be recognized in the acts of a man who seeks to gratify himself.

The fear of eternal punishment is useful, Pomerius claims, for fear can prompt a man to seek virtue, which alone can strengthen a man when he is called upon to defend himself at the Last Judgment.

Echoing Saint Augustine, whom Pomerius venerated and whose theology he admired, Pomerius extols charity as "the end of heaven's precepts" and "the life of virtues." Charity makes obedience possible. "Without it no one has pleased God," writes Pomerius; "with it no one has been able to sin nor will he be able."

The number four, says Pomerius, "is consecrated to perfection." There are four principal virtues: temperance, prudence, justice, and fortitude. These virtues are gifts of God, and they are given only to those who live by faith. The other virtues spring from these principal four. Temperance, fortitude, and justice are the virtues of one who seeks to perfect himself in the active life; prudence "enlightens reason" and enables reason to govern the appetites. Prudence and wisdom are one; through prudence one is able to acquire that knowledge by which the human soul is perfected. Fear, desire, sorrow, and joy, provided that they accompany virtue, are good emotions; and here Pomerius refers for support to Augustine and describes the saint as the "holy bishop Augustine, keen in mind, charming in eloquence, skilled in human learning, zealous in ecclesiastical labors, celebrated in daily disputations, self-possessed in every action, Catholic in his exposition of our faith, penetrating in the solution of problems, prudent in the refutation of heretics, and wise in explaining the canonical writings. . . ."

At the close of this book, Pomerius apologizes for what he fears is the "wretchedness" and "excessive wordiness" of the work, but he declares that he is more concerned with matters of faith than with matters of style. But if a man can be known by the life he espouses and the spirit he exhibits, Julianus Pomerius had no cause for misgivings.

DE TRINITATE

Author: Saint Anicius Manlius Severinus Boethius (480-524)
Type of work: Theology
First transcribed: Unknown

Principal Ideas Advanced

It is a matter of Christian belief that there is one God and three divine persons; by appeal to philosophy we can show that a denial of plurality of nature is compatible with the assertion of a plurality of Persons.

The category of substance, though "substance" does not mean the same thing when predicated of God and creatures, saves the unity of the divine nature.

The category of relation enables us to speak of the plurality of Persons without in any way prejudicing the unity of the divine nature.

The *De trinitate* is one of several theological treatises written by Boethius; others deal with the way in which names are predicated of the Persons of the Trinity, with the Incarnation (*De duabus naturis*), and the goodness of creatures (*De hebdomadibus*). If the *Consolation* is a philosophical effort which indicates that its author was not only well acquainted with the best of ancient philosophy but also had assimilated it to a remarkable degree, the theological treatises represent a contribution to the Scholastic manner of doing theology, a manner which relies heavily on philosophy as its instrument. That Boethius recognized he was not the first to attempt this method is clear enough, but equally significant is the request he makes of Symmachus, his father-in-law, to whom he dedicated the *De trinitate:* "You however must examine whether the seeds sown in my mind by Saint Augustine's writing have borne fruit." The great work of Augustine's which bears the same title as the present treatise of Boethius is doubtless referred to here. Saint Thomas Aquinas, in his commentary on this work of Boethius, sees the following significance in this reference to Augustine: Augustine had said that there are two ways to discuss the Trinity, either by appeal to authorities or by arguments (*rationes*); the great bishop himself employed both methods, some Fathers rely mainly on authority, but Boethius proceeds mainly by arguments.

This procedure of argument which Boethius employed is an adumbration of what we think of as the Scholastic method. One who uses this method does not hold that he can deduce from truths naturally known such revealed truths as the Trinity of Persons in the divine nature. Rather, accepting as fact that such a truth has been revealed (Scripture would be the main source culled for what has *de facto* been revealed), Boethius will appeal to philosophy and devise arguments which proportion the revealed truth to a mind steeped in philosophy or natural wisdom. "So I purposely use brevity and wrap up the ideas I draw from the profound inquiries of philosophy in new and unaccustomed words which speak only to you and to myself," Boethius writes in the preface to the *De trinitate*.

In the first chapter of the treatise, Boethius states that it is a matter of Christian belief that the Father is God, the Son is God, and the Holy Spirit is God, but from this it does not follow that there are three Gods. There is only one. Again, Boethius is not concerned to fashion arguments which will show that this has been revealed, that the Church says this is so, and that the Fathers have shown it to be so revealed. He assumes all that, and if he could not, there would simply be nothing to discuss. Attempting to understand the Trinity of Persons in the Godhead is not a problem which would occur to the philosopher, Boethius writes; it is a problem for one who firmly believes it on the authority of God, and if he has a philosophically trained mind his meditation on what he believes can take the form of bringing natural truths into conformity with faith. In reasoning about this revealed truth, Boethius writes, he is not out to show that we can see that there must be three Persons in God; that is the starting point, not the conclusion. Consequently, the arguments Boethius formulates will not provide a basis for assent to the doctrine of the Trinity. He concludes the treatise by saying, "If with God's help I have furnished some support in argument to an article which stands by itself on the firm foundation of faith, I shall render joyous praise for the finished work to Him from whom the invitation comes. But if human nature has failed to reach beyond its limits, whatever is lost through my infirmity must be made good by my intention." Obviously, such an effort, if unavoidable since faith is given to a rational creature, is paradoxical in its results. One cannot deduce the Trinity from naturally known truths; the employment of philosophical arguments to approximate to an understanding of the Trinity can never end by making faith superfluous. Yet this effort must be made. "If I am right and speak in accordance with the faith, I pray you confirm me," Boethius writes in another treatise; "But if you are in any point of another opinion, examine carefully what I have said and if possible join faith and reason: *et fidem si poterit rationemque coniunge.*"

The arguments which Boethius brings to bear on Christian belief in the Trinity have, as we shall see, a distinctively Aristotelian cast. Thus, in the first chapter, when Boethius sets out to explain why Catholics say the union of three Persons in the Trinity consists of an absence of difference, he goes on to a give a philosophical explanation of three kinds of difference, an explanation which is based on Aristotle, although its intermediate source is doubtless the *Isagoge* or *Introduction to the Categories* of Aristotle which was written by the Neoplatonist, Porphyry, an introduction which Boethius translated into Latin and on which he wrote two commentaries. Boethius wants to deny that there is a difference *as God* between God the Father, God the Son, and God the Holy Spirit; but difference as we use the term comes about in three ways, and he wants to show that none of these senses of "different" can be applied to God. Things are *generically* different, *specifically* different, or *numerically* different and, since difference is a correlative of sameness, Boethius spells out what "sameness" means. Things may be *generically* the same; for example, man and horse share the common form of animality; things may be *specifically* the same; for example Cato and Cicero share the common form of humanity; finally, we have *numerical* sameness when the same thing is called by different names; for example, Tully and Cicero. Two things are numerically different because of their accidents. Here the first chapter ends, and Boethius now digresses before applying these considerations to the Trinity.

In Chapter 2, Boethius gives the Aristotelian division of theoretical philosophy into physics, mathematics, and theology. What Boethius says here had a great influence on later thinkers to whom the writings of Aristotle were largely unknown and for whom Boethius' remarks could not function as a shorthand statement of something quite familiar to a student of Aristotle. For our immediate purposes, it is sufficient to note that the mark of the objects of theology is that they are free from matter and motion, and we must avoid appeal to the imagination in speaking of them. Generally speaking, things owe their being to form, and material things are compounds of form and matter. Something which is not simply form is not its own essence, but that which is form alone is identical with its essence. Now God is pure form and is His own essence. Boethius goes on to argue that if forms like humanity have accidents attached to them, this is due to the subject or substratum of the form. For example, we say "Man is white," but it is not humanity that is white; if this accident is attached to humanity, it is because of the subject of the form. Now, if God is pure form and is His own essence, there will be no substratum for the divine form and, consequently, no accidents will attach to God. But numerical difference has been explained in terms of accidents. Therefore, there can be no numerical difference in God.

God is complete unity, then, because no difference or plurality of the admitted kinds can be applied to Him. And yet, as Boethius is quick to point out in Chapter 3, we say the Father is God, the Son is God, and the Holy Spirit is God, and we have used the term "God" three times; but since three is a number, numerical difference seems to be involved in speaking of the God whose nature does not allow of numerical diversity. In replying to this difficulty, Boethius distinguishes two kinds of number. There is, on the one hand, the number with which we count and, on the other, the number in things. The difference between these two kinds of numbers is discussed by alternately using abstract and concrete terms; for example, "unity" and "one": a thing is one, and unity is that whereby the oneness of the thing is denoted. So, too, with "duality" and "two." But in speaking of the same thing, we may say one coat, one garment, one vestment, and the verbal repetition does not multiply the thing being discussed. In somewhat the same way, when we say the Father is God, the Son is God, and the Holy Spirit is God, we use the term "God" three times, but this need not be taken to mean that we are enumerating three Gods.

Having shown that the Father, Son, and Holy Spirit must be the same God because none of the species of difference available can be true of God, Boethius goes on to say that, nevertheless, the Father is not the Son, nor is the Son the Father, nor is either the Holy Spirit. Thus, the oneness of the divine nature is not taken by Christians to exclude the difference of Persons, and where there is difference there is number. But thus far the only source of numerical difference has been the substratum, and there is no substratum of the divine form. Boethius notices that this is something he must discuss but first, in Chapter 4, he wants to examine how particular predicates are applied to God.

Boethius invokes the Aristotelian

doctrine of categories and asserts that there are ten categories which can be universally predicated of things: substance, quantity, quality, relation, place, time, condition, situation, activity, and passivity. As predicated certain of these (substance, quantity, quality) are substantial predicates; the rest belong to the class of accidental predicates. Speaking quite generally, Boethius denies that these terms can mean the same thing when predicated of God as they do when predicated of creatures. "God" predicated of God seems to denote a substance, but Boethius suggests that we think of it as a supersubstantial predicate. When we say of God that He is just or great, such predicates, since they are not meant to assert a composition of the divine substance and an attribute, must be looked upon, respectively, as supersubstantial quality and quantity. In short, God is justice and He is greatness. In the remainder of the chapter, Boethius goes through the rest of the categories, and the upshot of his discussion is the denial that any of them has application to God. His conclusion is that the only category which is applicable to God is substance, although He is not therefore a subject; that is, the term "substance" as applied to God will not mean the same thing it does when it is applied to a creature.

The category of relation was conspicuously absent from Boethius' examination of the categories in their applicability to God. In Chapter 6, Boethius turns to relation, and he remarks that the whole of the previous discussion was leading up to this. The thing about relative terms is that they are quite adventitious and do not alter the substance to which they are applied. For example, if a man is called a master, this is because of his relation to a slave; and if the slave dies or runs away, the man ceases to be a master, but this does not alter his substance in any way. From this Boethius wants to conclude that the category of relation does not increase, decrease, or in any way alter the substance to which it is applied. Boethius is not in a position to say that if "Father," "Son," and "Holy Spirit" are predicates of relation, they will not introduce any difference into the divine nature itself, although they indicate a difference of Persons in that nature.

Boethius brings his discussion to a close in the sixth and final chapter of his treatise, and he summarizes his results. It is the category of substance that preserves the unity of the divine nature; it is the category of relation which brings about the Trinity. There are some things predicated of the divine nature and some things which are predicated of the persons taken singly, but these latter will always be relative.

It is perfectly clear, when we read the *De trinitate,* that Boethius' method is as we described it earlier; that is, what is assumed as given, as a matter of simple belief, is the truth that there is one God and three divine Persons. In his treatise, Boethius appeals to philosophy, and principally that of Aristotle, to elucidate the content of that belief. Thus he shows that the divine nature is such that it does not permit any diversity, because if we look to the kinds of difference which have been distinguished by philosophers, it is clear that none of them is applicable to God. And yet we believe that there is a plurality of Persons. Boethius thereupon recalls the doctrine of categories and finds in the category of relation an explanation of the diversity of Persons which does not prejudice the unity of the divine nature. Is the effect of this a proof that there is one divine nature and three divine Persons? Not at all. That article of belief remains an assumption accepted on divine faith; it is simply a datum of faith. But the truths of faith are accepted by men; and since men are rational, they must meditate on what they believe. If a man is trained in natural wisdom, philosophy, he will employ the meanings of the terms in question which have been explored by philosophers and try to elucidate the content of his faith. That such an attempt must always fall short of comprehension of its object is the concluding point of the *De trinitate.*

Something must be said, by way of conclusion, of Boethius' use of Aristotle. The Aristotelian division of philosophy into theoretical and practical is accepted by Boethius and mentioned in the *Consolation,* his first commentary on Porphyry, and elsewhere; moreover, the division of theoretical philosophy sketched in the second chapter of the *De trinitate* is unequivocally Aristotelian. The criteria or principles of the division are matter and motion, and insofar as objects involve formally different relations to matter and motion they constitute diverse sciences. Thus, the objects of physics are forms in matter and such compounds are subject to motion; the objects of mathematics are forms considered apart from matter and motion although they do not so exist; the objects of theology are objects, forms, which exist apart from matter and motion. There are many difficulties to this doctrine, but it is substantially that of Aristotle. Elsewhere, namely, in his first commentary on Porphyry's *Isagoge,* Boethius speaks of the various theoretical sciences as concerned respectively with naturals, intelligibles, and intellectibles; and these are treated as three groups of existents. God and soul are intellectibles; intelligibles are spoken of as intellectibles which drift into matter, and soul is again mentioned; naturals are bodies. What emerges are two contrasting ways of speaking of theoretical sciences, and the second strikes one as being more Neoplatonic than Aristotelian. This raises the much discussed question of Boethius' personal preference as between Plato and Aristotle. The *De trinitate* gives the impression that Boethius is fundamentally Aristotelian. And yet, on the major question dividing Plato and Aristotle, that of the ontological status of universals, Boethius will give, in commenting on Porphyry, what he calls an Aristotelian version of universals, but he adds that he is doing so because this seems fitting in dealing with a text which is an introduction to Aristotle. The way in which he puts this suggests to many scholars that Boethius himself preferred the Platonic philosophy, and there is indeed much Platonism in the *Consolation.* Perhaps the question could only have been answered by Boethius himself in his projected reconciliation of Plato and Aristotle. What must be said, nevertheless, is that in his writings Boethius gives sometimes an Aristotelian emphasis and sometimes a Platonic one, and it is difficult to know how finally Boethius saw the compatibility of what are, as they stand, conflicting views. With respect to the *De trinitate* and the kind of theology it represents, the important point is not which philosopher Boethius preferred, but the fact that he stresses the necessity of appealing to philosophy in order to achieve the elucidation of religious truths.

Boethius' actual contribution to the theology of the Trinity is perhaps less important than the philosophy he passed on to subsequent thinkers in developing his theology. Through his translations as well as through such works as the *De trinitate,* Boethius was, until the latter part of the twelfth century, one of the main conduits whereby ancient philosophy came down to Scholastic thinkers. Thus, even apart from his intellectual contributions, which were considerable, Boethius has historical importance as a bridge between the wisdom of the pagans and the faith of the Middle Ages.

R.M.

THE CONSOLATION OF PHILOSOPHY

Author: Saint Anicius Manlius Severinus Boethius (480-524)
Type of work: Spiritual instruction
First transcribed: 524

Principal Ideas Advanced

When we ask why the wicked prosper while the innocent suffer, we must realize that just as good luck is not happiness, so bad luck is not unhappiness.

True happiness is found not in terrestrial things but by striving for God, the sovereign good.

All things work together for good, and neither the existence of evil nor chance nor free will pose real problems for the doctrine of divine providence.

In sum, a correct view as to the nature of man, of human happiness, and the order of the universe will console us in times of adversity.

Boethius wrote *The Consolation of Philosophy* while awaiting execution for a crime of which, he assures us, he was innocent. The life that was drawing to this melancholy close was lived in a time when much that was known and familiar was ending and the nature of what was to come was at best obscure and did not seem especially promising. For Boethius lived on the threshold of the Dark Ages and his life might seem to write finis to the slow decline of the empire of the West. There is nothing imaginative or strained in linking Boethius with the larger facts of political history, for his public life was that of a statesman and he was a member of a Roman family that had been in the councils of emperors before. His father had been a consul and two sons of Boethius held the same office. He himself was a consul under Theodoric the Ostrogoth, and the eminence he attained seemed only to provide him with a height from which to fall. Theodoric was a Christian but an Arian, and ultimately Boethius was accused by Theodoric of conspiring with Justin, the emperor of the East, who, like Boethius, was

Catholic and opposed to the Arian heresy. Boethius protested his innocence but was cast into prison without benefit of trial and was executed in 524.

As we shall see, *The Consolation of Philosophy* is directly concerned with the meaning of Boethius' situation after he has been thrown into prison. He brought to his meditation on his undeserved misfortune a mind that had long been nurtured on philosophy and theology. One of the amazing things about Boethius is that, despite his quite active public career, his private life was devoted to study to such a degree that he had set himself the task of translating into Latin the complete works of Plato and Aristotle, after which he intended to show the ultimate compatibility of the two philosophies. His forty-four years of life were not sufficient for the accomplishment of this task, of course, but he did begin his momentous task, and we have from his pen a number of translations of works of Aristotle, works which he also commented on, sometimes more than once. His Aristotelian translations are all of logical works, and he is also credited with a number of independent works on logical subjects. Besides the *Consolation,* Boethius also wrote a number of theological treatises, one of which, the *De trinitate,* is discussed in the present work. If Boethius' public life appears to be one lived at the termination of a political period, his private life, his intellectual efforts, point into the future. This contrast is doubtless the intent of the famous description of Boethius as the last of the Romans and the first of the Scholastics.

As the foregoing indicates, in *The Consolation of Philosophy* Boethius meditates on the misfortune which has befallen him and tries to discover its meaning. What he is after is a truth which will console him and enable him to accept an undeserved fate; it is in philosophy that he seeks this truth. This reliance on philosophy is something which has seldom failed to puzzle readers and their reaction is succinctly expressed in Johnson's remark, quoted by Boswell, "Speaking of Boethius, who was the favorite writer of the Middle Ages, he said it was very surprising, that upon such a subject, and in such a situation, he should be *magis philosophus quam Christinus.*" Surprising indeed, for where better than in the example of Christ could one find a model of innocence oppressed? Some critics have thought to find hidden Scriptural references in the *Consolation,* but others have been so struck by the absence of Christian categories in this work of Boethius that they have argued that he was not a Catholic and could not have been the author of the theological treatises attributed to him. However, we have the word of Cassiodorus Senator, a contemporary of Boethius, that Boethius did indeed write those theological works. And no one doubts he is the author of the *Consolation.* The puzzle remains, consequently, but from it we can conclude something of no small importance. However difficult it is to understand why Boethius in the difficult straits he found himself did not avail himself of the consolation of Christianity, the fact that he could then compose a book so purely philosophical in character (that is, independent in its arguments of truths known by faith) is a dramatic proof that he recognized a distinction between philosophy and faith, philosophy and theology. Although he was a Catholic, in the *Consolation* Boethius attempts to show that truths available to pagan and Christian alike can make evil and misfortune tolerable; in any case, the ultimate source of reassurance for man is acknowledged to be God.

The Consolation of Philosophy is divided into five books, in each of which a prose section alternates with a verse section. This literary form, we are told, has a history that can be traced back through Martianus Capella (who composed a work on the liberal arts in this form), to Varro, and on to a Greek origin in the Menippean satire. Quite apart from its content, on which we shall concentrate, the *Consolation* enjoyed an almost unparalleled fame during the Middle Ages as a work of art. The meters of its verse are varied and the result highly esteemed; the style of its prose passages is a thing of beauty. One is reminded of the *Apology* of Plato—but with this overwhelming difference: Socrates did not compose that immortal dialogue before death; Plato did, and in retrospect. The *Consolation,* on the other hand, was composed by the victim in his cell. This increases the enigma of Boethius. That a man, particularly a man of Boethius' talent and background, should have the thoughts expressed in the *Consolation* is understandable enough; that he might write them down does not unduly strain the imagination, but that he should rise to the literary heights of the *Consolation* in doing so is undoubtedly a great demand on our credulity. Yet the facts seemingly permit no grounded skepticism.

The overriding question of the *Consolation* is simply this: What is the rational explanation of the fact that the innocent suffer while the wicked not only go unpunished but prosper? Can there be any rational explanation of this unreasonable state of affairs, an explanation which will reveal that it is not after all unreasonable but tolerable? Book One opens with a poem in which Boethius laments his situation. Having unburdened himself of his plaint, he goes on, in the prose section, to describe the entry into his cell of a majestic woman, her eyes flashing, her manner assured and authoritative. She is, it developes, Dame Philosophy, and she chides Boethius for seeking solace in the poetic muses who will only increase his sorrow and self-pity. It is time not for feeding his sorrow, but for seeking its remedy; and where else, she asks, will this be found but in philosophy? Dame Philosophy reminds Boethius that he should know this, since he has spent time under her tutelage, and his spirits begin to lift ever so slightly. Philosophy will not abandon him in his hour of need, nor is she surpised at what has befallen him, since she has witnessed it many times before. She mentions the exile of Anaxagoras, the hemlock given Socrates, the torturing of Zeno, and many other instances where devotees of philosophy have been, though innocent, accused. Boethius cannot refrain from cataloguing his contributions to the public weal, and he asks Dame Philosophy why it is that the sovereign harmony which is apparent in the cosmos is so sadly absent from the affairs of men. Dame Philosophy is distressed to find that Boethius is overcome by grief, and she offers to lead him gradually back to sanity and a true view, moving from rhetorical persuasions to stronger, more solid arguments.

Before she can begin her therapy, Dame Philosophy poses a few questions which will enable her to determine Boethius' exact state of soul. She asks him if he would say that the world is merely the arena of chance and caprice or that it is ordered and directed. Boethius replies that he cannot bring himself to believe that the world depends on blind chance; he holds it to be the handiwork of God, who also directs and governs it. This salutary judgment of Boethius gives Dame Philosophy a starting point, but she goes on to observe that it appears to her that Boethius has allowed his passions to obscure his mind and prevent his seeing the true goal and end of nature. Of man Boethius can only say that he is rational and mortal and Dame Philosophy finds this knowledge so minimal that Boethius' despair is comprehensible. If he has so far forgotten his own nature, she tells him, it is little wonder that he weeps.

Book Two concerns itself with an examination of fortune or luck. This topic is introduced when Boethius describes his present plight as a misfortune and professes surprise at what has befallen him. But, says Dame Philosophy, fortune is by nature capricious, both in the way in which it elevates and the way in which it depresses. The goods of fortune are not things attained by man; they simply come his way. Boethius' difficulty is that he does not see that his prior state, when he was the recipient of good fortune, was just as irrational as his present unfortunate condition. Since he lived in a time of great unrest, Boethius should have been impressed by the inconstancy of luck and learned thereby to seek happiness within, in an arena where his own efforts can play a role. To be honored by others, Dame Philosophy points out, is not constitutive of true happiness; Boethius, who had the good fortune to be so honored, was misled into believing that his happiness was bound up with honors. Fortune, good or bad, is something capricious and beyond man's control, and if good fortune cannot bring true happiness, neither can misfortune destroy it. Fortune is consistently inconsistent, and misfortune is ethically more useful than good fortune, for it forces a man to ask where true happiness lies.

A more affirmative task is undertaken in Book Three, but the note struck in the second book recurs again and again. Happiness cannot be a matter of riches or honor or worldly power. Nor can carnal pleasures of whatever sort make a man happy. The true good, that in which human happiness lies, cannot be found in terrestrial things. When we consider the marks of the good, Dame Philosophy says, we discover that they must all be found in one substance and that this substance must exist outside the material world. God is the sovereign good and He is also true human happiness. All beings aspire to rejoin their source and since all things have the same source, God is the universal or common end of everything in the universe. God is the governor of the world, and Boethius is urged to turn his eyes from earth to Heaven if he would find consolation in this darkest hour.

But this sunny view develops clouds as the Fourth Book commences. The idea of a benevolent God as the source of the universe, who continues to direct each thing in it, seems to be contradicted by the existence of evil. Dame Philosophy must be able to solve the problem of evil or the foregoing is as naught, and thus she bends her best efforts to the task. The view that God is a benign governor of the universe implies that the good are rewarded and the evil punished. Obviously, to suppose that this is indeed the case would require a manner of viewing things which would assess the apparent prosperity of the wicked as only apparent and the apparent suffering of the virtuous as something less than unhappiness. Dame Philosophy urges Boethius to the heights where he may gain the proper perspective. Boethius is dubious but willing. Dame Philosophy observes that if it can be shown that it is the virtuous who are potent, it must follow that the bad are weak. Now he is powerful who can attain the end he seeks, she argues, but the end sought by all men is happiness. But who can attain this good if not the virtuous, and who fails to attain it if not the vicious? Thus, it is good men who achieve the object of their desires and evil men who fail to achieve it. The change of perspective here follows on the judgments made in the second and third books. The claim that happiness cannot consist of honor, fame, riches, and bodily pleasures must be stringently applied and one must see that though wicked men may enjoy any or all of these things, they are not thereby happy. Since happiness is what evil men seek, in being committed to pseudo-goods, they are powerless to attain that which they truly seek. (One hears the echo of Plato here.) What we must realize, says Dame Philosophy, is that the wicked are not and cannot be happy. How silly then to envy them! What they require is our pity.

Boethius is able to acquiesce to these conclusions, and Dame Philosophy is heartened to discover that his sanity is returning. What Boethius must come to see is that whatever happens does so because God wills it, and consequently one realizes that everything is ultimately ordered to the good. Both good and bad fortune have edifying roles. From this it follows that, in a profound sense, there is no bad fortune for the virtuous and that even good fortune is not in itself truly good.

The final book of *The Consolation of Philosophy* takes up the question of the compatibility of providence and human free will. If God directs all things, if His providence encompasses every occurrence in the universe, it must encompass the acts of men as well. But human acts seem to have their source within man. Thus, it seems that we must say either that free human acts escape the providence of God or that being included, they are not really free. Dame Philosophy attempts to show the compatibility of providence and free will by beginning with the case of chance events. Aristotle's definition of the chance event is accepted as adequate. Aristotle taught that when a determined cause, which is such because of its relation to a determined effect, also brings about an unintended result, that result is said to be a chance result; and if the event is referred to the cause, the cause is not a determinate explanation of the event. If I dig for water and strike oil, the discovery of oil is the result of my digging for water, but since the discovery of oil is unintended, it is a chance event. Such an event is indeed accidental to my intention and unforeseen by me, but this does not prevent its being foreseen and intended by God. In somewhat the same way, Dame Philosophy suggests, we can find a compatibility between our undeniable certainty that we are free agents and the fact that our free acts come within the scope of providence.

The Consolation of Philosophy has now reached its conclusion. Boethius has altered considerably from our first view of him. At the outset, he was a sobbing, complaining, broken man, who was convinced that everything had turned against him, that the world, from being a fairly reasonable whole, had turned into an incomprehensibly absurd place. Dame Philosophy has led him gradually away from the view that external events, what other men can confer, can constitute happiness. Good luck is as absurd, finally, as bad luck. Happiness is not thrust upon us; it is something we must earn, and we can earn it only when we have a clear view of what it is. It is something beyond this world, and it is precisely this world which leads us to see that. A reversal of fortune can be a stroke of good luck if it leads us to reassess the nature of luck, if it prompts us to reflect that the world is a whole whose order demands a Governor. Contemplating that governance, our sense of values changes. The wicked are not happy; the unlucky virtuous man is not thereby less virtuous, less truly happy. Although we cannot comprehend this truth in all its amplitude, we know that in this world all things work together for good. But we can see this only if our aspirations are not terrestrial. Boethius is consoled when he has relearned the truth that human values are not the values of the universe, that reality is not measured by our wishes but that we must desire real values.

It is said that, in the Middle Ages, the fame of *The Consolation of Philosophy* was second only to that of Scripture, and we may be sure that this fame did not repose solely on the undeniable literary merit of Boethius' work. Surely it is not an exaggeration to say that the *Consolation* is a wonderful summary of the Greek view that philosophy is a way of life and that moral practice must be grounded in philosophical theory and in metaphysical commitment; moreover, the fact that its author was a Christian led him to foreshadow the medieval conviction that there is a natural or philosophical base for the Christian faith. *The Consolation of Philosophy* is a veritable monument of Western literature, and just as one who has not read it is to that degree culturally deprived, so no one can read it without profit.

R.M.

THE RULE OF SAINT BENEDICT

Author: Saint Benedict (c.480-c.547)
Type of work: Monastic rule
First transcribed: c.530

Principal Ideas Advanced

Monastery brethren should be humble; they should follow the Rule *and submit themselves to the considered judgment of the abbot, who is the father of the community.*

Reverence in prayer is essential; God must be addressed in purity of heart and humility.

Moderation, not excessive abstinence, should be the general ascetic practice.

The brothers should be obedient to their superiors.

The brothers ought to be occupied in manual labor and in sacred reading, as well as in meditation and worship.

Saint Benedict was born in Nursia (or Norsia, a Sabine town). His unhappy experience with the schools of Rome and with the decadence of the city led him to seek seclusion in Enfide and then in Subiaco, where he lived as a hermit in a cave. His reputation for holiness and spiritual self-discipline impressed even the rude mountain folk and they came to him for counsel.

Benedict became the superior of a monastery at Vicovars, but he was still unpracticed in the art of building and maintaining a monastic community, and his mode of discipline was such that the monks attempted to poison him. He was forced to leave Vicovars and return to Subiaco. His experience with monastic life increased as he founded a series of monastic cells, each with thirteen monks. Finally, in or about the year 530, he went to Monte Cassino, where he gradually evolved a monastery by the application of principles which have influenced Western monasticism for centuries.

Saint Benedict's *Rule,* composed shortly after his arrival at Monte Cassino, was the product of his long and humbling experiences with the monasteries at Vicovars and Subiaco. The most distinctive features of the *Rule* are its emphasis on moderation in ascetic practices (as contrasted to the extreme austerity of the Eastern religious communities), its insistence on humility and obedience, and its call for a combination of spiritual and physical effort. Benedict's *Rule* is one of the basic four religious Rules, the others being the Rule of Saint Basil, the Rule of Saint Augustine, and the Rule of Saint Francis.

Realizing that just as the spiritual community which is the Church derives its inspiration and unity from God, the Father, Saint Benedict was careful, in his *Rule,* to make explicit the qualities which the abbot of the monastery must possess if his community is to prosper spiritually. Thus, Benedict wrote, "An abbot who is worthy to rule a monastery should always remember what he is called and realize in his actions the name of a superior. For he is believed to be representative of Christ in the monastery, and for that reason is called by a name of his, according to the words of the Apostle: 'Ye have received the spirit of the adoption of sons, whereby we cry Abba, Father.'" Benedict reminds the abbot that at the Judgment "there will be an examination of . . . these matters," and the saint declares that the abbot himself "should do everything in the fear of the Lord and in observance of the Rule. . . ."

In instructing the abbot, Saint Benedict stressed precisely the same point which, in his directions to the brothers, he made paramount; namely, that it is by deeds rather than by words, although words are important, that a man will be measured and judged. Thus, concerning the abbot, Benedict says, "To intelligent disciples let him expound the Lord's commandments in words; but to those of harder hearts and ruder minds let him show forth the divine precepts by his example."

The abbot is not to love some more than others, except to the degree that love is compelled by the obedience and good works of some of the members of the monastic community.

Obedience to God and to one's superiors, obedience to the *Rule,* the performance of good works and useful labor, and the constant exercise of humility: these are the requirements which Saint Benedict puts upon abbot and brother alike.

Benedict was aware of the difficulty of governing men, especially when that government was to be directed by spiritual concern and to spiritual ends. Thus, the principles of teaching and counseling are explicitly spelled out, and in his clarification of such matters Benedict himself exhibits the art of gentle persuasion, regulated by divine order and modified by compassion and respect for one's fellowman. According to Benedict, then, "the abbot in his teaching ought always to observe the rule of the Apostle, wherein he says; 'Reprove, persuade, rebuke.' He must adapt himself to circumstances, now using severity and now persuasion, displaying the rigor of a master or the loving-kindness of a father." But the abbot is to be no sentimentalist: those who are disobedient are to be punished. In fact, the saint outlines the circumstances under which admonishment, corporal punishment, or excommunication would be appropriate.

In writing of the appointing of an abbot, Benedict endorses the principle that the superior be chosen as "with one heart" by those who, after careful consideration and with the fear of God to humble them, have the responsibility for selection. The sole criterion of selection is to be the "merit of life and learnedness in wisdom" of the prospective abbot; considerations of rank or birth status are to be dismissed as irrelevant.

The abbot must regard himself as one chosen to help, rather than to command, the community; he must know the divine law; he must put mercy before quick judgment; he must be moderate in his demands; he must not be troubled, anxious, or obstinate.

But the abbot does not bear the entire weight of responsibility for the spiritual well-being of the monastery; the brothers have duties—to God, to the abbot, and to one another—which Saint Benedict describes with care and understanding. In the first place, no one is to gain easy admission to the monastic community; each applicant must undergo the trials of repeated application and periods of testing as a guest and novice. An elder brother is appointed to observe the behavior and attitude of the candidate. If the rigorous demands placed upon him do not dismay him and weaken his spirit of perseverance, if the "insults" of the brothers do not cause him to lose heart, if he attends to the *Rule* and shows every evidence of obeying it with humility and joy, if he understands the purpose of the community to be that of seeking to perfect oneself for the moment of coming into the presence of God—then, after months of trial, if he vows to God in the presence of all the brothers that he will be faithful and steadfast, he may be received into the congregation.

Benedict declares that just as one

customarily addresses men of high position by adopting an attitude of humility, so one should, in praying to God, who is Lord of all men, approach Him with humility, reverence, and purity of heart.

The saint does not neglect specific details of community life. He suggests that the brothers sleep in one room, if that be possible; or, if there are too many for that arrangement, that seniors be placed in charge of groups of ten to twenty brothers. They should sleep clothed, "but without knives . . . lest they injure themselves in sleep," and they should rise quickly, but with modesty, when the time comes: "And when they rise for the service of God let them gently encourage one another, because the sleepy ones are apt to make excuses."

Benedict maintains that the monks should have no personal property whatsoever: "neither a book, nor tablets, nor a pen—nothing at all." All property should be common, for "it is not allowed to the monks to have bodies or wills in their own power." In distributing necessaries, however, the need of each is to be taken into account.

According to Saint Benedict, who knew from experience the importance of exercising the whole man, "Idleness is enemy of the soul. And therefore, at fixed times, the brothers ought to be occupied in manual labor; and again, at fixed times, in sacred reading." The saint goes on to outline the day, assigning certain periods to labor, others to reading, rest, meditation, and prayer. He writes that those who work away from the monastery should observe the hours as he has outlined them.

Benedict's *Rule,* which acknowledges the contribution to monastic discipline made by Saint Basil's Rule, is a document which both practically and spiritually testifies to the common sense and religious dedication of its saintly author, and it is no wonder that this remarkable prescription for the monastic life brought about a refreshing and inspiring change in the monasteries, thereby justifying those who over the centuries have maintained that the communal life is an important part of the living Church.

PASTORAL CARE

Author: Saint Gregory the Great (c.540-604)
Type of work: Pastoral theology
First transcribed: 591

Principal Ideas Advanced

The difficulties and responsibilities of pastoral care will lead a prudent man to shun the episcopal state; nevertheless, a qualified man must in conscience accept the burden of office when he is legitimately called to it.

It is a pastor's serious responsibility to live in such a way that he is both an inspiration and model for his flock.

Because men differ widely in temperament, training, and social position, in the care of souls the pastor must study individual differences and treat people accordingly.

When Saint Gregory was acclaimed successor of Pope Pelagius II by the clergy and people of Rome in 590, he tried to decline the office because he was conscious of its responsibilities and his own unworthiness. In replying to the Archbishop of Ravenna, who chided Gregory for his attitude, the new pope published the *Liber regulae pastoralis* as an explanation of his reluctance to accept the burden of the papacy. The work describes the responsibilities and difficulties of the priesthood and, more particularly, of the episcopal state.

The book is divided into four parts. The first describes the type of man who should be made a spiritual ruler; the second part gives directions for the bishop's conduct. In the third section, Saint Gregory gives methods for dealing with persons of different characters and social positions. The last section is a brief exhortation to the pastor to be on his guard to live in accordance with the dignity of his office.

Though Saint Gregory used the occasion of his elevation to the papacy to put the *Pastoral Care* in its final form, he had probably been working on it long in advance. Gregory had been a monk, and he was acquainted with Saint Benedict's *Rule*. The title Gregory gave his own work, *Liber regulae pastoralis,* suggests that the new pope conceived of his book as a rule for secular clergy which would be a counterpart of the much admired rule of Saint Benedict.

The *Pastoral Care* enjoyed a widespread popularity from the beginning, enhanced as it was by the prestige of its author. Saint Gregory himself sent copies to the Archbishop of Seville, to Saint Columban, and to other bishops. Saint Augustine of Canterbury carried the work to England. The Emperor Maurice (582-602) had it translated into Greek. Alcuin, head of Charlemagne's palace school, wrote to the Archbishop of York in 796, "Wherever you go, let the pastoral book of Saint Gregory be your companion. Read and re-read it often, that in it you may learn to know yourself and your work, that you may have before your eyes how you ought to live and teach." It became customary for bishops to receive a copy of the *Pastoral Care* at the time of their consecration. In the ninth century, King Alfred the Great had the *Pastoral Care* translated into Saxon, and he used the work as a means of reform of the Church. Thus the book became one of considerable formative influence in Christian history. Frederick Homes Dudden, an authority on the life and works of Saint Gregory, says, "The maxims of Gregory have moulded the Church. . . . The ideal which Gregory upheld was for centuries the ideal of the clergy of the West, and through them the spirit of the great Pope governed the Church, long after his body had been laid to rest beneath the pavement of Saint Peter's."

Holding that "the government of souls is the art of arts," Gregory insists that only men of tried virtue are fitted to rule others. Because of the prestige attached to spiritual office and the power of pastors to influence the ideals and actions of others, the burden of government should be dreaded by the prudent man.

"No one does more harm in the Church than he, who having the title or rank of holiness, acts evilly," Gregory writes. The author is suspicious of the man who actively seeks a position of authority. This was not the way of Christ, who refused the glory of earthly kingship and chose the ignominy of public disgrace. "It is common experience," notes Gregory, "that in the school of adversity the heart is forced to discipline itself; but when a man has achieved supreme rule, it is at once changed and puffed up by the experience of his high estate." Of itself, government of others poses dangers, because it forces a man to divide his interest among many things, until he finds to his confusion that he is doing nothing well. A similar snare into which the unwary pastor may fall is engaging in pointless activity, "when there are abundant resources at hand, and things can be done which subjects admire just because they are done."

Despite these dangers, the man who has the qualifications for pastoral rule is obliged to accept the responsibility of office when he is called to it legitimately. The office is for the community, not for the office holder. Recalling Christ's injunction to Saint Peter to feed His sheep, Gregory says that the qualified man who refuses to feed Christ's flock has no true love for the Supreme Shepherd.

Formerly, men could more safely aspire to the bishopric, since the bishop ran a far greater risk of martyrdom than the rank and file Christian. Gregory warns that in his own day there is great danger that a man may deceive himself and, while professing to be disinterested, actually find his greatest satisfaction in lording it over others.

In the second part of the work, in which Saint Gregory outlines a rule of conduct for the pastor, he attempts the difficult task of showing how to harmonize the life of contemplation with that of the ministry. He describes those whose pleasure is in being too busy and who "regard it laborious not to be labouring in earthly concerns." The pastor owes it to his flock to keep his life serenely centered on things eternal, "for when earthly cares occupy the pastor's mind, dust, driven by the winds of temptation, blinds the eyes of the Church." The first means to attain this goal of a harmonious active and contemplative life is purity of thought, by which Saint Gregory means a habit of mind which instinctively rejects whatever is either evil or irrelevant.

The art of effective preaching must be assiduously developed by the pastor. Gregory warns him to avoid a "slovenly manner," observing that the force of the message is lost if the audience is offended by a careless presentation. The preacher also errs if he fails to take notice of the practical needs of his hearers. Gregory has a high esteem for preaching, as well he might, living at a time when religious knowledge depended almost entirely on oral transmission. Preachers, he says, beget thought in their hearers' minds, and the subsequent development of that thought is dependent on the nature of the seed planted by the speaker of the Word.

Gregory wants pastors to excel in compassion for the sufferings and weaknesses of their flocks, thereby making themselves so approachable that their subjects will be willing to reveal their hidden secrets to them. The good should find in the pastor a comrade, but the evil should fear his stern correction. The pastor must steer a middle course between a too-rigid discipline and excessive indulgence.

In the third section of the *Liber regulae pastoralis,* which gives directives for dealing with nearly forty different classes of people, Gregory shows himself to be a keen practical psychologist. The forty classes of people are paired off in opposites: men and women, young and old, poor and rich, hale and sick, slothful and hasty, and so on down the list. The first principle laid down is that adjustment must be made to individual differences. "Gentle hissing that calms horses, excites young puppies," observes Gregory.

Attitudes and behavior patterns which became dominant in medieval culture can be detected in this section of the work in which Saint Gregory describes how different groups should be treated. For example, subordinates are to be taught to obey an unvirtuous superior, because obedience to authority is divinely ordained. Not only must the subject obey, but he is to guard carefully against judging a superior rashly.

Among the principles which guide Saint Gregory's advice is that of the social responsibility of human behavior. For Gregory, the moral quality of human actions is greatly conditioned by their effect on one's neighbors. Thus, the taciturn are warned that they may err seriously by default in not sharing their knowledge with the ignorant. Fasting is prescribed, but Gregory insists that it should issue in almsgiving to the poor. The wealthy are to understand clearly that they are the custodians of wealth whose real owners are the poor and needy. Almsgiving for those blessed with an abundance of material goods is presented as a strict obligation of justice, "for when we administer necessities to the needy," Gregory explains, "we give them what is their own, not what is ours; we pay a debt of justice, rather than do a work of mercy." The same principle is applied to those endowed with goods of the mind: "By withholding the word of preaching from sinning brethren, they are hiding the medicine of life from souls that are dying." Marriage and celibacy are likewise treated largely in terms of their relationship to the good of society. The person who foregoes marriage and then fails to use his freedom from the burdens of family life to serve others is condemned by Gregory for his selfishness.

Gregory's *Pastoral Care* is significant for its emphasis on the importance of interior motivation in human behavior. Though Saint Gregory was eminently practical, and his directions treat largely of external actions, he teaches clearly that it is the motive that makes actions fully human and wins for them final praise or blame.

The advice of the *Pastoral Care* is embellished with so many examples from Holy Scripture that the meaning is at times almost lost in rhetorical verbiage. To the modern reader the examples often seem farfetched, since Gregory delighted in allegorical interpretations of the Scriptures, an achievement in which he became, as in so much else, a schoolmaster of medieval Europe.

The final section of the *Liber regulae pastoralis* is a brief exhortation to the pastor to keep a careful watch over his own soul, lest he be ruined by success. Success in preaching, Gregory shrewdly observes, can easily ruin a man who may deceive himself that he practices all that he preaches. Of course, he should strive to practice what he preaches, but let him look less to what he has done than to the good he has left undone.

During the pontificate of Saint Gregory, it looked as if the Church in the West might succumb to the onslaughts of wave after wave of barbarian invasions. Many times during the feudal period, and long afterwards, Saint Gregory's picture of the ideal bishop must have seemed a hollow mockery. That the ideal was kept alive can be credited in part to Saint Gregory's *Pastoral Care.*

Sister M.E.

DIALOGUES

Author: Saint Gregory the Great (c. 540-604)
Type of work: Hagiography
First transcribed: c.593

Principal Ideas Advanced

Italy has had many saints whose miracles testify to their holy lives.

The true value of the lives of the saints was in their virtue, not in their wonderworking.

Knowledge of the lives of the saints helps make a man humble and gives him a longing for Heaven.

It has been said that the Middle Ages began the day Saint Gregory the Great was born. Certainly his *Dialogues* illustrates many cultural aspects of medieval life. The work became a source and model for medieval hagiography, a genre which included much of the popular history, theology, philosophy, poetry, and fiction of the period between the decline of Rome and the revival of learning which was well under way in the twelfth century.

The *Dialogorum libri* consist of four books of anecdotes of the lives of saints. Books One and Three are collections of short tales of Italians who were reputed to have been men and women of extraordinary virtue. Book Two is given entirely to an account of the life of Saint Benedict (c.480-c.547), who was recognized already in Saint Gregory's time as a figure of signal importance in the development of monasticism. The fourth book, intended by the author as a discussion on the immortality of the soul, is hardly more than a collection of anecdotes. These differ from the stories of Books One and Two only in being loosely related to a general theme.

In the dialogues the author presents himself in conversation with Peter the Deacon, a member of the papal household. Peter plays the role of eager investigator of the marvelous. Throughout, Gregory dominates the conversation. Besides formulating the questions which Gregory wants to answer, Peter does little more than make complimentary comments on Gregory's replies. In answer to Peter's request at the beginning of Book One, Gregory sets out to show that Italy, too, has had her wonderworkers, and that the miracles which testify to holiness have not been wanting in the Italian Church.

It was while Gregory was pope that he compiled these wonderful tales. One of his aims was to counteract the prevailing mood of pessimism in the Rome of his day. The city, along with the entire territory surrounding it, had been the victim of waves of barbarian infiltration, attack, and plunder for almost two centuries. Gregory himself, as he reveals in other of his writings, believed that almost complete destruction of Christo-Roman civilization was imminent. At the same time he understood that if civilization did survive, the future of the West lay with the barbarian peoples. It was with a view to their pastoral care that Saint Gregory realized the didactic value of such tales as he collected in the four books of the *Dialogues.* The work reveals only one facet of Gregory's life and work, and any evaluation will fall far short of a balanced picture if it fails to consider that this man who wrote four books of marvelous tales of the saints was the same realistic administrator who composed the *Pastoral Care.*

Unlike Saint Augustine's *City of God,* which attempted to vindicate the place of the Church in society, Gregory's *Dialogues* attempted to illustrate Christian living at its finest in terms that an unlettered people would understand. Saint Augustine was still writing for an educated elite; Saint Gregory had come to terms with the barbarian invasions and wrote for an audience that could learn a moral lesson from a legend but which would have been helpless in the face of the refinements of philosophical thought. That one of the most able administrators of the Church's long line of popes should have chosen anecdotes of visions, miracles, and prophecies, many of them with little or no basis in fact, is indicative of the cultural level of the sixth century. Equipped with little scientific explanation of the universe, men were ready to attribute to direct divine causality events which are now easily referred to in terms of specific secondary causes. The miracles, visions, and prophecies which became the stock in trade of European storytelling for centuries were not accepted primarily as explanations, but as illustrations. They were taken as signs of divine approval of a holy life. Modern historians recognize that the *Dialogues* are not strict records of fact. They are, however, a storehouse of information about prevailing customs, manners, and beliefs of the sixth century.

Evident throughout is the characteristic medieval love of the marvelous. Through the prayers of the holy men and women presented by Gregory for the edification of the faithful, the dead are raised to life, animals speak, broken dishes are mended, food is supplied, the weather is controlled, lamps burn without oil, and a host of other wonders great and small occur.

Saint Gregory was not content to relate marvels. He continually draws lessons from the miracles, and he emphasizes the truth that the real worth of a saint's life is found not in his miracles, but in his virtues. The former are merely testimony of a holy life.

Many of the stories preserve the simplicity characteristic of the folk tale. Typical is the story of the monk who had a tame bear which brought his sheep home at a certain time each day. When some envious monks killed the animal, its master was overcome with grief and rage. Gregory relates, "When the bear did not return at the usual hour, Florentius became suspicious. He waited till sunset, and still there was no sign of the bear. What a misfortune! In his great simplicity he called him 'brother bear.' The next day, going out to see what had happened to his sheep and shepherd, he found the bear dead. A careful inquiry soon brought to light the perpetrators of the wrong. . . . Distracted with grief, [he] pronounced a curse on the monks then and there. . . . 'I hope to God,' he exclaimed, 'that before they die they will be punished in the sight of all for killing my bear who never did them any harm.'" The sequel of this story shows the evil monks who killed "brother bear" struck with leprosy, while Florentius weeps for the rest of his life because he has fallen into the terrible sin of cursing his brother monks. Gregory draws the moral that "it may be that almighty God brought this about in order to prevent Florentius from ever again presuming to hurl the weapons of malediction in a state of anger."

In Saint Gregory's tales of diabolic activity can be found a concept of the Devil which was to prevail in European culture for centuries. The Devil is portrayed as actively engaged in plotting the ruin of men. He takes possession of bodies and souls, and his apparitions are frequent. Sometimes he appears in terrifying forms. Saint Benedict is reported to have described him as enveloped in fire, with flames darting from his eyes and mouth. At other times the Devil is a mischievous creature who plays harmless tricks to try the patience of the saints.

Book Two of the *Dialogues* has a special historical interest as the only near-contemporary source for the life of Saint Benedict. Because Saint Gregory was writing to edify and did not have the critical sense of the modern biographer, the work has long presented a problem to historians, who have been at a loss to know how far it can be trusted as a source of historical data. Today there is a consensus that the portrait of Saint Benedict drawn in the *Dialogues* is consistent with what is known from other sources, particularly from the *Rule* which he drafted and which became the great model for subsequent monastic legislation in Western Europe. Benedict is portrayed as a strong-willed abbot with a profound knowledge of human nature and a boundless charity.

Book Four of the *Dialogues* makes a direct attempt to handle some doctrinal questions. At the close of Book Three, Peter remarks, "Considering how many there are within the fold of the Church who doubt the existence of the soul after death, I am urged to beg you for proofs from reason showing that the soul will continue to live on forever." Philosophical argument is not Saint Gregory's forte, though he does attempt to explain the immortality of the soul. For the most part, Book Four is another collection of anecdotes that do little more than illustrate orthodox views on the nature of the soul and its activities. Peter's persistent interrogations include many questions about the problem of eternal punishment. Where is Hell? Is it eternal? Or is God merely threatening eternal punishment? How can Gregory reconcile an eternal Hell with God's mercy? How can infinite punishment be decreed for a finite fault?

For several centuries Saint Gregory's popularity depended more on the *Dialogorum libri* than on any other of his works. In the East there are references to him as "Gregory of the Dialogue." In the eighth century the work was translated into Greek at the order of Pope Zacharias. Translations were also made into Anglo-Saxon and French. There is no work of the period which better reveals the popular religious attitudes of the sixth century. Tales such as those Gregory collected were copied and enlarged upon, finding their way into medieval drama and song, as well as expression in the sculpture and stained glass of the cathedrals. In these tales men found an assurance of God's concern for human striving and suffering, as well as a graphic portrayal of a Christian moral ideal expressed in terms the unlettered man could readily understand.

Sister M.E.

HISTORY OF THE FRANKS

Author: Saint Gregory of Tours (c.543-594)
Type of work: History of the Church in the Merovingian era
First transcribed: c.575-594

Principal Ideas Advanced

All men are caught up in a cosmic drama between good and evil forces, in which the supernatural order constantly intervenes on one side or the other.

During the Merovingian era, with its intellectual, artistic, and moral poverty, the Church battled constantly against barbarism, cruelty, ignorance, and heresy.

To maintain sufficient order for the preservation of society, it was necessary for the Church to join with the state against the divisive forces of the self-seeking nobility.

Gregory of Tours began his *History of the Franks* shortly after his consecration as Bishop of Tours in 573. He came from a great Gallo-Roman family of the region, one which had long provided civil and episcopal leaders for Tours, and he had doubtless grown up with full awareness of the issues and personalities which dominated the period of the *History*. It would be vain, however, to look for an explicit analysis of either in his work, for he concerns himself purely with the headlong rush of events as he observed them and often participated in them. The *History* is narrative rather than descriptive in nature, and it is up to the reader to untangle the many threads of events so that they may be arranged in a meaningful pattern. Events and personalities appear in a confusion similar to that in real life; they are recorded without concern for cause and effect.

Gregory himself deplored his lack of sophistication and the necessity for writing in the common speech of the day. At times he veered from his intention of writing simply, in favor of the elaborate diction and obscure allusions of the few decadent Latin literary stylists still writing at that time. Yet on the whole, Gregory tells his story artlessly and straightforwardly, in a barbarous Latin undergoing evident changes in syntax, grammar, and spelling. He is not known for imaginative use of language or for subtlety or insight, but his achievement is no doubt all he ever meant it to be: a sincere account of an age almost bereft of literary men and so of historical record, told as truthfully as Gregory was able to tell it. His sources were the few available to a man who was born into an embattled time and had never traveled beyond the boundaries of Gaul; he refers to the Bible, Frankish epics, legends and annals, and Latin patristic literature. However, the real value of the history does not lie in the reliability of the sources Gregory managed to amass, but in his own observation of events and his familiarity with the great personages of his time.

The first three books of the *History* cover the years from the creation of Adam through the reign of Clovis, first of the Merovingian kings. The Fourth Book sets the stage for the events of Gregory's own lifetime, and it is of importance for understanding those events, even though the material is not reported with the reliability and vividness of the later eyewitness accounts. A generation before Gregory, Clovis's son Lothar (died 561) had managed by treachery and good fortune to unite all the territories that had been divided among Clovis's sons at his death. The unity of Gaul, so painfully achieved, was at once destroyed when Lothar died. The Frankish custom was to divide the father's kingdom among all his sons as though it were a piece of private property and not a nation. At the time of Gregory's consecration as bishop, a precarious balance of power existed among the four sons of Lothar. Within two years, the balance had been destroyed and Gregory's episcopate was engulfed in the currents of treachery and armed conflict which marked the entire Merovingian era.

Gregory's loyalty lay with the northeast corner of Gaul, Austrasia, ruled by King Sigibert (died 575). Sigibert's greatest rival was his own brother, Chilperic (died 584), the villain of the *History*. Chilperic's neighboring kingdom, Neustria, was the more romanized of the two territories, and her kings were able to foster a stronger loyalty to the Merovingian house. Austrasia was rawer and less stable. Its nobles never ceased to dream of reducing their rulers to a merely constitutional power. The issue inherent in this conflict was the central government's authority over the diffused, feudal power. Gaul had a strong imperial tradition, and this spirit of external, collective organization fused with the inward, ethical convictions of Christianity. The bishops formed a link between the order of imperial Rome and the interior morality and spirituality of Christianity, and they were largely responsible for the maintenance of both during the chaotic period of the invasions. The sentiments of the bishops were clearly on the side of peace and order, as represented by strong royal power, and Gregory was no exception to this rule.

In the self-seeking nobles, who themselves were a raw, nonaristocratic group of royal henchmen risen from the ranks, Gregory saw the enemy of any civilized order that Church or state might hope to establish. The military might and personal integrity of the young King Sigibert was the single hope for holding the restive Austrasian nobility in check, and it was Sigibert alone who could have confined the ambitions and intrigues of the vicious Chilperic.

Rather than contract the sort of mean alliance for which his brothers were notorious, Sigibert chose to marry Brunhild, the beautiful and cultivated daughter of the King of Spain. Chilperic, not to be outdone, insisted on marrying Brunhild's older sister, who was immediately done to death by his paramour Fredegund. Fredegund then became queen and achieved a lifelong ascendancy over Chilperic. She encouraged him to carry to even greater lengths his already serious quarrel with Sigibert. Brunhild was understandably enraged by her sister's murder, and Sigibert was determined to avenge Chilperic's continual armed incursions into Austrasia. Militarily, Chilperic was no match for his brother, and Sigibert soon swept him from the field. Just as Sigibert was on the verge of becoming the ruler of all the northern Franks, Fredegund's assassins struck him down and the politics of Gaul were again in chaos. Gregory had been Bishop of Tours for scarcely two years.

The diocese of Tours was taken from Austrasia and joined to Chilperic's kingdom. Gregory was obliged to spend nine years in contention with his hated sovereign until the latter's assassination. Meanwhile, his sympathies still lay with the unhappy royal house of Austrasia.

In the confusion that followed her husband's assassination Queen Brunhild had inexplicably run off to Rouen and married Merovech, Chilperic's grown son. It may have been that she wanted to establish her authority over the Austrasian nobles by a firm tie to another member of the Merovingian house. But her choice of Fredegund's hated stepson was a dangerous one. Fredegund was intent on removing all the heirs to the Neustrian throne except her own sons, and Merovech, as Chilperic's oldest surviving son, had long been on her mind. If Brunhild had been hoping for a strong man's sword to fight her battles with Chilperic and the Austrasian nobility, she was to be disappointed. The marriage had been performed at great personal risk to all concerned, especially to Bishop Praetextatus of Rouen. He had baptized Merovech and was devoted enough to him to celebrate his marriage to his aunt Brunhild, in defiance of Chilperic and of canon law. All involved save Brunhild were to suffer on account of her mistaken judgment.

To avoid the vengeance of his father, Merovech sought sanctuary in the Church of St. Martin's at Tours, while Brunhild fled back to the Austrasian court. Gregory, true to his episcopal trust, stood firm for the fugitive despite Chilperic's demands that he be expelled. Ultimately, Merovech was tricked into leaving St. Martin's, a move which ended immediately in his death. Gregory was punished by the destruction of territories belonging to St. Martin's Church. Still Fredegund was not content. She had Bishop Praetextatus tried and exiled for a time from his diocese, despite Gregory's courageous efforts to defend him. Both bishops, throughout the conflict, were firmly aware of their rights, and they resisted to the death the royal encroachments made upon the episcopal office. In return for his frank denunciation of Fredegund, Praetextatus was struck down by an assassin as he said Easter Mass in his cathedral, not a man among his clergy daring to come to his aid. No doubt Fredegund would have rejoiced to see Gregory meet a similar end, and it is a measure of his courage that he continued to speak out against her crimes and to remain the friend of her rival Brunhild.

Her misadventure with Merovech having been terminated without harm to herself, Brunhild began to rebuild her authority in Austrasia. Her hopes were centered on her five-year-old son Childebert II, who had been provided with a guardian from among the nobility. Brunhild had long since alienated the nobles and they wanted one of their number to be in charge of the young king, with the title of Mayor of the Palace. Once it had been the case that the mayor had represented the Frankish king against the nobles, but after Sigibert's death, the mayor's office existed solely to curtail or undermine the royal power. Brunhild was convinced of the right of the central government, with its overtones of the old imperial grandeur, to do all that was necessary to destroy its opposition. Fortunately for Brunhild, Sigibert's brother Guntram, the weak and vacillating King of Burgundy, chose to ally with her, throwing the balance of power against Chilperic and Fredegund. The latter were at that time engaged in the brutal but profitable oppression of all western Gaul. Their tyrannous reign was marked by epidemics and natural disasters, which Gregory feels were clearly marks of divine displeasure. Knowing that the Austrasian nobles still chafed under Brunhild's rein, Chilperic made common cause with them, but in 584 his intrigues were cut short by yet another assassin's dagger.

From this time on, the struggle for power was between Fredegund and Brunhild, with Guntram of Burgundy weakly intervening first on one side and then on the other. The two queens engaged in continual attempts at mutual assassination, and tides of intrigue and civil chaos surged across their tormented countries. Guntram died in 593, naming Brunhild's son, Childebert II, as heir to Burgundy. It appeared that Brunhild's dream of a united Frankish monarchy was on the verge of accomplishment.

As Gregory viewed the scene just before his own death in 594, he had reason for optimism, since it seemed that the house of Austrasia was once again in the ascendancy. But there was in store for Gaul no such imperial peace as Brunhild envisioned. In the end, Fredegund, who died peacefully in her bed (597), triumphed over her rival. Brunhild was defeated and tortured to death (613) by Fredegund's son, who lived to reign as King of France, as did his own son after him. The Merovingian house then began its descent into weakness and decay, dominated by the Mayors of the Palace and the free aristocracy, from whose ranks were to spring the ancestors of Charlemagne. Not until his reign were the hopes of Brunhild for a united empire and Gregory for Christian peace and order to be realized.

B.J.R.

THE ETYMOLOGIES

Author: Saint Isidore of Seville (c.560-636)
Type of work: Encyclopedia; philosophy of education; philosophy of government
First transcribed: 630

Principal Ideas Advanced

Ignorance is a major obstacle to right faith and good morals.

It is easier to know the nature of a thing once one knows the etymology of its name.

Natural law is law which applies most properly to unfallen man; lex gentium *is the law now in force in nearly all the nations.*

A king is bound to be just; if he fail in this obligation, it is right that he lose his throne.

In the work of preserving at least some elements of classical Greco-Latin culture through the five hundred years of the Dark Ages, none played a more important role than Saint Isidore of Seville, the last of the Latin Fathers and Doctors of the Church. His major work was the *Etymologies,* a rather large "desk encyclopedia," which abbreviated what the most learned man of his age thought most worth knowing (or at least, believing). For the better part of a thousand years it was *the* standard reference work, and it gained for its author rank next to the four great Doctors of the Western Church, Ambrose, Augustine, Jerome, and Gregory the Great, and the title, "The Schoolmaster of the Middle Ages." Next to the Bible, no book was more widely read. There are nearly a thousand medieval manuscripts of this work still in existence, and even in the Renaissance it was found useful, having been printed ten times between 1470 and 1529.

In a manuscript copy of the *Etymologies* found at Trinity College, Cambridge, one can read a verse which sums up what this work meant to one of its medieval readers:

> This booke is a Scoolemaster to
> those that are wise,
> But not to fond fooles that learning despise,
> A Juwell it is, who lifte it to reede,
> Within it are Pearells precious in
> deede.

Isidore came of a remarkable family, for he and his two brothers, and his sister all played important roles in the life of the Church in Spain, his sister Florentiana as the religious superior of over a thousand nuns in forty convents, his younger brother Fulgentius as Bishop of Astigi, his elder brother Leander as Bishop in the Metropolitan See of Seville, and Isidore as Leander's successor at Seville. (And all four were canonized as saints.) The times were ones of disintegration and transition in Spain, of disintegration of the institutions and classical learning of the Western Roman Empire, and, after a century and a half of Spain's being the battleground of barbarian tribes, of transition to a new national civilization blending racial elements, the Hispano-Gothic kingdom. And no one met the challenge of these times more adequately than Leander and Isidore, especially in the establishment of the rule of law through the part they played at the national councils of Toledo and Seville—regarded by Lord Acton as the earliest examples of parliamentary government—from which issued the most significant elements of Visigothic legislation.

Isidore's main interest, however, was in education, for with the arrival of the barbarians had come an almost unbelievable intellectual decline. A contemporary of Isidore's, Saint Gregory of Tours, lamented, "Woe to our times, when the study of letters is dying out among us." And it is of this period that Lord Acton wrote, "Europe lay under the grasp of masters the ablest of whom could not write their names." Isidore believed that if this state of affairs were allowed to continue, it would prove of incalculable harm to the Church, for "ignorance nourishes vice and is the mother of all errors." He made it his mission in life, and the motive, we learn from his friend Braulio, of all his literary activities "to restore the monuments of the ancients, lest we sink completely into barbarism." To further this goal Isidore compiled and wrote prodigiously. In addition to his major work, the *Etymologies,* he wrote commentaries on Sacred Scripture; two volumes of *Sententiae* which were the first systematic treatment of ascetic, moral, and dogmatic theology (and the forerunner of the *Sentences* of Peter Lombard); *De ecclesiasticis officiis,* a study of the liturgy and an explanation of the origin and purpose of various offices in the Church; *Adversus Judaeos,* which answers objections brought by the Jew against the divinity of Christ; *De natura rerum,* a collection of treatises on physics; and an important history of the barbarian nations that invaded Spain.

The encyclopedic *Etymologies* is divided into twenty books, each devoted to one or more special topics, and treating each particular subject by giving a brief explanation of what was known about it, preceded by an etymological derivation of the Latin or Greek name of that subject. The first three books deal with the liberal arts, the trivium (grammar, rhetoric, and dialectic) and the quadrivium (arithmetic, music, geometry, and astronomy). Book IV ("on Medicine and Libraries") gives an alarming account of the medical beliefs of Isidore's day, and concludes with a chapter which explains why the doctor must know the seven liberal arts well. Book V deals with law (no part of Isidore's writing was more influential) and concludes with a very brief résumé of the six epochs of the history of the world from creation to the year 627. Books VI, VII, and VIII include a discussion of ecclesiastical books and offices, an abbreviation of dogmatic theology, and a discussion of the Church and of the sixty-eight heretical sects. These first eight books constituted a survey of what the secular clergy was supposed to know.

Book IX treats of languages, peoples, and kingdoms, and it is clear that Isidore regarded the races of northern Europe as savages; he characterizes the Germans as "fierce and unconquered, living by hunting and plunder, the depth of whose barbarity is apparent in the hideousness of their speech," the Saxons as outstanding pirates, the Franks as particularly fierce, the Gauls as sharp-witted, and the Britons as stupid. Book X is an alphabetically arranged etymological dictionary of about one thousand words whose origins interested Isidore. Book XI treats of men and monsters, Book XII of beasts and birds, and Book XIII of the world and its parts. The last seven books treat of such diverse topics as physical geography; public buildings and roadmaking; stones and metals; agriculture; the terminology of war and of jurisprudence; ships, houses, and clothing; food and drinks, domestic and agricultural tools, and furniture. (The last few books give an excellent picture of what city life was like in Isidore's time.)

In the course of these twenty books, Isidore treats of approximately seven thousand subjects, giving first the etymology of the name of each. He includes a great many quotations from no fewer than seventy-five Christian and pagan authors, his favorites being Cicero, Lactantius, Lucan, Lucretius, Ovid, Pliny, Varro, and Virgil, together with a few quotations from Suetonius, whose *Prata* (now lost) probably inspired Isidore's general plan as well as many of its details. So highly regarded was the *Etymologies* as a depository of classical learning that it may well sometimes have superseded the use of the individual classics themselves.

One may well wonder why it was that Isidore gave so much attention to etymologies of words. He himself tells us, "Knowledge of the etymology of a word is often useful or even necessary in understanding it. For when one sees whence the name comes, he more quickly understands its power [*vis*]. For every investigation of a thing is easier once its etymology is known." This explanation is not very clear, but it is likely that Isidore had something like the following in mind (at least this sort of explanation was meant to justify attention to Isidore's etymologies in the Middle Ages): since words are signs of our concepts, and concepts are in their turn signs (formal signs) of things, words can refer to things only through the medium of the mind's conception of them. The way in which words signify thus depends on the way things become known to us: we name as we know. Given that we tend to know, and name, first what is concrete and sensible, and that we tend to use the same name for what is later and more abstractly known, it may be that we can trace the path of human knowledge and understanding of some reality in tracing the meaning of a word. As J. S. Mill wrote, "Etymology is slight evidence of what the idea now signified is, but the very best evidence of how it sprang up."

So, for example, it may be useful for one concerned with understanding the Aristotelian use of "matter" to know that the etymology of the Greek word for matter (and of the English word through its Latin root) has something to do with *wood:* the abstract philosophical meaning of this word may become easier to grasp once we establish its early definite concrete meaning. (And even if the derivation was a mistaken one, as were so very many of Isidore's, some lesson about a later abstract meaning may have been learned.) And it may be that knowing the etymology of "philosophy" to be "love of wisdom" permits us to see a certain constancy behind all the definitions that have been given of "philosophy," including Isidore's own "knowledge of human and divine matters, together with a desire to live well" —a definition which combines fields which only later, in the Middle Ages, would be carefully distinguished: philosophy, theology, and liberal arts.

That part of Isidore's encyclopedia which exercised the greatest influence on later times was his discussion of law and government. Saint Thomas Aquinas, for example, quotes Isidore about one hundred times in the *Summa Theologiae,* and about ninety of those times in the Second Part, which treats of moral and social questions. Isidore worked from the theories of Roman law as he found them in the textbooks of Gaius and Ulpian, in the Theodosian Code, and in the *Sentences* of Paulus, supplemented by the Christian writing up to his own time, especially that of Saint Augustine.

Of special interest is Isidore's teaching on natural law. "Natural law," he writes, "is common to all peoples and is in force everywhere by an impulse of nature [*instinctu naturae*] rather than by definite statutes." (Isidore was departing from the tradition, found expressed in Ulpian, according to which natural law was common to all animals and was grasped by an animal instinct.) Examples of natural law for Isidore included the union of man and woman, the education of children and their right to inheritance, the payment of debts, and the repulsion of aggression by force. But also included as "natural" were property in common and equal freedom for all. Private property and slavery are introduced by the *lex gentium,* the law "in force among nearly all nations." Following St. Augustine, Isidore sees slavery as a punishment for sin, but a remedial punishment intended to correct the evil tendencies of sin in human nature. And presumably, had there been no sin, private property would not have been necessary; and even government would not have been called for, being only useful as a divinely appointed remedy for sin. Generally speaking, Isidore followed the Church Fathers in their way of fitting the Ciceronian conception of the natural law together with the doctrine that man is in a fallen state. The solution adopted was to speak of a natural law appropriate to man in *puris naturalibus,* in a relatively ideal pure state of nature; and to contrast natural law institutions with those appropriate to men under the *lex gentium.* But this makes some "natural laws" purely hypothetical, and it was only in the Middle Ages that the issue was resolved in favor of speaking of "natural law" as a hierarchy of more or less easily knowable precepts, knowable, though perhaps with some difficulty, in the very state of fallen nature in which man found himself; and in the high Middle Ages, *lex gentium* was well on its way to becoming international law.

Isidore's ideas of kingship had an important bearing on and foreshadowed later medieval theory, and they formed a striking contrast to the absolutistic theories then prevailing in the Eastern Roman Empire. The king, Isidore says, is bound to the promotion of justice: "He does not rule who does not correct. The king holds his title by doing right; he loses it by sin. There is an ancient proverb: 'You shall be king if you do right; if not, you shall not be king.' " And Isidore goes on to define the chief virtues of the king as justice and the *pietas* which tempers justice. The king's law should be "honest, just, possible, according to the nature and custom of the country, suited to the time and place, useful and also clear, lest anyone by its obscurity should be deceived, written not for the benefit of any individual, but for the common good of the citizens . . . and should be sanctioned both by those of high birth and by the common people."

One will scarcely find originality or the results of independent investigation in Isidore—though perhaps we ought to think of him as being original when he gravely informs us that "because the surface of water is always *aequalis* (level), the name *aqua* (water) has been given it"; or when he tells us that *nox* (night) is derived from *nocere* (to injure) because "night injures the eyes"; or that *lapis* (stone) is derived from *laedat pedem* (injures the foot). Isidore was content to be an echo of tradition; and if it is possible to be shocked when we see how inadequate an echo he sometimes was, we must remember that in his day no one had more manifold interests, was more widely read, or more diligent in compiling, as he put it, "flowers from different meadows."

R.L.C.

THE ASCETIC LIFE

Author: Saint Maximus the Confessor (c.580-662)
Type of work: Dialogue on the spiritual life
First transcribed: c.630

PRINCIPAL IDEAS ADVANCED

God became man for the sake of man's salvation; He showed men the way of life, and gave them commandments for their salvation.

The fundamental commandments are these: Love God, and love one another.

Love, self-mastery, and prayer are the virtues which one who would devote himself to God must acquire.

Men have no compunction who do not fear God and keep His commandments.

Saint Maximus the Confessor, Maximus Homologetes, was born in Constantinople of a noble family. He was a student of the works of Aristotle and the Neoplatonists, and his subsequent writings reflect his admiration of Pseudo-Dionysius and Origen. The *Liber asceticus* (translated as *The Ascetic Life*) is a characteristic expression of Maximus' conviction that it is through the attempt to imitate Christ as the Incarnation of the Word that man can achieve salvation. The Incarnation is the concrete expression of that divine charity which stands as the creative center of the Christian spirit.

Maximus was active in the struggle against the Monothelites, who argued that Jesus had but one will and operation. The climax of Maximus' opposition was his participation in the Lateran Council of 649 which condemned Monothelitism. Maximus, a simple monk and neither a priest nor a superior, then found himself in opposition to Emperor Constans, who had issued a decree favoring Monothelitism. In 653 Pope Martin I was arrested for denying the position endorsed by the emperor; Maximus was arrested soon afterwards. The monk was exiled to Bizya, and then to Perberis, where he remained six years. In 662 he was tried again at Constantinople by a Monothelite council; he was anathematized and punished by having his tongue cut out and his right hand amputated. He died in exile at Lazica in August, 662.

The Ascetic Life is a dialogue between a young novice and an old monk. The young man begins the discussion by asking, "Please, Father, tell me: What was the purpose of the Lord's becoming man?" The answer is that the Lord became man for our salvation. The old man explains that man sinned in Paradise and progressed in evil until he was lost in despair. God, then, the only-begotten Son, the Word, took flesh "by the Holy Spirit and the holy Virgin," and He showed the way of life which man should strive to imitate. He promised man resurrection and eternal life, and He sent the Holy Spirit to help man to keep the commandments.

The young brother asks to have the commandments of Our Lord made clear to him, and the old monk again stresses the importance of faith and the keeping of the commandments; he insists that those who free themselves from material things will be given the power to imitate the Lord. The commandments are many, the old monk agrees, but they can be summarized "in one word": "Thou shalt love the Lord thy God with thy whole strength, and with thy whole mind, and thy neighbor as thyself." To love in this way one must renounce the things of the world. "What things do you mean, Father?" the young man asks, and the old man replies, "Food, money, possessions, acclaim, relatives and the rest."

The old monk agrees that it is difficult to love envious and hateful men, but the Lord would not ask the impossible. If one can rid himself of love for pleasure and material things, the love even of one's enemies is made easy. The Lord resisted the temptations of the Devil and loved His enemies in order that men might learn the way of the Lord. Love is the power by which one is able to resist temptation.

The brother asks, "And what should one do, Father, in order to be able to devote oneself continuously to God?" and the old man answers that one must "possess these three virtues: love, self-mastery, and prayer. Love tames anger; self-mastery quenches concupiscence, prayer withdraws the mind from all thoughts and presents it, stripped, to God himself."

When the young brother asks why he has no compunction, no remorse because of his failure to love God and his neighbor with his whole heart, the old man replies that the absence of compunction is the result of failing to fear the punishment of God. But if one attends to the descriptions of the awful fire which awaits those who do not fear God and obey His commandments, compunction is felt immediately. It is not enough to avoid doing evil; one is in danger if one fails to love one's neighbor, even one's enemies. Nor is it enough to have faith, for "The devils also believe and tremble," and "Faith without works is dead in itself."

The old man repeatedly goes to Scripture to find passages which illuminate his claims concerning what God demands and what awaits those who defy those commandments.

The brother finds that he has indeed been moved to compunction by the strong and insistent words of the old monk, and he entreats the old man to tell him what he ought to do to achieve salvation. The monk replies by quoting Scriptural passages which tell of God's power and loving-kindness. Man cannot attain salvation by himself, but if he asks for forgiveness, seeks to do what the Lord asks, loves the Lord and his neighbor, and forgives his brother for his sins, then he can rely on God's charity. Christ has shown man the way; the task of imitating Him is man's responsibility. If men encourage one another in the practice of charity and in the performance of good works, salvation is possible. With the practice of charity comes illumination, and by that illumination a man can be guided. "Let us then love one another and be loved by God," enjoins the old monk; "let us be patient with one another and He will be patient with our sins," and he adds, ". . . the Lord bestowed on us the method of salvation and has given us eternal power to become sons of God. So finally then our salvation is in our will's grasp."

By doing penance, the old monk advises the young brother, our souls are detached and we are freed from the grip of the passions. "Let us emulate the holy athletes of the Savior," says the monk; "Let us imitate their tireless course, their flaming eagerness, their perseverance in continence, their holiness in chastity, their nobility in patience, their endurance in long-suffering, their pity in compassion, their imperturbed meekness, their warmth in zeal, their unfeignedness in love, their sublimity in lowliness, their plainness in poverty, their manliness, their kindness, their clemency."

The old monk concludes his exhortation by telling all who are brothers in Christ to flee the world and the world's ruler, the Devil. "Let us lay hold on the author of life, let us rejoice in the fountain of life," he declares, and he closes the book with a prayer of thanksgiving for the mercy of the Lord.

THE LADDER OF DIVINE ASCENT

Author: Saint John Climacus (c.570-649)
Type of work: Mystical theology
First transcribed: c.640

Principal Ideas Advanced

The man who really loves God will renounce everything and follow Him.
If a man loves God and desires the monastic life, there are three paths open to

him: complete retirement and solitude, living in silence with one or two others, or living in a community.

The goal of all monks is the rank and state of the incorporeal beings.

To achieve this goal the monk must practice obedience, chastity, and constant prayer.

Saint John Climacus, whose *The Ladder of Divine Ascent* was one of the first mystical treatises produced by Christian monasticism, entered a monastery on Mt. Sinai when he was sixteen. Nineteen years later he retired to a place called Thola, five miles from the monastery, and lived there in solitude for forty years. At the end of his voluntary seclusion he was made abbot of the monastery. What little we know of his life is taken from a brief biography written by Daniel, a monk of Raithu, which usually prefaces the extant texts. Daniel wrote of him: "His whole life was unceasing prayer and unexampled love of God; for day and night he contemplated Him as in a mirror in the purity of integrity, and he could never have enough of this contemplation."

The Ladder of Divine Ascent was composed upon the request of the Abbot of Raithu, a monastery on the Gulf of Suez at the southern tip of the Sinai peninsula. He wrote to Climacus: "And by this letter of ours we appeal to your masterly virtue to describe for stupid people like us what you have seen in divine vision like Moses of old on that same mountain, and to send us a book like the divinely written tablets, for the instruction of the New Israel, which has only recently, I might say, escaped from the spiritual Egyptians and from the sea of life." Not to be outdone in Christian humility, Climacus replied: "It is typical of you and of your holy soul to ask for words of direction and instruction from me who am unlearned and stupid in deed and word, for you have ever made it a habit to show us an example of humility." *The Ladder* was written to communicate the spiritual and intellectual fruit of a lifetime of meditation. It was written specifically for monks, professionals of the spiritual life, and there is much in it that is not immediately applicable to the ordinary life of men. The book is organized into an account of thirty steps which symbolize the thirty hidden years of Our Lord.

One of the central concerns of *The Ladder* is to define the essence of the monastic life. In the sixth century Christian monasticism was still young, and in the absence of a long tradition it had to be carefully directed by men of intelligence and practical wisdom. Climacus wrote: "A monk is he who strictly controls his nature and unceasingly watches over his senses. A monk is he who keeps his body in chastity, his mouth pure and his mind illumined. A monk is a mourning soul that both asleep and awake is unceasingly occupied with the remembrance of death."

Monastic life is for Climacus the concerted attempt of men to triumph over this world and live for God alone. Following from this definition the central problem for the monk is the overcoming of the world, and Climacus devotes most of his book to explaining specific methods for subduing the passions, bringing the will to perfect obedience, and ridding the mind of all thought of self. The way is not easy. Those who wish to ascend to Heaven while still in the body require constant suffering, especially in the early stages of their renunciation. The beginner should remember, however, that any man who still has an attachment to anything visible is not yet delivered from grief. To be attached to the world is to be miserable. Monasticism is the orderly liberation of men from the tyranny of temporal life.

Climacus has many practical suggestions for those attempting a life of perfection. He cautions the beginner not to despair when he is distracted from his prayers: "Unbroken recollection is proper only to an angel." A man who is often a prey of despondency should never attempt a life of solitude, for despondency is a "constant companion of the hermit." However, he writes, the communal life has difficulties all its own. Those living in silence have only the devils to fight against, but those living in a community must struggle with human beings as well as with devils. The cravings of the flesh are linked, and the man who has mastered one of them has a good chance of overcoming all of them. The man who masters gluttony can achieve the highest degree of chastity, but the man who attempts to rid his mind of impure thoughts will never succeed if he is still devoted to food. Climacus recommends frequent vigils for those who are attempting to overcome the flesh. Vigils sap the strength of the passions and calm troubled minds: "A monk who denies himself sleep is a fisher of thoughts, and in the stillness of the night he can easily observe and catch them."

God resists the proud, Climacus writes, but the meek and humble of heart find quick access to Him. There is no barrier to the life of perfection more serious than pride: "A proud monk has no need of a devil; he has become a devil and an enemy to himself." The proud are corrected by falling into sin. Sin and suffering remind the proud man that he must constantly correct himself if he is to lead a good Christian life. The proud man has a turbulent soul, but in meek hearts the Lord finds rest. The proud man is irritable, but meekness, says Saint John, "is a rock overlooking the sea of irritability, which breaks all the waves that dash against it yet remains completely unmoved." A humble monk will not meddle with the holy mysteries, but a proud one will always be questioning what he can never know and finding fault with those around him.

Climacus was a careful observer of human nature and many of his comments reveal a practical insight into the workings of the mind. He tells the monk to devote the first fruit of the day to the Lord, "because the whole day will belong to whoever gets the first start." In discussing blasphemy his advice is to imitate Christ in all things and pray constantly for God's help. "For how will you catch, or contend and grapple with one who bursts into the heart suddenly like the wind, utters words quicker than a flash, and immediately vanishes?" Inherent in such an observation is the assumption that evil is spiritual and can be fought only by a pure spirit. The devils distract us from God with impure thoughts and a multitude of images, Climacus warns; the monk must therefore master the mind as well as the body, for he is constantly involved in a war with the powers of darkness.

A monk who has fallen from his

high calling must practice repentance. He should confess his sin immediately and do penance. "While a wound is still fresh and warm it is easy to heal," Climacus writes, "but old, neglected and festering ones are hard to cure." Terror at the thought of death is evidence of unrepented sin. Climacus suggests the remembrance of death as a means to avoid falling into sin.

The Ladder contains many stories about monks whose lives were notable. Isidore of Alexandria was a fierce and arrogant man when he came to the monastery. Perceiving his character, the abbot directed Isidore to stand at the gate of the monastery and say to everyone who passed: "Pray for me, father; I am an epileptic." In this way the man was taught humility, and after seven years at the gate he died with a will perfectly disposed to God. Saint Menas was a particularly holy man. In order to test his patience the abbot left him lying prostrate when Menas came to request a task. After a long time the abbot found him as the abbot had left him, perfectly happy. Upon being asked how he had occupied his mind Menas replied that he had recited the entire psalter from memory. The abbot knew that Menas had great patience and had acted as he did for the edification of the other monks. On the third day after the death of Menas the entire room in which his coffin lay was filled with fragrance. Upon opening the coffin they found sweet-smelling oil "flowing like two fountains from his precious feet."

For Climacus the highest point in the life of a monk is the practice in solitude of "holy quiet." The preliminary task of solitude is disengagement from all the affairs of the world. The second task is "earnest prayer," and the third is "inviolable activity of the heart." The result of the solitary life should be dispassion. The dispassionate man is he "who has made his flesh incorruptible, who has raised his mind above creatures and has subdued all his senses to it, and who keeps his soul in the presence of the Lord, ever reaching out to Him even beyond his strength." Through dispassion we come to know the love of God which has no end and in which we will continue to progress, "continually adding light to light."

The Ladder of Divine Ascent is remarkable for its compact, aphoristic style. Climacus can reduce a complicated idea to a single sentence: "The healthy do not go to a hospital." Through the use of images he is able to communicate truths that would otherwise lack dramatic impact: "Dried up mire offers no attraction for swine, and in exhausted flesh demons no longer find anywhere to rest." His favorite technique is that of the metaphor. Repentance is a contract, he writes; a penitent is a buyer of humility; deliberate silence is the mother of prayer. Like Our Lord, Climacus spoke in parables.

The Ladder of Divine Ascent has exerted a great influence upon Greek, Russian, and Slavonic spirituality. It was read and copied in the Kievan Monastery of Caves, the oldest Russian religious house. A group of monks gathered on Mt. Athos in the fourteenth century with the central purpose of practicing "holy quiet" as defined by Climacus. It was a popular work in Serbian and Orthodox monasteries. From the earliest days of the

Middle Ages *The Ladder* was read by a much wider circle than the monks for whom it was originally intended. It will continue to be of interest to students of Byzantine monasticism and Christian spirituality in general.

D.M.R.

ECCLESIASTICAL HISTORY OF THE ENGLISH PEOPLE

Author: Saint Bede (c.672-735)
Type of work: History of the Church in England
First transcribed: 731

Principal Ideas Advanced

Biographies of the saints reveal the importance of holy lives to the development of the English Church.

The history of the early English Church is the history of the great conflict between the body of long-isolated Celtic Christians and the newly-converted Anglo-Saxon Christians.

The achievement of political and religious union by the English people made possible the Northern Renaissance.

The Venerable Bede came late to the writing of the *Historia ecclesiastica gentis Anglorum.* Many other of his works preceded it, and some prepared the way for its style, method, and particular greatness. The scope of Bede's learning is indicated by the subjects that engrossed him during a lifetime of prolific writing: grammar and metrics, Scriptural exegesis, histories of saints and monastic foundations, mathematics, and natural science. His interest in the last is evident in the work *De temporum ratione,* a treatise on the historian's problems in accurate dating, and it bore fruit when he was obliged to reckon the chronology of the *Ecclesiastical History.*

Not only was Bede concerned to date his material accurately, but he was also methodical and scrupulous about investigating and reporting his sources. Letters, hagiographies, both oral and written traditions of the major English Churches, as well as reports of eyewitnesses, were Bede's materials, and he is careful to indicate exactly which source he relies on for specific information. Often he transcribed into his narrative whole copies of written sources, which otherwise would have perished. He used Saint Guildas's (died 570) *De excidio et conquestu Britanniae* and references to Britain in available patristic works for his brief account of the pre-invasion Church. The plan and scope of the work was doubtless suggested by Rufinus's Latin translation of the *Ecclesiastical History* written by Eusebius of Caesarea (c.260-c.340). The Abbot Albinus of St. Augustine's monastery at Canterbury urged Bede to write an inclusive history, not simply a local one. It was through Albinus that the Northumbrian Bede learned of the traditions and records of the southern Church centered at Canterbury.

Though he was a Northerner and of the race of the invaders, St. Bede has often been commended for his impartiality toward individual saints of the Celtic and Southern traditions. It is true that he occasionally revealed prejudices against those who used the Celtic Easter dating system or in favor of Christian kings like Edwin or Oswald. Still, his objectivity is notable, especially since his object was not merely to inform but also to edify: "For if history relates good things of good men, the attentive hearer is excited to imitate that which is good." With Bede's objectivity and careful estimation of sources went clarity, conciseness, and austerity of Latin style, which set a precedent for other writers of the period. In view of the flowery and obscure Irish rhetoric of the period, which was much imitated in England, the salutary influence of Bede's own directness and simplicity should not be underestimated.

St. Bede's history falls into five books, the first of which recounts what little was known of the achievements of the Celtic-Roman Church before it was driven into the West and cut off from the continental Church by the invasions. The latter half of the first book tells the story of Saint Augustine's commission by Pope Gregory the Great to go as a missionary to the Anglo-Saxons. Augustine arrived in Kent in 597, converted King Ethelbert shortly afterwards and established a bishopric at Canterbury. Gregory, in his *Responsiones,* specifically directed Augustine to use whatever good customs he found in other churches, to assume authority over the British bishops, and to sanctify for the Church pagan temples and ceremonies so that the rude converts would not be too abruptly wrenched from their traditions. Augustine evidently took the recommendation to exert authority much more to heart than he did the advice to be flexible regarding the customs of others. He irrevocably alienated the Celtic bishops, who had come to him ready to acknowledge his leadership if only he greeted them with respect. Bede takes care to record that Augustine's curse upon the recalcitrant Celtic bishops was fulfilled in a bloody defeat of the Celts by the barbarians.

Books II through V cover the period from the death of Pope Gregory to 731, a few years before Bede's death. Throughout the massive detail of the history, certain trends and representative events stand out clearly. The seventh century was a critical period in England, marked as it was by the successive rise and fall of Christian and pagan kingdoms, as well as by the continuing hostility of old Celtic Christians toward the hated Anglo-Saxon invader, Christian as he often was, and toward the customs of the Canterbury Church which had naturally become identified with the people it had been established to convert.

Augustine had been commissioned to set up another archdiocese at York, but it was years before this could be accomplished. In one of his greatest stories, Bede tells of the Witan of 626 at which Edwin (585-633), King of the Northumbrians, brought together his chief followers to see if they might all become Christians together. His own high priest, Coifi, urged that the missionary Paulinus (c.584-644) be heeded. Of the paganism he had adhered to before, Coifi said, "I have long been sensible that there was nothing in that which we worshipped; because the more diligently I sought after truth in that worship, the less I found it. . . . I advise, O king, that we instantly abjure and set fire to those temples and altars which we have consecrated without reaping any benefit from them." Upon receiving leave of the king, Coifi rode off at once to cast his spear into the local temple and then burned it with all it contained. In this way Northumbria became Christian (627), and Bede declares that complete safety and Christian peace prevailed through northern England during the years of King Edwin's reign. Oswald (c.605-642), who succeeded Edwin after the latter's assassination, carried on the tradition of fervent Christianity in the north, with the help of St. Aidan, his bishop. Bede regards Oswald highly, just as he does Edwin, and is strongly critical of the British Christian kings who allied themselves with the pagan Penda of Mercia against Oswald.

The ascendancy of pagan Mercia, lying across the middle of England as that territory did, further divided the national Church. This trial was ended by the victory of the Northumbrian King Oswy (c.612-670) over Penda in 654. Once more the Northern and Southern cultures could communicate freely. The cause of national and religious unity had been significantly advanced. It was King Oswy again who furthered the eventual reconciliation of the Celtic and the Anglo-Roman elements in the Church by holding the great Synod of Whitby in 663, in which the spokesmen for the Celtic and the Roman dating systems publicly debated the issues that divided them. King Oswy opened the proceedings by declaring "those who served one God" should keep the same rules and the same "celebration of the divine mysteries." When both spokesmen had set forth their arguments and authorities at length, Oswy asked them if they accepted the authority of St. Peter. Each man answered that he did. Since the pope was the authority for the practices cited by Wilfrid (c.634-709), the advocate of the Roman system, Oswy decreed that it was to the representative of the keeper of the keys that they owed obedience and not to the Celtic bishops. All present agreed and resolved to conform to a single rule.

The spirit of unity achieved under Oswy's guidance was developed and institutionalized during the time of the Archbishop of Canterbury Theodore of Tarsus (c.602-690). He came to England as a foreign scholar, already an old man, and it was to him that many factions found it possible and often necessary to submit. Theodore was the first archbishop in England with nationally recognized authority, which he used to initiate the holding of synods, to weld together the ecclesiastical structure of the nation before its political counterpart existed, and to make Canterbury a center of English learning. Through contact with Canterbury began the great Northern Renaissance in which Bede was to play so prominent a part.

Theodore's school was run briefly by Benedict Biscop (628-690), a scholar who spent his life studying the varying monastic rules of the continent and collecting books for the monasteries he himself founded at Wearmouth and Jarrow in Northumbria. The Celtic monasteries provided priests and bishops for their areas and were both poor and austere. The Benedictine monasteries, like Bede's own Jarrow, were strictly enclosed, with no pastoral duties, so that the monks' time was free for prayer, scholarship, and teaching. In the North, the artistic influences from the Celtic houses of Iona and Lindisfarne were able to contribute to the Benedictine cultural awakening, while in the South ecclesiastical culture was exclusively Anglo-Latin. Thus, in Northumbrian culture, particularly in so far as it was dominated by the achievement of Bede, Celtic and English features of the Church were reconciled.

Bede's influence spread far beyond the walls of Jarrow, where he had lived as a student and later as a monk, taking "delight in learning, teaching and writing." The historical account of his death was written by an eyewitness in the simple, direct style which Bede himself had done so much to promote. The monk who wrote it shows the same love and reverence for Bede's devout and gentle character as Bede exhibits in his stories of great saints in the *History*. Up to the last day of his life, Bede was busy translating the Gospel of Saint John into the vernacular speech. When he knew the time had come for him to die, he gathered up his few poor belongings, and he told those around him: "Run quickly, call the priests, that I may distribute to them such gifts as God has given me." Having dictated his last sentence and stripped himself of his last possessions, Bede lay down upon the floor of his cell. There he died, after singing the antiphon of the Ascension, *O Rex gloriae*.

The example of Saint Bede's holiness and scholarship had its effect, both directly and indirectly, on the future of the medieval Church. His pupil Egbert became Archbishop of York, and Bede advised him on how best to fulfill his episcopal labors. Egbert and his brother King Eadbert of Northumbria collaborated in building the great cathedral school at York, which soon outshone Jarrow itself. For the next fifty years York was the great intellectual center of the West, and it was at York that Charlemagne was able to find a scholar and teacher, Alcuin (735-804), gifted enough to spark the Carolingian Renaissance. Through Alcuin runs the connection between Bede and the learned Hrabanus Maurus (died 856), German abbot and scholar. Perhaps Bede's most lasting contribution was the convention of dating events *"anno Domini,"* from the time of the Incarnation according to the previously little known chronology of the Eastern scholar Dionysius Exiguus (sixth century). Along with the *Historia ecclesiastica,* this system spread rapidly over Europe, where even in his own lifetime Bede enjoyed a great reputation.

B.J.R.

CONCERNING RHETORIC AND VIRTUE

Author: Alcuin (c.735-804)
Type of work: Educational and moral treatise
First transcribed: c.794

Principal Ideas Advanced

Rhetoric, the art of speaking well, teaches men to deal effectively with public questions.

Competence in rhetoric depends on knowledge of principles and practice.

The qualities of a good rhetorician are at the same time the virtues of a good man.

There is a difference, but no conflict, between natural virtue and Christian virtue; the distinctive virtue of the Christian is charity.

The impetus which Charlemagne, King of the Franks, gave to the movement of intellectual recovery and advance known as the Carolingian Renaissance was furthered by the establishment of a palace school. To staff this establishment, men of learning were recruited and brought to the Frankish court from Italy and England. Among these scholars was Alcuin of York, whose *De rhetorica et virtutibus* is representative of the literary and educational production of the period.

Alcuin became head of Charlemagne's palace school, a heterogeneous group of scholars, teachers, and students, including, besides Charlemagne himself and his sons and daughters, adults as well as carefully chosen youths destined for posts of responsibility in the royal administration.

Trained in York, the leading intellectual center of England at the time, Alcuin was heir to the intellectual tradition of Saint Bede and the Jarrow school, which had excelled, according to early medieval standards, in Biblical and Patristic scholarship. Both Jarrow and York had also been able to preserve something of the classical literary tradition as this had been transmitted by such writers as the philosopher Boethius and the monk-educator Cassiodorus, in sixth century Italy, and by Isidore of Seville in the seventh century.

Alcuin's *Rhetoric* can hardly be called an original work; it is rather an early medieval equivalent of both a teacher's manual and a student's text. Alcuin was a popularizer, whose aim was the pedestrian one of providing a practical tool for transmitting the classical rhetorical training to students of the palace school. Although the work has almost no literary merit, it holds, nevertheless, an important place in the history of Western European educational theory and practice, as an apt illustration of the effort to assimilate the classical rhetorical tradition to Christian philosophy.

The *Rhetoric* is in the form of a dialogue, as are Alcuin's other educational treatises on grammar, spelling, and dialectic. Alcuin, a cultured and highly trained teacher, was faced with the problem of instructing a group of students, some of whom, like Charlemagne, must have been of outstanding talent, but whose ignorance of the liberal arts was surpassed only by their zeal for learning. Many, including Charlemagne, could neither read nor write. Alcuin's educational treatises show him struggling to find the most effective teaching methods. The dialogue form promoted an atmosphere of friendliness and fellowship and made the students active participants in the teaching process. The technique was at the same time a regular literary device among classical authors, including Cicero, some of whose writings Alcuin knew well.

In the *Rhetoric* Charlemagne acts as interlocutor, and Alcuin as instructor. Alcuin's part of the dialogue is largely a tissue of extracts from an early minor work of Cicero, the *De inventione,* which was an exposition of the theory and practice of oratory. There are also in Alcuin's work sizable borrowings from Cicero's more mature work, the *De oratore.* Knowledge of the *De oratore* came to Alcuin only secondhand, through the *Ars rhetorica* of a fourth century rhetorician, Julius Victor. Four-fifths of Alcuin's *Rhetoric* can be traced directly to the texts of Cicero and Julius Victor. In places the *Rhetoric* is hardly intelligible, because Alcuin frequently juxtaposes sentences from different sections of Cicero's *De inventione,* thereby destroying the unity of the original work. But if we remember that Alcuin intended his book to be a tool in the hands of a skilled teacher, his faults of composition appear less serious, and the work becomes more understandable.

Rhetoric as a branch of learning meant many different things during the Middle Ages. Sometimes it was identified with, and at other times distinguished from, grammar, logic, law, literature, and philosophy. Alcuin's *Rhetoric* shows the concept of the art held by a leading educator of the late eighth century.

The work opens with Charlemagne's statement that rhetoric's value is in dealing with public questions. This pragmatic view leads the king to request instruction in an art which he sees as eminently useful to himself. He observes, "It seems absurd not to know the rules of an art when the necessity of using it confronts us daily."

Following Cassiodorus, Alcuin accepts the classical definition of rhetoric as the art of speaking well. To speak well, two things are necessary: knowledge of the principles of public speaking, and practice.

The five integral parts of the art of rhetoric, as set down by Cicero, are outlined: invention, or the devising of subject matter, arrangement, style, memory, and delivery. Alcuin next shows that rhetoric deals with legal cases and public questions. In discussing these categories, he demonstrates the intrinsic relationship between the art of speaking well and both law and politics. Any legal case, whether demonstrative, persuasive, or judicial, has seven parts: the person, the thing done, time, place, manner, motive, and ability or capacity. The art of rhetoric trains a man to build his case on whichever of these seven parts provides the most convincing evidence.

Charlemagne asks Alcuin to explain the different parties in law courts. In explaining the roles of plaintiff, defendant, witness, and judge, and in discussing the matter of premeditated and impulsive action, Alcuin shows that the men of his day were acquainted with some refined Roman concepts of legal procedure.

Returning to the problem of effective speaking, Alcuin gives directives for each part of a speech. Special attention is given to the introduction, which must use every available technique to win the good will of the listener. Deduction and induction, as the two processes of argumentation, are discussed reluctantly by Alcuin, who says that "these types belong rather more to the art of the dialectician than to that of the orator." Discussing style, Alcuin advises the student to avoid ambiguity and to use words that are concrete, specific, and familiar. Indispensable to the acquisition of effective style is deep and extensive reading in the ancient authors.

All this part of Alcuin's work, together with the brief remarks on memory and delivery which follow, is merely a transcription of early Ciceronian theory of rhetoric. Before he brought the dialogue to a close, however, Alcuin addressed himself to a question which gives the *De rhetorica et virtutibus* some small claim to originality, while at the same time it indicates a major problem with which the medieval intellectuals struggled. As Cicero had related rhetoric to law, Alcuin wanted to show the relationship of the art of rhetoric to Christian wisdom. His attempt is as curious as it is unsuccessful. While discussing temperance as a guiding norm in effective speaking, Charlemagne is made to ask for an explanation of the four virtues which Alcuin has called the roots of all the others. Charlemagne wants, further, an explanation of the difference between the ancient philosophers and the Christians in their understanding of virtue. Alcuin admits, "I am caught in a dilemma. Brevity demands a few short remarks, and this difficult subject requires a great many." Alcuin's "few short remarks" inform Charlemagne that the difference between philosophers who cultivated virtue and Christians is in the latters' faith and baptism. While prudence, justice, courage, and temperance satisfied the philosophers of old, love of God and of neighbor is the highest virtue for the Christian. When Charlemagne asks, "What is the due order of the soul?" Alcuin answers that the norm for a Christian's actions is love. The soul must love what is higher, that is, God, and rule what is lower, that is, the body. Love will also direct it to "nourish and assist its fellow creatures." Finally, concludes Alcuin, "the soul, cleansed and exonerated by these devotions, will fly back from this troubled and wretched life to eternal peace, and will enter into the joy of the Lord."

As the dialogue began with an effort to show the practical value of rhetoric for the man of public affairs, it concludes with an attempt to relate the art of effective speaking to that of effective Christian living. Under both aspects, it reveals the key position of rhetoric in the medieval educational ideal. Until the rise of Scholasticism in the twelfth century, rhetoric was seen by men like Alcuin as the integrating discipline. It was intrinsically related to law, politics, and ethics. The trained rhetorician was supposed to have become an articulate, liberally educated man. Alcuin even dared to think that practice in the art of effective speaking would somehow aid a man in becoming a better Christian.

For centuries, rhetoric, as taught by Alcuin and developed and modified by later educators, influenced not only the art of speaking, but the writing of letters, petitions, legal documents, and the other forms in which Western Europeans have expressed and transmitted their ideas.

Sister M.E.

THE LIFE OF CHARLEMAGNE

Author: Einhard (c.770-840)
Type of work: Biography
First transcribed: c.830

Principal Ideas Advanced

Charles the Great is the supreme example of a good and successful Christian king.

He fought long wars that more than doubled his realm, promoted education, charity, and architecture, aided pilgrims to the Holy Sepulchre, and loyally served the Pope of Rome.

Charles the Great (742-814), ruler of an empire encompassing France, Germany, the Lowlands, northern Italy, Bohemia, and Hungary, was undoubtedly the greatest prince of the Dark Ages and one of the most important monarchs of all time. His stature was as apparent to his contemporaries as it is to modern men. Fortunately this great king's life was preserved for posterity by a friend named Einhard whose *Vita Caroli magni* is one of the principal sources of information concerning Charles's reign.

Einhard (sometimes spelled Eginhard) was born in East Frankish Germany about 770 of parents of some substance. When the boy was ten or eleven years old his father sent him to the famous monastery of Fulda where he remained for the next twelve years and received his education. An abnormally small man, Einhard, who was never a priest, a monk, or a missionary, was summoned about 793 to Aix-la-Chapelle (Aachen), the court of Charles, King of the Franks. Here the young man gained a reputation for learning and soon became an intimate of the king, remaining with him until the end of the reign. He thus knew Charles during the last twenty years of his life, but it seems clear that he never held any great office under this monarch. Einhard served Charles's son and heir, Louis the Pius (778-840) in a more responsible position, although perhaps somewhat less faithfully. Late in this reign Einhard retired from court life and devoted himself to the monasteries of which he was a lay abbot and to the great shrine he erected at his own residence, Seligenstadt. Here he died in 840. He was the author of several treatises, including a description of his shrine's foundation in *The Translation of Saints Marcellinus and Peter*. The actual date of the composition of his greatest work, which has come to be called *The Life of Charlemagne,* is uncertain, but it is thought to have been compiled between 830 and 833, or more than fifteen years after his subject's death.

Einhard declares in his preface that he composed this biography lest the glorious life of this most excellent king and his illustrious deeds be lost in oblivion. He also offers a more personal motive by stating that he wishes to honor the monarch who protected him in his youth and was his friend and patron for almost two decades. Einhard apologizes for his lack of grace in composing a Latin treatise, declaring that although he is only a barbarian himself, he feels qualified to write this book for he was personally well acquainted with his subject. This is certainly true, and yet it is also apparent that Einhard used his position as an official of King Louis to pursue his research in the royal archives.

Since this is the first medieval biography of a lay figure, Einhard did not find it convenient to use the various lives of the saints as models for his own study. He therefore turned to ancient Roman classics and used them, in particular the works of Suetonius (69-140), as his guides and exemplars. Some scholars have suggested that Einhard employed whole passages from Suetonius in describing the appearance and characters of his own ninth century contemporaries; this charge seems a bit exaggerated. More important and certainly more obvious is this Carolingian historian's wholesale adoption of Suetonius's biographical style. This method demands that both praise and blameworthy characteristics of the subject be included and that his biography be recorded topically through a description of his ancestry, his public and private life, his physical appearance, his death, and the omens which prefigured his fall.

Einhard followed Suetonius's plan rather closely in tracing Charlemagne's ancestry from the famous Charles Martel, who defeated the Moors at the battle of Poitiers (Tours) in 732. The son of this Charles was Pepin, who, like his father, was the Mayor of the Palace of the Merovingian kings. Since the mayor actually controlled the kingdom, Pepin sought and received papal approval in 752 to rule as actual sovereign himself, sending the last of the Merovingians, Childeric III (743-752), off to monastic retirement. In 768 Pepin died leaving two sons, Charles and Carloman, to divide his kingdom. After Carloman's death two years later, Charles was unanimously elected King of the Franks, which title he held and extended until his death in 814.

Einhard says it would be folly to write of Charles's birth or early life because no witness remains to give him reliable information about these events. Therefore, the author presses on and offers an account of his hero's deeds at home and abroad, of his character, and lastly of his admiration and death. Einhard makes it clear how much of Charles's life was spent in the saddle waging war to create and defend his empire. In fact, a third of the biography concerns reports of the king's military campaigns against his diverse enemies, who included the men of Aquitaine, the Lombards, the Saxons (who were his greatest foes, demanding constant attention for thirty-three years), the Spaniards, the Bretons, the Bavarians, the Slavs, the Avars or Huns, and the Danes. As a result of such activity Charlemagne more than doubled his realm in his forty-five-year reign and created an empire stretching from the Elbe to the Pyrenees and from below Rome to the English Channel. The most famous event of all these conflicts was, of course, the death of Roland, the Count of Brittany, at the Pass of Roncesvalles, probably in 778. Einhard is our only historical source for this legendary hero, and he gives him but scant attention, perhaps because he wanted to minimize the effect of this great defeat.

The author moves on, declaring that the purpose of his work is not to record the incidents of Charlemagne's wars but rather the manner of his life. Thus we learn of Charlemagne's diplomatic successes, especially with the famous Haroun al Raschid (786-809), who sent Charles an elephant as a present and also granted him possession of the Holy Sepulchre in Jerusalem. These negotiations were clearly more important to the Franks than to the Moslems, who never mention them in their archives. The king was also proud of his palaces, his great bridge over the Rhine at Mayence, and his beautiful church at Aix-la-Chapelle, modeled after San Vitale in Ravenna. Einhard says Charles excelled all the princes of his time in wisdom and greatness of soul and that he possessed extraordinary constancy in good and evil fortune alike. Clearly there is little he finds worthy of censure in such a man's history.

Concerning the king's private life, Einhard relates that Charlemagne had four wives and several concubines and that he had his children, both male and female, carefully instructed in the liberal arts. He never allowed his daughters to marry, however. One of the illegitimate children, a hunchback called Pepin, once rebelled against him, and Einhard blames the queen for the sedition in the realm. This might be construed as a warning to the wife of Louis the Pious, for she was causing similar troubles while Einhard was writing.

Charles himself was tall, fair haired, with a large nose and eyes and a rather prominent stomach. His health was excellent except for his last four years, and then he raged at his physicians, who urged him to forego his favorite roasts and eat boiled meat instead. He rode well and especially delighted in swimming, sometimes having a hundred friends and nobles bathing with him in his great pool. He usually wore a linen shirt and breeches beneath a tunic, hose on his legs, and shoes. Over all he affected a blue cloak and always had his sword about him. In winter he added a coat of animal skins. It was only rarely that he would wear the Roman costume. He was temperate in eating and drinking and knew Latin and some Greek as well as his native tongue. Charles spent much time studying in the company of men such as Peter of Pisa and Alcuin of York (735-804), who encouraged him in grammar, rhetoric, dialectics, and especially astronomy. Einhard, who gives us all these details, says the king's favorite book was Saint Augustine's *City of God*, and Einhard also includes the famous tale that Charles kept tablets under his pillow to practice forming letters, but never met with great success in writing. The king was also very much interested in the old Frankish customs and he caused the Frankish laws and songs to be compiled and recorded for posterity and even began a grammar giving Frankish names to months and winds.

Einhard writes that Charles was most dedicated to the Church and lavished gifts upon pilgrims, shrines, and popes. It is reported by Einhard that Charlemagne did not wish to be crowned Roman Emperor by Pope Leo III in 800. Charles was supposedly so angry that he said he would not have gone to church that day, Christmas Day, had he known what was to happen. Einhard is the principal source for this surprising royal reaction; other contemporary accounts demonstrate that the royal thoughts had been directed to the imperial ideal some time before this. It is unlikely, however, that Charlemagne wished to receive any sanction from the pope; years later, in 813, Charlemagne crowned his son Louis as emperor without any papal blessing or consent.

Having followed Suetonius as a mentor thus far, Einhard continues by briefly relating Charlemagne's death from pleurisy on January 28, 814. He was seventy years old and had reigned for forty-five years. The author then goes on in classical fashion to detail the omens which portended this tragedy, events such as an eclipse, the fall of a palace gallery, the royal vision of a ball of fire, and the flaming destruction of the great Rhine bridge. The biography closes by quoting the emperor's will, which left the realm to Louis and a third of the treasury to the Church. Moveable property and even the imperial library were to be sold and the money devoted to charity.

In some ways Einhard's biography remains disappointing. The author offers no theory of history or causal explanation for many of the events he records. His research in the archives of Louis the Pious prompted him to quote only one imperial document, Charles's will. There are also glaring omissions. Charles's famous slaughter of thousands of pagan Saxons is passed over in silence, and no details are offered regarding his involved negotiations with the papacy. There are a few errors of place and date, and Einhard, like some of his contemporaries, had a confusing method of counting. Thus, while Charles ruled from October 9, 768, until January 28, 814, a little more than forty-five years, Einhard gives this as forty-seven by regarding both terminal years as complete.

More important, however, is Einhard's apparent lack of any deep psychological understanding of his subject or any unique political insight into the events he records. Absent, for example, is any analysis of the energy and governmental ability of the emperor who, largely by the force of his personality alone, held together the diverse parts of his extensive realm. Einhard evidently also missed the significance of the intellectual revival we now call the Carolingian Renaissance and the importance of Charles's own belief that he was called by God to be a Christian Ruler, a new David, governing both Church and State. He does not evaluate, much less criticize, his hero, but rather offers a vivid impression of a living person. Perhaps he was too close to his subject to judge him, or maybe Suetonius's example did not urge him to study broader problems. His faults are those of most medieval historians and chroniclers, but he must be given credit as being one of the first. Einhard's book was evidently quite popular in its own day and even among later medieval readers. For all its faults, Einhard's *Life of Charlemagne* is undoubtedly one of the great books of the Middle Ages.

E.J.K.

LIFE OF ALFRED

Author: John Asser (died c.910)
Type of work: Biography
First transcribed: 893

Principal Ideas Advanced

Alfred (849-899), King of the West Saxons, is probably the best loved of the early English monarchs, by virtue of his zeal for learning, personal piety, and courage in fighting the Danish invaders, who almost constantly threatened the English.

Becoming King in 871, amid popular acclamation, Alfred threw himself unstintingly into the affairs of his kingdom, fighting Teuton marauders, furthering his own learning, ministering to the needs of his people and encouraging the cause of scholarship and education.

Despite chronic illness and occasional military setbacks, Alfred succeeded in consolidating his kingdom, building monasteries, translating several significant Latin works into Anglo-Saxon, codifying laws, dispensing justice, and performing countless acts of Christian charity and religious devotion.

According to J. A. Giles, the translator, the *Life of Alfred* "is ascribed on its own internal authority, to Asser, who is said to have been Bishop of St. David's, of Sherborne or of Exeter, in the time of King Alfred." There is not the slightest doubt as to the genuineness of this work, although late nineteenth century scholarship had cast some doubt regarding its authenticity. Many of the facts of Alfred's life as recounted by his biographer were new, but a number of them were also to be found in the older *Saxon Chronicle* and in other manuscripts.

One outstanding characteristic of this work is the certitude with which John Asser, Bishop of Sherborne, presents his data. Not only did he know Alfred intimately for a number of years, but he loved and admired him. His portrait of Alfred tends to be a little one-sided for he says little of whatever faults Alfred may have had; this partiality is certainly true in comparison, say, to Einhard's *Life of Charlemagne,* where the monarch's faults and virtue are candidly drawn.

Asser establishes Alfred's birth in 849, in Wanating, Berkshire. Alfred's mother was Osburga, a noblewoman by birth and nature, and an extraordinarily pious person whose fervent Catholicism was probably a strong influence on young Alfred, even though she died when he was six. Asser says very little more about her, except to remark that she would read to her children verse stories in Anglo-Saxon, the language Alfred used in everyday affairs. Alfred's father was Ethelwulf, also a devout Catholic, who in 853 sent his son to Rome, despite the rigors and great dangers of long distance travel. In Rome, Pope Leo IV "anointed for king the aforesaid Alfred, and adopted him as his spiritual son." In 855 Alfred visited Rome a second time, accompanied by his father, now a widower. They stayed a year. On their way back to Wessex father and son were handsomely received in France as guests of King Charles, and Ethelwulf brought back to England Charles's daughter Judith, a child bride of thirteen who became Alfred's stepmother. A marriage of political expediency, it nonetheless profoundly shocked the English.

But Ethelwulf faced even more serious trouble than his marriage, fomented by his unscrupulous and rebellious son Ethelbald, who had been plotting to gain control of Wessex. To avoid open rebellion Ethelwulf, perhaps sensing his approaching death, surrendered control of Wessex to his son, but retained control as underking of the four remaining regions: Kent, Sussex, Essex, and Surrey. Judith and Ethelwulf were married two years, when he suddenly died, but he had taken the necessary steps to insure his being remembered in masses and prayers. He left a handsome sum of money to Rome to be used for the purpose of buying oil for devotional lamps, and a smaller sum to the pope himself to be used as he saw fit. Judith, soon after the death of Ethelwulf, was wed to Ethelbald, who had inherited his father's crown, but for his action he "drew down infamy upon himself." The people were no more pleased with the son's marriage than they had been with the father's. Within two years Ethelbald was dead, and Judith found herself widowed for the second time. She was then almost eighteen.

In relating his facts the author sometimes digresses interminably. He apologizes several times for this fault, admitting that he must get on with his story of Alfred. The biography is also punctuated by a recital of the innumerable and exhausting battles which occupied so much of the attention and abilities of the English. Alfred's lack of formal education, the dearth of schools in southern England at that time, and the generally low level of literary achievement in comparison with what had been accomplished elsewhere in England can be directly attributed to the demands and conditions of the almost incessant warfare. Life in ninth century England was measured by success or failure in battle.

Young Alfred, we are told, loved wisdom and learning from his earliest years and demonstrated a great aptitude and fascination for telling stories. Clearly he was different from his brothers. But he did not learn to read until he was twelve. Asser emphasizes Alfred's remarkable intelligence and especially his retentive memory, demonstrated in his recital of numerous Saxon poems. His biographer affirms again and again that Alfred was in God's particular favor and protection.

Alfred was enthusiastically crowned king in 871 when his brother, King Ethelred, died. But he no sooner became king than he had to exchange his crown for a battle helmet. The Danes and Vikings were again at war, pillaging, looting, burning monasteries, and slaying hundreds of priests. Despite truces and treaties with these "pagans," as Asser calls them, Alfred was seldom unoccupied with some kind of military operation or fortification. He was once forced to hide for weeks in the marshlands of Somerset, which became his base for guerrilla action against the enemy. For a time he was almost totally dependent on the goodwill of the local peasantry for supplies and information.

Although Asser paints a nearly ideal portrait of his subject, he nonetheless suggests that God made the king suffer some physical torments that "he might learn there is one Lord of all things." Asser complicates the image of Alfred by admitting that Alfred brought about his own suffering when, as a young man, he was reluctant to bend a sympathetic ear to the petitions of his people. Unfortunately, concrete details are lacking, and modern scholarship has failed to turn up any evidence suggesting that the king was in any way lax or deficient in his obligations. Apparently Asser saw no inconsistency in asserting that although the king was lacking in attention to his subjects' petitions, he was beloved by all. Later Latin manuscripts by William of Malmesbury and Simeon of Durham, among others, testify to Alfred's popularity and unimpeachable character.

Alfred's health was a matter of serious concern to himself as well as to his contemporaries. At the age of twenty he married a noble Mercian lady, Ealhswith, and during the wedding festivities he was seized with an "overwhelming pain," a manifestation of a mysterious disease which had plagued him since childhood.

An interesting episode attests Alfred's strongly religious and ascetic character, despite his suffering. One day while on a hunting trip, he turned off the main road to pray at a small chapel. He implored God, not to free him from pain, but to grant him lesser maladies in place of the torments which periodically wracked his body. He also prayed that he might be spared blindness and leprosy, for these afflictions would render him contemptible to his people.

Asser refers persistently to Alfred's intense devotion to the Catholic Church and to his struggles to overcome sin. But he gives very few concrete instances of these struggles. The biographer does tell us, however, that the king, fearing God's wrath, would rise "at cockcrow" in order to pray unseen in churches and before the relics of saints.

Alfred's children (there were at least six; one became a nun, and one daughter was given in marriage to Baldwin of Flanders) enjoyed an education superior to their father's. In his unrelenting quest for improving his own mind and mastering Latin, and in his passion for furthering the cause of education and scholarship in general, Alfred invited scholars from distant parts of England and from the Continent. Among them were such famous men as Grimbald, a monk from northern France; John, a European priest (possibly from West Germany) whom Asser describes as a "priest and monk, a man of keen mind, deeply versed in literary scholarship and writing, with skill in many forms of art"; and Asser, a priest from the community of St. David's, in Pembrokeshire. To help build and decorate beautiful churches and monasteries the king procured the services of some of the finest craftsmen in Europe, paying them from his personal funds. All these intellectual activities were aided by the relative peace England enjoyed from 886 to 892 while the Vikings were plundering France and Germany. But in 892 Alfred was again forced to take up his sword to fend off Danish invaders; for four years he fought relentlessly. Asser does not mention the king's role in building England's first warships, but later chroniclers substantiate the claim that Alfred contributed, in this manner, to England's developing might. Intriguingly, Asser refers to certain "mechanical inventions" by which Alfred taught his people to build houses, but we never learn just what these inventions were.

Near the end of his life Alfred vowed to offer up to God "half of his services, both day and night, and half his wealth, such as lawfully and justly came annually into his possessions." To help him divide his day accurately he invented a system of what seem to have been four-hour candles arranged in groups of six so that an accurate division might be made between night and day. Even when he traveled, in peace or war, he seems to have had with him a lantern specially constructed to hold such candles.

A later hand inserted into Asser's biography October 26, 900, as the date of the king's death. Others later set the date in 900 or 901, depending on the method of computation. But the consensus of modern critical opinion places the date as October 26, 899.

Although Asser does indicate that Alfred requested Werefrith, a bishop well versed in Latin, to translate the *Dialogues* of "Pope Gregory and Peter, his disciple, from Latin into Anglo Saxon . . . ," there is no further note of any other translating arranged by the king. Completely lacking are references to the king's famous translations of the works of Bede, Boethius, and Orosius. Doubtless they belong to Alfred's last years. Asser's last recorded date in the king's career is 887. From internal evidence we know that the date of the manuscript can safely be assigned to 893, but Asser survived the king by ten years. We learn from other manuscripts that Alfred even compiled a *Handbook* for his own use; interestingly, a copy of the manuscript is known to have existed as late as the twelfth century. Of Alfred's attempts to translate the Psalter from Latin into Anglo-Saxon, and of his accomplishment in formulating a just code of laws for his people, nothing is said.

Notwithstanding the additional materials of King Alfred which have come to light since the tenth century, Asser's interestingly written and absorbing *Life* remains an indispensable document in understanding and evaluating Alfred's position in English history.

J.P.F.

HOMILIES

Author: Aelfric (c.955-1020)
Type of work: Spiritual homilies
First transcribed: c.990-992

Principal Ideas Advanced

Life is a constant warfare between virtue and vice, and victory is made possible through the grace of God made available by the redemptive power of Christ.

The transitory nature of man's life on earth demands that he devote all his energies towards the life to come.

Salvation depends upon faith, good works, the Christian virtues, and above all, love of God and Man.

Aelfric completed his first vernacular work, the *Homilies* (sometimes referred to as the *Catholic Homilies*), during the century before the Norman conquest. His writings are of a practical nature; besides the homilies, we find pastoral letters, lives of saints, and Biblical translations. It was his conviction that his prime objective was the salvation of souls through exhortation to the unlearned, and that his talents were for the common people. "It is good and right to minister to God's poor," he writes, "and especially to the servants of God, but it is greater to speak heavenly lore to the unlearned, and to feed their souls."

The idea for the *Homilies* was conceived about the year 987 at the Abbey of Cernel: "Then the thought came to me, I trust through God's grace, that I would translate this book from Latin into English; not from confidence of great learning, but because I saw and heard of much error in many English books, which unlearned men in their simplicity esteemed great wisdom; and I was grieved that they neither knew, nor had the gospel teachings in their language, except those who knew Latin, and except the books which King Alfred wisely turned from Latin into English." The *Homilies* is a series of sermons for the Sundays and principal feasts of the Church calendar. They are addressed to the laity in an attempt to teach the doctrines of the Church. Aelfric does not seek to add anything to the teachings current in the English Church, but only to adapt the material to the limitations of his audience. The terminology of late tenth century England is frequent: "The town-reeve, Hippolytus, said to the deacon. . . ," in the "Homily for Feast of St. Lawrence," and "There was a thane, called Ananias. . . ," in the "Homily for the Feast of Pentecost."

The first series of homilies was completed by 991; the second, by 992. Each part has a Latin preface addressed to Archbishop Sigeric (flourished 990), and an English preface describing the origin and plan of the work. Each volume runs through the Church year; neither is dependent upon the other. The first series has a greater proportion of Scriptural and exegetical material dealing mainly with Creation and Redemption. Legends and the history of the English Church make up the bulk of the second series. Aelfric based both series upon the writings of Augustine, Bede, and Gregory, among others. While he acknowledges his debt to these writers, it is obvious he freely adapted their writings to the needs of the common people of the England of his time. They are exhorted to practice the virtues of industry, patience, and moderation, virtues appropriate to their station in life. He avoids complex theological approaches to Church teachings, and the sermons abound in wise maxims calculated to aid the uneducated in working out their salvation.

Each homily begins with a text from the Scriptures which, if not quoted exactly, is accurately paraphrased. There follows a step-by-step explanation of the passage, and then a conclusion which describes the practical application of the lesson to the lives of the hearers. With minor exceptions, quotations from the Vulgate form the basis for the sermons. Aelfric's commentaries are for the most part traditional, echoing the teachings of the early Church Fathers, as was customary in his time. To these he adds practical applications and comments. The homily for the Second Sunday after Pentecost exemplifies Aelfric's method. The Scriptural reading for the feast is taken from the Gospel of Saint Luke and narrates the parable of the rich man, who has all the material comforts, and Lazarus, the poor sick outcast who lies at his gate. Aelfric writes that there is a certain mystery attached to the meaning of this parable, but he uses Pope Gregory's explanation as the explication and the basis for an exhortation. Gregory tells the story of a certain monk who came upon a leper desirous of someone to carry him to a certain destination. The monk bore the leper in his arms until the diseased one revealed himself to be the Christ. Thus, the admonition that what one does for the poor in His name is done unto Him is borne out. It is typical of Aelfric to refer continually to his sources by name, as he does here in the case of Gregory. Such expressions as the following, which appears after the Scripture reading for the Fifth Sunday in Lent, "We will expound this gospel according to the authority of Augustine and Gregory," are common throughout the *Homilies*.

At times Aelfric picks a seemingly unimportant part of the Scriptural reading as the basis for his didactic lesson. In his commentary for Shrove Sunday, the Gospel of which deals with the blind man of Jericho, he tells his audience that the word "Jericho" means moon, and he uses the phenomenon of the waxing and the waning of this celestial body as a symbol of the decay of our mortality. How foolish it is, in view of the transitory nature of our lives, to love voluptuousness and material pleasures, writes Aelfric. Another such example is to be found in the homily for the Epiphany in which Aelfric writes of the wise men's being led by a star, the significance of which has been attested by the astrologers of the time of Christ. The word "astrologer' is cause for a digression condemning as false what men call destiny, and warning all that God predestines no man to evil. Just as the wise men were guided by a star, we are led to our home, Heaven, by obedience, continence, and humility.

Whether Aelfric is expounding a text or apparently digressing on one particular word or groups of words, his sermons never fail to exhort and admonish. His general explanation of the parable of the workers in the vineyard, in a homily for Septuagesima Sunday, is that the workers in the story who arrive at different hours and receive the same pay represent, respectively, the Patriarchs, the teachers of the Law, and the Prophets, and, finally, the apostles in our time, all having been sent by God to cultivate the morals of the people. There follows the application of the parable to his own day. Some are good from childhood, keeping faith with the Law, while others go astray but by the grace of God return to the right way, some in middle age, others in old age; all receive their reward, Heaven. Be not discouraged by sin, says Aelfric; there is time to repent.

Aelfric believed that men had need of good instruction, especially in his own day, for he was convinced that the end of the world was approaching. He devoted many of his sermons to accounts of the constant warfare between virtue and vice, and he held out encouragement to those weary of the fight for good by reminding them that Christ, their Redeemer, had overcome the Devil and his cohorts.

The homily for Palm Sunday reminds the people that the palm is a sign of the victory of Christ, who overcame the devils and rescued mankind. Further, says Aelfric, we must adorn ourselves, as with palms, but we will use good works, and, finally, we will deliver the palms victorious at the end of our days.

The first homily in the first series is a long narration of the Creation, the Fall of the angels and man, and the coming of the Redeemer. It is filled with warnings from Aelfric concerning the transitory nature of this life, and it concludes: "Men, most beloved, consider this discourse, and with great care eschew unrighteousness, and merit with good works the eternal life with God, who alone ruleth to eternity." The theme for the feast of Saint John the Baptist is the taking of Heaven by violence; chastity overcomes nature by violence; pride is traded for humility by violence; drunkenness, for soberness. The medieval concept of life as a conflict between virtue and vice is developed by Aelfric, who believed that vices are overcome by corresponding virtues.

In order to insure salvation, writes Aelfric, one must be on the alert against superstition, which is unchristian. Accordingly, in the homily for the feast of the Circumcision the author inveighs against diabolical customs: "Now foolish men practice manifold divinations on this day, with great error, after heathen custom, against their Christianity, as if they could prolong their life or their health, while they provoke the Almighty Creator." Some persons regulate their journeys by the moon, Aelfric reports, while others follow equally foolish customs, all of which are accursed. Any man who manipulates God's creatures with diabolical charms is a Christian in name only. He who directs a curse or malediction against another endangers his own soul and makes use of his tongue, not for the praise of God as it was intended, but in the service of the Devil, God's enemy.

Superstition, witchcraft, magic, and sorcery are all attacked by Aelfric in his sermons as having their origins in the devils. The true Christian does not depend upon these pagan practices, he writes, but only upon good works, faith, and the Christian virtues. Further, a man must have the spirit of God in him or his works will show the spirit of the Devil. Above all, man must be motivated by love. In the homily for the feast of Saint Stephen, Aelfric speaks at great length of Stephen's suffering and death, and goes on to illustrate how Stephen forgave those who persecuted him. The spirit that moved Stephen was love of God and his fellow man: "Let no man trust in alms-deeds, or in prayers, without the aforesaid love; for so long as he holds black malice in his heart, he cannot in any way delight the merciful God." Love is a key teaching of Aelfric, not the love of God in prayer only, but love proven in good works.

That Aelfric's *Homilies* were a success is attested by various imitations of them which appeared long after the Norman invasion of 1066. Aelfric himself chose the homiletic style for his *Lives of the Saints,* which appeared in 998. The *Homilies* contain sermons that are usually fresh and instructive, calculated to stimulate attention and interest. They are replete with sound common sense, and the subjects treated have a direct bearing on the way of life of the times in which he lived. Aelfric attempts to explain clearly every difficulty, and he overlooks nothing which could help to bring out the thought and spiritual overtones of the Gospel passages for the Church year. The avoidance of ecclesiastical idiom, the frequent use of Old English terminology, and the use of alliteration and Old English ballad rhythms, all assist the *Homilies* in carrying out Aelfric's purpose; namely, to instruct the unlearned members of the English Church of his day.

F.J.T.

BOOK OF PROVERBS

Author: Otloh of St. Emmeram (c.1010-c.1070)
Type of work: Spiritual instruction
*First transcribed:*c.1062-1066

Principal Ideas Advanced

[*The little collection here represented, not without some importance in the history or education, shows the traditional interest of medieval writers in the didactic and especially the apophthegmatic. The* Libellus proverbiorum, *on the author's own statement in his short prologue, culls from sources both sacred and profane. Otloh aims to produce a work for young students ("parvi scholastici") for use after a reading of the psalter.*]

In no one's judgment—least of all in his own—would Otloh of St. Emmeram (Latinized as *Othlonus*) be regarded as one of the great and commanding figures in medieval literature. Yet he was a man of genuine ability, a somewhat prolific writer, a traveler, and a scholar. Born about 1010 in the diocese of Freising, Germany, he was early destined by his parents for a study of the liberal arts. His earliest studies were in the Bavarian monastery of Tegernsee, and later he studied at the cloister of Hersfeld. He himself tells us how at quite a tender age he began to teach himself the art of writing, quite unaided by any mentor. Seemingly, the educational regimen of the times preferred some extensive progress in reading before writing was attempted. Otloh's self-taught efforts thus caused grave concern among his superiors because of his unacceptable method of grasping his pen. But dire predictions that he would never write well notwithstanding, he yet succeeded so capably that, even in boyhood, he was set to copying manuscripts.

His father had seemingly had in mind for him some established and highly remunerative priestly post, while Otloh himself had early decided upon the life of a monk. After sundry difficulties he was received by the Abbot Burchard, of the Monastery of St. Emmeram in Ratisbon, a place some distance from his boyhood environment. He remained there for a time as a guest, underwent a severe illness, and finally, in 1032, was accepted as a monk. In later years he had a four-year stay at the Monastery of Fulda, and a one-year stay at the Monastery of Amorbach, returning to St. Emmeram in 1067 or 1068, where he died not long afterwards, in or about the year 1070.

His writings are impressive in bulk, display a good contemporary Latinity, and show no little breadth of interests. Largely, they are contained in Volume 146 of Migne's *Patrologia Latina*, though his *Life of Saint Boniface* is in Volume 89 and his *Amorbach Sermon* in Volume 93.

Prior to 1032, at St. Emmeram, Otloh had written his *Book in Meter on Spiritual Doctrine;* this work included certain *opuscula* at the close of the thirty-ninth chapter: *Discourse to the Greedy or Proud,* in hexameters; *Verses on the Sequence of the Holy Spirit,* in hexameters; *Verses on the Gospel "When Jesus was born,"* in sapphics; *Metrical Discourse to the Blessed Trinity,* in hexameters; and *Verses on the Day of Judgment,* in elegiac couplets.

The thirty-year period between 1032 and 1062, at St. Emmeram, was marked by the following: the *Dialogue on Three Questions,* the *Life of Saint Nicholas,* the *Life of Saint Alto,* and the *Life of Saint Wolfkang*. Perhaps to these years belongs his *Book on the Confession of My Deeds,* a work which has since been lost.

During his sojourn at Fulda, 1062-1066, Otloh produced the *Book of Visions,* the *Life of Saint Boniface,* the *Manual on the Admonition of Clerics and Laymen,* and the *Book of Proverbs.* His *Amorbach Sermon* presumably belongs to 1067, during his stay at the Monastery of Amorbach.

Finally, the following are assigned to the period after 1067 or 1068, when he had returned to St. Emmeram: the *Life of Saint Magnus,* the *Book on the Spiritual Course,* the *Book on His Own Temptations, Varied Fortune, and Writings,* the *Story of a Miracle,* the *Letter on the Reasons for the Permission of Things Good and Things Evil.* To this period, too, may be assigned a doubtfully ascribed fragment, certain discourses and sermons, and certain unnamed and lost works. Otloh's language of publication was, of course, Latin; but it is to be observed that he issued a *Theodiscan Discourse* in German, accompanied by a Latin paraphrase.

The *Book of Proverbs* (*Libellus proverbiorum*), the especial concern of the present pages, follows a long tradition of the proverbial and the sententious, wherein we may distinguish the "proverbial" as pithy and brief sayings of popular origin and the "sententious" as sayings likewise pithy and brief but of conscious literary production. Thus, "Haste makes waste" one would designate proverbial; while the pungent and quotable utterances of a Greek Thucydides, a Roman Tacitus, and a British Macaulay or Chesterton are better labeled *sententiae.*

In ancient Rome proverbial and sententious utterances are not far to seek. There are indications of early rustic lore epitomized in proverb and apothegm; and Cato the Elder, father of Roman prose, almost surely enclosed sayings of homely wisdom in his now lost *Precepts to His Son.* Current under Cato's name, though not by him, were the *Poem on Morals* and the *Distichs of Cato,* the latter probably a work of the third or fourth century of our era. The *Comedies* of Plautus and Terence abound in quotable sayings. But the most impressive single collection surviving from ancient Rome is that of the mime-writer Publilius Syrus, of the time of Cicero and Caesar. There remain some seven hundred versified lines. These probably include many accretions to the original collection by Publilius, and it is noteworthy that the very name of Publilius itself was long lost, so that his collection came to be referred to as "the proverbs of Seneca."

Yet the actual writings of Seneca, like those of Lucan and Tacitus and other authors of the Silver Age (A.D. 14 to 180), provided a rich field for the excerpter of *sententiae* and found themselves richly represented in medieval *florilegia* or "cullings of flowers." The same medieval fondness for the didactic contributed to the continuing popularity of the satires of Horace and Persius and Juvenal and to the fables of Phaedrus and Avianus and Romulus.

In the Christian era itself we encounter, in the sixth century, the Irish monk Saint Columbanus, who composed various didactic works, among them his *Letter to Hunaldus* and his *Precepts of Living* or *Monostichs.* In the ninth century Sedulius Scotus compiled a collection of sayings from classical authors. Wipo, born about the close of the tenth century, included in his writings certain moral proverbs; these are interestingly phrased in such a way that the end of the first half and the end of the second half of each line rhyme—thus, "Decet *regem* discere *legem,*" or "Caritas non *ficta* odit de*licta,*" or "Mundi con*temptus* a Deo est in*ventus.*" For the last of these, the effect may be suggested by the English: "Contempt of the *world* by God was un*furled.*" Then, born about 972, was Egbert von Lüttich, who won no little fame through his *Laden Raft* (*Fecunda ratis*), a collection of axioms divided into two books, *prow* and *stern,* respectively. Following him, Arnulf, an eleventh century monk, put out between 1054 and 1056 his *Cleric's Delights* (*Delicie cleri*); here there are many versified *sententiae,* gathered for the greater part from the Sacred Scriptures.

Hence, Otloh, in his *Book of Proverbs,* is in a well established tradition. The opening lines of his own *Prologue* to the collection are instructive (and let us note again that to him the *Sententiae Publilii Syri* are by the philosopher Seneca): "Recently, when I had read the *Proverbs* called Seneca's, arranged in alphabetical order, I marveled at first that such great wisdom could have resided in an unbeliever, wisdom such as is found in certain of those proverbial sayings. Then I was in no small measure roused to an imitating of him in a like piece of work, that is to say, by gathering both from profane and sacred writings, and likewise from my own, some proverbs suitable for the edification of the faithful. For if this same Seneca, without any faith or hope for the attaining of eternal life but delighted solely with upright living in the present life, strove both to correct his own ways and to instruct others unto correction, how much more should I do likewise—I who believe that God is everywhere present and is promising eternal life to those who love Him!"

He is pleased with the thought of

the *utility* of short and meaningful words of wisdom: "And how pleasant and delightful it should appear to every man to have ever in mind and memory some brief words of quite compact sententiousness by means of which he may be corrected!" And he indicates a use of his own collection: "Now with the words of the proverbs here gathered any young pupils, should this be some one's desire, can be aptly instructed after a reading of the psalter. For they are of briefer and clearer sense than the fabled sayings of Avianus, and likewise more useful than certain utterances of Cato—both of which authors almost all masters are wont to read for the first instruction of the young. . . ."

Otloh's collection, to be sure, is not one of "proverbs" in the sense of "pithy and brief sayings of popular origin," but rather a gathering of *sententiae;* however, in him, as in his predecessors, no consistent attempt is made to distinguish *proverb* and *sententia,* and the word predominantly employed is, of course, *proverb.* Further, the tradition of an alphabetical arrangement of the items used was established in Publilius, though the alphabetization did not carry beyond the first letter of the word; thus, of the forty proverbs in Otloh's "B" group, the first begins with "Beati" and the last with "Bestia."

A very definite arrangement, therefore, alphabetically in reference to the first letter of the quotation, is observed. Thus the *Book of Proverbs* has twenty "chapters." In terms of the English alphabet, "I" and "J" are not distinguished, nor are "U" and "V." There are no chapters for "W" or "X" or "Y" or "Z," though (in certain of the codices) there are entries under the seldom used "K."

Within each chapter except "K" (which has only three items) there is a fixed tripartite division: first, excerpts from the *Sacred Scriptures;* second, various prose excerpts from writers sacred and profane; third, varied excerpts in meter.

For the first set, both the Old and the New Testaments are represented, with the preference given to the Old Testament. Excerpts from the *Psalms, Proverbs, Ecclesiastes, Wisdom,* and *Ecclesiasticus* are frequent; other Old Testament books occur as well. In the New Testament, *Gospels, Epistles, Acts of the Apostles,* and *Apocalypse* all appear.

As to the second and third divisions within the chapters, not all the excerpts, of course, are readily indentifiable. The prose excerpts, however, clearly stem from a variety of sources. In the second division, the profane authors employed include Sallust and Seneca; sacred writers include Saint Jerome and Saint Gregory the Great. Nor does Otloh neglect to cull from his own writings—"by gathering," he had said in his prologue, "both from profane and sacred writings, and likewise from my own." Thus, the fiftieth chapter as a whole of his *Dialogue on Three Questions* reappears in the *Book of Proverbs,* distributed according to alphabetical needs, as between the second and third divisions within various chapters.

The third and final division of each chapter, the metrical portion, is commonly introduced by a couplet, usually in hexameters. But under "A" there are two couplets; under "B" a set of three verses; under "I," two couplets; "K" has a total of only three *sen-*

tentiae, and the third of these is a single-line hexameter; "Q" has an elegiac couplet; "V" has two couplets. Following such heading verses are single hexameter lines, many of them displaying leonine rhyme. Horace and Juvenal and Cato appear here, and there are many hexameters from Otloh's own writings, and certain versified Scriptural items.

All in all, Otloh has left in his *Book of Proverbs* a slight work, perhaps, yet one of interest and value—not undeserving of the two-line hexameter with which he concludes his prologue:

This do you students observe and
  equally you, too, their mentors:
This do you boys and you youths
  devotedly read, I beseech you.

W.C.K.

PROSLOGION

Author: Saint Anselm of Canterbury (1033-1109)
Type of work: Dialectical theology
First transcribed: 1063-1078

Principal Ideas Advanced

One argument can be formulated which, without having recourse to Scripture, by itself suffices to prove that God exists and is the highest good, a being in need of nothing other than Himself, whereas all other existents need Him both to be and to be good.

The word "God" means that than which nothing greater can be thought; whoever knows what the word means must agree that something in reality corresponds to this concept.

This argument enables us to understand that God is all we believe Him to be: self-subsistent, creator of all else, incorporeal, omnipotent; in short, whatever it is better to be than not to be.

Saint Anselm called this work the *Proslogion* to indicate its relation to another and earlier writing of his own entitled the *Monologion.* In the early work he was engaged in monologue, soliloquy; in the *Proslogion* he addresses himself to others. The title under which we know the second work is, however, an afterthought; earlier Anselm called it *Fides quaerens intellectum:* faith seeking understanding. The rejected title is actually more informative, at least concerning the method of the work, for Anselm presupposes in himself and in his reader a firm belief in the truths of the Christian faith. The *Monologion* was written in response to a request by Anselm's fellow monks of the Norman monastery at Bec that he gather reasons for the truths of faith which would depend neither on Scripture nor on the Fathers of the Church for their cogency. This Anselm attempted to do and, in the earlier work, he set down three proofs for the existence of God. Afterward, so he tells us in his preface to the *Proslogion,* he found himself wondering if a simpler way of meeting the original request could be found, a reasoned approach to the central truths of faith, an approach that even the most humble and unlearned could grasp. For a long time he felt this hope was doomed to frustration, and he had all but despaired of realizing it when the proof which is the heart of the *Proslogion* suddenly came to him. That proof, called, since Kant, the Ontological Proof, is advanced as a justification of what its author already believes.

I do not seek to understand in order that I might believe, Anselm argued; rather, I believe in order that I might understand. Yet, so cogent and persuasive did Anselm take his proof to be that, having formulated it, he could say: if I did not choose to believe, I could not understand God not to exist.

The style of the *Proslogion* is personal, almost intimate. Anselm insinuates himself into the mind and heart of the reader by addressing him directly, by pleading for divine assistance in the eloquent prayer which makes up the whole of the first chapter, and then by continuing in a heightened style which derives from and compares well with that of the Augustine of the *Soliloquies* and, above all, the *Confessions.* It is Anselm himself who pointed out that Augustine was his mentor and guide, though Anselm shares none of the Platonic presuppositions of the great Father.

The ontological argument receives its first statement in the second chapter, where God is described by Anselm as that than which nothing greater can be thought. From this description Anselm deduces the existence and the attributes of God. But if God is that than which nothing greater can be thought, Anselm asks, why is it that we read, "The fool has said in his heart, there is no God"? To deny that God exists involves thinking that the being than which nothing greater can be thought does not exist. That is, the atheist at least grants mental existence to that than which nothing greater can be thought. Is he justified in denying an objective correlative to the concept?

It is important to realize that Anselm had no desire to erect into a general rule the validity of passing from idea to reality. This is clear from the *Proslogion* and is clearer still in his reply to his critic Gaunilon (monk of Marmoutier; died 1083), who objected that he had a very vivid concept of the isles of the blessed and yet found that doubt as to the real existence of the isles was compatible with the idea of them. In reply, Anselm points out that it is possible to have an idea which requires no referent. Before he paints, for example, the painter has an idea of a picture, but that idea is certainly no argument for the real existence of a picture yet to be painted. There is only one instance where it is valid to move from concept to reality, Anselm insists, and that is when the concept is of a being than which nothing greater can be thought.

One who would deny that God exists, Anselm argues, agrees that God is that than which nothing greater can be thought. But, having accepted this idea of God, the critic is led inexorably to the admission that God exists, for if that than which nothing greater can be thought enjoys only mental existence, it cannot be that than which nothing greater can be thought, since existence is closer to perfection than mental existence. Consequently, to have the concept of that than which nothing greater can be thought entails the assertion that such an entity exists. It is impossible to know what "God" means and also to deny that He exists. That is why Scripture calls the one who does so a fool.

Operative in Anselm's proof is the axiom that it is better to be (to exist) than not to be. If it is better to be than not to be, then that than which nothing greater can be thought must also be. Moreover, such a being must be whatever else it is better to be than not to be, and the *Proslogion* goes on to show what attributes, on this basis, God must have. "What then, Lord God, than which nothing greater can be thought, are you? What else than the greatest of all things, alone existent through Yourself, who made everything else from nothing? For, whatever is not thus is less than can be thought. But this cannot be thought of Thee, for what good could be lacking to the highest good from which is every good? Therefore you are just, veracious, blessed and whatever it is better to be than not to be, since it is better to be just than unjust and blessed rather than unblessed."

The *Proslogion* then goes on to show that God is intelligent, omnipotent, merciful, unchanging, eternal, and beyond our comprehension. These attributes are shown to attach to the triune God and, in summation, the *Proslogion* argues that God is principally goodness.

Saint Anselm has been called the father of Scholasticism, and the method of the *Proslogion* indicates that in his appeal to dialectic he is indeed a forerunner of the great theologians of the thirteenth century. It is therefore of some interest to note the opposed attitudes of Bonaventure and Aquinas *vis-à-vis* Anselm's ontological argument. Bonaventure defends the argument, and in doing so he distinguishes between knowing and knowing plus assent. According to Bonaventure, one can understand what the proposition "God does not exist" means, but one cannot know the proposition in the sense of assenting to it. Bonaventure, like Anselm himself, wanted to make "God does not exist" as unthinkable as "The part is greater than its whole."

Thomas Aquinas mentions and waives the difficulty involved in agreeing that "that than which nothing greater can be thought" is a noncontroversial meaning of "God." But, he argues, this meaning is not in itself warrant for the assertion that God exists. Thomas does not agree that Anselm has shown that the prohibition against arguing from concept to reality can be suspended, for the idea of even the greatest *existent* thing is not an assertion that such a thing exists. In modern times, Descartes accepted as valid an argument for God's existence very like that of the *Proslogion,* while Kant felt that all classical arguments for the existence of God are versions of the ontological and thus, like it, invalid.

Anselm stands at the threshold of the golden age of Scholasticism and is somewhat eclipsed by the stature of his successors, but the method of the *Proslogion* and of many of his other works is one that has been refined and altered but never essentially changed. That method, which was employed by Augustine but has subsequently been neglected, seeks to justify the truths of faith by allowing reason with its natural power and acquisitions to range over those truths and to establish them on rational grounds, either by showing their consistency or by showing that they are not in flat contradiction with what is known naturally. If anything, Anselm is more sanguine about the scope and power of this "dialectical" method than were later thinkers. In the *Proslogion* he argued, in effect, that "God exists" is a self-evident truth, since knowledge of what the term means forces assent to the proposition. Whatever their judgments on its validity, most subsequent philosophers exhibit interest in Anselm's ontological argument.

R.M.

LIBER DE CORPORE ET SANGUINE DOMINI

Author: Lanfranc (c.1005-1089)
Type of work: Theological polemic
First transcribed: c.1080

Principal Ideas Advanced

The Christian belief in the Eucharist holds that at the words of consecration in the Mass the substance of bread and wine is replaced by the substance of the Body and Blood of Jesus Christ although the appearance or accidents of bread and wine remain.

The effort of Berengar of Tours to maintain that there is no such transubstantiation is particularly insidious because he twists the words of such authorities as Saint Augustine to make it seem that they hold with him, whereas a careful and honest reading of the authorities indicates that Berengar contradicts the traditional teaching of the Church and Fathers.

Berengar actually sets his own reason and arguments above tradition, authority, and the judgments of ecclesiastical councils.

Lanfranc, the teacher of Saint Anselm, and Anselm's predecessor as Archbishop of Canterbury, wrote the *Liber de Corpore et Sanguine Domini* to refute the heresy of Berengar of Tours concerning the nature of the Eucharist. Like his pupil Anselm, Lanfranc may be thought of as taking a moderate position with respect to the controversy which raged over the propriety of using dialectic or, generally, philosophy in the discussion of matters of faith. The title of Lanfranc's work is almost a generic one; it was the title of a ninth century work by Paschasius which Berengar attacked, and many others who wrote in opposition to Berengar used the same title. The prestige of Lanfranc as theologian and churchman tended to focus attention on his reply to Berengar.

Lanfranc was born in Pavia, Italy; he was trained as a lawyer and then came to France, where, in Normandy, he devoted himself to learning. When it became clear to him that he had a religious vocation, he repaired to the recently founded monastery at Bec, where eventually he opened a school. Men of high caliber were attracted to the school, Anselm notable among them, but also the future Pope Alexander II. Lanfranc, who was drawn into the controversy stirred up by Berengar over the nature of the Eucharist had an opportunity to defend his own views at Rome and was ever after an adversary of Berengar's teaching on the Sacrament of the Altar. In order to understand the nature of the *Liber de Corpore et Sanguine Domini* we have to understand something of the controversy between the Dialecticians and the Anti-Dialecticians and, more particularly, we have to know something of the doctrine advanced by Berengar of Tours.

In the eleventh century two extreme positions with respect to the use of dialectic in discussing matters of faith arose. It is not an easy matter to say what precisely brought this about. The documents which were made use of by the "Dialecticians" were ones which had been around for a long time, being principally the early books of the *Organon* of Aristotle and the commentaries on them by Boethius. But, while always there, these works seem to have waited for the modicum of peace and leisure attendant on Europe's emergence from the Dark Ages to exercise the fascination that led to the great debate. In the school at Chartres, which was opened at the end of the tenth century, the use of dialectic as a tool in discussing Christian belief was always modest and controlled, but the concentration on the study of logic in the schools induced an attitude that has come to be called rationalism. That is, men began to think of human reason as bounded by no limits and the art of logic was the only guide of its limitless reach. There seemed to be no question, no doctrine, which could not be clarified and served by the application to it of logical analysis. It appeared that matters of faith were being brought to the bar of natural reason in such a way that only what squared with natural reason, aided of course by logic, could pass muster as true and acceptable. Great men, among them some who were to be canonized saints, spoke out against this tendency, and in the process they seemed to proscribe the study of logic itself. Few were more outspoken on the subject than Saint Peter Damian. He had taught school himself at one time and so could speak of dialectic as one who had managed to extricate himself from its charms. Peter Damian goes so far as to say that the contradictories of the most basic natural truths are possible to God. Saint Bernard of Clairvaux also raised his eloquent voice against the Dialecticians. Thus, the foes of dialectic and eloquence seem often to have been most reliant on dialectic and eloquence in their attacks. This paradoxical circumstance is something of considerable importance, for the extreme Anti-Dialecticians, by the very quality of their opposition, give the charter to the more moderate theory on the employment of philosophy by the man of faith. Lanfranc and Anselm are both representatives of the moderate position. Berengar of Tours is the very type of the Dialectician, the rationalist, who in his devotion to logic calls into question fundamental tenets of the Christian tradition.

The doctrine of the Eucharist certainly provided a belief well calculated to strain the credulity of the rationalist. The traditional doctrine, the teaching of the Church that Lanfranc defends, is that at the words of consecration in the Mass the substance of the bread and wine is replaced by the Body and Blood of Jesus Christ while retaining the appearances or accidents of bread and wine. Berengar rejected this doctrine and, when he was attacked for it, appealed to the authority of John Scotus Erigena. Scotus Erigena, in the ninth century, had attacked a work of Paschasius which, as we have mentioned, bore the same title as Lanfranc's. Thus, Lanfranc entered the controversy by refuting Scotus Erigena's position and attacking Berengar's appeal to it. Berengar was hailed before a number of councils to answer for his views. In 1055 at Tours and again at Rome in 1059 he retracted his views and signed a formula of faith. But he later repudiated his earlier retractions, attacked the formulas he had signed, wrote a book against Lanfranc, was condemned several more times, and signed several more recantations. But he kept reversing himself until the Council of Bordeaux in 1080, when the matter seems to have been definitively settled and Berengar retired.

Berengar sought to base his dissident views not only on the authority of Scotus Erigena but also on that of Saints Jerome, Ambrose, and Augustine. Briefly, what he taught was that the bread and wine do not become the Body and Blood of Jesus Christ, for the bread and wine remain and are but the sacramental signs of the presence of Christ's Body and Blood. Thus, apparently, Christ is really present in the Sacrament of the Altar, but the substance of the bread and wine is not replaced by the Body and Blood of Christ. There is no transubstantiation.

Lanfranc's *Liber de Corpore et Sanguine Domini* is a work in twenty-three chapters in which he undertakes to refute Berengar by taking up the various authorities to which his adversary appealed and showing that, far from serving Berengar's view, they bolster the view Berengar is attacking. Lanfranc quite evidently does not have much respect for his adversary, and he details the occasions in which Berengar went back on his written retractions. What deeply troubles Lanfranc is not so much the original error as Berengar's apparent contempt for authority which led him to retain his own view at all costs and in the face of the unmistakable condemnation of the Church. Something more than disingenuousness is involved here, and Lanfranc finds Berengar almost diabolical. However, although there is strong invective in the *Liber de Corpore et Sanguine Domini,* there is also an indication of how dialectic can be used sanely, an attitude toward philosophy which sees it as an aid to understanding what is believed but not as the absolute measure of what has been revealed. The impression one gets from reading Lanfranc is that Berengar has abused a worth-while instrument. Thus, there is no strident attack on dialectic as such; indeed, Lanfranc takes permissible delight in pointing out fallacies in Berengar's argument. What Lanfranc objects to in Berengar is the latter's desire to comprehend everything by means of logical arguments and, in the process, to reject tradition and authority. That neither reason nor authority need be rejected is the message of Lanfranc, as it is the message of Saint Anselm and of the great Scholastics who were yet to come.

R.M.

CUR DEUS HOMO

Author: Saint Anselm of Canterbury (1033-1109)
Type of work: Theological dialogue
First transcribed: 1098

Principal Ideas Advanced

It is possible to abstract from the historical existence of Christ and prove by necessary reasons that, given man's sin, God had to become man in order to redeem man and make it possible for him to attain the goal to which he is destined by God.

For the man of faith, belief precedes his search for arguments which bolster his faith, but the arguments that he devises can be convincing to those without faith and show them the evidence for the truths the Christian believes.

While the Incarnation may seem principally to be called for by the justice of God, God's becoming man is the greatest instance of the divine mercy.

The intention of Saint Anselm in the *Cur Deus Homo,* as the title indicates, is to show why God became man; he proposes to prove by necessary arguments that man's salvation would be impossible without the Incarnation. If God's honor seems to demand that He not let mankind perish, since man is destined by God for beatitude, why did God choose to become man when He could have achieved the same result otherwise, by a simple act of will, for example? Anselm proposes to deal with the question posed just that way, and his claims for the answer he will provide are striking. He states in the preface his purpose and the method he will follow. Having noted that the work is divided into two books, he writes: "The first contains the objections of those who reject the Christian faith, because they feel it contradicts reason, as well as the responses the faithful make to those objections. Making abstraction from Christ as if nothing were known of Him, this book proves by necessary arguments the impossibility that any man be saved without Him. In the second book, by an identical method, proceeding as if nothing were known of Christ, it is demonstrated by arguments and truths no less evident that human nature was made so that one day the whole man, that is to say, body and soul, would enjoy a blessed immortality; that it is necessary that this end be realized and this only by a God-

Man; and that it is necessary that everything we believe about Christ was actually realized."

Anselm undertakes the discussion of these matters in the form of a dialogue with one Boso, a fellow monk who had been among those urging Anselm to commit his thought on these matters to writing. Boso's first remark casts light on the nature of the "necessary arguments" referred to above. "Just as correct order demands that we first believe the profound truths of the Christian faith before we presume to submit them to a rational investigation, so it seems to me it would be a matter of negligence on our part if, once confirmed in faith, we did not strive to understand what we believe." His faith does not depend on such elucidation; even if none were forthcoming, the firmness of his faith would remain unaltered, yet Boso pleads with Anselm to discuss why an omnipotent God assumed a nature so infirm and base as is human nature. After suitable modest hesitation, Anselm adds that perhaps the question requires a sophisticated inquiry into the concepts of power, necessity, and will but Boso suggests that his master need only speak of these to the degree necessary for the present inquiry. Anselm's final scruple has to do with his inability to construct arguments commensurate in their beauty with the subject, Christ, whose beauty surpasses that of the sons of men. Boso allays this fear with the confident challenge of the devoted disciple that anyone who thinks the work insufficiently beautiful is free to attempt to write one more beautiful.

Once Anselm has made clear his diffidence, that he is not rushing precipitously into a discussion of so difficult a point, he wants to make clear how what he is going to say should be understood. Any explication he gives which is not confirmed by a higher authority, even though it seems to him to be firmly founded on reason, should be regarded as certain only in the sense that he accepts it until God grants it to him to see more clearly. If he seems to reply satisfactorily to Boso's questions, Anselm says, the reader should constantly remind himself that one wiser than Anselm could respond yet more satisfactorily. Finally, any explanations given are, after all, human ones, and it must be understood that the profound reasons for what they are to discuss will ever remain obscure.

Thus far Anselm does not reveal himself as a rationalist, although he suggests in the preface that, quite apart from faith, by abstracting from the historical existence of Christ, he will attempt to come up with arguments which will prove that Christ must have existed. When the dialogue begins, we seem to be faced with an instance of Anselm's method which is best summed up in his own phrase: *fides quaerens intellectum,* faith seeking understanding. That is, he has something to investigate rationally here precisely because he already believes it; if he did not believe it, there would simply be no problem. Boso's first speech seems to stress that Anselm, presupposing faith, will attempt to construct arguments which will manifest, elucidate, and justify that faith.

And yet it is Boso who casts a somewhat different light on the necessary arguments Anselm will propose. Boso will take the part of those who have not faith (it is felt that Anselm's target here is not so much those who have absolutely no faith, but Jews and

Moslems) and he suggests that, while Anselm seeks reasons for what he believes, these others want reasons in order to believe. Despite this different orientation, the same arguments can serve both functions; namely, to elucidate a presupposed faith and lead to a faith not yet possessed. Boso, however, will undertake to apply the test of sacred authority to whatever Anselm says.

Anselm continues to comment on the nature of the work he is writing. Boso gives as an objection of the unfaithful that it is an offense and outrage to God to affirm that He entered into the womb of a woman, was born from a woman's body, that He grew, took nourishment, and was subject to all the woes that flesh is heir to. On the contrary, Anselm replies, the affirmation of the Incarnation provides an opportunity to praise the mercy of God. The unfaithful would be well-advised to consider the propriety (*convenientia*) of the fact that just as all men fell as a result of the disobedience of one man, so all men are saved by the obedience of one man; that just as the sin which was our downfall had its origin in a woman, so it is fitting that the author of our justification be born from a woman; that just as the Devil seduced man with the fruit of a tree, so it is fitting that sin be conquered on a tree. Pretty pictures, replies devoid of necessity, Boso retorts for the unfaithful; such considerations cannot prove the assertion that God must become man. Arguments from propriety or fittingness (*convenientia*) seem to the unfaithful to constitute a fiction, and Anselm is going to have to place in evidence the rational solidity of the truth; that is, a necessity which proves that God could and should lower Himself in the manner affirmed. Only after such necessary arguments will arguments from propriety be in order. Anselm then proposes the following as a necessary argument: mankind, the most precious work of God, would be totally lost and God's plan for man wholly frustrated if man had not been redeemed by his Creator. Later Anselm says something of import concerning the meaning of "necessary" applied to such arguments. Addressing himself to Boso, he says, "Since in the present inquiry you are taking the part of those who will believe nothing except on the basis of a rational demonstration, I want us to be in accord in this that, speaking of God, we allow nothing which in however small a measure admits impropriety and set aside no argument, no matter how small, on the condition that no stronger argument can be opposed to it. For, when it is a question of God, if the least impropriety entails an impossibility, the least argument, so long as it is not rebutted by a stronger, is accompanied by necessity."

The foregoing remarks indicate that it is no easy matter to state precisely what Anselm conceives his method to be. At times he speaks of the possibility of coming up with "necessary" arguments for believed truths, while at other times he seems clearly to indicate that without the illumination of faith he would have neither the occasion nor the desire to seek such arguments. Yet the arguments he seeks, once attained, should have force for those who do not come to them with the gift of faith. Finally, the necessity claimed for these arguments is of a decidedly minimal sort. What cannot be gainsaid takes on necessity when we are speaking of God.

Commentators continue to discuss the compatibility and consistency of these various remarks by Anselm on his procedure. We shall not here attempt to provide an interpretation nor adjudicate those which have hitherto been offered. But it may be well, in closing these methodological remarks, to revert again to that justly famous maxim of Anselm which stands as a motto to all his work: *fides quaerens intellectum.* Saint Anselm of the *Cur Deus Homo* is a man of Christian faith who feels the irresistible pull to meditate on what he believes, to adduce reasons for it, to clarify it in terms which make it accessible to every man. If he sometimes seems to suggest that there are arguments which must propel one into faith, it seems correct to say that this was surely not Anselm's true view. A clear description of the task of the theologian must await a later day, but however he describes what he is doing, Anselm in the *Cur Deus Homo,* as elsewhere, lovingly meditates on the truths of faith and what he has to say will be accounted precious by any believer.

As has been indicated above, the First Book of the *Cur Deus Homo,* is devoted to presenting and refuting the objections of the unfaithful. Anselm argues that, since God has destined man for a given end, His purpose would be frustrated if He did not redeem man once he had fallen. But why could not this have been accomplished by someone other than God? Could not God have created a man without sin who might accomplish the task? But if this had been done, mankind would have been so indebted to that person that it would have become his collective slave, and man is the slave of God alone.

However, if the faithful say that God has redeemed man, saving him from Hell and the Devil, it is objected that God could have accomplished this by a simple command. And what conception of the Devil permits us to see him as a rival of God, as an alternate possessor of men? To say that God debased Himself and became man seems to fly in the face of reason; to say that God suffered seems to contradict the notion of divinity.

Anselm, in reply, says that, of course, it is impossible for the divine nature to suffer, but Christ, who is true God and true man, has suffering attributed to Him insofar as He has a human nature. So, too, Christ's obedience to the Father, obedience even unto death, is the debt human nature owes divine nature because of sin. To sin is to fail to render to God what is due Him; the creature sins whenever his will is not in submission to the divine will. To make satisfaction for sin, it is not enough to restore what one has withdrawn; because of the object of the offense, it is necessary to give in compensation more than one has taken away.

Anselm now returns to the question whether it would be fitting for God to remit sin by simple mercy without requiring that the debt incurred be acquitted. To do that, that is, simply to dismiss it, would be to fail to punish the sinner, and this would be a violation of order. But God cannot be conceived as introducing disorder into His Kingdom. Moreover, if God did not punish the sinner, He would treat the sinner and one who does not sin equally, and that seems unjust. But does not God ask us to forgive one another? Anselm says that this precept is given lest we assume the divine prerogative of punishing. But is God bound by the demands of justice? Anselm retorts in the following way. It does not follow that if God lies, lying is just; rather we should say, if God lies, God is not God.

Now it would be intolerable, for the order of the universe, if the creature took away from the honor of God and did not restore what he had taken away. That, in sum, is why God does not simply dismiss sin by a simple and merciful act of His will. God's honor demands the punishment of sin. But what can increase or diminish the honor of God? Anselm agrees that, considered in itself, the divine honor can be neither increased or diminished. The creature is said to honor God insofar as he plays the role assigned him in the universe and to dishonor Him when he does not play this role.

Anselm finds another reason for the salvation of man in the fact that the places of the fallen angels may be filled. This is one of the lengthier discussions of the First Book. Then, arguing that man must satisfy for his sin in a manner commensurate with his offense, Anselm goes on to show that man is himself incapable of making the recompense needed. This follows from the gravity of sin. Man, consequently, is in an impossible situation. He cannot be happy unless he renders to God his due; in the state of sin he cannot do this and his incapacity does not excuse him. From such considerations it follows that man can be saved only by Christ, by God become man.

The Second Book of the *Cur Deus Homo* attempts to prove the assumptions of the concluding argument of the preceding book. Anselm will prove that man was indeed created in order to enjoy perfect happiness and that death comes to him only because he has sinned. The beatitude for which he is destined entails that the body will be resurrected. God, having fashioned man for the end of beatitude, must bring man to that goal. The necessity in question here must not be construed as a constraint on God, however; it is a necessity that He imposes on Himself, so to speak, by the desire involved in the creation of man. Anselm now takes up one by one the various points made by Boso in Book One when Boso first stated the misgivings of the unfaithful concerning what Christians believe about the Incarnation. Anselm sets out to prove the satisfaction demanded for man's sin can only be made by a God-Man and that it is necessary that one and the same person be perfect God and perfect man. Moreover, the God-Man must be a descendant from Adam and the son of a Virgin. The death of this incarnate God must be something freely chosen; if He partakes of our weaknesses, this participation is not constitutive of misery. Ignorance is not one of our weaknesses He shares. The death of the incarnate God far outweighs in significance the sins for which that death makes satisfaction. In the course of offering proofs for these and other statements in the twenty-two chapters of Book Two, Anselm discusses the way in which Christ was and was not obliged to die for our sin.

Anselm's approach to the Incarnation may seem to stress the needs of divine justice, but in Chapter 20 of the second book he brings his discussion to its close with a eulogy of the divine mercy: "With respect to the mercy of God which seems to you to evaporate when we consider the divine justice and the sin of man, we find that it is so great and so conformed with His justice that it cannot be conceived to be greater or more just. For can one conceive conduct more merciful than that of God the Father saying to the sinner condemned to eternal torments and deprived of the power to redeem himself: Take my only son and offer Him in your place? Or the Son Himself [saying]: Take me and redeem yourself? For that is indeed what He says to us, when He calls us to the Christian faith and attracts us to it." Anselm, accordingly, sees a perfect compatibility of the justice and mercy of God as they manifest themselves in the Incarnation.

Disputes about the accuracy of Anselm's own descriptions of what he was doing in the *Cur Deus Homo* may continue, but the believer will find in the arguments brought forward many powerful defenses of the fittingness of the Incarnation. Whether these arguments can be accepted as proving *a priori* what is accepted on faith is, to say the least, doubtful; but given the faith, Anselm's arguments provide a fruitful source of meditation because they represent, we may be sure, fruits of meditation on the part of Anselm.

R.M.

SIC ET NON

Author: Peter Abelard (1079-1142)
Type of work: Problematic sourcebook for theologians
First transcribed: c.1122

Principal Ideas Advanced

Since the books of Scripture and the writings of the Fathers present us with a number of seeming contradictions, the task of the theologian is to employ dialectic to dissolve these oppositions.

Dialectic, as the technique which enables one to discern the many meanings and uses of words, can do much to clear away these contradictions.

The canonical books of Scripture, unlike the writings of the Fathers, are infallible, but both kinds of books contain copyists' errors and even factual errors in matters unimportant to the great truths of faith.

Conflicting authoritative statements concerning 158 statements of faith are collected to induce doubt in the reader, for doubt will make him inquire, and inquiry, by overcoming doubt, will bring him to the truth.

Peter Abelard's *Sic et non* (*Yes and No*) has long been regarded as an extremely important document in the history of the development of the Scholastic method and yet, significantly enough, its contents are simply a compilation of the writings of others, a selection from Scripture and the Fathers and even the pagan philosophers. Only the prologue to the selected passages is a completely original work and, in proportion to the whole, it is quantitatively negligible. Nevertheless, this work is not only a thesaurus or compendium of texts; there is a form which binds the disparate elements together, as the title indicates. To many questions which we ask, Abelard writes, the answer we must give would seem to be, if we consult authority, both yes and no. Scripture and the writings of the Fathers appear to give contradictory answers to the most fundamental problems of Christian faith. Abelard discusses the reason for this in his prologue, and he makes his claim evident by bringing opposing authorities to bear on the 158 propositions which make up *Sic et non*. The problematical method was not original with Abelard, but no one before him carried it out with such verve and thoroughness.

The question inevitably arises as to Abelard's intention in this work. It may seem that he is merely ringing the changes on the theme that if you appeal to Scripture and authority, you can prove anything *and* its opposite. In order to see that this is not what Abelard intended, it is imperative to understand his contribution to the growth of theology (the very word became current with him) by considering the work of his predecessors, Abelard's other theological works, and his more or less immediate influence. Against this somewhat diffuse background, we will find that in method Abelard is in the mainstream of Scholastic theology and that in content he is not as unorthodox as was once thought.

In a unique fashion for a Scholastic figure, the very person of Abelard is taken to be a factor in any effort to grasp the intent of his teaching. Abelard's contribution, that in terms of which he is praised or blamed by his contemporaries, depending on their persuasions, is his insistence on the utility of logic or dialectic in approaching the documents of faith. He goes so far as to link up logic and the Divine Logos of John's Gospel: "Since the Word of the Father, Our Lord Jesus Christ, is called Logos in Greek, just as he is sometimes called the Wisdom of the Father, many things pertain to him by that science which is connected with him by its very name, logic being derived from logos: one is called a Christian from Christ and logic is properly named from logos. . . ." The rules of logic, which are the laws of natural human reason, are of aid when we attempt to understand what we firmly believe. Such a contention seems hardly to go beyond the remarks and practice of Saint Anselm (1033-1109). Yet Abelard was the object of prolonged and fervent attack by Saint Bernard of Clairvaux (1901-1153), who felt that Abelard was subjecting faith to the measure of what man can naturally understand in such a way that, if matters of faith could not be proved by reason, they must then be rejected as false. Abelard, whatever his intention, managed too often to convey the impression that he wished to convert the Augustinian motif of Anselm from *credo ut intelligam* to *intelligo ut credam*. Yet the difference between Anselm and Abelard has been judged to be less one of doctrine than of personality. It has been suggested that Anselm was the contemplative monk who made unobtrusive use of dialectic to explore beliefs lovingly meditated on, whereas Abelard was first and foremost the dialectician, a man of intellectual combat to whom struggle and victory in the form of the refutation and rout of his opponents were the breath of life.

It may seem that to make appeal to Abelard's personality to explain or extenuate the ambiguity and enigmatic effect of his teachings is to go from the obscure to the more obscure. The career of Abelard was a dazzling one. He studied under Roscelin (c.1050-c.1120) and William of Champeaux (1070-c.1121), prominent figures in the early twelfth century controversy over the status of universals, but Abelard quickly came to question and then to refute his teachers. He shortly opened his own school, apparently by popular demand, first at Melun, then at Corbeil. When he turned to study theology under Anselm of Laon (died 1117) and William of Champeaux, his status as student once more swiftly converted to that of teacher. He opened a school on Mount St. Geneviève on the left bank of the Seine and eventually became head of the cathedral school of Notre Dame. At the apex of his career, he met Héloïse, and the romantic drama he chronicled in *Historia calamitatum* took place. Although he had secretly married Héloïse (for the future of a theologian known to be married would have been bleak), agents of her uncle emasculated him, and Abelard and Héloïse repaired to monastery and convent, respectively. There he resumed his career as a theologian, but works of his were condemned in 1121 at the Council of Soissons and in 1141 at the Council of Sens. After the latter council's decision, Abelard set out for Rome to appeal, but he never reached his destination. The last year of his life was spent in a monastery of Cluny; and Peter the Venerable, who knew him during this year, was full of praise for the virtue of this incredible monk.

Abelard's own story of his fall from the height of fame to at least momentary infamy does little to clarify the reasons for the fall. He remains an enigma: at once an exemplary monk and a contentious dialectician; a teacher whose charm and erudition captivated generations of students, and a student who seemed always destined to be contemptuous of the masters whom he dethroned. Handsome, arrogant, egocentric, he had a salutary daring in his efforts to show that one does not defend the Faith by calling into question the validity of the instruments of defense. Although it is easy to understand how Abelard, because of his stormy personality, was attacked for what Anselm, too, had practiced, an appeal to his personality does not provide us with a complete key to his writings. That key must be sought in the works themselves.

The prologue to *Sic et non* must be compared with two other works of Abelard, the so-called *Introductio ad theologiam* and the *Theologia Christiana*. When taken together, this trio of works gives us an understanding of the purpose of Abelard's effort as a theologian, and we are thus prevented from misconstruing the import of *Sic et non*.

The prologue to *Sic et non* is famous as an expression of Abelard's views on the use of logic in theology, but quite conflicting interpretations have been put on what he says there. Abelard begins with the statement of a truth which would have made itself felt by any student of Scripture and the Fathers. Our authorities often contradict themselves and one another, Abelard points out. Are these contradictions real or apparent? It is not for us to call these authors liars or deceivers, he writes, and applies to them that utterance of the Lord, "He who hears you, hears me; he who despises you, despises me." The defect, Abelard suggests, is rather on our side, then; our weak minds cannot grasp the sense of the passages.

If there is a defect on our side, Abelard continues, if we must always refrain from calling the sacred writers and the Fathers liars, there is nonetheless reason for the difficulties we meet in their writings. Apparent contradictions are frequent, and we must ask why this is so. A major impediment to our understanding the writings of authorities is their unconventional use of language and their use of ambiguous words. If a word has many meanings, it is quite clear that unless we know what meaning is intended, the passage in which it occurs cannot deliver up to us its proper significance.

Abelard's remarks are hardly revolutionary, but coming from the pen of Abelard they constitute, in effect, dialectic's charter as the instrument for understanding matters of faith. The dialectic Abelard knew and practiced has been called a *sprachlogik* to indicate that what might appear to be mere grammar is part and parcel of what Abelard means by logic or dialectic. The hope that he places in this application of logic to authority is summarized in the following statement from his prologue: "It is easy to arrive at a solution of most controversies if we are able to show that the same words have been used with different meanings by different authors." There are textual difficulties which arise from the variation of vocabulary for stylistic reasons and from the intentional use of bad grammar to communicate more efficaciously with the unlearned or to come closer to the truth to be expressed. The rule to follow, Abelard writes, is this: the usage of men rather than any *a priori* view of linguistic priority must govern the art of teaching.

With respect to Scripture itself, Abelard continues, we must not attempt to define or comprehend it when our efforts to understand it fail. He makes a distinction, hitherto imperfectly respected, between the books of Scripture and the writings of the Fathers: the latter are not infallible, as the authors themselves tell us. The practice of the Fathers makes it clear that there is no point in giving equal weight to whatever can be plucked from their writings. Their works often contain controversial opinions with which they do not agree and which may indeed be heretical. Some of the Fathers called attention to this practice in order to defend themselves against criticisms that came their way. Moreover, Abelard adds, men like Augustine corrected or retracted passages they had written, and they wrote not to give the last word, but simply to express views which were to be judged rather than uncritically accepted. Finally, Abelard writes, some works attributed to the Fathers were not written by them; a kind of textual criticism is necessary, therefore, before anyone can make proper use of the documents.

Although Abelard opposes the fallibility of the Fathers to the infallibility of the Scriptures, there are qualifications made in the opposition. Both the Scriptures and the writings of the Fathers come to us through the efforts of scribes and are equally subject to secretarial errors. Sometimes, too, the sacred writers uncritically adopted human opinion; for example, Joseph is called the father of Christ. Moreover, there are factual mistakes and errors, but these are never in matters important to faith.

Having indicated the subjective and objective difficulties which produce seeming contradictions, Abelard proposes to show that there are such contradictions by adducing authoritative and conflicting statements concerning 158 questions pertaining to faith. Over and above his view that we must employ dialectic if we are to attain to an understanding of authority, Abelard believed that there was a distinct advantage in seeking out such difficulties. By listing and sharpening conflicts of opinion, he believed that his reader would be provoked to more intensive investigation of the truth of the matter. He quotes Aristotle to the effect that it is useful to doubt, and he then expresses himself thus: "By doubting we are led to inquire and by inquiring we are led to the truth." The nature of the doubt Abelard advocated has been variously understood. Some interpreters have felt that he was defending total skepticism, but this view does not seem to be defensible. Abelard wanted to distinguish between the fallible authority of the Fathers and the infallible authority of the books of Scripture recognized by the Church. Although the Scriptures are infallible, their true meaning is not always readily apparent. An appreciation of the multiple meanings of words, of stylistic variations, of grammatical errors knowingly made so as to convey more graphically the truth in question, and even of factual errors given in support of matters of less import is necessary if one is to arrive at the infallible truth of Scripture. But what one brings to Holy Writ, what dialectic presupposes and cannot confer, is faith. Abelard could write to Héloïse that he had no wish to be a philosopher if this entailed opposing St. Paul and that he would spurn being Aristotle himself if such a condition would set him in opposition to Christ. The final recourse, the rock on which all else must be constructed, is Christ and the Christian faith.

The prologue to the *Introductio ad theologiam* gives ample evidence that Abelard had no desire to call into question or to jeopardize the Faith by his use of dialectic; he believed that the failure to clarify the Faith dialectically would leave the simple faithful open to the blandishments of heretics. As for his attitude toward the authority of the Church, there is no evidence that Abelard did other than accept the condemnations that came his way. True, he suggests that the propositions rightly condemned were not taught by himself, but he does not question the right of the Church to be the final arbiter in matters of faith. It is, of course, another question whether Abelard, despite his intention, taught things contrary to the Catholic faith. Recent scholars tend to feel that his doctrine was not always in conflict with orthodoxy when it was thought to be, but by even the most irenic estimate there remains a good number of teachings which certainly go contrary to the Faith. For example, in reacting against the tritheistic heresy, according to which the doctrine of the Trinity entails that there are three Gods, Abelard tends to overlook the real differences in the Persons of the Trinity. Moreover, he became so impressed by the accomplishments of pagan thinkers—and this at a time when there was as yet imperfect access to Aristotle as well as Plato—that he speaks of some of them as saints and suggests that the supernatural order somehow grew out of their natural achievements.

Sic et non is a compilation of seeming contradictions from various authorities, and it was designed to provoke inquiry on the part of students so that by seeking to overcome the difficulties they would arrive at the truth. That it was not intended as an attack on authority or as an attempt to reduce the truths of the Faith to the level of natural reason is corroborated by the interesting fact that none of Abelard's adversaries made use of *Sic et non* in charges against him.

Abelard divided theology into three main parts: faith, the sacraments, and charity. It is possible to see the propositions of *Sic et non* as roughly following that division. Propositions 1-58 are largely concerned with faith; 59-135 with the sacraments; 136-158 with charity. Examples of propositions of the first group are: that faith should be bolstered by human arguments and the opposite; that faith is concerned only with hidden things and the opposite; that only God is to be believed and the opposite.

Abelard's influence on the later Middle Ages is somewhat hidden because of the two condemnations of his writings. His indirect influence through his students was of course great, and the impetus he gave to employing all the resources of human understanding to approach the truths of faith was deep and lasting. If anything, it must be said that his effort was premature. Abelard lived just before the time when the writings of pagan antiquity began to flood into the West, principally the hitherto unknown writings of Aristotle together with Arab commentaries, interpretations which presented unprecedented dangers and opportunities. We can only imagine what Abelard might have done had he lived seventy-five or a hundred years later. When we consider the impact on him of Aristotle's so-called *logica nova,* we have to ask what Abelard would have done if the rest of the philosopher's works had been available to him. These are interesting but inconsequential questions. Abelard teaches as much by his excesses as by his genuine contributions; any attempt to understand what he taught must inevitably be affected by his enigmatic personality as the lionized teacher, the lover and husband, the maimed monk and abbot, and the controversial dialection and theologian. With all his fascination and daring originality, Abelard remains an indispensable link in the development of the method which would flower so wonderfully in the theological *summae* of the thirteenth century.

R.M.

ON THE STEPS OF HUMILITY AND PRIDE

Author: Saint Bernard (1091-1153)
Type of work: Ascetical and mystical theology
First transcribed: c.1121-1125

Principal Ideas Advanced

Truth is attained only through the practice of humility, a virtue which may be defined as that which enables a man to see himself as he truly is and thereby to become aware of his own worthlessness.

There are three degrees of truth to be attained: truth in ourselves, truth in our neighbors, Truth in its essential nature; that is, God.

The search for truth involves the progressive elimination of pride in oneself, the development of compassion for one's neighbor, and the achievement of purity of heart; in other words, one seeks humility, charity, and contemplation.

The ultimate aim of the progressive elimination of pride and the acquisition of the corresponding degrees of humility is to achieve the fullness of love.

It is not surprising that Saint Bernard of Clairvaux's first written treatise should be entitled *On the Steps of Humility and Pride.* He was a true son of Saint Benedict, the founder of Western monasticism, and Saint Benedict had devoted Chapter 7 of his *Rule* to a detailed treatment of the virtue of humility, treating it as a ladder consisting of twelve steps that lead upward to Heaven.

Saint Bernard's treatise (*De gradibus humilitatis et superbiae*) was written at the request of one of his former monks, Godfrey, a relative, who had accompanied Bernard to Citeaux in 1112 and afterwards to Clairvaux. The substance of the treatise was taken from a number of brief addresses which Bernard had given to his monks. As part of the daily routine of a Cistercian monastery the monks met in the chapter house. During the chapter meeting a section of the *Rule* of Saint Benedict was read daily; then the abbot would comment on and explain the section read.

There is little doubt that Saint Benedict's *Rule* had a special appeal for Saint Bernard, for he had joined the new order of Cistercians because he was attracted to the simplicity and the austerity of their observance of Benedictine spirituality, a simplicity which he contrasted to the more moderate observance of the Benedictines of the famous Abbey of Cluny, for example. In the eyes of Bernard Cluny represented power, authority, wealth, extravagance, and therefore pride. It was not likely that Cluny would attract this young nobleman, fleeing from worldliness and its temptations to the wilderness of Citeaux and mature enough to know the power of that which he was renouncing.

Bernard came from a noble Burgundian family; he turned his back on rank, wealth, power, and the opportunities for a distinguished worldly career in order to become a simple Cistercian monk, entering Citeaux along with thirty companions in 1112. In 1115 Stephen Harding, Abbot of Citeaux, sent Bernard to found a new monastery in a lonely little valley on the borders of Burgundy and Champagne. This monastery became renowned as Clairvaux, the "Valley of Light." In the twelfth century Clairvaux, because of Bernard, now its abbot, became famed for being the center of a new school of mysticism, from which radiated a spiritual influence which was to affect not only the Benedictines of all observances, not only France, but all of Christendom, and was to make of Clairvaux's modest abbot a figure who rivaled in importance the pope himself. Before Bernard's death one hundred and sixty monasteries were to take their origin from the Abbey of Clairvaux.

Bernard was responsible for reforms not only among the Benedictines but also among the secular clergy of his time. A humanistic scholar, one of the best Latinists of the Middle Ages, he left his imprint on almost every phase of medieval culture: Gregorian chant, Gothic architecture and art, politics, ecclesiastical discipline, and theology. He played a crucial role during the schism of Anacletus II (died 1138); and he was as valiant in his efforts against heresy as against schism, attacking both Peter Abelard (1079-1142) and the brilliant Bishop of Poitiers, Gilbert de la Porrée (1076-1154) as well as the Manichaeans of Languedoc. He preached the Second Crusade at Vezelay and devoted his last years to writing a book on the reform of the Catholic Church, especially of the Roman Curia, his *De consideratione* (1149-1153). Bernard was canonized twenty-one years after his death in 1153, and was proclaimed a Doctor of the Church in 1830.

On the Steps of Humility and Pride falls into two main parts, a long introductory section (Chapters 1-9), which deals with the essential meaning of the virtue of humility and explains its advantages, and a second section (Chapters 10-22) which, in brilliant and graphic fashion, depicts the twelve degrees of pride. From an examination of the degrees of pride the reader is expected to become deeply conscious of the corresponding and opposed degrees of humility.

Bernard approaches his topic through a consideration of truth, for humility is the highway that leads man to Truth; that is, to God. This emphasis on truth has led some students of Bernard to consider these opening chapters to be a statement of the saint's epistemology, but the author was more concerned with spiritual progress than with the theory of knowledge. The road Saint Bernard proposes to follow is long and arduous, but the man who seeks perfection along this way is assured of being consoled by Christ Himself. Christ, who is the Way, the Truth, and the Life (John 14:6) has promised to reveal the truth to the meek and humble of heart. Consequently, the beginning of man's ascent toward the vision of God is the recognition of his own unworthiness; in other words, one needs humility, which Saint Bernard defines as the virtue that enables a man, through the truest kind of knowledge, to discover his own unworthiness and wretchedness.

Humility can be viewed as the first stage toward the perfect enjoyment of truth. Love is the second stage, and pure vision, rejoicing in its power, is the third. Bernard, like so many thinkers of his time, discovered trinities wherever he looked. Truth, accordingly, has a three-fold location. Man seeks truth in himself, in his neighbors, and in its own pure and essential nature. One must not forget, however, that Bernard, deeply steeped in the Augustinian tradition, never thinks of Truth as being a cold and abstract essence, but as a vibrant, subsisting, and personal reality: God Himself.

Bernard's treatment of these three degrees of truth constitutes the most important part of this introductory section; in fact, though less interestingly written than the second section, these chapters contain his most distinctive and significant ideas. Again and again Bernard reveals both his sure and profound knowledge of human beings and also his deep compassion for man's weakness and failings. Starting, as he so frequently does, from the Greek dictum "Know thyself," Bernard insists that the search for truth begin with serious self-scrutiny. The discovery of one's own wretched condition, one's own pettiness and shortcomings, is a sure antidote for one's tendency to judge others; such a discovery prepares a person to be understanding of and compassionate to his fellowmen. Bernard makes it clear that if men examine the faults of their neighbors without first examining themselves, they are all too easily moved to anger and contempt, and are then more ready to condemn their neighbors than to pity or assist them.

Self-examination, therefore, naturally leads to the second level of truth, where men look for truth in their neighbors, "when from the realization of their own shortcomings they discover those of other people and learn from their own painful experience to sympathize with those who suffer." Finally, through a process of purification, which includes repentance, a desire for righteousness, and the performance of works of mercy, men reach that direct vision in which the third degree of truth consists. Thus, through humble effort and loving sympathy, the Christian rises to the stage of the enraptured vision of God.

It is, however, in the second part of this treatise that Bernard's acute powers of observation and his genius in literary expression are most fully displayed. Literature is filled with attempts to personify virtues and vices through a series of character sketches. All too often the effort fails; either the characters are too individualized to reveal depth or universality of moral insight, or the characters become wooden and lifeless as a result of the author's trying to give them too much ethical or religious significance. Bernard's sketches have probably never been surpassed. He was not concerned, however, to depict the vices of mankind in general or to hold up to ridicule or scorn the sins of the world; rather, he wanted to show the special dangers that beset men who profess to live a particular vocation, that of monks. The solemn warnings that Saint Bernard desired to give through these sketches never prevented him from being lively, humorous, and interesting in style. Behind his loving sternness are keenness of observation, a wealth of experience, and a store of humor that make it impossible for the reader to put down the book once he has come to this section. There are frequent touches that make the reader quite certain that Bernard is at times describing monks he has actually known and observed. For example, when he depicts the third degree of pride, foolish merriment, he writes as follows: "His gestures are those of a buffoon, his look that of a coxcomb, his step that of a dandy. He is always making jokes, and never loses a chance of laughing. . . . A bladder swells when it is full of wind, but if a small hole is pricked in it and it is squeezed, it creaks as it collapses, and the air does not rush out at once, but is gradually expelled and gives out frequent intermittent sounds. In like manner when a monk has filled his mind with vapid and vulgar thoughts, the flood of folly which cannot, owing to the rule of silence, find full and free vent, is thrown out from his narrow jaws in guffaws of laughter. He constantly hides his face as if ashamed, compresses his lips, and clenches his teeth. He laughs loudly without meaning to do so, and even against his will. And when he has stopped his mouth with his fists he is frequently heard to sneeze."

The intent of this second section of the work is to examine step by step how moral perfection can be diminished and lost. The way down is easy, beginning with curiosity, continuing through thoughtlessness, foolish mirth, boasting, eccentricity, conceit, arrogance, presumption, and hypocrisy until at last, having rebelled and having left the monastery, a monk embarks on a life of vice and finally reaches the state of habitual sin.

Saint Bernard was too masterly a guide of souls and too consummate a literary artist to end this work on a note of pessimism and to conclude his treatise with a description of the man who has replaced the holy fear of God with contempt for God. In the final chapter, recalling miracles wrought by faith, recalling how Saint Peter, who denied the Lord, was yet forgiven, he concludes on the lofty level of humility and love, placing his confidence in his faith in God and in the deep and abiding power of silent prayer.

J.H.R.

TREATISE CONCERNING THE PURSUIT OF LEARNING

Author: Hugh of St. Victor (1096-1141)
Type of work: Philosophy of Christian education
First transcribed: c.1127

Principal Ideas Advanced

Since the pursuit of wisdom, known as "philosophy," includes both secular and religious learning and leads ultimately to God, it is the way to human perfection and happiness.

Human learning falls into four general categories: theoretical, practical, mechanical, and logical.

All learning is of some benefit, but while learning should be broad, it should also be discriminating and ordered to proper ends, since the less good should not impede the better.

Full wisdom is affective and voluntary as well as cognitive, and it is attained by five steps: study, reflection (meditation), prayer, performance of good works, and contemplation.

The Sacred Scriptures may have one, two, or all of three possible meanings: the "historical," which includes the literal; the "allegorical" in which one thing represents another; and the "tropological" or moral; in each case the direct meaning intended by the author should be preferred, and any interpretation should be conformable to faith.

Hugh of St. Victor's *Treatise Concerning the Pursuit of Learning* was probably the most influential educational treatise composed in the high Middle Ages. Born in 1096, the oldest son of the Count of Blankenburg in Saxony, Hugh was educated at St. Pancras, a monastery of the Canons Regular of St. Augustine in Hamersleben. Hugh was an eager student, and eventually he took the Augustinian habit despite parental opposition. Later, on the advice of an uncle who was Bishop of Halberstadt and had earlier studied under William of Champeaux, he traveled first to the Abbey of St. Victor at Marseilles and then to the Abbey of St. Victor at Paris, both of which followed the rule of the Augustinian Canons Regular. He spent the rest of his life—first as a student, then as a teacher, and finally as distinguished master—at the famous monastic school of St. Victor in Paris, where he died in 1141.

An inspiring and fertile writer, Hugh of St. Victor is noted as a proto-Scholastic because of his extensive use of secular learning and natural reason as well as of divine revelation and faith in his many works, which were written chiefly on theological, mystical, and Scriptural topics.

Much of Hugh's thought is semi-Platonic, in accordance with the trend at St. Victor's, but some is Aristotelian, and all is partly Christian. One of his most important treatises was his *Didascalicon de studio legendi* or *Didactic Treatise Concerning the Pursuit of Learning,* written in the late 1120's. His purpose, he tells us, is to present a reasoned plan of study, an account of what should be learned, in what order, and in what manner. After a general discussion of philosophy, or the pursuit of wisdom, in which learning is the first phase, Hugh discusses secular learning and then theological or divine learning. Although his plan was apparently designed primarily for monks and clerics, it was applicable to any Christian in a position to pursue it.

In his *Didascalicon* Hugh was able to draw on sources such as Saint Augustine, Cassiodorus, and Isidore of Seville, as well as Saint Jerome, Boethius, and Remigius of Auxerre. But his view of philosophy and its proper content had a new breadth and unifying quality that, without losing sight of Christian truths and objectives, sanctioned both a more liberal education and a wider use of natural reason. That his work was most influential is indicated by its survival in almost a hundred manuscript copies, dating from the twelfth through the fifteenth century. It is referred to in such subsequent pedagogical treatises as those of John of Salisbury and Vincent of Beauvais.

According to Hugh of St. Victor, wisdom in its full sense (as cognitive, affective, and voluntary) is man's ultimate proper goal: the sum of his perfection and happiness, the means whereby he becomes united with God. Philosophy, the pursuit of wisdom, investigates the ideas and causes of all things, human and divine. Philosophy is both a discipline (science) and an art (an applied science). It illumines, perfects, and even deifies man, since its ultimate object is "that Wisdom which, wanting in nothing, is a living Mind, and the sole primordial Idea or pattern of things. . . . This Wisdom bestows upon every manner of souls the benefit of its own divinity and brings them back to the proper force and purity of their nature." This integral wisdom is achieved in knowledge and virtue, "in which two consists our sole likeness to the supernal and divine substances."

Cognitive philosophy or learning, according to Hugh of St. Victor, may be divided into four main categories: theoretical, practical, mechanical, and logical, each in turn divided and subdivided into component parts. Hugh's scheme of knowledge, one of his most distinctive contributions, involves the division of philosophy into four classes: (1) theoretical or speculative philosophy (theology, the *quadrivium,* and physical philosophy), (2) practical or active philosophy (personal, private, and public), (3) mechanical philosophy (manufacture, commerce, agriculture, hunting, medicine, the theater), and (4) logical philosophy (grammar and the logic of discourse).

Theoretical philosophy, according to Hugh's analysis, includes theology, mathematics, and physical philosophy. Theology considers God and the soul: completely spiritual substances. Mathematics considers abstract quantity and is subdivided into (the *quadrivium*) arithmetic, geometry, astronomy, and music. Arithmetic concerns multitude or numbers in themselves; music, multitude in relation to other multitude; geometry, immobile magnitude; astronomy, mobile magnitude. Music is of three kinds. One is the music of the universe, as in the mutual relations of the heavenly bodies, those of the seasons, and those of the material elements. Another music is that in man, as in the growth of the body, the virtues of the soul, or the bond between the two in their "sympathetic relationships." Finally there is instrumental music, or music proper. Physical or natural philosophy is equivalent to what we now call "the sciences," and it investigates the natures, causes, and effects of things as they exist in the visible world.

Practical philosophy, which considers norms for the actions of men, Hugh divides into solitary or moral philosophy, which is concerned with individuals and individual ethics; private, or managerial, or economic philosophy, which is concerned with the conduct of family or corporate business; and political or public philosophy, which concerns states and is today known as political science.

While many authors accept only three divisions for philosophy, namely, the theoretical, the practical, and the logical, Hugh adds what he calls mechanical philosophy, which consists in those "manual" arts which alleviate the weaknesses and supply the needs of man's present life. Hugh lists seven mechanical arts: fabric-making, armament, commerce, agriculture, hunting, medicine, and theatrics. Most of these mechanical philosophies (or arts) are broader than their names suggest. Thus, hunting includes fishing and the work of those who prepare and serve food and drink, while theatrics includes all forms of public entertainment, such as racing, boxing, and wrestling.

Although logical philosophy was the last branch of cognitive philosophy to be developed, it should be the first studied, Hugh argues. Logic is equivalent to the *trivium,* and includes grammar and argumentation, the last of which is divided into dialectic and rhetoric. Sophistry, incidentally, is concerned with *false* argumentation. Hugh further argues that the works of literature: "all the songs of the poets—tragedies, comedies, satires, heroic verse and lyrics, iambics, certain didactic poems and fables and histories," are "appendages to the arts" or "by-products of the arts" rather than the arts themselves, and are to be studied only as secondary and subsidiary to the arts proper.

Since all studies have use and benefit, Hugh argues, they are to be cultivated as far as time permits, although the pursuit of learning must be kept within reason and cultivated in an ordinate manner. In a famous passage, Hugh says: "Hold no learning in contempt, for all learning is good. At least read a book, if you have the time . . . since in my judgment there is no book which does not set forth something worth looking for, if it is taken up at the right place and time. . . . Nothing, however, is good if it eliminates a better thing. If you are not able to read everything, read those things which are more useful." And elsewhere he writes: "There are those who wish to read everything. Don't vie with them. Leave well enough alone. . . . The number of books is infinite: don't pursue infinity."

For the effective pursuit of philosophy and attainment of full wisdom, there are five steps: study, meditation (or reflection), prayer, pursuit of good works, and contemplation. Study or reading, the main part of learning, which is completed by meditation or reflection, is the subject of the *Didascalicon.* Study and meditation are the preliminaries; perfection is achieved by the three steps following. Hugh says: "There are four things in which the life of just men is now practiced and raised, as it were by certain steps, to its future perfection—namely study or instruction, meditation, prayer, and performance. Then follows a fifth, contemplation, in which, as by a sort of fruit of the preceding steps, one has a foretaste, even in his life, of what the future reward of good works is."

Aids to learning are humility, seclusion, scrutiny (earnest consideration), poverty, and foreign soil. In connection with humility, Hugh says: "The wise student gladly hears all, reads all, and looks down on no writing, no person, no teaching." Concerning eager inquiry, he says: "I would that our students possessed such earnestness that wisdom could never grow cold in them." Among obstacles to study are carelessness, imprudence, and bad luck, the last of which is exemplified by illness or lack of a suitable teacher.

Under the heading of Sacred Scriptures, Hugh includes Church "decretals," or canons, and the writings of Church Fathers and Doctors, as well as the Old and New Testaments proper. According to Hugh, there are three senses or possible interpretations of the Sacred Books: the historical, the allegorical, and the tropological. The historical sense includes the literal: "We call by the name of 'history' not only the recounting of actual deeds, but also the first meaning of any narrative which uses words according to their proper nature." In allegory one thing signifies another, while in tropology a moral message is discovered. In Scriptural interpretation the author's meaning is to be sought, the literal meaning is to be given preference, and interpretations are to be consonant with sound faith: "When therefore we read the Divine Books. . . , let us prefer above all what it seems certain that the man we are reading thought. But if this is not evident, let us certainly prefer what the circumstances of the writing do not disallow and what is consonant with sound faith. But if even the circumstances of the writing cannot be explored and examined, let us at least prefer only what sound faith prescribes."

D.D.M.

NOAH'S ARK

Author: Hugh of St. Victor (1096-1141)
Type of work: Mystical theology
First transcribed: 1125-1131

Principal Ideas Advanced

God's house is the whole world, the Catholic Church, and every faithful soul.

God dwells in the human heart by knowledge and by love.

There are two visible arks and two invisible arks: Noah's wooden ark and the ark that Christ made through his preachers are the visible arks; wisdom built through meditation on the law of God is the third ark; and grace builds the fourth, by joining the virtues into a single charity.

Hugh of St. Victor, born in Flanders, or perhaps in Lorraine, spent most of his life as an Augustinian Canon Regular at the monastery of St. Victor in Paris. He achieved a considerable reputation as a dogmatic theologian, and in his *Eruditionis didascaliae* he proposed a division of philosophy into four classes: the theoretical, the practical, the mechanical, and the logical. His interest in epistemology and dialectic also led to his systematizing the dogmatic works of the early Fathers. As head of the school at St. Victor (from 1133 until his death), Hugh became the chief critic of the view of Abelard, and as the champion of the dialectic method Hugh brought about the eventual victory of the orthodox theology. His principal theological work is his treatise *De sacramentis Christianae fidei,* but he is perhaps best known for his mystical writings, which enjoyed wide distribution. Of the mystical writings, the masterpiece is undoubtedly *Noah's Ark,* which Hugh began to compose about ten years after entering St. Victor.

The *Noah's Ark* is not so much a single work as it is three related spiritual treatises. The first (which is to be emphasized in this review) is the *De arca Noe morali,* in which Hugh concerns himself with the problem occasioned by "the instability and restlessness of the human heart," a problem to be solved only by discovering how to attain to the love of God; the second is the *De arca Noe mystica* (or the *De pictura arcae* or *De reformatione arcae*), in which Hugh attempts to show, by a colored diagram of the Ark, how all history combines to support the Church in her attempt to restore to men the image of Christ and the love of God; the third treatise is Hugh's *De vanitate mundi,* in which Reason and the Soul converse, with reference to the image of the Ark, concerning man's attachment to the things of this world. *Noah's Ark,* considered as a whole, is a lively and intellectually informed image of the soul's endeavor to be carried by the ark (which is, in one important sense, the Church) *in time* but in such a manner that the soul will at last be free of vanity, the cause of restlessness, which only charity, as an expression of God's love, can conquer.

At the beginning of *De arca Noe morali* Hugh explains that he has been asked to explain the cause and the cure of the instability and restlessness in the human heart. His answer is to be based on reason and authority, and he has composed his treatise, he tells us, for those who are ignorant of the ideas it contains.

Hugh contends that had Adam not sinned he would have been able to see, love, and cleave to God, and thereby to enjoy immortal life; and the author claims that "the one, true good of man" is "the full and perfect knowledge of his Maker. . . ." But man did sin, and thus the human heart, divided by earthly desires, no longer knew the peace that comes from contemplating God, and the heart became restless and lost its stability. The only remedy for the disease of restlessness, which is the result of loving the world, is to attain to the love of God; but to attain to the love of God, one must learn the way. The ensuing account is designed to suggest the way to the love of God.

Hugh explains beautifully and economically the difference between the love of God and the love of the world: "The difference between the love of God and the love of the world is this: the love of this world seems at the outset sweet, but has a bitter end; the love of God, by contrast, is bitter to begin with, but is full of sweetness in its end." It is vitally necessary, then, to love God—but where is He to be found?

To love God, one must know Him, Hugh writes. And once one has come to know God, love is inevitable, for "so great is the beauty of His loveliness that no one who sees Him can fail to love Him." The problem, then, is to find God's house, the place where God dwells; and it might seem that no amount of searching would reveal the place. But: "God's house is the whole world; God's house is the Catholic Church; God's house is also every faithful soul." There is some hope, then, of coming to God's house; but to do so one must realize that God is in the world "as ruler of His kingdom"; He is in the Church "as head of the family in His own home"; and he is in the soul "as the bridegroom in the wedding-chamber." All men, says Hugh, are in God's house, but if a man is in His house only because of his human condition as the product of God's Creation, he is there with the Devil; if a man is in the house through faith alone, "there is still chaff on [the] threshing-floor"; "But if you are in the house of God through love, blessed are you, for not only are you *in* the house of God, but you yourself have begun to *be* His house. . . ."

Hugh then writes that God lives in the heart both by knowledge and by love, but he suggests that, in this case alone, knowledge and love are one in that to know God is to love Him, and one cannot love Him without knowing Him. Knowledge and love are different, however; knowledge provides the object of faith and love, and love provides "an adorning colour. . . ."

In what is perhaps the most moving passage of *Noah's Ark,* Hugh sings that "God is become everything to you, and God has made everything." The learned theologian is here seen as the joyful mystic, aware of the unity of all that God has made: "This one is all, and this all is one." An ecstatic accounting is given; the house of God is the heaven, the sun, the moon; the mountain, the desert, the land: "It is the net, the vine, the field. It is the ark, the barn, the stable, and the manger." So Hugh continues, in a magnificent abundance of praise and understanding, and having suggested how everything wonderful and spiritual relates to God, Hugh argues that "it was for this . . . that the whole of Scripture was made. For this, the Word was made flesh, God was made humble, man was made sublime."

The image of God's house, of the spiritual building which is everything that man needs to know and love, is Noah's ark. The figure is used for the instruction of the soul. The ark represents the Church, Hugh explains; and the Church is the Body of Christ.

After elaborating on the passage from Isaiah 6:1, in which God is described as "sitting upon a throne, high and lifted up," Hugh explains, by means of elaborate imagery, how the ark, which represents the Church, reaches from the head of God ("that which was before the foundation of the world") to the feet of God ("that which is to be after the consummation of the age"), because the Church extends through time. Although the ark, in time, is buffeted by storms, God will guide it (the Church) "to the haven of eternal rest."

Hugh makes it clear that when he writes about the ark he means to be commenting on several levels at once. God's house, he has explained, is the world, the Church, and the soul. The ark, which is an image of God's house, can be interpreted literally as the wooden boat which Noah built; but the ark is also the *Church,* "that which Christ made through His preachers"; the *wisdom* which meditation makes possible; and the single *charity* which results from the joining together by grace of many virtues. The ark, then, says Hugh, must be built within ourselves, and we must learn within ourselves how to enter it and live within it.

Hugh enters upon a detailed analysis of the literal ark, and he discusses its shapes, doors, spaces for storage, and other features. He then compares the ark of the Church to Noah's ark; here units of time replace units of space, and the various stories of the ark signify ranks of believers. He relates the number of stories to numbers of significance to man: the number of elements, the number of senses, the three wills of man. Everything which Hugh discusses is developed for its spiritual meaning.

In his discussion of the ark of Wisdom, Hugh emphasizes the spiritual value of meditation and contemplation. Right thoughts build the inner ark, and the ark must be covered on the outside with the pitch of gentleness and on the inside with the pitch of charity. Man cannot forever remain in a state of contemplation, however; there must be a door of action, which is to be used only when necessary, and a window of thought through which the soul can fly. Hugh examines the various kinds of contemplation and the steps by which wisdom rises toward the wisdom of God. The tree of wisdom, writes Hugh, is "sown through fear . . . watered by grace . . . dies through grief . . . takes root by faith . . . germinates through devotion . . . shoots up through compunction . . . grows by longing . . . [and] is strengthened by charity." These eight steps correspond to the eight beatitudes. But there is more to be considered about the tree: it "grows green through hope"; it "puts out its leaves and spreads its branches through caution"; it "bears fruit through virtue" and "ripens through patience"; the fruit of the tree is cut off by death, but the tree itself "feeds by contemplation," and the contemplation is of God, who is food for the tree.

Finally, there is the ark of Grace by which man, caught in the flood of concupiscence and threatened by the reptiles of fleshly thoughts, is enabled, through faith, to return to God.

Reason, conversing with the Soul (in *De vanitate mundi*), remarks, "We must be in the ark until wickedness be done away, and until the waters of the flood abate." Through his inspired imagery Hugh of St. Victor has made vivid for all men the account of that perilous spiritual journey which comes to a successful close only through the grace of God.

HISTORIA CALAMITATUM

Author: Peter Abelard (1079-1142)
Type of work: Spiritual autobiography
First transcribed: c.1135

Principal Ideas Advanced

Abelard suffered adversities of body and spirit because of overweening pride and self-confidence in his intellectual superiority and in his pre-eminence as a master-teacher.

The bodily mutilation inflicted on him combined with the bitter persecution by his monastic brethren and malignant opposition of jealous ecclesiastics brought him to Christian humility and a true evaluation of his former fruitless life.

Marriage, according to the teachings of pagan philosophers and Christian Fathers, is incompatible with the demands of a dedicated intellectual and philosophical career.

Theological problems can be illuminated through the application of man's reasoning powers.

Religious women in view of the inadequacies of the female nature and the difficulties which they encounter living a monastic life according to the Rule *of St. Benedict require the skilled spiritual guidance of men.*

The *Historia calamitatum* (*The Story of My Adversities*) holds a unique place in medieval literature, for men of that era were not accustomed to reveal their inmost life to a reading public. In this little autobiographical pamphlet Abelard gives us the only reasonably full treatment of his extraordinary life up to the time that he decided to flee the Abbey of St. Gildas in Brittany, where his unruly monks constantly threatened his life. In the course of his narration Abelard lays bare his inmost soul in all its pride, consuming ambition, lustful intentions toward Héloïse, and its gradual transformation toward Christian humility. He reveals throughout this spiritual odyssey the workings of Divine Providence in his soul, leading him through the suffering of bodily mutilation and persecution along the path of self-knowledge and peace of soul.

It became evident very early in his youth that Abelard's talents lay with letters rather than with military prowess. His father, with commendable open-mindedness, furthered the education of his eldest son, who normally would have been expected to embrace a knightly career. Instead of the tournament and the joust Abelard engaged in lively contests of disputation with the eminent logician William of Champeaux (c.1070-1121) concerning the nature of universals. He bested William in these philosophical debates, thereby earning William's hatred and the jealousy and envy of his fellow students. Whether he taught at Mehun, Corbeil, or Paris, Abelard attracted flocks of students, together with the unceasing opposition of William, who continually strove to silence him.

Having scored a resounding success as a teacher of logic, Abelard grew dissatisfied with philosophy and sought instruction in theology from the most prominent theologian of the period, Anselm of Laon (died 1117). Abelard's judgment of Anselm's ability found expression in several uncharitable and tart metaphors; for example, he once stated that Anselm's tree was heavy with foliage, fair to behold from afar, but lacking any fruit. Dissatisfied with a theological method which sought light on the mysteries of the Faith through supporting quotations from Holy Scripture and the comments of the Church Fathers, Abelard advanced the novel idea that reason and logic could help to illuminate these mysteries. When challenged to demonstrate his theory, he prepared an exegesis on an obscure and difficult passage in Ezechiel. He then expounded his explanation of this text to a growing number of Anselm's students who abandoned the older theologian for the newcomer. As a result Abelard harvested the old man's bitter envy and hatred. Anselm encouraged two of his clerical pupils as they persecuted the young upstart with even more vigor than had William of Champeaux.

Abandoning what he judged to be the arid intellectual atmosphere of Laon, Abelard returned to Paris where, as a teacher of divinity, he equalled and bettered his earlier achievement as a philosopher. This unqualified success made him famous, wealthy, and swollen with pride in his ability as "the one philosopher in the world." At this juncture he gave himself up to his passions and withdrew from philosophers and theologians in order to lead an unchaste life.

Here Abelard presents us with the chief point of his story: "And while I was laboring under my pride and lust,

God's grace procured a remedy for each, though I did not desire it, first for my unchaste life by depriving me of the organs by which I led it, then for my pride nursed by my scholarship . . . through the burning of the book which was my special glory." The rest of the autobiography elaborates these two critical parts of his story, that of his relation with Héloïse and that of his subsequent career as a fugitive and unlicensed teacher of theology.

So confident had Abelard become in his renowned status and his personal charm that he felt no woman could resist him. He set out to seduce Héloïse, the one woman whose intellectual gifts and attainments, combined with extraordinary beauty, made her in his eyes the most fit object of his desire. Narrating with undisguised frankness how he took deceitful advantage of her uncle, the Canon Fulbert, to gain access to the house, Abelard then dwells on the transformation of his cynical desire for Héloïse into deep and ardent love. When she gave birth to their son, Astrolabe, Abelard determined to marry her. Here he gives us insight into Héloïse's intellectual capacity and profound love for him by citing the numerous arguments by which she protested against the proposed marriage. Briefly, Héloïse argued that the marriage would completely destroy Abelard's career as a clerical teacher of philosophy and theology. She insisted that marriage is incompatible with the demands of the intellectual life. She bolstered her position with profuse arguments from classical literature, Holy Scripture, and the Fathers of the Church. But Abelard persisted in his demands, and the lovers were married.

In order to protect his wife from the abuse of her uncle Fulbert after their secret marriage, Abelard had her installed in a convent at Argenteuil. Fulbert then revenged himself on Abelard by arranging to have him castrated. Abelard, having reflected on the impossibility of any future married life, entered the Abbey of St. Denis. Here he aroused the animosity of the monks by chiding them for their worldliness and openly doubting that their cherished founder, Saint Denis, was in truth identical with the Areopagite.

Again resuming the teaching of theology, Abelard wrote for the use of his students a reasoned theological tractate *On the Unity and Trinity of God,* which, because it approached the problem of the Trinity through rational and philosophical exposition, was immediately assailed by his enemies, whose vigilance never ceased. Abelard failed to prevent the condemnation of the work in a council at Soisson, and he was later constrained to cast the book into the fire. Having been completely humiliated by this turn of events, Abelard, writing in the *Historia,* laments the injustices inflicted on this work and reputation, and he claims that the criticism injured him far more acutely than had his physical mutilation. Despite his bitterness, the monks of St. Denis forced him to return to them and submit to their domination.

Temporary refuge came when Abelard secured permission to establish himself in a wilderness which he called the Paraclete, the Comforter. But he could not escape the students, and they flocked to hear him, building their quarters around his so that the Paraclete took on the guise of a semimonastic community of scholars. Because he was unlicensed to teach and because of the condemnation of his theological treatise, Abelard lived in constant fear of arrest as a heretic. To escape the plots against him, he accepted a prelacy as Abbot of St. Gildas de Rhuys, located in bleak and distant Brittany.

Chastened further through the furious and constant threats to his life made by the completely depraved monks of this monastery, Abelard now arrived at the culmination of his spiritual evolution. In his account he views his former career in terms of the beneficent providence of God drawing him away from pride, lust, and worldly ambition toward Christian humility and true wisdom. He gives expression to these thoughts in his reflections on the reasons for offering spiritual guidance to Héloïse and her nuns, whom he has had installed in the abandoned Paraclete. His love for Héloïse has ripened into a deep solicitude for her and her nuns' spiritual welfare. Even when slander rises up in an attempt to frustrate this work by insinuating that he has lustful intentions toward the community, Abelard can now view the criticism with the detachment of one who at last realizes that whatever the future holds for him nothing can now separate him from the love of Christ.

The *Historia calamitatum* concludes with Abelard's declared but as yet unfulfilled intention to flee for the safety of his life from St. Gildas. After his escape he enjoyed another brilliant period as a teacher of theology in comparative peace at Paris. Saint Bernard of Clairvaux, however, had become concerned about the effects which, in his opinion, Abelard's rationalistic methods in the teaching of theology were having on young and impressionable minds to the detriment of their faith. He consequently challenged Abelard to defend his views at a Council to be held at Sens. Bernard then proceeded to prejudice the assembled bishops against Abelard in a secret meeting with them prior to the scheduled debate. When Abelard discovered that the issue for all practical purposes had already been decided and that he would be condemned and excommunicated, he fled Sens and headed for Rome, where he hoped to defend himself at the Papal Court. But age and ill health caught up with him and constrained him to stop at Cluny, where Peter the Venerable ultimately secured his reconciliation with the Church and with Bernard. Here Abelard achieved his fullest spiritual maturity, and in 1142 he died with a reputation among the monks for genuine sanctity.

The reading of the *Historia calamitatum* should be supplemented by that of the letters which passed between Abelard and Héloïse. In these the mature spiritual views of Abelard find immortal expression as he strives to persuade Héloïse to subordinate her undying love for him to the love of God. Here, as Étienne Gilson has so signally demonstrated, two souls reveal their inmost spiritual natures and stand forth as two of history's most extraordinary personalities.

R.H.T.

ON THE NECESSITY OF LOVING GOD

Author: Saint Bernard (1091-1153)
Type of work: Ascetical theology
First transcribed: c.1126-1141

Principal Ideas Advanced

Man is made in the image of God, and hence for man to become most truly himself, he must become more like God, who is Love and whose life and substance are love.

Ultimately the reason God should be loved is God Himself; the measure of loving God is to love Him beyond all measure.

Man by nature loves himself, that is, he seeks his own good; the problem of human love, therefore, consists in reconciling this love of self with the love of God for His own sake.

The re-education of human love consists in moving from the lowest degree of love to the highest, a process of purification in which the grace of God plays an indispensable role.

The four degrees of human love are the following: (1) *man loves himself for his own sake;* (2) *man loves God, but for man's own sake, not for God Himself;* (3) *man loves God, not for man's own sake, but for God Himself;* (4) *man loves himself only for God's own sake.*

Saint Bernard of Clairvaux, when he wrote his treatise *On the Necessity of Loving God* (*De diligendo Deo*) for his friend Aimeric, Chancellor of the Roman Church, was directing himself to a problem that preoccupied his age. He was also proposing a solution to a problem that Christianity had posed with remarkable acuteness and for which Christian thinkers in all ages have sought solutions: namely, if man by nature is necessarily directed toward seeking his own good, if he loves himself for his own good, how can he be expected to obey the Scriptural injunctions to love God above all things and to love God for Himself alone?

A creature such as man, deficient in so many ways, needing help and completion from other beings, dependent on other beings for his continuation in existence, such a creature must use his powers of thought and action in order to perfect and to complete himself. This rule seems to be inscribed in the very metaphysical core of every finite being and especially within man, for being in a sense infinite in his power to know and love, he is open to an infinitely greater development than any other being. One might say that since man's capabilities are infinite, they bespeak and require an infinity of fulfillment. There is another way to see the uniqueness of man's problem. He appears, as a Christian, to be involved in a contradiction. It would seem that man's love must be self-centered, a self-interested love; and yet there is demanded of him a wholly disinterested love: that he love God above all things for the sake of God and that he love all other things for the sake of God. What becomes of the self? Is not this demand expecting the impossible of man? Is man psychologically capable of such disinterestedness? Is not such an other-directedness a violation of man's metaphysical need to seek his own good? It was in an attempt to resolve difficulties such as these that Saint Bernard wrote his short but brilliant work *On the Necessity of Loving God.*

Saint Bernard sets out to explain why and how God should be loved. At the very beginning of this work, in a sentence that has become almost proverbial, Bernard gives his answer in brief; he spends the rest of the treatise explaining what the following succinct statement means: "The reason for loving God is God Himself; the measure of loving God is to love Him beyond measure."

To appreciate the originality of the answer which Bernard gives, it is necessary to show the place of his solution in the history of ideas. Among the ancients, Plato, Aristotle, Cicero, and Ovid had all written on love and friendship. However, during Bernard's day very little of Plato's work was known in the West, and Aristotle's discourse on friendship would not be discovered for another century; as a result of these lacks, Cicero and Ovid enjoyed an influence which was far larger than their originality or their importance justified. Neither one of them was up to the task of solving a Christian's problems on the meaning of human love, although Bernard does draw upon Cicero in developing his own doctrine. Other sources, however, played a more significant role in helping Bernard and his disciple and friend, William of St. Thierry (died c. 1148) to develop a fully articulated doctrine of love and of Christian charity, or, one might say, an ascetical, mystical theology. These sources were the Scriptures, wherein it is written, "God is love" (I John, 4:16); the Rule of Saint Benedict; the writings of the Fathers, especially those of Saint Augustine; and a source wherein actual examples of highly developed Christian love might be found, the *Lives of the Fathers of the Desert* (*Vitae patrum*).

The eleventh and twelfth centuries were an age of the cloister, as the thirteenth century was to be the age of the university. Within these cloisters learned and saintly men such as Saint Anselm, Hugh of St. Victor, Richard of St. Victor (died c. 1173), Saint Bernard of Clairvaux, and William of St. Thierry strove to develop schools of the love of God, wherein a group of monks, under the guidance and instruction of their abbot, might learn better what was to be loved and how they were to love.

It was to seek such a school of perfection that the young Bernard, brilliant and talented son of a noble Burgundian family, went with thirty noble companions to Cîteaux, where they asked to become members of the newly organized Cistercian order. This was in 1112 when Bernard was twenty-two years of age. Three years later his spiritual formation was so advanced that Bernard was sent by his abbot to found a new monastery in a little valley on the borders of Burgundy and Champagne. The new abbey was called Clairvaux and it was to be Bernard's home for the rest of his life. His father and brothers also entered Clairvaux and the abbey's growth was so phenomenal that new houses had to be established continually. Before his death, Bernard had sent forth monks to found 160 Cistercian communities.

His saintliness and his wisdom soon caused Bernard to be involved in high matters of Church and state, until this "last of the Fathers," as he has been called, was to achieve a personal power and influence second to none in Christendom. He labored for the reform of the Benedictine order in all its branches, and for the reform of the secular clergy; he fought heresy and schism, and he was largely responsible for the launching of the ill-fated Second Crusade.

Throughout all this activity, however, Bernard remained essentially a mystic; and his writings, especially his *Sermons on the Canticle of Canticles* (1135-1153) witness to the high level of his contemplative life. He died in 1153 and was canonized in 1174.

The doctrines developed by Bernard, as well as those of his close friend and fellow Cistercian William of St. Thierry, were to have an important and permanent influence within the Church and were to continue to be of general significance down to the present time. Nowhere are Saint Bernard's teachings on love expressed with more clarity and at the same time with more spiritual unction than in his little treatise, *On the Necessity of Loving God.*

By what title does God deserve and claim our love? An eminent one, says Saint Bernard, for out of the superabundant generosity of His love He has called us into existence and has willed for us all we need in order to achieve our perfection. In short, God has first loved us. We are His, body and soul, and this being so, we should be eager to know what we are and to realize that we possess this love, not of our own power but as a gift from God. Though a Christian has many other reasons for admitting that God should be loved, the works of Christ, for example, even the unbeliever must recognize that he owes all he possesses to God. Bernard states this idea with clarity and fervor: "Here first see in what measure, yes, how beyond measure God has deserved to be loved by us; He who (if I may repeat in a few words what has been said) first loved us Himself—He so great, yet He loves us greatly and *gratis;* we, so small and sinners such as we are. . . . My God, my Help, I shall love You according to Your gift to me, and according to my measure, which is less, to be sure, than justice demands but clearly not less than I am able to give."

Before examining further Saint Bernard's positive doctrine of love, it is important to recall that although he developed it in the quiet of his cloister, he did not develop it in ignorance of other views on love which were current in his time. Saint Bernard was a vigorous fighter for what he held to be true, a polemicist of no mean quality. One of his contemporaries, Peter Abelard, with whom Bernard was publicly to disagree on more than one occasion, had developed a doctrine of human love which Bernard found quite unacceptable.

Abelard's doctrine of pure or disinterested love was unique in his time. According to this doctrine, true love is directed exclusively to the person loved, and it admits of no thought of gain or reward for the one who loves. Abelard goes so far as to say that in loving God, we are not to love Him because He loves us; we are to love Him even under the hypothesis that He might cease to love us. God is to be loved merely because He is good in Himself, without any reference to the fact that He is our beatitude. William of St. Thierry was to point out the absurdity of asserting that man could be united to God by love and not at the same time by beatitude or happiness.

Bernard had views that came close to Abelard's but Bernard's doctrine, taken as a whole, is quite different from that of Abelard. Bernard, for example, writes: "For not without reward is God loved although He should be loved without thought of the reward. . . . True love finds satisfaction in itself. It has its reward but it is the object it loves. . . . How much less does the soul that loves God seek anything besides God as the reward of her love! If she seeks anything else, it is clearly something else and not God that she loves." God, then, is loved because He is good; but He is at the same time man's reward. The problem for Bernard, however, is not to separate love and reward but to see whether he can maintain at one and the same time the natural necessity of man to seek his own good and man's ecstatic love of God for His own sake.

Saint Bernard's answer to this dilemma was his doctrine of the four degrees of love. The first is that whereby a man loves himself for his own sake. Bernard, mystic though he was, recognized the frailty of the human condition. He does not claim however, that love is by essence carnal; he admits only that it is at the carnal level that love, deformed in man through original sin, begins the process of re-education; it is here that the purification of love begins, a purification that will progressively enable human love to become once again fully itself. Nature is weak and feeble and is impelled by necessity toward self-preservation. "It is carnal love by which before all other things man loves himself for his own sake," he writes. Carnal love, which could easily become selfish in addition to being love of self, is kept in bounds by the command to love one's neighbors as oneself. One cannot love oneself to excess if he keeps in mind the good of his neighbor, which is to say, if he is aware of the fact that his own good is bound up with the good of others.

It is not difficult to see how Bernard moves from the level of carnal love to the second degree of love. If man loves himself, he ought to love that which produced and which protects him. Thus, carnal man, who initially loved no one except himself, begins to love God, at least insofar as God is good for man. This is the second degree of love, to love the other and especially to love God, although at this point the love continues to be self-centered. To go beyond self-interest, a man must move higher, to the third degree of love, whereby a man loves God, not because of what God does for man, but solely for God Himself. God is loved because He is good and sweet. At this stage, too, comes a true love of one's neighbor; for man no longer loves his fellow man for what he can get from him, but because his neighbor is a creature of God and therefore belongs to God.

The fourth and highest degree of love is that degree wherein a man does not love even himself except for the sake of God. This ecstatic condition is one which belongs principally to the future life, but it is possible that favored souls attain it briefly from time to time, even in this life. In short, it is the love which the blessed possess, and even they will not enjoy it to the full until their bodies are united to their souls after the resurrection.

It is Bernard's teaching that man's love has diverse objects, himself, his neighbors, and God. One begins with the love of self; then through the grace of God man comes to love God in the second degree, but for self-centered reasons. Through familiarity, however, God becomes better known to man and, learning of God's sweetness, man comes to love Him for Himself. Finally, perhaps in this life, perhaps only later, man reaches that loftiest degree in which there exists a perfect union of man's will with God's will, the ecstasy of beatitude.

Underlying the magnificent development of these degrees of love lies a well-worked-out doctrine of man as the image of the Word of God. Through original sin the soul, which was like God, has become unlike Him. What the human soul needs, therefore, is to become unlike its present self and more like God and thereby more truly itself.

It is now possible to understand how Bernard meets and disposes of Abelard's doctrine and reconciles the love of God with the love of self. If man is an image, then the more faithfully it mirrors that of which it is the image, the more true it is to itself. Now God is love, and the life He lives is a life of love; in fact, the very substance of God is love. Man, therefore, can be himself fully and truly only when he loves God for God's sake; that is, as God loves Himself. Man's love of himself is like God, too, since God first loved us.

What has made and continues to make the doctrine of Saint Bernard so attractive to Christians is its unique reconciliation of man's actual weakness with his transcendent destiny. A slave to his passions, his eyes turned at the beginning toward himself and toward the physical goods of this earth, man responds to the divine invitation to become a friend of God, and without ever doing violence to his deepest desire to be fully himself, comes to realize, with the help of divine grace, that he can be truly himself only by becoming more and more like God. In this realization man will be aware that it is impossible to separate love and beatitude or happiness when love is directed wholly toward God, who is man's beatitude; thus, Abelard's antinomy disappears. There is no need to choose between a pure love of God and man's happiness, for man's happiness consists in that pure love of God. Man will finally come to abide in that state, "when God alone is loved in the highest possible degree; because, now, we do not even love ourselves save for His sake, so that He Himself is the reward of those who love Him, the reward eternal of those who love for all eternity."

In this treatise, as in all his treatises, Saint Bernard reveals himself to be a traditional thinker rather than an innovator, and his tradition is the tradition of the Fathers of the Church. He was not a writer of *summae* nor a builder of complex theological systems. He was a saint whose vocation, in spite of incessant demands made upon him, was to live the life of a Cistercian monk within the walls of his abbey. Yet, though he was deeply in debt to Sacred Scriptures and to the continuing patristic tradition, he was nevertheless able to produce thoughts of striking originality and arguments of vigor and acuteness to maintain his positions.

Above all he was a monk and a mystic, and his mysticism grew and deepened with the passing years of his life. The full power of his mystical theology, lived, explained, but never really systematized, is best exemplified in his *Sermons on the Canticle of Canticles,* but even in this early and brief work, *On the Necessity of Loving God,* the origins of his mystical doctrine may be traced and the richness of what is to come may be brilliantly anticipated.

J.H.R.

THE TWO CITIES

Author: Otto of Freising (c.1111-1158)
Type of work: Philosophy of history
First transcribed: 1143-1147

Principal Ideas Advanced

Through divine providence, God guides all His creatures, as He also controls and protects them.

Ever since the Incarnation "the faithless city of unbelieving Jews and Gentiles" has been unimportant in the eyes of God and Man.

From the time of Christ the City of God has been localized in the Church.

Otto of Freising was a high-placed German cleric, a grandson of Henry IV, nephew of Henry V, half brother of Conrad III, and uncle of Frederick I. He lived shortly after Henry IV had humbled himself before Pope Gregory VII at Canossa, and when Frederick I had recovered imperial power and was asserting his claims to Northern Italy. In this time of troubles Otto wrote *The Two Cities: A Chronicle of Universal History to the Year 1146 A.D.* in order to "display the miseries of the citizens of Babylon and also the glory of the kingdom of Christ to which the citizens of Jerusalem are to look forward with hope, and of which they are to have a foretaste even in this life."

The *Chronicle* is divided into eight books. The first covers the period from Creation to the beginning of Rome; the second carries the account forward to the Nativity; the third, to Constantine's establishment of the Christian Roman Empire; the fourth to Odoacer and the end of the Roman Empire in the West. The fifth continues the history to the Treaty of Verdun (843), which divided the Empire of Charlemagne; the sixth, to the death of Pope Gregory VII (1085); the seventh, to the year 1146; and the last book, which is an integral part of the work, deals with the future.

The significance of this book-by-book division is that in this way Otto foreshortened his account of history as others had not done. Thus, the last four books cover only three centuries, while the first four cover all the rest of past time. More important for Otto's philosophy of history is his division of universal history into three great periods: (1) from Creation to the founding of Rome; (2) from the founding of Rome to the Nativity; (3) from the time of Christ to Otto's own time. Otto interpreted the Book of Daniel to mean that the Roman Empire must be the last secular empire and that it would be replaced by the Church, which would grow into not only a spiritual power but also the greatest of earthly kingdoms.

The Two Cities is a work of relatively high historical quality, especially in its later books. Otto speaks of the "art of the historians" in terms that sound quite modern. The function of the historian is to find and tell the truth. Otto excludes the apologetic aims of Saint Augustine and Orosius. "It is our intention," he tells the reader, "to set forth, not after the manner of a disputant, but in the fashion of one telling a story, a history, in which on the one hand the varying experiences, on the other hand, the progress and achievements of the citizens of Babylon, shall be interwoven." Otto does not try to picture all popes as blameless men, nor is he harsh in his treatment of heretics. He tries always to present an account of the last that is vivid and interesting as well as accurate and truthful.

Otto used remarkably good historical methods for his age. He let the reader know what sources of information he employed. He did not follow any one or two sources slavishly, and he explained why he selected one source in preference to others. Moreover, he frequently employed such saving expressions as *fertur, dicitur,* and *asserunt.*

The title of Otto's work, *The Two Cities,* suggests an intentional similarity to Augustine's *City of God.* In the Prologue Otto tells the reader: "In this work I follow most of all those illustrious lights of the Church, Augustine and Orosius, and have planned to draw from their fountains what is pertinent to my theme and purpose," and in Book VIII he speaks of "the blessed father Augustine, whom we have undertaken to imitate." Despite his intention to imitate the *City of God,* Otto wrote a work which differs considerably from Augustine's. Otto is more the historian, and Augustine more the rhetorician and theologian. Otto uses his sources more critically and judiciously than did Augustine, and Otto takes a narrower view of history since the time of Christ than did his predecessor. "The faithless city of unbelieving Jews and Gentiles still remains," he tells us, "but, since nobler kingdoms have been won by our people, while these unbelieving Jews and Gentiles are insignificant not only in the sight of God but even in that of the world, hardly anything done by these unbelievers is found worthy of record or to be handed on to posterity." Thus Otto expressed a hardening Christian attitude toward those outside the fold of Christendom.

The two cities originated with the expulsion of Adam from the Garden of Eden. Cain and Abel are "the first citizens of the two cities of which I have undertaken to treat." The two cities will continue through the course of history, and they will exist in eternity after the end of time. Otto sees three stages clearly manifest in their history: (1) before Christ; (2) since Christ; (3) after time has ended. The City of God is abject in the first stage, increasingly prosperous in the second, and fully blessed in the third. The

City of Evil is wretched in the first stage, and in the second "so much the more wretched as it was the more inexcusable after the truth had been made manifest," while in the third stage of eternity it will be condemned and therefore most wretched.

Otto describes the two cities at the beginning of his chronicle: "For, inasmuch as there are two cities—the one of time, the other of eternity; the one of earth, earthy, the other of heaven, heavenly; the one of the devil, the other of Christ—ecclesiastical writers have declared the former Babylon, the latter Jerusalem." In the time before Christ, citizens of the two cities are distinguishable only as the good and the bad. But Babylon became the representative of the earthly city, or the City of Evil, whereas Jerusalem became the womb of the City of God. Not many Jews, however, were citizens of this latter City, for they too resisted God: "You can find no one of the kings of Israel and very few of the kings of Judah that were citizens of Jerusalem."

After Christ, the City of God is localized in the Church. In the prologue to the fifth book Otto tells the reader that henceforth he will write the history of only one city, the Church, "for although the elect and reprobate are in one household yet I cannot call these cities two, as I did above; I must call them properly but one—composite, however, as the grain is mixed with the chaff."

Although Otto's purpose is not apologetic, he defends the providential view of history against those who claim that God neglects the world. His argument is that every wise and good man cherishes what he has made. Similarly, he concludes that "we are privileged to understand clearly that God does not neglect His world, as some claim, but rather that by His omnipotent majesty He created things that were not, by His all-wise providence guides His creatures and by His most kindly grace preserves what he guides and controls."

Otto seems to have believed that the end of history was near. He thought that history moved geographically as well as chronologically, and that all things moved from east to west. Since Spain was the western edge of the world for him, he believed that the geographic limit of history had been reached and the chronological end was not far away.

It is frequently observed that Otto of Freising's *The Two Cities* was the most important philosophy of history between Augustine and Bossuet. Such claims are hard to measure, but no scholar denies that his work was widely used, frequently transcribed, and quoted many times as an authoritative work in the Christian tradition.

T.P.N.

SPIRITUAL FRIENDSHIP

Author: Saint Aelred (1109-1167)
Type of work: Spiritual instruction
First transcribed: c.1150

Principal Ideas Advanced

Unlike charity, which is universally extended to all, friendship is reserved for those to whom we can give our entire confidence and from whom we can receive their entire confidence in return.

Since friendship is so excellent, it is important to distinguish it from its counterfeits, as regards origin and practice.

In a Christian perspective, genuine human friendship is a preparation for divine friendship, and more precisely for friendship with Christ.

The Latin literature of the Middle Ages is an unknown land for most modern Catholics, even for the professional scholars among them. The legend of "the dark ages" dies hard. Thus, although the literary beauties of ancient Greece and Rome or their later reflections in the Renaissance have been assiduously studied, the centuries in between have been largely ignored.

An acquaintance with the little-known writer Saint Aelred would go far to dissipate such ignorance. Aelred is a fine example of a Christian humanist, even though he is found in the "gothic barbarity" of misty Yorkshire in mid-twelfth century. One would hardly expect to find in this unlikely place what we have here; namely, a truly magistral treatise on love, under its double form of love of God and friendship for men.

The earliest biography of Aelred, whose name also appears under several variant forms, the most common of which is Ethelred, was written shortly after his death. Predictably, it is cast in the traditional mold of those times, including the indispensable early predictions of future sanctity and the foretelling of his date of death. However, some truly personal traits do manage to shine through, and they reveal a rich personality, worthy of being better known.

Aelred was born at the beginning of the twelfth century, near the borders of England and Scotland. His family was of Saxon origin and was related to the ruling dynasties of both these kingdoms. His father was a priest. In an age in which violations of the law of ecclesiastical celibacy were widely tolerated, his family handed down the charge of the local church from generation to generation. It is difficult for us today to form an accurate picture of such a situation. We tend to think of it as a rebellious and irreligious atmosphere. It was not; it was both pious and, for the times, cultured. Aelred's father finished his days in a Benedictine monastery, and one of Aelred's sisters became a contemplative nun.

Aelred received an excellent education at the local school. It was there that he learned the elegant Latin in which he was to write his later works.

He completed his education at the court of Scotland, where he was raised among the young princes, to whom he always remained strongly attached. King David the First, son of Queen Saint Margaret, entrusted to Aelred the general running of his palace, and, though Aelred was still quite young, the king was preparing to have him elevated to the episcopacy.

These royal plans, however, were blocked by a decision of Aelred. He felt called by God to leave the life at court and to enter the recently founded Cistercian abbey of Rievaulx. It was a difficult decision from many points of view. In particular, for a person so sensitive to the joys and consolations of friendship, this separation from his closest and dearest friends must have cost a great deal. Nevertheless, Aelred severed these ties, which bound him to all that was best in the secular society of his time, and entered the monastery in 1133.

In 1141 Aelred was named master of novices, and the following year he was chosen to be the first abbot of Revesby in Lincolnshire, a daughter foundation of Rievaulx. Five years later he was elected abbot of Rievaulx itself, a post which he was to fill for twenty years, until his death in 1167. Abbot of Rievaulx was a heavy charge. At Aelred's death the monastery held 640 members. Besides this abbacy he had the care of the daughter abbeys of Rievaulx, six in England and eleven in Scotland.

Nor was Aelred's influence restricted to these monasteries. He was often consulted in ecclesiastical and secular disputes. He became a sort of English Saint Bernard. In the schism of 1159, it was Aelred who persuaded King Henry II Plantagenet to recognize the legitimate pope, Alexander III.

His last years were made more difficult by several long and painful illnesses. Of all his virtues, the ones which most impressed his contemporaries were his patience and his kindness.

Aelred's writings fall into two groups, the first mainly historical, the second mostly sermons and ascetical treatises. Among these latter is the work under discussion, *Spiritual Friendship.*

The sources of this work are not difficult to discover. Aelred himself indicates them for us in his prologue: first of all, Cicero and his treatise *De amicitia;* second, the Bible; third, the Fathers of the Church, especially Augustine and Ambrose; and last, though it is not explicitly mentioned, Aelred's own personal experience.

Aelred begins his treatise with an account of his spiritual adventures. He tells us how, as a young student, he first made the acquaintance of Cicero's work. It filled him with admiration, even though he felt incapable of living up to the ideal it proposed. Once he had entered the religious life, however, his attention became focused on Holy Scripture, and he began to test and criticize his previous opinions in relation to Scripture. He also sought out what the early Fathers of the Church had to say about friendship. As a result of this seeking he conceived the great ambition to love truly in spirit, but he did not feel the strength to do so. It was this ambition which made him resolve to write about spiritual friendship, in an effort to lay down for himself, "the rules of a chaste and holy love."

Following the example of Cicero,

Aelred presents his treatise in dialogue form.

In the first dialogue he proposes to discuss the nature of friendship, its origin and its causes; in the second, its advantages and its excellence; and in the third, how and between whom friendship can be preserved intact to the end.

The first dialogue is set in a monastery depending on Rievaulx. Aelred has come on an official visit, and now, after the noise and bustle of a general assembly, his young friend, the monk Yves, approaches him for a private conversation and requests him to speak about spiritual friendship, a subject about which Yves has many question and doubts. Yves has read Cicero on friendship, but what he says seems incomplete to the young monk. After all, he argues, Cicero was a pagan. He had no knowledge of Christ and of His salvation. Aelred agrees and proposes, therefore, to discuss that friendship "which begins in Christ, develops according to Christ and is brought to its perfection by Christ."

Aelred begins with Cicero's definition: friendship is an accord on things both human and divine, accompanied with benevolence and charity. "Would we not judge that those who think the same about human and divine things and who have the same will with benevolence and charity have reached the perfection of friendship?"

Yves is willing to accept the definition, but he does not understand what "that pagan" means when he used the words "benevolence" and "charity." Aelred interprets "charity" as meaning a sentiment in the soul, and "benevolence" as the translation of this internal sentiment into acts.

And so the dialogue progresses, Yves providing doubts and objections, Aelred responding each time or taking Yves's questions as a basis for further developments. To Yves genuine friendship seems such a difficult thing that he despairs of ever attaining it. Aelred answers that just the effort toward friendship is salutary. He adds further that friendship is a *virtue,* and a Christian should never despair of obtaining a virtue, with God's help. The virtue of friendship is not that of charity, of course. Charity is universal; it extends to all, even to enemies. Not so friendship; its domain is restricted to those to whom one can give one's entire confidence and from whom one can receive entire confidence in return.

These definitions lead to a discussion of true and false friendships and of the difference between them, since even the counterfeit presents many attractions. Aelred distinguishes three types of friendship: carnal, worldly, and spiritual. He describes in bold strokes and colors the course of carnal friendship, born of passion, intoxicated with physical beauty, seeking bodily satisfactions, using friendship as a justification for any sort of crime, and finally ending with the same abruptness and ease with which it began.

Worldly friendship is essentially inconstant, because it is based upon personal interest and profit. Changes of fortune, therefore, can shake its foundation and put an end to it. However, Aelred remarks with considerable psychological insight, such friendships, though originally entered into out of a hope of gain, sometimes eventually result in a complete and satisfying accord, at least in purely worldly matters. It remains, nevertheless, an inferior form of friendship, which hardly merits the name.

Spiritual friendship, the only true friendship, develops, according to Aelred, not from any prospect of temporal gain or profit, but out of its own worth and from the desires of the human heart. This sort of friendship is its own reward. It seeks no profit other than itself. True charity excludes from friendship anything vicious or sinful. Thus, the often cited description of friendship, "to will and not to will the same," becomes a sweet and sincere accord in all that is good.

In the second part of this dialogue, Aelred passes on to the question of the origin of friendship. He finds this origin in nature, in experience, and in law. In the manner of the Middle Ages, Aelred finds throughout nature vestiges and images of the Divine Unity. Every form of being seeks a sort of society with its like. Aelred discovers the first vestiges of social life even in minerals and vegetables. He traces it further among animals and even among the angels. Is it possible, he asks, that man alone in the whole universe is an exception to this law of nature, that he was created to be *alone?*

Prior to man's fall into original sin, friendship and charity would have been extended without discrimination to all, but after the Fall friendship became impossible between good men and evil men. Experience, then, taught men to be cautious; men learned that one could not trust everyone indiscriminately and that friendship was to be given only to good men. However, since evil men also felt the natural need of society with others like themselves, they also entered into relationships modeled on true friendship. It is this fact which necessitated the formulation of the laws and precepts of true friendship in order that the counterfeit might be avoided. Aelred compares friendship with wisdom and assures Yves that true friendship, like true wisdom, can never be abused. If what appears to be friendship or wisdom is abused, this abuse is simply an indication that the supposed friendship or wisdom is not genuine, but a counterfeit. Pushing his praise of friendship to the limit, Aelred does not hesitate to substitute it, at its best, for charity in the famous statement of Saint John: "He who abides in friendship, abides in God, and God in him."

So ends the first dialogue. The two other dialogues which make up this work take place several years later. The dear friend Yves is dead, and Aelred's interlocutors are now two other monks, Gratian and Galterus. After a few brief preliminaries to set the stage, Aelred passes immediately to the first point of this dialogue, the fruits of friendship. In a lyrical period, strongly reminiscent of Cicero, he sings its praises, emphasizing especially the isolation of the man who lives without friends and the security of the man who lives with them. The presence of friends makes prosperity more enjoyable and adversity more bearable.

In a more characteristically Christian perspective, Aelred proposes genuine human friendship as a preparation for divine friendship and more precisely for friendship with Christ.

At this point Galterus invites Aelred to comment on the limits of friendship, there being such a diversity of opinion on this particular point. Aelred says that friendship can never justify the transgression of one's duty, and he supports this admonition with a series of examples drawn from the Bible. This does not mean, Aelred hastens to add, that friendship is something exotic, reserved to some sort of perfect or near-perfect stoic; it is for what we would call ordinary good people. Not only would injury to the interests of the state or of a third person be excluded from the duties of friendship, but any sort of evil, whatever its form.

Aelred repeats here some ideas which he had previously expressed to Yves in the first dialogue on the three types of friendships, and he develops in greater detail his description of friendship based on self-interest. He concludes this dialogue with a summary on the limits of friendship and then, with his two interlocutors, he plans a rendezvous for the following day.

Whereas the first two dialogues present a general *theory* of friendship, the third one describes its *practice*. Aelred describes the choosing of friends, testing of them, admitting them to one's friendship, and, finally, being in perfect accord with them. It is regrettable that we are unable to describe each of these steps in detail, containing as they do much psychological insight as well as human warmth.

The considerations regarding the practice of friendship lead Aelred into a discussion of the delicate *art of giving*. One should grant a friend without delay all that is not incompatible with duty, but in this regard not everyone has the same possibilities. The manner is most important; one should give as God does: freely, liberally, gladly, even anticipating the request by a watchful attention to one's friend's needs. At this point one of Aelred's monks objects: How can monks, who have surrendered, by their vow of poverty, the right to receive or give anything, practice this duty of benevolence, which springs from friendship? Aelred replies that voluntary poverty in reality confers upon friendship an even greater stability, by abolishing the unfortunate distinction between *mine* and *thine*. Besides, monastic life itself affords many occasions for assisting one's friends, especially by mutual good counsel and admonition.

A further question arises: Should one seek to advance one's friends toward honors and dignities? Aelred replies, making a distinction full of humanity and good sense: "Many are worthy of our love but do not deserve promotion." It would be a grave fault to lay upon their shoulders a burden which exceeds their strength. Aelred further illustrates this distinction in a prolonged comparison between Saint John and Saint Peter. John was the beloved disciple, the preferred friend of Our Lord, and he received from Him the custody of Our Lady. Still it was to Peter that Jesus committed the keys of the Kingdom of Heaven and the primacy in the Church. Aelred extends this comparison through several paragraphs of reminiscences, recalling in particular two dear friends, who seem to have resembled Peter and John. This is a touching revelation of Aelred's own heart. It shows us that he is no mere theoretician regarding friendship. He speaks of what he has himself experienced.

In a final flight, Aelred summarizes all that he has said previously, emphasizing especially the manner in which friendship, begun here below, gradually leads to love of Christ. Looking forward to its final consummation in glory, Aelred sings: ". . . then this friendship, to which here below we admit only a few, will flow out toward all and from them will flow back into God, for then, 'God will be all in all.' "

E.L.B.

DECRETUM GRATIANI

Author: Johannes Gratian (c.1100-c.1178)
Type of work: Canon law
First transcribed: Between 1139 and 1151

Principal Ideas Advanced

An equilibrium between charity and justice must be achieved in canon law through dialectical legal science applied to the Sacred Canons.

The development of ecclesiastical polity, spiritual and juridical, known as the Gregorian Reform was destined to create in the Church an entirely new constitution for it, implementing its supernatural character and enabling it to educate and discipline its members; the *Respublica Christiana* was made real and actual in its operation. For the first time since the ancient *Sacrum Imperium Romanum* had imposed its laws in Europe, a true commonwealth came to function in human affairs. From it not only the Church was to benefit, but also emperors, kings, and statesmen, who were to learn the lessons which they applied in chanceries throughout the civilized world as governments arose out of the welter of barbarian custom and Roman ruin. The most important impetus in this process derived from the *Decretum Gratiani*, its *fons et origo*.

For a thousand years, the Church had contented itself with a familial constitution under *Papa* and *Patriarcha*, whose principles of government were charity and the *Mos Patrum*, "The ways of the Fathers," the custom handed down from the Saints. It was refined and found in the Sacred Canons drawn from Holy Writ, the General Councils, the writings of the Fathers of the Church, the decisions and rules of regional and local councils. Sanctioned by the holiness of their origin and the long use made of them, the Sacred Canons cultivated unity and virtue in Christian people, educating them and directing them in the ways of Christian ideals, and reducing these ideals to particular practices with a flexibility which provided for large variety and particular need.

At the beginning of the eleventh century, however, a new tide flowed. The Church found herself faced with an invigorated Holy Roman Empire of the German people and, beyond it, with apt kings whose royal servants were extending household government into governments of royal realms. The possibility was that the Church would be overcome by the imperial and feudal systems, until the movement born in the monastery of Cluny in the tenth century began providentially to flower into those saints and actions called, after the most outstanding pontiff of the eleventh century, Saint Gregory VII, the Gregorian Reform.

It soon became apparent that the principle of charity and the *Mos Patrum* were insufficient to rescue the Church from the feudal and imperial involvement. The Roman pontiff had to begin the exercise of an effective jurisdiction over every man's actions if he were to become the defender of every man's rights; any man must be able to appeal to the Bishop of the Catholic Church. Charity and the *Mos Patrum* will ever remain the animating soul of ecclesiastical governance; bishops and popes must continue to be Most Reverend Fathers in Christ. United to this soul, a political body was created in the following centuries incarnating justice and Roman Law, the *ratio scripta* (written reason) of right in human affairs. First attempts were made to systematize and universalize the Sacred Canons in the outstanding labors of Saint Ives of Chartres and Burchard of Worms, who were only the greatest of many colleagues in this work.

The critical moment happened when Master Gratian appeared on the scene with his carefully compiled schoolbook, to be known forever as the *Decretum*. What Gratian himself called it we do not know. His immediate disciples and their students had a variety of titles for it, *Decreta, Corpus decretorum, Liber decretorum,* even *Corpus juris canonici,* the last a title which was used for centuries to designate the entire legislation which was the fruit of the *Decretum. Decretum* the book was to be called, though it might lead to some confusion among the unwary, since it never was official, never promulgated; nor could it be, for it was a schoolbook, an instrument of dialectic to be used in making lawyers and judges. The book quickly got another name which it has retained until this day, a name doing much more justice to its content and purpose: *Concordia discordantium canonum* (*The Concordance of Discordant Canons*); *Decretum* is handier, and perhaps use, if not papal authority, sufficiently promulgated it. When, after a hundred years, Bartholomew of Brescia brought together the best comments on it to form the *Glossa ordinaria,* it was axiomatic that "What the Gloss does not know, the court does not know": *"Quod non agnoscit glossa, non agnoscit forum."*

Master Gratian became in medieval fanciful symbolism the third in a trinity made up of three uterine brothers, Peter Lombard, the father of theology; Peter Comestor, father of history; and Gratian, father of law. Whatever poetic fancy is lovely in this symbolism, it does not correspond to fact. Little is known of the great Master. He was born at Chiusi, a city in Tuscany, became a Camaldolese monk, and so lived an eremetical life according to the Rule of Saint Benedict at the monastery of Saints Nabor and Felix. He taught in Bologna. He died sometime before 1179. The chronicler Martin of Troppau tells us that Gratian composed the *Decretum* in 1151. More recent scholars say it was 1139. Actually, Gratian seems never to have finished composing his work, a factor which accounts more than anything else for the lack of a definitive edition of it. An authentic version of the *Decretum* probably never existed. Today, in the edition of Emile Friedberg, the work occupies 1,468 columns in quarto, in eight-point type, about one-fourth of this space being devoted to the editor's notes. Its practical importance centuries after it was written is attested by the fact that at least seventeen incunabula editions exist. The most influential edition, which became standard, was that produced in 1582 by the scholars and lawyers known as the *Correctores Romani,* who synthesized a century and more of critical work on the text and printed under orders of Pope Gregory XV in 1582. This work was again resumed in the eighteenth century, which saw some *parti pris* editions by Gallicans. In the early nineteenth century Emile-Lous Richter produced the edition which the Abbé Migne printed in his *Patrologia Latina,* tome 187; it was this edition which Friedberg improved later in the century and which is standard at present. These latter two editors, differing from the Romans, who wanted a critical text, tried to establish an authentic text, but were doomed to fail. Scholars are presently trying to get at least an *editio princeps.* All this interest and labor testifies that the *Decretum,* eight centuries old, still possesses its value. Today it remains the foundation in the *Codex juris canonici.* The careful study of the *Decretum* with its *Glossa ordinaria,* still is, and forever shall be, the best initiation into the superb, profound art which the skill of canonists exercised to form the medieval Church. Canonists today neglect it at their peril and the Church's loss; historians of Church and state who wish to understand either medieval or modern society cannot proceed without it.

The intimate reasons for the great wealth of the *Decretum* may now be pointed out. The *Decretum* is the mighty river formed by the meeting of four streams in the intellectual flood of the twelfth century. Immediately preceding Master Gratian, Europe had witnessed the long-drawn-out controversy between Papalists and Imperialists over the Investure Struggle, preserved for us to some extent in the *Libelli de lite.* Here, excellent dialecticians had examined and debated the very foundations of Church and state; spiritual and civil life had been vigorously examined, and the juridical result was a thorough search of the *Mos Patrum* and the clarification of the jurisdiction of the Roman pontiff. A second stream was the new hermeneutic, the technique of exegesis and interpretation to be used in applying the *auctoritates,* as the Sacred Canons were called, to specific questions created by the problems and the legislator, the conditions and qualities of persons, time, and place. Its principal proposal by Saint Ives of Chartres, which came to be the supreme norm in making the "concordance of canons" and remains so today, was the establishing of equilibrium between charity and justice. The French theological movement, a third stream, brought to the Master the developed science of *solutio contariorum,* the "Solution of Contraries," originated by Abelard. Finally, the mighty force of Roman Law, that *mare magnum,* was making itself felt in Bologna where Gratian lived and taught. The internal coherence of the Justinian Code was being investigated, and men came again to know, and in pure intellectual excitement to revel in, the juridical maturity of the most profound legal culture the world has ever seen. This enabled them to formulate, develop, stress the coherence of the Sacred Canons, and an *ius canonicum* came to exist alongside the *ius civile*. The great tradition of the Roman Jurists again flourished. The Glossators' example was followed: *distinctiones, causae* and *quaestiones* were the particular intellectual instruments used to analyze and synthesize the Sacred Canons. Bologna was the center of one of the greatest intellectual excitements the world has ever seen, and this in the field of law; in civil and canon law, streaming from Irnerius and Gratian, the world found the juridical principles and methods which it has used ever since with astounding success to solve the problems of empires and societies whose existence the Glossarists and Decretists never dreamed of.

Master Gratian's book introduced students to all these wonders. It came to be received in three distinct parts. The first part contained 973 *capitula*, or chapters, as the canons came to be known, arranged to treat 101 *distinctiones*, the first fifteen handling law in general; the sixteenth to the twentieth, pontifical and conciliar law; then eighty-one on clerics and the clerical state, containing the first law *de personis* ever written. The second part is thirty-six *causae*, or cases, fictitious situations created by the Master. It has 2,576 *capitula*. The thirty-first *causa* has seven *distinctiones* and is the first complete treatise *de paenitentia*, the determination of responsibility and rehabilitation of the offender. The third part is the least satisfactory of the *Decretum*. It is only a chaplet of canons dealing with *sacramenta*, holy things. A later Decretist thought Gratian was taciturn in this part, because "Holy things must be spoken of with sobriety; of such it is dangerous to say even true things." It contains five *distinctiones*, and 396 *capitula*. To all this, one of Gratian's disciples, setting out to improve upon the work of his Master, added what in all humility he called his chaff, the *Palaea*; he has since been called Paucapalaea, Pocopalia in Italian, "Little Chaff," we would say in English. The chaff was all accepted, however, and is always printed with the *Decretum* where he inserted it.

The *Decretum* of Gratian formed the minds of the great race of canonists who worked in two areas, the chanceries and the schools. From the chanceries arose the jurist popes who ascended the papal throne during the late twelfth and throughout the thirteenth centuries, and by their flood of decretal letters (1,971 in about seventy years) furnished the materials for Saint Raymond of Penafort's *Quinque libri decretalium*, which is the first codification of law subsequent to Justinian's, the fruit of the marriage of the *Decretum* with Roman Law. In the schools, the Scholastics brought legal science to its fullest development in the *doctores utriusque juris*, (doctors of civil and canon law). Justice with charity was again possible in the world, and the *Respublica Christiana* had in its hands the instrument needed to replace the sword Rome used *parcere subjectis, debellare superbos*, "to spare the conquered, to tame the proud."

The *Decretum* of Master Gratian has special interest even for those who live in countries of Anglo-American jurisprudence. No one has spoken more eloquently that F. W. Maitland: "English law was administered by the ablest, the best educated, men in the realm; nor only that, it was administered by the selfsame men who were the 'judges ordinary' of the church's courts, men who were bound to be, at least in some sense, learned in canon law. At one moment, Henry has three bishops for his 'archjusticiars.' The climax is reached in Richard's reign. We can then see the king's court as it sits day by day. Often enough is was composed of the archbishop of Canterbury, two other bishops, two or three archdeacons, two or three ordained clerks who were going to be bishops and but two or three laymen. The majority of its members might at any time be called upon to hear ecclesiastical causes and learn the lessons in law that were addressed to them in papal rescripts. . . . It is by 'popish clergymen' that our English law is converted from a rude mass of customs into an articulate system, and when the 'popish clergymen', yielding at length to the pope's commands, no longer sit as the principal judges of the king's court, the creative age of our mediaeval law is over. . . . Viewed therefore from one point, the effect produced on English law by its contact with the romano-canonical learning seems immeasurable, or measurable only by the distance that divides Glanville's treatise from the *Leges Henrici*."

J.A.M.

THE BOOK OF SENTENCES

Author: Peter Lombard (c.1100-c.1160)
Type of work: Theology
First transcribed: c.1150-1152

Principal Ideas Advanced

What is proposed for Christian belief may be discussed under four major headings: God; Creation; Incarnation and Redemption; and the Sacraments and the four Last Things; namely, death, Judgment, Hell, and Heaven.

Peter, the author of the *Book of Sentences* (*Sententiarum Libri IV*), was born in Lombardy in Italy. He taught in the Cathedral school in Paris from about the year 1140 until he became bishop of the city in 1158 or 1159. He died in or about 1160. Peter was educated at Bologna and Rheims and in the school of St. Victor in Paris. Commentaries on the Epistles of St. Paul and on the Psalms were composed by Peter, and he cast light on the text by collecting passages from elsewhere in Scripture and from the Fathers. These writings may be looked upon as way-stations to his masterpiece, the *Book of Sentences,* which he completed around 1150-1152. Within twenty years of its composition, the *Sentences* became an integral part of the process whereby one became a Master of Theology. The candidate was expected to comment on the four books of the *Sentences* in a way which would exhibit his competence in the field. Most great Scholastics, such as

Alexander of Hales, Saint Bonaventure, Duns Scotus, and William of Ockham, left such commentaries. Saint Thomas Aquinas in 1254-1256 commented on the *Sentences,* although the importance of the commentary as an endorsement of Peter is somewhat eclipsed by the fact that Thomas later felt a need to compose his *Summa theologiae* to introduce a better order into the treatment of theological topics.

What accounts for the phenomenal success of the *Sentences?* At the time of its composition, there was definitely a need for a systematic compilation of orthodox doctrine on the whole range of theological questions. This is not to say that the method employed in the *Sentences* was originated by Peter himself. It can be shown that the texts of the Fathers gathered around a given point were known to Peter from previous compilations. The parentage of the *Sentences* may be traced back to Cassiodorus Senator by way of Strabo, Alcuin, Bede, and Isidore of Seville. Most prominent in the immediate background were theological monographs such as that of Saint Anselm and, earlier, those of Saint Augustine himself. However, the success of Peter's textbook was due to its usefulness, not its originality. It achieved prominence and, except for the Bible, became the most referred to book in thirteenth century theology. The student of theology, having finished his Biblical course, immediately followed with the composition of lectures on the *Sentences.* The number of such commentaries on the *Sentences* later committed to writing is almost unbelievable. The book was copied almost as often as the Bible. It is sometimes thought that Saint Thomas's *Summa theologiae* took over the role of being *the* book to be commented on, but this does not seem to have been the case. There are, of course, many excellent commentaries on the *Summa,* but commentaries on the *Sentences* continue to be written. We are speaking, then, of a work of immense historical importance in medieval theology.

There are four books of the *Sentences,* and they deal, respectively, with God, Creation, Incarnation and Redemption, and, finally, Sacraments and the Last Things; namely, death, Judgment, Heaven, and Hell. Lombard's procedure is to distinguish a doctrinal point or question and then bring to bear on it authorities with opposing views. Peter refers to Scripture, of course, and the Councils, but also to the Fathers and, principally, Saint Augustine. It is maintained that ninety percent of Peter Lombard's quotations are of Augustine, and obviously this does not leave much room for the other Fathers. Peter often quotes Hugh of St. Victor and Abelard, and it is thought that both these men were his teachers. The method of the *Sentences* bears obvious kinship with that of Abelard's *Sic et non.*

There are forty-eight distinctions in the first book of the *Sentences* and Lombard entitles the book, *De mysterio trinitatis* (*On the Mystery of the Trinity*). Lombard asks what the purpose was on the part of those men who wrote on the Trinity, and he appeals to Augustine to reply that what they want to teach is the message of Scripture; namely, that in the one divine nature there are three divine and equal Persons: the Father, the Son, and the Holy Spirit. Continuing to rely on Augustine, Lombard says that the order to be observed in discussing the Trinity demands that we first establish the doctrine on the basis of Scripture and then try to devise arguments for the defense and utility of faith in that doctrine. True to this order, Lombard goes on to cite Scriptural passages in which the doctrine is proposed for our belief. In Distinction Three, he asks how the Creator can be known from creatures and, after appealing to Saint Paul (Romans 1:19), Peter gives a succinct summary of Augustine's teaching on the vestiges of the Trinity in creatures and on the soul as the image of the Trinity.

After devoting some space to the generation of the Son from the Father, Lombard turns in Distinction Nine to the question of the source of the distinction of Persons in the Trinity. The generation of the Son from the Father does not prejudice His being coeternal with the Father, as many texts from the Fathers are adduced to show. In the following Distinction, the Holy Spirit as the substantial term of the love of the Father and Son becomes the topic of discussion, and Peter asks whether the Holy Spirit should be thought of as proceeding principally from the Father or from the Son. The discussion of the third Person of the Trinity continues through Distinction Eighteen.

Once the equality of the Persons has been established, Peter, having devoted several Distinctions to the meaning of the term *Person* and to the various modes of speech employed in expressing the doctrine of the Trinity, speaks of attributes appropriate to Persons and of things which are predicated of God temporally. (In reading the first book, the reader becomes conscious of repetition and circularity, and if he is acquainted with the order and precision of the *Summa* of Aquinas he may feel a trifle impatient.) The book closes with a treatment of some essential attributes of the divine nature, such as omniscience, omnipotence, and the divine will.

Book Two is entitled, "Concerning the Creation and Formation of Corporeal and Spiritual Things together with Other Pertinent Matters." The forty-four Distinctions of this book range from a treatment of the fact that there is but one source of the being of all things to man's possibility of sinning. Distinctions Two through Eleven deal with the angels, their creation, the fall of some, their order and distinction, and their function in the universe. Distinctions Twelve through Fifteen treat of the work of the six days of Creation, and the remaining Distinctions deal with man. Grace, Free Will, and Sin are the great topics of what may be called Lombard's treatise of man.

"Concerning the Incarnation of the Word" is the title of the third book of the *Sentences,* and by the time Lombard gets to the end of the forty Distinctions of the book, his attention has turned to questions of morality. Influenced by Augustine as always, Lombard asks whether the Father and Holy Spirit could have assumed flesh as the Son did, and he then goes on to discuss the nature of the union of human nature and the Second Person of the Trinity. He asks how such statements as the following are to be understood: "God was made man," "God is man." Authorities are brought to bear on the question as to whether it is proper to say that Christ is a creature, whether He was always man or came to be man, whether as man Christ is pre-eminent in wisdom and grace. The role of Christ as Mediator and Redeemer is discussed, as well as the way God used for actually redeeming man from sin.

The moral discussions of the third book of the *Sentences* may be said to begin with the twenty-fifth Distinction; here Peter discusses the theological virtues of faith, hope, and charity; the seven gifts of the Holy Spirit, the Ten Commandments, and their relation to the two precepts of charity.

The fourth book of the *Sentences* does not bear a title but, as we have said, its principal concern is with the sacraments. It contains fifty Distinctions and from Distinction Forty-three until the end, Lombard treats the four Last Things. Penance and Matrimony, of the sacraments, receive the most extensive consideration.

Whatever criticisms must be made of the lack of detailed order in the *Sentences* and of the repetitions within individual books, the general outline of the *Sentences* is that which we find in the *Summa* of Aquinas as well. The theologian organizes the body of revealed truths by first discussing God and then creatures, and when he comes to man, he treats of sin and redemption. It is only natural, then, to turn to the Incarnation and Redemption by Christ and of the means He has left men to share in the divine life; namely, the sacraments. With general success, Peter Lombard makes use of this fundamental framework to build an impressive array of authoritative texts and arguments from the Fathers, chiefly Saint Augustine, around a series of questions and points of doctrine. The result is at once a developed doctrine and an invitation for further discussion, and this invitation, as we have seen, was accepted frequently and with enthusiasm by an amazing number of medieval theologians.

The modest textbook composed by Peter Lombard in the middle of the twelfth century was destined to have an impressive history. The fact has to be recognized, but there remains reason to marvel at the fact. In explanation of the incredible importance the *Sentences* took on, David Knowles suggests that it was due in large part to a happy combination of circumstances. Men were ready for such a compilation and, although the style and method of the *Sentences* have little originality, Peter Lombard, in adopting the method developed by Anselm and Abelard, produced a textbook of sufficient scope to make it a convenient object for subsequent speculation. Peter Lombard's lack of daring, his solid good sense, and, one might add, his carefully maintained proximity to Augustine, assured him safe passage through the shoals of ecclesiastical appraisal. Furthermore, the *Sentences* antedate subsequent divisions of theologians into factions and schools, and Peter Lombard's work played the role of the common point between quite different doctrines. Peter Lombard, a compiler, a popularizer of a method already developed by his teachers, and no candidate for the title of original thinker, was nonetheless, because of the *Sentences*, an influential figure in the development of Catholic thought.

R.M.

THE LETTERS OF SAINT BERNARD OF CLAIRVAUX

Author: Saint Bernard (1091-1153)
Type of work: Pastoral epistles
First transcribed: c.1119-c.1153

Principal Ideas Advanced

Humility, charity, and courage are virtues which every monk should seek to acquire.

Action in the world is necessary if the Church is to survive and prosper.

Every man is important, but error concerning theological matters must be detected and condemned.

The reading of *The Letters of Saint Bernard of Clairvaux* is both an illuminating and refreshing experience. The reading is illuminating because the letters of Saint Bernard, Doctor of the Church, are the letters of a master politician and churchman, a twelfth century Abbot of Clairvaux who had a hand in the making of popes, who dealt with emperors, who challenged and vanquished those he took to be enemies of the Church, and who promoted a crusade against the Turks. The letters fill out the portrait of this powerful and saintly man, for they are not mere footnotes to history but part of history itself, traces of decisive action which changed the course of events within the Church and the world. At the same time, the letters are refreshing because the man they reveal, one who speaks afresh through his public and personal letters, is a full-bodied figure, a distinctive person of spiritual insight and courage but also a man of human passions, subject to anger and laughter, a man of compassion but also a man of principle and justice.

Saint Bernard was born in the castle of his father, Tescelin Sorrel, a Burgundian nobleman, at Fontaines-les-Dijon, in the year 1090 or 1091. Bernard's father was reputed to be a religious man; and Bernard's mother, Aleth, daugher of Bernard, Lord Montbard, was a pious woman who dedicated her seven children to God. Aleth died when Bernard was nineteen, and rumor has it that he led a somewhat lively and worldly existence for some time afterwards. In the year 1112, however, Bernard entered the religious life, accompanied by some thirty of his friends. The place he chose was the house of Cîteaux, founded in 1098 by Robert of Molesme, ordered by the Rule of Saint Benedict, and under the guidance of Saint Stephen Harding (died 1134). Three years later, in 1115, Bernard and twelve others were sent to form a new house in Champagne. As Abbot of Clairvaux, Bernard was encouraged by William of Champeaux, Bishop of Chalons-sur-Marne, and Bernard's fame began to grow, partly as a result of his intense dedication to his calling and partly because of his intelligence, common sense, and eloquence. He imposed strict discipline upon brothers, and he himself practiced a course of such extreme asceticism that his health was affected. However, his understanding and character were such that both at Clairvaux and in the world of Church and state he was respected and consulted. Much of the advice he gave is preserved in the hundreds of letters which he wrote over the years.

Although Bernard was frequently appealed to for advice, as the letters to kings and popes, as well as to men of lower station, testify, the first momentous occasion which tested his personal integrity and political acumen occurred in 1130, when, a few hours after the election of Innocent II as pope, Peter Leonis secured the election of himself as anti-pope, under the name Anacletus II. Bernard opposed Anacletus and plunged into the tumultuous controversy that surrounded the disputed election; largely due to Bernard's persuasive powers the canonically elected pope, Innocent II, triumphed.

Ten years later, in 1140, Bernard undertook the task of challenging the views of Peter Abelard, and Bernard's insistence at the Council of Sens that Abelard was placing too great a reliance on human reason led to Abelard's retreat: an appeal to Rome. Abelard's views were condemned on July 16, 1140. (The balance of Abelard's life was spent, at the invitation of Peter the Venerable, at Cluny; Abelard and Bernard were later reconciled through Peter's intercession.)

In 1146 Bernard instigated a crusade against the Turks, but the crusade was unsuccessful. Bernard's reputation as a leader was secure, however; during his lifetime sixty-eight Cistercian monasteries were founded, and his mystical writings, which include *On the Necessity of Loving God* and *On the Steps of Humility and Pride,* were very influential during the Middle Ages.

The Letters of Saint Bernard of Clairvaux (1953) is an edition of the letters as freshly translated by Bruno Scott James. James includes 469 letters which are regarded as authentic, and he has attempted, despite a paucity of evidence, to arrange the letters chronologically. An index correlates the new arrangement with the traditional order.

Some conception of the range of character which the letters exhibit may be gained through comparing characteristic examples of various types. In a letter written near the end of his life, to Baldwin, Bishop of Noyon, Bernard shows the sense of humor which, no doubt, enabled him to survive the controversies and practical difficulties of a busy and demanding calling; he writes, in part, "I am sending you the small boy who is bringing this letter to eat your bread, that I may find out how mean you are from the sort of welcome you give him. But you have no cause for tears or lamentations, he has a small stomach and will be content with little. I shall be grateful if he returns wiser rather than stouter."

A quite different tone pervades the letter which Bernard wrote in 1145 to the Roman Curia, upon the election to pope of Bernard Paganelli, Abbot of the Cistercian monastery of St. Anastasius; Bernard expresses his dismay at learning that a man of contemplation has been called upon to be a man of action. Beginning his letter with the blunt question, "God have mercy on you; what have you done?", Bernard declares, "You have recalled a dead man from the grave and restored him to his fellow men. You have plunged once more into crowds and cares a man who had fled from both." Bernard suggests that the new pope may have had difficulties in the past: "Did he leave Pisa so as to receive Rome? Did he, who could not endure the responsibility of being second in charge of one church, covet the lordship of the whole Church?" And Bernard then asks, "What reason, what counsel, made you, as soon as the late Pope had died, suddenly rush upon this rustic, lay hands upon him when in hiding from the world, and, throwing away his axe, mattock, or hoe, drag him to the palatine, place him upon a throne, clothe him in purple and fine linen, and gird him with a sword. . . ? Had you no other wise and experienced man amongst you who would have been better suited for these things?" Bernard concludes, however, by asking that the Curia "comfort with your fervent support what is clearly the work of your hands," and he closes with the following injunction: "Whatever things are true, whatever things are seemly, whatever things are of good fame, suggest them to him, persuade him of them, encourage him to do them, and the God of peace will be with you."

In a letter to the Curia concerning the doctrines of Peter Abelard, Bernard has this to say: "Read, if you please, that book of Peter Abelard which he calls a book of Theology. You have it to hand since, as he boasts, it is read eagerly by many in the Curia. See what sort of things he says there about the Holy Trinity, about the generation of the Son, about the procession of the Holy Spirit, and much else that is very strange indeed to Catholic ears and minds. . . . And if you then consider that I am rightly disturbed, do you also bestir yourselves . . . and let him who has scanned the heavens go down even into hell, and let the works of darkness that have braved the light be shown up by the light. . . ."

Many of Bernard's letters are quite naturally concerned with monastic affairs and discipline. Much of the advice which he gave to fellow abbots and monks was of a practical nature, but practical or not, the advice was always tempered by a steadfast spiritual emphasis. Bernard's interest in others was not merely dutiful; it arose naturally from one who saw himself and his brothers as forming one family in Christ. To the monks at Clairvaux, during his absence from the monastery, Bernard wrote, "Your own experience can tell you how much I am suffering. . . . You are suffering from the absence of one person, but I am suffering from the absence of each and all of you, and this is something quite different and much more hard to bear. I cannot but have as many anxieties as I have sons at Clairvaux. . . ."

Although there is a great deal of interest to be found in Saint Bernard's letters to royalty and the popes, particularly in the letters directed to Pope Innocent II, with whom Bernard was so influentially associated, the affairs of Church and state, insofar as they involved political and military matters, are not as attractive and moving as are the personal affairs of Bernard as the busy and very human Abbot of Clairvaux. One more glimpse at the man himself is afforded by the last letter in James's collection, the letter addressed to Arnold of Chartres, Abbot of Benneval, and written near the end of Saint Bernard's life; perhaps Bernard's patience was wearing thin, the result of prolonged suffering, but the spirit of the man prevails: "I have received your charitable gift in the spirit of charity, if not of pleasure. What room can there be in me for pleasure when suffering claims me completely for her own? The only sort of pleasure I have is in eating nothing. . . . even sleep has left me. Weakness of stomach is the whole of my trouble. . . . Support, I beg you, with your prayers a poor wretch destitute of all virtue, so that the enemy who lies in wait for me may find no place where he can grip me with his teeth and wound me. I have written this with my own hand so that . . . you may recognize how well I love you. But I would have preferred to have been a man of God in a world than to have been the one to write first."

A reading of Saint Bernard's 469 letters provides some sense of what it was to have been a man of God in a world of suffering and intrigue; for that reason the letters are of contemporary relevance.

POLICRATICUS and METALOGICON

Author: John of Salisbury (c. 1115-1180)
Type of work: Political and educational theory
First transcribed: 1159

Principal Ideas Advanced

Rulers should act in accordance with the divine plan and law for the common welfare, physical and spiritual, of the community, subject to the moral guidance of the Church.

Governmental officials (courtiers) should live in an exemplary and serious manner, avoiding excessive waste of time in "frivolities," shunning vice, and seeking wisdom by continued study and reflection.

Education, whose ultimate objective is wisdom, human and divine, cognitive, affective, and practical, should begin with a thorough study of the arts of verbal expression (grammar) and reasoning (logic), which are the foundations of all learning.

The study of grammar should include not only a solid grounding in formal grammar, but also study and imitation of the classical authors; while that of logic should be based on Aristotle's complete logical works (or Organon*), preceded by Porphyry's* Introduction.

John of Salisbury (c.1115-1180), whose name is prominently associated with the twelfth century Renaissance, was a leading twelfth century humanist, political and educational theorist, and Churchman. Born at Old Sarum, evidently of humble parents, John was early marked as "promising ecclesiastical timber." For twelve years, from 1135, he studied the liberal arts and religious subjects at the leading educational centers of his day, Chartres and Paris, under leading masters of the time, such as Thierry of Chartres, Peter Abelard, and Gilbert of Poitiers. After service at the papal court, John became secretary (1154) to Archbishop Theobald of Canterbury, next to the king the leading personage in England. In 1159, Salisbury completed and dispatched to Chancellor Thomas à Becket, and through him to the royal court, his companion-treatises entitled the *Policraticus* and *Metalogicon*. When Becket became Archbishop of Canterbury shortly thereafter (1161), John continued as Archepiscopal secretary and Thomas's influential adviser, until Becket's murder in 1169. Later (1176), on the invitation of Louis VII of France, John, evidently *persona non grata* with Henry II, left England to become Bishop of Chartres, where he served until his death four years later.

The *Policraticus* and *Metalogicon* are twin, related treatises, jointly presented to Thomas à Becket in 1159, and designed to present John's ideas concerning government and the life and education of governmental officials.

The *Policraticus* or *Statesman's Book* has been hailed as "the earliest elaborate medieval treatise on politics" (R. Lane Poole) and the "first attempt to produce a coherent system which would aspire to the character of a philosophy of politics" (John Dickinson). It actually consists of two distinct parts. One part (about two-fifths of the book), which has been translated by John Dickinson as *The Statesman's Book,* consists of principles concerning rulers and government; the remaining part, which has been translated by Joseph B. Pike as *Frivolities of Courtiers and Footprints of Philosophers,* discusses the way of life proper for government officials, who are warned to avoid wasting their time with trifles and follies, and are urged to seek wisdom by learning and virtue.

The *Metalogicon* or *Defense of Logic* is, in a broad sense, a plea and prospectus for a thorough study of (1) grammar or the arts of reading, writing, and speaking, and (2) logic proper, demonstrative, probable, and sophistic. According to John, the study and imitation of the best literature, the classics, is an indispensable part of the study of grammar; and he recommends the method of study used by Bernard of Chartres, who based his teaching on the classical authors. For the study of logic proper, which is the main concern of the book, John endorses an extensive study of the logical works of Aristotle.

John's humanism is amply attested by the recurrent, almost continuous flow of quotations and anecdotes from classical sources. Much of the work, and particularly the part of the *Policraticus* translated by Joseph Pike, is a mosaic of extracts and stories from classical and Scriptural sources. Among John's favorite classical authors are Virgil, Horace, and Cicero; while Justinian's *Corpus,* or codification of Roman law, is used extensively in the *Policraticus,* and Aristotle's *Organon* in the *Metalogicon*.

The *Metalogicon* is a natural continuation of the *Policraticus*. The final part of the *Policraticus* encourages the study of philosophy, or the quest of secular and divine wisdom through study and reflection; the *Metalogicon* implements this suggestion by explaining how the groundwork for philosophy must be laid by a thorough study of grammar and logic. The exhortation to the pursuit of wisdom was apparently intended for the personal admonition of Thomas à Becket as well as for the court at large.

According to John's *Policraticus,* the state or commonwealth is comparable to a body, of which the ruler is the head; the priesthood, the soul; the military and tax-collectors, the hands; and the laborers, the feet. All parts are interdependent "members one of another." The ruler represents both the secular leader and the divine ruler, God. The authority and power of the ruler and his government proceed ultimately from God and the divine will, and are transmitted through the Church, as is symbolized in the royal coronation ceremonies. It may even be said that the ruler is a minister (or servant) of the Church, as temporal objectives are subordinate to eternal ones. Subjection of the prince to the judgment of the Church is exemplified by the deposition of King Saul by the Prophet Samuel, and the submission of Emperor Theodosius to St. Ambrose of Milan. Yet the supremacy of Church officials may be only a "moral" supremacy, rather than a strictly "legal" one.

The divine plan, according to John, is to be found in a universal and abiding "natural law," imbedded in the nature of things and discernible by natural reason. The ruler is bound by natural law, and he must act in accordance with it, not only to promote the political prosperity of his state, but also in order that his authority may be real and binding. If the ruler violates the divine law in certain matters, his subjects are not bound to obey him, at least insofar as he disobeys the divine law, and if he tries to force his subjects to disobey God's law, or if he becomes a serious threat to religion, he may even, in extremity, be assassinated, although ordinarily tyranny is to be borne in a spirit of patience and penance. Sanctioned by examples from the Scriptures, tyrannicide is accordingly licit in extreme cases, though it is a "last resort," and it is never to be performed by anyone who is bound by an oath of fealty to a tyrant, or who would sacrifice justice and honor by his act.

Succession to the throne, writes John, should be determined by both heredity and election, with fitness and divine approbation important factors to be considered. Among qualities a ruler should possess are learning, knowledge of the law, prudence, and solicitude for the welfare of his subjects. He should carefully guard and administer justice, yet temper it with mercy, and he should both promote religion and assist the weak and needy. The ruler should seek incorruptible and spiritual ends as well as temporal and material ones. The liberty of individuals and particularly their freedom of speech should be respected by princes and defended by citizens themselves at all costs.

John maintains that government officials or "courtiers" should avoid unprofitable and scandalous dissipation of their time and energies in "frivolities," and should seek after cognitive and practical "wisdom." Of the "frivolities," some, though licit, are less desirable than others and thus are a nocuous waste of time when indulged in to excess by those who have weighty responsibilities. As examples of such activities, John cites hunting, gaming, sensuous music, "spectacles," and drama. Among other follies, sinful and therefore positively forbidden and always illicit, he names magic, sorcery, and divination, and he warns that one of the most detestable and pernicious vices found among courtiers is flattery.

Instead of frittering away their time with such "trifles," rulers and government officials would do better to seek after wisdom by the pursuit of learning, or "philosophy," the quest of wisdom, human and divine, and its implementation through the practice of virtue, or applied wisdom. The reading of worth-while literature not only elevates one's thoughts and enlightens one's mind, John argues, but it also helps to liberate one from slavery to carnal desire. As St. Jerome says, "Love the scriptures and you shall not love the lusts of the flesh,"—here meaning by "scriptures" writings in general. The courtier should seek wisdom through knowledge and virtue. In this pursuit a certain detachment from wordly concerns and activities is of great assistance, while covetousness, ambition, gluttony, drunkenness, and sensuality are obstacles.

In the *Metalogicon* John writes that the knowledge necessary to wisdom is to be obtained in large part through education. The basic studies necessary as a foundation and key to all learning are the arts of verbal expression and reasoning; namely, grammar, rhetoric, and logic, known collectively as "logic" in a broad sense; whence, *Metalogicon:* a treatise in defense of logic. Since rhetoric is included both in grammar and in logic, these two form the basic arts. Grammar is the gateway and cornerstone of learning, according to John; one should study not only the formal grammatical rules and principles but also the works of the classical authors. Love of good literature is to be fostered, and the habit of reading good books should be inculcated as a lifelong source of solace, refreshment, and strength.

Logic is even more closely associated with philosophy, since it is the means of ascertaining that truth which is philosophy's goal. Just as the great works of the greatest authors are to be made the basis of the study of grammar, so Aristotle's books on logic, known collectively as the *Organon,* are to be studied directly in that subject, of which Aristotle is the acknowledged master. First, the student of logic should study Porphyry's *Isagoge,* or *Introduction to the Categories of Aristotle,* as "the right kind of introduction, remarkable for its easy brevity"; then one should read Aristotle's *Categories* or *Predicaments,* which discuss simple terms or "the various kinds of words and how they signify things"; next, the *Interpretation* relative to the various types of "propositions," or terms combined into statements; next, the *Topics,* concerned with "the sources of probable arguments" and "how proofs may be constructed"; next, the *Prior Analytics,* which discuss syllogisms; next, the *Posterior Analytics,* which treat absolute proof or incontrovertible demonstration; and, finally, the *Sophistical Refutations,* which expose merely specious, empty, and fallacious reasoning.

John contends that the student and scholar, as well as the teacher and man of learning, should keep his eyes and purpose fixed on pursuing that wisdom which is eventually identifiable with God. He should avoid distractions such as vain-glorious ambition and greed for lucre, as well as trivial pedantry and frivolous curiosity, which lack direction and purpose. The successive stages of ascent in the cognitive process are sense-perception, including both sensation and sensory imagination; discursive reasoning; and intuitive understanding, to which may be added divine revelation, grace, and faith. The successive steps of learning or "philosophy" are reading, study (learning), meditation (reflection), and persevering application (virtue).

D.D.M.

BENJAMIN MINOR and BENJAMIN MAJOR

Author: Richard of St. Victor (died 1173)
Type of work: Mystical theology; spiritual instruction
First transcribed: c.1160

Principal Ideas Advanced

Every rational spirit has two powers, reason and the affections; the reason leads to truth, and the affections lead to virtue.

Every man loves wisdom, but not all desire to be righteous; nevertheless, before coming to wisdom the soul is chastened by righteousness.

To be able to contemplate heavenly things, the mind must know itself and prepare itself inwardly; God can then act upon the soul.

Benjamin minor and *Benjamin major* by Richard of St. Victor, the disciple of Hugh of St. Victor and himself prior of the Abbey of St. Victor, is an allegorical discussion of the ascetic discipline by which the soul prepares itself for the "divine shewings" which come to the ecstatic contemplative. The account is allegorical; the powers of the soul are symbolized by figures drawn from the story of Jacob. Rachel, one of Jacob's two wives, is the image of truth and the search of wisdom; she is beautiful but sterile. Leah, the other wife, is fruitful but ugly ("blear-eyed"); she represents the discipline of virtue and the desire for righteousness. Benjamin, ". . . a youth, in ecstasy of mind" (Psalm 67:28, Vulgate), is the contemplative, whose nature and discipline Richard is to explore.

Richard addresses himself to the young men of St. Victor's Abbey. The "sermon" is to be about youth, about contemplative youth, and, in particular, about Benjamin, whom many know, says Richard, "some by learning and some by experience." Jacob, who is the figure of man as rational spirit, has two wives, Rachel (wisdom) and Leah (righteousness); he quite naturally loves Rachel, who is "well favoured," for all men love wisdom. But not all who love wisdom attain it. Righteousness, on the other hand, is not equally desired by all men, but those who can come to love righteousness perfectly will then be righteous. To lovers of the world, the demands of righteousness are entirely unreasonable, for righteousness asks that men love their enemies, bear their suffering, and abandon the pleasurable life which the world of the senses provides. Leah, then, is regarded as "laborious" and even stupid.

Every rational spirit, says Richard, has two powers: reason, which seeks truth and offers right counsel; and the affections, which seek virtue and from which holy desires spring. The affection cannot be directed toward righteousness without great labor; hence, Leah is regarded as laborious. The contemplation of the highest wisdom is a great joy; hence, Rachel is considered to be delightful. Just as Jacob, having hastened to the marriage-bed of Rachel, found that he was embracing Leah there, so the rational spirit, eager to know the joys of contemplation and hungry for truth, finds that it must first be laboriously chastened by the demands of righteousness.

Imagination is the handmaiden of reason, writes Richard; and sensation is the handmaiden of the affections. The reason could not function without the knowledge of things which the imagination provides, not could the affections direct themselves were the senses not operative. In the allegory, Bilhah is the imagination, Rachel's maid; and Zilpah is sensation (the senses).

The handmaidens have their vices, Richard warns his young listeners: "Bilhah is garrulous and Zilpah drunken." The affections (Leah), which should be directed toward higher things, sometimes attach themselves to things of the flesh and of this world, for the senses (Zilpah) lead the affections to carnal pleasures and make the affections drunk with joy and lust. The imagination is also wicked, for it uncritically and wastefully pours out fantastic images which obscure the truth: Bilhah, who talks too much, thus misleads Rachel, who would know the truth.

The sons of Jacob and Leah are the seven virtues, although only as virtues and as ordered are they properly to be called "Jacob's sons." The affections, hope and fear, joy and sorrow, hate, love and shame, are such that they may be either ordered or disordered. Reuben, the "son of vision," represents the first of the virtues, fear of the Lord; Simeon, the second son, represents the second of the ordered affections, sorrow or contrition because of sin; Levi, who hopes for pardon, is ordered hope; and Judah, who confesses a pure love, is the ordered affection of love: "Judah represents to us ordered love, love of heavenly things, love of God, love of the highest good."

At this point in the development of the allegory Richard begins the course of spiritual instruction for the sake of which *Benjamin minor* was written. Just as Rachel, observing Judah, begins to long for children and for the love which Judah exhibits, and thus desires to have vision in order that she might know what she is to love, so the rational spirit with its powers of the affections and reason desires to know what it will, upon knowing, be compelled to love. Yet, as Richard of St. Victor writes, "Everybody knows how difficult or almost impossible it is for the carnal mind still untaught in spiritual studies to raise itself to an understanding of unseen things and fix its eye upon contemplating them."

Since the intelligence is not initially capable of contemplating invisible and incorporeal things, the imagination must be called upon. (In the allegory, Rachel calls upon her handmaiden to bear her first children.) The first stage of mystical contemplation, then, is that which the use of the imagination makes possible.

There are two kinds of imagination,

Richard states: animal imagination and rational imagination. The animal imagination is undisciplined and vague; it reviews actual experience. The rational imagination constructs new possibilities from fragments of visible things; by the rational imagination one can consider future goods and evils. The rational imagination, in turn, may combine with reason to produce new visible things, or it may combine with the intelligence to produce the unseen. (Bilhah, the imagination, Rachel's handmaiden, has two sons, Dan and Nephtali, who represent respectively these two combinations.)

Richard continues to develop the various combinations by which the spirit ascends in its contemplative training. A summary statement in *Benjamin major* sets forth the six kinds of contemplation which Richard develops allegorically (as well as by direct exposition): "There are six kinds of contemplation divided from each other and subdivided. The first lies in the imagination and is according to the imagination only. The second is in the imagination but according to reason. The third is in the reason according to the imagination. The fourth is in the reason and according to the reason. The fifth is above reason but not contrary to it. The sixth is both above reason and contrary to it."

The summary statement is evidence of Richard's logical mind, but only a reading of *Benjamin minor* and *Benjamin major* can lead to an appreciation of the spiritual dedication with which Richard adapted his allegory and his logical scheme to the training of those who sought to discipline themselves in contemplation in order that they might know God in the darkness of the final ecstasy. Richard writes of the "interior joy" that comes to those who are drawn by the sweetness of the unseen, and he repeatedly warns those who seek such joy to beware of the "waves of fleshly desires. . . ." He warns his listeners that their virtues will become vices unless their affections are not only ordered but also moderate. Discretion (Joseph, Rachel's first-born) is, thus, a central virtue; discretion teaches the soul in such a manner that the soul finally acquires self-knowledge, from which, through contemplation (Benjamin), the rational spirit is raised to the vision of God, the invisible.

The heights of contemplation are not to be reached, however, Richard avers, unless the grace of God makes the final knowledge possible; one must follow the truth, then, and the truth is Christ. The death of reason (Rachel) is the birth of that contemplation (Benjamin) which transcends reason and is contrary to reason. Human reasoning cannot grasp such mysteries as the Trinity and the truth concerning Christ's Body, but in a moment of divine revelation human intelligence is not only transcended but radically confounded.

In *Benjamin major* Richard extends his remarks concerning mystical contemplation, but his inspiration is now Psalm 131:8, Vulgate, where there is reference to the "ark of thy sanctification" (*arca sanctificationis tuae*). Richard writes that "the contemplation of truth begins in this life but is carried on perpetually in the next." The ark of sanctification is "that wisdom which overcomes evil"; it is the wisdom which the sanctifying grace of contemplation provides.

Richard distinguishes contemplation from meditation and thinking. Thinking is the ordinary activity of the mind which has no end in view; meditation is the deliberate progress toward the end; contemplation, untoiling and free, comes to the end without labor. Richard defines contemplation as "a free and clear vision of the mind fixed upon the manifestation of wisdom in suspended wonder." He then defines the six kinds of contemplation, as previously noted. Richard is naturally concerned most of all with the fifth and sixth kinds: contemplation beyond reason but not contrary to it, and contemplation beyond and contrary to reason. To rise to such levels of contemplation a person must, in effect, rise above himself; he must exceed his ordinary spiritual limits. What is contrary to human reason, however, is not contrary to divine reason; nevertheless, ordinary reason, and especially the imagination, cannot grasp what is given on the sixth level of contemplation.

Richard contends that a man may pass into a state of ecstasy, of mystical knowing and love, at any of the six levels, although such a state is more common on the fifth and sixth levels. In ecstasy the mind is abstracted or alienated from all things present; alienation is a mode of contemplation (the others being enlargement and raising) which occurs only by divine grace. Ecstasy is caused by greatness of devotion, great wonder, and exceeding exultation; thus, there are three modes of ecstasy, each of which has its distinctive and rewarding character.

To the soul which longs for a renewal of that grace whereby ecstasy is possible, Richard speaks in exultant language, declaring that the minstrel who makes the soul dance with joy and rise above all earthly things in ecstasy of mind is the heart's own exultation, and he advises: "Let us therefore endeavour with great alacrity of mind to rejoice in the Lord, let us stir ourselves to sing to him with heart-felt devotion. . . ."

DE CONTEMPTU MUNDI

Author: Pope Innocent III (Lothario Conti, c.1161-1216)
Type of work: Ascetical treatise
First transcribed: c.1195

Principal Ideas Advanced

The pride of man can and should be dissipated by the consideration of his wretched earthly condition: from conception to the grave he exists in a continuing state of misery and unhappiness, regardless of whether he is rich or poor, master or slave, married or celibate.

Human happiness is forever vitiated by physical and moral evil: the physical evils which are the major enemies of human happiness are temptations, unexpected sorrows, ever imminent death, sickness and disease, and human cruelty and injustice; the moral evils (for example, greed, drunkenness, impurity, and pride) which beset the well-being of man stem chiefly from his desire for power, pleasure, and honor.

The ubiquitous specter of death and judgment, and the eternity of Hell and its punishments hover over the life of man and increase his uneasiness here on earth.

De contemptu mundi, sive De miseria conditionis humanae (*On the Contempt of the World, or On the Misery of the Human Condition*) was written by Lothario Conti while he was a cardinal deacon in semi-retirement from curial affairs during the pontificate of Celestine III (1191-1198). It is a medieval essay in form and is divided into three books, all of which have as a backdrop the vanity of earthly things. Men are but pilgrims of the earth, finding here no lasting home. The earthly life is shot through with difficulties which contribute to the frustration of man's situation.

Some contextual understanding is needed to appreciate the value and the role of this work in the history of Christian thought. First of all, Pope Innocent III is primarily known for the work of his pontificate (1198-1216), which is judged by many to have been the apex of the medieval papacy. Having been schooled at Paris and Bologna in theology and Roman law, and possessing great native ability, political, diplomatic, and administrative, he was well prepared, despite his mere thirty-seven years, to assume the duties of Successor of Peter upon the death of Pope Celestine III. During his eighteen-year pontificate, Innocent wrestled with the problems of freeing Rome and the papal states from the yoke of factions, of completing the withdrawal of Italy from German domination, of carrying on the crusade against the infidels, and of purifying Europe from heresy. He felt a mission to organize Christendom both in its public institutions and in each person's private life. To realize such organization, he sought to form a powerful hierarchy and to inspire a deep piety in the souls of men. During all his years as pope, Innocent III was concerned intensely with reform. Perhaps the crowning event of his pontificate was the fourth Lateran (twelfth ecumenical) Council in 1215, which treated at length the question of clerical reform.

In the light of this history, it is somewhat remarkable that Lothario Conti's small work, *De contemptu mundi,* written some three or four years before he became the Pope Innocent III of historical fame, has received so much celebration during the centuries that have followed. This book's renown and its widespread influence upon the religious life of Christians in the Middle Ages is witnessed in a variety of ways. Numerous copies of its different versions and editions were housed in the libraries of medieval Europe. It was cited in a number of the theological works of the thirteenth century, especially in the *Summa universae theologiae* of the English Franciscan philosopher and theologian, Alexander of Hales. Francis Petrarch, the Italian poet, made reference to it, as did Geoffrey Chaucer (c. 1304-1400) in his *Canterbury Tales.* Saint Bernadino of Siena (1380-1444), the noted Franciscan preacher, quoted *De contemptu mundi* extensively in his sermons. Finally, its influence is attested by the fact that the early Jesuits employed it assiduously as a meditation manual. Two translations of it were published in England in the sixteenth century bearing the titles *The Mirror of Man's Life* and *The Drum of Doom,* though in both of these the papal authorship remained unnamed. Although it is not easy to find another work of this type which was as widely propagated during the Middle Ages, it too fell into oblivion by the end of the seventeenth century. Of Pope Innocent's three pre-papal treaties (the other two being *On the Four Kinds of Marriage,* and *On the Sacred Mystery of the Altar*), *De contemptu mundi* was certainly the best known and most influential.

Christian pessimism viewed the world as ugly, and by depreciating the world, this pessimistic form of thought hoped as well to temper the pride of man. It was this cynical mentality that inspired Cardinal Lothario's work. While keeping references to classical literature and to the Church Fathers to a minimum, he laced his three books with quotations from the Old Testament and the New. Part of the merit of the book rests in the cardinal's selection of texts.

Viewing myriad facets of human existence, the author gathered together and described in detail the miseries, sufferings, and sorrows of man from his entrance into life until his death. Book I opens with an examination of physical evils, with Chapters 1-8 considering the abased condition of man from his beginnings. The child, for example, is conceived from mud and blood, made of the most vile matter, defenseless, with an intelligence which hardly differs from that of the beasts. The animals which we look down on are able to walk from the start, but proud man is not even able to crawl. The sadness of childhood is evinced by the cries of the newborn infant. The first vesture that man has to cover his nudity is nothing but a thin bloody skin. Indeed, in comparison with the other creatures, man is decidedly inferior. The trees of the forest and field can produce fruit, but man yields nothing but phlegm and dung.

In a similar manner, Cardinal Lothario writes of the inconveniences of old age, of the vanity of knowledge and of human occupations, of the shortness of life, and of the misery of the poor and the rich, the serfs and the lords, the married and the celibate. For the most part, the author is quite matter-of-fact in his presentation. There are moments, however, when his portrayals become especially vivid. Such is the case in his depiction of the married woman with her eccentricities, her caprices, her love of toilet, and her strong will. What a pity, the cardinal bemoans, that one never knows beforehand just what kind of person one is marrying. Other things, such as animals and clothing, a man can examine, test, and approve before buying. Such is not the case with a wife. She is hardly known to the prospective husband before the wedding, yet, whatever she is and whatever she becomes, she remains his wife for life.

In the other phases of life, the cardinal writes, man does not cease to be tormented. Sleeping, he is aroused by nightmares; awake, he is buffeted by the reverses of fortune, by sickness, and by sudden sorrows. He does not grow in general well-being but his nature is constantly deteriorating. Whatever joy he comes upon is short-lived. In closing Book I, Cardinal Lothario leaves us with a most somber impression by enumerating some of the dreadful punishments which the cruelty of man has invented for the torture or execution of his brothers and by citing from the Jewish historian Flavius Josephus (c.37-c.95) a gruesome tale of a demented mother who devours her own child.

The forty chapters of Book II concern the unhappiness of man because of moral evil in the world. Since the moral evil which exists is rooted in man's undue desires for power, pleasure, and honors, he himself is responsible in part for his progressively worsening wretchedness. By skeletal outlines of the condition of the drunkard, the parvenu, and the proud man, the author makes his point. In more detail he describes the smallness of the man who seeks worldly advancement unscrupulously. (There is little doubt that such men had come under the author's eye in real life.) The man who begins by desiring but a little wealth soon finds that his desires are never satisfied; the man who starts by desiring a modicum of pleasure soon discovers that he can seek nothing but pleasure. Man is never satisfied with a little; he must always have more. Since man's unquenchable desires will not be quieted by any earthly thing, he finds himself growing increasingly miserable. In his catalogue of vices, the youth cardinal includes sexual deviations practiced by men of various stations in life, and the folly of pride, ambition, and vanity. Throughout he admonishes those who have ears to hear his words of warning.

In Book III, which is a very brief and standard treatment of the subject, Cardinal Lothario concerns himself with the eternity of the pains of Hell and the irrevocable condemnation of the damned. No longer does penance or amendment of life avail; the darkness and fire of Hell and the loss of God are without end.

In the preface to *De contemptu mundi,* the cardinal explains that, if requested, he will at a later date describe the dignity of human nature as blessed by Christ. As in this present work he has attempted to humble the proud, so in his proposed treatise he will exalt the humble. Because of the fact that the second work was never realized, we are left with a one-sided, dismal picture of the human condition. In reading this ascetical treatise, then, we ought to be aware that for proper balance, it needs the complementary hopeful description of the glory of man redeemed by Christ, a work which the cardinal anticipated but never brought to reality.

J.J.F.

DE SACRO ALTARIS MYSTERIO

Author: Pope Innocent III (Lothario Conti, c.1161-1216)
Type of work: Liturgical treatise
First transcribed: c. 1197

Principal Ideas Advanced

The ceremonies of the Mass are filled with symbolism and allegorical meaning, and familiarity with these meanings will enrich the Christian's understanding and intelligent participation in this great Sacrifice.

The ceremonies of the Mass have developed through the centuries and their format can still be improved.

The Mass is the central and most valuable act of the Christian life.

Pope Innocent III's treatise *De sacro altaris mysterio* (*On the Sacred Mystery of the Altar*) is ranked among his most significant writings. Like *De contemptu mundi,* this work was composed while Lothario Conti was still a cardinal deacon in semi-retirement during the reign of Pope Celestine III (1191-1198). While *De contemptu mundi* may well be the more famous of these two treatises, *De sacro altaris mysterio* is surely the more valuable because of the wealth of information that it contains.

Essentially, the treatise is a long commentary on the Mass, with particular relevance for the history of the liturgy and for sacramental theology. Cardinal Lothario accurately portrayed the liturgy of the Mass as it was celebrated in Rome in the twelfth century. Replete with listings and symbolical interpretations of the rubrics, customs, vestments, and Mass appointments of the time, this work became the basis for most of the commentaries on the Mass of the later Middle Ages, many of which were but paraphrases of it.

While the treatise truly abounds in symbolism and Scriptural allusions, with every word, gesture, movement, and accessory given a symbolical or allegorical meaning, it cannot legitimately be dismissed as merely an example of the richly imaginative interpretations of the Mass which were in vogue at that period of the Middle Ages. Historians of the Mass claim that it has unparalleled value in giving them a clear picture of the Eucharistic rites and ceremonies in use in Rome in the twelfth century. Moreover, some of the doctrinal statements made by Cardinal Lothario have become the classic forms for the assertion of Church dogma in the centuries that have followed. For example, as recently as 1947, in the encyclical letter of Pope Pius XII on the sacred liturgy, *Mediator Dei,* the pope, writing on the participation of the faithful in the offering of the sacrifice of the Mass, recalled the words of Cardinal Lothario in *De sacro altaris mysterio:* "Not only do the priests offer the Sacrifice, but also all the faithful: for what the priest does personally by virtue of his ministry, the faithful do collectively by virtue of their intention."

In the early Middle Ages, the Mass was looked upon as a holy drama, a play performed before the eyes of the participants. All the while additions were being made to the ceremonies. Signs of the cross were multiplied and the kisses of the altar became more numerous. The symbolical positions of the hands of the celebrant and his head bows were prescribed. Distinction was made in the dramatization between the Gospel side of the church (or the altar) and the Epistle side. All these developing usages made a bid for the curious and fascinated eyes of the Christian people and obtained allegorical signification. Less and less importance was given to the meaning of the words of the ceremony, and more and more concentration was directed to the dramatic and symbolical force of elements like loud and soft tones of prayer. The meaning of the ceremonies was often abstracted entirely from the course of the on-going sacred action. Some traditional ceremonies acquired a fixed significance, with little thought given to their particular status in the liturgical action. The spirit of this period is caught in a didactic poem of the times which outlined the minimum that each priest should know about the Mass: what the sacrifice is, and what the altar and chalice, water and wine, and the signs of the cross signify.

New images of Old Testament origin were introduced into the allegorizing of the Mass. Re-enacted were the exodus from Egypt, the revelation of the commandments, the conquest of Amalec at the prayers of Moses pleading with outstretched arms, and the entrance into the Promised Land under the leadership of Joshua. The bishop, dressed in his sacred vestments as in the armor of war, represented a general; the lector the herald; the bells and chants the fanfare of war. This type of symbolism, joined with the traditional allegory of Christ's Passion, resulted in a bewildering number of variegated meanings, to which one could scarcely apply the title of explanation of the sacred mysteries.

A healthy reaction to this increasing overloading of the interpretation of the Mass with so many diverse elements, and, at the same time, a high point of rememorative allegory is found in the *De sacro altaris mysterio* by Cardinal Lothario. Except for an abundantly practical number-symbolism, he restricted himself almost entirely to the traditional meanings derived from Christ's life and Passion. These he presents distinctly and in a simple style, highlighting many of his interpretations with quotations from the Scriptures.

The great compiler of medieval liturgical allegory, William Durandus (1237-1296), acknowledges in his noted *Rationale divinorum officiorum* that he took Pope Innocent III as his guide for the explanation of the Mass.

Cardinal Lothario divided his treatise into six books. In Book I he treats the order and the role of the different ministers and participants in the Mass, from the bishop to the choir. The origin and significance of rubrics and vestments are examined in detail. Book II concerns the ceremonies of the pontifical Mass with its processions, the use of incense and kisses, and the various tones of chant proper to the different parts of the sacrifice. The canon of the Mass is explained in detail in Book III. In Book IV the cardinal focuses his attention on the sacramental aspects of the Eucharist and considers such issues as transubstantiation, the form of consecration, the method of concelebration, and other related questions. The ends of the Mass and a continuation of the discussion of the symbolical meaning of the various signs of the cross used at Mass form the bulk of the fifth book. In Book VI Cardinal Lothario concludes with an examination of the final parts of the Mass, the breaking of the host, the *Agnus Dei,* the kiss of peace, the communion verse, final prayer, and the last blessing. To catch a feeling for the type of commentary the author elaborated within the framework of these six books, we will allude to a few examples from his many chapters.

The Mass is called "that banquet of the Church in which the father kills the fatted calf for the son who returns to him, setting out the bread of life and the wine mingled with wisdom." In considering the transubstantiation the cardinal notes that what was bread when Our Lord took it into His hands was His Body when He distributed it. Because of the threefold repetition of the names of the saints in the canon, the author argues that the canon of the Mass was not composed by one man at one time, but was gradually built up by different men at different times. At the same time he suggests that, even in his time, the prayers in the Canon of the Mass might easily be improved.

In Cardinal Lothario's treatise we find for the first time a determination of liturgical colors for specified days, along with their respective significance. Lothario's rules are more or less those still in effect today: white is the festive color (in seeking a reason he even referred to the whiteness of the clouds on the day of Christ's Ascension); red is for martyrs' days and Pentecost; black is for days of penance and of the Masses for the dead; and green is for days without a festal character. The interest in colors and the zeal in explaining their meaning were both typical manifestations of the spirit of the Gothic period. In interpreting the significance of the liturgical vestments, the cardinal combined a moral meaning with the relationship between the priestly garments and the properties and attributes of Christ's Person.

In speaking of the pontifical buskins, Lothario asserts that they are fastened at the knees, lest the preacher become weak-kneed. The bishop's miter signifies knowledge of the Old and the New Testament: its two points stand for the two Testaments and the two bands that extend from it represent the spirit and the letter of the word of God. The reason that the pope did not use a crosier, the cardinal maintains, was that Saint Peter had sent his to Eucherius, the first Bishop of Trier, whom he had missioned there to preach the Gospel.

The gradual of the Mass is allegorically interpreted by the author as an echoing of the penitential preaching of Saint John the Baptist, or as the transition from the Old Testament to the New. Therefore, despite the content of the gradual, Cardinal Lothario contends that it should be sung not festively but gravely.

The cardinal explains how the custom of concealing the Mass paten from the offertory until before the priest's communion was transferred from the solemn to the nonsolemn Mass. The rubrics demanded that in the nonsolemn Mass the paten be slipped part way under the corporal and covered with the purificator. Allegorically the cardinal took this practice to represent the Disciples of Christ hiding themselves at the beginning of His Passion.

In his conclusion, Cardinal Lothario warns his readers not to take his commentary as a full and complete account of the great sacrifice of the Mass. Though it is true that his treatise is not an exhaustive treatment of the subject, it forms, contrary to the opinions of some of his commentators, a definite contribution to the history of the liturgy of the Mass.

J.J.F.

THE EXTANT WRITINGS OF SAINT FRANCIS OF ASSISI

Author: Saint Francis of Assisi (c.1181-1226)
Type of work: Theology, monastic rules, religious songs
First transcribed: c.1200-1226

Principal Ideas Advanced

Men should serve and love God by loving their enemies, by refusing to seek wordly wisdom and fame, by praying to God and confessing to Him, and, in general, by seeking the good and avoiding evil.

Nature reflects its Creator; hence, men should love the world and the creatures that inhabit it.

As might be expected of a man whose vocation it was to preach to the world, Saint Francis of Assisi often had to let his pen speak for him when his tongue could not. Some of the writings were set down by his own hand, while others were written by Brother Leo, who was both biographer and secretary to the saint. Some of the writings were in Italian, but most were in Latin. The Franciscans in Quaracchi produced a critical edition, *Opuscula sanci patris Francisci Assisiensis,* in 1904; this collection, based on a fourteenth century manuscript, carefully defines the extant works justifiably attributable to Saint Francis of Assisi.

Among the prose works accepted by the Quaracchi edition are six letters, the *Testament,* and the rules of the Order of St. Francis. (The *Rule of the Poor Clares* and the *Rule of the Third Order of St. Francis* are no longer attributed to Saint Francis himself.) Those with whom Saint Francis is known to have corresponded are Saint Clare and Sisters of the Poor Clares, Gregory IX, Brother Elias of Cortona, and Saint Anthony of Padua. These letters have to do with the spiritual life in general and with matters pertaining specifically to the Order.

When in the Orient, Francis contracted an eye disease which left him almost blind as he grew older. He eventually had to confine his preaching to letters, and in the last days of his life he sent out five letters or "circular epistles": a letter to all Christians, a letter to a Pentecost Chapter he was unable to attend, a letter to all clerics, a letter to all guardians, and a letter to all superiors. There is nothing actually new to the Franciscan scholar in any of these letters; they are, in fact, variations on the constant theme which threads its way through the Rules and Admonitions: ". . . to serve and love God, to live a life of conversion, to fast—also in a metaphorical sense to fast from sin and crime—to love and help our enemies, not to seek worldly wisdom or exalted positions, to pray much, to confess and approach the altar, to try to do good where we have been doing evil." In the letter to the Pentecost Chapter and in the letter to the clerics and guardians, Francis especially exhorts great reverence for the Holy Eucharist, and "if a number of priests are together only one mass is to be said, which the others can be content at being present at"; Francis advises the priests "to pick up every piece of paper on which holy words may be and to preserve such with reverence; the Office is to be said with more regard to inner devotion than to melody of voice, the sacred vessels and the altar-cloths should be kept shiningly clean, and the most holy sacrament should be preserved with reverence. And when it is offered on the altar in the mass, all shall kneel down, praise and glorify God, and the church bells are to be rung so that all near can participate in this giving of praise." In his letter to all authorities, Francis exhorts persons of high position ("all podestàs, consuls, judges and rectors") to approach the altar humbly, as common men, keeping in mind that earthly power pales before the power of God.

The First Rule of the Order, written by Francis at Rivo Torto, is no longer extant and no attempts to reconstruct it have been successful. According to Francis's *Testament*: "I had it written with few and simple words, and our Lord the Pope confirmed it for me." Much of the First Rule was made up of extracts from the Bible and consisted of passages from Matthew 10: 9-10; 12: 21; 16: 24; and Luke 9:3. To observe the gospel was Francis's aim. It is generally agreed that the *Regula prima* which has been preserved was basically the rule of Rivo Torto with the addition of admonitions, alterations, and expansions.

Among the first additions to the original rule are an entire collection of writings of Saint Francis called the *Admonitiones*. They briefly but succinctly cover the matters considered to be important for the attainment of salvation, as seen through the eyes of the simple yet knowing ascetic whose religious rule of life was as unusual when compared with that of other orders as his own life was when compared to that of other men. The *Admonitions* contain the following chapters, whose headings indicate Francis's concerns: I. On the Lord's body; II. On the sinfulness of self-will; III. On perfect obedience; IV. That no one should strive after command; V. That no one should be exalted, but should glory in the Cross of the Lord; VI. On following after the Lord; VII. That wisdom must be followed by work; VIII. To envy no one; IX. On charity; X. To hold the body in subjection; XI. To not participate in the effects of another's sin; XII. On signs of the Lord's spirit; XIII. On patience; XIV. On poverty of spirit; V. On peace; XVI. On purity of heart; XVII. On being an humble servant of God; XVIII. On sympathy with our neighbor; XIX. Of a good servant of God; XX. On the good and bad Brother of the Order; XXI. On the empty and gossiping Brother of the Order; XXII. On correction; XXIII. On humility; XXIV. On real charity; XXV. And blessed the servant of God who loves and fears his Brother as much when he is away from him as when he is near him, and says nothing behind his back which he could not in charity let him hear; XXVI. That God's servants ought to honor clerics; XXVII. On virtues, that put vices to flight; and finally, XXVIII. Not to boast of your virtue.

During the years of rapid growth of the Order, Francis added legislation to the *First Rule* as new circumstances arose. He codified these additions in 1221 to guarantee some uniformity of life in the greatly expanded Order, and presented the new document to the General Chapter of the Order in June, 1223, where it underwent several alterations. On November 29, 1223, Pope

Honorius III solemnly approved this final version of the *Rule.* This is the *Rule* which has continued to govern members of the Franciscan First Order of men since 1223. Its twelve brief chapters and simplicity of legislation make it one of the shortest of religious rules of life. Through the centuries disputes, sometimes bitter, broke out within the Order regarding the observance of some of the precepts of the *Rule,* especially those pertaining to the vow of poverty. The Holy See clarified these disputed points in a series of bulls and approved the separation of dissident factions in the three major branches of the First Order, namely, the Order of Friars Minor, the Order of Friars Minor Capuchin, and the Order of Friars Minor Conventual. All three branches observe the *Rule* according to their own particular form of government and constitutions. The Second Order of women and the Third Order Regular and Secular follow the *Rule* as a spiritual guide but do not formally profess it.

Before treating the third portion of the *Regula prima* which includes what may be technically classified as religious poetry, attention must be given the *Testament* of Saint Francis. Written near the end of his life, it is a poignant rehearsal of his own joyous conversion to a life of penance and a sad foreboding of the trials which lie ahead for those Brothers who would wish to live in strict accordance with the rigorous life of poverty which was his legacy to them: "And let not the Brothers say: 'This is another Rule'; for this is a remembrance, an admonition and an exhortation, and my Testament, which I, Brother Little Francis, make for you my blessed Brothers for this, that we may observe in a more catholic way the Rule which God has put before us. . . . And I make it a firm precept of obedience for all my clerical and lay Brothers, that they do not apply glosses to the Rule nor to these words by saying, 'They ought to be understood thus'; but as the Lord gave it to me to tell and write the Rule and these words purely and simply, so are you to understand simply and purely and observe unto the end with holy operation. . . . And I, Brother Francis, your little one and servant, as far as I can, confirm to you within and without this most holy blessing. Amen."

Incorporated within the rules of the Order were certain *lauds* or songs of praise which Francis encouraged his Brothers to use in their preaching to attract men to the love of God in a joyous manner. Four of these songs of praise are preserved, three written in Latin and the fourth, the famous *Sun Song,* in Italian. The three Latin *lauds* deal with praises to the Blessed Trinity, to the virtues, and to God the Creator. Included among these documents is the well-known blessing of Saint Francis (beginning "The Lord bless thee and keep thee . . .") addressed to Brother Leo.

At the end of his *Rule,* there is a chapter of deep poetic feeling in which the soul of Francis seems to speak unfettered by the strictures of lawmaking and formal regulation. Entitled "Prayer, Song of Praise and Thanksgiving," it is a poetic summation of all that has gone before in prose.

The final, and probably most famous extant piece of writing from the hand of Saint Francis is the "Sun Song or Song about Creatures." Written in Italian from his sick-bed, the masterpiece is one in which Francis poured forth his admiration for all God's creatures. Francis loved nature directly, as a reflection of its Creator, and symbolically, as it reflected its Creator's attributes. Both of these views are present in the "Sun Song," which offers praise first to God the Creator of all things, and then, in particular, to "Brother Sun," "Sister Moon," "Brother Wind," "Sister Water," "Brother Fire," and "Mother Earth." Partially blinded by the fierce Italian sun, and suffering tremendous physical pain, Francis's senses nonetheless seem even more keenly sharpened as he brings forth one image after another, each more beautiful than that which preceded it. Two more verses were to be added to "Sun Song" before its completion, the final one being in praise of Sister Death, "from whom no living man can escape." It is characteristic of Saint Francis, whose life was one great irony, to praise the sun which blinded him, the wind and the water which buffeted him, the fire that seared his flesh, the earth which bruised him, and finally death, which was for him the final joy of his life.

SUMMA DE CREATURIS

Author: Saint Albert the Great (c.1206 or c.1193-1280)
Type of work: Systematic theology
First transcribed: c.1240-1243

Principal Ideas Advanced

Four philosophic principles were co-created with the world and function as the basic sources of the whole of the created universe: matter, Heaven, angelic nature, and time.

The human soul is both a substance having its own being (Plato) and also the animating form of the human body (Aristotle); its principal parts are active intellect and possible intellect.

The moral virtues are not simply means but are good and desirable for their own sake.

The *Summa de creaturis* (*Summary of Doctrine Concerning Created Things*) of Albert the Great is actually a group of six treatises, only three of which have been published and none of which has appeared in any language other than Latin. Treatises *On the Sacraments, On the Incarnation,* and *On the Resurrection* exist as yet only in manuscripts, although the Cologne Institute of Albert the Great under the directorship of Bernard Geyer projects publication of these treatises within a critical edition of Albert's *Opera omnia.* The Institute has thus far published a fourth part of the *Summa de creaturis,* the treatise *On the Good.* The last two treatises, *On the Four Coevals* and *On Man* have existed in printed form since 1651.

Albert's lifetime nearly coincides with the thirteenth century, the "Golden Age of Scholasticism." His total literary production covers at least forty years. The dominant figure of his time, he was well traveled, a keen observer of nature, the most prolific writer and the most influential teacher of the century. The one learned man of the "Golden Age" to be called "the Great," he was cited by the name even before his death—a most unusual occurrence in medieval authorship when the test of time was thought necessary to establish an "authority." The first impression of Albert's encyclopedic production is its aspects of compilation and syncretism. We find Christian Father and pagan philosopher, Aristotelian and Neoplatonic sources: Saint Augustine, Boethius, the Pseudo-Denis (c. 500), Aristotle (384-322 B.C.), Avicenna (980-1037), Averroës (1126-1198), Alfarabi (died 950), and, through the anonymous *Liber de causis* (c. 900), Proclus (410-485) and Plotinus (203-269) head the cast of contributors to Albert's writings. Still to be determined precisely is the influence, if any, which Saint Thomas Aquinas, whom Albert taught and outlived, had upon his teacher; this influence, at present, appears to be small.

Albert's primary philosophical importance rests upon his accomplishments as a scholar rather than as an original thinker. Along with such men as Robert Grosseteste and Roger Bacon, Albert resolved the problem common to the Latin world of the time—namely, the problem of handling the pagan Greek and Arabian learning just being introduced into Western thought—by leading the movement to synthesize this learning with Christian tradition. Rather than simply criticizing the new doctrines, Albert and his colleagues felt that scientific knowledge and philosophy were good in themselves, worth being sought by Christian men, and that they had to be acquired in order to be used. Albert's attitude towards science was different, however, from his attitude towards philosophy: science, concerned with "things of nature," was to be learned from nature, while philosophy, concerned primarily with ideas, was to be sought in books. Albert achieved, then, in his philosophic writings, a systematic ordering and interpretation of the ideas expressed by the philosophers; his writings, consequently, represent a huge source book of Greek and Arabian thought, blended with the world view of his Christian heritage. This very same characteristic of Albert's writings, however, also poses a problem as to his interpretation. For example, his *Book of the Causes and Procession of the Universe* (*Liber de causis et processu universitatis*), a metaphysical work describing the basic structure of the whole of reality, proclaims that its author is merely presenting an explanation of the "peripatetics" and that the doctrine is "not necessarily" to be taken as his own. And, indeed, it is often difficult to decide what part of Albert's writings is his own and what he is merely reporting.

The treatises composing the *Summa de creaturis* are among Albert's earliest works, dating from about 1240-1243. There are many problems in dating Albert's work, some of them stemming from the fact that, apparently, many of the earlier writings were revised at various times by Albert himself. Thus, both the treatises of the *Summa* and the *Commentary on Lombard's Sentences* date from the decade 1240-1250, the material of both works being interrelated: the *Commentary* resulted from Albert's teaching and reading of the *Sentences* as a Master at the University of Paris, and also stemmed from his lecturing in various German convents before 1240; the treatises of the *Summa* apparently were the fruit of "disputed questions," formal exercises held during the academic year by the master.

The treatise *On the Four Coevals* discusses the items which have coexisted from the beginning of the created world: matter, Heaven, angelic nature, and time. These four have coexisted (are "equally old") as the number of principles or sources of created entities.

According to Albert, matter is the principle of that which can come to be or pass away, the universal subject of mutable being. Albert indicates his awareness of what will become a characteristically Franciscan position: that matter enters into the composition of *all* things, except God. Albert first notes that even this position cannot maintain that matter is really the same for spiritual and nonspiritual entities, and he later takes a stand against such "universal hylomorphism." Rather, he argues, while all except God are composite beings, this composition is best expressed in the terms of Boethius: a composition of that which is (*quod est*) and the essence by which it is what it is (*esse, quo est*).

Heaven is the principle of the nongenerable immutable body as well as the source of generation and corruption upon the earth. Albert takes over the Aristotelian-Ptolemaic view of the universe as an ordered hierarchical procession from God in the form of concentric spheres. The earth is at the center of ten heavens whose only "alteration" is movement in place: counting "upwards" from the sphere of the moon, there are the loci of the moon, sun, five planets, and the firmament of the stars, each endowed with a variety of local movements. The "aqueous" heaven mentioned in Genesis as "the waters above the firmament" is endowed with uniform circular movement; and the empyrean heaven is of the nature of light: immobile, universal, the primary cause of generation and corruption and movement in the whole universe, the abode of angels. Beyond this heaven is the infinite power and being of the triune God who limits, envelops, and exceeds all creation.

The theory of four terrestrial elements is thus completed by a causal nexus to the heavens; this astronomical view of a universe of causally related entities then gave rise to an astrological attempt to understand these relations. Astrology, in the sense just described, is an important science for Albert in the sense of an ordered, reasonable attempt to understand the causal relationships between heavenly bodies and earthly events. This astrology, or "astronomy" (the words are interchangeable for Albert), was not to be confused with any sort of black magic. The *Speculum astronomiae* (*Mirror of Astronomy,* probably one of Albert's works) appears to have been written to safeguard and distinguish the science from necromancy. The largest problem Albert had to face was reconciling the natural causality of the heavenly and earthly bodies with the voluntary, free causality of man. While the body of man is subject to this causal influence, his soul is from God alone; thus human reason and will are free. Yet man may consult heavenly movements to discover when natural events are most propitious for his free initiation of some action.

The third principle, the angelic nature, is the principle of spiritual beings which do not arise from matter or from the heavens. Angels are relatively simple since they are not composed of matter and form, but distinguished from God as composed both of what is and of essence.

Albert's discussion of time is an example of how theologians and philosophers may take different views about the same topic: the theologians consider time as the measure of any sort of change, even of the spiritual activities of thought and will; the philosophers consider time more strictly, as the measure of motion. In the first sense, time is the co-existing measure of the duration of all created things. In an analogous way, "aeviternity" is the measure of those incorruptible beings which had an origin, while "eternity" is the "measure" of God or, better, is the divine essence, the ever-present "now."

The treatise *On Man* discusses, in order, the soul and its definition, the sense powers of the soul, the nature of dreams, the intellect, the will, freedom, and memory, and ends with a brief account of the "habitations" of man: Paradise, the world, and the universe as a whole. Plato's definition of the soul can be reconciled with that of Aristotle by calling upon a formula used by Avicenna: the soul may be considered either with respect to its own being or in its relation to the body. In itself, the soul has a being of its own (Plato) and is therefore included in the category of substance; but the term "soul" (that is, *anima*) is taken from its function as life-principle of an organic body (Aristotle). The soul, as in the case of angels, is relatively simple, as without quantitative extension, but, as with all things other than God, it is composed both of subject (*quod est*) and essence (*esse, quo est*). Its principal parts correspond to this composition: possible intellect to *quod est,* active intellect to *quo est.*

The discussion of the intellect is complicated by the fact that the philosophers have divided the intellectual powers in apparently incompatible ways. Alexander of Aphrodisias (c. 190) speaks of potential, habitual, and active intellects; Averroës of possible, active, and speculative intellects. Algazel (1058-1111), Avicenna, Alpharabi, and Aristotle have slightly different arrangements. Albert settles the problem by describing these divisions as a many-to-one analogy. The intellectual states are all ordered to the speculative intellect, which is intellectual perfection; with respect to this state, active intellect is efficient cause, possible intellect is recipient, habitual intellect is preparation for perfection, while the other terms describe subdivisions of these. Albert takes exception to the position espoused by the *Summa* of Alexander of Hales, the view that the active intellect is the innate habit of first notions, a likeness of the First Cause; he shows that Avicenna is wrong in identifying the active intellect with the intelligence that rules the sphere of the moon; and he concludes that Averroës is correct in saying that the active intellect is joined to man, is without parts, and, while not itself possessed of intelligibles, causes intelligibles to come to be in the possible intellect from phantasms. But even Averroës must be corrected, writes Albert, for in describing the active intellect as "separate" one means only that the active intellect is not any part of the body; it is, however, a part of the intellectual soul.

The world in which man lives is created and not eternal. Aristotle, not having the concept of creation, proved only that the world could not come to be through generation. In his later *Summa theologiae,* Albert maintained that the noneternity of the world cannot be proven but must be accepted on faith. But in the present treatise he marshals a number of philosophical arguments which he believes are sufficient to establish the point.

Moral good, the virtues, and especially the cardinal virtues of fortitude, temperance, prudence, and justice are the subject of the treatise *On the Good.* Virtue is not simply a "useful good," that is, a means, but it is a *bonum honestum,* good and desirable for its own sake. Albert's ethical theory is the least analyzed part of his thought and appears to be an area of fruitful scholarly study; the publication of this treatise and others projected should aid future work.

F.J.C.

THE THREE WAYS

Author: Saint Bonaventure (Giovanni di Fidanza, 1221-1274)
Type of work: Spiritual instruction
First transcribed: c.1250

Principal Ideas Advanced

The interior life of man consists wholly in the union of the soul with God, and all asceticism and mysticism merely chart the paths that this dynamism within the soul follows in its hierarchical ascent to its Creator.

The return of the soul to God is accomplished by a threefold act: purgation, illumination, and perfection, which are carried out by means of meditation, prayer, and contemplation, and which result in peace, truth, and love, respectively.

Purging itself of the material and sensible world which scatters its forces, and concentrating its gaze on its life as spirit, the soul responds to the grace and light of Christ and rises upward toward ecstatic union with its God, a union which is beyond knowledge and is a foretaste of that definitive union which awaits on the other side of death.

The *De triplici via* of Saint Bonaventure is not a speculative treatise, but a manual or handbook which directs the soul desirous of traveling the three ways of the spiritual life. The distinction of the three ways is already found in Pseudo-Dionysius, but it is in the works of Saint Bonaventure that the three ways are considered in detail. Behind this spiritual guidebook, however, stands a great speculative synthesis, and it is only in the light of the intellectual and mystical forces at work within the tradition that the lines of the *De triplici via* take on luminous depth and vital tension.

The first principal source for St. Bonaventure's ascetical and mystical theology was Saint Augustine. For both of these Doctors of the Church the goal of all speculation is the same: the knowledge of God and the knowledge of self. For both, the material world mirrors its Creator, leads the soul to the truth within itself and finally to the Truth which lives above the individual soul. Saint Bonaventure's *Christus, unus omnium magister* found its inspiration in Augustine's *De magistro*. But other sources are clearly present. The Bonaventurian ascent of the soul to God strongly resembles Plotinus's hierarchical return of the soul to the One, and Bonaventure's stress on the incomprehensibility of God recalls Dionysius the Pseudo-Areopagite. With Saint Bernard, Saint Bonaventure is more inclined to love than to speculation, and his mysticism shows his kinship with Saint Victor. Nevertheless, Saint Bonaventure was more than just another scholar and mystic within the Augustinian or Platonic tradition. The inspiration of Saint Francis of Assisi was at work in his thought and his asceticism; the spirit of Saint Francis pervaded his Augustinianism and transformed it into a new synthesis, so that in a very real sense Bonaventure can be said to have begun a new school.

To Saint Bonaventure, Saint Francis was a "man of desires," for whom the soul encounters God in the depths of that deathless desire for the good which drives man ceaselessly to strive after happiness. The second moment of this encounter is God's response, which is also an act of love externally and definitively expressed in the Passion and Death of Christ; an act of love not for an abstract human race but for each individual person. For Saint Francis, as for Saint Bonaventure, "God is love," and this love is expressed supremely in the Passion of Christ. Bonaventura, the "Seraphic Doctor," was well aware that no matter how much a soul desires and seeks the Creator, an infinite abyss between God and man remains until God comes to man. In the *Itinerarium mentis in Deum* Saint Bonaventure tells us that he found the answer on Mount Alverna where Saint Francis received the Stigmata. The act whereby God crosses eternity and unites Himself to man is the suffering and death of Christ, who is the beginning and the end of the life of man, his love, truth, life, and peace. It is only in the light of the "Poverello" of Assisi that the *De triplici via* can be understood.

The first step of the soul toward its God can be taken only after it has searched the labyrinths of its heart and found there only need, torment, desire; each man must see himself as a "man of desires." The soul then moves on to the realization that the love of creatures can never exhaust its desire: ". . . the love of creatures is of no use; and if it is of use, it does not refresh; and if it does refresh, it is not sufficient." From this intuition the soul reaches out beyond knowledge to God, who is wholly desirable. The unaided intellect in this life cannot see God, and the will can grasp Him only by an act of love. In the union of the soul with God the will has soared above the intellect; the ecstatic experience is an experience of pure love: He whom the soul loves, "is not sensible . . . is not imaginable . . . is not intelligible, but is wholly desirable." Finally, at the highest point of its striving, God comes to the soul on the Cross: "The cross is the key, the gate, the way and splendor of truth. . . ."

A great difficulty for the reader of the *De triplici via* and the other works of Saint Bonaventure is their typically medieval character. *The Three Ways* abounds with the rich and elaborate symbolism which was prevalent in the Middle Ages but is of little relevance to modern man. But to consider this symbolism as the artificial and arbitrary trappings of a mentality completely foreign to our own is to lose all possibility of a true understanding of the medieval masters. All through the Christian tradition—already found clearly expressed in St. Augustine—runs the conviction that the world of nature mirrors, to a greater or lesser degree, the perfections of its Creator, that material things are signs and symbols pointing to a loving God. For Saint Bonaventure the world of nature is a book in which man reads about God. Adam was able to read this book perfectly, but with the Fall man lost the key to understanding it, and the book of nature became a book written in an unknown language which no one could understand and for which no dictionary could be found. Man now strove to know and love creatures for themselves. Once man turned from God he looked for a meaning for the world within the world itself. The true meaning of the universe lies beyond the world, and man, left to his own lights, could no longer see the signs in nature which would have directed his mind to it. But with the suffering and death of Christ the key to the book of nature was restored to us, for the key to reading the book of nature is the Cross. The symbolism of the universe reappears, and everywhere the soul finds the footprints, the vestiges, the images of its Creator. But to achieve a true understanding of the world and through it to return to God is still a difficult journey, for the ways are tortuous and the distractions many. If a man wishes to return to his Creator, he requires an asceticism. This is precisely what is offered him in *The Three Ways.*

The first obstacle to man's advance along the ways of perfection is the lack of awareness of his true state and, as a consequence, the absence of desire for deliverance from misery. The soul, then, must at the beginning turn inward upon itself and upon its woeful condition. In every murky shadow it finds negligence, concupiscence, and wickedness. Man must continue to hold his woeful state before his mind, meditating carefully upon it to the point of anguish and terror. At this point the soul turns from itself and rising upward gives voice to an excruciating wail which deplores its misery, begs for mercy, and adores its God. Prayer is born of anguish and with prayer the soul makes its first ascent toward its God. "Prayer," Saint Bonaventure tells us at the beginning of the *Itinerarium mentis in Deum,* "is the mother and origin of the upward striving of the soul." This much the man of desire can do: pray constantly, knock unceasingly. The soul has now reached the limits of its own capacity; it can do no more. In darkness and fear it waits for the coming of the Bridegroom.

The second moment of the mystical ascent now begins. Christ comes to the soul. The darkness and anguish fall away before His light and truth, which lift the soul away from the pull of the world of creatures, and the last part of the journey begins, not to end until the soul has been transported into the very heart of the Trinity.

The task, however, is not yet finished. Under the influence of grace man must set about uprooting from his life the effects of original sin, which consist essentially in the disruption and disorder which shatter the unity of man's nature and personality. The soul must undertake the reordering of all its faculties, a laborious work which is nothing less than the total reform of the self. The first evil to be attacked and uprooted is passion or concupiscence, which is the source of all other evils and the principal effect of original sin. With the Fall man turned inward on himself and became the center of his universe. All other creatures had meaning only insofar as they contributed to the fulfillment of man's desire for power, pleasure, and possession. In meditating upon this evil and in seeing its application in his own activity and that of other men, the soul becomes aware both of the extent to which concupiscence grips the human heart and of the labor entailed in rooting it out; in most cases even the best efforts of a man's life are motivated by the thirst for favor, honor, glory, position, wealth, leisure, carnal pleasure, and distraction. The struggle against concupiscence amounts to a revolution within the self. The soul and heart of man must become, for the first time, other-centered; the focus of his attention must shift from himself to others and ultimately to the Other. This change in direction requires the laborious task of chipping off the old order of values and acquiring a new one; the re-establishing of the true relationship of man to his fellow men, the material universe, and God begins at this point. Man has a destiny, and it is in fulfilling that destiny that he finds his happiness. In Pauline terminology, the struggle against concupiscence is the effort of the soul to put off the "old man" and put on the "new man," which is Christ.

At first glance *The Three Ways* may seem to have little relevance for modern man, filled as it is with a seemingly abstract and impersonal mode of thought, an exaggerated use of symbols largely unknown to our age, and an excessively artificial construction which quickly wearies the mind. But this is a superficial view; if we believe this, we have failed to penetrate beyond the style, the symbolism, and the framework to the religious heart of the saint himself; we have not understood the expert psychological analysis of the spiritual life; we have failed to grasp the dynamic forces at work within the soul, which are based on a logic not of the mind but of the heart. In the *Hexaemeron* Saint Bonaventure tells us that our logic is Christ. Does the Seraphic Doctor address himself to modern man? Each modern man must answer that question for himself. But the man Saint Bonaventure is addressing is the man whose soul is filled with desire, needs, torment, misery, and despair. Saint Bonaventure's message is as ancient as the human heart and as contemporary: God is love, and man is both the expression and the object of that love.

A.G.

COMMENTARY ON ARISTOTLE'S *DE ANIMA*

Author: Saint Albert the Great (c.1206 or c.1193-1280)
Type of work: Philosophy of spirit
First transcribed: c.1256

Principal Ideas Advanced

There is but one soul or substantial form in each man, a rational soul which is the principle not only of intellectual but also of vegetative and sensitive operations.

The human soul is simple, spiritual, and immortal.

It is erroneous to say that there is but one agent intellect for all men: each man has his own agent intellect.

Saint Albert the Great, *Doctor Universalis,* was perhaps the most learned man of the high Middle Ages. His writings, collected into 38 quarto volumes, cover all those areas of human thought in which his master Aristotle was interested, and in addition, Scriptural exegesis and the fields of theology, dogmatic, moral, and mystical. Nor was his tremendous ability and learning lost on his contemporaries, a remarkable sign of their respect being the fact that, contrary to usual practice, he was quoted as an authority while still living: "He is cited in the schools just like Aristotle, Avicenna, and Averroës, and while he is still alive is counted as an authority, unlike any other man," complains Roger Bacon, who was far from being Albert's greatest admirer. Today most people know Albert as the teacher of Saint Thomas Aquinas, and as one who contributed significantly to the development of science in his time. In 1941, ten years after Albert's canonization, Pius XII declared him patron saint of all those who devote themselves to natural science.

But perhaps the major contribution of the "Stupor and Miracle of his age," to use the phrase of Ulric of Strasbourg, to the development of medieval philosophy (and theology, indirectly) is his series of commentaries on the writings of Aristotle, a good example of which is found in the work under consideration, his commentary on Aristotle's *De anima* (*On the Soul*). For at a time when some Church authorities were banning the works of Aristotle and many were, on theological grounds, generally fearful of the vast philosophic and scientific literature recently translated from the Greek and Arabic, Albert welcomed Aristotle as one of the greatest of all philosophers, as being of incomparable value in coming to know man and the universe better, and for his contribution to a deepened understanding of the philosophical presuppositions of Christian belief. His harshest words were directed against those who denied the value of philosophy: "There are ignorant men who try in every way to combat the use of philosophy, above all among the Preachers [Dominicans] where no one opposes them. Like unreasoning animals they blaspheme what they do not understand." And being aware of the difficulties of these works in translation, Albert gave the years of his maturity to making them clear (along with some Neoplatonic writings wrongly identified as those of Aristotle) with the professed purpose of making Aristotle intelligible to the Latins: his plan was to write a book for every book Aristotle had written, had planned to write, or should, for the intelligibility of his position, have written. As Albert writes in the beginning of his commentary on the *Physics* of Aristotle, "It will be our method in this work to follow the order and opinion of Aristotle and to say what seems necessary to understand his proofs, even though his text makes no mention of these. And besides this we shall sometimes digress, pointing out doubts and making clear what in Aristotle is obscure. . . . Proceeding in this way we shall go through the books by number and name as Aristotle did. And we shall add to the imperfect books and even omitted books which Aristotle did not write, or which if he wrote them, have not come down to us." Only when Albert had finished was there a detailed statement of an Aristotelianism explicitly consistent with Christian theology. His aim being to act as "middle man" between Aristotle and the reader, as one who by amplifying the spare language of Aristotle would make it easier to come to know the position of "the master of those who know," in Dante's phrase, he made extensive use of the Greek, Arabic, and Jewish satellite literature; he was no less widely learned in these expositions of Aristotle's thought than he was in the thought of his Latin predecessors.

In the Middle Ages philosophy was taught by "reading" the text of a "master." Such "reading" generally included two phases: first, the literal exposition, which divided and subdivided the text to make clear the schema of the book and the order of argumentation, and then proceeding from part to part, word to word, making clear the underlying opinion. The second phase began on the occasion of obscure or difficult matter, difficult either because of the obscurity of Aristotle's opinion or because of objections and difficulties already raised to the opinion; finally, "disputed questions" were raised and treated at length.

Albert's typical commentary on Aristotle is often called (and sometimes dismissed as) "a mere paraphrase." But "paraphrase" is surely misleading if it brings to mind nothing more than the notion of some sort of elementary and abbreviated restatement or rewording of some given original material. For although it is true that, unlike Aquinas, Albert did not keep the text of Aristotle explicitly distinct from his interpretation, it is also true that the text of Albert represents a reading and understanding of Aristotle that could come only from the widest reading of the relevant literature, and no one showed a more comprehensive reading of the Arabic and Jewish Aristotelians. Nor did Albert regard Aristotle as inerrant: "He who believes Aristotle to be a god ought to believe that he never made a mistake. But whoever thinks him to have been a man must admit that he was liable to make mistakes as the rest of us are." It is also worth noting that, unlike Aquinas, Albert explicitly and often disavowed any intention of giving *de jure* approval to everything he wrote in this commentary form. For he wanted first and foremost to get the best possible reading and understanding of Aristotle and to avoid making what might very well turn out to be premature judgments on the value or truth of this or that point of Aristotle's teaching.

When Albert began his commentary on Aristotle's *De anima,* he was heir to more than 1,000 years of controversy on the nature and properties of the human soul. It is doubtful whether, outside a few passages from the Bible, any writing had been subject to a greater number of learned commentaries than those passages in which Aristotle set down his teaching on the nature and properties of the human soul. And in the thirteenth century the *De anima* became a focal point of especially intense controversy, for if the doctrine of Aristotle was inconsistent with personal human immortality, as Averroës had held, it appeared that any attempt to "baptize" Aristotle was doomed to failure.

The problem which exercised philosophers and theologians was this: How is it possible to reconcile the unity of man with personal immortality, to understand the soul of a man both as form and as mind-substance? According to Aristotle, every living thing has a substantial form called a "soul," which is to the living thing what the shape of a statue is to the statue. When the statue is destroyed, its shape does not continue to exist. And neither does the soul of a dog when it dies. But when a man dies, Christians want to maintain, his soul does remain in existence; but how can a substantial form have the characteristics of an independent substance? If the human soul is the (only) substantial form of the human composite, is not the soul so closely bound to the body that existence independent of the body, personal immortality, is made impossible? If however the human soul is a spiritual substance, and so clearly immortal, how can it do for a man what the soul of a dog does for the dog; namely, be a principle of extension of matter in three dimensions, making it a body, and the like? And if the spiritual human soul cannot be such a principle, then at least one other substantial form, a *forma corporeitatis* seems to be demanded; but then, given a plurality of substantial forms, how can a man be regarded as *one* being?

Likewise, could one accept Aristotle's statement that the agent intellect is "separable, not acted upon and unmixed with the body"? Does this not imply one agent intellect for all men (even though this would mean that it is not proper to say that it is the individual man who knows)?

It was the opinion of Albert, and of his disciple Thomas Aquinas, that what Aristotle wrote in the *De anima,* when rightly understood, could be seen to be consistent with personal immortality; and that whatever the textual difficulties, there is at least no inconsistency between the basic principles of the Aristotelian philosophy of nature and whatever truths are believed by faith. The weight of scholarly opinion seems to favor an understanding of Albert's teaching which makes it contradict Aquinas on no major issues as regards Aristotelian rational psychology.

According to Albert, the intellectual soul is the only substantial form of the human body. Among its powers are those which enable it to be the principle of vegetative and sensitive operations, together with others which enable it (though not 'naturally') to act independently of the body. This soul is a subsistent but not a complete substance; unlike a separated substance (an angel) the soul is so imperfect that a body with external and internal senses is a necessary condition of intellectual operation in its natural state. (After death the soul is in a preternatural state, and its way of knowing is not "natural.")

The nature of the intellect, by contrast with that of a sense power, which is only passive, is two-fold: the possible intellect is like a screen, initially blank, but capable of "receiving" any picture whatever; the agent intellect is like a light which shines on the phantasms (which come ultimately from external sensation), illuminating them (making what is only potentially intelligible to be actually intelligible), and making it possible for them to be received on the screen of the possible intellect, and thus known.

There is not only one source of illumination, only one agent intellect for all possible intellects, Albert claims. Rather, each possible intellect is illumined by its own proper agent intellect. Albert writes, using another light-metaphor, "Since there are even bodily eyes which see by the light existing in them, as the eye of a cat or of an owl can see in the dark without the aid of an outside light, even more so can the intellectual 'eye' see by the light existing within itself: so the light which understands is not separate from the substance of the soul."

In addition to his commentary on the *De anima,* Albert wrote a work called *De intellectu et intelligibili* (*On the Intellect and its Object*), a further and more developed treatment of intellectual knowledge in the state of union with the body and of how the intellect rises from sensible objects in time and place to the contemplation of higher, more divine objects. In his treatise *De natura et origine animae* (*On the Nature and Origin of the Soul*) Albert speaks of the operation of the intellect when after death the soul is separated from the body; this consideration helps to clarify the nature of the intellectual soul, its spirituality, immortality, origin, and the nature of its union with the body. Saint Albert also published a treatise *De unitate intellectus contra Averroistas* (*On the Unity of the Intellect against the Averroists*), a dispute first held in the curia before Pope Alexander IV in 1256, written like a Scholastic "dispute question" (first stating thirty objections to the position taken, then thirty-six contrary arguments, then a general outline of the position defended, and finally answers to the thirty objections).

The very nature of the goal Albert set for himself, to make Aristotle intelligible to the Latins, perhaps precludes his making one of the half dozen major contributions to the development of human thought. But there is little doubt but that he succeeded magnificently in achieving his own aim, as the history of philosophy in his own time and in the next few generations following his work attests. As a result of his efforts obscurantist opposition to philosophy as found in one of its most eminent exponents was stilled, and the foundations for fruitful development were more firmly laid down.

R.L.C.

ON BEING AND ESSENCE

Author: Saint Thomas Aquinas (1225-1274)
Type of work: Religious metaphysics
First transcribed: 1254-1256

Principal Ideas Advanced

The essence of a composite (material) being is constituted of both the matter and the form, and not of the form alone.

The essence of a simple substance, such as an angel or a human soul, is purely formal, with no matter whatsoever in it.

All created substances agree in that their essences are other than their acts of existence.

Every creature receives its act of existence.

In God alone are essence and existence one, since His essence is to exist.

The *De ente et essentia* of Saint Thomas Aquinas is an opusculum composed when he was around thirty years of age. This small treatise is one of his first written works and his first truly metaphysical effort. Because it is a youthful work, it is perhaps stylistically inferior to Thomas's later, more mature works, but it is well worth the effort of close study because of the historical insights which it affords into the developing philosophy and theology of its author.

The *De ente et essentia* is traditionally divided into four general parts: (1) essence in composite substances; (2) essence in simple substances; (3) essence in accidents; and (4) the relation between essence and the logical predicables, genus, species, and difference.

The explicit and positive purpose of the treatise, as is evident from the above titles, is to delineate and define the metaphysical structure and role of essence. The negative and immensely more important result, in terms of Saint Thomas's later writings, in his assertion that whatever *essence* is, it is not the same as the *act of existing*. "From this it is clear," writes Saint Thomas, "that the act of existing is other than essence or quiddity, unless, perhaps, there is a being whose quiddity is its very act of existing." Because the *De ente et essentia* contains the first formal statement of this principle, the treatise is important in the history of religious metaphysics. The work was a challenge to the time-honored and hallowed philosophies of the preceding centuries. Although it is brief and disconcertingly sketchy, it suggests the quality of the writings which Saint Thomas would go on to produce in his rich and productive mature years. One important distinction, that between *what* a thing is and the irreducible fact *that it is,* raises the *De ente et essentia* from the status of being simply a historical curiosity to that of standing as the first enunciation of a classic and revolutionary metaphysics. Because the book is so brief, little is brought forward in its pages as evidence for Thomas's radical insight; indeed, the distinction is stated as if it were an intuition or a hazarded guess. In his later works, Saint Thomas developed, enriched, and strengthened this insight with additional evidence. He demonstrated how the primacy of the act of existence catalyzes the universe into an intelligible order, a process which had been totally unseen by men before him. Thomas's metaphysical vision enabled him to see that the ultimately real and perfect character of reality is the fact of existence. The *De ente et essentia* is his report of the first faint glimmer of that vision, unclear and uncertain, but unmistakeable.

Saint Thomas begins his inquiry into the meaning of being and essence by advancing the theory that essence in a composite substance (a material being) is itself composite. A theory previously held stated that the essence of a thing is the same as its form. Indeed, certain texts in the *Metaphysics* of Aristotle apparently support the latter position. But Saint Thomas argues that the form alone cannot constitute the essence of material beings, because by itself the form does not express entirely *what* these things are. Since the quiddity of material things includes both form and matter, both form and matter contribute to essence in material things.

But it is when Thomas moves into a consideration of essence in separate substances, that he brings forward his insight into the act of existence. Prior to St. Thomas, it was the approved doctrine that *all* creatures are composed of matter and form, for only by virtue of such a composition might the proper distinction be drawn between God and creatures. God is simple; creatures are composed, specifically of matter and form. Thus, corporeal creatures are composed of corporeal matter and form, and spiritual creatures are composed of spiritual matter and form. This theory derived from the *Fons vitae* of Avicebron (1021-1058), a Jewish philosopher who lived in Spain. To the mind of Avicebron, composition meant only one thing: composition of matter and form.

Saint Thomas did not take issue with the position that all creatures are composed. What he did assert, however, was that such a composition need not be an essential composition; that is, of matter and form. Instead, Thomas theorizes in the *De ente et essentia* that separate substances (such as angels) are essentially simple; their essences are simple forms. The composition which distinguishes these beings from God is that they receive their existence, and consequently, are composed of essence and existence. God alone is absolutely simple, composed neither of matter and form, nor of essence and existence. He *is* existence (thus, the cryptic Bibilical text, "I AM WHO AM"); His essence is the same as His being, His essence is to exist.

Therefore, God is the source of the reality of the universe. But not, as some had theorized, in the manner of a form. Rather, Saint Thomas insists in the *De ente et essentia,* God *is* His own existence, and creatures *have* their own. God is the cause of the being of creatures, specifically the efficient cause, and He produces them from nothing. He does not give them something of Himself.

This theory of creation was at once a revolutionary doctrine and a brilliant insight. For centuries, indeed from the time of Plato, philosophers had considered the form (*what* a thing is) to account for the fact of the thing. But Thomas first clearly saw that this view neglected a whole dimension of reality, completely other from form and essence. The order of existence, which he first clearly enunciated, is not only other from essence and form, but it is the very perfection of essence and form, since existence is the ultimate actuality of all things. Existence is at once all-necessary and elusive. Men of philosophy had previously failed to detect this great metaphysical principle of existence because existence is inconceivable. Essences correspond to concepts, and whatever is conceivable is in some way an essence. But to the act of existing there corresponds no concept; hence, conceptualistic philosophy simply did not know of this ultimate perfection, because it was entirely beyond the conceptualistic order.

Indicative of the fact that Saint Thomas had not clearly established in his own mind the ultimate structure of his metaphysical system, are the logical digressions scattered through the *De ente et essentia.* He inquires, in several texts, about the relation between real essence and essence as in the logical categories of genus, species, and difference. How does the essence of a real man (matter and form) correspond to the logical essence of man expressed by the definition, "rational animal"? His answer is that the mode of essence as it exists in the mind (an idea or concept) is of its nature universal; while essence as it exists in the world of composite things is always particular, since a composite essence includes a form which is received into limiting and individuating matter.

In the *De ente et essentia,* Saint Thomas sketches only the briefest outlines of the monumental synthesis which he would later work out. But in this little work the light of his genius is clearly evident. He had yet to develop his method of exposition, nor had he yet mastered the Aristotelian corpus; but it is apparent that, even at this time, Thomas was saying something new to his contemporaries.

Just exactly what was new in this doctrine of *esse* may be gained by attending to the changes which it brought about in the structure of philosophy. First, the Thomistic doctrine of existence provided Saint Thomas with a basic and functional distinction between God and creatures. God is subsistent existence; creatures, in every instance, receive their existence and are thus composed of existence and essence. Further, God causes *esse,* not in some formal way, but efficiently, so that creatures properly exist in their own right. Second, the doctrine of existence liberated Thomistic philosophy from the ponderous and ultimately unintelligible theory of spiritual matter. Angels and human souls can be simple substances, yet still be composed and distinct from God, for they are composed of a simple essence and an act of existence proper to that essence. Third, the doctrine rendered the divine nature somewhat more intelligible by giving a more understandable interpretation to the "existence" texts of the Old Testament.

Finally, the doctrine of existence provided an excellent *a posteriori* method for arguing to the existence of God. If all creatures receive their existence from outside themselves, they must receive it from some first cause, whose existence is unreceived. To quote Saint Thomas's own words in the *De ente et essentia:* "Everything, then, which is such that its act of existing is other than its nature must needs have its act of existing from something else. And since every being which exists through another is reduced, as to its first cause, to one existing in virtue of itself, there must be some being which is the cause of the existing of all things because it itself is the act of existing alone. If that were not so, we would proceed to infinity among causes, since, as we have said, every being which is not the act of existing alone has a cause of its existence."

One last lesson can be gathered from Saint Thomas's little treatise, *On Being and Essence*. In holding up this insight, which was certainly revolutionary, Thomas did not throw out as useless the old and accepted metaphysics. Though he emphasized the primacy of the act of existence, and though it made a profound and fundamental difference in his world view, he still insisted that essence is a real constituent of being and plays an indispensable role in the internal dynamics of metaphysical structure.

Though act is the perfecting principle, passive potency is necessary in order to explain the tremendous diversity and multiplication of God's creation. In a very true sense, the genius of Saint Thomas lay in his ability to evaluate a concept or a theory purely on its objective merits. To him the source, whether Arabian, Jewish, Greek, or patristic, made no difference; his only requirement was that the notion in question agree with the real world as he saw it. Thomas's philosophy is, in a sense, an eclecticism, though a responsible eclecticism, because he realized that the truths of all men and of all ages are good and honorable.

J.P.W.

TREATISE ON THE LAWS AND CUSTOMS OF ENGLAND

Author: Henry of Bracton (died 1268)
Type of work: Codification of common law
First transcribed: Before 1259

Principal Ideas Advanced

Justice in English law operates by the dialectical refinement of custom in the courts.

This practice preserves in the law the liberty of the person and the principle that to be just, government must be legal.

Henry de Bratton, today and since his death in 1268 known as Bracton, wrote his treatise *De legibus ac consuetudinibus regni angliae* (*Of the Laws and Customs of the Kingdom of England*) in the height of that magnificent sunburst of legal achievement which had dawned when, about the year 1100, Irnerius began teaching Roman Law in Bologna. Thanks to the creative genius of the medieval jurists of these centuries, the legal systems of the civilized world today subsist in three forms: the civil, canon, and common laws.

Bracton is responsible for the prevalence of the *common law* throughout the jurisdictions of the present and former members of the British Empire and the United States; his work made it possible for all these people to accept and develop "the practice of the courts of the kings of England," created by royal judges and lawyers: the corpus of law which is known as Anglo-American jurisprudence. The second universal law known to the world is the *canon law* of the Roman Church, Catholic in its principles, its doctrine and spirit, Roman in its techniques. By the *civil law* is understood all those systems which derive, through lawyers known as Glossarists and Post-Glossarists, from the *Codex juris civilis* of Justinian; it holds throughout the world today outside the Anglo-American jurisdictions. Henry de Bratton rightly takes his place in legal history with Irnerius and Gratian, the two key figures in civil and canon law. By a curious irony which Bracton made possible, today the Catholic populations of the world are ruled by a pagan law, whereas vast stretches of non-Catholic peoples are ruled by the common law, founded and structured principally by Bracton and his colleagues, who were Catholic priests. Both civil and common laws, however, proclaim their rationality, and this they have in common with each other, that the one has been called *ratio scripta,* "written reason," the other *ratio non scripta sed tradita,* "reason unwritten and handed down."

Bracton is responsible for the principle of Anglo-American law that "Law is reason," as James I in 1607 said to his Chief Justice, Sir Edward Coke, and that it was, in Coke's famous reply, "artificial reason . . . the golden metewand and measure to try the causes of the subject, and which protected his majesty in safety and peace." Bracton was, as well, the foremost of those "popish clergymen with their foreign jurisprudence" who, as Sir William Blackstone so patriotically protested, had nothing to do with good English law. F. W. Maitland, the greatest English legal historian, knew deeper and better than Blackstone when he said, "It is by 'popish clergymen' that our law is converted from a rude mass of custom into an articulate system . . . . the effect produced on English law by its contact with the romano-canonical learning seems immeasurable. . . ."

In this process, Bracton with his treatise was the key figure; he did his work at a moment between the time when English custom under royal tutelage had grown for better than a century, and just before Parliament and baronage, jealous of royal writ to make right, were to begin the hedging about of royal power by petitions for "redress of grievances" which were to turn into statutes. In no other country could Bracton have done his work; nowhere else was it possible for such a work to play the part it was to assume in England. The reasons were many for the fortunate circumstances in which Bracton found himself. Of most importance, England had by Bracton's time experienced what no other European people had known, a series of strong kings beginning with the Conqueror in 1066; his son Henry I, the "Lion of Justice"; and Henry II, who made himself the protector of every man's right; even Richard, John, and Henry III had preserved the machinery of royal government intact and efficient—too efficient to suit the barons. Good administration, armed conflict even, had eliminated from England any real threat to secular government which was not royal; by Bracton's day, when he sat on the bench, and long before, no man had to answer for his land in any court other than the king's; strong kings had made strong peace, and the king's writ ran throughout the land. The justice of great lords was withering on the vine; the justice of the Church in the Courts Christian, once on the verge of extending itself into every area of life, had been severely restricted, as a Roman cardinal had shortly before Bracton's day learned when armed barons clashed their weapons and cried out, "Nolumus mutare leges Angliae," "We shall not change the laws of England." One single civil and criminal justice was more and more to occupy the minds of men, the justice of the king's courts.

But the justice of the king's courts was, before Bracton, the "crude mass of custom" that Maitland called it. Without Bracton's work, and there was no one else to do it, it could have no future, and it was only a matter of time before a strong government, then in the offing, under the English Justinian, Edward I, would find in Roman Law that fitting handmaid of strong government which it always has been, and indeed was created to serve. So at least it must seem to us, when Bracton, probably forced to obey the papal injunction forbidding priests to sit in profane tribunals, had to leave the king's bench together with the other priests, the last of the sacerdotal justices who had served English kings and received bishoprics and preferment in reward for devoted, competent service. The new judges were inexperienced and needed the help of Bracton's skill. Bracton knew well what the custom of the king's court was. He was a protégé of William Raleigh, a man fabulous for his strenuous judicial work, who received the bishopric of Winchester for his reward, only to begin quarreling with his royal master. Raleigh remained Bracton's legal paragon, and he was probably the first English judge to be famous for his legal craftsmanship.

From 1245 until late in his life, certainly for twenty years, Bracton sat steadily on the king's bench. He received ecclesiastical preferment for his services, became in approved fashion of the time a pluralist, and died as chancellor of Exeter Cathedral. There, for three hundred years, in a chantry he had provided in his will, masses were daily sung for his soul. In that same cathedral, since 1923, is a stone inscribed "To the memory of Henry of Bratton, temp. Henry III, Author of the first systematic treatise on the laws of England, Chancellor of this church . . . this stone was placed on the site of Bratton's altar."

A "systematic treatise" on the laws of England had to be different from anything that Bracton, with what Roman and canonical learning he had, and it was considerable, was acquainted with. He knew the written work of Azo and Vacarius, the former an advocate in Rome whom the English retained when they wanted the best, the latter a teacher at Oxford in Henry II's day. It was of the textbook kind, as was the canonical *Summae* and *Apparatus* known to him. Bracton could not proceed to write a schoolbook or a "hornbook," as the common law lawyers today call their rudimentary treatises. He lacked a *Codex juris* to comment on, to parse and construe.

Nor did English kings use decretal letters as did Roman pontiffs, who were trained and polished jurists, to teach their subjects, judges, and plaintiffs alike the lessons of law learned in the schools. Bracton had only two things, writs and cases: writs, whereby actions were begun (originating, so "original"), were royal commands in stylized formula to sheriffs, setting forth the matters which the king wished to be determined and the manner of determining them. Of the cases which had been heard by royal judges, recording the procedures and rules they followed in these determinations, thousands upon thousands were to be found in the particular court "rolls" available to Bracton. Royal judges had long observed in the king's courts the papal injunction to the Courts Christian that a case once decided was to be a model for similar cases. A gigantic task was involved; Maitland describes it: "Imagine fifty rolls, each composed of twenty or thirty membranes, each membrane as long as one's arm, as broad as a span, each membrane covered back to front with writing, whereon are no headnotes, no catch words, nothing to guide the eye save the names of the counties in the margin." From these rolls, Bracton counted about 2,000 cases which he marked, 500 of which he had transcribed into what Sir Paul Vinogradoff has called "Bracton's Notebook," which Vinogradoff discovered in 1884, and which F. W. Maitland, Bracton's most profound admirer, edited and printed beautifully at his own expense in 1887.

The analysis of the writs which originated the cases and the cases themselves chosen as typical and best judged make up the *De legibus*. Practically all the cases were tried by two judges who thus owe their fame to Bracton: William Raleigh and Martin Pateshull. We cannot tell whether this was because they were Bracton's idols, which we know, or because he happened to possess the particular rolls which contained their work, but we can suspect the former to have been the case. For Bracton never mentions his colleagues, of whom he had small opinion, as he lets the reader know, and he had great respect for the *vetera judicia,* the "old judgments."

The book, unhappily, was never completed, though it almost was; why the abrupt condition, we do not know. An order went out in 1258 to Henry de Bracton to bring in the rolls he had; either this order, or old age, or pressing business deprived us. But Bracton had written a readable, comprehensive description of actual thirteenth century law; no one would make the attempt again until Sir William Blackstone. Copies are plenteous, and they present all the problems arising from the literary career of a popular, useful work written for and used by judges, practitioners, and students. In this century, Professor Woodbine of Yale worked at solving them in his edition; Professor Thorne of Harvard was engaged in 1964 in the arduous task of translating them for the Selden Society. The one edition of the Notebook is F. W. Maitland's in 1887. Translations of some of the rolls Bracton used can be found in the publications of the Selden Society, Volumes 53, 56, and 59.

Thus it was that Bracton formalized for us the inherent genius that has always informed the common law. He not only made a *jus commune* comparable to the *jus civile* and *jus canonicum,* he also structured into it the fundamental principles which have always guided the common law. A Schoolman would have a deductive law applying principles to individual cases, but Bracton taught the common law lawyer to start with the analysis of the case; the individual right is determinable, not dictated; each man is to have full say for himself and a way to say it. Common law has later in its life tended toward archaism and formalism, but it has always rescued itself, not by extrinsic means but by its own principles.

The most celebrated contribution of Bracton's formulation of common law to politics is the principle that government must be legal. Bracton and his contemporaries, popes, emperors, king, lawyers, lords, freemen, and even serfs, knew no other kind of government than government under law: government not outside, not beyond or above law, but government serving, obeying, protecting right. When in later times, the necessity of government's being legal in order to be just became obscured, common law lawyers trained in Bracton kept that principle of government alive for it. In Bracton they had learned that "the king must be under God and the law, for the law [lex] makes the king [regem], not the king [rex] the law [legem]." And "the king must attribute to law what law attributes to the king, power and domination." Our Lord Jesus Christ Himself and His holy Mother, he tells us, did not put themselves above the law, but subjected themselves to it.

Bracton, excellent legal craftsman that he proves himself to be, able to excite even modern critics, was more than a craftsman. He was a true man of law. He knew how to use the civilians and the canonists. Sir Paul Vinogradoff describes best the use that Bracton made of them when he said that Bracton had "the definite plan of using, as it were, Roman bricks for the construction of an English edifice; . . . his use of civilian jurisprudence remains a remarkable monument of the scholarly interest and of the ingenuity of an English lawyer bent on rationalizing the law and customs of his country."

When Bracton's legal career was blighted by the pope's forcing him off the royal bench, the root and branch grew a different and greater flower in the *De legibus*. Owing to this learned priest, today "the practice of the king's courts" rules men thankful to call themselves free, made free and learned in freedom, its principles and processes, by this "popish" clergyman, with his foreign and native jurisprudence.

J.A.M.

THE MIND'S ROAD TO GOD

Author: Saint Bonaventure (Giovanni di Fidanza, 1221-1274)
Type of work: Spiritual instruction
First transcribed: c.1259

Principal Ideas Advanced

The first step in ascending to union with God is contemplation of the sensible world as showing forth God's power, wisdom, and benevolence; the second, the realization of the reflection of God in our very observation, enjoyment, and understanding of the external world; the third, the contemplation of the divine image in the natural powers of our own minds; the fourth, the contemplation of the First Principle in the soul of a man reformed by faith, hope, and charity through divine grace; the fifth, the contemplation of divine unity as Being itself; the sixth, the contemplation of divine goodness in the Trinity.

When the six steps have been traversed, the soul enters the peace of mystical ecstasy.

Saint Bonaventure introduces *The Mind's Road to God* (*Itinerarium mentis ad Deum*) with an autobiographical prologue, in which he reports that in 1259, soon after he had become Minister General of the Franciscans, he retired to the solitude of Mount Alverno, near Assisi, to meditate and pray. In so doing he was following the example of Saint Francis of Assisi, the founder of the Order, who in this same "quiet place" had had his celebrated vision of the Crucified Seraph. The vision was repeated for Saint Bonaventure. He takes the six-winged Seraph as a symbol, which he proceeds to interpret allegorically, at the same time giving the outline of his treatise, for the *Itinerarium* proves to be a development in detail of the meaning of the allegory. The reason for the subtitle of the treatise, "The Mendicant's Vision in the Wilderness," thus becomes apparent. The wings of the Seraph symbolize the stages of illumination in the mind's progress toward God: the first pair represents contemplation of the physical world; the second, contemplation of the mind and soul of man; the third, contemplation of God in His essential traits and in His goodness—all as symmetrically ordered as a Gothic rosace.

This use of symbol and allegory to convey religious ideas was in accord with a tradition, one of many in diverse fields, which originated in antiquity, was highly appreciated in the Middle Ages, and continued into the Renaissance. By its allegorical method of interpretation and also by its use of Biblical texts to illustrate the application of each symbol and to reinforce each point as it is made, the *Itinerarium* is thoroughly representative of its time.

The first two chapters of the *Itinerarium* are concerned with showing how, by contemplation of the universe with the senses and imagination, one can discover in the properties of physical objects and in the conditions for our knowledge of them manifestations of God's attributes. In this connection one recalls that observation of nature was more important to the Franciscans than to the Thomists, and that Roger Bacon, too, was a Franciscan. The empirical interests of the Franciscans kept open the paths which finally led to Renaissance science.

Saint Bonaventure distinguishes three moments in sensory observation. First, external objects are apprehended by the senses. Man has five senses like five doors, through which enters into his soul cognition of everything in the sensible world. The "external sensibles" generate "similitudes" which enter the external organ, pass thence to the internal organ, and thence again to the apprehensive power. Second, apprehension is attended by delight if the sensible object is appropriate.

Sense delights in its object by reason of beauty (*speciositas*) in sight, sweetness in smell and hearing, and wholesomeness in taste and touch. All delight is by reason of proportion, and proportion is of the nature of excellence (*pulchritudo*). Third, an act of judgment follows as to the reasons for the delight which sense takes in the object. Judgment, then, is an action which causes the "sensible species" to enter the intellective power by abstraction.

Bonaventure's epistemology, though formulated in thirteenth century terms, differs from the Scholastic view in that his view assimilates all knowledge to aesthetic contemplation; he holds that the source of all truth is direct experience, from its initial degree in observation of the world of nature to its ultimate degree in the enlightenment of mystical experience.

It was obvious to Bonaventure that the universe is the handiwork of God. He finds the attributes of the Creator shining forth in created things; all is testimony to the power, wisdom, and benevolence of the Maker. He invites us to contemplate with awe the masterpiece of divine art in its magnitude and order, with its plenitude and multitude of creatures in their diversity of genus, species, and individual; to admire with gratitude the beauty of stars and stones, plants and animals.

The view of the physical universe as showing forth divine handiwork in its order and complexity and adaptation of means to ends is the basis of the traditional argument from design for the existence of God. It is noteworthy that Bonaventure, though a master of Scholastic dialectic, does not attempt to offer an argument from design, and that he does not give elsewhere in the treatise any of the other traditional proofs for the existence of God. It seems likely in the context of the *Itinerarium,* which is in its central purpose the description of a *via mystica,* that the reason Saint Bonaventure does not resort to arguing God's existence is that he is convinced of it on extralogical grounds; that is, by mystical experience which provides him with direct and unassailable knowledge of God. He does not attempt to construct an argument, but is satisfied to draw an analogy, taken from aesthetic experience, between the product of the human artist and the product of the divine artist. He develops the analogy: The world was fashioned by the hand of God; He has left His marks (*vestigia*) upon it; as we can come to know the personality of the human artist through appreciation of his works, so we can learn something of God's nature by contemplation of His creation.

The first and second chapters of the *Itinerarium* carry the theme that God is like man; the third and fourth, that man is made in the likeness of God. Chapter 3 concerns contemplation of the powers of the human mind: memory, understanding, and will. In these threefold and unified powers, Bonaventure finds the image of the eternity, truth, and goodness of the Trinity. He divides philosophy into corresponding branches: natural (metaphysics, mathematics, physics), rational (grammar, logic, rhetoric), and moral (monastic, domestic, political). Chapter 4 considers man in his moral life. Divine grace assists the soul to go beyond the light of reason and acquired science to a high level of contemplation in faith, hope, and charity—a passage from rational activity to affective experience. In considerations of the moral consciousness are traditionally found the makings of the moral argument for the existence of God; but here again there is no argument. Bonaventure is entirely preoccupied by the progress in the mystic path of the soul which has been purified, illumined, and perfected by the theological virtues.

In Chapter 5 Bonaventure deploys the ontological concepts which medieval philosophy inherited from Plato and Plotinus, and Greek philosophy in general. It is always pointed out that the ontological proof of the existence of God is an *a priori* argument, that it makes no appeal to experience. This is logically the case, yet psychologically not so. The proof is made to look like a syllogism; it claims to develop the implications of the definition of God; but the concepts which it invokes grow out of mystical experience. The similarities on which the argument from design relies can be seen in the cheerful light of day, whereas the motives which the ontological proof tries to express spring up in the dark night of the soul. The appeal of the argument from design—even Hume and Kant, who rejected it because of the logical weakness which they found in it, acknowledged its appeal to their feelings—is more generally felt because it expresses a more frequent experience. On the other hand, the ontological proof is not so popular and has been more vehemently criticized (it has been found invalid by many philosophers, notably by St. Thomas Aquinas and Kant) because it is motivated by more esoteric experience.

In their accounts of their experience, mystics agree, with what William James noted as "eternal unanimity," that the experience is ineffable, for it transcends ordinary sensory-rational consciousness; that, as their consciousness passes beyond the differentiations of sensory images and intellectual concepts, it becomes concentrated into a pure unitary state; that the bliss which they enjoy is inexpressible, immeasurably greater than any mundane happiness; that the knowledge which they attain is ultimate truth. All attempts to communicate this knowledge must necessarily fail, for everyday language is inadequate to accomplish it.

The mystics in their ineffable experience know God as pure Being. The appearance of ontological expressions in the utterances of the mystics can be understood when it is borne in mind that these words say nothing empirical; they have no descriptive content. "Being," "reality," "oneness," these are contentless terms, to which the mystic resorts because his experience is such that there is nothing he can say about it in ordinary language. The impossibility of ascribing attributes to God leads to the consequences of negative theology; sometimes the mystic attempts to express God's ineffability by attributing to Him pairs of contradictory qualities.

Their unitary experience reveals God to the mystics as the One. He is declared to be unique; and there are many modes of uniqueness: supreme greatness, supreme perfection, and others. If the mystic is concerned to remain within the bounds of orthodoxy, he must somehow accommodate to the theological conception of God his own knowledge of an absolute God. Hence, we often find in the writings of the mystics a distinction between a personal God with the traditional attributes, and the Deity or the Godhead completely devoid of attributes. The doctrines of the Trinity and the Incarnation compound the difficulties.

The transcendence of the experience makes God the *ens realissimum* in contrast to the material world and everyday experience, which the mystic despises or at least holds to be of inferior value. The ontological terms can take on the force of value terms. Because of the blissfulness of the experience, God is the most perfect Being, the *summum bonum,* the object of all desire. In this use, the terms have an almost purely evaluative force. This fusing of the orders of reality and value, this superimposition of the axiological hierachy upon the ontological hierarchy, is a motive which appears with particular clarity and strength among the mystics, becoming sometimes even a dominating motive, as in the metaphysics of Plotinus and Spinoza.

In Chapter 5 Bonaventure explains that, if we wish to understand God in the unity of His essence, we must concentrate our minds on pure Being. There is a passage with a strong Eleatic flavor; it runs thus: Only Being is intelligible; non-Being, which is nothing at all, cannot be thought except as the privation of Being. Then follows a passage with Platonic ingredients: Pure Being is divine being, beyond all particulars, all universals, all genera; when we try to look at this light, we are blind because we are accustomed to the shadows and phantasms of the sensible world. The chapter concludes with an expression of intense emotion carried by ontological language.

St. Bonaventure produces an effect of climax by using his adjectives dramatically; first of all, positively: Pure Being is primary, eternal, and most perfect; then in contradictory pairs: Being is first and last, eternal and most present, highly one and all-inclusive; finally as thesis, antithesis, and synthesis: Because Being is eternal and most present, it is at the center and at the circumference of all; because Being is highly one and all-inclusive, it is all in all.

Bonaventure does not arrange the ontological concepts into a logical proof (invalid or valid) because he needs no proof. In using ontological language he is trying to find expression for what is to him all-absorbing and completely satisfying experience. Though in his other works he is primarily a theologian, here he speaks as a mystic who has been inflamed to his very marrow by the love of God.

In Chapter 6 is the only passage in his book where Bonaventure feels that he must argue a point. He attempts a dialectical demonstration of the doctrine of the Trinity, trying to show that the three Persons are necessary in order that the eternal goodness may diffuse itself more freely. But he soon gives up, conceding that the mystery of the Trinity is incomprehensible; it produces in us helpless wonder (*stupor admirationis*). He adverts to the doctrine of the Incarnation but it, too, baffles comprehension; it is beyond even wonder (*supermirabilis*). He disposes of these stumbling blocks for the mystic by consigning them to faith, for he accepts the orthodox Christian position as a matter of course.

The final chapter returns to the subject of mystical experience. After ascending the six steps of illumination, the mind rises above the sensible world and itself and passes to the sabbath of repose in God. Saint Bonaventure has only one remark to make about mystical experience itself: that it is most secret, known only by those to whom it has been granted.

This elegant little treatise presents many facets of interest. For the historian of ideas it is a summary of thirteenth century knowledge, reflecting in its score of pages the entire age. The student of philosophy finds in it a concise and masterly exemplification of Scholastic metaphysics. Furthermore, it illustrates an exegetical method much in use in the Middle Ages. It affords the observer of human nature an encounter with a personality distinguished by acuity and profundity of mind and by ardor and generosity of temperament. To all readers in our distraught time it gives a glimpse of the serene strength of the mystics.

CHRONICA MAJORA

Author: Matthew Paris (c.1200-1259)
Type of work: Historical chronicle
First transcribed: 1235-1259

Principal Ideas Advanced

King Henry III of England is to be criticized for exacting excessive taxes and for his favoritism towards foreigners.

The capture of King Louis IX of France at Damietta by the Moslems was a unique and shameful moment in the history of France.

The popes have not conducted themselves properly in involving themselves in secular affairs and in demanding English gold.

Western Christians have been grievously threatened by the Moslems and the Tartars, who are beastly infidels.

Economic depression, the rising cost of living, poor crops, and famine add to the misery of the times.

In 1235 a Benedictine monk by the name of Matthew Paris was commissioned to continue the *Chronica majora* of St. Albans Abbey in England. This chronicle, initiated in the twelfth century by an abbot of St. Albans, portrays the outstanding events upon earth of the "People of God," beginning with Creation. The purpose was to present a universal history, depicting the fulfillment of God's plan for mankind through a narration of the everlasting conflict between the two worlds of Augustine: the world of God and the world of man. The historical importance of this work is that it covers the events of Christian Europe with special emphasis on England from 1216 to 1273. Matthew Paris, beginning in 1235, revised the earlier parts of the chronicle and brought them into line with his concept of historiography. He then composed the section dating from 1235 to his death in 1259.

The part of the *Chronica majora*

actually written by Matthew Paris is by far the most important section of the entire work. It is the major source for the history of England during the reign of King Henry III (1207-1272), and it is a source for the affairs of Christian Europe during the same period. The author has recorded and commented on the great events of his age and has accurately mirrored the public opinion of his time. Since he was not a professional historian of the twentieth century type, but only a poor medieval forerunner, he can be forgiven for expressing biased judgments based on local and personal feeling and also for including hearsay and rumor as factual information. Despite such weaknesses, this Catholic writer ranks as the most outstanding of English medieval historians and one of the few in the Middle Ages who can rightly be called a conscious writer of history. In fact Matthew Paris was only obeying the command of his king, who told him to write "a plain and full account of all these proceedings, and insert them in indelible characters in a book, that the recollection of them may not in any way be lost to posterity at any future ages."

The chronicle of Matthew Paris can best be divided into three general parts: English affairs; non-English affairs; and a miscellany, which includes material on a multitude of subjects from natural phenomena to economics. The wealth of information contained on England is woven about two institutions: the monarchy in the person of Henry III and the Abbey of St. Albans. Considerable detail is given to the affairs of the author's abbey, including information on monastic politics, relations with neighbors over property rights, conflict with papal envoys, visits of the king, and impressions of the many travelers who by stopping at the abbey became sources of information for Matthew Paris. Of greater importance is the England of Henry III. The author in part presents a biography of the king, describing his marriage to Eleanor of Provence, the struggle with France over the continental claims of the Plantagenets, the developing conflict between Henry and Simon de Montfort over Gascony, the constant attempts of the king to raise revenue and the resulting hardship on the country, the continual negotiations with the various popes concerning the Hohenstaufens and the kingdom of Sicily, and finally the contest between Henry and his barons, culminating in the Provisions of Oxford (1258) and temporary baronial supremacy.

Matthew Paris presents many anecdotes concerning the king and the great of his kingdom. He excels in writing eulogies for deceased nobles and churchmen. In telling of the birth of a son to the king, the author reveals his gift for description: "On the night of the 16th of June, a son was born at Westminster to the king by his wife Eleanor. At this event all the nobles of the kingdom offered their congratulations, and especially the citizens of London, because the child was born at London; and they assembled bands of dancers, with drums and tambourines, and at night illuminated the streets with large lanterns." Matthew is particularly harsh on the king because of his monetary exactions upon the people, and his favoritism for men from the continent. The public mind is revealed, when the chronicler writes that "many people agreed with the prophecy of Merlin, . . . declaring that this king Henry was truly a 'lynx penetrating all things with its eye'; that is to say, peering into and penetrating the purses of all."

In 1251, the king is strongly criticized for his favoritism towards foreigners. Matthew describes how a Poitevin priest was allowed to pelt Henry and others with turf, stones, and green apples and was then permitted to squirt grape juice into their eyes. The author remarks: "Such are the persons to whom the king of England intrusts the care and guardianship of many thousands of souls, rejecting such a vast number of learned, prudent, and proper men as England has given birth to, who know the language of the natives and how to instruct the ignorant."

On continental affairs, Matthew Paris gives considerable information about two of the great lay rulers of the thirteenth century: the Holy Roman Emperor Frederick II (1194-1250) and the saintly king of France, Louis IX (1214-1270). Frederick's conflicts with the papacy and the Italian city-states are described, along with his interest in the Moslem world. Louis of France is seen in his relations with the king of England and on the ill-fated crusade to Egypt. One of the great moments of the chronicle is the meeting of the two kings, Henry and Louis, in Paris. On the English king's departure Louis is quoted as saying: "Would that the twelve peers of France and the barons would agree to our wishes; we should then be inseparable friends." The saddest moment comes when Louis is captured at Damietta by the Moslems: "Never has it been found in any history that a king of France had been taken prisoner, especially by infidels, or defeated, except this one; and if he alone had been preserved in safety and honour, and all the rest had fallen, the Christians might have had some means of recovering breath and avoiding shame."

The actions of the papacy are treated in great detail. Facts are given concerning three popes: Gregory IX (1227-1241), Innocent IV (1243-1254), and Alexander IV (1254-1261). Needless to say, Matthew treats the popes rather harshly because of their deep involvement in secular interests and because of their demands for English gold. In 1245, the Council of Lyons and the excommunication of Frederick II are highlighted. The author describes with thinly disguised delight the conflicts between the two mendicant orders: the Dominicans and Franciscans. There is also information concerning the vicissitudes of the University of Paris.

Of even more curious a nature is the material concerning the Holy Land, the Moslems, and the Tartars. The chronicler narrates the difficulties of the French nobles in Palestine and the repercussions resulting from the fall of Jerusalem in 1244. Mention is made of developments in the Latin Eastern Empire and the conflict between the Greek and Latin churches. Early in his section of the chronicle Matthew Paris gives a brief and obviously prejudiced biography of Mohammed (570-632), together with a summary of Islamic doctrine and practices. Several times the Tartars are discussed by the writer. The great fear and mental unrest of the Western Christians caused by these mysterious invaders from the East is revealed in Matthew's description of the Tartars: "The men are inhuman and of the nature of beasts, rather to be called monsters than men, thirsting after and drinking blood, . . . they clothe themselves in skins of bulls, and are armed with iron lances; they are short in stature and thickset, . . . they have no human laws, know no mercy and are more cruel than lions or bears. . . ." Later on in the chronicle he states that further information could be obtained "by making diligent search of St. Albans."

Finally, isolated facts are given concerning the Iberian Peninsula, Scotland and Wales, and Scandinavia. The Christian attitude towards the Jews is well shown, with the author describing mutual acts of violence and the attempts of King Henry to force money out of them. Matthew Paris frequently describes climatic and natural disasters, such as floods and earthquakes. In one place he tells of a great ocean storm that "suddenly broke forth by night, and a fierce storm of wind arose, which caused inundations of the rivers as well as of the sea, and in places, . . . drowned great numbers of people, destroyed flocks of sheep, and herds of cattle, tore up trees by the roots, overthrew houses, and ravaged the coast." The author tells of economic depression, the rising cost of living, poor crops, and famine. He comments in 1251 on the arrival of crossbills and on the presentation of water buffaloes to the king's brother. The buffalo is described as "similar to the ox, well adapted for carrying or drawing burdens, a great enemy to the crocodile, fond of the water; and provided with large horns to defend himself."

From the above examples it is possible to see the wide range of information contained in Matthew Paris's written record. For a man of the Middle Ages he reveals a universality of interest which is remarkable. The extensive range of factual matter and opinion makes this work a major source not only for medieval England but for the medieval Christian world in all of its ramifications during the thirteenth century. At the end of his section of the chronicle there is a drawing of Matthew Paris dying. He is quoted as saying: "Into your hands I commend my spirit. Make me safe, O Lord God of Truth." The dying man's elbow rests upon the *Chronica majora.* No better final picture can be given of this great Catholic medieval historian: a union of God, Truth, and Matthew's masterpiece: the *Chronica majora.*

R.J.K.

DE VERITATE

Author: Saint Thomas Aquinas (1225-1274)
Type of work: Philosophy of truth
First transcribed: 1256-1259

Principal Ideas Advanced

Truth in general is the conformity of being to the intellect.

The proper object of the intellect is truth; the proper object of the will is the good.

God has knowledge in the highest degree.

In the *De veritate,* Saint Thomas Aquinas speaks for the first time in his own right. Certainly, this is not the first of his works, but it is the first work in which he puts forth without hesitation his own thoughts and his own opinions on the problematic questions of his day. In doing this, he does not abandon the prodigious learning of Saint Augustine, nor does he cast aside the profound thinking of Aristotle. These two intellectual geniuses were his models and inspiration in the very beginning of his educational career, and they remained such until the end. However, there were points on which the developed mind of Saint Thomas Aquinas did not agree with his masters. There were other points on which he had deeper insight into the problem in question. There were still other points in which his wider literary contact gave him a broader view and consequently the possibility of a more synthetic understanding. In the *De veritate,* one will find the first evidences of this independence of thought. Thus, the *De veritate* is the first Thomistic treatise. It is a philosophical masterpiece which is the product of Saint Thomas's independent and creative thinking.

The questions of the *De veritate* are disputed questions. In the thirteenth century a master of theology at the University of Paris was expected to hold disputations several times during each academic year. On the first day, one of the students, under the direction of the master, would present the problem of discussion and indicate a position in answering it. Those in attendance would present objections and difficulties which the student would then attempt to answer. On the next day, the master himself would present the proceedings of the previous day by stating the objections which were advanced and giving his own resolution of them, and by giving his own solution to the problem and offering proof for it. The articles of the *De veritate* represent the efforts of Saint Thomas in the academic disputations which were held while he was the master of theology at the University of Paris. Each article is at one and the same time his summation of the first day's proceedings and his own personal presentation and solution of the problem under consideration.

The *De veritate* is a very early work in the writing and teaching career of Saint Thomas, coming as it did during his first professorate at the University of Paris from September of 1256 until July of 1259. It is not an immature or amateurish kind of work, however, but the product of a true professional in every sense of the word. At the time of its composition, the University of Paris was the crossroads for the meeting and merging of diverse strains of thought, the pivotal point for the intellectual encounter of minds that were steeped in traditional viewpoints. Saint Thomas was in the midst of this melee, possessed as he was with the traditional Christian way of thinking, and his *De veritate* emerges as an adjustment of this traditional Christian way of thinking to the advancement of these other philosophies and terminologies.

The subject matter of the *De veritate* falls into two major divisions. The first section extends from Question 1 through Question 20, beginning as it does with a discussion of the nature of transcendental truth and then proceeding to an elaboration of the various kinds of knowledge. The first section, then, can be said to treat of the intellect and its proper object, which is truth. It is this section which gives this work of Thomas its traditional title; namely, the *De veritate* (*Of Truth*). The second section extends from Question 21 through Question 29. Thomistic scholars usually divide this second section into two divisions. The first includes Questions 21 through 26, which treat of the will and its proper object, which is the good. The second division includes Questions 27 through 29, which treat of grace and justification. There is a certain amount of unity, then, in the development of the *De veritate*. For the relationship of the two rational powers of intellect and will to their proper objects is examined. Other problems are considered, but they can easily be linked in some way to the general major considerations of the intellect in its acquisition of truth and the will in its pursuit of the good.

When one first peruses the *De veritate,* it may appear that there is no real unity at all in its contents. In fact, one could readily admit that it does not have the unity of a systematic treatise in which there is the development of a single theme. Such an admission, however, does not affect the value and the greatness of the *De veritate,* for this work is simply the record of an academic event which was peculiar to the Middle Ages. It fulfills its purpose of recording for posterity the views of one of the great masters of the era concerning the great questions of the era.

The first major division of the *De veritate,* Questions 1 through 20, is certainly the largest. In the very first question Saint Thomas Aquinas begins by defining truth in general as the conformity of being to the intellect. He then proceeds to give some characteristics of truth in general.

Question 2 becomes specific as it takes up the first of a series of particular applications of what was discussed about truth in general. It begins the treatment of truth and knowledge as it is present in God, and this consideration extends over the next five questions, discussing in order the divine Ideas, the Word of God, Providence, Predestination, and the Book of Life. It is quite easy to recognize how these various topics are associated with knowledge and truth in God.

Questions 7 and 8 turn to a consideration of the second of a series of particular applications of what was discussed about truth in general. They consider knowledge and truth as it is present in angelic nature, covering almost the same material that was covered in the section concerning God, but noting the likenesses and the differences between angelic knowledge and divine knowledge.

In Questions 10 through 20 Saint Thomas Aquinas takes up the third particular application of what was discussed about truth in general; namely, the problem of knowledge and truth as it is present in man. In sequence he considers the following topics: the mind of man as an image of the trinity, the nature of a teacher, the nature of prophecy, the nature of rapture, the nature of faith, the nature of the distinction between superior and inferior reason, the nature of synderesis, the nature of conscience, the nature of the knowledge of the first man, the nature of the knowledge of the soul after death, and the nature of the knowledge in the soul of Christ. Again, it is quite evident how these different topics are variations on the general theme of the human intellect and its proper object of truth.

The second major division of the *De veritate,* Questions 21 through 29, cannot be fitted so easily into a coherent outline. The rational power of the will and its pursuit of good in general is the theme of Questions 21 through 26, but the specific application of this theme in particular cases is not as precise. In sequence, Saint Thomas Aquinas discusses the nature of good in general, the nature of the appetite for good, the will, freedom of the will, the nature of sensuality, and the nature of the passions of the soul.

The final three questions of the *De veritate* could be looked upon as an appendix, containing as they do a discussion of grace, the justification of sinners, and the grace of Christ, in that order. None of these topics has any direct bearing on either the intellect in its acquisition of knowledge or the will in its pursuit of good. Yet there are several indirect relationships which Saint Thomas makes and which therefore justify their inclusion in this particular work.

The *De veritate* is truly a masterpiece of Catholic literature. Its style is succinct and its Latin is compact. Occasionally there is obscurity, but overall there is profundity. For a person who desires to understand the depths of Saint Thomas's mind, a thorough acquaintance with the *De veritate* is as necessary as an acquaintance with the *Summa theologica* and the *Summa contra Gentiles.* For it is in the *De veritate* that many of the chief principles and conclusions of the complexus of Thomistic thought are initially presented and developed.

M.K.R.

SUMMA UNIVERSAE THEOLOGIAE

Author: Alexander of Hales (c.1175-1245), and others
Type of work: Systematic theology
First transcribed: c.1245-1260

Principal Ideas Advanced

The soul has an innate knowledge of God; we can be more certain of God's existence than of the existence of creatures.

The likeness of God, innate to the soul, consists of the primary notions of the first being, the first true, and the first good, in the light of which the soul is able to know created being, created truth, and created goodness.

A description of the soul and its powers in Augustinian terms as an image of God is compatible with Aristotle's philosophical description, since the different approaches, although viewing the soul from different aspects, are similar.

Although traditionally ascribed to Alexander of Hales under the title *Summa Fratris Alexandri* (*Summa of Brother Alexander*) this "Handbook of Theology" is actually a compilation of a number of authors. Modern scholarship dates the composition of the *Summa* partly before (most of the first three books) and partly after (the entire fourth book) Alexander's death. Even the parts composed during Alexander's life may not have been written entirely by him, although it is likely that he edited and approved what was written. In any event, the *Summa* does represent a school of thought to which Alexander, John of La Rochelle (died 1245), William of Meliton (c.1245), and Saint Bonaventure, among others not identified, contributed. Like most of the theological *summae* of the thirteenth century, that of Brother Alexander is "great" in topics covered, in references to *auctoritates,* as well as in size. Roger Bacon in commenting on the bulk of the work wrote that the Franciscans "attributed to Alexander a great *Summa,* heavier than a horse, although it had not been done by him but by others." In the work traditional division of topics is made: God, Creation, Angels, Bodies, Man, the Soul, Evil, Sin, the Incarnation and Redemption, Law and Precepts, Grace and Virtues. The treatment is, of course, intended to be "summary" and not at all a complete exposition of each topic.

Although Alexander taught as "master" in the faculty of Theology at the University of Paris from about 1220 until his death, he did not enter the Franciscan Order until he was fifty. Then, since he was already teaching at Paris, he provided the Franciscans with their first chair at the University and initiated the Franciscan School of Theology. This *Summa,* therefore, represents the original thinking of Franciscan theology and philosophy: Augustinian in tone and context, employing not yet completely understood and barely assimilated Aristotelian categories whenever possible, but always using Augustinianism as a check and reference point.

Alexander was among the first masters to teach from the compilation (*Sententiae*) of Peter Lombard. Unlike the extended commentaries on Lombard's *Sentences* by later masters of theology, the text of Alexander's *Commentary* which has come down to us is, for the most part, little more than a series of lecture notes which, apparently, were developed in class but recorded as a series of references. The form of the text, however, already reveals the style to be followed by the later great *summae* of most of the masters: a statement of the question, a series of arguments against the intended position, a statement of the position of the master with its justification, and, finally an answer to the arguments and objections raised in the beginning. A similar structure of both content and form characterizes the *Summa of Brother Alexander* with, however, an important difference: this *Summa* does not simply cite references, but includes quotations of more or less complete arguments from the "authorities" to support or even to establish its conclusions and solutions. At the same time, the authors of the *Summa* add little or no development of these arguments, probably in line with its "summary" status as noted above. A first impression of this work is that it is similar to the theological writings of Albert the Great, although on a much reduced scale: a sourcebook of Christian theologians and mystics, with Aristotle (or at times the pseudo-Aristotelian *Book of Causes*) as the main representative of the pagan philosophers.

The syncretic aspects of the *Summa* is exemplified in its treatment of knowledge of God's existence and in its discussion of the human soul. Proofs for God's existence in the tradition of Saint Thomas Aquinas have always avoided an *a priori* approach, seeing this as incompatible with human knowledge which can proceed only as far as it is led by sensible things. Consequently, it is with some surprise that we find in the *Summa of Brother Alexander, a posteriori* arguments along with *a priori* approaches, including the ontological argument of Saint Anselm, all quoted with approval. This gathering together of apparently incompatible approaches to knowledge of God has been interpreted by some scholars as a simple eclecticism. The surprise and the judgment of simple electicism, however, may be unjustified, for, apparently, the *Summa* tries to reconcile the two approaches by including both within an Augustinian theory of knowledge. The Augustinian light of truth which the soul finds within itself and in which are contained all those things which are true becomes formalized in this *Summa* and is expressed as basic, primary notions: that of "first being," that of "first true," that of "first good." The mind is innately equipped with these first notions which together are the likeness of God in the soul. In the light of these notions, one may either regard sensible being and recognize that such being is not eternal, is caused, has a cause, or one may contemplate the notions themselves and thereby be assured that there exists a transcendent being, God. Sensible experience of changeable being may provide knowledge of God as Cause; but such experience may also be the occasion for the soul to become aware of those innate notions whereby it can know Good as Being, Truth, and Goodness, and thereby be assured that He exists. For example, becoming aware of the presence in us of the notion of the first good, we see that The Best (the *optimum*), since it *is* the best, must truly exist. In the very understanding of that which is "best" we must include "existence," since the best is that than which nothing is better. But actual existence is better than potential existence; and both are superior to nonexistence. Therefore, that entity than which nothing is better necessarily and actually exists. Although similar to the ontological argument of Saint Anslem, the argument in the *Summa* adds this consideration: our ability to argue in an *a priori* manner about God rests upon the possession of these innate notions which, as natural to the soul, avoid the problem of arbitrariness in our original concept of God. Insofar as this source of knowledge of God is *a priori* and the ground of other knowledge, we can have a more certain knowledge of Him than of creatures; insofar as these innate notions carry their own guarantee for necessarily asserting actual existence, the soul reflecting upon them cannot fail to know that God does truly exist.

The *Summa* presents and accepts seven definitions of the soul, which are distinguishable one from another only insofar as they view the soul from different aspects; the soul is understood from its cause ("the soul is a God-like breath of life"); from its relation to a body ("the soul is a certain substance which participates in reason and is suited to rule the body"); or from its powers ("the soul is a spirit which is intellectual, rational, always living, always in motion, and capable of a will for both good and evil"). In general, the powers of the soul are one with the substance of the soul, since the soul could neither subsist (be a substance) nor be understood except by its powers, nor could its powers be understood without reference to its substance. But since in the soul, as in all entities except God, being and activity are not one and the same, so the essence of the soul, which expresses its being, and the powers of the soul, which express its activity, are not one and the same. The distinction between substance and essence is rooted in the distinction of Boethius between that which is (*quod est*) and that by which it is (*quo est*), a distinction which the *Summa* retains, regarding it as the most basic of all distinctions and as the ultimate source of distinguishing between God (in whom *quod est* is the same as *quo est*) and all creatures (in which these principles form a composition).

The rational powers of the soul may be divided in different ways according to the pseudo-Augustine treatise, *On the Soul and the Spirit,* or according to Damascene or Aristotle; but the divisions are not incompatible, for the cognitive functions may be related, for example, to different intelligible objects (reason, intellect, intelligence: the division of psuedo-Augustine); to the process of abstraction (material, possible, and agent intellects: the division of Aristotle); or to different cognitive attitudes about propositions (opinion, certitude, and memory: divisions of pseudo-Augustine and Damascene). Augustinian illumination and Aristotelian abstraction are accomodated as the *Summa* appears to identify the agent intellect with the presence in the soul of the innate first notions, a divine likeness, the light in which knowledge of all things becomes possible. The description of the agent intellect as the soul's own power bears witness to the inroads which the newly discovered Aristotelian philosophy was making in the first half of the thirteenth century. At the same time, however, the *Summa of Brother Alexander* anticipates, although in a less than systematic and complete way, the central position which St. Bonaventure came to occupy as a stronghold and rallying point of Augustinian thought, especially among Franciscan philosophers and theologians.

F.J.C.

SUMMA CONTRA GENTILES

Author: Saint Thomas Aquinas (1225-1274)
Type of work: Theology
First transcribed: 1259-1264

PRINCIPAL IDEAS ADVANCED

It is a task of wisdom to present the truths of the Catholic Faith and to refute the errors opposed to them; these truths cannot fully be understood or compre-

hended, but knowledge casts light on truths of faith and shows that arguments advanced to oppose such truths are not conclusive.

A consideration of the divine nature, and of the creatures God has made suggests that God is the end to which all creatures tend.

The *Summa contra Gentiles* is divided into four books, and to discover what Saint Thomas's intention was in writing we can hardly do better than to consult Chapter 2 of Book I, in which this point is discussed. Thomas begins by saying that nothing is more perfect, sublime, useful, or satisfying than for a man to devote himself to the pursuit of wisdom, for wisdom deals principally with divine things, and the pursuit of wisdom is conducive to eternal life. Saint Thomas goes on to say that in his book he intends to manifest the truth of the Catholic faith and to eliminate errors contrary to that truth and that, in doing this, he will be engaged in a sapiential task.

There is a legend to the effect that the *Summa contra Gentiles* was composed by Thomas as a missionary manual for Saint Raymund of Peñafort, who sought to convert the Moors in Spain. Scholars are unanimous in treating this legend skeptically; they point out, among other things, that if this had been indeed the intention of Aquinas, he certainly did not devise a very practical instrument for facilitating a missioner's task. As a matter of fact, it seems unlikely that Thomas had any such immediately practical purpose in mind. The positions he refutes in the course of the work were not chosen solely because some contemporary held them; indeed, many of the positions Thomas is concerned to refute were held by men long since dead, and it seems a little otiose to attempt their conversion *ex post facto*. The truth is that the *Summa contra Gentiles* is a work of wisdom and that the task of the wise man is to order. Thomas wished to present the truth of the Catholic faith in an orderly fashion, and since every science proceeds by considering opposites, just as medicine is concerned with both health and sickness, so in dealing with the truth, Saint Thomas must take error into account and use established truth to refute the contrary error. There is good reason to believe that the title under which his work has come down to us, a title which has caused so much speculation as to the purpose of the work, is not authentic. Scholars tell us that the work ought rather to be titled, on the manuscript evidence, *On the Truth of the Catholic Faith*. In short, the work is a presentation of Catholic theology, a sapiential and chiefly contemplative effort, and should not be treated as a manual of apologetics or *vademecum* for missionaries.

The books of the *Summa contra Gentiles* are divided into chapters; this practice distinguishes this work from the *Summa theologiae* and *Disputed Questions*, both of which employ the articles as the basic unit. Saint Thomas compares Books I and II of *Summa contra Gentiles* in the following manner. Aristotle has said that operation is of two kinds, immanent and transient. Thus, in the first book Thomas has dealt with activities immanent to God; in the second he discusses the effects of God's transitive action; namely, creatures. In the first chapter of Book III, Thomas writes, "Since in Book One we treated the perfection of the divine nature and, in Book Two, the perfection of His power, insofar as He is the maker and lord of all, we must in this third book treat of His perfect authority and dignity, insofar as He is the end and director of all things." In the fourth book, Thomas discusses the Trinity, the Incarnation and Sacraments, the resurrection of the body, and the last things. Before examining selected topics from these four books, it is best to consider the methodological chapters with which Saint Thomas begins the *Summa contra Gentiles,* for these early chapters cast considerable light on the nature of theology and on its distinction from philosophy.

In Chapter 3 of Book I, Saint Thomas makes an important distinction: "There is a twofold manner of truth in those things we say about God. For some things are true of God which surpass in every way the capacity of human reason, for example, that God is one and three. Some things, however, natural reason can grasp, like 'God exists,' 'God is one' and other similar truths which even philosophers have demonstratively proved, led by the natural light of reason." The distinction of these two kinds of truth concerning God follows from the fact that, since the principle of demonstration is the quiddity of the substance concerning which we want to demonstrate something, if there are different ways of knowing a substance, there will be different ways of knowing things about that substance. Our mind, in the present life, begins to know in reliance on the senses and it can know what is not sensible only insofar as knowledge of it can be gotten through what is sensed. Now it happens that we are able to know some things about God by way of sensible things, but this kind of knowledge is oblique and surely not comprehensive or exhaustive. Thus, there are some truths about God which are closed to the natural reason.

Although there are these two kinds of truth concerning God, one that can be attained by natural reason and the other which exceeds the capacities of man, Thomas goes on to argue that it is fitting that *both* have been revealed by God. Why, if there are truths concerning God that a man can learn by his own power, did God reveal them to man? Saint Thomas enumerates three reasons why this was done. The first is that, while such knowledge is possible for man, the fact is that very few men attain it since there are any number of impediments to the pursuit of truth: some men are constitutionally indisposed to a life of study; others do not have the time for such study since their days are taken up with securing the necessities of life; finally, some are lazy. In short, the truths concerning God accessible to natural reason are not evident truths which anyone might discover in a brief time. Saint Thomas writes "Many things must be known prior to that knowledge of God which reason can undertake; practically the whole of philosophy is ordered to knowledge of God and because of this, metaphysics, which treats of divine things, is the last part of philosophy to be learned. So then it is only with a great deal of effort that inquiry will arrive at the aforesaid truth. A second reason why such truths have been revealed is that, the few who have achieved philosophical knowledge of God have done so only late in life; but knowledge of God is important not only late but also early in life. The third reason is that in attaining some truth concerning God philosophers have mixed with them many errors." Faith gives fixity and purity to such truths, and thus Thomas sees a fittingness in the fact that God has revealed not only what is beyond our capacity but also what in principle is within it.

Thomas now turns to the second kind of truth about God; the kind we cannot grasp because of our connatural mode of knowing which entails reliance on the senses. Is it fitting that a man should believe things which are beyond the reach of his reason? Man is destined for something far beyond the present life, and it is imperative that this goal be set before his mind. Philosophers regarded their task as that of leading men away from the things of this world to the contemplation of divine things; revelation that gives truer knowledge of what the philosophers recognized, for we know God truly only when we believe Him to be above everything that is possible for man to think concerning Him. Now it is brought home to man in a forceful way that he cannot understand God when things are proposed for man's belief that exceed his powers of understanding. Revealed truths about God also have the effect of quelling presumption, since one who has a tendency to trust himself, to consider himself the measure of what he does or does not know, is humbled by the recognition of the limits of his capacity. Thus there are benefits to be derived from believing truths concerning God which we cannot understand.

But does not this readiness to assent to what men do not and cannot know indicate a certain weakness of character? No, Saint Thomas argues, there are occasions for faith which, while they do not make evident the truths of faith, make assent to those truths a rational act. Thus, one may be moved by witnessing the miraculous cures of the sick, the raising of the dead, the altering of the courses of the heavenly bodies and, even more marvelous, by the spectacle of simple and ignorant men, upon reception of the gifts of the Holy Ghost, being rendered wise in one fell swoop. It is not by the promise of pleasure, indeed it is despite torture and impending martyrdom, that huge numbers of persons not only the simple but also the wise, gave their assent to those truths of the Christian faith which they cannot understand. Saint Thomas remarks that such phenomena of faith cannot be dismissed as chance occurences; the only explanation is to be found in the hand of God, the more so since they were predicted by His prophets. Saint Thomas finds in the wonderful conversion of the world to the Christian faith the most striking sign of its truth; this assent has never been easy, and yet it has been given under the impetus of God's grace.

Saint Thomas is concerned to show that there is no contradiction between natural truths and those presented to faith. He argues that both kinds of truths come from God; natural truths are discovered insofar as God, the author of our nature, provides us with the means of grasping them; supernatural truths are known insofar as they are revealed by God. These truths, natural and supernatural, are consistent, for God would be in contradiction with Himself if He were the source of conflicting truths. Further, Thomas continues, the contrary of truth is falsehood, and two truths, though their immediate sources differ, cannot be in conflict. The human mind, which comes to know by dependence on the senses, finds traces of God the Maker in sensible things and is able to affirm certain truths concerning Him. Truths of faith cannot be understood in this life; the essence of faith is that it is an assent to what is not seen. Nevertheless, human reason ought to attempt to bring to bear on truths of faith what it can know of God independently of faith: "It is nonetheless useful in reasoning of this kind, no matter how weak it be [that the human mind exercise itself] so long as it does not presume to comprehend or demonstrate, since nothing is more gratifying than even a minimal and imperfect consideration of the highest things."

In Chapter 4 of Book II of the *Summa contra Gentiles,* Aquinas compares the way the philosopher and theologian consider creatures. Christian doctrine includes truths about creatures, since some similitude of God is found in men and since errors about men can result in errors concerning God. This indicates that the theologian's treatment of creatures differs from the philosopher's: "For this reason the philosopher and the man of faith [the theologian] consider creatures differently, for the philosopher considers those things which pertain to them according to their own nature, for example, that fire rises. The man of faith is solely concerned with that in creatures which pertains to them insofar as they are related to God, for example, that they have been created by God, are subject to God, and the like." Thus, what faith tells us about creatures is no substitute for the knowledge we gain of them by studying them in themselves.

As Saint Thomas makes clear in Chapter 9 of Book I, the man of faith brings to bear on the truths he believes the truths he knows naturally. In short, the theologian employs philosophy to cast what light it can on the truths of faith. This sometimes takes the form of the refutation of arguments which opponents of the faith use to show that the tenets of faith are false. Such arguments the man of faith knows to be fallacious, and he must show they are. There are other arguments which are merely likely and may provide an occasion for meditation and solace to the faithful but would do little to refute an adversary. Saint Thomas warns that it is important not to present the second sort of argument as if it were of the first sort, for this would give one who lacks the faith an occasion for deriding it. In a more positive way, he continues, truths of philosophy may be employed to confirm the truths of faith, to refute adversaries who employ philosophy, and by a mounting number of such arguments to display the truth of faith.

It has often been debated whether the *Summa contra Gentiles* is a theological work. The doubt reposes partly on the fact that the first three books deal with truths which are accessible to reason; only the fourth seems to consider truths known through revelation. It is now generally held that this difference in no way calls into question the theological character of the work as a whole. The starting point of Aquinas is always what has been revealed. Moreover, the contrast in Chapter 4 of Book II, cited above, is taken to be conclusive proof that Thomas regarded what he was doing as theological. His task was to manifest the truths of faith and to oppose errors contrary to those truths. The order of the work is a theological order; Thomas begins with God and goes on to creatures, but this route is not that which can be taken by the human mind unillumined by faith. Only one who accepts Christian revelation, by which God has revealed Himself to men, can begin with God and go on to view creatures in the light of his knowledge of God. The philosopher, on the other hand, must advance to knowledge of God in the light of his knowledge of creatures. It may be said that Thomas is clearer elsewhere as to the character and method of theology, but it does not thereby follow that his method in the *Summa contra Gentiles* is wholly obscure.

The *Summa contra Gentiles,* despite the title by which it has come to be known, is not a polemical work; it is not a manual for missionaries; it is not concerned with the actual errors of the historical situation in which Saint Thomas found himself. Like the *Summa theologiae* it is addressed to believers and offers to them a presentation of the truths of faith argued for with reasons which vary in quality, reasons which employ philosophy to clarify the nature of the body of doctrine proposed for our belief. Moreover, philosophy is employed to reject errors opposed to faith. The work, in short, is a sustained meditation on revealed truth, presented in an orderly fashion and with reference to those truths which are knowable apart from faith. Far less complex and a good deal shorter than the *Summa theologiae,* the *Summa contra Gentiles* is a work of essentially the same kind as the later *Summa.* A comparison of parallel treatments in the two *Summae* reveals that those in the *Summa theologiae* are more terse, more effective, more cogent. In the *Summa contra Gentiles* Thomas regularly gives a sizeable number of arguments for the same point, and this method indicates that no one argument is particularly conclusive. On one major point of doctrine, however, the *Summa contra Gentiles* is more subtle and complete and that is in its presentation of the proof from motion for the existence of God.

By way of conclusion, it may be said that if Thomas had not written the *Summa theologiae,* the *Summa contra Gentiles* would loom as a much greater achievement than it now appears to be when it is compared with the later work. This is not to say, of course, that the *Summa contra Gentiles* is a negligible factor in the study of the doctrine of Thomas Aquinas, but only that it is almost never the center from which one attempts to grasp the thought of the Angelic Doctor on a particular point. Its literary form makes it an easier work for the modern reader to follow and this ease is augmented by the nature of its discussions. Yet one who may find it a valuable introduction to the theology of Saint Thomas will want to go on to the more mature work, composed, ironically, for beginners, the *Summa theologiae.*

R.M.

ON KINGSHIP

Author: Saint Thomas Aquinas (1225-1274)
Type of work: Political philosophy
First transcribed: 1260-1265

Principal Ideas Advanced

Since unity of peace is the fundamental requirement of political society the rule by one man will be the most effective form of government.

What the good king has and the tyrant lacks is friendship, the greatest worldly good.

The duties of the king include promoting all the material conditions which are conducive to leading a good life, but especially should the ruler preserve the harmony of peace according to which men can progress in a virtuous life.

Since man's last end exceeds his temporal end, kings must be subject to priests, in matters relating to the ultimate end.

The Reverend Ignatius Thomas Eschmann, O. P., in his revision of Gerald B. Phelan's translation of Saint Thomas Aquinas's *De regno, ad regem Cypri* refers to this work as an authentic fragment. Aquinas apparently wrote it early in the 1260's as a gift to Hugh III of Antioch-Lusignan (1267-1284), King of Cyprus. In the time between the death of Aquinas in 1274 and his canonization in 1323 parts of the original work were lost, but Dominican editors made up for this by tacking on to the authentic part a work of Thomas's friend Tolomeo of Lucca (died 1327) entitled *De regimine principum* (*On the Governance of Rulers*). This title, quite popular in the later Middle Ages for works of the genre of which Machiavelli's *The Prince* (written 1513) is but a Renaissance example, came to be used as the title of the combined work, giving rise to the erroneous tradition that Aquinas was the author of a long work on *The Governance of Rulers*. Thus, while this work is in no sense a full statement of Thomistic political theory, or even a sample of Thomas's mature political thought, it nevertheless represents the reflections of a great Christian theologian on the social nature of man and his need for direction in society. It also represents a moral ideal according to which any ruler, monarch, or prime minister, might pattern his regime.

Man is, for Thomas, who follows Aristotle on this point, a social and political animal. He is destined by nature to live with others since he cannot satisfy his needs adequately living by himself. He needs society to help him take care of physical wants, but, more important, he needs others to live virtuously, to give him his education, and to help him attain his final end, God. But when many are working together they require direction in order to attain the unity of peace; otherwise, each man seeking only his own individual good is brought into conflict with others seeking their individual good. Therefore, there must be some governing power directing a society to its common good if there is to be a just society. There may be rulers who direct people for the good of the ruler, but according to Aquinas, this perversion of monarchy, the good rule by one man, is tyranny. Saint Thomas again reflects the influence of his reading of Aristotle's *Politics* in his division of governments by numbers and justice into *aristocracy* and *oligarchy, polity,* and *democracy,* the latter being given to a form of rule "which comes about when the plebian people by force of numbers oppress the rich. In this way the whole people will be as one tyrant."

The purpose of government determines what will be the best kind of government, for the form of government which promises to be most efficient in attaining that end will be best. Aquinas argues: "Now the welfare and safety of a multitude formed into a society lies in the preservation of its unity, which is called peace. If this is removed, the benefit of social life is lost and, moreover, the multitude in its disagreement becomes a burden to itself. The chief concern of the ruler of a multitude, therefore, is to procure the unity of peace." Since it is obvious that what is itself unified can best bring about this unity, it follows that "the rule of one man is more useful than the rule of many."

In the context of his argument it is apparent that Aquinas is concerned to fix or locate responsibility in one man. He is not defending hereditary monarchies as such, but forms of government, be they feudal, democratic in our sense of an elected chief executive, or dictatorial in the benevolent sense, wherein one man takes the initiative and responsibility for promoting the welfare of society. According to his medieval experience this was, for Aquinas, a limited monarchy, for he says: "Then, once the king is established, the government of the kingdom must be so arranged that opportunity to tyrannize is removed. At the same time his power should be so tempered that he cannot easily fall into tyranny."

There is in this treatise *On Kingship* quite a preoccupation with the evils of tyranny. Writing as a theologian to a ruler Saint Thomas extolls the virtues of a good king and the rewards such a ruler will receive from God, but he is also very much concerned with the temptation any ruler might face to be selfish and inconsiderate. Thomas stresses the claim that the corruption of the best form of government results in the worst form of government, and he warns the ruler about the disadvantages of bad rule.

The great loss a tyrant suffers is friendship. In passages which are magnificent in their simplicity Saint Thomas extolls friendship as the greatest of worldly goods: "Friendship unites good men and preserves and promotes virtue. Friendship is needed by all men in whatsoever occupations they engage. In prosperity it does not thrust itself unwanted upon us, nor does it desert us in adversity. It is what brings with it the greatest delight, to such an extent that all that pleases is changed to weariness when friends are absent, and all difficult things are made easy and as nothing by love."

However, should a tyrant come to control one's community, Thomas advises, it would be better to endure the evil one knows than to precipitate violence with its risk of a greater tyrant who might succeed in gaining power after a revolution. Aquinas recognizes the justice of deposing or restricting an evil ruler, but this measure should not be presumptively assumed by private persons, but only by "public authority."

Just how this resistance could come about in a well-controlled tyranny Aquinas does not specify, but the impression is left that he believed it better to pray to God for a redress of grievances than to precipitate the suffering of a civil war, though the door is open to the deposing of an unjust tyrant who has broken his covenant and thus has released his subjects from obedience.

Reflecting on the rewards a king, as a good ruler, might receive, Saint Thomas insists that more is needed than simply worldly glory. Since the glory of this world depends on the opinion of men, who are fickle, it is too perishable a good to reward a good ruler adequately. Rather, if a king were to seek glory, he might submit to the temptation of hypocrisy, seeking the acclaim of men instead of deserving it. A good king should look to God for his reward, since only in God can there be a satisfaction of human desires.

In the Second Book Aquinas takes up some of the duties of a king, and he notes that a ruler can learn something of the requirements of the kingly office by reflecting on the works of God in creating the universe. Assuming that the king is the founder of a city or kingdom, Thomas has the opportunity to speak of geopolitical and sociological conditions as they might characterize an ideal community. He notes the importance of a "suitable place which will preserve the inhabitants by its healthfulness, provide the necessities of life by its fruitfulness, please them with its beauty, and render them safe from their enemies by its natural protection." Aquinas did not judge the role of a political leader to be of the laissez faire variety. He believed the king had to work actively to promote the good life of his people, and the good life included their psychological as well as their material well-being. In the sections that follow there is presented a number of insights into medieval thought on medicine, anthropology, and general sociological matters.

Thomas remarks, for instance, on the problems that arise with merchants: "Since the foremost tendency of tradesmen is to make money, greed is awakened in the hearts of the citizens through the pursuit of trade. The result is that everything in the city will become venal; good faith will be destroyed and the way open to all kinds of trickery; each one will work only for his own profit, despising the public good; the cultivation of virtue will fail since honour, virtue's reward, will be bestowed upon the rich. Thus, in such a city, civic life will necessarily be corrupted."

Aquinas insists that man's last end is a spiritual one and Christian men need the care provided for the faithful "by the ministers of the Church of Christ." The chief priest of this ministry is the Roman pontiff, and Aquinas writes: "For those to whom pertains the care of intermediate ends should be subject to him to whom pertains the care of the ultimate end, and be directed by his rule." This remark reflects, of course, a medieval view of Christendom as a *sacral* society, a state of affairs which no longer exists and which is not considered by such contemporary Thomistic political philosophers as Jacques Maritain to represent a desirable state of affairs, implying as it does the immaturity of political societies with respect to their autonomy. Nevertheless, in Thomas, the work of the ruler to promote the good life of his people in such a way that they are able to enjoy this world and their progress toward the attainment of heavenly happiness is encouraged.

It must be remembered that Thomas was writing as a Christian theologian to a Christian king in the thirteenth century. There are certain principles which are operative in his thinking which are true for all time, but there are other factors which historically will never be repeated. In reading such a treatise one must appreciate the perennial aspects but resist any tendency to take some feature out of context and say that this is an ideal which should be reconstituted today. As Eschmann remarks: "Above all, let the reader be careful to study St. Thomas' answers to St. Thomas' own problems; let nobody expect him to solve other and later questions of political science and practice." Properly read, *On Kingship* can serve as an interesting introduction to Saint Thomas's political thought.

D.J.F.

ON THE POWER OF GOD

Author: Saint Thomas Aquinas (1225-1274)
Type of work: Dogmatic theology
First transcribed: 1265-1267

Principal Ideas Advanced

Power, meaning an active principle of operation, is most perfectly predicable of God.

Action is nothing other than communication of that by which an agent is in act; and since God is purely and absolutely act, the communication of act is eminently befitting of Him.

The creative power of God, which is the same as His essence, causes things to come to be from nothing; because of the absolute perfection of God, His action is productive of being simply, presupposing no subject, indeed, producing the very subject itself.

The relations which exist between creatures and God are nonmutual; that is, they are real predicamental accidents in the creature but only logical in God; creatures are really related to God, but God is not so related to creatures.

Saint Thomas Aquinas's *On the Power of God* is a massive and masterful theological treatise. In keeping with the style of his *Disputed Questions,* Saint Thomas did not organize this work along any strict line of method. That is to say, there is no strict concatenation of questions, so that the reader might proceed from the beginning to the end in uninterrupted sequence. Instead, the topics treated are many and varied as they spring from the spontaneous character of the inquiries which these disputed questions report. The general subject of the *De potentia Dei* is God; specifically, God considered from the point of view of His processions, internal and external. The term "external procession" refers to the manner in which creatures come forth (proceed) from God; the "internal processions" of God are those mysterious and eternally subsistent relationships which are the Divine Persons.

Traditionally, the *De potentia Dei* has been divided into three sections; (1) questions (articles) dealing with the power of God in general and the creative power of God in particular; (2) questions concerning the manner of divine preservation, and what things are to be preserved after the renewal of the world; (3) questions pertaining to the nature of the Trinity, the relations between the Divine Persons. The first set of questions, or book, presents a profound metaphysical analysis of divine power, its scope, and the nature of the creative act of God. The second book inquires specifically into the dependence of creatures on God for their continued being, and into the phenomenon of the miraculous intervention of divine power in the world. The third book is an exhaustive and monumental trinitarian theology, and in it Saint Thomas sets down some of his greatest writing. Indeed, this treatise on the Holy Trinity stands as perhaps his highest accomplishment. It is theology in the purest sense; namely, an inquiry into the very nature of God as Three Persons in One. (Important parallel readings from St. Thomas's other writings would be: *Summa theologiae,* I, 25-48, and *Summa contra Gentiles,* II, 1-31.)

The *De potentia Dei* is principally a theological work, and the topics treated generally concern matters of revelation, for Saint Thomas was not willing to let revelation remain unscrutinized. His theological genius lay in the fact that he could probe into the mysteries of the faith to the very limits of human possibility, and yet never lose his profound awe before the things of God, nor his respect for their essentially mysterious character. Moreover, Thomas had a substantial respect for the power of human reason guided by the principle of true philosophy, and he used for his historical model the achievements of Aristotle. He was convinced that the mysteries surrounding certain articles of faith did not render them irrational; rather, they were simply removed beyond the grasp of human reason during this life. Though man might not entirely comprehend these mysteries, he might, by intensive investigation, at least demonstrate that they involve no contradictions.

The *De potentia Dei* is, then, an example of Saint Thomas's conviction of the harmony of faith and reason. Within the scope of this work are raised myriad problems which occur to the thoughtful mind attending to the fact of God and His relation to the world. The order of the work is theological; that is, no attempt is made to demonstrate the truth of the proposition that God exists. Rather, God as an existential given is simply assumed, but it should be pointed out that the metaphysics of efficient causality, which is central to Saint Thomas's treatment of the creative act and creaturely dependence, is an implicit and powerful suggestion of the necessity of God's existence, if not a demonstration of it.

Saint Thomas begins the treatise

with an analysis of the nature of divine power: What is divine power? What is its source in God? To what is it directed? The power of God, Thomas responds, is the same as the essence of God; this is so because God is purely and absolutely perfect and actual. Such an entitative condition precludes any composition of any sort whatsoever, either of substance-accident or of essence-existence. It is the nature of an active principle to be unlimited in itself, limited only by its reception into a potential principle. Thus, act is of itself fecund and diffusive, overflowing, and therefore creatures, because of the latent power within their forms, can act and cause. The divine nature, then, being supremely actual, is supremely powerful, omnipotent: "Now God is act both pure and primary, wherefore, it is most befitting to him to act and communicate his likeness to other things: and consequently active power is most becoming to him. . . ."

But though God is all-powerful, commensurate with His being completely and perfectly actual, His active power, so rich and fecund in its possibility, is not necessarily directed outside Himself. He is the sufficient object of His own power, just as He is the sufficient object of His own knowledge and His own love. The universe did not spring from the divine power as from some cosmic cornucopia driven by its own internal productivity to the delivering up of things. The universe came to be, observed Saint Thomas, only because it was freely willed by the Creator.

The fact of creation, says Saint Thomas, is indisputable. Our senses give constant testimony to the existence of things. But the question might validly be asked, has this universe *always* been, even though created? Such a question was not a mere dialectical subtlety for Saint Thomas, because it was the explicit opinion of Aristotle that the world is eternal. Saint Thomas answered that from philosophy we may not strictly decide for either the temporal or the eternal position; that is, merely from the point of view of reason, it is a moot question whether the world is temporal or eternal. Thus, Saint Thomas believed that Aristotle was not in serious philosophical error in holding the eternity of the world as a probable philosophical conclusion. Thomas enters into a detailed discussion of this question in his opusculum, *De aeternitate mundi contra murmurantes* (*On the Eternity of the World Against Those Who Are Murmuring*). But in the *De potentia Dei,* which is a strictly theological work, there is no room for such philosophical probabilities. It is certain, insists the author, that the world came to be in time, that it had a beginning. The difficulty for the Christian thinker is to explain its *coming to be,* not its *duration.*

Before the world, says Thomas, there was only God. By means of His active power, at the free command of His omnipotent will, and ordered by His perfect knowledge, the universe came into existence. The universe, we say, proceeded forth from God. Yet, God made it from nothing, not from some subject which preceded the Creation, nor from something of Himself. Where there was only God before, suddenly there was God and His creation. This activity of God causes no change—not in Him, nor in the creation—since there was nothing which could substand the change. He was the same prior to and posterior to the Creation, having relinquished nothing of Himself to His creatures. Rather, simply by the sheer fact of His immense power, the universe began to exist.

More than this, Saint Thomas continues in the *De potentia Dei,* the continued existence of the universe depends entirely upon the conserving power and presence of God. A rough analogy to this divine conservation is the intramental existence which man confers upon his own ideas. They exist only when he attends to them; when he ceases to think of them, they pass again into nothing. Man's greatest active power produces ideas which remain within him; God's infinite power produces things which come to be outside Him. But the dependence is infinitely more final and absolute. Should God cease to attend to the created universe, instantly it would lapse into the vast nothingness from which it had emerged. The divine power not only produces the actors that populate the universe, but it is also the very stage upon which they live and play their parts.

To the mind of Thomas, this relationship between the created universe and God is a relationship of total dependence, so that it is entirely expressed by the fact that the creature proceeds wholly and totally from the power of God. This being so, it is necessary to posit a real predicamental relation in God, since He is in no way *ordered to* creatures. The only *ordering to* which is in God is the triple manner in which He is to Himself, expressed in the sacred mystery of the Holy Trinity.

This mystery of faith comprises the subject for the third book of the *De potentia Dei.* In its series of questions, Saint Thomas takes up the difficult task of showing, as well as human reason may show, that the mystery of the Holy Trinity implies no contradictions. This task he accomplishes through his theory of subsistent relations, whereby he applies the terminology of Aristotle's metaphysics, sublimated by his own insight into the act of existence, to this capital truth of the Christian faith. This effort on the part of Saint Thomas is truly the supreme height to which human reason has been borne. Whether he has succeeded in best stating the conditions of this one great truth of faith is beyond the judgment of man. But it is certainly a testament to Saint Thomas's conviction that the universe is ultimately intelligible, since it has proceeded from an eminently intelligible God.

The *De potentia Dei* of St. Thomas Aquinas, then, stands as one of his theological masterpieces, both from the point of view of the excellence of its subject, and of the masterful execution of the work itself. This series from the *Disputed Questions* presents Thomas the theologian at his best.

J.P.W.

OPUS MAJUS

Author: Roger Bacon (c.1214-1294)
Type of work: Philosophy of science and theology
First transcribed: 1268

Principal Ideas Advanced

By knowledge the Church is governed, the faithful are regulated, the conversion of unbelievers is secured, and those who persist in malice are held in check.

Theology is the mistress of all the sciences, but without the other sciences theology cannot attain its end.

Through reasoning, conclusions may be drawn, but only experience guarantees the certainty of conclusions.

In Europe during the thirteenth century, a century more noted for its interest in philosophy and theology than in natural science, an Englishman named Roger Bacon produced the *Opus majus,* a work concerned with what the author called *scientia experimentalis,* or the science of experience. Because of his interest in the inductive method of knowledge Bacon is considered to be a pioneer in the development of scientific thought.

Bacon prepared himself for his life's labor with an education obtained from two great medieval centers of learning: Oxford and Paris. Upon returning to England he joined the Oxford Franciscans and began to pursue his interest in science and language. It appears that, as a result of his study, Bacon decided to write a great work on philosophy, in which he would correlate the learning of his time and demonstrate how it could be practically utilized in the service of the Church. In 1266 Pope Clement IV (died 1268) provided further incentive by asking Bacon to send the finished product to Rome. Before beginning his *summa,* Bacon composed a prospectus, which was to serve as a basic outline for the projected masterpiece. Seemingly he never wrote his *summa,* but the prospectus became known as the *Opus majus,* and presents an insight into what his great work would have been like.

For the purpose of investigation the *Opus majus* can be divided into seven different sections, each treating a particular aspect of human knowledge. The work as it is arranged is basically an odyssey from the obstacles to truth, through the natural sciences, to the culmination in moral philosophy. Part One begins with Bacon's claim that the unity of knowledge if properly understood can be of great advantage to God's Church, to the civil community, for the conversion of unbelievers, and for resisting the enemies of Christendom. At once he turns to a rather lengthy treatment of various obstacles which prevent man from grasping truth. He writes that since "truth veiled lies hidden in the deep and is placed in the abyss," it is necessary to recognize and banish these obstructions from the human mind. The obstacles are threefold: the submission to weak authority and custom, the influence of prejudice, and basic human frailty. Bacon cautions the student not to believe everything he hears or reads; he should recognize deficiencies in earlier writers and with "all modesty" and "consideration" correct whatever errors he finds. This is the goal which he has established for himself. Bacon warns strongly concerning the danger of ignoring the three obstacles to learning: "For where these three bear sway, no reason influences, no right decides, no law binds, religion has no place, nature's mandate fails, the complexion of things is changed, their order too confounded, vice prevails, virtue is extinguished, falsehood reigns, truth is hissed off the scene."

In the next part Bacon discusses the position of philosophy and its relationship to theology. Recognizing theology as the queen of sciences, he regards it and the other sciences as interdependent. Philosophy for Bacon is an expression of the wisdom of God on the human level. Since truth, no matter where it is found, belongs to Christ, Christians should seek it in the thought of all philosophers, poets, and thinkers. The aim of philosophy is "that the Creator may be known through the knowledge of the creature, to whom service may be rendered in a worship that gives him honor, in the beauty of morals, and in the integrity of useful laws. . . ." Reflecting a dispute dating from the Fathers of the Church, Bacon defends the right of Christians to seek truth among the writings of pagan and non-Christian thinkers. Whether these individuals be prophets of the Old Testament or pagan Greeks, the wisdom found in their words has been given them by God. It is evident that Bacon was influenced by the Augustinian theory of knowledge, for he posits that such thinkers have been illumined by a divine light from God. As for the Greeks, beginning with Thales (c. 640-546 B.C.), the "first of the wise men," God gave them life "to complete philosophy through experience." Thus, for Roger Bacon philosophy is a continuing human experience, an experience which demands discipline. The purpose of the Christian thinker is to use the wisdom of the past and to correct and advance it, until a great synthesis is achieved. The truth discovered in philosophy can ultimately contribute to a better understanding of the Divine Truth as found in theology.

Having shown the relationship between theology and philosophy, Bacon turns to a study of five valuable aids for philosophy, which make easier the discovery of true wisdom: language, mathematics, optics, the science of experience, and moral philosophy.

Bacon condemns medieval intellectuals for their lack of interest in learning foreign languages and for their total dependency on Latin. A knowledge of Greek and Hebrew, he insists, are necessary to understand fully the wisdom contained in the ancient philosophers and in Scripture. (His contemporaries, depending mainly on badly translated copies of the originals, suffered the danger of corrupted texts and false interpretations created by the translators.) Bacon adds that a knowledge of languages is also necessary for the welfare of the civil commonwealth. A training in languages is also helpful in business and commerce, in securing justice, in converting unbelievers, and in repressing those who refuse conversion. Such benefits are more likely to be brought about by the arguments of learned men than by force or violence.

Bacon emphasizes the great loss suffered by Christian scholars because of their linguistic ignorance.

Bacon considers mathematics to be the foundation of all purely scientific knowledge, and he criticizes his fellow Latins for their neglect of this science. Ignorance of mathematics, he says, accounts for their lack of progress in the natural sciences. Mathematics is for Bacon the key by which the prison of ignorance can be opened. He attempts to prove that mathematics is the most basic human science, since its truths are innate; it is the earliest science, and it proceeds from the simple to the complex. The remainder of Part Four is devoted to showing how mathematics can aid man's understanding and can lead to practical accomplishments for humanity and the Church. Bacon also shows how mathematics is the basis of logic, geometry, and the study of the physical universe.

In order to demonstrate the contribution mathematics can make to sacred subjects, Bacon establishes it as the basis for music, a corrected calendar, astronomy, and chronology. Since "the whole course of history is traced through times and generations and ages from the beginning of the world to Christ the Lord, . . . " it is necessary to set the approximate dates of such great events as the Deluge and the years of Christ's life. Furthermore a knowledge of this science will aid man in comprehending the influence of the stars and planets upon world affairs. Finally, mathematics enables man to understand the world through the science of geography. The commonwealth of the faithful must have a clear knowledge of the size and form of the world, the habitable and unhabitable parts, and the location of the various continents and regions. Such a knowledge would contribute towards the development of philosophy, theology, and the Christian Church. Bacon proceeds to describe the various regions of the world, including Africa, the Near East, Russia as the land of the Tartars, Cathay or modern China, and Europe. Thus, mathematics becomes the key not only to the "natural" but also to the "divine" sciences.

The next section reveals a particular interest of Roger Bacon: the science of optics. While for much of his information he depended upon Ptolemy (127-151) and Arabic scholars, his treatment does reveal knowledge gained from his own original experimentation. Beginning with a theory of knowledge, Bacon develops a theory of vision, which explains how the images seen by the eye impress the brain and provide man with the basis for his natural knowledge. The section includes an anatomical study of the eye and its operations, including the influence upon perception of light, distance, and the object seen.

The most interesting and perhaps important section is Part Six, in which Bacon explains his "science of experience." His purpose here is "to unfold the principles of experimental science, since without experience nothing can be sufficiently known." The basic thesis is that while man can reach knowledgeable conclusions through the use of reason, he can not fully understand and comprehend unless the reasoned proof "is accompanied by its appropriate experience." Experience itself must be based on experiment: "He therefore who wishes to rejoice without doubt in regard to the truths underlying phenomena must know how to devote himself to experiment."

The experience which man undergoes is of two types: one is gained through the external senses and the other is obtained through the inner faculties by divine inspiration.

Having explained his science of experience, Bacon complains that his contemporaries are totally unfamiliar with his method and that it is necessary for him to "disclose its excellence and its proper signification." This science is to investigate by means of experimentation the notable conclusions reached by reason in all other sciences. Experiment must be utilized to provide a more complete understanding of the principles attained by reason. To illustrate this method Bacon adds a section in which he applies his method to the rainbow, to the prolonging of life and the hindering of old age, and to the new practical developments, such as explosives and magnets. Finally there is in this science an utilitarian aspect for Christianity. It can promote conversions by revealing the falseness of various superstitions and the illusions of magic.

In the final part of the *Opus majus* Roger Bacon treats of moral philosophy, which he calls the noblest of the five natural sciences. This is the active science "which instructs man as to his relations to God, and to his neighbor, and to himself, and proves these relations, and invites us to them and powerfully influences us thereto." The various laws of human conduct are established by this moral science. Such laws are necessary because of bodily frailty, "which seizes upon the substance of the soul and makes it foolish, and causes it to forget its natural longing and search for the perfection that befits it. . . ." In discussing the relations between subjects and their ruler, Bacon affirms that the prince must frame laws based on justice and "he must do this with the consent of the nobles and of the people. . . ." Next the author takes up personal conduct as it relates to the public good. For this part he relies heavily upon the Roman writer Seneca (c. 4 B.C.-A.D. 65), who is described as the "wisest of men, who was granted a revelation by God to few." A series of long quotations are given from Seneca concerning the effect and importance of the various virtues and vices in human affairs. Perhaps for Bacon this Roman exemplifies the ability of unaided human reason to arrive at a code of human conduct.

Bacon then turns to the subject of religion. A plea is presented for belief in one true religion, which contains the wisdom necessary for the salvation of the human race. He gives a comparison of the various religions in order to demonstrate the superiority of Christianity. It is the most practical because it provides both temporal blessings for man's needs in this world and spiritual aids for the attainment of eternal life. Here the treatise ends abruptly, without a conclusion.

It must be emphasized that much of Bacon's thought was hardly original. He borrowed many of his ideas from the great thinkers of the past. The *Opus majus* is sprinkled with the great names of the past and reveals the profound encyclopedic range of Bacon's knowledge. Among the Greeks and Romans, Plato (427-347 B.C.), Aristotle (384-322 B.C.), Seneca, Sallust (86-34 B.C.), and Cicero (106-43 B.C.) seem to be Bacon's favorites. The Scriptures and the Church Fathers are heavily quoted, along with the two great Arabic thinkers, Averroës (1126-1198) and Avicenna (980-1037). Bacon also utilizes such early medieval writers as Cassiodorus (480-575), Boethius (c. 480-524), Alcuin (c. 735-804), and the Venerable Bede (c. 672-735), among others.

While Bacon was in the tradition of the medieval Catholic intellectual by subordinating all human endeavors to theology, he merits particular appreciation in the modern world for his emphasis on the importance of scientific learning, a method based on experience and experiment, and on the practical utility to be obtained from advances in the natural sciences. By his life and work Roger Bacon proves that the scientific revolution of modern Europe was no sudden development out of a vast waste land, but that it was based in great part on the inconspicuous and prodigious labor of such medieval thinkers as himself.

R.J.K.

ON SPIRITUAL CREATURES

Author: Saint Thomas Aquinas (1225-1274)
Type of work: Theology
First transcribed: 1266-1269

Principal Ideas Advanced

Spiritual creatures are essentially simple; they are purely actual in the order of essence, with no admixture of matter.

Every angel is a species in its own right, for since there is no matter in angelic natures, they may not be multiplied as individuals of a single species.

In spiritual creatures, there is a composition of potency and act; however, this potency is not matter; rather, the simple essence is potential as related to actual existence.

The human soul is both the form of the body and a subsisting spiritual substance.

The power of understanding (possible intellect) and the agent intellect are distinct powers of the soul, individually possessed by each individual man.

This work is one of the *Quaestiones disputatae,* or Disputed Questions, written by Saint Thomas. Each set of such questions is a polished and reworked account of a series of classroom disputations conducted by the author. As was the custom in the great universities during the high Middle Ages, a regular part of the classroom regimen consisted in such disputations. The disputants were students, who defended points of doctrine against the objections of masters and bachelors. At the end of the series of disputes, the master conducting the disputation (in the case in point, Saint Thomas) would offer his *determinatio* or solution to the questions raised. The entire series would then be edited, ordered, and prepared by the master for transcription. Thomas conducted a great number of these classroom disputations, possibly one a week for extended periods over several years.

The *De spiritualibus creaturis* (*On Spiritual Creatures*) is a complex and an extremely important work. In general, it deals with problems concerning the nature of spiritual substance. The work is composed of eleven articles which can be divided into four broad groups: (1) spiritual substance in general (I, II); (2) the human soul *as* a spiritual substance (III, IV); (3) the powers of the human soul (IX, X, XI); and (4) separate spiritual substances, or angels (V, VI, VII, VIII). These problems are treated at length many times by Thomas, both because of their intrinsic importance in Christian doctrine, and because of the controversies regarding their solutions which raged in Thomas's time. Important parallel Thomistic readings on these subjects would be: (1) *Treatise on Separate Substances;* (2) *Disputed Questions on the Soul;* (3) *Commentary on the* De anima *of Aristotle;* (4) *Summa theologiae,* I, 50-64 (treatise on the angels); I, 75-89 (treatise on man).

The thirteenth century was a time of tremendous theological and philosophical ferment and change. The emergence of Aristotle in the West, as a result of the Latin translations of his works by the Dominican scholar William of Moerbeke (1215-1286), brought about a tension between adherents of Aristotelianism and of Augustinianism. The new interest in and fascination with Aristotle, exhibited by such men as the Franciscan, John of La Rochelle (died 1245), and the Dominicans, Thomas Aquinas and Albert the Great, in many instances ran directly counter to the traditional Neoplatonic and Augustinian theology.

These two currents of thought, namely, the Neoplatonic Augustinian and the Aristotelian, generated two theological schools, each of which had a set of standard positions which were held rather uniformly by all its members. The Augustinian school drew its inspiration and doctrine in the main from Saint Augustine, his principal commentators, and the Spanish Jew Avicebron (Ibn Gabirol, 1021-1058). Avicebron's treatise, *Fons vitae* (*The Source of Life*), was widely read and very influential; it was an important source of Neoplatonic doctrine for the thirteenth century schoolmen.

Characteristic positions of this Augustinian school were that all creatures, both spiritual and corporeal, have a material component; that the heavenly bodies are animated; that there is in corporeal substances a plurality of substantial forms; and that the human intellectual soul is identical with its powers. Saint Thomas, as an Aristotelian, takes issue, in his *De spiritualibus creaturis,* with the positions, and he advances against each a contrary theory supported by authority and by closely reasoned arguments.

To the mind of Thomas, the central fallacy of the Augustinians was their theory of spiritual matter. Following Augustine and the general Neoplatonic tradition, these men argued that the main difference between God and creatures was the composite natures of creatures; composite in every instance, that is, of matter and form. Corporeal creatures were held to be composed of corporeal matter and form, while spiritual creatures were held to be composed of spiritual matter and form. Against this theory, Thomas pointed out that they failed to see that not every potential principle was a material principle: "And hence it does not have to be the case that every thing which is in potency in any way whatever must get its potentiality from the pure potency which is matter. And on this point Avicebron seems to have been deceived, in his book *Fons vitae,* since he believed that everything which is in potency, or is a subject, has this character somehow from prime matter."

Thus, for Thomas, there were two orders of created spiritual substance; namely, the angels and human souls. The opinion of the Neoplatonists, that the celestial bodies were animated in the sense of possessing spiritual souls after the manner of human bodies, appeared erroneous to Thomas. There was in his mind no doubt that the heavenly bodies were moved through the agency of spiritual substances (the separate substances of Aristotle), but this union of angel and heavenly body was one of mover to thing moved, not of soul to body.

This distinction is of central importance. The human soul, and for that matter every soul, in united to its proper matter in such a way that it is an intrinsic source of the being of the composite. On the other hand, the heavenly body does not exist in virtue of its connection with a spiritual substance; it exists in virtue of its being informed by a substantial form. Its relation to the spiritual substance is necessary in order for it to move in a circular manner, which is beyond the power of any natural body. In short, the celestial bodies subsist in themselves, independent of spiritual substances; but their circular motion through the heavens is a result of the action of a spiritual substance.

Saint Thomas's whole discussion concerning the relation of spiritual substances to celestial bodies, because it is couched in the geocentrism of Aristotle and the Alexandrian astronomer Claudius Ptolemy (flourished c. 130), might appear to some to be inconsequential. However, this is not quite the case, since Thomas's theory has ramifications which reach well beyond the limited scope of this astronomical point. For example, whether or not the heavenly bodies were to be considered animated would make a capital difference in Saint Thomas's doctrine of the angels. Underlying this whole discussion in the *De spiritualibus creaturis* is Thomas's conviction that the angelic nature is purely formal and spiritual, having no intrinsic relation to matter, or, at best, related to matter only as an extrinsic efficient cause of motion.

In taking up the matter of the spiritual substance which is the human soul, Saint Thomas was participating in a controversy which was raging during the thirteenth century. It was the opinion of Aristotle that the human soul is one, the sole substantial form of the body. On the other hand, the traditional Augustinian and Neoplatonic position was that the human being is the subject of three distinct souls, each of which supposedly perfected man in a progressively higher degree, culminating in the rational and properly human soul. This trinity of forms was advanced by the Augustinian school as a reflection in man of the Holy Trinity.

In response to this position, and in concern with Aristotle, Thomas formulated his theory of the unicity of substantial form, which posited that in man (and for that matter, in all natural substances) there is only one substantial form, which stands in a relation of act to potency as regards matter. Again, this was not a quibbling distinction for Saint Thomas. Bound up in this theory is a wealth of metaphysics. To his mind, the Augustinians failed to grasp two important facts. First, they did not see that among several actual principles, the essentially more excellent immanently contains the perfection and power of the lower; and second, they did not see that the primary effect of substantial form is the communication of substantial being to the composite (hence, Thomas's frequent dictum, *"Forma dat esse"*). Thus, according to the first of Thomas's insights, more than one soul in man is superfluous, since the human soul can do all that the sensitive soul and the corporeal form can do. And according to his second insight, the presence of three actual substantial forms in a man seems contradictory in the light of the primary function of form, namely, the conferring of being upon the substance. One human soul is sufficient to actuate one human being; further substantial forms seemed to Saint Thomas unnecessary.

Another common position of the Augustinian school was that there is no distinction between the soul and its powers. It is the soul itself which knows, loves, and senses, rather than a really distinct intellectual potency, a rationally appetitive power, the sense powers. Such an explanation fails, says Saint Thomas, because it does not take account of our conscious experience of the various powers of the soul passing from a condition of potency to act, and back again, intermittently. Further, the powers of the soul are distinguished by the objects which move them, as contrasted to the Augustinian theory that the powers of the soul are somehow intrinsically specified, and that human sensations are not passions, but rather actions of the soul.

Thus, for Thomas, if the sense of sight is identical with the soul, then, when the human being is not *seeing*, he is not truly *being* human. If, on the other hand, the sense of sight is a power really distinct from the soul itself, its intermittent conditions of potentiality and actuality would not affect the essence of the soul, which remains constantly actual. Moreover, this view seemed to Thomas to conform to his experience of the fragmentary and sporadic nature of the conscious life: "And hence, since in no creature is its own activity its own actual being, but this is proper to God alone, it follows that the active power of no creature is its essence; but to God alone is it proper that His essence is His power."

In the *De spiritualibus creaturis*, Thomas also considers two positions which are not strictly Augustinian, but Arabian-Aristotelian; these are the problems of the possible intellect and the agent intellect, problems which receive numerous treatments in Thomas's other works, but are included here because they pertain especially to that spiritual substance which is the human soul. It was the opinion of several of the great Moslem Aristotelian sages that men understood by some sort of a participation in the powers of the agent and possible intellects. To the mind of Saint Thomas, it was absurd to hold a separated possible intellect; for, since the possible intellect is the very power of human understanding, it seemed to him contradictory to have the very thing that constituted man as man separated from man.

However, regarding the opinion that the agent intellect is separate from man, Saint Thomas is more tolerant in the *De spiritualibus creaturis.* Several of his Augustinian contemporaries had adopted this view, construing it to be the same theory as the Divine Illumination theory of Saint Augustine. Thomas, reverently interpreting Augustine, did not hold such an opinion to be indefensible. But he argued that such was not the opinion of Aristotle.

The *De spiritualibus creaturis* is, therefore, primarily a brief defense by Saint Thomas of several of his theories against the assertions of the Augustinian and Neoplatonic school. Most of the topics treated in this work are more fully handled in his other writings. But this set of questions forms a clear and nonpolemical statement of the Thomistic doctrine of spiritual substance.

J.P.W.

ON FREE CHOICE

Author: Saint Thomas Aquinas (1225-1274)
Type of work: Philosophy of free will
First transcribed: 1268-1269

Principal Ideas Advanced

An inclination follows upon every form; since the human form is intelligent and rational, the human will, which is the inclination which follows this form, is a rational inclination.

Because the human intellect knows universally and hence is not directed naturally to any particular, the will as the consequent inclination is undetermined to any one singular.

The will is moved in two ways: first, it is specified and thus moved by an apprehended form in the intellect; second, it exercises itself; that is, it moves itself to action in a certain sense.

The will is not moved necessarily except by the absolute and perfect good; no particular good necessarily moves the will.

The treatise *On Free Choice* is actually the sixth question of the *Disputed Questions on Evil,* written by Saint Thomas Aquinas. The problem of human freedom is a central concern for every Christian moralist. Around the problem of human freedom revolve a number of related problems concerning punishment, reward, praise, and merit, matters which make up the subject matter for moral theory. Moreover, the Christian thinker is committed to a theory of freedom by the very fact of his religion, which teaches that it is by free acceptance or rejection of God's plan that man gains or loses eternal beatitude.

Thus, for Saint Thomas, there is no

question as to whether or not man is free. The truths of faith demand that the Christian thinker hold to human freedom. But the deposit of faith does not explicitly define in what sense man is free, or, put another way, the dogma of human freedom does not describe in detail the psychological processes which determine or terminate in the free act. This is a significant area of speculation for the Christian philosopher-theologian, and Saint Thomas formulates a unique and satisfying theory, in keeping with the systematic lines of his new Aristotelianism.

It must be borne in mind that Saint Thomas never used the term "free will"; he always spoke of "free choice." To his mind, the will *in its nature* is not free. Every power which is end-seeking has a certain inherent tendency toward the end which will perfect it. Thus, of its nature, the will is necessarily directed toward union with God. But the human being, in this life, reaches God by a tremendous number of intermediate acts, which stand as means to this ultimate end. Because none of these means is the perfect good which is God, who is the natural end of the will, the will is not necessarily moved by any one of them. Rather, the will acting in concert with the intellect makes rational options for this or that individual action, and it is in this rational choosing that the human being is free.

It must be remembered that Thomas was an "intellectualist," meaning that he considered intelligence to be the primary and most perfect human perfection. This conviction carried over into his theory of human freedom. Man is ultimately free, Thomas insisted, because man possesses intelligence. Only an intellectual being can be free in any meaningful sense. It is because man has intellectual knowledge, which is universal and directed to the whole of being, that the human will can be indeterminate in its options. Man is free, to the mind of Saint Thomas, because man is rational. The action of the will, whereby man opts for one thing or another, necessarily depends upon conscious rational advertence. Action which is not counseled by reason is neither human nor free.

This emphasis on reason is not intended to derogate the role of will in human freedom, for the will as the power or tendency to choose is absolutely necessary to human free activity. But what Saint Thomas emphasizes is that it is the *man* who is free, not the will or the intellect. Man is free in that he makes choices, and he is free because he is reasonable and because he tends toward those things which he knows to be most reasonable. The will and the intellect as human powers are intimately intertwined in the phenomenon of human action; each contributes its own specific character to human action. The intellect contributes rationality, and the will contributes tendency, moving power. The product is a free choice, which is a reasonable and active option.

Saint Thomas shows in this treatise exactly what human freedom consists in. His conception is definitely not the conception of many modern thinkers. For them, human freedom or "free will" means an absolute and spontaneous unlimitedness, a complete lack of restraint or restriction. But, according to Thomas, human freedom, far from being unlimited, is conditioned by many things: by passions, habits, violence, and ignorance. In so far as the reason of man is clouded or encumbered by such limitations, so will the freedom of his action be impaired.

Nor, for that matter, is freedom the *sine qua non* of human existence. It is not an absolute and ultimate character of the human person. It is, rather, one of many powers which man is capable of exercising. Intelligent, rational men may, but need not, freely choose. Indeed, that one action which is the ultimate end of man and his sole reason for existence, union with God in the beatific vision, is not free. When the human will is confronted by the unimaginable splendor of God, it may not reject this vision. But the act of beatific union is still eminently human because it is rational and voluntary, in the sense that the will moves man toward the union.

This theory of Saint Thomas, succinctly expressed in the sixth question of the *De malo,* is in full accord with the demands of faith. For, man is truly free, and he is responsible for his acts. He is free and responsible for his acts because he possesses a rational soul. Because man can know intellectually and immanently desire and tend, man can opt for one thing in this life or another. The options are a result of his intelligence and will power acting in concert.

But yet another difficulty concerning human freedom arises for the Christian theologian. The foregoing analysis concerns natural man; that is, man considered purely from the standpoint of his unaided nature. But the Christian revelation adds an entirely new dimension to human nature, because that revelation tells of the divine operation in the world by grace. Grace is absolutely necessary for man to make a salutary act. Grace has the effect of giving impetus to human action. Thus, Christian theology has the additional difficulty of explaining how it is that man may act freely under the influence of divine grace.

This problem was one of the central issues in a famous theological debate which raged during the centuries succeeding the life of Saint Thomas, a debate concerning the relation between divine knowledge and human freedom. The debate centered around two principal positions formulated by two Spanish Thomists, the Dominican Domingo Bañez (1528-1604) and the Jesuit Luis de Molina (1536-1600). For that matter, the dispute has never been adequately settled, and the problem remains one of the wounds in Thomistic theology even to this day because the debate has begotten so much bitterness.

Nonetheless, the doctrine of Saint Thomas regarding human freedom remains one of the classic formulations. It emphasizes the important fact of the substantial unity of man, and it insists that the activity of man flows from the whole rational person. Thomas's insistence upon the reasonable character of all truly human action preserves both man's dignity and man's destiny.

J.P.W.

ON THE SOUL

Author: Saint Thomas Aquinas (1225-1274)
Type of work: Philosophy of the soul
First transcribed: 1269-1270

Principal Ideas Advanced

The human soul, the substantial form of the body, is united to the body directly and immediately.

The soul is present wholly in the whole body and wholly in every part, since it is the very actuality of the whole and of each of its parts.

Each man possesses a possible intellect and an agent intellect, which, as powers of the soul, are distinct from the soul.

Saint Thomas Aquinas's treatise called *On the Soul* is an exhaustive inquiry into the nature of man, the union of his soul and his body, and the powers proper to him. In this work, the author does not proceed in a strictly philosophical manner; that is, he does not begin by analyzing living beings in general and then proceed argumentatively to the essential difference of man. He does use such a philosophical order in his *Commentary on the* De anima *of Aristotle,* but in the *Disputed Questions on the Soul* the order is more theological, similar to that in his treatise on man in the *Summa theologiae.*

This treatise is a report of a series of actual debates (hence, the title, *Quaestiones disputatae de anima*); the only formal order in such medieval classroom disputations was the intrinsic order of each actual question (article). The order among the various questions was purely a matter of the exigencies of the time and occasion of the disputation. The extremely formalistic character of the disputations of later and decadent Scholasticism is completely foreign to these thirteenth century classroom exercises. In the later Scholasticism, the dispute became an end in itself, and logic became the measure of truth in all cases. Thus, the able disputant was one who could begin with one thesis and then, by means of perfect deductive logic, assemble a concatenation of arguments leading to foregone conclusions.

Indeed, the very manner of the statement of questions emphasizes the difference between these two ages. In the dynamic metaphysical exchanges of the thirteenth century, of which this series is an example, the question was always introduced as, for example, "*whether* the soul . . . ," opening the matter to a real dialectical scrutiny. However, during the period of decline, the statement of the thesis would begin, "*that* the soul . . . ," all those present being fully cognizant of the outcome, which outcome was inescapable because the structure of the arguments which led up to it would be logically flawless. In a word, the thirteenth century was metaphysically dynamic, with meaningful questions being asked, and varying solutions being hotly upheld; but within several centuries, the questions had become categorized, the answers settled, and the case finished. What remained for the student of philosophy was not the man-universe encounter which had brought such great joy to Saint Thomas and his contemporaries in the morning of university learning. Rather, what was left was simply the mastering of the formulae, which expressed a tidy universe reduced to complete and exhaustive intelligibility.

The *Disputed Questions on the Soul* is, then, a treatise on man. Important parallel readings from other works of St. Thomas would be: *Summa theologiae,* I, 75-89, *Summa contra Gentiles,* II, Chapters 56-90, De *spiritualibus creaturis,* and *Commentary on the* De anima *of Aristotle.*

The series of problems which Thomas takes up in his *Disputed Questions on the Soul* are for the most part occasioned by the disputes which raged during the thirteenth century concerning the nature of man. There were at that time three principal philosophical positions regarding man and his nature: (1) the Augustinian and Neoplatonic school, (2) the moderate Aristotelian school, and (3) the Averroist-Aristotelian school. The Augustinians derived their principal doctrinal positions from Saint Augustine, and the Neoplatonists, Proclus (410-485), Plotinus (204-270), and Avicebron (1021-1058). Representatives of this school were the thirteenth century Franciscans, notably Saint Bonaventure. The moderate Aristotelians, best represented by Saint Thomas Aquinas, drew inspiration from Aristotle as guided and corrected by the Faith. Finally, the Latin Averroists held as their authority Aristotle as interpreted by Averroës (1126-1198), the great Moslem Aristotelian commentator. Probably the greatest among these adherents was the Parisian arts master, Siger of Brabant (flourished 1270).

The Augustinian school was the entrenched philosophical and theological orthodoxy. Certain of its conclusions had been approved doctrine for nearly a thousand years. Thus, the emergence of Aristotle in the West, about midway through the thirteenth century, and the philosophical revolution which the discovery of his works portended, caused the older Augustinians to regard the new Aristotelian school as dangerous, or, at least, suspect. This suspicious attitude by the old order, that Aristotle's philosophy was ultimately incompatible with the truths of faith, led finally to the Paris condemnations of 1270.

Central to the disputes among these three factions was the theory of the nature of man. This was so, because any formulation of a philosophy of man during the Middle Ages required a consideration of spiritual substance, union of spirit and matter, the problem of intellection, and the possibility of man's being a one (*unum per se*). These particular problems were precisely the points of contention among the various schools. In his *Disputed Questions on the Soul,* Saint Thomas presents his position on these points of controversy.

It must be pointed out that the disagreements among the various schools of the thirteenth century were not absolute. The schools shared a common fund of truths given by the teaching authority of the Church. All three agreed that man is in some sense both material and spiritual, that man knows things, and that the rational soul of man is immortal. But between each of these doctrinal poles, there was to be found a whole spectrum of differing shades of interpretation. For instance, granted that man is both spiritual and material, is he two substances? Or, if he is one substance, what sort of union can link spirit and matter? Further, granted that man has a rational, immortal soul, is this the *only* soul actually in man, or does he not need a living principle for every level of life; namely, vegetable, animal, and rational?

The great theoretic triumph of Saint Thomas's philosophy of man is his assertion that the rational soul, a subsistent thing in its own right, is also the sole substantial form of the body. There is implicit in this theory a beautiful economy, since it salvages the spiritual nature of the soul and does away with the cumbersome multiple forms supposed by the Augustinians. However, this position begets one great theoretic problem; namely, the substantial unity of man. If the soul is a subsistent thing (*aliquid subsistens*), it must be a substance, since only substances can subsist. But if it is a substance in its own right, and constitutes another substance (man) in its formal union with the body, how can man be said to be a one? These two considerations, then, are the central foci of Thomas' *Disputed Questions on the Soul:* (1) how can the subsistent soul be the substantial form of the body, and (2) how can the resultant composite be a substantial unity?

Saint Thomas begins his *Disputed Questions on the Soul,* then, by asking how the soul can be a form (meaning a determining principle of matter), and yet be called a particular thing. In other words, how can the soul be both a principle of a thing (this man), and a thing in its own right? Thomas answered that we must simply consider two facts about the soul: First, it performs intellectual operations, and must, therefore, be a spiritual and subsistent thing: "Consequently the human soul's mode of existing can be known from its operation. For, inasmuch as the human soul has an operation transcending the material order, its act of existing transcends the body and does not depend on the body." Second, it is the source of life in man, since it confers living existence on the composite, which is the function of a form: "Moreover, vital activity [vivere] is the act of existing [esse] of living things. Consequently the soul is that which gives the human body its act of existing. Now a form is of this nature. Therefore the human soul is the form of the body."

In insisting that the soul is the substantial form of the body and a principle of the composite man, Saint Thomas avoided the Platonic extreme of viewing the soul as completely apart from the body and related to it only as a mover. At the same time, by insisting that the soul is something subsistent, Thomas provided a context for arguing to its immortality.

The human soul, then, as a spiritual substance with an act of existence proper to itself, is, at the same time, the substantial form and actual determining principle of the body. Moreover, this union of body and soul is immediate; that is, the soul is the direct and sole formal actuality of the body. This point is breached by Saint Thomas, not simply as an interesting possibility, but because it is the explicit position of his Augustinian adversaries. Alexander of Hales and Saint Bonaventure, following in the

Augustinian and Neoplatonic tradition, taught that every composite is the subject of several distinct forms, each of which confers upon it a different mode of substantiality. Thus, by a gradual preparation, the body becomes suitable or proportioned to a rational soul, which finally informs the preceding series of forms and matter, through the mediation of these anterior forms. To the mind of Thomas, this simply could not be the case. If it is true that the substantial form of a composite is that which confers substantial existence upon the composite, there can be only one such substantial form in a substance. To have more would be to have a number of substances.

Against the Averroists, Thomas asserted that in each man there is one possible and one agent intellect. To posit a common possible intellect would be nonsense, tantamount to removing from the existing man that which specifically makes him a man; namely, the power of understanding. Moreover, in each man there is an agent intellect, necessary because the world which surrounds him, contrary to the opinion of Plato, provides the objects for his knowledge. This world, being material and singular, is only actually *sensible,* requiring some sort of illumination or sublimation to be intellectually known. This is the reason Saint Thomas, following Aristotle, posited the existence of the agent intellect.

Moreover, the rational soul, which is the substantial form of man, is distinct in the real order from its numerous powers. Because of the existential role of the form in the composite, Thomas felt it impossible to identify the soul with its powers. That is, since the primary function of the soul is to confer substantial existence upon the composite, for it to be identical with its powers would be to have the composite passing in and out of substantial actuality. For, if actually being a man is the same as actually thinking, when the man is not thinking (which seems to be a fact of experience), he is not actually being man.

The *Disputed Questions on the Soul* is an extremely thought-provoking metaphysical inquiry into the nature of man. It was a radical departure from other thirteenth century theories of man, because Saint Thomas reinterpreted the Christian notion of man in terms of existential metaphysics. To say that Thomas's theory of man was a simple Aristotelianism is to slight both Aristotle and Saint Thomas. Without question, the Angelic Doctor borrowed much from the Philosopher, both methodologically and terminologically. But the central dynamism which set Thomas's thought apart from his predecessors and contemporaries as something new was not Aristotelianism; Saint Thomas's principal contribution was his insight into the unique and irreducible character of the act of existing.

J.P.W.

ON THE VIRTUES IN GENERAL

Author: Saint Thomas Aquinas (1225-1274)
Type of work: Moral theology
First transcribed: 1269-1272

Principal Ideas Advanced

Virtues are habits which confer upon man a skill in acting well.

Virtues inhere in the intellect, the will, or the sense appetites.

Virtues by their nature are rather permanent and constitute almost a "second nature."

Good actions which man performs, if repeated, cause the coming into being of natural virtues; on the other hand, the divine power infuses man with supernatural virtues which are beyond his own power to attain.

The treatise *On the Virtues in General* is one of five discussions of the virtues to be found in the *Disputed Questions* of Saint Thomas Aquinas. The five are: (1) *On the Virtues in General,* (2) *On the Cardinal Virtues,* (3) *On Charity,* (4) *On Hope,* and (5) *On Fraternal Correction.* These five works taken together form a thorough and detailed theology of the moral life. *On the Virtues in General,* as the first segment of this series, considers the common or general nature of virtue. Here Saint Thomas inquires into the psychological reality of virtue as a habit, the parts of man that are properly perfected by virtues, and the causes of virtue in man. In the succeeding treatises, he applies these judgments to the individual virtues, illuminating the nature and role of each.

Important parallel readings in the works of St. Thomas would be: *Summa theologiae,* I-II, 49-67, and *Commentary on the Ethics of Aristotle.*

In this general treatise on virtue, Saint Thomas is continuing his program of reinterpreting received Christian theology in terms of Aristotelian metaphysics. The theory of virtue had been a cornerstone of Christian morality since the time of the early Fathers. Thus, Thomas's contribution was to articulate carefully the metaphysics of virtue; that is, he attempted to determine precisely what virtues *are* in the metaphysical sense, to trace their causal origin, and to designate exactly what powers of man are subjects of virtues.

Saint Thomas begins his analysis by stating that virtues are a kind of *habit,* and in so doing he reverts to the definition which Aristotle gave in his *Categories,* that a habit is a disposition which is difficult to dislodge. In metaphysical terms, habits are qualities, actual accidental perfections which reside in the soul or in its powers. The effect of the presence of a habit in a man is twofold: first, the perfection of the power in which it inheres by the conferring upon this power the skill to perform a determined activity; and, second, the permitting of this activity to be done with ease. Thus, a habit is a skill or facility of action which perfects man and which is relatively permanent.

There are in man, according to Aristotle and Saint Thomas, many habits, and habits of several different types. There are, first, habits in the speculative intellect, whereby the mind gains a certain skill or expertise in *knowing* reality in a particular way. For instance, the habit of metaphysics gives the metaphysician the skill of seeing a whole new dimension in the real world that the nonhabituated person simply misses. Those habits which reside in the speculative intellect, and which facilitate specialized knowledges, are called *sciences*.

There are also habits which reside in man's appetitive powers whereby he gains a facility or expertness in *acting*. Thus, a man is benevolent, or magnanimous, or courageous as a result of the inherence of operative habits in his will or irascible appetite; he is, for example, readily and easily benevolent, and this facility for acting benevolently is difficult to dislodge. Such operative skills are called *virtues*. This meaning of virtue—as an operative habit—is the keystone and beginning of St. Thomas's involved and exhaustive analysis of the moral life of man.

Virtues, then, are habits of action, specifically of *good* action. Virtuous action is action in accord with the nature of man, which is precisely what the moral good is. The very derivation of the term, Saint Thomas points out in the *De virtutibus in communi*, suggests this notion of natural power of action, since the word *virtus* (virtue) comes from the word *vis*, which means strength, force, or power.

Thus, virtues are habits which perfect man and render his action more potent, swift, sure, and enduring. The reason these virtues are necessary, Thomas continues, is that certain of the powers of the soul, because they are undetermined to any one specific action, need some extrinsic specification. This need applies to any of the powers which Thomas categorized as "both active and acted upon." A power both active and acted upon, for example, would be the possible intellect. In the absence of its object it is purely passive, but the presence of its object reduces it to a condition of actuality. This feature is characteristic of any simply passive potency. What distinguishes operative potencies is the fact that when they have been reduced to a condition of act by their objects, they then exercise an activity proper to themselves. Thus, after the possible intellect has been made actual by the presence of the sublimated phantasm, it performs its own proper activity; namely, it "says" or expresses that which it knows, forming a mental word. Similarly, the will, after being reduced to actuality, performs its own proper activity; namely, tending toward an object.

Characteristic of powers which are both active and acted upon is the fact that they are not determined to one particular mode or activity. Therefore, the intellect, whose adequate object is the entirety of being, can perform its activity across the whole broad expanse of being. Sciences, then, are needed as determining channels to narrow down the effective possibilities of the intellect and increase its power to act in some specific area (for instance, in knowing geometrically, or metaphysically, or theologically).

By the same token, the appetitive powers can be similarly habituated. But such habituation enables them to perform actions and motions, to move the body to desire or appetite with swiftness and unerring skill. These habituated powers are virtues, and for Saint Thomas, they are real accidents of quality which perfect man and enable him to act well and with ease. Indeed, so helpful are habits, so strong and native, that Saint Thomas called them "second natures," for activity which flows from habits is so befitting and is done with such nonviolent ease that it seems to flow from man's very nature.

In the *De virtutibus in communi,* Saint Thomas states that virtues can inhere in three different powers of man: in the intellect, in the will, and in the sense appetites. Virtues perfect these powers in the sense of conferring upon them a certain specific skill and ease in acting well. Thomas then takes up the question of the manner of the formation of virtues; that is, what is the efficient cause of their coming to be? Put another way, are virtues connatural, part of the very natural equipment of every man, or are they acquired? Virtues as perfections of powers both active and acted upon, are not natural, according to Saint Thomas. If they were natural (a part of the natural equipment of man), every man would possess all the virtues, which is clearly contrary to our experience. The difficulty, then, is to determine what is the causal source of the coming to be of virtues; that is, how do we acquire them?

Man acquires virtue in two ways, according to Saint Thomas. First, he may acquire it naturally, by his repeated actions. The virtue of courage, for instance, is acquired by acting bravely in many instances; after a time, brave action becomes "second nature," and a man can then be said to possess the virtue of courage. In other words, through repeated action, a certain skill and facility in acting a certain way is acquired, and this is precisely the virtue. Thus, for the courageous man, there is no advertent and conscious effort to be brave in the face of danger; he simply *is* brave, because he has acquired this particular operative skill. The habit is permanent and no conscious effort is needed to bring it into play.

Second, man acquires certain virtues by a direct infusion from God. Activities which man cannot of himself perform in order to acquire a virtue must be superadded. For example, man, of himself, cannot exercise supernatural faith. But because God confers upon his intellect the virtue of faith, man is able to believe in the truths of faith and to exercise this act of believing with ease and intensity.

Therefore, there are two basic types of virtue; namely, those naturally acquired by repeated action, and those acquired by divine donation. Saint Thomas was certain that some virtues were natural to man, since the pagans, especially Aristotle, had been well aware of the psychological fact of virtuous habituation. Aristotle, in fact, had compiled an exhaustive table of the virtues in his *Nicomachean Ethics.*

In considering these questions on the virtues, Saint Thomas outlines the broader points of his moral philosophy and theology The moral life, to his mind, is the virtuous life. The moral man is the man who acts well; that is, in accord with his nature. He is enabled to act consistently in such a manner by the virtues which he possesses. But Thomas would not subscribe to the Stoic notion that virtue is for its own sake; rather, he held, virtue stands as a means to man's end. Yet in a certain sense, virtue *is* its own reward, because the product of acting well is the development of virtue, which in turn begets good action.

Nor do the virtues completely stifle man's freedom, for true liberty consists in acting in the right manner for intelligent reasons. The virtues which a man possesses do not cloud the mind nor harshly regiment activity; on the contrary, they liberate him, since they facilitate truly human action by enabling him to use his powers in the best way. Moreover, the virtue which is central to the moral life, namely, prudence, is nothing other than correct *reasoning* about what is to be done. Thus, the very keystone of the moral life is a virtue in the intellect which permits man correctly and reasonably to choose a course of action.

This treatise on the virtues is a central work in the theology and philosophy of Saint Thomas Aquinas. In it he delineates the very heart and core of his moral theory. The work contains a series of questions rich from the point of view of doctrine, and it is more detailed than any other of his investigations of the subject. Before the moral theology of Saint Thomas can be mastered this treatise must be carefully read, for the work is a key to an understanding of his ideas on the good life.

J.P.W.

SUMMA THEOLOGIAE

Author: Saint Thomas Aquinas (1225-1274)
Type of work: Theology
First transcribed: 1266-1273

Principal Ideas Advanced

Since God has revealed Himself to man, a science of which God is the subject is possible; this science, Sacred Doctrine or theology, will treat of all things with reference to God.

Theology should first treat of the divine nature and then of the three Persons in that nature, after which it can treat of creatures, angels first, and then man.

Man, the image of God, has within himself, thanks to free will, the principles of his own acts, and we must treat of the virtues (and opposed vices) whereby human acts are perfected.

Christ, the Incarnate Word, is the way whereby man can attain to his supernatural end, union with God; the sacraments are the means devised for his salvation.

Saint Thomas Aquinas wrote the *Summa theologiae* not for the initiate but for beginners in theology, and in doing so he produced a work which is incontestably the finest achievement of Scholastic theology. In it all previous theology comes to fruition; in a sense it marshals and orders the sum of human knowledge in the light of faith; it is a monument not only to the man who wrote it and the century in which he lived but, one can say without presumption, to the Church itself. At the council of Trent it occupied a place of honor along with the Scriptures and for the popes and theologians of subsequent ages it has gained a place of honor and esteem which make it a document wholly unique. Scholars have been carried away by its majestic and serene order, by its complexity which somehow adds up to simplicity, and by its subtlety which makes its arguments at once suitable material for the prepared beginner and fruitful objects of prolonged meditation for the professional theologian.

Theology did not stop with the writing of the *Summa theologiae;* some questions which were open for discussion at the time of its composition have been closed, and some dogma has been defined contrary to the opinion of the Angelic Doctor, but it is no doubt necessary to say that just as the *Summa* brings together into a commodious yet supple texture the threads of previous theology, so too it is a continuing point of reference for subsequent theology even into our own times. Its author, "whose doctrine the Church has made her own," has been elevated above the ranks of other theologians of all time; he is not simply another thirteenth century master; he is not simply the greatest Dominican theologian; he is not merely the inspiration of one school among several; he is, in the title the Church has given him, the *doctor communis,* the Universal Doctor, everyone's teacher, and in the *Summa theologiae* this teacher operates at the peak of his capacities.

In his prologue to the *Summa,* Saint Thomas sets as his task the treatment of those things which pertain to the Christian religion in a manner which is tailored to beginners in the study. Why was such a work necessary? Saint Thomas writes: "We have thought that novices in this study are much impeded by what various authors have written, partly because of the multiplication of useless questions; partly because things necessary for beginners to know are not treated in the order in which they can be learned but in an order required by the books being exposed or by the occasion of disputation; partly because frequent repetition of the same things induces in the minds of the listener loathing and confusion." Thus, Thomas aims at achieving as brief and lucid an exposition of the subject as the material permits.

Just what is the subject matter of the *Summa theologiae?* What is the Sacred Doctrine of which the first question of the First Part of the *Summa* treats? Interpreters have thought to find a certain ambiguity in the use of the phrase "Sacred Doctrine" in this first question; it seems to cover Scripture, the Faith, and reasoning about what is believed. The answer is to be found in Thomas's work.

Saint Thomas argues that beyond the philosophical sciences which had been developed by pagans, it is necessary that man have knowledge revealed to him by God. Man is ordered to God as to his end and in order to direct himself to his end he must have knowledge of it; over and above what man can learn by reason unaided by revelation, revelation of truths which cannot be so attained is required. Saint Thomas argues that it is fitting that even those things which men can know apart from faith be revealed in order that such knowledge be had easily and without error. Sacred doctrine is a science whose principles are accepted on faith, which is to say that they are known not because of their clarity and evidence but as revealed by God. The formality under which everything is considered in this science is that it has been revealed. The subject of the science is God as He has revealed Himself to men: "Everything in Sacred Doctrine is treated with reference to God (*sub ratione Dei*) either because [the topic] is God Himself, or because it is related to God as principle or end. Hence it follows that God is truly the subject of this science." Needless to say, God can be the subject of a science, in the technical sense of that phrase, only because He has chosen to reveal Himself to men. As Saint Thomas says elsewhere, philosophical theology does not treat of God as its subject but as a cause of its subject.

The principles of Sacred Doctrine are those truths revealed by God; it is not the theologian's task to prove these principles (indeed he cannot); he accepts them on divine authority and strives to conclude other truths from them. As a wisdom, however, Sacred Doctrine must defend its principles against attack, and in doing so it employs philosophy; moreover, it employs philosophy, that is, humanly acquired truths, to deduce other truths from what has been revealed. (These methodological remarks indicate something of supreme importance: the beginning theologians to whom Saint Thomas addresses his *Summa* must already know philosophy, since philosophy is instrumental in performing the task of Sacred Doctrine.)

The *Summa* is divided into three parts, and the second part is subdivided into two parts, the first part of the second part, and the second part of the second part, and usually editions of the *Summa* appear in four volumes based on this division. There is also usually a fourth part, the *Supplement,* for despite his hopes and despite the systematic whole so often praised, Saint Thomas did not live to complete his *Summa.* The *Supplement* garners from Thomas's commentary on the *Sentences* of Peter Lombard treatments of those topics which would have completed the third part in Thomas's design. The First Part of the *Summa* treats of God in Himself; the Second, the moral part of the work, treats of God as the end of the creature; the Third treats of God as the way whereby creatures return to their principle, God Himself.

Apart from doctrinal linkings within each part of the *Summa,* the penultimate unit of the work is the question, which in turn is subdivided into articles. The first article of the first question of the First Part of the *Summa* (which, incidentally, is the convention whereby reference is made to a point of doctrine in the work) adequately illustrates the technique employed. An article poses a question, in this case, "Is it necessary for there to be some other teaching beyond the philosophical sciences?" Immediately after the statement of the point up for discussion, Saint Thomas will indicate that a yes or no answer seems called for because of certain arguments or authorities which are then listed. These arguments or authorities are often called objections, which is perhaps an unhappy way to describe them. After the enumeration of arguments suggestive of a negative answer to the question, Saint Thomas says, "On the contrary," after which there follows a single authority stating an answer in opposition to that of the just listed arguments. Next, Thomas says, "I reply." What follows is called the body of the article, and in it we have Thomas's view as he wants to express it. Once he has done so, he turns to the opening arguments and treats each of them singly, and in doing so he expands and furthers the doctrine of the body of the article. The literary form of the question embodies a kind of dialectic which is controlled by the principles of the science. In the opening arguments, the so-called "objections," Saint Thomas is able to make use of the teaching of his predecessors, and his doctrine is presented within a tradition but also as adjudicating real or apparent divergencies among previous theologians. The selection of the "objections" (three is the average number for an article in the *Summa*) is clearly a matter of great importance; moreover, the order in which they are listed is almost never a random one. The order of the *Summa* reaches down into its smallest parts. So too, the question, which is a cluster of articles, is an ordered whole. The number of articles to a question varies greatly in the *Summa,* but the order in which the articles appear within a question is always important, and commentators have always wisely insisted on this importance. Obviously, then, the order of questions in each part and the order of the parts themselves are the result of careful thought on the part of Aquinas. One can begin to appreciate the reason for the awed praise of this work which, while showing this great conscientiousness concerning the most orderly arrangement of its least parts as well as its greatest, does not thereby become something mechanical and lifeless. From its beginning to the point at which it ended with his life, the *Summa* of Saint Thomas breathes the life of the intellect, exhibiting one of the keenest minds of Western civilization bringing to bear on the truths of Christian revelation all the powers of his own genius as well as the accumulated resources of the preceding centuries.

There are 119 questions in the First Part of the *Summa* which, as we have said, deals with God Himself. We can say more accurately now that it deals with God and the emanation of creatures from Him. It has become customary to think of clusters of questions as treatises; thus, Questions 1-26 of the First Part are called the Treatise on the One God; 27-43, the Treatise on the Trinity. The first twenty-six questions, incidentally (with the exception of the first, of course), are taken to treat of what Thomas calls the *praeambula fidei;* that is, truths concerning God which have been discovered or could be discovered by philosophers; that is, by men without benefit of divine revelation. Thus, in Question 2, Saint Thomas asks whether God exists, and in article three presents the famous *quinque viae,* the five ways of proving that He does exist, proofs which are taken to be valid and independent in their cogency from the faith. God's existence having been established, Thomas goes on to discuss such topics as God's simplicity, His perfection, His goodness, infinity, immutability, eternity, and unity. After the Treatise on the Trinity, Thomas speaks of the procession of creatures from God, who is the first cause of all being. With Question 50, the treatment of the angels, the most perfect of God's creatures, begins. This discussion continues through Question 64. Corporeal creation is next considered, and Thomas, relying heavily on Saint Augustine, discusses the works of the six days mentioned in Genesis. The so-called Treatise on Man begins with Question 75 and continues through Question 102. There is a heavy reliance on philosophy, and the thought of Aristotle, already prominent, becomes here even more so. Saint Thomas's treatment of God's governance of creation takes up the remainder of the First Part.

In his prologue to the Second Part Thomas says that, having treated of the exemplar, God, we must now speak of His image, man, insofar as the latter is a principle of his own works, thanks to free will. The first part of the Second Part of the *Summa* contains 114 questions, which move from a discussion of man's ultimate end, the principles of human acts, the goodness and badness of human acts, through a discussion of the emotions (which are the matter of the moral virtues), habits and virtues, the gifts of the Holy Spirit, the fruits of the Holy Spirit, and sin, to the treatises on law and grace.

The first part of the Second Part treats of common aspects of morality; the second part goes on to more detailed considerations, and it comprises 189 questions. Thomas first considers the special matter of the particular virtues, and he then goes on to discuss various states of life. In treating a given virtue, he discusses the vice opposed to it in order to make for a better grasp of the virtue itself. Aiming at a discussion of virtues, Thomas sees seven basic headings: the three theological virtues, faith, hope, and charity; and the four cardinal virtues, temperance, fortitude, justice, and prudence. In the course of his treatment he discusses in detail the gifts of the Holy Spirit. Mention should be made of the treatment of the contemplative life (see Questions 179-182) which, in the opinion of John of the Cross, succinctly states the heart of the matter.

Saint Thomas finished only ninety questions of the Third Part of the *Summa,* which deals with Christ, who is described as the means whereby man can achieve eternal life: "Because Our Lord and Savior, Jesus Christ, by the testimony of the angel, has delivered His people from their sin, He showed the way of truth to us in Himself, the way whereby we can attain by resurrection to the happiness of immortal life, we must, if we are to complete the task of theology, having considered the ultimate end of human life and the virtues and vices, turn our consideration to the Savior of all and to the benefits He has bestowed on mankind." The Third Part treats of the Savior Himself and of the sacraments whereby we gain salvation, and it ends with a discussion of the Sacrament of Penance, which is completed in the Supplement.

This, then, is the grand schema of the *Summa theologiae,* a panoramic view which begins with God, first as He was known or could have been known even if He had not chosen to reveal Himself to men (although such knowledge is facilitated and saved from error precisely because God did reveal Himself). The suggestion here is that the Christian, reflecting and meditating on what God has revealed, will naturally and inevitably try to bring it into relation to what he knows apart from revelation. The mystery of the Trinity, which is known to us only because God has revealed it, is approached not only by way of what Scripture, the Fathers, the Councils, and the Church have said concerning it, but also with reference to such philosophical notions as nature and person.

It is difficult to single out any one treatise of the *Summa* for special mention, but if Thomas is called the Angelic Doctor, this appellation may be due, at least in part, to the magnificent treatise on the angels (and in part, of course, to Thomas's exemplary purity). The moral part of the *Summa,* while it moves from common to more special considerations, retains a level of discussion which enables its treatments to survive vast social changes and speak to us with continuing meaning today. It is common and understandable to lament the fact that Thomas was not given the time to finish this work, for the treatments of the Incarnation and Passion of Christ sustain the high level and precision of the earlier portions of the work.

It is said that, in his last hours, having been granted a vision, Thomas said of everything that he had written that it was but straw. Doubtless from the vantage point of special revelation and, later, from the vantage point of the beatific vision, all that men have said in the obscure knowledge of faith will seem mere babbling, but this side of paradise, the *Summa theologiae* is surely the greatest achievement of any theologian, for in this monumental work the essentials of Christian belief are presented in an orderly and lucid fashion, for beginners and adepts alike, and with a conviction in which men will continue to see revelation, intelligence, and spiritual commitment.

R.M.

THE HYMNS OF SAINT THOMAS AQUINAS

Author: Saint Thomas Aquinas (1225-1274)
Type of work: Devotional hymns
First transcribed: Thirteenth century

Principal Ideas Advanced

[*Saint Thomas Aquinas sets forth in the language of hymns precise and clearcut dogma on the Blessed Sacrament.*]

Saint Thomas Aquinas, the "Angelic Doctor" (*Doctor Angelicus*), born in the kingdom of Naples about 1225, died at the age of forty-nine years, on March 7, 1274. A member of the Order of Preachers (Dominicans), he led a life of teaching, writing, praying. So magnificent are his monumental works, the *Summa contra Gentiles* and the *Summa theologicae,* that the reader would at first hardly associate him with the gentle and lyrical task of hymnody. Yet in 1263, following the directive of Pope Urban IV, he drew up the Mass and Office for the Feast of Corpus Christi. Four great hymns of his were here included; a fifth, the "Adoro Te Devote," a part of the Thanksgiving after Mass, was in 1570 inserted in the front of the Missal by order of Pope Pius V.

The metrical principle employed by Thomas is *accentual* (not *quantitative,* according to the classical tradition); that is to say, the rhythm depends on a patterned sequence of stressed and unstressed syllables. In addition—again unlike traditional classical verse—Thomas employs a patterned rhyming system. The meters themselves vary.

The "Lauda, Sion, Salvatorem" ("Praise, O Sion, the Savior") is basically in trochaic dimeters—when we understand that foot-designations are commonly in "dipodies" or "double feet," so that a "trochaic dimeter" means four individual trochaic feet. The basic rhyming system is a, a, b, c, c, b. The hymn was liturgically set for the sequence of Corpus Christi and throughout the octave of the feast. The verse scheme was one much favored by an earlier distinguished hymn writer (died between 1172 and 1192), Adam of Saint Victor.

The beautiful twelfth and concluding stanza runs to ten rather than six lines (stanzas ten and eleven have, each, eight lines), with a rhyming scheme of a, a, a, b, c, c, c, b:

Bone pastor, panis vere,
Jesu, nostri miserere:
Tu nos pasce, nos tuere:
Tu nos bona fac videre
  In terra viventium.
Tu, qui cuncta scis et vales,
Qui nos pascis hic mortales,
Tuos ibi commensales,
Coheredes et sodales
  Fac sanctorum civium.

The *in terra viventium,* "in the land of the living," in Heaven, is effectively re-echoed by the *ibi,* "there," of verse eight—as well as by *commensales,* "table companions," *coheredes,* "coheirs," and *sodales sanctorum civium,* "associates of the blessed citizens."

The "Pange, Lingua, Gloriosi" ("Sing, my tongue, the mystery of the glorious Body"—with verse two added in the translation) recalls in its opening verse the "Pange, lingua, gloriosi" by Venantius Fortunatus (530-609), Bishop of Poitiers. The meter is trochaic dimeter, with each second verse catalectic. The six-line stanzas rhyme as follows: a, b, a, b, a, b. Liturgically, it has been used in Vespers for Corpus Christi and throughout the octave of the feast and is likewise a processional hymn. The last two stanzas, beginning with the verse *Tantum ergo Sacramentum,* are, of course, familiar from the Benediction service.

The element of patterned rhyme, along with assonance and alliteration, were most effectively used by Saint Thomas. We must recall that the current pronunciation was not that of classical times. Thus the sounds of 'e-long' and 'e-short' and 'ae' and 'oe' were all alike. With this in mind, we can appreciate the extraordinary effect of such a stanza as the third, the sense of which is: "On the night of the Last Supper,/Reclining at table with His brethren,/After full observation of the Law/In respect of foods prescribed,/As food to the group twelve in number/Himself He gives with His own hands:

In supremae nocte cenae,
  Recumbens cum fratribus,
Observata lege plene
  Cibis in legalibus,

Cibum turbae duodenae
Se dat suis manibus.

In the "Sacris Solemniis Juncta Sint Gaudia" ("With the sacred solemnity let our joys be joined") the meter is asclepiadic and glyconic—recalling the *Odes* of Horace—though still on an accentual principle. The basic rhyming system is a, a, a, a, though sometimes the fourth line does not have the end rhymes; there is also a rhyming scheme within lines. The liturgical use has been at Matins on Corpus Christi and throughout the octave. The hymn proclaims a deep sense of joy and exultation, suggested, for example, by the wondrous opening verse of stanza six: *Panis angelicus fit panis hominum,* "The bread of angels becomes the bread of men."

The "Verbum Supernum Prodiens" ("The Word supernal going forth") is set in iambic dimeter, the meter so much favored by Saint Ambrose, the "Father of Latin Hymnody." The rhyming scheme is a, b, a, b, though a, a, a, a, in stanza four. It has been set liturgically for Lauds on Corpus Christi and throughout the octave. Stanzas five and six, opening with *O salutaris hostia* ("O saving Victim") are familiar from the Benediction service.

There is a wonderful compactness of thought in the fourth stanza—"Born, He gave Himself as our companion,/ Dining He gave Himself as our food,/ Dying, He gave Himself as our ransom,/Reigning, He gives Himself as our reward:

Se nascens dedit socium,
Convescens in edulium,
Se moriens in pretium,
Se regnans dat in praemium.

The Reverend Matthew Germing, S. J., in his *Latin Hymns* (1920), remarks: "These wonderful lines express in concise lyric form the whole economy of redemption."

The "Adoro Te Devote, Latens Deitas" ("I adore Thee devoutly, hidden Deity") is expressed in trochaic trimeter catalectic, with an anacrusis in the opening stanza. The rhyming scheme is a, a, b, b, but a, a, a, a in stanza six. Profound faith in the Real Presence of the God-Man in the Blessed Sacrament is sounded throughout the poem, with profound hope of the Beatific Vision in the last stanza: "Jesus, whom veiled I now look upon,/Let that, I pray, come to pass which I so thirst for,/So that, beholding Thee with face unveiled,/I may be blessed in the vision of Thy glory":

Jesu, quem velatum nunc aspicio,
Oro, fiat illud, quod tam sitio,
Ut, Te revelata cernens facie,
Visu sim beatus tuae gloriae.

W.C.K.

DE PRIMO PRINCIPIO

Author: John Duns Scotus (c.1264-1308)
Type of work: Religious metaphysics
First transcribed: c.1300

Principal Ideas Advanced

It can be proved that there is a First Principle which is the first eminent cause, the first efficient cause, and the first final cause.

Then, by invocation of the notion of aseity, the transition can be made from the possibility to the actuality of the First Principle.

Not all the attributes which faith attributes to God can be shown by reason to belong to Him.

In the *De primo principio* (*On the First Principle*), John Duns Scotus, the "Subtle Doctor," as he was appropriately called, sets out to show by reason alone, in the familiar Scholastic manner, that God exists and that He has some of the attributes which by faith we attribute to Him.

Duns Scotus begins with a prayer: "Lord Our God who when your servant Moses asked you as the truest teacher what name of yours he might tell to the sons of Israel replied, knowing what the moral intellect could grasp, revealing your blessed name, 'I am who am.' You are true being; you are total being. This, if it be possible, I wish to know. Help me, Lord, who inquire to what degree knowledge of that true being you are can be attained by our natural reason beginning from that being which you have predicated of yourself." The theme is familiar from Saint Anselm: the *De primo principio* is another instance of faith seeking understanding. But if Duns Scotus's work has much in common with the efforts of his predecessors, it has peculiarities which mark it as a product of its time, a time when the grounds for great syntheses such as that of Saint Thomas Aquinas came in for questioning. Duns Scotus lived at the beginning of the period of dissolution; great as he is, he stands on the downward slope of a curve that reached its height a generation earlier.

The first striking characteristic of the *De primo principio* is its method. The work reminds some scholars of Euclid's *Elements* and others of the procedure *more geometrico* of Spinoza, for Duns Scotus's work also seeks to proceed "geometrically," through logical steps. Because of the rigor of its method, it is well to see at least the skeleton of the work.

The *De primo principio* is made up of four chapters. In the first chapter, Duns Scotus, having pointed out that being involves order, gives four divisions of essential order. These amount to definitions to which he makes constant appeal in the sequel. In the second chapter, the author attempts to prove sixteen propositions concerning the relations between things essentially ordered. In Chapter 3, he argues that a First Principle of all things exists in terms of three types of essential order.

Duns Scotus's essay provides a succinct statement of that proof for God's existence which he gave in his *Oxford Commentary on the Sentences*. He argues that there is one nature which is the first efficient cause, the first final cause, and first cause by way of eminence. Nineteen propositions are presumably proved in this chapter. Finally, in Chapter 4, Duns Scotus purports to prove ten propositions expressive of the divine attributes.

By essential order Duns Scotus means the order of things which are either prior or posterior. What is prior is eminent and independent; what is posterior is exceeded and dependent. The prior is not dependent upon the posterior, but the posterior cannot be without the prior.

Duns Scotus then divides the order of dependence. Such an order can be simple, comprising cause and effect, or it can be more complex, with subordinate causes leading to an effect.

The simple order of cause to effect may be by any of four kinds of causes: material (the matter), formal (the plan), efficient (the agency), or final (the purpose).

Duns Scotus then goes on to explore the relations between things essentially ordered. The sixteen propositions which he attempts to establish in the second chapter are as follow: (1) Nothing has an essential order to itself; (2) In any essential order a circle is impossible; (3) What is not posterior to A cannot be posterior to what is posterior to A; (4) What is not ordered to a final cause is not an effect; (5) What is not effected is not ordered to a final cause; (6) What is not effected is not materially caused; (7) What is not materially caused is not formed, and conversely; (8) What is not caused by extrinsic causes is not caused by intrinsic causes; (9) The four genera of causes are essentially ordered in causing the same thing; (10) If two things are related to the same cause, it is either a proximate or remote cause; (11) Not everything caused proximately by a cause is the cause of what is mediately caused by that same cause; (12) Everything is essentially dependent either on a cause or on a proximate effect of a cause; (13) Not everything which is exceeded is essentially dependent on the eminent; (14) Not everything which is dependent is exceeded by that on which it depends; (15) No plurality is to be posited unnecessarily; (16) Everything ordered to an end is exceeded.

These preliminaries accomplished, Duns Scotus states the task of the sequel in another prayer: "Lord Our God, who have called yourself first and ultimate being, teach your servant to prove by reason what he holds most certainly by faith, that you are the first efficient cause, the first by way of eminence and the ultimate end. Of the six foregoing essential orders, it suffices to select three, two of extrinsic causality and one of eminence, and, if you grant it, to show that in these three orders there is some one nature absolutely first. I say one nature because in this third chapter these three primacies will be demonstrated not of a unique singular, of something numerically one, but something one in quiddity and nature. We will speak later of numerical unity." We have arrived at the point where Duns Scotus shows that there is a first efficient cause, an ultimate final cause related by way of eminence to its effects. He argues that these three primacies pertain to one nature; then he demonstrates that what is first in these three ways is something numerically one.

The proof of the existence of God is given in the first two conclusions of Chapter 3: (1) among beings there is some nature which is efficient cause; (2) some efficient cause is absolutely first. In proof of the first proposition, Duns Scotus proceeds as follows. Something can be effected; therefore, there is something which is efficient.

The consequent is proved from the nature of correlatives. The antecedent is proved in two ways. First, something is contingent; that is, something whose being follows on its nonbeing and which cannot therefore be from itself (*a se*) or from nothing. Duns Scotus adds that to say that such a thing came from itself is just another way of saying that it came from nothing, since before it came to be it was not. Thus, that which can be effected must come from something else which makes it be. Second, there is some nature which is mobile or mutable, because it lacks some perfection which can be in it. The term of a motion can begin and thus be effected.

We cannot help noticing the stress which Duns Scotus puts on possibility in these proofs: what can be effected is related to what can effect. That this emphasis is intended is clear from Duns Scotus's criticism of those who would argue that there is some nature which is efficient cause from the fact that something has been effected or has come to be or is the term of a motion. "But I prefer to state premises and conclusions in the mode of possibility," he writes, "since if the actual facts are granted, their possibility will be conceded, but not conversely. But as actual these are simply contingent, however manifest, whereas as possible they are necessary and can properly pertain to being understood quidditatively, whereas otherwise they would pertain only to existent being." This procedure entails that, having arrived at the possibility of a first efficient cause, something Duns Scotus proves in his second conclusion, he must then show that there actually is such a cause. This he attempts to do in his fourth conclusion: the absolutely first efficient cause actually exists and some actually existing nature is such. That to whose nature it is repugnant that it be from another, if it can be, can be only from itself (*a se*), but it is repugnant to the absolutely first efficient cause that it be from another and it can be. Duns Scotus attempts to make the transition from the possibility of a first efficient cause to its actual existence. He argues that the absolutely first efficient cause is of itself (*a se*) possible. But what is not by itself (*a se*) cannot come to be by itself because then nonbeing would make something be, which is impossible; moreover, it would then cause itself and so could not be said to be wholly uncausable. (We can appreciate why Duns Scotus was called subtle.) The notion of aseity, being by or of oneself, is such that when it is shown to pertain to a nature, that nature is not just possible but actual. If it were only possible, it would not yet be. How could it come to be? From nonbeing? That is impossible. From itself? Then it is not wholly uncaused. Thus, aseity is a possibility which is incompatible with anything other than its actuality. Another way of arriving at the same conclusion is given by Duns Scotus: it would be absurd if the universe were lacking the highest possible grade of being.

Duns Scotus proceeds in exactly the same way in arguing from the orders of eminence and finality. He shows that a first in each of these orders is possible and then, summarily, with a brief reference to the way in which transition was made from the possibility of a first to its actual existence in the order of efficient causality, Duns Scotus concludes to the actual existence of something first by way of eminence and of something which is the ultimate final cause.

The next step is to show that these three primacies pertain to some one nature. Then Duns Scotus goes on to show that what is first in these three ways is something numerically one. With respect to the divine attributes, Duns Scotus argues that the First Principle is simple, infinite, intellectual. The key divine attribute is infinity, and he feels that if he had started with infinity as an attribute, the others would be much easier to deduce.

Duns Scotus claims that reason alone can prove that a great many perfections must be attributed to God. But many of the perfections we know by faith to be God's elude efforts at rational proof: "Beside the foregoing which are predicated of you by philosophers, Catholics often praise you as omnipotent, immense, omnipresent, just, merciful, exercising over all creatures but especially over intellectual creatures a watchful providence, all of which will be treated in the following work." The reference here is thought to be to the *Theoremata,* although the authenticity of this work is still questioned.

The full impact of Dun Scotus's teaching cannot of course be felt by studying this one work; the *De primo principio* should be read in conjunction with Duns Scotus's commentaries on the *Sentences* and his other works. The *De primo principio* certainly provides no reason for supposing that Duns Scotus was attempting to deflate the claims of reason and to question the scope that had been given to reason in such syntheses as that of Saint Thomas Aquinas. On the contrary; we are here impressed by the anticipation of rationalism in the rigorous, almost mathematical, procedure exhibited by the Subtle Doctor. There is, of course, a highly significant difference from Thomas in that Duns Scotus shows a preference for taking possibility rather than the contingently actual as the starting point for an argument to Gods existence. The course of the argument from possibility to actuality, reminiscent of the ontological argument of Saint Anselm, provides sufficient basis for continuing to call Duns Scotus the "Subtle Doctor."

R.M.

OPUS OXONIENSE

Author: John Duns Scotus (c.1264-1308)
Type of work: Scholastic metaphysics
First transcribed: c.1302

Principal Ideas Advanced

Metaphysics is the universal science which considers transcendentals as such; God is the goal but not the subject of metaphysics; being is the subject.

It is possible for man to know God naturally; one can have a quidditative notion of God, a univocal concept, a concept based on pure perfections, and a concept known through intelligible species of creatures.

God's existence can be demonstrated through proofs based on God's triple primacy (efficient causality, finality, and pre-eminence).

It can be shown through natural reason alone that there is but one God.

Some truths about God can be learned naturally, although indirectly, without the assistance of the Uncreated Light.

Natural reason cannot prove, either by a priori *or by* a posteriori *proofs that resurrection is necessary; faith alone can guide man in the consideration of immortality.*

In the medieval period it was the custom for all philosophers and theologians to comment on the *Book of Sentences* of Peter Lombard. Peter Lombard, Bishop of Paris, who died about the year 1160, was a prominent figure in theology, and his textbook had become a standard work in the universities. The commentary of John Duns Scotus, however, takes on greater proportions than an ordinary commentary. In the *Opus Oxoniense* Scotus took great pains to make his commentary on the *Sentences* a critical and well-organized body of philosophical thought; the result is a masterpiece of metaphysical reasoning.

During the time from 1293 till 1297 Duns Scotus was engaged in studies at the University of Paris. After completing his studies at Paris, Duns Scotus returned to Oxford, where he produced the *Oxford Commentary* on the *Sentences*. The main sections of this work were completed before the author died. Following his death, however, zealous disciples attempted to complete this valuable work and the resultant inconsistencies have produced many serious textual problems for Scotist scholars. The solution of these problems will depend ultimately on the completion of the critical edition of the works of Scotus.

The most important question that can be asked concerning the *Opus Oxoniense* is in regard to its character. Scotus was interested in producing a new synthesis of philosophy and theology. It was his plan to outline and define the true nature of philosophy and theology, and to establish the relationship of these two disciplines. At the same time the "Subtle Doctor" was aware of the vast patrimony from which he could draw a wealth of tradition. Saint Thomas Aquinas had recently given the works of Aristotle new vitality; the Franciscan school itself was rich in the philosophy of the Augustinian school; new translations of Aristotle were available; the works of the Arabian thinkers demanded attention. Scotus attempted to develop a new synthesis wherein this rich patrimony would be an instrument in the search for truth, and, at the same time, the truths of the Catholic faith would be retained and enhanced.

Scotus defines metaphysics as "the transcending science," for it is concerned with "transcendentals"; that is, with ideas about matters beyond the science of nature. "Being" is transcendental, says Duns Scotus, when it is considered in general, prior to any particular determination. Predicates which apply to God, predicates such as "wise" and "good" are transcendental because, as applied to God, they are infinite.

"Being" has primacy among the transcendentals because nothing can be more common than "being."

Duns Scotus considers whether the subject of metaphysics is being or God. He concludes that God cannot be the subject of metaphysics for, as Avicenna had argued, "no science proves its own subject," and metaphysics is capable of proving that God exists. There is a science which has God as first object, however, and that science is theology. The first subject of metaphysics, then, is being, although in demonstrating the implications of being, metaphysics illuminates matters which have to do with God as the highest cause; consequently, God is the end or goal of metaphysics.

Duns Scotus proceeds in scholastic fashion, by asking a question, considering pro and contra positions, criticizing solutions other than his own, advancing his proposed resolution of the problem, and working out the implications, relative to the views of others, of his own solution.

It was necessary to settle the basic question as to whether it is possible to know God. Thus, Duns Scotus asks "whether the intellect of man in this life is able to know God naturally." He mentions the arguments for the contra position: God cannot be known because He cannot be sensed; the intellect cannot grasp the most evident, and hence most blinding, truths; the infinite, as infinite, cannot be known; knowledge of God must terminate with what is "beneath Him." Yet Aristotle has claimed that man's true happiness consists in precisely that knowledge which the above claims deny. Before considering the four contra points, however, Duns Scotus presents his own observations on the nature of the question.

Scotus argues that even when knowledge of God is the knowledge of what He *is not,* such knowledge is, at the same time, knowledge of what He *is,* for a denial makes sense relative to an affirmation. Furthermore, there is no need to distinguish between existence and essence when reasoning about God, for His essence is such that from a consideration of it the intellect can come to knowledge of His existence.

Scotus's next point is particularly interesting methodologically; he argues that there is no need to distinguish between the truth of a proposition about God and the question of His existence; one has to understand the proposition in order to determine its truth, but once one has grasped the meaning of the subject term "God," one knows the truth-value of the proposition.

Other arguments are advanced to show that Scotus is interested here in the possibilities of a purely natural inquiry; he wants to know whether the unaided reason can attain to knowledge of God through purely natural means.

After considering the denial made by Henry of Ghent, Duns Scotus presents his own opinion. He argues that it is possible to know God not only incidentally, that is, as having a certain property, but also quiddatively, that is, as conceived by Himself, as *what* is characterized. Second, God is known not only by analogy, that is, as "wholly other" than creatures, but also univocally, that is, in some sense peculiar to Himself. However, Scotus adds, in a third statement, no human being can know God in His essence. But, he adds reassuringly, in a fourth point, there are nevertheless "many concepts proper to God" which can be known. A method of building up concepts applicable to God is outlined in a fifth statement; namely, the method of joining together ideas, "intelligible species," learned through abstraction from creatures. Thus, by joining together the idea "good," the idea "highest," and the idea (or intelligible species) "act," one can construct an idea applicable to God alone; namely, the idea of the "highest good which is pure act."

Each of these points is carefully defended by Scotus, who exhibits throughout his work an incisive logical acumen.

The Subtle Doctor is now able to challenge the four contra statements presented earlier. The intellect is not confined by sense knowledge, he argues, for the intellect has an abstractive power by which it proceeds to general ideas. It is true that the intellect is blind to the intuitive aspect of God, and it is assuredly difficult to learn what is "most evident" in nature; nevertheless, there is no reason for supposing that things are absolutely unintelligible. In response to the third claim, that the infinite as infinite cannot be known, Scotus replies that an infinite intellect could know it; he does concede, however, that a comprehensive knowledge of the infinite as infinite is not possible to finite minds. Finally, in answer to the suggestion that knowledge of God must end with knowledge of what is "beneath Him," Scotus contends that knowledge of God does not end with knowledge of some *creature* beneath God, but with knowledge of some intelligible concept which is "beneath God" only in the sense of being less perfect in intelligibility than the essence of God itself.

Scotus concludes the section concerning man's natural knowledge of God by maintaining that although God is uniquely singular, He can be known by abstraction of predicates, although "indistinctly."

Scotus's next basic question is "*whether in the realm of beings something exists which is actually infinite,*" and he answers in the affirmative after a meticulous, technical examination of the relative and absolute properties of God. He refers to the "threefold primacy" of God: the primacy of efficient causality, the primacy of finality, and the primacy of pre-eminence. Each of these primacies admits of three conclusions: "(1) Something is first, (2) It cannot be caused, (3) It actually exists in the realm of beings." Thus, Scotus comes to nine conclusions; the three which come under the primacy of efficient causality are: "Among beings which can produce an effect one is simply first . . ."; "Among those things which can produce an effect that which is simply first is itself incapable of being caused"; "Such a being actually exists and some nature actually existing is capable of such causality." Similar triads are defended in demonstrations based on the primacy of finality and the primacy of pre-eminence. Scotus's conclusion, then, is as follows: "In the realm of beings there actually exists a being which has a triple primacy, and this being is infinite. Therefore, some infinite being actually exists." Scotus maintains that this concept of God as an infinite being is "the most perfect absolute concept we can have of him. . . ."

Scotus asks whether there is but one God, and he answers that natural reason can establish the unicity of God by arguing from the respects in which

God is infinite and by drawing out the implications of His status as a necessary and omnipotent being. In general, Scotus's procedure is to argue that God would not be infinite, necessary, or omnipotent were there more than one God; in each case a *reductio ad absurdum* is devised to show that a multiplicity of Gods involves a contradiction.

The question is asked "whether any certain and unadulterated truth can be known naturally by the intellect of a person in this life without the special illumination of the Uncreated Light," and Scotus again comes to grips with the opinions of Henry of Ghent, who argues that knowledge of certain truth depends upon attending to God Himself as the sole exemplar. Scotus argues that although sensible things, by the examination of which one seeks to acquire certain knowledge, are often in motion, they are not always in motion; furthermore, one acquires knowledge of the "nature" of objects; hence, of that which is unmoving. The soul might appear to be mutable, in that the knower is affected by the motion of what he knows and sometimes changes his mind; but it is possible for the soul, once truth has been made evident through the relations of terms, to rest with the truth. Finally, Scotus maintains, knowledge is possible through the intelligible species, which function as the secure and immutable grounds of knowledge.

The vital question as to whether man can know by natural reason that there will be "a general resurrection of mankind" is also considered by Duns Scotus. In this case, the pro arguments are first presented, for Scotus finally takes the contra position. He considers both *a priori* and *a posteriori* arguments for the immortality of the soul, but he is satisfied with neither kind of argument. The *a priori* arguments are based upon the propositions that man is essentially intellective, that the intellective soul is immortal, and that the human soul will be restored to the body. Scotus assents to the first proposition, and he agrees that natural reason is sufficient to demonstrate the truth of the claim that man is essentially an intellectual being, but he denies that natural reason can support the other two propositions. The arguments in support of the second proposition, namely, that the intellective soul is immortal, are "persuasive probable arguments," but they are not conclusive; there is even less of a case for the third proposition. It is not enough that men desire resurrection or that moral justice seems to demand it; natural reason cannot establish resurrection on such grounds. Duns Scotus contends that men should be grateful for the divine gift of faith, whereby they are able to be certain of eternal life even though natural reason is not able, in this case, to construct a conclusive demonstration.

One might expect to find that a philosopher as logically disciplined as Duns Scotus tends to lose sight of the object of his faith and that his work therefore fails to give evidence of any spiritual joy; a reading of Scotus's *Opus Oxoniense*, however, is sufficient to provide evidence for the contra position: logical subtlety is not incompatible with maintaining a sense of the divine and with enjoying an exhilarating response to the spiritual significance which the created world yields to the inquisitive natural reason.

DE POTESTATE REGIA ET PAPALI

Author: John of Paris (c.1255-1306)
Type of work: Philosophy of Church and state
First transcribed: 1303

Principal Ideas Advanced

Man is not only ordained to a good end which can be acquired through nature, that is to a life of virtue, but he is further ordered to a supernatural end, which is life eternal.

The people are not bound by divine law to be under one supreme monarch in the temporal sphere, for, according to a natural instinct which is from God, citizens in a community can, as a consequence of living in common, choose various rulers according to the needs of their community.

While the ruler needs the priest in spiritual matters, the priest needs the ruler in temporal affairs; that which one does not have, the other has.

John of Paris, a member of the Order of Preachers, was prompted by the struggle between King Philip IV of France (1268-1314) and Pope Boniface VIII (c. 1235-1303) to write the treatise *De potestate regia et papali.* This conflict marked the ability of the rising national state to challenge successfully the universal authority of the medieval Church. This Church-state conflict, as a part of the birth of modern Europe, called for a rethinking of the old theories concerning the relations between the spiritual and temporal powers, and for the advancing of new ideas, more compatible with the realities of the fourteenth century. The result was a great literary outflow. While much of this outflow was polemical in nature, John of Paris, writing between 1302 and 1303, succeeded in dealing comprehensively with the whole question of the authority of the Church and state, and with the great philosophical issues involved in the debate between these two powers.

In the introduction John of Paris states that his purpose is to refute the errors of those who claim that it is contrary to the nature of the Church to possess material goods, and of those who hold that the pope must have the full lordship over temporal authority and property. John's task is to discover the *via media* between these two extremes.

The treatment begins with an examination of the origins of Church and state. Since man is ordered to both a natural and a supernatural end, means have been provided to aid him in the attainment of his goals. To provide for man's supernatural end was the function of Jesus Christ. Even before dying on the Cross, Christ aided man by instituting the sacraments and establishing a human agency: the Church, with priests for administering the sacraments. John of Paris limits the Church to this purely spiritual role upon this earth. The natural end of man is within the jurisdiction of the state. To establish the origin of the state, John relies upon the Greek philosopher Aristotle (384-322 B.C.) who claimed that since man is a social animal, the individual must unite with other men to form a state for the benefit of all involved. John defines the state as "the perfect rule of the greater number regulated by one for the common good," and he concludes that the rule of one is better than that of many, because under one peace is more secure and the common good is better served.

Having laid separate foundations for the Church and the state, John compares both societies with regard to status, power, and priority. The status of the Church is one of unity and universality, because the mission of the Church is the salvation of all mankind. The mark of the state is diversity. Since divine law has ordained no supreme ruler for the temporal sphere, lay people by a natural instinct, which is from God, are free to choose various forms of government according to the needs of a varied human society. John offers several proofs of his thesis, one of which is based on the fact that the temporal order is not dependent on one common source for its needs and that various forms of government exist because of the differences in climate, language, and geography.

Regarding the authority of both institutions, John attributes to the Church a purely spiritual and verbal power, which has been interpreted as a form of indirect authority. The state has power over all temporal affairs within its own boundaries; by nature this authority is physical, and physical means must be used to enforce it. Turning to a concrete example of this division of powers, John denies that the pope could absolve the French from allegiance to their ruler. The denial is based upon the idea that the feudal oath is a natural obligation between the ruler and the ruled. The Chuch is thus regulated to the spiritual realm; the state, to the temporal area.

In the matter of priority, according to John, the Church takes precedence in regard to dignity, because of its supernatural end; while the state is prior in time, in that rulers antedate priests. John emphasizes that the spiritual is not the cause of the temporal, but that both authorities come immediately from the same divine source. In summation he writes: "Therefore the priest is the greater ruler in spiritual affairs, just as the prince is in the temporal realm, although naturally speaking the priest is greater, in as much as the spiritual is greater than the temporal."

While John has separated and made distinct the two powers, he must still allow for co-operation between them, since both have the end of man as their common goal. The result of this consideration is a theory of dependency, which reads as follows: "While the ruler needs the priest in spiritual matters, the priest needs the ruler in temporal affairs; that which one does not have, the other does have." In order to illustrate this dependency John examines the various powers of the Church, such as consecration, administration of the sacraments, correction of sin, and infliction of ecclesiastical punishment. Only in the correction of sin and the application of censure is there permitted a form of co-operation between the spiritual and temporal spheres. The Church uses spiritual means, the state uses physical methods. The Church can compel through the use of such spiritual punishments as excommunication, but only the temporal officer can impose any physical punishment.

The treatise then turns to a key problem: How would this relationship of dependency apply to a king or pope who has violated the status of one of the two realms?

If a king should commit spiritual wrongs, says John, he must first be warned by the Church. If he remains incorrigible, the pope can excommunicate him. This is the limit of the pope's direct action, but indirectly or *per accidens,* the pope, with threat of spiritual censure, can influence the subjects to act against their ruler. If the ruler should offend in only temporal matters, it is the duty of the barons and peers of the kingdom to take action. These in turn can call upon the Church to apply her spiritual censures. John of Paris then applies the principle to the pope. If the pontiff should become a source of scandal to the Church, the Holy Roman Emperor can bring about his deposition. If he offends in purely temporal affairs, the emperor can either admonish or punish the offending prelate. The emperor, however, is the only one who can thus chastise the pope, since the emperor shares a form of universal jurisdiction with the spiritual ruler. Thus, while John of Paris separates the powers of the Church and the state, he allows for a mutual dependency in which each has an indirect means of acting in the other realm.

John then considers the Church and state as separate institutions. In the state, the ruler receives his power from both God and the people. The function of the people is to choose the ruler or his house. Relying once more on Aristotle, John feels that the ruler must promote the common good and the virtuous life of his subjects. The ruler's powers are limited, since he does not govern according to his own will but according to the laws which the citizens or others have formed. If the king should offend in temporal affairs, he can be deposed by his subjects. John not only makes the ruler responsible to the people for his acts, but the author also provides criteria for deciding when revolution is justified.

For the Church there is the twofold problem of the relationship of property and of the pope to the Church. The universal Church is the proprietor of the Church's property, while the pope, as only the administrator of this property, must not deal arbitrarily with his trust. The pope cannot compel, although he can request, that private goods be contributed to the Church. While John of Paris accepts the pope's position as the visible head of Christ's Church on earth, he lays down certain conditions for the exercising of judgment upon him. If a pope should abuse his authority by committing criminal acts or by using his spiritual power to disturb society, the Church can proceed against him, and the secular ruler can resist him with his sword, but the sword cannot be used "against the pope as pope, but against him as an enemy of the common good." It is further implied that the pope could be deposed by a general council, though John's personal opinion is that the cardinals as a body could depose the recalcitrant pontiff.

In his treatise John of Paris reveals himself as an original thinker, who because of his wide erudition was able to marshal supporting evidence from a multitude of sources to add credence to his own rational conclusions. He tends to avoid extremes and to seek a middle position. John's influence upon the world of religious and political thought has been both positive and negative. His ideas furnished ammunition to the conciliarists of the fifteenth century, who attempted to place the government of the Church under the control of the General Council and in the seventeenth century the Gallican movement in France looked upon John of Paris as an early champion of its ideas.

Today a more constructive influence can be assigned this French Dominican in the area of Church-state relations. John's theory, which precluded any direct power of the Church in the temporal realm and yet provides for a *per accidens* or indirect means for Church action, seems to conform with contemporary thought on this problem of the two powers. Whether or not John of Paris should be given any credit for such modern developments is not important; what does matter is that at the beginning of modern Europe there was a Catholic thinker who was able to intepret the changing relations between Church and state in a rational and realistic manner, even though the interpretation was not always consistent with the Church's doctrine. He had the foresight not only to recognize and accept change, but also to provide a theoretical basis for new conditions in an ever-changing world.

R.J.K.

THE LIFE OF SAINT LOUIS

Author: Jean de Joinville (1225-1317)
Type of work: Biography
First transcribed: 1309

Principal Ideas Advanced

King Louis IX of France (1214-1270) was a masterly, dignified, and firm monarch, whose guiding principle was to observe justice in all things, with regard both to his subjects and to outside powers, in accordance with the will of God.

Louis was a saint, a man who considered his own eternal salvation and that of his subjects as the paramount objectives of his life; he was extremely devout and idealistic, abstemious and mortified, and given to good works.

As a man, Louis was an amiable, friendly, loyal, and humorous companion; an affectionate, tolerant husband; a dutiful son deeply attached to his pious, competent mother, Blanche; a fond father and a loving brother; yet not without human failings and foibles, and on occasion injudicious and rash, as well as subject to strong gusts of grief and anger.

Jean, Lord of Joinville, was an honest, upright, hard-headed, proud feudal knight, partly worldly, partly religious, who became a trusted lieutenant of King Louis IX on the latter's first crusade to Egypt and remained his lifelong friend.

The author, Jean, became Lord of Joinville and Seneschal (a chief administrative officer) of Champagne by inheritance in 1243. He was conscientious and reliable, practical and prudent, as well as honest and brave—a knight and feudal lord imbued with chivalric concepts and class consciousness.

Joinville participated in Louis' first crusade (1248-1254) and accompanied the king to both Egypt and Palestine. On this crusade, the chief topic of his *The Life of Saint Louis,* Jean became Louis' trusted aide and confidant. After returning to France, Joinville devoted most of his time and energies to the administration and reconstruction of his estates and to his duties as Seneschal of Champagne, with only occasional attendance at the royal court, where he was, however, cordially received. He declined to accompany Louis on the king's second crusade, which Joinville condemned as foolhardy, and he survived his king, who died at Tunis in 1270, by forty-seven years. Joinville completed *Le livre des saintes paroles et des bonnes actions de St. Louis* in 1309, a dozen years after its hero's canonization.

Joinville's *Life of St. Louis* is principally a biography of St. Louis, but it also contains useful information concerning the latter's crusade to Egypt and gives some autobiographical information concerning Joinville himself. The *Life* is reminiscent and anecdotal in form and it is the earliest known example of a biography written by a gentleman who employs the French vernacular. Its main contributions are the vivid picture it presents of St. Louis IX, its historical information concerning the crusade to Egypt, and its pictures of the life of the French aristocracy in the thirteenth century.

Louis IX was profoundly influenced by his saintly and capable mother, Queen Blanche of Castile, who ruled France from the time of her husband's death in 1226 until 1236, when Louis reached his majority; she also reigned during her son's absence on his first crusade. Blanche, who assidiously and strictly saw to her son's upbringing, reportedly said that she would rather see him dead than guilty of a mortal sin.

After extensive preparations, Louis IX set out on his first crusade in 1248, with Joinville among his many followers. Delays and insubordination weakened the French army, which, despite the initial successes of taking Damietta at the main mouth of the Nile and repulsing an Egyptian army, was unable to move on Cairo. A brief chance for victory after having effected a surprise crossing of the Nile was frustrated by the rashness of the king's brother, the Count of Artois, who lost the flower of the French cavalry and disconcerted the operation. Shrewd Moslem strategy which employed water barriers, disrupted French supplies, and took advantage of French discomfort and the toll of disease did the rest, so that the trapped crusaders were forced to surrender to the Egyptians in 1250. Many of the French were slain or enslaved, but the fortitude and firmness of Louis as well as the payment of a huge ransom and the surrender of Damietta brought about the release of the king and many of his followers.

Louis now repaired to Palestine, where he spent four years (1250-1254) encouraging the Westerners and building up the defense of such Crusader strong points as Sidon, Jaffa, Caesarea, and Acre. It was only on learning of the death of his beloved mother and regent in late 1252 that Louis decided to return to France.

Louis became a recognized model of sanctity, justice, and charity. After several years of peaceful and successful rule, he decided to go on another crusade, despite the opposition of Joinville, and he died of fever and dysentery soon after the landing at Tunis. Joinville says: "Of the journey that he made to Tunis would I recount and say naught since I was not there, thank God."

The sanctity and sensitivity of Louis IX did not prevent him from being "every inch a king," a competent and effective ruler. He was practical, decisive, and firm, even with his beloved wife, Margaret of Provence, and his favorite, Joinville. Although extremely devout, fond of the company of religious and willing to concede to churchmen on minor points, he was careful to guard his essential rights and duties as king. Thus, he refused to accede to the request of his bishops that he order the confiscation of the property of excommunicated persons, unless their cases were submitted for judgment by his own courts. His great political principle was the careful provision of justice, as shown by his personal interest and participation in its administration, his invitation of appeals from dissatisfied suitors, his careful supervision of his courts, and his detailed instructions to his officials on this subject. A frequently quoted passage from Joinville describes Louis' passion for justice and personal participation in its administration: "Often in summer, after Mass, he would go and sit in the woods at Vincennes, and lean his back against an oak-tree, and bid us sit around him. All those that had business came there to speak to him, not hindered by guards or anyone else. And then he would ask them with his own mouth: 'Is there anyone here who has a cause (case)?' And those that had suits would stand up. Then he would say: 'Be silent all of you, and your cases shall be settled one after the other.' And then he would call my lord Peter of Fontaines and my lord Geoffrey of Villette and would say to one of them: 'Decide this case for me.' And when he found anything to correct in the words of those who spoke for him or for others, he would speak the correction with his own mouth."

The same principle of justice also governed Louis' foreign relations. Thus, he gratuitously concluded peace with the hard-pressed Henry III of England and ceded disputed territory to the English king. His paternal solicitude for his subjects was manifested on various occasions, as when he refused to abandon his companions on a damaged ship off Cyprus and declined to leave behind the long overdue sailors he had sent to gather fruit at Pantelleria. His lack of prejudice is manifested by his support of his low-born but wise counselor, Robert de Sorbon, and his caution to his son Philip III to defend the rights of the towns as natural allies against the aristocracy.

The saintliness of Louis IX is manifest throughout Joinville's narrative. Apparently the king was speaking the truth when he said that he would rather be a leper than seriously offend God. He refused to allow Moslem threats of death and torture to persuade him to grant to the enemy any concessions which would offend God. Louis insisted that his agreed debts to the Moslems be paid in full and that restitution be made for accidental deception. He was frugal and abstemious in drink, indifferent as to food, and simple in attire. He ordered the feeding of six-score poor people daily; he personally attended lepers, distributed alms to numerous persons, and maintained institutions to care for the sick and needy. He attended Mass daily and participated in the recitation of the Divine Office. His guiding principle is summarized in his instructions to his son, Philip: "My first teaching is that you fix your heart on loving God, . . . and avoid anything that is displeasing to Him."

As a person, Louis was pleasant and affable, frequently lighthearted and even mirthful. He was devoted to his mother, his wife, his brothers, and his children. On learning of his mother's death while he was still in the Holy Land, Louis was so overcome with grief that he was unapproachable for two days and finally had to be reproached by Joinville for his excessive sorrow. Louis also had a sense of humor and frequently joked with Joinville, so much so, in fact, that when Jean saw Louis in a vision after his death, the king was laughing. Yet Louis could be stern, as is attested by his wife's refusal to vow a pilgrimage even to save lives without her husband's permission, because he could be "so wayward," as she put it.

Despite his virtues, Louis IX was not free from indiscretions and even follies. Joinville regards as among these faults Louis' excessive deference to his mother, his inflexible determination to go crusading, and his rashness in needlessly exposing himself to danger, as in the landing at Damietta.

Jean, Sire de Joinville, both in his manner of writing and in the things he tells us about himself, shows himself to be a proud, class-conscious aristocrat with a cherished code of manners and ethics. He is a strictly honest narrator of the truth as he conceived it. His account shows that he was faithful in meeting his obligations to his king and his responsibilities to his own subjects and followers. His ideal is the "prudhomme" or "prudent man." Although a practical man and a not over-scrupulous realist, he respected the sanctity of his master and kept the faith.

The life of the aristocracy and even of monarchs in the thirteenth century, as we glimpse it in Joinville, was difficult and fraught with dangers. Yet it was supported by a warm faith in God and eternal life, by a stoical resignation to hardships and death, and by respect for the Church and loyalty to the overlords, the chivalric code, and Christian ideals.

D.D.M.

DE MONARCHIA

Author: Dante Alighieri (1265-1321)
Type of work: Christian political philosophy
First transcribed: c.1313

Principal Ideas Advanced

In order to achieve and maintain that peace and order necessary for man to fulfill his prime function of speculation, the will of a universal monarch must reign.

A reasonable survey of history and the Scriptures testifies to the right of the Roman people to provide the universal monarch.

The temporal authority of the Roman monarch comes directly from God and not through the pope, who is the agent of spiritual authority, because the monarch is an agent separated from the spiritual by the temporal end he serves.

Dante Alighieri begins Book I, "Whether Temporal Monarchy Is Necessary for the Well-being of the World," of his *De monarchia* with a search for a universal end and principle of temporal government. The end of human society, he states, is discovered through the common capacity of the individuals composing it. Because their differentiating characteristic and distinguishing capacity is intellect, speculation is their primary function. Because universal peace is necessary to speculation, the basic principle and universal end of government is to provide the best means for achieving and maintaining peace.

Dante argues from this principle that a monarchy is necessary for the well-being of the world, for a monarch can most effectively order his subjects toward peace. Harmony on earth can be achieved only when temporal government becomes a reflection both of the kingship of God and, in each human being, of the ordering of the various faculties under the kingship of the intellect. Leadership is, therefore, natural in each household, community, petty kingdom, and thus, by implication, in a universal society. While petty monarchs are necessary in the world, they should be ordered with reference toward one monarch or monarchy, and their obligations to this monarch should take precedence over obligations among themselves. In proving monarchy as the best system of government, Dante concludes that man is best disposed when he most resembles God. Since God is one, man, whom He made after His own image, inherits God's unity. Hence, the human race is best ordered when all its movements and motors are directed by one monarch or mover toward the ultimate function of man, speculation.

The peace and order necessary for speculation depends upon justice, says Dante, and justice depends upon a supreme judge. The supreme judge is synonymous with the universal monarch who can accomplish the purest possible justice on earth, which depends upon the domination of one will or a minimum of opposition: ". . . when with Justice is intermixed a minimum of its opposite, both as to disposition and operation, there Justice reigns." Indeed, the monarch, because he would be in a position to satisfy all material want, would be the least stained by cupidity. The monarch would also be the most charitable, for charity, which brightens the will as cupidity clouds it, resides in the will in inverse proportion to cupidity. It is necessary, because he is closest to all men, who approach lesser dependent princes through him, that the monarch be the best disposed towards charity. The monarch is the universal cause of man's well-being or ability to exercise his primary function.

Freedom of the will is proportionate to order and peace, claims Dante, for judgment is necessary for order as freedom is necessary for judgment. Since the monarch is the instrument of purest justice, he is indispensable to individual liberty. A monarch exists for individual liberty and is, therefore, the chief servant of the laws protecting it. The monarch is the epitome of individual liberty because his will is free from cupidity; freedom of will is synonymous with individual liberty.

Unity is the keynote of Dante's argument for monarchy. One agent for one end, he insists, is better than two for one end; the evil of uselessness makes rule by one better than rule by many. (This principle does not outlaw petty princes to whom the monarch may delegate authority in petty matters.) Goodness, continues Dante, subsists in unity, while sin resides in disunity or lack of integrity. Disunity, which is to unity as discord is to concord, diverts man from his final end. Concord of wills is the ideal state for man to realize his end. Such concord necessitates a directing will: "Nor is this directing will a possibility unless there is one common Prince whose will may dominate and guide the wills of all others." Dante detects in Christ's birth divine approval of a universal monarch. Christ picked a time of unity, concord, or peace, the time of the Roman Emperor Augustus (63 B.C.-A.D. 14), in which to be born.

In Book II, "Whether the Roman People Rightfully Appropriated the Office of Monarchy," Dante becomes immoderately chauvinistic. After having proven the necessity of universal monarchy, he proceeds to prove that the Roman people should inherit it. He believes divine providence to have been behind the Roman conquest, which ended the disunity the world suffered since the fall of Adam. The claim of the Roman people to universal monarchy is a right, insists Dante, because it is in accordance with divine will, which can be investigated through visible signs.

The first sign of Roman right is nobility, which resides in virtue and ancient wealth. The Romans inherit their nobility from Aeneas, the father of the Roman people, who himself was noble of soul and inherited the nobility of three continents, Europe, Africa, and Asia, through his progenitors. Dante attempts to make Aeneas uniter of the world's nobility through progenitors with whom other peoples can identify and through Aeneas's marriages: the first to Creusa, who inherited the nobility of Troy; the second to Dido, who inherited the nobility of Carthage; and the third to Lavinia, who inherited the nobility of the Albanians and Romans. "This last consort was of Italy, most excellent region of Europe," Dante comments.

The second sign of Roman right is established by miracles. The Empire was brought to its perfection with the aid of miracles recorded by Roman historians. Livy (59 B.C.-A.D. 17) records the dropping of a shield from heaven into Rome, "the chosen city of God." Livy also records the saving of Rome from the approach of the Gauls by the warning cry of a goose. This incident was also recorded by Virgil (70-19 B.C.). Livy also tells how Rome was saved from being sacked by the Carthaginians by a sudden hailstorm.

Conquest itself is a right of divine will, continues Dante. The Roman conquest, the purpose of which was to establish right or justice throughout the world, further establishes their right to universal monarchy. To prove that the Romans were so disposed Dante cites examples of individual Romans who labored for the common good. He cites, among others, Cincinnatus (c.519-c.439 B.C.), Fabricius (died 250 B.C.) Camillus (died 365 B.C.), Brutus (c.85-42 B.C.). The government of the Empire, as directed by such individuals, offered a defense rather than a domination of individual liberty throughout the world. If the Romans had such a noble purpose in conquering the world, Dante argues, the means they used must have been just or else the conquest would have been a contradiction and frustrated justice.

Dante concludes that the Roman people were God's natural means to divine similitude or unity among men. Because nature produced many people with different talents ordained for diverse activity, ". . . there is no doubt but that nature set apart in the world a place and a people for universal sovereignty; otherwise she would be deficient in herself, which is impossible. What was this place, and who this people, moreover, is sufficiently obvious. . . . They were Rome and her citizens or people."

Dante concentrates on establishing the reality of divine sanction in the remainder of his second book. The judgment of God can be detected in the outcome of contests of individual combat, under which, in a passage beginning with the contest between Aeneas and Turnus for the unification of Italian peoples and concluding with the contests between a multitude of Greeks and Romans for sovereignty, Dante includes wars, under which he classifies multitudinous individual combats. Wars, he insists in a moment of extreme idealism, should be waged in love as a means to discover God's will. The spirit of God is present in such wars until they become struggles of bitterness and blood and the spirit of God is replaced by Satan's. The judgment of God was manifest in Roman victories over all other contestants for the empire; namely, the Assyrians, the Egyptians, the Persians, and the Greeks. Divine sanction, continues Dante, can also be established by faith in Christ's birth, which confirmed Roman right to divine authority: "Now Christ willed to be born of a Virgin Mother under an edict of Roman authority, according to the testimony of Luke, his scribe, in order that the Son of Man, made man, might be numbered as a man in that unique census. This fulfilled the edict. It were perhaps more reverent to believe that the Divine Will caused the edict to go forth through Caesar, in order that God might number Himself among the society of mortals who had so many ages awaited His coming."

Having established Roman right to universal monarchy, Dante explored the source of such authority in Book III, "Whether the Authority of the Roman Monarch Derives from God Immediately or from Some Vicar of God." In the Middle Ages the source of temporal power was a controversial question. Dante held that temporal authority came directly from God, and he grouped his opponents, those who believed that the temporal monarch was dependent upon the pope as the channel of divine authority, into three classes of men. The first of these is the pope, the vicar of God and successor to Peter, and his supporters, whose claim to hold the key to temporal authority, Dante concedes, is based on zeal rather than pride. The second class opposed to direct derivation of temporal authority is the irrational, and the third Dante terms "Decretalists," who depend upon the Decretals (papal decrees which form the groundwork for the ecclesiastical law) for authority superior to all secular law. Dante dismisses the second class as unworthy of argument and the third class with the argument that the Decretals are, as minor Scriptures, inferior to the Old and New Testaments and the councils of the Church. Decretals he describes as administrative traditions rather than as sources of divine authority of the Church. Those whose faith resides in traditions, he implies, become like the Pharisees.

Dante concentrates his defense of direct derivation of temporal authority against the first class by refuting their various arguments for delegating authority to temporal governments. Dante first refutes his opponents' sun and moon argument, the claim that the sun symbolizes the pope, the moon the universal monarch, and light the authority the former bestows upon the latter. Dante insists upon the impossibility, because they preceded man in creation, of these heavenly bodies' being ordained as examples for earthly government. He also charges his opponents with confusing authority and light. Dante refutes his opponents' argument from the precedence in birth of Levi, the father of the priesthood, over Judah, the father of temporal rulers, by pointing out that they confuse authority and birth. He refutes their argument based on the deposition of Saul by Samuel by claiming that Samuel was not vicar of God, but a special envoy. The pope, as vicar of God, he continues, must function within the boundaries of his jurisdiction, while a special envoy, like Samuel, is not thus bound. He refutes the argument based on the adoration of the Magi by reminding his opponents that the Christ Child was God and that the vicar of Christ is not. God, he insists, did not give all His authority to His vicar. In rejecting the argument based on Christ's entrusting Peter with keys of His Kingdom, Dante reminds his opponents that the power to bind and absolve is limited by nature and the laws of God. Peter, for example, would not be able to absolve an unrepentant sinner. Since Christ insisted that His Kingdom was not a temporal one, temporal authority would lie beyond the jurisdiction of Peter and his successors. To refute the argument that Christ's command to His disciples "He that hath no sword, let him buy one" implies temporal jurisdiction, Dante interprets the command as merely a warning against persecution and contempt. Against the claim of temporal power through the Roman Emperor Constantine's (c. 288-337) donation to the pope of the city of Rome and various imperial dignities, Dante asserts that such a donation was not within Constantine's right; the monarch or emperor reigns to preserve rather than divide the empire. Against the argument from the crowning of Charlemagne (742-814) by Pope Hadrian I (pope, 772-795), Dante cites the restoration of Pope Leo VIII (pope, 963-965) by Emperor Otto (912-973). Against the argument from reason that all men, to reflect the unity of God, should be reducible to one type and that, since the pope cannot be subordinated to another, the emperor must be subordinated to the pope, Dante maintains that official positions must not be confused with a standard for the genus. Popes are the measure of popes and emperors the measure of emperors. Both leaders must find a ground of unity beyond themselves yet related to the authority they share. This standard is God Himself. Having rejected all the arguments of his opponents, Dante concludes that temporal authority comes directly from God: "Imperial authority derives immediately from the summit of all being, which is God."

Dante concludes *De monarchia* with a reflection on the dual nature of man. Man's mortal nature is directed toward an end, as is his immortal nature. Happiness on earth is the mortal end of man, and eternal happiness, the immortal end. The means to the former, which is conducive to the latter, is made known to us by human reason. The means to the latter, however, is made known by the Holy Spirit, who has revealed to us supernatural truth through the Scriptures. Man, in order to achieve both ends, must be guarded from cupidity. Two agents must guide him, the universal monarch in the temporal sphere and the supreme pontiff in the spiritual. Having established in divine authority the universal Roman monarch and having reasoned, Dante admits, to the point of absurdity, Dante very briefly indicates the election of the monarch by "heralds of divine providence." The procedure of electing the monarch is not worked out, quite possibly because to do so would be beyond the limits of this theoretical work.

J.J.M.

THE DIVINE COMEDY

Author: Dante Alighieri (1265-1321)
Type of work: Religious allegorical poetry
First transcribed: c.1320

Principal Ideas Advanced

Dante reveals how he awoke in a dark wood, where he was prevented from climbing the mountain by a leopard, a lion, and a wolf.

Virgil appears and leads him by another way through the earth to Hell, where the poets witness the punishments of the unrepentant sinners in the nine circles that lead to the frozen lake, the abode of Satan.

Throughout the journey Dante sees many classical, historical, and real persons, including many of his political enemies and unworthy prelates.

Coming to the surface of the earth, Dante and Virgil begin their ascent of the two terraces and seven cornices of the mount of Purgatory until they reach the Earthly Paradise; and Virgil returns to Limbo.

Beatrice then guides Dante through the nine heavenly spheres to the Primum Mobile and finally to the Empyrean, where Saint Bernard leads Dante to the throne and vision of the Trinity.

It is generally agreed that Dante entitled his epic *Commedia,* and that Boccaccio about forty years later glorified it with the adjective *Divina.* This epithet first appeared in print, however, in the sixteenth century editions of the poem.

Dante Alighieri emerges from the medieval world and stands at the threshold of the Renaissance in the execution of this poem. It is a synthesis of the outlook of the Middle Ages and at the same time a reflection of the slowly rising new attitudes.

Dante's theology is thoroughly Catholic; Saint Thomas Aquinas is the poet's chief theological source, and the influence of Saint Augustine and Saint Bonaventure is also apparent. The form of the poem is typically medieval in its cosmology, its allegory, the use of the dream vision, symbolic and mystical numbers, and the verse form.

For Dante, as for his contemporaries, all astronomical calculations were made by the Ptolemaic system, which was based on the assumption that the earth was the center of the universe. Thus, in the poem the earth is the center around which move nine spheres or heavens at increasing speeds. Surrounding the ninth sphere, the Primum Mobile, is the motionless, timeless, and infinite Empyrean, which is the dwelling place of God. The fall of Lucifer and the wicked angels from the heavens to the earth created a funnel-shaped pit penetrating to the center of the earth with the apex at the center. This pit is Hell, which is divided into nine circles of decreasing size. The mass of the earth displaced by the formation of Hell forms a mountain called purgatory, which consists of seven cornices of punishment. On the top of this mountain is the earthly Paradise that was inhabited by Adam and Eve before the Fall.

In its literary form, the *Divine Comedy* is an allegory of the human soul's journey in its search for God. Dante himself commented on the nature of allegory and on the *Commedia* specifically in his epistle to his patron Can Grande della Scala, the Imperial Vicar of Verona. The poem may be read on four levels: the literal, the allegorical, the moral, and the anagogical. In the literal sense, the poem indicates the states of souls after death and recounts the imaginary journey of Dante through Hell, Purgatory, and Heaven. As an allegory, according to Dante's own words, the *Divine Comedy* treats "man as by freedom of will, meriting and demeriting, he is subject to Justice rewarding or punishing."

Dante employs the mystical number *three* and its multiples in both the structure and the rhyme scheme of the poem. It consists of three books: Hell (Inferno), Purgatory (Purgatorio), and Heaven (Paradiso). Each book contains thirty-three cantos, and Hell has one introductory canto making a total of one hundred, the square of the "perfect" number. The rhyme scheme invented by Dante and called terza rima comprises a unit of three verses woven together by the rhymes of the middle line. An extra line rhyming with the second line of the last terzina closes the canto.

The inspiration provided by the figure of Beatrice may be considered a transitional element in the poem between the medieval and the Renaissance attitudes. Following in the medieval tradition of the courtly lover, Dante idealizes Beatrice, who becomes a symbol of earthly and heavenly perfection. It is she who has prompted Virgil to go to Dante's rescue, and it is Beatrice herself who becomes Dante's guide through Paradise. She is, for Dante, Divine Revelation, the image by which he perceives the Church, Divine Grace, the Blessed Virgin, and even God Himself. But Beatrice is not only a "God-bearer"; she is a real person whom Dante met at the age of nine and who died in the year 1290. In the poem this earthly, human affection is sublimated; but it is a very real emotion, and Beatrice is not a type but an individual.

Dante's allegory is not limited to the personification of abstract virtues and vices; he uses real people and places. The greater number of his figures are symbolic images, and he takes pains to make his details graphic and his descriptions geographically and scientifically accurate, as far as possible. His gallery of sinners indicates his awareness of the struggle for worldly power and for personal gain, and the mystic poem is peopled with souls full of "the business and passions" of the world. The realism of Dante's vision included the political turmoil and partisan temperament of the Renaissance.

Another significant reflection of Dante's modernity was his reverence for classical antiquity and particularly for Virgil. Dante indicated that the Latin poet was his guide not only in this poem, but that he was also his inspiration and teacher in the art of poetry. In Canto I of the "Inferno" Dante greets Virgil with the lines: "Thou art my master, and my author thou,/From thee alone I learned the singing strain,/ The noble style, that does me honour now."

The character Virgil is not the Virgil who was looked upon by the Middle Ages as the unconscious prophet of Christianity, but the real Virgil, the poet and scholar who celebrated in his epic the destiny of Rome. In the allegory, Virgil is the personification of philosophy and human wisdom, the best that man can be with the aid of human reason without the aid of divine grace.

The Renaissance is also foreshadowed in Dante's use of the vernacular for this serious work rather than Latin, even though Latin was considered at that time to be the only proper vehicle for dignified writing. The Tuscan dialect that Dante used in the *Divine Comedy* and that he considered appropriate for great literary work became the basis of modern Italian.

As the son of a noble family, Dante had received an excellent education, and the range of his knowledge is evident in the comprehensive scope of classical, Biblical, and historical references and images that enhance the pages of the *Commedia.*

The story opens in the year 1300, the thirty-fifth of Dante's life. He awakes to find that he has strayed from the right path and that he is lost in a dark wood. In the literal interpretation of the poem Dante is always himself, the poet, the scholar, the politician, and the lover; it is Dante himself who experienced the life of sin for which he later repented. He is recognized by the various souls as the Florentine. In the allegory, Dante is the symbol of every Christian who is seeking God and who must go from the dark wood of error to the mount of salvation, the City of God. The poem tells of Dante's desire to climb the mountain, the image of repentance and of the soul's ascent to God. However, he is hindered by the appearance of a leopard, a lion, and a she-wolf, identified as lust, pride, and avarice. Suddenly the soul of Virgil appears and bids Dante take another way because the power of the wolf will continue until the Greyhound, "the Master-Hound," will come and be the deliverer of Italy. Virgil promises to lead Dante through Hell and Purgatory so that he might understand the nature of sin and the need for penance. "A worthier spirit" will come to lead him to Heaven and the contemplation of divine truths.

The poets then pass through the Gate of Hell where they read the terrible inscription: "Lay down all hope you that go in by me." In the Ante-Hell they find the souls of the Futile running perpetually after a whirling standard. They proceed to the First Circle called Limbo, where the unbaptized and the virtuous pagans are enjoying a natural existence. Virgil, Homer, Ovid, Lucan, and Aristotle are among the many illustrious pagans catalogued as inhabitants of this circle.

As the poets descend to subsequent circles the cavity in the earth narrows, and the punishments of the impenitent sinners are increased in kind and intensity. The punishment is suited to the crime, so that, for instance, the gluttonous are wallowing in mire, drenched with continuous rain, and lacerated by Cerberus, the three-headed dog.

In the next four circles the poets find themselves among the incontinent: Circle II, the lustful; Circle III, the gluttonous; Circle IV, the avaricious and the prodigal; and Circle V, the slothful and the angry.

The travelers are then conducted to the City of Dis, the first division of nether Hell where the sins of the lion, violence, are punished. In Circle VI are the heretics, and in Circle VII are the violent and the bestial: tyrants, murderers, suicides, squanderers, and those violent against God, nature, and art. The remaining circles contain the sinners who have offended through the sins of the wolf: simple fraud and complex fraud. Circle VIII, called Malbowge, is divided into ten trenches containing the panders and seducers, the flatterers, the simoniacs, the sorcerers, the barrators, the hypocrites, thieves, counselors of fraud, sowers of discord, and falsifiers. Circle IX is the frozen Lake of Cocytus, reserved for those guilty of treachery and malice. In its four divisions are (1) traitors to their kindred, (2) traitors to their country or party, (3) traitors to their guests, and (4) traitors to their lords or benefactors. Fixed in ice at the center of the earth is Lucifer, who is continuously devouring the souls of Judas, Brutus, and Cassius. The poets then leave the horrors of Hell and follow the stream of Lethe until they reach the base of the mount of Purgatory.

The whole tone of the book changes as the two poets emerge from the depths of the Inferno. In Purgatory there is hope, for the sinners here are penitents; eventually they will reach Heaven. There are three main divisions of the mountain: (1) Ante-Purgatory, from the base to the gate of Saint Peter; (2) Purgatory proper, seven cornices bounded above by a ring of purifying flame; and (3) Earthly Paradise, the summit.

In the two terraces of Ante-Purgatory are those who failed to avail themselves of the means of grace in good time. They died imperfectly prepared, repenting in *articulo mortis,* and are obliged to wait for a period of time before being admitted to Purgatory itself. All souls must approach by the three steps of Penitence—Confession, Contrition, and Satisfaction—to Saint Peter's Gate. Here the Angelic Warden inscribes the forehead of each soul with the Seven P's, standing for the seven capital sins. The letters, which are placed on Dante's forehead, are erased one at a time as he leaves each terrace of Purgatory.

In Pugatory proper the punishments are purgative, not penal, and cleanse the soul from the stain of sin. As the poets ascend the mountain, the punishments become decreasingly severe since the arrangement of the terraces is based on their reference to disordered love. Thus, in the first three terraces the sins of perverted love, pride, envy, and wrath, are expiated; in the fourth, the sin of love defective or sloth; and in the last three, the sins of love excessive: avarice or prodigality, gluttony, and lust.

Passing through the purging fire, the poets arrive at the earthly Paradise, the summit of the mount of Purgatory, which Adam and Eve had to abandon because of their sin. This garden represents the "blessedness of this life, which consists in the exercise of man's natural powers." Here Beatrice replaces Virgil as guide; she rebukes Dante for lack of devotion but leads him into Eden where Dante beholds a vision of the Church and the Empire.

Then Beatrice bears Dante into Paradise and they begin the journey to the throne of God. In the first three spheres are the souls who have attained beatitude, but not the highest. On the Moon Dante finds those inconstant in vows; on Mercury are those ambitious of the active life who were deficient in Justice; and on Venus are the lovers or those who lacked Temperance. Going beyond the shadow of the earth, Dante finds on the Sun the souls that exemplify Prudence: theologians, teachers, and historians; on Mars, the warriors, those who had practiced Fortitude; on Jupiter, the Just; and on Saturn, the contemplatives, those who were noted for their Temperance. Taken together the souls on these heavens exemplify the four cardinal virtues. Dante then ascends the Celestial Ladder and arrives in the eighth heaven, the sphere of the fixed stars. Here he is examined on the three theological virtues and is given a vision of man's redemption, the triumph of Christ, and the new Adam.

In the ninth sphere, the Primum Mobile, where all nature, time, and motion begin, Dante receives a vision of the angelic hierarchies and of the Creation. He is prepared for the celestial vision by a temporary blindness and finally enters with Beatrice into the Empyrean, the true Paradise. Here Dante beholds the saints in Heaven seated on tiers which form the petals of a snow-white rose. Beatrice takes her place among the Blessed and Saint Bernard comes to show Dante the Blessed Virgin and to beg her assistance as he brings Dante to see the True Light, the Blessed Trinity. Then Dante's powers fail, for he is absorbed in the love of God.

So many of the elements of the poem are realistic that the question of the reality of Dante's vision is a perennial one. Is the poem a personal record of a mystical experience, or is it a statement of personal conviction? Most critics hesitate to give an unqualified opinion, but most agree that the *Divine Comedy* belongs to the literature of mysticism.

This brief outline of the narrative or "story" of the poem hardly indicates the complexity and richness of the poetry. Neither does it begin, nor could it, to suggest the multiple interpretations that each figure contains. Barry Ulanov, in commenting on the complexity of the opening canto, has epitomized something of what happens in the reading of the *Divine Comedy*. "For Dante, in this hundredth part of the work alone, has linked his personal history to biblical events and events in his own lifetime, to the Creation, to the Trojan War, to Aeneas and his creator Virgil. Upon all this he has superimposed an allegory, sometimes personal, sometimes universal, always obscure, which is the despair of the literal-minded and the delight of the imaginative, but for all full of meaning."

Sister M.R.M.

THE LITTLE FLOWERS OF ST. FRANCIS

Author: Unknown
Type of work: Biographical legends and anecdotes
First transcribed: c.1320

Principal Ideas Advanced

Saint Francis of Assisi conformed the acts of his life to those of Christ.

Saint Francis elected poverty, and he gathered about him a brotherhood of men who lived with the joy which the love of God makes possible.

Saint Francis preached to the birds and the animals, and they were moved by the simplicity of his spirit.

Saint Francis, through his stigmata, reached the heights of the spiritual life.

The Little Flowers of St. Francis (*I Fioretti*) is an episodically arranged literary account of the Franciscan movement; the work is a collection of legends and anecdotes centering about the life of Saint Francis and written with simplicity and pious naïveté by an unknown writer of the Middle Ages. About a century after the death of Saint Francis an account of the Franciscan tradition was written in Latin by Brother Umberto di Santa Maria and entitled *The Deeds of St. Francis and His Companions.* Some fifty years later an anonymous friar of unquestioned literary skill, possibly Ugolino de Monte Giorgio, translated more than half of Umberto's work into Italian, called it *I Fioretti* (*The Little Flowers*), and added five new chapters entitled "The Considerations on the Holy Stigmata." Further chapters were added to *I Fioretti* during the century following its Italian translation. Thus, the "author" could more accurately be termed "editor," for the tales are based upon such diverse accounts as reports by eyewitnesses and companions of the saint, secondary reports by those who heard of the saint from others, and written documents such as letters and historical treatises.

The work was designed to satisfy the desire of those who wished to know more of Francis the *man*. Unlike the traditional biographies, which emphasize the remoter qualities of sanctity, *The Little Flowers* is composed of the homely, the unconventional, and the humorous, as well as the miraculous, all recorded in a manner so simple and direct as to suggest the very spirit of the saint about whom the work centers.

It would be a mistake to accuse either *The Little Flowers* or its subject of a simplicity without substance. The simplicity of the tales and of the saint they mirror is the simplicity of a profound and unquestioning faith. On one level the tales may be regarded as elaborations of folklore, but one has still to account for the unique spirit which transcends the direct accounts of Francis's sermons to the birds and animals, his visions, and the miracles. That the simple may stand with the sublime, that the two may in spirit be one, is the central truth of medieval religious faith.

I Fioretti begins with the familiar comparison of the life of Saint Francis with that of Christ: "First, it is to be considered that the glorious Messer St. Francis in all the acts of his life was conformed to Christ the blessed: in that as Christ, at the beginning of His preaching, chose Twelve Apostles to despise every earthly thing and to follow Him in poverty and in the other virtues; so did St. Francis, at the beginning, choose for the foundation of his Order twelve companions, possessors of most high Poverty. And as one of the Twelve Apostles of Christ, being rejected of God finally hanged himself by the neck; so likewise one of the twelve companions of St. Francis, whose name was Friar Giovanni della Cappella, apostatised and finally hanged himself by the neck. And unto the elect this is a great ensample and cause of humility and of fear; considering that no man can be certain that he will persevere unto the end in the grace of God." In these few sentences lies a fair example of the style of the piece—direct, succinct, ingenuous, and frequently accompanied by a moral.

As would be expected of a collection based on the accounts of associates in the Order and those whose knowledge of Francis began with his public life, *I Fioretti* begins with the founding of the brotherhood and some sketches of Francis's early companions in the Order. Many of the tales particularly involve Friar Bernard, Francis's "First-born son" (the first friar to join him), Friar Leo, the beloved "little sheep of God," Friar Masseo, and, of course, Saint Clare, Francis's cousin who gave her life to the pursuit of Lady Poverty by founding an order for women, the Poor Clares, of which Francis was the spiritual head. Tales as plain as the mere recounting of a sermon by Francis on the nature of joy are characteristically juxtaposed with straightforward recountings of miraculous apparitions and supernatural phenomena. That the medieval mind found both equally important testifies to its sophistication in religious matters; the entire tone of *I Fioretti* reflects the paradoxical merging of the profound and the naïve.

Among the most familiar tales is that of Francis's sermon to the birds, in which he is supposed to have quieted a flock to the extent that they allowed him to preach to them of God's goodness: ". . . and, as St. Francis spake these words unto them, all those birds began to open their beaks, and to stretch out their necks, and to open their wings, and reverently to bow their heads even unto the ground, and to show by their motions and by their songs that the holy father gave them very great delight . . ."; thereupon, Saint Francis blessed and dismissed them, and they flew into the air in the formation of a cross, bursting into song in order to carry the message of Francis to the four corners of the earth, just as, so the moral tells us, Saint Francis and his friars, committing themselves to the care of God, carry His word to all men.

A less familiar but deeply humorous encounter with a flock of birds is related by John R. H. Moorman in *A New Fioretti,* a collection of early stories about Saint Francis, not included in the original *Fioretti,* and translated within our own century. In this instance the birds flew away in fright when Saint Francis tried to preach to them, whereupon he reproached himself for his impudence in trying to force "irrational creatures to obey him as if he, and not God, were their creator." Both accounts reveal the humility and the power of the saint.

Another legend involving the animal kingdom, with which Saint Francis felt such affinity, is that of the wolf of Gubbio. It seems that into the village of Gubbio there came a fierce wolf that devoured not only animals, but men and women as well. The people begged Saint Francis to subdue the animal, and blessing the wolf and addressing him as his brother, Saint Francis did indeed admonish and tame the beast. The wolf, we are told, "lifted up his right fore-foot and put it with friendly confidence in the hand of St. Francis, giving thereby such token of fealty as he was able." The people of the village rejoiced, and they fed the tamed wolf until he died, "whereat the citizens lamented much, because as long as they saw him going so gently through their city, they recalled the better the virtue and sanctity of St. Francis."

Saint Francis's power to subdue was not confined to animals, as is shown in the story of his encounter with the Sultan of Babylon. Going boldly with his twelve companions into the land of the Saracens, from which no Christian had previously been permitted to escape alive, Francis and his band were captured and beaten, but their lives were spared and they were brought before the sultan. Inspired by the Holy Spirit, Francis began to speak, and so fervent was his preaching that the sultan was converted.

Much of *I Fioretti* deals with the lives of the friars associated with Saint Francis and with their own miracles, temptations, visions, and ecstasies. In these tales the master stands side by side with, rather than overshadows, the disciples—as Saint Francis himself would doubtless have wished.

I Fioretti technically ends with the accounts of miracles, but there follows a consideration of the Stigmata which is equal in value to all that which preceded it. In a lengthy preface we are told:

> *Because the said Stigmata were five, even as the wounds of our Lord Jesus Christ were five, there-*

fore this treatise will have five considerations.

The first consideration will be touching the manner in which St. Francis came to the holy mountain of Alvernia.

The second consideration will be touching the life which he lived, and the conversation which he held with his companions on the said holy mountain.

The third consideration will be touching the seraphic vision and the imprinting of the most sacred Stigmata.

The fourth consideration will be how St. Francis descended from the mountain of Alvernia, after he had received the sacred Stigmata, and returned to Santa Maria degli Angeli.

The fifth consideration will be touching certain Divine visions and revelations made after the death of St. Francis to holy friars and to other devout persons concerning the said sacred and glorious Stigmata.

Since the Stigmata mark the peak of Saint Francis's spiritual ascent, and many miracles were worked through them, a concrete and thorough perusal of this aspect of the saint's life is as important as a reading of the more legendary aspects. Though included as part of the whole study, the account of the Stigmata was a surety, whereas the tales of *I Fioretti* themselves, though based on fact, are undocumented as regards specific authoritative detail.

Through the need of a people eager to know intimate details about a beloved figure, details that sentimental or unimaginatively factual biographies could not supply, was born a sincere compendium of stories, the more sweet because of their innocence, yet as factual as human memory could render them. The perfume of these "little flowers," persisting through the centuries, makes their unknown author's words at the closing of his work come alive with hope: "And this sufficeth as touching the fifth consideration of the glorious and most holy Stigmata of our father St. Francis; whose life may God give us grace so to follow in this world that, by virtue of his glorious Stigmata, we may merit to be saved with him in paradise. To the praise of Jesus Christ and of the mendicant St. Francis. Amen."

J.S.

THE TREATISES AND SERMONS OF MEISTER ECKHART

Author: Johann Eckhart (c.1260-c.1327)
Type of work: Mysticism; catechetical sermons
First transcribed: c.1308-1327

PRINCIPAL IDEAS ADVANCED

True obedience is the highest virtue; one should freely do the will of God.

The more a man strives, through submission to God, to be receptive of the Divine inflowing, the happier he is.

The Son of God, the Word, is the just man by whose being justice itself is made known to men.

Johann Eckhart, "Meister" Eckhart, born in Hochheim, near Gotha, Germany, is a controversial but influential figure in the history of Christian mysticism. A Dominican teacher, Eckhart was Prior of Erfurt and Vicar of Thuringia before going to Paris in 1300 and becoming a master of sacred theology in 1302. He held official posts in the Dominican Order in Germany, and he gained fame as a preacher and teacher in Paris, Strassburg, and Cologne. The orthodoxy of some of his ideas was challenged by the Archbishop of Cologne, but Eckhart was cleared after a preliminary investigation in 1325. The archbishop persisted, however, and some of Eckhart's writings were condemned in the court at Cologne. A subsequent appeal by Eckhart to Rome led to the condemnation, in the Papal Bull of 1329, of some of Eckhart's ideas. Nevertheless, Meister Eckhart made a full profession of faith, and his reputation as a mystic and theologian has grown steadily over the years.

Until recently, Eckhart's fame has rested primarily on his German works, the sermons and treatises written in medieval German. In 1886 the Latin works were discovered, but it was not until 1958 that a selection from the Latin sermons and tractates was published in an English translation (by James M. Clark and John V. Skinner).

The first item in the Clark-Skinner translation is a German sermon, "On the Just Man and Justice." The text is from Wisdom 5:16: "Justus in perpetuum vivet et apud Dominum est merces eius." The just shall live forever, Eckhart explains, for the just man is one who is "conformed and transformed into justice," and justice is found in God: "The just man lives in God and God in him." The reward is with the Lord, Eckhart continues in his explication, because if one is just, one is with God in justice: "St. John says, 'The Word was with God.' He says 'with' and therefore the just man is like God, for God is justice. Hence if someone is in justice, he is in God and he is God."

The just man, Eckhart continues, is the Son of God. The Father, who is justice, "begets His Son as the just one, and the just one is His son." Wherever one finds a just man, just to the extent that one finds justice there, one finds God, and the just man, insofar as he is begotten by justice, is with the Word, as the Son. "The Father hastens and rushes to the end that we may be born in the Son and become the same as the Son is," writes Eckhart, and he insists that works which are impelled by justice must be the result of God's having moved man, through the Son, in the soul itself. The Holy Spirit is also revealed in the soul when the Son is revealed there, for, says Eckhart, "It is the nature of the Holy Spirit that I should be burnt in Him and should be completely consumed in Him and become entirely love."

It is interesting to compare this expression of an idea which is central in Eckhart's theology—the idea that all virtues spring from justice, which is God—with the more formal expression of the same conception in the Latin treatise, "The Commentary on St. John's Gospel." The German sermons were designed to be nontechnical presentations of edifying commentary on Scripture; the Latin sermons and treatises were directed to those who, like their author, were trained in Scholastic theology. But just as the German works, for all their emphasis on a complete devotion to God, show the mind of the theologian at work, so the Latin writings, which take advantage of every persuasive device known to the trained intellectual, reveal the passionate heart of the mystic.

Commenting on John's passage, "In the beginning was the Word," Meister Eckhart, by the use of adroitly chosen Scriptural passages, compares John to "a mighty eagle" who "drank of the Word itself in the bosom of the Father" and argues that the Apostle, who "drank from its very source in the Lord's breast the draught of heavenly wisdom" used the passage cited to "commend unto us the divinity of Christ and the mystery of the Trinity."

Eckhart then offers fifteen propositions which may be asserted as included in the meaning of "In the beginning was the Word," among them the following: the Word issued from God; therefore, it existed previously in God; the Word proclaims the nature of its source; it is distinct in person but not in substance; the Word is the living expression of the divine idea, and it thereby possesses creative power; it is the light in the darkness for men.

To illuminate his account, Eckhart then offers fifteen propositions about the "just man, in so far as he is just, in relation to the justice which begets him." The parallelism is drawn between the just man and justice, on the one hand, and the Word and God the Father, on the other: the "just man" *is* the Word. Among the conclusions drawn are the following: The just man is "*in* justice"; he is the concrete expression of the abstract; the just man "is the 'word' of justice, by means of which justice declares and manifests itself . . ."; the just man is the "son" of justice. The subtlety of Meister Eckhart's thought is seen in the twelfth proposition: ". . . the just man in justice itself is no longer begotten, nor is he begotten justice, but is unbegotten justice itself"; here the effort to preserve the unity of God despite the Trinity of Persons is evident.

Returning to the German works, one finds that much the same single-minded devotion which in the Latin sermon leads Eckhart to probe the depths of the concept "the Word" leads him, in his *Talks of Instruction* (c. 1297), to make the radical effort of transforming theological principles to edifying principles of Christian action. The *Talks,* we are told by the author himself, is a collection of "the talks that the Vicar of Thuringia, the Prior of Erfurt, Friar Eckhart of the Order of Preachers, had with those spiritual children who asked many questions when they sat together at collation."

The theme of the *Talks* is that virtue resides in the will, provided that the will is just. Since the just is whatever conforms to God's will, perfect obedience is the principal virtue. Eckhart quotes with approval Saint Augustine's pronouncement: "The true servant of God has no desire to be told or given what he likes to see or to hear; for his first and highest endeavour is to hear what pleases God most." Eckhart declares that all men are inclined to sin, and it sometimes seems as if God has hidden Himself, but those who detach themselves from the concerns which are an expression of self-will are rewarded with a new confidence in the power and love of God. One's external works should be harmonized with the internal ones, for it is the internal effort to find and obey God which pleases God most.

Eckhart's *Book of Divine Consolation* is a work in the German vernacular, addressed to Queen Agnes of Hungary (c.1280-1364), and probably intended to console her in her grief over the murder of her father, Albert, Duke of Austria and King of Germany, who was murdered by his nephew John. *The Book of Divine Consolation* or, as it is sometimes called, the *Liber Benedictus,* is one of the works which was said, in the Papal Bull of 1329, to contain heretical opinions. Eckhart's defense had been that the views he expressed were in accord with the ideas of Saint Bernard and Saint Thomas, and he declared that his accusers were not familiar with Scripture. Undoubtedly, Eckhart's paradoxical style, designed to express what only mystical experience can fully realize, contributed to his difficulties with his critics; as a theologian he moved easily from the abstract to the concrete, and he saw the two united in God, who is at once Father, Son, and Holy Spirit. To the extent that his language, like that of other mystics, encourages pantheism and obscures the Truth, the works of Eckhart must be handled with caution; but Meister Eckhart's insights as a mystic have given him a secure place in the history of Catholic thought.

Once again, in *The Book of Divine Consolation,* Eckhart relates goodness to the good man, and the author maintains that goodness, justice, and wisdom have all been shown in the Son. Consolation comes from submitting oneself to God; if one does the work of justice, he gains an internal strength that will sustain him in the state of external injury. If one loves internal things, says Eckhart, the loss of external things will not be painful. He who remains unconsoled must still be bound to creatures and far from God, but he who loves God and does the work which God's love demands will achieve that inner joy which overcomes all external suffering.

The emphasis on the joy that comes from giving oneself to God is also found in Eckhart's sermon "On Detachment," in which he claims that "the more man strives to be receptive of the Divine inflowing, the happier he is, and whoever can place himself in the highest preparedness for it also dwells in the highest happiness." To make oneself receptive, says Eckhart, one must be "uniform with God," and to be uniform with God, one must submit to God, not to creatures.

Again, in the sermon "The Nobleman," Eckhart declares that every man is body and spirit; the outer man is the "old man" who clings to the world, but the inner man is "the new man . . . the nobleman," who is the man of spirit. There are six stages of inward growth: living according to the example of good and holy men, living according to divine doctrine, withdrawing from one's mother and binding oneself to God, undergoing all temptation and pain for God, living in peace with oneself, and finding transformation through being drawn into the divine image and becoming a child of God. Blessedness comes from contemplating God and knowing that one knows God. In contemplating God "unveiled," writes Eckhart, "the soul receives all her being and her life, and draws all that she is from the ground of God, and . . . knows nothing but being and God."

MEDITATIONS ON THE LIFE OF CHRIST

Author: Saint Bonaventure (1221-1274) and an unknown Franciscan friar of the fourteenth century
Type of work: Mystical biography; manual of devotion
First transcribed: c.1330

Principal Ideas Advanced

Christ's life is a model for that of a Christian, and prayerful consideration of His words and deeds arouses devotion and is a principal means of growing in virtue.

In meditating on an event in the life of Christ, one should imagine it as taking place before one's eyes, and for this purpose one should not hesitate to add details which are not found in the Gospel accounts.

Through prayer one can enjoy an experimental knowledge of God which excels the knowledge attained by rational investigation.

Less than a third of the book accepted for centuries as Saint Bonaventure's *Meditations on the Life of Christ* is actually the work of Saint Bonaventure himself, but this fact does not detract from the importance of the work or from the influence it has had on the theory and practice of prayer and on the popular art forms of the Middle Ages.

The *Meditations* is a literary counterpart of the mystery and morality plays, which drew not only their inspiration but also many dramatic details directly from this work. Traces of the work, or at least of the type of piety it embodies, are also discernible in the *Spiritual Exercises* of Saint Ignatius Loyola, founder of the Jesuits in the sixteenth century. This distinction alone would make the work one of significance, since the *Spiritual Exercises* has exerted a profound influence on the ascetical life of the Church down to the present. The *Meditations on the Life of Christ,* in its turn, was greatly influenced by the devotional and mystical writings of the Cistercian abbot and reformer, Saint Bernard of Clairvaux. Thus, the work forms a link uniting two important schools of spirituality.

In the *Meditationes vitae Christi,* only the section on the passion of Christ is the work of Saint Bonaventure. All the rest was written by an unknown Franciscan friar of the early fourteenth century. Designed as an aid to prayer for nuns, the book was originally written in Italian, but it was translated almost immediately into Latin, and then back again into various vernaculars.

The work embodies much of the

traditional popular piety of the period. In contrast to ascetical writings of the early centuries of the Church, which emphasized the divinity of Christ and His doctrinal teachings, this fourteenth century manual of devotion concentrates on His humanity. Its aim is less to instruct than to inspire.

Saint Bonaventure, to whom the work was so long attributed, was Minister General of the Franciscans, a leading religious order founded early in the thirteenth century and remarkably adapted to the needs of the Church in the growing urban centers. A contemporary of the incomparable Dominican, Saint Thomas Aquinas, Saint Bonaventure was known, as was Saint Thomas, as one of the leading theologians of the University of Paris.

Although not entirely Saint Bonaventure's own writing, and certainly not typical of his philosophical and theological thought, the *Meditations* is an effective exponent of his theory that prayer should be a kind of experimental knowledge of God, a knowledge far excelling that attainable by rational investigation. This idea of prayer is perfectly consistent with Saint Bonaventure's teaching that the purpose of philosophy and all lesser sciences is to lead to devotion. The pseudo-Bonaventure who incorporated Saint Bonaventure's work in his own book saw meditation on the life of Christ as an indispensable step to higher contemplation. More than that, it was an exercise never to be abandoned. To despise such loving consideration of the humanity of Christ would be a sin of pride.

The *Meditations on the Life of Christ* consists of a series of graphic sketches of scenes from the Gospel, interspersed with moral applications and exhortations to virtue. These latter are geared to the feminine audience for whom the book was intended, a fact which helps explain the author's persistent and clumsy attempts to evoke a particular type of emotional response. While the narrative generally follows the pattern of the New Testament accounts of the life of Christ, the work is embellished with much imaginative material. Early in the work the pseudo-Bonaventure explains that he will use his imagination "as long as we write nothing contrary to truth, justice, and sound doctrine, or against faith or morals." The reader is advised to distinguish between those passages which are based on Holy Scripture and those which are the product of imagination. That it was within the power of the ordinary reader to make this distinction between history and legend was probably an unwarranted presumption on the part of the author. He seems, moreover, to have been unaware of the inherent danger of abuse in a method of prayer that gave such large play to the imagination. The writer's aim was to help others grow in the loving imitation of Christ through meditation on His life and virtues. "If you wish to gather fruit from these things," he writes, "imagine that you are actually present when the Lord Jesus says or does them; as if you heard with your own ears, and saw with your own eyes, and attend with your whole mind and heart, intently and joyfully, putting aside for the moment all other cares and solicitudes."

A large proportion of the book is composed of selected texts from the mystical writings of Saint Bernard. The author of the *Meditations* is careful to acknowledge his debt; wherever he borrows long passages from the famous Cistercian, he consistently credits his source, explaining that he uses the words of Saint Bernard, "for they are not only spiritual and heart-stirring, but full of beauty and of exhortation to the service of God."

Prayerful consideration of the life of Christ, practiced regularly, is advocated as the most necessary and likely means for leading the soul to perfection. From a frequent and habitual meditation on Christ's words and actions, the soul, moved by love, learns to adopt His attitudes. In this way the follower of Christ learns what to do and what to avoid in every circumstance of life.

The moral teaching of the *Meditations* reflects the importance of poverty in the Franciscan spirituality of the period. The follower of Christ must not encumber himself with superfluous goods, "for a soul burdened with a supply of temporal things cannot ascend to God."

The first part of the *Meditations* gives a picturesque account of the birth, infancy, and childhood of Christ. An introductory meditation is in the form of an allegory, in which Mercy and Peace plead with God against Truth and Justice for the salvation of mankind. "And when [Mercy] had long and frequently importuned the Lord, . . . He at length replied: 'Go, call your sisters, Truth and Justice, whom you behold arrayed against you, and let us hear them likewise.' " Many of the details found in these meditations became in time traditional elements of the Christmas story and reflect the same love of realism that characterized the art of the period. The Child's Mother is described nursing Him, and wrapping Him in her veil. The ox and ass are shown breathing over the Infant to keep Him warm, "as though they had the use of reason, and knew the poor little Child was cold."

In the meditations which have as their subject the public life of Christ, the author states his intention to treat only the outstanding features, the principal events, but when he comes to the sacred passion, he asserts that nothing should be omitted. The reader is reminded that his conscience will tell him how his own life falls short of the ideal set forth by the example of Christ. Again poverty is singled out as a virtue especially exemplified in the life of Christ and proposed for imitation. Saint Bernard is quoted at length in order to add the weight of his authority to that of the author. In a later meditation which incorporates Saint Bernard's teaching on charity, the value of the soul is shown to be the measure of its charity. In the soul of one who excels in charity, God dwells with delight and shows something of His glory.

The meditations on the passion and death of Christ, which constitute the portion of the work written by Saint Bonaventure, describe in detail the physical and mental sufferings of Christ. It was especially this aspect of the life of Christ which captured the medieval mind and heart and, even more, the medieval imagination. The reader is again reminded to banish all distracting thoughts and to make himself present at the scenes as they unfold before him. From the prayerful consideration of the sacred passion the soul will receive "a new compassion, a new love, new consolations, and consequently, as it were, a new state of soul, which seems to be a presage and share of eternal glory."

The considerations on the passion

are followed by meditations on the resurrection of Christ, His appearances to His disciples, His ascension, and the descent of the Holy Spirit upon the disciples at Pentecost.

Throughout the book the attempt is made to correlate the mysteries of the life of Christ with the feasts of the Church, showing that the pseudo-Bonaventure recognized a relationship between public worship and private prayer, though it is evident that he looks especially to the latter as a means of achieving union with God. What is significant by its absence in this attempt to relate the meditations to liturgical prayer is any evidence of an understanding of the centrality of the Eucharist and the sacraments in Christian worship.

A closing exhortation summarizes the spirit and purpose of the entire work: "You see now how this meditation on Christ in His Humanity is corporeal in deed, in fact, but spiritual in mind. . . . By adopting this habit, you will steady your mind, be trained to virtues, and receive strength of soul. . . . Let meditation of Christ's life be your one and only aim, your rest, your food, your desire, your study."

The popularity of the *Meditations on the Life of Christ* is attested by the hundreds of extant manuscripts in Latin and various vernaculars. Late in the nineteenth century the work was still being published in popular editions as an authentic writing of Saint Bonaventure.

Today scholars are agreed about the work's authorship. They also recognize that the book in no way adequately represents the Franciscan school of spirituality. It does, however, illustrate the popular devotional mentality of the late thirteenth and early fourteenth centuries, and it shows one significant form of reaction to the speculative theology of the period.

Sister M.E.

THE LITTLE BOOK OF ETERNAL WISDOM

Author: Blessed Henry Suso, O.P. (c.1295-1365)
Type of work: Spiritual instruction
First transcribed: c.1330

Principal Ideas Advanced

Christ died for our sins; meditation on this redemptive act reveals it to be not only an indication of how much God loves man but also a pattern of the Christian life.

In order to live well, we must learn how to die; we prepare for our physical death and the judgment to follow by dying spiritually to the things of this world.

The *Little Book of Eternal Wisdom,* which is without a doubt an authentic work of the fourteenth century Dominican mystic, Henry Suso, forms part of a larger work, *The Exemplar,* which purports to bring together Suso's writings in a master or model edition because of the diffusion of pirate and inaccurate copies. *The Exemplar* contains a life of Suso whose authenticity is widely rejected; the *Little Book of Eternal Wisdom;* the *Little Book of Truth;* and a collection of letters. Because it is highly doubtful that Suso himself edited his own works in *The Exemplar,* we need not think of the *Little Book of Eternal Wisdom* as part of a larger literary whole. If there were any doubt of this, the fact that Suso himself wrote an enlarged and rearranged Latin version of it, the *Horologium sapientiae,* would satisfy us that the work was considered by Suso himself to be independent.

The literary form of the *Little Book of Eternal Wisdom* is that of a conversation between Suso, described as the Servitor of Eternal Wisdom, and Eternal Wisdom. Suso says in the Prologue that nothing is attributed to Eternal Wisdom which is not found in, or consonant with what is found in, Scripture. This is not to suggest that the book is not based on personal experiences of his, but, as he points out, his conversations with Eternal Wisdom were not carried on by means of physical speech or imaginary answers. The answers given in the book are simple because they are addressed to simple souls who still have bad habits to overcome.

Suso points out that some men are drawn to God even unknown to themselves. They are kept from sin, they develop a correct appraisal of worldly affairs, and then one day they recognize that what their hearts pine for, what they are unable to find in any created thing, is the Eternal Wisdom itself. Such a soul is then desirous of knowing more and more about God in order that the quality of its love for God can increase. How do we come to know God? The answer to this question sets the stage for most of the following meditations: "According to the natural order, we follow the highest emanation of all beings from their first principle through the noblest beings down to the lowest, but the return to the first principle takes place through the lowest to the highest. Therefore, if you desire to gaze upon my uncreated divinity, you must first learn to know and love me in my suffering humanity, because that is the quickest way to eternal happiness."

For the Christian, Christ is the pattern of life, and everything that He did has an exemplary character for his followers. Suso singles out the Passion of Christ as the series of events on which meditation is most important and fruitful for the soul that would achieve true happiness: "No one can arrive at divine heights or taste mystical sweetness without passing through my human bitterness." To attempt to scale the heights without imitating the Passion of Christ is to risk a fall to the lowest depths. The worldly soul recoils from the thought that it must somehow repeat the terrible sufferings Christ endured. What gives the soul courage is the thought that in this effort to overcome worldly attachments we are assured the help of God's grace. What is the essence of the imitative suffering asked of one who seeks perfect union with God? "Break off your pleasure in useless seeing and frivolous hearing," we are told; "love and take pleasure in those things which formerly were repugnant to you; for my sake give up all pampering of your body. Seek all your rest in me; love physical discomfort; endure wrongs willingly; desire contempt; renounce your concupiscences; die to all your lusts. These are the rudiments of the school of wisdom, read from the opened, wounded book of my crucified body."

It is a strong doctrine Suso teaches in the *Little Book of Eternal Wisdom*. Christ died for our sins and endured the humiliations prior to the Crucifixion, but not because He was incapable of redeeming man except by such suffering, for since the Incarnation was not absolutely necessary for man's salvation, the horrible sufferings Christ endured could hardly have been chosen because they were needed. The traditional theology has always taught that the Passion of Christ was chosen with an eye to the man He was saving; that is, Christ acts in a way proportioned to our understanding. His suffering and death show us the horribleness of sin and the extent of God's love for man. As a measure of love the Passion of Christ is an object of tearful joy for the devout soul; so, too, his own sufferings undertaken and accepted in imitation of Christ can be a joyful weaning from the world in order that one can seek union with the God who loved mankind so much that He gave his only Son. Without this parallel, it is difficult to understand Suso's insistence on the need for suffering.

Souls are drawn to God when they learn that nothing in this life can constitute true happiness. God's loveableness is manifest in the sufferings of Christ, and by meditating on them we will find not only how much God loved man but also a pattern for our life. The Christian must give himself entirely to God through Christ, freely and forever; his life must become one of redemptive suffering: "By being satisfied with the bare necessities of life you will have your hands truly nailed to my cross. Take up good works cheerfully and perseveringly; this will shackle your left foot. Restrain and stabilize your fickle mind and wandering thoughts in me; then your right foot will be fixed to my cross."

Suso's devotion to the Blessed Virgin is manifest when he treats of her role in Christ's Passion. The way of the Cross and the sorrows of Christ's mother blend, and Suso wants to learn from Mary the proper attitude toward Christ's sacrifice. She remained loyal to Him to the very end, identifying herself with His death, and she will assist us in our efforts to imitate Him.

The first twenty chapters of the *Little Book of Eternal Wisdom* form Part One of the work; Chapters Twenty-one through Twenty-four make up Part Two; the twenty-fifth and last chapter is the whole of Part Three. The first part contains meditations on the Passion; the second teaches how to die, how to live, how to receive Christ lovingly in the Blessed Sacrament, and how to pray heartily. The death in question is spiritual as well as physical death; it is by a spiritual dying to this world while we live that we come to our physical death prepared for what lies beyond. How then should one live? True life is an interior life, and to lead it we must keep ourselves detached from all men, disengaged from external images, and elevated to the contemplation of God.

The final chapter of the *Little Book of Eternal Wisdom* lists one hundred points of meditation which one should devoutly recall each day. These points cover some aspect of the suffering and death of Christ. They are grouped in fives and tens, and usually a group is followed by a prayer. At the end of the book, Suso gives permission for copying the final chapter independently of the rest of the book. That chapter is at once a résumé of what has gone before and a practical devotional exercise.

A mystical writer of the stature of Suso is scarcely in need of any recommendation or praise. The *Little Book of Eternal Wisdom* has been a popular handbook of the aspiring soul for centuries. While in many ways dated, as, for example, in point of style, it remains a powerful and persuasive call to interior life. Few authors have been able to see the Passion of Christ as a pattern for Christian life, but Suso contends that the sacrifice of the God-Man must be repeated by those who glory in His name. Unless they take up their crosses and follow Him they cannot be His disciples. This is the fundamental, the simple message of the *Little Book of Eternal Wisdom.* If its message seems harsh and uncompromising in our age of comfort, this can hardly be laid to medieval excess. It is Christ who first calls into question our concern for comfort, our ceaseless quest of evanescent pleasures, our attachment to creatures. Like every great spiritual writer, Suso is able to show that his message is finally a repetition of the message of Christ.

R.M.

THE SPIRITUAL ESPOUSALS

Author: Blessed Jan Van Ruysbroeck (1293-1381)
Type of work: Mystical theology
First transcribed: 1343-1351

Principal Ideas Advanced

There are three different levels of Christian life, the active, the interior, and the contemplative.

On each of these levels God's love is available to all in sufficient amount for their salvation and those who do not advance beyond the active or interior life should neither trouble themselves on this account nor disparage those who do go higher.

There is a perfection proper to each life, but as it is attained and practiced the soul is drawn to a more complete love of God, and hence a higher life.

In the ascent to God the whole man is to be perfected, body, soul, and spirit, for nature, which is the bride of God, was made in His image and reflects His glory.

Blessed Jan Van Ruysbroeck's *Spiritual Espousals* was the fruit of a life dedicated to God from early childhood. At the age of eleven he had put himself under the guidance of his uncle, John Hinckaert, a saintly priest in Brussels who was trying to live a life modeled on the simplicity of Apostolic days. His mother followed him to Brussels, entered a religious house, and died shortly after. Ruysbroeck served at the collegiate church of St. Gudule for twenty-six years with his uncle and Francis Van Coudenberg, a canon. He lived a humble life of prayer, contemplation, study, and the cure of souls. He first became prominent sometime before 1344 (the date is uncertain) when he attacked the heretical doctrines of Bloemardinne (died 1335), a woman who was proselytizing for the Brethren of the Free Life. She had been teaching that the flesh was the creation of the Prince of Darkness and that since the spirit created by God was unfortunately imprisoned in the flesh during this life we should let the flesh do what it will so that it will not trouble the spirit in its worship of God. Ruysbroeck recognized the utter incompatibility of this essentially pre-Christian dualism with the fact of the Incarnation, and he never ceased to advance the idea, in opposition to dualism, that the material world as well as the spiritual had been sanctified by God and must be dedicated to Him. In 1343 he left Brussels with his uncle and Van Coudenberg, retiring to the nearby forest of Soignes with the intention of living a simple monastic life. They were joined by unexpected disciples, and in 1349 they organized themselves into a body of Augustinian canons in the hermitage of Groenendael. Ruysbroeck was elected prior, and under his guidance the priory became a center of spiritual life for the region of the lower Rhine. He became known for his saintliness, and he attracted many disciples, among them John Tauler (c. 1300-1361) and Geert de Groote (1340-1384). Through Groote he influenced the Brethren of the Common Life, who took *The Spiritual Espousals* as their rule.

Although Ruysbroeck tries to tell the reader nothing of himself, the *Espousals* reveal him to have been a man of natural curiosity and homely wisdom. In his description of the mystical life he often refers to nature: the habits of the bee, ant, and bat; the motion of the planets and action of boiling water. At Groenendael he was familiar with the orchard, kitchen, infirmary, and library. It was his habit to wander in the forest with his writing tablet, and late in life he declared he had written nothing that had not been directly inspired by the Holy Spirit.

The Spiritual Espousals is divided into three books treating the active, interior, and contemplative life. Each book is divided into four parts based on the text "Ecce Sponsus venit, exite obviam ei": *Ecce,* the work of vision, *Sponsus venit,* the many comings of the Bridegroom, *exite,* the soul going forth on paths of virtue, *obviam ei,* the embrace of the soul and the heavenly Spouse.

Ruysbroeck begins his discussion of the active life by observing that to see spiritually we need God's grace, a will turned to Him, and a conscience free of sin. These are the prerequisites for a holy life in the world. Preventive grace, which operates both from within and without, reminds man that his home is not in this world. It operates from without through sickness or loss of possessions and from within by meditation on the Passion and the brevity of our earthly life. However, when man has done all that he can "then there is need of the immeasurable riches of God, that they may finish the work." Unless the light of grace shines into the soul it will not be able to advance in perfection.

The second point in the active life, writes Ruysbroeck, is the realization that God created the world out of love in order that rational beings might know His glory. God Himself, through Christ, taught men how best to know Him, and we must imitate Christ in all things. We should be particularly concerned to imitate His humility, charity, and suffering in patience. He was humble in His desire to take on human flesh, and as a man He was obedient to the older dispensation, to the commandments, and to the Jewish conventions of His time, whenever they were appropriate. Christ's charity was adorned with all virtues, coming, as it did, from "the boundless well of the Holy Ghost."

In describing the Passion of Our Lord, Ruysbroeck demonstrates a considerable talent for dramatic narrative when he tells us that Christ "was stripped mother-naked." Christ's first coming was to man in the active life. His second coming is daily in man's soul: "When a man contemplates his littleness in the depths of his being he becomes a valley of humility and Christ, the Sun of righteousness, makes him 'fruitfull in perfect virtues and in good works.'" The third coming of Christ is in the hour of death as the Judge.

The third part of the active life, according to Ruysbroeck, is the soul's going forth into the world strengthened by humility and love, from which all other virtues come. If man desires to keep the virtues he acquires, he must "rule over his soul as if it were a kingdom." The culmination of the active life is to meet with Christ in the world. We meet Him if we are inclined to Him in all things and put everything below our duty to the Father. The highest form of meeting God in the world is when the soul "loves and rests above all gifts and above herself and above all creatures, [for] then she dwells in God and God in her." This highest form of the active life leads naturally to an interior life of yearning for God.

The three conditions for spiritual seeing in the interior life are God's grace possessed with inner zeal, a heart bare of alien images, cares, and distractions, and a turning of all one's resources to a flowing into the unity of God. There are three unities in man by nature. The highest unity we possess is beyond intellectual comprehension. It is the direct possession of God through the Holy Spirit. The second unity is that of our superior powers: "We possess this unity in ourselves above our powers of sense; and from this come memory and understanding and will and all the power of spiritual acts." The third unity is that of physical strength. All physical acts flow from this unity, and in it the soul takes the form of the material life and animates the body. "These three unions exist naturally in man, as one life and one realm. In the lowest man is sensual and animal . . . ; in the middle union man is rational and spiritual; in the highest man is preserved in his essence. And this exists naturally in all men." Ruysbroeck ends the first part of Book II by stating that to begin a fruitful inner life man should be "unimpeded by earthly love and sorrow, by gain and loss; by exaltation and by depression; by the cares of others; by joy and by misery; and that he be not preoccupied with any creature."

The first coming of Christ in the life of yearning for God is an inward coming in which He "draws man with all strength upwards to heaven, and urges him to have unity with God." The second manner of inward coming is a flowing of divine gifts into the highest power of the soul, illuminating it and making it rich. At this point there must be a flowing back into God of all the gifts that God gives to it. Ruysbroeck often uses the verb "flow" to describe the growing reciprocal love of God and the soul as the soul advances in perfection. The third manner of the inward coming of Christ "is an inward stirring or touching in the unity of the spirit, where the highest powers of the soul have their dwelling and flow out and come back again."

Ruysbroeck discusses at length the first inward coming of Christ. He likens the fire of God's love driving the soul upward to a fire beneath boiling water, and says that whenever the heart falls back the fire of the Holy Ghost drives it upward again. In his ascent to God the contemplative must preserve that singleness of the heart which binds together body and soul, heart and sense. From singleness comes inwardness.

In the beauty, power, and simplicity of his comparisons Ruysbroeck reveals a poetical genius with its roots in the common life of man. In discussing the different manners of the first inward coming in the interior life, he relates them in a natural progression with the seasons of the year. In one particularly fine passage his prose equals the most inspired passages of the Bible: "So when the summer is near and the sun is high, the earth's humidity is drawn up first through the roots and then through the trunk into the branches of the tree; and from this come leaf and blossom and fruit. When Christ, the eternal Sun, mounts high and ascends in our hearts, so that summer comes there and they are made fair in virtues, in just the same manner he gives light and His heat in our yearning, and draws the heart away from all multiplicity of earthly things, and makes singleness and inwardness, and causes the heart to swell and to put forth leaves with inward love, and to flower with a yearning devotion, and to bring forth fruit with praise, and to keep the fruit forever, in humble sorrow because it is not more."

The second manner of the first inward coming Ruysbroeck likens to a rain of consolation that makes all virtue double itself. He again gives the spiritual state a concrete reference by relating it to the third sign of the zodiac, Gemini, in which the sun is quickening the work of nature. In the third manner man feels "an inward need and command in the heart that it should go out towards a higher unity." He likens this manner to the sun in Cancer, burning with its hottest heat as it draws to fullness all the crops of the earth. In this manner the soul experiences a tempest of love which is an "inward impatience." It is in the tempest of love that a man is sometimes "drawn up in the spirit" so that truths may be communicated to him that will be useful "to other men or to the times that are yet to come." This was the state in which the prophets of the Old Testament foresaw the coming of Christ. The tempest of love is one of the most crucial points in the development of the mystic, for while in it he may be deprived of his senses from without by a single temptation of the Devil.

In the fourth manner of the inward coming, Ruysbroeck writes, the sun is in Virgo and all its work is complete. The soul that was so recently battered in a tempest of love now feels itself to be exiled. God takes Himself away to teach the heart humility and urge it on even further in the way of perfection: "When these men who have passed out of the tempest into calm are in this way deprived of all comfort, and, as it seems to them, are finished with the anguish of love and are forsaken by God and all His creatures, it is then that they are well able to gather in their harvest of every kind, for the corn and the wine are now ready, ripe and timely, for they have stood long in the sun." At every turn Ruysbroeck sees the natural world as a vast analogue for the life of the spirit.

As he describes the continuing ascent of the liberated man Ruysbroeck turns to metaphors involving water to clarify the relationship between the soul and God. The second manner of inward coming is compared to a fountain with three streams. The grace of God is a well of water, and each stream of grace flows to one of the three different unities man possesses by nature. God is compared to a sea, "ceaselessly flowing into each one of His elect, according to the needs and worth of each." The third coming, which has already been described as a "touching," is beyond the understanding of reason, although reason continues to function.

One of the hallmarks of Ruysbroeck's mysticism is his view that as the soul advances in perfection it loses none of its faculties or powers of perception. The whole man advances, not simply one aspect of his consciousness. At this point the soul is brought face to face with the divine clarity of God which is the Word Himself. Though reason must "remain standing outside the gates, the spirit's power of loving will pass on, for this power is impelled and compelled as is the understanding, and it is blind, and it will know enjoyment, and to enjoy is more to savour and to feel than it is to understand. Therefore love will press on where understanding is locked out." Finally, in the fourth coming of Christ, the soul is led by love to rest in "that state of naked being in which God gives Himself, in all His riches, without mean." God's giving here is direct and unimpeded in any way, by methods or means.

Ruysbroeck is careful to distinguish what he calls the false "natural rest," advocated by the Brethren of the Free Life, from the genuine resting in God which is the life of the contemplative. The passive waiting "which they feel and have in themselves in emptiness" is not the contemplation of the Godhead, but rather a purely selfish abandoning of will in order to achieve peace of mind. The surest sign that theirs was not a genuine mysticism Ruysbroeck found in the fact they would not stir themselves to perform acts of charity or attend the "exercises of Holy Church." The system expounded in the *Espousals* never gives the contemplative any grounds for drifting from a basic Christian life of faith and good works.

Ruysbroeck begins Book III, the life of contemplation, with a summary of the conditions necessary for spiritual sight in this most advanced state. At this point the contemplative must be ordered in all virtues from without, but "empty of all outward works as though he performed nothing." He must live in a continual inner dependence upon God. He must have lost himself in a darkness from which he can never find himself in any natural way. In this darkness the mystic finds "an incomprehensible light, which is the Son of God," and he "feels himself to be that very light by which he sees, and nothing else." There are no manners of Christ's coming in the contemplative life, for beyond all exercise of virtue and all works of the creature He is His only work "in the highest excellence of the spirit."

The going out of the soul in the contemplative life is the activity of pure love, which is "an everlasting work without beginning." God contemplates Himself and all things, and in His contemplation all creatures have an everlasting life, "outside themselves, as it were in their everlasting exemplar." The final ascent of the soul, through the Holy Spirit, to the "delectation" or complete enjoyment of the Godhead is shrouded in the mystery of God's contemplation of Himself. Ruysbroeck says that as God is "a living depth" He goes into the Son who returns the Father's wisdom to Himself, and from the meeting of Father and Son springs the Holy Spirit. It is important to note here that these distinctions do not apply to or have any meaning in the dimension of time. The Father has gone to the Son, the Son has returned to the Father, and the Holy Spirit has sprung from that meeting from all eternity. These are not acts in time but constitute the very structure of infinity itself. Man "sees without measure as God does, the riches which are God, in the unity of the living depths where man possesses Him according to the manner of His uncreated being." The Prior of Groenendael lived an outwardly uneventful life in an undistinguished corner of Europe. What can be seen from one point of view as a paradox of Christianity was for Ruysbroeck literally true: "He who finds his life will lose it, and he who loses his life for my sake, will find it."

D.M.R.

THE CLOUD OF UNKNOWING

Author: Unknown
Type of work: Mystical theology
First transcribed: Second half of the fourteenth century

Principal Ideas Advanced

Every man who has truly and deliberately forsaken the world is called by God to the way of contemplation; this higher way involves reading, meditation, and prayer; it cultivates the will and concentrates the attention on God in his unity.

A guide can encourage a man in the pursuit of this way and by analogies and images can suggest what the process of contemplation is.

Since God is unknowable, the contemplative state is one of unknowing; acceptance of this dark state will prepare one for impulses of the soul, surgings of love toward God, and perhaps even brief, piercing visions of Him.

The mystical state is a God-given grace; it is not the product of any human effort.

The Cloud of Unknowing is one of the earliest and perhaps the most polished of English mystical treatises. In seventy-five short chapters of prose, it describes that "solitary form and manner of living" in which one may "learn to lift up the foot" of his love and "to step towards that state and degree of living that is *perfect,* and the last state of all."

Highly specialized and other-worldly though the topic is, a decidedly personal quality informs the work and is part of the reason for its success. The form is a pseudo-dialogue. The author speaks directly to his reader, explaining, cajoling, commanding. Then, from time to time, he imagines questions or expostulations bursting from his reader and to these he makes reply. The interplay of two individual personalities animates the whole presentation.

The author specifically addresses a man of twenty-four years, one who has clearly made progress already in the spiritual life and is probably a member of a religious community. Now this young man has had a sudden penetrating experience of the inexorable swiftness of time and of his own helplessness in pursuing perfection. He is not seeking the life of "true contemplatives," for the outward form of his life may still be active. What distinguishes him is the "inward stirring under the privy spirit of God."

The abiding attitude of the author toward this "ghostly friend" blends awe, tenderness, and stock terms of disparagement. He points out the singular love which God has directed toward the young man, creating "a leash of a lovely [loving] longing," by which God has "how sweetly and how graciously . . . privily pulled thee to the third degree and manner of living, the which is called *"singular."* He brusquely demands meekness from this "weak wretch," whom he accuses of having a "weary wretched heart and sleeping sloth."

The author is peremptory at moments, but he is far from presuming a superiority over his client, in either goodness or wisdom. He distinguishes "them that have been in customary sins (as I am myself and have been)" from those who "never sinned deadly with an abiding will and advisement, but through frailty and unknowing." The humility which he insistently preaches conditions his expression: "But now thou askest me and sayest: 'How shall I think on himself [God], and what is he?' Unto this I cannot answer thee, except to say: 'I know not.' " Here the author is himself in the same state of unknowing as is his young friend.

Although the author writes for one particular person, he also expects others to read his treatise. Indeed, his only fear is that his work will be picked up by the idly curious or carpingly critical.

The work was popular, judging by the number of extant manuscripts. In the seventeenth century its language was brought up to date by a Benedictine monk, Father Augustine Baker. With renewed accessibility to the general reading public, the book became established as one of the classic English works on mysticism and is esteemed by both Protestants and Catholics.

Part of the appeal of the work lies in the self-evident authority with which the author writes. Attempts to identify him have, most scholars feel, proved futile. But one can deduce that he was probably a priest, possibly a member of a religious order, and clearly unusually well read in the general theological and mystical works of the day, including Saint Gregory, Saint Bernard, Albertus Magnus, Saint Thomas Aquinas, and Richard of St. Victor. His principal inspiration is the Syrian monk Denis or Dionysius the Pseudo-Areopagite (probably fifth century). Dionysius's phrase "The most godly knowing of God is that which is known by unknowing" and his image *"caligo ignorantiae"* provide the central doctrine, the title, and the controlling metaphor of this work. Like Dionysius, the author of *The Cloud of Unknowing* stresses the transcendence of God and, hence, the action of the will rather than that of the intellect. While he does not abolish thought, he does point out, "By love may he [God] be gotten and holden; but by thought never."

The Neoplatonic influence and the broad literary and doctrinal background tend to set *The Cloud of Unknowing* apart from other English mystical treatises. But this work in other respects departs from the Near-Eastern traditions and is markedly English. It provides a personal, not communal, way of perfection. It incorporates humor and satire. It is direct, warm, and homely, not austere. Not to an aristocracy of intellect or social class does the author speak but to "all that have forsaken the world in a true will." This universality of intended audience is characteristically English, as is the insistence that the mystical state is a God-given grace, not the product of any human effort.

The homeliness just mentioned appears in the images chosen by the author to suggest the sublime mystical state, images taken for the most part from everyday life and hence commonplace and graphic, but not decoratively pictorial. The contemplative is to look in the mirror of God's word, wash at the well of confession, smite down thoughts, grope toward God, knit himself to God, melt all distractions to water, shear away desire, and stalwartly step over distractions. The author speaks of the congealed lump of sin, the gamesomeness of a father with a child, the double-edged dreadful sword of discretion, the nakedness of intent, and those hells' calves, the devils. The cloud itself hovers over all, its darkness emphasized, and contrasting with the occasional beam of ghostly light. The following passage typifies the combination of imagery and paradox and suggests the two voices heard in the work: " 'Where then,' sayest thou, 'shall I be? Nowhere, by thy tale!' Now truly thou sayest well; for there would I have thee. For why, nowhere bodily is everywhere ghostly. . . . For I tell thee truly that I had rather be so nowhere bodily, wrestling with that blind nought, than to be so great a lord that I might when I would be everywhere bodily, merrily playing with all this aught as a lord with his own."

Besides the transcendent nature of the mystical experience, what the author must struggle to express is the unity of that experience, a unity so great as to defy discursive thought and ordinary language. Thus, the author asks that concentration be on a single word, rather than on a sequence or a scene. Words suitable as focal points for concentration are: "God," "love," "sin," "help." One can use one of these words as a tamper to push down memory, as a hammer to beat on the cloud. In a typical comparison, borrowed from Scripture but freshly applied, this monosyllabic prayer is likened to a man's cry of "Fire!" which no one, even his enemy, even though it be midwinter's night, can resist.

The author is insistent in arguing that the figure of the cloud is but a metaphor. Do not think, he warns, that this cloud is "any cloud congealed of the vapours that fly in the air, or any darkness such as in thine house on nights, when the candle is out." Darkness is "a lacking of knowing." In the same vein, the author ridicules those who take literally "in" or "up" or "under." Ludicrous similes illustrate that the appropriate inwardness requires no pious expression or posture: "Some set their eyes in their heads as though they were sturdy [stupid] sheep beaten in the head. . . . Some hang their heads on one side, as if a worm were in their ears." Those who literally look upward mistakenly think that they will find a hole in the firmament through which they can look.

The denial that bodily activity and bodily images are beneficial in contemplation distinguishes the author of *The Cloud of Unknowing* from such a contemporary mystical writer as Walter Hilton. Much of the triumph of the book lies in the author's powerful use of the resources of language to create a vivid, comprehensible, and evocative picture of the way, without compromising the intangibility and transcendence of that way and its goal.

The result is one of the finest treatises on mysticism, a forthright and practical work, without any mechanical steps or complex philosophical categorizing, the more useful and immediate for being written in the vernacular. Himself helping to establish what is now the traditional understanding of the mystical life, the author presents it as one of infused prayer. Never losing sight of his conviction that contemplative vision is a free gift, springing "unto God as a sparkle from the coal," the author expounds comprehensively the dispositions which must be cultivated to enable one to receive this gift.

J.K.W.

ON HIS OWN IGNORANCE

Author: Petrarch (Francesco Petrarca, 1304-1374)
Type of work: Christian epistemology
First transcribed: 1367

Principal Ideas Advanced

Contemporary Aristotelians wrongly assert that all true knowledge must be derived from logic and empirical investigation, with faith excluded as an avenue to truth.

In fact, true wisdom requires that reason be joined with faith, and that the resulting truths be endeared to the souls of hearers and readers by all the resources of eloquence, so that men will not only know what virtue is in the abstract but come to love it and, accordingly, not only understand but abhor sin.

All human wisdom is finally only relative, and the greatest of goods is to be simply a virtuous man, even if one is ignorant of what is taken to be earthly wisdom.

Though Petrarch's open letter *On His Own Ignorance and That of Many Others* arose from a particular incident, its larger interest lies in the conflict between the ideals of early humanism and the burgeoning Aristotelian scientific philosophy. The book itself, in the form of a lengthy letter, was addressed to a friend but intended for wider circulation, as was at that time often the practice. Petrarch recounts with mingled shock and sorrow that four "young men" had declared in formal legal terms—though at a dinner party—that Petrarch was "certainly a good man but a scholar of poor merit." The point of the statement was that Petrarch knew little or nothing of that which was genuine knowledge, the newly rediscovered Aristotelian scientific philosophy which was much studied at the University in Padua, where Petrarch was then residing. The four accusers' names are preserved in a marginal note to an early manuscript copy in Venice; all four are men of importance, two of them members of the high nobility, the third a wealthy merchant, and the fourth the court physician. Thus their sentence, in whatever spirit intended, quickly became common knowledge in important circles in Venice, where Petrarch had been living. The incident took place in 1366, when Petrarch was the most famous scholar in Italy. Nevertheless, the attack was clearly not to be shrugged off, for it represented the challenge of the new generation to the ideals of Petrarch's own. Hence probably his emphasis upon their being "young" men, though in fact they seem to have been in their thirties at the time.

The letter is dated January 13, 1368, but Petrarch asserts that he wrote it late in 1367 to while away the time while traveling in a barge on the Po. He apologizes for the loose organization as due to the circumstances of composition. Obviously, he could have had little recourse to books if he actually wrote the book on such a journey. Nevertheless, a modern annotated edition has well over two hundred footnotes tracing the literary and Biblical references in some eighty-five pages. It is thus quite possible that Petrarch was being elaborately casual about a work, supposedly written in a period of enforced tedium, on which he must have expended more pains than he cared to say.

Petrarch begins with a direct attack. These men have professed themselves to be his friends, and have visited him and praised him, but their attack shows they actually envy him. Though he disclaims order and method in what he calls a rambling letter, a "talk," Petrarch follows his initial remarks with a series of rhetorical questions showing that his critics cannot envy him for any of those goods of fortune that are commonly envied by men. Nor can they envy his learning or eloquence or virtue, for they say he has no learning, and any eloquence and virtue he may have they despise, after the new fashion. It can only be his fame, Petrarch concludes, that has drawn their envious hostility.

His four erstwhile friends have set out to show that the grounds for his fame are insufficient. If the world at large, even kings and popes, have praised and favored Petrarch, the four would answer that the world is not good at judgment. The fact is, Petrarch claims, three of the four have little or no learning, and the fourth possesses only a collection of oddments and curious details without order or meaning. If Petrarch is eloquent, they count this a proof he is not wise. Petrarch ironically agrees: "How could the style of a person who knows nothing at all be excellent, when theirs amounts to nothing, though there is nothing they do not know?" Thus his enemies regard their case as proved: Petrarch is "a good man without learning."

Though this remark is intended as condemnation Petrarch takes it as the highest praise, for in goodness is all true value. If goodness is granted, no matter how laughable virtuousness may be to the new generation and "their god Aristotle," Petrarch professes himself content to acknowledge his own ignorance.

The title of this book, or letter, however, mentions two elements—his own ignorance *and* that of many others. At this point, then, Petrarch turns to his opponents and their essays to prove that they are, if not so eloquent, at least as ignorant as he. (The reader cannot fail to see that the work is not by any means as casual in organization as Petrarch insists in the dedication.) The four men had sought in the guise of friends to show up Petrarch's ignorance, especially of Aristotle, whom they followed in all questions. They took the philosopher's voice as final and felt that the only questions on which knowledge could be attained were those of which their master had spoken. The only method that could lead to true knowledge, not merely opinion, was for them logical and empirical. Aristotle, however, says Petrarch, was necessarily ignorant of "the two things without which there can be absolutely no happiness: faith and immortality," Aristotle and the other pagan philosophers—Petrarch quotes Saint Augustine—"shaped their happy lives for themselves, just as it pleased each of them," since they had no certain knowledge on these points. Aristotle's genius blinded later ages to the errors which Petrarch's opponents adopt with the same blind confidence as his truths. Even Cicero, though he sometimes rose to sublime heights in speaking of God, many times falls into error on the same subject. This Petrarch converts into a lengthy *a fortiori* argument to show that if even the best of the ancient writers, Cicero, often erred, the faith which his opponents smile at is the only recourse that will provide lesser men from worse error. If they leave faith to one side and employ only human reason, "is this anything else," Petrarch demands, "than seeking the truth after having rejected the truth?"

Those who have rejected faith as an avenue to truth defend many erroneous propositions, but among them one that Petrarch finds "particularly damnable: the claim . . . that the world is coeternal with God." This opinion he attacks, at first with bitter indignation, then with more measured arguments drawn from Saint Augustine and Cicero, who had already addressed themselves to the same topic. In all this Petrarch is, of course, offering implicit comment on the charge that he himself has no learning, though he continues to profess that it is true. In fact his real fault is, as he puts it, that he does not "adore Aristotle." Petrarch finds that the style of Aristotle's surviving works does not commend them to his judgment or his memory. The repellent dry style of Aristotle's ethical writings never enkindles in the reader a love for virtue. Thus, Petrarch asks, "What is the use of knowing what virtue is if it is not loved when known? What is the use of knowing sin if it is not ahborred when known?" The true moral philosophers are those who, like Cicero or Augustine, have joined eloquence to wisdom and actually made their readers love virtue and hate vice. The moral philosophers who write in Latin and thus can be read in their own language (Petrarch had no command of Greek) are obviously more likely to move their readers than is Aristotle. Indeed, the ancients uniformly regarded Plato, not Aristotle, as the prince of Greek philosophers. The reason is not hard to see: Plato had the great gift of eloquence whose importance only the "crazy and clamorous sect" of Aristotelians would dispute. Even they, perhaps, praise Aristotle because in commenting upon him they have made him, so to speak, their own property. Averroës is an example of the militant Aristotelians who think that to praise their master sufficiently they must cry down everyone else. (However, P. O. Kristeller showed in 1952 that Petrarch is not here attacking the Averroists of Padua but only the more general Aristotelian tradition of the time.) Aristotle lacked Christian revelation, and his epigones now think it necessary to smile at Christianity as an empty fable because Aristotle knew nothing of it. Petrarch comments: "In the judgment of such people nobody can be a man of letters unless he is also a heretic and a madman besides being impertinent and impudent, a two-legged animal disputing of four-legged animals and beasts everywhere in the streets and squares of the city." The preoccupation of the contemporary Aristotelians with matters susceptible of empirical verification. like the description of animals, is a recurrent object of criticism throughout the present treatise.

As he approaches the close of the work, Petrarch gradually lets his indignation and emotion appear. This, too, may not be as spontaneous as he claims it to be, for it belongs to the rhetorical pattern of the invective which, broadly speaking, Petrarch follows. His opponents' highhanded rejection of the truths of faith provokes him to angry irony in reply. Though his fame is indeed a burden because it draws the attacks of the envious, he writes, it seems the world will not permit him to lose it. Nearly universal judgment seems not to regard him as being quite so ignorant as his one-time friends make him out to be. Only in Venice, where the prevailing evil is the worst of evils, too great freedom of speech, can trivial persecutors freely besmirch him: "So sweet does the word Freedom sound to everyone that Temerity and Audacity please the vulgar crowd, because they look so much like Freedom. Thus the night owls insult the evil with impunity; so do the ravens the swan, and the monkeys the lion; thus the nasty rend the honest to pieces, the ignorant the learned, the cowards the brave, the bad the good." (The reader observes that just as the imputation of ignorance is silently refuted by the panoply of learning throughout the treatise, so the splendid climax of indignation refutes by its sheer effectiveness the charge that eloquence is valueless.) As a parting shot in this section Petrarch recalls that Mark Antony wrote a book, *On His Drunkenness,* in which he confessed himself the greatest of all drunkards except for one other named person. Petrarch acknowledges, "I am the greatest of all the ignorant, but I will not except only one other man—there are perhaps four others."

For the rest, Petrarch is content to affirm, in a more serious mood, that he knows nothing; but he does this expressly in the spirit that Socrates had affirmed the same thing. Truth is not something that can be mined from the earth, it must be "approached with the steps of genius on the ladder of grace." The question at issue between himself and his four opponents must be decided by posterity (or oblivion). At any rate, after ages will not be driven by the passion of envy that motivates his enemies. Adopting the Ciceronian rhetorical tactic of *Omittam* (I shall pass over), Petrarch glances briefly at many other arguments that he might have brought forward in his defense. He prefers, however, to conclude simply by asking the friend to whom he is writing to continue to love him, if not as a man of letters, then as a good man, as a friend.

J.B.G.

THE DIALOGUE OF SAINT CATHERINE OF SIENA

Author: Saint Catherine of Siena (1347-1380)
Type of work: Mystical theology; devotional meditations
First transcribed: c.1370

Principal Ideas Advanced

The soul exercises through prayer; and through prayer, which leads to proper self-knowledge, the soul comes to know its complete dependence on God.

Knowledge of God is beyond human understanding.

Love (that is, Charity) is the central force of human life; suffering alone is not so important as the contrition which it should encourage; through the virtue of love, pain and suffering have rewards in the spiritual life.

Of Christ God made a bridge by which fallen man could travel to Heaven.

In the fourteenth century Christendom was visited by a deadly plague. The ancient walled city of Siena, in the mountainous region of north-central Italy, suffered the loss of some 80,000 persons in 1348, the year after Saint Catherine's birth. Her twin sister died at birth, and of her twenty-four brothers and sisters only twelve reached maturity. Thus, death and suffering were an intimate part of Catherine's daily life.

It is recorded that Saint Catherine experienced levitation at five and a vision of Christ at six; she dedicated her virginity to Christ at the age of seven. At sixteen she became a member of the Dominican Third Order and spent three years in religious seclusion and more than usual asceticism; she then ministered to the poor and the sick. Her biography tells of her praying for invisible stigmata (a petition so consonant with her unique fusion of a rich spiritual life and a spirit of self-renunciation); she was permitted to suffer the pain of Christ's wounds without bearing their marks.

So pure and strong a spirit lived in a time of disease and institutional decay. The moral state of the papacy and, consequently, the secular clergy, was at a scandalously low level; this was the period of the residence of the popes at Avignon. A number of heresies were spreading rapidly throughout Europe. Yet the work of Saint Catherine gains in clarity, power, and beauty by the contrast of its picture of the beauty of the soul in a state of grace against such political corruption and such ugliness of sin.

In her *Dialogue,* a great saint has treated the elements of Christian theology in a simple, almost colloquial and yet most vivid, manner. The work is presented in a series of colloquies of unequal length between God and the human soul, on whose beauty in a state of grace she constantly dwells. It has been called by Edmund Gardner "the mystical counterpart in prose of Dante's *Divina Commedia.*" Especially for the modern reader the subtitle is: "The Book of Divine Doctrine given in person by God the Father, speaking to the mind of the most glorious and holy virgin, Catherine of Siena, and written down as she dictated it in the vulgar tongue, she being the while entranced and actually hearing what God spoke in her."

The first colloquy is entitled "A Treatise of Divine Providence," in which a soul asks God for help—for the self, for the reformation of the Holy Church, for men in general, and for all things worthy. Lifted by its great and yearning desire for the honor of God and the salvation of souls, and rising in mystic ecstasy, the soul exercises itself through prayer, which leads to proper self-knowledge. Life is intuited under the forms of Beauty and Love, and through proper self-knowledge the soul learns that knowledge of God is beyond all human understanding. But grief naturally accompanies this ineffable love of God—grief for one's own sin and for the sins of the world—yet pain and suffering are to be borne in patience; for through the virtue of love, suffering and the contrition which accompanies it becomes effective in the spiritual realm.

The second colloquy is a treatise on discretion, which is presented in a parable (of which there are several in this treatise) as the only child of self-knowledge; wedding with charity, discretion has as many descendants as a tree has branches: "But that which gives life to the tree, to its branches, and its roots, is the ground of humility, in which it is planted, which humility is the foster-mother and nurse of charity, by whose means this tree remains in the perpetual calm of discretion." The road to Heaven having been broken through Adam's disobedience, God made of His Son a Bridge reaching from Heaven to earth and constituting a union of man with God; and Catherine reports God's words: "For I told thee, if thou remember, that upon the Bridge, that is, upon the doctrine of My Truth, were built up the stones, based upon the virtue of His Blood, for it is in virtue of this Blood that the virtues give life." Those who ignore the

Bridge are damned and deprived of the vision of God; by contrast, the blessed rejoice in God and share the experienced beatific vision.

The third colloquy is a treatise on prayer, instructing on the soul's advance by degrees, for (as God is reported as saying), "the more the soul tries to loosen her affection from herself, and fasten it in Me with the light of the Intellect, the more she knows; and the more she knows, the more she loves, and loving much, she tastes much." This treatise is not only a presentation of the tenets of orthodox theology but an emphasis appropriate to Catherine's Dominican spirituality; the stress on knowing is essentially Thomistic. Faith is fashioned through personal experience, but purification of the soul is not accomplished by the will alone; the question of how imperfection is lost and perfection is acquired is answered: "By perseverance seasoned with the most holy faith." The final confirmation of faith is experienced in the mystical and humanly incomprehensible union with the Divine.

The fourth colloquy is a treatise of obedience, which puts into practical terms much of what has preceded. It first tells where obedience is to be found, and that it is the key with which Heaven is opened: the soul should fasten it by means of a cord to her girdle. (Saint Francis is praised for his poverty and Dominic for his learning.) Then God tells the soul: "Look at my glorious Thomas, who gazed with the gentle eye of his intellect at My Truth, whereby he acquired supernatural light and science infused by grace, for he obtained it rather by means of prayer than by human study." The work recapitulates its major themes in ending on a note of mystical rapture.

What informs the *Dialogue* as a whole is a powerful conviction in love purified as the central force of human life; that is, charity, a divine fire that is acquired through the use of the intellect. (Catherine's emphasis bespeaks her life as a Dominican, for her intellectualism is to a considerable degree Thomistic, but Catherine's approach to the knowledge of God is more intuitive than that of Saint Thomas.)

The *Dialogue of Saint Catherine of Siena* is the culminating work of a life that uniquely synthesized contemplation and action; Catherine was deeply involved in ecclesiastical events, and in several hundred letters of beauty and great interest, (often compared with those of Petrarch) Catherine gives evidence of a life of powerful action. The *Dialogue* is informed by its consistent concern with the purifying effect of love (a theme which Dante treats in another fashion in his *Commedia*), and by a characteristically vivid and usually colloquial style. Her style is marked by a profusion of metaphors (vine, plough, bridge, sea), only a few of which are continued and developed.

R.J.S.

REVELATIONS OF DIVINE LOVE

Author: Julian [Juliana] of Norwich (c.1343-after 1413)
Type of work: Mystical treatise
First transcribed: c.1393

Principal Ideas Advanced

Julian desired a more perfect knowledge of Christ's suffering and death that she might better love Him and her fellow Christians.

In the course of sixteen "shewings" she beheld directly the extent of His suffering and love.

After some twenty years' meditation upon her experiences, she understood that their purpose was to confirm her in Christ's infinite love for all men.

The *Revelations of Divine Love* is one of the outstanding achievements in the tradition of English devotional literature that flourished during the thirteenth and fourteenth centuries. This outburst of devotional writings, especially in the latter century, has been attributed to the new religious zeal introduced from Italy by the friars as well as to the emergence of the devout layman in letters, the latter either coincidental with or resulting from the general replacement of Latin by the vernacular on the Continent as well as in England. It was this tradition which was largely responsible for the continuance of a native English prose from Alfred through to the Renaissance.

The sixteen "shewings" which Dame Julian describes took place on May 8, 1373. The first fifteen occurred from four until nine in the morning, and the last appeared that night. The experiences were probably first set down shortly afterwards, for a shorter version than the one generally known survives in a mid-fifteenth century manuscript, in which it is possible to feel a freshness of detail lacking in the expanded version. The latter, which is three times longer, could not have been written earlier than 1393, for she speaks of having spent twenty years in prayer pondering the meaning of the visions before receiving a "ghostly understanding" of them. The greater length has been achieved by subjecting the revelations to instructive analysis and commentary. It is ironic that the "first English woman of letters" should describe herself as a simple creature "that cowde no letter," but this admission need not be interpreted too literally. Against the possibility that she may have had to dictate her experiences, there is the no less strong one that she was merely referring to either a lack of literary polish or an ignorance of Latin. Certainly the work indicates the author's fairly extensive familiarity with devotional literature.

At thirty years of age, Dame Julian writes, she desired three gifts of God: "mind of His Passion," "bodily sickness," and "three wounds." These last were the wounds of "very contrition," "kind compassion," and "steadfast longing toward God." Shortly thereafter she was seized by an illness wherein her life was despaired of by those attending her and in which she felt her body die. (The details about her condition and surroundings are scanty, but in one version she mentions her mother as one of the ministrants, which suggests that she might not have entered reclusion as an anchoress until after her mystical experiences.) Suddenly the pain left her, and she felt a desire for the second of the three wounds so that, through union with His blessed Passion, she might fulfill her longing for God. It was compassion, not personal revelation, she desired, but "Suddenly I saw the red blood trickle down from under the Garland hot and freshly and right plenteously, as it were in the time of His Passion when the Garland of thorns was pressed on His blessed head who was both God and Man, the same that suffered thus for me. I conceived truly and mightily that it was Himself shewed it me, without any mean." In quick succession she experienced fourteen more "shewings" of Christ's passion, His victory over sin, and the grace secured for mankind thereby.

After the fifteenth "shewing" she underwent tormenting doubts about the reality of her visions; and falling into a sleep, she was visited by an apparition of the Devil. That night she beheld a final vision which confirmed her belief in all of the others and assured her that she would not be overcome by the adversary. This was the last of the revelations, but after almost twenty years of meditating upon them, she received a full understanding of their import: *"Wouldst thou learn thy Lord's meaning in this thing? Learn it well: Love was His meaning. Who shewed it thee? Love. What shewed He thee? Love. Wherefore shewed it He? For love. Hold thee therein and thou shalt learn and know more in the same. But thou shalt never know nor learn therein other thing without end."*

The general character of the *Revelations* is less theological than devotional. Although the experiences described are essentially personal, they have been recorded in such a way that the book can serve as a manual for general meditation. "Because of the Shewing," Julian explains, "I am not good but if I love God the better: and in as much as ye love God the better, it is more to you than to me." The approach throughout is didactic rather than ecstatic; like all mystics who have chosen to share the fruits of contemplation, the author is more concerned with elucidating the meaning of her experience than with reproducing that experience and her impressions of it. This instructive mode at times even attenuates the particular revelation by subjecting it to a markedly artificial enumerative analysis, especially the triad, a predilection she seems to have absorbed from the Pseudo-Dionysius. This becomes especially noticeable in the expanded versions, wherein even the passage of time seems to have encouraged analytical reflection.

Each "shewing," the author writes, manifested itself in three parts: "bodily sight," "word formed in mine understanding," and "spiritual sight." Thus, she begins each account of a revelation with a description of the apparition itself. The account of the dying Christ is presented in graphic detail; she conveys to us a direct impression of the flowing blood, the discoloring of the flesh, and the transformation of the face. At other times she communicates instead a summary statement of the revelation, for example, "I saw God in a Point. . . ." The latter mode is employed when the "shewing" is itself an insight into God's nature instead of a direct beholding of His person. This is more frequently the case than not.

After each "shewing," she generally, though not always, was made aware of its import by a statement which she attributes, sometimes directly, to God. This acknowledgment in turn is followed by the illumination of the "shewing," wherein she is especially concerned with clarifying its spiritual and moral significance to those who have not enjoyed personal revelation. Her didactic purpose becomes manifestly clear when she begins her third part in so typical a fashion as, "In which Shewing I understood six things. . . ," or "I saw four manner of dryings. . . ." The author's focus is strongest upon this last aspect of the revelations, which is evidenced not simply by its disproportionately lengthy treatment (between the fourteenth and fifteenth revelations and after the sixteenth the expanded versions supply a commentary upon the significance of the revelations that is at least equal in length to the treatment given the revelations themselves), but conversely by a handling of the revelations themselves that is often so sketchy as to leave some of them obscure to the reader. Thus, despite the fact that she distinguishes clearly among sixteen separate revelations, there seems often to be a distinction without a real difference.

Nevertheless, it is possible to perceive a pattern to the series of "shewings" which corresponds to the three wounds she had originally desired. The first eleven bring her progressively deeper into participation in Christ's Passion, during which process she is made to realize with increasing awe and gratitude the enormity of the guilt that required this sacrifice and the love that inspired it. It is worthy of note that she demonstrates very little of that pathological disgust with sin which often permeates medieval treatises of moral instruction. Rather, she is filled with joy at the limitlessness of God's forgiveness and His assurance that all will be made well: *"For since I have made well the most harm* [Adam's sin], *then it is my will that thou know thereby that I shall make well all that is less."* Her direct experience of Christ's suffering and death, instead of producing self-loathing for her own unworthiness and that of mankind in general, ultimately inspires her with a greater zeal to return that divine love and to share it with her "even-Christians." In the eleventh "shewing" she beholds Mary at the foot of the Cross.

In the remaining visions she beholds God in His glory and the goodness of His works. Here the possibility of distinguishing precisely between those which answer to the second and third wounds respectively is less certain. Since she has been mindful of her fellow-Christians throughout, for her whole purpose is to communicate the revelations to them, her compassion for them has been operative throughout her meditations upon the "shewings"; and she feels "oned" with them in her longing for the union with God, which is the culmination of this spiritual experience. There is no feeling of exclusiveness in the extraordinary grace she has been permitted: when she explores the ingenious, but not original, concept of "Christ the

Mother," He is not her mother but ours. Her sense of sharing all this love and goodness only intensifies her joy and peace in it.

In an age which not infrequently saw private illumination as a liberation from the mediating needs of the Church, Dame Julian makes abundantly clear the orthodoxy of her faith and her complete submissiveness to the Church and its teachings. Her direct revelations, she often assures us, have been a special grace, and they serve only to deepen her faith.

If the contemporary reader experiences any disappointment with the *Revelations,* his feelings will probably stem from the author's relentlessly analytical approach and the almost complete absence of autobiographical and psychological detail. He must admit, however, that interest in personality is a modern characteristic and that, for a medieval reader, it would have been merely intrusive and even inimical to the purpose of the work to singularize what was expressly meant to be generalized. Again, if the depiction of the individual apparitions is often wanting in its visualization, the critic must acknowledge that the author was attempting to describe what is essentially ineffable. Despite the frequent obtrusiveness of its didactic approach and its diligently sustained impersonality, the entire work is nonetheless infused by love, joy, and comfort, which, enhanced by a homely and vigorous style, make the book one of the monuments of mystical writing. Dame Julian's style is characteristically a simple one; but when the occasion warrants it, for example, in her encounter with the Devil, or her vision of God in His glory, she can range with ease and conviction from the forthright to the sublime. And the frequent assurance of God's love and wisdom remains indelibly in the reader's mind: ". . . *all shall be well, and all manner of things shall be well.*"

R.S.B.

ON THE EDUCATION OF A GENTLEMAN

Author: Pier Paolo Vergerio (1370-c.1444)
Type of work: Philosophy of Christian education
First transcribed: 1393-1404

Principal Ideas Advanced

Free men, at least those of the upper classes, should be well educated in both liberal studies and practical studies appropriate to their state of life.

A generous curriculum should be provided, emphasizing literature, history, and moral philosophy (ethics), as well as the traditional liberal arts, and embracing practical subjects such as physical education and military training.

Academic and physical education should take account of and adapt itself to individual differences; and it should utilize natural tendencies in the student, avoiding extremes of severity or indulgence.

Training in natural morality, together with inculcation of respect for parents and religion, as well as for authority in general, is an essential part of education.

Pier Paolo Vergerio, the leading educational theorist of the Italian Renaissance, was born at Capodistria in the neighborhood of Trieste on July 23, 1370. After a broad education, which included advanced studies in the arts and the law at the leading North Italian educational centers of Padua, Florence, and Bologna, Vergerio took up teaching. In the period from 1390 to 1406, he taught rhetoric and logic at Padua and Florence, and he also served as tutor to the Princes of Carrara. During this time, probably about 1400, he composed his *De ingenuis moribus: On the Education of a Gentleman,* which attested his practical good sense as well as his intellectual attainments and tastes. The versatility and competence of Vergerio were also evidenced by the fact that he served as Papal Secretary for about a decade (from 1406) and took part in the Council of Constance (1414) as Secretary to Emperor Sigismund. He died at Budapest in 1444 or 1445.

Vegerio was the author of several works, including a treatise, *On Restoring Church Unity, Life of Petrarch,* and *History of the Princes of Carrara,* as well as other biographical works, and several letters, poems, and plays. But his chief claim to fame is his *De ingenuis moribus.*

The *De ingenuis moribus: On the Education of a Gentleman* or *On Good Manners and Liberal Studies* was the most popular and influential, as well as the earliest, of over a dozen Italian Renaissance treatises on education, as is evidenced by the fact that it went through at least twenty editions by 1500, and at least forty editions by 1600. The *De ingenuis moribus,* a comprehensive, reasoned, balanced presentation of humanistic concepts as applied to education, was highly praised by subsequent humanists such as Jovius, Bembo, and Sabellico. It is a treatise on the education of the laity and written by a layman; it stresses the study of classical literature and history in classical terms, deplores the neglect of the study of Greek, advocates the study of the natural sciences, and endorses the inclusion of such subjects as physical education and military science along with the liberal arts in the curriculum. It also omits making the study of theology the culmination of the curriculum as had been the case in earlier treatises, and it does not emphasize the study of logic, although it includes it. It advocates the use of what we would today call educational psychology, as well as adaptation of both curriculum and educational methods to individual students. Finally, both arguments and methods are more in the supernatural.

According to Vergerio, a good education is one of the most valuable and lasting bequests a father can give his son. A most important part of education is character training. The young have many natural good qualities which can be utilized, such as a facility for emulation, alertness, a sense of pride, and friendliness; but at the same time, youthful impulses, such as loquacity, liberality, and strong passions need to be kept within proper bounds. In moral training, the best teaching is by reference to examples, the lives of past heroes and the conduct of the teacher, who should be selected with this fact in mind.

Sexual purity should be inculcated, Vergerio insists; and he suggests the avoidance of occasions for sexual indulgence, such as being in the company of women or bad companions, dancing, drinking wine, and overeating. Respect for divine ordinances and reverence for church services, as well as submission to one's parents and the constituted authority should be instilled, along with good manners, such as courtesy, hospitality, and reasonable care as to one's appearance.

"Liberal studies" are those which are worthy of a free man (*liber*). Such studies "call forth, train, and develop those highest gifts of body and mind which ennoble men." Learning (literature, letters) is praised by Vergerio in classical terms: the study of letters is of benefit in public affairs and is an aid in private negotiations; it is essential for a life of study and writing; it is a distraction from the pitfalls and snares of evil and vice; it provides recreation in a busy career and interest in a life of leisure; it is solace for the lonely and insurance against ennui for the aged, and it makes men possessors of all that is known, so that knowledge will not perish.

Among "liberal studies," those most highly recommended by Vergerio are history, moral philosophy, and rhetoric or "eloquence," as well as literature. The full curriculum includes grammar, logic, rhetoric, poetry, music, arithmetic, geometry, astronomy, the natural sciences, and ethics. It is a pity that Greek is not also studied, Vergerio adds. Distinct from the liberal arts are professional studies such as medicine, law, and theology.

As to educational method, Vergerio continues, the teacher should make use of competition, rewards, and praise to attract students, using threats and punishments only as final resorts, and then only to a limited extent. It is not necessary that all subjects be studied by all students; the courses chosen should be suited to the individual and his talents. Moderation should be the rule in deciding how much one will try to teach at a given time, and subjects once introduced should be mastered before hurrying on to new ones. What is studied should be reviewed and discussed with others. The scholar should follow a schedule and budget his time. Libraries should be sacrosanct for study only and should provide clocks by which scholars could be made aware of the flight of time.

Physical education should also be provided, and military training should be included at least for such princes as those whose responsibilities include the conduct of war. Bodily exercises, even as academic studies, should be adapted to the needs and capabilities of individuals. Physical stamina and endurance should be developed, and youths should also become accustomed to hardships and deprivations and to the thought of dying. Extensive physical education is a necessary basis for military training, Vergerio adds, and he writes that the latter should include training in the use of arms and the art of horsemanship, military strategy, tactics, and the art of generalship, all subjects whose learning is completed by practice, experience, and observation.

Recreation is necessary, Vergerio claims, for "The string that is ever stretched will end by breaking." Games which develop bodily skills and strengthen the will such as "the sharp exertion of ball-play," are to be preferred, but for some less energetic students milder exercises such as walking or riding will suffice. Humor, song, or even complete rest are other forms of recreation, but dancing and drinking intoxicating beverages should be avoided.

Although education is a parental responsibility, Vergerio writes, it should also be a matter of "public regulation." Education "is a matter of more than private interest; it concerns the state"; and Vergerio observes, "I would wish to see this responsibility extended. Parents should be made to realize that it is best to have their children educated away from home, for they are then less likely to be subjects of undue parental indulgence or prey to other influences which hinder study."

Vergerio's *De ingenuis moribus* clearly reflects the humanist emphasis of the Italian Renaissance, and it turns the attention of its readers to the individuality of students and to the necessity of relating the liberal studies to the problems of man. At the same time, it is interesting to note, the work perpetuates the values of the Church without succumbing to the fault of those who, in the past, had emphasized the study of theology to the detriment of the training of the student as a whole man.

D.D.M.

OF LEARNED IGNORANCE

Author: Nicholas of Cusa (Nicolaus Cryfts or Krypffs, c.1401-1464)
Type of work: Mystical theology
First transcribed: 1440

Principal Ideas Advanced

God Himself is the "infinite order" and in Him all opposites exist simultaneously as one uniform and simple essence which He shares with creatures only by the link of causation.

Since the infinite, which is absolute being, is relative to no known thing in the finite order, it cannot be known except by inexact analogies or by the via negativa.

The underlying unity of the cosmos may most accurately be viewed in terms of God's creative activity, which bestows existence to a differing degree on each created being.

The cosmos (or finite order), insofar as its nature allows, imitates the infinite order, and at the same time the cosmos exists in microcosm within every individual part of itself.

Nicholas of Cusa wrote *Of Learned Ignorance* (*De docta ignorantia*) in an age dominated by skepticism, individualism, and the disintegration of established institutions and philosophies. Early in his career Nicholas turned from the study of law to the study of theology, but he did not, on that account, cease to concern himself with contemporary affairs. He took a prominent part in the Council of Basel (began 1431), and at first he was an enthusiastic believer in the principle that the council outranked the pope. Perhaps because of the council's indirection, Nicholas soon changed his views, and during the remainder of his life he was a strong supporter of papal supremacy. Nicholas also played a major role in the temporary reunion of the Greek and Latin Churches (1448), and for this accomplishment, among others, he was made a cardinal. As Papal Legate to Germany, he tried to unite the lax German clergy in a thoroughgoing reform. He was fully aware of the problems the Church faced as it moved into the modern period, and in his writings this concern is reflected as a strong impulse toward synthesis and unity, transcending the barriers of logic and tradition that divide mankind.

Though notable for his originality, Nicholas borrowed heavily from the thought of the past, particularly from Neoplatonism, which had been cast into the shade by the rising of the Aristotelian sun in the thirteenth century. Nicholas chose to deal with the relation of the mind to reality, a problem that had grown stale after absorbing the energies of medieval thinkers for over four hundred years. Other Renaissance philosophers largely ignored epistemology in their desire to affirm human conduct alone as the proper sphere of man's investigation. To them it did not seem necessary to complicate their inquiries with the problem of knowledge, a problem which appeared to defy solution.

Since Nicholas is dealing with a problem that engrossed ancient and medieval thinkers, he is obliged at times to use old terms such as "form" even while he deviates from the original conceptions behind them. While he agrees with the medieval philosophic "realist" that only form is intelligible, he denies that the forms (quiddities or "whatnesses") of particular objects can be known in their purity by the human mind. Nicholas shares with Saint Augustine and Saint Thomas Aquinas, both philosophers and Doctors of the Church, the conviction that God comprehends within Himself the being of the universe. Unlike them, however, Nicholas finds it unnecessary and improper to advert to the "ideas," or exemplars, in the mind of God. Instead, he asserts the simplicity and indivisibility of the divine essence, which is *the* Form. In this context, "form" is not an epistemological term. Divine Form is responsible for the *being* of particulars, and we cannot know that being perfectly. The view of an ordered ascent of natural reason and of the intellect enlightened by faith, a view propounded by Saint Thomas, can, of course, no longer stand, for man is able to advance only by effecting a relative and uncertain diminishment in his overall ignorance.

Nicholas united elements of the old Thomistic order with a point of view even older, the Platonism to which Christian philosophers had first been attracted. The Platonic realist is generally in the following position: he must link the particular object to a universal concept, which in turn must be linked to the human mind. The process of knowing is described as an intuitive "correspondence" between the universal, or idea in God's mind, and the soul of the knower. The latter is conformed by imitation to the shape of the divine exemplar.

Conceptualists (moderate realists) had only to deal with two terms: the particular object, composed of form and matter, and the mind. The knower "abstracts" the indwelling form, then unites his mind with it, instead of achieving an intuitive resemblance to a divine idea. Nicholas agreed that form and matter cannot exist separately in creation, but he denied the ultimate validity of the "abstraction" process. As an Aristotelian, Saint Thomas Aquinas, no less than Nicholas, sought unity in the created and uncreated orders, but he tended to look for that unity in the activity of the mind, while Nicholas chose to affirm unity in terms of God's creative act and unique nature.

For Nicholas "act" and "potency" (potentiality) are not merely synonymous, respectively, with being and the privation of being, as they were for the older tradition. He endows the two concepts with a dynamic quality. In the infinite order, act and potency can exist simultaneously. Infinite being is itself the realization, the "act" of all potential. Potentiality in the finite order is limited by act and determined by it, as all act outside God is limited by potentiality. The two analogous attributes in God are of another order and are not subject to change or limitation. Every created being is composed of potency and act and that which links the two. Diversity in creation is accounted for by varying combinations of act and potency, which allow no two particulars to be identical. Thus, there exists a hierarchy of being, the members of which participate in the being of one unique Act, Himself the fullest in being and the terminus of the scale.

There is no absolute movement except in God and God must be understood as embracing contraries in Himself. In Him, movement is the rest which contains all movement, just as potency contains act. Since God's essence is simple and undifferentiated, there is no need to assume a "connection" which would reconcile opposites. In intellectual natures, the movement or "connection" between potency and act is understanding; in corporeal things, the movement is existence.

There are clearly, in Nicholas's system, two distinct orders of reality. God, in His infinite order, is the supreme reality, but in the finite order, reality is composed of particular individuals. Particulars are unique because they have realized to the limit of their own natures the possibility of God-communicated being. Their uniqueness solves the problem of individuation that so vexed the medieval realists, but it poses another: In what way are things alike? Nicholas states that no form is in two or more things; God is Form, and He shares that honor with no created being. The unity of things lies in their connection with God, not in their embodiment of common form. God is the Form of being, but He is not immanent in His creation. As the Form of being, He may also be given the title of "Form of all forms." Nicholas uses the word "form" to mean extent-of-being, and being, in the finite order, is nothing more nor less than existence-caused-by-God. There is no need to assume either a multitude of separate forms immanent in the world or a multitude of forms present in the mind of God, for an explanation of God as Form accounts for both the diversity and the unity of creation.

God is at once the "minimum," the least He can be and remain Himself, and the "maximum." He cannot be made less by reducing some part of His essence so that it might form the universe; God is totally separate from the finite order where limitation of being is always possible. The link between finite and infinite, two orders so far apart that there is not even any proportion by which they can be related, is *causation,* the creative act by which God made the inferior order. It is this created order which imitates the being of God, however imperfectly, in a "contracted" manner.

According to Nicholas, the universe exists in individuals by contraction. The universe is a series of unities, a scale of increasingly restricted being. The first unity is itself uncontracted (God); the next three are contracted in a descending scale and exist in the finite order: the universe, humanity, and man. In these "contractions" one sees a resemblance to the medieval universals, the genera and species, but it is only a resemblance. Contraction is not specifically a means to knowledge; it does not make the particular perfectly intelligible. Both being and truth are restricted, limited by their contraction in the finite order. Insofar as particulars *are,* they resemble God, but they are not part of Him, because they can never be one with the infinite order. Here there are clear Neoplatonic overtones. Resemblance, not immanence, is the basis of creation, just as it is the basis of knowledge. Yet for Nicholas the universal does not have an objective, eternal reality outside the object or the mind, as it does for the Platonist.

In such a theory, based on the mystery of the penetration of divine being into the finite order, the "form" of the Neoplatonists and the Scholastics has no meaning. In the system of Nicholas "form" is only a name for contracted being. Contraction, not form, is the link between being and knowledge. Everything presented to the reason is contracted, and it is the reason which distinguishes what are called species or universals. In the singular, the universal becomes explicit. The medieval roles of universal and particular are here reversed: thus, it is the particular which gives existence and meaning to the universal, not the universal to the particular.

In only one sense can universals be said to be pre-existent: they exist by contraction in individuals, including the individual intellect. The "beings of reason," the universals formed by the understanding, are products of comparison or *analogy.* The intellect is equipped with innate principles of judgment, as well as with information from the senses, and thus it has a working basis for drawing analogies. The intellect compares its sense perceptions with its innate principles of order, and it thus produces an "abstracted form." Such a form, which is a product of the fallible intellect, is by no means the perfect fusion between knower and known envisioned by the Platonists and the Aristotelians. The "world of resemblances" produced in the intellect is the result of correspondence by contraction. All creation is the image of one Form, and each contraction of that Form is unique. The concepts of form and contraction preserve and unite the principles of order and being in the universe while they allow a pragmatic, if nonexact, knowledge of that universe.

Nicholas makes it clear that the only knowledge possible for man (natural or redeemed) is relative, experimental, and practical. The kind of knowledge available to man allows him to function properly in his environment, though it does not offer him the possibility of metaphysical certainty. Judgment by analogy gives man "working truth," but ultimately he remains ignorant, since he cannot know the quiddities of material things, the secret of their being and of their relationship to God.

What is expressed in Nicholas's philosophy is not pure skepticism, but an unwillingness to attribute certainty to human knowledge, a knowledge which Nicholas regards as no more than a recognition of degrees of likeness. The only thing of which man can be sure is his ultimate ignorance. God is the Lawgiver for nature, and the latter can be perfectly understood only by the perfect understanding of God.

Since we know creation only by the guesswork of analogy, writes Nicholas, we are limited in theology by our finiteness and thus cannot know the infinite God. Our aim must therefore be to transcend imperfect conceptualizations, not to concentrate on forming them as ends in themselves. We will never be able to comprehend the coincidence of contraries, either in creation or in God, and so Aristotelian logic is of little use in the knowledge of either. Nicholas would not, however, simply because of our insurmountable ignorance, have us refuse the challenge to approach God; he proposes the ancient *via negativa,* the road of negation, as the only possible way to divine truth. Among negative affirmations about God, the truer ones are those "which eliminate greater imperfections from the infinitely Perfect." One can seek to know truth most surely by the path of mystical darkness and unknowing.

God can be known, though darkly and uncertainly, by one whose virtue and faith have conformed him to God's nature. Since one must know to love and love to know, man must perform this paradoxical operation to unite himself to God, who unites in His divine nature both truth and goodness. In the system of Nicholas there is ultimate union of the good, the true, and the real in God, and, to a lesser extent, there is the same union in the soul that knows God, though it must always be restricted by its finite order from absolute identity with the truth and being that is God. In this way, individuality is strictly maintained, even in the mystical union between God and man.

Though Nicholas initially separates the hierarchy of knowledge from that of being in the finite order, he unites them again in the infinite order (God), thus preserving both man's capacity to know and the union of all being and knowledge in a transcendent God.

The final vision of Nicholas achieves much the same unity as did the vision of Plato before him. Like Plato, Nicholas declares that we love an absolute through contemplation, and knowing it and loving it, are obliged to live virtuously in accordance with the object of our love and contemplation. Nicholas is thus more faithful to the spirit of classical Hellenic thought than were the secular Renaissance moralists who transferred wisdom from intellect to will. Such skeptics felt that man's proper study was man, not physics or metaphysics. This idea is a kind of secular medievalism, reminiscent of the Augustinian emphasis on the will as the source of man's dignity and the center of his proper activity. Since we cannot *know* the truth, let us *do* the truth. Wisdom thus becomes divorced from prudent conduct; the scales of being and knowledge are totally divorced.

Even as the modern period began, it was clear that the most daring and influential thinkers of the day preferred to embrace the new secular, skeptical attitude as their own, while Christian philosophers occupied themselves with Scholasticism and the problems posed by the Reformation. Neither the Church nor the world took up the synthesis of Nicholas by which reason, religion, and experimental science might have found common metaphysical ground and ultimate reconciliation.

B.J.R.

ORATION ON THE DIGNITY OF MAN

Author: Giovanni Pico della Mirandola (1463-1494)
Type of work: Philosophy of man
First published: 1486

Principal Ideas Advanced

The chief dignity of man consists, not in any position, however lofty, accorded to him; but in his spiritual freedom to ascend to the level of the angels themselves or to descend to the level of the brutes.

Truth is to be sought from all quarters; philosophers and theologians of every culture have caught at least a glimpse of the truth and added something precious to the stock of wisdom available to the wise.

The great thinkers, including often the poets, have concealed the riches of their wisdom under the appearance of simple stories; only the philosopher can descry them and draw out the fullness of their meaning.

The work now generally known as the *Oration on the Dignity of Man* arose in remarkable circumstances. The young Giovanni Pico della Mirandola, twenty-four years old, published a series of nine hundred theses on which he invited the learned world to dispute publicly with him. He had studied thoroughly not only such more ordinary subjects as Latin and Greek and Scholastic philosophy, but also the Hebrew and Arabic languages and the philosophic and religious learning in those tongues. The theses themselves are correspondingly ambitious. They are separately published in full in his collected works, but the *Oration* gives some idea of their variety and scope. One of them, the boldest of all, proclaimed the essential unity of Plato and Aristotle; Pico justly asserts that this particular thesis might easily have been subdivided into six hundred or more specific theses according to the number of the points on which these philosophers are commonly thought to disagree. Of the other theses, many were taken from the arcane lore of Hermes Trismegistus, from the teachings of the Chaldeans, and from the mysteries of the Hebrews. Still others were original with Pico himself, like the inner concord of Plato and Aristotle; these embraced such diverse fields as natural philosophy and divinity. He also offered to show that certain of the Scholastic Doctors, such as Thomas Aquinas and Duns Scotus, in fact agree on points on which hitherto they have been thought to be of divergent opinions.

Pico's magnificent program was, however, not to be realized. When the theses were actually published in December, 1486, Pope Innocent VIII suspended the disputation, which was to have taken place in Rome in the following month, until the theses were examined for orthodoxy. The commission of examiners found some of them to be heretical; Pico's efforts to defend these in writing led to further imbroglios with the papacy, and the disputation in fact never took place. Pico had intended to open it by delivering an *Oration,* which has become famous almost independently of the dramatic circumstances of its origin. The words, "on the dignity of man," were added by later editors to describe the best known part of the *Oration*.

The *Oration* falls into two parts, according to the usual pattern for such works. The first part presents a general topic; in this case, the praise of philosophy; the second introduces more specifically the issue at hand; in this case, the necessity for so many and such varied theses, with Pico's defense against the predictable charges of foolhardiness and ostentation.

The first theme of Pico is the wonder that is man. He begins, with set purpose, obviously, by drawing on "Abdala the Saracen," Hermes Trismegistus, a Persian saying, and the words of the Biblical David, instead of the more usual Scholastic and Christian citations that would be expected. Thus, he tacitly illustrates from the very outset that the truth may be found in the most diverse traditions. Pico denies that the glory of man lies in his being placed by God at the center of created things. On the contrary, Pico asserts that man's glory is his freedom. Man alone of all creation is not fixed in a definite position. The plants, the animals, even the angels, are already from the start what they must be. Man's place depends on himself: by the action of his human faculties, especially intellect and will, he can rise to the level of the angels, or he can sink incomparably below the most savage beast. Pico imagines God saying to newly created man, "We have made thee neither of heaven nor of earth, neither mortal nor immortal, so that with freedom of choice and with honor, as though the maker and molder of thyself, thou mayst fashion thyself in whatever shape thou shalt prefer. Thou shalt have the power to degenerate into the lower forms of life, which are brutish. Thou shalt have the power, out of thy soul's judgment, to be reborn into the higher forms, which are divine."

Man is thus a "chameleon," in Pico's word, and in this light Pico explains the otherwise puzzling references in the old mystery religions of the Greeks and Hebrews to metamorphoses. Their teachers used this mysterious phenomenon to symbolize the "rebirth," as Pico has called it, of the soul into the world of the "higher forms." He here employs for the first time in the *Oration* an assumption that he later on defends at length: that the teachers and lawgivers of old taught, not openly and by appeal directly to reason, but darkly and symbolically, so that they could be truly understood only by the initiate.

To justify his contention that man can sink to the level of the brutes requires little proof. But the contention that man can rise to the level of the highest angels is initially less obvious. Pico undertakes to show this by comparing the powers of the three highest among the nine orders of angels, the Seraphim, Cherubim, and Thrones, to the powers of man. Man may analogously "lead the kind of life," as Pico actually says, that these highest angels do: "The Throne stands by the steadfastness of judgment." This order corresponds to the fullness of the active life, in which man may take upon himself after due consideration the care of lower things. If man turns from the active to the contemplative life, "considering the Creator in the creature and the creature in the Creator," he will blaze with the light of the Cherubim, whose life is contemplation. The deeper the contemplation of God the more vivid the love for Him, and so man comes finally to the office of the highest order of angels, the Seraphim, whose life is to love. So, by Jacob's Ladder, which Pico also interprets symbolically, man rises from height to height. He learns that the lessons of philosophy alone cannot fully quench the fires of wrath and violence that burn in him, that for this he must trust to the mistress of philosophy, which is theology. When he has arrived at this stage man is ready for progressive initiation into the religious mysteries.

Pico expresses the resulting harmony of all man's forces and their gradual growth to exultation in a fashion that insists upon the share that all the earlier religions have had in the divine truth: "Thereupon Bacchus, the leader of the Muses, by showing in his mysteries, that is, in the visible signs of nature, the invisible things of God to us who study philosophy, will intoxicate us with the fulness of God's house, in which, if we prove faithful, like Moses, hallowed theology shall come out and inspire us with a doubled frenzy." Finally "we shall no longer be ourselves but shall become He Himself Who made us."

Pico now proceeds to show successively that the Delphic oracle of Apollo, the teachings of Pythagoras, the lore of the Chaldeans, and the doctrines of Zoroaster all offer, when rightly understood, the same message of purgation, illumination, and perfection. The reader learns that sometimes a good deal of sympathetic interpretation is required. Pythagoras, for example, "will first enjoin us not to sit on a bushel, that is, not by unoccupied sloth to lose our rational faculty. . . . Then he will point out to us two things particularly to beware of: that we should not make water facing the sun or cut our nails while offering sacrifice. But after we have, through the agency of moral philosophy, both voided the lax desires of our too abundant pleasures and pared away like nail-cuttings the sharp corners of anger and the stings of wrath, only then may we begin to take part in the holy rites, that is, the mysteries of Bacchus we have mentioned, and to be free for our contemplation."

The praise of philosophy, then,

which is the subject of the first half of the *Oration,* is chiefly this: that it enables man to achieve his destiny of freedom by rising to those heights of contemplation that are only open to him who has gradually been initiated into the secrets of philosophy, which in turn prepare him for the divine study of theology.

It remains for Pico to show why he, a man only twenty-four years old, should have set forth so many and varied theses to defend. He asks that he be judged not by his youth but by the success or failure of the enterprise. It is in the nature of the case that if he succeeds at all he must succeed wholly, for his contention is that all peoples and religions of which records remain have shared in the discovery of truth. If, then, it is praiseworthy to defend convincingly ten theses, why should it not be praiseworthy to defend nine hundred? He reviews not only the Christian and Hebrew authors but also the Arabian philosophers, through whom, as Pico plainly says, Greek philosophy finally came to the Latins. Even the writings of heretics, which sought to combat sacred truths, served indirectly to strengthen it by causing defenders to spring up who make truth shine the more brightly.

Not only does Pico draw his theses from many sources, but he adds that it would be shameful to content himself with defending others' propositions without adding something of his own. Besides proposing theses in natural philosophy and divinity, he refers to a group of theses which in effect constitute his own original approach to the problems of philosophy. Here, too, he feels he should not be condemned for bringing forward a new method in philosophy, but should be judged solely according to how he fares in disputation. Still further themes are drawn from magic—not what is commonly referred to as black magic, which every Catholic Christian must abhor because of its dependence on demons and damned spirits, but that magic (white magic, as it was sometimes called) which is in fact a lofty branch of philosophy.

Pico thus arrives at a most important statement, not only for its bearing on his methods of exegesis, but for his understanding of truth as well. Citing Scriptural authorities, he argues that Moses received not only the revelation now written down in the Pentateuch, but a profounder revelation as well, revealed to a priest and transmitted by priests, always only in oral form, until the troubled fortunes of Israel made it imperative that the other revelation also be reduced to writing, which was done in seventy volumes. It is by the light of this more recondite revelation that the "guileless story" of the Pentateuch is to be understood. The story was sufficient for the simple people, and the deeper revelation was not profaned by being exposed to the uncomprehending gaze of the vulgar. Thus it is that superficial or apparent contradictions among philosophers cannot infrequently be resolved by recognition of the deeper meaning underlying both. Though Pico does not draw out the implication, it becomes clear that he regards philosophical formulations differently from the way the Scholastics regarded them. The Scholastic sought a maximum of clarity, a sharpness of definition, that would make a word or a proposition, so to speak, a capsule of meaning, a meaning that had so much and no more content. A word was as nearly univocal as possible and thus meant much the same to all who used it in controlled discourse. For Pico, on the other hand, the word was rather a sign or symbol, not so much delimiting a clear content of meaning as pointing in the direction in which the able exegete might find a richer and fuller meaning. The exegete's art therefore consists in drawing out as fully as possible the inexhaustible fullness of meaning latent, but not expressed, in language. From this vantage point one understands why Pico in this *Oration* often speaks of the poets as true philosophers and theologians; he even announces the intention, unhappily never fulfilled, of writing a treatise to be called *Poetic Theology,* in which he would show among other things that "Homer concealed this philosophy [of the stages in the soul's progress toward illumination] under the wanderings of his Ulysses, just as he concealed all others."

In concluding, Pico asks a sympathetic hearing for those truths whose discovery has cost him so much toil and study. The *Oration* ends with a summons to the disputation which was to have decided Pico's success or failure.

J.B.G.

THE IMITATION OF CHRIST

Author: Saint Thomas à Kempis (c.1380-1471)
Type of work: Spiritual instruction
First published: 1486

Principal Ideas Advanced

Man's chief endeavor should be to meditate on the life of Jesus Christ and to conform one's life to His.

Men should be humble; they should disdain honors, wealth, and human glory.

A clear conscience and holiness of life are more important than the pursuit of knowledge.

To achieve union with God, an unconditional surrender of the heart to God is necessary.

The *Imitation of Christ* is a treatise on the spiritual life, written by Thomas à Kempis, and first published anonymously. Two hundred years after its publication a controversy arose as a result of the attempt to establish Jean Charlier de Gerson (1363-1429), Chancellor of the University of Paris, as the author, and although this attempt met with some success for a time, it is generally conceded today that Thomas à Kempis is the author. Thomas was born at Kempen, in the diocese of Cologne in 1379 or 1380. When he was fourteen he began school at Deventer, Holland, remaining there seven years. While there he came under the influence of the "New

Devotion," a revival in the Low Countries of the fervor of the first Christian communities. From Deventer he went to Wildesheim, where he joined the Brothers of the Common Life. He entered the Canons Regular of Wildesheim, was clothed as a novice in 1406, and ordained in 1413. In 1441, Thomas completed and signed his name to a codex, which is still extant; it consists of the four books of the *Imitation of Christ* and nine minor treatises. He died on July 25, 1471. Thomas's work has always been regarded as a Christian classic; it has been issued in innumerable editions and translations, and in the number of its readers is said to be surpassed only by the Bible.

The *Imitation* is divided into four books, the first three of which deal with the spiritual life, largely from an ascetical point of view. The fourth is a small treatise on the Blessed Sacrament.

It seems that in writing his book Thomas had primarily in mind the members of his own congregation. It is clear that he is speaking to religious contemplatives. And yet his appeal is so universal that no Christian reader will feel that the directions and exhortations scattered so profusely throughout the work are not addressed specifically to him. The work is eminently practical. Throughout the entire four books there is hardly any theoretical reasoning or any proposing of special theories of spirituality. In fact, Thomas seems to have had little use for theorizers; what he is encouraging here is work and virtue, and while he regards man's immediate and ultimate destiny as the love of God, he is practical enough to realize that this love can be attained only by effort, accompanied, of course, by grace.

Thus, the whole first book can be regarded as equivalent to the purgative way, a preparation, a cleansing of the soul. Thomas is tireless in urging self-humiliation and self-abasement. He constantly insists on the passage of time, the emptiness of horrors, the vanity of human glory, and the worthlessness of wealth; he urges all men to love God by faithfully adhering to His divine will.

This urging is all done with an unction, a gentleness, a conviction that cannot but have its effect on the reader. Some have thought that Thomas goes to an extreme in favoring a kind of anti-intellectualism; their judgment is based on such assertions as, "It is better to feel compunction than to be able to define it." But if passages of this sort are carefully considered in their context and against the intellectual background of the times, it will not be difficult to dismiss the charge of anti-intellectualism, especially if we consider that Thomas does not condemn learning and apostolic works as such, but only learning undertaken out of motives of vainglory: "After all, God takes into account not so much the thing we do, as the love that went to the doing of it." And again: "No reason why we should quarrel with learning, or with any straightforward pursuit of knowledge; it is all good as far as it goes, and part of God's plan. But always what we should prize most is a clear conscience and holiness of life." Such passages express Thomas's pure asceticism.

It will be easier to dismiss the charge of anti-intellectualism against Thomas if we recall the extreme lengths to which his intellectual contemporaries went because of the extravagance of late Scholasticism. It was probably to provide his clerical readers with some antidote against the virus of exaggerated intellectualism and out of a worshipful simplicity that Thomas wrote with such determination in opposition to the pride and vanity of the schools and insisted on the practice of an unreserved humility in the presence of Omniscience.

If a sensitive reader finds the *Imitation* somewhat irritating, it is not because of any harshness on the part of the author or any intolerance in his manner of speech but because, as he relentlessly holds the mirror up to nature, the reader cannot but behold the reflection of his own features, distorted perhaps by selfishness and pride. But Thomas does not threaten, browbeat, or even plead. He is never unkind, and he seems to have the greatest faith in human nature, in spite of the ugliness he sometimes beholds in it. He does no more than propose the ideal, confident that the soul itself will take the proper measures to remove this ugliness and promote the beauty of the supernatural.

Are there passages of self-revelation in the *Imitation*? Monsignor Ronald Knox, in the introduction to his translation of Thomas's work, finds only one passage (I, 25) that can be identified as an "echo of autobiography." But there are other passages which, although not autobiographical, are personal enough to lead the reader to believe that the author is speaking not merely from observation, but from actual experience. In spite of the intense emotion of some of these passages, the expression is always reserved and sober. Thomas never descends to mere sentiment, even when he speaks with a feeling that is vibrant. Although there is a complete absence in his work of what we have come to call pietistic spirituality, the book is completely suffused with devotion. It is perhaps its solid devotion that has made the *Imitation of Christ* an enormously popular handbook for five centuries.

Thomas à Kempis never tires of exhorting the soul to a complete and an unresisting union with God, and he ceaselessly tells the Christian that this union can be achieved only through an absolute surrender of the heart to Him. Thomas represents God as speaking: "The only way for such as these to reach the real freedom of the unencumbered heart, to be favored with happy and close friendship with me, is this: they must first make an unconditional surrender, and daily offer themselves to me. Without this, no fruitful union with me can be formed, none endure."

In this dialogue, which Thomas presents as taking place between the "Beloved" and the "Learner," the reader can hardly think other than that Thomas speaks from personal Christian experience even though he never gives explicit indication that this is the case. But when he writes that fears, hesitancies, weaknesses, even antagonisms must be bravely and generously overcome, the reader knows that he is in contact with one who has walked the path himself; has climbed its steepness; has followed it through morass and swampland and been muddled in the process; and has finally achieved the heights where, from his peak of victory, he sends signals and words of encouragement to those who are struggling after him.

The Fourth Book deals exclusively with the Blessed Sacrament; it can be united with the three preceding books if the Blessed Sacrament is considered as a means devised by God for producing the union between man and God. The author is earnest in recommending frequent communion, and he insists once more that the grace of devotion is won by humility and self-denial. Thomas's book can well serve both for preparation and thanksgiving in receiving Holy Communion.

W.J.Y.

THE LADDER OF PERFECTION

Author: Walter Hilton (died 1396)
Type of work: Spiritual direction
First published: 1494

Principal Ideas Advanced

There are degrees of prayer and contemplation which depend upon the gift of God's grace and the co-operation of the soul in using this gift.

The soul must experience a twofold reformation in its progress toward perfection: (1) a reform of its fallen nature brought about by a turning away from sin; (2) a higher reform of feeling effected by the gift of Divine Love within the soul.

The Ladder of Perfection, published in 1494, is one of the best examples of the devotional literature of the fourteenth century. Although this work was written for the guidance of an anchoress and emphasizes the relationship of the soul to God rather than to one's neighbor, it had a wide circulation among the devout living in the world. The elevated thought and clarity of style combined with insight and common sense account for its popularity during the fifteenth century and for the many modern versions that have appeared during the nineteenth and twentieth centuries.

Walter Hilton was a Canon Regular of Saint Augustine at the Priory of St. Peter at Thurgarton near Southwell. He had many contacts with the Carthusian Order and a great admiration for its ideals.

The treatise is divided into two books that follow a gradual unfolding of the means a soul should use to progress from purgation to illumination and union with God. In commenting on Hilton's place in the school of Richard Rolle of Hampole (c.1300-1348), a Catholic mystic, Alice D. Greenwood notes that the disciple "supplied both system and corrective to Rolle's exuberance of feeling." These are apparent in the sequence, the distinctions, and the readily understood figures, especially the ladder or scale that supplies the framework for the journey of the soul to

God. Hilton reinforces his observations with references in Latin from the Bible, especially from the Epistles of Saint Paul and the Psalms, and from the works of Saint Augustine and Saint Gregory the Great.

Hilton first makes a fundamental distinction between the active life of love, which is shown outwardly in good works and is suited to all men living in the world, and the contemplative life, which he defines as "perfect love and charity inwardly experienced through the spiritual virtues, and in true knowledge and perception of God and spiritual things." This state, the author declares, belongs to those devoted exclusively to the service of God. He then distinguishes three degrees of contemplation which progress from the love of God enkindled by simple devotion to union with God through knowledge and love. Clear knowledge and perfect love of God can be achieved only in Heaven.

Humility in every degree of prayer is one of the virtues Hilton emphasizes here and throughout the work. Man must forget himself and concentrate on ascending to God through love. Faith joined to humility supplies the future contemplative with the essential attitude for reformation by the practice of all virtues. Humility enables a man to see himself as he really is and to despise his nothingness. This necessary virtue can be acquired by meditation on the humility of Christ in His humanity. Hilton here admonishes the recluse not to be concerned with the faults of her neighbor, but to turn the light of humility into her own soul.

Hilton's explanation of the virtue of humility as one of the foundations of the spiritual life is the occasion for his denunciation of heretics and hypocrites. In several sections of the work he interrupts his comments on the love of God to condemn in severest terms those who prefer their ideas to the teachings of the Church. Such persons, Hilton claims, lack humility and consider themselves superior to others. The severity of his remarks is due to the disturbances caused by John Wycliffe (c.1320-1384) and his followers, the Lollards. Although Hilton does not make a specific reference to this group, he is believed to have had first-hand knowledge of their teachings from his association with a group of examiners comissioned to investigate the heresy of the "poor preachers," as the Lollards were popularly called. In stating that heretics cannot savor truth since the interior powers of their souls are like rotten teeth, Hilton uses one of the most unpleasant figures in the work. The hatred he had of heresy also accounts for his repeated exhortations to believe in the articles of faith and in the sacraments and to obey and submit to the Holy Church humbly without criticism.

In suggesting means to attain contemplation, Hilton proposes three practices: (1) the reading of Holy Scripture, (2) meditation, (3) constant prayer. The first must not be an intellectual exercise, but a filling of the mind with God's message. The various forms of prayer from fixed vocal prayer to prayer of affection are explained in the framework of the ascent of the heart to God. The sanity of Hilton's teaching is evident here in his caution not to abandon vocal prayer too soon. Ascending to a higher form of prayer before the soul is prepared may result in straining the mind and injuring bodily health. Hilton is, however, equally insistent that the soul be flexible in adopting the form and kind of prayer that may aid it in ascending most quickly to God. There can be no inertia in attempting to scale the ladder. Distractions and temptations during prayer are not sinful unless one willingly yields to them. They may indeed be occasions for God's rewarding the soul who is faithful to duty and prayer and perseveres amid hardships. Hilton gives the following specific directives for overcoming temptations: (1) trust in Christ and His Passion, (2) ignore the temptations, and (3) seek advice from a wise man.

However, in addition to reading, meditation, and prayer, there is yet another requisite for achieving contemplation. A person must understand not only the powers and virtues of his soul but also understand his sins. This self-knowledge is imperative as the soul ascends the spiritual ladder, since man must recognize the necessity for turning from sin to virtue. Hilton constructs the false image created in man by the seven deadly sins: the head of pride, the back of covetousness, the breast of envy, the arms of anger, the belly of gluttony, the legs of lust, and the feet of sloth. This figure must be reformed into a new man in the likeness of Christ, by the recollection of His humanity and sufferings, by the pursuit of all virtues, and by earnest prayer.

Book II is Hilton's reply to the request of the anchoress to learn more about the image that was described in the first part and the directions for destroying the false image in the soul. The practices for attaining the highest contemplation of divine things are more fully described here than in the first part; the notion of ascent is strengthened.

The major distinction in this section is made to explain the difference between the soul that has been reformed by faith alone and without difficulty, and the soul that has been restored by faith and experience with difficulty and great spiritual effort. The restoration of the soul from sin to grace either by baptism or penance is the first step toward the reforming of the false image. Even great sinners can be reformed in Christ provided they humbly surrender their wills to God, amend their ways, and sincerely ask God's grace and forgiveness. However, souls reformed in faith alone frequently make little advance in the spiritual life because they are satisfied with this first state instead of seeking the higher one of reformation in feeling. The resulting stagnation is dangerous since the soul must either advance or relapse into sin.

Hilton chastens those souls who fail to attain to contemplation because of their rigidity in adopting and adhering to a certain rule of life in the early days of their conversion and in never thereafter deviating from or changing their devotions or practices. Such persons concentrate on themselves, whereas true reformation is grounded in charity, and, finally, is the result of the grace of God allied to man's effort. Grace is given to the soul that is truly humble, that follows God's grace rather than its own inclinations, and gives all the credit to Him. Thus, complete reformation is attained by very few, for it is achieved only after great concentration and self-denial.

Man's striving to attain contemplation is compared by Hilton to a soul's journey to Jerusalem. It is inaugurated by reformation in faith based on humility and submission to the laws of the Church. The departure is marked by spiritual and, when necessary, bodily activity. Use any spiritual activity that will help you to love Christ, Hilton writes; change devotions and methods when necessary and when grace prompts the soul. Hilton lists the chief enemies encountered on the journey: bodily desires, foolish fears, deceitful evil spirits, flattery, vanity, and any other experiences that withdraw the soul from the love of Jesus. The remedy for these evils is the practice of humility and the love of Christ.

Hilton sustains the image of the spiritual pilgrimage by describing the dark night as the purgation of the senses, a self-knowledge, a trial that brings the faithful soul to the threshold of Jerusalem. He cautions the soul not to be disturbed by this darkness which accompanies death to the world and is the gateway to contemplation and reformation in feeling. The soul, advancing to perfect love of God, must use this self-knowledge, not as an end in itself, but as a means to attain a higher knowledge. God gives this higher knowledge of Himself gradually as the soul becomes able to bear it. The soul is weaned from the milk of the imagination to the solid food of reason strengthened and illumined by the Holy Spirit.

Purity and peace are the companions of the reformation in feeling, Hilton writes; the soul arrives at the contemplation of the Godhead united to the manhood in Christ. In this degree all poetic images of God such as fire and light, are elevated to a spiritual sense. Divine Love opens the spiritual eyes of the soul to see God by the infusion of a special grace. This grace cannot be attained by study or by one's own efforts. Various writers on the spiritual life give this awakening names according to their own experience of this grace. It is called spiritual rest, inward stillness, peace of conscience, wakeful sleep of the spouse, reformation in feeling. The special emphasis given to the nature of rest in God in this experience does not exclude the love of creatures, but keeps them in correct subordination.

The special grace of the contemplation of God is sometimes withdrawn from a soul either by God Himself, as a testing of the soul, or because of the weakness and corruption of human nature. The soul must recognize that this special grace does not always continue at its highest intensity; the human soul could not sustain it. As in the beginning of the climb up the ladder, perseverance in prayer is also essential here, even if it is difficult. The soul must strive for mastery of the body so that the heart and lips are always in harmony. Often grace calls the soul to abandon vocal prayer and to see and experience God in Holy Scripture, where God who is Truth is hidden "under the precious cloak of beautiful language." Holy Scripture can be understood in four ways: the literal, the moral, the mystical, and the heavenly. Humility, the handmaid of truth, will keep the soul from going astray in interpreting the Scriptures.

At an even higher stage, writes Hilton, there is a spiritual vision of God, not as He is in Himself, but in His secret and merciful operations and in His awful and just judgments. Grace enables the soul to recognize, too, the various degrees in the Church Militant and also the nature of the angels. The soul progresses from an understanding of the nature of the angels and their ministry to knowledge of the human and divine nature of Christ and, finally, to an awareness of the Blessed Trinity. Souls moved by such grace, Hilton concludes, learn more in one hour of prayer and contemplation than from all that is written in a long book.

Sister M.R.M.

ENCHIRIDION MILITIS CHRISTIANI

Author: Desiderius Erasmus (c.1466-1536)
Type of work: Devotional manual
First published: 1503

Principal Ideas Advanced

Life in the world is a continual war with the Devil, who lies waiting to betray us.

The Christian should use prayer and knowledge as his chief weapons in the war of life.

Unless we pray with pure hearts our prayers will not even approach God, and no mere repetition of words can be a prayer unless the soul of man is lifted up to Him.

If the Christian refers all things to Christ he will overcome the Devil and transform the world.

In a letter to Abbot Volz, Erasmus wrote of his *Enchiridion militis Christiani:* "Let this book lead to a theological life rather than theological disputation." Erasmus felt that for too long Christian philosophy had been out of touch with life, and his intention in his handbook for the militant Christian was to provide an easily understandable and practical guide to Christian living. The book is divided into two parts. The first consists of an analysis of the human condition, a summary of the aids to which the Christian has recourse and an examination of human consciousness as it is involved in the struggle for perfection. The second section includes a listing and discussion of twenty-two rules for living a Christian life and a brief statement of special remedies for particular vices.

Erasmus manifests incredulity at the general conduct of Christians. "It seems that life is a drinking bout rather than a war. We clothe ourselves with boudoir trappings rather than armor." However, if a baptized Christian gives himself to this world he violates a contract made with God. Nor can there be any hope of escaping unnoticed, for "The same Person witnesses our struggle who will one day reward us." Erasmus begins his discourse by reminding the reader of the obligations that Christians must fulfill if they are to please God. For him the issue is one of utmost seriousness:

"We do not fight for praise but for Life itself." In the battle of life victory depends not on chance but on God, and only if we heed His call can we be victorious. At the first attack of the Devil through a temptation to sin we should lift up our minds to God. An excellent bulwark against evil is the reading of the Bible. Erasmus also thinks that reading the pagan poets is a good preparation for the Christian life because of their natural goodness. He recommends Plato but has harsh words for Aristotle and the Scholastics, "who surpass the pagans of antiquity in the subtlety of their distinctions." For Erasmus philosophy must be rooted in the life of man, and any undue attention to abstract distinctions is suspect. He advances the Fathers of the Church as models of practical piety. His emphasis is always on the spirit rather than the letter of Christian law. Abhorrent to him is the idea of a man merely going through the motions of a Christian life and never realizing a genuine love of God. The wisdom of the world must be forgotten by him who would be truly wise.

According to Erasmus, man is composed of spirit, soul, and body. The body at the Fall came under the law of sin "whereby we are inclined to evil." The spirit is "the original pattern of the divine mind wherein the eternal law is engraved by the finger of God, the Holy Spirit." The spirit binds us to God. The soul is between the body and the spirit and is like a country convulsed by revolution in that it sometimes inclines toward the body, sometimes toward the spirit. The soul "really constitutes us as human beings" and is "neither good nor bad in itself." Reason, which is a function of the soul, should be king in man and rule over the senses and the passions, which are not to be destroyed, but rather, subdued. The wise man will know himself and submit all things to the judgment of reason.

Erasmus's first rule for Christian living is to rely on the Scriptures. There is nothing in Holy Writ that does not pertain to salvation. He enjoins the reader to act upon the Word of God and suffer no delay. "The kingdom of heaven does not belong to the lazy." Many people fear the active pursuit of virtue "because it involves relinquishing so many things we have come to love and because it demands incessant struggle against those three really formidable elements, the flesh, the devil, and the world." Erasmus analyzes such fears: "If you take a little time to think it over, it becomes quite apparent that there is no manner of life in this world that is not crowded with difficulties and hardships. Take a man in high political position. No one in his right mind would aspire to such a position if he was aware of the difficulties that beset such an office. What an endless parade of scraping and bowing to woo the good will of those above you! What an interminable suppression of disdain and concealment of despite for those with whom you must work! Need I mention the vicissitudes of the military life? The risks and dangers encountered by businessmen are well enough known. Take the state of matrimony. The cares and miseries flowing from domestic difficulties are incredible. Only those who are married can really appreciate and understand how real they are. Regardless of the vocation you may have chosen, there are difficulties on all sides. The life of man is filled from beginning to end with tribulation, and, besides, the virtuous suffer right along with the guilty. If these are the difficulties you fear, you will find that they actually serve to increase your merit. Without virtue, you will have to put up with them anyway, and with greater trouble and no reward at all." Since man must suffer, he should imitate Christ and refer his suffering to God.

Again and again Erasmus insists that Christ must be the only goal of life. All things, even knowledge, are useless unless they are referred to Him. The author directs the reader to seek the invisible. The things we see with our physical eyes are mere shadows of reality. Since this is so, unless the various forms of religion are filled with a spirit of fervent devotion they become empty and meaningless. "The cowl of St. Francis will not benefit you after death, if during your life, you did not imitate his personal integrity." Most Christians allow externals to dominate their religion. If external things were a source of true holiness, the Jews should have been the most religious people in history, for they lived with God Himself.

Erasmus's frequent criticism of the misuse of ceremony led many to think that he agreed with Luther. Erasmus, however, did not advocate the disestablishment of "forms," but rather suggested that without a fervent dedication of man to God the forms would lose their efficacy to establish the life of God in man. On the other hand, when a fervent man commits himself to an act of prayer or receives the sacraments, the external actions, the words, become a perfect symbol of the life of grace that animates his soul, and the external order becomes part of a perfect offering of man to God.

To live a holy life we must go to Christ Himself. Imitate "not . . . that which is most popular, but . . . that which is most perfect." We are all unified in Christ. As members of the Mystical Body we should always be willing to help weaker souls and never envy those who are more perfect. Christians should attempt to surpass each other only in meekness and good deeds. The fact that we are weak does not mean we should stop trying to attain the highest religious ideals. If we remember that God loves us, we will not be afraid to attempt the most difficult tasks. Temptation does not mean that God is abandoning us, but rather that he is trying to teach us to prefer Him above all things.

Erasmus has specific and practical suggestions for the Christian faced with temptation. He directs us to fasten our attention on a holy task. If this is impossible, we should turn interiorly to God. After the temptation has passed we should give all the credit to God if we have triumphed over it. To take pride in overcoming temptation is folly since without God we are incapable of living holy lives. If we have been tempted to be greedy, we should give more to charity; if to be gluttonous, we should fast. For each particular temptation we should make an attempt to exercise the corresponding virtue. We should treat each battle with sin as if it were the last, for no sin is trivial and all are harmful. The man who triumphs over sin has far greater pleasure than the man who indulges in it. Erasmus asks if we would rather live with the saints or with the damned. Every time we sin we take the Devil for our master. Therefore, since we do not know when we are going to die, we should turn to God as soon as we are tempted and never allow ourselves to fall away from Him.

Erasmus concludes his *Enchiridion* with a discussion of special remedies for particular vices: "When lust tempts you, fight immediately with these weapons: First of all, think of how rotten, how unclean, how utterly unworthy of human dignity lust is. It puts the divine in us on a level with the animals." The Holy Spirit will not dwell in an unclean soul. God sees all things. "Would you do in the presence of heaven's court what you would be ashamed to do in the presence of the lowest of human beings?" Nothing is more painful than the sting of a sinful pleasure once gone; nothing pollutes youth faster than lust. "If you are old nothing is more monstrous, nothing more provocative of scornful laughter than impurity." If we are tempted by avarice, we should consider how wealth destroys peace of mind and quietness with never-ending cares. Avarice indicates a lack of faith in Christ, who provides so liberally for the birds of the air and for all other creatures. If we are ambitious, we should think of how peaceful and calm is a private life compared to the lives of those who are always in the public eye.

The Cross should always be before us, writes Erasmus. As a remedy for pride we should remember that God has given us all we have. Pride is the vice that Christ condemned most. As a remedy for it, we should remember how great God is and how he can destroy a man: "If He levels the hills and did not spare the angels, will He allow *you* to raise your head in pride?" In the last analysis, says Erasmus, there is no better way of reconciling yourself with God than to reconcile yourself with your brother. See Christ in all men. Refer all things to Him and a virtuous life will follow.

Between 1514 and 1518 there were eight Latin editions of the *Enchiridion*. Within a century it had been translated into English, Czech, German, Dutch, Spanish, French, Portuguese, Italian, and Polish. The Bishop of Basel carried it with him continually. The book has had a lasting influence in the Church of England, even to the present day. The down to earth piety of the *Enchiridion* modified the tone of Calvinism in the low countries. It was carried into the New World by Spanish explorers, and Indians were reading it before the end of the sixteenth century. It was one of the most popular books of the Renaissance and two different English translations since 1960 indicate its continuing appeal.

D.M.R.

THE PRAISE OF FOLLY

Author: Desiderius Erasmus (c.1466-1536)
Type of work: Moral satire; Christian humanism
First published: 1511

Principal Ideas Advanced

Life is worth while only when it is pervaded by folly; the happiest men are the most foolish.

Among those presumed to be wise, the theologians are the most pretentious fools.

The Apostles must have been fools, for they lived by simple faith, and they were ignorant of theology.

Desiderius Erasmus, born in Rotterdam, was the illegitimate son of Gerard of Gouda. When he was fourteen he was orphaned, and about four years later he was sent to a monastery at Emaus, although he did not himself choose the cloistered life. He was able to leave the monastery in 1491 because of the intervention of the Bishop of Cambrai, and the following year Erasmus was ordained. The young man, who was to be renowned as a humanist scholar, began his intellectual training as Latin secretary for the bishop; and he then undertook intensive studies at the University of Paris, where he felt oppressed by the humorless and pedantic atmosphere. In 1498, while in England, he made the acquaintance of the man whose learning and temperament would influence the whole course of his life, Sir Thomas More. More encouraged Erasmus to continue the creative work which eventuated in the book of proverbs, *Adagia* (1500); and John Colet (1467-1519), lecturer at Oxford on the New Testament, who was part of the Erasmus-More circle, turned the attention of the young scholar to Biblical commentary. Erasmus's *Enchiridion militis Christiani* appeared in 1503; the work reflected both the scholarly discipline and the Christian conviction of its author, and it became an influential statement of that distinctive combination of respect for classical learning and Christian piety which came to be known as Christian Humanism.

Partly as a result of More's influence and partly out of enthusiasm for the didactic possibilities of such "fool" literature as Sebastian Brant's *Narrenschiff* (*The Ship of Fools,* 1494), Erasmus decided to write a book in praise of folly, but of that folly which distinguishes the Christian from those persons, both in and out of the Church, who think more of their wordly reputations than they do of their devotion to God. He decided to call his book *Moriae encomium* (*The Praise of Folly,* but a pun on the name of his friend More).

In his later career Erasmus had some difficulty in keeping to a course which would not alienate him from those who were defending the Church against the criticism of Luther; he was often under attack by theologians who were fearful that his views might represent, if not heretical opinions, at least attitudes disrespectful of the Church. However, he managed to convince the popes, at least, that he was a scholar, a critic, and a searcher after truth, not a Protestant either by conviction or manner; and Luther, who had at first looked upon Erasmus as an ally because Erasmus was also critical of abuses within the Church, eventually realized that he had no friend in

Erasmus, for the humanist wrote a number of critically damaging treatises against the position of the Protestants and against Luther in particular. But that phase of Erasmus's career was in the future; his lively satire on current manners and sins, *The Praise of Folly,* was welcomed with delight even by many of those within the Church, such as Pope Julius II, who were targets of his uncompromising commentary. Others, who found Erasmus's pointed moral comments too painful to be laughed off, charged the author with attempting to undermine the Church. On the whole, however, the book was able to do its work of calling attention to the harmful practices and customs which weakened the society of which Erasmus was such a vital part.

In *The Praise of Folly* the only voice to be heard is that of Folly herself. She declares that her appearance alone is enough to banish cares and make everyone glad. She has come to eulogize herself, and she compares herself to the ancients who, in order to avoid being called philosophers, described themselves as Sophists. Folly realizes that there will be those who will criticize her for praising herself, but it is better to praise oneself and present oneself without disguise than to hide one's foolishness behind the discourse of paid flatterers. It is discouraging, she declares, to find that many of those who belong in her camp, for they are themselves fools, hide their foolishness behind their Latin and Greek. They call themselves philosophers, but they can hardly hide their asslike ears, and they deceive no one but other fools with their archaic, contrived jargon.

Folly tells her audience that she is the illegitimate daughter of Plutus and the nymph Youth, and she states proudly that Plutus begot her while he was drunk with nectar and in the heat of youth. Folly was nursed by Drunkenness and Ignorance, and she is attended by Self-love, Flattery, Forgetfulness, Pleasure, Laziness, Madness, Sensuality, Intemperance, and Sound Sleep.

Folly insists that she be regarded as "the alpha of all the gods," for she is the "dispenser of all goods to men. . . ." Were it not for Folly, no one would be conceived; any man, no matter what his pretensions, must "for a few minutes be silly and act the fool" if life is to be generated. The sacred fountain of all life, after all, is the generative organ, "that foolish and ridiculous part that cannot even be named without laughter. . . ."

Life is worth while, says Folly, only when it is lightened by foolishness and youthfulness. Men are by nature one part reason, five parts passion. Anger and lust overcome reason whenever the latter attempts to control the passions through moral prohibitions. Man was given reason so that he could rule over the other animals, but life was tolerable only by hearkening to Folly: man took woman to himself, and woman is, of course, a fool—that is why she finds life so delightful.

Some persons maintain that friendship and marriage are the greatest goods in life, but what friendship or marriage would be possible were it not sustained by Folly? In fact, all society depends upon flattery and other foolishness. Men can tolerate others only because they love themselves, and there is nothing more foolish than that.

The greatest blessings of life are the outcome of Folly's work. What but foolishness would lead a man to spend his days and nights in pursuit of fame? Even the philosophers, who are scornful of the fool, are themselves the greatest fools of all in supposing themselves to be wise. Socrates, who was not so foolish as to think himself wise, nevertheless foolishly pursued his practice of philosophy and ended by drinking hemlock.

The happiest men, says Folly, are the most foolish; namely, the morons and simpletons. The fools, moreover, are honest, but the wise men say one thing and mean another. What men are happy?—Those who foolishly suppose their wives are faithful, who love hunting, who are continually constructing new buildings, who futilely seek "some fifth essence," who gamble, and who tell fantastic stories.

Among the happy fools are those who seek by mechanical means to achieve all the goods of this life and an eternal reward afterwards. They gaze on pictures, venerate mere objects, burn candles, utter rote words, and seek to escape the consequences of their sins by giving away a little money. Such fools are encouraged in their superstitious practices by priests who are hungry for profit.

Foolishness is everywhere, Folly declares. One sees it in the nobility, where title is everything; one sees it in actors, singers, and poets, who suppose that they are the greatest of men. Each nation thinks itself to be the greatest of all nations. Self-love leads to flattery, and flattery makes every fool happy.

But one could go on forever telling of the kinds of folly to be found among men. After all, even those men who seem to come closest to wisdom are really fools: the grammarians, poets, authors, scientists, lawyers, and theologians. But it is dangerous to attack the theologians, says Folly, for they hide behind ingenious scholastic arguments, and they invent new words by the use of which they explain mysterious matters. Theologians spend their days asking curious questions, but it never occurs to them that those who knew Christ did not know or seek the answers to such questions. The Apostles were busy baptizing people, but they did not know the theology of baptism; they worshiped in spirit, and they failed to realize that a picture of Christ, "with two outstretched fingers . . . and . . . three sets of rays in the nimbus attached to the back of the head," would have done just as well, as an object of worship, as Christ Himself. They went about in ignorance, in a kind of simple piety, because they did not enjoy the advantage of having studied Aristotle and the Scotists.

The Apostles won debates with the pagan philosophers and Jews, says Folly, because the Apostles used their lives as examples of their faith. Peter and Paul, although they were untutored, managed to do without the subtleties and sophistries of the learned theologians.

Monks are honored as devout men, but they seem to honor illiteracy, and they go about begging from door to door. Moreover, they regulate everything, even to the last detail of their clothing. They quarrel with members of orders other than their own, and they take pride in petty accomplishments and in outdoing one another in the extravagance of their ascetic practices.

Scholars spend a great deal of time dwelling on the significance of certain names and inventing theories by which they hope to fathom the mysteries of the Divine. Rhetoricians of the Church devise elaborate regulations and conventions by which to hide the emptiness of what they say. The popes, cardinals, and bishops attempt to follow the practices of the princes of the state; the bishops forget that they must aim at a pure life and care for their flocks; the cardinals do not remember that, as successors of the Apostles, they are expected to do good works; and the popes do not recall that they are intended to imitate Christ, "His poverty, tasks, doctrines, crosses, and disregard of safety. . . ." Pomp and ceremony have been substituted for the service of God through humility and self-mortification.

If one goes to Scripture, Folly declares, one finds there many passages in which the fool is honored. Christ Himself said to the Father, "Thou knowest my foolishness," and He condemned the wise: "I will destroy the wisdom of the wise and I will reject the prudence of the prudent." Paul said, "God has chosen the foolish things of the world," and "It has pleased God to save the world by foolishness." Christ, who was the wisdom of the Father, took on human foolishness in order to save men from their foolishness.

The conclusion must be, says Folly, that Christianity has a certain relationship with folly. It is folly so to love that one is drawn out of oneself and becomes thoroughly preoccupied with what is outside. The pious, who are fools in the eyes of those who cannot share their love, will be absorbed by the Highest Mind; they will be happy through union with the Highest Good. Those who have a foretaste of this highest happiness of union with God act as if they were mad; they are inspired fools in their eagerness to return to that blessed state.

Folly refuses to sum up her teachings; she declares, "I hate a student with a memory," and she bids her devotees to "live and drink. . . ."

For those with no sense of irony, Erasmus's *Praise of Folly* is a puzzling, frivolous, and even impertinent work. But for those who see in Erasmus both the earnestness of a satirist who wished to scold the hypocrites and selfish charlatans who corrupted society and the Church, and the sincerity of a Christian critic who sought to emphasize anew the honest charity and simple piety of Christ and His Apostles, this little book will serve as an expression of that divine foolishness by which man abandons worldly concerns and attains the happiness of knowing God.

THE PARACLESIS

Author: Desiderius Erasmus (c.1466-1536)
Type of work: Exhortation to Christ's Doctrine
First published: 1516

Principal Ideas Advanced

Men are attentive to the affairs of other countries and to wonders from foreign lands, yet they neglect the affairs of salvation and the greatest wonder of all, the Doctrine which comes from Heaven itself.

Because Christ intended a wide dissemination of His Doctrine, all men and women, regardless of class or status, should have access to the Sacred Writings.

The purest sources of the Philosophy of Christ are the Gospels and the Epistles piously and prayerfully reflected upon.

Only these Books can re-create for Christians the living image of Christ Himself.

The *Paraclesis* by Desiderius Erasmus of Rotterdam has a twofold importance. First, its exhortations to Christianity to regain its vibrancy by a return to the Faith's original sources are as timely today as they were in the sixteenth century; second, it is an excellent statement of the Northern humanist position in the broad spectrum of the Renaissance.

The surging force dominating the European intellectual climate during Erasmus's years was a rebirth of learning encouraged by and dependent upon the generous patronage of a commercially affluent, urban middle class. Misunderstood and often condemned by a Church psychologically conditioned to a static agricultural society, this emerging middle class in turn rejected the Church and extracted from classical times an ideology which stressed man and his physical world, a view well geared to the middle class ideal of material success and social mobility.

This ideology of humanism, in which man replaces God as the chief center of interest, had its beginnings in Italy with two identifiable trends. The first can be characterized as an overwhelming awe of classical works which manifested itself as a "great manuscript hunt" by which many Greek and Latin manuscripts were recovered. Unfortunately, the Italian humanists, by a slavish imitation of the style of the ancients, made their own work sterile and transitory, thereby becoming, in effect, the prisoners of their finds. The second trend manifested itself in a contempt for the spiritual and for the Church. The humanists, in embracing a secular philosophy of life rooted in classical paganism, toppled the medieval Christian ideal by an extreme worldliness which cast off all restraints upon private morals.

A shift in trade patterns from the Italian city-states to the Atlantic coastal areas caused the decline of the Renaissance in an Italy now bereft of its financial base. Its reappearance in northern Europe, while maintaining continuity of interest in the classical writers, included some differences from the Italian form. Instead of the visual arts, the North excelled in literature. The explanation for this lies in the *Ciceronius,* written by the greatest of the Northern scholars, Desiderius Erasmus. A devotee of freedom, Erasmus refused to be tyrannized by classical culture and insisted that the wisdom of the ancients be interwoven with the learning of his day. Latin, from his pen, became a living, flexible language in a natural style which could only have been Erasmus's own.

The salient difference, then, between the Italian and the Northern Renaissance was the direction and purpose given to humanism by the Northern scholars. Erasmus and his contemporaries confronted a degenerated Scholasticism wandering in the labyrinths of finespun arguments regarding the meaning of terms, but no longer interested in the finding and testing of truth. This contagious effeteness among the Church's intelligentsia combined with the immorality prevalent in clerical ranks to create apathy among the laity. Church ceremony became tediously formal and lacked the spark of sincerity necessary to enkindle piety. The Church seemed to oppose, not worldliness, but the things of the world.

The middle class, however, was molding a society which would no longer be inert, in which education would not be limited to the clergy, in which earthly life would no longer be merely a waiting period for salvation, and in which the individual would no longer subordinate his interests to those of the group. The Northern scholars, led by Erasmus, were determined, not to revolt against the Church in Italian fashion, but to purge the Faith of the useless conventions and conformities which were the breeding ground of ritualism and apathy. Through the philosophy of humanism, these dedicated men hoped to connect the laity more directly with the magnificent dogmas of Christianity, thus bypassing the hair-splitting of the self-interested Schoolmen. By inculcating in the laity a renewed sense of participation in the Church, true piety would be stirred within the hearts and souls of all of her members. Only in this manner could she maintain a vibrant faith and a continued influence in a changing world.

That this true piety was Erasmus's goal in life is beyond doubt. An early education received in schools staffed by the Brethren of the Common Life, a lay teaching order founded by Gerard Groote (1340-1384), a Netherlands ascetic, left a deep impression upon the young Erasmus. Instilled in him by the Brethren was a dualism of practical piety and a love of the New Learning. He also acquired from them a distaste for sterile abstract theorizing, a deep love of the classics, and the realization that the good life can be achieved only through the study of the Scriptures.

This dualism was finally harmonized in Erasmus's mind by his experiences in England. Under the influence of the English humanists, especially John Colet (c. 1466-1519), Erasmus suddenly became aware of an abyss that had developed between the uneducated common man and his faith because theology, instead of providing desperately needed answers for the common man, had become the private preserve of the aloof Schoolmen who consecrated it to quibbling. He believed that a reacquaintance with the original sources of Christianity's dogmas would renew the common man's appreciation of his faith and restore his piety. To gain this end Erasmus determined to utilize the philosophy of humanism to highlight the doctrine of Christ and then supply a practical application of that doctrine to everyday life.

He devoted himself, therefore, to a modern translation of the New Testament. He intended not only to publish the Greek text, which predated Saint Jerome's Vulgate, but also to furnish a new Latin translation designed to correct the errors in the Vulgate. The finished product, from the press of the printer Froben at Basel, Switzerland, in 1516, was a disappointment because of the haste with which it was published. Yet the very essence of the Northern Renaissance movement longed at that moment for just such a work, and its importance derived from its ability to satisfy an intellectual hunger. Erasmus, however, would devote much time to corrections in the future editions.

The fusion of Erasmus's piety and humanism is easily detected in his introduction to his New Testament. Most aptly named, "Paraclesis" comes from the Latin "paracletus," meaning to exhort or to encourage, and certainly the prime purpose of this introduction is to revitalize Christian interest in the very source of Christianity's dogma, the New Testament itself. The "Paraclete" is also another designation for the Holy Spirit, who is the font of all Truth and without whose intercession, writes Saint Thomas Aquinas, the most noted of the Scholastic philosophers, no truth of any kind can exist.

In good classical style, the *Paraclesis* opens with an appeal to the Greek incantations, to the Delphic power, "if there be any," but especially to Christ Himself, for the eloquence to plead His case well. Again, in the closing paragraphs, Erasmus pays tribute to the ancients for discovering much of Christ's doctrine, even though their efforts are ridiculed by Christians because Christ taught these same things so much more fully.

The theme to which Erasmus consistently returns is the neglect, by the world of men, of the Truth in the Philosophy of Christ. He admires the study by the Platonists, Pythagoreans, Academicians, and others of the doctrines of their sects; but he deplores the lack of study devoted to the truths of Christ, the Teacher sent from Heaven; he comments on men's avid interest in the affairs and accomplishments of distant lands; but he laments their unconcern for the Doctrine of Christ which proceeds from Heaven itself; he emphasizes the incongruity of the rereading of letters from close friends and the familiarity of the various monastic orders with their man-made rules, while the Rule of Christ, the Gospels, remains unread and virtually unknown.

The *Paraclesis* is indeed significant for its humanistic appreciation of the worth of each and every man as a whole individual and not merely as an insignificant member of a medieval spiritual proletariat. "This Philosophy accommodates Itself to all. . . . It is not kept from the least thus that It may be admired by the great. Nay rather the further you have made progress in Its riches, the more are you moved by Its majesty. For the little, It is little; for the great, It is superlatively great. It rejects no age, no sex, no fortune, no condition. . . . It in no way restricts anyone, unless he restricts himself by contemning himself."

Another facet of the Renaissance, optimism regarding man's reasoning ability, shines forth in Erasmus's work when he declares himself to be "in serious disagreement with those who do not wish the Divine Letters to be read by the ignorant when they have been translated into the vulgar tongue, as if either Christ taught what is so involved that it can scarcely be understood by a handful of theologians; or as if the defence of the Christian religion were founded on the fact that It be unknown." This declaration is followed by the very famous passage which begins "I should like all women of low estate to read the Gospels . . ." and includes Erasmus's fervent wish that "the yeoman might sing them at his plow, the weaver chant them at his loom, the traveller beguile with them the weariness of his journey."

To Erasmus, each and every man could be a theologian, for to him the theologian was not the practitioner of artfully constructed syllogisms but anyone "filled with the Spirit of Christ" who would teach, preach, and exhort to a life of love, charity and virtue; ". . . he it is . . . who is the true theologian, even if he be a ditchdigger or a weaver." Theology, practically applied, is a key; theology confined to the realms of abstract thought is a barren waste.

Erasmus closes the *Paraclesis* with a predictable critical comment on relics: "If anyone should point out a footprint made by the feet of Christ, how we Christians should bow in reverence; how we should adore. . . . If anyone were to place on exhibition Christ's cloak, whither should we not travel on earth to be permitted to kiss it? But suppose you present all His goods, there will be nothing which represents Christ more clearly and truly than the Gospels . . . the Gospels bring to you the living image of that sacrosanct mind, Christ Himself, speaking, healing, dying, rising. In a word They make Him so present that you would see less were He before your eyes."

Many of Erasmus's exhortations in this work were later to become the arguments of the Reformers, and, in fact, the thesis has been advanced that Martin Luther did no more than carry out the theories of Erasmus. Still a distinction must be made between carrying out a theory and carrying it to an extreme. Although Erasmus supported the practical reforms of Luther as they affected the daily conduct of men, and also strongly opposed any repression of the Reformers by the Church, he and Luther were poles apart on the fundamental questions of dogma. Erasmus was a moderate who desired an evolutionary reform within the Church itself. A violent frontal attack by a headstrong Luther would serve only to entrench the ultra-conservative Church elements and destroy the area of flexibility created by the humanists and through which they hoped, with time, to conquer. Moreover, Erasmus could hold no brief for a doctrine which eliminated the humanist belief in the goodness of man.

The *Paraclesis* remains still a persuasive argument in favor of the reading of the Word of Christ for the restoration of an understanding of and an enthusiasm for His doctrines. In our day, when a major complaint against Catholics concerns their apathy and indifference to their religion, the renewed interest in the works of Erasmus should come as no surprise. His writings were needed to restore piety in the sixteenth century; they are as desperately needed today.

E.S.F.

UTOPIA

Author: Saint Thomas More (1478-1535)
Type of work: Political philosophy
First published: 1516

Principal Ideas Advanced

The evils that beset Europe [in More's day], and especially England, are traceable to abuses of the right of private property, greed for gain among the wealthy, and laws which worsen the evils they seek to regulate.

The institutions of Utopia, an ideal commonwealth, are based on community of property and thus ensure a fair share of the society's goods to all its members.

The same rational institutions assure freedom from most of the evils of war, religious toleration, and means and leisure for every citizen to develop his capacities as far as possible.

The words "utopia" and "utopian" now belong to the familiar vocabulary of Western man. As with many such names that enjoy so wide a diffusion (*Rabelaisian* or *Machiavellian,* for example), its meaning has become a good deal blurred in the course of time. The author of the *Utopia* was canonized as a saint in the Catholic Church in 1935, and a chair of philosophy is named after him in the present-day University of Moscow. What Thomas More actually meant by his little book can only be decided by a close look at the known facts concerning its origin and early reception, taken in conjunction of course with the text itself.

It is clear from the *Utopia* itself that the book had its origin as a kind of *jeu d'esprit* begun in the course of an English embassy to the Netherlands in mid-1515. The part written in the Netherlands, as we learn from More's good friend Erasmus, was the present Book Two, the description of Utopia proper. Erasmus also states that after his return to England More added the present Book One, which mainly describes the evils of contemporary England. This broad and general account of the *Utopia's* genesis has now been refined upon in important ways by Professor Jack Hexter. Professor Hexter, followed in this by more recent scholars, has shown by internal evidence that a part of the present Book One was also written in connection with the description of Utopia that now constitutes Book Two. What More in effect did was to intercalate the description of the England of his day into the existing work. The original form of the work was a narrative introduction, to provide a framework or setting, and then a systematic account of the institutions of Utopia, an account put into the mouth of a traveler recently returned from Utopia, one Raphael Hythloday.

The importance of this reconstruction of the book's development is clear. In the *Utopia* as originally planned and written, the institutions of Utopia are described in wholly admiring terms. Since Hythloday is the only speaker in the whole body of the work, and he is enthusiastic about Utopia, the account is of course strongly favorable in its overall effect. Now the distinctive institution of Utopia is of course the fact that all property is held in common, so that money plays no role in the internal life of the Utopian state. It follows then that what More intended to stress in his original version was a criticism, not only of private property as such, but of the evils that it brought inevitably in its train.

With the later addition of all that part of Book One except the framework, the focus is less clear. The evils that beset the England of More's day are the evils of a Christian country, while Utopia is described as it was before missionaries arrived. Thus, criticism of contemporary England inevitably implied some criticism of the working of religious institutions; this new point was perhaps never quite perfectly integrated into the original book with its single sharp focus. It seems clear, nevertheless, that Thomas More saw the criticism of private property, and not of religious institutions, as the main point of the book, apart from the attractive and fanciful overlay of verisimilitude that he ingeniously provided.

More was, if anything, at pains to stress the learnedly playful character of his *jeu d'esprit*. The name *Utopia* itself comes from Greek elements meaning *nowhere;* the Utopian alphabet has a teasing distant kinship to Greek, and the officers of Utopia tend to bear Greek names. The learned reader was expected to catch occasional echoes of Plato's ideal commonwealth, the *Republic,* and also of his *Laws.* More confined his readership to those who had a good command of Latin, for the book was of course written in that language and no English translations appeared during More's lifetime. (The first was the rather diffuse version by Ralph Robynson in 1551.) The Latin, moreover, is not easy. Rare, even very rare, words are used, and the author was not averse to displaying his familiarity with obscure authors and phrases. All in all, the *Utopia* was clearly intended as a kind of witty fable for readers who would not simple-mindedly strive to transplant the ordinances of Utopia onto the more stubborn soil of contemporary Europe.

The later addition, Book One, is in dialogue form and not broken into sections; the original part, describing Utopia itself, is a continuous discourse by Hythloday (whose name means roughly "teller of idle tales") and is divided into nine chapters. Each of these has a heading to indicate its contents, but the longer ones are pretty loosely organized (as befits a traveler's tale) and touch on a wide variety of topics.

The book begins with an account of how More, coming from the cathedral after hearing mass in Antwerp, came upon a friend of his, Peter Giles of that city, engaged in earnest conversation with a stranger whose dress and manner made More rightly take him for a seafaring man. More joined them and the now three-sided conversation grew so interesting that More suggested they all adjourn to the garden behind his house, where they might continue more at leisure. It soon appears that the stranger, Hythloday, has also spent some months in England, to which country the conversation turns. Some of the principal evils are discussed, and the conversation leads to two broader problems which occupy almost the entire latter half of Book One. These social problems contrast so strongly with the serenity of Utopia, which he has recently visited, that Hythloday is prevailed upon by his companions to give that account of Utopia which, with a due pause for the midday meal, occupies all but the very last page or so of Book Two. It is worth adding that Book Two is about twice as long as Book One.

Installed now in More's garden, Hythloday, Peter Giles, and More soon find themselves considering the severe unemployment in England and its possible causes. Hythloday is generally the most active speaker, even in Book One, and the author gives the More of the dialogue the role mainly of questioner and interlocutor, a rather neutral role in which he at first mostly plays Boswell to Hythloday's Johnson. All agree that the swarms of unemployed, or "masterless men," are an object of dread as well as pity, for their desperate circumstances often drive them to desperate courses. Some of the unemployed are peasants who have been driven, with their families, off the lands they once farmed so that these could be converted to pasture. The price of wool had risen so much in recent times as to make this a more profitable use of the land, a use moreover that required much less labor and made most of the former tenants economically superfluous. Sheep, once so tame, had become "eaters of men." The dispossessed peasants were joined by a still more dangerous group, a swaggering idle rout of serving men who had been dismissed by the lords whose retinues they once swelled. These serving men, unlike the peasants, were not accustomed to any useful work and lived by terrorizing the countryside. The number of the destitute had far outrun the charitable facilities traditionally available. Indeed, even the monasteries, which in the past had freely and generously relieved the poor, had now sometimes predatory abbots who turned honest farmers off the land to convert it to more profitable uses; the same could be said of the bishops in their capacity as great landowners. Many landowners who left the peasants farming the land turned to rack-renting to increase their profits.

This somber discussion leads naturally to the first of the two general topics discussed in Book One, the administration of justice. Here the author More (one must always remember that he is not necessarily identical with the Master More of the dialogue) seems quite understandably to have felt himself to be on delicate ground. The desperate situation in which the masterless men found themselves led them to theft and other crimes as their only recourse, and they did not stop even at assault or murder. All three men agree of course that some means must be found to punish these crimes, but steadily greater severity of punishment had been followed not by the cessation of crime but actually by an increase. The author therefore chooses to make the More of the dialogue demand of the indignant Hythloday whether he could possibly devise a better system of punishments than that being used. It is Hythloday, then, (not the author), who answers that he would be hard put to it to find a worse system. He points out that if almost any offense is made a capital crime the deterrent disappears. A hungry man who has stolen a loaf of bread will be executed if caught just as a murderer will. He therefore often will be tempted to add murder to theft in order to make detection and the bloody course of justice more difficult. Hythloday argues that punishment must be proportioned to the crime, with the severest punishment reserved for the most serious crimes. Only so can order be gradually restored in the present difficult circumstances. More positive steps must be taken too, by which gainful employment can be retained or found for as many of the able-bodied poor as possible.

Advice such as this, even if it is good, may not always be acted upon, or even received in the spirit in which it is meant. Indeed, it could even redound to the discredit or disgrace of the counselor, however good his counsel. Thus arises the general topic which occupies about the entire last fourth of Book One, the duty of counsel. It happens that by 1516, when Book One was being completed, Thomas More was under increasingly heavy pressure from King Henry VIII to accept responsible positions in the government administration; while his conscience enforced upon him the duty to further the public good, he had already reason to know that Henry did not always welcome advice that ran counter to his own wishes. This biographical fact does not appear directly, of course, in the dialogue; but one notices that for the first time the More of the dialogue takes the initiative, so to speak. Hythloday insists upon the duty of the best citizens to place their wisdom and learning at the disposal of their sovereign and, through him, the whole of the body social. More, however, asks some very pointed questions. Suppose, he says, that the pliant courtiers who surround even the best of kings have proposed an ingenious plan for unjustly raising taxes or for enforcing obsolete and long neglected laws, and suppose that a good counselor raises his lone voice against those who pander to the king's wishes. What kind of reception would such a counselor get? More asks. Hythloday has to concede that it would be a cool one indeed. Under continued pressure from More he further concedes that by such ill-advised insistence a counselor might lose whatever credit he would otherwise have with the king and be unable to exercise any influence thereafter. The conclusion seems inescapable that there cannot be a duty to offer advice which is certain to be ignored.

Hythloday is once again struck by the contrast that all this offers to the happiness and order and wise government that he had seen in distant Utopia. His companions urge him to tell them more at large of the institutions of Utopia, and this, after the midday meal is eaten, he gladly does.

Book Two begins with a rather circumstantial account of the forms of social organization in Utopia and of the place itself. It is a large island, situated, we are told, between India and America, and below the equator. On the island are fifty-four cities, each with a surrounding territory or "shire." The most centrally located is the capital, Amaurote. The cities are of uniform size, with about six thousand households each, and are located about a day's journey apart. In the cities each group of thirty households elects a ruler, called the "syphograunt," who serves for a year. Larger groups of households also elect a higher official, called a "tranibore," who, though his term is for one year, is under normal circumstances re-elected. The tranibores in turn elect a king, who serves for life but whose office is not hereditary. The main forms of social organization are communal. Not only the schools of various kinds but also the dining rooms are common to groups of households. Common warehouses carry ample stocks of all the goods required for a household. A household has only to request what food and other supplies it requires and these are furnished. All contribute by their several kinds of work to the production of these goods and all are therefore entitled to have their needs met in return. Money has no place in the commonwealth; it is kept only for such uses as hiring foreign mercenaries in case of war. Wars are regarded as an evil except insofar as fought for defensive purposes or for vindicating the Utopians' right to colonize nearby unimproved land when their own population on the island exceeds the prefixed size of the island's cities. The Utopians if obliged to go to war take extreme measures to make the war short and relatively bloodless for their citizens (the war being on their side just). With their stores of money, they not only hire mercenaries, as has been mentioned, but they also offer an immense reward to anyone who will murder the ruler of the opposing state. This provision places the ruler, and not just his subjects, in direct danger in wartime, and thus the measure makes him hesitate to embark on a war that might well cost his own life. In general, the Utopians prefer to use traps and stratagems in war rather than to sacrifice human life unnecessarily. To emphasize the lack of esteem in which gold is held in peacetime, the Utopians use it for the lowest purposes; namely, the manufacture of chamberpots or (symbolically) chains.

Life is so arranged that every citizen of Utopia can realize his own abilities as fully as possible. The majority of boys follow their fathers' professions, an inclination More seems to have regarded as natural. Those who prefer another trade may follow it, and they are transferred to another household whose head can teach it to them. If he wishes, a boy may learn more than one trade and then follow either when and as he desires, subject only to the overriding claims of the public good. Certain youngsters with marked talent are given opportunity for various kinds of intellectual work, but they are subject to return to physical labor if for any reason they do not work out well. Rotation between city and country work is also encouraged, so that work remains as meaningful as possible. One is also free to travel about the island, staying at another city a day's journey off and taking one's meals there. In this case, however, one has still the duty of working his share for that day in the city he is visiting.

Labor is as little irksome as possible in Utopia. Because no one has a superfluity, six hours' labor in a day is enough to produce ample amounts of everything needful. The Utopian does not have to regard labor as the central fact of his daily life, because the short working day leaves him plenty of leisure for games, developing skills, study, music, and the other arts.

Possibly because of this broadly diffused culture the Utopians are characterized by another quality which, while not specifically named, permeates all their activities and forms of organization; namely, rationality. If occasionally there are individual offenders, their deviation seems not to be dangerous, for the citizens themselves understand and support their institutions, which they know to be not only different from those of other countries, but also better. The same spirit of measure and reasonableness is applied to one of the problems that might be foreseen as arising from the widespread pursuit of understanding, that of maintaining toleration.

From the prefatory material to the *Utopia* we learn that a bishop is ready to set out to christianize Utopia, but at the time of Hythloday's visit the Utopians had merely a natural religion. It had for all men a few premises, which More felt no reasonable man, and therefore no Utopian, could deny: that God exists, that His will is unchanging, and that He will reward good and punish evil—which implies the survival of the soul beyond death. Otherwise a man was free to believe as he would. Those of less intellectual power were likely to see some physical entity as God, such as the sun or the moon, but others of better abilities attained to the purer concept of a single spiritual God, boundless and beyond the comprehension of man. A heretic was thus one who denied one of the few fundamental premises on which all Utopians would normally agree. He was not punished for his unbelief, this being beyond his present power to change. But he was forbidden to disseminate his belief, and he was encouraged to discuss the matter with learned men who saw further than he in this question.

Their churches have a dim, religious light, but only because the Utopians have found empirically that for most men such surroundings are best suited to worship. Religion being so largely a personal matter, their priests do not occupy an especially prominent place in the commonwealth as a whole; they are "exceeding holy, and therefore exceeding few." The religion of Utopia, the subject of the book's concluding chapter, therefore is in some points similar and in other points dissimilar to Christianity. However, even when it differs from Christianity, it is not incompatible with it. Utopian religion is apparently presented as a noble pediment reared by reason alone, ready to be crowned by Revelation when the bishop who is about to set out arrives. Hythloday and those who were with him had already seen a keen and sympathetic interest in Christianity evinced by the Utopians.

Presumably More's contemporaries avoided misconceptions that have sometimes arisen in later times concerning his meaning. The prefatory materials written by friends and included in the definitive edition published under More's supervision in 1518 show that contemporaries understood that private property, not religion, was the central concern of the book. Nevertheless, the later intercalation of the greater part of Book One did introduce other topics that somewhat detract from the singleness of interest, though they doubtless increased its interest for readers of More's day. The additions also introduced the technique already referred to, by which More dissociates himself from opinions that he probably shared, preferring to let these be advanced and defended by Hythloday. No doubt we are to understand in this way the last page of the book where the More of the dialogue demurs at Hythloday's sharp criticism of the institution of private property; on reflection one sees that the author has not seen fit to give the More of the dialogue either the space or arguments with which to refute Hythloday.

J.B.G

COMMENTARY ON THE *SUMMA THEOLOGICA* OF ST. THOMAS

Author: Saint Cajetan (Cardinal Thomas de Vio, 1469-1534)
Type of work: Theological commentary
First published: 1507-1522

Principal Ideas Advanced

The Summa theologica *of Saint Thomas Aquinas is for beginners—beginners in theology, not in philosophy.*

Reading the Summa *well calls for close attention to the order of questions and articles and to the precise reasons as expressed in the precise language of Saint Thomas; and it also calls for using objections that have been or can be raised to force a deepened understanding of the text.*

Regarded by most scholars as the major work of the greatest of Thomist theologians, this celebrated *Commentary on the* Summa Theologica *of St. Thomas* was written by Cardinal Cajetan during a period of fifteen years when he was otherwise occupied with high administrative duties in his order and in the Church. Among those duties were acting as Master General over 30,000 Dominicans at a time when reform was imperative (a reform Cajetan accomplished by insisting strongly on poverty and on at least four hours a day of study for every Dominican), and later acting as Papal Legate to Germany where he preached a crusade and was engaged in the fruitless attempt to persuade Luther to return to the Church.

This is the first commentary on all parts of the *Summa.* And it has been the most influential, both by reason of its influence on the development of the Thomist vocabulary and by reason of the direct influence it had on later Thomists such as Francis of Vittoria, Domingo Bañez, the Salmaticenses, and John of Saint Thomas.

In his preface to the Prima Pars, Cajetan writes that what strikes him about the *Summa* is the contrast between its apparent easiness and its real depth: repeated readings of this work seem to increase rather than to decrease the difficulties. Because the work is difficult it has been subject to varying and incompatible interpretations, and even to thoroughgoing attacks, principally those of Duns Scotus and his followers. In the face, then, of such difficulties and attacks, Cajetan planned no simple paraphrase of the words of Saint Thomas, no mere *Abbreviatio* (a short condensation or summary of the key ideas or conclusions), but rather a full-scale textual analysis and, where the matter and the occasion called for it, an answer to any who had taken positions in opposition to those of Saint Thomas.

To the objection that the work could hardly be so profound if Thomas intended his *Summa* for beginners, Cajetan answers that the *Summa* is indeed intended for beginners, not by reason of its ease or superficiality, but by reason of its avoidance of secondary matters, its lack of repetition, and its beautiful order: it is a text, after all, for beginners in *theology,* which presupposes a thorough grounding in *philosophy.* Cajetan proposes to write a commentary which will take Thomas out of the hands of obtuse and incapable interpreters, will answer his critics, and will multiply his disciples. Cajetan will also add considerations on matters which are not necessarily of the greatest importance but which have contemporary interest or are less well known. "Weigh my reasons," he writes, "try to refute them if this seems necessary. I reserve the same right, so much the more as specifically personal attacks are not in issue."

Cajetan's exposition is both formal and magisterial: "formal" in that it is an explanation and outline of the text, usually opening with a reason for the precise title and location of the article, followed by a discussion of key terms, presuppositions, and useful distinctions; "magisterial" in that Cajetan raises and solves the difficulties he or others have seen, starting with the easier ones and going on to those which are harder. He intends to explain the very *littera et mens,* the very words and intentions of Saint Thomas; and for exact understanding, he uses both internal and external rules of criticism, clarifying obscurities either by a close examination of the text in hand or by interpreting one text in the light of another. Often remarking on the progression of thought from one of Thomas's works to another, Cajetan gives particular attention to dissipating what are apparently internal contradictions in the writings of Thomas, either those which adversaries have found or, more usually, those which he himself has found.

The greatest strength of Cajetan in his treatment of the most difficult philosophical and theological questions lies in his wide familiarity with Aristotle. On the most diverse points recourse to the works of Aristotle is customary for Cajetan; and his comments are competent, for he had already written extensive literal commentaries on the major works of Aristotle. Cajetan gives a great deal of attention to spelling out which Aristotelian principle it was that inspired such and such a solution of Saint Thomas.

Other major sources for Cajetan are the writings of Plato, Porphyry, Boethius, Avicenna, Alfarabi, and Algazel; he is always careful to present opinions, whether of friend or of foe, exactly, objectively, and fairly. He strongly favors texts from the New Testament over those from the Old Testament, and he almost invariably interprets them in their literal sense. The appeal by Cajetan to the authority of the Church Fathers is less frequent than one might expect; though he knows the classical doctrinal texts, he seems not to have studied their works extensively.

Cajetan is sometimes reproached for being obscure. The reproach is justified to this extent: Cajetan does not make use of the concrete images favored by Saint Thomas; his own images are of the interior rather than of the exterior world, psychological rather than physical, based on observation of men rather than of the physical world. And then, too, there are times when he is hunting out the errors of the Scotists, the followers of the "Subtle Doctor," and he is obviously willing to match subtlety with subtlety, for he was a dialectitian of considerable power. Cajetan's language throughout is well-ordered and careful—and usually quite dry: "as rare as a rose in Cajetan" is proverbial.

There are some inconsistencies of practice in Cajetan's commentary. After his commentary on the Prima Pars he tends to proceed more independently of the text, he does not comment on each and every article, he usually does not attempt to put arguments in form, and the length varies from a simple remark to a complete exposition of the text. He is very insistent in the preface to his commentary on the Secunda Secundae that neither his own personal authority nor that of contemporary moralists should have any place in the discussion of the difficult moral issues treated, where an error would have serious practical consequences for salvation. As a moralist who refused to subscribe to a narrow formalism which consisted in nothing more than holding to the letter of the law and applying the principles of Saint Thomas mechanically to the individual case, he himself was accused of laxism, though today one might well interpret what he was doing as pioneer work in moral psychology.

In the preface to his commentary on the Tertia Pars, Cajetan notes that he intends to add to his commentary on the text of Saint Thomas some considerations addressed to confessors of matters useful for salvation and to give special attention to defending Catholic doctrine on the Incarnation and the sacraments against the attacks of the Lutherans. He does not comment directly at all on the articles of the *Supplement* to the Tertia Pars, only "raising some useful doubts" about confession, indulgences, Holy Orders, and Matrimony.

Though Cajetan can hardly be said to treat the authority of Saint Thomas lightly, he does not always follow the opinion of Thomas: "Who will not doubt that Aquinas has not sometimes departed from the truth, he who proposed so many thousands of questions on matters divine and human, theoretical and practical, always raising objections on both sides of every question?" He is willing to concede that pious opinion on the Immaculate Conception is probable. And he does not follow Saint Augustine and Saint Thomas on the reality of the dove at the Baptism of Christ; to their high reasons of fittingness, he places emphasis on the "*sicut* columba" (like a dove), and concludes: "It appears more reasonable in my opinion to follow the literal text." He also abandons the position of Thomas on the impossibility of salvation for infants who die without Baptism of water, maintaining that if the faith of the parents in the Old Testament was sufficient to save an infant, God would be no less merciful in the New Dispensation.

Cajetan, most especially in his later life, showed himself to be a transitional man, one raised in the traditional philosophical and theological culture of the Middle Ages, but one who found himself in the full intellectual and religious revolution of the Renaissance and the Reformation. He was very familiar with the positions of the humanists and the Averroists, for he had studied and taught for seven years at Padua in his youth, during the course of which time he became familiar with Scotists as represented by Trombetta; with the Averroists as represented by Vernias, Pomponazzi, and Niphus; and with the humanists as represented by Pico della Mirandola (whom he once bested in a public dispute). As is well known, near the end of his life he became convinced that the immortality of the soul could not be demonstrated philosophically. And at the Lateran Council, when it was proposed in its decree against Averroism, that all public professors of philosophy be asked to justify in their courses the conclusions of Christian faith, Cajetan voted *non placet.*

Perhaps his originality and independence are best manifested in his commentaries on Scripture written near the end of his life. Cajetan was firmly attached to the literal sense, and he had no fear of adopting an interpretation "a torrente doctorum sacrorum alienus" (differing from the consensus of the holy fathers), provided it conformed to the doctrine of the Church. This led him to judgments which appeared rash to some of his contemporaries: his allergorical interpretation of the first chapters of Genesis and his questioning of the rightness of the traditional attribution of the authorship of the Epistle of the Hebrews, of the Second Epistle of St. Peter, and of other books. But it is clear that the work of Scripture scholars in the nineteenth and twentieth centuries has confirmed the rightness of Cajetan's attempts to apply, so far as possible, the techniques of science to the search for the literal and primary sense of Scripture.

R.L.C.

ON EDUCATION

Author: Juan Luis Vives (1492-1540)
Type of work: Philosophy of Christian Education
First published: 1531

Principal Ideas Advanced

Scholarship should aim at serving such useful purposes as furtherance of the common good and the glorification of God.

The study of nature (the natural sciences) should be stressed because most of our knowledge originally derives from experience or induction from particular observations to generalizations, and because all knowledge of things eventually leads to their divine source.

The study of history is a most important source of practical wisdom because it provides us with the experience of mankind through the ages.

Both Latin and the vernacular languages are to be studied and utilized: Latin as the universal language for communication between diverse peoples as well as a key to valuable learning and literature; the vernaculars as practical means for the dissemination of learning and popular communication.

Juan Luis Vives, born in Valencia in 1492, scholar, educator, humanist, and philosopher, was one of the most brilliant, versatile, and original thinkers of the Renaissance. After undertaking his initial education in Valencia, he studied at Paris from 1509 until 1514. He then went to Bruges in the Spanish Netherlands, which became his "second fatherland." About 1518, Vives became tutor to young Cardinal De Croy, and both taught and studied at Louvain, part of the time under Erasmus. From 1522 to 1528 most of his time was spent in England, where he was a protégé and friend of Wolsey and More, as well as of Henry VIII and Catherine of Aragon. He was also tutor to the Princess Mary, but lost the king's favor when he declined to support the royal cause in the divorce proceedings against Catherine, after which he was banished and his pensions were discontinued. In the meantime he had married Catherine Valdauras, the young daughter of a Spanish family in Bruges, and he spent the rest of his life in that congenial city writing on various topics. He died in 1540 at the age of 48.

The gifted Vives was author of numerous works on a wide variety of topics. He is regarded as a founder of modern psychology because of his treatise *De anima* (*On the Soul*), and as an early sociologist because of his treatises on marriage (*On the Husband* and *On the Duties of a Christian Woman*), as well as because of his advocacy of public welfare provisions in his *On the Aid of Paupers,* and his critical treatise *On Common Property*. He denounced war in his *On Concord and Discord Among Men,* and he wrote *On the Beginnings, Schools, and Praises of Philosophy* as well as *On the Truth of the Christian Faith*. His pious and devotional works were very popular, and one, his *Introduction to Wisdom,* saw fifty editions. His most successful work was an elementary Latin textbook which went through ninety-nine editions. He was the leading pedagogical theorist of the sixteenth century, and besides lesser tracts composed the most extensive and progressive treatise on education that the world had yet seen.

The *De tradendis disciplinis,* or *On Education* is actually the second part of a general treatise *De disciplinis* (*On Learning*). In the first part the author discusses *The Causes of the Corruption of the Arts* (or *Learning*), and he criticizes current abuses such as excessive deference to ancient authority, neglect of observation, and undue fondness for epitomes.

The *De tradendis disciplinis* (literally, "The Transmission of Learning") consists of five books: On Educational Origins, On Schools, On Language Studies, On Higher Studies, and On Relations of Learning and Life, to which Vives adds an Appendix on Scholars. In many ways this epochal work sums up the best of medieval and Renaissance educational theories on the one hand, and, on the other, it anticipates many modern advances in the philosophy of Christian education. The book is the most comprehensive treatise on its subject down to its own day, remarkable for its insight and practicality, as well as its breadth.

According to Vives' *On Education,* nothing is more excellent than learning, since it distinguishes man from beasts, makes him truly human, and even raises him towards God Himself. The knowledge of the things of nature leads to the knowledge and love of God, their Creator, man's chief end and good. Nature is a great book in which we learn of God. Nature, rather than authority, is the chief font of human knowledge. Although we should profit from what earlier authors have to tell us, we should use a critical approach to their teachings. For experience, particularly rational or controlled experience, is the principal source of the arts.

Language is the key to learning, Vives contends. He argues that Latin should be mastered as a universal language, but it is more valuable as a means to content than because of any inherent virtue. The vernacular languages should also be studied and used in instruction and for popular communication. Language teaching should be enlivened by interesting incidental information. The so-called "paperbook method" of collecting notes concerning various features of the materials being studied is a useful aid to learning. Another is repetition; another, discussion by the students. Vives concedes that some knowledge of Greek is useful, but he argues that only certain gifted students should be expected to master it.

Languages are studied, Vives writes, not for themselves, but in order that we may be able to read what is written by their use. There is a hierarchy among authors, he suggests; some are to be memorized, some to be read but not memorized, while still others to be kept for possible reference. Among ancient authors particularly recommended by Vives are Virgil, Lucan, Horace, Persius, Martial, Ovid, Livy, Valerius, Maximus, Terence, Seneca, Caesar, and Cicero; among "modern" authors Linacre, Lebrixa, Erasmus, Politian, and L. Valla. Also useful in particular fields are Tacitus, Palladius, Vitruvius, and Quintilian.

Vives writes that poetry is "lofty, sublime, and brilliant," with "a certain great and elevated spirit," and "a harmony which corresponds to the melody of the human soul," while containing "the seeds of all kinds of knowledge" scattered through it. Among recommended Greek authors are Homer, Aristophanes, Euripides, Hesiod, and Pindar.

Following a solid grounding in language and literature come higher studies, Vives writes. The latter include logic, nature study, philosophy, rhetoric, the mathematical quadrivium of arithmetic, geometry, astronomy, and music, and applied arts such as husbandry, architecture, and navigation. Finally comes the acquisition of practical wisdom through experience, and the study of history and moral philosophy.

Logic provides us with a method of investigation, and since it is closely related to the study of languages, the study of logic directly follows the study of languages. The best textbook in logic would be one covering the logical treatises of Aristotle.

Next, Vives claims, should come "Nature Study," which is particularly congenial to youth, as concerning concrete, observable realities. A general descriptive introduction should be provided for all, while further inquiry into causes or detailed scientific studies should be pursued by those capable of undertaking them. Among the nature studies, by which most youths will whet their appetite for learning, are geography, astronomy or meteorology, biology, botany, ichthyology, and mineralogy. Observation rather than disputation is the key to such studies, which provide a continual source of interest throughout life.

Vives then points out that when the study of natural things penetrates beyond phenomena or observable things to their causes, it becomes "First Philosophy," which ultimately leads to the first and final cause: God. Basic philosophical works to be studied are the *Physics* and *Metaphysics* of Aristotle. For rhetoric, the basic authors are Cicero and Quintilian; while a principal means of acquiring eloquence is through the imitation of the masters of literature.

The mathematical sciences as described by Vives include arithmetic, geometry, astronomy, and music, as well as acoustics, perspective, and optics; the principal scientists in those areas are James Faber, Jordanus Nemorarius, John of Canterbury, Rafael of Volterra, Euclid, Archimedes, Bradwardine, Ptolemy, and Georgius Valla.

Scholars should seek to acquire some knowledge of auxiliary and practical arts, such as husbandry, architecture, navigation, pharmacy, and dietetics. Thus, Carolus Virulus, headmaster of a school in Louvain, used to inform himself concerning the occupations of whatever fathers were coming to visit his school; in this way he was able to entertain them at dinner and to question them about their specialties.

Basic for the study of medicine, writes Vives, is anatomy. One must then become familiar with various remedies. Some physicians should be primarily clinical physicians and researchers, rather than regular practitioners. The leading medical authors, according to Vives, are Galen, Hippocrates, Celsus, Psellus, Nicander, Avicenna, Razes, and Averroës.

After having learned the natures of things, the student should seek to acquire practical wisdom: the skill of adapting means to ends. A principal way to such wisdom, Vives suggests, is through experience: both personal experience and, even more important, the experience of mankind in general. The latter kind is acquired through the study of history: "Where there is history, children have the advantages of old men; while where history is absent, old men are as children, since history, following the definition of that wisest of men [Cicero], is 'the spectator of time' and 'the light of truth.'" Not only is the reading of history delightful and entertaining, Vives writes, but it is also the main source of knowledge for many branches of learning.

In the study of history, we should not concern ourselves unduly with wars and battles, Vives cautions, but we should limit ourselves to the essential facts, such as the information about contestants, dates, locations, and outcomes. History should concentrate its main attention on "peaceful affairs," such as virtuous acts and their rewards, wise councils and sayings, and achievements in the arts and sciences. In studying history, one should first read general works that provide a general overview or survey; then one can profitably turn to more specific works. For early history, one should supplement the historical books of the Old Testament with the works of such Greek historians as Herodotus, Xenophon, Arrian, Polybius, and Plutarch; and one can then study such Roman historians as Livy, and Tacitus, together with the Gospels and Acts of the New Testament. Christian historians recommended by Vives include Eusebius, Cassiodorus, Jerome, and the authors of the *Historia tripartita,* Bede, Isidore of Seville, Paul the Deacon, and Einhard, as well as Procopius. More recent historians (from Vives's point of view) include Biondo, Gaguin, Pius II, Sabellico, Trithemius, Bruni, and Peter Martyr.

The practical examples of history are to be interwoven with the general principles of moral philosophy. The latter provides a rule of reason for public and private life, in that it includes ethics for individual moral guidance, economics for private associations such as the family, politics, and laws for the state. Among the writers which Vives endorses for these studies are Plato, Aristotle, Cicero, and Thomas More, as well as Xenophon, Erasmus, and Patritius.

In commenting on laws, Vives asserts that they are provisions of justice as perceived by reason and decreed by those who have leadership in the community. One of the conditions of laws is that they be accepted by the majority of people.

With respect to scholars, their final objectives in learning, according to Vives, should be the benefit of the community and the glory of God, not empty and fleeting present honors, favors, and riches. Scholars should give good example, refrain from envy, and live in unity and harmony with their fellows. With respect to the writing of books, Vives has some good advice: "One who intends to become an author must read much, reflect much, write much, correct much, publish very little. The proportion in these activities, unless I am mistaken, is expressed numerically as follows: Reading: 5; Reflection: 4; Writing: 3. Emendation brings the last named number to 2; and from these two actual publication by a scholar should be counted as 1."

D.D.M.

THE PRINCE

Author: Niccolò Machiavelli (1469-1527)
Type of work: Political philosophy
First published: 1532

Principal Ideas Advanced

Political power is a principle in itself, ordered by laws as objective as the laws of any other nature.

The ruler who would attain to power or maintain himself in it must make the study of the objective principles of political power his chief concern.

The study of political power has its corresponding art; it is not a mere speculative or contemplative knowledge of power which the prince must seek, but a knowledge which will give him mastery over the processes of power.

Machiavelli's essay *The Prince* spells out, on the basis of Machivelli's considerable political and diplomatic experience and reflection, the chief indications which he would offer a prince concerning both the nature of political power and the principles of the art of ruling.

Machiavelli plunges immediately into his self-appointed task by delimiting the range of his interests. He distinguishes all forms of political dominion into republics (aristocratic or oligarchic republics) and principalities (rules of one man). He will not discuss republics, he says, because he has done so elsewhere; the reference is to his commentary on Livy (*Commentary on the First Ten Books of Titus Livius,* 1512).

Machiavelli will limit himself to the systems of one-man rule. These, he notes, may be hereditary or newly established, especially by the force of the ruler himself. Hereditary states will not preoccupy him very much; they are readily maintained if only the ruler has wit enough to follow the customs of his predecessors and meet emergencies as they arise. New principalities will concern him more, for they present the difficulties with which the prince must cope.

The first class of newly acquired or established principalities comprises those which are added to the already existing principality of a ruler. The problems which these present seem to be properly of a diplomatic order. The task of the prince is to make himself and his rule acceptable in the new realm with the minimum expenditure of force and effort. His first task must be to reconcile those in the new realm whom he has injured by his acquisition, whether peaceful or by force; his second must be to rid himself of those who, from within the newly acquired realm, have aided him to power. The first he can gain by suavity and reassurances; the latter he must destroy, for he can never hope to satisfy their demands so long as he remains under obligation to them. Barriers of language, culture, and religion may interpose themselves between the new prince and his fresh possessions. The prince is counseled not to disturb the established patterns so far as this is possible. He is urged to go, if possible, to live among his new subjects; if not, to establish colonies among them from among the population of his other realm; these are far better than garrisons, for colonies support themselves while garrisons require to be supported. The prince must make himself the leader of the less powerful elements within the new realm and in the surrounding provinces, and the enemy of the stronger elements. His model in this must be the Romans who had mastered this aspect of the art of rule to perfection.

Machiavelli warms to the subject of his predilection: principalities entirely new, established by the arms and ability of the princes themselves. Here the art of rule is deployed in its full extent. And the best teaching in this matter is to be gained by the study of great men who have achieved eminence in this difficult art. Among men who thus acquire power by their own efforts Machiavelli makes certain classifications. There are those who do so by valorous actions; they gain power with great labor, but maintain and retain it with relative ease. There are those who acquire power with the help of others, and those who rely, to the greatest possible extent, on their own resources. The first inevitably come to a bad end; they are not so much in power as in the power of another. Eventually, only the second survive. But among the second, there must also be distinguished those who rise to power by fortune; these have a hard path: they come easily to power, but must encounter great difficulty in maintaining it. They have neither the knowledge nor the proper virtues necessary for power. The men who really interest Machiavelli are those who rise to power and hold it by their own talent; and to these most of his observations directly apply. And it is to be noted that those who claim to find Machiavelli's ideal in Cesare Borgia are obviously mistaken; for Machiavelli cites this man as an example of one who came to power through the fortune of another, his father, the pope, and failed eventually because of this dependence, though his own talents meanwhile were developing. As an example of one who rose by his own talent Machiavelli cites Francesco Sforza. A very special case is composed of those who rise to power by crime and preserve it by cruelty. These, if ethics and politics were identical, should perish; but they do not necessarily. The criminal origins of their power can be assuaged by the order they may bring. As for cruelty, it may be well- or ill-used, and this makes all the difference. Those who use it well may long survive in power.

A special type of principality Machiavelli calls *civil.* In this, one rises to power by favor of his fellow citizens, through neither fortune nor talent alone, but by a combination of shrewdness and good luck. His situation may seem fortunate, but it is beset with problems. If he has come to power by action of the great, he stands in position to offend the people; if by favor of the people, he surely stands to offend the great. Rare must be his diplomacy indeed; and a short reign, and not too quiet, can be foretold him. His greatest hope lies in making himself indispensable to all, if that is possible.

A very special class of principalities is the *ecclesiastical.* Such principalities have a rare instrument at their command: they can bring their exercise of power under the aegis of the sacred and thus invest the one with the awe belonging to the other. So far as they are under that aegis Machiavelli protests that he can say little about them. He does, however, point out that the papacy, the greatest of such principalities, came to its position of power through the combination of many factors, not the least of which was the political talent of the popes themselves. Machiavelli is reluctant, ostensibly, to examine such principalities too closely; nevertheless, it is clear that he considers their sacred character simply an added advantage in the process of securing power and corresponding consensus and sees no fundamental difference between them and earthly and temporal principalities.

Chapters 12 to 14 of *The Prince* are concerned with a matter which Machiavelli clearly considers of supreme importance in the art of gaining and maintaining power: military affairs. He has absolutely clear insight into the fact that in the last analysis power rests on force. As a consequence, the basic skill in the ruler is skill in arms, and this skill includes both actual field ability and military diplomacy. He discusses the various kinds of troops which a prince may have at his disposal, and he devotes very special attention to the matter of mercenaries. He reviews this problem from its earliest appearance in classical times and finds abundant instructive examples on which to draw in every period, most especially from the contemporary scene in Italy. His analysis of the military, fiscal, logistic, and psychological aspects of the employment of mercenary troops is masterly, and indicates that though he was himself a clerk, a member of the learned profession, he had a strong bent in the military direction and a very considerable knowledge gained, no doubt, from many opportunities for observation. His conclusion is clear: mercenary troops must be considered by their nature the most treacheous instrument of policy which the prince can assume. He does not say that it is entirely possible to avoid their use. What he does say is that the prince who is determined or forced to employ them should do so with full knowledge of the kind of instrument he is using and should appreciate at every moment that this is potentially his most threatening enemy. He mercilessly accumulates example upon example of the perfidy of mercenary troops, their reluctance in battle, their facile transfer of allegiance.

He goes on to discuss auxiliaries, mixed, and native troops. These are types of military forces for which he finds the examples both in ancient times and in the practices of his own day. Of the three, he undoubtedly feels that native troops are best from the psychological point of view, but he notes the difficulty in raising and maintaining native forces at the peak level of strictly military competence. The prince, in other words, can never count on having a perfectly secure military instrument at hand. He must be resigned at all times to working with an instrument of dubious character. But this is no more, for Machiavelli, than a supreme test of his skill in the game of power; for the most politic of his skills must be, in the last analysis, controlling these volatile forces upon which his own power so precariously rests.

On one point, however, Machiavelli is firm and unyielding: the military preparation of the prince himself. Here he insists that there is no substitute for the personal skill and competence of the prince. The military art is the one the prince must practice beyond all others: he must know skill at arms; he must understand problems of strategy and tactics; he must understand the analysis of terrain and the problem of logistics. Furthermore, the prince must understand military psychology, the temper of his troops, the characters, both strengths and weaknesses, of his captains, how they may be controlled and bent to his interest even when they are manifestly seeking their own. The prince, as always in Machiavelli's view, must study the past; he must learn from those who have gone before him, for this is the very essence of history and the true school of the human spirit.

The matter of chapters 15 to 19 is more delicate, though hardly more important from the point of view of the art of power than the military concerns. These chapters are occupied with the character of the prince; not, however, from the moral or ethical point of view, but from what might almost be called a functional point of view; that is, one which concerns his efficiency as a prince. This section might well be called a masterly analysis of a role-psychology. Machiavelli begins with a review of the things for which men and particularly princes are most often and widely praised or blamed. He recommends what might be called a power morality. The most basic of the rules of this morality must be that the prince must see things as they really are, and not as people propose them to be. His eye must be single and fixed on the actuality. For this reason, he cannot take as his own, uncritically, the norms of the many; nor must he be afraid of departing from the popular norms when the demands of power indicate. If he cannot do this and form in himself an absolute independence of action, he will surely fail as a prince, however "good" a man he may be by the standards of morality. And these Machiavelli finds to be, as they are actually applied, most vacillating in themselves. Princes are praised and blamed for the most extensive variety of causes and with a complete inconsistency of pattern. The prince who would seek to guide his conduct by such norms would be inviting disaster and political ruin.

Machiavelli's examination of the bases of praise and blame proceeds by the ancient method of opposites. A prince may be characterized now as liberal, now as stingy; one as bountiful, another as rapacious, and so forth. The prince is not to disregard these dichotomies; neither is he, however, to take them in any literal sense, but he must employ them dialectically to determine his own pattern of conduct. Machiavelli suggests for special treatment the pair of opposites: generosity and meanness. The worst thing would be for the prince to accept any common interpretation of these terms. He must see them, rather, in their reality and in their appearances and must balance these against each other. Thus, it must always be to the prince's advantage to appear generous and to avoid every indication of meanness; he should not, however, be seduced into undervaluing the reality of those two dispositions of soul. Actual generosity, practiced on a scale which might meet with anything like popular approval, might well spell his ruin. Meanness, on the other hand, when it comes to involve the husbanding of resources, so as to insure independence of action and power to carry through enterprises to which the prince's hand has been set, is a virtue to be praised. So, too, with the duality of cruelty and clemency; a like balance between reality and appearance, loss and gain must be established by the prince, without too much concern to follow, in establishing this balance, the view of the many or even the common view of the learned. And so, too, must it be with regard, finally, to the prince's word, whether he keep it or not and when. The prince, in a word, is the most subtle moralist of all. Not only good and evil, but appearance and reality of good and evil are the matter of his dialectic. He has a fixed point from which this dialectic can be conducted, but it is not that of the ordinary man nor even of classical morality and ethics. It is that of the art of power. And since, as a prince, the whole reality of his person is in this art, without which he is not this character at all, this fixed point is the center of the real for him and the only point of reference he can take seriously.

In this light, the most celebrated chapter of *The Prince,* the eighteenth, entiled "In What Manner Princes Should Keep Their Word" and in which are found, according to some commentators, the most extreme forms of moral perfidy, which have made the term "Machiavellian" one of opprobrium, demands re-interpretation. The last thing Machiavelli is advocating is moral perfidy in matters of truth. What he is inculcating is the "realmoralitat" of the order of power. At no time does he imply that this is a universal point of view, such as must be the point of view of a transcendental science such as classical ethics. At no point does he offer the indications made here as a real alternative to classical transcendental ethics. Outside the dialectic of appearance and reality mentioned above, Machiavelli's words cannot be understood. Within that context they have a perfectly clear but by no means transcendental meaning. If any question can here be raised concerning Machiavelli's view, it is this: does he try to substitute a role morality for a transcendental morality? But he must be exonerated of the charge that he does, for to do so would be to violate the premises of his discourse. He neither affirms nor denies one at the expense of the other, but accepts both as part of that order of things, "come stanno le cose," which is the constant context of all of his remarks.

The chapter devoted to the problem of fortresses (Chapter 20) is something of an interlude, in the position which it occupies; a more fitting place for it might have been in the sequence devoted to military matters. Be that as it may, in the age in which the art of fortification reached a new peak in Italy and engaged the talents of some of the greatest architects, the chapter was instructive by reason of the advanced point of view it represents. Machiavelli was already aware, in a distant and dim way, of the fluidity with which the development of new weapons would endow warfare. The pros and cons of the fixed position are argued with skill from a politico-military point of view.

The theme of the proper personal and role endowments of the prince is resumed in the following chapter and preoccupies the attention of the succeeding pages until the reflective and hortatory chapters which bring the work to a close. The twenty-first chapter takes up the matter of the prestige of the prince: what advances and what undermines it. Foremost in Machiavelli's mind is the concern for great enterprises. Here he exhibits a keen insight into the role of the ruler as "entrepreneur," a concept which gained increasing force with the loosening of the feudal structure of Europe. To be appreciated, this idea must be set in contrast with that of the medieval lord, who is not the initiator of great enterprises but the guardian of an established order. In no other place, perhaps, does Machiavelli's "modernity" appear in more striking fashion. Equally modern, perhaps, is his insistence on the prince's skill in internal affairs; that is, his administrative talent. Steadfastness in attitude is also an element of prestige; the prince must be a true friend and also a true enemy. Neutrality is not his role, in Machiavelli's view; the neutral prince inherits the enmity of all parties. A talent for calculated risk is high on the list of the prince's attributes; he is deluded if he hopes always to follow a safe course. His prudence lies in weighing the disadvantages of each choice and taking the least bad as the good. Finally, though he himself may not be bound to them, the prince should be ready to reward those who excel in the conventional virtues and, at the same time, to salute suitably all those who show excellence in any of the arts which contribute to the common wealth. All these practices and attitudes, readily enough cultivatable, must create a favorable image of the prince in the minds of his people.

Machiavelli's administrative acumen

comes to the fore again in what he has to say about the prince's skill and prudence in the selection of his ministers. The first opinion of a prince, he notes, is based on the men he has around him and who represent him. Wisdom in the selection of these men is second only to skill in war. Machiavelli demands selflessness of the minister as a *sine qua non;* and he makes it the first rule by which the prince can evaluate the candidates for his favor. And, prudently, Machiavelli cautions the prince not to be niggardly in this instance, but to make sure that the ministers have occasion to enrich themselves. These are golden chains of attachment to himself which he is permitting the minister to forge.

Machiavelli reserves his sharpest warnings to the prince for the matter of flatterers. No doubt there is a good measure of personal experience behind these words. In any case, it is evident that the flatterer represents for him a low form of human life, a parasitical form which, having no creative power but grafting itself onto another living thing, destroys eventually the very life on which it feeds. Machiavelli notes that flattery is an insidious poison; it is difficult to resist because such resistance involves a high degree of self-knowledge and self-criticism. Flattery feeds on the complacency of the flattered. To free himself from it, the prince must have an unprejudiced eye for his own character and be relatively free from forms of self-delusion. The best protection against flattery is to make it clear that plain speech is welcome on all matters; yet not from all. Rather, such speech is a privilege which the prince may accord only to counselors whom he has chosen for their wisdom. The prince should listen to the advice of such men, but only when he asks for it. Yet he should reserve his judgment, for in the last analysis the decision is his. To put himself completely in the hands of another is to surrender that power which is the entire *ratio* of his own life.

Machiavelli takes the cases of many of the princes of Italy who had fallen from power as evidence of the rightness of his own views and counsels. In Chapter 24 he cites concrete instances of such decline and relates them directly to the failure of the princes concerned to tread the paths he had traced out. This chapter is a prelude in turn to the passage on fortune in human affairs and the means by which it may be countered, which constitutes another of the most famous passages not only in Machiavelli's writings but in the whole of the literature of political wisdom. He recognizes the influence which men accord to fortune in human affairs; but in the ultimate event, he holds, it is the will of man which prevails. Machiavelli creates here the great image of fortune as a raging river in flood which none can withstand; yet he counsels that in peaceful times one may raise levees against the flood and barriers against the tides of fortune. Fortune, he holds, is a coward; she directs her strongest blows against those places where no defenses against her have been erected; where she encounters the sage provisions of human prudence, she retreats.

Many commentators have long thought that the chapter which stands at the end of *The Prince* does not constitute an integral element of the whole. Despite all the philological evidence which may be adduced to the contrary, there will always be a certain persuasiveness to this view. The exhortation to the princes of the House of Medici to place themselves at the head of a movement to free Italy from the barbarians who afflict her by their presence is sincere, indeed, but rhetorical. Some may protest that these two characteristics cannot belong to the same passage but they fail to see clearly the complexities of human sentiment and expression. It is sincere, for there can be no doubt that Machiavelli bitterly resented the servitude to foreign power in which Italy lay. The rhetoric lies in the fact that he addresses the Medici as her potential liberators. This is counter to the political wisdom which breathes through the whole work. In a word, Machiavelli should have known better, and did know better, than to expect anything of the kind from these princes. Yet he selects them as the targets for this heartfelt plea. This is a situation which it would be foolish to try to simplify or to clarify completely, but despite the problem of the ending, *The Prince* remains as a masterpiece on the art of power politics; and, in perhaps a somewhat negative manner, it plays its part in the development of the critical debate concerning the relation of the state to the concerns of the Church.

A.R.C.

THE DIALOGUE BETWEEN THE SOUL AND THE BODY

Author: Saint Catherine of Genoa (Catherine Fieschi Adorna, 1447-1510) or possibly Tommasa Vernazza (1497-1587)
Type of work: Spiritual biography
First transcribed: c.1500-1548

Principal Ideas Advanced

Union with God is achieved through a series of purifications of body and soul.

In the earlier stages, these necessary purifications are actively assumed by the person; they involve various bodily mortifications, denials of the interior senses, and deprivations of the spiritual appetites.

In the later stages, man's spiritual nature is the victim of passive mortifications sent by God to effect perfections impossible for the spirit to achieve unaided.

"Spoken between a Soul, her Body and Self-love, and between the Spirit and Natural Man, all of which was verified in Saint Catherine." So does the author of the *Dialogue* introduce the characters who will play out the drama of the spiritual biography of Saint Catherine of Genoa. It appears certain in the light of modern investigation that Catherine herself did not write the *Dialogue,* at least in the form we now possess. Baron Friedrich von Hügel, a great authority on Saint Catherine, has assigned the authorship of the *Dialogue* to Tommasa Vernazza, the daughter of one of Catherine's closest disciples, Ettore Vernazza—a girl who was Catherine's god-child, who knew her and many of her followers and the quality of their "spirituality" intimately, and who entered the same convent which had refused Catherine because of her tender age. Von Hügel claims that there, in 1548, thirty-eight years after Catherine's death, Tommasa, in religion known as "Battista," wrote the *Dialogue,* which came to be called ". . . of St. Catherine" because in it Catherine's thoughts and teachings on the spiritual life were distilled and transcribed. Certain other views hold to the theory that Catherine dictated the *Dialogue* in secret, as it were, that out of humility she wished it not to be published, and that the present version (made at a later date, perhaps between 1548-1551) is but a composite of at least two versions of this dictation. But to whom Catherine dictated is unknown. A number of close disciples, as well as her confessor of later years, are proposed as possible candidates. The other work commonly ascribed to Saint Catherine, *The Treatise on Purgatory,* was more surely of her own composition, but it too underwent editing at some later date. It is agreed, however, that in the *Treatise* and in the *Dialogue,* the saint's doctrine is adequately and accurately set forth.

The *Dialogue*'s literal attention to biographical details of Catherine's life is minimal. Rather, these details are used as the stamped pattern upon which are woven the threads of that other life-story, the spiritual biography of a mystic soul, in order to indicate the evolution of Catherine's spiritual life in union with God and, in so doing, to present to the world Catherine's legacy to the fund of ascetical-mystical theology.

Briefly, the schema of the *Dialogue* is this: Part I describes Catherine's initial good will, combined with a quite imperfect desire for spiritual perfection; her lapse for a time into a life occupied with material considerations; her "conversion"; her gradual progress in virtue, especially in humility and prudence, underwritten by her active mortification of the interior and exterior senses; and the many sufferings attendant upon all these stages.

Part II continues to describe the purification process involved in Catherine's movement towards mystical union with God; the renewed and more interior suffering of the soul, coupled with rejoicing at God's manifestations of love towards her; and the soul's growing understanding of divine things.

Part III is taken up with the soul's seeking to learn more from God about His "pure love"; the soul's ecstatic outpourings of love; and descriptions of the soul's transformation in mystical union with God.

The biographical details of Catherine's life which correspond to the earlier sections of the *Dialogue* are these: Catherine Fiesca, in obedience to family wishes, renounced her own desires for the religious life and, at the age of sixteen, married Giuliano Adorni. The Adorni were Ghibellines, the aristocratic Fieschi Guelphs, and this marriage was intended to help make for peace between the two factions. For some five years after her marriage, Catherine lived quite ascetically, avoiding even the many legitimate pleasures of her society. Coming out of retirement because of family pressures, she turned for a time to more normal and even relatively "worldly" social pursuits until her "conversion" in 1474. Following this, Catherine, now with a more refined sense of interior motivation, entered on a life of intense and prolonged prayer, supported by heroic penances and charitable works among the poor and infirm.

This life of prayer and penance lasted for thirty-six years following Catherine's conversion. Except for the last ten years when she was very ill, she spent many hours in daily prayer, endured long periods of fasting, denied herself every conceivable bodily comfort, and busily engaged herself in hospital work with victims of incurable disease, whom she tenderly and patiently cared for, overcoming great repugnance for the naturally offensive character of such work. She literally wore herself out in serving others, which led to her final long illness and death in 1510.

In part I, the characters engaged in conversation as the drama begins are the Soul and the Body, who come together for a journey through the world. Because Self-love resides in each, he is called to join them as arbiter to any dispute which may arise between them. Soul, knowing her spiritual nature, her own mettle and destiny ("God has created me for love and delight"), forces her spiritual mode of existence upon Body, whose needs lie but in "raiment, food, drink, sleep, service, and something in which to take delight," thus breaking the delicate balance reason would establish between them. Body revolts. Goaded by Self-love, Body quickly and insidiously brings about Soul's corruption. No longer motivated by her lofty aspirations, Soul grovels in misery outside the world of spirit, whose atmosphere is necessary to her survival. Enslaved, but full of self-justification for her gross disorientation, Soul and her companion, Body, travel on, and "fearing their earthly tastes might be disturbed, they neither spoke of them nor could bear to hear a word of them." Soul suffers the beginning of an abundance of suffering and anguish that will be hers before the journey's end, seeking rest yet turning from God in Whom she could find perfect rest.

God then takes pity on Soul, and aided by His special grace, she throws herself upon His providence towards all His creatures, abandoning her "sinful" ways and asking for nothing but what His goodness will provide. Her "conversion" has taken place. (Chapter VII. The author calls it a "conversion." We must not understand this as a movement from belief in one cult to belief in another, but more as a "reconversion," often described by the saints as a moment in time after which they undertook the pursuit of holiness and union with God with complete determination, *no matter what the cost to themselves*—with a holy vengeance, one might say.)

At this point in the *Dialogue* begins the long but most necessary purification of Soul by God, designed to effect the complete eradication of all that is not spiritual in man. This purifying action is initiated with a series of interior illuminations, under the light of which Soul sees her own immense poverty of spiritual goods. Humility is born in her, a virtue that will grow to full flower by journey's end. Thus armed with self-knowledge and a richer understanding of God's patience with sinners, Soul is strengthened against despair. Of most profit to Soul at this stage is the experiencing of God's "pure love" poured out on her, effecting a purification of all her lower affections for base things and thereby deepening her attraction for things divine.

Body, perceiving the near demise of his reign over Soul, will have none of this. With consummate craft, he reminds Soul "that after the love of God comes love of thy neighbour, which should, in bodily things, begin with thine own Body." He protests against this neglect of himself and of his needs by Soul, but she, resolute, presses on, insisting upon his subjection to her.

Then God, burning away Soul's self-love, gives her a painful and prolonged knowledge of all her sins, and of their evil effects. But to make life bearable for her, since this knowledge could not have been endured for long, God sends her many consoling interior visions. These visions are "rays of love," or "wounds of love," their pain arising from Soul's realization of the *limitations* of her own love in response to the *limitless* love of God.

Natural Man (another name for Body—later used as a synonym for "creature," to refer to the whole person; that is, body *and* soul) victim of neglect, and weakening visibly from the mortification Spirit inflicts on it, again cries out for consideration (the author probably wishes to distinguish Soul, as used generally, from the most interior part of the soul, called here "Spirit," which corresponds to the *fundus animae* of other mystics). God answers by sending consolations—spiritual joys to Spirit, and emotional raptures to Natural Man. Thus refreshed, Natural Man thinks that on this kind of food he can indeed survive the journey. But Spirit deals him the last, fatal blow. For she resolves not to seek or crave or relish even *spiritual* delights, realizing that it would be as easy to become too attached to these as it was to become too attached to sensual pleasures. Gradually, Natural Man, through service to other creatures, especially the sick, is disciplined by Spirit, and finally surrenders to it, feeling therein great peace. Now Spirit can say at last, "Henceforth I will not call her a human creature, for I see that she is all in God and without Natural Man."

Part II continues the conversation between God, the Soul, the Spirit, and Natural Man, carrying the reader deeper into Spirit's mystical experience. For Spirit, having done all she can *of herself* to effect her desires for union with God, is now the *passive* victim of the loving yet painfully burning action of God's love, searing yet cleansing, blinding in its brightness, yet illumining the deepest recesses of Spirit's understanding. Saint John of the Cross, whose works on spiritual transformation are unexcelled, writing later in the same century says in the *Dark Night of the Soul,* Book I, Chapter 3, ". . . however greatly the soul itself labours, it cannot actively purify itself so as to be in the least degree prepared for the Divine union of perfection of love, if God takes not its hand and purges it not in that dark fire. . . ." God acts on passive Spirit by purgations of the memory, intellect, and will, so that these spiritual faculties, seemingly rendered useless with respect to their natural activities, can be prepared to accept God as their object. This frustration in their activities results in Spirit's suffering intensely in each faculty separately and in all together. But so "secret" and "subtle" is God's work in Spirit that when He shows her, in consideration of her weakness, how far along the path to union with Him she has already been drawn, and when

God allows her to see the sins she has left behind and the virtues she has now acquired, she is truly amazed and eager to suffer even more, if need be, in order to advance further towards Him.

And so periods of refreshment, lovingly sent by God, follow periods of pain alternately, and when refreshed, Soul "was left with love for God alone, and in Him was all recollected." Purified now in Body, Soul, and Spirit, Catherine approaches the door of Divine Love, behind which awaits union with God.

In Part III, the door to loving union with God is slowly opened. Spirit and God converse on the nature of Divine Love. Body at this stage, "without strength, and almost without food," is somewhat "as the Soul was when she was without God, that is like a dead thing." But God directly provides for Body's sustenation by sending people to care for him, so that Spirit may freely enjoy God's gifts of interior rapture. Soul, divesting herself of every last measure of self-love, responds to God's gift of Himself to her with exclamations of love. Yet nothing she can put into words can approximate the inner delight she is experiencing: "I know not how to tell these words or this feeling of love, nor can I tell them for the words are not like others. This love opens my heart and pours into it news so gracious that all within it is on fire and burnt away."

In the remaining chapters, Soul is more and more engrossed in God as He reveals Himself to her, sharing His Love and Wisdom with her, "all of which was verified in Saint Catherine," as the author of the *Dialogue* reminds us.

R.L.C.

SPIRITUAL EXERCISES

Author: Saint Ignatius Loyola (1491-1556)
Type of work: Spiritual instruction
First published: 1548

Principal Ideas Advanced

Since man was created to reverence and serve the Lord, it is fitting that he undertake certain spiritual exercises by which he can rid himself of inordinate affections and order his life in accordance with the divine will.

The salvation of the soul can be sought by meditating upon man's true end and on sin and Hell (First Week); by contemplating the Incarnation and the life of Christ and by electing to live as He would have us live (Second Week); by contemplating the Passion and thereby strengthening ourselves in our struggle against the inordinate affections (Third Week); and by contemplating the Resurrection and Ascension of Christ our Lord and thereby gathering hope by which we can seek to obtain God's love by loving Him.

Although written for the most part in 1522, the *Spiritual Exercises* did not appear in book form until 1548, when in Latin translation (from the Spanish) it was officially approved by Pope Paul III and published in Rome. The book is a summary of the meditations, reflections, and inspirations received by Ignatius after his conversion in 1521 while he was convalescing from wounds suffered at the siege of Pampeluna. While the substance of the *Spiritual Exercises* was written at Manresa, where Ignatius spent a year in retreat (1522-1523), and is the work of an unlettered soldier, the book was enlarged and frequently revised during the next twenty years. In the meantime the author studied intensively at Barcelona (1524-1526), Alcalá (1526-1527), Salamanca (1527-1528), and Paris (1528-1535), where he acquired his master of arts degree and enough theology to be ordained priest at Venice in 1537. (The Society of Jesus, first formed by Ignatius and six fellow students in 1534, received its name at Venice in 1537 and was approved in 1540.) Thus, by the time the *Spiritual Exercises* was submitted for papal approval it had enjoyed the benefit of constant practical use and critical revision. Its orthodoxy, therefore, has been proof against hostile attack, and its psychology, or practical knowledge of the human soul, has resisted every unfriendly approach.

The *Spiritual Exercises* is not a unified work in which a single theme is developed, nor is it an ascetical treatise which can be consulted for definitions, comparisons, attitudes, influences, and analyses. It is a collection of directions, a manual intended for the use of a retreat director rather than for the guidance of the exercitant. In fact, it was at first carefully kept out of the hands of such individuals because even Ignatius thought that its directness and conciseness would puzzle rather than enlighten the inexperienced exercitant.

The purpose of the book is unequivocally stated: "Spiritual Exercises whereby to conquer oneself, and order one's life, without being influenced in one's decision by any inordinate affection." Ignatius did not demand that inordinate affections be entirely absent at the time of decision, only that they not influence that decision. A discipline of the self by contemplating matters that tend to encourage ordering one's life according to the divine will is necessary; the exercise of the spirit through ordered contemplation will enable an individual to resist attachments to matters which conflict with man's true end, which, according to Saint Ignatius, is "to praise, reverence, and serve God our Lord . . ."; by this means man can save his soul.

Thus, insisted Saint Ignatius, everything on earth is created to assist man in his worship of God. All things are means designed to help man in attaining his end, and they are valuable to him only insofar as they assure him of this help. To make use of them for any other purpose would be a misuse. Some things appeal to man, others repel him, but to be reasonable and consistent, a man must choose things, not on the basis of their appeal, but only insofar as they help him in his worship; and he must avoid things only insofar as they hinder him in his worship. This, of course, is a truth which needs pondering and exploring, but it holds the answer to man's happiness in this world and the next: "It is therefore necessary that we should make ourselves indifferent to all created things, in all that is left to the liberty of our free-will, and is not forbidden . . . and so in all other things, desiring and choosing only that which leads us more directly to the end for which we were created."

Once an individual has accepted the Christian idea of man's true end, he is ready to begin the "First Week" of the exercises. The word "Week" is used to mean a period of spiritual exercise; the actual length of time to be spent varies according to the matter to be contemplated and the capacity of the exercitant. For example, the Second Week involves twelve days of contemplation if one spends the days, as suggested by Saint Ignatius, in contemplation of the principal events in the life of Christ through the events of Palm Sunday. The exercises are designed to take some thirty days to perform, but this period is usually shortened in actual practice to six or eight days in annual retreats. Each of the four Weeks has its specific content and objective.

The First Week is taken up with a consideration of various aspects of sin. Sin is defined as a failure to obtain the equilibrium necessary to make the right choice between alternatives which consist, on the one hand, of the loss of one's eternal destiny, and, on the other, of the attainment of that union with God, which, even here below, was planned and desired by the Creator and which is consistent with the destiny of man as a child of God. The malice of sin in various contexts is considered: the sin of the angels, the sin of our first parents, and the sin of a soul after the Fall. A second exercise is a further meditation upon sins in which one begs for "great and intense sorrow and tears for my sins." Finally, after two other exercises of contemplation and prayer with the same concern, there is added, as a fifth, a meditation on Hell, which completes the study by having the exercitant behold the ultimate effects of sin and thus strengthen his will.

After the First Week the soul should be enlightened concerning man's true end; the exercitant should have resolved, from a contemplation of the nature and consequences of sin, to submit himself to further spiritual discipline. But the passions remain, says Saint Ignatius, and he suggests that they are not so much to be exterminated as controlled and directed. To achieve this dual purpose, a second fundamental area of meditation is proposed: "The Kingdom of Christ." By contemplating a temporal king chosen by God, a person may appreciate the call of the eternal King, who demands even greater courage and loyalty than any knight gives to his military leader. It must be remembered that Ignatius was a soldier, as was practically every able-bodied man at the time in a Spain which for seven centuries had been carrying on a crusade against the Moslems. The crusade was brought to a victorious end in 1492, when Ferdinand and Isabella, the "Catholic Kings," drove the Moors from the last of their strongholds in Granada. Christ is presented as the divine Leader, to follow whom is to attain peace and to love whom is to attain eternal happiness. Once the retreatment has been captivated by the irresistible attraction of this divine Leader and has sworn allegiance to Him, it remains only for him to study His plan, its strategy and tactics, in order to find the model and guide for his whole life.

The Second Week, then, involves a

study of the life of Christ and, at the same time, a thorough self-examination—not so much an examination of conscience as an examination of motives and potencies. The exercitant is asked to consider three classes of men, "each of which has acquired ten thousand ducats." The first class "would wish" to be rid of the affection for money, but will not choose the means; the second actually do wish to be rid of the affection, but do not wish to part with the money; the third wish to be rid of the affection but in such a way that the use of the money will depend on God's will. The exercise encourages the third way, both in regard to money and to any other thing to which a person may become attached.

Meditations on the life of our Lord are then resumed and continued to the beginning of His Passion, a consideration of which constitutes the matter of the Third Week. But before the Second Week of the exercises is over, the exercitant is called upon to reflect on "Three Modes of Humility." In this exercise the zenith of perfection is proposed. The first Mode of Humility is to humble oneself and obey the law of God, and to resolve never to commit a mortal sin or to deliberate about doing so. The second Mode of Humility is to be indifferent to riches, honor, and longevity of life, and to resolve never to commit a venial sin or to deliberate about doing so. The third Mode, the "most perfect humility," is reached when the first two Modes have become habits of the soul and when, seeking to imitate Christ, the worshiper of God desires poverty, reproaches, and "to be accounted as worthless and a fool for Christ, Who was first held to be such. . . ."

Saint Ignatius considered the state thus attained to be the perfect disposition for making the "Election"; that is, the choice of a state of life or, if a permanent state (such as marriage or the priesthood) has already been chosen, a reformation or rearrangement of one's life according to the principles proposed in the foregoing meditations.

The "Rules for the Election" are directed to the retreat-master rather than to the exercitant, and the director is expected to explain to the exercitant the conditions necessary for making a sane and proper choice.

The Third Week consists of contemplations on the Passion of our Lord. The structure is much simpler than that of the Second Week. The purpose of the contemplations is to familiarize the exercitant with the sufferings of our Lord in the hope that the recollection of them will give him the courage he needs to meet the obligations he has assumed in his election. Some rules are given for the practice of penance, not only during the exercises but during any subsequent period of the exercitant's life.

The Fourth Week begins with a meditation on the Resurrection of our Lord and His appearance to His Blessed Mother, continues with meditations on the Mysteries of our Lord's life, and ends with a meditation on the Ascension of our Lord into Heaven. The purpose of the Week is to strengthen the exercitant in the resolves he has taken by reminding him that there is no such thing as defeat for the Christian: he who remains faithful in the service of the Divine King has certain triumph awaiting him.

The last exercise is the "Contemplation for Obtaining Love." Not a structural part of the *Spiritual Exercises,* it seems to be given for the benefit of the exercitant after he has left the atmosphere of the retreat and has returned to the ordinary activities of life. Some commentators have mistakenly considered this final exercise to be the culmination of the *Spiritual Exercises,* but Ignatius could hardly have intended it to be so, for in the early directories he suggests that the contemplation might be given at any time in the Fourth Week, or even in the Third. It seems rather to be an easy form of mental prayer, a practical suggestion for achieving the facility, so much recommended by Saint Ignatius in his correspondence, "of finding God in all things."

The mere reading of the text of the *Spiritual Exercises* will produce little or no effect on the reader, for the book was written to be practiced, not scanned. Saint Ignatius acquired no style during the years of his education, and except for clarity the *Spiritual Exercises* has no literary merit.

The book is not an ascetical treatise. Even when Saint Ignatius speaks of spiritual consolation, he leaves the reader in doubt as to whether he is speaking of those who are limited to the ascetical life or is including those of the mystical life as well. The value of the book consists in the masterly manner in which the exercises are designed to produce the maximum spiritual benefit for the effort expended. There is nothing sacramental about the exercises; they do not produce the grace they signify. But they are constructed so as to prepare the exercitant for receiving veritable outpourings of grace, which God provides for those who prepare themselves.

Since its approval by Paul III, the *Spiritual Exercises* has been approved by successive pontiffs. Pope Pius XI declared Saint Ignatius to be the heavenly patron of spiritual retreats and exercises. The *Spiritual Exercises* has provided the most widely used framework for retreats in the Catholic Church throughout modern times.

Two translations into Latin of the Spanish text of the *Spiritual Exercises* were presented by Ignatius for papal approval. The first, a literal version, was probably prepared by Saint Ignatius himself; the second, a more elegant rendering, was done by André de Freux. Both translations were approved by Paul III. Centuries later, a literal translation of the original Spanish text into Latin was made by Johann Philipp Roothaan (1785-1853), then General of the Society of Jesus, and was published in 1852. Its purpose was to give to the modern reader as much of the sense of the original Spanish as possible.

W.J.Y.

TREATISE ON THE PASSION

Author: Saint Thomas More (1478-1535)
Type of work: Spiritual counsel
First published: 1557

Principal Ideas Advanced

The honors and glories of this world are but trifles, and man must resist the evil councils of those who would have him forfeit his salvation for the sake of this world's goods.

Man stands in debt to Christ, for by His Passion and death He redeemed man and by His steadfast love He puts to nought the fickle love of those flatterers of this life.

The writings of the saints, the Scripture, and the faith of the Church testify to the efficacy and the truth of the Holy Eucharist.

The Passion of Christ gives courage to the faint of heart, the fearful, and the weary to whom Christ, through His Passion, shows the way.

The *Treatise on the Passion* was the product of Thomas More's twelve-month imprisonment in the Tower of London. Following Henry VIII's break with Rome, More resigned the chancellorship in 1532 as a sign of his disapproval. In 1534, the year Rome declared the marriage between Henry and Catherine of Aragon valid, Henry's Parliament passed the Act of Succession by which the heirs of Henry and his new queen, Anne Boleyn, would be recognized as the legitimate heirs to the throne, and the Act of Supremacy by which Henry and his heirs were declared heads of the Church of England. All the king's subjects were required to take an oath to uphold the Act of Succession. In 1534 More was ordered to Lambeth before the King's Commissioners to swear to uphold not only the Act of Succession but also the Act of Supremacy. More, who was ready to accept the former, refused to accept the Act of Supremacy on the grounds that to do so would jeopardize his soul. He was four days later committed to the Tower where he was to remain for twelve months of deprivation and hardship, tempted by offers of compromise, but sustained and encouraged by his lifelong devotion to the Passion.

During the year-long imprisonment More wrote numerous letters and two books, the *Dialogue of Comfort* and the *Treatise on the Passion.* The many references to the Passion in his letters from the Tower show his preoccupation with this period in the life of Christ. Every year on Good Friday it had been his custom to gather his family together for a reading of the Passion, during which he would interrupt from time to time with pious exhortation. When Cromwell questioned him on the Act of Supremacy, More answered that he did not have time for this new statute, but rather preferred that "My whole study should be upon the passion of Christ and mine own passage out of this world." Again, on his last journey, bearing a cross in his hand, he refused water saying, "Christ in his passion was given not wine, but vinegar to drink."

The treatise begins in English and continues in Latin, a fact for which no satisfactory explanation has ever been advanced. Mary Basset, More's granddaughter, translated the Latin section of the work. It is generally believed that the manuscript, at least the final sections, was probably seized by the high officials and then, by some means not now known, came into possession of the More family.

The English portion, three times the length of the Latin, begins with a consideration of Creation, the Fall of the angels and of man, the Redemption, and some incidental questions. More reflects upon the conspiracy of the high priest, the betrayal of Judas, and Jesus' washing of the feet of the disciples. There follows a commentary upon the institution of the Holy Eucharist. At this point the Latin section, translated by More's granddaughter, begins the study of the Passion proper with the leaving of the Upper Room and the journey to Gethsemane. The unfinished introduction is a comment upon the quotation, "We have not had a dwelling city, but we seek the city that is to come." The author reflects that we spend too much time on the things of this world.

Then follows a series of considerations called by More "Points." His first Point concerns the Fall of the angels. Angels were created by the Trinity, not because of God's need for them, but out of His goodness. Lucifer, rejecting the grace of God which permitted him to gaze upon his Maker, looked down and, beholding his own beauty, declared, "I will be like unto the highest." After his defeat at the hands of Michael, Lucifer and his followers were cast out, deprived of hope and comfort, and condemned to punishment, each according to the degree of his former gifts.

More warns the reader of the horrible peril there is in the sin of pride, an abominable sin in the sight of God, which has as its end disobedience, rebellion, and, finally, rejection by God. If God was so angered by the pride of the angels, who on this earth can say that his state is so high that he has not cause to tremble? The mightier the prideful man is, declares More, the mightier his torments; we are fools if we pride ourselves on the material things of this world. More's admonitions carry much weight since it was almost at the height of his temporal power that he was imprisoned. He concludes his first Point with a prayer asking God, who had crushed the angels in His wrath, to grant him meekness through the merits of the bitter Passion and salvation.

More's second Point touches upon the Creation and Fall of man. It is his belief that God created man in order to replace the numbers of the lost angels, and thereby enraged the proud and hateful Lucifer. The Devil then chose the woman Eve as the weaker of the two human beings, and through her, brought about the downfall of both. Man, too, shares the blame, for God gave the woman to him as his companion; Eve needed Adam and he should not have left her to the mercy of the tempter. More declares that this incident should serve as a reminder to every man of his obligation to keep watch over his fellows. The stubborn failure of Adam and Eve to call upon God for forgiveness was greater than their sin itself, More writes. Man should thus consider well how foolish it is for him to follow the suggstions of the Devil. Further, he must remember that no man can enter Heaven except in virtue of the fact that Christ has paid his ransom. This second consideration ends with a prayer that God may grant Thomas, through the merits of the Passion, the courage to resist the suggestions of the Devil so that he might remain steadfast and not seek to preserve his life at any price.

The restoration of mankind is the subject of More's next Point. God, seeing the wretchedness of man after the Fall, a wretchedness caused not by an obdurate heart but by the subtle suggestions of the Devil, had mercy on His creatures. Through His wisdom a way was found whereby man, asking pardon, would be rescued from bondage and enhanced with honors. No one, man or angel, has sufficient merit to proffer satisfaction for an insult to the Creator; therefore, recompense must be made by one who is both God and man, namely Christ, the Son of God and Second Person of the Blessed Trinity: "He lived and preached on this earth and was finally betrayed and put to death . . . . He pacified the wrath and indignation of God against man."

There are some, says More, who raise the question as to the need for redemption, since only Adam and Eve had sinned. Such questions should be rebuked, for, as Saint Paul says, who is man to dispute with God? Further, we are part of Adam, just as the fruit is part of the tree. The revelation that a Savior would come was given to Adam, Noe, Abraham, and all the old Fathers and Prophets, and by them to the Jews. Scripture tells us that as by one man sin came into the world, by One Man was it pardoned.

More next raises the question: since a single drop of Christ's blood would have been sufficient to save all, why was so much suffering necessary? He answers that since man is impressed by suffering, it was used in order to show him how much he is beholden to Christ. Is it not true then, he asks, that all men are saved the moment they are born? And he replies that the purpose of man's redemption is to restore him to his state before the Fall and not to transport him immediately to Heaven. The concluding prayer begs that through the Passion we may partake in the Redemption.

The three-point discussion ends here; this study has been, in truth, a preamble to the consideration of the Passion itself. More has prepared the background for a meditation on the last days of Christ by tracing through Scripture and tradition original sin, its causes and its consequences. Against such a background the Passion proper is much more meaningful. As a source for his consideration, the author uses the *Monatessaron,* a concordance of the four accounts of the Passion according to the Evangelists.

The treatise now continues with a series of chapters reflecting upon events immediately preceding the crucifixion. The first chapter consists of five lectures—each ending with an appropriate prayer—concerned with Christ's activities as the days of the Unleavened Bread approached. He reminds His disciples that the Son of Man is to be betrayed and crucified. The Trinity, More writes, had prepared men for the happenings of which Christ warned His followers, by the words of the Old Testament prophets and by the incidents in the history of the Jewish people. Thus, the safe passage of the children of Israel through the Red Sea signifies man's safe passage through the Devil's wiles by means of the waters of Baptism, a sacrament having its efficacy through "the red blood of Christ that he shed in his bitter passion." The stories of the unleavened loaves and the Pasch are further examples from Jewish history. Christ knew His hour; man, even though he be a king, cannot. Therefore, it behooves him to work out his salvaton while he can, before the messenger of death comes unannounced. Even as Christ predicted these things, Judas and the council of the high priests were meeting to bring these evil things to pass. With a topical reference to his own circumstances More reflects that men, meeting in evil council to bring wickedness to pass, should not glory in their wiles, for it is the Devil who not only convenes the council but also brings its deliberations to pass.

The last lecture contrasts the steadfast love of Christ with the fickle love of the world which vanishes in the face of hardship. Beware of those who say they love you, writes More—those who flatter, who sit at your table with words of praise, but who in adversity desert your ranks. More prays that he might escape that cruel tyrant, the Devil, and that he be given the grace not to "give mine assent to follow the sinful device of any wicked council."

After describing the preparations for the Last Supper by Saints Peter and James, and the washing of the disciples' feet, the narrative turns to the institution of the Eucharist. Christ longed to eat the Paschal lamb with the Apostles, for the time of His death was at hand when He would offer Himself to the Father as the Paschal Lamb who was slain for the sins of the people and for their redemption. The Eucharist, which Christ would leave to the faithful, would be the new Paschal lamb. In the institution of the Eucharist Christ stresses that "this is My Body which will be delivered up," to emphasize that his words constituted no mere figure of speech. His command, "Do this in remembrance of me," says in effect that this act of consecration was not merely for the Paschal night alone, but for all time. There are some, writes More, who would have the faithful believe that Christ meant the Eucharist to *represent* His Body and Blood, while the elements remained bread and wine. Others claim that it would be impossible for Christ's real body and blood to be in many places simultaneously. The author regards these people as doubting God's power to perform a miracle and lacking in willingness to carry out His command. There are two aspects to be considered here: the very substance of the Body and Blood of Christ, and the accidents of the bread and wine, such as whiteness, redness, and flavor. The accidents, after the consecration, remain without the substances of which they were originally the accidents. This metamorphosis is possible through the limitless power of God, which gives us in the Eucharist the selfsame Body and Blood which were sacrificed on the cross.

In his arguments More shows his grasp of the principles of the Scholastic philosophy which was an integral element of the humanism of his day. He concludes his treatment of the Eucharist with the comment that although we consecrate the species of bread and wine separately, yet in the Blessed Sacrament the "blood [is] with the body, that is in the form of bread, and the body with the blood that is under the form of wine."

After giving a brief history of the reception of the Blessed Sacrament under both species, and of the diverse names by which it is called, More concludes with an admonition as to the spirit and devotion with which the

Holy Communion should be received. Since this is the most excellent of all the sacraments, he writes, we must believe with the faith and humility of the centurion of the Scripture even those things which seem to rebel against our senses. The writings of Ambrose, Gregory, Justine, the Scripture, and the faith of the Church from her beginnings all testify to the truth of this most Holy Sacrament.

Here the manuscript continues in Latin. It begins with an account of the journey to Gethsemane. This section, slightly less than one-third of the entire work, abounds in Scriptural quotations taken from Matthew 26, Mark 13, Luke 22, and John 18. Upon leaving the Upper Room Jesus and His followers went up to the Mount of Olives. Here the symbolism of the olive, which signifies peace, must encourage us, writes More, to lift up our hearts from time to time from the daily business of the world. It is appropriate that Christ should pray for peace, for He came to reestablish peace between God and man. Some may wonder that Christ, the inspiration of martyrs, should face death troubled and with a heavy heart, but More sees this suffering as consolation to our own faint and feeble hearts.

The work ends with a description of the arrival of Judas and the seizing of Christ. The lesson of Judas is a pointed one for those in high office, says More. Judas, a leader among Christ's followers, is brought low by avarice. How many others have suffered his fate?

In the midst of the discussion of the apprehending of Christ in the Garden of Gethsemane the treatise ends abruptly. Both the Latin and the English editions conclude with the note, "Sir Thomas More wrote no more of this work, for when he had written this far, he was in prison kept so strait, that all his books and pen and ink and paper were taken from him, and soon after he was put to death."

The *Treatise on the Passion* is the last significant work of one of the great lights of English humanism. Its importance lies in the light it throws upon the character of Thomas More, who at the height of temporal power renounced everything for the sake of a matter of conscience. Any consideration of the meaning of his tragic end is incomplete without a reading of the *Treatise on the Passion.* In its writing More found comfort and courage; the reader finds new strength in the exercise of his faith.

F.J.T.

THE LYFE OF SIR THOMAS MORE, KNIGHTE

Author: William Roper (1496-1578)
Type of work: Hagiography
First transcribed: 1553-1558

Principal Ideas Advanced

Saint Thomas More's life was characterized by great, though unobtrusive, holiness and by unfailing serenity and cheerfulness.

More served the king loyally in all matters, and he held the highest administrative office in the realm, that of Lord Chancellor.

Though most unjustly executed for fidelity to his conscience and the universal Church, More died praying that he might be joined one day with his judges and the king together in Heaven.

William Roper's *The Lyfe of Sir Thomas More, Knighte* is more a book of reminiscences than it is the traditional biography. It is nonetheless one of the earliest works that endeavor to set out the life of a private man in some depth. Roper apparently composed the book during the short reign of the Catholic Queen Mary. Presumably the publication was deferred because the new reign brought a change of religion that made the publication of Roper's little book impossible, as it had of course been under Henry VIII and his strongly Protestant son Edward VI, whose death in 1553 had brought Mary to the throne. The book survives in at least thirteen manuscripts, indicating its considerable circulation. However, it remained unprinted until 1626, when it finally appeared abroad, in Catholic Paris.

Roper states at the beginning that he lived upwards of sixteen years in the house of Sir Thomas More, whose elder daughter Margaret became Roper's wife. Thereafter, as the account shows, Sir Thomas called his son-in-law "Son Roper," in the friendly fashion of the time. Roper had plenty of occasion to see More from every side, yet he writes some two decades after his father-in-law's death in a tone full of the deepest and most unqualified admiration. His narrative is nevertheless saved from the excesses of a sentimental adulation by a homely anecdotal vein, with a good deal of convincing dialogue, and toward the end, by the pathos and the grandeur of his theme.

Roper's short account (about seventy average-size pages) is continuous, without chapter divisions of any kind. It necessarily lacks the kind of unity one finds in the modern interpretive biography. Roper's approach is respectful and external, as befits his relation to More; about his subject he is rather interested than curious. Thus, there is no psychological approach, and what seem to us the critical early years are passed over in a few sentences at the outset. This is doubtless partly due to Roper's having only his memory on which to rely and also to his being most familiar with More's last sixteen years, during which he had lived with his wife in More's house. It is the martyrdom of Sir Thomas More that provides the climax and the justification for this book, and the book is to some extent a historically attested saint's life, but it is a good deal plainer than most hagiographical writings. The other element that goes into shaping the book into a powerful whole is the so-called *de casibus* tradition, which governed the accounts of the rise and the fall of great men. This genre was then a favorite one, best known perhaps in the poetical "tragedies" of the *Mirror for Magistrates,* a volume almost exactly contemporary with Roper's own. For Roper, however, the fall of More no doubt illustrated, not the power of fortune over men's lives, but the mysteriousness of God's providence.

Roper passes quickly over More's birth and education—his brief years at Oxford followed by the study of law, as desired by his father, Judge More. After More read law he retired to a Carthusian monastery for more than four years, where he lived in prayer and retirement but without taking vows. Roper here and often elsewhere laconically recites the sequence of More's early life without essaying any causal connections. We know, however, from other sources that More was ultimately advised by his confessor to marry. His wife, whom he chose over her younger and fairer sister because it would have been a disgrace to the elder sister if the younger married before her, gave him in the course of time three daughters, one of whom, Margaret, or Meg, became Roper's wife, and one son, who died young. More then entered upon a political and legal career. In the former capacity he soon attained the unlucky distinction of becoming, as a member of Parliament, the spokesman for the Parliament in resisting certain unwarranted demands made of the Commons by King Henry VII. The king could do nothing against the intrepid "beardless boy" who had foiled his plans, but he imposed an unwarranted fine on old Judge More, who was imprisoned till he paid it. The young man's disgrace was complete, and he retired from Henry VII's court to enter the practice of the law. Had Henry not died soon after, More later said, More would have fled abroad, so restless was the king's desire for vengeance.

In his legal work More soon did extremely well. He became one of the undersheriffs of London and derived large income from his fees. Meanwhile the promising young humanist King Henry VIII had come to the throne, and a golden age seemed promised for England's young intellectuals, who, like More, were steeped in the New Learning. The king grew uncommonly fond of More because of More's charm, learning, and wit, and More began to have royal commissions pressed upon him—the Lord Treasurer's office; embassies, including one to the Netherlands in 1515 that was to produce the *Utopia;* and the Chancellorship of the Duchy of Lancaster. The king went so far as one day to drop in unexpectedly at More's house for dinner, after which he walked in More's garden with his arm on his host's shoulder. Family and friends were delighted with this striking sign of the king's favor. More, however, a keen student of human nature, replied to his son-in-law with words that Roper still remembered well close to forty years later: " 'I thank Our Lord, Son,' quoth he, 'I find his Grace [the King] my very good lord indeed; and I believe he doth as singularly favor me as any subject within this realm. Howbeit, Son Roper, I may tell thee I have no cause to be proud thereof, for if my head could win him a castle in France' (for then there was war between us), 'it should not fail to go.' "

From this point forward the narrative seems subtly to change tone. Having grouped in the earlier part of his narrative the incidents of More's rise to fortune and favor, Roper, with apparent artlessness, introduces a more somber mood. We find More telling Roper that there are three ills for whose correction he would gladly give his life: the wars among Christian princes that trouble the peace of Europe, the heresies that afflict the Church, and the ominous business of the king's projected divorce. More wrote many controversial works against heresy in the 1520's and 1530's—the only ones among his writings that Roper even briefly mentions. The last of the evils mentioned, which was to involve More fatefully, seemed to More and most informed contemporaries to arise from the ambition of Cardinal Wolsey. In 1521 and again in 1524 Wolsey had sought the papal throne, only to be circumvented each time by the Spanish Emperor Charles V. Wolsey then sought revenge by raising doubts in the mind of the king concerning the validity of the king's marriage to Catharine of Aragon, the aunt of Charles V. Catharine had first been married to Henry's elder brother; upon her husband's death, and following due papal dispensation, she married her brother-in-law, who soon thereafter became Henry VIII. More was one of many counselors from whom Henry sought support for his divorce as being "incestuous." More was of course sorely troubled by the predictable political repercussions from affronted Spain, but especially by the possible challenge to papal authority in the king's request to have the marriage annulled. For reasons which Roper leaves aside as apparently not pertinent to his narrative, the pope refused the divorce, thus provoking a crisis of the greatest magnitude and one that proved most anguishing to Thomas More, a faithful Catholic and a true Englishman. Meanwhile, More was being forced ever closer to a direct confrontation with this issue. After the fall of Wolsey, about which Roper has almost nothing to say, the king offered the great post of Lord Chancellor to More, in 1529. The king expressly charged More "first to look unto God, and after God to him"; More accepted, though Roper adds that one of Henry's motives was to bring More over to his side in the matter of the divorce. More discharged the office for three years, but finding the king determined upon the divorce, he was permitted, thanks to the earnest intercession of the Duke of Norfolk, to resign the Lord Chancellorship. Though his income had been very substantial More had always been generous to his own large family, who all lived in his house, and to his numerous petitioners and the poor generally. He therefore found himself at once relatively poor, a prospect he accepted with a whimsical equanimity which his wife (his second wife, whom he had married to give his children a mother's care after his first wife's death) apparently did not share. (Roper mentions that in over sixteen years of domestic life together he never once saw Sir Thomas "in a fume.")

Thereafter difficulties of a more serious kind gathered fast about More. The king, well aware of the reservations that had brought More to resign the Lord Chancellorship, forced the issue. In 1534 the king put through the House of Lords a bill charging More, among other great men of the realm, with misprision of treason. The hearings appealed to More's very real sense of gratitude to the king, and then resorted to threats, which Sir Thomas dismissed as "for children." On his return to his house he was very cheerful; More explained that in the hearings he had taken such a clear stand that he could not subsequently retract without losing all honor. "At which words," says honest Roper, "waxed I very sad."

Roper makes it clear that More, a very capable lawyer, sought to limit the point at issue as narrowly as possible and so to define the question at issue in his case as to avoid as much as possible broad confrontations of principle. While never shrinking from death if it had to come, More did not court martyrdom in the least. He defended himself ably, and the Crown was compelled to the shabby expedient of suborning witnesses. These false witnesses were one after another refuted so long as reasonably fair judicial procedures were maintained.

His friends meanwhile besought him to accommodate himself somewhat to the king's insistence that he subscribe the Oath of Supremacy, by which the king would be acknowledged spiritual head of the Church in England, and the pope's supremacy accordingly denied. To his friend the Duke of Norfolk, who sought to remind him that the anger of the king meant death, More answered, "Is that all, my lord? Then in good faith is there no more difference between your Grace and me, but that I shall die today, and you tomorrow." When the day arrived on which the chief prelates, and More alone among the laymen, were summoned to take the fateful Oath of Supremacy, More suddenly leaned over and broke the silence by whispering, "Son Roper, I thank our Lord the field is won." Though Roper professes at that point not wholly to have understood, he still remembered many years later his father-in-law's decisive acceptance of the grace to resist the king's pretensions.

Upon More's saying he was unable to sign, he was remanded to the Tower of London. Though he resisted still for legal reasons, More was finally convicted of treason on the sole testimony of one false witness who swore that More had denied formally the king's supreme headship of the Church. Roper, who was himself a trained lawyer, gives a clear and careful account, of perhaps disproportionate length, of the shameful trial and Sir Thomas's noble and measured defense. When his accusers told him that in his refusal he stood alone against "the bishops, universities, and best learned of this realm," Sir Thomas More answered: "If the number of bishops and universities be so material as your Lordship seemeth to take it, then I see little cause, my Lord, why that thing in my conscience should make any change. For I nothing doubt that, though not in this realm, yet in Christendom about, of these well-learned bishops and virtuous men that be yet alive, they be not the fewer part that be of my mind therein. But if I should speak of those which already be dead, of whom many be now holy saints in heaven, I am very sure it is the far greater part of them that, all the while they lived, thought in this case as I think now. And therefore am I not bound, my Lord, to conform my conscience to the council of one realm against the general council of Christendom." When at last pronounced guilty of treason, More reminded his court that Saint Paul had consented to the martyrdom of Saint Stephen and approved of it, "and yet be they now, both twain, holy saints in heaven," so he prayed that he and his judges "may hereafter in heaven merrily all meet together, to our everlasting salvation." Roper is careful to state his authorities for his painstaking report of the trial and conviction.

More expressed to his loved daughter Margaret, Roper's wife, his desire that his suffering be on the eve of the feast of Saint Thomas and the octave of the feast of Saint Peter. The next day he was told that this was indeed the day on which he was to suffer. With dignity and joy he came to the scaffold and even uttered in that dreadful place a last pleasantry or two. He asked the prayers of those present and declared that he died in and for the faith of the Holy Catholic Church. "So passed Sir Thomas More out of this world to God."

A fitting epitaph is quoted from the Emperor Charles V, who, hearing of the execution, told the English ambassador that had he such a servant as Sir Thomas More he would sooner have parted with the fairest city in his dominion than have lost so worthy a counselor.

J.B.G.

JERUSALEM DELIVERED

Author: Torquato Tasso (1544-1595)
Type of work: Religious epic
First published: 1575

Principal Ideas Advanced

Inspired by the angel Gabriel and the directions of Peter the Hermit, Godfrey, aided by the valiant knights Tancred and Rinaldo, leads the First Crusade's attempt to rescue Jerusalem from the Saracens.

Although the leaders are harassed by storms and fire, dilatory amours, chivalric expeditions, enchantments and Satanic deterrents, as well as by the amazing military feats of the Amazon virgin Clorinda, Christianity is finally triumphant over the forces of paganism.

Tasso's *Gerusalemme liberata* (*Jerusalem Delivered*) is justly described as the first Christian epic. The author's early and rigorous Jesuit training in religion and the classics not only molded his character but also prompted his attempt to weld together the worlds of the pagan epic and chivalric romance.

The opening *in medias res,* the invocation to the muse, and the statement of the theme: "The sacred armies and the godly knight/That the great sepulchre of Christ did free/I sing" are all Virgilian in character. The legendary and historical heroes, Godfrey, Tancred, and Rinaldo are embodiments of the spirit of chivalric romance. But the focus of the work is on the religious level; its theme is redemption, both external and internal. Peter the Hermit is a powerful, although minor, character. His voice directs the choice of Godfrey as leader; he is the father confessor and guide of the Crusaders. His advice, faithfully executed, causes the final triumph over the Turks.

Tancred and Rinaldo are lured from their quests by the wiles of the voluptuous sorceress, Armida. Allegorically, the effects of passion and sensuousness on the virtuous are represented by the knights' lapse from their code of honor, and in Erminia's unfortunately doomed love for Tancred. Both knights are redeemed by the forces of good and are ennobled by their rejection of degrading passions. Armida voluntarily denies her powers of sorcery and joyfully accepts Christianity and Rinaldo's love, now sanctified by Christian marriage. She represents a powerful figure associated with Counter-Reformation symbolism, Mary Magdalen, an alluring, sensuous beauty, prostrate at Christ's feet, begging for salvation. In a larger context, all the pagan and sensuous elements of the Renaissance world, which Tasso so admired, are refined and sanctified, in proper Counter-Reformation spirit. Tasso was torn between his nostalgic delight in the Renaissance spirit, particularly reflected in Ludovico Ariosto's *Orlando Furioso* (1516) and his respect for the *dictum* of the Renaissance critics that the epic poem should elevate and inspire the reader. His characters are almost excessively noble; even his villains excite pathos rather than scorn. Solyman, one of the pagan leaders, after losing his young son in battle grieves so intensely that he leaves the battlefield and wanders aimlessly, thereby exciting the reader's pity and sympathy.

The instructive element of epic poetry is bolstered here by the pervading motif of the "vanity of human wishes." Time and again, Tasso lyrically creates an illusory world, perfect except for its transitoriness. The lovely Fortunate Isles remain only a dream; Armida's enchanted garden vanishes in a puff of smoke. One of the poem's attractions for Spenser was this sense of the transience of beauty and human glory. He translated segments of it for his *Faerie Queene,* especially the lines: "So, in the passing of a day, doth pass/The bud and blossom of the life of man."

The melancholy note of the poem is not surprising even in an author as young as Tasso. Only thirty at the time of the epic's completion, he was very much a part of the excitement and color of life at the court of Alfonso of Ferrara, which world is captured in the glitter of the chivalric episodes. But disillusion is also here; Tasso's own father had lived precariously on court favor, and Tasso depended on patronage for survival.

But more alarming than the whimsical fortunes of court favor is the looming specter of madness. Romantic legend regards Tasso's seven-year confinement as an attempt to separate him from his beloved Leonora, sister of Alfonso. Facts, however, belie this fancy. She died in 1581 and Tasso was not released until 1586. The legend also discounts the evidence of Tasso's persecution mania, his erratic conduct, and, especially, the fanciful world of the poem itself, in which some of the descriptions seem haunted images from the realm of hallucination.

The author's introduction of monsters and wild episodes was excused as necessary invention, novelty added to the epic form. Tasso was acutely sensitive to criticism, and he was extremely anxious to preserve "correctness" in his poem. He justified the use of "marvellous" elements as representing the "*deus ex machina*" convention, and he insisted on the need for the many episodes to vary the main plot.

However, his main difficulty lay in the creation of unity within the poem. Contemporary critics frowned on the lack of the classical unities, the many bewildering episodes and the presentation of a trio of heroes. For both Godfrey and Tancred there was a historical justification for inclusion; Rinaldo was introduced as a graceful compliment to Tasso's patron, since this legendary figure was allegedly the ancestor of the Duke of Ferrara.

Tasso tried to rectify this criticism in a later version of the poem published in 1593, but it never achieved the popularity of the 1581 edition. In reality, the unity of the work is preserved, despite its episodic structure, since the central theme of redemption is constantly in focus. Peter serves as an integrating element from his early direction of the expedition, until his final counseling on the need to rescue Rinaldo from his enslavement in Armida's palace of pleasure. Godfrey reigns supreme as commander of the force, despite the more interesting adventures of Tancred and Rinaldo. Most of the chief adventures within the epic are Rinaldo's; he emerges as the center of the heroic band, particularly when the success of the Crusade depends on locating him and persuading him to spearhead the final attack on Jerusalem.

Those who find themselves bewildered by the frequent introductions of new adventures can still trace the poem's unifying theme, the triumph of the First Crusade. Indeed, Tasso's greatest achievement is his fusing of the various levels of allegory and other literary genres. The poem combines the varied adventures of the romantic epic popularized by Ariosto with the more formal demands of the Virgilian epic, while an echo of Provençal song hovers over the whole: Rinaldo's devotion to Armida recalls the conventions of courtly love. The pastoral world, first evoked by Tasso in his *Aminta,* appears in Book VII, when Erminia seeks shelter and solace in a shepherd's cottage. She grieves about her unrequited love for Tancred and carves on the trees, as she guards her flock of goats, songs and sonnets dedicated to him. She lives as a simple milkmaid, and slowly her life in such rustic simplicity brings with it a sense of conciliation and security. She is now ready for the acceptance of her fate: that she may serve as Tancred's nurse and friend, but that her love for him will never be fulfilled. Her passion for Tancred, which had caused her to abandon honor and self-respect, has been thus purified.

Erminia's is not the only love which is refined within the epic. Surprisingly, Tasso was accused of a lack of seriousness of purpose because of the many love stories unfolded in the poem. Actually, he explores various types of love and allegorically warns of the dangers of surrender to passion. He reiterates the necessity of ennobling love; some of the finest episodes in the work involve descriptions of selfless, idealized love.

Clorinda, the pure maiden, moves through the story with a flame-like intensity. She is a Galahad without an evident grail; she is thoroughly dedicated to her accepted knightly code. She is the only one who moves to rescue the two young lovers about to be executed under an unusually harsh decree, and she offers her services to fight against the Crusaders, in her determination to free them. It is Clorinda who leads the adventurous band which sallies out of Jerusalem to burn the Crusaders' scaling ladders and engines. She valiantly covers their retreat, sacrificing her own life. Unlike Tancred, who deviates from his quest because of his love for her, a pagan, she remains faithful to her vows, and, ironically, it is Tancred himself who accidentally and mortally wounds her (Book XII). By then she has discovered her Christian origins and earnestly begs him to baptize her before she dies. By this baptism, their love is idealized; the despised pagan is Christianized and the dilemma of their romance is resolved. A spiritual reunion may be contemplated, and Tancred is now free to return to his task, chastened and newly strengthened by her example.

Even in tiny segments of the poem, Tasso manages to convey this sense of spiritual regeneration through love. The first book includes a catalogue of the great warriors assembled for the Crusade; among them is a curious pair, Edward and his wife, Gildippe, "In bond of virtuous love together tied," who are so united that they choose to serve in the Crusade together. They die together in the last campaign, a symbol of lasting union and idealized love.

The most affecting episode of selfless love is that described in the second book. Aladine, the pagan ruler, has removed an image of the Blessed Virgin to a pagan temple, and he later discovers that it has been stolen. Enraged by this flouting of his authority, he orders all Christians killed, thus hoping to execute the criminal. To prevent this slaughter, a young maiden, Sophronia, volunteers to die at the stake, claiming she is the thief. Her shy lover, Olindo, now firmly declares his love for her and insists that he is the guilty one. Each proclaims the other's innocence and Aladine then decrees that both should be burned. Just as they are preparing to die, with Sophronia stoically accepting her fate, and Olindo lamenting their never being able to marry, Clorida protests the injustice of the execution and insists that the image has been removed by Mahomet. The noble sacrifice planned by the two lovers is blessed; they are allowed to marry and their generous act is immediately rewarded.

This triumph of the idealized over the sensual is symbolic of Tasso's successful reconciliation of his nostalgic admiration for the waning Renaissance with his intense desire to produce a refined epic. In a sense, his *Jerusalem Delivered* is a swan song, the last epic to celebrate the chivalric romance. Tasso Christianized his beloved but unorthodox predecessors and satisfied his rigid conscience by endowing his poem with the requirements for a Virgilian epic. His completed work, and its revision, reflects the tide of late Renaissance critical opinion on the epic. Tasso represents those critics who believed in the pre-eminence of the epic in literature. The whole purpose advanced for the writing of literature might be summed up in the key words, "to delight and to instruct." Tasso confidently felt he had accomplished this purpose by delighting his audience with the fabulous adventures of his Crusaders and by enriching them through the exemplary lives and noble sacrifices of his heroes.

The modern reader can still be charmed by episodes such as the Satanic parliament (especially when he compares it with Milton's description) and the rescued knights' account of Armida's sorcery which had transformed them into fish. The creaky supernatural "machinery" of the poem which allows Michael the Archangel or special guardian angels to ward off pagan attacks can easily be tolerated. Less easy to accept, however, are such incidents as Erminia's binding Tancred's wounds with her hair when no other bandage was available. The main difficulty, however, which faces today's reader cannot be laid to Tasso but to Fairfax's famous translation, in which the glorious world of the author's lyric gift is lost. This surging lyricism, which allows Venetian gondoliers to sing Tasso's verses while plying their gondolas through the canals is lost in this banal translation. But Fairfax is not wholly to blame for this loss; the polished, subtle, and sophisticated Italian of the original is impossible to duplicate, and the conveying of Tasso's lyric soaring would require another poet of his own stature.

Read for its lyric charm, or as the attempt of a young poet to chronicle the triumph of Christian love, the poem maintains a surprising vitality nearly four hundred years after its completion.

E.M.

THE SIX BOOKS OF THE REPUBLIC

Author: Jean Bodin (c.1530-1596)
Type of work: Political theory
First published: 1576

Principal Ideas Advanced

Sovereignty is the quality that distinguishes a state from other societies.
Sovereignty is perpetual and inalienable.
In a "well-ordered" state sovereignty resides in a single monarch.
The state can tolerate more than one religion on the grounds of public policy.

During the religious wars in sixteenth century France hundreds of books and pamphlets were written on political theory to justify the claims of one group or another. The only work of enduring value in this time, however, was Jean Bodin's *Six livres de la république,* published in 1576, four years after the Saint Bartholomew's Day Massacre. Both Catholics and Huguenots believed that France could tolerate only one religion; each was fighting to exterminate the other. In time a group of Catholics, derisively dubbed *les Politiques,* began to insist that religious unity was not necessary for political unity. Bodin adopted this view.

Not a great deal is known about Bodin's personal religious views. He studied to be a Carmelite, but left the religious life to earn a law degree. He practiced law and held various minor government positions. Bodin was a scholar who personally experienced the vicissitudes of life, including imprisonment, under weak rulers dominated by cliques of powerful, ambitious nobles. His masterpiece, written in these circumstances, stresses the need of authority, unlimited by an aristocracy, residing in the king's hands. Thus, Bodin worked out a theoretical justification for France's two greatest needs of the time: religious toleration, and a sovereign ruler powerful enough to keep the peace.

Bodin's work is built on the model of Aristotle's *Politics,* but it is much more discursive. In the first book he treats of the family, types of domestic authority, and citizenship before getting to an analysis of sovereignty in the eighth chapter.

Bodin is the first to take a modern view of sovereignty. It is, he says, the power to make and enforce laws without the necessary consent of others. It is supreme power over subjects and citizens, a power unrestrained by human law. Sovereignty is perpetual, in the sense that it is not held for a limited period of time. It is not alienable, nor can it be delegated. Although the sovereign is not accountable to his subjects, he is, in Bodin's opinion, accountable to God and subject to the natural law. He writes: "But may it not be objected that if the prince forbids a sin, such as homicide, on pain of death, he is in this case bound to keep his own law? The answer is that this is not properly the prince's own law, but a law of God and nature, to which he is more strictly bound than any of his subjects. Neither his council, nor the whole body of the people, can exempt him from his perpetual responsibility before the judgement-seat of God. . . . Those who say without qualification that the prince is bound neither by any law whatsoever, nor by his own express engagements, insult the majesty of God, unless they intend to except the laws of God and of nature, and all just covenants and solemn agreements."

Sovereignty is an essential attribute of the state, says Bodin. It must reside somewhere, or else the society is an anarchy instead of a true state. The location of sovereignty determines the form of government. If it resides in the king, the government is a monarchy and other bodies are advisory. If it resides in the estates or in a parliament, then the government is aristocratic. If it resides in some kind of popular institution, then the government is a democracy. Government, then, is the apparatus through which the sovereignty of the state is exercised. Bodin admits the need of many corporate and administrative bodies, but he insists that they exist only by the sovereign's permission, and whatever powers they exercise are derived from him.

Bodin sets down several specific "true attributes of sovereignty," the first of which is the power of the prince to make laws that are binding on his subjects as a group and also individually. Among his other attributes are the prince's right to make war and peace. He also has the power to institute the great officers of state, though the appointment of lesser officials should be left to subordinates. Another attribute of sovereignty is that the prince should be the final resort of appeal from all other courts: "Even though the prince may have published a law, as did Caligula, forbidding any appeal or petition against the sentences of his officers, nevertheless the subject cannot be deprived of the right to make an appeal, or present a petition, to the prince in person." The sovereign also has the right of coinage and the right to levy taxes and impose duties on goods. In short, the sovereign has dictatorial life-and-death power over his subjects but he must not violate natural or divine laws.

After having described sovereignty

in seemingly quite absolute terms, Bodin proceeds to limit it somewhat. First, the sovereign cannot violate the laws of God or nature. ". . . the sovereign prince cannot remit any penalty imposed by the law of God, any more than he can dispense any one from the operation of the law of God, to which he himself is subject. If the magistrate who dispenses anyone from obedience to the ordinance of his king merits death, how much more unwarrantable is it for the prince to acquit a man of the punishment ordained by God's law? If a sovereign prince cannot deny a subject his civil rights, how can he acquit him of the penalties imposed by God. . . ." Bodin does not provide any legal way to bind the sovereign in this respect, but he becomes specific in saying that the sovereign cannot violate property rights and must abide by his word. Respect for property rights requires the sovereign to obtain consent of his subjects or their representatives to taxes. Nor can the sovereign alter the royal succession or alienate any part of his domain. There is also a class of long established laws or customs (which Bodin looked upon about as we look on our Constitution), the *leges imperii,* which cannot be violated by the king, for to do so would create anarchy and destroy sovereignty itself.

Bodin's advocacy of religious toleration put him in the unpopular camp of the *Politiques,* described by a contemporary as "those who preferred the repose of the kingdom or their own homes to the salvation of their souls; who would rather that the kingdom remained at peace without God than at war with Him." He was one of the first advocates of religious toleration, not on grounds of principle but of prudent public policy. His argument is that if two religions teach different doctrines, both cannot be true. But even if the sovereign is convinced of the truth of his own religion, his attempt to force others to believe with him will only drive them to hardened opposition and even to civil war.

Bodin's concept of sovereignty and of toleration was a sharp departure from medieval theological-political speculation. Another departure was his discussion of the relation of physical environment to national characteristics, a subject on which Montesquieu was to offer a classical treatment in his *Esprit des lois* in the eighteenth century. Bodin argued that Northern people are big and strong, but slow of mind and body. Southern people are smaller, quicker, and more acute of mind. The ideal type, politically, says Bodin, are those who live in the middle regions, such as France, as their accomplishments in thought and action have proved.

The *Six Books of the Republic* made three important contributions to modern political thought: (1) the definition of sovereignty as the supreme legal power in the state; (2) the advocacy of religious toleration as prudent public policy; (3) the analysis of the influence of climate and other factors of physical environment on national characteristics.

THE WAY OF PERFECTION

Author: Saint Teresa of Ávila (Teresa de Cepeda y Ahumada, 1515-1582)
Type of work: Ascetic theology
First published: 1583

Principal Ideas Advanced

The inordinate desires of selfish pride and pleasure can best be restrained by a life of humility and poverty; by constant humility and poverty one is able to devote himself to the most worth-while Christian vocation; that is, a life of prayer.

The three essential elements of the life of prayer are: first, love of neighbor; second, complete detachment from the things of this world; third, genuine humility; of these three humility is by far the most important since it alone entitles us to merit the holy presence of God.

The way of the soul to perfection is one of constant struggle: the closer one is admitted into the friendship of God, the greater the temptations and sufferings He permits one to undergo.

The Life of prayer and contemplation is the only road of ascent of the Mount of Carmel at whose summit the soul will find the goal for which the soul was created; namely, union with its divine Master.

Saint Teresa of Ávila is recognized everywhere as the most gifted teacher of all who seek the way of perfection. She is also hailed because she gave to the public, through her simple, colloquial yet graceful style, her competence in spiritual matters, and her candor, some of the great secrets of the life of Christian perfection by prayer and contemplation. The life of Christian perfection of which Saint Teresa writes is the life of struggle of the soul against the tempter in the course of the soul's ascent of Mount Carmel. On the summit of the mountain the soul meets and achieves union with its Lord, thus receiving but a taste of the joys to come in Heaven.

Of all mystical writers to be found in Christian literature, Saint Teresa of Ávila alone is able to communicate the deepest spiritual insights in the most direct, apt, and simple form readily understandable to readers from every walk of life. To this day her works are widely read in Spanish and in a multitude of other languages. It is notable that Teresa wrote all her works in obedience to the commands of her religious superiors, while at the same time pursuing a most active life of hardships and challenges thrown up in her work of founding convents of her order of nuns, the Discalced Carmelites.

Teresa of Ávila entered the Order of our Lady of Mount Carmel at the age of eighteen. Through prayer she attained to the highest degree of mystical life, and she was so enlightened in theological matters that her writings gained her the title of Doctor of the Church, conferred by Popes Gregory XV and Urban VII. Saint Teresa is the only woman in the Church ever granted such an august title.

The book called *Way of Perfection* contains the most valuable counsel to those who aspire to religious service of

God through contemplation. In this work Saint Teresa deals expressly with the life of prayer. She wrote it out of obedience to her superiors who were quick to notice her extraordinary talents. Of all her writings, this book is the one most concerned with ascetic theology. Mysticism is not to be found in its pages except for scattered passages which occur almost at random. Teresa follows her own bent in this book: it is quite rambling in style, but this very fact, perhaps, attests her great psychological gifts. She was writing to a specific public; namely, the nuns of her order. Everything in the book is part of a meaning which, though it follows its own peculiar inner connections, nevertheless is firmly guided by the author's pre-eminent consideration that this be an intimate yet practical guide to the perfect living of the vocation of a cloistered contemplative nun.

There are to be found here many ideas already set out by the saint in her *Life,* completed in 1565, just before the present work was begun. However, the emphasis and presentation of these ideas differs here from their appearance in the *Life,* since Teresa avoids many contextual references and incidents from her own life which she deemed too personal to appear in a work meant to be a manual of practical advice for all her sister companions of the Order.

Written with the desire to teach the nuns of Carmel to love prayer as the most effective means of attaining virtue, the *Way of Perfection* has as its two-fold principal reason for being composed both a negative and a positive aim. Negatively, the end in view was to check the inordinate passion for the individual "freedom" which a militant Protestantism was abetting. Positively, the author felt that it could and should be made quite clear that excessive worldly desires could be best overcome by the contemplative life lived in humility and poverty.

In its structure, the book is divided into a prologue and fifty-two following chapters. Its three opening chapters contain an injunction to the nuns of Carmel to pray that God might extend His protection to include all defenders of the Church, especially its preachers and theologians who are charged with maintaining true doctrine.

The importance of strict observance of all the Rules and Constitutions of the Carmelite Order is emphasized in Chapters Four through Fifteen. Moreover, the saint stresses three essential ingredients of the life of prayer. The first of these, love of neighbor, refers, in the context at hand, to one's companions in the convent. Repeated stress is put on the second ingredient; namely, the necessity of complete detachment from the world in even the most inconsequential matters. Finally, and most important of all since it includes the two preceding virtues, genuine humility must be incorporated as habitual in the life of the contemplative. With respect to the first of these three elements, Teresa presents a minute treatment of how Carmelite nuns are to live in the convent, and how disorders in the convent are to be prevented and remedied. Here she displays her marvelous knowledge of the psychological problems of the cloistered life. It is obvious that her counsel is the result of her mature thought, which was the consequence of many years of convent experience.

Concerning the second ingredient of the life of prayer, many detailed injunctions are given as means to the attaining of perfect detachment from worldly distractions. Carmelite cloistered nuns are to be interiorly free from attachment to relatives, friends, confessors, nun companions in the convent, all honors and presents, and, last but most difficult of all, from themselves.

Humility, Teresa tirelessly repeats, is the key to habitual prayer and to the aforementioned two elements in the life of prayer. Humility is essential here, for if we exaggerate our own merits, we exclude the possibility of self-detachment. In the spirit of humility we are strengthened to face all truth squarely, including the truth about our genuine worth. Assuredly, declares Saint Teresa, if we seek the three virtues of fraternal love, detachment, and humility, then our soul will have dominion over all created things and will be truly a "royal soul."

At this juncture the saint develops more fully the contents of the aforementioned elements of the life of prayer. She uses the famous simile of the chess game to depict the mysterious way in which the contemplative soul is checkmated by the King of Love, Jesus. It is made abundantly clear in Chapters Sixteen through Twenty-six that the only road to mystical contemplation lies through the practice of the three aforementioned elemental virtues which permit genuine prayer in a life devoted to continued self-conquest and self-sacrifice. The notion that contemplatives are constantly given spiritual favors by God is dismissed as a ridiculous piece of ignorance. Rather, Teresa writes, those devoted to prayer receive few and passing favors, and these are granted only as aids to move the devotee to greater virtue.

The author treats several other questions at stake here, meanwhile agreeing with theologians of mysticism that a soul in grave sin cannot experience true contemplation. Such queries as whether all souls can attain to the state of contemplation, or whether one can be a perfect Christian without contemplation, are examined. In the course of these chapters the writer insistently rejects the idea that contemplatives have spiritually succeeded so well that they should not expect further sufferings and temptations. Contemplatives suffer *more* than those whose vocation keeps them actively engaged in the world. God puts his friends, the contemplatives, through the severest trials, for the closer one approaches God, the more arduous becomes the path of spiritual ascent.

In the latter half of the *Way of Perfection,* Chapters Twenty-seven through Fifty-two, one theme alone is paramount: the Lord's Prayer. These chapters are presented in the form of a commentary on this prayer taken clause by clause. Incidentally, in passing fashion, the topics of recollection, quiet, and union are mentioned, but they are not nearly as thoroughly treated here as in the saint's later work, *The Interior Castle.*

Towards the final portion of her commentary on the Lord's Prayer, Teresa again affirms the value of the life of prayer. She describes excesses to be avoided; namely, a lack of humility and a sense of presumption of virtues which one does not really possess. She describes such defects as signs of a crippling timidity stemming from acute sensitivity. Excessive sensitivity to the evil of one's sins must be overcome, because sensitivity may well end in the utter spiritual defeat of despair.

This spiritual treatise is concluded by the author with an exhortation in which she begs her nuns to seek the love and fear of God, two mighty fortresses which Satan cannot reduce to surrender.

J.B.L.

THE ASCENT OF MOUNT CARMEL and THE DARK NIGHT OF THE SOUL

Author: Saint John of the Cross (1542-1591)
Type of work: Mystical theology
First transcribed: c.1584-1587

Principal Ideas Advanced

In order to become perfect, the soul of man must undergo purgation of the senses and of the spirit.

The purgation of the soul can be likened to a dark night into which the soul must be plunged in order that the Divine Light may take up its abode within this darkness.

The dark night actively takes place in the senses and the spirit when the soul, through meditation and co-operation with habitual grace, empties itself of all impurities and creature attachments.

The dark night passively takes place when the soul, prepared in the described manner, allows God to act upon and take possession of it.

The *Ascent of Mount Carmel* and the *Dark Night of the Soul* are two treatises on the attainment of spiritual perfection by the sixteenth century Spanish Carmelite mystic and Doctor of the Church, Saint John of the Cross. Written largely as guides for those already involved in the pursuit of the spiritual life, the treatises presuppose the fundamental principles of ordinary Christian living and concentrate on the achievement of the extraordinary. It is Saint John's thesis that the soul, consisting of both sensual and spiritual parts, must be cleansed of all imperfections before it can attain union with the All-Perfect. This cleansing or purgation is achieved by the soul's undergoing a journey through the "dark night" of spiritual annihilation, with faith as the guide, to the morning light of perfection which is union with God. The first three parts of the thesis are contained in the *Ascent of Mount Carmel* while the fourth and last part is contained in the *Dark Night of the Soul.* Saint John himself tells us: "The first night of purgation is of the sensual part of the soul, which is treated in the present stanza, and will be treated in the first part of this book. And the second is of the spiritual part; of this speaks the second stanza, which follows; and of this we shall treat likewise, in the second and the third part, with respect to the activity of the soul; and in the fourth part, with respect to its passivity.

"And this first night pertains to beginners, occurring at the time when God begins to bring them into the state of contemplation; . . . And the second night, or purification, pertains to those who are already proficient, occurring at the time when God desires to bring them to the state of union with God. And this latter night is a more obscure and dark and terrible purgation. . . ."

The plan of both books is an explication (stanza by stanza, line by line, and often phrase by phrase) of the text of one of the most famous of Saint John's many poems, *En Una Noche Oscura* ("On a Dark Night"). In writing of mystical experience, Saint John himself realized that he was trying to put into words that for which language was inadequate, for who can describe the indescribable? The symbolism of poetic metaphor best suited the subject matter and, fortunately, was also best suited to the talents and temperament of Saint John himself. As spiritual director for souls seeking perfection, he often jotted down thoughts and phrases which he later used as bases for spiritual instruction. It was Saint Teresa of Ávila, his contemporary and mentor, who enjoined him to set down in writing the details of mystical experience. The resulting poetry soars with the ardor and passion of one aflame with the love of God. The language of the mystic often bears similarity to that of the romantic poet; the mystic and the romantic poet alike speak in passionate terms of suffering love and of the wish for annihilation of self in union with the beloved. Many of the lyrical clichés of love poetry find their way into mystical poetry, but the significant difference is that the romantic lyrical poet sings to his lady, while the mystic sings to God.

The *Ascent of Mount Carmel,* then, prepares the soul for its final stage of desired union. This preparation consists of the soul's forming a detachment from creatures by mortification of the senses. The first and second books treat of the obstacles to the understanding; the third book treats of the obstacles to the memory and will. Saint John compares these divisions to the three stages of night: "These three parts of the night are all one night; but, after the manner of night, it has three parts. For the part, which is that of sense, is comparable to the beginning of night, the point at which things begin to fade from sight. And the second part, which is faith, is comparable to midnight, which is total darkness. And the third part is like the close of night, which is God, the which part is now near to the light of day."

As long as the soul has affection for any creature, it is susceptible to desire and imperfection. These desires cause two serious evils in the soul; namely, they deprive it of the Spirit of God, and the soul wherein they dwell is wearied, tormented, darkened, defiled, and weakened. Imperfections, no matter how slight, will keep the soul from attaining the liberty of complete union, since they imply attachments to matters outside God.

In order to surmount the temptations to the senses, the soul desiring to conquer them should strive to imitate Christ, to renounce and completely reject every pleasure to the senses which is not solely for the love of God, to mortify and calm the four natural passions (joy, hope, fear, and grief), and generally to mortify the concupiscence of the flesh, the eyes, and the pride of life: "So that the soul that has denied and thrust away from itself the pleasures which come from all these things, and has mortified its desire with respect to them, may be said to be, as it were, in the darkness of night, which is naught else than an emptiness within itself of all things."

As the first part of the *Ascent* deals with the senses, the next part deals with the spirit, citing faith as the proximate means of ascending to union with God. Saint John contends that even as the lower part of the soul (the senses) must be in darkness with regard to temporal considerations, so must the spirit "be blinded and darkened according to the part which has respect to God and to spiritual things, which is the rational and higher part. . . ." Thus, the spirit will be as a blind man, led by pure faith. By means of the three theological virtues, the three faculties of the soul are perfected (faith perfects the understanding by causing an emptiness or darkness within it; hope perfects the memory, since in relating to that which is not possessed, it, too, produces emptiness; and charity perfects the will by obliging us to love God above all things). The spiritual person is ready to leave meditation and reasoning and pass on the road to contemplation when he recognizes three main signs: (1) he can no longer meditate or reason with his imagination; (2) he has no desire to fix his meditation on fixed objects, exterior or interior, and (3) he takes pleasure in being alone, waiting patiently upon God.

The remainder of the second and third books treats extensively the dangers to spiritual progress encountered by the soul who gives too much attention or attachment to visions, apprehensions, and all which is externally a threat to his primary aim. Here Saint John proves himself as capable of discoursing on the proper use of rosaries, novenas, statuary, oratories, and church architecture as he is on the less concrete areas of devotion.

Saint John speaks at great length of joy and Christian duty, and he states that "the will must never rejoice save only in that which is to the honour and glory of God; and that the greatest honour we can show to Him is that of serving Him according to evangelical perfection; and anything that has naught to do with this is of no value and profit to man." After listing the false "goods" in which the will should not rejoice, Saint John lists those things which should be a cause for rejoicing. This part of the treatise stops abruptly, apparently unfinished.

The fourth and last part of this study in mystical perfection, the *Dark Night of the Soul,* deals with the soul who has put into practice the pattern of darkness laid down in the *Ascent* and now waits for the invasion of the Light: "Into this dark night souls begin to enter when God draws them forth from the state of beginners—which is the state of those that meditate on the spiritual road—and begins to set them in the state of progressives—which is that of those who are already contemplatives—to the end that, after passing through it, they may arrive at the state of the perfect, which is that of the divine union of the soul with God."

After discussing some of the imperfections to which beginners on the way to perfection are subject (pride, avarice, luxury, wrath, spiritual gluttony and envy, and sloth), Saint John tells of three principal signs whereby the spiritual person may know that the aridity arising from purgation of the senses is the desired end and not the product of the aforementioned sins or imperfections. These signs are: (1) the soul finds no attraction or sweetness in any creature whatsoever, (2) the memory is ordinarily turned upon God, with "painful care and solicitude," thinking itself remiss in that it finds no pleasure in the creatures of God, and (3) the soul can no longer meditate in the imaginative sphere of sense. The best way for such souls to prepare themselves to receive the union with God that is to follow is to leave themselves utterly pliable and receptive to the infusion of His presence, "for contemplation is naught else than a secret, peaceful and loving infusion from God, which, if it is permitted, enkindles the soul with the spirit of love. . . ." This state of contemplation does not follow immediately or necessarily upon the purgative contemplation of the beginner; indeed, to very few does it come at all. So great is the Presence of God that preparation for His infusion causes the soul much pain, just as does the infusion itself, for the soul of man, however perfect, is a flimsy vessel to contain the Absolute. When, then, by purgation and prayer, the soul has rendered itself empty and completely devoid of self, God is free to enter in and possess it with His love. In summary, Saint John cites ten steps of the mystic ladder of divine love by which the soul mounts to God. These are: (1) the soul languishes, (2) the soul seeks God without ceasing, (3) the soul works with fervor and fails not, (4) the soul endures habitual suffering because of the Beloved, but without weariness, (5) the soul desires and longs for God impatiently, (6) the soul runs swiftly to God and touches Him again and again, (7) the soul becomes vehement in its boldness, (8) the soul seizes God and holds Him fast without letting Him go, (9) the soul burns with sweetness, and (10) the soul becomes wholly assimilated to God.

Saint John of the Cross was respected by laymen as a poet and by churchmen as a mystic and teacher. The *Ascent of Mount Carmel* and the *Dark Night of the Soul* show that both appraisals of Saint John's unique gifts are correct.

J.S.

THE INTERIOR CASTLE

Author: Saint Teresa of Ávila (Teresa de Cepeda y Ahumada, 1515-1582)
Type of work: Mystical theology
First published: 1588

Principal Ideas Advanced

The incomparable beauty and dignity attached to the human soul is like that of a transparent crystal; the mystical life of the soul, wherein it enters itself to find God at its center, may be compared to a castle formed of crystal into seven rooms or mansions.

The seven mansions of the soul devoted to serving God through a contemplative life of prayer are best accorded logical structure in terms of the three-stage progress into which the mystical life has been traditionally divided.

In the first stage of the mystical ascent to God, the soul endures a period of preparation or purgation; the second stage is one of illumination, in which the soul passively receives divine enlightenment with respect to all things; following these two probationary steps, the soul enters upon the third and final stage of perfection; namely, mystical union with its Divine Master.

In a letter to the Bishop of Ávila, Saint Teresa, author of the *Interior Castle* wrote that, "the best prayer and the most pleasing to God is that which brings on improvement, showing itself in good works, and not the enjoyment which only serves for our own satisfaction." This down-to-earth formula dominates all her writings and, no doubt, accounts for the great popularity they have always enjoyed both in her native Spain and throughout other Christian lands.

Saint Teresa spent her life in the Order of Our Lady of Mount Carmel, which she entered at the age of eighteen. She devoted her life to contemplative prayer, but in obedience to her superiors she simultaneously endured an active life of trials and challenges attendant upon her duty of founding new convents of Discalced Carmelites throughout the Spanish Kingdom. In her mystical life she reached the summit of perfection, and she so clearly and theologically correctly described the prayerful life of the soul that Popes Gregory XV and Urban VII conferred upon her, the only woman so honored in the Church, the eminent title of Doctor of the Church.

The *Interior Castle* is a treatise on mystical theology, written in Teresa's colorful, peculiarly personal style. In it she describes the various stages which, in her spiritual experience, a soul encounters in its transformation in God. The saintly author is very careful to examine minutely her personal experiences to insure that they form a consistent whole and to safeguard this whole from any deviation, large or small, from the traditional theology of the Church, and the revelation of God found in the Bible.

Mystical theology, traditionally, is divided into three stages which are called the preparative, the illuminative, and the unitive life. In the first stage, that of preparation, the devoted soul is purged of sin and ingrained imperfection by the usual means of the sacraments and freely undertaken chastisement of unruly desires and passions. The mental life of the novice is spiritually clarified and focused by constant reflection on the Life of Christ. This beginning of the life of prayerful contemplation can be accomplished by the ordinary aid of God's grace without any unusual divine guidance.

In the second or illuminative stage there is accomplished the further purification of the soul and enlightenment of the mind in what is, by this time, an obediently receptive soul.

Here God intervenes and carries out the cleansing of the soul by means of severe outer and inner sufferings. The passive soul is raised to the level of contemplation, and it finds itself rising with less and less difficulty now that it has achieved a habitual readiness to meditate on the holy thoughts which are before it. The severest trial encountered on this level is the so-called "dark night" of the soul in which it feels totally abandoned to its own nothingness by its divine master. Yet this emptiness is only apparent, for actually God is very close to the soul, exerting this most powerful means to wipe away its least imperfection.

The unitive or third stage is entered upon following the two probationary stages. Here the soul is aware, even in the midst of the most keen spiritual persecutions from outside and within, that it is God's own, that its will and His will are one. Extraordinary phenomena indicating the contemplative's arrival at the third stage are not at all necessary and are often never experienced.

In the "interior castle," the first two rooms or mansions comprise the life of preparation, the third and fourth belong to the illuminative, and the last three are the mansions of the unitive life.

If one compares this book with others like it, one is struck by the relatively small space devoted to the stage of preparation. Since this stage is often a most difficult one for the person embarking upon a life of prayer, Teresa's brief treatment of it, in this world-renown treatise on the subject, needs some explanation. The accepted reason given for her brevity with regard to perhaps the most difficult stage of the contemplative life is that she herself was spared, by God's grace, from the more gross forms of sin. In her youth, she was given to a certain girlish vanity, yet she never was a victim of the sins of the flesh or of intractable wilfulness.

The *Interior Castle* is a brilliant treatment of mystical theology in even its subtlest points, and, furthermore, it is one of the saint's best works from the point of view of its clarity of style and its firm logical coherence. In addition it shows on every page the indelible imprint of her vivid personality and unique spiritual experiences.

The author describes the beauty and dignity of the soul, comparing it to a castle fashioned in the form of a transparent crystal sphere containing seven rooms or mansions. In the center mansion God, the King of the soul, makes His dwelling. The surrounding mansions form stages of increasing closeness to God's holy presence. Without the crystal dwell, in loathsome darkness, hideous reptiles, which represent the souls who are turned away from the life of holiness.

In order to progress from the first to the second mansion, the soul must be ready to endure the raging might of Satan. The best armor in this battle with the tempter is perseverance and confidence in the power of Christ's Cross to overcome even the worst evils. Having undergone the severest purgation, the soul now passes through the third and fourth mansions, comprising the stage of illumination. Here the soul, passive to the divine light, perfects itself in prayerful humility and perfect detachment from the world and every trace of selfish will.

At last the contemplative soul, passing with assurance through the deeply formative stages of the fifth and sixth mansions, enters the seventh mansion, wherein it achieves mystical union with its master. During this progress the soul continually suffers the most intense trials which God permits in order to strengthen its ardor and increase its fervent longing for that which alone can fully satisfy its holy craving; namely, union with its Lord.

In the seventh mansion the soul must be courageous in the presence of its King, for He grants it extraordinary favors in the form of spiritual ecstasies which must be carefully distinguished from illusionary raptures. This state of joy, the most complete granted to the loving soul on earth, nevertheless is but preparatory to the ineffable bliss of the Beatific Vision which awaits the contemplative soul in Heaven, the end of its mystic voyage.

J.B.L.

POLITICAL WRITINGS

Author: Saint Robert Cardinal Bellarmine (1542-1621)
Type of work: Political philosophy from Catholic perspective
First published: 1586-1593

Principal Ideas Advanced

The one mystical body of the Christian commonwealth has a soul and a body; the ecclesiastical power is the soul, and the civil power is the body.

The pope has jurisdiction over the spiritual and the temporal orders: direct jurisdiction over the spiritual, and only indirect over the temporal—though this latter may extend to the very deposition of an insubordinate monarch.

Political power comes from God, is first resident in the civil multitude, and is only then transferred to ruling personnel.

Certainly there was no one in the Church in the thick of a greater number of religious controversies than was Saint Robert Bellarmine, the "Hammer of Heretics." There have even been those who found it difficult to believe that so voluminous and powerful a work as the *Controversies,* Bellarmine's major work, was written by one man, and they apparently suspected that "Robert Bellarmine" was the pen name of a whole battery of Jesuit theologians. And though Queen Elizabeth made it a capital crime to possess Bellarmine's writings and ordered that lectures be given against him at Oxford and Cambridge—it is even the case that in 1600 a *Collegium antibellarminianum* was established at Heidelberg by one David Parée—no one thought of him as anything other than scrupulously fair, moderate in statement, and even in temper. A striking example of his fairness is found in his going out of his way, on one occasion, to defend Calvin against a charge made by Saint Peter Canisius of a fundamental error in the theology of the Blessed Trinity; and a Hungarian Jesuit complained bitterly that Bellarmine was making things easier for the heretics: "The Lutherans and Calvinists will have no further need of Luther's and Calvin's books: they can find all they want here [in Bellarmine's *Controversies*]."

The political writings of Bellarmine are generally recognized as the classical *locus* of the political theory to which his name is usually attached, the indirect power theory of the superiority of ecclesiastical to civil authority, the theory that the State is not directly but only indirectly subordinate to the Church. This theory is most adequately stated in the first volume of his *Controversies,* "On the Temporal Power of the Pope." Also worth reading on the topic is his "On the Laity," a treatise "on the political magistracy," found in the second volume of the *Controversies.* Thereafter he defended this position in the three major political conflicts in which he engaged: in the Venetian dispute over clerical exemption from prosecution by the civil power; in his fight against the royal absolutism of James I of England; and against the absolutist and Gallican ideas of William Barclay and Roger Widdrington.

The first statement of the position Bellarmine was defending had been made by Pope Gelasius I in 494, when the pope identified for the Byzantine Emperor, Anastasius I, the respective roles of pope and prince: "Two there are, august Emperor, by which this world is ruled on title of original and sovereign right—the consecrated authority of the priesthood and the royal power." Saint Thomas Aquinas had developed this doctrine by distinguishing, along Aristotelian lines, between the nature and finality of ecclesiastical and civil authority, and he had argued that the pope's power touches the very substance of temporal matters, but indirectly, only at the point where the civil law itself touches matters that are not "indifferent": the divine law, natural and positive. This is to say that the pope may intervene in temporal affairs as an interpreter of the natural law, and on matters touching the faith and law of the Church itself. This power of intervention extends, under some conditions, even to absolving subjects from allegiance to their sovereign: ". . . as soon as sentence of excommunication is passed on a man on account of apostasy from the Faith, his subjects are *ipso facto* absolved from his authority and from the oath of allegiance whereby they were bound to him."

Bellarmine regarded his own view as Thomistic and traditional, as a "middle view" between the excesses of the hierocrats, who said that the pope has direct power even in temporal matters, and the regalists, who would deny to the pope any power of intervention in political matters. Bellarmine writes, "We understand by jurisdiction of an indirect kind the jurisdiction which the pope has over the temporal in relation to the spiritual; properly and of itself his jurisdiction regards the spiritual." Bellarmine thus earned for himself the enmity of both sides: of the ecclesiastical conservatives (notably Pope Sixtus V), who wanted to say that political power originated in the fact of sin and not in the law of nature and that authority is given to the prince only with the approval of the pope; and of the monarchists, who saw in the "indirect power theory" a threat to the very stability of their thrones. Like other Jesuits of his times, Bellarmine, for his part, saw in a moderate form of papal sovereignty the best hope of salvation for the Christian world; and he regarded that sovereignty as the consequence of two simple truths: the fullness of jurisdiction given by Christ to the successor of Peter to lead souls to eternal salvation, and the fact that the acts of temporal rulers, if completely unchecked and unguided, might possibly hinder the work of the Church.

A favored way of giving his reader an intuitive glimpse of the relations Bellarmine saw between the two powers was his use of the body-and-soul metaphor of Saint Gregory Nazianzen: "The two powers in the *Ecclesia* [the one Christian commonwealth] are as flesh and spirit in a man." It is possible that flesh and spirit exist separately, as in angels and brute animals, but when they "make one person, there is necessarily a relation of subordination" of flesh to spirit. Now when the actions of the flesh are, on occasion, a bar to the ends of the spirit, the spirit "gives commands" to the flesh that may either inhibit its action (as when fasts are commanded) or encourage its action (as when a martyr's death is commanded). Bellarmine's use of this metaphor lets us see how dependent he was on a medieval unitary concept of Christian society: the "person" in whom the two powers were united was one social reality, one *Ecclesia* or "Church," composed of ecclesiastical and civil powers: "In this mystical body of the *Church,* the ecclesiastical power is as the soul and the political power as the body." He held to the view, it appears clear, that the religious division introduced by the Protestant Revolution was merely a passing phenomenon, that Europe would soon again be a Christian unity, and that a strong position taken by the pope could act as a catalyst to reunion. The crux of the matter was the pope's putative power to depose kings: if the pope could make effective his claim to depose heretical monarchs, desire for stability on the part of the populace would lead to their insisting on a Catholic king, one whose throne was not under papal attack. Bellarmine found examples of effective deposition in the Middle Ages: of Henry IV by Gregory VII; of Otto IV by Innocent III; of Frederick II by Innocent IV. These popes did depose kings; therefore, they must have had the power to do so. As well say, Bellarmine insisted, that no man may for any cause be deprived of his life or goods, as that no king may for any cause be deposed. What Bellarmine failed to realize, as we from our privileged position of hindsight realize, was that medieval circumstances were exceptional, that in effect the Church played so strong a role in the political sphere not so much because of the necessity for carrying out spiritual functions but because of its role as the only strong social and cultural force left after the collapse of civilization. Both earlier and later there was no need and no right to depose: only the temporary imperfection of civil society, the disorder of a political vacuum, had ever created such a transient need and makeshift right.

According to Bellarmine, though, the pope cannot by his ordinary and regular power depose kings as he can depose bishops; the pope cannot make civil laws nor annul those made; he cannot judge temporal things. But when, to his mind, the salvation of souls calls for special intervention, special intervention is thereby justified, though no more than is necessary: the pope is first to use paternal correction, then to deprive the recalcitrant nation of participation in the sacraments by ecclesiastical censures, and only finally, when all else has failed, to release subjects from their oath of fidelity and deprive the ruler of all dignity and royal authority, "if the case calls for it." (Bellarmine insisted, though, that deposition was not equivalent to execution: "It has never been known, from the beginning of the Church to our own day, that any sovereign pontiff has put to death, or approved that others put to death any prince whatsoever be he heretic or pagan or persecutor.") Although a defense of the papal power to depose rulers seems strange to us in the twentieth century, it is useful to remember that the denial of that papal power was, for Bellarmine, the denial of the sovereignty of the spiritual in men's lives, the denial of the reach of the spiritual into the temporal order. It is also useful to remember how easy it was in the sixteenth century to confuse the person of the prince with the power and office of the prince, to confuse the prince's personal duties to religion with either the duties of one whose actions ought to be directed to the secular common good or with the religious duties of men organized in civil society. Bellarmine laid down principles which can be used to argue that civil society is ordered to a merely natural and temporal end, and it is these principles, without their overlay of confusion, which may very well be valuable today.

What upset one of Bellarmine's readers, King James I of England, even more than Bellarmine's doctrine on the "indirect power," was his doctrine on the origin of civil power. James wanted to maintain the exclusive rightness of the monarchical form of government: that a king had an inalienable and God-given right to govern, independently of any human agency, and that a king's power was absolute and that he could not be made to answer for his acts by any judge, that he was forbidden to do only those acts which by divine law were denied to any human being. Bellarmine's doctrine on the nature and origin of the civil power shattered all three of these pretensions of the "divine right" theory, and his view is best expressed in his "On the Laity," a short work whose main intent was to establish the legitimacy of civil government against the antinomian tenets of Luther, Calvin, and the Anabaptists.

Bellarmine's position is summed up in his own words: "Firstly, the political power considered in its universal essence . . . proceeds immediately from God alone . . . secondly, this power has for its immediate subject the whole multitude . . . thirdly, this power is transferred from the multitude to one or several by the same law of nature."

Political authority exists not because individuals freely decide to pool their personal and natural rights and transmit them to some ruler, but because man is such that he cannot attain his perfection outside civil society. Natural law establishes civil authority, and its properties do not depend on human consent. In whom does civil authority first reside? Since all men are equal, authority first resides in the civil multitude as its first subject. But the multitude, not usually being able to exercise this authority directly, usually transfers it to one or more men according to the traditions of the society; the particular determination of governing personnel is not given by natural law, but by *jus gentium,* which builds upon common practice and custom. Thus, it is the multitude which gives itself a king, or consuls, or other rulers, and it can for sufficient reason transform one form of government to another. Once the determination of ruler has been made, the multitude owes its ruler obedience, and his orders are binding in conscience no less than are the orders of the pope. Thus, according to Bellarmine (and to the dismay of James), there are two notable differences between civil and ecclesiastical power: the former resides immediately in the multitude, and, considered in its particular forms and scope, is not of divine right; the latter has for its immediate subject one single man and is of divine right in its particular form and scope.

R.L.C.

AN INTRODUCTION TO THE DEVOUT LIFE

Author: Saint Francis de Sales (1567-1622)
Type of work: Devotional manual
First published: c. 1608

Principal Ideas Advanced

The way of perfection is meant for all men, for sanctity is compatible with any legitimate occupation and is spurious when it conflicts with one's earthly duties.

The everyday practice of humble virtues is the most direct road to sanctity, for by it the habit of virtue is more solidly established than by occasional heroic sacrifices.

It is through the will, informed by charity, that a man unites inward belief with outward conduct, thus integrating his soul and body, his faith and his life.

True devotion is perfect charity so dominating a man's life that he does perpetual good in obedience to his love of God.

Saint Francis de Sales apparently wrote *Philothea,* or *An Introduction to the Devout Life,* for the benefit of a French noblewoman, Madame de Charmoisy, yet its appeal proved to be universal, even in his own lifetime. His manner is never pompous or abstruse; he instructs practically and simply, teaching a sanctity which never divorces itself from the common temptations, sufferings, and joys of the human condition. Saint Francis's humor is seldom tart, and when it is, he directs it against those who pretend to a virtue when they do not truly possess it. For those who know their state and humbly and faithfully seek to remedy it, Saint Francis has only compassion and generosity. Just as in his pastoral life he relied more on love and example than on sternness, so in the *Philothea,* his attitude is one that constantly reflects the words of Christ: "Take my yoke upon you and learn from me . . . For my yoke is easy and my burden light." (Matthew 11:29-30.)

In his emphasis on the primacy of the will, under the influence of charity, as the fundamental basis of the spiritual life, Saint Francis borrows the intuition as well as the very words of Saint Augustine. "Your soul," says

Francis, "has a noble will which can love God . . . your heart can find no repose save in God alone, and can be subject to no creature." The soul, then, must maintain itself in perfect balance between the Creator and the rest of creation. Such a balance is in accord with both reason and religion and it is this balance that we call sanctity, brought into being by true devotion.

The *Philothea* is chiefly directed to the practical training of the will, strengthening it in its contest with enemies which would enslave it. The book falls conveniently into two parts. In the first, which conforms to the purgative way of the mystics, Saint Francis teaches a systematic method for the detaching of the soul both from its sin and from its tendency to find sin attractive. In the second, similar to the illuminative way, he devotes himself to establishing the habit of virtue. The second part ends with a brief note on the place of contemplative prayer in the devout life, but this suggestion of the unitive way remains only a suggestion. It is not until the great *Treatise on the Love of God* that Saint Francis treats of matters beyond the beginner in the spiritual life. The *Philothea* confines itself to the problems that such a beginner might reasonably expect to encounter, and those problems are always understood in terms of the adjustment of fallen man's will to divine realities.

As men we must exert a supreme effort to "possess our souls" in patience, that is, to make will sovereign over circumstance. The difficulty is great because material creation, the order of human events, is always unstable. Saint Francis, like the ancients, sees man as a microcosm of creation, subject to the same upheavals as nature. If we are to achieve that precarious balance between creation and God called "evenness of spirit," we must "ever remain content and unmoved in looking, seeking, and longing after our God." In himself, if he mirrors the dynamic stillness of God, man successfully reconciles all the fluctuations and extremes present in the rest of creation, of which he is at once the symbol and the flower.

If a man is truly to possess his soul, he must, above all, have both purity of vision and steadiness of purpose. Purity of vision implies temperance and balance in evaluating reality. All things must be looked upon in their proper proportion, "enjoyed" if they are spiritual and merely "used" if they are corporeal. If a man reverses this order, he denies reality, and his passions tempt him to possess and abuse creation. Steadiness of purpose is not a matter of mere affections or the pursuit and enjoyment of heavenly consolations. It is pure faith, which is the application of the will to an end known to be higher than the visible or sensible ends perceived by the wisdom of the world.

Saint Francis takes great pains to define the relationship between the world and the believer. Above all, the Christian must love the things of the world purely, not impurely. He must never give to creatures that love which belongs only to God. Persons and objects must never be substitutes for God; they must never be wrenched out of their proper and real context to serve ends that they were not intended to serve. The same thing is true of vain desires, like the wish for raptures and visions in prayer. Especially are desires vain if they contradict the divinely revealed order of values, in which eternal concerns of the soul are superior to the claims of the flesh. Both religious and worldly vain desires distract and disintegrate the soul, preventing it from achieving the integrity and harmony possible only in sanctity. The pleasures and goods of the visible world are the supreme distraction. If they dominate the soul, they cause it to reflect their own division and strifes.

Yet most Christians must find their way to God through life in the world. The progress of their souls is inextricably linked with the events and situations in which they find themselves, just as the sacramental bread and wine bear the presence of Christ. Saint Francis, gentle as he was, advocates no mere worldly, mediocre attempt at sanctity. Much of the *Philothea* is directed toward the right use of the world's goods to avoid every occasion of sin implicit in the possession of those goods. Marriage, to Saint Francis, does not condemn a person to second-rate spirituality. It is a state altogether good and holy, as long as its benefits are not inordinately used or its responsibilities allowed to distract the soul from its serene attitude toward God and His creation. Riches possessed in a spirit of detachment and charity are not barriers to sanctity, nor is poverty a guarantee of it. The poverty of the religious life is often admired because it is the result of a dramatic vow. But Saint Francis sees greater profit in the despised, involuntary poverty that is the lot of the average man, for it has no consoling romantic aura.

In both wealth and poverty, one has the opportunity to do good works. Saint Francis insists always that the claims of faith unsupported by works are weak. For him, interior devotion must be perfectly united to outward conduct, as the good tree bears good fruit, and as man's soul acts in union with his body. The devout life envisioned by Saint Francis is designed to achieve this perfect psychological unity and it does so chiefly through the practice of obedience—obedience of the body and passions to the will, and of the will to God.

The spiritual life begins in the school of obedience, where the will must be trained, whether a man is in the cloister or in the world. Superiors must be obeyed in important matters, and, if perfection is being sought, one should follow "even their wishes and inclinations" without murmuring or losing one's cheerful serenity, identifying one's obedience with that of Christ's on the Cross. Charity itself is obedience to the commands of grace; we prepare ourselves to obey these commands perfectly when over and over again we bend our will to another's for the sake of God. Thus, our charity to our neighbor blends with our love of God and our openness to divine influences in prayer. Only theoretically would Saint Francis differentiate between the practice of virtue in the spiritual life and the practice of prayer; in reality they are aspects of one unified experience.

In the practice of virtue, consistency and habit are of greater importance than the magnitude of individual acts. Even devout souls are tempted to anger, envy, folly, deceit, affectation, and impurity, and it is part of their progress toward perfection that these weaknesses be slowly and surely eliminated. Yet we must never lose sight of the end, for the achievement of virtue is meaningless without reference to the love of God. Our end must always be "to serve and love God truly," a purity of intention which allows no hypocrisy or self-righteousness to corrupt the devout soul. Patience, next to charity, is the key to the practice of heroic virtue. Patience is obedience to the will of God as it is expressed in the great and small trials of a man's life. The absence of this virtue severely flaws the quality of one's devotion.

The possession of our souls in patience prevents us from falling into anxiety, which Saint Francis calls the soul's greatest enemy apart from sin itself. It paralyzes the heart and does not allow it to practice even those virtues which it seemed to have mastered before. "Anxiety," he says, "proceeds from an ill-regulated desire to be delivered from the evil we experience, or to acquire the good to which we aspire." Yet the effect of anxiety is just the opposite. We lose our serenity, the real good we enjoyed previously, and experience only trouble, in a frame of mind which prevents our suffering from profiting us spiritually. Saint Francis urged that anxiety be countered with patience and faith and that God be trusted without confusion, despair, or self-love.

Prayer and the sacraments are the sources of patience and faith in the spiritual life, for God alone provides the unshifting foundation for serenity in the midst of man's exterior and interior worlds of mercurial flux. The technique for prayer advocated by Saint Francis reveals his concern for uniting the inner life with the outer life. He begins with a consideration of God's omnipresence, seeing God as a part of all life and event. Each of the mind's faculties is enlisted in the great enterprise of meditation. The imagination draws a picture of the mystery being reflected upon. From this scene and all it represents, the reason draws a meaning and a message which in turn spur the will to make specific resolutions for virtuous action. Again we see the intention to blend action and contemplation perfectly in the devout life.

Saint Francis strongly recommends, besides formal prayer, the frequent turning of the mind to God throughout the day's activities. This turning serves to order the distracting and confusing events that sweep up those who live in the world, and to give those events an eternal significance. Saint Francis does not admit of a proper life apart from God's order of existence. Creation and the process of living itself abound in spiritual revelations capable of being understood by the devout soul. A proper reading of these perpetual little epiphanies encourages us to live again the life of Christ, a life constantly informed by the presence of the sacred and renewed by participation in it.

B.J.R.

THE AUTOBIOGRAPHY OF A HUNTED PRIEST

Author: John Gerard (1564-1637)
Type of work: Memoirs of a missionary priest
First transcribed: 1609

Principal Ideas Advanced

John Gerard and three other English priests entered England secretly in 1588 to undertake missionary work among the persecuted Catholics.

Courageous members of the Catholic nobility offered the missionary priests the security of carefully constructed hiding places.

Gerard was captured in 1594 as the result of betrayal by an informer, but he escaped from the Tower of London after having been tortured several times.

The failure of the Gunpowder Plot in 1605 led to Gerard's flight from England in 1606.

The strength and courage of Catholicism in England during the Elizabethan age is made clear by Gerard's experience.

Four English priests landed unnoticed on the west coast of England one night late in 1588. Their mission was the spiritual care of the persecuted Catholics, a priestly work forbidden in Elizabethan England. Two of them were soon captured and executed; the third, after eighteen years of heroic labors, was captured, tortured, and executed. The fourth, though also captured, escaped from the Tower and continued his work until 1606 when he returned to the continent.

The lone survivor of this party of four was John Gerard, second son of Sir Thomas Gerard and Elizabeth, daughter of Sir John Port. After a brief stay at Oxford he completed his education on the Continent. He was ordained to the priesthood and had entered the Society of Jesus only a few months before he and his three companions "set out for home," all fully aware that torture and execution would be the probable epilogue of their homecoming. On the advice of others, Gerard recorded in Latin for private circulation his years of missionary activities. It is an exciting chronicle, in an unassuming style, of the remarkable sacrifices made by the English Catholics, as well as by Gerard and other missionary priests, in the effort to keep the Catholic faith alive in England.

Although the Latin manuscript has often been consulted since its writing in 1609, the first complete English translation of Gerard's autobiography did not appear until that of Philip Caraman, published in 1952. A translation was edited in 1881 by John Morris, S.J. and published under the title of *The Life of John Gerard,* but Morris engenders some confusion by calling it the "third edition, rewritten and enlarged." Gerard had written prior to this memoir a narrative of the Gunpowder Plot, and in 1871 Morris edited and published this English manuscript under the title, *The Condition of Catholics Under James I,* prefixing to it a life of Gerard based extensively on the autobiography. This combined work is the book which Morris calls the first "edition." When this work was reprinted in 1872, Morris corrected some errors in the *Life* and called it the second "edition." Only the 1881 *Life* may be properly called an edition of the autobiography, but even in this translation Morris omitted some parts, and his extensive editorial notes interrupt the flow of

Gerard's account. Caraman's editorial work in the 1952 translation, published by Pelligrini and Cudahy, is highly professional. Persons and places are identified (Gerard, of course, could not name his friends) at the bottom of the pages, and historical and explanatory annotations are included. The translation, too, is an improvement over the earlier one by Morris; Caraman renders Gerard's simple, unaffected Latin into lively, familiar English.

In the *Autobiography* Gerard constantly refers to the nobility and the gentry as his associates. This association was a dictate of necessity, not of choice. Since functioning as a priest was forbidden, Gerard and the other missionaries had to labor quietly and unobtrusively, using the homes of wealthy recusants (Catholics who refused to attend Protestant services) whose social position and wealth provided protection. Most readers will be deeply impressed by the great and frequent sacrifices the English gentry willingly made to practice their religion, thereby showing that the Catholic faith was far from dead as Elizabeth's reign neared its end. The homes of the nobility became centers where both the household and less socially favored neighbors could practice their faith. Gerard's own rank and education, his knowledge of falconry, hunting, cards, and the ways of the gentry, and his dress as "a gentleman of moderate means" allowed him to pass as a friend of his host or hostess; his identity was known only to his friends and his protectors.

Gerard faced the constant danger of either being tracked down and captured by pursuivants or betrayed by informers within the households. So the homes where he lived were provided with ingeniously constructed hiding places, where one or more priests and friends could hide safely though with considerable discomfort. Gerard frequently escaped capture by secluding himself in these shelters. On one occasion he remained in hiding four days without food while searchers stripped the walls; later he survived nine days in a "priest-hole." Much, then, of Gerard's long years of priestly work must be credited to the master designer and builder of most of these shelters, one Nicholas Owen, a Jesuit lay brother known as "Little John." The lives of all the Jesuits and many other priests were in his hands. Eventually captured and mercilessly tortured, Owen was executed after the authorities despaired of getting any information from him.

The reader's interest in Gerard's quiet but intensive and effective work among the English Catholics is quickened by accounts of his thrilling escapes and then by the story of his capture in the spring of 1594, the result of betrayal by an informer employed by the family then harboring him. He was first examined by England's chief inquisitors of Catholics, and his innate kindness deserts him when he describes Richard Tofcliffe ("a cruel creature" who "thirsted for the blood of Catholics") and Richard Young ("a veteran in evil"). Refusing to reveal the names of those who sheltered him, Gerard was chained up for three months. But friends bribed Young, and the captive was moved to a better prison, where he had considerable freedom with fellow prisoners and visitors, and his good work continued.

Three years after his capture Gerard was moved to London's famous Tower and there he was examined by a board of five high-ranking Elizabethan officials, among whom were two of England's most renowned personages: Edward Coke, then Attorney General, and his rival, Francis Bacon. Ordered by the board to be tortured, Gerard fainted eight or nine times during the first day in the torture chamber. Although threatened with torture twice daily until he confessed, Gerard was tortured only once more. After three weeks, he tells us, he was able to move his fingers again. His trial was postponed, and "In my enforced rest," he writes, "I turned more to my studies. . . ." In October, 1597, he escaped from the Tower, an episode that is one of the great adventures in history.

Following his flight, Gerard remained quiet for "a few days" and then took up residence with loyal friends "near my second prison." But the intense search for him led him to change residences frequently. Twice he was nearly captured; once the search for his hiding place was abandoned only when his pursuers captured another fugitive whom they took to be Gerard. Finally, established in a new quarter in the country, Gerard resumed his work, for, as he observes with a touch of English humor, "Now . . . our life was safe and undisturbed."

Gerard continued his work in England for nearly nine years after his escape from the Tower, making visits to London, where he had "many opportunities of meeting men of rank," and "was able to strengthen them in their faith, and direct them, and, in some cases, bring them back to the Church." The Gunpowder Plot (1605) ruined his work and that of his fellow laborers. Expecting relief from James I, the Catholics found themselves burdened with greater hardships than ever and their struggle was broken. Goaded beyond patience, a small group of young Catholics imprudently involved themselves in a plot that was easily detected and then used to destroy the hopes of the Catholics. The search for Gerard now became relentless. Father Edward Oldcorne, his companion when he landed in England, was captured, tortured, and executed. By now, Gerard writes, "nearly all my friends were either in prison or so distressed that they could hardly look after themselves." Since it was now a time "for lying quiet, not for work," he decided to cross the Channel. He commended his friends to different priests and made arrangements for his departure. On May 3, 1606, he left England as an attendant in the retinue of the Spanish Ambassador and the Ambassador to the Netherlands. At the port the diplomats at first "took fright" and refused to let him join them, but suddenly they changed their minds and he safely crossed the Channel with them.

His spectacular departure, which must have required the help of many important persons while authorities were on the alert to seize him, is related briefly and soberly as if it were simply another routine incident in a busy life. Gerard makes no claim to the role of a hero or a saint. But he was a rare person, holy and charming. The countless sacrifices of his friends, who made every effort to protect him in his priestly labors despite the mortal dangers involved, reveal the depth of their love and respect for him.

Gerard never returned to England. He spent the remaining thirty years of his life in Flanders and Rome.

W.L.L.

TREATISE ON LAWS

Author: Francisco Suarez, S.J. (1548-1617)
Type of work: Political theology
First published: 1613

Principal Ideas Advanced

Men enter political society in order to live together in peace, justice, and happiness.

The first subject of political authority is the civil multitude, which generally transmits to some designated personnel its power to rule, retaining, however, the power to depose.

Church and state are distinct societies, but the rulers of the state, being subjects of the pope by baptism, owe him obedience; thus, there is an indirect subordination of state to Church.

Jus gentium is a branch of customary law which has for its object the promotion of the moral and political unity of all men, though its use does not require a single world community.

What Francisco Suarez wrote on the first page of his first treatise in dogmatic theology, *On the Incarnate Word,*—that he has taken on himself the task of "explaining the doctrine of St. Thomas with exactness and clarity" —he might well have written of his *Treatise on Laws,* a 1200-page expansion of the nineteen questions of Saint Thomas's discussion of law. But determining the sense in which Suarez may legitimately be called a follower of Saint Thomas may give pause. Suarez was far from being an uncritical sectarian, so far, indeed, that he was more than once accused "in high places" of holding opinions opposite those of Saint Thomas. (The Council of Trent had shortly before recommended that Saint Thomas's *Summa theologiae* be made the official textbook in the schools; and the founder of the Jesuits, Saint Ignatius Loyola, had strongly recommended the study of Thomas.) Though the weight of scholarly opinion would lead one to conclude that Suarez should be referred to as an eclectic rather than as a Thomist, part of his difficulties stemmed from the fact that he was a good teacher who lived at a time when most teachers were incompetent: "The custom in this country [Spain] is to teach by dictation from copy books, to hand down the doctrine almost exactly as it has been received." His own lectures, Suarez continued, are always "presented with a certain air of novelty which comes from the scheme I follow, my manner of explanation, the type of proofs I use, my manner of solving difficulties, the problems I raise at points where others do not raise them. . . . Thus my doctrine is not novel; but it becomes novel in its presentation and in its departure from the routine of the copy books."

There is a sense in which Suarez might be thought of as the first important modern theologian. None of his predecessors or contemporaries went so far as he in treating scientifically, in their fullness, the principal questions of theology, speculative and practical, emphasizing all the opinions given on the subjects by heretics as well as by Catholics, together with the principal arguments given on each side, and analyzing as exactly as possible all the relevant patristic and conciliar documents. His analytic and historical procedure enabled him to raise problems only implicitly touched on or treated not at all in Saint Thomas or his major commentators; and Suarez offered the reader the opportunity of putting his hand on an inventory of work that had been accomplished in theology up to his time.

Of course, such a procedure has its defects: Suarez's detailed analysis of opinions, his lengthy criticisms of the objections of adversaries, and his fragmented presentation of his own theses constitute a risk to the clarity of the whole and to the patience of the reader.

The *Treatise on Laws,* Suarez's major work in political theory, is divided into ten books: on the nature of law in general, on eternal and natural law and the jus gentium, on positive human law, on canon law, on penal law, on the interpretation and change of laws, on custom, on privilege, and on divine positive law. Second in importance to the treatise is a work written at the request of Pope Paul V to answer King James I of England: *Defense of the Catholic and Apostolic Faith Against the Errors of the Anglican Sect, with an Answer to the Apology for the Oath of Allegiance and to the Admonitory Preface of His Most Serene Majesty, James, King of England.* (James caused this work to be burned by the common hangman and forbade its perusal under the severest penalties.)

Three other relatively minor works are of importance in coming to know the full scope of Suarez's political theory: *The Work of the Six Days,* a commentary on the first three chapters of Genesis, in which Suarez speculates about the political situation of men in a state of sinlessness; *On the Three Theological Virtues,* which includes considerations of colonization and of war; *On the Justice of God,* in which the author treats at considerable length of commutative, distributive, and legal justice.

Suarez's point of departure in political theory, like that of Aristotle's and Saint Thomas's, is the natural sociability of man, which leads him to live not only in families but also, in order to preserve peace and to permit human progress, in political society; and Suarez agrees with Aquinas that even had man not sinned, he would have lived in political society for the sake of good order and greater happiness for self and family.

According to Suarez, the formation of civil society calls for the intervention of the human will. Civil society appears when there is formed "a certain political union, which does not take place without a pact, express or tacit, of helping one another, and not without subordination of individual families and persons to some superior or leader of the community, without which the community could not exist." This pact Suarez often calls a "consensus," and thus he may be said to be speaking of a "consensual" rather than of a "contractual" society. (The term consensus actually denotes a double-consent theory: the formation of a given political community depends on human consent, as does the establishment of the government. In both cases men give their consent not out of enlightened egoism but because of the social character and needs of human beings.)

The common good of the "political mystical body" is conceived by Suarez rather narrowly as being the good of the individual only in this life and only as related to the good of the whole community: "that men live in the order of peace and justice, with that sufficiency of material goods which is required for the decent sustenance of bodily life, and that moral probity which is necessary for peace, justice, and external welfare."

How then does it happen that some one man (or group of men) has the power to rule, the power to bind consciences to obedience? According to the divine right theory, the power of the ruler comes directly from God, and designation of the rules is divinely effected; according to the designation theory, though ruling power is directly from God, it is men who designate the person who is to receive this power.

Suarez was an exponent of the transmission theory, according to which the civil multitude is the first bearer of civil authority and it is this multitude which (usually) designates some person (or persons) to rule and then transmits to them the ruling power; thus, neither is the power of the king directly from God (as is the power of the pope) nor is the ruler directly designated by God. Nor is it necessary that a ruler have given to him a certain quantum of civil power, as is the case with the pope's God-given powers. Suarez writes: "Primarily the supreme civil power, considered in itself, is given immediately by God to men assembled into a city or perfect political community; this does not take place by a peculiar and, as it were, positive disposition or by a donation entirely distinct from the production of such a nature; it takes place by way of a natural consequence from the first creation of such a nature: therefore as a result of such donation this [supreme civil] power is not placed in one person or in any peculiar group but in the whole complete people, or in the body of the community."

According to the transmission theory, the power of the people is, in a way, superior to that of the governing personnel, for the people retain the power to depose, though this power can rightly be exercised only in case of extreme provocation such as high treason or extraordinary mismanagement. Suarez is closer to Hobbes and farther from Rousseau than was Bellarmine or the leading Scholastics of the time, because for him authority is transmitted to the monarch: the right given the ruler is no less absolute than the right given the owner of private property, though the latter can be abridged by one who, in a desperate emergency, needs someone else's goods to preserve his life.

It should be noted that Suarez was not recommending democracy. He thought of monarchy as the "best form of government" (though it is as a rule expedient, given man's character, "to add some element of common government"), but he was very much concerned with limiting the claims of absolutistic monarchs whose position had been strengthened on the occasion of the Protestant Revolution by the desires of religious leaders on all sides to use coercive government to promote religious belief.

Suarez also held a rather moderate theory (at least by contrast with some of his Jesuit confreres, such as Juan de Mariana, 1536-1624) of the legitimacy of tyrannicide: if the ruler is not the legitimate ruler and if there is hope of restoring the legitimate ruler, the usurper can be considered an actual aggressor, a public enemy, and can be killed by any citizen; but if the ruler be both a tyrant and the legitimate ruler, he can be overthrown only by representatives of the people who originally placed him in power.

The relations between Church and state were of course much controverted in Suarez's time. His position was that they are distinct and independent societies, and that there is no direct or intrinsic subordination of one to the other. But the actions of civil authorities may either help or hinder the work of the Church, and it is, of course, preferable that they help. Now the state, as such, is utterly indifferent to the ends of the Church, but not so the persons who exercise the ruling power, for the rulers are baptized persons whose ultimate end is supernatural, and thus they, as individuals, are subject to the jurisdiction of the Church. And so it is that the power of the Church over the state is indirect, touching its rulers not *qua* rulers but *qua* persons who happen to be baptized. Nonetheless, this power is as extensive as the most ardent hierocrat could wish: the pope can exempt clerics from civil jurisdiction without the consent of the civil authorities; can oblige rulers to use temporal power for spiritual ends; can abrogate civil laws; can intervene in civil cases; can inflict coercive penalties both spiritual and temporal on kings; can depose kings; and can use force against infidel rulers to oblige them to respect the conscience of Christian subjects. Of course, such power can be legitimately exercised only when and insofar as the best interests of the Church demand it.

Suarez made a considerable contribution to the development of the Thomistic theory of natural law (though he clearly tends towards voluntarism and subjectivism in contrast to Aquinas's intellectualism and realism). Especially valuable is Suarez's discussion of "intrinsic change" in the natural law. It is a precept of natural law that that which has been borrowed should be returned; but if that which has been borrowed is a knife and the man from whom it was borrowed has become a homicidal maniac, the knife ought not to be given back. But this is not to say that the precept has undergone change; rather the precept, as formulated, was inadequately formulated for application in some circumstances. So, also, "Thou shalt not kill" is inadequately formulated for many purposes unless it be taken implicitly to include such qualifications as: on one's own authority, as an aggressor.

The distinction between natural law and jus gentium also received considerable development and elaboration from the pen of Suarez. The natural law prohibits what is intrinsically evil, the jus gentium does not; thus, for example, the obligation to observe treaties once made is a precept of the natural law, but the obligation not to refuse an offer of treaty duly made and for reasonable cause, is a precept of jus gentium. It is not enough to see jus gentium as simply a civil law that happens to have been adopted by many states; or to say that jus gentium differs from civil law (which is written) in being established through custom. One must, rather, see jus gentium as prohibiting acts which go counter to the desired "moral and political unity of all men."

This unity does not lead men to form a single political community—this is scarcely possible, and much less is it advisable—for, following Aristotle, Suarez spoke emphatically of the difficulty of governing rightly a too populous social body and, *a fortiori*, of governing the whole world. But he did emphasize, even at a time when all one could see were violent struggles and disputes between nations, the solidarity that exists among men and the consequent obligations which limit civil sovereignty, and in this he was a precursor of Hugo Grotius (1583-1645) and Samuel, Freiherr von Pufendorf (1632-1694). "Although a given sovereign state, commonwealth, or kingdom may constitute a perfect community in itself, consisting of its own members," writes Suarez, "nevertheless each one of these states is also, in a certain sense, and viewed in relation to the human race, a member of a universal society. . . . For even though the whole of mankind may not have been gathered into a single political body, but may rather have been divided into various communities, nevertheless, in order that these communities might be able to aid one another and to remain in a state of mutual justice and peace (which is essential to the universal welfare), it was fitting that they should observe certain common laws, as if in accordance with a common pact and mutual agreement. These are the laws called jus gentium."

R.L.C.

LETTER TO THE GRAND DUCHESS CHRISTINA

Author: Galileo Galilei (1564-1642)
Type of work: Letter on Scripture and science
First transcribed: 1615

Principal Ideas Advanced

The inspired authors of Scripture present the knowledge needed for the salvation of souls.

These authors did not intend to teach us about scientific matters but rather they accommodated themselves to the common way of speaking in referring to natural events.

God gave reason to us and expects us to use it in reading the book of nature and learning its laws from our experience.

To use Scripture in scientific matters is to risk endangering the reputation of the validity of Scriptures in religious matters in the eyes of those outside the faith who see the scientific errors involved.

As Stillman Drake, the translator of Galileo's *Letter to Madame Christina of Lorraine, Grand Duchess of Tuscany, Concerning the Use of Biblical Quotations in Matters of Science* comments in his *Discoveries and Opinions of Galileo* (1957): "Ignorant men were powerless to injure science, but they could seriously damage the Church. In order to prevent such a calamity Galileo undertook a struggle which involved him in great personal danger, while his enemies acted not only in complete safety but even with the prospect of gaining glory."

When Galileo wrote his famous letter on Scripture and science the Copernican theory was already over seventy years old. In that sense it was not a new theory but it was far from being an established one. When in 1543 Nicolaus Copernicus (1473-1543), the Polish astronomer, published his *De revolutionibus orbium coelestium,* which described the sun as the center of our planetary system and the earth as moving around the sun as well as rotating daily on its axis, there was no opposition in Catholic circles. True, Martin Luther (1483-1546) and John Calvin (1509-1564), the Protestant reformers, reacted negatively towards the new astronomy, but for the most part it was regarded as a hypothesis to better unify and order the movements of the heavens. Such a great astronomical observer as Tycho Brahe (1546-1601) could accept it in part, and reject it in part, keeping the earth at the center but having the other planets move around the sun, which in turn moved around the earth; and Francis Bacon (1561-1626), philosopher of science, rejected it altogether. It is not surprising that at the beginning of the seventeenth century the older Ptolemaic theory was still in favor, especially since it was intellectually allied with the philosophy of Aristotle (384-322 B.C.), still generally taught in the universities.

When in 1610 Galileo developed his version of the newly invented telescope, he made one discovery after another: the moons of Jupiter, the phases of Venus, the rough surface of the moon, the rotation of sunspots around the sun. This evidence confirmed his acceptance of the Copernican theory and encouraged him to become with Johannes Kepler (1571-1630), Brahe's assistant and successor, a most articulate and controversial defender of Copernicanism. However, as might be expected, the very campaign to win adherents to the new astronomy provoked opposition, especially from the Aristotelian-minded professors, who judged the triumph of Copernicus would further undermine the authority of their master. These were the men who, in the opinion of Giorgio de Santillana, author of *The Crime of Galileo* (1955), began the maneuverings which eventually led to the condemnation of Galileo.

The Council of Trent (1545-1563) signalized the Counter-Reformation on the part of the Church. One result of this period of reform was a greater sensitivity on the part of Catholics to the Protestant charge that they were not as respectful as they should be to the words of Scripture. While it would be an exaggeration to speak of Catholic fundamentalism, the tendency was now more in this direction than it had been during the time of Copernicus. Thus, scruples about the harmony between certain passages of the Old Testament, such as Joshua 10:12 ("Sun, stand thou still, stand thou still") and the new astronomy began to disturb some who had become excited by Galileo's discoveries. Such a person was the Grand Duchess Christina.

Christina of Lorraine was the mother of Grand Duke Cosimo II (1590-1621), a Medici and as ruler of Tuscany at this time, Galileo's patron. When Galileo's protégé, the Benedictine monk Benedetto Castelli (1578-1643), who taught mathematics at the University of Pisa, was invited to dine at the Ducal Court, his conversation about the moons of Jupiter (which Galileo, their discoverer, had named the Medicean Stars) impressed Christina. She wanted to know more about the Copernican theory, but having been exposed to religious objections against it she had doubts about reconciling Scripture with it. Father Castelli reported the discussion to Galileo and this provided the latter with the opportunity for answering the murmurings against Copernicanism on the grounds of revelation.

The letter was not simply an answer to the Grand Duchess. Galileo knew from his friends in Rome that the machinery of the Inquisition had been set in motion; hearings were being held and testimony taken. The Congregation of the Index was considering the advisability of banning both the work of Copernicus and a book by Father Paolo Antonio Foscarini, a Carmelite priest, who had just written a pamphlet arguing that Copernicanism was not contrary to Scripture. Father Foscarini had sent a copy of his work to Robert Cardinal Bellarmine, S. J., one of the leading theologians of the Counter-Reformation and himself a great controversialist against James I of England concerning the divine right of kings. Bellarmine replied courteously that he believed Foscarini and Galileo would be more prudent if they treated the Copernican theory as merely a hypothesis. Bellarmine argued that the theory could thus serve the purposes of the astronomers and not run the risk of irritating either the Scholastic philosophers or the theologians.

Galileo, however, would not settle for such a compromise. The Copernican theory was not a hypothesis for either Copernicus or himself. It represented the truth, and for the Church to compromise on the truth in the name of truth was a contradiction. As a loyal son of the Church Galileo was attempting to do more than protect himself; he was trying to save the Church from making a blunder.

Galileo begins his letter by noting the nature of the opposition which has arisen and he comments that the traditionalists, writing in defense of their positions, sprinkled their writings with quotations from the Bible. These men, he says, would have been better off to have followed the advice of Saint Augustine, who urged moderation in difficult matters of interpretation lest one conceive a prejudice against what might turn out to be the truth. Galileo explains the substance of the Copernican theory and he is concerned to show that Copernicus offered it to Pope Paul III (pope, 1534-1549) in his letter of dedication as the truth, not as a mere hypothesis. Galileo observes that Copernicus was a priest extremely well respected for his work and consulted by Pope Leo X (pope, 1513-1521) about calendar reform; furthermore Pope Paul III accepted the work without objection. It was only in the early seventeenth century, then, that the objection was made that the Bible teaches that the sun moves and the earth stands still. Galileo affirms that the Bible speaks the truth, but he adds, "I believe nobody will deny that it is often very abstruse, and may say things which are quite different from what its bare words signify. Hence in expounding the Bible if one were always to confine oneself to the unadorned grammatical meaning, one might fall into error . . . even grave heresies and follies."

Galileo indicates that he has in mind passages which speak of God in an anthropomorphic way. He notes that the inspired authors write in a popular way, accommodating themselves to the ordinary forms of speech. He makes the key point that the purpose of Scripture is "the service of God and the salvation of souls." It is not the purpose of Scripture, he insists, to make scientific pronouncements about whether the heavens move or stand still; the Holy Spirit was not trying to teach astronomy when he inspired the authors of Scripture.

In his polemic with the critics of the Copernican theory Galileo masterfully uses authorities to strengthen his arguments. Saint Augustine, who devoted a great deal of attention to the problems of interpreting the Bible, particularly in his controversies with the Manicheans, is Galileo's favorite author, but Tertullian, Saint Jerome, and Saint Thomas Aquinas are cited as well. Nor are all his authorities ancient. Galileo shows his knowledge of more recent Biblical scholars by quoting from Thomas de Vio Cardinal Cajetan, Cosme Magalhaens (1553-1624), and Didacus à Stunica, who had published in 1584 a *Commentary on Job,* in which he showed that the mobility of the earth was not contrary to Scripture. There is no doubt about Galileo's pugnacious personality, and in such a controversy as this he used his authorities with the skill of a master debater.

There was more at stake than winning a debate; Galileo's concern was with respect to his Church's position and the new developments in astronomy. To ban Copernicus would be to become involved in forbidding work in astronomy, an impossible consequence: "To carry out such a decision it would be necessary not only to prohibit the book of Copernicus and the writings of other authors who follow the same opinion, but to ban the whole science of astronomy. Furthermore it would be necessary to forbid men to look at the heavens. . . . And to prohibit the whole science would be but to censure a hundred passages of holy Scripture which teach us that the glory and greatness of Almighty God are marvelously discerned in all his works and divinely read in the open book of heaven." Galileo's point is that intelligent men cannot be content to look at the stars as do brutes and idiots. Learned men will seek with all their ingenuity to penetrate the structure of the heavens.

Turning to the question whether the Bible teaches that the sun moves and that the earth stands immobile in the center of the heavens, Galileo argues that this is the ordinary way of speaking, a way which common people understand. Even if on the scientific astronomical question all the experts were in agreement in favor of the Copernican position, it would still be necessary to speak as the Bible does in order that the common man may understand and not have his ordinary experience contradicted.

Galileo was not arguing for an official approval of the Copernican theory, but rather that religious authorities make no commitment in scientific matters on the basis of Scriptural texts. To do so would pervert the purpose of Scripture, Galileo writes, and he quotes with approval an epigram which Stillman Drake says was made originally by his contemporary Cardinal Baronius (1538-1607): ". . . the intention of the Holy Ghost is to teach us how to go to Heaven, not how heaven goes."

Quoting Saint Augustine on the dangers involved in using Scripture for purposes for which it was not intended, especially when those outside the faith can see the error of such usage, Galileo emphasizes the discredit such a practice brings on religion. Those who do this usually do so because they have failed in other arguments and must resort to Scripture as a last resource. "If I am correct," Galileo writes, "it will stand them in no stead to go running to the Bible to cover up their inability to understand (let alone resolve) their opponents' arguments, for the opinion which they fight has never been condemned by the holy Church." He was correct that the opinion he held had never been condemned, but that was 1615. Within a few months his statement was false.

In 1616 Pope Paul V (pope, 1605-1621) asked a committee of theologians for a ruling on the Copernican matter. These eleven consultants to the Holy Office ruled that the proposition that the sun is the center of the world and altogether devoid of local motion was "foolish and absurd philosophically, and formally heretical inasmuch as it expressly contradicts the doctrines of Holy Scripture in many places." The second proposition on which they were asked to rule, namely, that the earth is not the center of the world, nor immovable, but moves as a whole, and also with diurnal motion, was declared to merit "the same censure in philosophy, and that, from a theological standpoint, it was at least erroneous in the faith." The Congregation of the Index placed the work of Copernicus, Foscarini, and of Didacus à Stunica on the *Index of Prohibited Books,* where they remained until the first part of the nineteenth century. Galileo was not mentioned in the decree nor were any of his writings up to that time condemned.

However, his friend Cardinal Bellarmine was directed to inform Galileo of the decree and forbid him from continuing to teach Copernicanism in any way. Whether or not the prohibition was as general as that is a controversial point, but the conviction in his trial of 1633 was principally for violating the prohibition of 1616 with the publication in 1632 of his *Dialogue Concerning the Two Chief World Systems.*

But Galileo was vindicated. Not only were the condemned writings removed from the *Index* after Copernicanism had won acceptance, but Pope Leo XIII (pope, 1810-1903) in his encyclical on interpreting the Bible, *Providentissimus Deus* (1893), wrote of the relation of Scripture and science in a way that sounded in parts like a paraphrase of *The Letter to the Grand Duchess Christina.* Galileo had achieved his objective.

D.J.F.

THE LOVE OF GOD

Author: Saint Francis de Sales (1567-1622)
Type of work: Ascetical and mystical theology
First published: 1616

Principal Ideas Advanced

Love is synonymous with charity or union with God.

Gratifying love as found in prayer is affective love; benevolent love, as shown in complete union of the human will with God's will, is effective love.

Benevolent love aims at a perfection of compliance and disinterestedness which is the death of the will, after which the soul begins the eternal union of Heaven, the beatific vision.

Examples of gratifying and benevolent love may be found by attention to Scripture, the Fathers of the Church, the liturgy, the Councils, the theologians, the mystics, the saints, the pagan classical writers, and nature.

Saint Francis de Sales, Bishop of Geneva, founder of the Order of the Visitation, and Doctor of the Church, still lives in his writings: his pamphlets, written to counteract error when he was a missionary among the predominantly Calvinistic people of the Chablais; his letters of direction to people of all classes of society; and his two great books, classics of the spiritual life, *An Introduction to the Devout Life* and *The Love of God: a Treatise.*

While *An Introduction to the Devout Life* initiates the soul to the fundamental methods of leading a life of charity or union with God, *The Love of God* complements the work of the former, directing the soul from the lower to the higher realms of the life of prayer of union. In both books Saint Francis uses the words charity and love as synonyms of the union between the soul and God, but the fire of charity burns with a more brilliant light as treated in the second book because there the author discusses the heights of mystical experience when God has taken complete possession of the soul.

In the latter work Saint Francis did not pretend to write anything original on divine love, his intention being merely to help sincere souls see the beauty and attractiveness of God as well as man's complete dependence on Him as a loving Father, who, in return for man's love and obedience, intends him to share His happiness eternally.

The author devotes the first four books of *The Love of God* to the theory of God's love and His attributes; the remaining eight are concerned with a consideration of the practical application of the theory, with Saint Francis explaining how divine love gradually transforms the soul, despoiling it of all selfishness, and leading it finally to the highest realm of intimacy to prepare it for the eternal union of the beatific vision in Heaven.

The author defines fundamental terms, and he treats of the human will's control over the soul's powers and the natural appetites. Other topics include the good and beautiful in God, man's natural craving for love, the beauty of human love, and the tendency to love God above all others as the supreme good for which man was created.

It is love in man which determines the activities of his emotions and passions, and whether the activities are good or bad depends upon the goodness or badness of the love from which they spring. Love has such dominion over the will that it makes the will exactly like itself. When love is carnal, the will is carnal; when love is spiritual, so is the will. But the will also rules over love, since the will loves only what it wills to love and from several loves can choose that which it prefers. Therefore, if man wants God's love to live and reign in him, he must kill self-love.

The supreme goodness of God, according to Saint Francis, is actually one single perfection, but is seen by the finite mind as multiple. It is as though the white light of God's infinite perfection shines through the prism of the created mind and is refracted into all the colors of the spectrum as love, power, mercy, justice, and the other virtues.

Because God has made it so easy for man to love Him—for man's most insignificant deeds are pleasing in His sight—it is easy for man to grow in charity. God never increases His love for a soul possessing charity without increasing the soul's charity too. And since "charity bestowed as a wage always exceeds . . . the charity given to merit it," the least act of charity in Heaven will be superior to the greatest charity possible in this life.

Saint Francis goes on to set down some practical applications. He warns that as long as life lasts, there is a possibility of losing God's love. Voluntarily to turn away from the Creator to His creatures causes a decline in charity and possibly even its loss. In this state of decline, or imperfect love, one may continue through habit to practice virtues he once performed in charity even though charity no longer informs them. Though it appears to be real, this "charity" is actually only the reflection of these virtues, and one may find this counterfeit as satisfying as the real virtues until some strong light shows the deception.

The soul that truly loves God rejoices in His perfection, and this love is complacent or gratifying love, writes Saint Francis. Man wants to possess the likeness of the things he loves and make them his own, as Saint Paul's love for Christ caused Christ to live again in him. Gratifying love leads to spiritual childhood, which exults in all God's excellencies as though they were its own. But because these excellencies are beyond man's grasp, he is, in reality, possessed by them, and they appear fully to satisfy the soul; yet, the soul goes on longing still, for the enjoyment of even higher good is forever desirable.

In contrast to gratifying love is benevolent love, which desires to give something to God. The realization that God lacks nothing fires the soul to the consideration of imaginary goods which it would like to give Him. Man would even die if by so doing he could procure for God something more. In this state of longing to give, Saint Augustine found himself crying out: "I am Augustine, Lord, and You are God. Yet were the impossible possible, that I were God and You Augustine, I should want to change places with you, want to become Augustine so that You could be God." This desire to give all inspires an intense yearning to praise and honor God as perfectly as possible, even as the angels and saints do in Heaven. This longing can become so strong that the creature may die in an act of pure charity. Of such a love Mary, the most perfect of God's creatures, died. In an infinitely higher degree than all creatures, however, Christ praises His Father, and it is in union with Him that the soul aspires continually to praise the Trinity. Though Chirst's human actions are infinite compared to man's, they are finite compared to the essential infinity of the Godhead. Finally, benevolent love finds its completion in the love of God for Himself, because God alone can provide what is His due. He alone can offer Himself infinite, adequate praise. The human heart longs to glorify the praise which God gives Himself, but gradually it experiences contentment in the realization that God's infinitely praiseworthy goodness can be suitably praised only by an infinite being. Man's incapacity to praise God perfectly then becomes a source of gratification that his Beloved is above all created praise.

This kind of love for God expresses itself in two ways, Saint Francis claims. Man sets his heart on God through affective love and serves Him through effective love. The first fills him with gratification, joy, and spiritual yearnings; the second leads him to firm resolution, courage, and absolute obedience to whatever God's will enjoins. Affective love of God is exercised in prayer, a prayer which, while not excluding petition, embraces the whole of contemplative activity. God talks to the soul and the soul talks to God in a secret conversation. Since the subject of this conversation is God Himself, it is synonymous with mystical theology, which is a profound attention to God's goodness for the purpose of achieving union with Him. Meditation, the first step in mystical theology, has to do with the things that make man good, that lead him to God; it does not exclude reflection on his problem when this serves to bring his mind back to God's goodness in order to praise His love and mercy.

According to the author, contemplation, the second step in mystical theology, is the artless, unceasing mental preoccupation with the things of God. Meditation is motivated by the desire to possess God's love, a love that once attained leads to contemplation. As meditation is reflection on the details of God's perfections, so contemplation is loving preoccupation with all of these in a single, loving, concentrated look. Contemplation, then, presumes that the soul has found God. It becomes spiritually inebriated with Him, alive to Him, united to Him. Normally, the way leading to this state is by hearing the word of God, speaking of Him, reading, praying, and thinking of His goodness, all of which results in an ever increasing love of Him. This love produces so secret an attentiveness as to give the impression of not being attention at all. Sometimes, there being no activity except in the will, the soul seems to be lulled to sleep; it no longer thinks of itself, but only of Him whose presence affords it delight. It has found its Beloved; there is nothing else to look for. Even though the intellect and memory may turn to irrelevant thoughts, in this contemplative state the soul never ceases to enjoy the happiness of being with

God. In spite of all external distraction, it manages to maintain tranquillity at least in its will; and, after the distraction, little by little, the soul's faculties are lured back to the supreme gratification which the will enjoys.

There are degrees of quietude depending partly upon whether the mind is extremely active, flexible, introspective, or self-conscious. According to Saint Francis, the soul may occasionally be conscious of God's presence through some inward delight, as was that of Saint Elizabeth at our Lady's visit. The soul may feel a charm, as though God were present without its being aware of the fact as such, as was the case with the two disciples of Emmaus. Sometimes the soul hears God speaking through inner lights and convictions to which it may or may not be able to respond. Finally, writes Saint Francis, the soul may simply know it is in God's presence, in spite of there being no indication whatsoever.

It is important to note that, according to Saint Francis, "more care is needed to become aware of God's presence than to remain in it." Once God's presence has been recognized, the realization of His presence may be continued through listening to Him, talking of Him, acting for Him, and putting the self completely at His disposal. Consent to God's permissive will is the highest quietude, free as it is from all self-seeking. The soul that has reached this degree of love has become so pliable that at times it melts, as it were, at the sound of God's voice and flows into Him to become one with Him. This state may even become ecstasy, and it produces complete absorption in God and makes the soul dissatisfied with everything that is not God.

Saint Francis cautions the reader that the love, which can produce so desirable a condition, does not free the soul from suffering. Because love penetrates the heart to its very depths, it wounds and causes pain. The very fact that one loves makes separation from the beloved an acute distress, the effect of an intense desire for an absent good. So God Himself at times wounds the soul He destines for a closer union, for after attracting it by giving it a wonderful awareness of His supreme goodness, He allows it to experience its own utter helplessness. The soul's love for God can never fully answer His love for it; its desires are forever incommensurate with its capacity; therefore, the soul suffers and even longs to be freed from this life to enjoy uninterrupted union with God.

Since freedom from this life is now impossible, Saint Francis adds, the soul ardently seeks an intimate union with God in prayer. Saint Francis describes in detail the various degrees of union with God in prayer, beginning with that in which the soul lends its efforts to achieve union and culminating in the supreme degree of suspension of the faculties and rapture, in which the soul is completely passive and so in love with God that death may result, as has been the case with some of the saints. An outstanding example of one whose life was caught up in God in a sort of permanent ecstasy is the great Saint Paul. But if it is said of Paul's life that it was "hidden in Christ with God," how much truer it is to say of Mary, the Mother of Jesus, that she is the supreme example of a life of love. Her Son's sorrows pierced her heart because of their intimate union, or rather actual interpenetration of heart, soul, and life. If Mary lived with her Son's life, she likewise died of His death, since a person dies as he lives.

After speaking of the heights of ecstatic love Saint Francis devotes some time to the discussion of what he calls compliant love and submissive love. Compliant love is born of the desire of the heart which has taken complacency in God to please Him in return and thereby to grow in His likeness. This love, moreover, flowing from benevolent love, has the wish that God be loved and adored by every creature. It consists, in conformity with God's declared will, in the keeping of His commandments, counsels, and inspirations, in all of which man plays an active part. Inspirations are described by Saint Francis as rays of grace bringing light and warmth to the heart to show it what is good and to supply it with energy to pursue the good. God's ways of inspiring are numberless and vary with individual souls. Proofs that one is following inspiration are perseverance, peace of soul, and humble obedience, in contrast to fickleness, impulsive anxiety, and stubborn willfulness.

Submissive love is the passive acceptance of trials and sorrows which are infinitely lovable when seen as coming from Providence. For love of the Cross, one runs to meet unpleasant things in order to please the Beloved. But the calm acceptance of toil and trouble permitted by God is a still higher degree of love, while the highest of all is the welcoming of trials, loving them, and embracing them only because God's will is seen in them. This last is love completely disinterested, ready for every impression of the divine will, like wax in God's hands. Such a love has no preferences of its own; it wants only what God wants. Sometimes God fills a soul with ambitious aims, which are meant to be unsuccessful in order that the soul acquire the virtue of disinterestedness. Again, while God hates sin, He occasionally permits it in order that good may come of it. But so perfect is this love that it will be exercised in the absence of all success, delight, or pleasure. Obviously, such love is not maintained without difficulties, and these God allows in order to test its purity. The soul which seeks God alone will persevere without any sign from God that it is pleasing to Him. This state is so painful, yet so salutary, that it produces in the soul an act of complete renunciation of itself into the hands of God, such as our Savior made of Himself to His Father on Calvary. The will at last freed from all preference can perform its highest function, the surrender of all effort to desire or choose for itself from among the things that God's permissive will allows; it can praise and thank Him for all that happens. This state is not so much one of compliance with God's will or one of passive acceptance, as it is a complete readiness on the part of the alert will to take whatever comes.

God has commanded man to love Him in this world that he may love Him forever in Heaven. But Saint Francis adds that the wholehearted love of God does not exclude the love of creatures, which are loved in and for God. Such love includes love of oneself and of all men because they are made in His image. Love of neighbor is love of God in man, or man in God, and it is so important that Saint Francis thinks the subject is deserving of an entire treatise in itself, for after all, the test of love of God is love of neighbor. Saint Francis concludes by claiming that there is one especially excellent apprenticeship of love; namely, Christ's passion and death, the fruit of His love for man.

Sister M.L.

ARS LOGICA

Author: John of St. Thomas (John Poinsot, 1589-1644)
Type of work: Logical foundations of science and metaphysics
First published: I, 1631; II, 1632

Principal Ideas Advanced

The liberal art of logic, which is simultaneously the speculative and demonstrative science of second intentions, is necessary as an instrument of the mind for the perfect state of the other sciences and is of value precisely insofar as it looks to them.

The task of the logician is the scientific investigation of second intentions of both formal and material import on the levels of the first, second, and third operations of the intellect.

The problem of the universal is solved in terms of a distinction between the nature which is denominated universal (which may be divided into the ten categories) and the second intention of universality which accrues to it as known and from which it is denominated (which is divided into the five predicables).

Science in the strict sense is achieved in demonstrations yielding necessary conclusions from self-evident premises; and these demonstrations are either in physical science, mathematics, or metaphysics, depending upon the degree of formal abstraction or mode of defining appropriate to the middle term in question.

The *Ars logica* of John of St. Thomas is a profound exposition of the logic of Aristotle, which goes beyond the stage of mere commentary to be in itself a significant development of logical theory. The excellence of the work assures us of an outstanding exception to the popularly accepted rule that from the fourteenth century on Scholasticism was decadent and Scholastics concerned ineffectively only with trivia. Not only in logic, but in philosophy proper, as well as in theology, John of St. Thomas, born Jean Poinsot, though a Scholastic in the seventeenth century, earned a place in the history of thought as one of the great teachers of all time. Admittedly a disciple of Saint Thomas Aquinas, and through him of Aristotle, John of St. Thomas was not content merely to repeat the words of his masters. We do find in his works, happily, a lucid exposition of Aristotle and Aquinas, but we find also significant philosophical and theological advances, the fruit of the patient, rigorous, profound effort that makes his works at the same time difficult and highly rewarding.

John of St. Thomas, like Saint

Thomas Aquinas before him, from whom John's name in religion was taken, was a Dominican monk and university teacher. His works in philosophy were published together, under the title of *Cursus philosophicus Thomisticus,* for the first time in 1637; while his works in theology were published together for the first time in 1888, under the title of *Cursus theologicus Thomisticus.* The best edition of the *Cursus philosophicus Thomisticus* is the edition edited by B. Reiser, O.S.B. This edition includes three volumes, the first of which is the *Ars logica.*

The *Ars logica* is significantly subtitled *De forma et materia ratiocinandi,* for it is divided into two parts: Part I, formal logic; and Part II, material logic. The distinction between formal and material logic, so clear to John of St. Thomas, is not so clear to most logicians today, who tend to restrict logic to formal logic alone. For John of St. Thomas, as we shall see, logic establishes the rules of discourse. These rules express the demands of certain relations between objects in the mind, relations through which these objects are ordered in discourse. There are some rules which govern the consistency or validity of discourse. Formal logic establishes these. There are other rules which must be followed if discourse is to have, over and above validity, a determinate degree of probative force or scientific status. Material logic establishes these. The *On Interpretation* and *Prior Analytics* of Aristotle are in formal logic; the *Categories, Posterior Analytics,* and *Topics* are in material logic. Part I of the *Ars logica* has two sections, the first for beginners in logic, the second for advanced students. The first section consists of a number of brief treatments, called *summulae,* of points in formal logic. The *summulae* are presented according to the order indicated by the three operations of the intellect: (1) simple apprehension, (2) composition or division, (3) reasoning. The second section consists of eight questions (*quaestiones disputandae*) divided into articles, in which the author explores on a highly sophisticated level some of the more difficult points out of the *summulae.*

Part II of the *Ars logica* is considerably longer than Part I, more difficult and philosophically more significant. It begins with a rigorous investigation into the nature of logic and of its proper subject, the logical being of reason known as the second intention. This is followed by a searching inquiry into the problem of the universal, with John's attempt to solve it as a moderate realist in terms of several sophisticated distinctions. Next comes a meticulous commentary on Porphyry's *Introduction to the Categories,* in which John develops the doctrine of the five predicables which has found its way into so many contemporary textbooks in traditional logic. This is followed by a deeply philosophical consideration of the subject matter of Aristotle's *Categories,* with separate treatises on substance, quantity, relation, and quality. After a consideration of the nature and division of sign and a treatment of the concept, John gets into the subject matter of Aristotle's *Posterior Analytics.* Here, in a relatively brief but exacting treatise, he goes into demonstration and its product, science, and into the unity and distinction of the sciences. The *summulae* making up the first Section of Part I have been translated by Francis C. Wade, S.J., in a volume entitled *Outlines of Logic* (1955). Major portions of Part II have been translated by Yves R. Simon, John J. Glanville, and G. Donald Hollenhorst in *The Material Logic of John of St. Thomas* (1955).

The *Ars logica* is a work of great proportions. First, it is a lengthy work, including many treatises. Second, except for the *summulae,* which are significant in their own way, the treatises are all developed on a profound level and each represents a contribution to logical or philosophical theory. Thus, there is always a danger in focussing on some of the treatises as though they alone represented the central ideas and significant contribution of the work as a whole. Those parts which must be left out when only a few are taken up are surely not all less significant than these others. Still, the depth and significance of the work as a whole can be forcefully suggested in a consideration of some few of the treatises. We can consider, for example, John's treatises on the nature of logic, the problem of the universal, and the specification of the sciences. In each of these John of St. Thomas, while attempting to remain scrupulously faithful to Aristotle, and especially to Thomas, goes beyond his masters to make his own contribution to the fields of logic and philosophy; and in each he presents a teaching which has had a deep and lasting influence on thinkers within the Thomistic tradition.

The question of the nature of logic is properly not so much a problem in logic as it is a problem in epistemology, but the question is nevertheless crucial for logicians. John distinguishes between natural logic, a native endowment of all men, and artificial or acquired logic. Logic is for discourse, and discourse is for science. Is natural logic sufficient to serve the needs of science? John answers in the negative, insisting that something over and above natural logic is necessary for a man if he is to acquire speculative science in more than an initial and imperfect state. This something, namely, acquired logic, is an intellectual virtue which is at the same time a science and an art. Possessed of acquired logic a man knows the rules of discourse and the necessity which they impose. Some logical rules are seen as self-evident, and others are seen as resolved back into the self-evident. Thus, logic is the demonstrative science of the rules of discourse. These rules of discourse are regulative canons according to which the intellectual operations (remotely) and the objects present in knowledge (proximately) are set in order. Insofar as logic looks to the production within the mind of ordered thinking and ordered thoughts, logic is a liberal act. The rules of discourse establish the relations of things in their existence as objects of thought and discourse in the mind. These relations, such as subject, genus, syllogism, are called second intentions. To say, as we have, that logic is the science of logical rules is to say it is the science of second intentions. As relations of the reason, second intentions are nonreal and are not worth knowing for their own sake. They are worth knowing only insofar as in a knowledge of them the mind grasps the rules of discourse needed to acquire scientific knowledge. Logic is of value, then, only inasmuch as it is useful; but as useful for the sake of knowledge, logic is a speculative science. For John, then, logic is the liberal art of sound discourse and, at the same time, the speculative, demonstrative, exclusively useful science of second intentions or rules of discourse.

How can the universal be real if only singulars exist; and if the universal is not real, is not nominalism forced upon us? John of St. Thomas faces this problem and offers a brilliant defense of the position of moderate realism. Taking his lead from Thomas Aquinas, John distinguishes between the nature in itself or the nature absolutely taken, which as such is neither singular nor universal, and the nature as it exists, either as singularized in things in a first existence outside the mind or as an object in a second existence within the mind. In its first existence in things a nature is multiplied from individual to individual. Still the nature is negatively one, even in these many singulars, for it involves no division by way of formal principles; in things it is numerically many but specifically one. In an act of abstractive insight the intellect sloughs off on matter, the principle in things of individuation and multiplicity, and holds the nature in its vision as an object positively one and nonrepugnant to being in many. Reflecting on the nature so conceived, the mind invests it with a determinate reference or relation to the many of which it can be said. This relation, a being of the reason (in fact, one of the second intentions investigated in logic), is precisely universality. Universality accrues in the mind to a nature which does not become less real as subject of the nonreal relation of universality. John calls the nature known the "metaphysical universal," which in intelligible content is identically the nature absolutely taken. He calls the relation of universality, which is distinct from the nature known while accruing to it and which is that from which the nature is denominated universal, the "logical universal." In an attempt to explain this logical relation, as all relations are to be explained, in terms of subject and foundation, he calls the nature to which universality as a relation accrues the "material universal," the positive unity and nonrepugnance to being in many of the nature as known the "fundamental universal," and the relation of universality itself the "formal universal." In effect John solves the problem of the universal on the basis of a distinction between the universal and its universality. Universality is nonreal, but the universal, that is, the nature to which as an object universality accrues, might very well be real. John's treatises on the predicables and the categories follow logically upon the treatise on the universal, for the predicables directly divide the relation of universality into its types.

For John of St. Thomas logic is an instrument of the mind looking ultimately to science. Accordingly, the *Ars logica* ends with a treatment of science, and one of the questions taken up is that of the division of speculative science into its types. John teaches that the speculative sciences are distinguished one from another on the basis of formal differences in objects; that is, on the basis of differences in objects as intelligible. To the extent to which objects are submerged in matter they are unintelligible; hence, to the degree to which they can be cognized in abstraction from matter they are intelligible. John sees three degrees of matter from which an object can be abstracted: (1) individual matter, (2) sensible matter, (3) intelligible matter. Abstraction from individual matter constitutes the formal object of physical science. Abstraction from individual and sensible matter constitutes the formal object of mathematical science. Abstraction from all matter constitutes the formal object of metaphysics. Each of these abstractions is an abstraction of an intelligible object from matter yielding an object formal to a given science. As such they are formal abstractions and are not to be confused with total abstraction, which is the abstraction of a universal whole or general object from its particular instances. Though each given degree of formal abstraction is proper to a given level of speculative science, total abstraction in all of its degrees is common to all the sciences inasmuch as all science is of the universal. The division of speculative science into physical science, mathematics, and metaphysics is only generic.

John of St. Thomas goes on to consider the principle according to which specific distinctions within each genus of science are to be made. The division of the sciences is made on the basis of differences in degree of formal abstraction from matter. John also goes on to show that this is the same as to say that the division of the sciences is based upon different modes of defining and upon formally different grades of middle term in scientific syllogisms. In his treatise on the specification of the sciences John of St. Thomas attempts as always to be authentically the disciple and interpreter of Saint Thomas. Whether or not in fact he has succeeded is vigorously argued on both sides. There is agreement, however, that in this treatise, as in so much of what he has done, John of St. Thomas has expressed and developed a position that has been a major influence on the majority of those who have come after him in the Thomistic tradition.

E.D.S.

DIALOGUE CONCERNING THE TWO CHIEF WORLD SYSTEMS

Author: Galileo Galilei (1564-1642)
Type of work: Astronomical theory
First published: 1632

Principal Ideas Advanced

The Ptolemaic system errs in asserting that the earth is the center of the universe; the fact is that the sun is the center around which the earth, planets, and stars revolve in circular (not elliptical) orbits.

Experiments practicable upon the earth are insufficient measures for proving the earth's mobility, since such experiments are indifferently adaptable to an earth in motion or at rest.

A study of celestial phenomena strengthens the Copernican hypothesis.

The problem of the ocean tides can be solved by assuming the motion of the earth.

In 1616 the Copernican theory that the sun, not the earth, is the center of a system of planets had been declared "false and erroneous," and Copernicus' book, *Six Books on the Revolutions of the Celestial Orbits* (1543), placed on the Index, despite Galileo's pleas. In 1624 Galileo tried unsucessfully to get the decree revoked, but he did receive permission to write on the two systems of thought, Ptolemaic and Copernican, as long as he remained in the realm of theory and did not try to decide in favor of Copernicus or claim that his theory represented reality. After a two-year delay with the censors in Rome, Galileo's *Dialogue Concerning the Two Chief World Systems* was published in 1632 at Florence with the full *imprimatur* granted in 1630.

The common and attractive style and the use of Italian rather than the scholarly Latin brought the book to the immediate attention of educated men all over Europe, a fate quite opposite to that of Copernicus' book, which remained a work for the specialist, and of Kepler's works, which were practically unreadable.

While not his major contribution to science, Galileo's *Dialogue on the Two Chief World Systems* is his best known and most influential work, best known because it was *cause célèbre,* the object of the most famous case of prohibition by the Sacred Congregation of the Holy Office (the Inquisition), and most influential because it became the focal point and inciting cause of a struggle to the death between the "new science" of experimental observation, which Copernicus and Galileo represented, and the Scriptural-theologico-scientific complex of Aristotelian-Ptolemaic cosmology common in the universities of that day.

In 1543 Copernicus offered both scientific evidence and argument for the rejection of the prevalent Ptolemaic astronomy, which claimed that the universe has the earth as its center, towards which matter tends from every point in space. According to Ptolemaic ideas, the earth is spherical and objects fall towards its center. The sun, moon, and stars are located in circular orbits around the earth and are prevented from falling into it by their attachment to transparent spherical shells. Everything enclosed within the terrestrial sphere, which has the moon's orbit as its outer limit (the Ptolemaic theory continues), is perishable and transitory, while the outer celestial sphere contains all that is eternal and unchangeable.

Despite repeated warnings by Augustine, Baronius, and others through the years, the predominant cosmology, described briefly above, was an uncritical mixture of Scripture, theological speculation and doctrine, and astronomy.

The *Dialogue* has three participants, Salviati, Sagredo, and Simplicio. The scene is Venice. Salviati, who in real life was Galileo's fellow student, fellow astronomer, and dear friend, defends the Copernican theory. Sagredo, another friend, a Venetian nobleman, quick of mind, solid in judgment and a good listener, defends the Ptolemaic cosmology. Simplicio, a figment of Galileo's imagination, represents Galileo's antagonists, the literal-minded, blind, and obstinate followers of Aristotle.

The first day of discussion begins with an analysis of Aristotle's picture of the universe, based on three dimensions, three types of motion (straight, circular, and mixed, with the circular being the most perfect), and two spheres, the incorruptible celestial sphere and the changeable terrestrial sphere. Aristotle's argument that heavy things fall to the center of the *universe* while lighter things move away from it is then exposed. Sagredo rejects this argument by showing that it begs the question and that it is more reasonable to believe that heavy things tend to the *earth's* center, without presuming that the earth's center is also the universe's center. After a digression on the Aristotelian notion of the incorruptibility of the heavenly spheres, Salviati notes that, were Aristotle alive, he would change his ideas when confronted with all the new discoveries. The existence of sunspots, for example, offers a fine argument against the incorruptibility of the heavenly spheres. But Galileo represents Simplicio as demurring: "Who would there be to settle our controversies if Aristotle were to be deposed? . . . Should we destroy that haven, that Prytaneum where so many scholars have taken refuge so comfortably; where, without exposing themselves to the inclemencies of the air, they can acquire a complete knowledge of the universe by merely turning over a few pages?"

A comparison is then made between the characteristics of the earth and moon, with particular attention to the question of reflection. Here Simplicio claims that the rugged surface of the moon is no proof of its changeableness; he argues that the mountains are only illusions, and that the surface is like a mirror. The first day's discussion closes with some comments on the admirable progress of human knowledge and its limitations when seen against God's infinite wisdom.

On the second day, after reminding the others that the previous day's argument tended to favor the view that the heavenly bodies are not incorruptible and that the earth is a movable and moving body, Sagredo suggests that the discussion continue by concentrating on the question whether, as a matter of fact, the earth is movable or immovable. Simplicio comments that he has heard many interesting points in support of the claim of movability, but he cannot resist the power of authority, even when authority runs counter to forceful arguments. Sagredo then tells of an Aristotelian philosopher who, upon being shown a dissected human nervous system, refused to give up the view that the nerves originate in the heart, and commented: "You have made me see this matter so plainly and palpably that if Aristotle's text were not contrary to it, stating clearly that the nerves originate in the heart, I should be forced to admit it to be true." Salviati adds an account of some Peripatetics (followers of Aristotle) who insisted that the invention of the telescope was inspired by a passage in Aristotle; as a text they cited a passage in which Aristotle wrote of seeing stars from the bottom of a well. Salviati contends that the followers of Aristotle do not do the great philosopher justice, for if Aristotle were alive he would not ignore the evidence of his senses.

The remainder of the second day is taken up with a variety of arguments, involving experimentation, observation, and computation, for and against the movement of the earth. Salviati argues that the diurnal motion is the earth's and not that of the remainder of the universe; although motion is relative, it is more reasonable to suppose that the earth moves than that the earth is stationary while "an immense number of extremely large bodies move with inconceivable velocities. . . ." Astronomical observations yield further grounds in support of the claim that the earth moves. Simplicio attempts to refute Salviati by citing passages from Aristotle, but Salviati analyzes Aristotle's arguments and reveals what he regards as errors, although he praises Aristotle's ingenuity. A long discussion ensues concerning the behavior of projectiles and the conclusions to be drawn from that behavior. Aristotle's claim that heavy falling bodies move proportionately to their weights is critically examined and rejected. As the discussion of the second day comes to a close, Salviati suggests that they go on to a consideration of the belief that the earth revolves around the sun once in the space of a year.

The third day of discussions begins with another critical attack by Salviati on men who first of all reach a conclusion and then adapt their observations to fit the conclusion. Sagredo adds that such men also accommodate the premises to the conclusion, and he agrees that knowledge about the world cannot be gained in this manner. A detailed examination of various methods used by astronomers to determine the altitude of certain stars is undertaken. Salviati then poses a dilemma to Simplicio. Aristotle maintained that the center of the universe is the earth and also that all celesial spheres moved about a common center. If Aristotle were forced by his experiences to confess himself mistaken about one of his claims, which one would he prefer to give up? Simplicio evades the question, and Salviati suggests that Aristotle would find denial of the first proposition—that the earth is the center—more palatable than denial of the second—that the universe moves about a common center. Since observations show that the sun is the center of the celestial revolutions, one must admit either that the earth also revolves around the sun or that the universe has two centers of revolution. Aristotle would find it intolerable to say that there are two centers; hence, he would conclude that the earth revolves around the sun.

A detailed explanation of the Copernican solar system is next offered, complete with sketches. A summary of what is known about each planet and its orbits is applied to the Copernican theory. Before the third day comes to a close, eclipses, annual rotations, retrograde orbits, sunspots, and lodestones have been discussed and related to the Copernican ideas.

The final section of Galileo's work, the part concerned with the discussion of the fourth day, was originally entitled, "On the Flux and Reflux of the Sea," but Pope Urban VIII asked the author to change the title so that the book would appear to be organized around a final explanation of tidal movements.

During the fourth day of the discussions, various theories proposed to explain the causes of tides are examined and rejected, among them the theory that the tides are the result of lunar attraction. According to Salviati, the earth's motion accounts for the diurnal, monthly, and annual tides, and he makes an ingenious effort to fit his theory to the observed facts. The dialogue ends with Sagredo's suggestion that they refresh themselves by taking an hour's ride in a gondola.

R.T.F.

THE SPIRIT OF ST. FRANCIS OF SALES

Author: Jean Pierre Camus (1584-1652)
Type of work: Spiritual biography
First published: 1641

Principal Ideas Advanced

Spiritual wisdom begins with trust in God rather than in self and ends in perfect forgetfulness of self for God's sake.

The charitable motive of an act, not its heroism in the eyes of men, is the entire measure of its worth in God's sight.

The freedom of every soul must be respected and cherished, never jeopardized by harsh arguments or force even in the name of truth.

In *The Spirit of St. Francis of Sales,* Jean Pierre Camus, friend and spiritual son of the saint, reveals the living example of the virtues taught in Saint Francis's *An Introduction to the Devout Life* (1609) and his treatise, *The Love of God* (1616). The sanctity of Saint Francis is characterized particularly by the union of faith and charity, the fusion of the contemplative and the active life, and the firm belief that the love which comes from God and which we pour out upon the world is the only valid measure of virtue, merit, and happiness. The works of our charity can never be separated from their divine motivations; to rely on faith without works is to mistake the command itself for one's obedience to it. If a man doubts that his works are united to his faith, he is more likely to exaggerate the "feeling" of faith, or the lack of it, in his spiritual life. He becomes concerned about the state of his soul, even though he wills to love God and manifests that will in his life. Francis, involved as he constantly was with the early Protestant reformers, emphasized the necessary union of faith and works as well as the dangers to the spiritual life wrought by excessive scruples and introspection.

Personal experience perhaps had its influence on the conviction of Saint Francis that a man must love God more and think about himself less. As a college student he suffered for an entire month from the belief that he was damned. His mental and physical health deteriorated rapidly under the stress of his despair. The agony was lifted only after he begged the Blessed Virgin to intercede for him. From that time on, he was free to think of matters other than the fate of his own soul. Throughout his life, Saint Francis believed and taught that one must not stay forever at the doorway to the devout life, fruitlessly dwelling on the fact of one's own salvation, but must always go forward in sanctity. The initial assent and submission to God's will are not sufficient for salvation; all through life one's actions must be inspired by charity and faith.

For Saint Francis, love crowns the activity of the will, though a whole spectrum of desires, passions, and affections also flow from the same source. The passions are not, in themselves, evil, but they are capable of being transformed into right desire only by charity and grace. To achieve perfection of motive, one must refer every act to the love of God. Camus quotes Saint Francis: "In charity lies the end of every perfection and the perfection of every end." The saint saw no reason for a bishop to complain that his time for contemplation was too much curtailed by the ceaseless demands of his flock. He himself was always at the disposal of anyone who wished to speak or write to him. "We must look upon the souls of men as resting in the Heart of our Savior," he said, referring the love of man to its ultimate end, the love of God. Since he was able to remain aware of the Presence of God whether he was alone in prayer or busy at his episcopal labors, Francis was never restless, impatient, or abrupt with those who constantly imposed on him. Despite his lifelong interior struggle against anger, his outward mildness and unhurried courtesy toward all was as great as though he were encountering in every man he met the Person of Christ Himself. The Bishop of Belley, wishing very much to know if Francis were as recollected in solitude as he appeared among men, had, in an excess of devotion and curiosity, peepholes bored in the door of his guest room, through which he spied on his saintly friend. He was much edified to see that Francis sat motionless in prayer and meditative reading for hours at a time and that his conduct when he thought himself alone was as holy as it always was in public.

Francis was able to combine the active and contemplative life successfully because he saw existence as one, the Creator never divided from His creation. The life of prayer is built upon the love of God's truth, in the mysteries of doctrine and sacrament as well as in the revelation of God in His works. The life of virtue begins with the recognition that God's will reveals itself to us under the veil of circumstance and that it must be loved without reservation regardless of its mystery and our failure to understand it.

Identity of one's will with God's can be achieved by any Christian, Saint Francis insisted. It is an identity effected by love and learned by constant practice throughout the trials of life. Francis advised the young Bishop of Belley and all those under his direction to love without regard to their own best interests but only in terms of God's concerns. Love of God means honoring Him for what He is and desiring the good that He desires, which is the love of creatures. "To desire anything otherwise than for God is to desire God the less," Francis maintained. Obedience to such a principle of charity prevents one from being excessively immersed in devotional practices or feeling undue disgust at one's own sins. This single unalterable absolute known to us on earth proves also to be the one absolute beyond temporal life and death, for it is participation in that love, not mere personal reward, that we must long for as the supreme reality of present and future life.

What the world flees as pain, the Christian is to bear willingly as the Cross of Christ, which transforms the obedient will and unites it to the will of God. The evil that comes from within us is sin, and we learn to overcome it by "mortification of the heart," rather than of the body. Repeated practice of the humble virtues required by charity and fidelity to one's vocation instruct the soul far more rigorously than do fasts and flagellations,

Francis claimed. Temptation is an evil presenting itself to us from without but seeking a home within us, that it may become sin. Yet temptation is not evil in itself, for it can be a great spur to virtue, urging the soul to greater effort and greater dependence on God. Suffering itself, the evil which the world's wisdom can never make us welcome as a blessing, is a source of eternal benefit to the devout. When endured without restlessness or any desire beyond the accomplishment of God's will, whatever that divine will may prove to be, suffering becomes a veritable ladder to sanctity. Indeed, a man must suffer in order to see reality in clear perspective, his attention undistracted from the Source of his being, the Life by which he is sustained, and the End for which he is destined.

Despite the fact that Saint Francis was often the victim of calumny and contempt, he was always faithful to his belief that the greatest blessing belongs to those who suffer for the sake of justice, and that these sufferers achieve a sacred and singular identity with the suffering Christ. Because Francis dealt so gently and courteously with the Protestants in his diocese of Geneva, more rigorous priests criticized him for laxness. The spirit of the times was not one of conciliation and tact on either side, but of harangues, misrepresentations, and personal slanders. Through this unchristian atmosphere of bitterness and bigotry, the charismatic presence of Francis moved like a wind fresh from Heaven.

As a newly ordained priest, Francis was assigned to the Chablais, an area that had become heavily Protestant. Against the advice of more experienced missionaries there, Francis refused to engage in vituperation and controversy. Instead, he preached his inspiring sermons in decrepit, freezing, nearly empty churches, and performed his priestly duties in the spirit of charity, even when physical abuse and contempt were his reward. When he left the Chablais four years later, the majority of the inhabitants had returned to the practice of the Faith, thus vindicating Francis's belief that the use of Christ's own methods, loving persuasion and example, are far more likely to win men's hearts than the harsh, worldly methods many religious men insist on using.

Francis believed that controversy, whether in sermons or in discussions with non-Catholics, is always a poor method of winning converts. A preacher can better move his listeners by a brief, simple message directed to their hearts than by a relentless, logical appeal to their intellects, especially if his words are supported by evidence of humility and charity in his own life. Francis was strongly against the possession of wealth by the clergy. and, as Bishop of Geneva, he practiced the poverty he advised for others. The example of charity, he believed, was as important in imparting faith to others, as were the words, however well-chosen, one used to convince them. Faith could come only by grace, Francis maintained, and not by proof, and, therefore, the priest must concentrate on acquiring the holiness of life that reveals the grace of God to others in such a manner that they desire it for themselves. Camus says of Saint Francis's universally recognized gifts of persuasion: "Cardinal du Perron used to say that if it were only a question of confounding the heretics, he thought he had found out the secret, but to convert them he felt obliged to send for the Bishop of Geneva."

Francis believed that we must imitate the gentleness of God in our efforts to convince others of His love. It is through the Passion that God most gently and yet most forcefully "constrains" our love. The very law of the mind's being is the freedom of its will. Therefore, it defends itself vehemently against threats of harshness, but submits itself willingly to love. In his direction of souls, Francis practiced his belief that the spirit must be free from excessive rules which constrict and disturb it. Obedience to the love of God should be sufficient to instruct and confirm one in all the virtues of the Christian life.

The aim of Saint Francis in creating the Visitation Order with Saint Jane Frances de Chantal was to effect in the lives of his nuns a purely spiritual conversion. Many of the Visitation sisters were in poor health and could not practice the austerities of other orders. They were enjoined to pursue instead an interior mortification, wholly motivated by love of God and neighbor and manifested in the perfection of humble virtues. Some mockingly called the order the "Confraternity of the descent from the Cross," since it was so deficient in the conventional techniques of monastic asceticism. But Francis taught that one can never truly judge another, since appearances are all too often deceiving. The merit of an action depends on the degree of charity in the heart of the one who performs it, he argued, and that charity can only come from and be judged by God Himself.

Saint Francis, and his devoted follower Camus with him, always returns to the primacy of charity in effecting the surrender of the will to God. Obedience can never be forced and God does not seek to force it. His gift of free will to men is one that allows men to imitate Himself. No man should seek to take from any other his freedom to dispose of himself and the allegiance of his soul, for God alone deserves to possess a man's soul. The marriage of man and God in a perfect, free act of worship should be facilitated but not intruded upon as though what God desires to win by love could be taken by force.

B.J.R.

CARMEN DEO NOSTRO

Author: Richard Crashaw (c.1612-1649)
Type of work: Devotional poetry
First published: 1652

Principal Ideas Advanced

The two most important events of human history are the Incarnation and the Crucifixion.

At the Incarnation Mary's acceptance of God's will counteracted the effects of Eve's disobedience and made possible the salvation of man through the Son.

At the Crucifixion the perfect sacrifice of the Son to the Father reunited men with Him.

These events in all their details are worthy of celebration in poetry.

The poems in *Carmen Deo nostro* are the result of Richard Crashaw's complete dedication of himself to God throughout a life of intellectual and spiritual achievement. The son of an Anglican divine noted for his hatred of the Catholics, Crashaw was attracted to Catholicism while at Cambridge, where he was a close friend of the poet Abraham Cowley (1618-1667) and the Anglican monk Nicholas Ferrar (1592-1637). Crashaw often visited Ferrar's religious house at Little Gidding and delighted in the ascetical life of fasting and prayer. He received his BA. from Pembroke College in 1634, and the following year he was elected to a fellowship at Peterhouse, then the focus of Laudian High-Church sentiment at Cambridge. Under Dr. John Cosin (1594-1672), Master of the College, the Latin service had been restored and the new chapel richly decorated with stained glass from the low countries. Crashaw was appointed curate and catechist of Little St. Mary's and spent his time in teaching, writing, music, and meditation. His sermons were admired and well attended. He was completely at home in his surroundings and in later years spoke of the University as a "little contentfull kingdom." However, it was not long before the bitter political and religious conflicts of the day erupted into open warfare. In 1644, during the confusion of the civil wars, he was deprived of his fellowship and escaped to France where he became a Catholic. However, his conversion was in no sense sudden. Throughout his years at Cambridge he had been increasingly drawn to the spiritual ideals of the monastic life, and a search for their fullest expression brought him inevitably to the Church. Cowley found him in Paris two years later, living in poverty, and introduced him to Queen Henrietta (1609-1666), who gave him a letter of introduction and sent him to Rome. He was discovered there a year later, again living in poverty, by Sir Kenelm Digby (1603-1665), English diplomat, naval commander, and scientist, who brought him to the attention of Pope Innocent X (1574-1655). A short time later Crashaw obtained a post as personal secretary to Cardinal Palotta. He complained, however, about what he considered the wickedness of the men in the Cardinal's retinue, and to protect him from their vengeance the Cardinal sent him to the Basilica-church of Our Lady of Loretto where he was installed as a canon. He was taken sick immediately thereafter, however, and died within a few weeks at the age of thirty-seven. He was an accomplished Latinist and Hellenist and had an intimate knowledge of Spanish and Italian. His skill in painting, engraving and music was admired in his lifetime. *Carmen Deo nostro,* containing his most significant religious poetry, was published in Paris three years after his death.

Crashaw was influenced by George Herbert (1593-1633), Anglican poet and divine, to dedicate himself to religious poetry. *The Temple,* Herbert's only book of poetry, was published in

1633 while Crashaw was at Cambridge. Although he was inspired by the poems, Crashaw's mature style was far different from Herbert's. The poems in *The Temple* are marked by a rhetoric of tightness and economy governed by logic, while Crashaw's poetry is characterized by the use of antithesis and paradox within a verbal structure whose chief end is exaltation and ecstasy, not insight. As Crashaw was drawn to Catholicism, he was swept up by that efflorescence of spiritual and imaginative energy we now call the Counter-Reformation. The saints of the period, Ignatius, Teresa, and John of the Cross among them, were figures of great intellectual power and strength of will, virtues that were accompanied by unusual mystical states: trances, visions, and raptures. Popular piety and the artistic tradition accepted these states as signs of great holiness, and human figures transfixed by the love of God became a characteristic feature of baroque style. In order to dramatize to the fullest the human encounter with the divine, the baroque sought picturesque effects in architecture and plastic and musical effects in poetry, whose structure gradually came less and less under the rule of reason. Behind the baroque vision is the idea that the entire created order has been sanctified through the Incarnation and aspires to be reunited with God. Man delights in the beauties of the temporal world, but only as they embody and help him attain the infinite. The immense longing of the created for the creator is the hallmark of baroque poetry, art, and architecture.

Contemplating the wounds of Christ, Crashaw wrote in "Sancta Maria Dolorum, or the Mother of Sorrows":

> O let me suck the wine
> . . . of this chast vine
> Till drunk of thy dear wounds, I be
> A lost thing to the world, as it to me.

Again, in "Mr. Crashaw's Answer FOR HOPE" he gives dramatic expression to his desire for union with God: "True hope's a glorious hunter and her chase / The God of nature in the fields of grace." Nothing is simply itself in the world of Crashaw's imagery. In "Sainte Mary Magdalene" her eyes are "sister springs / Parents of sylver-footed rills!" Her tears speak: "We goe to meet / A worthy object, our lord's FEET." The sensory world is enticing, but he knows it to be a world of appearances only, constantly impinging on the divine that is the truly real. In his poetry God is the being who encompasses and gives meaning to all the contrarieties of earthly existence. In "To the Name Aboue Every Name, the Name of IESUS," he writes: "SWEET NAME, in Thy each Syllable / A Thousand Blest Arabia's dwell." "In the Gloriovs Epiphanie of Our Lord" expresses the same idea: "O little all! in thy embrace / The world lyes warm, & likes his place." In the same poem he writes: "To THEE, thou DAY of night! thou east of west / Lo we at last haue found the way."

In his dwelling upon duality and paradox as the defining features of temporal life Crashaw was closer to Henry Vaughan (1622-1695), the Anglican poet and mystic, than to any other English poet of the seventeenth century. The dualities, the paradoxes, he perceives, lie at the heart of the Christian view of life. Man is born in this world but is destined for the next; man gains himself by losing himself, sleeps to wake, dies to live, and in the holy sacrament of the altar consumes bread that is not merely bread, but the bread of life, Jesus Christ who is one with the Father. In "The Office of the Holy Crosse" he writes of the Crucifixion: "The captiue world awak't & found / The prisoners loose, the Iaylor bound." The freed prisoners are men liberated from original sin and Satan is the jailor who is bound. In the same poem he sees a paradox in Christ's bearing of the cross: "Lo the faint LAMB, with weary limb / Beares that huge tree which must bear Him." From Christ's eyes "the sun himself drinks Day." Paradox in this sense is a seemingly contradictory belief or statement that is, in some mysterious way, true. The belief that one gains his life by losing it is certainly contradictory if viewed with the eyes of reason alone. However, reason without faith is the wisdom of this world that Saint Paul says must be overthrown if we are to be united with God. Nicholas of Cusa, cardinal, theologian, and mystic, expressed the same idea when he wrote: "The wall of paradise is built of contraries, nor is there any way to enter but for one who has overcome the highest spirit of reason who guards the gate." Eyes that are springs and tears that speak are fit symbols of the major Christian paradox, the willing death of God that men may attain to a spiritual life in eternity, united with the being who in Himself resolves all paradoxes, the being to whom Crashaw's poetry is designed to lead the reader.

It is precisely this, the experience of the divine, that Crashaw's poetry attempts to induce in the reader. His poems ask us to contemplate an object such as the crucifix, or an event such as the Epiphany, realized, of course, in all the concrete details of the wise men and their gifts, while the poet uses meter, assonance, and alliteration to create an atmosphere in which the analytical intellect is put to sleep and the soul may glimpse, at last, the glories of Paradise beyond the wall of contraries. Crashaw wrote perhaps his most inspired poetry in the conclusion of "The Flaming Heart," his poem to Saint Teresa:

By all thy dowr of LIGHTS & FIRES;
By all the eagle in thee, all the doue;
By all thy liues & deaths of loue;
By thy larg draughts of intellectual day,
And by thy thirsts of loue more large than they;
By all thy brim-fill'd Bowles of feirce desire
By thy last Morning's draught of liquid fire;
By the full kingdome of that finall kisse
That seiz'd thy parting Soul, & seal'd thee his;
By all the heau'ns thou hast in him
(Fair sister of the SERAPHIM!)
By all of HIM we haue in THEE;
Leaue nothing of my SELF in me.
Let me so read thy life, that I
Vnto all life of mine may dy.

Although Crashaw is best known for his ecstatic flights, it would be wrong to ignore those poems that proceed from a less exalted mood. Devotional poetry is not noted for variety of tone, and yet Crashaw at times expresses a whimsical humor that one does not expect. In "Temperance, or the Cheap Physitian" he satirizes the man who is too anxious for his health:

Go, take physic Dote upon
Some big-nam'd composition.
Th'Oraculous DOCTOR'S mystik
bills;
Certain hard WORDS made into
pills,
And what at last shalt' gain by
these?
Only a costlyer disease.

A delight in verbal exaggeration for its own sake is evident in his address to man in "Death's Lectvre at the Fvneral of a Yovng Gentleman: "Come man / Hyperbolized NOTHING! know thy span." In his poem to the Countess of Denbigh, the Duke of Buckingham's sister who befriended Crashaw in Paris and eventually became a Catholic, he describes her temporary inability to decide between Anglicanism and Catholicism:

Plead your pretences (o you strong
In weaknesse) why you chuse so
long
In labour of your selfe to ly,
Not daring quite to Live nor Die.

Such lines remind us that Crashaw was as much a self-conscious artist as Spenser, Herrick, or Milton and that even his ecstatic passages were based firmly on the linguistic training of Renaissance humanism.

Crashaw's artistic evolution was marked by a movement from formalism to improvisation. His early poems are characterized by formal patterns of meter and rhyme. As a young man his sense of form was conditioned by the composition of Greek and Latin epigrams based on verses in the Bible, a literary exercise that was part of his schooling. He studied the craft of emblems, symbolic representations of moral and spiritual states that were accompanied by verses explaining their meaning, and the pictorial quality of his mature poetry can be traced to this influence. In his later poetry, especially in the odes, he improvised rhythms, altering the length of lines at will, although in general he continued to use the rhymed couplet. The result of these improvisations is a lilting music reminiscent of Cowley's odes and the pindarics of the late seventeenth century that owed so much to Crashaw. The effect of "Prayer, an Ode, which was Praefixed to a little Prayer-book giuen to a young Gentle-Woman" depends upon the smooth alteration of contrasting rhythms, as in the lines:

It is an armory of light
Let constant vse but keep it bright,
You'l find it yields
To holy hands & humble hearts
More swords & shields
Then sin hath snares, or Hell hath
darts.

The genius of such poetry is that it suggests overall design but never limits itself in order to achieve such a design.

Crashaw's impression on his Anglican contemporaries is expressed by Cowley in the elegy he wrote for the young poet: "Poet and Saint! to thee alone are given / The two most sacred names of earth and heaven." Crashaw's poetry was also praised by the poet Alexander Pope (1688-1744) and attracted the attention of some discerning eighteenth century critics. However, it was inevitable that the Age of Reason would not look with favor upon the ecstatic outpourings of a Catholic mystic, and his work was temporarily forgotten. Coleridge acknowledged the influence of the "Hymn to St. Teresa" upon the second part of his "Christabel," and some scholars think Shelley was familiar with Crashaw's poetry. His reputation grew slowly throughout the nineteenth century, but it was not until the early twentieth century when critical interest in the metaphysical poets revived that he was given his due in the literary world. Crashaw has received more attention in the past thirty years than he did in the preceding three hundred, and he is now regarded as one of the finest devotional poets in the language.

D.M.R.

CURSUS THEOLOGICUS

Author: John of St. Thomas (John Poinsot, 1589-1644)
Type of work: Theological commentary
First published: 1637-1662

Principal Ideas Advanced

Saint Thomas has a greater authority in theology than anyone other than Saint Augustine.

One does well to have a "master" in beginning to study theology (and even philosophy): one is enabled, then, to stand on his master's shoulders and to identify more distinctly at least some avoidable errors; it is in this way that theology (and even philosophy) becomes a co-operative enterprise.

Near the end of the golden age of Spanish Scholasticism lived a man whose assimilation of the philosophy and theology of Saint Thomas Aquinas was regarded by some contemporaries as so thorough that they called him a "second Thomas." This man was John of St. Thomas, or John Poinsot, who taught philosophy and theology for seventeen years at the Dominican College in Alcalà and then taught theology for thirteen years at the University of Alcalà, where he lectured to the largest classes in Spain. These lectures formed the basis for the eight volumes of his commentary on the *Summa Theologiae* of Saint Thomas. The *Cursus theologicus,* as John's work is entitled, together with his briefer commentaries on Aristotle's philosophy, has had an influence on nineteenth and twentieth century Thomism second only to the commentaries of Cardinal Cajetan.

The *Cursus theologicus* is not a commentary on each and every question and article of Saint Thomas's *Summa,* for John followed the then usual practice of discussing only those parts of the *Summa* about which controversy was currently going on in the schools, or which had not, to his mind, been satisfactorily explained by earlier Thomists. Unlike Cajetan, who wrote detailed analyses of the title, logical structure, and presuppositions of each article considered, John of St. Thomas proceeded by writing relatively autonomous "disputations," sometimes two or three on a single key question of the *Summa,* and sometimes only one, treating a problem discussed by Saint Thomas in a dozen questions of the *Summa.*

Three volumes are devoted to questions treated in the Prima Pars of the *Summa;* two volumes treat of issues taken up in the Prima Secundae; one on topics in the Secunda Secundae; and two volumes on questions in the Tertia Pars.

The first volume is one of the most significant, for in addition to three preliminary treatises addressed to "tyros" in theology this volume contains the twenty disputations corresponding to the first fourteen questions of the Prima Pars. The first disputation on the certitude of the principles of theology, a sketch of apologetics, deserves special mention as does the second, a luminous treatment of the nature, object, properties, and scope of theology. Also valuable and influential are the eighth, on the existence of God in things, the four treating of the beatific vision, and the twentieth on *scientia media.*

Volume II has eleven disputations completing John's treatment of God considered in the unity of his nature. Volume III has fourteen disputations on the Trinity and the angels. The twelfth, on the divine processions, and the seventeenth, on the missions of the divine persons, are especially highly regarded, subsidiary as they are to John's profound treatment of the gifts of the Holy Spirit. This latter treatise manifests a mastery of the subject which, it is agreed, has never been equalled.

In the last two volumes on the Tertia Pars, John follows the Scholastic practice of commenting only on the first twenty-six questions of Saint Thomas's treatment of the Incarnation, the later ones being thought to present no great difficulty once the earlier, more fundamental ones had been analyzed. John's treatment of the sacraments is especially noteworthy for his defense of their instrumental physical causality. Only the first four volumes up to the treatise on the gifts of the Holy Spirit were edited and revised by John himself; the others were edited from John's lecture notes by his friend Ramírez.

John's style is simple and clear, though somewhat diffuse. He was not timid about inventing Latin barbarisms if a barbarism would help make his ideas lucid. Clarity was his single and exclusive literary objective; and every other aspect of composition, including, on occasion, grammatical propriety and stylistic felicity, was subordinated to it.

The disputations are usually composed of two or more articles. Each article ordinarily includes the following elements: statement of the question: *Utrum* (whether) . . . ; the reasons why the question is appropriate; various opinions of Scholastics on the issue; John's own opinion, stated in one or more theses; discussion of the relation between John's position and that of Saint Thomas; the making of distinctions and the specifying of the presuppositions and principles on which John's solution to the question rests; finally, a reply to the arguments of the Scholastics with whom John disagrees.

John was himself a Scholastic, a Schoolman, by his very title not an isolated individual but a member of a professional community with a strong sense of tradition. His education had impressed him with the importance of making his first approach to truth as a disciple, and since he realized that

Plato was a disciple of Socrates, Aristotle of Plato, and Saint Thomas of Saint Albert, he firmly believed that unless one established oneself in the tradition of the perennial philosophy, one would make the same mistakes repeatedly.

What discipleship meant to John he spelled out in one of the three preliminary treatises of Volume I addressed to tyros. (The other two treatises are outlines and explanations of the order and parts of the *Sentences* of Peter Lombard, and of the *Summa theologiae* of Saint Thomas: "The principal and most efficacious means for discovering and penetrating the thought of the Angelic Doctor consists above all in coming to know the order he followed in the composition of the *Summa*.") Entitled "Treatise on the Approbation and Authority of the Doctrine of St. Thomas," this work is divided into two disputations, in the first of which John reviews the signs of approval given in papal documents, in Canon Law, and in the liturgy, and he concludes that Saint Thomas stands with Saint Augustine in having received a degree of approbation higher than that given any other theologian. The second disputation is devoted to answering those who claimed to have found errors in Saint Thomas, and it concludes with a chapter discussing what it is that leads to a true understanding and discipleship of Saint Thomas.

This defense of Saint Thomas, John tells us, is not "to vindicate some private person but to vindicate the judgment of the whole Church and of its Apostolic approbation. And so what is received and defended is not Thomas himself but what is found in Thomas." The Church has not only permitted the writings of Saint Thomas to be published, has not only approved the establishment of a "chair" in one or more universities, has not only established him as a Doctor of the Church, but also has given to all his works a sort of general approval granted only to one other; namely Saint Augustine. One could, of course, according to John, adopt without any sort of censure a philosophical opinion contradicting that of Saint Thomas, so long as this was done without contempt for what was generally approved by the Church.

To be a faithful disciple of Thomas, John says, one must follow his doctrine as true and catholic, and what is equally important, contribute with all one's powers to its development. It is not a condition, but rather a goal, of discipleship, that one never depart from Thomas, for one must at all events hold on to what one sees of the truth. But many claim to be Thomists and yet disagree with one another—can all be disciples? What are the signs of true discipleship? There are five, claims John, and the best is that one accept and continue the work of those who, in the course of time, have clearly been followers of Thomas. And the disciple will bend every effort to defending and developing Saint Thomas's teachings. Nor will he ever use Thomas's texts only to bolster his own personal opinion. He will not only see Thomas's conclusions as sound, but he will also attempt to see that Thomas's reasons, whether demonstrative or dialectical, are "proper." And finally, a disciple will find himself in accord with common tradition in the interpretation of Saint Thomas's text.

A true disciple himself by these criteria, John could declare on his deathbed: "For thirty years I have neither written nor taught anything which I did not judge consonant with the teaching of the Angelic Doctor." He devoted his energy to the fight against what he believed to be the betrayal of truth and of Saint Thomas in the writings of Gabriel Vasquez (c. 1549-1604) and Francisco Suarez (1548-1617), both of whom claimed to be Thomists but who, by John's standards, were philosophical and theological eclectics.

It is clear that one cannot reasonably expect to find novelty and originality in the writings of John of St. Thomas, for he believed that theological progress consists less in finding new conclusions than in perceiving better reasons for conclusions already held. A dialectical proof of a proposition will be improved by finding a new middle term which leads to demonstrative certitude. The effect, then, of what John recommended is the displacement of the frontiers of the probable and the certain and the opening up of new areas to probable demonstration. An eloquent witness to the value of this method is his brilliant treatise on the gifts of the Holy Spirit, a model of the value of Thomist methodology. There are only a few instances in which John holds opinions, which are today commonly rejected, as being true and Thomistic, as, for example, his placement of the formal constituent of Deity in the actual intellection of God by Himself.

John recognized, of course, that in philosophy the only appropriate place for the exercise of authority is that of assisting in the crucial choice of a first teacher; that is, of pointing out that the philosophy of St. Thomas is an apposite means to philosophical formation and occupies a privileged position with respect to theological approbation.

John does not recommend that the assent to philosophical propositions rest on ecclesiastical faith rather than on evidence. Authority in philosophy can pertain only to the realm of the practical. What he had in mind was this: the Church, recognizing the practical importance of intellectual *mores,* of what one is used to hearing, recommends beginning one's study with Saint Thomas; after a period of apprenticeship some will find, as John did, that the more deeply Thomas is studied, the more evidently does philosophical or theological truth shine through his words. If one does not agree with Thomas, it is probably because one has been badly taught, John believes. He grants critics the right to disagree with Saint Thomas, however, provided they do not scorn the right of the Church to approve Thomas as a philosopher and theologian whose writings are coherent and harmonious with her own teachings.

R.L.C.

DISCOURSE ON UNIVERSAL HISTORY

Author: Jacques Bénigne Bossuet (1627-1704)
Type of work: Philosophy of history
First published: 1681

Principal Ideas Advanced

God shines forth in history; only the willfully blind can fail to find Him working His marvels, using men and empires to do His will in history.

The Judeo-Christian religion has made continuous, steady progress in history, while a succession of worldly empires has crossed the stage of history, each accomplishing its divinely ordained purpose and then coming to an end.

The Church triumphs over idolatry and all errors.

Bossuet was a prominent French bishop who was appointed tutor of the French dauphin, son of Louis XIV, in 1670. He prepared his *Discours sur l'histoire universelle* for the dauphin's instruction, for it was commonly believed in the seventeenth century that future rulers could learn much of statecraft from studying the successes and failures of their predecessors.

But it is evident that Bossuet had a larger audience in mind. He considered himself the defender of orthodox Roman Catholic teaching against both Protestants and skeptics, and it is against them, especially the latter, that the *Discours* was directed. This is an unfinished work, taking the reader from the creation of Adam to the reign of Charlemagne, which Bossuet considers the end of ancient history and the beginning of the "last epoch," or modern history. In coursing from Adam to Charlemagne, Bossuet concludes, the reader has learned "all the secrets" of universal history—probably the principal reason why Bossuet did not complete the work, which was apparently to center on France and culminate in the reign of Louis XIV.

The *Discours* is divided into three books, treating respectively of general history, religious history, and the history of empires as related to religious history. In the first book Bossuet divides the past into "ages" and "epochs." There are seven ages in world history, the last beginning with the birth of Christ, whereas there are twelve epochs, each beginning with "some great event, to which everything else is related." These epochs of universal history begin respectively with Adam, Noah, Abraham, Moses, the taking of Troy by the Greeks, Salomon, the founding of Rome, Cyrus the Great, the conquest of Carthage, the birth of Christ, Constantine, and Charlemagne.

The second book deals with the religious history of the Jews and Christians from Abraham's calling to the conversion of the Gentiles. Bossuet bases this book almost exclusively on the Bible. In the third book he describes the history of ancient empires, tracing their rise and fall in broad strokes and seeing them as instruments of divine providence whereby God prepared the world for the coming of Christ. Thus God used the Assyrians and Babylonians to punish His chosen people, as He used the Persians to reestablish the Jews, Alexander the Great to protect them, and Roman rulers to safeguard their religious freedom against Syrian kings.

The purpose of Bossuet's *Discours* is to justify the ways of God to man against the skeptics of his time. "The freethinkers," he writes, "declare war on divine providence and they find no better argument against it than the distribution of good and evil which seems unjust and irrational, since it does not discriminate between the good and the wicked. It is there that the godless ones entrench themselves as in an impregnable fortress from which they throw bold missiles at the divine wisdom which rules the world, falsely convinced as they are that the apparent disorder of human affairs is an evidence against this very wisdom." A proper understanding of history will correct this view, Bossuet argued, for then "you will see only wisdom where you saw disorder."

The distinctive feature of Bossuet's *Discours sur l'histoire universelle* is the all-important role given to divine providence. He uses both Biblical revelation and historical events to demonstrate that providence is the ultimate efficient cause of the historical process. God not only sustains and directs the entire series of secondary causes, but frequently interferes directly, suspending their natural effects or enabling them to produce results beyond their natural powers. Evidence of this direct interference is found in miracles, prophecies, and theophanies. The third book is especially replete with references to providence, with God using worldly empires to effect His designs. The classic example is His using the Romans to prepare the world for the coming of Christ and the spread of Christianity, as well as to test the early Christians and purify their faith in martyrdom. Bossuet holds that it is evident that "it is He who forms kingdoms, in order to give them to whomever He will. . . . He knows how to make them subservient, in His own good time and order, to the designs He has upon His people."

Bossuet holds that there is no such thing as chance or fate. "What seems chance to our weak minds is part of a design conceived in the eternal mind, uniting all causes and effects in one single order." Were we to grasp the whole of history, the pattern would become clear and each "chance event" would fall into place. No one can use his mind or will to thwart God's design. "There is no human power," Bossuet insists, "that does not minister, whether it will or not, to other designs than its own." These are the designs of God, who created time and history, and is in perfect control of these creatures.

Although Bossuet appears to accord an overweening importance to divine providences, he does not eliminate secondary causes as influencing the course of history. Men and empires, individual events and particular happenings all influence history. Bossuet warns his readers that they must search for hidden factors, as well as for great ideas and outstanding men who have brought about changes at each stage of history. However, these causes do not operate independently. They are the secondary causes through which providence operates. "The long sequence of particular events, which make and unmake empires," Bossuet tells us, "depends upon the secret orders of divine providence. God from the highest heavens holds the reins of all the kingdoms of the earth. . . . Thus it is that God reigns over all nations. Let us talk no more of chance, or of fortune, or talk of them only as names with which we cover our ignorance."

Bossuet's *Discours sur l'histoire universelle* was, until the twentieth century, the last important Catholic statement on the meaning of history. It is generally criticized for having attempted to prove too much. Bossuet makes divine providence to the image and likeness of Louis XIV, an arbitrary, willful God who interferes with the natural course of events capriciously. Such a view of providence somewhat caricatured the standard Christian concept of the intellectual God whose will is done through freely acting persons and other secondary causes.

Voltaire admired Bossuet's "lofty, vigorous" style, but he condemned him for devoting so much space to a minor tribe of ancient history, the Jews, while ignoring the Chinese, Indian, and Moslem empires, which included many more people than Bossuet's Christendom. The use of the adjective *universelle* was unfortunate, for Bossuet did not write a discourse on *universal* history. Rather he wrote a discourse on Judeo-Christian history. To him and to most Christians of his age this was the only history that mattered.

The *Discours* was an influential book. Sainte-Beuve called it one of the "three great monuments of Christian literature in the seventeenth century." About two hundred editions, impressions, or printings of the book have been made. It was first translated into English in 1686, and one version or another appeared in most of the European languages. Its influence was cut short by advances in historical scholarship and Biblical criticism, both of which made Bossuet's sweeping claims appear unscholarly. But it is still recognized as a masterful statement of a Christian view of history in the seventeenth century, and as a work whose influence was strong for two centuries after its publication.

T.P.N.

THE HIND AND THE PANTHER

Author: John Dryden (1631-1700)
Type of work: Religious didactic poem
First published: 1687

Principal Ideas Advanced

Man must place all his confidence in knowledge gained through faith, in an infusion from divine sources, rather than in his own insufficient rational faculties.

Private interpretation of Scripture leads only to inconclusive debate; man must have an ultimate authority on which he can rely: the Roman Catholic Church (represented in the poem by the gentle Hind).

The Hind, which has been preyed on in England by various beasts (Protestant sects) but is now protected by the Lion (King James II), debates with the Panther (the Anglican Church) and attempts to win it over to reconciliation by showing the futility of the Anglican policies (trying to balance reason and private interpretation of Scripture with authority and tradition); however, the Hind and the Panther cannot finally agree.

In *The Hind and the Panther,* John Dryden presents not only a defense of the Roman Catholic faith and an attempt to consider the possibility of reconciliation between the Anglican and Roman Catholic Churches, but also a description of the skeptical position that led him to place his confidence in faith over reason, and, in particular, in a religion that claims infallibility. A conservative in politics as well (he was a Tory), Dryden desired a secure religious position to relieve the anxiety of uncertainty. He makes clear such a desire in the lines: "Rest then, my soul, from endless anguish freed: / Nor sciences thy guide, nor sense thy creed./ Faith is the best ensurer of thy bliss." His position is that if one accepts faith as his guide, then "Vain is the farther search of human wit. . . ." He need not rack his reason to try to understand such mysteries as the Trinity or Transubstantiation.

In *Religio Laici,* a poem written in 1682, Dryden had espoused the Anglican position while presenting his fideistic philosophy, but that same philosophy led him from the via media of Anglicanism to the dogmatic but more secure Roman Church. Having been converted to the latter by 1686, Dryden states in *The Hind and the Panther* (1687) that Anglicanism "wants innate authority" because it has rebelled against the Fathers of the Church and against Tradition. It thus is vulnerable to attack from other Reformers, such as the Presbyterians and Baptists. With the old authority gone, Anglicans attempt to rely (at least partially) on private interpretation of the Bible, but so long as each man may interpret for himself then "Our airy faith will no foundation find. . . ." By attempting to reform, Anglicanism had put itself at the mercy of other Reformers and is reduced to a "mere mock queen of a divided herd. . . ."

While Dryden's own skeptical-fideistic philosophy is interwoven into its structure, the three-part poem is basically organized around the relationship between Roman Catholicism (the Hind), and the various Protestant sects in England, particularly Anglicanism (the Panther). The first part of the poem gives a general description of the situation, in which the gentle Hind and her young have been prey to various beasts (for example, the Bear stands for the Independents, the Boar for the Anabaptists); but the Hind is now protected from the beasts by the Lion (King James II, himself a Roman Catholic). Dryden, in voicing his displeasure at religious persecution and violence, ironically develops the point that man was distinguished from the beasts by being created with "mercy mix'd with reason."

Three major portraits dominate the first part of the poem. One, of course, is that of the Hind, who is characterized succinctly in the famous opening lines of the poem: "A MILK-WHITE Hind, immortal and unchang'd,/ Fed on the lawns, and in the forest rang'd; / Without unspotted, innocent within, / She feared no danger, for she knew no sin." In contrast to this gentle, humble animal, Dryden develops at length a portrait of the Wolf (Presbyterianism), a beast with gaunt belly and famished face, with "predestinating ears," who has a hatred for kings, and advocates commonwealths and presbyteries. The third portrait is of the Panther, whom Dryden represents as the most attractive of the Hind's enemies, and in fact one which is often confused with the Hind herself (by the extreme

Reformers) because most like her. The Panther is "fairest creature of the spotted kind," and "least deformed, because reformed the least." However, the Panther cannot control others after she herself has rebelled.

Dryden treats the Panther in a mild manner, reflecting the hope (held by James II and many other Roman Catholics) that she and the Hind might be reconciled. This possibility is encouraged when, at the close of the first part of the poem, the Panther acts mannerly towards the Hind and desires conversation. The Hind readily agrees.

As he announces in his preface to the poem, Dryden attempts to give to the first part, which is a general discussion, "the majestic turn of heroic poesy" (high style, with its aim being to move the reader). Therefore, he uses such devices as epic similes and catalogues and the poetry is imagistic and figured. The second part, concerned with matter of dispute between the Hind and the Panther, is made "plain and perspicuous" (low style, to persuade). The third part, which is conversational, containing fables that the Hind and the Panther narrate, is to be "more free and familiar" than the previous two. Thus, Dryden attempts to present the basic religious situation in three episodes with three different levels of style.

The second part of the poem begins with the Panther showing sympathy towards the Hind, telling her that "times are mended well,/ Since late among the Philistines you fell"; but the two soon fall into dispute over the question of the Real Presence in the sacrament of Holy Eucharist. This leads to the question of Infallibility, with the Hind holding that it resides in the joint decrees of the pope and the General Councils. Further points of dispute are private interpretation of Scripture, and the value of Tradition. The Hind criticizes the halfway position of the Panther "Pretending Church authority to fix,/ And yet some grains of private spirit mix . . ."; and claims that an authoritative guide on earth is needed since "discord cannot end without a last appeal." The Hind claims that she herself is that authority—the other churches clearly make no claim of infallibility—and then states that she alone possesses the marks of the true Church as set forth in the Nicene Creed. Finally, in lines that develop in emotional intensity, the Hind invites the Panther to return to Christ's Church (herself) and be welcomed with open arms, as the Prodigal Son was welcomed on his return. But the emotional spell is broken with the approach of night, and the Hind once more shows sympathy and charity by inviting the Panther to be her guest that night rather than to chance traveling in the dark when evil-minded beasts might do her harm. Thus, this last invitation parallels the former one: the Hind is seeking reconciliation, inviting the Panther to find true rest with the true Church.

In the third part of the poem, the sympathy betwen the Hind and the Panther breaks down, with the Panther showing the malice and disdain it had been concealing, and the Hind becoming much more biting in her comments on the Panther. Some scholars are of the opinion that Dryden has this tension develop because this part of the poem was written about the time that James II's attempts to form an alliance with the Anglicans against the nonconformists and his attempts to get the Anglicans to repeal legislation discriminating against Roman Catholics had failed. In any case, the Hind becomes sharper with the Panther, saying that many who may act as her supposed followers and friends do so only for "a little coin" or for "Fat bishoprics. . . ." The Panther replies that many of the Hind's converts followed her only to be fed; the Hind counterattacks. Their dispute then concerns itself with satiric commentary on contemporary political-religious situations: the Panther tells the fable of the swallows who decided not to cross the sea to escape the coming winter (Roman Catholics who would not flee from England to the Continent) and who, because of the foolish advice of the Martin (Father Petres), died when winter came. In this fable Dryden satirizes the Jesuit adviser to James II, Father Petres, for advising the Roman Catholics to stay in England even after James II's rather rash attempts to manipulate members of the House of Commons to repeal anti-papist legislation. This same Father Petres had encouraged the king in these political maneuvers. Seemingly in favor of moderate policies on the part of the king, Dryden prophesies in this fable the possible new persecutions that could come to the Roman Catholics if James continued his rash manipulations.

Upon hearing the Panther's fable, the Hind is willing to admit that every church has its extremists (adding that the Panther's has more than hers), but rebukes the Panther for retaining the Test Act of 1678 against the king's request for repeal. The fable the Hind tells concerns extremists within the Anglican Church, represented by well-fed doves, who grudge the small fare that the chickens (Roman Catholics) are able to partake of, so they slander them, then find the Buzzard (Bishop Burnet) to lead their attack. At last, the keeper of the birds (King James II) proclaims all birds free (the Declaration of Indulgence, 1687), and the Buzzard loses his power. This last part of the poem ends with no reconciliation, but it does present criticisms and satires on extremists in both churches, and it shows that both the Hind and the Panther are for moderation. With regard to the fate of the Roman Catholic Church, the poem ends with these lines on the Hind as she retires to rest after the fables are told: "Ten thousand angels on her slumbers wait/ With glorious visions of her future state."

Though *The Hind and the Panther* quickly passed through many editions, it was more notorious than popular (as could be expected with a predominantly Anglican or at least Protestant audience): most people read it to disagree with or condemn rather than praise it. Various suggestions were made that Dryden converted to Roman Catholicism only for financial reward or favor from James II, but Dryden remained true to his new faith even when Protestant rule returned with William and Mary after the death of James, and because he would not take the oath of allegiance to the new rulers he lost the pensions he had been receiving from the crown since the time of Charles II. Thereafter, he had considerable difficulty raising money, and sustained many attacks on his work and his character. It is therefore likely that his real motive for conversion was his skeptical-fideistic philosophy which moved him towards a religion in which he felt he could rest secure.

F.P.C.

THE AUTOBIOGRAPHY OF SAINT MARGARET MARY ALACOQUE

Author: Saint Margaret Mary Alacoque (1647-1690)
Type of work: Spiritual autobiography
First published: 1726

Principal Ideas Advanced

In an age permeated by Calvinism and Jansenism, God chose to remind men of His love and mercy.

He made use of a Visitation nun of Paray-le-Monial, France, Saint Margaret Mary Alacoque, as His instrument in revealing to all men the love of His Sacred Heart for them.

In the three Great Revelations, our Lord, after reassuring her of his love for all men and for her in particular, complained of the ingratitude shown His Heart and asked for a public reparation by means of the establishment of the Feast of the Sacred Heart and an act of solemn consecration to It on that day.

The Autobiography of Saint Margaret Mary Alacoque is the work of a Visitation nun of Paray-le-Monial, France. Written in obedience to her director, Father Francis J. Rolin, S.J., and intended for him alone, the *Life* is completely devoid of literary polish. It describes candidly and simply the extraordinary condescension and intimate relations of the Second Person of the Blessed Trinity with one of His lowly creatures. There are no dates recorded in it, no names of persons, with the exception of that of Blessed Claude de la Colombiere, S.J., who was occasional confessor of the nuns from 1675 to 1676. Several times in the work, Saint Margaret Mary expresses her extreme repugnance to her task, but our Lord assured her of His help and told her He wished His graces to her to be made known to all men. She was to be the "channel" for communicating them, and their publication would make His graces "open to every kind of examination and test."

Necessary to an understanding of the account is the age in which the saint lived. Calvinism with its doctrine of predestination and Jansenism with its excessive stress on the holiness of God discouraged souls from approaching Him. From her earliest childhood, our Lord chose and prepared Margaret Mary to be an instrument that would be heroically responsive to the graces He would give her to draw men to the forgotten human love and tender mercy of the Christ of the Gospels.

When Margaret Mary was only four years old, our Lord treated her as His bride, inspiring her at that early age to make a vow of chastity, even though she understood neither the word "vow" nor the word "chastity." Quite soon thereafter, however, she gained some realization of her dignity as spouse of Christ. This awareness made her scrutinize her interior and exterior acts with a fidelity that appalls men of less spiritual insight, who are unable to comprehend, as the saints do, the gravity of the slightest offense against an infinite God. Because of her attraction to prayer, Margaret Mary often withdrew from games with other little girls; she endured patiently the trials of illness and the persecutions of relatives. Whenever she allowed herself even ordinary pleasures, she felt ungrateful to God and imposed upon herself penances for these "crimes." Her accounts of her great fear of offending God and of doing her own will in preference to His, and of her continual internal and external sufferings, make uncomfortable reading for the less sensitive. In addition, she wrote of the conflict between her higher and lower natures that caused her to seek enjoyments which she always afterwards regretted. However, to those who can penetrate beneath the surface, the saint appears just as she truly was, a great servant of God, whose only desire was to love Him and to express her love by suffering in order to be like her divine Spouse in His crucified life. She was selected by our Lord Himself, with much resistance on her part, to be the apostle of the public devotion to the Sacred Heart, a devotion which, in imitation of Christ's love for men, entails sacrifice. In conforming herself to His choice for her, she finally found true happiness and peace.

Her memoirs reveal that Margaret Mary was deeply attracted to obedience because she was convinced that in no other way could she please God. Her unusual home situation, in which her mother, Madame Alacoque, after her husband's death, had surrendered all her authority into the hands of Margaret Mary's grandmother and two aunts, gave the young girl ample opportunity to practice this virtue. Since everything in the house was under lock and key, she was required to ask permission not only of her mother, but of these "three persons," as she calls them, each time a need arose. Her charity always disregarded secondary causes and saw God's hand in these restrictions. The saint's desire for the religious life, implanted in her by her Spouse met with violent opposition from her family, especially her mother, whose illness the rest of the family blamed on the daughter. At last, having won their consent, Margaret Mary did enter the Monastery of the Visitation in Paray. Upon her first visit to the parlor there, she heard the words, "It is here that I would have thee to be."

Once in the cloister, the young postulant looked upon the Mistress of Novices as Jesus Christ on earth, and in her dependence she was happy. While reserving for Himself the care of her prayer life, our Lord insisted on an exact submission to her superiors in every other matter. For Margaret Mary, obedience was inextricably joined to self-renunciation. In proof of this, she relates numerous incidents. There was the occasion when Saint Francis de Sales, founder of the Order of the Visitation, appeared to her and corrected her sternly for having gone beyond the intention of her mistress in exceeding a permission for a penance. He told her that obedience, not austerity, was the foundation of the Visitation. Again, when she had taken the discipline beyond the allotted time, our Lord Himself voiced His displeasure and told her that the extra strokes had been for the Devil. When Margaret Mary was on the verge of being dismissed because of her extraordinary ways, Christ repeated His injunction about the value of submission and emphasized that she was to do nothing without the consent of her superiors, even when their commands should contradict His. A few times, the saint writes, she was sent to ask our Lord to cure her bodily ailments in order that the healing might be a sign that He was at work within her. Cures always followed at once.

Since prayer was to be of such importance in Margaret Mary's life, it was fitting that our Lord should make Himself her Master in it. All her requests to learn the different methods of prayer from human teachers came to nothing. Having once asked the Mistress of Novices to teach her to pray, she was told to place herself "like a blank canvas before a painter." Not knowing what to do, she heard an inner voice whisper, "Come, and I will teach thee." The saint enjoyed the gift of passive prayer, a gift that even those who experience it cannot explain. After her profession she describes it in this way: "I saw and felt Him close to me, and heard His voice much better than if it had been with my bodily senses." Again she said, "He deigned to converse with me sometimes as a friend, at other times as a spouse passionately in love, again as a father who dearly loves His only child, or under other titles." Often during times of community prayer, her superiors, to try her virtue, would bid her do manual work, and if she asked to make up her prayer later, she was told that she could make it up equally well while working. During her profession retreat, she was given the charge of looking after a lively ass and its foal all day long every day of the retreat. But our Lord, who is everywhere, gave her an especially deep understanding of His Passion and Death in the midst of this occupation so that she had never been happier in His presence. One day while she was picking hemp with the other sisters and had withdrawn a little into a courtyard to be nearer the chapel, the Heart of Jesus appeared to her surrounded by seraphim, who sang, "Love triumphs, love enjoys, the love of the Sacred Heart rejoices." These blessed spirits invited Margaret Mary to unite her praise with theirs and made an agreement with her that they would represent her before the Blessed Sacrament that she might offer homage unceasingly.

Frequently the saint refers to the "two sanctities" that our Lord held constantly before her, the one of love and the other of justice. The sanctity of love made her suffer for the souls in purgatory, that of justice made her offer herself as a victim for sinners, especially for the unfaithful souls among those consecrated to Him. Saint Margaret Mary took upon herself the most excruciating chastisements to avert the punishment of God from individual sinners as well as from whole religious communities.

All of Christ's exceptional gifts to Margaret Mary had as their purpose to make her the messenger of His love for men. He had singled her out to be the "beloved disciple" of His Sacred Heart in an age when men had lost sight of the human, personal element of that love. Though devotion to the Heart of Jesus had been known to a few before her time, it was she who, with the help of Blessed Claude de la Colombiere, had the unique mission of making this devotion public. The visions and "Great Revelations" granted her have had a transforming effect on countless lives and are among the reasons for the revivifying of devotion to the Blessed Eucharist today.

In the first of these Great Revelations, after our Lord had disclosed His great love for all men and for her in particular, He told her she must be the means of spreading to all human hearts the infinite charity He had revealed to her.

In the second Great Revelation, Christ complained to the saint of the ingratitude that men showed in return for the excessive love that had driven Him to become incarnate and to redeem His creatures. He pleaded with her to make reparation to Him in the Sacrament of His love.

Finally, as in the previous revelations, our Lord renewed His appeals for love in the third Great Revelation and requested the establishment of a special feast to honor His Heart on the Friday after the octave of Corpus Christi. He desired that on that day all would communicate and make a solemn act of reparation.

From these revelations and the specific request of our Lord stemmed the universal practices of the nine First Friday, reparative Communions, and the Holy Hour.

Saint Margaret Mary's story of her life ends abruptly, for with the departure from Paray of Father Rolin, S.J., who had bidden her to write it, she felt no longer bound to continue it. The little book, unfinished and lacking in style, nevertheless is read as a classic by Christians everywhere, for its contents tell the amazing story of the incomprehensible love of God for men.

While there is much to marvel at in the life of this saint, even the skeptics must admit that the mental balance she maintained in the face of the most virulent opposition from others and her own doubts about the origin of her visions was little short of miraculous. Indeed, her sanity was questioned by some, but her superiors were reassured when Father Colombiere, a wise director of souls, declared that her virtues, especially her obedience and humility, were proof of the authenticity of her revelations. While the Church has established the practices asked by our Lord of Saint Margaret Mary, it does not require of any of its members that they accept a private revelation of this nature, despite the many proofs demanded to show the saint's sincerity and holiness both during her life and after.

Sister J.M.

THE NEW SCIENCE

Author: Giovanni Battista Vico (1668-1744)
Type of work: Philosophy of history
First published: 1725; definitive edition, 1744

Principal Ideas Advanced

The key to the knowledge of history lies in the structure of the human mind, its "modifications."

The modifications of the human mind are differentiated on a dual basis, the one analytical, the other temporal.

History is the temporal movement of the human spirit.

The human mind acts out and expresses this conscious movement in its civil institutions.

The rationale of historiography is the reflective recovery of the movement of the human mind from the finite to the infinite, from sense to idea, from passion to wisdom.

The *New Science* of Giambattista Vico is variously looked upon as the last and greatest achievement of the spirit of Italian humanism or the first fruits of the spirit of Romanticism. From either view it constitutes the greatest single rebuke to the spirit of the Enlightenment. And it is looked upon finally as the first great document of modern man's sense of history in the profound sense of the historicity of his own being and existence, realizing all the historical longings of the Renaissance and by the same token anticipating the historicism of the romantic age.

All Vico's work before the appearance of the *First New Science* (1725) is considered by historians of ideas and was looked upon by Vico as preparation for that work; and all his subsequent effort, until his death and the posthumous appearance of the definitive version the *Second New Science* in 1744, the perfecting of that labor. The version of 1744 is universally considered to transcend all earlier forms; hence, when the *New Science* is spoken of *simplicter,* it is this version to which reference is being made.

Vico speaks of the method of the *New Science* as geometrical. This should be understood to indicate his persuasion as to the certainty of its conclusions, which he considered to be superior to that of mathematics. He had already in earlier criticisms of the Cartesian philosophy rejected mathematics as normative among the sciences. His own method may best be called hermeneutical; for it resides in the reconstruction of the principles and patterns of past cultures on the basis of the analysis of documents in the light of aesthetic and expressive principles. The central principle of all culture is language; language, however, is not to be restricted to the written word, but is to include the full range of expressive forms from "real words" to the most refined and abstract philosophical discourse.

The general structure of the work falls into five books. The whole is preceded, however, by a symbolic picture upon which a commentary is composed which serves to indicate the "idea of the work." Vico summarizes this commentary in the following fashion: "Last of all, to state the idea of the book in the briefest possible summary, the entire engraving represents the three worlds in the order in which the human minds of the gentiles have been raised from heaven to earth. All the hieroglyphs visible on the ground denote the world of nations to which men applied themselves before all else. The globe in the middle represents the world of nature which the physicists later observed. The hieroglyphs above signify the world of minds and of God which the metaphysicians finally contemplated."

The first book is entitled "Establishment of Principles" and falls in its turn into four sections. Here it becomes apparent that the basic movement of Vico's exposition is a series of recapitulations. The basic insights are stated in diverse forms which serve to corroborate one another. Thus, the first section of the book of principles is devoted to the reconstruction of the chronology of the ancient Occidental world. It is obvious that this undertaking presupposes all that Vico will eventually seek to establish in the subsequent books; such a reconstruction could only be the result or product of the *New Science.* In this section Vico takes issue with such earlier authors who had advanced theories about the chronology of ancient Western culture. By the range of his references Vico lifts the veil slightly upon the vast and heterogeneous reading which underlay the composition of the *New Science,* the authors cited ranging from the classics to the most contemporary classicists and Biblical and Gentile antiquaries. Here, too, Vico reveals his preference for the pattern which will shape his own thought and which he ascribes to the antiquities of the Egyptians; they had identified the three ages of preceding time: that of the Gods, that of the heroes, and that of men; the three corresponding languages, hieroglyphic, symbolic, and epistolary; and he remarks that the division of Varro, whom he respects immensely, reduces to this pattern.

The second section of this first book is called that of "Elements." Here occur the great "dignita" or maxims by which Vico's thought is guided and in which his profoundest insights are expressed. These elements are axioms for the treatment of particular matters in the reconstruction of "poetic" wisdom; in themselves they represent dense compactions of reading and reflection molded, as were the axioms of Spinoza's *Ethics* to take on the form of "self-evident" propositions from which the argument could take its point of departure. This section and its spirit and flavor may best be indicated by citing a few of these elements: "Because of the indefinite nature of the human mind, wherever it is lost in ignorance, man makes himself the measure of all things"; ". . . whenever men can form no idea of distant and unknown things they judge them by what is familiar and close at hand . . ."; ". . . every nation has had the same conceit that it before all other nations invented the comforts of human life and that its remembered history goes back to the very beginning of the world . . ."; "Uniform ideas originating among entire peoples unknown to each other must have a common ground of truth."

As the list of these elements grows, however, it again becomes clear that the method of recapitulation and corroboration is at work; in this form are synthesized the author's insights into the world of classical and prehistoric culture and the principles of universal history which are later to be deployed in more open exposition.

The third section is called that of "Principles." This section is fundamental to the whole work, for here appears that most basic of all the insights of the *New Science,* inimitably expressed by Vico in his own quasi-prophetic and archaic manner: "But in the thick darkness enveloping the earliest antiquity, so remote from ourselves, there shines the eternal and never failing light of a truth beyond all question:

that the world of civil society has certainly been made by men and that its principles are therefore to be found within the modifications of the human mind."

Vico goes on to identify the principles of civil order as those things which all men have agreed on; these three principles prove to be: religion, marriage, and burial. These principles will provide recurring and controlling motifs for the entire undertaking of poetic wisdom.

The fourth section of the first book is dedicated to "Method." The essence and the quality of this book may be immediately indicated by the statement in paragraph 347, a statement which contains the essence of the Vichian method: ". . . in search of these natures of human things our science proceeds by a severe analysis of human thoughts about the human necessities or utilities of social life which are the two perennial springs of the natural law of nations. . . . our science is therefore a history of human ideas . . . and takes its start when the first men began to think humanly and not when the philosophers began to reflect upon human ideas. . . ."

The second book contains the heart of the *New Science* and represents Vico's supreme achievement in terms of his own science. It is a synthesis of "poetic wisdom," the re-creation, on the basis of documents viewed as expression, and hence from within, of the world of ideas of primitive man, according to the doctrine of the modifications of the human mind, a doctrine which regards man as dominated by the poetic consciousness. Vico indicates the basis of this undertaking in the axioms of the second section of the first book on *Principles,* especially Axiom 202, which indicates that all the histories of Gentile nations had fabulous beginnings through the poetic, that is, the spontaneous, imaginative, passional consciousness of the first men. Vico proceeds by giving a definition of wisdom in the manner of the philosophers; it is "the faculty which commands all the disciplines by which we acquire all the sciences and arts which make up humanity." And immediately the definition of poetic wisdom follows: it is the wisdom of the theological poets. This wisdom he also denominates "metaphysics." In somewhat Scholastic fashion, he then proceeds to give the divisions of poetic wisdom, by the same token structuring the entire second book of the *New Science.* Because the wisdom of the ancients was that of the theological poets, the first sages of the Gentile world, and because the origins of all things must by nature have been crude, the beginnings of poetic wisdom must be traced to a crude metaphysics. From this "as from a trunk, there branches out from one limb logic, morals, politics and economics, all poetic; and from another physics, the mother of their cosmography and hence of astronomy, which gives their certainty to its two daughters, chronology and geography, all likewise poetic. We shall show clearly and distinctly how the founders of Gentile humanity by means of their natural theology (or metaphysics) imagined the gods; how by means of their logic they invented languages; by morals, created heroes; by economics founded families and by politics, cities; by their physics established the beginnings of things as all divine; by the particular physics of man, in a certain sense created themselves; by their cosmography fashioned for themselves a universe entirely of gods; by astronomy carried the planets and constellations from earth to heaven; by chronology gave a beginning to measured time; and how by geography the Greeks, for example, described the whole world within their own Greece."

This is the enterprise which Vico carries through in the succeeding sections and chapters, bringing it to a close with this masterly summation: "We have shown that poetic wisdom justly deserves two great and sovereign tributes. The one, clearly and constantly accorded to it, is that of having founded gentile mankind. The other . . . is that the wisdom of the ancients has made its wise men, by a single inspiration, equally great as philosophers, lawmakers, captains, historians, orators and poets. . . . And it may be said that in the fables the nations have in a rough way and in the language of the human senses described the beginnings of the world of sciences which the specialized studies of the scholars have since clarified for us by reasoning and generalization. From all this we may conclude what we have set out to show, that the theological poets were the sense and the philosophers the intellect of human wisdom."

The third book, entitled the "Discovery of the True Homer" may best be considered a monograph study in which the force of the method developed and the accumulated lore of the second book are brought to bear upon the crucial and vexed problem of the Homeric poems and their status in the history of Western culture. Vico begins his treatment with a consideration of the reputation for esoteric wisdom which Homer enjoyed and of which Plato, according to Vico, is the supreme author. Nowhere does Vico find this confirmed in the Homeric text but finds, on the contrary, that Homer is entirely what Vico had anticipated, a figure from the heroic age of poetic wisdom: "Such crude, coarse, wild, savage volatile, unreasonable or unreasonably obstinate frivolous and foolish customs . . . can pertain only to men who are as children in the weakness of their minds, like women in the vigor of their imaginations and like violent youths in the turbulence of their passions; whence we must deny to Homer any kind of esoteric wisdom. These are the considerations which first gave rise to the doubts that put us under the necessity of seeking out the true Homer."

Vico then takes up in turn all of the salient problems about Homer: his fatherland, which he places in the "west of Greece and a little to the south"; the age of Homer: "after the Trojan war, to the extent of 460 years, or until the period of Numa"; notes his marvelous faculty for heroic poetry, marked by the twin features of popularity and heroic sublimity. These assertions are sustained by proofs both "philosophical" and "philological."

The fourth book entitled "The Course of Nations," returns more directly to the argument of the second book, though not without advertence to the significance of the discovery of the "True Homer." It returns, however, with a new purpose, opening a new dimension of Vico's thought. This is the purpose of raising the matter of the second book to a philosophical level, a level of intellectual expression and reflection in which what had there been observed as matter of fact under the rubric of the "certum" is now raised to the level of the "verum" of universal and necessary truth. Therefore, in this book all that had before been asserted under the form of the content of poetic wisdom is now asserted under the form of universal principles or rules governing the movement of all nations through their historical life and giving to that life articulation, progress, and meaning.

Here the triadic principle takes over completely as it had first been adumbrated in the book of principles. The divisions of wisdom are maintained, transposed to the entire institutional and disciplinary structure of the consciousness of nations. Vico intones the triadic litany: three kinds of natures (comings to be in time): poetic (or creative), heroic, and human (intelligent, benign, and reasonable); three kinds of custom: religious and pious, choleric and punctilious, and dutiful; three kinds of natural law: divine, heroic, and human; three kinds of languages: mute religious acts and divine ceremonies, heroic blazonings, and articulate speech; of characters: hieroglyphic, heroic, vulgar; of authority: divine, heroic, and human. Vico brings this section to a close by defining the "royal way" by which all nations come to rest under monarchies, and launching an attack on the political system of Jean Bodin. The latter had defined the course of political forms as monarchical, tyrannical, popular, and aristocratic; Vico believes that his testimony entirely refutes this argument, bringing the process to rest as he does in the monarchical form.

The fifth and last book of the *New Science* is entitled "The Recurrence of Human Things in the Resurgence of the Nations." This book is in reality a hymn to the eternal and inexhaustible fecundity of the human spirit, which is not in the last analysis, in Vico's view, subject to any iron law of time, but achieves, rather, a constant renewal of itself in time. This claim illustrates how different is Vico's theory of recurrence from any necessitarian view. Necessitarian views chain the spirit of man to a cycle which it does not itself renew but to which it is outwardly bound. Vico, by his theory of recurrence, asserts the power the human spirit has of renewing itself, or rediscovering within itself the eternal springs of life. Thus, at each point at which it reaches an exhaustion of the form which it itself had created, it does not perish in the shipwreck of that form but discovers in it the power to renew itself. In doing so, it initiates again the rhythm which Vico has delineated and passes through the patterns of the divine, heroic, and human, though under heavily invested forms, since its past experience is by no means shed, but provides, rather, the immediate matrix for its self-renewal.

To this power of self-renewal Vico gives the name of *ideal eternal history* which realizes itself in time and in the temporal careers of individual nations and of all nations taken collectively. The principle of divine ideal and eternal history is Providence, which has ever in view the realization of the basic and constitutive values of the human spirit.

Vico is not content however to define the great principle of recurrence in such abstract terms merely; he is concerned also to identify it with the reconstitution of social life on basic principles which, reappearing in diverse times, establish the ideal identity of human life in all times and hence its divine basis. As one such principle he cites the "eternal principle of fiefs" and the "recurrence of Roman law in feudal law." These instances make it possible for him to indicate that the movement of the human spirit in history is not merely backward upon itself, but forward upon the line of its constitutive values, since the past experience of nations is raised, in periods of recurrence, to become constitutive elements of the renewed order. The human spirit is continually enriching itself even as it perpetually renews itself upon its eternal principle.

A.R.C.

THE GLORIES OF MARY

Author: Saint Alphonsus Mary de' Liguori (1696-1787)
Type of work: Mariology
First published: 1750

Principal Ideas Advanced

Through Mary all blessings come to men, for it was through her submission to God's will that Christ was able to come into the world to save men by His perfect sacrifice.

As Mary accepted the Incarnation of God willingly, so she freely offered Him the life of her Son at the presentation in the temple, thus committing herself to a living martyrdom.

When Mary commended herself to the will of God, she spoke for all humanity and became the spiritual mother of the human race.

Mary willingly offered her Son to God because she wanted men to be reunited with Him; she is our greatest advocate before Christ and we should have recourse to her in all our difficulties.

The Glories of Mary is divided into two parts. The first section consists of a series of discourses, exempla and prayers based on the Salve Regina. In the saint's own words: "It treats of the various and abundant graces which the mother of God bestows on her devoted servants, in several discourses of the Salve Regina." Part two "treats of her principal Festivals; of her dolors in general, and of each of her seven dolors in particular; of her virtues; and lastly, of devotion to be practiced in her honor." Saint Alphonsus declares that the purpose of his book is to inspire in men a love of the Virgin. He is particularly dedicated to revealing her compassion for men and her intercession for sinners. As Jesus is King of the world, so Mary is Queen, the Queen of Mercy. The chief duty of the father is justice and the chief duty of the mother is mercy. During the wedding at Cana it was in response to a request by His mother that Christ turned the water into wine, even though it was not yet time for either His ministry or His miracles.

As a mother loves her children, so Mary loves us, writes Alphonsus, and she will intercede for us with the Father. As Saint Alphonsus writes of the Blessed Virgin, his love for her causes him to break into utterances notable for their intensity: "I am ready to renounce all the kingdoms of the earth, to be admitted among the lowest of thy servants." Mary is our mother not according to the flesh, but by love. Because the saints loved God greatly they performed acts of charity toward men, but who has loved God more than Mary? Mary knows our necessities and prays for us even before she is invoked.

Mary is the ark in which he who takes refuge will never suffer the shipwreck of eternal ruin. She is our life because she obtains final perseverance for us even in the face of suffering and death, and she does so even for those who do not invoke her, provided they love God. She renders death sweet to those who have recourse to her. Souls defended by her frustrate the devils who then can claim no power over them. The Church often invokes Mary as "refuge of sinners" and "star of the sea." Saint Bridget said that no sinner is so vile but that if he humbles himself before her, he will obtain pardon.

Each discourse in *The Glories of Mary* contains a summary of the reflections of the Church Fathers and the theologians on the Blessed Virgin, so that the reader finds in this book not only the opinions and prayers of Saint Alphonsus, but also the prayers of the saints and the faithful that constitute the living tradition of devotion to her. Mary is the mother even of sinners, providing they wish to repent. The sinner is often hated and abandoned by men, but he will never be abandoned by Mary if he makes even the slightest gesture of devotion to her. We "sooner find salvation by recurring to the mother than the Son; not because Mary is more powerful than her Son to save us, for we know that Jesus is our only Saviour, and that by His merits alone He has obtained and does obtain for us salvation; but because when we have recourse to Jesus, considering Him also as the judge to whom it belongs to punish the ungrateful, we may lose the confidence necessary to be heard; but going to Mary, who holds no other office than that of exercising compassion towards us as a mother of mercy, and defending us as our advocate our confidence will be more secure and greater."

In discussing the benefits of the Blessed Virgin's intercession Saint Alphonsus was deliberately challenging the Jansenists who at that time were teaching that devotion to her was an idle superstition. If, the saint asks, Saint Paul prayed for his companions, and Saint Stephen for his persecutors, and if Saint Peter promised to pray for the faithful when in Heaven; if, in short, the saints can pray for us, then why may we not implore them to intercede for us? And of all the saints, who but the Queen of Saints can most effectively intercede for us with God? Mary is the second Eve, who crushes the head of the serpent, ironically, through her humility. The cedar and the vine are her symbols because serpents shun them, and the oil is the symbol of her mercy. Mary obtains salvation and all good things for us not through the mediation of justice by means of merit, a mediation that is Christ's, but by the mediation of grace through prayer.

Saint Alphonsus makes it unmistakably clear that it is one thing to say God cannot grant favors without the intercession of Mary, and quite another thing to say that He will not. To believe, therefore, that all graces come through Mary is not to limit the power of God, but rather to say that He has chosen to pour graces to mankind through the perfect vessel He has prepared from the beginning of time. Mary's prayers to God are the prayers of a mother and are therefore most powerful. The authority in mercy that a wife has over her husband is the authority that Mary has over the justice of God. The power of the Blessed Virgin extends even into purgatory. Saint Alphonsus cites the Church Fathers to prove that there is a traditional belief to the effect that Mary descends at times into purgatory to lead to Heaven the souls that were devoted to her on earth. Devotion to the Virgin is the most certain sign that we will be saved.

Saint Alphonsus was one of the very greatest writers of prayers, and the prayers that appear at the end of each of the discourses have often been used in novenas and other devotions. *The Glories of Mary* contains one of the most beautiful morning offerings ever to be written: "O Jesus Christ, Incarnate Word, I desire to prepare a dwelling for Thee within myself, but I am incapable of this work. O Eternal Wisdom, prepare my soul to become Thy temple by Thy infinite merits. Grant that I may attach myself to Thee alone! I offer Thee my actions and the sufferings of this day in order that Thou mayest render them pleasing in Thy divine sight, and that tomorrow I may not come before Thee with empty hands."

Part one ends with a collection of prayers addressed to the Virgin by various saints.

Throughout his reflections on the sorrows of Mary, in the second part of the book, Saint Alphonsus takes the position that each insult to Jesus was an insult to her, and all that He suffered, she suffered in her heart. The basis for his conclusions is not theology, although he was a theologian, but rather the incontrovertible fact that she was His mother. From the time that Saint Simeon held the baby Jesus in the temple and prophesied that He would be persecuted by men, Mary suffered in her heart. In addition to her spiritual suffering she was forced to endure great physical hardship during the flight to Egypt where she and Joseph and Jesus lived in extreme poverty. She experienced an increasing agony of heart during the three days He was gone from her, while He was teaching in the temple and she thought He was lost. But when she met her own son on His way to Calvary, a young man covered with blood and wounds from head to foot, wearing a crown of thorns, and bearing the cross to which He would be nailed, and when she considered that He was not simply her son, but her God, a perfect Being, she suffered to the very limit of her being. When Christ was crucified, she was crucified in her heart, as any mother would be who witnessed her son so tortured. But Mary suffered even more because her son was God Himself and she loved Him with a perfect love. Mary, then, is the Queen of Martyrs because she has had to suffer more than any other martyr has had to suffer.

He who loves Mary should imitate her virtues, writes Saint Alphonsus. Mary was humble; the more she saw herself enriched, the more humble she became, remembering that all comes from God. She was emptied of herself; hence, she was filled with the love of God. She was constantly helping, unasked, those who were in need, as she did at the marriage of Cana and when she went to assist her cousin Elizabeth. She repaired, through her faith in God's will as revealed by the angel Gabriel, the loss Eve caused by her incredulity. She had perfect faith, and perfect hope in the promises of God. She is the mother of chastity, for she was the first to offer her virginity to God without counsel of others. She lived in poverty all her life in obedience to Christ's teaching that we ignore the riches of the world. Finally, she was obedient to God in all things whatsoever. God having prepared such a perfect vessel for Himself, the salutation of the angel Gabriel in Luke can be seen to be particularly meaningful: "Hail, full of grace, the Lord is with thee. Blessed art thou among women."

The Glories of Mary concludes with a series of devotions to be practiced in honor of Mary, meditations for the various feasts by which the faithful celebrate their devotion to her, together with ejaculations and acclamations in her praise.

In his "Petition of the Author" that begins the book Saint Alphonsus wrote, "Thou knowest that to see thee loved by all as thou dost deserve, and to offer thee some token of gratitude, I have always sought to proclaim thee everywhere, in public and in private, and to inspire all men with a sweet and salutary devotion to thee. I hope to continue to do so for the remainder of my life, even to my last breath. But I see by my advancing age and declining health that the end of my pilgrimage and my entrance into eternity are drawing near; therefore, I hope to give to the world, before my death, this little book of mine which may continue to proclaim thee for me."

Saint Alphonsus was, however, not to end his pilgrimage for another thirty-seven years. He lived to be ninety-one, and in that time his life was threatened so often that he received extreme unction eight times before he actually died. He was the eldest son of a noble Neapolitan family and was well on his way to a brilliant career as a lawyer when in 1723 the loss of a case prompted him to reject the life he had been living. In the same year he was peforming an act of charity in the Hospital for Incurables when he was surrounded by a light and heard a voice that said to him: "Leave the world and give thyself to Me." In September of the following year he became a priest. He founded the Congregation of the Most Holy Redeemer, whose chief purpose was to conduct missions among the poor of the province of Naples. Saint Alphonsus labored with the goatherds of the mountains, men who were illiterate, sometimes simpleminded, and who had been abandoned by society. In 1762 he was made bishop of a small Neapolitan diocese inhabited largely by people uninstructed in the Faith. For thirteen years he labored among the lowest class of Italian society, and his life was often in danger. During a famine in 1764 he saved the life of a syndic who had been seized by a mob by offering himself in the victim's place. Awed by the rescuer's fierce dedication, the crowd abandoned its evil intention. In 1768 Alphonsus had an attack of rheumatic fever that left him paralyzed for the rest of his life. Despite his suffering he continued to live a life of complete dedication to God, fasting, carrying on the daily activities of his office, and praying long into the night. For the last three years of his life he was deaf, nearly blind, and tormented by diabolical apparitions over which he finally triumphed. He died a holy death on August 1, 1787.

In addition to performing his pastoral duties Saint Alphonsus wrote more than sixty books and has been declared a Doctor of the Church. His *Moral Theology* is considered a classic in the field and is still studied in seminaries. He was a poet and musician and wrote many hymns, some of which are still in use. He experienced levitation, read the secrets of hearts, foretold the future, and was present in spirit at the death of Pope Clement XIV. The incidents of his life are unusally well documented, nor has the slightest doubt ever been cast upon their authenticity.

D.M.R.

TWO DISCOURSES ON UNIVERSAL HISTORY

Author: Anne Robert Jacques Turgot (1727-1781)
Type of work: Philosophy of history
First published: 1750

Principal Ideas Advanced

Natural phenomena follow fixed cycles, but man continually progresses.

Different societies have progressed at different rates, but the pattern of progress is always the same.

Every society passes through three stages: the mythological, the philosophical, and the scientific.

Christianity has played an important part in cultural progress.

Turgot is usually remembered as the reform minister in the early part of Louis XVI's reign, whose administration was cut short by the court circle opposed to his reforms. He is also remembered as an associate of the Physiocrats and Adam Smith, and an opponent of the existing mercantilistic system.

It is sometimes forgotten that he was also a brilliant philosopher and theologian, called by one authority "easily the greatest intellect of the Enlightenment." He studied at the Sorbonne for the priesthood, where he acquitted himself brilliantly, but on finishing he decided he should not be ordained. In 1750, when he was only 23, Turgot delivered two lectures on universal history, in which he tried to reconcile the Christian view of history as expressed by Bossuet with the thought of the Enlightenment. Arnold Toynbee maintains that these two lectures are more important than Lord Acton's lifetime of work. The first lecture is *On the Advantages that the Establishment of Christianity Have Given the Human Race,* and the second is *On the Successive Progress of the Human Spirit.*

Turgot is concerned throughout the first lecture with showing how Christianity has promoted human progress, which for him was a matter of intellectual and cultural rather than material gain. The coming of Christ and the preaching of the Gospel changed history, not in the way Saint Augustine stressed, but in promoting social and cultural progress. The old cruelties and barbarisms, such as killing unwanted infants and treating women as chattels, came to an end. The teaching of Christ limited despotism, so that, for example, Ambrose made Theodosius do penance before admitting him back to Church, and even the French king Louis VII was brought to task for his sins. Christianity protected the unprotected; for example, when the missionary Las Casas reported abuses by Spanish conquerors against the Indians he obtained imperial protection for them. So, too, the Church promoted liberty and the pursuit of learning, instilled noble ideals, promoted justice, and practiced corporal works of mercy.

In promoting social and cultural progress, the Church was simply adapting men more and more perfectly to natural law. Thus, Christianity takes on the aspect of a natural religion, spreading gentleness and charity, and making the world a better place. Turgot attempts to reconcile his Christian God with the secularized view of progress held by the "enlightened" thinkers of the time. He keeps God as creator of all things, and he tries to keep a place for Providence. But for him Providence is not the intervening God of Bossuet, but rather the design of God realized in a natural way by men following their individual desires and even their passions. Mankind is like "an immense army whose movements are directed by a mighty genius," always moving onward and forward, each soldier playing his part and not knowing the overall strategy of the commander.

Turgot has also secularized the goal of history, for Christianity's great value, he declares, is realized in making the world a better place, promoting religious respect for liberty and property and justice, increasing wealth and knowledge, and thus augmenting the happiness of all.

The author uses a typical rationalist argument to support his case for human progress. Natural phenomena, such as the weather, animal life, and even man's physical life, follow fixed cycles. But men, considered as rational beings, follow a progressive pattern. Progress, for Turgot, consists in the accumulation of knowledge. Such progress is certain, because each generation's increase of knowledge is passed on to succeeding generations. Moreover, progress is continuous and determinate because the law of cause and effect does not permit regressions in cultural and social life to follow increases of knowledge.

Because nature is uniform, Turgot maintains, progress works out for all societies. But the rate of progress differs from one society to another, because circumstances vary and "circumstances develop the talents of members of society or relegate them to obscurity. To the infinite variety of these circumstances is due the inequality in the progress of nations." Thus, the rate of progress differs, but the pattern is always the same. All nations, for example, were once in a barbarous stage, and all colonies will achieve independence when sufficiently developed—as he said, in 1750, that America would.

In these two discourses on universal history Turgot writes pre-history by conjecture, which has held up rather well under later archeological and anthropological findings. Men begin in a hunting society, Turgot tells us, and from this they enter a pastoral society. Then they settle in agricultural societies, and then into communities under a monarch and with a system of law. A division of labor and trade takes place, and the nation enters its historical period.

Turgot divides the historical period of each society or nation into three stages. The first is the mythological, in which men attribute all historical phenomena to the deities. The second is philosophical, in which men explain historical events as resulting from the operation of imaginary concepts or entities. The third and final stage is one in which effects are associated with true causes, in which the regularity of nature is discovered, and men lead truly rational lives.

It is difficult to estimate the effect of Turgot's *Two Discourses on Universal History*. He was read and eulogized by Condorcet, who in turn advanced the most widely read progress view of history in the Western world. Condorcet based his work on Turgot's, and for more than a century this was the most widely adopted philosophy of history in Europe and America.

T.P.N.

LES SOIRÉES DE SAINT-PÉTERSBOURG

Author: Joseph Marie de Maistre (c.1754-1821)
Type of work: Apologetics
First published: 1821

Principal Ideas Advanced

Religion is the mother and queen of the sciences.
If the just man suffers, it is not because he is just but because he is man.
Evil, pain, and suffering were introduced to the world through original sin.
Like a good father, God punishes men, whom He loves, for their own good.
Divine Providence rules history, and the existence of evil and suffering is only an apparent denial of this fact.
The arguments of the eighteenth century philosophes against Divine Providence are superficial sophistry.

Joseph de Maistre was a Savoyard who occupied a prominent position in the government of Piedmont. When revolutionary French troops invaded Piedmont, de Maistre fled with the king and the royal government. He moved about Europe according to the fortunes of war until, in 1802, he went to St.

Petersburg as ambassador extraordinary of the king of Piedmont. There he stayed fourteen years with little to do, for most of the time he was representing the ruler of a nonexistent kingdom.

At St. Petersburg Joseph de Maistre wrote his two most famous works, *Du Pape* (1819) and *Les soirées de Saint-Pétersbourg. Du Pape* was a challenging ultramontane argument against French Gallicans in favor of unlimited papal authority and infallibility. Its influence was immediate and extensive, but in time its arguments were seen to be extreme and it was no longer read. *Les soirées de Saint-Pétersbourg,* on the other hand, deals with questions of lasting significance, and it has continued to be read down to the present time.

Evenings at St. Petersburg is set on the banks of the Neva River where a spirited young French knight, a grave Russian senator, and a wise count (de Maistre) engage in eleven discussions on theological, moral, philosophical, and political questions. The three men represent respectively, the apprentice thinker, the companion, and the master discussing, as the subtitle indicates, "the temporal government of providence." The conversations are more or less casual discussions, progressing in Socratic fashion, turning the subject over and over, obtaining new views from various perspectives, saying some very wise things, and saying them in very readable fashion.

The conversation opens when the senator proposes a discussion of "the prosperity of the wicked and the misery of the just." Before they are finished the three have explored the whole range of God's action in relation to His creatures. They have raised the question of the utility of suffering, the problem of the justice of punishments meted out to the innocent, the question of the goodness of an all-powerful God. The count's answers are taken from the shelves of standard Catholic theology, but they are presented in nontechnical fashion, and are interlaced with a pungent, sometimes flaying analysis of eighteenth century thinkers like Locke, Voltaire, and Rousseau, and, as Father Raymond Corrigan has put it, "The stature of the *philosophes* shrinks visibly under the withering criticism of de Maistre."

Although the discussions are presented in ordinary language, they are based on a lifetime of reading and acute observation. Besides quoting frequently from the Bible, de Maistre cites seventy-five authors, ranging from Greek and Roman classical writers through the Fathers, Saint Thomas Aquinas, and early modern writers, down to men of the Enlightenment and of his own day.

Throughout the *Soirées* run certain basic Catholic ideas which de Maistre put flatly before the world as an adequate explanation of the mysterious problem of evil. If the just man suffers, it is not because he is just, but because he is a man. Evil men may prosper in a material way, but it is not because they are evil. Virtue itself is never punished, and evil itself is never rewarded. These are mistakes that critics of Divine Providence have failed to make.

De Maistre argues that evil entered the world as the result of sin; by suffering man expiates sin, both his own and that of the human race. In one of the conversations de Maistre tells his friends how, though a good father does not chastise the yardman for using coarse language, nevertheless he does punish his son for the same offense.

He chastizes his son because he loves him and because he wants to raise him properly. In the same way does God punish His children, and for the same reasons. Often enough, in the mysterious working of Providence, "there are just punishments of which the agents are most guilty." An outstanding example is the French Revolution, by which Providence used guilty revolutionists to punish the privileged class of the Old Regime for their failure to rule justly. Suffering is justified because it expiates sin and serves to heal human perversity.

De Maistre dismisses the *philosophes* of the eighteenth century in devastating generalizations. He concludes the eighth conversation by observing: "All the *philosophes* have a certain ferocious and rebellious pride which puts up with nothing; without exception they detest all distinctions which they do not like; they admit no authority which offends them; they admit nothing above if it is hateful to them. They freely attack anything, even God, because He is their master."

Such sweeping statements are modified and made more specific when de Maistre analyzes the writing of such individual thinkers as Voltaire and Rousseau. Voltaire is accused of "diabolical cleverness" and Rousseau of having only "dreamy half-visions." De Maistre dismisses Rousseau as "one of the most dangerous sophists of his century," whose sonorous phrases are apparently profoundly wise, but on analysis their wisdom disappears and they remain only collections of words. But he reserves his bitterest remarks for Voltaire, branding him as blasphemous, insulting, profaning: "He is mediocre, cold, and often—who will believe it?—dull and unpolished. . . . Voltaire's great crime is the abuse of his talent and the deliberate prostitution of a genius created to praise God and extol virtue."

Les soirées de Saint-Pétersbourg was important in the apologetics of the time for putting rationalists on the defensive, whereas they had held Christians on the defensive throughout the Enlightenment. De Maistre did the negative work, namely, discrediting the rationalists, that made possible the romantic movement of the early nineteenth century. Critics are generally agreed that although he overstated his case against the rationalists, de Maistre's arguments are fundamentally sound and are phrased in such engaging language that *Les soirées de Saint-Pétersbourg* will long endure as a masterpiece of Catholic thought.

T.P.N.

ESSAY ON INDIFFERENCE IN MATTERS OF RELIGION

Author: Félicité Robert de Lamennais (1782-1854)
Type of work: Apologetics
First published: 1817-1823

Principal Ideas Advanced

Religion is necessary for a peaceful, orderly society.

All real legislation is derived from God, who is the governor of the society of men.

At great personal sacrifice, the clergy render such important social services as comforting the afflicted, visiting the sick, and protecting the weak.

There can be only one true religion, and it can easily be distinguished from false religions.

Religious certitude is grounded not on individual reason but in the general reason of the human race.

Tradition is ultimately derived from the testimony of God or from revelation.

Revelation is composed of the primal revelation, the testimony of God at creation; the Mosaic revelation to Israel; and the revelation of Christ, continued by the Catholic Church.

Abbé Félicité de Lamennais was the most brilliant as well as the most tragic figure in the Catholic Church in the early nineteenth century. During the period of the Bourbon restoration (1815-1830) he brilliantly fostered a new apologetic in keeping with the intellectual and aesthetic tone of the post-revolutionary era. His *Essay on Indifference in Matters of Religion* was enthusiastically received by French bishops and laymen when the first volume appeared in 1817, but the following three volumes made orthodox Catholics uneasy because of the new ground Lamennais adopted for his apologetic. Nevertheless, he was warmly received by Pope Leo XII in 1824, the year after his Essay had been completed, and it seemed that he was the most brilliant new star on the Church's horizon.

After 1824, however, Lamennais turned to the problem of Church-state relations. Here he adopted the unpopular and premature view that the Church should renounce the arrangements of the Old Regime and adapt itself to certain accomplishments of the French Revolutions. He and some younger associates, notably Jean Lacordaire (1802-1861) and Charles Montalembert (1810-1870), established the journal *L'Avenir* in which they espoused the principle of "a free church in a free state." French bishops condemned the journal, and Lamennais decided to appeal to Rome. Pope Gregory XVI rejected the appeal and condemned certain teachings found in *L'Avenir*. Lacordaire and Montalembert accepted the condemnation, but Lamennais was unable to do so. He left the Church and remained until his death in 1854 a pathetic and tragic figure, one whose teaching was ahead of his times, but who refused to bow to proper ecclesiastical authority. Nevertheless, his *Essay on Indifference in Matters of Religion*, published while he was in the Church, remains one of the most important apologetic works of the nineteenth century.

In his essay Lamennais is concerned not with the "indifference" of persons to religion, but with doctrines or systems which are indifferent to religious truths or hold that one religion is as good as another. Moreover, he is more concerned with the effects of religion on society than on individual persons. His apologetic is not so much to justify Catholic doctrine for the individual as to show its good effect on society, for "everything proceeds from doctrines: morals, literature, constitutions, laws, the prosperity of states and their calamities, . . . without religion there is no society."

The first volume opens with an examination of three kinds of indifference: (1) that held by atheists who believe religion necessary for the common people; (2) deism, which holds religion necessary for all, but rejects revelation; (3) Protestantism, which recognizes revealed religion, but holds that only certain fundamental truths need be believed.

In the second part of the first volume Lamennais breaks away from the older apologetic approach. Here he is more concerned with the social effects of Christianity than with its effects on individual persons. The health and stability of society depend on its obeying the laws God has made known to men. The object of legislation is not private interests, but justice, and justice is the order ordained by God. Governments should secure the tranquillity of order, while religion teaches and governs the interior man. Governments prevent and punish crimes; religion cultivates virtue and teaches morality. Lamennais ends his first and most important volume by concluding that if there is a true religion it is of infinite importance; he promises to prove in the subsequent three volumes that there is a true religion and that it can be distinguished from false religions.

In the second volume Lamennais argues that the individual has no rational ground for being certain of anything, for the senses and reason are often deceptive and men have no way of knowing when they are mistaken. Nevertheless, men are in fact certain about many things: "All men, without exception, believe invincibly thousands of truths which constitute the necessary bond of society and basis of human life." This certitude is grounded in the *sensus communis,* the common consent of the human race. The common consent of mankind affirms the existence of God, the Creator of all things, including truth and certitude. Therefore, the truths He has revealed are certain.

Tradition is ultimately derived from the primal testimony of God or from later revelation, the author claims. Tradition, therefore, provides firm ground for human certitude. Primal revelation has "infinitive certitude" and is "infallible," because it is the testimony of God himself. However, particular societies as well as individual persons can err. Since religion expresses the relations between man and God, since the natures of God and man are constant and do not vary, and since religion is the expression of the relations between them, there can be only one true religion.

In his excellent study of Lamennais, Alec R. Vidler paraphrases Lamennais' reasoning on this point: "Men can recognize the true religion by the same means as they recognize all other truths, namely authority, tradition, the testimony of the human race, which derives from God's primal revelation. Included in the primal revelation were the following truths: the existence of one God, immaterial, eternal, infinite, almighty, the creator of the universe; the necessity of worship, prayer, and sacrifice; the moral law; the existence of good and evil spirits; the fall of man and the need for redemption and a redeemer; the immortality of the soul and the eternity of future rewards and punishments."

In the third and fourth volumes Lamennais demonstrates that the *sensus communis* of mankind testifies to a religion which bears the marks of Roman Catholicism: unity, universality, holiness, perpetuity. Deviations from this religion resulted from human weakness consequent upon the fall of Adam. So God was called upon to give a second revelation through Moses to Israel, and a third revelation through Christ. "Since Jesus Christ," Lamennais asks, "what authority dare anyone compare to that of the Catholic Church, heir of the primordial tradition, of the first revelation and the Mosaic revelation, of all the truths known in antiquity of which its teaching is the development? Going back to the origin of the world, it reunites in its authority all authorities."

LECTURES ON THE PHILOSOPHY OF LIFE

Author: Friedrich von Schlegel (1772-1829)
Type of work: Philosophy of man
First published: 1828

Principal Ideas Advanced

The proper object of philosophy is human consciousness: in itself, in its relationship to God, and in its relationship to the world.

Man's nature is threefold, consisting of body, soul, and an active and animating spirit which is wedded to the soul.

After the Fall human consciousness was disrupted, and the soul was unable to reconcile body and spirit or to maintain a balance between its two chief modes of activity, the analytical reason and inventive fancy.

In order to re-establish the original harmony of human consciousness man must give an internal assent to the will of God.

Friedrich von Schlegel's *Lectures on the Philosophy of Life* contains his final reflections on the nature and destiny of man. As a young man he had been the prophet of the romantic movement in Germany. In 1798 he inspired the formation of the "School of Romanticism" with the philosopher Friedrich Schleiermacher (1768-1834) and the poets Novalis (1772-1801) and Ludwig Tieck (1773-1853). In the same year he and his brother August Wilhelm began to publish the *Atheneum,* a review dedicated to advancing the principles of romanticism. In 1797 he published *The Greeks and the Romans,* and a year later his *History of the Poetry of the Greeks and Romans* was published. Both books were widely read and influenced Goethe and Schiller, among others. During this period Schlegel's philosophic outlook bordered on complete subjectivism. He wrote: "The deepest truth known to me is that erelong my present truth will change." Josiah Royce called this attitude "courageous fickleness." The horrors of the Napoleonic wars, however, sobered Schlegel's radical individualism. He dedicated himself to the study of Hindu religion and philosophy, and in 1808 he published *On the Speech and Wisdom of the Indians,* a book that is still considered a classic in its field. In the same year he and his wife were converted to Catholicism. He was appointed secretary in the state chancellery at Vienna and in 1809 accompanied Archduke Charles to war, issuing proclamations against Napoleon and editing the army newspaper. As a result of his experiences in the war he became increasingly opposed to an unqualified individualism in both philosophy and politics. His *History of the Old and New Literature* was published in 1815, the year of Napoleon's final defeat, and established him as the leading literary historian of his generaion. Schlegel reinterpreted his ideas in the light of Catholic Christianity and his *Lectures on the Philosophy of Life* published the year before his death, are the fruit of that reinterpretation.

For Schlegel philosophy must proceed from the entire life of man. The author begins with the totality of human life as it is expressed in religion, history, art, and literature. Implicit in his approach is the idea that what man is in his essence can never be explained by reference to external reality alone. Having accepted the whole of human life as his reference, Schlegel rejects the exclusive approach of the rationalists that would admit as evidence only what is "demonstrable" in the scientific sense. Anything that is part of human experience is worthy of the philosopher's attention. Philosophy is thus for him not the "dead and lifeless cogitation of abstract ideas," but rather an examination of the various dimensions of life in the light of the whole, an examination whose chief purpose is the revelation of the inner life and final destiny of man.

For Schlegel, if an idea has no reference to life, it is useless. The ideal toward which he constantly aspires is the perfect thinking of which man was capable before the Fall. He writes, "If all thinking were a living cogitation —if the thinking and the loving soul had remained at unity in their true center, then the external methodical thought and the internal productive thinking, meditating, and invention, would not be separate and divorced— at least they would not come into hostile contact with each other, but rather would be harmoniously combined in the living cogitation of the soul."

According to Schlegel, the philosophy of life must be a philosophy of God, for the experience of God is the highest dimension of life. Philosophy is an applied theology whose purpose is not to prove the existence of God or the eternal verities but to reveal the unity of life under God.

Schlegel saw in nature a significant revelation of God, as did his contemporaries in England and America; nature is a song of praise composed in living imagery. The entire created order gives praise to God, but since the Fall the praise is imperfect. Earth is akin to man, and man may have a communion with it. Schlegel writes: "Beneath the vast tombstone of the visible world there slumbers a soul, not wholly alien, but more than half akin to our own." The physical world is "a ladder of resurrection, ascending . . . to the highest pitch of earthly glorification, in which nature, too, has a promise that she shall partake." With the perfection of man at the end of time nature will be restored to the harmony that existed before the Fall, and it will give again perfect praise to God. Nature is a "symbolical being," and man reads in its life his own. Nature provides man with the symbols by which he can express his own inner life; at the same time, through these same symbols, nature tells him something of the divine.

Schlegel divided human history into three ages, each with a particular purpose in the unfolding of God's plan for the world. He assigns twenty-five centuries to primeval history, that period in which men lived haphazardly, barely able to endure earth's rigors, and in which their religious beliefs were a chaos of fantastic conceptions created by the fancy loosed from reason. The chief purpose of this period was to give men a sense of the unity of life on earth, a sense of the abiding realities and the natural symbols which can be used to express them. Fifteen hundred years are allowed for the Hebraic-Greek preparation for the coming of Christ. For Schlegel the Greek contribution lies chiefly in the realm of philosophic thought and in the artistic achievement that provided for a more accurate understanding of the self and of the world than had hitherto been possible. Operating upon the mythic foundation provided by primeval history, the Greek philosophers reached beyond myth for an objective view of the universe, but in the end they failed; having stepped beyond myth, the Greeks could no longer accept the myths as answers to the ultimate questions. Without revelation the Greeks were unable to formulate more adequate answers for a now far more sophisticated civilization.

The ultimate failure of Greek thought leads naturally to a consideration of the other main stream of Western civilization, the Hebraic. The Hebrews were a prophetic people, looking constantly to the future, and hence progressive. The secret of their progress was, of course, God, who had set them apart from other people. The Hebrews' recognition of God's action in their history added a third element to what had been a dualism in the thought of early man and provided them with an eschatology which gave them a belief in, not simply a hope for, the future. When the Greek love of thought was combined with the spiritual genius of the Hebrews in the early days of the Church, the result was a Christian civilization that lasted for fifteen centuries.

For Schlegel the Middle Ages represent the beginning and not the final flowering of Christianity. During this time the soul of man for the first time since the Fall became thoroughly steeped in God and aware of the ocean of infinity that surrounded him. Finally, Schlegel considers the two hundred years from the Renaissance to his own time as a separate period whose chief characteristic was the restoration of science. Unfortunately the flowering of modern science took place outside the interpretive center of Christian civilization which had begun to break down in the Renaissance. Because of this divorce between science and faith, science was hailed by many as a new religion. However, lacking a solid center in the experience of life itself, science was unable to provide a cultural synthesis. The result was first a deifying of reason in the Enlightenment and then a deifying of nature in Schlegel's own time, the Romantic Period.

According to Schlegel, the alternate deification of reason and nature is the chief intellectual error of fallen man and manifests itself in varying strength in all periods of human history. With this idea Schlegel rose above the intellectual experience of his own day and presented a comprehensive view of Western civilization from the Christian point of view. In his philosophy of life Schlegel hoped to provide an intellectual center about which man could refashion his disrupted spiritual life. He saw in Neoclassicism a rebellion of reason against love, and in Romanticism a rebellion of the fancy against the reason. His conception was that philosophy, "honoring that which has been given from above and that which is existent from without, must neither raise itself in hostility to the one, nor attempt to interfere violently with the other."

Schlegel was one of the originators of that school of thought in modern intellectual history that has emphasized the whole man occupying an emblematic universe. One can find echoes of his ideas in all the romantic thinkers from Coleridge to Emerson. In psychology the Gestalt theory of Kohler and Koffka is deeply indebted to the tradition amplified by Schlegel. The work of Cassirer, Kerenyi, Jung, and Wilhelm would have been impossible without the intellectual labors of the German romantics. More and more as modern man exhausts the possibilities of rationalism he is turning, in the twentieth century, to a symbolical-religious view of the universe. The modernity of Schlegel's thought is remarkable. The religious and intellectual catchwords of our day—symbol, kerigma, pleroma, encounter—are all prefigured if not actually discussed in his work, as is the increasing interest in the religion and philosophy of India. Twentieth century thinkers continue to explore the intellectual worlds Schlegel helped to discover.

D.M.R.

THE HISTORY OF ENGLAND

Author: John Lingard (1771-1851)
Type of work: History; philosophy of history
First published: 1819-1830

Principal Ideas Advanced

True historical writing must be based on original documents and sources contemporary with the events described.

The historian is not concerned with defending causes.

The historian must detach himself from the scene he is describing and try to view it as an unconcerned observer.

John Lingard was born in 1771 of a family that was intensely English and loyally Catholic, and at an early age he indicated the desire to study for the priesthood. English Catholics were divided into two camps during Lingard's youth. The Ultramontanists, supported mostly by the Irish, were bellicose and doctrinaire. The Cisalpinists were conciliatory and cautious. Lingard tended to adopt the Cisalpinist view, though in an independent manner, a position which dictated the kind of history he was to write.

Since Catholicism was proscribed in England in the eighteenth century, Lingard went to the English college of Douai in Belgium to study for the priesthood. Here he distinguished himself as a brilliant scholar in all fields of study. Before his ordination, however, he and the other students at Douai were forced to flee to England. In 1795 Lingard was ordained at York, one of the first to be ordained a Catholic priest in England since the Reformation. Until 1811 he taught seminarians of Douai, re-established on English soil, first at Tudhoe, then Crook Hall, and finally at Ushaw. In 1811, however, he retired to a parish at Hornby, where he had time to write his famous *History of England from the First Invasion of the Romans to the Accession of William and Mary in 1688*.

Lingard's original purpose was to write a handbook for students, in which he would dispel the myths that had been woven into English history by the Whig-Parliament-Protestant writers against the crown, tories, and Catholics. This could be done, he believed, only by going to the original documents to show how they had been misquoted or ignored. As his research proceeded, Lingard abandoned the idea of a handbook in favor of a multivolume opus. Besides using the English State Paper Office to find manuscripts and documents, he explored the archives in Paris, Milan, and Rome for materials relative to English history.

The first three volumes, going to the death of Henry VII, were published in 1819. They were widely acclaimed not only in England but on the Continent as well. The only criticism came from such Ultramontinist Catholics as Bishop John Milner (1752-1826), who charged Lingard with compromising with Protestants. Milner did not understand that Lingard wanted to write history, not apologetics: Lingard had said that he wanted to write "a book which the Protestants would read." The eighth and final volume appeared in 1830. (Later editions were published in ten volumes, but do not cover any more ground. Hilaire Belloc continued the story, starting with Volume XI and published under the authorship of "Lingard and Belloc.") During Lingard's lifetime five editions appeared. In each new edition the author incorporated new findings made by himself and other researchers in English history.

In the "Preliminary Notice" or preface to the 1849 edition, Lingard spelled out the rules he had devised for writing history: ". . . to admit no statement merely upon trust, to weigh with care the value of the authorities on which I rely, and to watch with jealousy the secret workings of my own personal feelings and prepossessions. Such vigilance is a matter of necessity to every writer of history, if he aspire to the praise of truthfulness and impartiality. He must withdraw himself aloof from the scenes which he describes, and view with the coolness of an unconcerned spectator the events which pass before his eyes, holding with a steady hand the balance between contending parties, and allotting to the more prominent characters that measure of praise or dispraise which he conscientiously believes to be their due. Otherwise, he will be continually tempted to make unfair use of the privilege of the historian; he will sacrifice the interests of truth to the interests of party, national, or religious, or political."

Lingard remains faithful to his self-imposed rules throughout his *History of England*—and these rules were formulated years before Ranke laid down similar rules for "scientific" history. Lingard never judges motives, and his interpretation of events is limited to the obvious. The few judgments which were challenged, such as his assertion that the Massacre of St. Bartholomew's Day was not planned, have all been vindicated. When the evidence is not sufficient to enable Lingard to come to a conclusion, as in the case of William II's death, the author does not try to speculate on what must have happened. The result is that Lingard's history has stood the test of time immeasurably better than Hume's Tory history or Macauley's Whig history, both of which were marred, in Linward's opinion, by *suggestio falsi* and *suppressio veri*. Throughout his work Lingard refers to partisan accounts of battles, court intrigues, and other such matters, but consistently dismisses them as unreliable.

Lingard's *History of England*, widely and enthusiastically received by scholars, was most influential on subsequent history writing, serving as a model of objective history written for its own sake rather than as propaganda.

SYMBOLISM

Author: Johann Adam Möhler (1796-1838)
Type of work: Comparative theology
First published: 1832

Principal Ideas Advanced

Symbolism consists of the scientific exposition of the doctrinal differences among various religious parties as these differences are shown in the public confessions or symbological books of the parties.

All differences in the doctrinal creeds of Catholics and Protestants can be traced to the differences in their views of human nature.

A study of the doctrines of the Protestants is of great value in helping the Catholic to appreciate and comprehend his own beliefs.

The achievement of real unity within Christianity is not an easy task, but a proper study of doctrinal differences can lead to the understanding that the contest of ideas between Catholics and Protestants springs from the honest efforts of both sides to uphold the truth.

Johann Adam Möhler's *Symbolism, or Exposition of the Doctrinal Differences Between Catholics and Protestants, as Evidenced by Their Symbological Writings* was in many ways a pioneering work in Catholic theology. The study of doctrinal positions taken by various religious groups initially attracted more interest on the part of Protestants than Catholics. But given the lively interplay of religious ideas in early nineteenth century Germany, it was inevitable that Catholics would soon take up comparative theology. Möhler was well prepared for this task. Prior to his ordination in 1819, he had studied widely in philosophy and theology, and he later became acquainted with Church history, a subject which he taught for some years at the University of Tübingen.

Möhler was careful to base his study of comparative theology on the best sources then available. His statement of the Catholic position was largely drawn from the decrees of the Council of Trent and from papal pronouncements and bulls condemning heresy and stating Catholic doctrine. Among the various sources of the Lutheran position, Möhler paid especial attention to the famous Augsburg Confession of 1530 and the larger and smaller catechisms of Martin Luther. With respect to the doctrines of Calvin and Zwingli, Möhler studied, among other sources, the various confessions of national Calvinist churches and the Thirty-Nine Articles of the Anglican Church.

In the opinion of Möhler, the really basic differences between the doctrines of Catholicism and Protestantism are attributable to their respective views of human nature. One of the most important questions relating to the nature of man is that of free will, a question that is in turn tied to a consideration of original sin. Catholics urge that man is free and therefore culpable for the first sin. Luther, on the other hand, tended to reject man's free will, and Calvin was determined to uphold the doctrine of predestination and yet somehow still see man as responsible for original sin. This latter task could be done only by postulating an absolutistic God who, since He is above the law, cannot sin. Thus, Möhler believed that because of their views of free will, Luther was forced to conclude that God caused the first sin, as Melanchthon actually declared, whereas Calvin had to postulate a totally arbitrary God in order to escape the difficulty.

Möhler also examined the differing views with respect to the effects of original sin. According to Catholic doctrine, man lost both his original justice and holiness and incurred the penalty of death, but he was not rendered totally corrupt. In the view of Luther, man lost both his fear of God and his confidence in Him, as a result, *was* rendered totally corrupt, unable to cooperate in his own salvation. Calvin's position was in essential agreement with Luther's although, according to Möhler, Calvin's view of man's situation was not quite as bleak as Luther's.

The different doctrines of justification, Möhler saw quite clearly, logically flowed from the position taken with respect to the effects of original sin. In the teaching of the Catholic Church, man retains his free will and the image of God. Thus, while justification comes only from the merits earned by Christ, man's salvation also requires free human co-operation with the grace of God. For Luther, man's role in salvation is purely passive: he can only accept the merits won by Christ which release him from the punishment, but not the guilt of sin. Calvin saw the process of salvation purely in terms of predestination.

Möhler was aware that both Catholics and Protestants believed in salvation by faith, but he was equally convinced that the two sides viewed faith in a different light. For the Catholic, faith is not merely an empty connection of ideas, for faith must be vivified by charity before man can earn salvation. For the Protestant, however, the mere acceptance of Christ's salvation is enough. Thus, to support his doctrine of faith, Möhler considered the question of good works. Here again there are important differences. Catholic doctrine insists on the necessity of good works, and it understands by good works the moral acts and sufferings of man justified in Christ. Luther, on the other hand, denied the existence of good works. Since man is totally corrupt, his every act is a sin. Calvin took much the same position. Works play no part in salvation; rather, works are, at best, mere evidences of salvation.

Möhler drew several important conclusions from his study of the different doctrines with respect to original sin and justification. He was convinced that Protestants had a different view of Christ from that of the Catholics. Catholic doctrine sees Christ as both Savior and Teacher. But since the early Reformers denied man's ability to obey God's law freely, they were forced to neglect Christ's role as teacher. Möhler also believed that the different groups possessed a divergent understanding of the relationship between religion and morality. For Catholics, religion and morality are essentially the same and equally eternal, whereas Protestants see them as separate: religion as eternal, morality as temporal.

While lamenting what he considered to be the errors of Protestantism, Möhler clearly saw that many of these errors flowed from basically good motives. Wishing to stress the power and freedom of God, Luther and Calvin did so by emphasizing man's decadence, thereby promulgating a view intended to promote in the believer a true dependence on God. But the reformer's position, Möhler thought, was overdrawn and destructive. The overstatement of God's power and of man's impotence leads inevitably to the fostering of human irresponsibility.

Möhler was also careful to examine the Catholic and Protestant views with respect to the sacraments. As he states it, Catholic doctrine defines a sacrament as an outward sign representing the conferral of justice and holiness. The use of outward signs is clearly based on the nature of man, who is not only a spiritual, but also a material being. Protestants, on the other hand, attribute no such significance to the sacraments and see no real connection between sacraments and grace. At best, for the Protestants, the sacraments are merely tokens to assure the believer in his faith, to quiet and console him;

they are not essential in the process of salvation. Thus, Möhler stated, Luther and Calvin retained as true sacraments only Baptism and the Lord's Supper, since only they could be construed as possessing a confirmative nature. But, Möhler goes on to maintain, Protestantism is forced by its own logic to reject even these two as true sacraments, for if salvation depends solely on faith, in the Protestant sense of that term, then neither Baptism nor Holy Communion is really necessary for salvation.

Given the divergence on the question of sacraments, Möhler found no difficulty in stating the disagreement between Catholics and Protestants over the question of the Mass. For Catholics, the Mass is a true sacrifice. The early Protestants objected to this belief on the grounds that to call the Mass a sacrifice is somehow to render the sacrifice of Christ on the cross incomplete.

Möhler also examined the divergence of opinion on the question of the Real Presence. Here the disagreement, as he saw it, was not only between Catholics and Protestants, but also among Protestants themselves. Whereas Luther denied transubstantiation, he still insisted on the Real Presence. Zwingli, on the other hand, saw Holy Communion as a mere remembrance of Christ. Calvin adopted a middle position. He argued that the bread remains bread, but that the believer partakes of Christ in a spiritual manner.

Finally, Möhler undertook to examine the divergent views with respect to the nature of the Church. For the Catholic, the Church is the visible community of believers, founded by Christ. It is both a human and a divine institution. It is infallible and the manifestation of the Word to the world. Moreover, Möhler stated, since truth is one, Christian truth is one, and in order to protect this truth the authority of the Church is necessary. Catholics do not deny that the truth is to be found in Sacred Scripture; but if Sacred Scripture is infallible, man is not. Thus, the Church is necessary as an infallible guide to the interpretation of Scripture. Tradition, which is the living Word, is also necessary for Christian truth, since without tradition it would be impossible even to establish the validity of Sacred Scripture. Since the Church is a visible authority, it requires a hierarchy based on an ecclesiastical ordination originating with Christ and perpetuated by Apostolic succession. Finally, stability within this hierarchy demands a head; namely the pope, whose powers are also ordained by Christ.

Möhler saw that the Protestant view of the Church is essentially different from Catholic doctrine. In stating that Scripture alone contains essential Christian truth, both Luther and Calvin were forced to conclude that the Holy Spirit guides each man separately in his interpretation of Scripture. Thus, according to this view, each man becomes a priest, and no outward authority or ordination is necessary; since every man, guided by the Spirit, is sufficient of himself, the whole idea of the Church is destroyed; there is no need for ecclesiastical authority, and the Church is no longer a visible institution. Instead, for the Protestants the Church becomes the invisible community of saints, and thus the reality of the hierarchy and the position of the pope is denied. There need be no visible head of an invisible community. Once again Möhler stresses the claim that the errors of Protestantism arose from laudable motives, but he insists that by stressing the divine elements of the Church and the absolute goverance of God, Luther and Calvin introduced a condition of anarchy into the Church.

Möhler was well aware that the doctrines of Luther and Calvin did not constitute the total teachings of Protestantism. Thus, in the second part of his study he examined the teachings of such other Protestant groups as the Anabaptists, the Methodists, the Socinians, and the Arminians. It has been said that Möhler's *Symbolism* forms a useful companion volume to Bossuet's *History of the Variations of the Protestant Churches* (1688). Indeed, this is so, for, like Bossuet, Möhler believed that once the principle of authority is denied, Christian doctrines will continually be perverted. Thus, Möhler wanted to show that although Luther and Calvin were sometimes reluctant to draw necessary conclusions from their own teachings, others were not. Despite the fact that Luther insisted on the necessity of Baptism and Holy Communion as sacraments necessary for salvation, his own teachings made the sacraments unnecessary. Möhler also pointed out that both Luther and Calvin denied the necessity of any authority in the Church save that of God, and yet both came to fear the anarchy inherent in their views, and both were finally forced to resort to the establishment of some sort of authority in their churches.

Möhler had a very deep appreciation of the "middle position" occupied by the Catholic Church. In his view it avoided both the extremes of rationalism and of mysticism. On the other hand, it was the tendency of Protestantism, impelled by its own principles, to adopt extreme positions that Möhler most condemned. Yet, Möhler was an understanding critic of Protestantism and insisted that most of its mistakes derived from the wrong application of good intentions.

As Möhler understood the science of symbolism, it had neither a polemical nor an apologetic aim, but at the same time it was impossible for doctrine completely to escape the elements of either polemics or apologetics. Möhler was aware that his study was one sided in that it dealt with only the differences, and not the similarities, between Catholicism and Protestantism. But although he knew that Christian unity was not an immediate possibility, he believed that his work could eventually contribute to such unity. A sound understanding of religious differences could lead to an appreciation of the earnest endeavors of both groups to uphold the truth.

P.T.M.

AN ESSAY ON THE DEVELOPMENT OF CHRISTIAN DOCTRINE

Author: John Henry Cardinal Newman (1801-1890)
Type of work: Theology; history of doctrine
First published: 1845

Principal Ideas Advanced

If one compares the content of faith of Apostolic times with that of later centuries, it would appear that Christians now count as objects of faith matters unmentioned in the primitive Church.

The difficulty this poses to the unity of Christian belief can be removed by the doctrine of development: any idea relevant to human behavior is articulated, its aspects distinguished, only gradually and in response to various circumstances of time and place.

Christian Revelation addresses itself to the minds of men, has its life there; just as men live in time and circumstance, so Christian doctrine has developed in time in response to diverse circumstances in a manner intended by its Author.

Newman completed *An Essay on the Development of Christian Doctrine* in 1845 and shortly thereafter (on October 9) was received into the Roman Catholic Church. There is nothing accidental in this sequence of events; the latter followed from the former, since, like every work but the *Grammar of Assent,* the *Development* was closely linked to Newman's personal life and work. No effort to sketch his personal religious odyssey could be successfully undertaken here, but it seems necessary to point out that, as a member of the Oxford Movement, Newman had joined in the great effort to redefine the Anglican Church as the local manifestation of the Catholic Church rather than as a Protestant church. The Roman Church was one that Newman had seen as guilty of additions to the ancient and Catholic faith and he, like others, was anxious to show that the Anglican Church was not guilty of such additions. The Oxford Movement, however, was not looked upon kindly by the Anglican bishops, and Newman, while ever obedient to his bishop, felt the difficulty which this official lack of enthusiasm entailed. Finally, with Tract 90, published in 1841, Newman's bishop asked him to cease writing, and Newman, together with a few friends, retired in 1843 to Littlemore; the historical research which issued in the *Development* and his own reception into the Roman Church followed.

In one of his letters Newman wrote that the subject of the *Development* could be stated as follows: "The difference and additions in doctrinal teaching observable in the history of the Church are but apparent, being the necessary phenomena incident to developing intellectual ideas." And that, abstractly stated, is precisely what the book is about. For Newman, Christianity could not be simply a private matter, whatever each man made of Scripture; it was something public and historical, and each man's private and personal reception of the Christian revelation had to be anchored to the objectively true Church. The great question became, how is the Christian Church in the nineteenth century, with its complicated protocol, its creeds, its theology, related to the primitive Church, to the Apostolic Church, and the Church of the ante-Nicene Fathers?

Newman claims that a study of Church history, a comparison of nineteenth century Christian belief with the New Testament, indicates that many great changes have occurred, if not in the substance of the Faith, at least in its articulations; if not in the essence of the Church, at least in its historical manifestations. The problem is not one which confronts the Church of Rome alone; it is also a problem for the Anglican Church and, indeed, for Protestants as well. The *Development* addresses itself to this problem, and it is a most orderly volume. In the course of it, Newman saw his earlier objections to the Church of Rome dissolve and disappear and, though he had for years felt ambiguous emotions toward that Church and an undeniable attraction to it, it was with real anguish that he recognized that his theory of development had led him to its threshold.

If ever a man came into the Church despite his feelings, despite his whole bent and background and emotional preferences, it was John Henry Newman. His case was complicated by his involvement in Anglican critiques of Rome, by his efforts to show that the Anglican Church was indeed a Catholic one, by his deep and affectionate ties to the other men involved in the Oxford Movement. In short, on the human level, Newman felt as if he were a traitor; he *knew* he was but going home, but he was far from *feeling* that way. One for whom religion is wholly inner and private cannot understand Newman, let alone admire him. David Swenson, for example, one of the men largely responsible for making the works of another great religious figure of the nineteenth century known to English readers, namely, Søren Kierkegaard, compared the Dane and Newman in the following way. Newman, he suggested, was looking for the objectively true Church in order that he might join it; Kierkegaard, on the other hand, was seeking so to live that others who lived likewise would constitute with him the true Church. That remark probably does justice to neither man, but it does point up the essentially Catholic outlook of Newman and the basically Lutheran outlook of Kierkegaard. If there is a point of contact between the two men it would doubtless be found by comparing Newman's notion of *realizing* Christianity and Kierkegaard's concept of Christianity as a mode of *existence*.

"This following essay is directed towards a solution of the difficulty which has been stated—the difficulty, so far as it exists, which lies in the way of our using in controversy the testimony of our most natural informant concerning the doctrine and worship of Christianity, viz., the history of eighteen hundred years." Thus writes Newman toward the end of his introduction to the *Development*. He wants to show that the increase and expansion of the Christian Creed and ritual and the variations which have attended the process are just what we should expect, that time is necessary for the full comprehension and perfection of the Christian message which is addressed to human hearts and minds and transmitted from generation to generation. In other words, Newman brings to the history of Christianity what he frankly calls the hypothesis of development, and he likens his method to that of Ptolemy and Newton. His theory of development is intended to account for the difficulty he feels when he juxtaposes the complex Christianity of the nineteenth century with the relatively simple faith of Apostolic times. The theory will commend itself precisely to the degree that it accounts for the facts.

Any idea which is of a nature to arrest and possess the mind may be said to live in the mind of its recipient; as living, it becomes an active principle of a process whereby its various aspects, implications and characters gradually emerge. "This process, whether it be longer or shorter in point of time, by which the aspects of an idea are brought into consistency and form, I call its development, being the germination and maturation of some truth or apparent truth on a large mental field," writes Newman. Insofar as such a living idea is involved in the wider arena of human life, it cannot but be affected by the other factors of human life; and it will destroy, modify, and incorporate within itself what it thus encounters. The development Newman has in mind is not an investigation worked out on paper; it is essentially a historical process.

With the same care he exhibited in the *Grammar,* Newman was concerned at the outset of the *Development* to define his terms. "Development," he observes, has three senses: sometimes it means the process, sometimes the result of a process, sometimes the corruption of something. Newman distinguishes these senses, not to rule any of them out, but to forewarn his reader that he will abide by common usage and use his key term in any of these senses. That having been said, Newman distinguishes eight kinds of development: mathematical, physical, material, political, logical, historical, ethical, and metaphysical. Are all these relevant to his task? He answers: "As to Christianity, supposing the truths of which it consists to admit of development, that development will be one or other of the last five kinds. Taking the Incarnation as its central doctrine, the Episcopate, as taught by St. Ignatius, will be an instance of political development, the *Theotokos* (Mother of God) of logical, the determination of the date of our Lord's birth of historical, the Holy Eucharist of moral, and the Athanasian Creed of metaphysical."

Newman's discussion of antecedent arguments which may be adduced in behalf of the theory of development is of moment. By "antecedent argument" here (one should consult the *Grammar* and its discussion of antecedent probability), Newman means something like the *a priori* considerations which lead us to expect a development of Christian Doctrine of the various kinds he has already mentioned. In a manner reminiscent of Anselm in the *Cur Deus Homo,* Newman attempts to abstract from the historical facts concerning the development of Christian Doctrine and to surmise what should be expected historically of an idea such as Christianity: "It may be objected that its inspired documents at once determine the limits of its mission without further trouble; but ideas are in the writer and reader of revelation, not the inspired text itself; and the question is whether those ideas which the letter conveys from writer to reader, reach the reader at once in their completeness and accuracy on his first perception of them, or whether they open out in his intellect and grow to perfection in the course of time." Moreover, Christianity addresses itself to all people of all times and places, and its principles will require very different application as the circumstances of the application vary. Every Christian of whatever stripe or hue develops the doctrines of Scripture, for example. Newman, in the following passage, gives a succinct statement of the need for theology: "When it is declared that 'the Word became flesh,' three wide questions open upon us on the very announcement. What is meant by 'the Word,' what by 'flesh,' what by 'became.' " In any attempt to reply to these questions, a process of investigation is involved; developments are involved. And the answers to the questions will suggest further questions, and at length a great number of propositions will be the result, propositions which cluster around the revealed sentence and which represent the development of its meaning, its aspects, its implications. Such statements of Scripture are, of course, mysteries, but a mystery is something which cannot be fully known, not what cannot be known at all. Furthermore, there is no determination in Scripture as to the desirable age of Baptism, and yet a question of such moment demands an answer. Thus, there is an antecedent probability in favor of development.

Newman goes further. There is antecedent probability that the Divine Author of Christianity intended its development. Revelation is addressed to the minds and hearts of men who live in time and in different locales; so much has been told them, but there are gaps which must be filled by what Newman calls development. That is, the full determination of the idea, all its aspects, must be worked out in time. This is not done by conscious attention to it so much as by response to difficulties and circumstances; and since the result is an integrated articulation of the central idea, it is not too much to say that these developments were contemplated by the Divine Author of the Revelation.

There is antecedent probability, further, for the fact that the Author of Revelation will provide an infallible authority to preside over these developments and discern true from false development. "Let the state of the case be carefully considered," writes Newman. "If the Christian doctrine, as originally taught, admits of true and important developments, as was argued in the foregoing section, this is a strong antecedent argument in favor of a provision in the Dispensation for putting a seal of authority upon those developments."

What Newman is led to propose is that although what Christians believe is all present *in ovo* from the outset of Christian Revelation, the implications, the articulations, and the aspects of that faith cannot be stated once and for all but can only gradually emerge in time in response to difficulties of time or place. There is an infallible authority which passes judgment on whether or not a candidate as a development is true or false. That is why the formal establishment of so many objects of faith which purport to be Apostolic must be assigned to the fourth, fifth, or later centuries. "In such a method of proof," writes Newman, "there is, first, an imperfect, secondly, a growing evidence, thirdly, in consequence a delayed inference and judgment, fourthly, reasons producible to account for the delay."

What are some of the historical instances which call for a theory of development for explanation? There is first of all the establishment of the canonical books of the New Testament. This canon seems to be established no earlier than the fourth or fifth centuries. Why did the Church pass judgment then? Because earlier, as a result of persecution, there was not sufficient time and leisure for research, discussion, and testimony. So, too, the doctrine of Original Sin does not seem formally fixed until the time of Pelagius and Augustine; but it is a doctrine at first held implicitly, then asserting itself, and at length fully developed. Again, the question of reception of Communion in one species is only gradually decided formally. Finally, there are the great Trinitarian controversies and those on the nature of the Hypostatic Union. Heresies provided an occasion for formal fixing of the object of Christian belief; before the difficulties there was no need for the precisions, but this does not suggest that we have wholly new data of faith. It was precisely those heresies which gave Christ a place beneath God which provided the attributes of the Blessed Virgin, Newman suggests.

One of the more lengthy discussions of historical instances of development has to do with the papal supremacy, and we may surmise that Newman had in mind his own and his countrymen's difficulties concerning that matter. In a manner that the previous discussions have prepared us for, Newman shows that the papacy does develop from the needs of the times and that the popes in various eras have viewed their function differently. But once more he does not take these variations to affect the essence of papal supremacy. We can imagine that Newman saw great local force in his ability to show that Anglicans could not balk at papal supremacy because it was a development unless they were willing to question their own Articles, most of which are also developments. What Newman was looking for is a universal theory which will demand consistency in testing the truth of developments.

What are the notes of a genuine development of Christian Doctrine? In the second part of his book, Newman distinguishes seven notes and goes on to apply each of them. The notes are as follows: Preservation of Type, Continuity of Principles, Assimilative Power, Logical Sequence, Anticipation of its Future, Conservative Action on its Past, and Chronic Vigor. In applying these notes, Newman is able to discuss a number of highly controversial issues. For example, the interpretation of Scripture; Penance, Purgatory, Meritorious Works, the Celibate Life, Devotion to the Blessed Virgin.

It is difficult not to be moved by Newman's conclusion, a paragraph in which he pleads with his reader to let the argument of his book speak for itself. Newman correctly expected the barrier his book was to create between him and his old friends, and it is almost as if he foresaw the long, somewhat bleak future that awaited him in the Roman Church. The theory of development this book developed did not meet a warm reception in the Catholic Church; Newman submitted the work for judgment, but this was not given because he had written the book as an Anglican. With the passage of time, the theory has been accorded an ever warmer reception and, while adjustments in it are doubtless necessary, it is clear that Newman, out of a sense of personal need as well as out of the necessities of the case, saw a difficulty that demands an answer and very likely an answer substantially like that he proposed. If it is true that all Christians of all times believe essentially the same thing, this cannot mean that at all times the articulations of the faith have been identical. We have seen in our own time definitions of articles of faith, definitions called for by the exigencies of the day or because discussion and research had finally been adequate. According to Newman's theory, this is the progressive assimilation of the idea we should expect; it is too large, so to speak, to be comprehended all at once. Its aspects must be made explicit, its facets developed. This is done in time and by men with the guarantee of an infallible authority. But the result is not something external and impersonal; it addresses itself to each of us and we must make it our own.

R.M.

ESSAY ON CATHOLICISM, LIBERALISM, AND SOCIALISM

Author: Juan Donoso Cortés (1809-1853)
Type of work: Apologetics, philosophy of history
First published: 1851

Principal Ideas Advanced

Theological error inevitably causes philosophical, political, and social error in any given society.

Liberalism is the midway station between Catholicism and socialism.

Theology is the light of history, the all-embracing science.

Deformed by original sin, "natural" man is a despicable being, unless cleansed by the supernatural grace of God.

Juan Donoso Cortés, Marqués de Valdegames, was a brilliant Spanish liberal who admired the French thinkers of the Enlightenment and believed that Spain was intellectually backward. Donoso served the Spanish government in various capacities, but his major concern was judging the intellectual and moral conditions of his age. He gradually turned away from liberalism, and in the last decade of his life was one of its most vehement and vociferous critics. The *Ensayo Sobre el Catolicismo, et Liberalismo y el Socialismo,* his only full-length book, sums up the conservative thought which he had expressed in many articles, letters, and speeches in the Spanish Cortes.

The *Ensayo* is the work of an orator; the book is full of so many rhetorical flourishes and overstatements that one imagines it as coming from the rostrum rather than from a quiet study. Throughout the book Donoso duels verbally with socialists, liberals, and liberal Catholics. Quotations from the *Ensayo,* therefore, tend to make Donoso seem even more extreme than he actually was.

Donoso condemned the "natural" man glorified by the liberals and socialists: "I know not if there be anything under the sun more vile and despicable than the human race outside the Catholic lines. . . . If my God had not taken flesh in the womb of a woman, nor died on the cross for the whole human race, the reptile I tread on would be less despicable in my eyes than man. . . . To believe in the nobility of those stupid crowds, it was necessary for God to reveal it to me."

This contemptuous view of man is theological rather than social, for it results from Donoso's appreciation of the enormity of original sin. He devotes many pages of the *Ensayo* to a study of the effects of original sin, which has destroyed right order in man's relationship to God and within himself. Original sin has resulted in sickness and death, he writes; it has turned the intellect from truth to error, and the will from good to evil; it is the source of rebellion, revolution, disobedience, tyranny, and all that is disordered in political and social life. According to Donoso, the transmission of sin to the entire human race "is one of the most fearful, most incomprehensible and obscure, of all the mysteries that have been taught us by divine revelation."

Political, social, and philosophical systems must be evaluated against the background of man's natural sinfulness. Liberals are in error, Donoso holds, when they say that the mind is naturally attracted to the truth. Between truth and human reason, Donoso tells us, there is "a lasting repugnance and an invincible repulsion," for the disordered intellect has an affinity for error and for the absurd.

Donoso argues that since Adam and Eve sinned before they had any children, Adam represented both the individual and the species; the solidarity of mankind thus has its natural beginning. The doctrine of solidarity has been obscured by modern individualist thinking, Donoso writes. According to Donoso, solidarity, "one of the most beautiful and august revelations of Catholic dogma," teaches the substantial unity of the human race, a unity extending vertically through all ages past and future and horizontally to all races and tribes. Membership in this community bestows responsibilities and a dignity that the isolated person could never possess. From this concept of solidarity, Donoso believes, one can deduce the permanency of nations, the inheritance of property, the unity of the family, and other such political and social ideas.

Liberal and socialist thinkers are both in error, Donoso argues, since both deny not only the God of Catholicism and the Christ of redemption but also man as deformed by sin and saved by supernatural grace. Nevertheless, Donoso admired the socialists for their boldness in accepting the conclusions to which liberal premises led. He was contemptuous of liberals for continually denying the truth without affirming the consequences of their denial. For this reason, he considered liberalism a halfway station on the road to socialism. The third possibility Donoso saw was a general return to Catholicism, not the "compromising" Catholicism of those trying to adapt their Church to modern institutions, but the "vigorous," "fearless" Catholicism of the past.

Donoso condemns the liberal School for being rationalistic, for admitting God but denying revelation, for favoring limited monarchy, and for reducing all questions of good and evil to a question of good or bad government, and he accuses the liberals of never affirming or denying anything absolutely. Eager to prevent the arrival of socialism or a return to Catholicism, liberals take refuge in discussion in order to create confusion and propagate skepticism. Donoso concludes that the liberal school "knows nothing of the nature of good or evil; it has scarcely any notion of God, and it has no notion of man whatever. Impotent for good, because devoid of all dogmatic affirmation, and for evil, because all intrepid and absolute negation horrifies it, it is condemned, without knowing it, to embark in the ship whose fortune carries it to the Catholic port, or the Socialist reefs." Although Donoso disagrees profoundly with the socialists, he grudgingly admires them for making bold, absolute denials and affirmations. In their manner they resemble Catholics, while in the content of their thought they resemble liberals: "Being, as they are, essentially theological, they measure the abysses in all their profundity, and are not wanting in a certain grandeur in the manner of proposing the problems and solving them." Socialists pervert right order by putting evil in society and making man the redeemer, whereas evil is in man, and God is the redeemer.

According to Donoso, socialism wants to tear down all forms of government, reject private ownership of property, and destroy the rights of the family in order to give free reign to all the passions and desires. Donoso considers this program wrong because it is based on erroneous theological assumptions about God and man. The social theories of the socialists are also absurd, for socialists do not understand the notion of solidarity; they would merge all men into a formless mass in the name of equality and fraternity. "In practice," Donoso exclaims, "they are yet Frenchmen, Italians, Germans; in theory they are citizens of the world, and like the world, their country is without frontiers. Madmen!"

Catholicism is seen by Donoso as having the answer to all human problems, for it is a synthesis of all truths. "It is a synthesis which embraces all, which contains all, and which explains all." Frequently in the *Ensayo* Donoso makes it clear that "liberal" Catholics like Montelambert were confused in believing that some modern institutions and ideas are good and should be adopted by the Church. Such modern ideas as that of separation of Church and state, or freedom of the press or religion he considers abhorrent, and those Catholics who advocate such principles are objectively untrue to their faith. Donoso considers both liberty and authority safe only within the Catholic system, for Catholicism enshrines both and limits both. The Church keeps authority from turning into tyranny, and liberty from becoming license.

The *Ensayo Sobre el Catolicismo, et Liberalismo y el Socialismo* caused violent polemics among European Catholics. Hailed by conservative Catholics, it became the biggest apologetic gun in the citadel they were holding against liberal Catholic thinkers. Liberals saw the *Ensayo* as containing certain basic heresies, and Donoso spent a large part of the remaining two years of his life defending his book against their attacks. Rome at length refused to condemn the *Ensayo,* which remains an important conservative statement.

As liberal Catholic thought grew stronger and more widespread, being accepted in Rome by the end of the nineteenth century, Donoso's influence waned. With the conservative revival of the mid-twentieth century, however, he again became important, and many basic social and political ideas of the *Ensayo* have been adopted by thinkers outside Catholic circles.

T.P.N.

THE IDEA OF A UNIVERSITY

Author: John Henry Cardinal Newman (1801-1890)
Type of work: Philosophy of Christian education
First published: 1852

Principal Ideas Advanced

Theology is theoretically and practically the only rationale for the successful operation of a Catholic center of higher learning.

A liberal education unifies science, the book of nature, and literature, the book of man, and requires the Church to refine the imperfections of each so that the disciplined student will be able to be a man of the world for the world.

The university is the place where universal knowledge is taught; the object of all learning is truth, and theology, as the study of the Ultimate Truth, forms the center of all learning.

John Henry Cardinal Newman's *The Idea of a University,* together with the appended *University Subjects,* is a collection of discourses and essays summarizing Newman's philosophical opinions concerning higher education and analyzing some of the subjects of the curriculum of the proposed Catholic University at Dublin, Ireland, to which he was appointed Rector in 1851. The first part is a series of nine popular but informed discourses or "lectures." The lectures were delivered before mixed audiences in Ireland to enlist financial and intellectual support for combating the growth of secularization at Oxford, Cambridge, and the University of London, as well as the nondenominational colleges established by the English government in Ireland. Originally entitled *Discourses on the Scope and Nature of University Education, Addressed to Catholics of Dublin,* the talks were delivered during May and June, 1852. The second part, first published as *Lectures and Essays on University Subjects* in 1858, is a grouping of ten varied lectures to the faculty of the Catholic University, Dublin. By 1873, the definitive edition of *The Idea of a University* was published, combining the lectures on the philosophy of Catholic university education with the essays on the university subjects to be taught at a Catholic university.

The Idea of a University is Newman's reply to the challenge to higher education which arose in England and Ireland in the 1850's concerning the aims, ideals, and curriculum of a Catholic university education. The discourses and essays are Newman's serious contribution to the educational and philosophic conflict then raging in the intellectual and political areas between the denominational and nondenominational theorists who argued for either total ecclesiastical or total secular orientation for higher education. Newman meets the ideological arguments in a patient and sincere explication written in a chaste, semiclassical oratorical style that became a hallmark of Victorian rhetoric. His cogent presentation of a philosophy of higher education together with his critical observation of some of the aspects of its curriculum have influenced the educational philosophy of all subsequent Catholic centers of higher learning.

Newman asks whether it is good sense to exclude the study of theology at the university level. Should the necessary emphasis on secular training neglect the higher training of the mind? What are the advantages of a Catholic university education beyond what is offered at secular universities? In reply, Newman extends the *via media* of his theological and autobiographical writings to champion the intellectual need for theology in the college curriculum as the *sine qua non* of a valid, purposeful respect for the branches of useful learning. He envisions a Catholic education as developing the student's entire personality, body and soul; he relates the Aristotelian premise of the primacy of knowledge to the Scholastic principle of perfection of soul.

Newman was distressingly aware that the educational practices and theories of the physical scientists and the rationalistic philosophers of his mid-Victorian day were creating widespread dissatisfaction among traditional educators and the more liberal innovators who sought to reconstruct an educational philosophy consistent with their times. He planned a university which would be for Catholics in Ireland what a perfect Oxford or Cambridge could become in England if the curricula were God-oriented. Thus, in his essays he insists that a religious-centered education be taken as the ideal, but, he adds, the Church should not discourage scientific investigation or in any way limit the pursuit of knowledge, the chief object of a university's existence. Newman declares that the essential task of theocentric education is to train men of the world for the world. While he opposes the liberalism of the Victorian scientist and pragmatist, he shows himself to be a liberal in his insistence on the primacy of learning prudentially based on Roman Catholic theology and philosophy.

Discourses I through V explicate the problem of relating theology to other fields of knowledge. In Discourses V through VIII he comments upon the relationship of theological knowledge to professional and nonprofessional learning, including religion. In Discourse IX Newman concludes with a detailed analysis of the role of the Church in higher education.

In the Preface to the series, Newman defines the university as a place where universal knowledge will be taught. Theology is a true science, he claims, and it should, therefore, be included in the curriculum of the university. A university has no right to exist if it permits students to concentrate exclusively on the study of advanced theories of science; on the other hand, if it stresses religious training to the exclusion of the scientific, it should close its doors. A university ought to be composed of a faculty gathered in one place to educate students to an appreciation of the harmony of all knowledge. "What I offer as my fundamentals," Newman writes, "are not the by-products of Revelation, supernatural study, or theological research affiliated with the Catholic Church; rather, my plans are rooted in wisdom, prudence and the testimony of antiquity and can be adopted by

Protestant as well as Catholic educators."

Theology is a branch of knowledge, Newman insists, and thus it should be respected and taught at the university. Without theology university teaching becomes unphilosophical and capricious. Since knowledge is the goal, the study of God cannot be excluded lest education be limited to secondary causes. The word "God" inspires a theology in itself which, once placed in the curriculum, cannot be overlooked in its relation to other subjects. How can we profess to know anything as true, Newman asks, if we bypass the "First Cause" and the "Last End" of all learning? Have we forgotten what theology means? Religion is not a sentimental feeling couched in prolixity, Newman insists, but an edifying conviction that faith is an intellectual act. Natural theology has greatly influenced our quest for learning; yet, God is more than nature and thus theology must be more than a study of nature. Subtly, Newman directs his pertinent comments to those in his Victorian audience who were affected by the serious decline in religious values. His argument is a logical rebuttal to Victorian secularists.

Theology, Newman points out in Discourse III, bears a positive relationship to other knowledge. Since the object of all learning is truth, the university curriculum cannot neglect the Ultimate Truth which is discernible in the various branches of all knowledge. The spokes of a carriage wheel (Newman uses an apt Victorian metaphor) are related to the hub and take their support from the strength of the center, which is Truth. Religious Truth is not, then, simply another arc in the wheel, but the actual hub, binding the arts and sciences to one another and giving purposeful meaning to the universality of knowledge. Remove the hub, Newman implies, and the arcs of learning will tumble from weakness into discord in their competition to become the new core.

Other subjects taught at the university, Newman argues in Discourse IV, have a bearing on theology and will create new intellectual hubs because of the very nature of truth (the mind's objective) and the capacity of the mind to search it out. Subjects other than theology will consequently form new pivots of student interest around which knowledge will develop. Since the mind cannot keep from questioning and systematizing, it will elect to center on one of the other branches of learning if theology is not allowed its central position in the university curriculum.

According to Newman, a university must teach the whole truth, and neither the secular sciences nor philosophy nor literature are, in themselves, the whole truth. Revelation, the written and unwritten word of God, furnishes facts unattainable by reason alone. To eliminate the knowledge supplied by theology and revelation is to narrow the function of the university. Natural theology and reason unsupported by the word of God tend to ignorance, Newman insists. He contends that the Fine Arts (painting, music, sculpture, architecture) and the secular sciences (physical and applied Geology and political economy) are handmaids of universal knowledge, but they cannot fully satisfy man's quest for truth. Theology alone can overcome the limitations of these subjects, since theology takes possession of them all and relates them one to another and each to the ultimate source of all truth.

Newman maintains that knowledge can and should be an end in itself, valued for its own sake without regard for the practical uses to which it can be put. Knowledge is like health; it is good in itself. When enriched by reason and theology, knowledge actually becomes a "philosophy" and has special power both as useful knowledge and as liberal knowledge. Useful knowledge often exhausts itself; liberal knowledge, since it is intellectual, exceeds the useful in that it is able to uncover more than the senses reveal and can thereby furnish ideas which supplement factual information.

Useful knowledge, Newman asserts, has benefited us in our time, but it has failed to make us better men or "gentlemen," which is the end of a university education. Whatever one's religious beliefs, the knowledge a gentleman needs is not to be equated with virtue, although refined cultural taste and a noble character may issue from much learning. Liberal education strives after intellectual excellence and the perfection of the reasoning faculty, and thus liberal knowledge should be sought as an end in itself. Newman regards liberal knowledge as involving seeking the "virtue" or perfection of the intellect through what, for want of a better term, he calls "philosophy" or "illumination." He defines the mission of the university as that of making possible the attainment of this illumination or intellectual culture.

In the three treatises which follow, Newman inquires into the "useful" nature of philosophic illumination. What, he asks, is the relation of the university goal to practical knowledge, to professional learning, to religious understanding? He concludes his analysis with a survey of the duties of the Church towards knowledge.

Too often, Newman suggests, a university is considered to be nothing more than a place for acquiring *information* about many subjects; the end of a liberal education, however, is *knowledge,* obtained through criticism. Enlargement of the mind is necessary if illumination is to follow. The greatest danger facing the Victorian system, Newman argues, is the overloading of the mind with a plethora of unrelated minutiae. Education is not recreation, but a preparation for further knowledge; a university should be a real "Alma Mater," loving its children for themselves.

According to Newman in Discourse VII, a cultivated mind is actually more "useful" than an uncultivated mind, for the liberally educated mind is a good in itself and gives the recipient a more creative sense of value than does a mere vocational training. Intellectual liberality encourages the student to descry realities and to accommodate himself to all situations and persons; it permits him to maintain that aplomb which is commensurate with genuine happiness.

Having witnessed the change which overtook Oxford University within the decade following his resignation, Newman speaks trenchantly from personal observation of the loss to Oxford's reputation as a cultural center by its acquiescence to the Utilitarian "march of the mind" encouraged by the Benthamites. Basically an apologist for romanticism, Newman abhors the cultural vacuity preached by the empiricists.

In Discourse VIII, Newman considers knowledge in relation to religion.

Since enlightened reason when properly exercised will lead the mind to a religious belief which is chiefly a code of morality and personal ethic, the Church has specific duties in education. Catholicism is distinguished from other religions by its fuller explanation of man's nature, origin, and end, and by its provision for a more adequate means for man's achieving his created purpose. Knowledge of God (theology) and the love of God's instruments (nature and man) keep us from those objects which may harm our rationality and spirituality. A gentleman's beliefs are all too often only the religion of reason (natural theology), which ignores the religious conscience; his creed is too often motivated by fear of God, not by charity. Too frequently, Newman argues, education and cultural refinement rationalize sin and avoid humility. Pride of intellect leads to a disdain for truth.

The secular university, says Newman scornfully, boasts of the gentleman-graduate: one who disdains conviction in favor of maintaining his social and intellectual balance. Many critics correctly see Newman's celebrated definition of a gentleman "one who never inflicts pain," as mild satire in the context of the discourse. Newman complains that too many educated men of nonreligious or denominational colleges (Protestant) are dilettantes, indifferent to religion and too full of pride to value intellectual virtue and humility. The implication is that if a gentleman lacks conviction, he will subscribe to philosophic shibboleths rather than offend by a doctrinal affirmation. Newman prefers virtuous edification to social composure as the mark of a university gentleman.

Newman argues in Discourse IX that the Church must implement its responsibilities toward the aquisition of knowledge by promulgating the sacred truths of revelation. Human reason can harm theological truth by minimizing religious experience and by adulterating the supremacy of the natural, moral law. In this final discourse, Newman minimizes his insistence on the need for making theology the core curriculum, and he devotes his lecture to an examination of literature and science, the universal objects of human study. Fearing that his audience may not comprehend the practical implications of his lectures, Newman appeals discursively to the commercial intelligentsia whose finances will ultimately have to endow the Catholic University at Dublin. He wants his philosophy of education to be construed as providing an incentive for a sound business investment.

There can be no conflict between Catholicism and the physical sciences when the activities of each are properly understood, Newman maintains. While there may be a jealous parochialism among religionists, scientists, and educators, there is basically no contradiction among their various disciplines, for all knowledge comes from God. Where differences existed in the past —and still do—the cause was due either to the exclusiveness of self-interest, or to the variety in method (induction for the scientist; deduction for the philosopher), or to self-imposed limitations on the subject matter (the scientist explains the logical order; the philosopher discusses the ontological order). The duty of the Church toward science is to keep the integrity of revealed truth from harm; the duty of the scientist is to search out the *whole* of Truth.

Literature, Newman continues, is more germane to man whereas science is more easily related to nature. A sinless literature, for example, would be a contradiction since it would hardly be a truthful record of human nature. Granting that the university is a place of intellectual preparation for men of the world, the Church can best fulfill its duty by encouraging men to accept the challenge of their nature as it is disclosed by the scientist and reflected in literature. Newman concludes as he began: theology is theoretically and practically the only rationale for the successful operation of a Catholic center of higher learning.

The dispassioned intellectualism of *The Idea of a University* and the succinct delineation of the curriculum in the *University Subjects* established Newman as the priestly director of the rebirth of Catholic writing in England. His clarity of approach, his humility of intellection, and his reverence for first and last causes made a profound impact on Catholic writers and on philosophers of Christian education.

E.A.J.

ENCHIRIDION SYMBOLORUM ET DEFINITIONUM

Author: Heinrich Joseph Dominicus Denzinger (1819-1883)
Type of work: Dogmatic theology
First published: 1854

Principal Ideas Advanced

[*Heinrich Denzinger's* Enchiridion Symbolorum *is a product of the great interest in theology and history which was so much a mark of intellectual life in nineteenth century Germany. The book is made up of a collection of historical documents important in the dogmatic development of Christianity. The documents cover the doctrinal history of Christianity from the first century until the middle of the nineteenth century and are presented with a high degree of scholarship.*]

Heinrich Denzinger's *Enchiridion symbolorum et definitionum* was first published in 1854. It was immediately regarded as a major work, important both for its historical and theological significance. Denzinger was certainly a scholar who, by his training, was capable of producing such a work. He had earned a Ph.D. degree prior to his entrance into the clerical life in 1838. After his ordination in 1844, he became professor of dogmatic theology at the University of Wurzburg, a position he held until his death in 1883.

Denzinger's work was in the best tradition of the German scholarship of the nineteenth century, an age of great German accomplishments in history, and also of great German interest in theology. It was only natural that the two studies, history and theology, should be combined, as they were in the minds of many of Germany's greatest thinkers, especially those of the Catholic faith, and Denzinger was an able follower in this tradition, a disciple of such distinguished forerunners as Johann Adam Möhler and Johann Ignaz Dollinger.

As a theologian imbued with a historical spirit, Denzinger wished to provide a reliable collection of sources in the doctrinal history of the Church; this he accomplished with his *Enchiridion symbolorum*. The work consists of a collection of original doctrinal documents, the chief decrees and definitions of Church councils, lists of condemned propositions, and other papal pronouncements. The documents are presented with all the requirements of sound scholarship. The sources from which the documents are taken are carefully noted, and whenever it is possible the documents are given in both Latin and Greek.

It is a mark of the importance of Denzinger's work that his compilation is still not out of date today, although it has been necessary to revise it continually in order to include in it documents which came into existence after Denzinger had completed his original collection. Moreover, there have been several translations of the work in order to make it available to those not familiar with Latin or Greek. Thus, the American student of today may profitably consult one of the two following books, both of which are based on Denzinger: *Sources of Catholic Dogma* (1957), translated by Roy J. Deferrari from the thirtieth edition of the *Enchiridion Symbolorum* and *The Church Teaches* (1955), edited by John F. Clarkson, S.J., John H. Edwards, S.J., William J. Kelley, S.J., and John J. Welch, S.J.

An examination of the documents included in Denzinger's work provides something of a brief panorama of the doctrinal history of the Church along with reminders of the struggles and conflicts which have marked the history of Christianity.

With respect to the documents which date from the early or primitive period of the Church, one should note first of all the numerous creeds with which the early Christians, in clear, restrained, yet simply eloquent language, expressed their beliefs. Denzinger's collection includes the Apostles' Creed, the Nicene Creed, the Niceno-Constantinopolitan Creed, and the famous Athanasian Creed. But in the study of the primitive Church there is much more of interest. One may find in Denzinger numerous documents in which popes and councils (notably those of Ephesus and Chalcedon) insisted on the primacy of the Roman See within Christendom. One will note, too, the great range of doctrinal disputes and heresies which were so marked a characteristic of the early Church, and one will also find many of the condemnations that were hurled at such unorthodox teachings as Nestorianism and Pelagianism. Especially numerous are decrees relating to the Incarnation and the Trinity, which, since they are the greatest and most profound mysteries of Christianity, naturally stirred up the greatest controversies. But decrees relating to other matters are also to be found: there are various pronouncements on the sacraments, especially the sacrament of Penance, around which more than one great dispute raged in the early Church, and there are also statements with regard to Extreme Unction, Confirmation, and Holy Communion. Other decrees deal with such matters as the virginity of the Blessed Mother of Our Lord, and the necessity of clerical celibacy.

During the Middle Ages the Church reached perhaps the highest peak of its influence over the Western world. Yet an examination of Denzinger's *Enchiridion symbolorum* provides ample evidence that there were still many matters around which doctrinal disputes could and did occur, and on which popes and councils saw fit to pronounce judgment. One continues to find a great number of decrees relating to the Incarnation, for example, and this fact serves as clear testimony that this difficult theological question had not yet been completely formalized. It was still necessary, too, to deal with the errors of various heretics, among whom the Waldensians and the Albigensians were the most prominent. In the decrees relating to usury and its evils one can find evidence of the Church's interest in the temporal world. From the frequency of the decrees on such clerical abuses as simony, it is evident that disciplinary matters were often of as great a concern in the Middle Ages as were doctrinal questions. Yet the Middle Ages was a constructive period for the Church and her doctrines. Much was then becoming settled and formalized; for example, a number of decrees in Denzinger relate to the form of the sacraments.

Beginning with the reign of Pope Boniface VIII in 1294 the Church entered into a new and dangerous period of her existence. This was the age of the great quarrels between the popes and the emerging national states. It was the age of new and dangerous heresies and of serious disruptions within Christianity, of which the Great Western Schism was the most prominent example. Denzinger's collection provides documentary evidence of many of these difficulties. Among other important texts, one may find Boniface VIII's "Unam Sanctam" condemning the French king, Philip the Fair. One may also find several of the decrees of the Council of Constance, which ended the Great Western Schism with the election of Martin V, condemned the heresies, and indeed the person of John Huss, and raised, in a particularly acute form, the danger of conciliarism.

Denzinger's *Enchiridion symbolorum* is particularly rich in documents which date from the period of the Reformation. Among the most interesting of these is Leo X's condemnation of the errors of Martin Luther. As might be imagined, the decrees of the Council of Trent are extensively reproduced. One may note especially the decrees on Sacred Scripture, original sin, justification and salvation. Also important are the decrees on the sacraments and the statements of the council Fathers with respect to the Mass. One may note, too, the decrees in which the council reaffirmed, in opposition to the Protestants, the truth of such Catholic doctrines as the existence of purgatory, the veneration of the saints, and the usefulness of indulgences.

The centuries which followed the Reformation and preceded the French Revolution were perhaps less dramatic for the Church, but they were no less dangerous. There were still heresies to be dealt with, some of them strikingly similar to Protestant doctrines. Thus, one may find in Denzinger some of the many papal pronouncements issued against the heresy of Jansenism, which rocked the French Church in particular. There was also the problem of meeting the threatened, and sometimes actual, secular domination of the Church by the powerful national monarchies. Thus, Denzinger's collection includes the condemnation of Febronianism, a teaching which threatened, particularly in Germany, to undermine the position of the papacy.

Denzinger's original collection concludes with the decrees and pronouncements of the early nineteenth century. But subsequent editions have continued to bring matters up to date, and it is probable that every few years will see a new edition of Denzinger's valuable work.

There are perhaps some characteristics of the documents contained in the *Enchiridion symbolorum* which may seem striking in the twentieth century. In an age in which there is much talk of limiting the power of the curia, Denzinger may appear to have included too many documents concerning the primacy of the papacy. In an age which is greatly interested in the ecumenical movement and prays for the eventual union of all Christians, Denzinger's documents seem all to be of a controversial, polemical nature. But Denzinger did not live in the twentieth century; he lived, instead, in an age in which there were continual and great controversies between Catholics and Protestants, Catholics and rationalists, and even among Catholics themselves. Studies of a polemical nature had not yet gone out of style in the nineteenth century. Denzinger's work was prepared with great diligence and careful scholarship. Certainly, he cannot be blamed for sharing the aims and ideas of his age. Armed with this understanding, the student of today can still hope to attain a better insight into the doctrinal history of the Church by consulting, if he will, the original documents contained in Denzinger's *Enchiridion symbolorum.*

P.T.M.

APOLOGIA PRO VITA SUA

Author: John Henry Cardinal Newman (1801-1890)
Type of work: Spiritual autobiography
First published: 1864

Principal Ideas Advanced

Dogma is necessary in religion; from dogma one learns that there is a visible Church, with sacraments and rites, the channels of invisible grace.

The early view (which the author held) that the pope is the Antichrist was in error.

The Church's infallibility is a provision of God to preserve religion in the world by curbing the excesses of free thought.

Once one accepts the authority of the Roman Catholic Church the intellectual difficulties besetting such doctrines as that of transubstantiation disappear.

For a score of years after becoming a Catholic (in 1845) and a member of the Roman Catholic clergy (in 1847), Father John Henry Newman had suffered from a series of critical attacks. He encountered opposition and frustration in his project to establish the Catholic University in Dublin, in the Achilli trial, which found him guilty of slander, and in his editorship of "The Rambler," undertaken at the request of his bishop and terminated by this superior after the second number. There was, moreover, the widely held view among Protestants that for years while in the Anglican livery and service Newman had been clandestinely working for Rome. As if that were not enough, a segment of the Roman Catholic clergy, including Monsignor Talbot and Cardinal Manning, questioned his orthodoxy and were regrettably captious in their criticism of what he said and wrote.

An unprovoked and unwarranted attack by the Anglican cleryman and novelist, Charles Kingsley, appeared to be another of the trials that had to be borne by Newman, but it proved to be a blessing in disguise. In the January, 1864, issue of "Macmillan's Magazine" Kingsley reviewed with fulsome praise James A. Froude's *History of England,* a work that is a thinly disguised panegyric of Protestantism. Using his review as a springboard for an attack on the Roman Catholic clergy, the critic singled out Father Newman as his scapegoat: "Truth, for its own sake, had never been a virtue with the Roman clergy. Father Newman informs us that it need not, and on the whole ought not to be; that cunning is the weapon which heaven has given to the Saints wherewith to withstand the brute male force of the wicked world which marries and is given in marriage. Whether his notion be doctrinally correct or not, it is at least historically so."

In the ensuing correspondence between Newman and Kingsley the latter consented to withdraw the charge but would not do so on the issue of its truth or falsehood. Newman's publication of the correspondence led Kingsley to publish a pamphlet of forty-eight pages, "What then does Dr. Newman mean?" In it Kingsley, using distortion and misrepresentation, set forth dozens of instances from Newman's writings as an Anglican and as a Catholic, examples of what he claimed proved Newman's deceit, dishonesty, and irresponsibility.

To leave this impeachment of his moral nature unanswered, Newman decided, would not be consistent with his duty to himself and, more importantly, to the Roman Catholic clergy. Here Newman's knowledge of the human mind and heart proved invaluable. He declared that he would answer the charges one by one lest anyone should say they were unanswerable. Yet such was not to be the substance of his reply. He would draw out the history of his mind; he would state from what external suggestions or accidents his opinions arose, how they developed from within, were modified, combined, changed. He would show how the doctrines he held for so many years were taught him partly by the suggestions of

Protestant friends, partly by the teaching of books, and partly by the action of his own mind. The result was Newman's moving spiritual autobiography and defense of the Faith: the *Apologia pro vita sua.*

For anyone to expose his innermost thoughts, his doubts, disappointments, frustrations, errors, and slanderous charges against others is an extremely trying experience. For the highly intelligent, affectionate, and shy future Cardinal it was an excruciating agony.

During his boyhood, Newman writes in his *Apologia,* he enjoyed reading the Bible, but he was not influenced by a definite creed until the age of fifteen, when through books given him by Reverend Walter Mayer he was attracted to Calvinism. The extracts from Saint Augustine and Saint Ambrose contained in Milner's *Church History* were to the fifteen-year-old boy a source of great delight. At the same age his reading of Newton's *Prophecies* convinced him that the pope was the Antichrist—a view that he was to hold until he was forty years old.

He acknowledges a significant debt to Dr. Hawkins of Oxford. It was he who taught Newman to be careful and exact in thinking and communication. He led Newman not only to rid himself of what remained of his Calvinism but to learn of and embrace the doctrine of tradition; namely, that Scripture was never intended to teach doctrine, but only to prove it. At this time the reading of Bishop Butler's *Analogy,* with its doctrine that probability is the guide of life, provided Newman with what was to be one of the fundamental principles of his later teaching.

Newman was on terms of the most affectionate friendship with Hurrell Froude from 1829 until Froude's death in 1836. In the *Apologia* Father Newman credits his friend with influencing him to look with admiration on the Church of Rome, to develop devotion to the Blessed Virgin, and to believe in the Real Presence.

Beginning in 1833 Newman, together with John Keble, Hurrell Froud, and a number of other Anglicans, became prominent in the Tractarian Movement, designed to uphold primitive Christianity, regenerate the Anglican Church, and resist and repel encroachments by the State on the prerogatives of the Church. His three cardinal principles as a Tractarian were: (1) the principle of dogma; (2) the truth of a certain definite religious teaching, based upon this foundation of dogma, namely, that there was a visible Church, with sacraments and rites, the channels of invisible grace; (3) the identification of the pope with Antichrist. Newman adds that although he has utterly renounced the third principle, he is firm and unchanged in his adherence to the first and second.

Newman's sincerity and candor do not permit him to be silent about many things that he wished he had never said. This applies not only to his equating of the pope with Antichrist but also to his slanderous attacks on Roman Catholics in general. Writing in the *British Critic* of 1840 against the controversialists of Rome he declared: "By their fruits ye shall know them. . . . We see it [the Roman Church] attempting to gain converts among us by unreal representations of its doctrines, plausible statements, bold assertions, appeals to the weaknesses of human nature, to our fancies, our eccentricities, our fears, our frivolities, our false philosophies. We see its agents smiling and nodding and ducking to attract attention, as gipsies make up to truant boys, holding out tales for the nursery and pretty pictures, and gilt gingerbread, and physic concealed in jam, and sugar plums for good children. . . . We Englishmen like manliness, openness, consistency, truth."

Such attacks he had made as a matter of duty because the prescription of such protests was a principle of the Anglican Church. Although he had acted according to conscience, one can realize the anguish that he suffered in having to iterate calumnies against the Church that he had now loved for many years.

It was primarily to prevent the conversion to Roman Catholicism of some members of the Oxford Movement that Newman wrote the fateful Tract XC. His thesis was that the Thirty-Nine Anglican Articles did not oppose Catholic teaching; they but partially opposed Roman dogma; and they for the most part opposed only the dominant errors of Rome. The storm of denunciation that followed led Newman to resign from the Movement. From 1841 to 1843 he was the target of attack from a host of Anglican ecclesiastics and laity.

In 1843 Newman made a formal retraction of the attacks he had made against the Church of Rome, and he later resigned from the Living of St. Mary's. Between 1843 and 1845 he lived in a state of almost monastic seclusion, praying, meditating, studying, endeavoring to attain certitude of religious convictions. During this period he abstained altogether from intercourse with Catholics, from their churches, religious rites, and usages. In October, 1845, he reached the state of certitude that he had been seeking and was received into the Roman Catholic Church.

On becoming a Catholic, Newman had no difficulty in receiving those additional articles that are not in the Anglican Creed. That there are intellectual difficulties besetting doctrines he does not deny. The doctrine of transubstantiation is such. He did not believe it until he became a Catholic, but he had no difficulty in believing it once he believed that the Roman Catholic Church is the oracle of God.

The Church's infallibility, he states, is a provision of God to preserve religion in the world, to restrain freedom of thought, which is one of the greatest of our natural gifts, in order to rescue it from its own suicidal excesses. He adverts to the view, widely held by his fellow countrymen, that following his conversion his own thoughts will no longer be his own property, that he will be restrained in a kind of cerebral strait jacket. "Nothing," he says, "can be presented to me, in time to come, as a part of the faith, but what I already ought to have received, and hitherto have been kept from receiving, (if so,) merely because it has not been brought home to me. Nothing can be imposed upon me different in kind from what I hold already,—much less contrary to it."

Newman then directs the attention of his countrymen to something he has had the opportunity of observing for nineteen years: the excellence, devotion, and self-sacrifice of the Roman Catholic priests. Their actions, their sacrifices, their self-abnegation can be explained in only one way—they believe what they profess.

As he concludes the *Apologia,* Cardinal Newman who, in Belloc's phrase, *was* Oxford, turns his thoughts to the Oxonians who were so dear to him and prays that they may all be united in Christ. On this note ends one of the world's greatest books of self-revelation.

J.E.F.

THE LIFE OF OUR LORD JESUS CHRIST

Author: Louis Veuillot (1813-1882)
Type of work: Biography, apologetics
First published: 1864

Principal Ideas Advanced

The Gospels are reliable inspired accounts of Christ's public ministry and of His miracles.

The Gospels are to be read in the literal, allegorical, tropological, and anagogical senses.

Miracles attest amply to Christ's divinity.

The greatest miracle of all was God's becoming man and living and dying for all mankind.

No man could have invented the life and words of Christ, for these are past human imagining and must be taken on faith.

Louis Veuillot was a self-educated, vociferous apologist for the Church in France during the middle fifty years of the nineteenth century. As editor of *Univers* he reached most French priests and many laymen. His journal became the leading voice of conservative Catholicism, a champion of papal infallibility, and severe critic of such "liberal" Catholics as Frédéric Ozanam and Bishop Dupanloup.

The Life of Our Lord Jesus Christ was written in answer to Renan's *Vie de Jésus* (1863). Veuillot was able to write his substantial biography in short order because his paper had been suppressed by Napoleon III's government in 1860 and was not allowed to appear again until 1867. Renan, the most literate and popular of the "higher critics," denied the possibility of miracles and considered Christ to be either a good social reformer or a self-deluded preacher. Opposing Renan's conception of a purely human Christ, Veuillot wrote a biography stressing the fusion of human and divine natures in the Person of Jesus, with special emphasis on His miracles and His message.

Veuillot writes that his larger purpose is to teach his age about the ways of God, for his age, he claims, is one of sophistry, rationalism, and intellectual confusion. "The science of the ways of God is the knowledge of Jesus Christ, and this knowledge is nowadays far more indispensable than ever," Veuillot states. His particular aim, he tells the reader, is to refute the modern sophists who think in the style of the ancient apostate Porphyry, who "pretended to honor Jesus Christ very much and called Jesus Christ a pious man and worthy of immortality." Even more forcefully Veuillot complains about Renan's "malicious book which unhappily signalizes the age in which we live." He does not write to convert such people, he claims, but rather for the sake of men such as he himself used to be, men who try to ignore the existence of God and to avoid questions concerning Christ's life and teaching.

Like other biographies of Christ, Veuillot's is based primarily on the Gospels. The problem of chronology is adroitly handled, and the commentary of the Church Fathers is interlaced into the narrative to explain Christ's teachings and the meanings of various miracles. The author explains to the reader that he really considers himself more a translator than an author, for with the Gospels as his source and many learned and saintly Fathers on whom to rely, "perhaps not an entire page belongs to him [Veuillot]." This statement is an exaggeration. The tone of the work is typical of Veuillot: highly polemical, strongly rather than reasonably dogmatic, attributing the lowest motives to those who doubt and the greatest sanctity to those who have never gone through the crucible of doubt.

The first sentence strikes the theme of the work: "There are in the Gospel two personages—God and man." And a sentence at the conclusion sums it up: "This Jesus thus given is the Son of Man and the Son of God—man and God at the same time: man born under the law, God to consummate and accomplish the law; man to serve, God to set free; man to bend under the yoke, God to conquer; man to die, God to triumph over death."

The author deals in a long preface with the problem of miracles, for he contends that he must vindicate miracles if he is to make his story of Christ's life credible. He maintains that the "sophists" argue that Jesus is not God because He has not performed miracles and that He has not performed miracles because He is not God. The claim that miracles are incredible, Veuillot insists, is ridiculous, since by their very nature miracles go counter to ordinary beliefs and must, therefore, be accepted on faith. But to accept by faith is not unreasonable, Veuillot claims, for there are many things we must accept as true without being able to understand them. Christ performed miracles so that men would know that He was divine and so that they would accept His teaching. Veuillot's opinion of the authenticity and purpose of miracles is summed up in a quotation he takes from Pope Saint Gregory: "The miracles of the Saviour are real, and at the same time they serve to teach us some truth. By those acts of his power, God points out to us certain things; he reveals to us from them other things, through the mysteries that his wisdom has placed in them."

The Life of Our Lord Jesus Christ is divided into nine books. The first three are strictly biographical, taking the reader through the first two years of Our Lord's public ministry. The next two deal with the education of the Apostles and with Christ's general discourses and parables. Book VI treats of the events leading up to the Passion; Book VII, the Eucharistic banquet; Book VIII, the Passion; and Book IX, the Risen Lord.

Veuillot's work is a standard treatment of Our Lord's life. Its popularity over other such biographies of Christ rests upon its unobtrusive use of authentic sources and the author's vivid narrative style. This work acquired additional authority from the preface written by Pope Pius IX, who addresses his preface "To Our beloved Son Louis Veuillot," and writes that "this new work presented to us gains peculiar lustre from the nature of the trials to which you have become subject; since, amid those trying circumstances, it is marked by that hunger and thirst for justice, that zeal and strength of mind, you always manifested in maintaining the combat you entered upon"—an obvious reference to the French government's suppression of *Univers.*

Veuillot's life of Christ went through many editions and was translated into several languages. Within the first decade after its publication seven French editions were issued, and the standard English version was translated from the seventh French edition in 1875 by the Reverend Anthony Farley. Veuillot has been called by some historians the outstanding Catholic layman of the nineteenth century, while others have claimed that he harmed the Church more than did any other layman. Veuillot's life of Christ, however, was not controversial, as were most of his other writings, and it was popularly accepted by Catholics of both liberal and conservative persuasions, and by many other Christians as well.

T.P.N.

THE AMERICAN REPUBLIC

Author: Orestes Augustus Brownson (1803-1876)
Type of work: Philosophy of Church and state
First published: 1865

Principal Ideas Advanced

The written constitution of the United States derives its vitality and legal force from an anterior, unwritten, and providential constitution which originally made it possible for the collective people to form a government.

The political destiny of the American republic is to complete the work of the Graeco-Roman civilization by eliminating the barbaric elements that undermined the older constitution and by achieving a true balance in the division of powers between the general and the particular governments of the states.

The religious destiny of the republic is to realize a relation between Church and state which respects the free movement of each within the sphere to which it is assigned by divine law.

Convinced that his views on political philosophy had reached their full development, Orestes Brownson announced in the Preface to *The American Republic* that he wished this work henceforward to be considered as "the only authentic statement" of his position on the subject. Writing some twenty years after his conversion to the Catholic Church, Brownson, acclaimed by *Americana* as "perhaps the greatest publicist America produced," writes that he especially wishes to address himself to his fellow Catholics, but speaks to all Americans, and hopes in his "old age" that he might be able "to exert an influence on the future" of the country he so dearly loves. Many are of the opinion that the full impact of Brownson's influence is yet to come. "In the latter part of the twentieth century," writes Russell Kirk in *The Conservative Mind,* "more attention may be paid to him than he has received in the past hundred years."

Throughout his work Brownson endeavors to establish that the dependence of creatures on their Creator leaves neither society nor government with an independent status. Accordingly, he announces that he has "labored to show the scientific relations of political to theological principles," which, he holds, are basic to all reality.

Brownson considers that it is important that nations as well as individuals heed the sage but difficult counsel given in the ancient precept, "Know thyself." Prior to the civil war, he reflects, the United States "lived the unreflective life of a child," but now "it has been suddenly compelled to study itself." The destiny of a nation is to realize the idea which Providence assigns to it, for, in a sense, every nation is a chosen people. He would have his fellow countrymen look beyond the written constitution to the "constitution of the American people themselves." This he calls the unwritten or providential constitution which expresses the creative act through which government participates in God.

Brownson conceives of a threefold communion with the triune God for the fulfillment of human existence: religion, society, and property. For the Christian, he says, religion is that communion "which binds man to God as his first cause," through God's creative act, "and carries him onward to God as his final cause," through the Incarnation. Society is viewed as man's "communion with God through humanity," and since society requires government, government becomes an important means of man's communion with God. Property involves man's communion with God "through the material world," or nature, a communion which forms the basis for his natural rights with respect to the use and ownership of property. Thus, man unites himself to his Creator through Church, state, and property.

Political writers, Brownson contends, generally deal with the origin of government without distinguishing between the historical fact of an existing state and the ethical right of government to govern. Historically, it can be said that governments developed from patriarchies, as society developed from the family. The transformation of the patriarchal system into Greek and Italian republics, and later into the Roman Republic and Empire, Brownson explains, "marks the passage from the economical order to the political, from the barbaric to the civil constitution of society, or from barbarism to civilization." The distinctive characteristic of barbarism, he explains, is that it exercises authority as a private right; civilization exercises authority as a public trust: "Republic, *respublica,* by the very force of the term, means the public wealth, or, in good English, the commonwealth; that is, government founded not on personal or private wealth, but on the public wealth, public territory, or domain, or a government that vests authority in the nation, and attaches the nation to a certain definite territory."

Brownson finds the social compact theory of the origin of government advanced by Thomas Hobbes (1588-1679) untenable. That men would voluntarily emerge from a previous existence in a "state of nature" would presuppose "modes of thought" possible only in men who have passed far beyond such a primitive state. That such consent could be unanimous, Brownson finds too fanciful to imagine. If the right of government derives from the consent of the governed, he asks, how can government exercise power over the many who never gave their consent? At best, he suggests, the social compact loses its binding force with the death of the individuals who formed it.

Whether sovereignty in the absolute sense be conceived as inhering in the individual or in the people collectively through a modified social compact, the result, Brownson argues, is state absolutism. To him neither individualism nor socialism sees the victory Christianity has won for modern society in overthrowing state absolutism and thereby securing the rights of individuals in keeping with the dignity of man. Man's dependence on his Creator limits the sphere and nature of human sovereignty to a secondary and derived sovereignty. Ethically, natural law is equated with moral law and is explained as transcribing the eternal law which the Creator imposes on man as a moral creature. Natural law, then, as man's "immediate participation of the divine light," authorizes society to institute government; it is the basis of all legitimacy in government, for it proceeds from God as final cause and prescribes man's moral rights and duties; it is divine law promulgated through human reason and binding on all men. Rulers derive their political authority from God through the collective people, and the collective people derive their authority from God through the law of nature. Because of the equality of men under the law of nature, as under the Christian law, political sovereignty vests in the collective people.

In seeking a basis for government that is purely human, Brownson points out, politicians have unwittingly sought a basis that is atheistic. In all legitimate government, there is movement and stability; movement derives from the human element, stability from the divine element. Civic virtues attain the rank of religious vitues with the recognition that the divine as well as the human element is involved in government. Religion, then, is brought to the aid of the state without confusing the separate spheres of Church and state.

Any form of government, says Brownson, may be constituted by a nation so long as it is "established and maintained by the national will." The essential constitution of all forms of government other than despotic or barbaric, he explains, is republican, but the wisest form of government within the republican framework for a given commonwealth cannot be predetermined. Thoughtful Americans look to the American system of government as better in itself than any other form, but they know that the providential constitutions of other countries may not require its adoption. America is a republic because it holds its power "as a trust to be exercised for the public good," and it is a territorial democracy "because all political rights, powers, or franchises are territorial."

Brownson emphasizes the importance of the question of the nature of the union that constitutes the United States. Whether it be a matter of a compact between several sovereign individuals, as held by the disciples of Jean Jacques Rousseau (1712-1778), or between several sovereign states for the purpose of forming a new state, as Americans have frequently contended, a compact between sovereigns, Brownson reasons, remains but a compact. Thomas Jefferson (1743-1826) had supposed the several states to be independently sovereign prior to the convention of 1787, but held that their subsequent ratification of the constitution made them one people as regards foreign nations, though individually sovereign as regards domestic matters. Daniel Webster (1782-1852) likewise conceded an independent sovereignty to the several states prior to the convention, but he regarded the ratification of the constitution as creating one sovereign state or nation with a supreme government that respects states' rights. Brownson finds Jefferson's and Webster's conception of the nature of the union in agreement with that of John C. Calhoun (1782-1850) according to which it is but a confederation of sovereign states. Thus, the right of a state to withdraw from a union conceived as a confederacy is unquestionable, though perhaps it would be unwise to exercise that right.

The sovereignty which was in Great Britain prior to the winning of independence might have passed to the states separately, Brownson grants, but as a matter of fact, he urges, sovereignty was recognized as having passed to the states as united. The mutually independent colonies constituted one people, as do the mutually independent states, and therefore, he concludes, the United States must be considered as one sovereign nation, not as a confederation of nations. Even the transitional Articles of Confederation, Brownson notes, speak of the states not as confederated but as united. "The instinct of unity," says Brownson, "rejected state sovereignty in 1787 as it did in 1861."

Brownson reflects that the wisdom of an inspired work is at times scarcely revealed to the workmen. The preamble to the constitution drawn up by American statesmen professes its ordination by "the people of the United States" and thus indicates that they thought of themselves both as "the people" and as existing within the states. They recognized that in the United States there are no sovereign people apart from the states and that there are no states apart from the union, but the nation first had to attain "full consciousness" before it could clearly see that the union of states was never intended as a confederation: "What binds is the thing done, not the theory on which it is done, or on which the actors explained their work either to themselves or to others. Their political philosophy, or their political theory, may sometimes affect the phraseology they adopt, but forms no rule for interpreting their work. Their work was inspired. . . ."

Brownson finds that the conventional division of powers between the general and the particular governments of the states, provided for by the constitution of government, accords perfectly with America's providential constitution. The general government concerns itself with general rights, such as making of treaties with foreign countries, and the regulation of foreign and domestic trade. State governments concern themselves with matters lying within their territorial limits, including the personal and private rights of their citizens. The method of dialectically organizing social forces, general and particular, Brownson calls the distinctive mark of the American system; it guards against the extremes of centralism, on the one hand, and disintegration, on the other hand. Neither can the general government oppress the people as regards private rights, nor can the state governments oppress the people as regards their general rights.

Prior to the war between the states, Brownson reflects, the American people talked boastfully of their dedication to democracy, but they failed to recognize democracy's three basic types: territorial, personal, and humanitarian. In the conflict "occasioned by the collision of two extreme parties," namely, the personal democracy of the secessionists and the humanitarian democracy of the northern abolitionists, the government rose to the defense of the nation's territorial democracy against the immediate threat posed by personal democracy. The fallacy of the secessionists, Brownson points out, was their failure to see that sovereignty is vested, not in the states separately, but in the union of states; the fallacy of the humanitarians was to look at state sovereignty as subordinate to the sovereignty of the general government. It was right, Brownson grants, that the humanitarians should seek the abolition of slavery, but wrong that they should petition the general government to deal with a matter pertaining to the personal rights of man. It was right that the Southern states should oppose the trend toward centralization of power within the general government, but wrong that they should tolerate "so barbaric an element as slavery." The government accepted the services of the humanitarians, but it was, in a sense, fighting a different war. Lincoln's anti-slavery policy, as the president personally assured Brownson, was reluctantly adopted to ward off the threat of foreign intervention in a war to preserve the unity and integrity of the American state. The Union victory was not a victory over the South, but a victory over personal democracy and for the territorial democracy of the American system. Personal democracy, Brownson points out, leads to disintegration, and he regards the defeat of the secessionist as its final elimination from the American scene. However, he warns, the tendency toward centralization of power that accompanies humanitarian democracy looms as the nation's future menace.

The political and religious destinies of man are considered as distinguishable but inseparable, for man communes with his Creator through all the media of his individual and social life. The political destiny of the United States, as Brownson conceives it, is to complete the work of the Graeco-Roman civilization by eliminating "the barbaric elements retained by the Roman constitution," and to realize a true balance in the division of governmental powers. The religious destiny of the nation is to make it possible to realize the proper relation between Church and state. Nowhere else in the world, thinks Brownson, is it possible to heal the breach between Church and state and thereby to achieve the free movement of each within its divinely constituted sphere. "The church wants freedom in relation to the state—nothing more," says Brownson. He makes a plea for "the utmost freedom" for all religions; it is sufficient that the principles of the state silently oppose false religions toward their elimination. A state constituted in harmony with the divine order, he says, "is carried onward by the force of its own internal constitution in a catholic direction." Brownson predicts that the steady growth in the Catholic population will be a significant factor in the future development of the country. Since the state bears the Church in its constitution, he suggests that the Catholic generally finds himself better prepared than others to understand the state's constitution, but he discerns "a more or less catholic truth" underlying the sectarian surface of nearly all Americans.

Though admittedly of secondary importance, the possibility of a continental destiny proves enticing to Brownson. That the American republic should someday encompass the continent that has given it its name, seems to him not unlikely. The initiative, he grants, would have to come from our neighboring states, for expansion by conquest is wholly incompatible with the American character. However, Brownson cautions the American people against concerning themselves about territorial expansion, and says that it will come as a matter of course and "as fast as desirable." He would have his fellow countrymen "devote their attention to their internal destiny, and the realization of their mission within." He entreats the country to assume its role of leadership in the New World and of influence in the Old, and he urges that it become the great military and naval power that its newly acquired position demands; in other words, he would have the American republic "yield to its destiny."

V.J.M.

THE MYSTERIES OF CHRISTIANITY

Author: Matthias Joseph Scheeben (1835-1888)
Type of work: Theology
First published: 1865

Principal Ideas Advanced

A mystery is a truth forever beyond the reach of reason and apprehensible only indirectly, through revelation and by means of analogy.

The triune relationship within the Godhead, though not rationally knowable, is the foundation and model for all creation, as well as being its source and end.

Men participate in the love of the Father for the Son through the action of the Holy Spirit, who Himself draws life and being from that love.

The mystery of the Incarnation unites God with man, the summit and summing-up of all creation, in a single dimension of existence, so that creation joins with the Son in offering up a continual and perfect holocaust of self-emptying praise to the Father.

The Mysteries of Christianity, by Matthias Joseph Scheeben, is a far-reaching attempt to view the whole range of theology in terms of the Christian mysteries, particularly as they operate in the everyday life of both the individual Christian and the entire Church. The mysteries are revealed as a systematic whole, "a great, mystic cosmos erected, out of the depths of divinity, upon the world of nature which is visible only to the mind." This final and definitive work of the great nineteenth century theologian explores the area where the science of philosophy meets that of theology and is transcended rather than contradicted by the latter. Revelation does not replace or overrule reason; it deals with those things reason could never arrive at unaided, no matter how advanced men's scientific knowledge might become.

The claim of Christianity to be a revelation of divine truth is strongly supported by its central mysteries. Without them, revelation itself would have been ultimately unnecessary and the highest fulfillment of man would lie no farther than the limits of his rational intellect. In order for a truth to be dignified by the name of mystery, it must lie beyond the potential knowledge available by the use of human reason and be capable of definition only by analogy, not by direct apprehension and comprehension of its essence. Only God Himself knows without mystery, and His essence can be known only in terms of mystery. Even when man observes natural phenomena, he is limited by his own nature, which is not equipped for a complete and instantaneous knowledge such as is proper only to the nature of God. A mystery can be known only with the aid of revelation and faith; even then theological statements about it are bound to fall short of adequacy.

The most sacred and obscure of the Christian mysteries, writes Scheeben, is that of the Holy Trinity. Reason may indicate to us that a creative and dynamic God exists, but it in no way suggests the nature of God's inner activity. God's activity is mysterious in a way that other features, such as omnipresence and freedom, are not. It is not directly through His relationships in the Trinity, a "closed order," that God has His links with creation: "Created nature cannot be conceived and explained apart from its relation to the divine nature, which therefore is the foundation stone and the keystone, as well as the center of the natural order of created natures." Although the nature of God dominates creation, His divine, interior, purely supernatural activity takes place outside the "natural" order. The triune aspect of God is a higher, truer, and more perfect representation of God's nature than is the rational idea of a God who can only be recognized and known through His creation.

The activity of the Trinity must be seen as "relations between persons." When the nature of one person is wholly and perfectly communicated to another, in a manner inimitable throughout the created order, the receiver assumes the very life and being of the giver, becoming a second self, a giver no less than a receiver, a being who is at once perfect and not one who is perfected. God's Word, His knowledge of Himself, unites with Him in a "sigh of love," as the Father and the Son communicate their divinity to a third co-possessor, whose personal characteristic is "an outpouring of love," not love itself, which is common to all three Persons. The third Person is willed to be distinct from the first two Persons and is "a bearer of the life which is poured forth into Him."

The terms used to define the divine nature must always be merely analogous and they must express a dynamic relationship between the Persons as well as preserve the distinctions between Them. One Person cannot be thought of as different from another without being seen as simultaneously the same, for "distinction in possession not only does not exclude common possession, but essentially requires it." Nor is one Person ever excluded from the work of another, although that work may be pre-eminently that of the other, as in the case of the Son's redemptive activity. The supreme relation of man to the Trinity is effected by the Holy Spirit, who draws man into participation in the life of the Trinity. Men are supernaturally caught up in the mutual love of the Father and the Son, the very outpoured love which in the Trinity itself assumes distinct personality as the Holy Spirit. The Son is born again in men and of the Father, and the Holy Spirit sustains in the temple of human bodies the breath of divine life which He received from the union of the Father and the Son. The Holy Spirit "takes possession [of us] for" the other two Persons, while they "give themselves to us in Him." Properly speaking, men do not share in the love of the Father and Son for the Holy Spirit, but the human relationship to God is an "imitation" of the Son's relationship to the Father, which issues forth in the Holy Spirit. It is the Holy Spirit who "is viewed as the natural channel conveying that [God's] love to the outside world." The Holy Trinity is, with regard to humanity, a "living root," which mysteriously interpenetrates the souls of men, perpetuating the interior supernatural activity of God in an outward expression of love for creatures.

The second great mystery of Christianity, according to Scheeben, lies in the creation of man and the gift of original justice. God gives men more than mere existence. He gives them what they need to attain their natural end; He gives them a share in divine life that can be understood only in terms of mystery. The gift of supernatural life was not necessary, nor was it the right of men to have it; God freely willed it.

What Adam initially possessed was only a seed of divine life, though it is often spoken of in terms of its fullness and intended end. Original justice was not static perfection, but a capacity for integrity and sanctity, the ultimate end of which was to be a transfiguration in Paradise. Integrity itself is rationally understandable; it predisposes one to sanctity, but it is not in itself positive, supernatural virtue. Sanctity, however, is the fulfillment of integrity, its supernatural complement, and sanctity is a mystery. Original justice, then, is a single gift but with two aspects, the supernatural element having been inended by God to flow smoothly and logically from that perfect natural order and harmony of all human functions which we call integrity.

Scheeben explains that since original justice is dominated by supernatural sanctity, it cannot be thought of as part of man's purely natural inheritance. It was only by a specific divine decree that this gift could have become linked with natural human generation. Such a link is provided by the constant activity of the Holy Spirit working concurrently with natural generation, perfecting what nature produces. God willed to pursue this common activity with Adam's race, sprung from him as one in nature as well as one in grace. Man summarizes visible creation and gives it a share in the mystery of divine life, which itself culminates in the mystery of the Trinity.

Sin is recognizable as a mystery, not by virtue of an exalted nature of its own, but because it displaces the supernatural activity of the Trinity in men's souls. According to the author, "Opposition to sanctity and the destruction of it constituted . . . the chief element of mystery in Adam's sin." Man actively sins in extinguishing the justice and life which God had established within him, and the "punishment" is imposed by the deprivation of "justice" which is consequent upon the sin itself. Just as goodness was perpetually present in the soul of man before the Fall, a state of habitual sin or habitual "dependence on creatures" dominates man after the Fall, simply because the life-giving supernatural spirit has been withdrawn.

Scheeben maintains that original sin had, as an inevitable consequence, the loss of the lower, natural aspect of man's justice, "integrity," and the supernatural aspect, sanctity, for which purpose integrity existed. As inheritors of a fallen nature, men receive not personal guilt but that "deformity which consists in the privation of obligatory justice," just as we would have received, undefiled and whole, both sanctity and integrity had Adam effected their permanence in the human nature he passed on to his posterity. Original sin's effects would not have been inheritable had it not been for the merciful love of God that intended Adam to be the father of an organically united human family possessing sonship to God as its supernatural inheritance.

The mystery of Adam, who was a son of God by adoption and not by generation, and his initial union with God is incomparably less than the mystery of the Incarnation. In the latter, Scheeben argues, the divine nature dominates and possesses a created nature so that a personal organic union, a hypostasis is effected. Nor was perfect holiness and beatitude achieved by the man Christ gradually; from the first instant of the Incarnation, Son and Father enjoyed a union unmarred by the possibility of sin. While Adam could only have begun the transmission of grace to his posterity, the Humanity of Christ, as "organ of the Godhead, is capable of uniting all other men to Himself, incorporating them in His own supernaturally holy life.

Scheeben points out that Christ means far more to the human race than Adam, its founder and first head, ever could have; Christ is the root, the soul and the ruling principle of the race as a whole, and "unfolds in each member," uniting all members to one another. The new Body exists implicitly since the Incarnation, but it must be vivified through the faith and baptism of individual members of the race. Christ gives to the human race a new and exalted vocation: a participation in the eternal praise and glorification of the Father by the Son. The Incarnation itself is a mystery which serves to connect the two great mysteries of the Holy Trinity and the blessing of creatures with divine grace, as well as connecting divine activity in an organic unity with the life of the entire cosmos. According to Scheeben, Christ "by His hypostatic union with a created nature . . . [became] the hypostasis of all creation and bears it upon His shoulders."

The priesthood of Christ the Mediator bridges the abyss between creator and created, infinite and finite, by associating the two in a single dimension of existence. Since man had sinned, Christ as Mediator had also to take upon Himself and His mission the character of atonement, but, according to Scheeben, Christ's mediation goes far beyond atonement and effects a supernatural union. The ultimate goal of the Incarnation is known only as a mystery, but we can assume that it is more than the mere redemption of fallen man and relates somehow to the willed activity of the Trinity in the created order. Thus, even had man not sinned, Scheeben writes, there is no reason why God might not still have chosen to become man in order to fulfill in this perfect and sublime fashion the union between Himself and His creation, at the same time adding a whole new dimension to beatitude. The sacrifice and suffering of Christ were not merely negative and propitiatory in nature, for they were a positive and creative contribution to the worship of God; Christ's suffering was more triumph than it was human abasement and extinction before an angry God. The mystery of the Incarnation thus casts light upon the other mysteries and on God's entire divine plan, which began for man with the solidarity of the race in one founder who was the human archetype of the Redeemer and High Priest to come. The redeemed human race, as the Body of Christ perfectly united with its Head and Founder, will be in Heaven an eternal "universal, total holocaust offered to God through the transforming fire of the Holy Spirit." According to the author, we maintain our unity with the humanity of Christ first through our identity with it as members of the same race, and second through contact with the "substantial" presence of Christ in Holy Communion.

Just as the mystery of the Incarnation depends on that of the Trinity, so also, does the mystery of the Eucharist. By the Eucharist, "our participation in the divine nature and divine life becomes a reproduction of the fellowship in nature and life which the Son of God has with His Father." While we are still immersed in physical creation, we are dependent on that creation both in our bodies and in our apprehension of reality. In the Eucharist, Scheeben writes, Christ "gives Himself up to us in His human substance, and through it in His divine substance," thus giving indirectly what He will give directly to us in the beatific vision. The Eucharist is the mysterious pledge of our supernatural destiny, a participation in the life of God. We are united to God in a manner typified by the process of Transubstantiation itself; the action of the Holy Spirit transforms the substance of the bread into the very sacrificial presence of Christ, and we ourselves by the same action are identified with the Lamb in both His sacrificial aspect and His risen, supernatural life.

The mystery of the Eucharist says Scheeben, depends upon the presence of Christ understood as existing on a plane higher even than that of the Transfiguration or Resurrection. In the Eucharistic state, the Humanity of Christ is entirely dominated by His Divinity, so that "it exists in a way that is naturally impossible even to a created spiritual substance," unrestricted by time and place, sharing a power and mysteriously elevated function proper to God alone. The distinction between the two natures of the Son indicates that we need not predicate of one of them all that we predicate of the other. Thus, the Body or Humanity of Christ is endowed with the purely divine power of indivisible and universal presence in the very depths of creation. His desire for union with the human race makes peculiarly appropriate the use of His own glorified, divinized Humanity as the instrument for entering and rooting to Himself the souls of men.

The mystery of the Church, Scheeben suggests, lies fundamentally in its incorporation into the life of the God-man; it confers upon men a new life and joins them in itself as the Body of Christ, and it does so pre-eminently through the sacrament of the Eucharist. It is through the nigh-maternal, sacramental intercession of the priest, representative of the Bride of Christ, that souls are born into the Faith. The unity of the Spirit as it permeates and binds together every member of the Body is reflected in "the unity of the pastoral power," culminating in the papacy. Scheeben thus argues that we must not artificially create a cleavage between the sacramental and the jurisdictional power of the priesthood, as has often been done in the modern era.

The mysteries of the Incarnation, the creation of man, the Eucharist, the Church, and the sacraments all share, according to Scheeben, the common marks of God's activity in the world: they are mysteries by virtue of the immeasurable depths of divine power that underlie and enrich them, and they are bound to visible, material phenomena that of themselves suggest the mystery which they both signify and contain. The divinity in creation exists only as a seed, to flower and bear fruit at the end of time. Its presence around us and in us, says Scheeben, blesses the material order and seals the role of the body in the ultimate destiny of the soul, all the while sanctifying the elements of the earth so that the earth becomes man's "spiritual mother," bearing to him supernatural food.

According to the author, the state of "sanctification and rebirth from God," as effected by the sacraments, is primarily to be considered as it opposes the mystery of sin. It is composed of two elements: one, the remission of guilt, is negative; the other, the elevation to union with God through sanctifying grace, is positive. The mystery lies in the fusion of these two processes, whereby contrition and faith mingle with the purifying grace of God to effect sanctification. The "real, intrinsic cause," writes Scheeben, is overwhelmingly divine grace, for no effort of man is capable of inevitably causing any action of God. "Faith prepares man for the reception of the precious gift of justification and induces God to bestow it," so that both elements join in co-operative activity. This is especially true in the "second justification," which is the dynamic growth of grace in the soul due to God-given merits possessed by the soul. The mystery of justification does not culminate with an initial act of faith and forgiveness, but in the mystery of glorification in Heaven.

Scheeben contends that the mystery of last things can best be comprehended as a mystery of transfiguration. Through the action of the Holy Spirit, men are reborn, even deified, by "participation in the nature of the Godhead," and this takes place on a supra-rational plane. The body is supernaturally raised above the state it enjoyed before the Fall; instead of mere integrity, the body, dominated as it is by the soul in union with God, becomes incorruptible and no longer subject to material conditions. Creation itself, by virtue of the Incarnation and the subsequent deification of man, is transfigured and by mystery raised above mere nature. The mystery of Hell is that of "negative transfiguration" in a supernatural fire that destroys and devours the substance of the creature in a manner analogous to the action of natural fire. This fire is the reverse of that fire of love which unites God to His chosen children.

According to Scheeben, the mystery of predestination lies deep in the development of God's plan for the universe, particularly in His plan regarding the Incarnation. Ultimately it is God who provides His creatures with that energy which they must possess to seek Him out; they cannot do good without the power given them by God. The mystery of predestination depends entirely on the supernatural, undeserved, and inconceivable end for all men that is willed by God and in the aid God is willing to give to attain that end. Secondary to this universal will to salvation, and stemming from it, is that particular predestination involving individual souls whom God knows will in fact arrive at the goal meant for all. God has pledged Himself to respond to *our* responses with grace; it is a mystery why some men are allowed to refuse Him while others seem not to be, as it is a mystery that those who do choose Him constitute the Living Body of Christ Himself.

B.J.R.

A GRAMMAR OF ASSENT

Author: John Henry Cardinal Newman (1801-1890)
Type of work: Philosophy of religion; theory of knowledge
First published: 1870

Principal Ideas Advanced

Inference, which follows upon premises, is of different sorts and is distinct in each case from assent, which is always unconditional; thus, assent to God may be reasonable and certain without depending upon a formal demonstration.

Human assent in religious matters is a complex affair involving both belief in the content of a proposition and also acceptance of the concrete, real existent intended by a proposition.

We assent to God as a concretely apprehended Person in the image of a loving provider, whereby the content of the inference to God and its notional acceptance can be related to our own moral being; the unique, irreducible commanding act of conscience provides us with the basis for such an assent.

To inquire into religion is not the same as to investigate religion: the former refers to a study of the evidences for God by one who doubts and does not assent to God; the latter is the approach of the believer who, while assenting to God, attempts to analyze the difficulties of human knowledge of God and the content of faith. John Henry Newman wrote *An Essay in Aid of a Grammar of Assent* to investigate the grounds of belief and assent in matters that cannot be understood fully or demonstrated formally. Few theists have, themselves, been as able to enter into the position of the doubter and the atheist and therein to elaborate a theory of knowing which describes the profound reasonableness of assent in matters that cannot be strictly proved. And reason there must be; Newman insisted that faith is not a sentimental response or feeling or even a will to believe. Faith in God must have a reasonable basis, but Newman objected to a limitation of reason to the logico-mathematical use of the Noetic School at Oxford and of the rationalistically influenced majority of Catholic thinkers of his day. On the contrary, Newman's observations of the religious mind at work, as well as of the types of faith exhibited by the vast majority of men in other matters, convinced him that the rationalists' criteria for the valid grounds of faith were much too narrow. Man is not a reasoning machine; he is a sensing, reasoning, feeling, believing, acting animal.

The approach of the *Grammar* is quite definitely that of the empiricist; Newman adopted the plain, historical account of human knowing proposed by John Locke (1632-1704) and then criticized Locke for not being empirical enough. He did not, however, feel that naturalism, such as that of David Hume (1711-1776), is the inevitable outcome of empiricism. Rather, he was convinced, an analysis of the workings of the human mind in concrete situations can provide an experiential basis for the assent to God. Central to Newman's thought is a notion of probability which he learned from Joseph Butler (1692-1752), a notion holding that probability is the guide of life and that human reason operates in scientific and in religious matters as well as in everyday affairs with probable reasonings and analogical suggestions, not feeling itself confined to strict Euclidean-type demonstrations. But probability is contrasted with formal demonstration, not with certitude. Newman took issue with the contentions that assent (belief) is conditional upon reasoning, that reasoning in concrete matters of fact can yield only an uncertain, doubtful response, and that thus the assent of faith can never reach more than a probable, conditional, uncertain status. Probability can lead to its own sort of certitude; and to support this position Newman introduces his central, sharply defined distinction between inference and assent: the assent to God can be reasonable and certain even though it is not based upon a formal demonstration.

Inference is of many types, Newman argues; the conclusion of an inference, as well as the act of concluding, is conditioned by the premises. Probability characterizes an informal type of inference which is distinguished from formal inference in that it receives its evidence and premises from experience rather than reason, proceeds nonmathematically through a cumulation of a number of nondemonstrative arguments, and is concerned with a concrete, existing being rather than with an abstract concept. Questions concerning the existence of God and His nature have to do with matters of fact, and a mathematical conception of reason simply cannot operate at this level. Besides, to demand that assent to God be the outcome of syllogistic argument would condemn the great majority of theists to unreasonableness. Newman argued from his own experience that there are minds which have reasonable grounds for an assent to God, even though they can provide no formal demonstration of His existence. Again, Newman felt that it was naïve to suppose that logical proof could compel assent from an individual whose heart was not prepared to make such an assent. The conclusion of a formal process of reasoning remains ineffective unless there is a response in the living mind that is making the conclusion. The religious mind sees much in the evidence that is invisible to the irreligious mind; in fact, the two minds do not have before them the same evidence at all.

Probable reasoning is constantly used in dealing with contingent facts. In such cases, we attain certitude by attending to the convergence of particular arguments. Each argument itself is no more than probable; but, as a strong cable can be woven from a cumulation of fragile strands, so a strong assent can be built on a cumulation of probabilities. Reasoning about complex matters of fact forces our minds to consider complex evidence, to make complicated inferences that cannot be captured in the mold of a syllogism, to consider the convergence of probable lines of reasoning, and to determine when it is "prudent" to give our assent. What Newman calls the "illative sense" is simply the mind as it is engaged in such a process bearing upon contingent, concrete matters of fact. Newman likened the illative sense to Aristotle's concept of *phronesis* (prudence); *phronesis,* however, concerns only moral, practical judgments, while Newman wished to extend the concept to include speculative truths, such as the notional content of the truths of faith.

Although inference, formal or informal, is a conditioned act, Newman writes, assent is an unconditional acceptance of an object and represents a passage from the consideration of evidence to the unequivocal response to the evidence as sufficient for internal conviction. The mind *concludes to* (infers) something only on the basis of the steps in reasoning; but the mind *assents* directly to the presented object. Notional assent and real assent agree insofar as they are both intellectually certain acceptances of proposed objects. They differ in their objects: the objects of the former are propositions; of the latter, real things, individual facts, existent beings intended by propositions. Newman distinguished these types of assent, not with the intent to oppose them, but to emphasize that the complex human act is a synthesis of notional and real elements. Notional assents function in our commitments as sources of content, controlling and critically containing our beliefs within bounds. Yet when the mind is concerned with the world of real existence, it is not satisfied with assent to content and meaning. By means of a concrete image, a real assent directs us to the real thing in its own being. The aim of the *Grammar* is to clarify the act of religious faith and to show that both the notional and real factors are indispensable elements of the religious act. There is a sort of circular movement in human thought as inquiry begins in real assents about particular facts, inductively generalizes the notional principles that ground inferences, and, finally, refers back to the existential order by means of the subsequent real assents. Real assents by themselves are not self-justified; they require the controlling critique of inference and notional assents. But the human mind cannot be brought to give its real assent merely on the basis of syllogistic argument and assent to content and proposition. In the *Grammar* Newman refers to his own "Tamworth Reading Room" article of 1841 in which he questioned the adequacy of scientifically grounded principles to insure our personal grasp of truth and moral activity: "First comes knowledge, then a view, then reasoning, and then belief. This is why science has so little of a religious tendency; deductions have no power of persuasion. The heart is commonly reached, not through the reason, but through the imagination, by means of direct impressions, by the testimony of facts and events, by history, by description. . . . Many a man will live and die upon a dogma: no man will be a martyr for a conclusion. A conclusion is but an opinion: it is not a thing which *is*, but which *we are 'quite sure about'*. . . . No one, I say, will die for his own calculations: he dies for realities."

Newman included our inference and assent to God among the other existential inferences and assents we make from the experience of self, in order to show that there is nothing extraordinary about the assent to God. We infer and assent to the existence of the material world and to other persons on the basis of sensations; such informal inferences are not cast into syllogisms but spontaneously move us beyond ourselves to the world as source of the experience. In a similar way, the informal inference and assent to God requires some initial data drawn from our experience. The inference to God is not a self-sufficient exercise in reasoning, an ontological argument; rather it is the attempt to work out the implications of our experience, including causal action, order in nature, design, the course of history, the obligation of conscience.

Newman did little more than mention the more metaphysical arguments to God. While not denying their validity, his reluctance to use metaphysics himself apparently stemmed from his own concern to analyze concrete human experience. His discussion of traditional arguments pointed out a difference between starting with the order of nature and with design. Without working out the implications of this distinction, he claimed that the common notion of design, as employed by William Derham (1657-1735), Samuel Clarke (1675-1729), and William Paley (1743-1805), was too bound up with the Newtonian science of the time, too mathematically considered, and too liable to result in a deistic or even finitist position.

Newman's own approach to God, consistent with his concern with the personal, concrete human experience, begins with the obligation of conscience. The commanding act of conscience is an irreducible form of personal self-awareness, bound up with the certitude of one's own existence. The obliging nature of conscience cannot be confused with taste, aesthetic fitness, good breeding, or social conformity. Reflection upon the moral commands of one's own conscience, inductively and in a non-*a-priori* way, generalizes the principle that conscience imparts commands which obligate us. As the recognition of duty in concrete affairs, conscience has the two-fold function of commanding and sanctioning. Under its aspect of commanding, conscience enables us to view the law as *coming from* a superior, personal source of our own moral tendencies. Under its aspect of sanctioning, it allows us to perceive that the notion of *future judgment,* a *Judge,* is involved in the feelings of conscience. Initially, such informal inference elicits from us a notional assent to the truth that God, an intelligent, moral agent, distinct from and superior to us, exists; subsequently, we can give real assent to this truth insofar as we realize that the proof begins in our own moral being and concerns the moral and personal being of God. Thus, we may assent complexly: we assent to God as a vividly apprehended Person, under images drawn from our experience of loving provider, father, judge, lawgiver—images whereby the content of the notional assent can be related to our own persons. Real assent is strongest when linking person to person; thus, Newman considered that the moral relation between ourselves and a Lawgiver was not only de facto in most men's religious experience, but actually essential in a theism which involves real assent and personal devotion.

F.J.C.

ON THE GENESIS OF THE SPECIES

Author: St. George Jackson Mivart (1827-1900)
Type of work: Christian evolutionary theory
First published: 1871

Principal Ideas Advanced

The evolutionary account of man's origin is scientifically sound, although philosophers and theologians may continue to argue about the religious implications of evolution.

Natural selection is not the primary causal mechanism involved in biological evolution; thus, natural selection must be supplemented by other more important and as yet unknown laws.

Natural selection implies a force that selects, an entelechy or vital force, superior to evolutionary phenomena, which directs evolution.

The belief in evolution and natural selection is not contradictory to the belief in God and divine creation; God may operate through natural laws.

Mivart was the first really competent biologist to offer a sound criticism of the weaknesses in Charles Darwin's theory of evolution. The fact that Dar win deals with Mivart's arguments at length in editions of *On the Origin of Species* published after 1871, and that Darwin made numerous comments about Mivart's criticisms (see *The Life and Letters of Charles Darwin*) clearly shows the great importance Darwin placed on Mivart's sustained and detailed attack on natural selection.

In his chapter "Specific Genesis," Mivart sums up what he considers to be the most telling scientific objections to an acceptance of Darwinian evolution. In opposition to Darwin, who claimed that minute variations were selected over a long period of time until a new species finally emerged, Mivart maintains that natural selection cannot explain the incipient stages of useful structures. He contends further that the fact that genetically widely different species have developed quite similar structures is unexplainable on the basis of natural selection of minute variations. Instances of similar structures in animals with no genetic affinity include the classic cases of eyes in both mollusks and vertebrates, and auditory organs in both fish and cephalopods. Numerous examples of "sports," new types or species which arise suddenly rather than after a long period of minute variations, argue against the primacy of natural selection but do not destroy it.

Mivart suggests that the concept of a species is still valid though we must now regard a species as being in a state of flux. He stresses the gaps existing in even the best of our fossil pedigrees; for example, evolution through the accumulation of minute variations is not evident in the case of the horse. (Today this argument is negligible since modern genetics has shown that new forms of life can appear more or less suddenly by quite natural mechanisms.) "Minutely intermediate forms" are more often than not missing in our fossil pedigrees, Mivart points out; the time necessary for such accumulations is much longer than that allowed for by Darwin. (The law of the disappearance of evolutionary peduncles because of their extreme scarcity and fragility answers the one objection; while the time argument is invalid today, particularly in the case of the evolution of man, whose ancestry is now known, with the discovery of *Zinjanthropus* by Leake, to extend back some three to five million years, instead of the few thousand years allowed by Darwin.)

According to Mivart, it is difficult to explain some facts of geographic distribution on the sole basis of natural selection, though "if it could be established that closely similar forms had really arisen in complete independence one of the other, they would tend rather to strengthen and support the theory." Homologies, organs, and systems with different functions but the same embryological origins cannot be explained by natural selection, Mivart writes, and "are inexplicable without admitting the action of what may most conveniently be spoken of as an internal power."

Mivart then claims that objections to natural selection based on physiological differences between "races" and "species" are still unanswered. He points out that definite breaks exist in the evolutionary stream which neither natural selection nor any other natural cause can bridge: the gaps between the inanimate and animate, between the irrational and rational. Thus, there are many outstanding phenomena in the world of life which the theory of natural selection does not explain or even attempt to throw light on.

The major importance of Mivart's work is attested in its serious reception by such scholars and scientists as Darwin, Thomas Huxley (1825-1895), and Alfred Russel Wallace (1823-1913). Shortly after its publication, *On the Genesis of the Species* was presented for ecclesiastical scrutiny in Rome by some English Catholics who rejected completely Darwinian evolution and natural selection, and who were "scandalized" by a Catholic scientist who accepted such an "atheistic and materialistic theory." While those who rejected evolution tried to have Mivart's book placed on the Index of Condemned Books, no official answer came from Rome except an indirect one: in 1876 an honorary doctorate of philosophy was conferred on Dr. Mivart by Cardinal Manning at the personal request of Pope Pius IX.

Patently, one of the main purposes behind *On the Origin of Species* was the refutation of the belief in the special creation of individual species by God's direct intervention. Since most Christians in the nineteenth century were committed to a belief in special creation, a conflict with the followers of Darwinian evolution was unavoidable. The lack of precision and clarity in terminology used by both the theologians and the scientists, coupled with an unwillingness to study seriously the weaknesses in one's own position or the strong points in the opponents views, added fuel to the fire of controversy. Atheistic evolutionists such as Thomas Huxley, Darwin's spokesman in England, and Ernst Haeckel in Germany, were just as outspoken and vehement as were the defenders of special creation such as Bishop Wilburforce.

To show what he regarded as the real situation, namely, that evolution is not necessarily atheistic and that a Catholic may accept this scientific theory without denying his faith, Mivart made two noteworthy points. First, he noted that many distinguished Catholic thinkers had accepted an evolutionary theory in some form or other, often quite primitive in its scientific conceptualization, among them two Doctors of the Church, Basil and Augustine. Second, after an examination of the concept of "creation," Mivart claimed that the concept had been used without precision and had been given different meanings by different thinkers. He presents three distinct definitions of the term: (1) the absolute origin of something out of nothing, which implies the direct action of the Creator, an action which falls outside the scope of science: *absolute creation;* (2) the origin of something new out of something previously created in the absolute sense and endowed with the power to evolve from one species into another: *derivative creation;* (3) man's making of something new out of material already present.

Having made these distinctions, Mivart compares the causal mechanisms of phylogeny with those of ontogeny. Since the birth and development of an individual is accomplished by mechanisms subject to the laws of nature, why cannot the same natural mechanisms operate in the birth and development of a species? In an earlier article in the *Rambler* (March, 1860), Mivart had stated: "Creation is not a miraculous interference with the laws of nature, but the very institution of those laws." Hence, the theologians speak of absolute creation (*ex nihilo*) about which the scientists can say nothing, either pro or con; while the scientists speak of a derivative creation (according to the laws of nature) about which the theologians can say nothing.

Mivart claimed that, in the confrontation of evolutionists and believers, "much confusion has arisen from not keeping clearly in view this distinction between *absolute* creation and *derivative* creation. . . . The greater part of the apparent force possessed by objectors to creation, like Mr. Darwin, lies in their treating it as if it were an assertion of absolute creation, or at least of supernatural action. Thus he [Darwin] asks whether some of his opponents believe that at innumerable periods in the earth's history, certain elemental atoms have been commanded suddenly to flash into living tissues. Certain of Mr. Darwin's objections, however, are not physical, but *metaphysical,* and really attack the dogma of secondary or derivative creation, though to some perhaps they may appear to be directed against absolute creation only."

Derivative creation is not a supernatural intervention, but rather the operation of natural laws under the directing influence of the Divine. In explaining or interpreting the ultimate mechanisms and causes behind evolution, those who believe in God will, by faith, claim that He acts through secondary causes, while the atheists will deny this. Yet neither can prove his belief experimentally. Thus, Mivart can conclude that, when "creation" is properly understood, evolution and creation are not contradictory.

The discussion in *On the Genesis of the Species* thus returns to the argument that natural selection is not *the* main causal mechanism behind evolution. His experimental work led Mivart to consider an internal force, somewhat on the order of Bergson's *élan vital,* as the dominant causal agent in the evolutionary process. Here Mivart leaves the strictly scientific realm to build an elaborate and detailed argument for the logic of positing an "internal force" for which we have no scientific evidence. The fact that some will object to this argument as a fancy revival of mysticism or vitalism is faced by Mivart with the question whether the theist is any more illogical or prejudiced than the atheist who believes in a *natural* internal force directing evolution (chance); both express a belief and a faith for which they have no scientific evidence.

Valid or not, Mivart's argument marks a midpoint between the chance-directed evolution of Darwin and the spiritualized evolution of Bergson. Mivart's theory allowed him to relate Intelligence (God) to evolution. Yet his argument was almost completely ignored by his contemporaries. Darwin had separated biology from metaphysics as a formal study by his experimental-evidential approach; Lamarck, who proposed the first complete theory of evolution fifty years before Darwin, had been both philosophical and scientific, as in his *Philosophical Zoology* (1809). Yet, along with this separation of science and metaphysics, the concept of evolution gave a new impetus to the dualism of Descartes. In the original Cartesian dualism, matter and mind were opposed. The entrance of evolution as a mode of thought introduced a new dualism of natural selection (matter) and the selector (mind). Materialists and scientists personified this selecting force as "Nature." Thus, the ancient concept of entelechy found a new expression.

Christians are free to accept the concept of evolution, Mivart believed, but he questioned whether his interpretation of "derivative creation" would be acceptable to the theologians, in spite of the distinct teachings of Augustine, Aquinas, and Suarez, to that effect.

The final section of *On the Genesis of the Species* deals with the evolution of man. Scholastic philosophy defines man as a rational animal; Mivart concludes from this definition that man's rationality and animality are distinct and therefore must have distinct origins. He does not object in the least to the evolution of man's body from a lower form of life, though he does insist on the direct "intervention" of God in the creation of the human soul. The Scriptural exegesis attempted by the author to support his theory is what scholars today would call "concordism" and is certainly unwarranted in the light of modern scholarship. Yet the view that man's soul has a distinctive origin remains valid, according to the Catholic doctrine approved by Pope Pius XII in the encyclical *Humani generis* (1950).

R.T.F.

HISTORY OF THE COUNCILS

Author: Karl Joseph von Hefele (1809-1893)
Type of work: Church history
First published: 1855-1874

Principal Ideas Advanced

The authority of an ecumenical council is based on the commission of Christ to the Apostles to teach and govern His Church, an authority that is passed down to the bishops through Apostolic Succession.

The general purpose for the convocation of an ecumenical council is the promotion of the well-being of the Church through the mutual consultation of its pastors.

No decree of a general council is valid or binding unless it receives the sanction of the pope.

The question as to whether pope or council is superior is really a false question, for a council represents the whole Church and the pope is neither inferior nor superior to the Church; he is, instead, within the Church and the head of the Church.

When originally published, Karl Joseph von Hefele's *History of the Councils* consisted of seven volumes which carried the story of the councils from the beginnings of Christianity through the fifteenth century. Hefele was himself unable to go further than this with the story, but Cardinal Joseph Hergenröther (1824-1890), another prominent German Catholic historian, added two more volumes, so that the final work covers the history of the councils through the Council of Trent, the last ecumenical council prior to the First Vatican Council of the nineteenth century.

The writing of a history of the councils was a very challenging work at the time Hefele put his hand to the task. It was fortunate, therefore, that he was in every way prepared for such an undertaking. Germany was the land of great historical writing in the nineteenth century, and Hefele had completely imbibed the historical methods and thoroughness of his teachers. Born in 1809, he was ordained in 1833, but prior to this had already studied at the University of Tübingen under the direction of the great German theologian and Church historian, Johann Adam Möhler. So great was Hefele's progress that when Möhler moved from Tübingen to the University of Munich, Hefele took over his teacher's position and filled it with great competence.

Hefele's work as a historian was, therefore, more than distinguished. His *History of the Councils* is lucidly written and marked by an unusually high degree of scholarship. Based almost solely on original sources, it treats not only of the ecumenical councils of the Church, but also of the more important synods and national councils that have been held through the centuries.

Hefele's study is remarkable for its honesty and objectivity, which is all the more impressive when one considers the kinds of delicate theological questions which can be raised by a study of Church history, particularly a study of Church councils. This tendency to analyze was especially so in the nineteenth century, and particularly in Germany where interest in theology and Church history was high and where the standard of both Protestant and Catholic scholarship was exceptional. Hefele's work as a historian, therefore, involved him in a good many partisan disputes not only with the Protestants, but also within the Catholic Church. The disputes came to a head in the First Vatican Council, over the question of papal infallibility. Since Hefele attended that council, initially as a theological expert and later as the Bishop of Rottenburg, it is advisable to examine some of the difficult questions which were raised there, for they had a significant bearing on both his life and his writings. It was, indeed, for the purpose of answering these questions that Hefele wrote his *History*.

Hefele believed that the origin of Church councils could be traced to the Synod of Jerusalem (about the year 52), which is recorded in the New Testament. Here Saint Peter, Saint Paul, and other Apostles met to reach a decision on the difficult question of the Judaizers: Must a convert to the Christian faith first accept Judaism and subject himself to the Mosaic Law? The assembled Apostles, under the leadership of Saint Peter, finally decided in the negative. Thus, in the opinion of Hefele, the authority of Church councils springs from their Apostolic institution. At the Synod of Jerusalem the Apostles acted on the basis of the commission they had received from Christ to teach and govern the Church. As the bishops are the successors of the Apostles, subsequent councils have met in the same way and with the same intention: to govern and teach the Church on the authority of the commission of Christ and under the guidance of the Holy Spirit. Hefele's research also reveals that the first recorded synods or councils met in the second century to deal with the Montanist heresy, but he believed, despite the lack of complete historical evidence, that some had probably met earlier to deal with the threat of Gnosticism.

Hefele was very careful to distinguish among the different kinds of synods or councils of which there are eight: (1) universal or ecumenical councils, which meet under the authority of the pope. Their decrees are made in the name of the whole Church and must be received by the whole Church because they have the force of law for all the faithful. But not every council called to be ecumenical, Hefele stated, necessarily becomes ecumenical; in order to so become, its decrees must receive the approbation of the pope; (2) general councils or synods of the Latin or Greek Church which meet only in the name of those Churches but whose decrees can become binding on all the faithful if the pope so decides; (3) national, patriarchal, or primatial councils; (4) provincial synods; (5) councils representing several provinces meeting together; (6) diocesan synods; (7) synods of residents, which occur when some high Church official, such as the Patriarch of Constantinople, calls together all other high officials who happen to reside in the city at that time; (8) finally, mixed councils, in which ecclesiastical and civil rulers of a kingdom or a nation meet in order to work out problems of Church and state.

A study of the various councils led Hefele to conclude that there are six common reasons for which councils, especially ecumenical ones, are usually called: (1) to deal with heresy or schism; (2) to decide between rival papal claimants; (3) to decide on some great Christian undertaking, such as a crusade against the enemies of the faith; (4) when the pope is suspected of heresy or other serious crimes; (5) when the cardinals have been unable to elect a pope; and (6) to reform the Church. Thus, it may be seen that the general aim for the convoking of an ecumenical council is "the promotion of the well-being of the Church through the mutual consultation of its pastors."

Hefele was convinced that councils and synods can be properly convoked only by the highest officials concerned. If it is to be a patriarchal synod, it must be convoked by the patriarch; if it is to be an ecumenical council, it must be convoked by the pope. Hefele did admit, however, that in the first few centuries of the Church some ecumenical councils were, in fact, convoked by the temporal protector of the Church, the emperor. But this, he believed, was the exception rather than the rule.

As far as the membership of ecumenical councils is concerned, Hefele stated that it usually consisted of the bishops, but that other ecclesiastics, such as experts in theology or canon law, were usually in attendance. Abbots and heads of religious orders also frequently attended and usually were allowed to vote, but their right to vote, Hefele stated, is based on ecclesiastical appointment, whereas that of the bishops is based on "divine right"; that is, by virtue of Apostolic succession. At some councils, especially those below the ecumenical level, laymen were in attendance, but they seldom had any determining voice. Hefele believed that the view of the Archbishop of Lyons in 517 was perhaps typical. He declared that "We permit the laity to be present, that the people may know those things which are ordained by the priests alone." In the early days of the Church, however, it was quite usual for kings and emperors, or their emissaries, to attend councils. But even when they had the right to attend, Hefele stated, they did not have the right to vote on the issues at hand.

Hefele took great pains to investigate the question as to who was the proper presiding officer of an ecumenical council. At first sight, he stated, the answer appears obvious: if the proper presiding officer of a diocesan council is the bishop and of a national council is the primate, then it would seem to follow that the proper presiding officer of an ecumenical council is the pope. But Hefele was forced to meet the challenge, urged by some historians, that occasionally the emperor presided over early ecumenical councils, and he met this assertion in various ways. He argued that in some cases the emperor had presided only in an honorary way, not in any real capacity. Moreover, he pointed out, even in instances where the emperor actually seemed to preside, such as at the Council of Chalcedon, he did so only in a material sense; that is, he maintained order and decorum. But Hefele's research revealed that on no occasion did the emperor take part in deciding the matters to be discussed, nor did he possess a vote, nor was he allowed to interfere in any way with the decisions of the council. Hefele believed that the words of Constantine best summed up the matter: "And I am a bishop. You are bishops for the interior business of the Church. I am the bishop chosen by God to conduct the exterior business of the Church."

The question as to who was the proper presiding officer of an ecumenical council was, indeed, an important one, for it touched on a still more debated issue; namely, what is the relation of the pope to an ecumenical council? This, of course, was an important question in the interplay of ideas between Protestants and Catholics, and to some extent it was a point of argument among Catholics themselves, especially when it became related to the question of papal infallibility. Hefele's position on this question was somewhat complex. He insisted, against the claims of the early Protestant reformers, that there was no validity to any claim that a dissenter might appeal to a council over the head of the pope. History convinced him that such an appeal had never been sustained. But even more than this, Hefele argued, the decrees of an ecumenical council can have no validity or binding force, unless they are confirmed and promulgated by the pope. But here again Hefele ran into a difficulty. His research revealed evidence that the decrees of the first eight ecumenical councils had been confirmed by the emperor, whereas the evidence was not nearly so strong that these decrees had always been confirmed by the pope. Hefele was convinced, however, of the necessity of papal confirmation, and he pointed out that the fourth ecumenical council, that of Chalcedon in 451, declared that papal confirmation was necessary to ensure the validity of conciliar decrees. Such a fact indicated to Hefele that the necessity of papal confirmation was a clear policy of even the early Church. Clearly, he pointed out, there could be no doubt that the decrees of all ecumenical councils subsequent to the eighth, the fourth Council of Constantinople in 869, had received the necessary papal confirmation.

But that was not the end of the matter. The councils of Constance and Basle asserted that a general council is superior to the pope, and the Protestants agreed. Hefele, however, argued that these assertions were not valid because the popes had never accepted or confirmed the decrees in question and had, to the contrary, specifically rejected them. In fact, Hefele stated, the question as to who is superior, pope or council, is a false question. Since a general council represents the entire Church, the question can really be reduced to: Who is superior, Church or pope? Seen in this form, Hefele was convinced, the question becomes absurd. The pope is neither inferior nor superior to the Church. He is the head of the Church and, as such, is within the Church. But if Hefele denied the assertion that the council is superior to the pope, he did admit that an ecumenical council could depose a pope. But not arbitrarily: a pope guilty of bad morals, for example, could not be deposed, for he would still remain within the Church. But a council could depose a pope guilty of heresy, for he who is guilty of heresy is not within, but is rather outside the Church, and therefore cannot be its head.

Hefele also tangled, as he had to do, with the difficult question of deciding what councils were truly ecumenical. The importance of this problem can be readily grasped if one considers the analogous question as to what writings can be truly considered as part of Sacred Scripture. Thus, the beliefs of Christianity depend a great deal on what writings are considered as the revealed word of God and on which councils are considered binding on the faithful. Hefele stated that a great number of councils were considered to be ecumenical without dispute, at least among Catholic historians. These are as follows: Nicaea (325), first Constantinople (381), Ephesus (431), Chalcedon (451), second Constantinople (553), third Constantinople (680), second Nicaea (787), fourth Constantinople (869), first Lateran (1123), second Lateran (1139), third Lateran (1179), fourth Lateran (1215) first Lyons (1245), second Lyons (1274), Florence (1439), and Trent (1545-1563). In doubt are: those of Sardica (343-344), Trullo (692), Vienne (1311), Pisa (1409), Constance (1414-1418), and the fifth Lateran (1512-1517). Hefele's research led him to conclude that the council of Sardica was not ecumenical and, in any case, it issued no important decrees. Nor was the council of Trullo ecumenical, for most of its pronouncements were totally unacceptable to the pope or to the Western Church. The council of Pisa was not ecumenical, and, in fact, few of those who participated in it thought that it was. On the other hand, the councils of Vienne and fifth Lateran were truly ecumenical, and their decrees received the sanction of the papacy. Most debatable of all, however, was the question of the nature of the councils of Constance and Basel. Here Hefele took a middle position. Both were truly ecumenical insofar as their decrees received the sanction of the papacy and did not prejudice its rightful power. But their decrees in favor of conciliarism were not valid and therefore could not be considered as true teachings of the Church.

Thus, even the question of what councils were truly ecumenical revolved around the issue of the relation of the pope to an ecumenical council. It would not be argumentative to point out that Hefele was occasionally ambiguous on this question. He clearly believed that an ecumenical council was not superior to the pope, and yet he granted to the council the power to depose a pope guilty of heresy, a power which clearly implied that a council was, at least in some respects, superior to the pontiff, in that it could judge him. It is somewhat singular, then, that when this question was solved once and for all by the first Vatican Council, with its definition of papal infallibility, Hefele found himself in the ranks of the opposition. Yet, once the council had made its decision, he accepted its decrees, an act which many of his critics argued revealed the victory of Hefele the bishop over Hefele the historian. But as Hefele himself pointed out, not to have accepted the dogma of papal infallibility would have been inconsistent with the thought of his entire life and, in particular, with the ideas expressed in his greatest and most important historical work. As a historian and as a bishop, he was convinced of the infallibility of an ecumenical council, an infallibility insured by the guidance of the Holy Spirit to which all must give allegiance. If such a council declared that the pope was infallible, Hefele could not but accept its decision.

P.T.M.

AETERNI PATRIS

Author: Pope Leo XIII (Gioacchino Vincenzo Raffaele Luigi Pecci, 1810-1903)
Type of work: Criticism of philosophy
First published: 1879

Principal Ideas Advanced

Among the principal causes of the bitter strife that afflicts the times are errors which arise in the schools of philosophy.

The chief remedy for this condition is belief in Almighty God and in the Christian religion and its diffusion throughout the world.

A second powerful remedy lies in the right use of philosophy, properly completed and strengthened by faith.

Of all the philosophical systems, that of Saint Thomas Aquinas, Angel of the Schools, is the most notable, as that philosophy is a bulwark and glory of the Catholic faith and, as such, should be restored and taught in all seminaries, colleges, and universities.

To understand the importance of Pope Leo XIII's encyclical *Aeterni Patris* in the life of the Church and the West, some idea must be gained of the kind of world in which it was written. When the encyclical appeared, the European mind was still haunted by the ghosts of the Cartesian and Kantian adventures with the soul and the mind of man, Hegelian optimism having failed to relieve the general moodiness of Continental thought. Scholasticism, despite the efforts towards its restoration by Gaetano Sanseverino (1811-1865), Josef Wilhelm Karl Kleutgen (1811-1883), and Matteo Liberatore (1810-1892), was but a wan Wolffian shadow of its golden, medieval self. In the secular universities of France and Italy, the study of philosophy was being more and more confined to the simple history of systems. The political and social life of Europe, furthermore, was vibrating to the pitch determined by the dominant schools of secular philosophy. The secularism and naturalism of a culture excited by a sense of its growing mastery over the material world favored the growth of moral and economic conditions that led to the revolutionary reactions of a later day.

Then came Leo XIII, whose efforts for reconstruction were to prove decisive. Already, in 1878, an old man of 68, Leo's reign was destined to stretch through twenty-five years of a glorious pontificate. Progressive and clearheaded despite sickness of the times, Leo, in his first encyclical, *Inscrutabili,* which appeared on April 21, 1878, spelled out the master plan of the work to be done: the reconstruction of the social order. Sixteen months later, on August 4, 1879, *Aeterni Patris* attacked society's disease at its root. Leo wrote, "Whoso turns his attention to the bitter strifes of these days and seeks a reason for the troubles that vex public and private life, must come to the conclusion that a fruitful cause of the evils which now afflict, as well as of those which threaten us, lies in this: that false conclusions concerning divine and human things, which originated in the schools of philosophy, have crept into all orders of the State, and have been accepted by the common consent of the masses."

The encyclical opens with a definition of the Church as the common and supreme teacher, engaged in an unending labor to instruct in the true religion and to contend against error. The Church has always regarded it as her duty to advance philosophy by every possible means. The pope, Leo reminds his readers, has made allusions to this subject in his first encyclical; now he must address the bishops on a mode of taking up the study of philosophy consistent both with the requirements of faith and the dignity of human knowledge. What follows is a very scholarly and incisive analysis of the role and the uses of philosophy for the thinking man of faith.

Leo writes that it must be borne in mind that the light of reason, as well as the superadded light of faith which renders reason more effective, has been placed in man by God. The history of pagan thought shows how efficacious the natural reason of man has been in discovering certain truths which God has revealed. Thus, it is altogether fitting that such truths be used in the service of religion, as Saint Paul and the Fathers of the Church have used them.

But there is a great danger to be

avoided in the uses of philosophy, Leo adds. Human reason dare not assume for itself excessive powers, for it is clear that some matters of religion are unattainable by reason alone. The attitude of the seeker after truth should be one of humility and gratitude to God. At the same time, philosophy should justly and confidently make full use of its own method, principles, and arguments, remembering always that since revealed doctrines are certain truths, anything warring against faith wars against right reason as well. The great truth for Catholic philosophers to remember is this: "Faith frees and saves reason from error and endows it with manifold knowledge." The history of philosophy makes this statement axiomatic, Leo claims, for philosophy is replete with cases of ancient sages who fell into the most appalling errors about divine and human truths so necessary for human welfare. But God raised up the mighty Fathers and Doctors of the Church who, while cherishing what was true and wise in pagan thought, sifted out what was erroneous. Of all these scholars, Saint Augustine holds the highest place for the power and beauty of his writings. Later, the Scholastics of the Middle Ages diligently applied themselves to their task by supporting theology with a prudent and excellent philosophy.

Leo XIII judges Saint Thomas Aquinas to be the prince of the Scholastics, indeed of all the Catholic Doctors, and argues that his judgment is supported by popes, general councils, universities, and even by many outside the Church.

Leo next proceeds to a consideration of the nature and remedy of the ills of society. It has come to pass, he writes, that novel and competing systems of philosophy were produced by philosophers of the sixteenth century who had no respect for the requirements of faith and who thus reached conflicting conclusions about the most important matters in human affairs. This condition has spawned great confusion among the masses of men. Even Catholic philosophers, quick to abandon patrimony, have striven to build up fanciful new edifices of thought. But carelessly constructed systems cannot escape instability and weakness. This is not to deny the service to philosophy that learned and able men render by their investigations. Yet great care must be taken lest such labors be wasted in mere erudition. The pope proposes the philosophy of Saint Thomas as the remedy: "Domestic and civil society even, which, as all see, is exposed to great danger from this plague of perverse opinions, would certainly enjoy a far more peaceful and secure existence if a more wholesome doctrine were taught in the academies and the schools—one more in conformity with the teachings of the Church, such as is contained in the works of Thomas Aquinas."

The teachings of Saint Thomas on the matter of civil order, then, could easily correct principles which are presently inimical to the peace and the public safety. Leo claims that the arts of learning would flourish again under Thomas, as they always do when drawing upon sound philosophy. Furthermore, if Thomas were studied, the physical sciences would be able to seek and find unity and purpose in the universe, and they would be supported in every way in the search for facts by a philosophy which guarantees the sensible world and its intelligibility to the human intellect.

The encyclical closes with the following unequivocal words regarding the system of Saint Thomas Aquinas: "We exhort you, Venerable Brethren, in all earnestness to restore the golden wisdom of St. Thomas, and to spread it far and wide for the defense and beauty of the Catholic faith, for the good of society, and for the advantage of all the sciences. The wisdom of St. Thomas, We say; for if anything is taken up with too great subtlety by the scholastic doctors, or too carelessly stated—if there be anything that ill agrees with the discoveries of a later age, or, in a word, improbable in whatever way, it does not enter Our mind to propose that for imitation to our age. Let carefully selected teachers endeavor to implant the doctrine of Thomas Aquinas in the minds of students, and set forth clearly his solidity and excellence over others. Let the academies already founded or to be founded by you illustrate and defend this doctrine, and use it for the refutation of prevailing errors. But, lest the false for the true or the corrupt for the pure be drunk in, be ye watchful that the doctrine of Thomas be drawn from his own fountains, or at least from those rivulets which derived from the very fount, have thus far flowed, according to the established agreements of learned men, pure and clear. . . ."

It is evident from a careful reading of *Aeterni Patris* that Leo XIII meant the encyclical to be something more than a mere recommendation or suggestion. It seems evident that the document was a clear exercise of apostolic authority directed toward the institutionalizing of Thomism in Catholic schools. *Aeterni Patris* in itself has all the earmarks of a papal prescription. The Leonine events which promptly followed the encyclical reinforce this view. They are as follows: (1) the brief *Iampridem considerando* (1879) restored the Roman Academy for the study of Saint Thomas and proclaimed the pope's intention of ordering a new edition of his writings; (2) the brief *Placere nobis* (1880) set up a commission of cardinals to edit the new edition; (3) the brief *Cum hoc sint* (1880) proclaimed Saint Thomas the Angelic Doctor of all Catholic schools and universities; (4) an exhortation was given to the Jesuits to follow Saint Thomas (1892); (5) an exhortation was given to the Franciscans to follow Saint Thomas (1893).

The editing of the writings of Saint Thomas got under way at once under the care of the Dominicans, vested with exclusive responsibility for the new edition, and by 1948 the editors had completed sixteen folio volumes. The editing aimed at giving not merely the sense but the very words of Saint Thomas through a method of textual criticism of the most painstaking sort, which involved working back through hundreds of copies to the apograph of each book. Comparison with one of the few autographs, that of the *Summa contra Gentiles*, has proven the method a complete success, as testified by experts such as Monsignor Grabmann and others.

The necessity of a definitive edition of the writings of St. Thomas as a propaedeutic to any meaningful restoration of the philosophy of the Angelic Doctor was a fact clearly seen by Leo XIII.

Although *Aeterni Patris* was not lacking detractors both inside and outside the Church, there is worldwide evidence that the plan and program of the foresighted and saintly Roman Pontiff Leo XIII has borne increasingly vital and abundant fruit in the increased study and appreciation of the works of Saint Thomas.

J.F.K.

IMMORTALE DEI

Author: Pope Leo XIII (Gioacchino Vincenzo Raffaele Luigi Pecci, 1810-1903)
Type of work: Christian social ethics
First published: 1885

Principal Ideas Advanced

Since it receives its authority from God, the state should publicly profess and favor the true religion.

The Church is supreme in religious matters while the state has charge of temporal affairs.

Rationalism and naturalism, which deny the authority of God and His Church, are sources of serious errors and dangers.

Catholics should participate in political life in order to Christianize and perfect the state.

Leo XIII had one of the longest and most influential pontificates of all time. A scholar, he had a wealth of practical experience, too, having served as governor of the papal cities of Benevento and Perugia for several years and as bishop of the latter for thirty-one. During his episcopacy Perugia was annexed to Piedmont, and as a result on numerous occasions he had to resist secular violations of the rights of the Church. Thus, when he was elected to the papacy in 1878, Leo was fully aware of the problems facing the times and was singularly well equipped to suggest solutions for them. These he presented to the world in a series of encyclicals whose depth, sanity, and appositeness did much to raise the fallen prestige of the Church and to provide the proper guidelines for it. Of these encyclicals *Immortale Dei,* the usual English title of which is *On the Christian Constitution of States,* is important because it states most fully Leo's views on Church-state relations, and as such it has guided Catholic theologians and preachers for half a century.

The reader, however, will be likely to misinterpret Leo if he does not keep in mind the historical situation in which Leo was writing and which indicates the kind of state he was talking about. Leo seems never to have adequately distinguished the paternalistic form of government common up to his time from the truly democratic form exhibited in states then starting to develop. Consequently, we may say that when Leo discusses the Christian constitution of states this is to be understood as referring only to paternalistic governments; that is, to those in which the rulers and subjects form two separate classes, even though sometimes the latter might share to some extent in the functions of the former. Thus, the pope's strictures against the separation of Church and state are valid in the case of a Christian paternalistic government but do not apply to contemporary pluralistic democracies—or even, for that matter, to any democracy whose citizens are all Catholic. In order, then, to understand fully the position of the Church on this question one would also have to consult later popes, such as Pius XII in his "Allocution to the Italian Jurists," of December 6, 1953. Similar remarks would hold for Leo's views on toleration.

Immortale Dei begins with Leo's claim that although the immediate and natural purpose of the Church is the salvation of souls, the Church is also the source of temporal benefits as various and great as if her chief end were to procure them. Despite this temporal concern of the Church, an old and hackneyed accusation leveled against the Church is that she opposes the civil powers and cannot help them in implementing the secular welfare and progress which is their proper end. This odious calumny, Leo points out, was long ago most capably refuted by Augustine in the *City of God*, but it continues to be levied. Moreover, novel theories, contrary to Church doctrine, have been advanced concerning the state. Leo feels duty-bound to compare them with the Christian view.

Man, says Leo, is by nature social since he can provide himself with his basic necessities and the means of mental and moral development only in civil society. To sustain itself, however, every state must have a ruling authority to direct the whole for the common good. Since both the ruling authority and the state have their source in nature, their power is derived from God. Any form of government is valid as long as it is capable of securing the general welfare. It is therefore treason against both God and man to resist legitimate authority.

The state, then, must make a public profession of religion. Every man is required by reason and nature to worship God, the source and end of his being. Society, the union of men living together, is equally bound to render Him due service by clinging to religion in both its teaching and practice, not to any religion it might prefer, but only to the one He has enjoined and certified with certain and clear marks. The rulers, then, should honor God's name and protect and favor His religion. In this way civil society which exists to achieve the common good helps its members to attain to that highest and immutable good all should seek.

It is not difficult, continues Leo, for an earnest and unbiased mind to find out which is the true religion. The prophecies and miracles, the rapid spread of the faith, the witness of the martyrs, all make it evident that the only true religion is the one Christ founded and entrusted to His Church to protect and propagate. This Church has one ruling head established by God Himself. Like the state, it is a society, but one which is supernatural and spiritual because of its end and the means it uses. Hence, it is distinct from the state and perfect in its nature and title. Just as its end is the noblest, so its authority is the most exalted and is neither inferior to nor dependent upon the civil power. This authority the Church has always claimed and exercised.

Thus, God has established two powers to rule men, the ecclesiastical and the civil, each supreme within its own province. To avoid any conflict of their authority God has marked out their right correlation to each other, which can be determined only by having regard to the nature and purpose of each. Since it is the function of the Church to lead men to Heaven, whatever is concerned with the salvation of souls or the worship of God falls under the power and judgment of the Church. The end of the state, however, is to provide for the well-being of men in this life, and civil authorities are responsible for securing that end. Such an arrangement does not detract from the rights or dignity of states; on the contrary, it adds to their permanence, luster, and perfection. History shows how such a Christian constitution of states made possible the most important of advances.

In the sixteenth century, however, declares Leo, a harmful and deplorable passion for innovation insinuated itself into the Christian religion, then into philosophy, and finally into all classes of society. As a result there later burst forth all those tenets of unbridled license which have been proclaimed the basis of a new conception of rights at variance not only with Christian law but also with natural law. Its main principle is that all men "are equal in the control of their life; that each one is so far his own master as to be in no sense under the rule of any other individual; that each is free to think on every subject just as he may choose, and to do whatever he may like to do; that no man has any right to rule over other men." God's authority is ignored, just as if there were no God, or as if individuals and societies owed nothing to Him, or as if there could be a government whose foundation, power, and authority did not come from Him. Thus, a state is nothing but a multitude which is its own ruler. The people being declared to be the source of all rights and power, the state is not considered to be bound by any duties toward God or any religion, and equal rights are granted every creed. All religious matters are referred to private judgment independent of all law. Every one has unbounded license to think and publish whatever he wishes.

In states founded on such principles it is the usual practice either to forbid the Church to do anything or to try to keep her in bondage. Such states treat the Church as equal or inferior to other institutions, the states ignore the marital regulations established by the Church. The states confiscate the property of the Church; they suppress her religious orders; they maintain that any rights or legal powers she may have are granted by them; and they provide a godless education for the youth.

All this follows, Leo declares, from the principle that sovereignty resides solely in the people, without any reference to God, a doctrine well suited to flatter and inflame the masses but lacking any reasonable proof and incapable of insuring public order and safety. Indeed, many have deduced from it that they may rightfully foster sedition. Likewise, the freedom to think and publish anything whatsoever is not an advantage for society but the source of many evils. True liberty perfects men but can have only truth and goodness for its object. If the intellect accepts false opinions and the will chooses what is wrong, both are corrupted and deprived of their proper perfection. It is wrong, then, to tempt men with anything opposed to truth and virtue; and it is even worse to protect and favor by law such behavior. Such doctrines the Roman pontiffs have always denounced, Leo states.

The Church does not condemn any form of government as such, Leo writes, for the Church thinks that wise and just rulers could insure the common good in any of them. "Neither is it blameworthy in itself, in any manner, for the people to have a share greater or less, in the government," Leo writes, "for at certain times, and under certain laws, such participation may not only be of benefit to the citizens, but may even be of obligation." The Church, then, is not hard, illiberal, or opposed to real and lawful liberty. She denies the equality of all religions, Leo admits, but the Church "does not . . . condemn those rulers who, for the sake of securing some great good or of hindering some great evil, allow patiently custom or usage to be a kind of sanction for each kind of religion having its place in the State. And, in fact, the Church is wont to take earnest heed that no one shall be forced to embrace the Catholic faith against his will. . . ." Indeed, the Church has always encouraged an honorable freedom, the pursuit of truth, and every striving for progress.

We can see, writes Leo, what then are the duties of individual Catholics. They should have a firm grasp of papal teachings and profess them openly when the occasion requires it, especially in regard to the "liberties" which are only a mask for the rejection of divine authority. They should conform their lives to the Gospel precepts whatever the difficulty. All should love, obey, and defend the Church. It is very important for the common welfare that all Catholics participate prudently in civic affairs and introduce laws based on Christian principles. In general, they should extend their efforts even to national politics, because, if they do not, men whose views are not conducive to the good of the state or of the Church will take power. Every one must determine for himself the means suited to his time and place, but all should have the same end: the Christianization of the state. Differences of opinion should not be allowed to cause dissension, but it must be remembered that views verging on naturalism or rationalism, views which exclude God and make man supreme, cannot be reconciled with Catholicism. In mutual charity, then, all should cease quarreling and should co-operate with the Church in preserving and propagating Christian wisdom. Catholics will thereby also confer the greatest benefit on civil society, which is being so seriously imperiled by evil teachings.

These, concludes Leo, are the main points he has thought it necessary to expound concerning the Christian constitution of states and the duties of individual citizens.

G.J.D.

RERUM NOVARUM

Author: Pope Leo XIII (Gioacchino Vincenzo Raffaele Luigi Pecci, 1810-1903)
Type of work: Social encyclical on capital and labor
First published: 1891

Principal Ideas Advanced

Those who undertake labor do so in the expectation of acquiring a living wage and private property; the Church, not the state, must act to insure that workers receive just reward for their efforts.

The rich and the poor can be united in a harmonious society if the Church recalls the two classes to their mutual duties.

The duties of the poor and the workers are to do their work conscientiously, to protect the property of their employers, to refrain from violence, and not to associate with those who would organize the workers for selfish ends.

The duties of the rich and the employers are to treat the workers as human beings, to treat them with dignity and to insure the satisfaction of their religious interests, to demand no more work than the worker is capable of performing, and to give the workers what is due them for their labor.

Pope Leo XIII wrote the encyclical *Rerum novarum* (also entitled, in English, *On the Condition of Workers*) to insure that the morality of the Church would prevail over the morality of socialism in the vital struggle to bring harmony and justice to the relations between capital and labor. Although the pope was concerned with the socialist threat to the free economy, Leo's defense of the natural right to private property was only part of his overall effort to bring about a state of affairs in which workers would be recognized as human beings of dignity and worth, entitled to a just return for their labor. The encyclical is properly entitled *On the Condition of Workers,* for it is not so much an attack on Socialism as it is a forceful and quietly revolutionary appeal for proper treatment of the laboring classes. In specifying the duties of capital and labor, as seen from the perspective of the Church, Leo anticipated the social concerns which later, in the twentieth century, would radically affect the condition of the workers.

Leo begins by emphasizing the right of private property, primarily land, a right which flows from man's rationality and is, therefore, one of the chief points of distinction between man and the animal creation. Leo writes that since man alone among the animals possesses reason, "it must be within his right to have things not merely for temporary and momentary use, as other living beings have them, but in stable and permanent possession. . . ." Basing his defense upon the laws of nature, Leo points out that a portion of land to be productive is dependent upon a human laborer, that the human laborer must change the condition of the land, and that he thus acquires the right to possess it. The natural duty of a man to provide for the future welfare of his family also argues for his natural right to accumulate property.

The right of private ownership of the individual and the family, the basic social unit, therefore precedes the state's right, advanced by the Socialists, to such property. The function of the state is to protect private ownership rights rather than usurp them. It is, in effect, the individual and the family which provide the state with whatever rights it has.

Arguing from a more practical standpoint, Leo cites private property as the basic incentive for the workingman and, because it enables the worker to partake in capital, the avenue to better productivity and a more equal distribution of wealth. (Men must recognize, however, cautions Leo, that there will always be a certain inequality in the distribution of wealth because there exists among men a natural inequality in the ability to earn it.) Leo implies that capital and labor are really one class separated by a degree of ownership rather than by any natural law, and he utterly rejects socialism as a means to human solidarity because it incites class warfare and deprives the individual of his natural right of ownership.

Leo concludes that the application of Christian principles to the relationships between employers and employees is the only feasible way to achieve human solidarity. Christianity, he writes, "teaches the laboring man and the workman to carry out honestly and well all equitable agreements freely made, never to injure capital, nor to outrage the person of an employer; never to employ violence in representing his own cause, nor to engage in riot and disorder. . . ." Furthermore, Christianity "teaches the rich man and the employer that their work people are not their slaves; that they must respect in every man his dignity as a man and as a Christian; that labor is nothing to be ashamed of, if we listen to right reason and to Christian philosophy, but is an honorable employment, enabling a man to sustain his life in an upright and creditable way; and that it is shameful and inhuman to treat men like chattels to make money by, or to look upon them merely as so much muscle or physical power."

In an attempt to revive Christian values in both the privileged and the underprivileged, Leo reminds the poor that suffering is part of life and cautions them against ideologies and practices which promise to abolish suffering; he reminds the rich that wealth cannot buy entrance to Heaven, that it can, indeed, hinder it. Because there is a difference between the right to possess private property and the right to use it, the employer is bound in practice by his duty to the human community. He is bound to alleviate human misery by freely sharing his wealth. Once Christian principles are applied to employer-employee relationships, many problems are easily remedied; conclusions may then be reached concerning the just wage, that which is sufficient to maintain a life in accordance with human dignity; the proper length of a working day, which varies according to the task; the cessation of work on Sundays to allow workers time for religious practices; and the proper fitting of the task to the worker, which includes humane conditions for children and women laborers.

By favoring a laissez-faire policy on acts of Christian charity, the virtuous potential of which diminishes when they cease to be voluntary and are enforced by state laws, Leo curtails the role of the state and relegates it to a protective force. Its prime function is to guarantee distributive justice, that is, justice toward each class, and it possesses the right to interfere in private matters only as a last resort to guarantee distributive justice. Leo XIII sanctions state interference in strikes only where there is "imminent danger of disturbance to the public peace. . . ." It is suggested that the state perform its prime function through private organizations, specifically workmen's organizations operating to heal the breach between capital and labor by promoting virtuous actions to guarantee distributive justice.

Workmen's associations or unions, which Leo believes would accomplish the ends sought by the ancient artificers' guilds of improving the quality of production and the conditions of the worker as well as preserving his human dignity, have a natural right to exist as long as their purposes are not bad, unjust, or dangerous to the state. Such associations are private societies housed in the public society of the state, and they have the sanction of the natural law, for to unite is a natural impulse of man. They should be orientated by religion to guarantee the application of those Christian principles essential for human solidarity. Leo believes that these Christian associations would prove an effective force against the socialism he rejects as a means to human solidarity. They would oppose and defeat similar associations of socialistic agitators endangering the natural rights of the individual. These private Christian societies would act like leaven and lead to the re-Christianization of states in which religion has suffered a grave setback. Christian action rather than the violence of strikes and the revolution preached by socialistic agitators would be the method used by these associations to achieve their goals.

It is interesting to note that Leo cites the distribution of work and pension and insurance plans among the purposes of workmen's associations; it is the task of the associations to make "an effort to arrange for a continuous supply of work at all times and seasons; and to create a fund from which the members may be helped in their necessities, not only in case of accident, but also in sickness, old age, and misfortune."

Leo's prescription of reasonable and charitable principles as guides for the operations of such associations is in keeping with the spirit of moderation which pervades his entire encyclical. The relations among members of such organizations should be harmonious with their common purposes, and officers of such associations should be appointed with discretion and work for the common purposes of their respective organizations rather than for themselves.

Leo XIII concludes his encyclical with an appeal for honesty between the classes. It is only by honest practices and the avoidance of the depravity of greed that right reason and the practice of Christianity can overcome the uneven distribution of wealth and heal the breach between classes. In advising moderation Leo is not supporting the *status quo* but attempting to guide mankind to a voluntary socialism continually dependent upon the independent will of the individuals composing the state. The value and beauty of the human community is dependent upon the goodness of each of its members, he concludes, and human solidarity achieved in this way is comparable to the symmetry of the human body. "Just as the symmetry of the human body is the result of the disposition of the members of the body, so in a State it is ordained by nature that these two classes should exist in harmony and agreement, and should, as it were, fit into one another, so as to maintain the equilibrium of the body politic. Each requires the other; capital cannot do without labor, nor labor without capital."

J.J.M.

A HISTORY OF THE CATHOLIC CHURCH IN THE UNITED STATES

Author: John Dawson Gilmary Shea (1824-1892)
Type of work: American Catholic Church history
First published: I, 1886; II, 1888; III, 1890; IV, 1892

Principal Ideas Advanced

The Catholic Church, an important factor in the history of the United States, has had a continuous existence from the period of explorations and discoveries through the colonial period, the Revolutionary War, and the birth and growth of the Republic.

The history of the Church in the colonial period is a history of repression and deportation, but by 1815 the hope of religious freedom brought new life to American Catholicism.

In the nineteenth century although the rapidly expanding Church was faced with internal disciplinary problems and with hostile criticism from the Protestant clergy, new dioceses were established and the Church continued to grow in strength and influence.

John Gilmary Shea, the outstanding American Catholic historian, was a contemporary and acquaintance of George Bancroft, Francis Parkman, Jared Sparks, and Justin Winsor. His reputation as a critical and impartial historian has fared better than that of most of his contemporaries. Although not a member of the New England school which dominated historical writing in the middle period of the nineteenth century, he was influenced by Bancroft to undertake the study of history; he was introduced to sound historical methods by the Jesuit antiquarian Félix Martin, and by Edmund Bailey O'Callaghan, editor of the indispensable collection, *Documents Relative to the Colonial History of the State of New York* (11 volumes, 1853-61). Shea's first major historical work to impress his contemporaries was *Discovery and Exploration of the Mississippi Valley* (1852), a volume dedicated to Sparks.

Shea was the first to write a detailed

and comprehensive history of the Catholic Church in the United States and hence he was compelled to discover and collect the primary sources. In the Preface to the first volume he describes the few written sources available and the documents he acquired "by many years of search and enquiry." In 1876 he started to put in order the papers and documents, accumulated since 1852, for his multi-volume history. He planned a five volume work, but he was compelled to settle for four, which he wrote under incredible hardships. The first two volumes were written mainly at night, after a hard day of office work. When he started on the third volume, he was an ill man, and the fourth volume was completed on his death bed. Yet, despite these obstacles, he wrote what authorities concede was a "monumental, critical, and impartial" history. The text is enhanced by illustrative maps, portraits, and facsimiles of signatures. Subsequent historians are greatly in debt to Shea for the sound start he has given them in nearly every aspect of the Church's history. Historians have been able to add to Shea's narration of events, but Shea's *History* retains a permanent value and Shea remains the dean of American Catholic historians.

The Catholic Church in Colonial Days (1886) covers the years 1521-1763 and is divided into six books. The first three cover the Church in the English, Spanish, and French colonies and territories up to 1690. The remaining three continue the account to 1763, when "Canada was humbled in the dust, her great missionary organization had been broken up and the Catholics in Florida saw no hope except in emigration," while in the English colonies prospects were gloomy beyond description.

Since Maryland was the center of Catholics in the English colonies, Shea devotes most of his space to this colony. Pennsylvania, however, became a haven in 1681, and the repressed Catholics of Maryland, together with new immigrants, sought homes there. Catholics also enjoyed some freedom briefly in New York during Governor Thomas Dongan's administration (1682-1688). Chapter 4 describes the deportation of the Acadians (1775), in disregard of "every principle of English law," to the English colonies which were reluctant to receive them. Isolated, ignored, and deprived of parish life, they either succumbed to the prevailing religious atmosphere of the colonies or sought freedom in escape.

The missionary activities in Maine and New York, narrated in the section on the French colonies, are superbly detailed, as are the activities of the missionaries in the other French and Spanish territories. Shea's work on the discovery and exploration of the Mississippi Valley, followed by his *History of the Catholic Missions among the Indian Tribes of the United States*, 1529-1854, by the editing of the *Jesuit Relations* and grammars and dictionaries of the Indian language, and by other writings, made him an authority in this area. (A bibliography of Shea's writings can be found in Peter Guilday's book, *John Gilmary Shea, Father of American Catholic History*, 1926.) Thus, Shea gave the readers of this volume the first scholarly presentation and appreciation of the tremendous activities of Catholic missions in this country during the colonial period.

The history of the Church from 1763 to 1815 is told in the *Life and*

Times of the Most Reverend John Carroll, Bishop and First Archbishop of Baltimore (1888). This is the best of the four volumes, mainly because of the remarkable person of John Carroll, who organized the Church after the Revolution and successfully directed it in its adjustment to the new opportunities offered by the federal constitution and by the freedom of religion gradually introduced into the new state constitutions. By word and by act Carroll gave to American Catholicism, a direction which became traditional.

After presenting a brief biographical sketch of Carroll which includes Carroll's return to Maryland from Europe in 1774, the author describes the status of religion in the colonies on the eve of the Revolution, the impact of the Quebec Act on the colonists, and the attitudes and activities of the Catholics during the Revolution (Carroll himself accompanied the American mission, which included his cousin Charles Carroll, to Canada). Then, after telling of Carroll's appointment as bishop of Baltimore, Shea recounts the development and administration of the Church in various sections. By 1815, when Carroll died, a remarkable change of mood had taken place: "Catholics were free; the days of penal laws had departed; professions were open to them, and in most States the avenue to all public offices. In the late war with England they had shown their patriotism in the field and on the waves."

The reviewer in *The Edinburgh Review* (April, 1890) declared this volume a "valuable contribution to national and ecclesiastical history," admirably fulfilling the promise of its title page, and he praised Shea's remarkable skill in illustrating the volume with pictures and facsimiles.

Shea intended to cover the history of the Church from 1815 to 1866 in three volumes, one each for the Atlantic States, the Mississippi Valley, and the Pacific Coast. Unfortunately, rapidly declining health and increasing burdens prevented him from following the plan. In a revised plan he covered all sections of the country, recounting the events from 1808 to 1843 in the third volume and from 1843 to 1866 in the fourth and last volume. Although these two volumes are rich in information, aptly illustrated, well documented, and a grateful source for future studies, the material is not well organized.

Since the four new dioceses of Boston (compromising all New England), New York, Philadelphia, and Bardstown, Kentucky, established in 1808 by the first division of the original Baltimore diocese, were not given the notice they deserved in the study of Carroll, the third volume starts with the events of 1808 and extends its survey to 1843, the date of the fifth Provincial Council. The approach is by a study of dioceses, starting with the diocese of Baltimore, and going on to other sections of the country. Two chapters are devoted to the first Provincial Council (1829) and the growth of anti-Catholic sentiment in the country. As one would expect, most of this large volume is concerned with the Atlantic section where Catholics were more numerous and where the early dioceses were established.

The diocese section approach did not lend itself to a clear and continuous exposition of the growth and the problems of the Church. The rapidly expanding Church was faced with internal problems of discipline (trusteeism and troublesome clergy), with faulty decisions made in Rome as a result of inadequate information about the young country, public controversies between Catholic and Protestant clergymen, and a growing hostility to Catholicism that erupted at times into violence. Since some of these problems, traversing as they did diocesan lines, needed further explication, an additional Chapter for this purpose would have allowed a better understanding of the impact of the social and political institutions of our national life on the attitudes and activities of the Catholics.

Yet the reader, introduced to the origins, problems, and expansion of one diocese after another, is given a clear and sound understanding and appreciation of the labors and growth of the Church, its institutions of learning and charity, its leading ecclesiastics, and, to a lesser degree, its prominent lay leaders. If there were no bishops during this period of the stature of Carroll, there were many able, learned, and zealous leaders in the hierarchy, such as Bishop John England (1786-1842) of Charleston, whose writings (five volumes) were published in 1849, Bishop Benedict Fenwick (1782-1846) of Boston, who founded Holy Cross College in Worcester (1843), and the saintly Bishop Benedict J. Flaget (1763-1850) of Bardstown. Of these three only Fenwick was an American by birth; the Church in America was in heavy debt to the generosity of European clergy.

Shea read the proof sheets of the fourth volume on his death bed, and he did not live to see it published. He was unable to write the usual preface with autobiographical data related to the writing of the work. In this volume he continued the same approach used in the previous one, that of treating one archdiocese or province (a group of dioceses) after another, and then the Western dioceses and vicariates. He describes their histories up to 1851, the year of the first Plenary Council of Baltimore, and then takes them, along with new archdioceses and dioceses, to 1866, the year of the second Plenary Council. The establishing of archdioceses was clear evidence of the rapid increase in the number of Catholics, most of them immigrants, requiring new parishes and new dioceses. New England, where the "most remarkable development of Catholicity" took place, is a good example of this growth. In 1808, all the New England states were part of the original diocese of Boston; in 1853, three more dioceses had been founded, Hartford (Connecticut and Rhode Island), Portland (Maine and New Hampshire), and Burlington (Vermont), and the diocese of Boston was limited to Massachusetts. All four dioceses were suffragans of the archdiocese of New York.

There is evidence of haste and the appearance of a rough outline in this last volume. Considering Shea's failing health and the period covered, this is easy to understand. To cover adequately one large diocese such as New York or Baltimore would have required a monograph. And Shea's plan did not allow for a continuous exposition of the major problems of the Church: the flood of immigrants, the tide of anti-Catholicism, education, the Civil War. The wonder is that he was able to accomplish so much, and one realizes what a wealth of notes, with references and sources indicated, he had gathered during his years of intense research—data which make the volume a source of much value for future historians engaged in writing biographies of Church leaders, or other works involving historical references to the Church.

Many able leaders emerged during this period and the biographical sketches of them are valuable. There were the two Kenrick brothers, Peter Richard Kenrick, Archbishop of St. Louis, and Francis P. Kenrick, Archbishop of Baltimore and a Scripture scholar; John Hughes, the first Archbishop of New York, "the most remarkable episcopal administration that New York has yet known," and one of the few leaders Shea does succeed in relating to the affairs of the city, state, and nation; John B. Purcell, Archbishop of Cincinnati, a leading educator and an influential spokesman of American Catholicism.

Shea's concluding chapter is on the Second Plenary Council of Baltimore (1866), which was a splendid manifestation of Catholic growth and unity after the Civil War. A more favorable attitude towards the Catholic Church was developing under the impact of the war, and it found public expression on the occasion of this Council.

W.L.L.

L'ACTION

Author: Maurice Blondel (1861-1949)
Type of work: Religious ethics
First published: 1893

Principal Ideas Advanced

The crucial problem facing philosophy today is the question of human action, its motivation, its limits, and its goals.

Human action must be seen as including the whole range of human activities, biological, psychological, social, metaphysical, and religious.

In human activity there is always a fundamental inequality between the objects or actions we will and the innate impulse or goal of our will; this disparity, evident in our physical limitations, is crowned by death.

Valid and useful as they may be, all the goals set up by the will are insufficient to satisfy the fundamental impulse of the will itself; this impulse is satisfied only by the Unique Necessary, God, with whom we seek to be one.

Maurice Blondel grew up in one of the richest periods of French culture, an age in which Proust and Gide, Peguy and Claudel, Matisse and Roualt, Debussy and Ravel were associates and friends. Of particular influence on him were his formative years at the École Normale, not so much because of his teachers but because of the impact of his fellow students. As an ardent Christian, Blondel was greatly disturbed to see his classmates giving up the solid foundations of their spiritual faith for the attractions of the philosophical fads of the day. These fads, very superficial in nature, involved their advocates in the abstract and the speculative to the point that they took no more than a spectator's role in everyday affairs. To Blondel this ivory tower attitude posed both a question and a challenge: "Does human life have a meaning, does man have a destiny, yes or no? . . . The problem is unavoidable and every man inevitably resolves it. Whether his solution is right or wrong, each one lives it out in his actions, and that is why we must study *action*."

As his studies advanced and he moved on to the Sorbonne, the topic of human action became primal in his thought and studies. It was the subject of his doctoral thesis, defended on June 7, 1893. Known by the abbreviated title of *L'Action,* the thesis is an attempt at a critique of life and the development of a science of human action. It became the keystone of Blondel's thought, the prime basis for his influence, and the source of all his later writings.

In examining the whole scope of human activity, Blondel begins by eliminating all suppositions, even the postulates of a moral obligation or natural necessity for acting. Such postulates, he feels, limit human freedom in such a way that mankind has tended over the years to construct a wide range of doctrines and beliefs as an escape from this so-called necessity. The true philosopher must examine these postulates, together with the doctrines and attitudes they have engendered, in order to learn critically whether they are valid.

With this premise as a procedural basis, Blondel examines the limitations various philosophies have imposed on the concept of human action. In every case, he finds that the artificial boundaries set up by a philosopher are necessarily transcended by the unwilling philosopher himself. Thus, a disparity is always present between the *volonte voule* and the *volonte voulante,* or between the object or act willed by the person and the primitive impulse or libido of the whole personality. In examining various human attitudes toward action, Blondel reveals a list of conditions necessary if the goal or act willed is to meet the demands of the voluntary aspiration. At the same time this disclosure demonstrates the wide scope of spiritual power latent in all human action.

The materialistic or naturalistic philosophy of action is the next step in the examination. Blondel attacks this pessimistic view of life as "willing nothingness" since it sees death as ending all; it is a type of motivation, or rather, a *lack* of motivation, which makes human action impossible. Moving on, he explores the different spheres of human activity and justifies the necessity of such activities as sense perception, the physical sciences, the development of freedom and individuality, the structuring of socio-economic constructs such as the family and society, as well as the erection of metaphysical and ethical systems. Each of these activities is based on an implicit act of the will, yet each of them is insufficient as an all-satisfying goal for the human mind and will. A simple but very important conclusion is then reached: the fundamental impulse of the human will cannot be fully satisfied by simple human activity.

This impasse marks a turning point for man. The physical, biological, and psychological limitations inherent in human nature are ultimately crowned by death. But "willing nothingness," as would be the case if death ended all, is irrational and incapable of acting as a motivation for human activity. In this apparent failure of the will to achieve its goal because of death Blondel finds a solution to the problem. The impasse of the will's seeming incapacity to achieve its goal is a vital proof that there must be something beyond death and that death is therefore only an apparent defeat. The goal of the will and the fact that this goal is not attainable in this life proves the immortality or indestructibility of voluntary action.

These arguments, concludes Blondel, lead us to posit an inner something which is responsible for our consciousness of this conflict, a recognition of the existence of a "Unique Necessary," a term later used by Teilhard de Chardin. Following the dialectics of human action, this postulate brings us to affirm the existence of God, an affirmation that lends a transcendent nature to our human activity. Not only do we seek to possess God, but also in some fashion to become God. And thus we arrive at the crucial question facing human action: "Yes or no, is man going to will to live, and even die for this, that is will he live and die by consenting to be supplanted by God? Or will he pretend to get along without God, profiting from his necessary presence yet without voluntarily accepting it, borrowing from him the power to get along without him, and infinitely willing without willing the infinite."

Blondel admits that every man sees this dilemma with a different degree of clarity and awareness, but each perceives it with sufficient light to be able to resolve the crucial problem of human action; namely, the disparity between the will and the object willed. Man must open himself to an action greater than his own lest the greatness of his desire and his willing be destroyed or consumed by the self-imposed limitations of his field of action.

Such a conclusion is basic but still not adequate because it is not distinct or concrete enough. Hence, the philosopher is led to consider the rites and doctrines of Christianity to determine if these might contain substance that will meet the demands of our primitive impulse. For Blondel, the Christian symbols, rites, and doctrines do portray externally the very essence of what we desire in our deepest being. They are a complete image of our real needs. Yet such an intellectual recognition does not imply an acceptance of them as true. This acceptance is a matter of faith and outside the scope of the philosopher.

Having examined the whole range of human experience, and arriving at the possibility of reaching a balance between the voluntary aspiration and our basic voluntary impulse, Blondel tackles the question of methodology. Such an examination, he maintains, is phenomenological. The empirical knowledge thus obtained, though, is not sufficient as a solution to the problem of human action. Knowledge leads to action, and action must follow our empirical knowledge if it is to be fruitful. Thus, faith, with the acceptance of the supernatural, is ultimately the key to our problem of action.

Having defended his thesis for the

doctorate, Blondel took a position at the Faculty of Letters at Aix-en-Provence. However the defense of his ideas was to continue for many years. Philosophers attacked his thesis because it went beyond the range of philosophy, while theologians attacked him for naturalizing Christianity. A serious and open-minded examination of his views clearly shows that both objections are baseless and that his works stand well within the framework of Christian and Catholic tradition. Despite the fact that his works were not translated, Blondel was able to contribute much to the renewal of creative thought within the Church. Through Laberthonniere, Bergson, and others, the influence of his ideas gradually spread. Gabriel Marcel and Teilhard de Chardin are only two of the important thinkers influenced by him. As a precursor of the more fully developed existentialist, phenomenological, and evolutionary writers of today, Blondel contributes the initial step in the development of what Teilhard called "human energetics," the science of human action and participation in the voluntary control of evolution.

R.T.F.

THE HOUND OF HEAVEN AND OTHER POEMS

Author: Francis Thompson (1859-1907)
Type of work: Religious and mystical poetry
First published: 1893

Principal Ideas Advanced

God's pursuit of man's soul is relentless and unceasing until man surrenders the objects of his earthly love in exchange for God's love; man's pursuer is also the object of man's search.

The poet looks upon external nature with the eyes of a child, and he sees God's love everywhere; childhood innocence prefigures the Mystery of the Incarnation.

The liturgy of the Catholic Church is a joyful and sublime gift from God; through an appreciation of liturgy, the happy and contented observer of nature develops insights into the Mysteries of the Incarnation, the Redemption, and the Mystical Body of Christ.

Although a century has passed since the birth of Francis Thompson, his reputation as the most mystical and religious poet of the Catholic Literary Revival has not been dimmed. Few reputable critiques and anthologies of Victorian literature fail to represent him, at least by his "The Hound of Heaven," a work regarded as a technical and thematic masterpiece which has, at least for some critics, a greater relevance today than it had when it was first published. Thompson's luxuriance of poetic diction, his propensity for romantic symbols and images, and his individualism of artistic vision may have repelled some of his nineteenth century readers, Catholic as well as non-Catholic, who deprecated his poetic craft as imitative of Shelley's pantheism and romantic ennui. The piquancy of personal suffering and the explication of sacrifice, which inspired his shorter nature lyrics and the longer religious odes, actually puts Thompson in debt to many post-Victorian poets.

The ambivalence between the opulence of his style and super-sensitivity to human joy and suffering has enabled Thompson to survive many subsequent sporadic aesthetic cults and to merit critical respect as the most talented Catholic contributor to the Literary Revival.

Thompson's poetry expresses, in emotional detail, fallen humanity's search for joy, truth, and spiritual reconciliation.

There is a growing interest in Thompson today. Commenting on his reputation twenty-five years after his death in 1933, *The New York Times* judged the tributes then being paid to him as equal to those ordinarily paid only after a century. A reputable critic of Catholic writers, Father Calvert Alexander, S.J., in his *The Catholic Literary Revival* (1935), estimates correctly that "[Thompson's] wealth of classical allusions, his exotic neologisms, the deliberate richness of his diction might be expected to jar painfully upon the susceptibilities of an age intolerant of any mannerisms but its own." Yet, Thompson survives because for all ages he embodies the marks of a true poet: rich imagination, metrical skill, and sublimity of thought.

Both artistically and inspirationally, Thompson belongs to the *fin de siecle* when there was an increasing demand for an escape from the multisided materialism of Victorian England. As a poet and essayist, he is easily identified with the Catholic Literary Revival, that persuasive movement that led writers to express their emotions of nobility and despair in accordance with Roman Catholic philosophy and theology. He ranks with Alice Meynell and Lionel Johnson as the apex of a triangular pattern dedicated to the artistic refinement of Catholic doctrine, dogma, and liturgy.

In retrospect, the Catholic Revival is closely associated with the secular history of the last half of Victoria's reign, when Catholic writing appears at first, as a literature of protest against the liberalism, anti-intellectualism, scientific naturalism, and romantic aestheticism of the time. Actually, the Revival was remotely connected to the Romantic Movement in its debt to the pantheistic philosophizing of Wordsworth, Coleridge, Shelley, and Keats and the practical theorizing of Ruskin and Arnold, who criticized the growing mechanization of society. The Oxford Movement, with Cardinal Newman's defection from Anglican cultural and religious apathy, was the immediate catalyst which inspired many young, imitative, Catholic-oriented visionaries to discover in Roman Catholicism the antidote to naturalistic monism and economic individualism. With confidence gained from the restoration of the Catholic hierarchy and the removal of civil disabilities against Catholics by the midcentury, the Church, under Newman's leadership, became a special topic for both the curious and the dedicated. A number of talented writers attracted public attention by reflecting in their publications the most fundamental concepts of Catholic teaching, though often in the poorest imitations of romantic literary technique. Thus, Aubrey De Vere, called "the Catholic Wordsworth," wrote songs in honor of the Blessed Mother and retold legends of medieval English saints; by celebrating nuptial love in *The Angel in the House* and *The Unknown Eros,* Coventry Patmore challenged Tennyson's domesticity and Keats's sensuousness; in blatant admiration of the melody and diction of Shelley's imagery, Thompson enjoyed temporary acclaim as the "Catholic Shelley" (his *Essay on Shelley* was posthumously published in 1909). Recent critical evaluations have shown these limiting Victorian tags to be only partially justifiable.

The artistic organizer of the Revival, it is now agreed, was Alice Meynell, who rallied Thompson, Johnson, Noyes, the young Chesterton, and other tyro literati to an appreciation of Catholic tradition as being more than merely a pertinent part of the historical past or as a emotional outlet for Decadent aestheticism. A writer of prominence herself, Alice Meynell envisioned the Catholic artist to be a deeply religious being living the religion which inspired his art. How fortuitous, then, as the Thompson biography reveals, that she was to become his literary patron by rescuing him from the literary limbo of London's streets.

Thompson's poetry appeared in three collections during his lifetime: *Poems* (1893), *Sister Songs* (1895), and *New Poems* (1897). His contemporary, Lionel Johnson, critically appraised these publications as "Magnificently faulty at times, magnificently perfect at others. . . . The ardors of poetry taking you triumphantly by storm; a surging sea of verse, rising and falling and irresistibly advancing. . . . He has the opulent, prodigal manner of the 17th century; a profusion of imagery, sometimes excessive and false and another profusion and opulence, that of Shelley in his lyrical choruses. . . . Beneath the outward manner a passionate reality of thought: profound, pathetic, full of faith without fear. . . . Words that if you pricked them would bleed . . . incapable of prettiness and pettiness . . . always vehement and burning . . . too fevered to be austere; a note of ardent suffering, not of endurance."

Often critically called the "Romanticist of the Catholic Revival," Thompson showed himself to be equal to the most erratic adventuring of any of the established romantics. Three catastrophes shaped his poetic artistry: he failed in his studies for the Catholic priesthood at Ushaw College; he disappointed his father, who was a doctor, by not completing his medical course at Owen's College; he failed to make a decent living as a writer in London when he left home in 1885. For three years, Thompson was a public charge, a drifter, an addict to opium and alcohol. Despite these buffetings, he did not cease to pray and to hope that his faith would not fail him. His critics are prompt to admit in re-evaluation that while he experienced the vagaries of the popular Decadents, he did not once renounce his spiritual idealism or Catholic heritage.

The account of his literary and physical salvation by the Meynells is almost legendary. In 1888 he sent some anonymous prose jottings and two poems, "The Passion of Mary" and "Dream-Tryst," to Wilfred Meynell, who, with his wife Alice, edited *Merry England.* Because of its unpromising appearance, the manuscript was at first pigeon-holed, but "The Passion of Mary" was published later in the year, with the hope that it would find its author. When Thompson saw it in print he agreed to meet the Meynells in a Drury Lane apothecary where he purchased his narcotics. Seeing him destitute and physically ill, the Meynells arranged for his recuperation at the Storrington Priory in Sussex. His famous "Ode to the Setting Sun," wherein he compares the sunset to the Benediction of the Blessed Sacrament, was composed here to celebrate his release from addiction. The promise of genius that the Meynells had hoped to see fulfilled was now realized.

From 1890 to 1894 Thompson lived happily with the Meynells and their children while he composed his lyrical *Sister Songs* (dedicated to Madeline and Monica Meynell) and "The Hound of Heaven." He entered the Capuchin Monastery at Pantasph, Wales, in 1894, eager to foster his developing interest in Church liturgy and to acquire a deeper understanding of the mystical insights of Catholic theology and philosophy. The *New Poems* attests the rewards of his transcendental research in their lucid and sincere explications of Catholic rubrics, thereby entitling Thompson to be called the poet of the modern Catholic Liturgical Revival. Having exhausted the exotic, imaginative rhetoric of his Shelleyan mentality in the earlier lyrics to nature, human love, suffering, and childhood innocence, Thompson now found in the symbolism of Church liturgy an increased comprehension of his Christocentric universe; the soon to be proclaimed papal encyclical of the Mystical Body of Christ is prefigured in his poetry of these years.

In 1896 Thompson returned to creative journalism in London, where he remained close to the Meynells and his new literary friend, Coventry Patmore. Thompson's death on November 13, 1907, was hastened by the overworking of a body that in youth had been sapped of its enduring energies.

Whether he was writing lyrics for children to enable them to appreciate the joys of their innocent years, or longer odes to stimulate his own desire for a richer love for Christ and His Church, Thompson was first and foremost a Catholic poet. His poetic attitude toward external nature and its creatures is reflective of his genuine faith in the supernatural and of his love for God. Despite his personal degradations, Thompson never fully relinquished his love and respect for the dignity of man or his faith in the intercessary powers of Christ's Mother to protect him from the despairs of human frailty. He continually stresses the duality of human nature in his lyrics of sacred and profane love. In the tradition of the Catholic Crashaw and the metaphysical Donne, Thompson declared that he wanted to be known as "the poet of the return to God," implying that there was no special glory in simply being another poet of "the return to nature." His insistence that society seek the Kingdom of Heaven, not through intellect, nature, or economic system, but through the only meaningful way, a return to spirituality, is basic in his religious lyrics. This underlying tenet is echoed in the concluding stanza of "The Kingdom of God," a short poem found after his death among his unpublished manuscripts: "Yes, in the night, my Soul, my daughter,/ Cry—clinging Heaven by the hems;/ And Lo, Christ walking on the water/ Not of Gennesareth, but Thames!"

To study his poetry and his biography is to realize how Catholic are his attitudes toward external nature, faith in the supernatural, and love of God the Father. For many readers, Thompson's fondness for allusions, his frequent allusions to little-known affairs and personal trivia, and the abundance of his radiant imagery may cloud the essential meaning: seek first the Kingdom of Heaven, the end of all earthly joy. Thompson, nevertheless, envisions the role of the poet to be that of using his craft for the sanctification of the soul, the uniting of the elements of God and man artistically. In his *Essay on Shelley,* Thompson recalls that "the Church was the mother of poets no less than of saints. . . . The palm and the laurel, Dominic and Dante, sanctity and song, grew together in her soil: she has retained the palm, but foregone the laurel."

By re-establishing the bond between the poet and Heaven, Thompson became the most gifted poet of the Catholic Revival. In "To a Poet Breaking Silence," he sets forth the subject matter pattern of his poetic ideal: "Ah! let the sweet birds of the Lord/ With earth's waters make accord; /Teach how the Crucifix may be/ Carven from the laurel-tree,/ Fruit of the Hesperides/ Burnish take on Eden-trees,/ The Muses' sacred grove be wet/ With the red dew of Olivet,/ And Sappho lay her burning brows/ In white Cecilia's lap of snows!"

Much of Thompson's poetry is associated with childhood in general and with the Meynell children in particular. His attitude is frequently that of a child looking with awe and élan at the magnificent splendor of the Eternal, never fully comprehending the mystery or for that matter, really wanting to. He wrote poetry from the child's point of view; he did not write children's poetry. The adult themes undercurrent in his lyrics and odes are hardly easy fare for children, although the imagery, song-like rhythms, and overall effects may at first reading have an appeal to the younger mind. He is often quoted as stating that he wished to be found after death "in the nurseries of Heaven." His poetry consequently reflects the restlessness of his personality, his material preoccupations, and his childlike faith in Christ's Redemption, the Sacraments, and God's Providence. As an adult, Thompson admired youthful innocence, and thus he thought of eternity as restoring the joys of that once happy state. His poetry is bright with childlike vision, but it is varied and mature in its intellectual implications.

The *Sister Songs* are poetic prayers begging that the child's beauty of soul may never be soiled by adult sin; Thompson contrasts his adult sinfulness with the child's sinlessness. He lyrically suggests the mystery of the Incarnation, when the powers of God were subservient to the will of man, and Christ's human soul waited upon the growth of His mortal senses. Children become for Thompson the Ultimate Beauty, unattainable but prefigured in the innocence of childhood; the children are Christ's brothers and sisters, playing with joyful innocence in the Nazareth carpenter shop.

Among the lyrics inspired by childhood are "Daisy," a blithe reminiscence of youthful delight in external nature; "The Poppy," dedicated to Monica Meynell, whose gift of the red poppy recalls the tragedies of life which children thankfully do not see; "Little Jesus," an imagined plea for the mercy of the Divine Child; "The Making of Viola," inspired by another Meynell daughter, in which the delicate subject of the procreation of soul and body is mystically and poignantly sung in a musical dialogue between God and His Angels; and "The Snowflake," in which the poet sees the Hand of God behind all the works of nature.

Written for Madeline (Sylvia) and Monica Meynell and given as a Christmas gift in 1891, the *Sister Songs* are choral odes in two parts: Part One invites the flowers and goddesses of Spring to join the poet in singing praises to the young girls' loveliness; Part Two singles out Monica for special tribute, since she nursed Thompson back to physical and spiritual health by offering him a living example of the intangible, mystical reality of Eternal Beauty, foreshadowed in the radiance of her own womanly beauty. Interwoven with elaborate imagery, Biblical and classical allusions, these impassioned melodies of childhood shimmer like multicolored Gothic windows by implying that earthly beauty and innocence is but a short-lived reflection of the Eternal. In comparing great things to small things, these boldly written lyrics express the poet's humble gratitude for the Incarnation and the Redemption.

"The Hound of Heaven" is acknowledged to be Thompson's classic; no other poem so completely expresses Thompson's desire to be the "poet of the return to God." While many critics have discussed this major work, the most knowledgeable explication is the analysis by Terence L. Connolly, S.J., in his *Poems of Francis Thompson* (1934). In his detailed notes, Father Connolly cites the poem as the greatest work of mysticism of our era, since it reverses the usual mystic process by depicting not man's pursuit of God, but God's pursuit of man. This "reverse pursuit" gives the work a unique stature among mystic poetry and accounts for the dramatic rapidity of the conflict. As Thompson describes the action, God's hunt for the soul is an awesome, terrifying, chilling experience. The variations on the refrain that run through the poem symbolize Thompson's spiritual excitement: no one will find peace of soul who does not first find God's love (Soul).

Father Connolly analytically suggests the comparison of "The Hound of Heaven" to a five act drama, with the poet's soul as the protagonist intent on fleeing from God's Love: I. Introduction (lines 1-15), the key-note theme, "I fled Him, down the nights and down the days . . ."; II. Rising Action (lines 16-110), the attempt of the soul to find escape in human love, nature, children; III. Climax (line 111), "Naked I wait Thy love's uplifted stoke!"; IV. Falling Action (lines 117-170), the retreat of the soul to God; V. Conclusion (lines 171-179), God's love is victorious as the mystery of life's suffering is revealed, "Halts by me that footfall. . . . Thou dravest love from thee, who dravest Me."

The poem is a masterpiece of poetic skill. The emotional variations are created by the effective use of the refrain, by deliberate contrasts of human love with Divine Love, and by the sense of dread which pervades the poem. When the crisis is passed, the reader can feel only relief. The diction also shows skillful control; it is elaborate but not artificial or constrained. The iambic meter is varied by contrasted and inverted phrases and assisted by a restrained use of simile and onomatopoeia. Although the central image of the hound as a symbol of the Divinity is not original, it has never before been more effectively employed. There are echoes throughout of the Old and New Testaments, of *Spiritual Exercises of Saint Ignatius Loyola* (Thompson read the work at the Capuchin Monastery), and the *Confessions* of Saint Augustine: "And lo, You at the heels of those who are fleeing from You, God of Vengeance and yet Fountain of Pity, turn us back to Yourself in wonderous ways." Unquestionably, "The Hound of Heaven" may be regarded as one of the finest examples of Catholic poetry to come out of the Victorian period.

Thompson's autobiographically inspired "Ode to the Setting Sun," written at the Storrington Priory, restates the central idea of "The Hound of Heaven." Here the sun is the symbol for the immanent love of God which is described as setting over past glories of past ages only to be found in the present of the Soul: "For there is nothing lives but something dies,/ And there is nothing dies but something lives./ Till Time, the hidden root of change, updries,/ Are Birth and Death inseparable on earth;/ For they are Twain yet one, and Death is Birth."

Other worth-while Thompson poems are "To The Dead Cardinal of Westminister" (exceptional metrical skill), "Lilium Regis" (musical cadence reflective of Wordsworth's "Solitary Reaper"), and "Envoy" (*New Poems*) with its memorable Thompsonesque lines, "Tell them ye grieve, for your hearts know Today,/ Tell them ye smile, for your eyes know Tomorrow."

Dedicated to Coventry Patmore, the mystical poetry of the *New Poems* was inspired by the religious atmosphere of the monastic life Thompson enjoyed at Pantasaph. The sixty-eight poems in this publication are more varied in range than are those in his other two volumes. The first section, "Sight and Insight," explains Thompson's belief that a poet should react emotionally and imaginatively to objects of beauty, seeking by "insight" the inner meaning behind external perceptions. Since Thompson was always a devotee of the romantic cult, as evidenced by his poetic and symbolic representation of his ardent love for external nature, the liturgy of the Church, which he came to understand at Pantasaph, supplied him with a completeness of artistic desire unknown before. Thompson's interests, however, remain quite close to the surface of the ritual, as is the custom among the romantics. From the Mass, the Eucharist, the Divine Office, the Office of the Blessed Virgin, the ceremonies of special feasts, and use of many sacramentals, Thompson drew inspiration for religious poems which expressed his newly experienced joy and his renewed faith in God. The profusion of appropriate images and the variety of symbols suggest that these poems must have been written in great haste while the poet was spurred on by an intense religious euphoria. So sensitive was his imagination to the rubrics and prayers of Catholic worship, that Thompson produced some of his most devotional lyrics at this time.

The celebrated "Orient Ode" is typical of Thompson's writing at this time; it reveals his love for the liturgy of Holy Saturday by depicting Christ rising like the sun in the East. In a profusion of luxuriant images steeped in Catholic connotations, Thompson compares the sun to the Blessed Sacrament in the Benediction service where the day is the priest, the sun is the Sacred Host, the East is the sanctuary, the West is the monstrance, and twilight is the assisting acolyte.

As the "poet of the Sacraments," Thompson uses many images to reinforce his own sanctity and to restore a mystical sublimity to English poetry. He transforms into lyrical poetry excerpts from the psalms, the antiphons, and the hymns of the Divine Office and the Little Offices of the Blessed Mother and the saints. Human love, Thompson is fond of repeating, is a reflection of the Divine, and all natural things sing the Glory of God. In rich, cadenced verses radiant with exotic and often involuted imagery, he was at last fulfilling his desire to be the poet of the return to God. The excitement of Church liturgy and the sublimity of the Mystical Body of Christ are introduced to remedy the vacuity of Victorian pantheistic monism. Thompson succeeds poetically in giving expression to the real significance of Christ's Redemption and in providing a new appreciation of the beauty of religious ritual. He is not an apologist or a didacticist preaching spiritual doctrine; he is a childlike, joyful participant in the Oneness of Christ and His Church.

The poetry of Thompson, from the earliest lyrics to the transcendental odes of his later period, indicates his growing appreciation for the Holy Trinity and the Church. He uses symbolic imagery to express the love and hope engendered by the promise of Calvary. Thompson's mystical sensitivity, his mode of poetic expression, and his dedicated faith are rooted thoroughly in Catholic thought and idealism.

Thompson summarizes his poetic credo in the essay, "A Renegade Poet," by declaring that "if religion is useful, so is poetry, since it is the teacher of beauty without which men would soon lose the conception of God." By creating beauty, the poet, as Thompson envisions him, is to restore the Divine Idea of things and to minister to his senses and his imagination as agents which are to bring him closer to God. His work is a critical challenge to the limiting nature worship of the romantics. Thompson gives Catholic coloration to Blake's oft-quoted quatrain: "To see a world in a grain of sand,/ And a heaven in a wild flower,/ Hold infinity in the palm of your hand,/ And eternity in an hour."

E.A.J.

EN ROUTE

Author: Joris-Karl Huysmans (1848-1907)
Type of work: Spiritual autobiography
First published: 1895

Principal Ideas Advanced

A Parisian aesthete (Huysmans himself), weary of his sensual ways and eager to find a more meaningful existence, converts to Catholicism.

Huysmans' fictional counterpart, Durtal, endures spiritual struggles during the period before his conversion; he embraces the Faith during his retreat at La Trappe; he struggles with his conscience again during his "Night Obscure"; and he decides to become a Trappist monk.

Observations of monastic life, Church art and architecture, the liturgy and plain chant, impress Durtal-Huysmans with their place in divine worship.

J.-K. Huysmans began his literary career with the naturalists shortly after the Franco-Prussian War. With Émile Zola and the circle of Medan he helped inaugurate this school of French fiction. Some fourteen years later he came to despise their aesthetic pretensions, and he openly castigated their "slop bucket techniques." In 1884 he crawled out of the trough wallowed in by Zola and his followers and engaged in a mad pursuit of beauty. The log of that quest is his novel *Against the Grain* (1884), an important precursor of *En Route*.

That *Against the Grain* was more than just another novel was seen by Zola, who recognized the book as a work undermining naturalism. Others read it with mingled amazement and indignation. Critics referred to its author as a "misanthropic impressionist" and to Des Esseintes, the fictional hero of *Against the Grain*, as "a lunatic and maniac of a complex sort." Some critics were kind enough to advise Huysmans that it would probably do him a world of good to be confined in a hydropathic establishment.

Only one critic, Barbey d'Aurevilly, who had no acquaintance with Huysmans at the time, saw the novel as it should have been seen. He drew attention to the humble pathos of the chief character, Des Esseintes, who brings the volume to a close, begging mercy "for the Christian who doubts and the unbeliever who would fain believe." Prophetically, D'Aurevilly summed up his criticism with the words: "After such a book, it only remains for the author to choose between the muzzle of a pistol or the foot of the Cross."

Eight years later, in 1892, Huysmans made his choice. With the naturalists he had been an agnostic; as a decadent he was a fervent worshiper of beauty and a dabbler in the occult. After his conversion he began to concern himself with mysticism and religious art. Though his naturalistic novels are devoid of spirituality, the novels Huymans wrote as a Catholic proclaim him, in the words of T. S. Eliot, ". . . a genius of faith."

Huysmans' religious novels are mainly psychological. They are devoted to what his main character thinks—his views on life, art, religion, ornamented with long and elaborate descriptions of anything intellectually stimulating to him. *En Route* is such a novel. This fictional account of Huysmans' conversion is generally regarded as his best work—far better than either *The Cathedral* (1898) or *The Oblate* (1903), his other Catholic novels. The importance of *En Route* was underscored several years ago when a group of eminent novelists, critics, and scholars (in *Ce Matin,* November 26, 1952) judged it to be one of the twelve greatest French novels of the nineteenth century.

En Route has Durtal, behind whom Huysmans lurks ill-disguised, in Paris in the last decade of the nineteenth century, wandering about in a materialistic wilderness, crying aloud for escape from the ennui and shallow purposelessness of his life. Art is not sufficient. Where to turn? Can the Church give him a reason for life? He allows his eye to study Christian art, and he begins to read the mystics. Constant attempts at prayer lead him to visit various Parisian churches; the beauty of their art affects him deeply. He ponders the truth of a religion that can inspire such art and engender profound feelings in his soul.

Many months later he awakens one morning and he is a believer. But how had he become a Christian? Durtal answers himself: "I don't know; all I know is that after being an infidel . . . suddenly I believe." He suggests, however, three principal causes: heredity (descent from a pious family), disgust with life, and most of all—art. "Durtal had been brought back to religion by art. More than his disgust with life even, art was the irresistible magnet which had drawn him to God." What he admired especially was the art of the Middle Ages: the early masters, plain chant, Gothic architecture, and the literature of the mystics.

But Durtal cannot change his sinful way of life. Though he attempts to conquer his exceedingly violent temptations of the flesh, it seems impossible for him to remain continent. The sin of sensuality ranks among the lesser mortal offenses, he tries to convince himself, but he cannot argue the matter lightly. He realizes his character is so base that any degree of lust in him is disastrous by its very nature. The forms and features of all the voluptuous women in his past haunt him. It seems that he cannot shake off the fleshy temptations that beset him.

Durtal confides his torment to an understanding priest for whom he has great regard, the Abbé Gévresin. The Abbé directs Durtal to the Trappists. After arguing with himself for weeks, Durtal decides, "There are many who go to Barèges or to Vichy to cure their bodies, why should I not go to cure my soul in a Trappist monastery?" Finally, trembling with anxiety, Durtal arrives at the monastery of Notre Dame de l'Atre. Here, during a retreat, he will attempt to unburden himself in the sacrament of penance. At the monastery he is immediately faced with the problem of confession. How can he lay bare the accumulated sins of a lifetime devoted to vice? At the thought of detailing all his hideous deeds of filth, Durtal is overwhelmed with shame. The penitent's ordeal, however, is understood by the Prior, who is as sagacious as he is kindly, and he defers hearing Durtal until the following day. On the morrow his confession is heard. Durtal is spared the anguish of entering into detail, as his confessor takes the view that the modesty of the confessional should be respected. Much relieved, Durtal makes a good confession, and the words of absolution bring him serene happiness. The next day he partakes of the Eucharist.

Shortly thereafter alternations of spiritual calm and chaos come over him. He feels unworthy of approaching again the altar rail. Might he not suffer a relapse? Many severe trials still await him. Years might pass, he fears, before his cure could be felt to be permanent. He can find peace only in the chapel. Here for the first time he hears true Gregorian Chant sung by the monks, and he is captivated by its magnificence: "This was at once flexible and ardent, sustained by such suppliant adoration that it seemed to concentrate in itself alone the immemorial hope of humanity and its eternal lamentation. Chanted without accompaniment, unsustained by the organ, by voices indifferent of themselves and blending in one alone, masculine and deep, it rose with a quiet boldness, sprang up with irresistible flight towards Our Lady, then made, as it were, a return upon itself forgiven, and dared then in passionate appeals to demand the undeserved pleasures of Heaven. . . ." No one, it is frequently said, has ever written so beautifully of the music of the Church as has Huysmans.

In the novel, church music and religious art salve Durtal's soul. His remaining days at La Trappe are the happiest that he can remember. Now that he has been restored in his Faith, he will return to Paris. He is convinced that he can remain master of his flesh, for he has learned to pray. But he does not leave in a state of bliss: "I have lived twenty years in ten days in that monastery, and I leave it, my brain relaxed, my heart in rags; I am done for. . . . I am still too much a man of letters to become a monk, and yet I am already too much a monk to remain among men of letters." On such a note of indecision the novel ends.

Whither will Durtal-Huysmans turn? A definite clue is given by Huysmans when back in Paris he is asked to give his views on literature and society. He noted that he cared little for the world of letters and less for the shams of society. For him, the way to happiness would be "to follow the canonical hours in a cloister, to ignore that which passes at Paris, to read books on liturgy and mysticism, iconography, and symbolism. To see as little as possible of men of literature and as much as possible of monks. . . ." A few years later Huysmans became a Benedictine Oblate.

Great books of the spirit have always stirred their readers. *En Route,* however, is different from other spiritual masterpieces. In no way does it recall Saint Augustine's *Confessions.* Nor does Huysmans' record of his conversion have the slightest affinity with Newman's *Apologia pro vita sua.* Only insofar as *Seven Storey Mountain* is concerned with the Trappist Order does *En Route* even remotely resemble Thomas Merton's work. Nevertheless, *En Route* recalls other spiritual autobiographies insofar as they resemble one another in their uniqueness: the innumerable pathways to God necessarily result in divergent religious autobiographies.

Huysmans' *Against the Grain* first cracked the wall of materialism that the author had erected about himself. *En Route* tells how its author co-operated with Divine Grace to demolish that wall. But how much of *En Route* is true? If *En Route* is more truth than fiction, why did Huysmans resort to the novel? Would not straight autobiography better have suited his purpose?

Durtal is unquestionably Huysmans himself. The priest who sends Durtal to La Trappe, Abbé Gévresin, is closely modeled after the priest who first received Huysmans into the Church, Abbé Mugnier. The letter that Abbé Mugnier received from the Prior of the Trappist monastery, to which he had written to secure permission for Huysmans' retreat, is transcribed word for word in the novel. The actual name of the monastery, La Trappe d'Igny, became in fiction Notre Dame de l'Atre.

Virtually every character in the novel had a counterpart in real life. Even physical aspects of the monastery were reproduced from actuality. Hundreds of other parallels could be listed, most of them drawn from a notebook into which Huysmans had entered his impressions while on retreat. Ninety percent or more of *En Route* is autobiographical.

There is hardly any difficulty in explaining why Huysmans chose the novel form. In the first place, it was the genre with which he had already achieved considerable success. Then again, it no doubt seemed to him that such a literary form would reach a greater number of readers who might remain indifferent to a spiritual autobiography. And, finally, Huysmans did not relish too strict an identification with his fictional alter ego Durtal; especially since, when Huysmans first began writing the novel, he had intended to entitle it *The Carnal Struggle.* The more he wrote, however, the more he decided that it would be best to minimize elements of sexuality. He wisely deleted most naturalistic expressions from his final copy.

En Route is not marred by any undue emphasis on the sensual, but the novel does display some of Huysmans' defects as a writer. Although in his style Huysmans was an extraordinary artist and innovator, what he lacked as a novelist was the ability to develop his characters with the power of a Balzac; nor did he have the subtlety of a Flaubert. Dumas' command of adventure and Hugo's romantic trappings are also missing. What he did have was an unparalleled genius for presenting in words whatever he felt or experienced. In his analysis of ill-defined states of emotion he is superb, to some extent anticipating Marcel Proust. Yet for Huysmans to be considered a highly significant author proper emphasis must be placed on the greatest of his books—*En Route.*

G.A.C.

THE POEMS OF ERNEST DOWSON

Author: Ernest Christopher Dowson (1867-1900)
Type of work: Religious and "Decadent" poetry
First published: 1896

Principal Ideas Advanced

Make the most of youth and love since beauty fades so quickly and the days of wine and roses are short; it is vain to hope that profane love will endure.

The poet has been faithful to his vows of love despite the temptations of other loves.

All men are exiles seeking a respite from earthly turmoil and the anguish of soul; all have drunk the dregs of life.

It is comforting to know the solace of prayer, Christ's Redemption, and the sacraments of the Holy Mother Church.

In his discursive study of Ernest Dowson, Mark Longaker opines that while Dowson was "never a Catholic poet in the sense that Francis Thompson, Alice Meynell, and his friend Lionel Johnson were," Dowson wrote, nevertheless, religious poetry of a high order. Among critical interpreters of the "yellow nineties" of the last century, it has become the scholarly fashion to list Ernest Dowson as a significant, although minor, contributor to the Catholic Literary Revival and the "Decadence" (the "Art-for-Art's sake" movement). Although below Thompson and Meynell in quantity and quality, Dowson made a commendable contribution to both movements. As a "Decadent" and a Catholic, Dowson surpasses the poetry of Johnson and Oscar Wilde in artistic excellence; he could correctly be termed a "Catholic aesthete."

Since he was a product of the turbulent last ten years of the nineteenth century, Dowson's literary reputation is not always adequately appreciated. The *Memoir,* for example, by his close friend and chief arbiter of Aestheticism, Arthur Symons, is not an honest evaluation of the poet's life or his poetic merit. Intent on justifying the importance of the English Aesthetic Movement in deference to its French counterpart, Symons plays down the significance of Dowson's spiritual proclivities. Subsequent critics, including Longaker, have more correctly revealed the prejudices of Symons' account.

Dowson's poetic work is encompassed within three small volumes containing less than a hundred poems: *Verses* (1896), *Decorations* (1899), and *The Pierrot of the Minute,* a verse play (1897). A thin collection of short stories and essays, *Dilemmas* (1895), completes his published output. The subject matter of Dowson's poetry is to be found in the experiences of his brief but intense life (he died at age 33) spent at Queens' College, Oxford, along the docksides of London's East End, in the rooms of the Rhymer's Club, in the cafés and market places of Paris, and on the French Riviera. It was probably while at the university (1891) that Dowson's conversion to Catholicism became a factual if not a dogmatic reality. Longaker rightly analyzes Dowson's adoption of Catholicism by stating that the poet was "sensitive to all forms of beauty, and impressionable to the influence of the spiritual quiet which comes to those who kneel before the high altar."

Aesthetic by temperament, Dowson fell in love with the external comfort of the Church liturgy only to discover within her sacramentals and sacraments that internal peace that his artistic nature sought in the vagaries of his tormented peregrinations. His short life fluctuated between his physical quest for "madder music" and "days of wine and roses," between habitual excitements and emotional quietude.

The two most influential elements illuminating his poetry are, then, the Church and the café, especially the Polish Restaurant in London's Soho district. Helplessly enamored of Adelaide Foltinowicz, the owner's daughter, he never married; inspired by the holy regimen of the Church, he never fully investigated her dogma or tradition. Instead, Dowson allowed his frustrations in both interests to quicken the ennui and nostalgia of his decadent love lyrics. Equally enraptured by the serenity of the Church and the innocence of maiden purity, he was too impatient to accept the discipline demanded by both. He preferred his love to be unrequited; he preferred the self-imposed sacrifice of denial. He was not, however, a martyr to either cause. Dowson's poetry is thus inspirationally ambivalent but thematically unified: the anguish of self-torment in search of satiation, physical and spiritual. He never wanted to slake his emotional thirst for love and beauty by the imposition of singular devotion.

Dowson's artistic credo is strongly derivative of the advice urged by Walter Pater in the conclusion to his study of the Renaissance: "Not the fruit of the experience, but experience itself is the end . . . to burn always with this hard, gemlike flame, to maintain this ecstacy is success in life." As such, Dowson allies himself with Lionel Johnson, Oscar Wilde, Arthur Symons, Aubrey Beardsley, the French Symbolists, and the contributors to *The Yellow Book*—all exponents of subjective, impressionistic literary aestheticism. Reacting strongly to Victorian sensibility nurtured by Tennyson and Darwin, these young aesthetes deliberately determined to reflect eroticism, hedonism, and emotional individualism in their artistic creations. They chose the bizarre subject, the sensuous and the sensual emotion, and the decadent thrill. They wrote of faded flowers, green wine, and tormenting love, thereby hoping to shock the complacent middle classes.

Actually, the religious indifference of so many of their literate countrymen coupled with the disintegration of nominal Protestantism compelled these poets to discover a new religion in art, beauty, and the sensational. Some few of the aesthetes carried their search for a more permanent metaphysic to the doors of Catholicism; Wilde, Johnson, and, especially, Dowson wrote religious poetry as devotees of the Art-for-Art's sake coterie. The green carnation and the faded rose vied with the sacraments, the life of Christ, and the Crucifixion as appropriate subjects for lyrical expression.

Dowson's choice of material and his lyric style reveal the influence of the elder Baudelaire and the youthful Verlaine in emphasizing delicate rhythms, musical cadences and demi-monde characters. So strong is the *symboliste* derivation of synesthetic verse that Dowson is frequently seen as an English Verlaine; in fact, the translations of Verlaine's originals into exquisite, musical English verse qualify Dowson easily for this critical distinction. He may be said to have lived as Pater's Marius, and to have written as Verlaine's Amanuensis.

Perversity, egoism, decadence, sentimentality, and self-pity become, therefore, the major emotional variants of Dowson's poetry; stylistic chastity and musical idiosyncrasy, their literary rhetoric. Dowson and his fellow aesthetes have been fittingly described by Arthur Symons as harboring a "new, beautiful and interesting disease." The reaction against Victorian artistic and emotional sterility which began with Pre-Raphaelitism and which culminated in the pagan outcries of Pater and Swinburne encouraged these productions of individual eroticism and religious sentiment so typical of the "Yellow Nineties" and Dowson.

Of all the poems, the oft-quoted lyric, "Non Sum Qualis Eram Bonae Sub Regno Cynarae" (I am not now what I was under the charm of the beautiful Cynara) is the most representative. It exhibits Dowson's aesthetic attitude in its insistence on experience as the end in itself, in its use of sensuous imagery and colorful diction, and in its fragile tone of hopeless love and emotional ennui. Without shame Dowson extols the basic erotic philosophy of the decadent movement: sense pleasure and human love can never be fully satiated; perhaps the ideal of love can be rewarding, but human weakness paradoxically precludes realization. The cadence of the lines, the simplicity of the diction and the bejeweled imagery of the "Cynara" are unmatched for excellence by any other example of aesthetic poetry. Despite the decadent imagery the lines retain a haunting emotional power: "I have forgot much, Cynara! gone with the wind,/ Flung roses riotously with the throng,/ Dancing to put thy pale, lost lilies out of mind." The monosyllabic refrain suggests the joy-in-pain plea of the emotionally overwrought, sensitive lover: "I have been faithful to thee, Cynara! in my fashion."

Critics have sought several identifications for Dowson's "Cynara." The title is derived from Horace's *Ad venerem* (Book IV, Ode I), in which a young lady is addressed in much the same manner. Perhaps the principal source of inspiration was Adelaide Foltinowicz, or a younger girl who may have symbolized maidenly purity to the poet, or, finally, the Church that taught him to be loyal to the ideal of love despite his human frailty.

Dowson knew clearly what he ought to be, but his habitual quest for unusual physical sensations, strong drink, hashish, and the company of morally questionable comrades determined the dark and tearful world of his soul.

A sense of frustration bordering on pessimism is recorded in many of Dowson's shorter lyrics. The haunting "Vitae Summa Brevis Spem Non Vestat Incohare Longam," in which Dowson echoes the Horatian lament that the days of wine and roses are not long but emerge only out of a misty dream and then retreat into hopeless forgetfulness, is typical of many of Dowson's *Decorations*. Life is too short, he rhapsodizes, for happiness to perdure. The "Amor Profanus" is a reverie of a romance with an imagined lover (the "Lalage" of Horace?) urging the *carpe diem* philosophy of the Latin poet.

In like mood and repeating similar images of faded roses (lost innocence) and old age (lost love) are "Dregs," "In Tempore Senectutis," "April Love," "Vain Hope," "Exile," and "Sapientia Lunae," showing through their titles their characteristic attitudes. The last mentioned lyric keynotes Dowson's verse play, *The Pierrot of the Minute,* wherein the young, pleasure-bent lover enjoys the anguish of rejection by the moon goddess. In the end, the youth languishes in the knowledge that earthly love cannot be consummated nor can immortality secure love's permanence in human form.

Dowson's imitations of Verlaine in the four poems, "After Verlaine," embody this same indifferent attitude toward lost love and virtue. Characteristically, Dowson does not despair; thus, his association with Catholicism is possible. Influenced by Horace and French contemporaries, Dowson never completely reaffirms their basic pessimism toward life and love. In his most typical aesthetic poems, Dowson is unwilling to make a conclusion about life and love; he appears wishing to find a more satisfying rationale than self or human sensitivity. His "A Last Word" best presages his hope for an adequate explanation to the nostalgia of fading beauty and the sentimentality of unrequited love: "Let us go hence, somewhither strange and cold,/ To Hollow Lands where just men and unjust/ Find end of labor, where's rest for the old,/ Freedom to all from love and fear and lust."

The goal so furtively sought in these decadent lyrics was eventually to be the Catholic Church. Chronologically, Dowson's poems date from his conversion. It cannot be said that he wrote exclusively under one or the other influence; his poems are a commingling of the mundane and spiritual. The personal struggle is apparent when his poems are viewed in totality. The outcome, too, is evident. While the opinion stated by Calvert Alexander, S. J., namely, that Dowson like Verlaine was perpetually falling short of his ideals, is certainly true, Dowson's ideals were much higher at the outset than those of many of his poetic forebears. It is, of course, to be regretted that the years surrounding his conversion are obscure, for we have no way of determining the strength of Dowson's religious convictions. Perhaps the Polish family with whom he was associated prompted his adoption of Catholicism. In any case, it is a matter of poetic record that Dowson always wrote with rare sensitivity and sympathetic understanding of Catholic matters. Especially does he show a conspicuous affinity for the rewards of the contemplative life and for those in religious life who are privileged to experience it. His Catholic lyrics manifest a personal desire to be faithful to Catholic worship and practice. That within his soul the conflict was to torment him ceaselessly is at once the mark of his genius as an artist.

Among the characteristic poems especially responsive to his adopted religion are "Nuns of the Perpetual Adoration." "Carthusians," "Extreme Unction," and "Benedictio Domini." Much of his own life is reflected in these simple and poignant lyrics written in language almost barren of image and aesthetic coloration. He writes with plaintive delicacy and restraint, yet adds physical warmth to his pictures. He admires the nuns: "These heed not time; their nights and days they make/ Into a long, returning rosary/ Whereon their lives are threaded for Christ's sake;/ Meekness and vigilance and chastity." The "hollow land" of his former desire might have been in the stillness of the monastic cell.

The rule of the Carthusians inspires this simple prayer in his imagination: "Move on, white company, whom that has not sufficed!/ Our viols cease, our wine is death, our roses fail./ Pray for our heedlessness, O dwellers with the Christ!/ Though the world fall apart, surely ye shall prevail." The impact is clear; the expression is aesthetic.

The outward signs of Christ's Grace are also hopefully considered: Penance and Holy Eucharist are singled out for poetic treatment over and over again. In "Extreme Unction," for example, Dowson pleads for "Vials of mercy! Sacring oils!/ I know not where nor when I come,/ Nor through what wanderings and toils,/ To crave of your Viaticum." In "Impenitentia Ultima" he confesses, "For, Lord, I was free of all Thy flowers, but I chose the world's sad roses,/ And that is why my feet are torn and mine eyes are blind with sweat,/ But at Thy terrible judgment seat, when this my tired life closes,/ I am ready to reap whereof I sowed, and pay my righteous debt." Plagued by the restless search for happiness amid sensuous activities, Dowson comes with childlike innocence seeking the supplication of Redemptive joy. There is a noticeable lack of bitterness and remorse in his aversion to the mundane or in his appreciation of the fitness of Christ's Passion and death.

In the poems explicitly religious in tone Dowson possesses a realization of the grandeur and justice of God, the mercy of Christ, and a remarkable understanding of the mission of the Church. His attitude remains, however, that of the defeated sinner. He was, after all, a devotee of the Decadence. That he raised a self-imposed wall between himself and his Church is not surprising; it is characteristic of the aesthetic imagination. It is as if these poets felt crushed by their self-styled wickedness and longed for eternal punishment to expiate the enormity of their evil. It is almost axiomatic of the Decadence to assert that decadent poets enjoyed this kind of premonition of punishment, glorying in their imagined and often very real sinfulness. Dowson, like Wilde, Johnson, and Baudelaire, frequently sought the emotional solace of the Church without making an intelligent appraisal of her doctrines or dogmas. Since the decadent poets were always seekers of sensation, not explicators of the real, and were childlike in their understanding, it is not surprising to find the symbol of the child woven into Dowson's poetic fabric. As little children these poets wished to enter Heaven, and they hoped that their ignorance of the Law would mitigate the justice of the Father.

Most typical of the naïve emotional attitude expressed in these poems is the ennui with self and the dissatisfaction with living which Dowson forced himself to endure. Paradoxically, his poetry brings together the beauty and the power of the sacraments with the sensual imagery of aestheticism. Some examples may be found in comparing the symbols in "Cynara" with "Carthusians": "I have flung roses, roses riotously with the throng" contrasts with "Our Cups are polished skulls round which the roses twine." His descriptions are striking: prayers as fragrant incense, the Church as a bride, Heaven as solitude, penance as soothing oil, evil as fallen plight, Mary as a sweet star are only a few of the many phrases so characteristic of the poetic language of the aesthete where profound intellections are symbolized with sensuous appeal.

As a Catholic aesthete, then, Dowson sought the thrill of uninhibited experience which Pater urged, and attempted, by the adeptness of his poetic image and decadent diction, to prolong the ecstasy. He was aware, however, that the feeling could not be sustained by continual emotional indulgence; such joy could be refined only by renunciation and sacrifice. He tried to be faithful to his Cynara—his Church, or his idealization of love—in his own fashion. The anguished melody of his lyrics is the tenuous hope that ultimate happiness must be accompanied by love and sacrifice. There is hope, he concludes, in the denial of self that satisfaction demands. The days of wine and roses are, after all, not too long! His association with the Church, however emotional and chaotic it may have been, is the antidote he found to the pessimism of the Decadence. Dowson's aestheticism, tinged by the ennui of his restless personality and blighted by his physical bohemianism, is soothed by his hope and faith in his adopted religious creed.

Dowson was also a clever and respected adapter of the fixed forms of French poetry. His villanelles and rondeaus are some of the best ever written in English. Worthy of specific comment are "Villanelle of the Poet's Road," "Villanelle of Acheron," and the famous "Villanelle of His Lady's Treasures," which contains the familiar concluding stanza: "I stole her laugh, most musical:/ I wrought it in with artful care;/ I took her dainty eyes as well;/ And so I made a Villanelle."

The café singer and the would-be saint combine in Dowson's poetry, reflecting the jaded, sensual preoccupation of the aesthete, and the devout, chaste longing of the Catholic, seeking Grace in a very human world.

E.A.J.

THE WOMAN WHO WAS POOR

Author: Léon Bloy (1846-1917)
Type of work: Semi-autobiographical novel; Catholic moral philosophy
First published: 1897

Principal Ideas Advanced

Physical poverty, though a source of suffering and torment to man's human nature, is nonetheless preferable to spiritual poverty, a burden more heavy and contemptible since it offends man's immortal nature.

Suffering is never without purpose or merit, since it shows man how to imitate Christ and unites him with his brothers in the communion of saints.

Through suffering, and especially through the deprivations and humiliations of poverty, which strips away all nonessentials, men can ultimately attain peace and joy; after the Incarnation man was restored the privilege of hope.

Described by the author as "a long digression on the evil of living, the infernal misfortune of existence, hogs lacking any snout with which to root for tit-bits, in a society without God," *The Woman Who Was Poor* by Léon Bloy is a semi-autobiographical novel of a nineteenth century French Catholic who is credited with laying the groundwork for the great Catholic Literary Revival which arose in protest against an age which smiled at belief based on faith rather than reason. The core of his irritability with the times centered about the spiritual upheaval taking place, especially among the intellectuals who rejected God as the Absolute Truth. If his statements seem harsh, his dicta without alternative, it must be realized that here was a "pilgrim of the Absolute" trying to hold the fort almost single-handedly against a multi-sided enemy. Modernism, with its emphasis on the limitations of human knowledge, had so robbed man of his rightful mystery that a new mounting had to be given the ancient gems of Catholic doctrine—something strong, harsh, and solid to complement the attractive luster with which scientific discovery and incipient humanism had lacquered the truth. Bloy was the craftsman inspired (as he believed, by God) to create the new setting in the world of Catholic letters, and, indeed, his style is not unlike that of the artisan who hammers and pounds—dealing his material heavy blows only so that what he makes of it may emerge strong, beautiful, and often exquisitely fragile. Impatient, indignant, contemptuous of mediocrity, Bloy set about his vocation of violence with almost prophetic certainty that scorn and indifference would be its only rewards. Nonetheless he willingly bore the loneliness of his own peculiar genius that God's Kingdom might reflourish in the blood of such martyrdoms.

The Woman Who Was Poor is considered by many to be Bloy's masterpiece. Its thesis is contained in the often quoted last lines of the book: "There is only one sadness . . . and that is—*not to be saints.*" The story concerns Clotilde (the "Woman") and her ascent toward sanctity through a life of earthly pain and anguish. The book is composed of two sections: Part One, "Flotsam of the Shadows," and Part Two, "Flotsam of the Light." We know flotsam to be a piece of wreckage or salvage floating on the water's surface, usually after a shipwreck. At one point Clotilde's husband presses her to him "as a shipwrecked man might cling to a piece of flotsam rendered luminous by the shimmer of the milky way." It would seem, then, that Bloy carefully chose this image to represent his heroine—commonplace, shabby, and insignificant until called on to fulfill her function; namely, to be an instrument of hope.

In Part One, "the Shadows," the conditioning for her vocation takes place; in Part Two, "the Light," she *becomes* the woman who was poor. The very phrasing of that title contains Bloy's ideal of poverty as a vocation. There were, he seems to say, women who were wives, and women who were mothers—but Clotilde was the woman *who was poor.* Significantly, Bloy withholds the bestowing of the title until it is properly won. Clotilde is a child of the deepest physical poverty from the beginning, but her spiritual depths are innate, untested, tremulous. Only after emerging serene from the flames which reduce her temporal life to a holocaust of ashes, after she becomes the woman who was *poor in fact,* may she receive that crown of fulfillment which is this title.

Clotilde is the child of a sanctimonious, hypocritical harridan whose practice of deception was so facile that she drove her husband to his grave believing he had maligned her virtue by accusing her of what was obvious infidelity. Clotilde's mother is now the consort of a despicably vulgar blackguard who would as soon violate the daughter himself as sell her body to another. This immoral pair form the framework of the only family Clotilde can lay claim to—a mire of squalor and filth both physical and spiritual. She is the fragrant flower on the dungheap of her environment—horrified and revulsed by it but incapable of knowing how to free herself—dependent upon the perception of a stranger to pluck her from it by the roots at last.

This stranger is an artist, Pélopidas Gacougnol, to whom her "foster father" has offered her services as a nude model, hoping to use her as a means of support, whatever the price. Pélopidas, discerning in Clotilde a woman of extraordinary simplicity and natural virtue, takes pity on her, clothes, feeds, and houses her properly, and temporarily puts an end to the shame and humiliation of her former station. Through him she is introduced to the world of ideas, religion, art, and some of the most fascinating figures of the day, the most prominent of whom is Cain Marchenoir, a thinly-disguised portrait of Bloy himself. She meets also Léopold, who will become her husband and whose child she will both bear and lose in less than a year's span. Finally, after experiencing the depths of human misery, persecution, and privation, Clotilde loses even Léopold; she is finally *completely poor*.

Bloy, who had himself experienced the same poverty of which he wrote so accurately, drew upon these experiences in the formation of this novel. Clotilde is a composite portrait of two women who were of great importance in his own life. The Clotilde of Part One is Anne-Marie Roulé, a prostitute with whom Bloy became passionately involved and whom he later converted. It was she who ultimately convinced him that his was a special calling from God. The Clotilde of Part Two is his wife, Jeanne Molbech, whose deep spirituality was the bulwark of his own life, as Clotilde's was of Léopold's (the second counterpart of Bloy in the novel, Marchenoir having died at the end of the first half). The death of Lazare, the son of Clotilde and Léopold, parallels that of Bloy's own child, André.

Bloy's characters, like the author himself, are often impatient, violent, and heartsore, but never without hope. Despite the profound abysses into which they are plunged there is never present a sense of despair, but rather an uplifting spiritual exhilaration and peace. The creatures "so cruelly beloved of God" can send up from the most inconceivable caverns of suffering this cry of joy: "Everything that happens is something to be adored."

Within the thread of the story Bloy weaves a mixture of his views on art, religion, society, and justice (as well as subdigressions on the role of woman, the figure of Eve, and the interrelationships of man with other members of creation as part of the redemptive whole), whence emerges a work of vivid textures. At once a romantic ("When Jesus should at last come down from His Cross, He might find her immediately, her who was defiled, as He followed the easy downward path from Calvary, leading as it surely did to the dwellings of the unbelievers and the unfaithful. She, for her part, might bathe and perfume His feet, like that great Magdalen who had been called the splendid Bride. But it would not be within her power—not with diamond claws!—to draw out a single thorn from His tortured brow!") and a naturalist ("This place stinks of God!"), Bloy reveals a literary style which is a paradoxical blend of the two major schools of writing clamoring for prominence in the nineteenth century. That the force of his personality and conviction could successfully merge two such opposing forms testifies to the genius that aroused hatred, discomfort, annoyance, and, deadliest of all to a writer, a "conspiracy of silence" among critics. It is said that from childhood Bloy had longed for martyrdom. Its fulfillment, though unbloody, was nonetheless real. Men of any age resent being told that their values are empty, their sights set upon that which is transient, their consciences drugged. Bloy said these things intelligently, fluently, and with the self-righteousness of one indisputably on the side of God against Mammon. Were it not for a handful of devoted disciples, among them Jacques and Raïssa Maritain, translations of his works might never have been made.

Because of his ruthless portrayal of circumstances as he saw them, Bloy was accused by his detractors of being incapable of writing two lines without the introduction of some bit of dirt. To this he is said to have replied, "I shall enter into Paradise with a crown of dung." Taken in the sense of being an agent of fertility, there is no better prophecy to describe this author who enriched the field of Catholic letters with his own lifeblood.

J.S.

THE STORY OF A SOUL

Author: Saint Thérèse of Lisieux (1873-1897)
Type of work: Spiritual autobiography
First published: 1899

Principal Ideas Advanced

Live in a manner consistent with your knowledge that you are a created, contingent being, a child of God dependent on your Father for everything, and then He will transform your soul, providing you refuse no sacrifice He asks nor any grace He offers.

The "little way" of salvation consists not in actively seeking great austerities nor in offering to God what He has not asked of you, but in accepting His will as it is expressed in exterior events and interior impulses toward virtue.

Suffering with and for Christ, properly viewed, is reason for rejoicing, since it allows us a share in the redemption of humanity and teaches us to find supernatural joy in loving the will of God even when it is not easy and natural to do so.

There is no conflict between the active and the contemplative life, for a soul in union with God participates in the process of redemption, experiencing simultaneously the beatific vision and God's own merciful search for souls to fill up with Himself.

In *The Story of a Soul (Histoire d'une âme)*, Saint Thérèse of Lisieux documents both her own progress toward sanctity and a design for the spiritual life universal in its appeal and revolutionary in its simplicity. So great is the relevance of this design to contemporary moral and spiritual problems, and so powerful an effect has her message and example had on the lives of ordinary men and women, that Saint Pius X called Saint Thérèse "the greatest saint of modern times." The book that her superiors had ordered her to write was, at her death, sent to other Carmelite convents and then offered to the general public. Within a few years it had been translated into many languages, and claims of miracles worked by her intercessions spread as rapidly as her fame.

Saint Thérèse did not intend to write a conventional autobiography but a history of God's dealings with her soul. The primary reality for Saint Thérèse was her absolute dependence on the love of her Father in Heaven. Thus, she felt a special kinship with the rest of creation, a kinship which reveals itself through the constant analogies she draws between God's action in nature and His action in the human soul. She often refers to herself as a "little white flower," thus acknowledging both her value and her poverty, her virtue and her contingency.

From early childhood Thérèse acted in accordance with the realities of the human condition as they were revealed to her by faith and by experience. She insists that there should be perfect continuity btween man's life in this world and in the next. Death should not grossly interrupt the pattern established during man's earthly life, but logically fulfill it. Ideally, man should be as true to the reality of his sonship to God as the flower is to the law of its nature. The fulfillment of this divine sonship is the act of the will made in faith and love which allows God to transform the soul and unite it to Himself. The life of Saint Thérèse was spent in maintaining within herself, often by the most dry and barren acts of faith, the spiritual attitude of complete surrender to the merciful action of God.

Thérèse's earliest memories were of the age when her awareness of God and love for His will first dawned in her soul. Her lively, stubborn temperament was responsible for the many corrections her parents and four older sisters found it necessary to give her. Yet despite the natural self-love which Thérèse declares she had in abundance, one correction was always sufficient to cure any fault. She was determined to imitate the high standards consistently upheld by those around her, and her stubbornness was thereby transformed into a strength of will which never deserted her.

The parents of Thérèse, Louis and Zelie Martin, had been drawn to the religious life before their marriage. Though their vocations are ultimately fulfilled outside the cloister, they lived in the world without allowing it to touch their hearts. The home in which Thérèse and her sisters grew up was not notably different in spirit and intention from the convents where they spent their adult years. The Martins took great care to seclude their daughters from the vanities of the world and to foster in them habits of industry, virtue, and spirituality. Thus, Thérèse knew a continuity in her environment and ideals. This outward blessing was not wasted upon her; she allowed it to help form within her an unshakable and singleminded faith. Almost from infancy Thérèse imitated the devoutness of those around her. She says of herself at the age of four: "Even at that time I possessed a very large measure of self-control. I made it a practice never to complain when my things were taken, and if at any time I were unjustly accused, I preferred to keep silence rather than attempt an excuse." She recognizes that this was easy and natural for her then, for there had not yet appeared any element of that supernatural struggle which would mark the rest of her life.

This joy in the practice of virtue ended very abruptly, for when the saint was four and a half years old her mother died of cancer. Thérèse did not reveal at the time how much suffering her mother's death caused her, but for the next ten years she had to fight against the onslaughts of sensitivity, fear, dejection, and spiritual dryness which were, at least partially, brought on by her great loss. Throughout these trials, she put into practice the religious instruction began by her mother and continued by her sister Pauline, who acted as her parent, governess, and confidante. Thérèse says of this period in her life: "I tried very hard to please [God] in all my actions, and was most careful never to offend Him."

After his wife's death, Louis Martin moved the family from Alençon to Lisieux, in order to be near relatives who could assist him in bringing up his motherless daughters. The change helped Thérèse to get over the initial violence of her grief; once more she was able to share the blessings of the Martins' serene family life. However, outside her home she was "an exile," overcome by her new timidity and sensitivity. She was very different from the gay, confident Thérèse of only a few months before.

By the time Thérèse had begun to attend school at a Benedictine convent, her interior life was centered on her longing for the Eucharist. Her sister Celine's First Communion affected her nearly as strongly as would her own, four years later. The greatest graces in her life were to be associated with her reception of the Sacrament. Though she never ceased to struggle against her extreme sensitivity, she looked to the Eucharistic Christ for the grace finally to overcome it. In a spiritual life based on faith rather than on emotional piety fed by sensible consolations, it is to be expected that the sacraments will assume central importance, and indeed they did in the life of Saint Thérèse. Her faults concerned her only in that they caused Jesus sorrow and interfered with the perfect union of love between them.

When Thérèse was nine, she suffered the loss of her second mother, Pauline, who left their home to enter the Carmelite convent at Lisieux. Thérèse says of her sorrow at that time: "In a flash I beheld life as it really is, full of suffering and constant partings, and I shed most bitter tears." She began to have constant headaches which culminated in a serious illness that lasted an entire year and almost took her life. The prayers of her anxious family bore fruit when the sick child experienced a vision of the Blessed Virgin and a simultaneous cure. Soon after her recovery, Thérèse received Holy Communion for the first time, and from that day on, her soul was at peace, despite the occasional trials of temperament that threatened its composure. She began to long for a suffering so intense that it would turn every earthly joy to bitterness and leave her attached to God alone.

By the time she was thirteen, her prayer was answered and her newfound peace was put to a severe test by a "martyrdom" of scruples which tormented her for two years. Her sister Marie had joined Pauline in Carmel, and Thérèse again had no "mother" left in whom she might confide. Her tears and her worries about her sins seemed to be out of control. Then, after receiving Holy Communion on Christmas Day, 1886, Thérèse had a "complete conversion," in which she says, "Our Lord accomplished in an instant the work I had not been able to do during years. . . . Love and a spirit of self-forgetfulness took complete possession of my heart, and thenceforward I was perfectly happy."

From this time on, Thérèse prepared to enter Carmel, though obstacles between her and her goal sprang up constantly. Her father took her all the way to Rome, where she begged Pope Leo XIII himself to intercede for her, but still she was denied entry to the convent because she was only fifteen. It did not deeply disturb Thérèse that Jesus seemed to be asleep in her boat, for she had long ceased to rely on spiritual consolations and favors to maintain her faith. When all her efforts had come to nothing, and Thérèse had abandoned herself and her future entirely into God's hands, permission was suddenly granted, and on April 9, 1888, she entered Carmel. Far from feeling joy and eagerness at the prospect of taking her vows, Thérèse went through a period of intense desolation, though she says, "I received unconsciously many interior lights on the best means of pleasing God and practising virtue." She believed that Christ Himself was prompting her from within, guiding and shaping her life from moment to moment. This conviction was to continue throughout her life in Carmel. Instead of raptures and consolations, Thérèse seemed more often to experience spiritual barrenness. Yet she was willing to live entirely by faith and she never let her aridity affect the intensity of her love or her constant practice of self-denial.

Young as she was when she entered the order, Thérèse cannot be said to have allowed the official Carmelite spirit to form her. The Carmelite ideal was the offering of oneself as a victim to the justice of God, begging God to punish the Carmelite victim instead of some obdurate sinner. Great austerities and penances were often practiced to achieve this ideal. Thérèse made considerable revisions in the spirituality presented to her. She believed God was essentially love, not justice, and that what He desired above all were souls who would allow Him to unite perfectly with them. Jesus had thirsted for souls on His Cross, and Thérèse felt that it was her vocation to quench that thirst. She planned to do so by loving God so completely that He would be able to pour out His love, through her, on the rest of mankind. All the asceticism of the "little way" was intended to break the dam men seem to have built against the flood of God's love into their souls.

In the convent Thérèse sought daily to become a martyr to "merciful love," and she practiced the heroic, consistent, unspectacular self-denial that has won her such fame. Everyday events were to her of eternal significance; she sanctified them by raising them to a supernatural level and investing them with her charity and self-forgetfulness. After much practice this habit of transforming little daily trials into sacrifices to be consumed on the altar of her soul became quite "natural" to her, and she conceived a positive joy in the suffering she was able to offer up. In all honesty Thérèse could say, "[God] has always given me what I desired, or rather He has made me desire what He wishes to give." Her own will had no preferences beyond the wish to love Jesus and never to offend Him.

At a time when her faith was lively and her joy in the religious life was calm and sure, Thérèse had the first hemorrhage that warned of imminent death from tuberculosis. Though she had always longed for Heaven and had no fear of death, suddenly all comforting assurances vanished. She was tormented by the fear that her faith had been an illusion and that her life had been a mockery which would end in nothingness, not in the eternity of love she had hoped for. "I have made more acts of faith during this past year," Thérèse writes, "than in all the rest of my life." For months, without consolation and in increasing bodily weakness and pain, she hung onto her faith by sheer will inflamed with an intense Love of Jesus. Offering her spiritual martyrdom for the souls of men without faith, she prayed, "Dear Jesus, Thy child believes firmly that Thou art the Light Divine; she asks pardon for her unbelieving brethren and is willing to eat the bread of sorrow as long as Thou shalt will it so. For love of Thee she will sit at that table of bitterness where these poor sinners take their food."

Thérèse's trials did not discourage her, nor did she feel that God had abandoned her, for she was sure He had sent her this cross only at her own desire and at a time when she could bear it. The years at Carmel had wrought in Thérèse a heroic charity; now she felt it necessary not merely to love her neighbor as she loved herself, but as God loves him, allowing His own love to live within her and reach out to embrace the world. Those around Thérèse knew themselves to be the recipients of a saint's love; they had no reason to suspect the degree of abandonment she felt. Since God did not allow her spiritual dryness to affect her sanctity, Thérèse was content. Her thirst for souls was growing stronger; the missionaries and priests of the world were close to her heart and she offered all her prayers, suffering, and sacrifices for them. Thérèse felt that true beatitude lay in sharing the saving love of God for man and thus participating directly in the Redemption. In Heaven, the contemplative experience would be perfectly fused with active charity. Shortly before she died, it is reported that she said, "I will spend my heaven in doing good upon earth." There are multitudes around the world who are convinced that she kept that promise and keeps it still.

The *Autobiography* scarcely mentions the author's physical illness. It is in the written reminiscences of the Carmelites who lived with her through her last days that one finds the story of her death. From the words recorded of Thérèse during those summer months of 1897 when she hung painfully between life and death, it is clear that her state of spiritual darkness persisted until the very end. According to all who were present, she bore her sufferings without complaint or loss of that joyful serenity she had fought so long to gain. On September 30, 1897, Saint Thérèse died, holding her crucifix before her as she spoke her last words: "My God, I love Thee!"

B.J.R.

THE PATH TO ROME

Author: Hilaire Belloc (1870-1953)
Type of work: Pilgrimage narrative
First published: 1902

Principal Ideas Advanced

The chief bond and central tradition of Europe is the Christian faith; Catholic Christianity is the mother of Europe.

If one is to see Europe in her pristine and untrammeled state, he must go along the little-traveled ways.

The Path to Rome is perhaps one of the most delightful of Hilaire Belloc's many books. It is the record of a pilgrimage made by the author from the small French town of Toul in the valley of the Moselle, to Rome, the first city of Christendom. Belloc describes the inspiration which moved him to go on pilgrimage: "Moreover, saying my prayers there [in the church at La Celle, St. Cloud, the town of his birth], I noticed behind the high altar a statue of Our Lady, so extraordinary and so different from all I had ever seen before, so much the spirit of my valley, that I was quite taken out of myself and vowed to go to Rome on Pilgrimage and see all Europe which the Christian Faith has saved; and I said, 'I will start from the place where I served in arms for my sins; I will walk all the way and take advantage of no wheeled thing; I will sleep rough and cover thirty miles a day, and I will hear mass every morning; and I will be present at high mass in St. Peter's on the Feast of St. Peter and St. Paul.' "

Belloc describes his subsequent journey to Rome in a most charming manner. The work is not a straight narrative, for the author takes many stylistic liberties, including digression, reminiscence, and sage and witty comment. The tone of the work is set in the first several pages when Belloc spoofs the traditional practice of book-writers of deprecating themselves in forewords and prefaces. After having read these introductory pages, the reader has an inkling that this is not to be a travelogue or guide-book in the ordinary sense.

The book does, in fact, catalogue the entire route of his journey. Belloc began on a summer evening in Toul, and set off up the valley of the Moselle. He then crossed over the Vosges Mountains, the plain of Belfort, and passed into Switzerland. Ahead of him were the mighty Alps, directly astride the straight line to Rome. After a harrowing attempt at a crossing in a storm, and a disappointing failure, Belloc finally entered Italy. He then proceeded down the peninsula to Rome, completing his pilgrimage, and discharging his vow.

Such a short summary lists the geographic highlights of Hilaire Belloc's walk. But it does not begin to capture the richness of the experience which he relates in this book. In the hands of a less gifted writer, this book would be a mildly interesting curiosity. But Belloc made it enthralling. He brought many things to the work which mark it as masterful.

He was, first of all, a sensitive man, sensitive to the world which surrounded him. This comes out time and again in the pages of *The Path to Rome*. He describes an old wall, a path, an evening, an ancient man, a French hill village in a manner which completely captivates. Few men were so open to the world.

Second, Belloc was a gifted historian. Not simply a compiler of research, he possessed a sense of history, a sense of what history is all about. This can be seen in all of his writing, where individual events and men are secondary to the larger patterns which work themselves out in the affairs of men. For example, in his book *The Crusades: the World's Debate,* Belloc repeatedly asserts that the failure of the Christian crusaders to seize the city of Damascus and thus acquire a defensible frontier condemned their efforts to ultimate defeat. This fact, he pointed out, overshadowed all the pageantry and colorful individuals of the Crusades. Such elementary factors, it was his belief, are the structure of history.

Third, he had a feeling for antiquity; and old things, however humble or inconsequential, to him were the stuff of history. Belloc was a man who actively felt within him the ancestral fires, one who loved the sight and feel of home country. His descriptions of revisitations of haunts of his youth in *The Path to Rome* are most moving.

Fourth, Hilaire Belloc was a devout and unapologetic Catholic. This strong faith which was his singularly prepared him for a sympathetic narrative on Catholic Europe. Belloc's histories have been criticized as too "Catholic," but it was his conviction that there is a living Catholic tradition, that the Faith is the architect and guardian of Western culture. This conviction and insight into the affairs of Europe gave Hilaire Belloc an extraordinary rapport with the European spirit. His conception of the Catholic tradition permitted him to look upon the remnants of medievalism in Europe as sacred reminders of a glorious past, rather than vestiges of the Dark Ages.

The last ingredient in this delightful potpourri is Belloc's charming and gentle wit. *The Path to Rome* is a concatenation of anecdotes which are uniformly amusing and pointed. This humor, more than any other of the writer's gifts, raises the book above an ordinary guide-book. He seizes any and all occasions to use incidents of his journey to poke fun at the social practices and mores of his time. No one escapes his mild barbs, not the Church, the government, the populace, or even himself.

In sum, *The Path to Rome* is one of those rare experiences in the realm of books, when the reader is both captivated and enlightened. The charm of the work is heightened by the very fine sketches done by Mr. Belloc himself, which are sprinkled liberally through the book. Hilaire Belloc is at his best here as story-teller, satirist, historian, and apologist for Catholic Christianity.

J.P.W.

PARISH LIFE IN MEDIAEVAL ENGLAND

Author: Francis Neil Aidan Cardinal Gasquet (1846-1929)
Type of work: Account of parish life
First published: 1906

Principal Ideas Advanced

In medieval England the parish church was the center of the life of the people, and the priest and other parochial officials managed many matters which were not strictly ecclesiastical.

Through sharing in the tradition of the Church, the parishioners were made familiar with the Christian faith.

Through the daily Mass and the administration of the sacraments, the Church extended its influence to every person in the parish.

Francis Neil Gasquet, born in London, became a Benedictine in 1866 and took the name of Aidan at that time. He was ordained in 1874 and served as abbot-president of the English Benedictines from 1900 to 1914; he was made cardinal-deacon in 1914 and cardinal-priest in 1920. It was ill-health which led to Gasquet's resigning the priorate at Downside in 1885 and undertaking the studies of medieval life for which he is best known.

Cardinal Gasquet (then Abbot Gasquet) begins his account of parish life in medieval England by explaining that no study would be complete which limited itself to the parson and his church, for the parish church was the center of life during the Middle Ages, and the priest and other parochial officials managed many matters which were not strictly ecclesiastical but which fell within the range of their action precisely because the parish church was the center of the community. Speaking regretfully, the author comments: "Religion and religious observances then formed an integral part of the English people's very existence in a way somewhat difficult for us to grasp in these days, when the undoubted tendency is to set God and the things of God outside the pale of ordinary worldly affairs, and to keep them out as far as possible." Both at the beginning and the end of his book Cardinal Gasquet quotes with approval a remark found in the *National Review* (the author is not identified): "In the Middle Ages the conscious sharing in a world-wide tradition bound the local to a universal life, and through art and ritual the minds of the poor were familiarised with facts of the Christian faith. By our own poor I fear these facts are very dimly realised to-day."

Gasquet explains that in the cities district clergy were appointed to preside at services in outlying churches, but such district clergy, appointed by the bishop, were not parish priests, for they belonged to the church of the bishop, and the bishop maintained direct government and care of the souls within his district; furthermore, the finances of the various churches within the district were not kept separate. The parish priests, however, were appointed to meet the needs of the country; they were originally chaplains of landowners, and although they were subordinate to the bishop of the see, they could be removed only by the process of canonical law. The parish was made up of a group of families "organized for the purposes of social order and the relief of needy brethren." The size of a parish was such that there were usually several parishes within a town, several manors within a parish, and several hamlets within a manor.

The parish was a "corporation," the author explains; and as a corporation, the parish was under the protection of the Church and free from domination by any lord of the manor or other worldly figure, however powerful. The strength of the parish came from the common religion which bound the worshipers as individuals into a body which sought to provide hospitality and relief for all who needed it. Tithing was an obligation which was generally met, and the tithes were of two kinds: *predial,* from the products of the land, and *personal,* from the profits of business and trade.

Cardinal Gasquet mentions the charge that one of the great abuses of the medieval Church was the assignment of tithes for purposes outside the parish, such as the building and support of cathedrals, monasteries, and colleges. But such assignment of funds was always with the approval of the bishop, and the complaints that did occasionally arise were dealt with in a way that assured ample funds for the parishes. It is Gasquet's conclusion that the paying of tithes was regarded "not in the light of a charge upon the land, but of a genuine acknowledgment to God of His supreme governance of the world, that all things were His, and that in His hands were the ends of the earth."

The first parochial churches were probably built by the nobles and landlords, who wanted to provide a place of worship for their tenants and serfs, but by the fourteenth century the parish church was the property of the parishioners, and it was their responsibility to build and maintain the edifice. The nave, that part of the church in which the people sat, was the responsibility of the parishioners; they had to see to its repair and maintenance; the chancel, which included the choir and presbytery, was the responsibility, generally, of the rector, and he was expected to use part of the tithe for keeping the chancel in repair. The author points out that the enthusiasm shown by the people in their work to maintain the nave was an expression of the deep respect which they felt for the church building as a structure dedicated to the service of God.

Cardinal Gasquet devotes a chapter to the description of the physical church, and he stresses the devotion with which the parishioners provided the church building with furniture and works of art—paintings, carved figures, stained glass windows—which would glorify the Lord, whose house the church was. The parishioners regarded the church as their own, and they supplied it with everything of wealth and beauty which they could afford for the place which was the center of their lives.

The head of the parish was a priest, a rector or vicar, the resident ecclesiastical head of the district. The word "parson" was often used to designate "the person of the place" who held the parochial care of souls. Other classes of clergy included the curates, chantry priests, chaplains, stipendiary priests, deacons, and subdeacons.

The parish, which included both the people and their parish priest, governed its own affairs, Cardinal Gasquet explains. Each adult had a vote in the management of the church and its accessories. The representatives of the people in parochial work were the wardens, or churchwardens, who were chosen by vote at annual parish meetings. The duties assigned to the churchwardens included the care of church monies, building, decorating, trading, and farming.

Second in importance to the churchwardens was the parish clerk, the "water-bearer," whose duty it was to carry the Holy Water on Sundays; on occasion he also assisted the priest at the altar, read the Epistle at Mass, and taught the children of the parish. The parish clerk also performed certain tasks connected with the general care of the church.

Other parish officials included the sexton, the schoolmaster, and the bell-ringer. When needed, a bookbinder, painter, carver, silversmith, gilder, or tinker would be hired by the parish officials to work for the parish in repairing or decorating the church.

Income for the parish was secured by the churchwardens through voluntary contributions, regular and specific collections, burial fees, payments for use of the best cross, pew rental fees, bequeathed monies, the sale of contributed articles, taxes levied on each household, contributions to the pope, and candle money. These various sources of income supplemented the regular tithes.

"From the cradle to the grave. . . ," writes Gasquet, "religion extended its care to every soul, and exerted its influence over man, woman, and child in every parochial district, mainly by means of the Church services and the administration of the Christian Sacraments." The parishioners faithfully attended daily morning Mass, and they were quick to complain if a priest was not available. The ringing of the Sanctus Bell let those whose business kept them from morning Mass know that the Sanctus at the beginning of the Canon of the Mass was being said and that the Elements were being consecrated and elevated. The parishioners were active and enthusiastic in their participation in Church festivals, and in all their worship they regarded the Church as providing the sense and order of their lives.

A description of parish amusements and of guilds and fraternities concludes Cardinal Gasquet's sympathetic account of parish life in medieval England. The account supports the author's claim that all life centered about the parish church during the Middle Ages in England, and one tends to share the cardinal's feeling of regret that with the change of social organization has come the diminishment of that spiritual enthusiasm and unity which made the Church the vital center of all medieval life.

THE HISTORY OF FREEDOM AND OTHER ESSAYS

Author: John Emerich Edward Dalberg Acton (1834-1902)
Type of work: Intellectual and religious history
First published: 1907

Principal Ideas Advanced

The goal of the state is to maximize the freedom to follow one's conscience; any other goal fails to put limits on the growth of the power of government.

It matters not so much who holds power—whether king or democratic assembly; what does matter is the effectiveness of the limitations on that power.

The main safeguard both of civil and of religious liberty is the distinction between Church and state.

The Church has less to fear from coming to terms with modern science than from the refusal to recognize its claims; scientific objectivity must never be sacrificed to religious interests.

Lord Acton is perhaps best known as the author of the dictum: "Power tends to corrupt and absolute power corrupts absolutely." This statement expresses the substance of Acton's lifelong work and, most notably, of the work under review, *The History of Freedom and Other Essays.* It was, of course, not power as such that Acton objected to, but the power to coerce others by threats. What may surprise the reader at first are the loci in which Acton found this corrupting power: not only in absolute monarchies but also in democracies; not only in pagan theocracies but also in the highest of Christian ecclesiastical circles, Catholic as well as Protestant: "There is no worse heresy than that the office sanctifies the holder of it. That is the point at which the negation of Catholicism and the negation of Liberalism meet and keep high festival, and the end learns to justify the means." A nineteenth century liberal, Acton believed that the solution was obvious: limit power by distinguishing and dividing it—above all, distinguish Church and state ("separation," he felt, was the wrong word). Make the maximization of liberty the goal of the state; and let the Catholic Church be reconciled to the fact that its highest interests in the long run, will best be promoted by encouraging the autonomous search for truth in science and politics.

Acton is in many ways a puzzling figure. Although one of the most renowned historians of his time he never published a single major work. A student of those problems which, as he put it, lie on the "wavy line" between Church and state, his standard of impartiality led him to offend most often those with whom he fundamentally agreed. A fervent Catholic who was never conscious of ever having "held the slightest shadow of doubt about any dogma of the Catholic Church," Acton nonetheless spent far more time fighting ecclesiastical authority than in fighting the avowed enemies of the Church; and he let it be known that his favorite theologian was a German Protestant, Richard Rothe. A man who was said to have known everyone in his day worth knowing, Acton seldom found firm allies—"I have never had any contemporaries"—yet it is in his work that modern Catholics can find a prophetic preoccupation with many of their major concerns.

The History of Freedom is a posthumous collection of seventeen of Acton's more important lectures, essays, and book reviews, one of five such collections, which gives a fair indication of Acton's views on freedom, on governmental morality (both civil and ecclesiastical), and on the proper stance of the Church in the modern world.

Throughout most of his life, Acton planned to write a major work on the history of freedom from ancient times to the present. Dubbed by a friend as "the greatest book that never was written," the proposed work was to have been based entirely on original sources and was to have taken note of all that scholars had written about liberty. But the better prepared Acton became, the more formidable appeared the actual writing, and all we have of his ideas on the subject, besides great masses of notes, is a pair of lectures delivered in 1877 and a long book review of Sir Erskine May's *Democracy in Europe* published the following year.

By "liberty" (or "freedom") Acton meant "the assurance that every man shall be protected in doing what he believes his duty against the influence of authorities and majorities, custom and opinion." And the best test of a country's liberty lies in the amount of security enjoyed by its minorities. On this definition, then, liberty is the necessary condition and guardian of religion. The first important step from government by coercion towards government by consent was taken by Solon in Athens when he gave the poor a voice in selecting magistrates and thus introduced an element of democracy into a world otherwise dominated by absolutism. With the decay of the Greek mythological religion, which served as a prop to absolutism, more and more democratic elements were introduced at Athens and mankind was given a first taste of the very worst of tyrannies, democratic tyranny: "It is bad to be oppressed by a minority, but it is worse to be oppressed by a majority. For there is a reserve of latent power in the masses which, if it is called into play, the minority can seldom resist."

In contrasting the contributions to the cause of liberty made by the Roman republic and by the tyrannical empire, Acton gives the palm to the empire; both poor and rich fared better than under the republic: Roman citizenship was extended, slavery mitigated, religious toleration introduced, and the Stoic notion of "natural" or "higher" law was sometimes influential. But the radical defect of the pre-Christian state lay in its concentration of powers and duties and allegiancies: "in morality, religion, and politics there was only one legislator and one authority."

It is in Christ's words, "Render unto Caesar the things that are Caesar's, and unto God the things that are God's," that Acton finds a charter for repudiating the presumed omnicompetence of the state. What belongs to Caesar, he argued, is precisely only as much power as is necessary for the promotion of liberty, itself the highest end of government, civil or ecclesiastical. But Constantine used Christianity to strengthen his throne, and as the guardian of the liberty and unity of the Church, he made the Church serve "as a gilded crutch of absolutism," an absolutism on the ancient classic model. The barbarians came from the north with a primitive republicanism and were converted, first the rulers, and through them whole peoples. The clergy, with their inheritance of Greek and Roman learning, became closely bound to the rulers as tutors and mentors and occupied a privileged role in the feudal societies. But, the question then arose, who was to have the dominating role, king or prelate? For four hundred years the conflict raged, and though the aim of both contending parties was absolute authority, it is because of this conflict in which neither won a clear victory that the rise of civil liberty occurred. It was Acton's lifelong view that liberty has grown out of the distinction of Church and state, for both had appealed to the people to judge between them, and "this doctrine of the divine right of the people to raise up and pull down princes, after obtaining the sanctions of religion, was made to stand on broader grounds, and was strong enough to resist both Church and king." In Acton's opinion the legacy of the Middle Ages includes these elements: representative government, "no taxation without representation," the virtual extinction of slavery, the right of insurrection defined as a duty sanctioned by religion, trial by jury, and local self-government.

In the sixteenth century Machiavelli paved the way for the triumph of absolute monarchy over the spirit and institutions of a better age "by a studied philosophy of crime and so thorough a perversion of the moral sense that the like of it had not been seen since the Stoics reformed the morality of paganism." The clergy now were, more often than not, dominated by monarchs, as they were in France, Spain, Sicily, and England. The Protestant Reformation was used by rulers on both sides as an occasion and an excuse for strengthening their own power, and under the influence of intense religious partisanship, horrible crimes, such as the massacre of Saint Bartholomew, were committed. The revival and development of the doctrine of natural law made little headway against the defenders of civil absolutism and the divine right of kings.

In the seventeenth century the mutual dependence of civil and religious liberty was discovered and taught by some of the smaller independent sects, such as the Quakers. But the advance toward freedom signaled by the Glorious Revolution of 1688 (which established the state on a contractual basis and made the king a servant who ruled only during good behavior), was shortly halted; and a hundred years later, though John Locke (1632-1704) and Baron de Montesquieu (1689-1755) were still read, their principles had not been effectively institutionalized.

It was then that America became the teacher of Europe. Acton's position on the American Revolution might be summed up in these words (from his review of Bryce's *The American Commonwealth*, included in this volume): "The story of the revolted colonies impresses us first and most distinctly as the supreme manifestation of the law of resistance, as the abstract revolution in its purest and most perfect shape. No people was so free as the insurgents; no government less oppressive than the government which they overthrew. . . . It teaches that men ought to be in arms even against a remote and constructive danger to their freedom; that even if the cloud is no bigger than a man's hand, it is their right and duty to stake the national existence, to sacrifice lives and fortunes, to cover the country with a lake of blood, to shatter crowns and sceptres and fling parliaments into the sea."

The French Revolution, though occasioned by far greater evils than those which beset the Americans, failed disastrously because "the passion for equality made vain the hope of freedom." And any revolution which takes as its goal happiness, prosperity, the promotion of virtue, or the progress of enlightenment—any goal other than liberty—will likewise inevitably fail, for "if any single definite object, other than liberty, is made the supreme object, the State becomes inevitably, for the time being, absolute."

And even where political democracy has carried the day against monarchy and oligarchy, absolutism is still greatly to be feared. Like Alexis Charles de Tocqueville (1805-1859) and John Stuart Mill (1806-1873), Acton was apprehensive that free play given the will of the majority would annul all the gains of freedom: ". . . the true democratic principle that every man's will shall be as unfettered as possible . . . [is] taken to mean that the free will of the collective people shall be fettered in nothing."

Several of the essays in this volume concern themselves with persecution, the most famous essay being "the Protestant Theory of Persecution." Here Acton maintains that though both Catholics and Protestants are guilty of persecutions, each is not equally guilty; for Catholics, unlike Protestants, did not justify persecution on dogmatic grounds, but only on grounds of practical expediency. Catholic rulers persecuted Protestants because Protestants tended to subvert social institutions, and the very safety of the state was thought, though wrongly, to call for persecution. But Protestant rulers persecuted on dogmatic grounds, maintaining that any government which tolerated heresy was responsible for the souls seduced: the state must punish even a nonsubversive but heretical minority, just as it punishes any other kind of criminal. The difference was one between a Protestant aggressive and a Catholic defensive intolerance, and even though the defensive intolerance was far bloodier, the aggressive intolerance was in principle worse. In his later years Acton rejected this position as based on a distinction which the facts of the case hardly bore out; he tended to say simply that any killing of heretics is murder and that murder is never justified.

One of Action's most influential essays is that on "Nationality." Monarchies, he begins by pointing out, have a natural community of interests, in that all monarchs are interested in preserving the character of royalty as inviolable; and dispossession of a hereditary crown would establish a dangerous precedent. But Poland in the eighteenth century did not have a monarch whose blood was dynastically royal, and there was no way for a Bourbon or a Hohenzollern to claim the country by marriage or descent, for the monarchy was elective; hence, Poland was partitioned. A nation was for the first time deprived of its political existence by the Christian powers. This gave birth to nationalism in Europe, the cry of nations demanding to be independent as states, the cry that the arrangement of states was unjust and unnatural. At the time of the French Revolution, a source of unity was sought and found in the physical, ethnological unity of the French people; and the only limits recognized were those set by "nature," which limits were, in order to avoid loss of territory, partly fictional. Napoleon, too, called into being nationalistic sentiments in reaction to his efforts to dominate Europe. The traditional monarchies made use of the popular feeling against the military domination and ideas of revolutionary France, but with the downfall of Napoleon the governments of the Holy Alliance undertook to repress the nationalistic spirit they had evoked in the struggle with France. There followed a period of reaction, not against bad government, but against government by foreigners. The further history of "nationality" is summed up: "Beginning by a protest against the dominion of race over race, its mildest and least-developed form, it grew into a condemnation of every state that included different races, and finally became the complete and consistent theory, that the State and the nation must be coextensive." For Acton, nationality is an essential but not supreme element in determining the form of the state. Just as he wanted to avoid absolutism by making Church independent from state, so he wished to weaken the sovereign power by dividing royalties. Associations were to be multiplied and definite groups of public opinion to be formed which would divide political sentiments. According to Acton, a diversity of nationalities in the same state is a "firm barrier against the intrusion of government beyond the political sphere which is common to all into the social department which escapes legislation and is ruled by spontaneous laws." If the establishment of liberty for the realization of moral duties is rightly taken to be the end of civil society, Acton argued that those states are substantially the most perfect which, like the British and Austrian Empires, include various distinct nationalities without oppressing them.

In his "Cardinal Wiseman and the *Home and Foreign Review*," Acton answers criticism by Cardinal Wiseman of a report the *Review* had contained, and then presents a defense of what he calls "Catholic Liberalism." The burden of his defense is that the ultramontanist tendency to subordinate everything, even scientific truth, to the immediate interests of religion, does more harm than good: "A discovery may be made in science which will shake the faith of thousands, yet religion cannot refute it or object to it." The ultramontane school of Catholic scholarship had earlier accomplished good work in answering the calumnies of anti-Catholic writers, but their work, Acton claims, was marred by partisanship and partiality. And today, he insists, only the disinterested search for truth which characterizes the liberal will serve the best interests of the Church. Only skilled, sound, careful scholarship will win respect; rhetorical apologetics has no role. Nor in the practical order should political principle or scientific discovery be objected to, hidden, or cried down because religious interest may be hurt: "How often have Catholics involved themselves in hopeless contradiction, sacrificed principle to opportunity, adapted their theories and their interests, and staggered the world's reliance on their sincerity by subterfuges which entangle the Church in the shifting sands of party warfare, instead of establishing her cause on the solid rock of principle."

In his essay on the Vatican Council, Acton tells a tale of malodorous ecclesiastical intrigue. His point of view was that of one who opposed defining papal infallibility on practical, not on theological grounds, believing that such a definition would serve to strengthen an autocratic authority that would use repressive measures extraordinarily ill-adapted to the modern world—a belief Acton later abandoned when he saw his predictions unconfirmed by history.

In his "Political Thoughts on the Church," Acton attempted a theoretical exposition of the relations between Church and state. His opponents were, on the one hand, the secular liberals and religious quietists who say that Christianity should have no influence on politics, and, on the other, the ultramontanists whose ideal was a theocracy, for Acton the most dangerous of all power systems. Acton's own ideal was that of the Liberal Catholic, "a free Church in a free State." It would always be unwise, he thought, for the Church to look to the state for favors, for these must be returned, often with interest; and if the Church is to be truly free, a free state is a necessary condition, for an absolutist state would hardly tolerate an independent Church.

R.L.C.

ORTHODOXY

Author: Gilbert Keith Chesterton (1874-1936)
Type of work: Intellectual and spiritual autobiography
First published: 1908

Principal Ideas Advanced

In his dissatisfaction with the thought of his time, Chesterton, who was a pagan at twelve and a complete agnostic by sixteen, invented a positive philosophy which turned out to be essentially identical with orthodox Christianity.

Chesterton found the progressivism and scientism based on evolution to be suicidal forms of thought because they involved either a skepticism concerning the mind's powers or a view of the will that is the negation of rational choice.

A listing of criticisms of Christianity reveals that it is accused of contradictory vices, but although Christianity does comprise opposites, it maintains them not in passive compromise but in furious tension.

Heresy, the choice of an original and idiosyncratic vision, is easy and dull; orthodoxy is difficult and exciting and the only guarantee of sanity.

Chesterton, the English man of letters and Catholic apologist, wrote *Orthodoxy* when he was thirty-five, and if it can be quickly classified as an attempt to convey to others his personal odyssey which brought him to Christianity, like all such attempts it is intensely personal and *sui generis*. Chesterton wants to show us what brought him to accept a doctrine which is not his alone but is common and for everyone. In approach, on the level on which it moves, it is much more akin to Newman's *Apologia* (a parallel he draws in the Preface) than to Augustine's *Confessions*. That is, *Orthodoxy* is not revelatory of the whole person who was Chesterton; there are no passages which lay bare the inner recesses of his soul. Rather, the book proceeds entirely on the level of thought, the dialectic of positions which led him to Christianity. "This book is the life of a man," he writes; "And a man is his mind." In short, the book is an intellectual and spiritual autobiography but one written out of the conviction that human life is lived most intensely in the life of thought. This was a conviction Chesterton shared with Newman; and in *Orthodoxy* as in the *Apologia*, the reader is struck by the energy, the passion, and the total conviction that are expressed in seemingly abstract disputes. And, of course, the man Chesterton was himself the denial of the claim that the intellectual life produces a dessicated personality, an inverted or misanthropic attitude. The author of *Orthodoxy* was a socially active friend of many of the great of his day, a frequent, lively, and respected debating partner of George Bernard Shaw, collaborator with Hilaire Belloc, and a novelist, poet, journalist, colorful lecturer, and radio personality. Like Belloc, Chesterton was drawn by the majesty and conviviality, the thought and the battles of the Church, and if he often seems at war with his own times, his criticisms were not leveled from the remote haunt of a recluse; he was always a participant, a man of endless energy (and massive physical bulk) who could never have been satisfied to be merely a spectator of the intellectual ferment of his time.

The style of *Orthodoxy* represents, perhaps, a highpoint of the peculiarly Chestertonian style. Chesterton seldom wrote long sentences, but one notices this only in retrospect and with some surprise because there is a flow and facility in his staccato sentences that is achieved without verbal connectives. The energizing force in his work is his thought, yet there are characteristic literary features of Chesterton's style. He made constant and delighted use of puns and was without apology for the practice.

A man who spent almost the whole of his life at the craft of writing would, of course, have a lively sense of language. "What on earth is the current morality," he writes characteristically, "except in its literal sense—the morality that is always running away?" Again: "Thus we may say that a permanent ideal is necessary to the innovator as to the conservative; it is necessary whether we wish the king's orders to be promptly executed or whether we only wish the king to be promptly executed." Finally, ". . . there must be something eternal if there is to be anything sudden." But the chief mark of Chesterton's style is his use of oppositions. He works toward a contrast as if he were to choose the one and reject the other, yet he seems constantly to end up with both. The sense of paradox, of the ultimate compatibility of the most unlikely opposites, is the soul of Chesterton's thought and is reflected in his verbal style. But the compatibility he found was not that of compromise, but of a difficult and passionate balance.

Obviously Chesterton does not and could not show the compatibility of every contrast; indeed, his critical rapier never seems to flourish more successfully than when he is advancing on an apparent instance of the kind of fusion he himself often effects. Early in *Orthodoxy* he tells of his youthful concern with the claim that martyrdom is simply suicide, since in either case one is setting aside his life. His rejection of this identification is echoed later when he tries to show the Christian advance over the pagan notion of virtue as measure and mean. The great difference between the martyr and the suicide, Chesterton argues, lies in the fact that the martyr lays down his life out of love for life and its values, while the suicide kills himself because he is disgusted and disenchanted with life. The fact that Christian burial is denied to suicides while martyrs are revered by Christians takes on symbolic meaning in *Orthodoxy*. Christianity demands that one emerge from himself and see himself as part of a meaningful universe such that the great intellectual task is to discover and accept one's place in the world. A man among men in a cosmos, a cosmos that cannot be explained in terms of blind forces: this is the central image of the personal odyssey Chesterton describes in *Orthodoxy*.

Chesterton, reacting against the tide of the age, invented a set of principles which went counter to those of the age, and he then discovered that what he had presumably created was nothing else than orthodox Christianity. His development, as he describes it, was one of reaction to the myths he thought prevalent in his time, and perhaps only Chesterton would have had the daring and clarity necessary to counter a heavy-handed scientism by an appeal to what he calls "the ethics of elfland." With that appeal the affirmative side of his development began, and he thereby profited from his initial negative reaction to the prevalent contemporary theories of man and the universe.

Chesterton takes the fairly innocent phrase, that a man should believe in himself, and attempts to show that no one believes more intensely in himself than does the madman. The cult of the rugged individual in economic affairs, itself deplorable enough, leads too easily to the cherishing of one's own views on larger matters. The contrast to orthodoxy (right opinion, true doctrine) is heresy and heresy, etymologically, means choice, the preference of one's private view over common facts and doctrine. Chesterton wants to employ the maniac as a symbol of self-reliance and of the demand for total rationality. He insists that no one is more reasonable than a madman, that in a sense his arguments are irrefutable. A man who feels that everyone is conspiring against him will counter the observation that many simply ignore him by citing the cunning of the plotters. His one argument explains everything, but it leaves everything untouched. The madman cannot be refuted by acceptance of the premises of his argument, but he can be led back to sanity by being brought out of the prison of self.

Chesterton suggests that intellectual sanity generally cannot be maintained by insisting on one point of view and twisting the facts to it; such attempts possess an austere logic and simplicity, and they may be, in their own terms, beyond refutation; but the stuff of life, the variety of being, cannot be confined within narrow logical categories. This is no argument for irrationalism, as the sequel makes clear, but it is an expression of impatience with the tendency to admit only one kind of evidence for rational conviction.

Chesterton holds that no view of life is founded on a single argument or on a single type of argument. Vital commitments spring from a congeries of arguments heterogenous in type which form a pattern whose intent is inescapable. What Chesterton objects to most strenuously in modern thought (he mentions Tolstoy, Nietzsche, Schopenhauer, and Shaw) is that it is suicidal, that it employs thought to call thought itself into question and is thereby on the road to the madhouse. But if dessicated, rationality ends in irrationality; the philosophy of will is pure chaos. Chesterton's point is the simple one that to inflate pure willing is to deny the nature of choice, for choosing implies a standard that measures will. Chesterton is critical of thought which insists on reason and yet is skeptical of reason because it has no objective standards which are indubitable, or which insists on will and by making will pure spontaneity destroys the nature of rational choice. He inveighs against these currents because they are enervating and unhealthy and do not account for the facts of human life.

It is at this point that Chesterton ironically introduces the code of the playroom, the world of toy cannon and fairy stories: "My first and last philosophy, that which I believe in with unbroken certainty, I learnt in the nursery." The viewpoint of the fairy story does not deny the facts of reason; it induces wonder about those facts. Grass is always green, and the fairy story, by speaking of golden grass, makes actual greenness a matter of wonder and delight. One understands that everything could very easily have been otherwise. The laws of nature become, from this vantage point, not obvious necessities but instances of what Chesterton unabashedly calls magic. The whole world might so easily not have been, and thus it is a matter for astonishment; the regularity of the world is not to be assigned to blind necessity but to a magician, and our first reaction to the world should be one of gratitude.

There is something disarmingly childlike in Chesterton's approach. He is saying that the world and human life are so much more than narrow theories permit them to be, that narrow theories end by consuming themselves with nonsense and that, finally, we have everything to gain and nothing to lose by returning to the attitude of the nursery, because that attitude does not create so much as it expresses an original and natural outlook on life. We do not begin life with a theory but with an attitude, and arguments which would shatter that attitude only shatter themselves; there are other arguments which manifest the truth and sanity concealed in the fairy story. Of course Chesterton's main aim is not to be hortatory but to reveal the path he himself took to orthodox Christianity.

Pure optimism and pure pessimism strike him as equally ludicrous, and Chesterton seeks a view which enables one to have what is valid in both. Likening one's attitude toward the world to one's attitude toward his own country, Chesterton suggests that only the loyal and patriotic have a standard for their criticism. It is a mistake to speak of being optimistic or pessimistic about the world: "The assumption of it is that a man criticizes this world as if he were house-hunting, as if he were being shown over a new suite of apartments. . . . But no man is in that position. A man belongs to the world before he begins to ask whether it is nice to belong to it. . . . To put shortly what seems the essential matter, he has loyalty long before he has any admiration." This fundamental loyalty to creation is the context of the desire to change it.

When Chesterton summarizes the objections which are made to Christianity, he finds that it is accused of contradictory things, often by the same critics. Christianity is pointlessly sanguine about life, and it is depressingly sad; it is too pacifist, and it is too bellicose; it is too drab, and it is too gay. Chesterton finds in such paradoxes of Christianity an expression of the tension of opposites; Christianity has conflicting characters and it possesses them, not by diluting them, but by keeping them in a delicate and difficult balance. He speaks of the "duplex passion" which is the key to Christian ethics. The Christian is to be proud, yet humble; reverent of life, yet disdainful of death; angry at sin, yet loving toward the sinner: "This is the thrilling romance of orthodoxy. People have fallen into a foolish habit of speaking of orthodoxy as something heavy, humdrum and safe. There never was anything so perilous or so exciting as orthodoxy. It was sanity: and to be sane is more dramatic than to be mad."

Orthodoxy is an untidy, uneven, rhetorical, and immensely alive document. In reading it, one is struck simultaneously by its clarity and its obscurity, its leaps and its connectives, its force and its weakness. But what it manifests throughout is the essential Christian folly which finally is the most fundamental reasonableness. It is tempting to draw a parallel between Chesterton and the Danish Lutheran, Søren Kierkegaard (1813-1855). Despite obvious dissimilarities, Chesterton and Kierkegaard both argue against the wise of this world on behalf of the basic wisdom of the plain man. Initially, both appear irrational, but they end by making us question our canons of rationality. They are champions of common sense against uncommon nonsense, nonsense unanchored in certitudes based on life. Such nonsense is productive of systems of thought which conflict with the world of ordinary life (where even the experts spend most of their time).

Chesterton's *Orthodoxy* is particularly interesting as the careful record of the conversion of a mind and spirit to Christianity. The power of the appeal of the Church makes itself felt most clearly when one who begins as the enemy of the Faith ends by embracing it with enthusiasm, as Chesterton did. Chesterton came to orthodox Christianity not because it was orthodox, but because he could not resist the excitement and the sanity which Christianity embodied.

R.M.

THE MYSTICAL ELEMENT OF RELIGION

Author: Friedrich John, Baron von Hügel (1852-1925)
Type of work: Mystical theology
First published: 1908

Principal Ideas Advanced

The mystical, the rational, and the social elements of religion exist in all men, and the balance of these elements in each individual person is what establishes his uniqueness as well as his degree of personal fulfillment.

An inclusive and truly Catholic Christianity must contain within itself a tension between transcendence (an interior, purely religious ethic) and immanence (the exterior, socially oriented ethic), and this tension is resolved dynamically by faith and action.

Sacrifice, the "vertical" relation of man to God, has always been conceived, along with communion, which is the "horizontal" relation of man to man, as essential to genuine and complete religion.

Since God, as Personality, is concrete, the Christian is necessarily committed to the created material object, the sacramental system, and the preservation and fulfillment of the individual personality.

Two underlying themes are everywhere apparent in Baron Friedrich von Hügel's monumental study *The Mystical Element of Religion;* namely, that spiritual and material reality are revealed in and through each other in a dynamic, constant interplay, and that the whole man must respond to the whole of reality. Both themes have their role in von Hügel's synthesis of science, philosophy, and religion, as understood in the modern and not the Scholastic sense. He is not interested in the formulation of some new all-inclusive system to explain man, but in the grounding of idea in the world of experience and action. Each order of truth must be explored by those whose vocation it is to explore it, and the only limitations on their inquiries should be those implicit in the discipline itself. Yet any such investigators, to be truly and perfectly human in their vocation, must bring not only their reason, intuition, or institutional loyalties to bear on their work, but also their entire personalities, for man, says von Hügel, is composed of senses, intellect, and spirit and is therefore obliged to work out his salvation amidst the complexities of creation, which he must resolve by the ultimately religious achievement of balance, order, and unity in his own personality.

Such a balance, von Hügel asserts, is impossible to achieve without God, both as experienced directly within the individual soul and as known indirectly through His action within other men, that is, through institutions, traditions, and formally communicated concepts. One must not be so subjective, von Hügel warns, as to suppose that the divine presence sensed or longed for in oneself exists without any confirmation in the real world outside the self. Cut off from its roots in a common body of belief and practice, the mystical temperament withers and dies for lack of nourishment. Nor must one be so objective as to rely completely on the forms and concepts established by other men for knowledge of the divine. In "the slow up-building of the personality" all previous responses to things and persons must be assimilated and unified in a total consciousness with which alone man is capable of a full, richly human love of God.

Von Hügel recalls that Hellenism, the first great force in Western intellectual history, plunged men into the search for order and unity in the midst of the chaos of experience. Ultimately, he continues, the Aristotelian concern for immanence confronted the Neoplatonic ideal of God's absolute unity, transcendence, and lack of specific qualities. Christianity, the second great formative movement in the West, established its ideal in the New Testament portrait of Christ. According to the author, "the careful reverence for the external facts of nature (so far as these are known) and for social religious tradition and institutions, and the vivid consciousness of the necessity and reality of internal experience" creates a new and more complex attitude toward the many and the one. During the medieval period of philosophical realism, mysticism and philosophy were united in a ladder of knowledge that rose from sense to spirit. But with the advent of nominalism, toward the end of the Middle Ages, the concern of philosophy became the knowledge of particular objects only, and mysticism was thus divorced from all other forms of science, a situation that tempts the mystic to regard himself as isolated from a world which is intrinsically evil and dangerous; a world from which the religious soul must be protected.

According to von Hügel, Western history since the Renaissance reveals the folly of religion's attempt to isolate itself from science and philosophy, as well as the folly of the latter two in their attempt to fulfill human personality in abstraction from its larger, religious dimension. The scientific view is marked by the "quantitative" and concentrates on what actually *is,* while the spiritual view is ethical or "qualitative" and concentrates on what *ought* to be. The single source of knowledge for science, says von Hügel, is the created universe itself, which gives the scientist his "passion for the thing as over . . . Person." The source of knowledge for religion is worship, which springs up "in a person towards a Person; a surrender to be achieved not in something, but in some one,—a some one who *is* at all, only in as much as he is living, loving, growing." Realism and nominalism are thus reconciled by the elevation of personality as the crown of being and by the inclusion within the fully developed personality of all the lower, but still significant material "accidents" of creation. There is a perceivable upward trend throughout all existence; it is possible to see the "ever-increased complexity of organization, the growing depth and interiority in the animate world—Plant-Life itself being already, very probably, possessed of a vague consciousness. . . ." Man, at the summit of the material universe, must be aware not only of his bonds with all that is below him but of the spiritual dimension of reality in which all creation lives, moves, and is. The individual must measure himself against the material "given" of the world and rebound to the divine, having been purified and stabilized by the impersonal discipline of science which serves to moderate and deepen the earnest but static and inflexible attitudes of "pure religion."

Since the three elements of religion (the mystical, the rational, and the social) are historically apparent, writes von Hügel, they can be found also in the developmental psychology of the individual. Childhood is marked by the acquisition of sense knowledge, a preoccupation with the external. Religion is grasped by the child uncritically as "Fact or thing," to be studied in art or learned in catechism. Youth is the period for reflection and for the rationalistic growth of "Question and Argument," which religion must answer reasonably with a broadly inclusive and flexible philosophy. If the institutional-social religion of childhood is properly fused with the humane and intellectually honest adherence of the mind during youth, the groundwork is laid for the faith of the mature man. Such faith is marked by will and action; it is the joining of the outward with the inward, contemplative man, embracing nature, man, and God in an act of mystical love. "We find here," von Hügel writes, "that all the activities of specifically human life begin with a sense-impression, as the first, the one simply *given* element; that they move into and through a central process of mental abstraction and reflection, as the second element, contributed by the mind itself; and that they end, as the third element, in the discharge of will and of action, in an act of free affirmation, expansion, and love." All of these stages, particularly the last, penetrate the personality, altering and broadening its cognitive base.

According to Baron von Hügel, man is dependent for knowledge of creation on his faculties of sense and intellect, but for the act of mystical knowing, what is required is *the whole person*, including all that has gone before to shape that person materially and spiritually. Nothing is wasted in, irrelevant, or unnecessary to fulfillment except sin itself.

Religion as a whole, the author insists, must begin with the study of facts concerning a divine revelation made in time through the Person of Christ; such a study demands an ultimate act of will and faith by which objective facts are interiorized and made one with the personality of the inquirer. In this fusion, the immanent is joined to the transcendent, communion is transformed into sacrifice, and the individual comes into mystical union with the Supremely Personal; yet the identity of the lesser personality is never pantheistically dissolved by participation in a reality greater than itself. Personality, whether present in the Holy Trinity or in the union of the soul with God, is revealed only in relation to *another* personality, never by annihilation of the other.

The mystical practice of Saint Catherine of Genoa serves as a clear illustration of the actual experience of the mystical state in conjunction with an active life of heroic charity and a firm sacramental union with traditional Christianity. It is possible to explore in the life of Saint Catherine a personality wholly developed intellectually, spiritually, and fraternally, whose union with God did not involve the sacrifice of a richly fulfilled human identity.

The childhood and young womanhood of Saint Catherine were unmarked by any signs of precocious piety; she was neither more nor less devout than most noblewomen of her time, though she had as a child desired to imitate her older sister and take the veil. After having been unhappily married for ten years to a frivolous and unfaithful young man of a family as rich and influential as her own, Caterinetta Fiesca Adorna experienced the complete and lasting religious conversion that began her mystical life. She began at once her life work of caring for the sick in a charity hospital, a work into which her husband was later drawn, upon his own conversion in 1473. Though he became a Franciscan Tertiary, and they were both surrounded by Franciscans at their hospital, Catherine herself never affiliated with any order, nor did she have a regular spiritual director or confessor for the first twenty-five years of her convert life, facts which set her apart from most Catholic mystics, though she shared with them and with all Catholics a devotion to the institutional Church, a devotion expressed by frequent and fervent reception of Holy Communion. This daily sacramental link with the historical-institutional side of Christianity she supplemented by the reading of Christian texts: the Bible, Dionysius the Pseudo-Areopagite, and the Franciscan mystic Jacopone da Todi (c. 1230-1306).

As it must be in the life of any mystic, the transcendental aspect of Catherine's religion was the dominant one, yet one need not look far to find the immanent aspect in her life also. For the first four years after her conversion, Catherine performed great penances in an effort to curb her natural appetites and self-will. From 1477 to 1499 her spiritual progress was marked by a tender, expansive love of God and by a general sense of contrition, rather than by hatred of particular sins. Her awareness of her own imperfections was swallowed up by a selfless and unaltering concentration on the love of God; nothing but duty could distract her when she was in the midst of contemplation.

When the plague struck Genoa, Catherine remained at her post throughout the disaster. She organized relief and treated the sick so tirelessly that she herself caught the disease and nearly died. By 1779, she and her husband moved into rooms in the hospital, leaving their own home behind them in order to devote themselves completely to their work.

Catherine's vigorous, healthy system at last began to break down under the combined stresses of overwork, bodily illness, old age, and the exhausting hours spent in contemplation. By 1499, the beginning of her "last period," her life was plagued by unusual psychophysical phenomena, mistaken by her devoted followers as supernatural favors, though she herself took care to draw a definite line between the value of the interior life of her soul and these peculiar, involuntary outward signs. "It is indeed in this last period of her life," writes von Hügel, "that we can most clearly see a deeply attractive mixture of personal suffering and of tender sympathy with even the humblest of all things that live." She at last found a regular confessor and spiritual director, Don Marabotto, who was able to help her over those years when her suffering was great and her strength failing.

Saint Catherine was quite aware of the need of the soul to utilize all that presents itself to both body and mind in order to assimilate material creation and at the same time to leap beyond its limitations. That she possessed her own soul as a perfectly disciplined unity is testified to by all who knew and followed her, von Hügel reports. Yet she had begun with a temperament so rich, volatile, strong-willed, and self-centered that only sanctity could have balanced and perfected it: "She became a saint because she had to; . . . she became it to prevent herself going to pieces: she literally had to save, and actually did save, the fruitful life of reason and of love, by ceaselessly fighting her immensely sensitive, absolute, and claimful self." Ultimately she had a passion for nothing except unity with God, and she could bear anything except that which separated her from that unity. Her contemplation was not marked by visions or images but was purely conceptual, experienced in an interior darkness, neither spatial nor temporal. She did not dwell on the humanity of the Gospel Christ, but on the Christ of the Holy Eucharist, who is known directly, through love.

In the mystical state, von Hügel writes, there seems to be an entrance into "Duration" (the experience of *quality,* not dependent on space) as opposed to Time (the experience of *quantity* and *movement* in space). "Duration" is that experience which is possible only when the whole person is alive and functioning at a peak level, rejecting all that interrupts his identity of will with the will of God. While quantity can move in space, quality can only be experienced. In both there is that permanent characteristic of the human soul, awareness of succession, or the knowledge of one thing at a time, rather than the perfect simultaneity which is a feature of God's own act of knowing. Union with God, the center of being, is won by moment-to-moment acts which are willed through love by the soul. The soul must *act, be,* and *love* in God.

Von Hügel claims that just as the ordinary human experience of time is capable of being transformed to the level of the divine, the consciousness of space, so elemental to our earthly life, is not lost when the mystic is united with God. To be known experimentally, and not by the *via negativa* of faith and mystery alone, God must be sought by the sacrifice of the false-self, which bars His entrance into the soul. In order to complete the mystical experience, God must be understood as "Other," seen at the same time as *outside* the soul (in His transcendental aspect) and as *within* the soul (in His immanent aspect). God's "place," von Hügel writes, is actually "a state, a disposition of the soul."

During her mystical experiences, Catherine was not able to judge her state of virtue clearly or to imagine any future growth in love; at such a moment of mystical union her love seemed to her to be perfect. Though she could look at her past and see the imperfections that had been outgrown, "I saw that . . . God continuously allows man to see his [momentary] operation as though it were without imperfection, whilst all the time He, before Whom the heavens are not pure, is not ceasing from removing imperfections from his soul." The process of this removal is, in the nature of things, painful, since when the soul attaches itself to anything but the End for whom it was intended, it causes itself suffering in the getting and in the relinquishment: "Such pain [is] everywhere automatically consequent upon deliberate acts of self-will." For the mystic, enveloped as he is in the fire of divine love, the process of union with God is experienced as both an unbearable joy at being in God's presence, and as an unbearable pain at being limited through his own faults from returning God's love. During her mystical unions with God Catherine felt a tender unity with the souls in Purgatory; it was as if they were all in the same "place." Catherine saw Heaven, Purgatory, and Hell not as material places, but as states of being which we begin to know during our earthly lives, according to the dispositions of our souls. The only joy greater than that of a soul wrapped in the fire of purifying divine love (Purgatory) is that of the soul enjoying a perfect union with the love of God in Heaven. The fire with which we symbolize the love of God "is always present: the impediment [our imperfect will to love God] simply renders this Fire painful —and that is all." Purgatory, then, is a dynamic process, a change of condition, by which the sins woven into the very fabric of the soul's being are consumed and transformed into channels of grace.

In the next life, after having battered away the locked doors of time, space, and materiality God's love makes direct entry into the soul. He is seen by the soul not darkly through a glass, but as a burning bush, into which the soul makes a voluntary, intuitive leap and in which all the soul's dross is consumed. In the state of beatitude, the soul remains joyfully within the fire of divine love. Even then, however, the soul retains something of the experience of suffering, for it never becomes God Himself; the gap between Creator and created is never entirely bridged, nor does the soul ever lose its sense of contingency in the face of God's fullness of being. Finally, von Hügel claims, the human personality passes into a state of freedom and perfected individuality which includes the progressive achievement and recognition of reality (spiritual *and* material) at previous stages in its development. It enjoys a purged and tempered individualism, an identity achieved by the desire to please a God whom one loves, and whose love brings about the progressive and perpetually dynamic transformation of the personality.

B.J.R.

THE SERVILE STATE

Author: Hilaire Belloc (1870-1953)
Type of work: Economic theory
First published: 1912

Principal Ideas Advanced

Men without property are reduced to a state of real, if not legal, slavery.
Industrialism is reducing most men to the servile state.
Socialism or any other form of collectivism will not afford freedom to the masses of men.

Distributism, or widespread ownership of property, is the only way of maintaining a society of free men.

With his friend Chesterton, Hilaire Belloc headed a group of English Catholic intellectuals, most of them converts, who wrote popularly on almost every moral and dogmatic issue facing the world in the first third of the twentieth century. They wrote against war, imperialism, industrialism, and other contemporary movements that they believed were contrary to human dignity and to the Catholic religion.

This group had definite economic views that came to be called "Distributism." Although he was primarily a historian and biographer, Belloc produced the "bible" of Distributism in his succinct book, *The Servile State.* This work was long considered a masterpiece of Catholic thinking about the problems created by industrialism, and was enthusiastically reprinted many times, even as late as after World War II. But it is now evaluated as advocating an ideal impossible of realization, one that turns its back on industrial and technological progress.

Belloc states his thesis forthrightly in the opening paragraph of *The Servile State:* "This book is written to maintain and prove the following truth:—That our free modern society in which the means of production are owned by a few being necessarily in unstable equilibrium, it is tending to reach a condition of stable equilibrium by the establishment of compulsory labour legally enforcible upon those who do not own the means of production for the advantage of those who do. With this principle of compulsion applied against the non-owners there must also come a difference in their status; and in the eyes of society and of its positive law men will be divided into two sets: the first economically free and politically free, possessed of the means of production, and securely confirmed in that possession; the second economically unfree and politically unfree, but at first secured by their very lack of freedom in certain necessaries of life and in a minimum of well-being beneath which they shall not fall."

The author's first concern is to describe the "servile state" of the ancient pagan world, in which slaves were propertyless employees forced to stay and work in their position. Then he shows that slavery came to an end under Christianity and that during the Middle Ages a system was arranged in which, as a result of the wide distribution of landed property, freedom was secured for the masses of men. He then demonstrates that this agrarian system came to an end, especially in England, by the development of capitalism, which concentrated productive property in relatively few men.

Belloc maintains that capitalism is, by its very nature, unstable "because its effects in denying *sufficiency* and *security* were intolerable to men; how being thus *unstable,* it consequently presented a *problem* which demanded a solution: to wit, the establishment of some stable form of society whose law and social practice should correspond, and whose economic results, by providing *sufficiency* and *security,* should be tolerable to human nature."

There are three solutions to this problem. One of these, advocated by various kinds of socialists, is "Collectivism." But this, the author argues, is only another form of the Servile

State in which workers are not free from the absolute control of the political officers of the community. The second alternative, which Belloc advocates is "property, or the re-establishment of a 'Distributive State' in which the mass of citizens should severally own the means of production." The third alternative, toward which England was drifting in 1912, according to the author, is the Servile State, in which those who do not own the means of production are compelled to work for those who do and, in return, are guaranteed a minimum security.

In the last chapters of his book Belloc tries to demonstrate that "the Servile State has begun." His argument is that both socialists and liberal reformers are driving the workers into a condition of enforced labor in exchange for minimum security. Beginning in 1906 the Liberal Party had succeeded in passing a series of "welfare laws" guaranteeing minimum wages, maximum hours, old age pensions, unemployment insurance, and other such measures. The fund for these benefits was created by contributions from the state, the employer, and the employee. Belloc argued that this procedure legally compelled the worker to toil in the industrial system in exchange for the promise of security in time of unemployment or old age. Therefore, he maintained, the Servile State was already beginning in 1912.

Belloc therefore concludes that "it is the very heart of my thesis that we are not, as a fact, approaching Socialism at all, but a very different state of society; to wit, a society in which the Capitalist class shall be even more powerful and far more secure than it is at present: a society in which the proletarian mass shall not suffer from particular regulations, oppressive or beneficent, but shall change their status, lose their present legal freedom, and be subject to compulsory labour."

T.P.N.

SAINT FRANCIS OF ASSISI

Author: Johannes Jörgensen (1866-1956)
Type of work: Biography
First published: 1912

Principal Ideas Advanced

The life of Saint Francis of Assisi was the life of a wise and simple ascetic chosen by God to help men of all times to attain salvation through imitation of his scheme for Christian perfection.

Saint Francis's formula for Christian perfection consists of three principal ideals which, like Francis himself, appear simple on the surface only to prove on closer examination to be profound.

The ideals of poverty, chastity, and cheerfulness are the cornerstone of the Franciscan Order, ideals based on the example of Christ Himself.

The flame which ignited the soul of Saint Francis made of him a burning torch which sent off sparks in all directions—especially into the souls of those who heard him preach and those who were his close associates in the brotherhood, until they too were aflame with his zeal and the Franciscan Order became a vast conflagration spread over the entire medieval spectrum, which, like a great sanctuary lamp in the universal Church, casts its steady and bright reflection even to our own time.

Johannes Jörgensen divides his study of the life of Saint Francis into four main segments: Francis the Church Builder, Francis the Evangelist, God's Singer, and Francis the Hermit. The biography is particularly noteworthy because of the lyrical quality of the narrative, a direct reflection of the lyrical quality of Saint Francis himself.

In Book I, Francis the Church Builder, a brief but thorough introduction to Francis's ancestry, social background, youth, and "conversion" is given. The son of Pietro de Bernadone, a wealthy Italian cloth-merchant of the Middle Ages, Francis had received the name of John at his christening (September, 1182), held while his father was absent on a journey. Upon his return *Ser* Pietro changed the John to Francis, a name then rare but not completely new to the region. There are many theories purported to explain the reason for the change, the most likely being that the senior Bernadone had a liking for things French (his wife, Lady Pica, was from Provence) and wished his first-born son to bear the name of the country for whose customs and people he had such admiration. Francis himself seems to have grown to share this admiration, for in later years he loved to speak the French tongue though he never could do so perfectly. "For him French was the language of poetry, the language of religion, the language of his happiest memories and of his most solemn hours, the language he spoke when his heart was too full to find expression in everyday Italian, and therefore his soul's mother-speech. When Francis talked French, those who knew him knew that he was happy."

As a youth Francis was well liked and well known for his *joie de vivre* and the readiness with which he parted with his money for the slightest escapade. He was generous to the poor as well as to the rich, an eager adventurer, a well-dressed dandy. For all of his worldliness we are told that he would not tolerate ribaldry or impurity in his presence: "Like all the pure of heart, Francis had great reverence for the mysteries of life."

Because of the degree to which he entered into the pleasures of the world, so much the more dramatic was his turning away from them. This "conversion" took place after a long illness, from which emerged the Francis who would eventually renounce not only the world but his very identity. Taking as his vocation the words of the text of St. Matthew in which Jesus exhorts His disciples to go forth and preach, heal the sick, and cleanse the lepers, and in which He enjoined them: ". . . do not possess gold, nor silver, nor money in your purses: nor script for your journey, nor two coats, nor shoes, nor a staff; . . . and when you come into [a] house, salute it, saying: Peace be to this house . . . ,"

Francis based the rest of his life on the literal application of these words. In the hands of some biographers this transformation is unsatisfactory and unconvincing. Jörgensen, however, presents his Francis as a man obsessed with God. Just as his passionate Latin nature caused him to plunge fully into the sweetnesses of the world, so, when his sights became set on higher goals, did it cause him to plunge just as fully into the pursuit of their attainment. His innately boundless generosity, heretofore manifested in the giving away of alms or clothing, now pricked him into remaining unsatisfied until he had given *all* for the love of God—not just his gorgeous clothing, his wealth, his inheritance, but also shelter, food, friends, and security—until he stood literally naked and unencumbered in his ascent toward that which is eternal.

Throughout his life, Francis held churches and the clergy in great reverence: "And then the Lord gave me and still gives me so great a confidence in priests, who live by the rite of the Holy Roman Church, that if they even persecuted me, I would for the sake of their consecration say nothing about it. And if I had the wisdom of Solomon and travelled in the parishes of poor priests, yet I would not preach without their permission. And them and all other priests I will fear, love, and honor as my superiors, and I will not look on their faults, for I see God's Son in them, and they are my superiors."

The commission from God to "go hence, Francis, and build up my house, for it is nearly falling down!" came to Francis after a long prayer that he might discover what God wished of him in his lifetime. A simple and literal man, Francis began the execution of this command with the rebuilding of San Damiano, a little field-church falling into ruin from neglect, where he had spent much time in prayer and meditation. He also restored other churches in his lifetime, but it was the symbolic interpretation of Our Lord's command wherein lay Francis's greatest contribution to the Catholic Church in particular and to the world in general.

Francis the Evangelist, then, began a simple life of prayer, preaching, and penance, and was eventually joined by other men inspired by his example to attempt a heroic life. We are told that their preaching always came back to three points: "Fear God, love God, convert yourself from bad to good." These bridegrooms of "Lady Poverty" soon found it necessary to take the form of a religious order to serve the growing number of persons desirous of joining the ranks of men seeking perfection through the imitation of Christ's life on earth, and thus the Order of Friars Minor was born. The original brotherhood led lives of such rigid simplicity and asceticism that there gradually emerged branches such as the Poor Clares (an order for women founded by Saint Clare) and the Third Order, for those who wished to follow the Rule but whose physical capacities or station in life would prevent its strictest observance. Poverty was the constant guiding principle of the Order: poverty of spirit and poverty of person. According to Francis and his followers, through voluntary detachment from the distractions of the world would come peace, joy, and eternal life.

There was no place for sanctimony or self-pity in these lives of renunciation. Francis despised any sort of negativism in the approach to holiness. In his own *Speculum perfectionis* he says: "For what else are the servants of God than his singers, whose duty it is to lift up the hearts of men and move them to spiritual joy?" In one of his directives to the brothers he states: "Let the Brothers take care that they do not present the appearance of hypocrites, with dark and cast-down mien, but that they show themselves glad in the Lord, cheerful and worthy of love, and agreeable."

The gentle spirit of Francis adapted easily to the role of God's troubadour. As God's Singer, he was often filled with such ecstasies of joy while preaching that he would start to dance on the spot. His favorite species of bird was the crested lark who wore a "hood" as did the brothers, but whose song was so beautiful and joyous that it uplifted the hearer's heart to God.

The songs of Saint Francis have come down to us in the form of hymns, verses, and prayers composed from the overflowings of his own joyous soul. The most well-known of these is the Sun Song, or Hymn to the Sun, one of the first examples of medieval Italian poetry.

The great personal magnetism of this humble man extended itself to all of nature—not only to men, but also to the beasts and the elements, his "brothers" and "sisters." The birds are supposed to have kept silent at his command in order that he might preach. In the Fioretti we are told that "after this, our holy father's word, all those little birds began to open their beaks to beat with their wings and stretch out their necks and bow their heads reverently to the earth, and with their song and their movements showed that the words St. Francis had said had pleased them greatly." His was not the sentimental love of nature by which he is so often misrepresented; his was an appreciative reverence of everything as reflecting divine and creative love.

Francis the ascetic was also possessed of a subtle sense of humor, a facet not surprising, but seldom stressed. His name for those who "tried out" the Order, usually for only a short duration, finding the way of life too severe, was "Brother Fly." Again, nearing death, Francis took great pleasure in composing and in having sung to him the verses of his Sun Song. He would call upon the brothers at various times to sing to him of Sister Death: "And now it was in vain that Brother Elias came and warned him not to give scandal by the constant singing—'There is a watch set below, and they do not think that thou art a holy man, when they hear singing and playing always in thy cell.' Francis had now for a long enough period submitted and yielded; now when he was about to die, he wanted at least to have leave to die in his own way. 'By the grace of the Holy Ghost,' said he, 'I am so completely united with my Lord and God, that I may well be allowed to be glad and rejoice in him!' "

The final phase of Jörgensen's biography, Francis the Hermit, centers about the last days of the saint, his stigmatization, and the suffering caused both by this phenomenon and his ensuing blindness. In addition there was the deep spiritual suffering caused him personally by the gradual change in the nature and purpose of the Order as he had conceived it. Because of its growth, alterations to the original Rule had to be made to accommodate the several types of persons being accepted for admission. Priests and men of learning were now a highly representative segment of the membership. Francis never opposed learning or the acquiring of it, as some historians have foolishly proposed. On the contrary, in the simplicity of his own wisdom, he saw the temptations to pride, envy, and vanity which often follow in the wake of higher learning, and he feared for the spiritual welfare of his brotherhood in this regard.

By the time of his declining years (he died in 1226) Francis had resigned the formal headship of the Order. Though the Rule had changed, his concepts never did. His Last Testament was the same in essence as his first. His final blessing to the brothers of that time and of time to come expresses perfectly the zealous spirit of the man who was even in his own lifetime called saint: "I bless them as much as I can—and more than I can."

Having undertaken a confessed labor of love based on his personal admiration for and devotion to Saint Francis of Assisi, Jörgensen, one of Europe's foremost writers of the twentieth century, adds a fuller dimension to his portrait because of his appreciation for Italy and his perceptive understanding of the Italian race—foreshadowed in his own *Autobiography*. This biography of Saint Francis is of particular importance both because of its lyrical artistry and because it is one of the most thoroughly comprehensive and documented pieces of scholarly research on the subject. It combines a highly readable style with scrupulously authenticated text. There is a set of notes to the text which constitutes valuable bibliographic data of sources in the German, French, Italian, and Latin languages. The notes are followed by an index of key words, names, and places.

J.S.

THE POEMS OF GERARD MANLEY HOPKINS

Author: Gerard Manley Hopkins (1844-1889)
Type of work: Religious poetry
First published: 1918

Principal Ideas Advanced

God created the world, and the beauty of the natural order reveals to us something of the Creator's beauty.

In all things there is a principle of individuality and selfhood expressing itself in design and pattern.

All true art attempts to express not simply exterior reality, but also the interior forms of things; outward beauty is a reflection of interior form.

The duty of the Christian artist is, through his work, to sanctify nature and offer it to God.

Although the poems of Gerard Manley Hopkins were not published until twenty-nine years after his death, he is now regarded as one of the foremost English poets of the nineteenth century, who, perhaps more than any other poet of his time, prefigured and helped to shape the poetry of the twentieth century. His life, like his art, was highly dramatic, but its drama remained hidden from all but a few close friends. The poet was the oldest of seven children in a family highly gifted in the arts. His father wrote poetry and published books on a wide variety of subjects, from a historical account of Hawaii to texts on arbitration and marine insurance. His father's sister was Gerard's first tutor and taught him Irish folk songs and Elizabethan airs. Two of his brothers had talent for sketching and contributed regularly to *Punch*. Milicent, the oldest daughter, driven by the same religious zeal that eventually drew Gerard to the Society of Jesus, eventually became a nun in the Church of England. Grace, the youngest daughter, was a competent pianist and harmonized a number of the airs composed by Gerard.

At the age of ten Hopkins was sent to Cholmondley's boarding school at Highgate, where he distinguished himself as a scholar and poet. "The Escorial," a poem dealing with the martyrdom of Saint Laurence, indicates his early interest in the heroism of the saints. The poem brought Hopkins a school prize, as did "A Vision of the Mermaids." Both poems express a passionate delight in sensuous beauty, and they are notable for their images and concentrated expression. In "A Vision of the Mermaids" Hopkins describes a sunset: "Plum-purple was the west; but spikes of light / Spear'd open lustrous gashes, crimson-white." He captures the essence of Saint Laurence's martyrdom in two lines: "For that staunch saint still prais'd his Master's name / While his crack'd flesh lay hissing on the grate."

An incident that occurred at Highgate indicates that even as a boy Hopkins attempted to imitate the heroism of the saints. To prove his endurance he determined to fast from all liquids for a specified length of time. Some days later the boy collapsed on the playing field with a black tongue, but only after having won his bet. At home it was his custom to fast regularly, so much so that his mother forbade him to continue the practice, although during Lent he insisted upon giving up desserts and sugar and limiting himself to meat once a day.

Such biographical details are important because they demonstrate unequivocally the poet's urge to asceticism and religious obedience. Some critics have maintained that Hopkins's decision to become a Jesuit was an unfortunate one, but the incidents of his childhood indicate that he had longings which could be fulfilled only in a demanding religious order.

Hopkins won a scholarship to Oxford and entered Balliol College in April, 1863. Three major currents of thought flowed through Oxford during the eighteen sixties. One was the spirit of rationalism in religion. Renan's *Life of Jesus* (1888), interpreting the Savior as a purely historical figure, was published in the year of Hopkins's matriculation and was a favorite of the undergraduates. Benjamin Jowett (1817-1893), classical scholar and challenger of religious orthodoxy, had thrown his weight with the liberal Protestantism of the day that was attempting to reconcile Christianity with the new developments in geology and anthropology by denying the divinity of Christ.

The second current, opposing the liberals, was a renaissance of the Oxford Movement begun by John Keble (1792-1866), professor of poetry; Edward Pusey (1800-1882), Regius professor of Hebrew; Richard Froude (1803-1836), a poet and fellow of Oriel College; and John Henry Newman (1801-1890), fellow of Oriel, poet, scholar, convert to the Church in 1845, priest, cardinal, and the most influential English Catholic of his time. The core of the Oxford Movement was a belief that the Anglican Church was more than a merely human institution and that it possessed privileges, sacraments, and a ministry ordained by Christ Himself. Having once accepted the validity of the apostolic succession, Newman was led inevitably to the Church as the one tradition that indeed possessed sacraments instituted by Christ. By 1863 the Oxford Movement had lost its original impetus, but Pusey remained enormously influential and through his followers continued to defend Anglican orthodoxy. Perhaps more important than any individual was an atmosphere electric with spiritual possibilities. During the height of the Oxford Movement students arranged altars in their rooms, and alarmed parents, fearing that their sons were "going over," wrote in consternation to the authorities. Although somewhat weakened by the eighteen sixties, this atmosphere continued to exert influence during Hopkins's Oxford years.

The third current of thought, one just beginning in the eighteen sixties, was the aesthetic movement, whose chief representative at Oxford was Walter Pater (1839-1894), scholar, critic, and novelist. Reacting against the incredible ugliness and squalor produced by the industrial revolution, a number of painters, poets, and scholars sought refuge in a superficial medievalism and in the ideal of a unique and bizarre beauty.

Hopkins was influenced by all three of these currents of thought. He studied Greek under Jowett, who said Hopkins was the finest student of that subject he had ever seen at Balliol. Pater also tutored him in Greek, and during the summer of 1864 Hopkins met several of the Pre-Raphaelites. However, his High-Church upbringing and his religious zeal led him to Pusey's camp. In 1864 Newman published his *Apologia pro vita sua*. The eloquence of his spiritual biography started a tide of converts once again flowing toward Rome. Hopkins and his friends read the book, which overnight had become the talk of England. In the same year he composed several poems dealing with repentance, expiation of sin, and the purification of the spirit through humiliation and pain. In "A Voice from the World" he wrote:

Steel may be melted and rock
rent.
Penance shall clothe me to the
bone.
Teach me the way: I will repent.

By 1865 Hopkins's tie with Anglicanism was tenuous, and in January of that same year he wrote the best of his pre-Jesuit poems, "The Habit of Perfection." The poem exalts the ideal of asceticism which he had held from the days of his early boyhood. He directs the senses to abandon the outer world and seek rather the purely spiritual:

Be shellèd, eyes, with double dark
And find the uncreated light:
This ruck and reel which you re-
mark
Coils, keeps, and teases simple
sight.

. . .

O feel-of-primrose hands, O feet
That want the yield of plushy
sward,
But you shall walk the golden
street
And you unhouse and house the
Lord.

And, Poverty, be thou the bride
And now the marriage feast be-
gun,
And lily-coloured clothes provide
Your spouse not laboured-at nor
spun.

During Lent Hopkins composed "Nondum" (not yet). In it he wrote:

Oh! till thou givest that sense be-
yond,
To show Thee that Thou art, and
near,
Let patience with her chastening
wand
Dispel the doubt and dry the tear;
And lead me child-like by the
hand
If still in darkness not in fear.

In June, Hopkins and William Addis, a close friend, visited a Benedictine monastery while on a walking tour. A Father Raynal spoke with them and maintained that Anglican orders were not valid. This conversation provided a crucial point for Hopkins, who had always been drawn to the sacraments as the center of his spiritual life. If Anglican orders were not valid, then Anglican communion was a sham. Like Newman years before, once Hopkins had begun to suspect that the Church of England had no claim to direct institution by Christ, he turned to the Catholic Church as alone having preserved unbroken the Apostolic succession. On July 24, Hopkins told a friend he had decided to become a Catholic. A month later he wrote to Newman, met with him, and shortly afterwards was received into the Church. Addis, as soon as he heard of Hopkins's conversion, sought a priest and was received on the same day.

In June, 1867, Hopkins left Oxford where he had distinguished himself with a Double First in *literae humaniores*. The following spring, during an Easter retreat, he decided to become a Jesuit. In September, 1868, he began his novitiate at Manresa House, just outside London, but before doing so he burned a number of poems in manuscript and did not write poetry again until he composed "The Wreck of the Deutschland" in 1875.

When Hopkins again began to write, he expressed himself in a style so completely individual that it resembles that of no other nineteenth century poet. However, many of the elements of his mature style were present in the poems he had written at Oxford. Most notable among these elements are his use of alliteration and compound words, and his frequent substitution of irregular feet within the iambic pattern. In 1874, while instructing in rhetoric at Manresa House, he began to formulate ideas on prosody that were eventually to become a theory of meter he was to call "sprung rhythm."

Describing his practice, he wrote: "To speak shortly, it consists in scanning by accents or stresses alone, without any account of the number of syllables." A similar system of scansion had been used in Old English poetry and in reviving stress scansion Hopkins was returning to the earliest form of English poetry. Besides his ideas on prosody, an increased awareness of God's glory in His creation helped to shape his mature poetry. His journals abound in prose descriptions of particular natural objects and phenomena. The principle of individuality in all natural objects he called "inscape," and he found in the philosophy of Duns Scotus a justification for what he had more perceived than thought of.

In December of 1875, five Franciscan nuns, exiles from Germany, were drowned when their ship, the Deutschland, went aground on the coast of Kent and was battered to pieces. In the poet's own words, "I was affected by the account and, happening to say so to my rector, he said that he wished someone would write a poem on the subject. On this hint I set to work, and though my hand was out at first, produced one. I had long had haunting my ear the echo of a new rhythm which I now realized on paper."

The poem is the story of the Passion and Redemption working themselves out in the lives of men. It is the story of Christ calling the souls of men to Him through sacrifice and suffering. Into it Hopkins poured all the passionate intensity of his longing for the divine. The poem opens with complete certainty of rhythm and idea:

Thou mastering me
God! giver of breath and bread;
World's strand, sway of the sea;
Lord living and dead;
Thou hast bound bones and veins in me, fastened me flesh,
And after it almost unmade, what with dread,
Thy doing: and dost thou touch me afresh?
Over again I feel thy finger and find thee.

Not out of the bliss of heaven springs redemptive grace:

Not out of his bliss
Springs the stress felt
Nor first from heaven (and few know this)
Swings the stroke dealt—
Stroke and a stress that stars and storms deliver,
That guilt is hushed by, hearts are flushed by and melt—
But it rides time like riding a river
(And here the faithful waver, the faithless fable and miss).

Rather, grace comes from Christ's Incarnation and Passion:

It dates from day
Of his going in Galilee;
Warm-laid grave of a womb-life grey;
Manger, maidens knee;
The dense and the driven Passion, and frightful sweat;
Thence the discharge of it, there its swelling to be,
Though felt before, though in high flood yet—
What none would have known of it, only the heart, being hard at bay.

The poem ends with a series of meditations rising to the majesty of the last stanza:

Dame, at our door
Drowned, and among our shoals,
Remember us in the roads, the heaven-haven of the Reward:
Our King back, oh, upon English souls!
Let him easter in us, be a day-spring to the dimness of us, be a crimson-cresseted east,
More brightening her, rare-dear Britain, as his reign rolls,
Pride, rose, prince, hero of us, high-priest,
Our hearts' charity's hearth's fire, our thoughts' chivalry's throng's Lord.

This poem, with which Hopkins broke a seven-year silence, ranks with Miltons "Lycidas" and Wordsworth's "Immortality Ode" as one of the finest short poems in the language.

From 1875 to the time of his ordination two years later Hopkins produced poems full of joyous wonder at the world's beauty. In "The Starlight Night" he wrote:

Look at the stars! look, look up at the skies!
O look at all the fire-folk sitting in the air!
The bright boroughs, the circle-citadels there!
Down in dim woods the diamond delves! the elves'-eyes!
The grey lawns cold where gold, where quickgold lies!

In "Duns Scotus's Oxford" he captures the spell of the town which he addresses as "Towery city and branchy between towers/Cuckoo-echoing, bell-swarmed, lark-charmed, rook-racked, river-rounded." In "Hurrahing in Harvest" fall is a season "barbarous in beauty." In the naturalness of its opening lines "Spring" captures the essence of the season: "Nothing is so beautiful as spring/When weeds, in wheels, shoot long and lovely and lush." Most of the short poems he wrote during this period are sonnets, and in them Hopkins permanently broadened the scope of the English sonnet.

During the four years following his ordination Hopkins filled various posts, chiefly in Liverpool and Glasgow. To one who loved natural beauty so deeply these cities were depressing. However, his chief concern was with the souls of men, and he threw himself into his duties with determination. Thus, his poems of this period are less concerned with the revelation of God in nature than with the problems of fallen men trying to lead a life of grace in a far from happy world. In "God's Grandeur" he asks:

Why do men then now not reck his rod?
Generations have trod, have trod, have trod;
And all is seared with trade; bleared, smeared with toil;
And wears man's smudge and shares man's smell.

In January, 1884, Hopkins was elected to a fellowship at the Royal University of Ireland in Dublin. His official duties involved the teaching of Latin and Greek and the preparing and grading of examinations for degrees. He left England in poor health and with the feeling that he was not prepared for the position. In an effort to be completely fair Hopkins was overly scrupulous in his marking of examinations so that the grading of each paper was an ordeal. Furthermore, he felt that to satisfy the obligations of his position he ought to publish scholarly papers, and to that end did research on a number of projects, none of which he completed. He became depressed and lonely, and he suffered moments of nervous exhaustion. In 1884 and 1885 he wrote a series of seven sonnets, untitled and undated, in which he expressed the despair into which he had fallen. In No. 45 he complained:

I wake and feel the fell of dark, not day.
What hours, O what black hours we have spent
This night! What sights you, heart saw; ways you went!
And more must, in yet longer light's delay.
With witness I speak this. But where I say
Hours I mean years, mean life. And my lament
Is cries countless, cries like dead letters sent
To dearest him that lives alas! away.

What tortured him most was the feeling that God had abandoned him. In his dejection he saw in himself the lot of the damned: "The lost are like this, and their scourge to be / As I am mine, their sweating selves; but worse." In these so-called "terrible sonnets" the grief of the soul, lost in its search for God, has never been more intensely expressed. In the last years of his life Hopkins wrote little poetry. In 1889, however, the year of his death, he completed "That Nature is a Heraclitean Fire and of the Comfort of the Resurrection," an elaborately ordered and triumphant poem in which he expressed the Christian belief in immortality through Christ.

In a flash, at a trumpet crash,
I am all at once what Christ is, since he was what I am, and
This Jack, joke, poor potsherd, patch, matchwood, immortal diamond,
Is immortal diamond.

Hopkins died of typhoid on June 8, after an illness of seven weeks. He was forty-four. He had led an obscure, hidden life. The first edition of his poetry (1918) took ten years to sell out, but there have been four editions since 1930, and Hopkins is now considered one of the wellsprings of modern poetry.

D.M.R.

ART AND SCHOLASTICISM

Author: Jacques Maritain (1882-)
Type of work: Thomistic philosophy of art
First published: 1920

Principal Ideas Advanced

Aesthetics in the philosophy of Saint Thomas is a study of beauty as it is found in three areas: in the artist, in the nature of beauty itself, and in the problems of morality.

Art is a virtue of the mind, a habitus of the practical intellect, by which the artist implants his ideas into selected materials.

The individual experiences beauty, not merely as a sensory pleasure but also as an intellectual delight.

The sovereignty of the artist is fulfilled in Christian wisdom.

Jacques Maritain's *Art and Scholasticism,* a classic in the field of aesthetics, examines the theory of art implicit in the philosophy of Saint Thomas Aquinas. It is a pioneer study of the nature of beauty in Christian philosophy and reveals Maritain's brilliance as a leader of modern Thomistic philosophy.

According to Maritain, who follows Saint Thomas, beauty is a rapture dwelling essentially in all experience and is endlessly sought by man. As he matures, man seeks more deeply for a philosophy of beauty. Aesthetics, according to Saint Thomas, is precisely that, a study of beauty in the world. As Maritain indicates, that study begins within the nature of the artist himself.

In Thomistic philosophy, writes Maritain, the artist is not merely a sculptor of statues or a painter of canvases. Rather, he is any individual who habitually makes things well. For instance, the shipmaker who builds good ships is an artist, as is the logician who constructs good arguments. Since the creation of an art object involves direction of the mind, the artist's work is *intellectual* in nature. His artistic labors are not of a speculative or abstract kind; they are not the labors of an Einstein or an Aristotle. Yet they are genuinely intellectual throughout the creative process from the initial inspiration, through the nurturing contemplations, and even into the solutions of practical artistic problems. Each stage of creativity makes its unique intellectual demands. Maritain stresses this mental nature in repeating the classic definition of art as "a virtue of the practical intellect."

The word "art" thus signifies a quality of individual greatness, a special kind of habit man has acquired through great effort. Art is, in fact, an inner spiritual improvement, a metaphysical increase in intellectual power whereby the artist is able to engender with vision and optimum efficiency. However, this spiritual quality is not precisely a habit, insofar as the word describes a repetition of routine activity, a semiconscious performance, but, rather, a "habitus"; that is, a fully conscious creative power within the individual. *Habitus,* thus, indicates the intellectual strength with which the artist is able to bring all his powers to bear upon the production of a great work. While, for example, habit suggests the routine activity one might observe in an elevator, *habitus* denotes the concentrated spiritual force one would find in a Michelangelo.

Standing in the Louvre and gazing

upward at the soaring "Winged Victory," a perceptive soul is seized with an experience of arresting joy and is suffused with pleasure, transfixed with the beauty that floods his being. A statue weighing tons, the "Winged Victory" seems to spring from the earth by its buoyant spirit, and the soul of man is pleased to behold it.

The very meaning of beauty is expressed in Saint Thomas's familiar phrase, "that which being seen, pleases." In contemplating a beautiful object, a person finds that his senses are filled with pleasure simply in beholding the object. Simultaneously, the intellect overflows with delight in a fluid preconceptual illumination. Maritain describes this aesthetic awareness as a "delight in knowing," an experience which is not simply sensory or emotional but also intellectual in character, a perception flooding the whole being. In thus perceiving beauty, man's intellect enters a dimension of reality which leaves the world of science and philosophy far behind. This perception of beauty, writes Maritain, is literally the winged victory of the soul.

By considering only the reaction of the beholder, some people have proclaimed beauty to be merely subjective in character. They would suggest that "beauty is in the eye of the beholder," thus subscribing to the ancient Pythagorean dictum that man is the measure of all things. On the other hand, Maritain points out, beauty must have an objective foundation, since it is based in the object of the intellect; namely, *being* outside the mind. Since beauty flows from being to the observer, it is objective in source; its roots lie in the reality of the outside world.

Three major qualities are discerned in the beautiful object, Maritain claims, continuing to follow Thomas. First, the spectator is enraptured because of the "integrity" or completeness of an object or being. Beauty is diminished whenever integrity is violated; the overall beauty of the "Venus de Milo" is lessened because of the statue's missing arms. The second quality is proportion or order within the parts; the fitting relationship of one part of the work to another, the *design* which is proper to the object. Beauty would be lacking in a painting composed of mere amorphous splotches evincing no intelligible pattern. "Clarity," beauty's third quality, bespeaks the brilliance or attractiveness of the object. For example, Leonardo da Vinci's "Virgin of the Rocks" projects a dramatic clarity which intensifies the enjoyment of the observer. On the other hand, clarity is lacking in a drab lackluster object; such an art work is not truly pleasing and, consequently, it is not beautiful.

Enamored of beauty, ancient philosophers rejoiced in thinking of the inner source of beauty as *splendor*. This idea, Maritain agrees, was correct up to a point, for the three characteristics of integrity, proportion, and clarity are seated within the heart of being. Certainly one may describe that inner throne as splendor. However, to fix more precisely the nature of that splendor, writes Maritain, one must penetrate deeply into the nature of that being of which it is the center. Accordingly, one discovers that root-principle which, when combined with matter, confers essential structure. It is the principle of *form*, the ultimate inner ground of both nature and the splendor which nature manifests. Thus, Maritain is able to demonstrate that the splendor of beauty is not a splendor of intelligibility or of order, but a *splendor of form.* Rodin's "The Thinker," for example, exhibits this splendor by recreating the impact of muscular tension surging from the inner form of the human body.

It thus becomes evident, Maritain claims, that one may approach the nature of beauty on several levels within Thomistic philosophy. Considered from the viewpoint of the observer, beauty is "that which being seen, pleases." On the other hand, when beauty is sought in external characteristics, it consists in the integrity, proportion, and clarity of the object. Lastly, one may indicate the inner causal source of beauty in the principle of form. In this manner Thomistic philosophy accounts for the finite aspects of beauty.

Beauty also presents infinite aspects. Saint Thomas, as a theologian, was well aware that finite beauty is a created beauty; it is a form impressed on matter by the infinite Artist who is, as Aristotle remarked, the Form of Forms. Hence, under myriad earthly appearances, finite beauty is a formal imaging of God, a finite utterance of the Divine Poet. Naturally, individual instances of beauty will differ one from another, for beauty is not a univocal perfection; it is not one identical reality somehow injected into various beings. On the other hand, neither is it something completely different, equivocally diverse and unique in each case. Rather, when one compares various instances of beauty, its analogous character comes to light and one begins to perceive similarities amid differences. In both the statue "David" of Michelangelo and a High Mass there is a mutual declaration of beauty. Each manifests its own proper proportion, integrity, and clarity yet in a manner befitting its own special nature. The "David," a being vibrant with energy, is simply different from the joyous expression of worship in the High Mass. Yet the solemn beauty of the latter is reminiscent of the young king. Maritain brings this similarity to mind when he describes the High Mass as "a dance in slow motion before the Ark of the Covenant." Because beauty is an analogous perfection, the finite things of beauty are created images of the divine analogue of beauty, the Poet of Infinity. Because He is, they are. Because He is Beauty itself, they are beautiful in themselves. Small wonder that Maritain gives utterance to the expression, "Poetry, my God it is Thou."

Art, like a jealous king, tolerates no interference, writes Maritain. A challenge to the sovereignty of art is a threat to its freedom. Yet the sovereignty of art seems to be endangered when morality pronounces some art works to be good for man, others to be harmful. Bristling at this invasion, the artist insists that he be free to follow the rules of art in order to be a true artist. Art, in his eyes, *is* for art's sake, and only by adhering to the rules of art is he able to safeguard its purity. Those external forces which would have him subordinate his art to the dictates of morality would simultaneously jeopardize his freedom and destroy his art.

Maritain contends that to measure these counterclaims between art and prudence it becomes necessary to explore the rules of art and their relation to the artist. Basically, the rules of art are the major conceptions that flow from the very process of art itself, from the process of forming matter according to a mental vision. In such a process both man and materials operate in certain ways, obeying physical and philosophical laws. Scholastic philosophy, which regards man as a reasoning creature, holds that human reason is the dominating force in the artistic process.

The rules of art, on the other hand, are not the separate techniques by which one guides the brush and the colors. Nor do they consist in mechanical innovations. Consequently, Michelangelo's device for fixing a candle in his hat so that he could see where his chisel struck as he worked late at night cannot be taken as an example of the following of the rules of art, for these rules are the larger conceptions, the governing laws by which the intellect regulates the process of bringing a work to fruition.

A basically inhuman force is lurking in the conception of the rules of art, says Maritain. These rules take precedence over the artist himself, working not for him, but for the perfection of the art object itself. They subject the artist to nonhuman criteria which demand that he sacrifice himself to meet the inexorable demands of the product to be made. Everything in his life, his thoughts, his plans, his labors, and his relations with his family and the outside world must be subordinated to the rules of art. The price is subservience but the guarantee is freedom, because the artist who obeys these rules sets himself free to seek greatness in his work.

It naturally follows, writes Maritain, that anything which seeks to control the artist, any external authority such as moral prudence, threatens the true freedom of the artist. How, then, is the tension between art and prudence to be reconciled? One procedure consists in delineating the proper field of each virtue. Another recognizes that while the surrender of one field to another would be ruinous, there is the possibility that both might recognize the demands of a higher principle of order. Thus, for example, one might consider the differences that arose between disciples of Christ; it is evident that Saint Peter did not consider himself subject to Saint Paul, yet both were willing servants of one Master.

In discussing the proper fields of these virtues, Maritain suggests that both art and prudence seek values through the human act; art aims at aesthetic and creative values while prudence is directed toward moral content. Art deals with beauty, an object of transcendental value, and in this respect has a marked superiority over prudence.

A more important consideration, however, rests in the nature of the higher principle which Thomistic philosophy designates as the ultimate principle in terms of which both art and prudence are ordered. This higher principle is wisdom—*sapientia*. Wisdom judges other disciplines and perfects the intellect in its understanding of ultimate causes. Wisdom is thus intrinsically superior to both art and prudence, being related to prudence as a king to his servant, and related to art as a higher kind of intellectual virtue. For the Christian there is a striking parallel here between the relation of wisdom to art and prudence, and the relation of Christ to His disciples. In the case of Christ, as in the case of wisdom, each is a principle which orders inferiors to a greater goal. Further, each is a principle in which the inferiors do not lose individuality but gain greater perfection.

Lack of wisdom is manifest in the

artist who merely carries out his commissions without regard for the purpose of the work in its entirety. On the other hand, the master artist who also possesses wisdom has a special comprehension of the order and purpose of his work. He is not only a wise artist but also a wise man. In the words of Jacques Maritain: "Thus Wisdom, placed as it is at the point of view of God, which equally commands the spheres of doing and making, can alone perfecty reconcile Art and Prudence."

Thus, Maritain concludes, a reconciliation of the problems of art and prudence can be effected in the person of the artist who, while devoted to the service of beauty, yet recognizes the guiding touch of wisdom. In this way the individual artist, reaching out to grasp the higher wisdom, attains both personal beauty and true dignity.

H.D.

THE INTELLECTUAL LIFE

Author: Antonin Gilbert Sertillanges, O.P. (1863-1948)
Type of work: Speculative and practical theology
First published: 1920

Principal Ideas Advanced

The intellectual life requires the organization not only of one's own interior life, but also of one's life in relation to others.

An intellectual vocation is similar to all vocations in that it is a sacred call from God, a call which men will be able to hear only by turning themselves inward to plumb the depths of their own souls where God's providence and gifts are linked up with natural liking and spontaneous impulse.

Study and devotion to the intellectual life are of value as means of extending and enriching human life, but the full richness and variety of human life must not be sacrificed to the intellectual life.

Antonin Gilbert Sertillanges's *The Intellectual Life: Its Spirit, Conditions, Methods,* which appeared in France in 1920 under the title *La vie intellectuelle,* combines a theoretical interest in describing the nature and character of the intellectual life with practical advice for the intellectual concerning the organization of his life and the spirit with which he should pursue his vocation. The book is permeated with the author's recognition of the intimate union existing between man and God. Seen in a Christian perspective, every man is a unique and incommunicable individual who has been given a sacred role which he alone can fill. The intellectual must never lose sight of the fact that Jesus Christ needs his mind to carry out His work on earth.

A recognition of this point, says the author, should strengthen the intellectual in those moments of frustration when, no matter how hard he tries, he cannot grasp the full truth of a situation, or having grasped it, cannot communicate it adequately. For his faith tells him that God asks a man to give only that which is in his power. Having done his best, he can leave the rest to God, confident that Divine Providence will not fail. Such faith not only helps one to persevere in the face of inevitable shortcomings, difficulties, and failures, but also to enjoy the very activity of study for its own sake.

In so far as the intellectual deals with the fragmentary truths of this world, he is engaged in an indirect communication with God, who is the ultimate Truth, manifesting Himself in the fragmentary truths of nature and of man. According to Sertillanges, the indirect communication with God which is the activity of study must make way at the proper time for prayer and recollection, for reading of the Scriptures, in a word, for man's more direct intercourse with God. After this more direct communication with the Divine, the intellectual can return to his study of the most trifling thing with the feeling that he is engulfed in the infinite eternity of the Infinite Being. Moreover, this relationship between finite truths and God points to the fact that mystery is an essential feature of the human condition. A human truth that is without mystery is a dead truth or, at best, an imitation of a real truth. Only in God does the living Truth exist without mystery.

The notion of a vocation as a sacred call from God to a unique individual to perform a unique task fits in with Sertillanges's emphasis on the central role of the individual in man's quest for truth. He maintains that a social life which includes receptions, visits involving further social obligations, and other features of an artificial life, is fatal to a life of study: "Solitude enables you to make contact with yourself, a necessity if you want to realize yourself—not to repeat like a parrot a few acquired formulas, but to be the prophet of God within you who speaks a unique language to each man." It is this solitude that must be protected.

Such solitude is not one that completely isolates a man from his fellow man and from the world. It is rather a solitude enriched by the individual's communication with his fellow man and with nature. There is a type of society that disperses one's spirit, scatters one's life, and blinds a man to the truth which is in him and to his intimate union with God. It is this type of society that is fatal to the intellectual life. However, there are other social relationships which nourish and deepen the individual soul and which help a man to find himself and the truth that is in him. This is the type of society which man must cultivate.

Sertillanges's concern with the importance of the intellectual's self-possession is also at work in his caution against an excessive devotion to reading. He presents two reasons for this position. First, he points out that there is much that is written that is not worth reading. The second and more profound reason behind this advice lies in Sertillanges's concern that a man may become so committed to reading that he becomes a victim of what he reads rather than a master of it. Again, the concern here is that a man not lose sight of the truth that is in him. The individual must avoid the development of a habit in which he will tend to prefer a familiarity with the thoughts of others to his own intellectual efforts.

When reading, Sertillanges says, the intellectual must strike a proper balance between passivity and activity. He must be passive in the sense that he must allow the writer's thoughts to sink into him. However, he must also react to the writer's work, for learning from another is not simply the acceptance of ideas from another, but consists also in the learner's personal reaction to these ideas. Sertillanges summarizes his views on this matter very nicely in the following statement: "The source of knowledge is not in books, it is in reality, and in our thought. Books are signposts; the road is older, and no one can make the journey to truth for us." A book is a help or stimulant to the reader's own thought; it should not be taken as a substitute for such thought.

Sertillanges also maintains that our primary interest in dealing with the conflicting and apparently contradictory views that are encountered in reading should be to discover the unity that underlies the differences and contrasts. This does not mean that we should simply ignore differences, nor does it mean that criticism and distinction have no place in an intellectual vocation. These activities are necessary, but they are necessary as means whereby the individual mind may come to a unified vision of reality. Those intellectuals whose interest is limited to distinguishing and separating various positions from one another are characterized by Sertillanges as intellectual gossips.

The importance of searching for a unified truth applies also to the intellectual's dealings with positions that he sees as being erroneous. The intellectual must certainly be interested in avoiding error and must point out errors when he finds them. However, such activities are not the end of his work. They are aids to the end of discovering the truth. To uncover the truth hidden in certain misinterpretations is much more fruitful than to be forever criticizing positions.

In discussing the question of the time which the intellectual should give to his work, Sertillanges maintains that study is similar to prayer in that both can permeate every moment of our lives, since both are essentially a desire, a state of being tending toward truth and open to communion with God. The desire that is study is not a constant worry and anxiety about learning. It is rather a habit of the mind, a second nature, as it were, nurtured and developed by discipline. Truth is everywhere. The intellectual must make study so much a part of his very being that he is always ready to receive and to see this truth not only in his study, but also in all his worldly contacts.

Sertillanges is aware of the fact that man, no matter what his vocation, must rest from his labors. He holds that one of the best ways to gain relaxation is so to balance one's work that a less tiring, but necessary, activity is able to afford relaxation from the more strenuous and demanding activities of the intellectual life. For example, one may relax from the demands of creative writing by sorting papers, perusing book catalogs, classifying manuscripts, tidying up one's study and books. This type of relaxation possesses a double value in that it not only avoids overstrain, but also serves to protect the moments of more intensive work from unnecessary distraction.

In addition to this sort of relative

rest from intellectual endeavors, man also requires a more complete rest, a rest which allows him to enrich other facets of his human reality and to enter into a communion with nature, his fellow man, and God which differs from that union with them which he may achieve in his study. The type of rest which Sertillanges has in mind is not to be equated with dissipation: "Rest is a return to our origins: the origins of life, of strength, of inspiration; it is a retempering." To the questions concerning the specific activities that suit this conception of rest and the specific amount of time that is to be given over to rest, Sertillanges answers with the admonition, "Know yourself, and proportion things accordingly." Whereas one man may find his rest in music, another may find it in conversation with friends or in walking through green fields. In trying to determine the proper amount of time to be given to rest, each man must try to find for himself that balance between rest and work which preserves the maximum momentum of a life of work with the minimum of fatigue.

Sertillanges's concern with achieving a proper balance between extremes is also evident in his treatment of the intellectual's field of work. Since all knowledge is interconnected and since it is impossible to know one field without some knowledge of its relations to others, the intellectual must work toward achieving a breadth of vision in his work. Moreover, any branch of study cultivated by itself and to the exclusion of all others is dangerous to the health and development of the human mind. For example, an exclusive pursuit of mathematics accustoms the mind to a univocal rigor that is not to be found in other sciences or in the concrete complexities of life. An exclusive concern with philosophy and theology inflates a man, making him a victim of magisterial pride. In short, although specialization is methodologically justified, it should never become the spirit that permeates our work.

Having thus presented his case in favor of widening and broadening our intellectual horizons, Sertillanges points out that breadth of vision is not an end in itself, but is rather a means to achieving a depth of vision into truth. A man must explore many areas in order to discover that area to which he is most suited. He must travel many paths in order to discover that task which Providence has marked out for him personally. Having discovered that task, the individual must center all his work on discovering the full depth and richness of truth that is hidden in it. This does not mean that once a man has discovered his area of concentration he must give up the study of other areas. It means simply that these other areas are to be given the time and energy commensurate with their secondary status, and they should be viewed in terms of the contribution which they can make to the major area of investigation. We must isolate in order to penetrate more deeply, and we must relate in order to understand more completely.

Finally, Sertillanges emphasizes the importance of writing and of creative effort in the life of an intellectual. Learning and preparation for the intellectual life are not wholly separate from the productive moments in this life. For writing helps to deepen, clarify, and organize the knowledge which one may possess. The intellectual grows by expressing himself. "Silence is a diminution of personality," Sertillanges writes. Hence, Sertillanges advises the intellectual to publish as soon as he can. Publication brings the joy of fruition to one's work. Deserved praise of one's work will stimulate him, while criticism will test him. Furthermore, by publishing, the intellectual avoids the dangers of stagnation inherent in perpetual silence.

Sertillanges's book was immensely popular in France during the 1920's and 1930's. It also seems to have enjoyed some popularity in American Catholic circles. It is unfortunate that it does not appear to be widely read today. For there is much in it, both in the way of theoretical description and practical advice, that is of value to any student or person embarking on an intellectual career, regardless of his religious commitment.

V.C.P.

THE POEMS OF ALICE MEYNELL

Author: Alice Meynell (1847-1922)
Type of work: Religious poetry
First published: 1875-1923; 1940

Principal Ideas Advanced

The poet attempts to celebrate the wonders of God's creation, but the final knowledge of even the simplest things will come only when the poet is with God.

Death and suffering are continuous with the joy and unfolding of life; sorrow purifies and ennobles man.

One senses the Real Presence through the transforming power which affects each individual person.

Alice Thompson Meynell was part of the Catholic Literary Revival which brought a new spirit of religious poetry to the nineteenth century, a spirit which provided a vigorous and confident answer to the skepticism and cynicism which marked the poetry of such writers as James Thomson and A. E. Housman. Alice Meynell was converted to Roman Catholicism in 1872, and her subsequent poetry is important as an expression of her religious sentiments. Together with Francis Thompson, whom she and her husband (Wilfrid Meynell) befriended, Gerard Manley Hopkins, Ernest Dowson, and Lionel Johnson, Mrs. Meynell contributed significantly to the body of enduring religious poetry.

The work of Alice Meynell is particularly interesting because it includes poetry *about* poetry, although it is certainly not confined to such self-conscious examination. Through a reading of such poems as "To Any Poet," "Pygmalion: The Poet to His Poetry," "The Day to the Night: The Poet Sings to His Poet," and "The Spring to the Summer: The Poet Sings to His Poet," one may gain certain insights into the problem which confronts the literary artisan who seeks to communicate religious values through poetry. (These poems are part of the first collection of Mrs. Meynell's poetry, *Preludes,* published in 1875; the other volumes are *Poems,* 1893; *Other Poems,* 1896; *Later Poems,* 1902; *Collected Poems,* 1913; *Ten Poems,* 1915; *A Father of Women, and Other Poems,* 1917; *Last Poems,* 1923; and *The Poems of Alice Meynell,* 1940, which contains four poems not previously collected and five poems not previously printed.)

"To Any Poet" expresses the difficulty and even despair which the poet feels in attempting to convey the sense and truth of life. "All the earth's wild creatures fly thee," says the poet to "any" poet; "Dumbly they defy thee;/ There is something they deny thee." After death, however, the poet will be reconciled with the life that flees from him, and he shall then know what now he vainly seeks: "Then the truth all creatures tell,/ And His will Whom thou entreatest/ Shall absorb thee; there shall dwell/ Silence, the completest/ Of thy poems, last and sweetest."

"Pygmalion" adapts the imagery of the myth to the poet's particular situation. The poet has made the poem, but it now has a life of its own, and there is a certain mystery about what it will say. The poet is proud of her accomplishment; at the same time she knows that she says more as poet than she can realize intellectually: "God knows. I chiselled each cold limb/ With loyal pain. He has given my mind/ Less light than my true hand; but dim/ Is life. I wait all I shall find,/ And all that I shall know, in Him."

When Alice Meynell writes of nature, love, death, friendship, and the aspirations of the poet, she fills her poems with clear imagery delicately cadenced to her mood. In "Parted," for example, she balances her expression of loss with her awareness of the continuity of life: "Although my life is left so dim,/ The morning crowns the mountain-rim;/ Joy is not gone from summer skies,/ Nor innocence from children's eyes,/ And all these things are parts of him."

True to the Wordsworthian dictum that the office of the poet is to "wipe away the veil of familiarity," Alice Meynell, observing with the eye of the poet, enables the reader to *see* what he does not see; that is, she opens the reader's eyes to the beauty, the implications, the significance of the world about him. She had not only this faculty of genuine perception but also the power to capture with a phrase the most elusive terms of thought.

"The Unknown God," for example, is no mere mechanical exercise, no mere display of metrical virtuosity with a touch of religious fervor. It is, rather, a fervent, sincere effusion of a poet to whom the Real Presence is most *real.* She tells of one who "went up/ And knelt before the Paten and the Cup,/ Received the Lord, returned in peace, and prayed/ Close to my side. . . ." She knows the Lord through him, the stranger, who kneels beside her; she confesses Him "here,/ Alive within this life; I know Thee near/ Within this lonely conscience. . . ."

Those who suppose that Alice Meynell is but another female poet, counterfeiting the intellectual's appreciation of the Divine, while indulging herself in sentiment, should turn to her searching poem, "The Two Questions," in which the conventional problem of evil is given a radical and metaphysical twist. She reports the complaint of one who declares that this is "a riddling world" and adds: "If pangs must be, would God that they were sent/ To the impure, the cruel, and passed aside/ The holy innocent!" But she, the poet, cries, ". . . Ah no, no, no!/ Not the clean heart transpierced; not tears that fall/ For a child's agony; nor a martyr's woe;/ Not these, not these appal." Not motherhood and its distress, not old age, "not the vile heritage/ Of sin's disease in saints;/ Not these defeat the mind./ For great is that abjection, and august/ That irony. Submissive we shall find/ A splendour in that dust." It is not these, the suffering which strengthens virtue and chastens the pride of the saintly, that "puzzle the will"; it is "the unjust stricken . . . the merited scourge . . . the liar in his snares. . . ." That is, it is the punishment of those who have sinned, the suffering that as a matter of fact sometimes visits "the impure, the cruel," that disturbs the poet and leads her to conclude: "The cowardice of my judgement sees, aghast,/ The flail, the chaff, the tares." It is justice, not mercy, that puzzles the will.

Other notable poems in which Alice Meynell expresses her highly individualized awareness of the Divine, the Real Presence, the Mystical Body, the Christ Child, are "Christ in the Universe" (". . . These abide:/ The signal to a maid, the human birth,/ The lesson, and the young Man crucified . . ."), "A General Communion" (". . . The devout people, moved, intent, elate,/ And the devoted Lord . . ."), "Unto Us a Son Is Given" ("Given, not lent,/and not withdrawn —once sent,/ This Infant of mankind, this One,/ Is still the little welcome Son . . ."), and " 'I Am the Way' " ("Thou art the Way./ Hadst Thou been nothing but the goal,/ I cannot say/ If thou hadst ever met my soul . . .").

Alice Meynell, like Wordsworth, was inspired by even the common and simple aspects of nature. This characteristic is but one facet of the religious romanticism which lies at the heart of her poetry, poetry which, paradoxically, is classical in its compactness and disciplined clarity. In several of his poems Wordsworth acknowledged his indebtedness to the unpretentious daisy, which was for him a source of consolation and edification; in her poem "To a Daisy," Alice Meynell also dwells on the eternal implications she finds in the flower. She writes, in part, "Slight as thou are, thou art enough to hide/ Like all created things, secrets from me,/ And stand a barrier to eternity." After death, however, the poet "from a poet's side shall read his book./ O daisy mine, what will it be to look/ From God's side even of such a simple thing?"

Thus, with these lines we learn that God was her Poet, that she hoped, through Him, to know what in this life she could only sense and sing through poetry. But as she herself acknowledged, although He gave her mind "Less light than my true hand . . ./ I wait all I shall find,/ And all that I shall know, in Him." Until one can, with her, read His book, one can at least, through her poetry, know the light which was given to her "true hand."

THE SPIRIT OF CATHOLICISM

Author: Karl Adam (1876-)
Type of work: Apologetics
First published: 1924

Principal Ideas Advanced

The goal of religion is the purification and sanctification of the inward man, with constant reference to the outward world of men and nature in which he functions.

God saves men in union with one another and with the Person of Christ, forming a single Mystical Body in which men reveal God's love and truth to one another.

The Church, conservative and united in doctrinal essentials, incorporates the truths men have perceived and tested in every age and place.

In *The Spirit of Catholicism* Karl Adam identifies modern man's need for two basic fulfillments: the social and the individual. The former is found in the ancient Western unity of the Mystical Body of Christ, through whose transcendental character men give themselves to, and are given, God. The fulfillment of the individual is ultimately to be won through sacramental union of the soul with God, independent of the personal merit or emotions of priest or bishop. In such a union, a man gains a sacred view of creation, time, and personality, as well as of his own unique position in the economy of the created universe. The assent of the individual, in faith and love, is as necessary to his own salvation as was the Blessed Virgin's consent to the Savior's birth. Yet belief in the unity of mankind through the Fall of the first man and its redemption through becoming one with the Risen Man is essential also. Men exist not merely as one family or as individuals united one by one to a God isolated from the whole of His creation, but "as one man." The purpose of Christ was clearly this: "That they all may be one, as thou, Father, in me, and I in thee." From the moment of the Incarnation, the Church existed as the One Man, who was Himself the kingdom He was later to proclaim. In the community experience of Pentecost the Church received the fullness of authority and power to incorporate men into herself as into Christ.

The intention of Christ was not to destroy the ancient Jewish faith, but to perfect and purify it, transforming it by a new universal law of love of God and neighbor. Of the law of Moses and the obedience men owed such a law, Christ said: "All things, therefore, that they [the Scribes and Pharisees] command you, observe and do. But do not act according to their works; for they talk but do nothing" (Matthew 23:3). He was not so much concerned to tear down the human institutions that bind men together in their worship of God, as he was to transform law and ritual by interior charity, without which the institutions are meaningless. Christ Himself founded the society of the Twelve, and the Apostles regarded this institution as so sacred a commission for the future that they at once elected a successor to fill the vacancy left by Judas. Adam warns against "the error of defining our Lord's teaching exclusively in terms of its novel elements," lest we endanger the firm historical and psychological continuity of Christianity, based as it is on the ancient form of monotheism and the search of all men for redemption in this world and the next. Because man is body and soul, he is led by visible things to the invisible; he is compelled to sanctify society and nature, as well as his own soul. In bringing Himself to men through other men, Christ affirms the need for the community of mankind to embody outwardly the very love and unity which bind each soul in the Church to God Himself. Individual commitment to Christ finds its complement, its fulfillment, in the fraternal love expressed in the social communion of the visible Church.

To conform perfectly to the intention of Christ, the Church must press toward the goal of holiness and universality, Adam writes. The Church must never be merely local or national, identified with one class or culture, for the Church belongs to all mankind and adapts herself to the legitimate rites in which each race searches out and appropriates the holy. Thus, the Church has developed "organically," not by successive veneers of alien ornament. The Church must never restrict herself to the forms and concepts of any age, even one hallowed by the historical evocations of the primitive Church or the imperial grandeur of the old Roman order. The New Testament itself is only a glimpse of the Christian life at one time in its history. Before the New Testament existed as a book, the Church had spread from one end of the known world to the other, unified in doctrine, tradition, and loyalty to Peter's successor in Rome. Now, as well as at Pentecost, the living Church is dynamically informed by the action of the Holy Spirit. Lacking that reverenced and preserved, cannot be Spirit, the letter of the Law, however interpreted without strife, division, and doctrinal confusion. Now, as in the beginning, it is the Holy Spirit, speaking through the apostolic Church, who seals us to Christ, not the words of the inspired document which was meant to nourish faith but not to create it.

The Church must fulfill both her sacramental and her educational or preaching functions if she is to unite men while sanctifying them. In the sacraments, God's grace is guaranteed to men, and through the preaching of the Gospel men are taught to know and love God. The Incarnation is the source of the Church's authority and message; it is a prototype of the union of God with His creation. God is revealed not in remote and solitary grandeur, but in the fullness of His Son's Humanity. It is God whom we see and love in the Blessed Virgin, in all the saints, and elsewhere in His creation. Out of His love for men, God gives each of them a role in his own salvation and in the salvation of his brethren. Always "there remains a human strand in the divine robe of our salvation, the 'be it done unto me' of Mary." The dignity and faith of the *Fiat* echoes in every prayer of one member of Christ's Body for another and in every individual act of will in response to divine grace.

The sacramental view of religion

involves a real transcendance of profane time. Adam claims that the liturgy of the Church's year captures the rhythm of human, historical, and universally meaningful event, transfiguring it in the light of the eternal: "The whole history of redemption, beginning in Advent with the hopes of patriarchs and prophets, and passing through the Crib and the Cross to the alleluia of Easter and the mighty wind of Pentecost" enriches everyday life with "new impressions, insights and powers." During the Passion of Calvary, the veil between the temporal and the eternal was torn in two, as it is for the Catholic at the Sacrifice of the Mass. The Church, which was present at the Last Supper and at the foot of the Cross, "eliminates time . . . and brings me into the closest historical relation to Jesus," writes Adam. As religious man has always sought to do, the Catholic is able to rise beyond the limitations of time, space, and personality to an eternal plane, transcending history without violating it, in a living communion with a living God, unmediated by the virtue of priest or Scriptual letter.

The two aspects of human life, the communal and the individual, cannot be separated in actuality as they are in theory. They blend most dramatically in the meeting of authority with conscience. An authority originating in Christ and delegated to the Apostles can never be purely democratic, Adam insists; it cannot merely reflect the consensus of the religious community at any given time. "It is God, and not man, who is the author of natural and supernatural reality," the author writes. Yet the faith of the community is the fruitful ground from which spring both new apostles and new testimonies to the life of grace. For the Catholic, the laws of the Church reflect the unchanging laws of God; consequently, they are not a burden but a life-giving revelation of our responsibility within the divine and human order of things. Only by an act of individual will can a man's conscience affirm such a revelation, and thus make the laws its own. No mere institution can force this affirmation upon an individual; it remains his right to commit his conscience where he wills, but with this act of obedience to the total vision of reality presented to him by Christ, the believer begins his spiritual life.

Since the Church is concerned to protect and encourage the communion of man with other men and with nature, she is also committed to the sanctification of the inward man in communion with God. In order to fulfill this duty, the Church must respect the integrity of human personality, allowing no cleavage between faith and reason, faith and works, or faith and art. Catholicism "teaches us not to destroy nature but to transfigure it," using for the Kingdom of God every human skill and talent. It is the whole man, not merely the rational or the intuitive self, who encounters God in the sacraments and in prayer.

There are countless ways in which Christ may be formed in the individual soul; and, Adam claims, the Church's calendar of saints gives evidence of that variety. The aim of all the Church's teaching and all her sacraments is to form in us "another Christ," "a new life in God"; yet this is done not in violence to the individual human personality, but in accord with the basic principles of its existence: freedom of will and dependence for life upon God. God does not approach us from without, as an intruder, but from the depths of our being and consciousness: "The new life rises out of this divine source within us which yet is not ourselves. It sets free all the good powers of the soul. I obtain a new desire . . . I am filled anew with God."

As God is reflected by His saints in an infinite variety, so the Church, as Christ's Mystical Body, is formed of many members, each with his specific role and virtue. Thus, there is no attempt made in the Catholic Church to standardize the pattern of perfection for all believers: they are not all to embrace poverty, not all to serve as priests, not all to have families, not all to be contemplative mystics, and not all to work at the world's business or on the world's terms. In service and charity to one another, the members of the Church fulfill their unique natures, seeing Christ in one another and in the entire Body. They do not expect the same sanctity in every member nor do they judge one another when sanctity is not apparent. "The Church is not only a gift to the faithful, but also a task for them," Adam writes. The Catholic does not expect that the Church while still in the world will be a field of wheat without tares. Instead, he accepts the Church as it comes to him through the hands of other men in other centuries, a work dynamically in process, rich with creative and constructive possibilities. A man is not made perfect with his initial act of faith, nor was the Church's form and work completed by the wind of Pentecost. The corporate and the individual life of grace demand, Adam concludes, "a compound of divinity and humanity," wherein the human personality is perpetually renewed and deepened by contact with the divine.

B.J.R.

ST. FRANCIS OF ASSISI

Author: Gilbert Keith Chesterton (1874-1936)
Type of work: Hagiography
First published: 1924

Principal Ideas Advanced

To understand Francis the Saint it is necessary to understand Francis the Man.

The author's approach will be to study the figure of St. Francis from the viewpoint of an outsider looking in, that is, from a realistic review of Francis of Assisi in relation to his times, to other men, and to God.

St. Francis emerges from this analysis as a true mystic and ascetic, joyous and serene in the somewhat eccentric pursuit of his vocation.

Chesterton defines "The Problem of St. Francis" (as he entitles the first chapter of *St. Francis of Assisi*) as the difficulty encountered by the modern writer in attempting to present a true picture of the saint which is both factual and real, as well as enlightened. To achieve this end, the writer cannot approach the subject from a strictly humanitarian aspect, for the motivating force of Francis's love for humanity was its Creator; nor can the writer veer too far in the opposite direction of defiant devotionalism, in which religion is so stressed that it would "take a saint to know a saint," so to speak, leaving the true joy that was the core of Saint Francis's asceticism an unintelligible abstraction to the modern reader. Chesterton proposes to avoid these two stumbling blocks by making his interpretation that of a modern enquirer already interested in and an admirer of Saint Francis, possessed of a certain amount of religious enlightenment which, in turn, enables him to evaluate the psychological aspect of Francis's extraordinary sanctity with more validity than previous biographers limited by their rationalistic blind spots; Chesterton cites Renan and Matthew Arnold, particularly. Chesterton argues that the first step toward the understanding of Saint Francis is to take the saint, as he took himself, literally.

When Francis called himself a troubadour and his brotherhood the *Jongleurs de Dieu,* he meant these terms in their truest sense; for a troubadour was first of all a lover, and Francis was so fired with the love of God that he loved all creatures for God's own sake; secondly, a troubadour was a wandering minstrel who sang the praises of his love throughout the countryside, and Francis and his band wandered not only from town to town preaching the love of God, but across seas and mountains as well. Clowns, buffoons, fools they seemed to many at first, in their ragged peasant costume, suffering insults and rebuffs with joy. Tumblers they truly were, for they turned values topsy-turvy; they loved all creatures with immediate personal involvement, and they preached in the clothes of poverty to enforce their message of detachment. "The reader cannot even begin to see the sense of a story that may well seem to him a very wild one," writes Chesterton, "until he understands that to this great mystic his religion was not a thing like a theory but a thing like a love-affair."

Born in the thirteenth century, Francis had come into a world which had made the transition from the long sleep which history has termed the Dark Ages to the fresh flowering of culture of the later Middle Ages. Chesterton contends that it is misleading to think of the Dark Ages as a useless period of superstition, enslavement, and suppression; it is better to think of it as a period of spiritual and intellectual purgation. The end of the Dark Ages came when civilization cleansed itself of the impurities of naturalism.

The worship of nature, first by the Greeks and eventually by the Romans, inevitably turned into a perversion *against* nature. Natural man as the measure of all things turned potential magnificence into effeminization. In Rome the desire for religious fulfillment turned the imagination towards gods who inhabited all forms of nature. When these gods became like men in their passions, especially in their sexual appetities, which can never be treated on the same level as the other natural appetites (for "When sex ceases to be a servant it becomes a tyrant."), all innocence in nature gave way to defilement. Neither heaven nor earth was left to the pagans, for they had ruined both. Their natural religion obscured the skies, the flowers, and the birds with erotic symbols and lascivious gods; thus, the pagans were forced to turn to supernatural religion.

After a period of expiation, medieval man emerged childlike, rude, and unlearned, but above all, *clean.* The rigid penitential period and the monastic movement left their marks of austerity, severity, and general unworldliness. Three primary medieval movements illustrate the temper of the times: (1) Slavery had turned into serfdom, which in many cases was the same as freedom; (2) Pope Gregory the Seventh imposed sweeping reforms within the Church; and (3) the Crusades stood for a tragically militant affirmation of faith. The point of all this historical background, then, is that "To anyone who can appreciate atmosphere there is something clear and clean about the atmosphere of this crude and often harsh society. Its very lusts are clean; for they have no longer any smell of perversion. Its very cruelties are clean; they are not the luxurious cruelties of the amphitheatre. They come either of a very simple horror at blasphemy or a very simply fury at insult. Gradually against this grey background beauty begins to appear, as something really fresh and delicate and above all surprising. Love returning is no longer what was once called platonic but what is still called chivalric love. The flowers and stars have recovered their first innocence. Fire and water are felt to be worthy to be the brother and sister of a saint. The purge of paganism is complete at last."

The earliest portion of Francis's life is told under the heading of "Francis the Fighter." As in all of Chesterton's works, there is more than one stratum of meaning to the most obvious words. Francis was indeed a soldier and a fighter, but the fight was ultimately to encompass something more significant than territorial wars. It was (to employ a paradox, of which Mr. Chesterton was the master) to grow universal by growing particular; by fighting "the good fight" to save his own soul, Saint Francis fought for the souls of those who would ultimately be saved through him and his brotherhood. Francis had an innate affinity for justice; to him all men were truly equal. Impetuous and fiery, "his life was one riot of rash vows; of rash vows that turned out right."

Francis entered into the gay and chivalrous life of soldiery with as much fervor as he was later to exhibit in throwing himself into the paths of asceticism. The first test of his bravery came not during battle, however, but at home when, recuperating from a recurrent illness which eventually forced him to forego hopes of a military career, he was meandering on horseback along a lonely road. From nowhere there appeared a leper advancing toward him. Fear seized Francis, for more than any battle or army, leprosy had always filled him with unfathomable horror. The turning point of his life came when Francis of Assisi leaped down from his horse and embraced the leper with swiftness and certitude. Some say the leper was Christ.

While praying in the church of San Damiano Francis heard the voice of Christ ordering him to restore His house which was falling in ruins. Francis took the command to mean *that very* church, which was in an advance stage of disrepair. In his great impetuous simplicity he sold all that he had plus his father's goods to buy the materials of restoration. This act of innocent piracy was to launch him on his career of poverty, for his father took him to a court of law demanding repayment. Francis gave back not only the money, but with a fervor characteristic of his temperament, stripped himself both of his clothing and his patrimony, declaring himself henceforth to be the servant of God alone. Francis "the builder" had laid the cornerstone, and the Church he would restore to splendor was that which was founded on Peter.

"Le Jongleur de Dieu" (Chapter 5) and "The Little Poor Man" (Chapter 6) provide a stubtle analysis, unique with Chesterton, which illuminates Saint Francis's asceticism. Valid in its logic, the account sets forth what others have left unsaid or have not fully understood. Briefly, Chesterton asserts that the essence of Francis's spirituality can be understood in terms of the troubadour-jongleur relationship mentioned earlier. Francis was very much a man in tune with his age. As a youth of wealth and popularity, he was acquainted with the language of the troubadours. Besides the element of sentimentalism in the medieval "Gay Science" of love, there was an element of almost excessive spirituality which could turn the love-object from an actuality into an allegory, thereby removing the risk of tainting spiritual love with animal passion. Though the object might be idealized, the passions of the lover remained nonetheless passionate. Thus, Francis was able to talk the language of the troubadour while addressing himself to his glorious and gracious Lady Poverty.

The jongleur was the jester or juggler, and sometimes a tumbler; at any rate, the jongleur was to the troubadour what the fool is to the tragic hero. The troubadour and the jongleur traveled and performed together, the troubadour singing his serious love-ballads, and the jongleur following to provide the leitmotif. Of the two, the juggler was the secondary figure or servant, and Francis found this latter position to be one providing the greatest freedom. In his life as a knight Francis was restricted by the bonds of money, position, and other men's opinion, but as the juggler he was the fool, the comic relief, of whom madness was expected. Tumblers take somersaults; Francis took a psychological somersault when he made the inward spiritual reversal from worldliness to poverty. Regarding God as the Author of all creation, Francis was no mere naturalist or humanitarian, but a mystic whose appreciation of the world had been made whole. By looking at the world topsy-turvy, he saw with gratitude the dependence of all things on the mercy of God.

Francis had the clarity of a visionary in his appreciation of everything in life as a gift both undeserved and unrepayable. By seeing God as the Origin of everything, Francis found that all things became extraordinary and nothing remained insignificant. "For a mystic like Saint Francis [things] spoke no longer in an unknown tongue. That is the meaning of all those stories, whether legendary or historical, in which he appears as a magician speaking the language of beasts and birds. The mystic will have nothing to do with mere mystery; mere mystery is generally a mystery of iniquity." Chesterton reasserts that "He who has seen the vision of his city upside-down has seen it the right way up." In other words, the feeling of literal dependence accompanies the view both of the Christian (who sees God as the object) and of the agnostic (who regards man as dependent upon the nature of things).

To the ascetic, man's dependence gives rise to gratitude and an infinite debt—a debt which only the generosity of an ascetic will refuse to stamp "unpayable." Saint Francis enthusiastically threw himself and his brotherhood into the payment of that debt; he served God positively, joyously, rigorously, and with the passion of a man in love.

The "Little Poor Man" was a man, maintains Chesterton, who would have been regarded as a "character" in any age; and in the Middle Ages, when so much was communal and based on anonymity, the stark individuality of Saint Francis was bound to stand out. Saint Francis held so magnetic a power over men that those who encountered his presence were never quite the same thereafter.

Relatively small in stature, and dressed in a poor brown tunic with a piece of rope to hold it together, Francis could not have cut much of a figure physically. Chesterton conjectures that Francis's Italian ancestry played a significant part in enhancing his temperament and demeanor. Passionate, enthusiastic, given to dramatic and highly-charged outbursts of fiery eloquence punctuated with frequent gestures and movement, Francis rose far above the level of spiritual mediocrity.

Francis saw everything individually, realistically, and factually. His friendship with men and animals alike was based on courtesy, a courtesy so sincere and spontaneous that it made kings of all men. By living in close imitation of Christ, Francis became, as it were, the Mirror of his Master, for men would accept in the figure of Francis what they had difficulty accepting in Christ. With the receiving of the Stigmata, Francis reached the summit of imitation. Saint Francis died before he was fifty, and the song of "God's Troubadour" became an echo perpetuated by the Order which he founded; for though, as Chesterton has written elsewhere, "Joy is the gigantic secret of the Christian," a man like Francis of Assisi could not keep the secret to himself.

J.S.

THE EVERLASTING MAN

Author: Gilbert Keith Chesterton (1874-1936)
Type of work: Philosophy of Christianity
First published: 1925

Principal Ideas Advanced

One of the best approaches to the study of Christianity is from the viewpoint of an outsider looking in.

The scope of this work is divided into two areas of time: the pre-Christian world and the post-Christian world.

By examining both of these eras from the viewpoint of an outsider, one concludes that Christ was divine and that the religion He founded is the true religion, the only religion which will endure to the end of time.

It is no surprise to a reader familiar with Chesterton to find that the author does the unexpected and approaches the study of supernatural religion from the natural level. According to Chesterton, the best possible way to understand the inside of Christianity is to look at it from the outside. In *The Everlasting Man* Chesterton presents the case for Christianity, and specifically for Catholicism, by means of logic, fact, and analysis, a study which at the same time refutes many of the heresies of his own and previous eras. The "Everlasting Man" is, of course, Christ, who, as Chesterton goes to great pains to point out, is strikingly different from any other founder of any other religion for this very reason; namely, that He claimed to be and *is* everlasting.

In his introduction to the plan of the book Chesterton first proposes the idea that next to studying a thing from the inside, the best method is to study it from the outside. Granting that closeness to a subject eliminates, or at least reduces, the possibility of objectivity, the author suggests that by making an imaginative effort to look at Christianity from the outside one will find to be true all the things traditionally said about it from the inside. His intention is to cause the reader to see Christianity as a whole against the background of historic events, and man as humanity against the background of natural things. By placing these subjects within their given perspectives, it is Chesterton's intention to show not only their general features, but also that transcendent quality which makes them different. Man is not merely a higher animal; Christianity is not merely a natural religion. The first part of the book, "On the Creature Called Man," is devoted to a study of humanity while it was pagan. The second part, "On the Man Called Christ," tells of the difference made by humanity's becoming Christian.

The point to be drawn by evolutionists concerning "The Man in the Cave," says Chesterton in speaking of primitive man, is precisely that he was a *man,* one who probably lived in a cave, of course, but a man, nonetheless, with all the faculties thereof. It was early man who drew portraits of animals on the walls of the cave, not the animals who drew pictures of man. However primitive his expression, however fumbling his methods, it was man acting *as man* who produced them. Chesterton points out that many early civilizations are prehistoric simply because they lacked the technique of writing or other methods of preserving information. But to assume that because these early societies are prehistoric they were not civilized, or that primitive arts were not art, is an error, Chesterton claims. In the primitive worship of the stars and nature forms was the yearning for religion, a yearning proper only to man.

Because man did not always know the direct way to God, he often chose wrong or misleading signposts. The comparative study of religions reveals many such signposts, according to Chesterton, but one must be careful in distinguishing religions. To compare Christianity with Confucianism, for example, "is like comparing a theist with an English squire or asking whether a man is a believer in immortality or a hundred-per-cent American. Confucianism may be a civilization but it is not a religion." It is the weakness of comparative religion, Chesterton contends, that no attempt is made to compare God and the gods. Even the pagans sensed the need for a being untainted by the natural lusts and frivolities they gave their gods. Remote, distant, even disinterested, their Supreme Spirit, Jehovah or Allah, was a being incomparable, serene, and pure.

Mythology was another of the wrong signposts, but it, too, peculiarly acknowledged the fact that it did not expect to be taken as the final answer. Men who allowed their gods to degenerate into profligates were well aware of the disappointing fall the gods had taken. But for a fall to be possible, there must be a height, and the awareness of the existence of this height haunted the heathens. In their daydreams, which grew into myths, they sought God or truth by means of a form of beauty. Chesterton writes: "In a word, mythology is a *search;* it is something that combines a recurrent desire with a recurrent doubt, mixing a most hungry sincerity in the idea of seeking for a place with a most dark and deep and mysterious levity about all the places found. So far could the lonely imagination lead, and we must turn later to the lonely reason. Nowhere along this road did the two ever meet." Indeed, Chesterton goes on to say, nowhere but in the Catholic Church did reason and religion ever meet and merge successfully.

The third wrong signpost or element of heathenism is demonology. In some cults where demonology has been practiced it has been found to have been adopted after a cult of deities has failed, the latter being too remote and the former more familiar. The placating of the dark gods through horrible sacrifices and unnatural rituals brought man to his lowest depths as man and doomed the civilizations which served these lower masters to eventual destruction.

The fourth and final signpost which proved false to man was what Chesterton calls "The Philosophers." Briefly, Chesterton maintains that these men were primarily concerned with thought, not with religion; to follow such thought as if it were a religion is to pursue it for the wrong end. The proper end of the long road of searching came for man with the birth of Christ.

In Part Two, "On the Man Called Christ," Chesterton describes the uniqueness of Christ from the day of His birth in the cave at Bethlehem. The author attempts to explain why the story of His birth has carried throughout the ages a power, a sense of drama, a human impact that no story of a pagan god can match: "There is something defiant in it also; something that makes the abrupt bells at midnight sound like the great guns of a battle that has just been won. . . . By the very nature of the story the rejoicings in the caverns were rejoicings in a fortress or an outlaw's den; properly understood it is not unduly flippant to say they were rejoicings in a dug-out. . . . There is in this buried divinity an idea of *undermining* the world; of shaking the towers and palaces from below; even as Herod the great king felt that earthquake under him and swayed with his swaying palace." Christ was more human than humanity, simple, yet infinitely complex, a Man who was truly a God.

Chesterton uses the Gospels to support his "rationalistic" approach to the divinity of Christ. The significant point of his argument is that Christ's ideas and teachings were strictly His own, depending upon neither the social order in which he lived nor the agreement of thinkers of His own day. His ideas were no more "suitable" to His time than they are to ours. As Chesterton remarks in wry understatement, "Exactly how suitable they were to his time is perhaps suggested in the end of his story." In other words, nothing has been altered by time, as some critics suggest, for Christ's teachings were apart from time, concerned with that which was eternal. His Church He founded on a rock, and like a rock the Church has endured, though buffeted by winds of heresy and waves of schisms. The keys given to Peter were to unlock the complex riddle of man's search. It was a complex riddle matched by a complex answer, for the Church was for the sophisticate as well as for the less learned. The Church united religion and philosophy; for her God not only died, but arose from the dead and walked, a proved God-Man, among men. The divinity of Christ, says Chesterton, saved the sanity of the world, for it "met the mythological search for romance by being a story and the philosophical search for truth by being a true story." As to the position of the Catholic Church, the author compares its members to messengers. A messenger does not dream about what his message might be, or probably will be; he delivers it as it is. The religion of the world, Chesterton tells us finally, "is divided by the line between the men who are bringing that message and the men who have not yet heard it, or cannot yet believe it." To the author of *The Everlasting Man,* that message gives new meaning to the world. "It is not a growth or a groping of blind life. Each [being] seeks an end; a glorious and radiant end, even for every daisy or dandelion we see in looking across the level of a common field. In the very shape of things there is more than green growth; there is the finality of the flower. It is a world of crowns."

J.S.

GOD AND INTELLIGENCE IN MODERN PHILOSOPHY

Author: Fulton J. Sheen (1895-)
Type of work: Religious epistemology; critique of modern philosophy
First published: 1925

Principal Ideas Advanced

The intellect provides the bond between brute matter and Infinite Spirit.

Much contemporary thought rejects the use of the intellect and endorses an intuitive method of arriving at knowledge of God.

The modern idea of God, as developed by the nonintellectuals, is that God is not static and aloof, but a changing being in the process of becoming.

Thomistic philosophy, which uses the intellectual approach to knowledge of God, argues that man is ranged with the angels and with God because of his intellect.

In rejoinder to modern philosophy, Neo-Thomism argues that God is Life and that He is in the world intimately; God is not an evolving process, for He is perfect.

Bishop Fulton J. Sheen's *God and Intelligence in Modern Philosophy* is both an explanation and a critique of modern philosophy's rejection of reason and its consequent nonintellectual conception of God. Bishop Sheen maintains that modern philosophy, because of its abandonment of the intellectual attempt to know God, has created a new notion of God, a notion which emphasizes the claim that God is not perfect, that He is *becoming*, that He is evolving and progressing as the world evolves. The result is that man acquires a new prominence in philosophy, for according to those who have lost faith in the power of the intellect, the divine is evolving in man, and God moves toward perfection because of man's efforts.

Dr. Sheen follows his initial account of the problem occasioned by modern philosophy's attack on the intellect with a careful analysis of modern philosophy's arguments for rejecting the proofs of God's existence. He then presents a careful exposition of the modern conception of God, as developed by the nonintellectuals. Then, in Part Two of his essay, Bishop Sheen gives the Thomistic answers to the claims of modern philosophy, and he concludes his book with a discussion of the extent to which the divine nature can be known through the use of the intellect.

According to the author, the three operations of the intellect are apprehension, judgment, and reasoning. The mind apprehends insofar as, without either affirming or denying, it grasps a point; the mind judges when it affirms some predicates of a subject and denies others; the mind reasons when it passes directly from one truth to another truth.

The criticism of the intellectualist position achieved its most effective statement, according to Dr. Sheen, in the philosophy of the French Academician Henri Bergson (1859-1941). Bergson maintains, according to Sheen's summary account, that the intellectual method places reliance on the idea or *concept*. But the concept, Bergson argues, is "naturally unsuited for life," for the concept is a symbol, not a reality; it solidifies movement and thus falsifies life; as a symbol of that which is abstracted from movement, the concept breaks up what, in reality, is continuous and successive. The only conclusion to be drawn, conclude those under the influence of Bergson's criticism of intellectualism, is that imagination is to be preferred to the intellect; aesthetics, not intelligence, provides the true vision of reality.

The critics of intellectualism, then, quite naturally reject the intellectual attempt to demonstrate the existence of God. As substitutes for rational proof, experience, intuition, and faith are offered by the modern philosophers. William James has been influential in defending the claim that religious experience is a nonlogical meeting of the consciousness of man with that of a "wider self." What religious experience provides in the way of grasping the active and the exterior, intuition provides for those who seek to know the contemplative and the interior; and faith, as the commitment to hypotheses not yet confirmed, has pragmatic value as an attitude which helps bring into being the reality hoped for: so argue the nonintellectuals at the forefront of modern philosophy.

Dr. Sheen maintains that the nonintellectual approach, in contrast to the intellectual, makes the self the source of what is taken to be knowledge of God; man seeks within himself for those truths which, according to the intellectual approach, can be found only in the external world of "movement, contingency, varied perfections, efficient causality and finality." (Here Dr. Sheen makes oblique reference to the grounds of the proofs composed by Saint Thomas.)

It is not surprising, then, Bishop Sheen writes, that modern philosophy describes the traditional theological view of God as one in which God is conceived to be static and aloof from the world's needs. God is not static and perfect, the nonintellectuals insist; He is a changing and evolving being. God is not an omniscient being who stands apart from the world and knows its perfection even as he observes every act of sinning man, say the modern philosophers; He is not transcendent but in the world; He co-operates with man and joins him in the struggle toward a better life. Dr. Sheen concludes his exposition of the modern notion of God with the following remarks: "The modern notion of God is on all sides that of an evolving God, who is either tending toward deity, budding off from the Divine Imaginal in one of the world systems, or else organic with a progressing world. He *is* not: He is *becoming*. . . . He is, therefore, helped by us, and without us would for ever remain unachieved."

In opposition to such a conception of God, Bishop Sheen first of all criticizes what he calls "philosophical lyricism," the tendency of modern philosophy to adapt scientific principles to its own nonintellectual mode of operation. Empirical science emphasizes the importance of hypotheses as useful tools, of mathematics as an expression of temporal and spatial co-ordinates, and of scientific laws as human interpretations of natural phenomena. Philosophy, exhibiting its "lyrical" tendencies, argues that the true is nothing more than the useful (pragmatism), that man is the measure of truth (humanism), and that the value of an idea is determined by its degree of instrumentality (instrumentalism); modern philosophy maintains, further, that time and space are ultimate and that mathematics and logic are identical; finally, modern philosophy contends that it is by intuition that man grasps what science, in its interpretation of nature, emphasizes: the quality of things.

Bishop Sheen argues that modern philosophy (anti-intellectual philosophy) has as its ideals increasing the richness of life, expressing the fact of change and progress, and emphasizing the movement toward unity in the evolutionary process. The author contends that the philosophy of Saint Thomas offers a better guarantee of these ideals than does modern philosophy. According to Saint Thomas, intelligence is the greatest immanent activity of men, and intelligence, then, is the highest form of life; because of intelligence, man is "ranged with the angels and with God. . . ."

As for continuity and progress, Scholastic philosophy long ago established them metaphysically; the intellect discovers the order within nature; the intelligence enables man to understand all things as "material realizations of the Eternal Ideas of God. . . ." By rejecting the intelligence, modern philosophy becomes a philosophy of the "block universe" and thereby defeats its own objective of affirming the principle of continuity.

The modern philosopher fails to find unity because he rejects the intelligence, which alone can uncover the fact of unity. Although the human intellect is imperfect, writes Bishop Sheen, it is capable of giving man the assurance that as he approaches God, he comes closer and closer to the source of unity and knowledge. The intelligence provides the bond of knowledge and love between God and the material universe; without the intelligence, no understanding of either evolution or unity is possible.

Dr. Sheen explains that "separability from matter" is the condition of intelligibility. The intellect is a spiritual faculty; it is uniquely capable of separating form from matter; it is through *abstraction* that ideas become intelligible. Thus, Thomistic philosophy, which conceives of the intellect as the faculty of abstraction, makes the knowing process itself intelligible; modern philosophy, on the other hand, is unable to account for the possibility of knowing. To deny the intelligence, the bishop writes, is to deny intelligibility.

It is sometimes supposed that traditional philosophy is opposed to common sense, but, Bishop Sheen maintains, the traditional philosophy "begins with common sense." In beginning with immediately evident principles, first principles, Thomistic philosophy uses as its basis naturally known principles, not suppositions, about which no one could be mistaken. The first principle is the familiar principle of identity, interpreted not as a pure tautology but as a principle having application both in logic and the world: *"Being is, non-Being is not."* Bishop Sheen maintains that the demonstrations of God's nature proceed from this first principle, and he argues that those who deny the necessity of first principles are neglecting the conditions of all fruitful use of the intellect. Although complete knowledge of the essence of God is not possible through intellect alone, it is possible, through the multiplication of metaphysical and moral attributes, to clarify one's knowledge of God. Such clarification is denied to one who refuses to proceed from first principles.

Bishop Sheen acknowledges, in a chapter entitled "The Value of the Non-Intellectual Approach to God," the value of religious experience and pragmatic tests, but he insists that an affective philosophy which relies on nonintellectual methods fails to make possible a public and communicable knowledge of God. *"The idea of God's existence is not true because it succeeds practically,"* Dr. Sheen writes; *"it succeeds practically because He exists."*

Following Saint Thomas, Bishop Sheen accepts the Scholastic arguments for the existence of God. "Thus," he writes, "from mutability we argue back to a First Mover, from dependency to an Efficient Cause, from contingency to a Necessary Being, from graded perfections to Perfect Being, and from ordered complexity to a Supreme Intelligence." God's essence and existence are identical: "He *has* no being; He *is.*" In the light of these arguments and conclusions Bishop Sheen criticizes the claim that God is organic with the world; he distinguishes between movement and the Mover, between effects and their Cause, and between the chronological problem of creation and the ontological problem: *"Creation is not change; it is a relation."* The conclusion of Bishop Sheen's very careful analysis is that God is not organic with the world; He does not change and move as the world changes and moves; He is not evolving, for He is perfect.

In answer to modern philosophy's charge that traditional philosophy regards God as static and aloof from the world, Dr. Sheen contends that "God is Life; . . . God is in the world intimately." Although God is perfect, He is not static, for He is Life, and the perfection of life is immanent, not transitive, activity. God is "Pure Spirit and Pure Intelligence," the author argues; "He is therefore Pure Life." Furthermore, as perfect being, God cannot be aloof from the world: "He is in the universe as the Power that brought it into being, as the Power which conserves it and as the Goodness which prompted it and towards which it moves." Modern philosophy's supposition that the perennial philosophy supports a static God is based on a misconception of the traditional philosophy.

In his concluding chapter, "The Spirit of Modern Philosophy," Bishop Sheen calls attention to principles propounded by both Aristotle (in his *Metaphysics*) and Saint Thomas (in *De veritate*), principles "whose sole claim to be accepted are their accord with common sense, and not their authority": "1. The Divine Intellect is a measure, not a thing measured. 2. Natural things are both a measure and a thing measured. 3. The human intellect is a thing measured, not a measure." What man knows, he knows because of the nature of things; man does not invent or create what is known, for God alone is the measure of all things. Modern philosophy, however, has divinized human intelligence and human nature; modern philosophy makes man, not God, the measure of all things. Such a perversion of traditional ideas exhibits a confusion of mind with Being, of Grace with nature, and of man with God. Bishop Sheen concludes with a summary judgment: "The wisdom of the ages and the epitome of our experience is given in the simple truth understood by the simple and forgotten by many a philosopher, that we are not 'God-makers but God-made.' "

A KEY TO THE DOCTRINE OF THE EUCHARIST

Author: Dom Anscar Vonier, O.S.B. (1875-1938)
Type of work: Dogmatic theology
First published: 1925

Principal Ideas Advanced

The Eucharistic doctrine can be seen in its true supernatural proportions only if it is studied in the light of the great sacramental doctrine of the Church, which analyzes the sacrifice in its sacramental setting.

The sacrifice is contained in the sacramental separation of the Body and Blood of Christ; this theory does away with the difficulties of those who attempt to find some explanation which involves actual suffering in Christ or some change in His heavenly state of existence.

Considered on the sacramental level, the sacrifice of the Mass is seen to be a representation of Calvary, not an integral part of it; the Last Supper is similarly regarded as the institution of the sacrifice of the Mass and not as the first act of the natural sacrifice which was offered on Calvary.

Dom Anscar Vonier's *A Key to the Doctrine of the Eucharist* is one of a number of works which appeared in the early decades of the present century on the nature of the sacrifice of the Mass. The exchange of views which took place in these volumes advanced divergent ideas about the nature of sacrifice in general, the essence of the Eucharistic sacrifice, and the type of change which took place in Christ in the Mass. This work of Vonier was a pioneer step in restoring the sacramental treatment of the sacrifice of the Mass to its rightful place of honor. Although Vonier claims only to "point out the true setting of the Eucharistic mystery in the economy of the supernatural life," and not to be concerned with apologetics, speculative theology, or devotion, he has written a volume which, from cover to cover, touches the fringe of speculative theology, besides giving devotional insights of eminent worth.

The first nine chapters of the book discuss in detail the meaning, the power, and the perfection of sacramental signification, and the harmony of the sacramental system. Following this, Vonier attempts to prove his thesis that "the sacrifice of the Mass, if it has any human explanation, must be explained in sacramental concepts." This thesis is demonstrated by appeal to the teaching of Saint Thomas and the Council of Trent, along with answers to objections from the Protestant camp or from Catholic sources. The book closes on a devotional and inspirational note, showing that it is the Mass which makes the difference between paganism and Christianity.

According to Vonier, the sacrifice occurs in the context of the salvation of mankind, of our union with Christ. This union, objectively, is brought about by the atoning and saving action of Christ on the cross. Subjectively, this union is perfect in the beatific vision in Heaven, inchoatively perfect in the life of charity on earth, and begun through contact with Christ by faith, which is the instrument by which we come into contact with Christ. The sacraments are external signs which are the guarantee and the reward of our faith; they are means by which the Christian can apprehend Christ not only mentally but also physically. But the sacraments are a special type of sign: They signify the cause of our sanctification, the passion of Christ, and thus are commemorative signs. They signify the form of our sanctification, the grace imparted, and thus are demonstrative signs. They signify the last end of our sanctification, life eternal, and thus are prognostic signs. They are also instrumental causes, bringing about what they signify. It is in this sacramental framework that the Eucharist is to be studied, and the student must not leave this context in investigating its meaning and efficacy.

Vonier, following Saint Thomas Aquinas, insists that the essence and celebration of the Eucharistic sacrifice is found in the consecration. Communion is related to this only as a further perfection, not as something essential to the sacrifice as such. The Mass, further, is not a natural sacrifice, since it is a sacrament. Natural sacrifices are known by experience, this one only by faith. The natural sacrifice takes place by the actual immolation of the victim; this, only by a representation of the natural sacrifice. Vonier is thus able to maintain the uniqueness of the Eucharistic sacrifice against the Protestant objection that the sacrifice of the Mass derogates from Calvary. The sacrifice of the Mass, according to Vonier, is in an entirely different order. Against the Jesuit theologian Maurice de la Taille (1872-1933), Vonier holds that the Mass is not part of Christ's natural sacrifice, for sacraments cannot be integral parts of natural happenings; they can represent the natural events, but they cannot complete them.

Is the sacrament of the Eucharist a sacrifice in any sense? Vonier answers according to the principle that the essence of a sacrament is to signify its effect. To find what is contained in the sacrament, one must first look at the sign which constitutes it; one must not attempt to determine the sign by stating first what is contained in it. For example, one should not say that the Body and Blood of Christ are on the altar and, therefore, that a sacrifice exists. Rather, one should take the signs and examine them to see whether they really signify a sacrifice. If they do, then there is a sacrifice, for the sacraments cause that which they signify. Here it is not a question of God's hidden omnipotence, of what He could do if He wished; it is a matter of His sacramental power, of what He actually effects through material signs. The question then is this: Does the Eucharistic rite signify Christ's death on the cross in the literal reality of that death? The Church replies in the affirmative: The external sign is the measure and guarantee of the internal reality.

Vonier takes up the question more directly: What is the essence of the Eucharistic sacrifice? Some theologians have placed the essence in something that happens to Christ's own Person. These are the ultra-realists, who proceed as follows: (1) Christ is produced on the altar through the consecration; (2) He is immolated and offered as sacrifice in some mysterious way. While there is no substantial error in this position since it safeguards the truths of the transubstantiation and the Real Presence, it is not Saint Thomas's way. He never asks what change happens in Christ's own Person. In fact, he denies any change at all in the heavenly Christ as a result of the Eucharistic action. According to Thomas, the Eucharistic sacrifice is not directly a mystery of Christ's Person, but rather a mystery of Christ's Body and Blood. Christ's Body is offered, Christ's Blood is offered; these are the inward meaning of the external sign in the sacrificial rite, and beyond these — the Body and Blood — the sacrament, as sacrament, does not go. Since Christ's Body and Blood are sacramentally separated on the altar, Christ's death, the separation of body and blood, is sacramentally represented on the altar.

It may be worth the effort to repeat the same thing in different words. The sacrifice of the Mass is found precisely in the fact that the separation of Christ's Body and Blood is brought about not by a fiat of divine omnipotence, irrespective of any precedent or human connections, but as a prolongation of the whole commemorative rite which historically and as an unbroken chain of remembrance is linked up with the dead Christ on the cross. Separation of Body and Blood on the altar, considered in itself, would not make a sacrifice; a mere figurative rite alone would never make a sacrifice. But the two together, one as the human act of commemoration, the other as the divine prolongation of that same act, make the Eucharistic sacrifice. The species present on the altar represent Christ's existence when it was nothing but sacrifice.

This explanation is the climax of Vonier's positive presentation. A consideration of how he answers some objections will serve to illustrate the theory further and to show its soundness. The Protestants reproach the idea of the Mass as a sacrifice, as a derogation from the infinite value of the unique sacrifice of Calvary. The essence of Vonier's reply is that the Cross, a true sacrifice, and the Mass, a true sacrifice, are one and the same sacrifice. It would be impossible to maintain this position if the Mass were a natural sacrifice, for then there would necessarily be two sacrifices; if Christ were again offered in his natural state, there would be a new sacrifice. But if the Mass is a sacrament, a representation of the natural sacrifice, there is no new natural sacrifice. But is the Mass a true sacrifice if it is a representation? Yes, it is, for the Mass is the Cross, as an image is the person depicted. The Mass is the Cross, because the fruits of the Cross are applied in the Mass. The Mass is the Cross, because the altar is an image of the Cross. The Mass is the Cross, because the priest is the image and instrument of Christ the priest.

All this is to say that the Mass and the Cross are one analogically; that is, they are simply diverse, and yet in some way the same. The image and its prototype are one by an analogy sometimes called the analogy of the model and the modeled. Also, when the effects of one thing are contained in and applied by another, there is another analogy operative, that of attrition, or of cause and effect. This analogy allows one to thread the delicate line between a Protestant denial of any sacrifice present in the Mass and an equally facile solution that says the Mass is an utterly different sacrifice from that of Calvary.

Holy Communion is intimately connected with the Eucharistic sacrifice. It is, first of all, the application of the sacrament to man. Second, it is a sacramental union with God, to be distinguished from other visitations of the Spirit outside the sacramental realm. The sacramental grace given is membership with Christ and the whole Mystical Body of Christ, for the sacrament signifies the society or body of the elect, just as it signifies the true Body of Christ.

Vonier also rejects the theory of a heavenly sacrifice. Sacraments have a future aspect, yet they are essentially transitory, in time. Sacraments are true prophecies of the eternal glories, yet they are instruments, part of the work Christ does here on earth, not permanent glories of the everlasting triumph. So it is with the Eucharist. Heaven is rather the consummation of all sacrifices, not a sacrifice itself. Immolation on earth involves the sacramental Christ; consummation in Heaven, the eternal Christ. The altar of Heaven in the Apocalypse is not the altar of holocaust and sacrifice, but of the Body and Blood of Christ, not of the Redeemer in glory.

Vonier thus presents a view of the Eucharistic sacrifice which he believes is strictly in the line of Thomistic theology. His basic principles are derived from and within the structure of sacramental theology, with emphasis on the fact that the sacraments are signs. In this, of course, Vonier was anticipating a revival which has characterized sacramental theology in recent decades, based solidly on the symbolic function of the sacraments. Nothing of what he says has been invalidated or found wanting by more recent investigations. These, rather, have shown that the theory so clearly outlined by the Benedictine monk is a safe and solid explanation of the essence of the Eucharistic sacrifice.

R.J.B.

THE HISTORY OF THE POPES FROM THE CLOSE OF THE MIDDLE AGES

Author: Ludwig von Pastor (1854-1928)
Type of work: History of the papacy
First published: 1886-1928

Principal Ideas Advanced

The papacy is a central institution in European history.

A knowledge of the history of the papacy is necessary for an understanding of European diplomatic and political history.

The popes and their curial assistants are human beings with human weaknesses and strengths.

The history of an institution or a state can best be studied in its archival sources.

Ludwig von Pastor was rigorously trained in the German school of historians who considered Leopold von Ranke (1795-1886) their model and ideal. As a youth, Pastor read Ranke's greatest work, *History of the Popes,* and met the semi-retired historian when Pastor was a graduate student. Bismarck's attempt to control the Church after 1871 led to much propaganda against the "Roman Church," which, Pastor thought, must be corrected by the true story.

Fortunately for Pastor, Leo XIII became pope in 1878. Whereas only limited access had been given in a few exceptional cases to the Vatican archives, they were made completely available for the first time to Pastor. (A few years later they were similarly opened to any qualified scholar.) This combination of events gave rise to Pastor's *History of the Popes,* which has aptly been called "the daughter of the Germany of the Catholic Center, of the Rome of Leo XIII."

The History of the Popes begins with the pontificate of Clement V in 1305 and concludes with the election of Pius VII in 1799, thus covering five centuries of papal history. The first volume appeared in 1886, and the last two volumes were prepared from Pastor's extensive notes and outlines after his death in 1928. Whereas the German edition appeared in fifteen volumes, there are forty volumes in the English translation. The first of these appeared in 1891, and the last in 1953.

Pastor tried to write modern scientific, objective history, following the advice of Pope Leo XIII to tell all the truth. In the volume dealing with Alexander VI and Julius II, he wrote in the preface: "I have said all, but said it like a son constrained to unveil the faults of a very dear mother." His presentation is sober, judicious, and objective. He presents as harsh a picture of Alexander II's morals, for example, as does any reputable Protestant historian, but at the same time he explains how this was apparently of little concern to the pope's contemporaries. He then goes on to show how Alexander was a most capable administrator and statesman.

The History of the Popes is based primarily on the Vatican archives, but Pastor also searched diligently through such archives as those of the Colonna, Ricci, and Gaetani families in Rome, and archival collections throughout Europe. He also read and used thousands of printed works. The result, as had been the case with Ranke, is that Pastor's *History of the Popes* is chiefly political and diplomatic history. Such matters as the papacy's relations with European states and papal elections take up a great deal of space, whereas less tangible matters that do not appear in documents and diplomatic correspondence tend to be slighted.

The work begins with a long analysis of the Renaissance, an analysis which has become a classic in historical literature. Pastor distinguishes between a secular and a Christian Renaissance. The latter is thoroughly compatible with the Church's teaching and attitude toward learning, and is personified by such persons as Saint Thomas More and Vittorino da Feltre.

The principal characters in these volumes—popes, members of the curia, secular rulers, and diplomats—are described in great detail as regards appearance, intelligence, strengths and weaknesses, and whatever else about them Pastor could extract from the sources.

The English volumes dealing with the suppression of the Jesuits (XXXVI-XXXVIII) have been criticized as being too sympathetic with the Jesuits, who were first expelled from the Bourbon countries and finally suppressed by Clement XIV. Curiously, no charges were made by the pope against the Jesuits, the bull simply stating that they were suppressed for the sake of peace within the Church. Pastor's tremendous weight of evidence that the Bourbon rulers used every pressure and threat possible to force the pope to suppress the Jesuits indicates that his treatment of this problem is fundamentally sound.

It is the general opinion of Church historians that Pastor's *History of the Popes* will long remain a masterful work to which scholars and students will turn for information and judgments about the papacy from 1305 until 1799.

PROGRESS AND RELIGION

Author: Christopher Dawson (1889-)
Type of work: Philosophy of history
First published: 1929

Principal Ideas Advanced

The cultural form and vitality of a society is determined by the religion which that society embodies.

The idea of progress became the religion of progress; as such, it led to the secularization of Western Culture.

Christianity provided the spiritual energy for the rise of Western civilization.

In historic Christianity, rather than in science and industrialism, the religion of progress finds its satisfaction.

Progress and Religion puts into the larger context of a philosophy of history the theme central to Christopher Dawson's *The Making of Europe* (1932) and his *Religion and Culture* (1948); namely, the idea that the vitality and growth of Western culture must be attributed primarily to Christianity as the source of the spiritual energy necessary to any creative advance. Dawson argues, in the present work, that the culture of a society is determined by the spiritual principle which moves it; and to the degree that a society attempts to progress without religion, just to that degree it tends to disintegrate and decline. This thesis is supported by a historical study of Western civilization, a study which leads Dawson to conclude that although medieval Christianity supplied a unifying religion of progress which drew Europe together as a cultural unity, the substitution of a secular religion of progress, a reliance on science and industry, led to disillusionment and cultural stagnation. The moral of this philosophy of history is that unless

Western civilization revives the religious center of its culture, the hope implicit in the characteristically Western religion of progress will be disappointed.

"Every living culture must possess some spiritual dynamic, which provides the energy necessary for that sustained effort which is civilization," Dawson writes in the preface; and that proposition, which is at once a generalization based on a study of history and a moral injunction based on a pervasive religious faith, is reiterated, in one form or another, throughout the book. The claim and the evidence combine to produce a forceful and provocative book.

Dawson begins by stressing the dominant place in Western civilization of the idea of progress. He argues that the belief in progress has been such an integral part of the faith of Western society that it has been accepted without question. In this respect the society of Europe can be distinguished from societies, such as those of the East, which have had at their centers the idea that man's state is static and that insofar as change is a fact of life, it is cyclical change, a matter of recurrence, not advance. It is now possible to recognize the omnipresence, in our society, of the idea of progress, because that idea is beginning to lose its influence; now what was once taken to be an eternal truth is seen to have been an article of faith, one which history has tested and found wanting.

In general, says Dawson, the idea of progress is simply the conviction that the world continues to grow better; in its most unenlightened form the idea is the uncritical acceptance of the benefits of a material civilization which has increased its productivity through scientific and technological advances (the very word "advances," Dawson might consistently argue, indicates the presence of the natural tendency to regard the solution of technological problems as signs of progress).

Men of the eighteenth century believed that progress was an undeniable principle fixed in the nature of things, and they were confident that changes for the better would eventuate, within a few decades, in a new age of "justice and enlightenment"; nineteenth century thinkers applied the idea of progress to social and economic affairs, and like their predecessors, they were confident that society could and would be transformed for the better. Now, in the twentieth century, there are deep-seated doubts which in their seriousness and probing go beyond the easy satire of those who have called into question the material values of Western society; more and more men are beginning to suspect that the industrial-scientific kind of civilization, for all its pragmatic success, is not satisfying the spiritual concerns, almost dormant, which alone can give rise to cultural traditions of true worth.

The idea of progress came into ascendency in the eighteenth century, Dawson claims, largely as a result of the dominance of the Cartesian movement. In arguing that reason alone is sufficient to yield the basic principles which science needs, René Descartes (1596-1650) had, in effect, sanctioned the dismissal of the experience and authority of Western culture. Eighteenth century scientists, scornful of the Cartesian effort to build science deductively, nevertheless shared Descartes' central faith in the complete reliability of human reason. Consequently, they tended to dismiss Christianity as an unenlightened appeal to superstitious fears. Nineteenth century political thinkers, impressed by the scientific method, a method which for all its pretensions still rested on the belief that man's intellect could make a new world out of empirical discoveries, began to venerate sociology as the science of society. Darwin's *On the Origin of Species* "put man back into nature" and forced men to conclude that reason is a product of the struggle for survival. This latter idea provided the basis for maintaining that nature itself has no moral dimension; if progress is to be made, it must be through human, scientific effort. The result has been a growing pessimism, the fear that science may not be enough to guarantee that progress in which everyone, until recently, had such abiding faith.

The historian has added to modern man's burden of doubt by questioning the belief in the unity of history. Hegel's idea that history is the manifestation of the ideal in time encouraged those who wished to rationalize their belief in progress; Spengler's emphasis on what he regarded as the individual personalities and life processes of cultures attempted to create unity out of relativity, and his philosophy of history supported those who had begun to disparage reason but had not given up their faith in the adequacy of science. Dawson's own view is that "a culture is neither a purely physical process nor an ideal construction"; although every culture is vitally affected by material factors, it "receives its form from a rational or spiritual element which transcends the limits of racial and geographical conditions." Those who have insisted upon the unity of history, a unity based either on physical process or ideal construction, have erred, Dawson insists; history has this multiple character, and if unity and integration are to be achieved, it is through the dominance and controlling energy of the spiritual factor.

Anthropological studies point out that those cultures which have not achieved and maintained a close and vital relation to their environments and thus have exhibited "biological inferiority" have declined in vigor and creativity. The comparative study of religions also shows, claims Dawson, that spiritual changes often have far-reaching effects in the material culture, but material changes do not add to the health and growth of a culture unless spiritual direction is afforded by religion. Thus, there is good reason to believe, Dawson maintains as he documents his case, that the religious factor is essential in the rise and growth of civilizations; and a corollary finding is that the character and vitality of a civilization is a function of its religious character.

Dawson examines the various world religions and the effects which they have had on the civilizations whose life-spirit the religions provided. In particular, following the central theme of his earlier books, the historian alludes to Christianity as the vital force responsible for the rise of Western culture and the unification of Europe. In this way, it might be said, the author makes his positive case for the beneficial effects of religion on culture: where a religion exists to provide spiritual incentive and direction, civilization rises and thrives.

The negative case consists in the claim that when a society becomes secularized, it tends to disintegrate and finally to disappear. The rise of the "Religion of Progress," when that religion, a secular faith, leads to a complete reliance on science and industry, as has increasingly come to be the case in Western society, marks the decline of culture. In chapters entitled, respectively, "The Secularization of Western Culture and the Rise of the Religion of Progress" and "The Age of Science and Industrialism and the Decline of the Religion of Progress," Dawson shows in detail how the faith in progress and science, to the exclusion of religion, has undermined Western society.

But the author, although not optimistic, is a man of hope. He believes that the spiritual element, although now depressed, will again become dominant. He does not argue for a theocratic state but for a society in which the Church makes a cultural community possible. If individual human beings are to be free citizens, if society is to be unified in such a manner that freedom becomes the natural condition of life, if Western culture is once again to grow through being vitally directed by spiritual energy, the Church and not the state must once again become, not the political center, but the cultural center of Western civilization.

THE AUTOBIOGRAPHY OF JOHANNES JÖRGENSEN

Author: Johannes Jörgensen (1866-1956)
Type of work: Spiritual autobiography
First published: 1929

Principal Ideas Advanced

The road of man in search of God is long and arduous, beset with doubts, temptations, discouragements, and adjustments.

The best way to travel this road is to trust in God's love and do all for His sake, wherein lies peace and spiritual fulfillment.

The proximate means for finding spiritual truth of mind and soul in this life is the Roman Catholic Church.

"For God's quern grinds slowly, slowly—year in, year out—two years, five years, ten years, fifteen years, it has not yet ground long enough.

"But if he who is being ground in the quern is a poet, it will happen now and then that a few verses will trickle out between the mill-stones, like blood. . . ."

These words of Johannes Jörgensen well summarize the tenor of his life. As artist and intellectual in nineteenth century Denmark, Jörgensen found that the same sensitivity which drew him so closely to the beauties of nature and produced the exquisite lyricism of much of his *Autobiography* proved unsatisfactory as a spiritual end. The tenets of Darwinism and rationalism, and the subsidiary currents of modern political and philosophical thought left him fascinated but equally unsatisfied. Finally, with his acceptance of Catholicism the initial thirst was quenched, but such complex torments then beset this soul so convinced of his own unworthiness that the account of his lifelong spiritual reformation and search for truth in both life and art seems, indeed, to have been written in blood.

Intellectually precocious, a potentially gifted poet before the age of twenty, Jörgensen, while abroad, enjoyed the student's bohemian life (which later caused him grave concern because of the time he had wasted), but later he married and began to eke out a living as a writer. Even while he was a student he attempted to find a personal spiritual orientation, yet he failed to discover any that would satisfy both his intellect and his heart. His acquaintance with the Catholic Church was made through various channels, but one of the most powerful influences in his conversion to its beliefs was Mogens Ballin, a devout and brilliant convert who introduced him to the militant viewpoints of writers such as Léon Bloy and Ernest Hello, among many. Despite a rigid Protestant upbringing and the seductive arguments of contemporary freethinkers, to say nothing of his feeling of personal inadequacy, Johannes Jörgensen was received into the Roman Catholic Church on February 16, 1884, and the most significant period of his life began.

It is apparent from his spiritual reminiscences (which are the sole content of Volume II of the *Autobiography,* Volume I being more prefatory in nature) that the pattern of struggle which preceded his conversion was not to abate with its accomplishment. With his surrender to God, there came to him no immediate joy, but an aridity of spirit and sterility of pen. One senses a foreshadowing of that "dark night" of which the mystics write, in these words describing the moments immediately following his baptism: "Nothing remained but a great void, a horrible disappointment. It seemed to me that I had been acting a part and I was profoundly ashamed of it. 'Oh, my God, have mercy upon me and send light into the tangled darkness of my soul!' "

Terrified that God demanded not only his soul, but its outpourings as well, he wrote: "Sometimes the thought flashed in upon me that I was not writing verses any more, that as a poet I was dead, *poëta mortuus.* 'For him who has given his heart to God, lyrics are no longer possible' (says the diary), 'for he has no longer a heart of his own, singing within him, or ought not to have one.' Consequently Christianity is synonymous for me with the death of lyrics. God demands my dearest, my only possession, that is, my song. He says, now as always: 'Leave all things and follow me.' Lord, Lord—whither? And for what?"

Despite his despair, some of his richest writings followed his conversion. Some of these had to do with Christian social doctrine, and for a time Jörgensen became actively involved in the Christian Democratic movement. Later, he devoted himself to the translation of the *Little Flowers of Saint Francis,* a task which brought him to Assisi for one of two events which were to influence his life profoundly. During his stay there, he became deeply ill and fell into a coma. While in this state, he was drawn to the very brink of eternity, where he received an extended vision of his final judgment. In this vision, he was adjudged the unworthiest of creatures due to his great lack of charity and inability to love anyone outside himself. The perception was so vivid that he was able to recall it in detail several months afterwards, and thus it is recorded. Thereafter, he regarded his life in terms of a "second chance" to remedy the ills of his egoism, and he strove to do so both in his personal affairs and in his writings.

The second event which left its mark on him occurred many years later. Though he was now middle-aged the torments of his soul still raged within him, giving him no peace. He was privileged to witness the ecstacy of a Belgian stigmatic, Rosalie Put, and to receive her blessing afterwards. He privately laid bare his heart to her, telling her of the doubts which had beset his whole life, hoping that some sort of answer would come to him through her whom God had chosen as a very special agent. Then, he writes, "It was no longer the Flemish peasant girl who was looking at me, it was *Another,* a fairer and a greater. *Rosalie was no longer Rosalie*—the infinitely painful, infinitely compassionate look with which she contemplated me was the look with which the Good Shepherd contemplates the lost sheep which has gone astray amongst the thorns of the world. . . . Cast down upon my knees I begged for a blessing for me and mine, *their* future and *my* future, and the hand with the wound of Christ made the sign of the cross over me."

Not all the suffering which pervaded the life of Johannes Jörgensen was of a spiritual nature; much of it stemmed from an innate personal sense of aloneness and a proclivity toward romantic melancholy. The artist in him found the home of its delight in Italy, which he called the "paradise of exiles," a phrase that had for him so many levels of meaning. It was Italy that gave his Catholicism refuge from his Protestant homeland; it was the healing warmth of the Italian sun which gave his creativity new life, and inspiration sprang from its sons and daughters and found its way into his writings. The best known of these works is his life of Saint Francis of Assisi, to whom Jörgensen was devoted and whose life he tried scrupulously to imitate (both Jörgensen and his wife were members of the Franciscan Third Order). When his faith or his health needed rejuvenation it was to Italy he turned, and its landscape and people alike moved his poet's heart as no other country could.

Apart from its spiritual value, the *Autobiography* is an exceptional literary diary, providing a vivid cross-section of the nineteenth and twentieth century world of letters. One is given, for example, a concrete glimpse into the explosive nature and temperament of Léon Bloy, who, as the result of a minor difference, severed a long friendship with Jörgensen. One is introduced to the spiritual quest of Strindberg, who sought the same answers that Jörgensen sought, but never succeeded in finding them. Other important figures shared the literary scene with Jörgensen.

As is the case in so many autobiographies, the persons whose influence was most deeply felt and cherished by the writer are given only cursory attention, as if to talk of them at length would tarnish or in some way mar their image. So it proves to be with the treatment of Jörgensen's wife, his children, and his spiritual confessor, for all of whom he felt the deepest affection. Other persons who were important in his life are treated with meticulous care and discernment.

However great its literary merits, the *Autobiography* of Johannes Jörgensen is an equally great spiritual chronicle. It lays open the heart, and, what is more important, the soul of an artist and intellectual whose life was devoted to the pursuit of truth, and who found that truth in the Catholic Church.

J.S.

THE CHRISTIAN EDUCATION OF YOUTH

Author: Pope Pius XI (Ambrosio Damien Achille Ratti, 1857-1939)
Type of work: Christian philosophy of education
First published: 1929

Principal Ideas Advanced

Education consists in preparing men to live so as to secure the end of human life; only Christian education is adequate to this task, for without Christ's teachings and example man is ignorant of his proper end and of the means whereby it is attained.

Educating is pre-eminently the responsibility of the Church by reason of its divine mandate to teach all nations.

The rights and responsibilities of parents in this area are prior to those of the state, since the end of the family is not only to beget children but to rear them as well.

The first duty of the state with respect to education is to protect the prior rights of Church and family.

The school is the creation of the Church and of the family and must, therefore, work in harmony with them, supplementing their educational efforts.

In his encyclical *The Christian Education of Youth (Divini illius magistri)* Pope Pius XI outlines the basic principles of Christian education and the important conclusions derived from them. His discussion includes practical matters as well, for the Holy Father explains the position of the Church on various modern educational practices. The essential aspects of Christian education treated are "who has the mission to educate, who are the subjects to be educated, what are the necessary accompanying circumstances, what is the end and object proper to Christian education. . . ."

The pope's introductory remarks emphasize the importance of having accurate ideas about education. Pius regards the special significance of rightly understanding the nature of education as arising from its intimate connection with man's last end. Education "consists essentially in preparing man for what he must do here below, in order to attain the sublime end for which he was created. . . ." Confused educators, then, form students who are in no position to achieve the end of human life. Arguing from this notion of the end of education, the pope maintains that Christian education alone is complete and perfect, since what a man must do has been revealed in the life of Christ. Christian education is, then, supremely important for the individual as alone clarifying how man is to live, but also, the Holy Father adds, for the family and for society as well, since their perfection comes from that of their members.

The problem of who has the mission of educating is solved in terms of two general principles: (1) education is essentially a social activity and (2) education is the joint responsibility of the societies into which man is born in accord with the respective ends of each. These societies Pius sees as three: the family, the state, and the Church. Their ends he represents as the generation and rearing of children, the temporal well-being of the community, and the eternal salvation of mankind. Since the same act can be ordered to each of these ends, there naturally arises the question of coordinating the educational roles of parents, state, and the Church. The problem is a complicated one. Pius assigns to the family priority of rights with respect to the state, because the family has been directly instituted by God for the purpose of generating and raising children. However, in view of its nobler end, the temporal well-being of the community, the state takes precedence over the family. Finally, the Church, looking as it does to man's supernatural end, is concerned with an order transcending that of the natural ends secured by the family and the state.

It is to the Church, the pope asserts, that education belongs pre-eminently since it is charged by God to teach divine truth to all men. The Church is, therefore, independent of all earthly power as to the source of its mission. The pontiff makes the same claim for the means the Church finds useful in promoting its educational aims. ". . . with regard to every other kind of human learning the Church has an independent right to make use of it, and above all, to decide what may help or harm Christian education." The justification of this latter claim is twofold: (1) as a perfect society the Church has an independent right to those things required to reach its ends, and (2) every form of instruction is of necessity related to man's last end, and, therefore, governed by divine law, of which the Church is custodian.

Because of this relationship of learning to the salvation of souls the Church encourages progress in the arts and sciences as useful. It is again by reason of the same relation that the pope asserts the Church's right of supervising what are often called secular studies. Since all learning leads to or away from the end of man, the Church must take an interest in the entire curriculum, not merely in religious studies exclusively.

This interest in all aspects of the education of every Catholic student should not be regarded as undue interference on the part of the Church. The pope points out that such watchfulness cannot but promote the public well-being by securing for its future citizens a properly ordered education. Pius does not see in the pre-eminence of the Church in education a threat to the rights of the family, state, and individual. He maintains that the supernatural order, the domain of the Church, in no way disturbs the natural order to which the educational rights of family, state, and individual refer. On the contrary, the supernatural "elevates the natural and perfects it, each affording mutual aid to the other, and completing it in a manner proportioned to its respective nature and duty."

The educational responsibilities of the family and of the state are also considered by the Holy Father. He emphasizes the priority of the family's rights, condemning the view that children belong first to the state and that the latter's educational rights are absolute. The right of the state he traces to the authority given it to promote the community's temporal welfare. Its educational mission, Pius points out, must refer to the state's proper end. To pursue further this question, the pontiff notes that the temporal well-being of society consists "in that peace and security in which families and individual citizens have the free exercise of their rights, and at the same time enjoy the greatest spiritual and temporal prosperity. . . ." The state's first duty with respect to education, the pope declares, is that of protecting by legislation the free exercise of the prior rights of Church and family. The state's educational efforts, then, begin with supporting those of the Church and family, supplementing them where necessary. Its own direct role is to insure a knowledge of civic duties and whatever measure of physical, moral, and intellectual development is necessary for individuals to discharge their social responsibilities.

Pope Pius notes the complete accord between this view of the relations between Church and state in the sphere of education and the view of Pope Leo XIII, who wrote extensively of the Church-state relationship. Leo is quoted as teaching that each of these authorities is supreme in its own domain, the boundaries of which are drawn in accord with their ends. He notes that "it may happen that the same matter, though from a different point of view, may come under the competence and jurisdiction of each of them." Education, Pius believes, is clearly such an area. The pope stresses the advantages of harmony between Church and state in education, arguing that since the good Christian is a good citizen, the state derives the greatest benefits by recognizing the Church's rights and co-operating with her.

Having shown that the Church's preeminence in education benefits the state, Pius asserts that the sciences also benefit from the Church's influence. The Church recognizes the freedom of the various disciplines, while at the same time preserving them from errors opposed to religious truth. The norm of conformity with revealed truth is thought by the pope to be relevant to freedom in teaching as well as to freedom of science. Teachers who propose what is contrary to divine truth violate the right of every Christian student to instruction harmonizing with religious doctrine.

In speaking of man, who is the subject of Christian education, Pius stresses man's weakness and disorderly inclinations resulting from original sin and the need for supernatural truth and divine grace to combat these defects. Without this supernatural assistance, the Holy Father declares, "It is impossible to control evil impulses, impossible to attain to the full and complete perfection of education." The pope condemns those educational systems which deny original sin and grace and which look only to human nature. Among these systems is that form of progressive education which insists upon unrestrained freedom on the part of children. The pope sees those who withdraw education from the guidance of divine law as making students not free men but slaves to pride and disorderly affections.

Sex education, when based upon the false assumption that youth can be protected by purely natural means, is also censured. Those who advance such practices are accused of failing to recognize the weakness of human nature and the fact that evil is more often the result of weakness than of ignorance. In this matter of sex education, the Holy Father warns that precautions must be taken lest an unwholesome interest arise and the door to vice be opened rather than closed. His Holiness criticizes co-education for mistaking "a levelling promiscuity and equality, for the legitimate association of the sexes." He points out that the significant differences in temperament and in abilities between boys and girls can be taken into account only when the sexes are educated separately.

The next major topic to which Pius turns his attention is the educational environment provided by the home, Church, and school. He passes over the role of the home and that of the Church in education, concentrating on the environment of the school. The pope stresses the fact that the school owes its existence to the family and to the Church and that its efforts supplement their educational contributions, particularly with respect to the arts and sciences required for society's temporal prosperity. The school must, then, work in harmony with the family and the Church, accomplishing those ends it has been assigned by them. The pontiff notes certain consequences of these principles. The school from which religion is excluded he condemns as not properly co-operating with Church and family. He also censures schools in which students are given separate religious instruction while following other courses with non-Catholics and taught by non-Catholic teachers. For a school to be suitable for Catholic students "it is necessary that all teaching and the whole organization of the school, and its teachers, syllabus and text-books in every branch, be regulated by the Christian spirit, under the direction and maternal supervision of the Church; so that Religion may be in very truth the foundation and crown of the youth's entire training. . . ."

The pope believes that the presence of different religions in a nation need be no obstacle to realizing this ideal. He remarks that the laws of various countries in fact make possible Catholic school systems, sometimes providing the financial assistance which distributive justice requires. Pius commends Catholics who promote such systems as engaged in an undertaking which conscience requires. He defends them from the charge that they wish to separate their children from the body of the nation, and he points out that the better Catholic makes the better citizen.

His Holiness outlines some of the

important advantages of Catholic schools. Secular learning does not come into conflict with religion to the detriment of education. When it is necessary to read false doctrine for the sake of refuting it, students are the more easily safeguarded. In order to take his place in society the Catholic student must be instructed in the arts and sciences, but in the words of Leo XIII: "Greater stress must be laid . . . on bringing into full conformity with the Catholic faith, what is taught in literature, in the sciences, and above all in philosophy, on which depends in great part the right orientation of the other branches of knowledge."

The last topic treated in the encyclical is the nature of Christian education. Pius defines it in terms of its end, "to co-operate with divine grace in forming the true and perfect Christian . . . the supernatural man who thinks, judges, and acts constantly and consistently in accord with right reason illumined by . . . the example and teaching of Christ." This aim, the enemies of the Church charge, leads to suppressing the natural faculties. It is inimical to social life and temporal prosperity, to progress in art and science. The pope replies by citing the great benefits, both personal and social, secured by those perfect Christians, the saints. Among others he mentions the founders of the great educational orders. Such, Pius counters, are the fruits of Christian education: full personal development and proportionate contributions to the common welfare.

R.J.G.

CASTI CONNUBII

Author: Pope Pius XI (Ambrosio Damien Achille Ratti, 1857-1939)
Type of work: Dogmatic theology
First published: 1930

Principal Ideas Advanced

Marriage is a sacrament ordained by God and therefore having divine mandate in its practical considerations.

Marriage provides benefits not only to the partners and their families but also to the whole society.

Modern life has developed false theories in regard to marriage, but these have been rejected by the Church.

To encourage Christian marriage, there is needed determination of individuals, adequate preparation, economic security, and civil recognition of Church laws.

Pope Pius XI, during his seventeen-year reign as Bishop of Rome, seemed especially concerned with the practical considerations of living the Christian life. Among his outstanding contributions to the Catholic Church teachings were his allocutions concerning family life, and in particular the two encyclical letters *Divini illius magistri* (*Christian Education of Youth*), written in 1929, and *Casti connubii* (*On Christian Marriage*), written the following year. Recalling Leo XIII's encyclical on marriage, *Arcanum divinae sapientiae* of eighty years before, Pius XI set out in 1930 to state the threats which modern society places upon marriage and to put before the whole Church a set of guides to help mankind combat those threats.

Casti connubii became one of the famed monuments of the papacy of Pius XI, and for nearly three decades following its publication it was unquestioned as the last word of the Church on all the subjects attendant to marriage. Later theological developments and the Second Vatican Council opened some parts of the encyclical's teachings to questions formulated out of advancements in the biological sciences as well as in the science of theology.

Pius XI drew on the past teachers of the Church, but particularly Saint Augustine, in formulating his encyclical. He made liberal use of Biblical interpretations also in dealing with the complex areas of marriage. He discusses the nature and dignity of Christian marriage, the advantages and benefits it gives to the family and society, the errors contrary to Gospel teachings on marriage, the vices opposed to conjugal union, and the principal remedies to be applied. Setting a tone of grief because of what he saw as society's attack on marriage, Pope Pius wrote, ". . . a great number of men, forgetful of that divine work of redemption, either entirely ignore or shamelessly deny the great sanctity of Christian wedlock." This comment creates the atmosphere for the encyclical, which is remanding in context and nature. Evils or errors which Pius XI saw in society were not to pass, and the problems he attempted to answer, especially in regard to indissolubility of marriage and birth control, remained problems long afterward.

In five sections, each dealing with one of his stated aims for the teaching, Pope Pius built a framework for discussion of these problems. He then proposed answers, many of which became commonly applied by private and public agencies in the years to follow.

As to the nature and dignity of Christian marriage, treated in the first of the five sections, Pius states the overriding idea "that matrimony was not instituted or restored by man, but by God." This, he said, is the doctrine of Holy Scripture, the constant tradition of the Church, and the definition of the Council of Trent. The pope writes, "For each individual marriage, inasmuch as it is a conjugal union of a particular man and woman, arises only from the free consent of each of the spouses; and this free act of the will, by which each party hands over and accepts those rights proper to the state of marriage, is so necessary to constitute true marriage that it cannot be supplied by any human power."

From God comes the institution and the laws of marriage, says the pontiff, and man fills his role by giving his complete co-operation.

The second section of the encyclical deals with the benefits of marriage, which Pius diligently lists in a hierarchy of values. The first of these is the child of the marriage, who "holds first place." The love, care, and education of the children of a marriage are reasons and benefits enough for such an institution to exist, said the pope, and he restates the idea of his earlier encyclical on education which gives the parents the prime responsibility for educating their children. A further blessing derived from marriage, and this again in accordance with the teachings of Augustine, is the conjugal fidelity and chastity of the married couple. Here the pope espouses the "liberty which fully belongs to the woman both in view of her dignity as a human person, and in view of her most noble office as wife, and mother, and companion." Pius discusses the relationship of man to woman, forbidding what he calls exaggerated liberty which does not care for the good of the family. He sets out the role of the mother and father, and he argues especially that the structure of the family always and everywhere be held intact. In further discussion of benefits, Pius XI explains the indissolubility of marriage and testifies that this is necessary to provide for the stability of the union and of the married couple themselves, to give each of the persons involved security and dignity, to establish a stable unit of permanence to provide for the upbringing of the children born of the union, and to increase the order of society as a whole. Finally, under the benefits, the pope studies the sacramental nature of marriage.

The pope's delineation of errors concerning marriage, an account to be found in the third and fourth sections of the encyclical, contrasts with the listing of benefits already put forth. Primary among the errors is the human denial of the divine institution of marriage. From this denial, either indirectly or directly, flow other errors besetting Christian marriage. It is in this section that the Catholic Church's teaching on contraception is contained; the pope forbids artificial and mechanical methods of birth control, but he points out the permissibility of "periodic continence," or the rhythm method of limiting or spacing conceptions.

"No difficulty can arise that justifies the putting aside of the law of God which forbids all acts intrinsically evil," writes the pope; "There is no possible circumstance in which husband and wife cannot, strengthened by the grace of God, fulfill faithfully their duties and preserve in wedlock their chastity unspotted." He adds, later, "God does not ask the impossible, but by His commands, instructs you to do what you are able, to pray for what you are not able that He may help you." To these admonitions, Pope Pius adds warnings against abortion as well as artificial contraception. Sterilization also is treated as a danger which might be promoted either as a private or as a public, governmental, measure. Sterilization of insane or criminal persons receives a strong condemnation from the pope.

Adultery and divorce are cited by the pope as additional threats to marriage, and he particularly cautions civil authorities against making laws which violate moral teachings. Mixed marriages between people of different faiths is counseled against as well. Despite the reasons advanced for civil divorce, even adultery, the pope is firm in his denunciation of the practice: "Opposed to all these reckless opinions," he states, "stands the unalterable law of God, fully confirmed by Christ, a law that can never be deprived of its force by the decrees of men, the ideas of a people, or the will of any legislator: 'What God hath joined together, let no man put asunder.' " The evils of divorce are listed as being in direct contradiction of the benefits, already explained in *Casti connubii,* of the indissolubility of the marriage vows.

Pope Pius XI devotes the final section of his encyclical to a consideration of remedies. Once again relying on the divine ordination of marriage, he presages future advances in science while at the same time he warns against blind following of scientific advances that do not take account of God's will. But of any natural remedy, he says, "God is the Author of nature as well as grace, and he has disposed the good things of both orders for the beneficial use of men." He warns against seeking to be independent of God's authority by exercising private judgment in matters as important as marriage. What Pope Pius proposes as a major remedy for all the ills he mentions is instruction and education, wholesome and not provocative. The pope asks all persons to be obedient to God's creation and God's laws.

Pius endorses marriage preparation efforts, either through private or general classes, and he attaches great importance to adopting proper procedures in choosing a marriage partner. In addition, he urges economic security as a foundation for a lasting marriage union, and he teaches married couples themselves to take great care that they remove or diminish any material obstacles before marriage, if possible.

The pope acknowledges the state's obligation to seek the common good of society by providing economic security if it is not available through the individual's own efforts: "If families, particularly those in which there are many children, have not suitable dwellings; if the husband cannot find employment and means of livelihood; if the necessities of life cannot be purchased except at exorbitant prices; if even the mother of the family to the great harm of the home, is compelled to go forth and seek a living by her own labor; if she too, in the ordinary or even extraordinary labors of childbirth, is deprived of proper food, medicine, and the assistance of a skilled physician, it is patent to all to what extent married people may lose heart, and how home life and the observance of God's commands are rendered difficult for them. . . . Those who have the care of the state and the public good cannot neglect the needs of married people and their families." Pope Pius points out that unmarried mothers are often helped (which he states is a just practice), but he adds that legitimate mothers are sometimes denied, or only grudgingly given, aid from the state.

Concluding the encyclical, the pope pleads that civil law should recognize ecclesiastical law in dealing with problems of marriage and family life. He prays that with his teaching, "fruitfulness dedicated to God will flourish again vigorously in Christian wedlock."

D.Q.

QUADRAGESIMO ANNO

Author: Pope Pius XI (Ambrosio Damien Achille Ratti, 1857-1939)
Type of work: Social philosophy
First published: 1931

Principal Ideas Advanced

In his encyclical letter Rerum Novarum, *Pope Leo XIII taught, as was his right and duty, the truth in detail with regard to the morality of the economic and social problems of his time.*

Now, forty years later, Rerum Novarum *is commemorated by a precise application of its principles to radically changed social conditions.*

Thus is provided Catholic social philosophy's sound remedy not only for present economic ills, but also for the widespread social disorders in which these ills thrive.

Quadragesimo anno (entitled, in translation, *Reconstructing the Social Order*) of Pius XI (pope, 1922-1939), is an example of the particular kind of papal document which has come to be known as an "encyclical" or circular letter. Published in Latin at Rome, the encyclical, because it is meant to speak to the entire membership of the Church, is then translated into all the languages of the faithful.

In these widely publicized papal statements devoted to political, social, and economic problems, the relation of these problems to Christian faith and morality is authoritatively defined in keeping with the traditional Catholic doctrine of the "power of the keys." This power, based on the words of the Church's Founder, "Blessed are you, Simon Bar-Jona! . . . I will give you the keys of the kingdom . . . ," (Matthew 16: 17, 19), both seats the pope as first among all the bishops of the Church, and grants him the ultimate authority to teach concerning all matters having to do with faith and morals. Moreover, the pope has both the right to speak concerning matters of faith and morals and the strict duty to teach the truth concerning them in keeping with the obligation placed on him by the divine command, "Go therefore and make disciples of all nations, . . . teaching them to observe all that I have commanded you . . ." (Matthew 28: 19, 20).

As the chief preceptor in the Church, however, the pope has the duty not only to teach, but also to see to it that his teaching, when touching upon temporal matters, is accurate in its grasp of actual conditions. To this end modern pontiffs have availed themselves of the thinking of the best specialists in the secular fields of learning to which they have occasion to refer.

Consequently, the "social" encyclicals, so-called because they grew out of the actual political, social, and economic conditions peculiar to their times, are noteworthy for their careful delineation of these conditions. Pius XI's *Quadragesimo anno* is an example of a social encyclical since it attempts to restate the social philosophy set forth by Leo XIII (pope, 1878-1903) in his letter on the condition of labor entitled,

Rerum novarum (literally, "Of New Things"). This restatement was needed in order that the principles of Catholic social philosophy as declared by Pope Leo might validly interpret the changed conditions of Pius XI's era.

On May 15, 1891, Leo XIII made public his encyclical letter on the condition of labor. This letter, a forthright statement of Catholic economic morality, strongly condemns the economic doctrine of laissez faire, a doctrine which divorces morality from the market place. Laissez faire is condemned by Pope Leo because, according to the Western tradition handed down from Plato and Aristotle, reality is a rational whole in which there is a moral order. This moral order stands above and governs the wholly subordinate realm of economic activity. It is this ordering of things which modern man must grasp intellectually and live actively, Leo contends, if he is to eliminate the socio-economic inequities of the time.

The chief goal of *Rerum novarum* is to provide principles of social reform. The practical effect of these principles would be, Pope Leo believed, two-fold: negatively, they would eliminate the evils of economic laissez fairism; positively, they would insert the economic order into a new social order founded on Christian morality.

In commemoration of *Rerum novarum* Pope Pius XI issued his encyclical *Quadragesimo anno,* on May 15, 1931. Literally, the Latin title translates as "forty years after," but the encyclical was given the formal title in English, "Reconstructing the Social Order." Upon its issuance Pope Pius's letter received a more instant sympathetic hearing than had *Rerum novarum.* Doubtless this warmer reception is attributable to the fact that the social order showed symptoms of even wider dislocations than it had in Leo's time. It was now the era of the great depression, and thinking men were rather acutely aware of the gravity of the social ills afflicting the entire industrialized world.

Pius XI declares that his encyclical *Quadragesimo anno* must precisely apply the principles of Pope Leo to social conditions which, though somewhat apparent in Leo's time, have by now clearly manifested their direction towards new and more gross forms of economic inequity. Intenisfied is the concentration of riches in the hands of the few who have captured control of the greater part of the supply of capital. Intensified too is the sophisticated use both of fiscal and legal techniques to expand monoplies, and legal and political devices to insure control over the total means of production throughout the international extent of the industrial economy. As a consequence, the social order finds itself divided into mutually hostile groups incapable, almost, of seeing any common good whatsoever. The middle class, though growing, expecially in America, tends to be unable to identify itself either with the leadership of the rich or with the brotherhood of the poor. By far the largest group in society, and the most rapidly increasing, is the vast, wretchedly oppressed, urban industrial proletariat.

Noting this oppression, Pius XI is alarmed at the almost complete disappearance of the spirit of *noblesse oblige* formerly associated with agrarian and mercantile paternalism. To Pius the economic aspect of society seems to resemble an impersonal mechanism of masses, managers, technicians, and the few holders of vast blocks of capital. Small wonder that the pontiff firmly points out that his task in *Quadragesimo anno* is to apply the principles of *Rerum novarum* to these greatly changed social conditions and needs. Pope Pius asserts, moreover, that by applying his predecessor's principles anew, he is seeking to save them from misinterpretation and subsequent invalidation.

In the forty-year period between the appearance of these two encyclicals the process of proletarianization had markedly intensified. This process, the chief social fact with which the pope had to deal, was considered by him to be a social and economic evil of the greatest magnitude. At this juncture, then, it was something of a world-wide event when Pope Pius XI not only reiterated Leo XIII's demand for a new order of things, but did so in the most vigorous language.

In no uncertain terms the author of *Quadragesimo anno* makes it clear that he is speaking on behalf of the oppressed workers of the world. Repeating Leo's assertion that ". . . it is only by the labor of the working man that States grow rich," Pius XI, while disavowing the violence of leftist extremism, nonetheless unequivocally puts himself and the Catholic Church on the side of those who seek to obtain simple social justice for all men. Basic to this end is the payment by the employer of a just wage, and wage contracts which exclude the possibility of a just wage are evil and must be changed. But above all capital and labor must co-operate for the common good of society as a whole. Both are individual, both have particular interests, but both are social as well. Capital, labor, and government are obliged to work together to settle the question of the just wage and the reasonable price. It must be clear to all men that all and each of them must receive an adequate share of the earth's goods, else there is no sound social and economic system.

In order that the individual worker escape proletarianization, the social order itself must be rearranged. Pope Pius, drawing upon the natural law philosophy of Saint Thomas Aquinas, declares that society can reform itself if only it restores the health of its organic life. It is a gravely sick society which permits the majority of its members to be confronted by a centralized state in which all political power is concentrated. To right this wrong principle of social organization, the principle of subsidiarity must be allowed to operate. This principle states that all authentic social groups should govern themselves in their own internal affairs; the best rule is "home rule." In addition, it is assuredly true that the state, taking care to foster the diverse forms of private initiative, must defend the new social order which can and should be built so that it is founded on the subsidiarity principle.

Society must be reordered and the economic order must be rearranged or, Pius's encyclical warns, the proletarian mass will ever remain such. The main presupposition of this right ordering is that there be social justice. Concentration of wealth, the pontiff alleges, has led to an unbridled struggle of a threefold character: struggle amongst the rich few for more money, struggle between the rich and the poor for control of the state, and struggle between state and state. Lust for gain and then for power has spread chaos through society. International relations are poisoned with economic imperialism. Into this chaotic situation it is imperative to introduce right order, and this can be done only by inducing all men to look to the common good which is social justice.

Some men, seeking to ameliorate economic evils, look to socialism as the means to social justice. But Pius XI strenuously insists that socialism cannot realize social justice. Neither in its mitigated nor in its communistic form can socialism realize this goal since it teaches class war and the abolition of private ownership. Christian social reform, as outlined in the papal plan, teaches neither of these aims. But it does declare that the individual's right to private ownership is not an absolute right since the state may find it necessary to take into its own hands certain forms of private property whose ownership by individuals would injure the common good. In this teaching Pius XI follows Leo XIII, and he is later reaffirmed by John XXIII (pope, 1958-1963).

In *Quadragesimo anno* Pius XI declares that, above all, the struggle for social justice must be crowned with that Christian charity which is described in the Gospels. From this imperative linkage of the struggle for a just society with supernatural charity, the pontiff draws two important inferences. First, the individual seeker after a just social order must join his effort to the Church's struggle for a better society, since the Church is the vehicle of supernatural charity which insures the fullest fruition of the Christian reconstruction of society. Second, this papal imperative that supernatural love be the ultimate motive in the struggle for a better social order makes it impossible for an agnostic or atheist socialism, no matter how close it approaches to Christian social reform in practice, to be in harmony with Catholic social philosophy. Socialism, if followed to its logical extreme, becomes communism, an ideology which denies God and places the individual at the mercy of the state. The social teaching of the Church, on the contrary, insures that man as a *person* in society should benefit both materially and spiritually.

In keeping with his final theme that man does not live by bread alone, Pope Pius XI concludes his encyclical with the assurance that a right ordering of human society is possible but only if the work of reconstruction is carried out under God.

Pope Pius XI's *Quadragesimo anno* has not gone unheeded. In 1961, on the thirtieth anniversary of the date of its issuance, Pope John XXIII published his now widely known encyclical, *Mater et Magistra* (English title: *Christianity and Social Progress*). In this letter John pays tribute to the social philosophy set forth by his predecessors, Leo XIII and Pius XI, and reaffirms the Church's struggle for a new social order based on social justice for all.

J.B.L.

THE SPIRIT OF MEDIAEVAL PHILOSOPHY

Author: Étienne Gilson (1884-)
Type of work: Study of medieval Christian philosophy
First published: 1931-1932

Principal Ideas Advanced

Medieval Christian thinkers utilized Greek philosophical systems in the construction of a philosophy that is distinctively Christian.

Reflection on Judeo-Christian revelation led to the discovery that some Christian beliefs could become objects of philosophical understanding; namely, beliefs in the existence of God, in the identification of God with the perfection of Being, in ex nihilo *creation, and in the utter dependence of beings on Being.*

The central theme of Christian philosophy is the relation of man to God; Christian philosophy is especially concerned with the kind of nature that is open to the grace that enables man to attain a transcendent end.

Christian philosophy flourished until the formulae of an otherwise rich variety of speculative approaches were permitted to obscure the common spirit of that philosophy.

The Spirit of Mediaeval Philosophy brings to the general reader the Gifford Lectures delivered by Professor Étienne Gilson over thirty years ago at the University of Aberdeen, Scotland. Professor Gilson has held many distinguished lectureships since that time, and the subsequent publication of those lectures in book form has met with unfailing success, but many look back to the Gifford Lectures as an unparalleled achievement in the interpretation of philosophical ideas. Professor Gilson undertakes to define the spirit of a philosophy which some say never existed. His announced task is to demonstrate the existence of a philosophy that is distinctively medieval. "In an effort to define" the essence of that philosophy, he notes in the Preface to his twenty lectures, "I found myself led to characterize it as the Christian philosophy *par excellence.*" Gilson's central thesis is that "the spirit of mediaeval philosophy is the spirit of Christianity penetrating the Greek tradition, working within it, drawing out of it a certain view of the world, a *Weltanschauung,* especially Christian."

The purely rationalist position, we are reminded, holds that the concept of a Christian philosophy is contradictory; it would mean the collaboration between reason and revelation, neither of which depends upon the other. Many Neo-Scholastics, Gilson explains, reject the notion of a Christian philosophy for the very same reason, but nevertheless acclaim Saint Thomas Aquinas as a true philosopher. Thomism is viewed as drawing out the implications of Aristotelian principles by a more rigid application of reason; it is a corrected and completed Aristotelianism. Thomism, according to these same Neo-Scholastics, is a philosophy because it is wholly rational, and it is compatible with the faith because it is true, but its truth no more entitles it to a Christian label than does the truth of a mathematics, a biology, or a medicine entitle any of them to a similar label. Thus there arises the question of the wisdom of further insisting upon the notion of a "Christian philosophy."

Gilson takes an experimental approach in considering whether a philosophy can retain its required rationality and yet be indebted to a revelation for some of its most penetrating insights. He points out the rich, speculative implications of both the Old and the New Testaments that enabled medieval Christianity to open up new perspectives to human reason and thus "to change the course of the history of philosophy." The idea of creation, for instance, was foreign to the classical philosophers of ancient Greece, but not to modern philosophers from René Descartes (1596-1650) to Immanuel Kant (1724-1804). Descartes's clear and distinct ideas, supposedly of rational origin, are found to accord finally with Christian ideas. Little would remain of the system of Gottfried Wilhelm von Leibniz (1646-1716) without its Christian elements, Gilson suggests, and the same could be said of Kant from the standpoint of his *Critique of Practical Reason* (1788). But if Christianity influenced modern philosophy despite the laborious efforts of its representatives to be purely rational, "the concept of Christian philosophy is not without a real meaning." Gilson quotes with approval the profound remark made by Gotthold Lessing (1729-1781): "The great religious truths were not rational when they were revealed, but they were revealed so that they might become so."

As far as the essence of philosophy is concerned, Gilson readily admits, a philosophy cannot be Christian, Jewish, or Mohammedan. If, however, revelation has helped reason to discover a body of rational truths, such truths can well be considered as making up the content of a Christian philosophy. Thus, for Gilson, the term "Christian philosophy" has a very precise meaning. He would not call a philosophy Christian simply because of the regulative role played by faith in that philosophy, for then any philosophy which leaves nature open to the influence of the supernatural could be called Christian. The Christian philosopher, as Gilson conceives him, would not pretend to reduce the contents of faith to understanding, but would ask if he might be able to know at least some of that which he believes. Saint Anselm's practice of seeking understanding through faith provides a method for the Christian philosopher. A believer becomes a Christian philosopher when his faith helps him to find among his beliefs some which can become objects of knowledge; thus the term "Christian philosophy" here relates to the construction of philosophy and not to its essential content. Gilson proposes to show that the great philosophers of the Christian segment of the Middle Ages clearly recognized that the construction of a true philosophy required a submission to the influence of religious faith. Their approaches were varied, but characteristics common to all of their systems entitle them to share the common name of "Christian philosophy."

Gilson sees the "most obvious trait" of the Christian philosopher as his choice of those philosophic problems which relate to the conduct of Christian life. The creative part of Saint Thomas Aquinas's philosophy had to do with such commonly discussed problems as "the existence of God, and the origin, nature, and destiny of the soul." The deepest of philosophical insights, Gilson finds, often originate in and are embedded in theological works: "In a word, faith has a simplifying influence on all Christian philosophers worthy of the name, and their originality shines forth especially in the sphere directly influenced by faith, that is to say in the doctrine concerning God and man, and man's relation with God." Revelation, then, unifies Christian philosophy by centering attention on significant matters to the subordination or virtual exclusion of matters of little importance. This, Gilson explains, is why a Christian philosophy has a strong tendency toward systematization. He writes: "Choosing man in relation to God as his central theme, the Christian philosopher acquires a fixed center of reference which helps him to bring order and unity into his thought."

The medieval conception of God as Being, a conception Saint Augustine derived from Exodus 3:14, reduces things to mere appearances in a much more radical way than Plato did. Christian metaphysics later found Aristotle's analysis of becoming and its necessary conditions most helpful, but beings that come into being are contingent for Christians in a much more radical sense than for Aristotle, for whom they do not depend on Being for their very existence. Along with the revealed truth of God as Being is placed the Creator God of Genesis I-1. The creative act of Being, then, confers an utter contingency on the sensible world; the whole universe is now suspended "from the freedom of a will that wills it," not "from the necessity of a thought that thinks itself," as for Aristotle. Things speak to Saint Augustine of their creator, *He made us,* but "the words of the ancient psalm," suggests Gilson, "never sounded in the ears of Aristotle." The efficient cause in Christian cosmologies will always be a creative cause, notwithstanding the Aristotelian language which thinkers like Saint Thomas Aquinas used. Thus, notes Gilson, in drawing distinctively Christian conclusions from Greek thought, Christian thought shows its indebtedness both to Greek tradition and to the "Divine Pedagogue."

Christian thinkers, Gilson continues, see causality as rooted in being. The causality of creatures is a secondary causality extending to the modes of being, for creatures are being by participation. Only God can cause the being of beings, for only God is the perfection of being. Goodness, an aspect of being, invites Being to communicate its actuality to possible beings. Communication is a mark of generosity; only perfect being is capable of the perfect generosity of the creative act. Since every effect in some way resembles its cause, all creatures resemble their creator, but intellectual creatures bear a much closer resemblance. A creature, then, is an analogue of its creator, but since there is no proper proportion between Being and being, the analogy is one of proportionality and bears on a similarity of proportions. Not only are creatures analogues of His being, but they are analogues of His desire, for He knows Himself as sovereignly desirable. God creates, then, that intellectual creatures may rejoice in His glory and participate in his beatitude. The Christian philosopher sees the world as "necessarily saturated with finality." Finalism for the Christian, Gilson concludes, is not naïve. Scientific explanations of the universe come and go, the author reflects, but "all things at bottom remain, for the Christian, as so many vestiges left by God's creative touch as it passes."

Christian optimism, Gilson points out, finds its basic principle in the first chapter of Genesis where the Creator pronounced His work as good, but there looms the inevitable problem of explaining the presence of evil in the world. Plotinus (c. 205-270), had simply identified evil with matter, but, we are reminded, matter in the Plotinian universe was not created. Saint Augustine sees in Genesis I:31 affirmation of the intrinsic goodness of everything. Creatures derive their mutability from their contingency, and their contingency from their *ex nihilo* creation. The beatitude open to intellectual creatures cannot be attained without free will, but from free will there follows the possibility of moral defection, or sin. Sin, an avoidable accident, violates the dependence that unites an intellectual creature with his Creator. Saint Augustine still finds much good in nature weakened by original sin, but the technical justification for this optimistic feeling awaits Saint Thomas and Duns Scotus. Original sin, for Saint Thomas, destroyed the good that God had added to human nature at creation; it did not destroy the good that properly belongs to that nature. Christian optimism, concludes Gilson, would refer the world to God and thus restore its integrity, and for this it seeks the help of God's grace. The author sees Christian asceticism as "but the reverse side of its optimism." "Not even the Middle Ages," he remarks, "knew any ruder asceticism than that of St. Francis—or any more absolute confidence in the goodness of nature."

All Christian philosophers, explains Gilson, have been concerned with rendering glory to God, but they have not always agreed as to the best way of accomplishing this objective. Nicolas de Malebranche (1638-1715), considering man's "claim to *independence*" as his most serious temptation, exalts the power and the glory of God at the expense of the efficacy of creatures. Gilson points to St. Augustine, notwithstanding the worthiness of his intention, as the ancestor of Malebranche and of all Christian thinkers who tend to depreciate the sufficiency of man in order to enhance the power and glory of God. The Augustinian doctrine of the simultaneous creation of all beings, including those that would at any time exist, emphasized the absolute dependence of creatures on God; the Stoic doctrine of "seminal reasons" is brought to the support of this doctrine. With Saint Augustine, an illumination grounded in the divine ideas accounts for our necessary judgments, and a moral illumination of virtues further emphasizes man's complete dependence on God. Gilson sees Saint Thomas and Duns Scotus as abandoning the Augustinian doctrine of seminal reasons and divine illumination of knowledge and virtue, all the better to follow the intention of Saint Augustine to render the glory to God that befits the perfection of infinite being. Saint Thomas makes use of the Aristotelian distinction between act and potency to support a doctrine of the efficacy of a secondary causality in creatures. He gives new significance to the Augustinian doctrine of illumination by conceiving the illuminating principle of man's intellect, his agent intellect, as his proper share in divine illumination.

Gilson shows that Christian thinkers have always linked the idea of divine providence with the idea of creation.

The possibility of creation, he explains, rests on the conception that God's eternal knowledge of Himself includes the creative Ideas by which He comprehends possible participations in His being. However, since God confers being on things not through any necessity of His nature but through His free decision that beings participate in Being, creation is a twofold movement; it is the giving of being and the providential directing of beings to ends that accord with their being. God wills to associate man with His beatitude, but man must freely will the means that accord with that noblest of ends. Because human acts arise from a man's free decisions, they are called personal acts. Intellectual beings, then, are called persons because the dignity of such beings more closely resembles the supreme dignity of a Personal God who is their Creator; the God that directs them to their end and associates them with His providence.

With regard to the matter of Christian anthropology, Gilson remarks that the problem of man's unity embarrassed Saint Augustine in view of his having accepted Plato's definition of man as "'a soul using its body.'" Averroës (1126-1198), the great Mohammedan commentator on Aristotle, finds no reason in Aristotle for thinking that there is any philosophical basis for a doctrine of the human soul's immortality. Accordingly, Gilson explains, Christian thinkers of the thirteenth and fourteenth centuries turned to an earlier Arab philosopher, Avicenna (980-1037) for an interpretation which would be more compatible with Christian thought. Avicenna distinguished between the essence of the soul as a spiritual substance and its function as form of the body. Thus, it seemed, both Plato and Aristotle could be brought to the service of Christian philosophy; the soul retains its substantiality and implied immortality, but it now becomes the form of the body. Saint Bonaventure unites the Avicennian doctrine with Solomon Ibn Gabirol's (c.1021-1058) doctrine of the hylomorphic composition of the soul, but Saint Thomas rejects both doctrines. Saint Thomas reasons that Avicenna, in excluding the soul's functions from the definition of its essence, makes the union of the body and the soul accidental. Substantiality, for Saint Thomas, belongs to the soul, but the soul needs to be joined to the body as form that it might turn to the least intelligibles embedded in matter.

As to the problem of Christian personalism, Gilson acknowledges that recognition of the individual by the Greeks, faulty though it was, helped to prepare the way for the Christian recognition of the person. Christian feeling for the worth of the human person, however, reacts against an underlying depreciation of the individual in Greek philosophy. For Plato, the idea of man is more real than the individual man, and, for Aristotle, the individual exists for the sake of the species. But in medieval Christian thought, the individual endowed with an intellect attains the dignity of a person because of its closer resemblance to a personal God.

It was the Delphic oracle, not philosophy, Gilson reminds us, that issued the precept to Socrates, *Know thyself*; but it was the Biblical teaching that man is created in the image of God that transforms the very problem of self-knowledge for Christians (Genesis I: 26-27). Although the moral emphasis of Socratism, Gilson readily admits, resulted in an anti-physicism for Christians just as it had for Socrates, it also helped medieval man to see that in the universal order of creatures he is superior to the brute and inferior to the angel. In seeking and loving the image of God within himself, the Christian seeks and loves his neighbor, for he too is the image of God. It is because man's soul is the image of God that all great Scholastic doctrines, notes Gilson, recognize that the soul's intuition of itself necessarily falls short of its object; accordingly, some seek in mysticism the final answers to their study of man. Christian wisdom, then, is seen as a twofold science embracing knowledge of self and knowledge of God.

As to man's knowledge of things, Gilson does not see that it is inevitable *a priori* that Christians be realists, but he notes that the Christian universe readily lends itself to the support of realist epistemologies. Generally, medieval thinkers neither wanted the innatism of Plato nor the threatening epistemological skepticism opened up by Matthew of Aquasparta's (c. 1240-1302) insistence that divine Ideas and not things give stability and necessity to knowledge. Unified truth, for Saint Thomas, truth in the absolute sense, resides in the divine intellect, but it is the human intellect's conformity with the entitative truth of sensible things that constitutes truth in the proper sense for man; the human intellect, for Saint Thomas, disengages its truth from sensible things. Duns Scotus limits the role of sense knowledge but seeks to rehabilitate the order of sensible things by showing that we rise to some kind of a knowledge of the divine Ideas from a knowledge of created things—a knowledge that requires a valid sense cognition. Thus the marked contrast between medieval anthropocentrism and the anthropocentrism of modern idealists. The former, Gilson considers, viewed the world as made for man and man for God; the latter, as in the thought of Kant, sees man at the center of things, not in the local sense of medieval thought, but in the radical sense that thought imposes laws on things.

In opposition to Plato, who had taken the intelligible Idea as the human intellect's natural object, Saint Thomas, the reader is reminded, agreed with Aristotle in contending that the proper object of the human intellect is the essence or nature of sensible things. Saint Thomas, Gilson cautions, is not saying that the natural object can be considered as adequately satisfying the intellect's capacity. Duns Scotus agrees that our knowledge directly bears on sensible things, but he insists that there is nothing natural about our present way of knowing; perhaps it is a punishment for original sin, or it may be simply that God desires for us in this life a measure of collaboration between sense and intellect. However, for Duns Scotus no more than for Saint Thomas does man's intellect directly apprehend the pure intelligible.

Whether we follow the Cistercian school of Christian love, Gilson observes, or the Thomistic, all human love becomes a thirst for God, the proper object of our love. According to Saint Bernard of Clairvaux, we are told "human love necessarily begins in egoism and carnality," but when the Christian comes to see that he is an image or analogue of God, he sees that in properly loving himself he loves not only the image of God within himself, but he loves others who bear the same image, and, finally, he loves the supreme Good which is the source of all created images. The more man seeks to become like God, the more perfectly he resembles God, and the more fully he realizes his essence. Finally, a love that seeks the Sovereign Good is rewarded by joy in the possession of the Good.

Gilson considers the notion of Christian liberty as it was clarified by medieval thinkers. Responsibility for attaining our last end presupposes a God-given freedom to accept or reject it. Aristotle had pointed out that man spontaneously wills happiness as his last end; free choice relates to means for attaining it. Boethius speaks of the decisive role of the deliberations of reason in free choice. Saint Thomas is assigned a position midway between Boethius's intellectualism and Duns Scotus's later voluntarism. With Boethius, Saint Thomas, to a point, sees the decisive role played by the judgment of reason, and does not mind calling free choice "free judgment," but he sees that free choice in the final analysis must be referred to the will, a point which Duns Scotus emphasizes. But the distinctively Christian conception of liberty pertains to that which distinguishes between a will that is morally indifferent and a will liberated by grace from servitude. The doctrine of Christian liberty, Gilson points out, is rooted in Saint Paul (Romans 6:2-23), developed by Saint Augustine, Saint Anselm, and Saint Thomas Aquinas. Grace strengthens the will and restores to it a measure of its original integrity. The blessed are conceived as completely delivered from the servitude of a will confronted with lesser goods, and in them freedom attains its maximum perfection.

The difference between the Platonic moral universe and the Christian, Gilson explains, is the difference between a universe ruled by a plurality of non-creative gods and one which is ruled by a creative God. The difference between the Christian moral universe and the Kantian is that the former rests on a Christian metaphysics which the latter lacks but needs. Christian thinkers of the Middle Ages worked out Cicero's classical conception of morality as the habit of acting according to the demands of reason and nature, but the laws that govern reason and nature in the Christian universe have their source in a creative God. As the proximate principle of his legislative deliberations, man's reason is an analogical participation in Divine Reason. Nature, then, takes on a sacramental appearance. The sinner turns from his reason and the eternal law that rules it, and only God can restore or re-create the order the sinner rejects. Thus, Christian thought sees the necessity for this special help called supernatural grace that restores the beauty of the soul and enables it to turn towards God as its proper end. The integrity of the soul before the Fall was itself a grace; supernatural grace restores a measure of the soul's lost integrity.

Greek moral philosophy, it is explained, interpreted the happiness that is man's last end in terms of the totality of his lifelong efforts in virtuous living. Thus, for Aristotle, expediency is seen as ruling the choice of means to that end. But Christians, we are reminded, have always seen man as inclining towards a transcendent end. Love, for Saint Augustine and Saint Thomas, Gilson notes, is the gravitational pull drawing back to their source the creatures that have issued forth from the generosity of the creative act, and such also is the world of Dionysius the Pseudo-Areopagite of perhaps the late fifth or early sixth century—a world in which the good circulates from the Good and back to the Good. Saint Augustine sees morality as depending on the internal movement of a will fixed on its transcendent end. It is the intention of the end that makes the will good, for intention is an act of the will in view of an end. Intention of the end also causes a deliberation of reason as to the means. This weighing of the means informs the conscience that obliges the will, but the choice belongs to the will. Thus, the author concludes that Christian philosophy, reflecting on the revolutionary notion of creation, rationalized the idea of moral law and duty centuries before Kant discovered their rationality.

The mystics, Gilson explains, were interested in what nature signified; the philosophers, in what nature is. Their philosophical view of nature accords with that of the Greeks—nature is conceived as the internal principle of a thing's operations. For Christian thinkers, however, the Creator's providential concern for all of nature leaves no room for chance. A miracle is but one creation added to another. As defined by Saint Thomas and Duns Scotus, nature is an order of secondary causes. Although a miracle transcends secondary causes wholly, it is completely rational, for it depends on divine reason. Christian philosophy, Gilson claims, is especially concerned with the kind of nature that is open to the miracle of God's grace. Thus, nature is conceived as a creation that is open to what God wills it to be. This passive possibility to receive the strength of God's grace is called "obediential potency." Nature, then, through obediential potency is open to the Beatific Vision. Pelagius's error was not that he denied grace, but that he considered nature as the only grace; he denied the need of a second grace or creation in addition to nature. The application of obediential potency to the problem of grace completes the systematic notion of a Christian universe.

Faith in the Gospel, in creation, and in the coming Kingdom of God, Gilson reflects, made the medieval synthesis of history possible. With Saint Augustine, Christian thinkers conceived of the existence of the world in terms of a progressive building up of the City of God. The philosophers were aware of the limitations of philosophy, but confident of its eventual integration with Christian wisdom. The Christianization of the world would be followed by the reign of the Antichrist, and then by the final triumph of good over evil. Christian thinkers of the Middle Ages, Gilson points out, were the first to provide the totality of history with an intelligible explanation. Moderns, he observes, have not always recognized their indebtedness to the Middle Ages in this regard. Auguste Comte (1798-1857) reminds him of an "Augustine turned atheist" with his three stages of development leading to "the religion of humanity." The philosophy of history propounded by Georg Wilhelm Hegel (1770-1831) withholds affirmation of the dogma of providence but proceeds to demonstrate its correctness. Medieval philosophy, Gilson says, expired before and not because of the rise of modern science; it was weakened and rendered ineffective by "the internal dissensions that afflicted it because it had forgotten its essence, which was to be Christian." It can scarcely be denied, he acknowledges, that the Middle Ages lacked a historical sense, but, he adds, "we must at least grant it the merit of assisting at the birth of a philosophy of history."

Since neither the Old Testament nor the New gave Christians a science of the world that is to be saved, they had to supply it for themselves; they needed a philosophy better to appreciate the nature that God has created and redeems by His grace. Platonism and Aristotelianism introduced them to the main problems of philosophy, to rational principles required for their solution, and to serviceable techniques. Christian philosophy essentially results in a "deeply considered affirmation of a reality and goodness intrinsic to nature, such as the Greeks, lacking knowledge of its source and end, only dimly foreshadowed." A Manichean, a Pelagian, or a Lutheran conception of nature would have made the appearance of medieval philosophy impossible. Mani (c.216-c.276) denied the goodness of nature; Pelagius (c.400) denied the wounds of nature and therewith the need of grace to heal the wounds; Luther (1483-1546) later viewed nature as intrinsically corrupt; but the medieval Christian conception of nature, with Saint Augustine, stands midway between Mani and Pelagius. The Greeks, then, made it possible for medieval Christianity to deepen and extend the rational principles which the Greeks had earlier employed so that those principles would yield their full truth; thus, the Greeks made medieval philosophy possible. The distinctive work of that philosophy was that Christian philosophers "pushed the problem of reality to the level of existence and thereby, for the first time, gave full significance to the concept of actuality."

V.J.M.

THE MAKING OF EUROPE

Author: Christopher Dawson (1889-)
Type of work: History of European unity
First published: 1932

PRINCIPAL IDEAS ADVANCED

The early Middle Ages created the cultural unity of Europe.

An understanding of medieval culture depends upon an understanding of medieval religion as effecting the conversion of the West.

The insistence of the Catholic Church on the supremacy of the spiritual over the temporal made the rise of medieval unity possible.

Although medieval unity was not permanent, it made subsequent cultural unity possible in Europe; the breakdown of the humanist culture suggests the need for a return to a spiritual ground of European unity.

Christopher Dawson describes history at its best as "the great corrective to that 'parochialism in time' which Bertrand Russell rightly describes as one of the great faults of our modern society." It is Dawson's contention that modern historians tend to judge the past with the standards of the present; they approach history from humanistic and nationalistic points of view. Consequently, such historians fail to understand the creative power of the age they call "the Dark Ages," and only a Catholic historian can appreciate, through his immersion in a living faith, the spiritual origin of the unity of the early Middle Ages.

Dawson's central thesis is that Europe as a cultural unity was made possible by the spiritual unity which rose in the early medieval period. As a historian Dawson seeks to show what forces brought about that early unity which, assuming a radically different humanistic direction, accounts for the creation of European culture, of Europe itself as a cultural unity.

According to Dawson, Europe is not a natural unity, and its cultural development results not so much from the convergence of various streams of culture, from the Mediterranean, Danube, Atlantic, and Baltic "channels of cultural diffusion," as from the emergence of a center of culture in the Aegean, which made the rise of Greek civilization possible. The Roman Empire, in introducing the city to continental Europe, became the transmitter of Greek culture and thereby brought about, the Hellenization of the West. The Romans "made the whole world into one city" and by introducing the Roman system of laws achieved a civic unity which the new era of Christian Rome inherited and spiritualized. Throughout the Dark Ages, Dawson contends, the efforts to return to the peace and order of the Roman empire "led the new peoples forward to the future and prepared the way for the coming of a new European culture."

The foundations of European unity are to be found in the Roman Empire, the Catholic Church, the classical tradition, and the barbarian invasions. The Romans provided the ideal of civic unity; the Catholic Church transferred the idea of citizenship to the spiritual order; the classical tradition added the intellectual element; and, finally, the barbarians supplied the human material, "the *gentes* as against the *imperium* and the *ecclesia*—the source of the national element in European life."

By the sixth century, as a result of the barbarian invasions, a fusion of the elements—Roman, Catholic, classical, and barbarian—had taken place. The Western peoples became Romano-Germanic in culture, and the Church provided the spiritual unity which kept the diverse cultures together. Nevertheless, Dawson points out, the leadership of culture passed to the East: "the 'Dark Ages' of western civilisation coincide with the golden age of Byzantine and Islamic culture."

The Byzantine culture was a new creation, not "a decadent survival from the classical past," but the center of a new cultural movement. Dawson chides historians for neglecting the study of the rise of Eastern culture and its influence on the West. The author points out that although the Byzantine culture was essentially religious and is best known through Byzantine art, it had a profound influence on society through its political and economic repercussions.

The institution of monasticism is credited by Dawson with having the greatest and most transforming cultural effect in both the East and the West. Although the monks were concerned only with the spiritual life and thus isolated themselves from all ordinary political and social activities, "these naked fasting ascetics became the popular heroes and ideal types for the whole Byzantine world." When, in the fifth century, the Roman Empire was disintegrating, the Eastern Empire seemed about to become thoroughly orientalized, "Graeco-Syrian in culture and Monophysite in religion," but that development was halted by Justinian, and the culture of the Eastern Empire brought Eastern and Western elements once again into unity. Throughout all of the creative effort of the Byzantine culture the emphasis on spiritual values, an emphasis which monasticism provided, is evident. Matter becomes the expression of spirit in such a crowning work of art as the Church of the Holy Wisdom at Constantinople, and in Byzantine liturgical poetry religious mysteries also find a form of expression in which East and West meet.

Despite the synthesis of Eastern and Western elements in the religious art of the Byzantine culture, the opposition of East and West in religion threatened the unity of the Empire. The coming of Islam led to the revolt of the subject nationalities and to the decreasing influence of Hellenistic culture in the East. Nestorianism, Monophysitism, Manicheanism, and Gnosticism contributed to the rupture between the Eastern churches and the Church of the Empire. During the ninth and tenth centuries Moslem culture, a cosmopolitan product, influenced the entire Islamic world.

Although the Byzantine Empire enjoyed a cultural renaissance during the ninth and tenth centuries, external forces—invasion by the Turks, Patzinaks and Kuman Tartars—reduced the Empire during the following three centuries, thereby allowing the Romanic-Germanic development of the West to provide the new unity of Europe. According to Dawson's account, the Byzantine culture failed to propagate the traditions of classical civilization, and it was uncreative because of the rigidity of the Byzantine church-state.

During the period of decline in the West as the result of the barbarian and Moslem invasions, the Church, precisely because it gave priority to spiritual concerns, kept the creative forces of Europe alive. The ideal which Saint Augustine described in his *City of God* (426) was influential in the papacy; the imperial tradition of the Roman Empire became the tradition of the Church, and Rome became the meeting ground of East and West. The monasteries were the centers of Christian life and the framers of the new spiritualized tradition. Ireland, at the close of the sixth century, became the leader of Western culture because of the influence of the monastic schools of Clonard, Clonmacnoise, and Bangor. Saint Gregory began the Benedictine world mission which, together with the Celtic monastic movement, made Anglo-Saxon culture dominant in the seventh century. In the eighth century the Anglo-Saxons were leaders in art, religion, scholarship, and literature. Thus Dawson credits the Anglo-Saxon monks "and, above all, St. Boniface" for the realization of "that union of Teutonic initiative and Latin order which is the source of the whole mediaeval development of culture."

The Carolingian age marks the period during which the Frankish dominions became the center of medieval culture. According to Dawson, the "ideal of the mediaeval Empire, the political position of the Papacy, the German hegemony in Italy and the expansion of Germany toward the East, the fundamental institutions of mediaeval society both in Church and State, and the incorporation of the classical tradition of mediaeval culture" are all historical aspects of the Carolingian period. The monasteries became agricultural and trade centers and contributed more than any other institution to the transmission of culture from the Carolingian age to that of the Saxon Empire.

The period of Viking invasions tested the new culture of Europe. Although the victories of King Alfred in 878 and 885 and of Odo and Arnulf checked the Vikings and prepared the way for the assimilation of the invaders, other forces, Saracen, Moslem, and Magyar, threatened Western Christendom. The final victory of the Christian West came not because of military superiority but because of the capacity of the new culture to absorb the invaders; new life was given to Europe by the Vikings, but new spirit and discipline, Christian in origin, countered the destructive aspects of the Viking ideal.

Dawson contends that the Carolingian Empire declined because "it embodied two contradictory principles, the universalism of the Roman and Christian traditions on the one hand, and the tribal particularism of barbaric Europe on the other." Nevertheless, Dawson argues, the Carolingian state contained within itself an ideal which survived the state and became the principle which undergirded medieval unity. The champions of the ideal were the Carolingian churchmen, and the ideal was that of a universal empire unified by the Christian faith. The state became a theocracy, and the Empire was clericalized. The claim that the spiritual transcends any temporal power originated with the papacy, and the state thus became an expression of the spirit and will of the Church, not because the papacy chose to assume temporal power, but because the ideal and the circumstances were such that power was thrust upon the Church.

Even during the dark age of lawlessness which followed the fall of the Carolingian Empire, the Church, despite its own weakness and disunity, kept the higher traditions of Western civilization alive. The tenth century was one during which a loosely organized feudal society threatened the values which had made a tentative unity possible; only the Church, through its intellectual, cultural, and social concerns, continued to champion the values of civilization. Thus, when Otto I came to power and insisted on a union of Church and state, the ideal was present and active in the Church. The unity of Christendom, by the eleventh century, had become that of a free society under the unified leadership of Roman Pope and Emperor. The unity of the West was thus a spiritual unity achieved in the medieval period because of the persistent spirit of the Roman Church.

Medieval unity was not permanent, however, but the spiritual unity which characterized the Christian North gave a strength to the West which later took the form of a cultural unity, a unity which held Europe together. In this later period, "the scholar and the gentleman took the place of the monk and the knight as the representative figures of Western culture."

Dawson concludes his account with the claim that the humanist and aristocratic culture of Europe is breaking down and the unity of Europe is threatened. The only solution, as Dawson sees the problem, is a return of that spiritual unity which made the rise of medieval unity possible and which contributed so vitally to the making of Europe.

DEGREES OF KNOWLEDGE

Author: Jacques Maritain (1882-)
Type of work: Christian epistemology
First published: 1932

Principal Ideas Advanced

Unity cannot be appreciated without an understanding of the distinctions which lead up, in a hierarchy of being and knowledge, to the ultimate unity of God.

Anything the mind truly knows, it knows in terms of being, first conforming itself to whatever level of intensity with which the essence known possesses being, and then integrating all its knowledge of the object to determine a concept which will adequately represent that essence.

The mind cannot be examined in a precognitive state, but only in terms of its connections with what it knows while it is involved in the process of knowing.

There is a distinction between the order of grace and that of nature, although grace constantly supports and permeates nature and is not totally separate from it.

Jacques Maritain, in his *Degrees of Knowledge,* sets out to vindicate the relevance of the Thomistic synthesis of knowledge and being for modern thought. He reveals Thomism not as a system to be arbitrarily imposed on science, philosophy, and theology, but as a flexible, pragmatic attitude toward material and spiritual realities. It is also an attitude toward our knowledge of reality, one that is securely anchored in observation and reason, but that can be extended into the less measurable or definable areas of metaphysics and theology. Augustinian wisdom, which had dominated the Church for nearly a millennium before Thomas, was "*religious* both in essence and mode," writes Maritain. Reality was not subjected to purely rational examination. Thomism, however, allowed for distinctions between the methods and areas of competence of science, philosophy, and theology. Thomas gave order to Augustine's theology and made it relevant to the lesser disciplines, enlarging their possibility for development according to their own valid mode of knowing. Thomism, unlike Platonic idealism, preserves and links a knowledge of things with a knowledge of minds. From the level of the physicist to that of the contemplative, there are unifying principles, an understanding of which closes the gap between science and Christian wisdom.

Knowledge on all levels, says Maritain, depends on the process of abstraction. The first level, that of experimental science or "prephilosophy," is that on which objects can neither exist nor be conceived without matter and thus must be viewed according to verifiable properties; objects on that level cannot be known "in themselves" or in their essence. The second level is that of purified "sciences of explanation," like mathematics, which refer to objects which, although existing in material form, can be conceived in abstraction from matter. The third, that of metaphysics, involves objects which can be conceived without matter and may even exist without it, objects such as the qualities of beauty and being.

Though it is fashionable to exempt science from the need for acquiring knowledge of essences, the truth is that science always depends on the process of abstraction, for nothing can be stated as known unless it applies in a sense broader than the single, material instance. The individual object existing in matter is not truly known and cannot be described merely in terms of itself and its appearance. Matter itself is unintelligible; what is known is the universal law or quality the mind draws from observation of the object. Science deals with specific things in contingent, not ideal, states, but with awareness of necessary laws and unchanging phenomena, which can be detached from the observed object. Our knowledge of being in general, says Maritain, assures us that there is a support or essence (unobservable to a greater or lesser extent) underlying those qualities we choose to abstract, investigate, or measure. On this essence depend laws, order, and stable relationships, with which science progresses.

Maritain insists that philosophical thought must not begin with a demand that the mind prove its ability to know. Instead, mind should first examine reality as it appears in sense experience and abstracted intelligible essences, and then periodically turn back to judge and test itself, its methods, and their validity. The mind can be studied only in the process of knowing, not in an isolated, ideal, precognitive state. Thus, the mind must always be understood in terms of its links with what it knows, not in terms of itself. In Aristotelian-Thomist "critical realism," epistemology develops of necessity alongside ontology, not as a separate science. The known and the knowing mind are apparent simultaneously to the intellect, which must have knowledge of its own being and function whenever it acts. However, the thing known exists in nature before it is known, just as the mind's knowledge of that thing as it is must rank before the mind's reflection on itself.

According to Maritain, there are two levels of existence in things as they are found in nature: the first is that being they enjoy in themselves as distinct from nothingness, and the second is the being that the soul perceives in them, or assigns to them, when it knows, during which process individual peculiarities are stripped away.

The "thing itself" exists in actual matter and its essence-as-we-know-it (the thing as an intelligible object) enjoys a "possible" existence in the mind. The latter is an immaterial *species* which is not subject to the individual restrictions of matter. It unites with another variety of *species* in the mind itself which has predisposed the mind to the laws and order of knowledge, while not being knowledge in itself. There is, writes Maritain, a conformity or correspondence "established between the being possessed by the thing and the being affirmed by the mind." Correspondence is a unique mode of being proper to the knowing mind in the moment of its knowing.

The definitive function of the intellect is to know, just as that of the essence is to exist. Knowledge is the perfection of being, its very crown; it is a super-existence in which being is raised to a new intensity without the creation of an entirely new being or product. The soul unites with the "presentative form" or intelligible aspect of a thing's being on two levels. The soul first intentionally submits to being acted on and informed, and then the soul performs its own characteristic, definitive function; that is, the soul becomes other than it *was* without becoming absolutely identified in essence with the object that it knows. It is able "to become a thing other than the self" without losing its own identity. The concept, or "uttered presentative form," says Maritain, is the sign, not the new product or new being, of the union between the knower and the known object's intelligible aspect. According to the author, "the concept . . . and object are indistinguishable, save that one exists only in the mind and the other exists at the same time in the mind and in the thing." The concept has no essence of its own; its meaning depends on the material thing from which it was derived.

Knowledge of such concepts as these is proper to a "philosophy of nature," which itself complements, or is the soul of, the experimental sciences forming its foundation. A philosophy of nature examines not only being as it can be detected beneath changing phenomena, but also the "ontological principles" which account for its mutability. Like experimental science, which employs myths or images to represent working hypotheses, a philosophy of nature utilizes myth in relating itself to physico-mathematical theories. The physico-chemical universe is a closed order which does not develop or progress into the realm of philosophy. It may, however, be the basis for a philosophy of nature which has one foot in the created, material order and one in the purely intelligible order. The level of metaphysics is higher still, according to Maritain, for its object is spirit alone, independent of matter and the experimental method. Science itself cannot be freed from matter as a basis and can never overlap metaphysics. Even concepts like "simultaneity," if they are to be usable by a physicist, must be reducible to concrete events and phenomena; they cannot be considered in their essence. Science is thus free from the concepts and imagery of common sense, as well as from those of ontology.

Metaphysics, with its own forms of knowledge, says Maritain, transcends "perinoetic intellection," or knowledge merely by signs which stand for differences between objects. Since the thing known by perinoetic intellection is dominated by the individuating power of matter, the thing is known "not by signs which manifest it, but by signs which hide it." In passing from science (perinoetic) to metaphysics, the author claims, we pass also into a region where the movement is not from the visible to the visible, but from the visible to the invisible. Even so, metaphysical knowledge is "a knowledge of things not by their essence but in their essence." It does not grasp essence intuitively or by direct perception, but by signs or properties. This latter procedure allows us to transcend the knowledge of merely accidental differences, though such differences are retained and relied upon even when one has passed to an awareness of universals on a non-material level.

While perinoetic intellection stops short at the boundary of essence, "dianoetic" intellection transcends limits of matter and individuality, attaining to a knowledge of signs that represent the essence of the thing known. It is based not upon differences but upon likenesses which, says Maritain, "are at once exterior signs and masks of the veritable properties." Dianoetic intellection depends on the idea that being-as-being has a real existence in itself and can be investigated on various levels, according to the degree of intensity with which existence is possessed by actual essence. The fact that an object exists comes first in our knowledge of that object. Being is the real object of metaphysics, and metaphysics is the crown of the philosophy of nature. Yet, unlike the latter, metaphysics does not terminate in things of the sense but in things of the spirit. Whatever the mind knows through dianoetic intellection is known in terms of being, first by ascertaining the degree or intensity of being (to distinguish), and then by integrating all known properties into a concept signifying essence (to unite). The concept that the mind knows is itself one, though the objects which it signifies are multiple in essence. Once grasped, the universal "bears within itself the possibility of being realized according to its proper significance," in subjects absolutely different in essence from the one initially known; it is thus that reason leads us to awareness of purely spiritual being.

In all created beings, essence is distinct from existence; the being of created things admits of varying degrees of intensity according to the determinations of their essences. Only in the case of God, whose essence it is to exist, is there ultimate identity of Self and Being, and such distinctions then cease to have any meaning. God is known to us through three degrees of "ananoetic" intellection, the first two in the realm of metaphysics and the last in the realm of theology. We may not seize the "object" of this form of intellection by apprehension of the properties of an essence *in* themselves, as by dianoetic intellection. We see only an obscured image of the transcendent reality, for the limitation natural to our minds does not allow direct and proportionate knowledge of a reality that is entirely of another order than our own. The being of God must not be thought of as limited by the inadequate concept of being to which human minds are able to attain. We know spirit, then, through analogy, and this method has several degrees, corresponding to its objects.

The first level of analogy is "circumscriptive" and concerns the knowledge of beings which are limited in being though they exist in an order beyond our own and are purely spiritual. Their goodness and beauty is not *our* goodness and beauty and cannot be conceived except through the inadequate means of analogy. The second level, that of "uncircumscriptive" analogy, includes knowledge of an unlimited God, who Himself circumscribes being; that is, He defines and terminates it. He is entirely beyond being as we know it, and the concept itself can be applied to Him only by analogy. While such metaphysical knowledge of God introduces distinctions, says Maritain, we must consider these to be the result of defects in our own cognitive mechanism, while the Object of our knowledge is one and simple in essence.

In passing from this second degree of ananoetic intellection to the third, or "parabolic" analogy, Maritain continues, we leave the realm of metaphysics for that of theology. It is in this transition that the bonds are forged between reason and faith. Through the former we are able to know God by His footprints left in nature and in our own intellects; through the latter, we know His essence, if only by faint analogies. We can apprehend a particular perfection of God, but our understanding of that perfection is conditioned by our bonds to a sensible, material order, utterly different from the divine order. This third degree of ananoetic intellection is a "superanalogy" (like that of the Father and the Son), and it depends entirely on the truths of revelation as accepted by faith.

To know God as He is, Maritain writes, we must be one with Him, for there can be "no duality of subject and predicate." Metaphysics does not reveal God as He is; only participation in His being can do that. God's sovereign personality, the "seal of transcendence," is what sets Him apart, even from our own human personality with all its endowments. Reason indicates a terminus of being in supreme personality that is also supremely individual; faith reveals to us, moreover, that within the single divine essence, there subsists three "relative personalities." Since we must grasp this essence only by analogy, we must first build up our knowledge by means of positive theology with its definite concepts and metaphors and then, at the very end, fall back on negative theology, by which the poverty of all our modes of intellection is recognized, and all concepts and metaphors are revealed as inadequate, if not, in fact, as wrong as they are right. At this point, negative theology becomes the mystical experience itself, which is borne up on all the knowledge which comes before it, both natural and supernatural. All the distinctions of this knowledge are fused and dissolved in this one experience of unity, which is, essentially, a participation in divine being and unity itself.

There are three forms of wisdom, as opposed to science, Maritain claims. The first and lowest is the ananoetic, metaphysical wisdom or natural theology, which is supreme in the natural order. The second is the knowledge of revealed mysteries or theology proper, which rationally develops what is known by faith. The highest, which is outside the realm of reason and in the realm of the supernatural, is the beatific vision, both as it exists in embryo during this present life and as it exists in Heaven. The beatific vision allows us to contemplate God in His "inwardness," in His very essence.

In the lowest or metaphysical wisdom, distinctions in the divine unity are known separately by means of concepts proper to limited creatures; that is, in terms of the images by which God makes Himself known in His creation. When God is known according to the second form of wisdom, by faith, His essence is known not in itself, but "according to" or "in virtue of" His essence, which is revealed through more or less accurate (humanly speaking) metaphors and concepts. Though the manner of knowledge is human, the object is supernatural; thus, the knowledge itself is disproportionate to the object.

Theology is not merely the result of natural reason at work upon the truths of faith, but the operation of a reason informed and dominated by faith upon those truths. According to Maritain, the final and most perfect wisdom is that of the mystical experience, in which the manner of knowing is at last proportionate to the object known, since it has joined itself to that object and has risen beyond the human limitations of sense and reason.

There are several conditions for this mystical experience, Maritain states. The first is sanctifying grace or the indwelling of the Holy Trinity within the soul. The second is the elevation of the soul to the same infinite order as its object, which is effected by a "connaturality" wrought by grace. In experiencing our own love of God (as we do through the Holy Ghost) we simultaneously experience God Himself. Finally, mystical knowledge is marked by Sonship to God, which puts us in the same order with Him, with the result that our knowledge of Him is proportionate to His being. The idea of this sonship should not be obscured by the use of purely natural terms or metaphors, for the relation is one enjoying the status of an "ontological reality," existing on a plane other than our natural one. In infused contemplation, says Maritain, we leap beyond all human modes of knowing, beyond all concepts; their existence in us is suspended in all but the lower forms of mystical experience, in which God is still known in terms of His effects on our soul. When He is known in Himself, all concepts and their relevance fade into obscurity, in a divine ignorance that is called negative theology or negative contemplation. Such contemplation is the seed, the foretaste, of union with God in Heaven. This mystical contemplation is the normal and proper development of redeemed human life, and the metaphysician longs for it even without knowing precisely what he longs for.

Just as there is a natural desire for contemplation on the part of the metaphysician, writes Maritain, so there is a "natural contemplation" whereby the philosopher ceases to employ his reason and actively loves the object he has learned to know with a purely natural human love. Metaphysics does not, of itself, demand union with God as a consummation, for such an achievement lies in the realm of grace, not nature. One does not, without grace, attain to the essence of God. The physical phenomena which often accompany mystical states exist because of nature and are not necessarily the effects of grace. According to Maritain, such ecstasies can be influenced easily by temperament, illness, or other forces. Without the restraining, guiding influence of faith, such experiences can be perverted into vagueness and pantheism, simply because the "mystic" is not then experiencing God as a Person. Mystics outside the Church cannot attain the true mystical union naturally, only when infused with grace. The poet as a natural mystic unites not with God but with the mystery of being in things. It is necessary to draw a strict line between the orders of nature and grace, while not forgetting that grace both surrounds and permeates nature by its action.

Practical philosophy truly knows, but cannot of itself produce, right action, Maritain writes. Speculative philosophy operates in the realm of intelligibles simply for the sake of knowing. Theology includes both practical and speculative thought, at once explaining and offering the experience of divine things. Saint John of the Cross pre-eminently used the vocabulary of the practical mystic. But ontologically accurate terms must sometimes give way to mystical language, so that both remain true in their own way. Thus, mystical theology is, says Maritain, at once the highest *activity* (speaking ontologically) and a hard-won state of *nonactivity* (speaking of the necessary suspension of all merely human modes of knowing.)

The suspension of ordinary modes of learning does not demand that all the previous modes of knowing be perverted, lost, or made irrelevant to life. Nor should it be thought that grace must destroy nature in order to perfect it. Instead, suggests Maritain, one must surrender the self as principal cause to Christ, who then fills the void from within, permeating nature and fulfilling it. The achieved result, which is to be transformed in God and participate "in equality of love with God," allows us to perceive at once the whole span, meaning, and end of human life. Saint John of the Cross always preserved distinctions between the natural and the supernatural orders; he did not believe that the latter invalidates the former. Thus, Maritain decides, one should not long for contemplation in order to know. Knowledge should come through reason and faith. Only when one passes beyond these highest human activities to love God mystically, does one suspend all human forms of knowledge, even while preserving them in the lesser regions of the soul.

In the thought of Saint John of the Cross, according to Maritain in his closing remarks, "everything is knitted together at the level of the human heart, it is disparity which is revealed to us, in order that, vanquished by love, it may lead us to unity." The multitude of distractions, of things known, must ultimately be renounced, if one is to love and know perfectly. But in our renunciation of love, we love these goods properly and in view of their relation to Being itself, as we have experienced it. The soul, as John of the Cross described it, must enter a dark night of the senses, in which even images and concepts of God are rejected while the Reality is awaited in purgative suffering. In the spiritual marriage, the soul shares with God the love and knowledge of His own essence, so that the soul may rejoice in offering God to Himself in a loving union of wills. The soul then experiences mystically the very life of the Trinity and the love of the three divine Persons for each other, which forms the highest state of knowledge possible for created beings.

B.J.R.

LITURGY AND PERSONALITY

Author: Dietrich von Hildebrand (1889-)
Type of work: Christian personalistic philosophy
First published: 1933

Principal Ideas Advanced

The spiritual formation of the individual who lives in accordance with the spirit of the liturgy is a transformation of the individual's personality; this transformation is not, however, the essential aim of the liturgy.

The prime intention of the liturgy is to praise God, to respond fittingly to Him; the second intention of the liturgy is to ask God's grace so that man may participate in the divine life.

The deepest and most organic transformation of personality in the spirit of Christ is not found when means for it are deliberately sought; the deepest transformation of our personality in Christ is brought about in an entirely gratuitous manner at that point where we respond to the world of values found in God, where our glorification of God is performed as divine service, as liturgy.

In *Liturgy and Personality,* the liturgy's formative power to constitute some of the deepest elements of personality is revealed by Dietrich von Hildebrand. Liturgy is defined by the author as the official public worship of the Catholic Church as found in the Holy Sacrifice of the Mass, the Divine Office, and the administration of the sacraments and sacramentals. The liturgy is the conscious and personal praising of God by means of spoken words and gestures which confirm and fulfill the interior love of God from which they flow. The liturgy is the most authentic human way of praising God since it is man's most conscious and fully awakened act performed in the divine presence.

Von Hildebrand is interested in tracing the mysterious, all-embracing, qualitatively expressed unity of the liturgy as the voice of the Church. This is an essential unity to be found by means of the philosophical procedure known as the phenomenological method which, the author believes, puts us in contact with metaphysical realities. Thus, even though the reasons for the introduction of the materials of the liturgy, such as rituals, symbols, and the like, have been merely fortuitous through elapsed centuries of time, through a study of these materials we can, by means of the aforementioned method, penetrate to the unchanging, metaphysically real essential marks of the liturgy. The author seeks to focus interest not on an historical analysis of the liturgy, but on the inner essence of the liturgy. The theme here is the liturgy insofar as it forms a supernatural personality in us, insofar as it transforms us in Christ.

Consequent upon his definition of the liturgy, von Hildebrand distinguishes the essential features of his conception of personality. Every man is a person. Every man is a subject, a conscious being which possesses itself and actively achieves itself by means of free choices. Not every man is a personality, however. In the true sense a personality is a man who can realize classical human attitudes. A personality is the complete, profound man who knows, loves, and wills more deeply and clearly than the ordinary man.

There are two essential parts to personality: the first part is a full and essentially spiritual organ which is a gift from God. This gift gives a man great powers of knowledge, love, and will-power. The second part is the link of the personality with the world of values. This second part is open to our will so that the man with this link can abandon his egocentric self to values. This kind of a man can live in truth, tuned to the objective Logos or Word.

The third important aspect of the personality is *style*. By means of style, that is, a way of speech, expression, and movement, the personality's outer being is a genuine projection of his inner being.

From the natural point of view not every man can become a personality. But transformed in Christ the natural man lives no more, for Christ now lives in him. Thus, a saint is a personality no matter what elements he naturally might have had to help him achieve a personality. In Christ the saint does not give up his individuality but becomes unique; that is, he fully becomes what God intends him to be. Indeed the saint alone is a personality in the true sense, because the saint alone is the true and complete man.

In speaking of the formation of personality, von Hildebrand distinguishes two fundamental elements. The two-fold first element consists in the natural ontological basis of personality. The natural basis is a pure gift of God which excludes our freedom. This foundation includes our natural inherited tendencies, and it exists in combination with our spiritual, personal reality. The supernatural ontological basis of personality presupposes the aforementioned natural basis. This supernatural foundation consists in the imitation of Christ by means of the divine life given in Baptism and partly restored and fortified through the sacraments. This foundation supports the life of the person in the Mystical Body of Christ, and it is the basis for the transformation of the personality in Christ.

The second fundamental element in the formation of personality is the intentional, or consciously attentive, contact with the world of values. The liturgy is treated by von Hildebrand only in its relation to this second element. He distinguishes several formative powers by means of which the values of the liturgy constitute personality.

One of the deepest formative powers of the liturgy is its spirit of communion. The liturgy, as the official prayer of the Church, provides a situation in which all participants are together in Christ. The liturgy is communal prayer; it unites us because in performing it we become aware of the ultimate supernatural unity of all men in Christ. Again, the communion of saints represents a new value over and above individual saintliness; it represents a new dimension of the glory of God and the Lordship of Christ. True personality is formed in the spirit of communion of the liturgy, because the inner walls of self-assertion are broken down by a "we" which has passed through the "Thou" of the God-man. The liturgy leads us through Christ into the presence of God, before whom there is no more cramping selfish isolation.

Another mark of the liturgy is its spirit of reverence. Reverence is the essential basis for the perception both of values and of the true relation to the world of values contained in God. Reverence is the mother of all virtues; it is a fundamental attitude toward being in which one gives the proper response to the majesty of values which are "messages" of God. In this context, liturgy forms personality by molding man's right relation towards God and all created beings. The liturgy uses wax, salt, oil, and the like, and in so doing it engenders in man a spirit of reverence toward all created things.

A further formative power of the liturgy, says von Hildebrand, is its spirit of response to value. One of the most essential elements of true personality is the consciousness that we owe to values a due response; that is, a response which is not up to our own choice. The liturgy embodies a unique value response in, for example, the Gloria of the Mass. In the Gloria the God-man offers Himself to the Father, and this offering presents us with the primal theocentric attitude. It is to be noted that true theocentrism does not exclude one's own person as unessential, for this attitude moves man to ask God, "Who art Thou and who am I?" The liturgy in the Mass breathes the spirit of including one's own person in a mutual relationship between man and God.

For von Hildebrand the two decisive features of true, or theocentric, personality are: first, a fundamental value-response attitude, that is, the living consciousness of the fact that an adequate answer is due every value; second, a clear grasp of the hierarchy of values. Assuredly the ultimate criterion of true personality is implied in the longing for God as the highest good. The liturgy takes account of the hierarchy of values in, to provide but one illustration, the structure of the liturgical year in which there is a hierarchical gradation of feasts.

A fourth fruit of the liturgy is the state of being awake which it engenders in man. Awakeness here means dwelling in the presence of God instead of in a state of routine bluntness. Awakeness is that true consciousness which is an indispensable element of personality. The liturgy is not a means to waking up; it is, rather, the highest form of awakeness. In its structure it is a state of being awake; for example, in the hours of the Divine Office the Credo is often repeated in a consciously focused affirmation of faith. Man formed by the liturgy is awake to the true value of all earthly goods such as, for example, that of water, which is used in Baptism and in the Mass.

The liturgy constitutes personality in still another way by its spirit of *discretio,* or the sense of distinguishing the law of the inner development of things. Through this sense of discrimination, the true personality distinguishes various levels in himself and responds according to the depth of the experience at hand. Thus, to cite but one case, the touching of a holy relic is seen by the man who lives in the liturgy as being a venerable nonliturgical form of piety which is quite secondary to the Church's official worship.

The spirit of continuity found in the liturgy is a further mode through which it forms a true personality. The power of continuity is the mark of every man as a spiritual person. The man with the spirit of continuity maintains "superactually" all truths and values, and he is not enchanted by novelties and glamour. This man does not live on the surface of the "now," but in his continuity he anticipates a part of eternity. Continuity is a special condition of the transformation in Christ, for Christ is the form of our soul just as our soul is the form of our body; consequently, our eyes must be superactually fixed on God.

The organic element in the liturgy is noteworthy here. In the present context the essence of the organic is an all-pervading fullness of meaning. The liturgy leads man down the path of value-response by unfolding to his spiritual eyes the glory of the Lord. Liturgical symbols and chants present to man the continued Epiphany of the Lord. In the liturgy everything is fittingly placed, and everything is seen in organic linkage, in the great connectedness of the relationship between God and man. Thus, the liturgy organically forms the classical spirit of true personality.

Underlying von Hildebrand's treatment of the topic of liturgy and personality is his philosophy of value. On the basis of this philosophy he asserts that all created values glorify God since they are traces of the Divine Being. Man, however, as an image of God opens the new dimension of personal being, and therefore his glorification of God, since it is conscious praise, is of a superior kind to that of impersonal being.

Man's true vocation and ultimate dignity consists in the adoration of God. Man reaches his fullest dignity, concludes the author, in sainthood, in the state of rendering the most authentic glory to God. But Christian theology asserts that only Christ can truly offer adoration to God since Christ alone is holy; therefore, the final and supernatural vocation of all men is transformation in Christ. By this transformation the divine life we received in Baptism is fully developed so that we stop living and Christ lives in us. Moreover by this transformation in Christ we attain a true personality. Thus endowed we can join more fully in the liturgy as the expressly uttered praise of God.

J.B.L.

EDMUND CAMPION

Author: Evelyn Waugh (1903-)
Type of work: Hagiography
First published: 1935

Principal Ideas Advanced

The apostolate of Blessed Edmund Campion was brief but most significant in the annals of the Catholic Church in England; he and his fellow priests trained on the Continent brought a much-needed clarification of the theological difficulties inaugurated by the establishment of the Church of England and the excommunication of Queen Elizabeth.

The mission of the Jesuits in England had no political motivation nor was it undertaken to proselytize, but to bring the comforts of their religion to Catholics during the persecutions of Elizabeth's reign.

The English Jesuit martyrs were, and are, the proof that there is no branch theory of the Church.

The reputation of Evelyn Waugh as a novelist is well established, and he has brought his craft and achievement as a novelist to synthesize into a "short, popular life" the information available in many books, articles, and papers on the Blessed Edmund Campion (1540-1581). The author has included a list of the chief works consulted and has acknowledged a special debt to Richard Simpson's biography.

The division of the book into four chapters gives a coherence to the work while it achieves a meaningful emphasis on the various phases of the life of Campion: The Scholar, The Priest, The Hero, The Martyr.

The narrative is interrupted occasionally to supply historical and political background, often in connection with a brief introductory biography of some associate of the Blessed; for example, we find an account of Pope Saint Pius V (1504-1572) and the situation created by his excommunication in 1570 of Queen Elizabeth I of England (1533-1603); the story of the founding and spirit of the Society of Jesus is accompanied by references to the suspicion of the English toward the Society. However, these sections are not digressions but an enrichment and an attempt to give to the uninitiate a picture of the complex situations in which Campion lived and died.

The death of Queen Elizabeth with its attendant physical suffering and mental horrors serves as a prologue to the story of Campion's life and provides a contrast to the last chapter of the book, the death of the Catholic martyr, with its physical cruelties but mental and spiritual exaltation. The author suggests a contrast of Elizabeth's last anguished thoughts and those that might have occupied her in 1566 during her six-day visit to Oxford. Campion, twenty-six years old, a popular Fellow of St. John's College, delivered a brilliant tribute to the queen and the vice-chancellor before defending a philosophical proposition in eloquent Ciceronian Latin. Later he engaged in an extempore debate and earned the patronage of William Cecil, Lord Burghley (1520-1598) and the chancellor of the university, the Earl of Leicester (1532-1588).

The queen's visit to Oxford was significant not only in her assurance of royal favor for scholars, but also in a more important respect, her search for qualified leaders for her Church. The Act of Oxford (1559) directed that Mass should be abolished and that penalties be imposed on anyone who ignored the prohibition. Many of the clergy who were the religious as well as academic leaders resigned their posts rather than submit. The new Church needed scholars and theologians to give it an aura of respectability and to defend its teachings. At Oxford, and particularly at Saint John's, Catholic feeling was strong, but the Protestant party was in the ascendancy.

In 1560 Campion received his B.A. degree and probably took the oath of supremacy. In 1568 he was ordained deacon of the Church of England, but the study of the Fathers of the Church aroused his doubts concerning the apostolicity of the Established Church. His Catholic sympathies grew and he did not attempt to conceal them. When in 1569 his term as proctor at Oxford was completed, he went to Dublin where the new laws against Catholics were hardly enforced. The home of Richard Stanihurst, one of his pupils whose father was Recorder of Dublin, was opened to him; and he became interested in the projected Irish University in whose foundation Mr. Stanihurst was engaged.

In Ireland Campion experienced a happy life in a cultured and affectionate household. He wrote two works: *De homine academico,* a picture of the ideal student and a preparation for his role in the Irish University; and *The History of Ireland,* his only complete work in English.

Campion's stay in Ireland was brief, however, since the status of Catholics was changed because of the Northern uprising and the excommunication of Queen Elizabeth in 1570 by Pope Pius V. In 1572, after traveling disguised from place to place, Campion went back to England. He left his own country shortly after for the English College at Douai in Northern France to join the Catholic refugees from England who had gathered there to study for the priesthood.

Chapter II begins with a history of the English College at Douai and a tribute to its founder and first president, Cardinal William Allen of Oriel (1532-1594). The continuity of the Catholic priesthood in England by English clergy was due more to the efforts and achievement of Cardinal Allen than to any other person. His training was directed toward making the young men missionaries and martyrs: it was counter-reformatory with concentration upon controversial texts.

Campion's stay at Douai was a remote preparation for his future apostolate in England, but he felt called to the discipline of the Society of Jesus and went to Rome to become a Jesuit after taking his degree at Douai in January, 1573.

In Rome the future martyr found a spirit of zeal for the practical and the moral. Both the saintly Pope Pius V and his successor Pope Gregory XIII (1502-1585), a skillful administrator, worked to resist the Turkish invasion and the heresy of the Reformers. The General Chapter of the Jesuits had been convened at Rome and had elected Mercurianus fourth General of the Order. Campion was sent to the Austrian Province where he made his novitiate at Prague and at Brunn in Moravia. Following this period of preparation he returned to Prague where for six years he was engaged in teaching.

Mr. Waugh gives here a brief history of the Hussite disorders (arising from the activities of John Huss, 1374-1415, a Bohemian religious reformer) and their baneful effects on the once flourishing country of the Bohemians and the University of Prague. This famous international university became a small provincial school. The monarchy was weakened by the hostilities which followed Huss's execution, and the country was absorbed in 1526 into the Empire by Charles V (1500-1558). The Jesuits went to Prague at the request of the emperor to aid the Catholic Church in that predominantly Protestant country. From 1574 to 1580 Campion was engaged in various educational activities in the new Jesuit school in the city of Prague, where the Society repeated the great success it had had in its educational system in other countries.

Edmund Campion was ordained priest in 1578. In addition to his work as a professor, after his ordination Father Campion also preached, heard confessions, and engaged in corporal and spiritual works of mercy. It seemed as though he were destined to spend his life as a scholar and teacher, but in 1580 he was summoned to Rome to prepare for a return to England.

The events that led to Father Campion's appointment were a series of difficulties experienced in founding an English College in Rome. The Jesuits were finally asked to maintain the college, but so many of the students then joined the Society of Jesus that an agreement was drawn up by which the Jesuits promised in return to send some of their English members back to England as missionaries.

Father Campion arrived in Rome on April 9, 1580, and remained there until April 18. He renewed his acquaintance with a fellow Jesuit, Robert Persons (1546-1610), whom he had known at Oxford and who was now appointed Father Campion's superior. The future missionaries were instructed regarding their vocations as Jesuits and the object of their mission: "the preservation and augmentation of the faith of the Catholics in England." They were forbidden to have contact with the heretics, to involve themselves in politics, and to engage in conversation against the queen, unless there was a justifying reason. One of the chief questions that needed elucidation was the problem of Elizabeth's excommunication. It was one of the important tasks of the Jesuits' mission to explain to their confused countrymen that they could perform the normal duties of citizenship and obey the royal authority except when it forbade the practice of their religion.

The group for England, numbering fourteen, traveled to Rheims. There they divided, setting out for England from various ports. Persons left first from Calais disguised as a soldier; and Campion, traveling as a jeweler, left shortly after with a lay brother. They arrived in London on June 24, 1580.

The first portion of Chapter III presents a picture of the relationship of England and Spain, Elizabeth's projected marriage to "the little frog," the Duke of Anjou (1544-1584), and the penalties and heavy burdens imposed by Elizabeth and Cecil's anti-Catholic legislation. This background is significant in view of the association of the Jesuits with a Spanish founder, the Catholicity of the French duke, and the severity of the penal laws.

The missionaries attended a meeting, later called the Synod of Southwark, to discuss the status of Catholics in England as well as to explain their own position.

Since informers for the crown were rampant in London, the priests dispersed to the provinces where they traveled as gentlemen of moderate means. In Catholic homes they spent a good part of the night hearing confessions; before dawn they said Mass, distributed Communion, preached, and then departed. Often they had to be hidden in "priest holes" that were constructed behind sliding panels, under eaves, and in other unsuspected places.

Father Campion's report tells of the poverty and hardships experienced by the Catholic people, and it praises their loyalty and constancy under every kind of personal insult and danger and exorbitant taxation. After a short meeting with Father Persons in Uxbridge, Campion continued for six months visiting Catholic homes in the provinces.

In the midst of his strenuous and dangerous journeys Father Campion found time to compose two important statements. The first, written in haste, was called by his enemies, "Campion's Brag." It is a perfect and thrilling statement of his love of England, of souls, and of God. It states briefly his reasons for being in England and the position of the Catholic Church and his own Society. The second was a reply to the Protestant pamphleteers and is entitled "*Ten Reasons,* for the confidence with which Edmund Campion offered his adversaries to dispute on behalf of the Faith, set before the famous men of our Universities." Printed on a press that had been hidden at Henley by Persons, the *Decem rationes* was placed in the pews of St. Mary's Church at Oxford. It became an immediate focal point of controversy and encouraged the informers to strengthen their efforts to find the Jesuits.

One month later Father Campion was arrested with two other priests at Lyford where he had stopped for several days to minister to a group of devout Catholics. The prisoners were brought in disgrace to the Tower of London by order of the Queen's Council. Here Campion was put in solitary confinement in a cell so small that he could neither stand up nor lie down. The queen had him brought to Leicester House and questioned him on his intentions concerning his allegiance to the throne and to Catholicism. When Campion refused to renounce his faith, he was sent back to the Tower and suffered the torture of the rack several times. Despite the rumors of his suicide, his apostasy, and the accusation of treason against his friends, Campion never broke down under the agony of the rack; there is no signed confession.

The prisoner was ordered to appear at four conferences held to dispute his "Brag" and *Ten Reasons.* Without a notary, pen and ink, or books Campion, who had been broken in health and mind by his imprisonment and torture, was permitted only to defend his works; he could not oppose his accusers. A few errors in Greek and an inaccuracy in quoting Tertullian were the only mistakes he made.

The Council decided to hold a trial and proceeded to manufacture evidence that Campion had planned to overthrow the government and murder the queen. Thirteen other priests and one layman had their names inserted in the margin of the accusation and were tried and convicted of the alleged crime although several of them had not been in Europe and some had never met before the trial. The proceedings were a mockery, and the prisoners were all found guilty although the witnesses for the crown had most of their testimony disproved.

Eleven days after the sentence was passed Father Campion and two other priests were dragged through the mud to Tyburn and there hanged, drawn, and quartered. The proclamation read at the execution declared that the priests were hanged for treason, not for religion. It was a last desperate measure to prevent Father Campion from being revered as a martyr. Yet, he had died with prayers for the queen on his lips.

Blessed Edmund Campion was only one of a large number of martyrs in Elizabethan England, but as Waugh writes, "it was his genius to express, in sentences that have resounded across the centuries, the spirit of chivalry in which they suffered, to typify in his zeal, his innocence, his inflexible purpose, the pattern which they followed."

Sister M.R.M.

THE GOOD NEWS—YESTERDAY AND TODAY

Author: Josef Andreas Jungmann, S.J. (1889-1962)
Type of work: Liturgical theology
First published: 1936 (as *The Good News and Our Proclamation of the Faith;* present abridgment, 1962)

Principal Ideas Advanced

The "good news" of the Catholic faith is the salvation of mankind through Jesus Christ.

Throughout the history of the Church the "good news" has taken physical expression by means of the liturgy.

Through study and practice of the liturgy, members of the mystical body of Christ on earth can best participate in the redemptive scheme of Christ.

Father Jungmann's original work on the theology of the liturgy, *Die Frohbotschaft und Unsere Glaubensverkündigung* (*The Good News and Our Proclamation of the Faith*), published in 1936, of which the present volume is a translation and abridgment, contains three main parts: Part One, The Situation; Part Two, Historical Reflections; and Part Three, Our Task.

In "The Situation," Father Jungmann points out that early Christianity was joyously fond of proclaiming the good news of Christ's redemptive plan in a simple but "whole-souled faith." The complexities of modern Christianity have made Catholicism today quite a different story, often superficial, monotonous and even burdensome, for the supernatural core has been obscured and even temporarily forgotten. By returning to the Scriptures and a study of the life and example of Christ, says Jungmann, the contemporary Christian can satisfy both intellect and emotion in his process of Christian formation, and he can emerge finally with the same feeling of joy in the practice of his faith as was experienced by his brothers in the early Church.

Catholic theology is based on an examination of the way in which God the Creator has planned for man to follow Him in order to achieve man's eternal End. Christ is the pivotal point from which mankind's fulfillment, both objective and subjective, radiates.

Father Jungmann briefly traces Christianity from its origin to the present for the purpose of showing that while Christianity was single-minded and idealistic, so were its Christians—strong enough to conquer a pagan world. From the start Christ was the central figure around whose life and teachings man's religious belief and instruction were centered. The writings of Saint Paul, the formation of the Apostles' Creed, and the works of the early Fathers of the Church all stayed within the framework of the same Christocentric pattern.

As man's worldly experience increased, writes Father Jungmann, so did his exposure to both knowledge and ignorance. From the well-spring of questions and criticism, attack and doubt, came the need for satisfactory answers; therefore, the areas of Catholic dogma and Scholastic theology were born. Without them, especially the latter, only answers which would satisfy the natural intellect could have been found. Theological science, however, transcends the natural.

Heresies over the dogma of Christ played a major part in the breakdown of the Christ-centered faith, the author contends. Paradoxically, the components in the figure of Christ as the Bearer of Grace became divided into (1) Christ and (2) grace. As Christ becomes more and more separated from the foundations of His own supernatural gifts, so Christianity becomes more and more secularized, cold, and remotely intangible to the humankind for whom it was founded.

Certain obvious changes took place in the life and liturgy of the Church as a result of the lack of emphasis on Christ as Mediator between Heaven and earth. According to Jungmann, "When proper attention is not given to the fact that we have access to the Father through Christ, when men become accustomed to see in Christ Himself primarily the appearance of God in the world who conceals Himself under the veil of the humanity, then forms of devotion will of psychological necessity be characterized by a sense of fear before the majesty of God, now directly encountered." Marian devotion ("to Christ through Mary") gained great momentum as a result of man's need for someone to intercede sympathtically for him. Lesser devotions of a merely pietistic nature also resulted, however, having a soporific affective value, but again losing sight of the positive lesson of the Incarnation.

Father Jungmann evaluates the results of the preceding analysis in terms of the trends in today's Christian formation. "Renewal in Christ," he declares, is the watchword of the times. The living of the liturgy is the key to the rediscovery of the joys of early Christianity. Orientation of the Christian life to its two central feasts (Christmas and Easter) lays the initial groundwork. Proper catechetical instruction, from the lower grades through maturity and even beyond, is a vital part of the life of the Church. Careful, solid presentation of dogma and doctrine will formulate indelible attitudes which will later enable the layman to make his religious beliefs an inseparable part of his own personality.

"Lived, but above all prayed, dogma will prove to be the best school," writes Father Jungmann, "and so far as prayer is concerned, the prayer of the Church—the liturgy—takes first place." Naturally, the highest expression of the Christian worship of God is the sacrifice of the Mass. Not only is it man's supreme religious expression of thanksgiving, but it is the most vivid and perfect reminder of the role of Christ as Mediator between man and God. The laity should participate in the Mass as actively as possible in order to appreciate the richness of this form of united worship. Whether by silently following the liturgy in a missal of the vernacular or whether by actual vocal participation, the ultimate religious satisfaction finds the Sacrifice of Calvary as its source. Other parts of the liturgy might well be shared by the layman, such as parts of the Divine Office.

With regard to the use of "devotions," Father Jungmann warns against certain dangers which may be encountered in their practice. There is the danger of mechanization in which the original inspiration deteriorates into a fossilized formula. One must also fight against an "egocentric narrowness of soul," in which the suppliant seeks to make God serve his ends by use of the particular devotional tool. We are warned, too, against devotional isolation, in which prayer becomes a thing apart from rather than complementary to one's daily life. All religious devotion has as its focal center the adoration of Christ, and as long as this is foremost, says Father Jungmann, the means to this end can be various and manifold.

In a brief discussion of ecclesiastical art, Father Jungmann comments that here, too, the results should reflect that "sacred encounter" which is the Incarnation. Christianity, he concludes, must be the formative principle of life, whether it be in the performance of moral duties in the work of one's calling, or in the apostolate. "In the long run, however," says Father Jungmann, "Christian culture will show signs of new life and become truly vigorous only when men bear the Kingdom of God so enthusiastically within themselves that they will not have to await a command to carry it with them into their places of work, their recreation, their social life and their solitude."

Included in this volume are essays by four Jesuit Fathers appraising the text and its theological significance.

J.S.

THE UNITY OF PHILOSOPHICAL EXPERIENCE

Author: Étienne Gilson (1884-)
Type of work: Philosophical history of philosophy
First published: 1937

Principal Ideas Advanced

In order to avoid repeating the mistakes of his predecessors, a philosopher should study the history of philosophy as a scientist studies specimens in his laboratory.

One mistake often repeated in various ways has been to attempt to order metaphysics by the methods of other sciences, a practice which, when pursued to its consequences, has led to skepticism.

The true starting point of metaphysics is the intuition that things exist.

In choosing *The Unity of Philosophical Experience* as the title for the William James lectures he delivered at Harvard University in the fall of 1936, Étienne Gilson was playing with the title of James's famous Gifford Lectures, *The Varieties of Religious Experience* (1902). Gilson's point is simple: philosophers are doomed to repeat each other's mistakes until they recognize the nature of philosophy and respect it as a science in its own right, having its own method.

Speaking of an ideal observer's being able to predict the breakdown of Scholastic philosophy in the middle of the fourteenth century, Gilson writes: "It does not even require a demonstration to make it clear; it is a flat truism that all attempts to deal with philosophical problems from the point of view, or with the method, of any other discipline will inevitably result in the destruction of philosophy itself. Yet such abstract statements usually fail to convince those who hear them, and sometimes even those by whom they are made. One of the greatest uses of history of philosophy is precisely that it brings us their experimental demonstration. By observing the human mind at work, in its failures as well as in its successes, we can experience the intrinsic necessity of the same connections of ideas which pure philosophy can justify by abstract reasoning."

Gilson contends that "the history of philosophy is to the philosopher what his laboratory is to the scientist; it particularly shows how philosophers do not think as they wish, but as they can, for the interrelation of philosophical ideas is just as independent of us as are the laws of the physical world. A man is always free to choose his principles, but when he does he must face their consequences to the bitter end."

Since Gilson is a historian of medieval philosophy, it is not surprising that his first case study is Peter Abelard's treatment of the problem of universals. In analyzing Abelard's position on the nature of our ideas and their relations to things, Gilson dramatizes the conflict between Abelard and his teacher, William of Champeaux (c. 1070-1121), and he shows how Abelard forced William to change his position affirming a substantial reality to the genera and species of our logical classifications. But, Gilson comments, in employing his dialectical skill to defeat his master, Abelard trapped himself, for he continued to attempt to resolve a metaphysical question as a logical problem. Seeking to determine what universals are, Abelard replied they are not things, but fictive entities like the imaginary cities we see in our dreams. Universals serve as representations in our minds of what is common to many things, but they have no reality proper to themselves except as ideas in the creative mind of God. Gilson's criticism of Abelard is that he began by mixing grammar and logic and then proceeded to make the mistake of "logicism" by attempting to answer a metaphysical question as a logical exercise by resorting to a psychological reading of the contents of his mind.

In his treatment of some early Moslem thinkers Gilson examines some of the difficulties which can arise between faith and philosophy. A religious thinker such as Algazel (1058-1111), the author of *The Destruction of the Philosophers* (1090) believed one had to be anti-philosophy in order to be pro-faith. Gilson notes this attitude will occur again in a Christian context, but there is usually an Averroës (1126-1198) around to reply with something like *The Destruction of the Destruction,* and such answers are often destructive of religion. Such a conflict breeds skepticism in philosophy and mysticism in religion, both attitudes suffering from lack of respect for the other as belonging to a different order of knowledge. Gilson calls this temptation to minimize reason in order to promote belief "theologism," and he analyzes its operation in a Mohammedan sect called the "Asharites" after their leader Al Ashari (873-935). Moses Maimonides (1135-1204), the greatest medieval Jewish theologian and philosopher, was their critic, and Gilson shows how the Asharites' denial of causality to creatures in order to promote the importance of divine causality was an interesting anticipation of the ideas of Nicolas de Malebranche (1638-1715). While not sharing the saint's views on causality, Gilson indicates Saint Bonaventure's tendencies towards making philosophy a branch of theology. Consequently, Bonaventure is also charged with *theologism,* especially in his development of Saint Augustine's theory that man's attainment of truth requires a special divine illumination. This attitude risks undermining natural knowledge, and this was a consequence reflected in the later Franciscan followers of Saint Bonaventure.

Gilson began his career as a historian of philosophy by searching for the medieval sources of René Descartes' thought. For a while he concentrated on the great Christian thinkers of the Middle Ages and wrote a number of special studies on men like Saint Augustine, Saint Bonaventure, Saint Thomas Aquinas, Saint Bernard, Abelard, and Dante. In his Gifford Lectures (1930-1931), published as *The Spirit of Medieval Philosophy,* Gilson again and again indicated he found Aquinas the high point of Christian thought for his resolution in the light of faith of various problems inherited from Greek philosophy. In his *History of Christian Philosophy in the Middle Ages* Gilson makes the 1277 condemnation of Latin Averroism at Paris and at Oxford a watershed in medieval thought. Since a few propositions taught by Aquinas were included in the condemnation, this had the effect of deflecting support for the synthesis Aquinas had made of reason and revelation, and from this event Gilson dates a growing loss of confidence in what could be established by reason. He notes a trend to transfer to the category of faith questions such as the existence of God and the immortality of the soul, which Aquinas considered were matters of philosophy. Gilson's tendency to view the work of William of Ockham (c. 1300-c. 1349) as representing "the road to scepticism" has been vigorously challenged by such Franciscan philosopher-historians as the late Father Philotheus Boehner (1901-1955) who charged Gilson with creating a "black legend" about Ockham and making him a sort of philosophical villain.

Gilson contends that Ockham's empiricism with respect to knowledge misreads reality: "He was convinced that to give a psychological analysis of human knowledge was to give a philosophical analysis of reality." This "psychologism," as Gilson calls it, leads to the conclusion that there is no more in reality than there is in knowledge: it is to mistake the map for the country, and in the long run it culminated in the skepticism of Montaigne (1533-1592) which came after the breakdown of medieval philosophy.

The human mind cannot rest quietly with skepticism, Gilson argues. A study of the history of philosophy reveals that after a period of philosophical defeatism a new champion emerges to defend the rights of knowledge. For the seventeenth century this was Descartes, and his special weapon was a method which he forged under the inspiration of mathematics. This discipline gave him a taste of certitude, and he demanded that philosophical knowledge measure up to his standards of clearness and distinctness or be rejected as false. To obtain such certitude Descartes took the apparently opposite course of choosing to doubt everything, even the existence of the world, in order to see whether there was something indubitable. The discovery of the certain came in his intuition of his own existence: "Cogito, ergo sum." Further analysis of the implications of his insight revealed to Descartes that he was essentially a mind, that he had an idea of God as all perfect (from whence he believed he could establish God's existence), and that using God's veracity he could demonstrate the existence of the extra-mental world.

In a series of brilliant chapters under the heading "The Cartesian Experiment" Gilson organizes the developments from Descartes through Benedictus de Spinoza (1632-1677), Gottfried Wilhelm von Leibniz (1646-1716), Malebranche to John Locke (1632-1704), George Berkeley (1685-1753) and David Hume (1711-1776) around the theme of "mathematicism." Gilson argues that Descartes' doubt led to Hume's skepticism: "Descartes had endeavoured to prove something that could not be proved, not because it is not true, but on the contrary, because it is evident." Starting in one's mind and then trying to establish that there is something existing corresponding to one's ideas is to found modern philosophy on a pseudo-problem.

In "The Modern Experiment" Gilson continues his philosophical analysis of the history of philosophy from Immanuel Kant (1724-1804) to various twentieth century trends such as Marxism and Fascism. Challenged by Hume, stimulated by the romanticism of Jean Jacques Rousseau (1712-1778), and impressed by the physics of Isaac Newton (1642-1727), Kant worked to save the validity of mathematics and physics, but he did so only at the sacrifice of metaphysics. This "physicism" led eventually to the idealism of Georg W. F. Hegel, (1770-1831) with the strong emphasis in German thought on practical reason or the will. Gilson handles the material of the history of philosophy to illustrate the inner logic of its movement. His skill is in being able to show how the insight of one philosopher provides the premises from which a number of philosophers draw their conclusions: ". . . it seems to result from the facts under discussion, that any attempt on the part of a philosopher to shun the consequences of his own position is doomed to failure. What he himself declines to say will be said by his disciples, if he has any;

. . . and anybody going back to the same principles, be it several centuries later, will have to face the same conclusions." Such, in one sense, is the unity of philosophical experience.

In the concluding section on "The Nature and Unity of Philosophical Experience" Gilson presents some of the laws he has inferred from his study of the history of philosophy. Despite mistakes which lead to skepticism, every instance of the death of philosophy has been accompanied by a renewal: "*Philosophy always buries its undertakers.*" Again, man, though frequently disappointed with what he has been offered, returns to metaphysics as if by nature, for he seeks the first principles or causes of what he experiences.

Though philosophers have often repeated the mistake of attempting to order philosophy by a method proper to another science, the solution to these mistakes seems simple enough: ". . . *no particular science is competent either to solve metaphysical problems or to judge their metaphysical solutions.*" In seeking to unify the multiplicity of our experience, says Gilson, we must not ignore *being* as the beginning of our knowledge and the first principle of our metaphysics. We begin our philosophy with the affirmation that things exist, and we go on to affirm that being comes from being, the root of our understanding of causality. These are the indemonstrable first principles from whence our science of metaphysics begins.

Gilson has achieved renown as a historian of philosophy, but he has also come to be regarded as a most articulate exponent of Thomistic metaphysics. His later writings such as *The Christian Philosophy of St. Thomas Aquinas* (1956) and *Being and Some Philosophers* (1949) are examples of his combination of historical exposition and metaphysical expression. *The Unity of Philosophical Experience* is a landmark in his career in his use of the material of the history of philosophy to underline his commitment to a metaphysics of existence and epistemological realism. Referring to having made this commitment very early in his career, in his recent autobiographical *The Philosopher and Theology* (1962), Gilson remarks "Unawares, I was already plagued with the incurable metaphysical disease they call *choisisme,* that is, crass realism. Today there is no intellectual infirmity more utterly despised, but I know well enough that one cannot get rid of it. A person like myself who suffers from this ailment speaks only about 'things' or about propositions related to things. . . ." Thus, there is a basic unity in Gilson's philosophical experience.

D.J.F.

THE LORD

Author: Romano Guardini (1885-)
Type of work: Life of Christ
First published: 1937

Principal Ideas Advanced

A biological treatment of the life of Christ tends to obscure the core of His Person, which is the mysterium Dei *or* Divinitatis; *similarly, a psychological description fails to reveal His personality in its fullness or even in its principal characteristics, for the personality of Christ also stems from and returns to the* mysterium Dei.

When the phenomenological method is used in examining the life of Christ, one becomes aware of a two-way movement in that life: the movement of God's making Himself man, and the movement upward from the human nature of Christ to the union with the Godhead.

The life of Our Lord Jesus Christ has been so exhaustively examined and recorded from every conceivable point of view that it would seem, at first glance at least, impossible to add a new dimension to our vision of the Savior. Nevertheless, in *The Lord,* Romano Guardini has been recognized, almost universally by the critics, to have achieved precisely this. His book, consequently, has quickly come to occupy a first place in the vast body of biographical literature concerning Christ.

In the preface to his work Guardini protests that he is essaying neither a psychology nor a biography of Jesus Christ. In fact, he goes further to add that in any strict sense both of these undertakings must involve fundamental contradictions. A psychology of Saint Francis, he affirms, is conceivable, at least to that point of his life where the mystery of his sanctity takes over the whole of his personality; similarly, a biography of Saint Francis is possible, because it is possible to place the Saint in a direct line of relation to his culture and his times and even to the more local and specialized features of his environment, though here again a limit must be recognized at that point at which his sanctity and its mystery make his life transcendent to all of these factors and relate it wholly to God. But in the case of Jesus both enterprises are doomed to failure, because the *mysterium Dei* is not the limit of His life, the term toward which His life verges, but is the very center of His life; hence, the *mysterium Dei* must be treated as the fountain from which all else flows. But since this fountain is wholly mysterious, is unseen and indeed invisible, the perspective we can gain on the life of Christ is wholly unique. It is a perspective defined by a whole range of phenomena whose source is hidden but which must nevertheless, to be intelligible, be deciphered in terms of that mystery. Consequently, without specifically adverting to the term, Guardini in effect proposes and practices a *phenomenological* method in his treatment of the life of Our Lord and Savior. Working wholly with the phenomena of that life, its appearance, His words and works, His sufferings, joys, conversations, and withdrawals, Guardini yet directs all of these to the essence; that is, the *mysterium Dei* which is the entire and sole key to their meaning. There is here a kind of "eidetic reduction" of this order of phenomena to its "essence," which is that *mysterium Dei.* When the book is considered from this point of view, one cannot fail to conclude that Guardini exercises and displays consummate skill in the application of this method, without at the same time offering any abstract or methodological definition of it.

Yet there would seem to be danger of a basic error in this statement. It might seem that the dynamic of his treatment of the life of Our Lord moves only in one direction, from the phenomena of His life toward the mystery. In fact, however, that dynamic is a two-way process; it is not only the movement of the phenomena directing our gaze to the mystery, but the power of the mystery seeking at every moment and at every point to fulfill itself historically in the phenomena, and in the man, Jesus Christ. Consequently, Guardini has to take account of this deeper and profounder movement. For Jesus Christ is not merely man who became God, as Saint Athanasius pointed out, but more importantly God who became man. Thus, in Guardini's work we are conscious of the author's constant effort to trace a dual movement, both dimensions of which have their concrete and historical locus in the life of Jesus Christ: the eternal mysterious God's *becoming* man, and Christ's progressively taking possession of and realizing Himself as God.

Within this dynamic perspective and method, Guardini's task becomes that of bringing an illuminating order to the welter of phenomena which, in a material sense, constitute the life of Christ. The principle of that order can only be the revelation of God in Christ; to this principle all else is subordinate and by it controlled. Thus, it is not Guardini's purpose to construct a *drama,* nor to recount a *history,* nor to compose an *epic,* nor, finally, to demonstrate a *proposition.* All these are modes of order and all have been used at one time or another with respect to and in the treatment of the life of Christ. Guardini's effort, however, is directed toward *pure presence;* his concern is to generate immediate and intuitive certitude of an ontal fact; namely, that Christ is God, that the mystery of God is here present and incarnated. In a certain sense, to embody this presence in a dramatic or epic form would be to disguise rather than to reveal the presence; for the work would divert attention from the pure actuality of Christ to the dramatic and epic movement and myth which sustains them. But in Christ there is no mythical element; His is wholly actual presence, the presence of God in man. His life is not a parable of divinity, it *is* divinity; His life is not a symbol, it is wholly ontal actuality. All this Guardini labors to make clear in the direct method of his presentation.

His external ordering of the life of Christ is simple in the extreme and does seem to have in its own right a dramatic order. He groups all of the works and days of the Savior according to a seven-fold order ranging from "The Beginnings" through message and promise, decision, the journey to Jerusalem, the last days, resurrection, and transfiguration to the fusing of "Time and Eternity." Yet it would seem to be a mistake if the revelation of the mystery of God were thought to reside in the extensive movement of this order. Rather, the revelation is an immanent process and, as such, is without extensive dimension, wholly and completely present in every movement of that ostensible dramatic process. This, also, Guardini labors to convey, lest it appear that at some moment of that process or movement, Christ was not God and God not revealed in Christ. The author's task is to make the wholeness of the revelation of the divine appear in the fragmentation of a life extended through time. But this cannot be done by any abstract logical formula; it can be achieved only by a kind of process of distillation. Within each of the moments of that ostensive movement he must bring all aspects to bear, by what he calls the converging lines of incomprehensibility, upon the indubitable presence of the Divine. In a sense, this process may be called incantational; for it is by the magic of his words that that presence is invoked.

The period of the beginnings in the life of Christ extends from the birth of Christ to the preaching of the Beatitudes. How, then, convey the presence of divinity here, how mark its pressure downward upon humanity, the straining upward of this humanity to identity with the Divine? The extreme simplicity of the material demands here the full power of the incantational imagination. In this phase, it may be said, the manner of presence of the Divine is *hiddenness*. That *presence* should be *hiddenness* would at first seem a contradiction, but the merely apparent character of this contradiction is established when we reflect that presence as hiddenness occurs also in the purely human personality. In the case of the human person, it is ultimately the presence as hiddenness which draws us on toward the person, whether we see him as friend, as neighbor, as citizen. He is always present, but the mode of his presence is not explictness, but hiddenness. And that which is hidden in him we sense to be what he most fully *is;* in the unfathomable, but ever present, friend we discover the subject of right which defines our duty and our liberty. In the years of the "hidden life," the Divine is present in every act of Jesus, in every word and gesture, by the mode of hiddenness. In the nativity, that mode is the debility of infancy; in boyhood, the mode of docility; in the first days of public life, the mode is one of expectation and almost of postponement, as depicted in the scene in the temple; in the Baptism, the Divine is hidden in the act of dedication to a future as yet undefined and obscure, but still so present as to dominate all else. Even in the calling of the Disciples, the quality of hiddenness is underlined; for to what does Christ call them but to a hidden mission and an unknown fate? And how does He present Himself to them but as an object of faith and hope and expectation, in which all that is believed, all that is hoped for, all that is desired, is present through its hiddenness? And finally, in the culminating moment of this phase, the preaching of the Beatitudes, the fullness of the hidden presence of the Divine is made apparent, for this wisdom Christ discovers not as an original or new revelation but as a presence hidden in the words already spoken through the mouths of the prophets of old. His is a wisdom which has been with His hearers always, but is for the first time rendered present and alive in Him. And correspondingly addressing the structure of self-presence in the Person of Christ, Guardini brings out very well the manner in which Christ carries His divinity; namely, as a hidden presence within Him, touching His own very identity—so that his neighbors said of Him, "But is not this the carpenter's son?" Hidden divinity present as promise: this is the burden of the beginnings, and it is this which the artless art of Guardini calls forth.

In the second phase of the extensive presentation of the life of Christ, a heightened tone emerges. The mode of the presence of the Divine begins to alter in both its dimensions: in Christ's own consciousness of self and in the forms of His power. The presence of the Divine might now be likened to the physical movement of youth in the young man or woman: life is undefined, but power and urgency stir within, imperious but still vague in their commands, present not as things alien, but as blood of one's own blood. Christ wanders here and there, seeking without what is only within, responsive to an inward command which expresses itself as the need for spatial movement. And His spirit is equally restive within; His mind ranges avidly, even feverishly, over all the dimensions of the human plight which constitutes the matter upon which His ultimate mission will be directed. The injustice of earth stirs in Him visions of the justice of God which inwardly urges Him; the sterility of human lives about Him drives Him to the fields for images of the eternal fertility of power and fruit which is the Godhead and which He senses so alive in Himself and which He would indeed impart to everyone He meets. He senses the Godhead within not only as pure presence but also as menaced by an unnamable thing which men call evil, even as the youth senses the life within him as something menaced by an unnamable thing which men call death. But, above all, that presence manifests itself, speaks within Him as a constant and imperious dialectic between the narrow confines of human existence and the promise of the fullness of being which the spirit of God moving within awakens. Rebirth becomes the symbolic word of this phase; man must suffer all the indignities of human existence, even the ultimate indignity, death, not for naught, but for all: as the passage to a new life, a life reborn, rebirth in water and the Holy Spirit.

Guardini calls the third phase of the extensive and ostensive ordering of the life of Christ in its words and works "Decision." This refers in the first place to the action of Jesus Christ Himself in respect to His own life. For what before was the mode of expectation and promise appears now under the form of an imperative to action and calls upon the constitutive energy of the person for its realization. He senses that the life of wandering, the ceaseless movement to and fro in response to the urgency of a mission not yet defined, has come to an end, but to an end which He Himself must bring about and by His decision open a new phase in the destiny He feels shaping up within Him. At a deeper level, however, this decision takes on greater dimensions than that of an act of Christ; it becomes the name of the mode in which divinity is revealed in human spirit, the way in which it must be revealed and present: as a choice and a decision on man's part directed toward a presence which is still hidden. The revelation of divinity and decision within the framework of human existence is the essence of this moment and the definition of the form of the purest existential amalgam of Godhead and humanity. It is in this moment that the divine-human life of Christ reaches its crisis, for at this moment Christ takes up His Godhood by His decisive act as man, and at the same time, the Godhood most fully becomes man by becoming the form and object of this decision. And yet this decision does not entirely or even significantly dispel the hiddenness of the presence of God; as a matter of fact, it deepens it, under a certain aspect. The presence of God now takes on the mode of destiny, but destiny is still the mode of hiddenness.

The hiddenness of God's presence as destiny is relieved by the local incarnation of destiny in the city of Jerusalem. The part this city had played in the history of Israel, which, under one of its deepest aspects, is the prefigure of the career of Jesus, is well known. This part is heightened and intensified by the fact that Jesus identifies Jerusalem as the place where His destiny, the revelation of His Godhead, is to be fulfilled. Jerusalem and that destiny become one thing. The mystery of the city and what it holds for him and the form of that destiny are one. But, even more immediately, that destiny takes the form of a journey or way, at the end of which lies Jerusalem. Decision places His feet in the way of destiny, which is the path to Jerusalem. But this, too, is much more than a figure; the form of the way is the very substantial form of the life of Christ and, through Him, of the Christian, and the manner under which, in existence, the presence of God is revealed concretely. For the concept of human life as pilgrimage, as march to destiny, is not an image or a symbol. In its turn, it is a name for the presence of God in the human spirit. But the way, which is the name Jesus assumes to Himself, is a mode of presence of the Divine in which darkness and light are closely interwoven as in a vast chiaroscuro canvas. All is light, for the decision has been made, the path taken, and there is no turning back; but all is darkness and hiddenness, for destiny does not reveal itself.

Presently, writes Guardini, even destiny passes from darkness to light, from hiddenness to the clear presence of an inescapable task. This is what transpires for Jesus in Jerusalem. Destiny becomes manifest; the form it must take is made clear: that form is death. Christ reaches the apex of Godhood, and God becomes completely man in this one transaction, the death which Christ must die. Christ is entirely God in the death He dies; God is entirely man in dying. This was the destiny which was revealed to Jesus as He entered Jerusalem in "glory," the glory of the Sabbath of palms. From this moment forward it is clear from every act and word recorded of Jesus, that He has grasped this fact and this truth clearly and fully; that is, in its full significance. His Godhood is death; He must really die, as every man dies, but the death He dies as man is the purest act of divinity. But the divinity of the death he will die relieves it of none of its black horror, a horror which is born of that hiddenness which is the essence of death even when God dies.

In many ways, the passages in which Guardini seeks to bring all this out clearly and concretely in the conscious and self-conscious actions and works of Jesus during the "Last Days" mark the high point of his achievement in this work. Most striking is the complete absence of moralizing in his treatment; at every point, the treatment is kept at the existential level. All is made to focus on one ontal point: the unity of

God and man in the supreme act of death.

Yet while the act of death is wholly the act of Jesus as man and as God, the consequence of that act is wholly on the level of the divine power. It is in the Resurrection and Transfiguration that the meaning of the death of God is revealed, the death that God dies, as man, in Christ Jesus. The meaning of that death is life. Here hiddenness passes away completely, and light and life take over. There is a death that is the greatest act of life: that is the death of the man-God Jesus Christ and the death of the Christian in Christ. But under the aspect of the transaction of death, this meaning of death is not apparent; it becomes apparent only as resurrection. But resurrection is not to be thought of as a transaction other than death. It is the death of the God-man Jesus Christ seen in its meaning and full reality. For Christ does not die and then rise; His death is already His resurrection, and His resurrection is but the inner and significant dimension of his death. Here the fullness of the Incarnation is revealed. Jesus as man and as God is He who transforms death into life, whose act of dying is a supreme act of life, who by dying calls eternal life into being. In this the entire meaning of the Incarnation is fulfilled.

Guardini is at pains to bring out the social nature of the death of Christ, though, like all Christian theologians, he is as yet inconclusive about the mode of this sociality, which must in some way be related to the mediatorial character of the Church. The death of Christ is universal death, and His resurrection is universal life. This is the essence of the sociality of the death of Jesus. Yet how is this character to be brought out? The juridical form, which has done yeoman service for so many centuries, clearly does not satisfy Guardini, for all his terms are existential and ontal. Yet to project these latter terms completely is too great a task. In this section, consequently, there seems to be a darkness and hiddenness which is now proper to the author's narrative and treatment. The fact would seem to be that the life of Christ cannot be dealt with as a self-enclosed whole; it leads necessarily into the consideration of the Church as the form of the sociality and continuity of the life-in-death transaction of Christ. But Guardini does not follow this path into the treatment of the Church. Instead, in the closing section of his work he passes over into the dialectical treatment of time and eternity. The tone of the work becomes eschatological. Here the absolute modernity of the treatment begins to falter. Guardini fails to see that the eschatological terms must be treated in terms of the historical reality of the Church and not naturalistically and projectively. The meeting of time and eternity achieved by Christ and through Christ is effectuated in the Church and not in a projective utopian schema. Nevertheless, when this lapse is recognized, one sees with admiration the manner in which Guardini handles the eschatological terms. With sound Scriptural footing he synthesizes the Johannine vision and the study of the God-man and His work into a persuasive whole. The Risen Christ is the true last thing; all are taken up and realized and given meaning in Him.

The power of this work is singular. Even more singular is the fact that this power stems from a single source: Christ, the Lord. Guardini has achieved here to a remarkable degree what modern Christianity has been striving to do: to grasp the actuality of Christ, the Incarnation as event, not merely *concept,* to relish anew that truth which the Church has never ceased to preach; namely, that our faith is wholly on Jesus Christ. In these pages, Christ comes to life in a most direct and concrete manner, relieved of all moralizing and devotional trappings, presented in dynamic and significant terms, and in such wise as to make possible that direct confrontation between Christ and the Christian which theologians have long recognized as absolutely essential to authentic Christian living.

A.R.C.

CATHOLICISM

Author: Henri de Lubac, S.J. (1896-)
Type of work: Dogmatic theology
First published: 1937

Principal Ideas Advanced

Justice rejects religious individualism and opposes the doctrine of Christian detachment.

The Fathers teach that redemption is the recovery of supernatural unity and the unity of men among themselves.

Catholicity, or universality, is primarily an intrinsic feature of the Church.

The beatific vision marks the completion of the mystery of unity to which Creation was the prelude.

God acts in history and reveals Himself through history, thus bestowing on it a "religious consecration."

There is no real contradiction between Christian personalism and Christian universalism.

Henri de Lubac is one of the most influential of the theologians in France who are bringing about a doctrinal and Scriptural renewal in the Catholic Church. He has frequently exposed the warped view of religion that developed in the modern age of individualism, showing that by Creation and by the Redemption all mankind are involved in a common destiny and that God did not intend any man to be "an island." The subtitle of this work states its theme: "A Study of Dogma in Relation to the Corporate Destiny of Mankind." Lubac bases his study almost exclusively on Scripture and the early Fathers of the Church. An eighty-page appendix of texts consists of fifty-five extracts, all but ten being patristic selections. Father Lubac has organized *Catholicism* with French lucidity. The first of three parts shows how the Catholic religion is eminently social in its dogma, its living constitution, its sacramental system, and its hope of eternal life. The second part deals with the historical problem of Christianity's place in universal history, the interpretation of Scripture, and the salvation of those outside the Church. The third part analyzes the present theological position and dissipates certain misunderstandings about personalism and about the twofold historical and social character of Catholicism.

Catholic dogma holds that God is the Father of all men: *unus Deus et Pater omnium,* as the first phrase of the "Our Father" makes clear, for this phrase postulates both monotheism and the brotherhood of all men. Thus, every sin or breach with God is at the same time a disruption of human unity, and redemption, as a work of restoration, is a recovery of the supernatural unity of man with God and the unity of men among themselves.

The Church is herself this reunion, Lubac argues, for fundamentally Catholicity is not a matter of geography or statistics, but an intrinsic feature of the Church. This unity is shown in personifying the Church as the "bride of Christ," the "chosen people," and the "son of God." "The Church which lives and painfully progresses in our poor world," Lubac maintains, "is the very same that will see God face to face. In the likeness of Christ who is her founder and her head, she is at the same time both the way and the goal; at the same time visible and invisible; in time and in eternity; she is at once the bride and the widow, the sinner and the saint."

The sacraments, the means of salvation, are instruments of unity. Penance effects the social reintegration of the sinner, and communion unites all the faithful in the Body of Christ. This unity is completed only in the beatific vision where "the saints dwell in fellowship and rejoice in common—*socialiter gaudentes;* their joy is derived from their community. . . . This is true unanimity, the very consummation of unity, both the image and result of the unity of the Divine Persons among themselves."

Christianity's concept of salvation is unique in asserting the transcendent destiny of man and the common destiny of mankind. It is also unique in its view of history, based on the Old Testament, completed in the New Testament, and given classic expression by Saint Augustine. In this view the City of God will triumph at the end of history, and meanwhile Christians must use time, working with the earthly materials but not for earthly purposes.

The reality typified in Scripture is not merely spiritual, Lubac insists; it is incarnate and historical. As the Fathers studied Scripture "they felt that, rather than giving a commentary on a text or solving a verbal puzzle, they were interpreting a history. History, just like nature, or to an even greater degree, was a language to them. It was the word of God. Now throughout this history they encountered a mystery which was to be fulfilled, to be *accomplished* historically and socially, though always in a spiritual manner: the mystery of Christ and his Church." Thus, Christian exegisis is historical in principles of interpretation and social in subject matter.

If the Jansenists were wrong in restricting salvation to the few, and if every man can in principle be saved, what need is there for the Church? This is ultimately a mystery, Lubac suggests, as is Christ's coming so long after Adam's fall, but it is enough "to know that 'she is by divine intention and Christ's institution the only normal way of salvation.'" Outside Christianity not all is corrupt, and the precise relation of individuals outside Christianity is known only to God, but salvation for humanity as a whole consists of receiving the form of Christ, and this is possible only through the Catholic Church, founded by Christ for this very purpose.

Christ's sacrifice would have sufficed of itself, Lubac writes, if God had willed to save us without our co-operation. But salvation in this way would not have been worthy of persons made to God's likeness, for it would be like salvaging a wreck rather than redemption with man's willing co-operation. Lubac concludes: "Humanity was to co-operate actively in its own salvation, and that is why to the act of his Sacrifice Christ joined the objective revelation of his Person and the foundation of his Church. To sum up, revelation and redemption are bound up together, and the Church is their only Tabernacle."

T.P.N.

ATHEISTIC COMMUNISM

Author: Pope Pius XI (Ambrosio Damien Achille Ratti, 1857-1939)
Type of work: Social theory
First published: 1937

Principal Ideas Advanced

Communism conceals within itself a false messianic zeal which informs all its doctrine and activity with a deceptive mysticism and communicates to all its adherents a zealous and contagious enthusiasm.

Communism denies God, the future life, and any difference between body and soul, matter and spirit.

Communism robs man of his dignity, his liberty, and all checks on blind impulse.

In contrast to communism, Catholic doctrine asserts the supreme reality of God, the immortality of the soul, and man's resultant personal and social rights.

The best program against the spread of communism is a renewal of Christian life, a true practicing of social justice and Christian charity.

Divini redemptoris was written in the backdrop of the "Popular Front" drive of the U.S.S.R. to enlist the democratic nations of the world in a common cause against aggressive nazism and fascism. There was fear among many Europeans and Americans that the "Popular Front" was a screen for Communist infiltration of the democratic countries. Pope Pius XI opens his encyclical on *Atheistic Communism* by reminding readers that the Papacy "has called public attention to the perils of Communism more frequently and more effectively than any other public authority on earth." Nevertheless, he believes, still another statement is needed.

"Hence," the Holy Father says in his introduction, "We wish to expose once more in a brief synthesis the principles of Atheistic Communism as they are manifested chiefly in Bolshevism [Communism in the U.S.S.R.]. We wish also to indicate its method of action and to contrast with its false principles the clear doctrine of the Church, in order to inculcate anew and with greater insistence the means by which the Christian civilization, the true *civitas humana,* can be saved from the satanic scourge, and not merely saved, but better developed for the well-being of human society."

The first principal section of *Divini redemptoris* condenses the theory and practice of communism into sixteen pregnant paragraphs. Here the pope explains that communism presents a false utopia "entrapped by delusive promises." As a form of evolutionary materialism it denies God's existence and man's spiritual nature, as "the class-struggle with its consequent hate and destruction takes on the aspect of a crusade for the progress of humanity." Communism strips man of his liberty and his human rights, including the right to ownership of private property; it makes marriage and the family artificial institutions dependent on a given economic system; and it denies parents the right of educating and rearing their children. Finally, "it subverts the social order, because it means the destruction of its foundations; because it ignores the true origin and purpose of the State; because it denies the rights, dignity and liberty of human personality."

Pope Pius XI explains the spread of communism as resulting from its alluring but false promises and its appeal to those who would do something to correct the evils of the great depression. Communism's appeal also rests on the fact that the world has been "already to a large extent de-Christian ized," to its shrewd and widespread propaganda, and to the relative silence of those who should have been exposing it.

The second principal section of *Divini redemptoris* contrasts the social and theological doctrine of the Church to communism. Here the Holy Father summarizes traditional Catholic teaching on God, man, the family, the nature of society, the social-economic order, and the role of the state as defender of divine and human rights. After explaining that God is the omnipotent Creator of all things and the just Judge of all men, that man has been endowed by God with the right to life and to bodily and spiritual integrity, as well as the right of association and the right to own and use private property, and that he has social duties corresponding to his rights, Pope Pius XI concludes: "The enslavement of man despoiled of his rights, the denial of the transcendental origin of the State and its authority, the horrible abuse of public power in the service of a collectivistic terrorism, are the very contrary of all that corresponds with natural ethics and the will of the Creator."

The third principal part of the encyclical deals with ways and means of combating communism. Beginning with the well-known verse from Saint James, "Be ye doers of the word and not hearers only, deceiving your own selves," the pope offers a constructive program to alleviate world ills and thus destroy the protest appeal of communism. He insists that there must be a renewal of Christian life, a detachment from worldly goods, and a realization of social justice and Christian charity. Justice requires that workers receive a living wage, economic assistance during unemployment, and old age insurance. Only the establishment of a sound economic order on these lines will make communism unattractive to the masses of men.

The final part of *Divini redemptoris* is a directive to priests and to their coworkers in Catholic social action. Pope Pius XI urges them to go to the poor and especially to laymen, who should be "the first and immediate apostles of their fellow workmen." The Holy Father says that besides this "individual apostolate" to bring truth to the worker and labor for his rights, Catholic action also requires organizations to disseminate propaganda on a wide scale so that the true fundamental principles of a sound Christian social order may be widely known. The pope also spells out succinctly the positive role of the state to create material conditions for an orderly society, such as supplying employment and seeing that "the wealthy classes . . . assume those burdens without which human society cannot be saved nor they themselves remain secure."

Divini redemptoris was addressed to the entire Church, and it mentions specifically the terrorism of communism in the U.S.S.R., Spain, and Mexico. It is cited commonly as one of the classic short critiques of the theory and practice of communism, and it has been published in almost all Western languages.

T.P.N.

MIT BRENNENDER SORGE

Author: Pope Pius XI (Ambrosio Damien Achille Ratti, 1857-1939)
Type of work: Social commentary
First published: 1937

Principal Ideas Advanced

[*Pope Pius XI, dismayed at the present sufferings of the Catholic Church in Germany, describes the nature and source of its persecution at the hands of the Nazi government of the Reich.*]

[*The two-fold principal aim of this papal letter is to comfort the suffering Catholics in Germany and to instruct them how to stand firm in the face of the war of persecution directed against them by the government of their nation.*]

[*The pope's instruction rests on the central proposition that true peace can come only from a moral life based on both the natural law and the Christian faith practiced in the Church.*]

Mit brennender Sorge (English title: *The Church in Germany*) of Pius XI (pope, 1922-1939), is an "encyclical" or papal circular letter addressed to the Catholic bishops of the world but in particular to those of Germany. Hence, this letter was published at Rome on March 14, 1937, in German rather than in Latin, the usual language of official papal documents.

Expressing his dismay and anxiety concerning the condition of the Church in Germany, Pope Pius XI recalls the events which have happened since the Vatican signed the concordat or solemn treaty of July 19, 1933, with the National Socialist government of the Reich. The pontiff mentions that he had grave misgivings about consenting to this agreement with the Nazi government which would be binding on Church-state relations in Germany. In these feelings he was confirmed, for, as soon as the concordat was signed, the German official press spread the story that this treaty represented a capitulation of the Catholic Church to the demands of Chancellor Hitler's government.

Continuing his narration of recent events in Germany, Pius XI asserts that scarcely was the ink dry on the concordat when the Nazi regime began a systematic and continued evasion of each of its provisions. The most serious evasion was doctrinal: the government equivocated on the term "Christian" in order to subvert Catholic teaching. Although it had pledged in the concordat to do nothing to hinder the Church in its teaching of traditional Catholic Christianity, nevertheless the Hitler government began, almost from the moment of the treaty-signing, to insinuate a new kind of religion into the minds of the German people.

A restoration of German paganism was openly advocated by Dr. Alfred Rosenberg, Reich Chancellor Hitler's educational adviser and plenipotentiary for *Weltanschauung*. Rosenberg publicly ridiculed traditional Christianity as a religion of the weak and timid, as a religion totally unfit for Germans. He preached a new gospel of German racial superiority.

Furthermore, with respect to Christian education an unceasing campaign was pressed by the Nazis to force the Church to surrender completely her role in the teaching of youth. The law of December 1, 1936, stated that all German young people were to be educated in the Hitler Youth, educated physically, spiritually, and morally according to the philosophy of National Socialism.

But ideological persecution was merely one side of a full-scale war, broadly described by Pope Pius in the opening paragraphs of his encyclical, waged against the Church by the government in Germany. On the political front the Hitler regime succeeded in persuading the Catholic bishops to disband the Catholic trade unions and to withdraw their support from the Catholic Centre party, the representative of the Church's point of view in the Reichstag, the national parliament. Consequently, when the government unleased its attack on the Church, the latter found itself deprived of effectively organized supporting groups. Concurrently with political attack the Church suffered actual physical violence. Clergy were arrested on all manner of charges, religious meetings and processions were set upon by young toughs of the Hitler Youth, and church property was destroyed.

To protest the various kinds of attacks fomented by the government, the German bishops issued a pastoral letter. In this public statement the bishops denounced the government's breach of the concordat and called for an end to the Nazi attack upon Catholicism and, indeed, upon religion in general. At this juncture, on Passion Sunday in 1937, Pius XI published his encyclical, *Mit brennender Sorge* (literally, "With deep anxiety"). Although this document was entitled to be freely distributed in Germany, the government of Hitler forbade its publication. Thus, it had to be smuggled into the country and secretly delivered to the churches to be read from the pulpit.

In his letter Pope Pius assures the German Catholics that he has exercised and will continue to exercise all the patience at his command so that there may be nurtured any little chance that good relations may return between the government in Germany and the Church. Then the pontiff addresses himself to the task of giving spiritual comfort to his German flock. He proposes to do this principally by teaching them the truth about Christianity.

The papal author deals point by point with the different errors of National Socialism concerning Christianity and its Founder, without, however, attacking nazism by name. He warns his flock against the pagan pantheism of the Nazi creed which seeks to equate God with the forces of physical nature. He asserts that in morality the exaltation of race, of the German people and state into the role of standards of morality, is condemned: "Only superficial minds . . . can make the mad attempt of trying to confine within the boundaries of a single people, within the narrow blood stream of a single race, God the Creator of the world. . . ."

The pontiff contends that true belief in God, the Creator of the world, the King and Lawgiver of all peoples, will be kept genuine only if supported by true belief in Christ, in whom God has fully revealed Himself. Therefore, a true knowledge of God's revelation can be had only in and through the unity of the Old and the New Testaments. It is sheer folly to listen to the vicious suggestions of the Nazis that the German Church must purge the revelation of God by eliminating the Old Testament because of its Hebraic authorship, and further, must reinterpret the New Testament in accord with "Aryan" or "Nordic" norms of faith.

True belief in God rests upon true belief in Christ, which, in turn, finds its foundation in true belief in the Church founded by Christ. This Church is one for all peoples and nations; one and indivisible in all essentials of doctrine. Yet the true Church fosters diversity and individuality of peoples by furthering education and all lawful progress.

Of course, says the pope, it is not enough to be passively a member of the Church since evils and temptations abound. Every member of the Church is exhorted by Pope Pius to "walk in the presence of the Lord" and to strive to perfect himself so that human scandals do not arise to be seized by enemies of the Church as opportunities to subvert her mission. Every member of the Church must live so that through their lives the unity and holiness of the Church will be apparent to all, especially to the enemies of true religion. This papal allusion is directed against the Nazi trials of members of the Catholic clergy on false charges of immorality and fraud.

Repeatedly the pope urges the Catholics of Germany to stand fast in their faith despite government-encouraged apostasy, especially of the young. The Nazi regime, Pius charges, has tried to create the impression that Christianity is a religion for weaklings and unpatriotic slackers; thus, it says that it is an act of sheer patriotism to leave the Church and devote all of one's energies to the building of the German Fatherland. To this claim Pius XI retorts with the advice that all Catholics resist false promises. Especially the Catholic intelligentsia must resist offers of worldly advancement which are contingent upon their repudiating their religion.

Finally, the pope sets forth the Catholic teaching of the primacy of the Bishop of Rome. The Catholic must remain faithful to this doctrine if his belief in the Church is to be pure and genuine. Arrayed against the truth that the successor of Saint Peter is the lawful head of Christ's true Church is the false attempt to break off the German Church from loyal attachment to Rome in favor of a German national church. The history of national churches in their slavery to passing political regimes should be enough to enable the true Catholic to utter a firm "No" to such an insidious invitation to weakness.

Turning to the true basis of morality, Pope Pius reminds his hearers that revelation in the Christian sense is God's word to man. As such it contains no whispers about blood and race. As a matter of fact, it is unconcerned with what may be a legitimate, proud confidence in the historic destiny of one's race or nation. Moreover, Christian revelation teaches that immortality means the life after death of the individual man, who will be given eternal reward or punishment. The Nazi creed has twisted immortality to mean the collective enjoyment of temporal life through the life of one's people or nation for some period of time in the future. Thus, to equate immortality with some period of time on earth is a perversion of the Christian meaning of the term, which refers to a supernatural existence after death.

Certainly it is ridiculous, asserts the pontiff, to claim that the moral order is grounded on the sands of merely human norms such as the "collective German soul." In contrast to Nazi theory, it is the doctrine of Confessional, that is, clear and definite Christianity, that the moral order is grounded on the eternal law of God. When the attempt is made, as it has been in Germany, to base education and social formation on a basis other than that of Christian culture, then the national state enters upon decline and decay.

Pope Pius notes that the present trend toward severing morality and law from its bond to true belief in God and His revealed commandments extends even to the natural law which has been written by the Creator in the hearts of men. He warns that if the attempt to cut morality loose from Christian faith succeeds, the end result can be only catastrophe. If the present secular leaders in power in Germany succeed in their suppression of the God-given rights of the person, the German nation will have suffered a calamity. This ruin can be avoided if it is clearly understood that the true public good within a state, as well as between states, is determined by the nature of man. The purpose of the community is conditioned by human nature; to reverse this order is a woeful error. The community is willed by God as the means to the full development of the individual, just as higher values which can only be realized by the community are, in the final analysis, willed by God for the sake of the individual.

Within the community the natural law operates so that education of children is a right and duty of parents. Parents are obliged to see that their children are educated in the spirit of the true faith, asserts Pius XI, and they have the right to see that their children are so educated. Laws, such as those the Nazi government has passed, laws which suppress this right of parents, are utterly immoral.

In the final portion of his letter, the pontiff gives voice to words of comfort and exhortation to youth, the clergy, and the laity. Speaking to the youth of Germany the pope exclaims that he particularly objects to the intentional systematic opposition set up between the purposes of education and the purposes of religion. To the clergy Pope Pius addresses words of exhortation to strengthen them in their time of persecution. He reminds priests that their duty is to serve truth, the whole truth. Bishops and priests particularly must take care to bring error out into the open and refute it in all its different forms. Speaking to the laity, Pope Pius sends them greetings and the exhortation to stand firm in their God-given rights and duties concerning the education of their children.

Pius XI closes his encyclical with a statement of his optimistic faith that the Catholic Church will triumph over its enemies. He declares his resolute trust that the German people will return unhindered to the service of Christ, the King of time and eternity, and they will realize the destiny which God has chosen for them. The German people will do this in harmony with all the right-minded people of other nations.

J.B.L.

CHURCH AND STATE

Author: Luigi Sturzo (1871-1959)
Type of work: Political and ecclesiastical history
First published: 1938

Principal Ideas Advanced

Church and state represent sacred and secular power, respectively; together they compose a basic diarchy of power.

The movement of the spiritual and temporal forms of power is toward a synthesis in which the claims to power are integrated.

As synthesized, the two powers, Church and state, remain distinct but exercise an integrating power within society.

The history of Church and state in the West is the history of the effort to realize the diarchy of power in a transforming synthesis.

Dom Luigi Sturzo's *Church and State* has become an intellectual landmark as a work which, supported by sound historical scholarship, presents a new integrative perspective on the relations of Church and state in the Western world. Sturzo himself had an eminent career in which the values of Church and state were personally realized. Ordained in 1894, he received his doctorate in theology at the Gregorian, Rome. He then spent some time as a teacher and journalist. In 1905, he was elected vice-mayor of Caltagirone, and during a fifteen-year period in that position he achieved many valuable reforms. As the founder of the Popular Party, later the Christian Democratic Party, he worked zealously for social and economic reforms favorable to the working classes. He was a political opponent of Benito Mussolini's Fascist regime, and was an exile until 1948, after which time he again became active in Italian politics and was a leading figure in the struggle against the Communists.

Church and State, which is a historical study of the basic diarchy of power comprising the temporal power, the state, on the one hand, and the spiritual power, the Church, on the other, is composed of three parts. The first is concerned with the growth and dominance of the Church from its earliest days until the breakdown of world Christendom after the "Babylonish Captivity" of the popes in the fourteenth century. The second part carries the historical account from the beginnings of Humanism to the period of nationalism and enlightenment in the eighteenth century. The third and final part presents the significant events concerning Church-state relations from the French revolution to the time of writing, the 1930's.

Sturzo's *Church and State* may be described as a Christian statesman's reply to the problem of the Christian presence in history. The view here presented takes its inspiration from Giovanni Vico's doctrine of the "ideal and eternal history" which is immanent in time. More concretely, the view holds that the divine presence which entered history through Christ and the Incarnation is now present in history according to the form and laws of historical existence and action. The spiritual presence does not introduce a new economy which is to replace that of history; at the same time, however, that presence introduces a wholly new and underived element, force, and dimension into history. This view is the root of Sturzo's doctrine of the "diarchy" which is manifest in the operations of Church and state.

The recognition of the basic diarchy of power creates a new problem for the historian. It is not the problem of reconstructing history from the point of view of theology, however, for the new view of history cannot be sustained if one aspect of the diarchy of power is emphasized at the expense of the other. The need, then, is not for a theology of history but for a formulation of a theory of history wide enough and dynamic enough to embrace in a complex unity this duality of presence without the undue subordination of one to the other.

Fundamental in Sturzo's thinking is the notion that the person is the existential point at which the introjection of the transcendent and immanent transpires—in the first instance in the person of Christ; in the second instance in the person of every Christian whose personality is, in turn, the projection of that Christ.

The Christian presence provides the historian with a fresh principle for a universal understanding of social form. The person whose actuality is revealed by the Christian presence forms the basic constitutive unit and principle not only of the Church but of all social institutions. Without the recognition of the person as the basis of social life, the "natural" processes of social life remain obscure. The person stands thus revealed as the basis of the entire social structure which rests upon a dual projection whose dimensions are seen in the Church and the state.

The Church and the state, Sturzo insists, are not two societies, as the older dualisms contended; they are, rather, dual principles, comprising a diarchy which makes possible the projection of the social dimension of the person. The individual person cannot be divided between two societies, for in his own nature he achieves a dual social projection which terminates in a complex unity, a synthesis of the secular and spiritual powers.

It is significant to note that the essence of the theory of the Popular Party, which Sturzo founded, was to restore autonomy to the Christian person and thus to restore the proper relation and balance between Church and state and, within the person himself, between Catholic and citizen. By its act of forbidding the Catholic to participate in the political life of the new Italy, the Church was substituting a principle of dualism for the principle of diarchy; the state, by making the status of citizen irrelevant to the confessional status, was committing the same error. Dualism, replacing diarchical law, was creating a situation of tension which could not be reduced at the level of Church and state as institutions confronting each other. The purpose of the Popular Party was to return the decisive power to its normal seat, the person, and thereby to emphasize that personal autonomy by which Church and state achieve a viable rapport.

Prior to his experience with Fascism, Dom Sturzo had placed his trust in the matter of the international community on the juridical principle. The mediation which would unite the nations, he believed, would be one of law. However, his experience with Fascism made clear to Sturzo that his trust in the juridical dimension was exaggerated. It thus became necessary for him to recognize that even at the international level social laws are operative which judicial considerations do not exhaust or even accurately reflect. In a word, Sturzo saw that a sociological problem underlies the problem of the international community. Thus, it became his intention to determine the relevant terms of sociological analysis applicable to the international order with the objective of providing a more secure context for international law.

Sturzo's basic discovery was that the sociological structure of the international community is governed by the same principle of diarchy which he had found to be operative at other levels of society. Devoid of Christian presence, the arena of international relations contains a sheer power struggle; nations, as secular powers, reveal themselves as motivated by nothing but the love for power, as Sturzo had discovered at first hand through his knowledge of the Fascist Party. The most obvious answer, it might appear, is that the direct countervailing principle must be the Church in her universal character, but to accept this suggestion is to assume that the Church remains untouched in her universal character by the national principle. In fact, Sturzo decided, this is not the case. The Church of the Patristic Age and that of the Middle Ages may have been unaffected by the national principle, but the Church of the twentieth century is not. As a consequence, the real problem was to find a mediatorial base for the diarchical system analogous to that which Sturzo had discovered in the person.

The mediatorial base, on the international level, Sturzo decided, could be none other than the nation itself. But the nation could serve as the base only if it had already achieved within itself the diarchical synthesis of spiritual and secular power.

For Sturzo, the mediatorial status of the nation was not an abstract logical principle but a concrete historical principle. The function of the nation, then, is to make possible the synthesis of powers; the necessity for such synthesis is constant, but the form is historical. In the days of the waning Roman Empire, it was precisely the vestigial structure of that empire in its juridical, administrative, and organizational features which offered the basis for that synthesis. In the Middle Ages it was the ideal of the Sacrum Imperium. In the modern age it could only be the nation as the primary seat of the synthesis which would then become effective as the basis of the larger synthesis at the international level. Once such a synthesis was achieved, the Church would be the Church of all nations not because she would then have moved herself to a level above the nations, but because she would provide the basis for a unity *within* nations upon which the unity of the world of nations could rest securely.

By these stages Dom Sturzo was led to realize that he had enunciated certain principles, those of the diarchy and its historical synthesis, which reached ideally far beyond the application they had in any limited context. The logical movement of his thought consequently made it necessary that these principles be projected against the entire field of their relevance, for only as projected in this way could their validity be tested. Thus, he was brought to undertake the writing of *Church and State*.

The field of the final relevance of the principles which Sturzo discovered is the entire career of the Christian presence in history. In *Church and State* the theory of the diarchy of Church and state is projected, in order to be tested, against the entire Western historical experience from the moment of that introjection of Christian presence to the moment of writing. Not that the time of writing closes the issue or the career of the Christian presence. Sturzo was well aware that in his monumental work he was composing only the first chapter of a work which history itself will necessarily continue.

A.R.C.

THE ORIGIN OF THE JESUITS

Author: James Brodrick, S.J. (1891-)
Type of work: History of the Society of Jesus
First published: 1940

Principal Ideas Advanced

The Society of Jesus owes not only its founding but also its particular character and motivation to Saint Ignatius Loyola; the love of God which was so dominant a motive in his life infused the Society as well.

Within a few years after Loyola founded the Society, Jesuits had taken the lead in the Counter-Reformation: Germany was saved for the Faith; Spain, Italy, and France were strengthened, and the vast missionary enterprise in the Far East was under way.

Loyola's guiding hand can be seen in all of these activities, and it was largely due to him that the Society succeeded in its task.

Father James Brodrick's *The Origin of the Jesuits* is the first of a projected multi-volume history of the Society of Jesus. It covers the years from the birth of Saint Ignatius Loyola in 1491 until his death in 1556. Although Loyola is the central figure in this work, it is far more than a biography of the founder of the Jesuits: it is a compact, extremely well-written study of both Loyola and the religious order he founded. The work first appeared in 1940, the four hundredth anniversary of the founding of the Jesuits, and it succinctly summarizes the vast amount of knowledge which had accumulated on the Society in its formative years. Father Brodrick also used to great advantage the Jesuit correspondence which had appeared earlier in the *Monumenta Historica Societatis Jesu.*

The book is divided into three parts: the first concerns the early life of Loyola up to the time he met the other men who came to join him in his religious enterprise. Born a Basque, Loyola exhibited all of the characteristic attributes of his countrymen —intensity, practicality, steadfastness, and uneffusiveness—and to these were added the "passionate orthodoxy" of the sixteenth century Spaniard, as well as the "clear-cut vision of human life as a battleground of God and the devil." As a young nobleman eagerly seeking worldly glory, Loyola had his life changed when he was wounded in the siege of Pamplona (1521). While recovering, he decided thereafter to seek his glory by winning souls for God. Brodrick points out that during this period Loyola had not yet achieved an interior virtue, although he had all of the outward manifestations of holiness. At Manresa he was changed; there, in seclusion, he experienced the conversion to holiness that he later wrote down in the *Spiritual Exercises.* The *Exercises,* Brodrick says, are based on the theme of self-denial: ". . . vigorous realist that he was, Ignatius saw in self-conquest and self-denial the indispensable preconditions of an active enduring love of our Lord."

Loyola then adopted a life of complete poverty and journeyed to Jerusalem to spend the remainder of his life. After a few months there he came to realize that in order to win souls for God he had to learn philosophy and theology. To this end, he returned to Spain where he studied Latin with a group of children. Then he enrolled at the University of Alcala and started his studies. In the Spain of the sixteenth century few people were safe from the jurisdiction of the Inquisition; Loyola was no exception. His apparently radical ideas and his completely ascetic manner of living aroused suspicion, and he was arrested and spent a few weeks in the prison of the Inquisition before he proved his orthodoxy and was released. He left Alcala and went to the University of Salamanca where he again collided with the Inquisition. He decided to leave Spain, and in 1528 he enrolled at the University of Paris.

The second part of Brodrick's work concerns Loyola's meeting and influencing the other men who eventually formed the Society of Jesus with him, and the book includes an account of the struggle to get the Society approved by the pope. In his relations with others and in particular with those whom he converted to his aims, Loyola exhibited another outstanding ability—that of learning from his mistakes. By applying this ability and by always using extreme patience, Loyola was able to win over his first two converts—Peter Faber, a Savoyard, and Francis Xavier, a Navarrese. Other students at Paris joined his group; most of the early members were Spaniards: Diego Laynez, Alfonso Salmeron, Nicholas Bobadilla, and Simon Rodriguez. In 1534, they pledged themselves to vows of chastity and poverty and decided to offer themselves to the pope for whatever purpose he chose to use them.

The group then set out to get papal approval of the Society as a religious order. As Brodrick points out, this involved some difficulty because with the rise of Protestantism and the desire within the Church for reform, there was strong opposition to the formation of another religious order. However, Loyola pressed for recognition. In 1537 Pope Paul III approved the ordination of the members of the Society, and in that year they decided to take a vow of obedience. During the years from 1537 to 1540 Loyola spent much of his time formulating and writing the constitution of the Society. In a brief but valuable commentary on this constitution, Brodrick points out that the purpose of the Society was to teach the Commandments to children. The function of the Society was at all times to be left to the discretion of the pope, and all Jesuits were to take a vow of obedience to him. The Society was to have an elected superior who was to be bound by an explicit set of reciprocal duties and rules between him and his fellow Jesuits. Finally, the Society was to be completely bound by a vow of poverty. After opposition was overcome, Pope Paul III formally established the Society in the Bull *Regimini militantis ecclesiae* in 1540, and the following year Loyola was elected the first superior of the Society.

The last part of this book deals with the history of the Society from 1540 to 1556 and is primarily a study of the expansive activities of its members. In missionary activities, Paschase Broet and Alfonso Salmeron were sent to Ireland, but they were unable to accomplish their aims and returned after a month. The greatest of all the missionaries was Saint Francis Xavier, to whom Brodrick devotes an entire chapter. Not only is the vast enterprise in India, China, and Japan detailed, but Brodrick also expresses in moving terms culled from Xavier's letters the tender filial and brotherly relationship between Xavier and Loyola. Xavier shines forth with Loyola as the moving spirit of the Society in these early years. In Europe the most important person to join the Society was Saint Francis Borgia, Duke of Gandia and grandson of both Pope Alexander VI and Ferdinand of Spain. Borgia contributed not only all of the resources of his patrimony but also great ability and foresight. It was Borgia who changed the fundamental mission of the Society to formal education by opening the Jesuit Colleges to all young men, not only the novices of the order. Another important convert to the Society was Jerome Nadal, who through his organizating ability became known as the "second founder" of the Society. He devised the preliminary *Ratio studiorum* to include the new educational methods of the sixteenth century, and Brodrick credits him with organizing the Jesuits as the main force of the Counter Reformation in Germany. The activities of Laynez, Salmeron, and Peter Canisius at the Council of Trent are clearly explained.

In the last chapter Brodrick concentrates upon Loyola as a father to his men. He does this by centering the story about Simon Rodriguez who, as provincial in Portugal, fell astray. Loyola's holiness was the chief factor in leading the errant Jesuit back to Ignatian ideals. Brodrick uses this incident to illustrate the outsanding aims motivating Loyola—concern for his brethren, devotion to the sick, and complete trust in God. It is upon this theme, with the death of Loyola, that the volume closes. Interestingly, Brodrick says little about the "military" nature of the Society, although the clearly commanding obedience given Loyola by the other Jesuits is always stressed. Rather, the bond of the Society, as expressed by Brodrick, is the overwhelming love of God. It is this love, as seen in the devotion of Loyola to his aims, in the selfless giving of Xavier to the conversion of the East, and in the vital, dynamic activities of the Jesuits in Europe, that makes the Society, as portrayed in Brodrick's book, appear to be the work of God.

J.M.S.

THE MONASTIC ORDER IN ENGLAND

Author: Dom David Knowles, O.S.B. (1896-)
Type of work: History of English monasticism
First transcribed: 1940

PRINCIPAL IDEAS ADVANCED

Monasticism was the most important factor in the spiritual and cultural life of the Church and society from the days of Gregory the Great to those of Bernard of Clairvaux.

The accumulation of wealth and involvement in worldly affairs distracted monks from their true aims and brought about a decline of their dominant culture.

Experience has demonstrated that only fidelity to its rule saves a religious order from decay and makes a spontaneous rebirth of true life possible.

Dom David Knowles is undoubtedly one of the greatest and most graceful of England's historians. His range of interests blankets the spectrum of historical and literary scholarship, and *The Monastic Order in England* is perhaps but the most famous of his many stimulating works. Born in Warwickshire in 1896, Knowles was educated at Downside Abbey, the home of several other distinguished monastic scholars, and Cambridge University. A Benedictine monk of Downside since 1915, he was ordained a priest in 1922. He has taught at various schools of his religious order and at his own university where he was chosen Regius Professor of Modern History in 1954. From 1956 to 1960 Professor Knowles also served as president of the Royal Historical Society.

The Monastic Order in England first appeared during the wartime summer of 1940 and was immediately hailed as the definitive work on its subject and as a lasting contribution to good historical literature. This study is an explanation and an analysis of the goals, lives, and activities of English monks during their most influential days, the period beginning with the career of Dunstan about 950 and ending in 1216 with the death of both the powerful Pope Innocent III and the infamous King John. In three subsequent volumes appearing in 1948, 1955, and 1959 under the title *The Religious Orders in England,* Knowles enlarged his work to include other and more recent orders and continued his analysis of their history up to the final dissolution of the English monasteries under King Henry VIII in 1539. Taken as a whole these four great volumes thus illumine the six centuries of the development, decline, and disappearance of organized religious life in medieval England. It is in the first volume, however, that the dominant trends are discussed and these concepts form the background for all subsequent English monastic history.

A monastery, Knowles explains, is basically a self-sufficient community governed according to the *Rule* of Saint Benedict by an elected abbot and having for its purpose the service of God and the sanctification of its members' souls apart from the life of the world. The *Rule* breathes a spirit of order and moderation, avoiding the extremes of clerical laxity and fanatical asceticism and providing a detailed and unvaried program for daily living within the cloister walls. Although apparently not part of Benedict's original conception, Western monasticism soon became a great social institution enmeshed in the affairs of medieval life —a reservoir of learning, a center of peace and charity, a home of men who continually interceded for their brothers in the world. Monasticism, which began as a flight from civilization to the desert, thus became an integral and influential part of society. Even so, England in the early tenth century could scarcely boast one such religious community. Yet once monasticism was revived it spread rapidly and by the dawn of the thirteenth century there were over 170 houses of monks, in addition to those of the canons. It is thought that the monks and canons may have numbered about fifteen thousand religious, or between one and two percent of the adult males in a total population of about three million. These religious controlled perhaps a quarter of the wealth of the country.

Knowles argues that the Roman mission of Augustine and his companions to Canterbury in 597 probably introduced monasticism into southern England; large parts of the northland owe their institutions to Irish missionaries. Gradually these two strains merged, and the eighth century saw the early flower of Anglo-Saxon monasticism in such men as the Venerable Bede. Internal disorder and Scandinavian invasion destroyed this culture, and by the time of Alfred (870-899) monasticism had ceased to live in England. Beginning about 940 Dunstan, Ethelwold, and Oswald revived the monastic ideal. In 972 a comprehensive statement of regulations, the *Regularis concordia,* was promulgated which set the tone for Saxon monasticism. It was drawn from the common usage of Western Europe, Dunstan's traditions at Glastonbury, and the training English leaders had received at Fleury with its Cluniac emphasis and Ghent with its reflections of the Lotharingian reform. The principal office of the monks was to be the solemn liturgy of the Church and intercession. This monastic life was not primarily a special vocation for individual perfection, but rather a perfection of the normal clerical life. The *Regularis concordia* had two unique features, the special deference paid to the monarch in prayers and elections and the suggestion that bishops who governed monastic cathedral chapters should themselves live as monks. Soon many monks were bishops and statesmen, and it may be that this close connection with the national life was one of the reasons for the relaxation of discipline which occurred before the Norman Conquest. At any rate, in the period between 950 and 1050, it was from the monasteries that there arose whatever was purest in English spiritual, intellectual, and artistic life.

According to Knowles' account, after the adoption of the *Regularis concordia* few continental influences affected English monasticism until the wholesale Norman plantation of William the Conqueror and his talented Archbishop of Canterbury, Lanfranc of Bec. Lanfranc, the "father of the monks," was the organizer of the English Church and the propagator of its monasticism. He introduced a new life and vigor into the English abbeys and infused them with the elaborate ritual and scholarly devotion of Bec, the intellectual mistress of northern Europe. Encouraged by the Conqueror, Lanfranc replaced Saxon abbots at their deposition or death with reforming Normans and introduced continental customs into the island houses. Ancient saints and laws were abandoned, great buildings erected, and many new foundations inaugurated. One Saxon tradition was honored and even enhanced, the institution of cathedral monasteries. In fact, within fifty years of the Conquest the number of cathedral monasteries rose from three to nine among the seventeen English bishoprics.

Anglo-Norman monasticism came to its full and glorious maturity in the early years of the twelfth century. Encouraged by the peace and prosperity of the long reign of Henry I and the early years of Stephen, the number of monks increased, treasure accumulated, libraries were organized, and even more new buildings were erected. The organization of English monasticism at this time was fairly clear. Abbeys, with a few notable exceptions, averaged about fifty to sixty members, most of whom were drawn from the class of wholly free landowners. Each monk engaged for four hours in the liturgical prayer of the oratory, four hours in reading or meditation, and perhaps six more in domestic, manual, or craft work. Each Benedictine abbey was autonomous. This was contrary to the contemporary trend of continental monasticism which had been greatly influenced by the centralizing constitutional and organizational genius of Cluny. Although Cluny enjoyed a favorable reputation among Englishmen (Henry I especially favored it) her English houses were of minor importance and her influence relatively slight except for that exercised through prominent individuals like Henry, Bishop of Winchester (1129-1171) and Gilbert Foliot, Bishop of Hereford (1148-1163) and of London (1163-1187).

Anglo-Norman monasticism fortified by Saxon skills, traditions, and mysticism and invigorated by Norman reform, discipline, and patronage dominated the culture of the land. Even so, the author writes, times were changing. Few men as yet realized that this period which witnessed the reformed and reforming papacy, the new and lettered hierarchy, the origins of the universities, and the coming of new religious orders, would also mark the end of the Benedictine Centuries and the paramount influence of the Black Monks. Rather, men judged it to be a time of joy for the English houses of Saint Benedict and these monasteries still claimed the affection of the people. The era of the Norman plantation was over and the Black Monks were prominent in the hierarchy of the English Church. Quarrels between the secular and regular clergy were somewhat muted and the rapidly increasing Austin canons were viewed as allies rather than competitors.

The white-robed Cistercians arrived in the north of England in 1128 and soon spread with incredible speed covering the landscape with their austerely beautiful architecture, the fields and moors with their *conversi* and their sheep. Ailred of Rievaulx, "the Bernard of the North," is supposed to have ruled a community of six-hundred-fifty at his death in 1167. The Cistercian rule with its *Carta Caritatis*, which would influence the constitution of all subsequent religious bodies, was intended for the few who had a special calling to lead truly penitential lives, and it stressed manual work and habitation far from the wiles and wealth of civilization. Yet the increasing numbers, property, and involvement in world affairs symbolized by Bernard of Clairvaux's own spectacular career as statesman of Europe brought to the Cistercians a very rapid decline from their own original standards. For a while the White Monks seemed to stem the tide of monastic retreat, but by Bernard's death in 1153 all specifically monastic influence on the policy of the Church at large ceased at once and forever.

Knowles' account presents a convincing picture of the last years of this whole period, which saw the quarrels of Henry II and Thomas Becket, the interdict of 1208-1213 during John's quarrel with the pope, the growing separation of abbots from their communities, the accumulation of monastic wealth and property, the increasing monastic possession of small and dependent priories, and even the emerging lack of suitable regular work for large numbers of the monastic rank and file. These were signs and causes of monastic decay. Perhaps in reaction, the number of canons rose and very strict orders like the Carthusians attracted attention. In 1215 the great Pope Innocent III tried to stabilize monastic discipline by decreeing that henceforth the black monks would be subject to periodic visitation. In effect, their complete independence was ended and they were now a canonically organized body, not a collection of autonomous houses. By this time English monasticism had become merely an element of importance but no longer the dominant spiritual or intellectual force in the country.

Thus has Dom David Knowles traced the rise, flourish, and decline of the English period of monastic supremacy. But this is only half the tale as it is only half his splendid book. There remains the life and activity of those monks whose influence and numbers he chronicled. In this second part Father David has analyzed the daily routine of the monk and the officers and personnel of his house. The contributions of monastic education, medicine, and art are also examined. Informing this whole section of the book is a description of the place of the monastery in society. This involves a consideration of what the *Rule* entails and a discussion of the political and economic requirements of feudalism and a statement about the implications of these interrelated systems. For example, the author traces the rise of control of Church property and spiritual rights by private owners and laymen. Some conclusions are revealing, as when Knowles points out the positive benefits that sometimes resulted from royal domination of supposedly free abbatial elections.

The English monasteries of this period did not produce any front rank spiritual leaders or treatises, Knowles points out. Most of the great monks of England appear to have been organizers and administrators rather than writers or thinkers. In a sense, however, this monastic culture was literary; it did not produce new discoveries in thought, science, or language, but it was concerned with preserving the traditions and recording the past. Its most distinguished contributions are in the fields of historiography, and men like Eadmer, Ordericus Vitales, and, most especially, William of Malmesbury, the greatest English author since Bede, created very sound and valuable contemporary histories. Interestingly enough, this group flourished in the first half of the twelfth century; the later years could not produce their like.

Unfortunately, as Father David points out, it is apparently impossible to evaluate the aspect of monasticism which matters most; namely, the spiritual life of the monks. This life does not naturally lend itself to analysis, and the English monks of this time made the task even more difficult by not leaving posterity any great corpus of spiritual testaments. While a historian can judge the external, social work of the monk in relation to the needs of medieval Europe, his spiritual life must be judged by his adherence to the *Rule,* as must the institution itself in every age. In the modern world monasticism has become again what it was in the beginning, a factor in the spiritual life of the Church working upon individuals and not upon society. But underneath such changes monastic life in its aim and ideal has continued without change; in its essence it is neither ancient, nor medieval, nor modern, but of every Christian age.

E.J.K.

THE CHURCH OF THE WORD INCARNATE

Author: Charles Journet (1891-)
Type of work: Ecclesiology
First published: 1941

Principal Ideas Advanced

The Church is a living entity to which we owe all that is because of the marvel of its mere existence.

The hierarchical power is the efficient cause of the Church in its twofold division into sacramental and jurisdictional powers.

Through the sacramental power the Church makes the living Christ really present to man.

Through her jurisdictional power the Church claims to exercise authority over truth and claims allegiance to its interpretations.

Charles Journet, professor of dogma at the Grand-Seminaire in Fribourg, Switzerland, attempts to explain the Church from the standpoint of what he calls "speculative theology." His attempt takes the form of an Aristotelian analysis using the four causes from which the Church results: efficient, material, formal, and final. The entire work is done in four volumes, one volume for each cause. The first two have appeared in English translation. These treat of the immediate efficient cause producing the Church in the world and of the nature of the Church as compared to the image of Christ the Head and of men the members.

A third volume treats of the end of the Church, in which God is considered as her "separated" common good, and of her interior order, which is her "immanent" common good producing her sanctity. The last volume deals with the Church as she was in the days of her preparation before the coming of Christ and with what she will be in her consummation in Purgatory and Heaven.

Journet realizes the inadequacy of much of the ecclesiology written since Vatican I. He tries to penetrate deeper than earlier scholars have into the intimate constitution and the essential mystery of the Church. This he does first in terms of efficient causality. The twin powers, sacramental and jurisdictional, in their union constitute the apostolic hierarchy, the efficient cause of the Church. This naturally leads him to a corollary study of apostolicity in the Church.

In *The Church of the Word Incarnate* Journet finds it dangerous to separate the mystery of the Church from her hierarchical organization. He points up the error clearly stated in 1939 by Pius XII about distinguishing between the juridical Church and the Church of charity. Journet believes all such errors can be avoided by explaining the Church in terms of the causes on which she depends. In this kind of approach the hierarchy is seen to represent no more than the efficient cause of the Mystical Body.

Journet takes the word "Church" in what he calls a *formal* or *ontological* or *theological* sense. This means the Church in her entirety, body and soul together. The word indicates the Church alone, a pure and uncontaminated idea, excluding all that is other than herself. It is in this sense alone that she can be called one, holy, Catholic, apostolic, Bride, and Body of Christ, the temple of the Trinity.

The word "Church" can also be taken materially in terms of a composition of both just men and sinners. We meet this meaning, Journet claims, in the empiricists, notably the historians, who tend to look at the Church from a purely descriptive and phenomenal viewpoint. This approach is also found among preachers and apologists who view the Church from a moral standpoint. Journet concerns himself entirely with the formal sense. This may help account for what otherwise would be a one-sided view of the Church as a power structure. He clearly distinguishes the Church, according to his "formal" view, from the persons making up the Church. It may be questioned, however, whether such a distinction is ontologically valid.

Journet attempts to synthesize the scattered insights of the past into one organic treatise. His principal sources are Saint Augustine and Saint Thomas Aquinas, in whom he finds the essential vision of the Church as the historical extension of the Incarnation. After considering the generative act of the Church in terms of successive divine regimes, Journet treats of the hierarchy in terms of its powers. These are the powers of order, considered as the ministerial cause of the Church, and the power of jurisdiction, viewed as a second ministerial cause.

The axis of the Church is cult which is built upon the first ministerial cause and depends on the sacramental power. This power is common to all members of the Church. But as the power of order or the hierarchic sacramental power, it is the ministerial power assuring the continuity of the chief acts of Christian cultus.

The second ministerial cause is the power of jurisdiction. This can be ordinary or exceptional, permanent or regular. This power, too, derives from Christ, the Head of the Church. As the head has its twofold action in the body (an interior motor action and an exterior directive action), so Christ exerts a twofold action upon the members of His Church. He enriches their souls and proposes two kinds of propositions, one to be believed and the other to be lived.

After the Ascension did action by contact with Christ disappear, leaving only action from a distance? Journet answers that Christ the High Priest left the visible hierarchy endowed with a sacramental power, a ministerial participation in His sacerdotal power with which the faithful can have sensible contact. This priesthood of Christ is participated in the Church only in an instrumental manner. It is not the same with His Kingship. So that men might not be deprived of the help of His living voice, He left a visible power, continuing to speak with authority in His name. This is the power of jurisdiction.

The power of jurisdiction is both extraordinary, directed to the foundation of the Church which is to endure till the end of time, and ordinary, directed to its conservation. This power has four chief divisions: formal, concerning the form or role of jurisdictional mediation; material, concerning the material character of measures ordered by jurisdictional power; final, the proximate end and thus the degrees of jurisdictional power; and accidental, the quality of assistance promised by God to the jurisdictional authority. This last involves the kind of obedience owed by the faithful to the magisterium.

The formal distinction is that between the declaratory power and the canonical power. The clearest manifestation of this permanent jurisdiction is the Roman pontificate. The relation between canonical power and political power is discussed by Journet at length. The declaratory power is the higher, but the canonical power which brings jurisdiction in touch with temporal things and is more affected by them implies complexity and contingency. Thus, the field of its influence has been variable. Since the resemblance of the Church to political society is analogical, the resemblance of her canonical power to the political power is also only analogical. The Church has definite rights. First of all, she has the right and duty to live within political society. Second, she has the right and duty of exerting a sanctifying influence on the life of political society. Journet devotes some 130 pages to the historical problem of Church-state relations.

By reason of the spiritual values invested in the temporal common good within a consecrational regime (a state with orientation to the sacred), the Church required that this temporal common good be defended by temporal means used in accordance with their own laws. Resort to the secular arm is not seen as being incompatible with the Gospel. Journet thinks that there is nothing to prevent us from making the Church responsible for resort to the secular power. The purity and sanctity of the Church always remains untouched. It is even a radical right for the Church to appeal to the secular, even if it becomes more and more difficult to assert this right in a pluralist society. He sees ecclesiastical penalties as analogous to the condemnations of the Gospel. The divine order, by its very nature, tends to overcome all adverse influences.

The jurisdictional power has as its first mission the proclamation of the Gospel (declaratory power) and for its secondary mission the effectual organizing of the conduct of those who welcome this Good News (canonical power). The Kingdom of God in its wholeness, that is, the divine order resulting from the insertion of the Trinity into history, cannot, in virtue of a divine intention given in the Gospel, reach its final perfection save by the integral functioning of the jurisdictional power. This involves a genuine legislative power and in consequence a judicial coercive power. Still, the Kingdom of God never takes up arms itself and never assumes responsibility for blood.

The accidental division of jurisdiction, taken from the quality of the assistance provided by God, produces the "proposition" of revelation and the "protection" of revelation, the "empirical existence" and the "biological assistance" of the Church.

The material division, taken from the nature of the things prescribed by the jurisdictional authority, is a division of convenience. It is thus a division into magisterial and disciplinary powers which can deal either with speculative or practical truth.

Christ entrusted to the Church certain exceptional powers (extraordinary powers) and certain regular (permanent) powers. The regular power involves the particular or episcopal jurisdiction and the universal or papal jurisdiction. The Savior poured out on the Apostles a hidden power which associated them in an exceptional way with the foundation of His Church. This enabled them to launch the Church on the world with an initial impulse sufficient to last her to the end of history. Journet departs from the traditional theory of Bellarmine and Suarez, which holds that Peter alone received episcopal consecration immediately from Christ and that the other Apostles received it from the hands of Peter. Journet holds that all the powers possessed by the Apostles came to them immediately from Christ.

Further divisions of jurisdiction do not arise from the divine institution but from the ordinances of Church law. Just as the power of order of deacons has been extended into the subdiaconate and into minor orders, so the power of jurisdiction has been extended. The Pontificate has given birth to the power of the cardinals, of the Roman Curia, the patriarachs, and other ecclesiastical offices.

The regular powers of the Apostles passed to the episcopate which, in the beginning, was sometimes unitary, sometimes collegiate. The episcopate was the authority instituted for a particular church, a local church. The two roles, that of looking after the preservation and propagation of spiritual life, and that of directing the belief and action of the faithful, belong to the bishop. The first belongs to him in virtue of the power of order and the second in virtue of the power of jurisdiction. The bishop possesses the fullness of the power of order. His jurisdiction over his local church is plenary, immediate, proper, and ordinary. It can be exercised even during a vacancy of the Holy See. By virtue of his union with the pope, the bishop receives certain powers by which he partakes in the sovereign jurisdiction over the universal Church.

Journet devotes the greater part of his work to a study of jurisdictional power. Yet this is not the more important of the two powers which give the Church existence and sustain her through the centuries. The more important is the sacramental power through which Christ acts on His members by way not of exterior movement but of hidden influx. Within this power in the hierarchy the power of order and power of jurisdiction are not independent. They are the two halves of a single hierarchy.

The adequate name, signifying the Church in the fullness of her reality, naming her by her efficient and conserving cause, is "apostolic." This is to maintain that she depends on a spiritual virtue residing in the Trinity and thence descending by stages, first into the humanity of Christ, then into the twofold power, sacramental and jurisdictional, of the apostolic body, and finally to the Christian people. Where the mediation, this chain of dependence, is found, there is found the true Church. Apostolicity means the dependence of the Church on her divine causes, and, above all, on the nearest of those causes, the apostolic hierarchy.

A more adequate understanding of the Church as composed in the image of Christ, the Head, and of men, the members, is thus achieved. For she is given life by a spiritual element essentially invisible (the formal cause or soul of the Church) and has a material element essentially visible (the material cause or body of the Church). From the soul of the Church there derives her unity. Her Catholicity derives from the body of the Church. The final cause of the Church is the origin of her sanctity and of her accidental modes.

The Church is the living abode of the Spirit of uncreated love. The Spirit is the infinite energy at her center, transcending her at all points. Journet writes that the Church is the abode of spirit, of love, and of created charity. The unique spirit of the faithful is the unique spirit of God. This spirit is maintained by powers "embodied" in the Church, the hierarchic powers of order and jurisdiction. This is the spirit of love and charity which attains in the Church an intensity unknown before and incapable of existence outside her visible frontiers.

L.W.R.

BASIC VERITIES

Author: Charles Péguy (1873-1914)
Type of work: Social philosophy; religious poetry
First published: 1943

Principal Ideas Advanced

It is necessary to maintain or return to certain enduring values (or basic verities), such as a regard for the dignity of work and the beauty of mysticism; these values are being eroded by the modern capitalistic bourgeoisie society.

Society's prime duty is to provide for the destitute; it can do so only through charity and fraternity—ideals alien to the modern spirit.

To counteract this spirit, society must undergo a revolution, one that is achieved through socialism, but a socialism which is Christian rather than materialistic, and which is actually a "religion of temporal salvation."

God gives freedom and shows tenderness to man; in return He asks that man show confidence in Him, that man trust in His providence.

Basic Verities presents selected prose and poetry from the *Cahiers de la Quinzaine* of Charles Péguy, the French journalist and crusader, who, in his uncompromising search for truth and for social justice, at first abandoned, but then returned to, the Roman Catholic Church. He reacted against religion as a young man in his teens, and declared himself an atheist; it was not until he was in his mid-thirties that he made known his return to Catholicism. Nevertheless, charity and compassion for humanity were values he held dear throughout his whole life. Almost entirely neglected by the general reading public during his lifetime, receiving attention mainly from the small group of socialists who knew of his bookstore and publishing ventures, he gained fame only after his death on a battlefield in World War I. It is fitting that he chose to serve as a French officer on the battlefield even though at his age of forty-one he probably could have been placed in the reserves.

Throughout most of his essays, Péguy repeats again and again two basic tenets: his hatred for the capitalistic bourgeois values of the modern world, and his burning desire to foster charity and justice—particularly for the poor, the weak, and the oppressed. He saw these two tenets as inter-related, because he believed that the modern world attempted to crush the old values, that it was a world of those "who believe in nothing, not even in atheism, who show neither devotion nor sacrifice for anything." He speaks of its sterility, disease, and unrest, and its constant straining after money. Christianity itself is stuck "in the mire of rotten economic, industrial morality. . . ."

Péguy felt that Christianity had lost its old spirit of community; it had become almost entirely a religion of the rich, and the rich were cut off from the poor. For Péguy, the charity of Jesus consists in the "spiritual, temporal and constant communion with the poor, the weak and the oppressed." But the rich did not, could not, understand poverty. The old communion, based on charity, was ruined by the bourgeois spirit.

Péguy's concern for the oppressed or poor is shown in his warm comments on the Jews and, in particular, the French peasants. He pities the Jews for the pains and lacerations they have suffered for centuries and for the basic inner conflict they have between policy and mysticism; a people of merchants, they are also a people of prophets. They must bear the trials God continually sends them and the constant fear that they will never be secure, that they must move on: "This people is always on camel back." He pays them great tribute, finding them "affectionate, firm, . . . unshakingly faithful to the mysticism of friendship."

In his appreciation for the French peasants, Péguy can look back on his childhood days in a poor parish where ancient values were still carried on.

But the world has changed radically in the thirty years since (that is, since around 1880). Then, the average parish was closer to one of the fifteenth, or even fourth century, than to the twentieth century. The people were gay, they had a decency of soul, a delicacy which could not be compared to the bourgeois contemporary tone. They loved work, and they had a respect for home and for respect itself. For them: "Everything was a rhythm and a rite and a ceremony from the moment of rising in the early morning. Everything was an event; a sacred event. Everything was a tradition. . . . Everything was an inner elevation and a prayer." These people were much more concerned with fraternity than with equality; they accepted inequality as an order or hierarchy which appeared natural "because it only meant the different levels of a common happiness." Péguy very carefully distinguishes between equality and fraternity. He has little concern for the first; it is the second which is essential to attend to the most serious social problem: destitution. Society has the primary duty of relieving the destitute; the matter of equality or the equitable distribution of goods is of minor importance beside this urgent problem.

Péguy did not simply lament the loss of old values; he called for a revolution to transform the modern world. This revolution was to be achieved through socialism, but a socialism which was "no less than a religion of temporal salvation" of humanity. (He had little respect for the political leaders of socialism of his day, feeling that they were bourgeois in spirit.) Charity and fraternity, of course, were at the base of this revolution; and a key aim was to achieve the restoration of the dignity of work.

Looking back on earlier generations of workers, Péguy says that for them: "Work . . . was joy itself and the deep root of their being. And the reason of their being. There was an incredible honor in work, the most beautiful of all the honors, the most Christian. . . ." These men perfected their work, took pride in it, as did the men of the Middle Ages who built the cathedrals. But the honor of work, the attitude that even a chair rung be "well made itself, in itself, for itself, in its very self," even the part that did not show, had been destroyed by the capitalistic bourgeoisie, who infected and sabotaged the working man when they began to treat his work as a security on the stock exchange. Then the worker himself started treating his work the same way.

As excerpts from his essays can only vaguely suggest, Péguy wrote in a simple and direct style that builds cumulatively through repetition and subtle redefinition or rewording. But Péguy also provides his readers with challenging aphorisms and paradoxes. For example, on the fundamentally revolutionary character of the struggle for justice and charity, he writes, "There is only one Lady in the world who has caused more wars than injustice: and that is justice. . . . Not only justice but charity itself is full of war." And on the search for truth: ". . . the life of an honest man must be an apostasy and a perpetual desertion." The honest man must be a "perpetual renegade," his life must be a "perpetual infidelity," because to remain faithful to truth he must be continually unfaithful to "all the continual, successive, indefatigable renascent errors," and to remain faithful to justice he must be continually unfaithful to "inexhaustibly triumphant injustices."

Though his prose is serious in tone, Péguy's poetry often reveals a lighter vein, particularly in his "God Speaks" poems, in which God the Father, while trying to maintain the role of the stern judge, cannot help showing the tenderness of a human father towards his erring children. The divine Father reviews the beauties of the world that He has seen, and then He concludes that "Nothing is so beautiful as a child going to sleep while he is saying his prayers." This is the one point on which the Blessed Virgin and He agree since she is for mercy whereas, as He puts it, "I, of course, have to be for justice."

God the Father explains that He is like a father that has the problem of teaching his sons how to swim: if he holds them up too often, they will not learn to swim by themselves, but at the same time he does not want them to swallow too much water. God must give men freedom to work their own salvations, because He does not care to be loved by slaves. It is important to God that man's love for Him be free.

What God wants in return for the freedom and tenderness He shows man is trust. He says that the man who does not sleep shows through his unrest and despair that he lacks confidence in God. He wants man to lie "Innocently in the arms of my Providence." To men He says of their business that they ought to leave it to Him for the space of a night while they sleep, and that the next morning "you might find it not too badly damaged perhaps." It is hope that God asks for, the willingness of men to abandon themselves to Him.

Even though He may comment on the weakness of man, God the Father, the supposedly stern judge, still tries to qualify the conduct of His weak children. He can remark that man is "not too bad" and that "When you know how to handle him, you can still ask a lot of him." And His Son has taught man how to win the Father over to mercy rather than justice simply with the opening words of the Our Father ("Our Father who art in Heaven . . ."): "Those three or four words that conquer me, the unconquerable./ . . . my son knew exactly what to do/ In order to tie the arms of my justice and untie the arms of my mercy."

Péguy's portrayal of God the Father is one that can make the reader smile, but it is also a portrayal that reflects Péguy's own basic compassion for humanity, a compassion that is consistently present throughout his poems and essays. Although he may castigate the bourgeoisie in his essays, his primary concern there, as in the poems, is love —whether it take the form of fatherly love, childlike trust, or brotherly charity.

F.P.C.

DIVINO AFFLANTE SPIRITU

Author: Pope Pius XII (Eugenio Pacelli, 1876-1958)
Type of work: Principles of Biblical studies
First published: 1943

Principal Ideas Advanced

The vastly changing and changed picture in the field of Scripture study calls for a completely updated set of norms to guide Roman Catholic attitudes toward the Bible.

Among these norms should be listed the recourse to original texts, the importance of textual criticism, the correct understanding of the Church's supervision of Scriptural interpretation, and the priority of a literal interpretation in preference to a merely allegorical or "spiritual" sense.

Most important of all, the Bible is to be interpreted according to the intention of the sacred writers and the mode of writing which they used.

Pius XII's encyclical on the promotion of Biblical studies, *Divino afflante Spiritu* ("By the inspiration of the divine spirit"), has merited, as few documents can merit in their field, the status of a *magna charta.* To say that of itself it sparked a revolution in Roman Catholic Biblical studies would not be completely the truth, since the stirrings of the movement had already been evident for some fifty years prior to the encyclical's publication. These approaches grew out of another pioneering church document, the encyclical of Leo XIII on Scripture, *Providentissimus Deus* ("God in His loving care"), issued in 1893. Leo gave to the Church a rather well-knit set of directives for arousing a properly intelligent attitude toward the Bible. The vitriolic rationalistic attacks on organized religion that had been spawned during the eighteenth and nineteenth centuries had regrettably led either to a weakly defensive position among some Catholic scholars or to an aggressive fideist and voluntarist attitude that spurned the works of human intelligence as inimical to the work of God. Nonetheless, even Leo XIII's encyclical left questions unanswered or proposed principles whose application remained in doubt when confronted with hitherto undreamed of results of research in archaeology, philology, ethnology, "lower criticism" (ascertainment of the correct text), and "higher criticism" (search for original sources and thus deeper understanding of the completed literary product).

The proximate occasion of *Divino afflante Spiritu* was a letter of the Roman Catholic Biblical Commission of August 20, 1941, rebuking the methods of an Italian priest, Father Dolindo Ruotolo, who wrote under the pseudonym, "Dain Cohenel." His short pamphlet, circulated largely among Italian ecclesiastics, violently attacked the attempts of certain Catholic Scripture scholars to apply scientifically historical norms to Scripture study while in no way departing from Catholic policies and beliefs. The rebuttal letter, out of which *Divino afflante Spiritu* developed, presented two main ideas which were to recur in the encyclical two years later: first, that the interpretation of the Bible requires all the resources of human and natural knowledge; and second, that despite the rationalism which destructively led to a reaction among believers for a spiritual and allegorical refuge, the heart of Biblical interpretation must come from a determination of what the inspired writers of the Bible meant to say, not from some quasi-foreign meaning attached to their words by pious commentators in search for devotional lesson material.

The first or historical section of *Divino afflante Spiritu* summarizes the work of earlier pontiffs, beginning with Leo XIII, whose *Providentissimus* is here explicitly commemorated on its fiftieth anniversary. Leo's doctrine, in summary, defended the truth of the Bible from attack. When the sacred writers spoke of the physical order, they either went by external appearances or used figurative language. The Bible is not to be taxed with error because of copyists' mistakes in the transcribing of Biblical texts or because the meaning of some Biblical passage remains ambiguous or still obscure. The inspiration of the Bible must not be limited only to passages where contradictions do not seem present; nor, on the other hand, may the Catholic admit that the inspired text teaches error as such.

But the fact of the Modernist heresy during the early years of the twentieth century definitely held back Catholic attempts to follow out the conclusions from Leo's principles, as criticism dogged the footsteps of definitely orthodox scholars whose scientifically oriented studies smacked of heresy to some suspicious officials. Thus it is that Pius XII's encyclical cannot point to any really monumental Scriptural advances in the intervening papal reigns. Its own doctrinal section, however, spells out a magnificently nuanced official attitude henceforth to be followed.

The encyclical first recalls the completely changed conditions of Biblical studies since the time of Leo XIII. Hardly a single place in Palestine had then been explored according to the methods of a scientific archaeology. A tremendous number of written documents have been discovered since the time of Leo, Pius remarks; and he points out that the documents contribute to the knowledge of the languages, letters, events, customs, and forms of worship of ancient times. Manuscript discoveries themselves provide a source of data calling for completely revised approaches. Yet the ancient writers, Pius comments, were ignorant of Greek and more often, of Hebrew, and thus the first task of the exegete (Scripture-scholar) is to learn the original Biblical languages in order to find precisely what the text considered to be inspired really says.

The encyclical points out that textual criticism had been used "quite arbitrarily" in introducing preconceived ideas into the interpretation of the Bible, but that criticism, the encyclical now adds, is outdated. Henceforth, textual criticism is to be considered as reliable and praiseworthy only in its scientific attempts "to insure that the sacred text be restored as perfectly as possible, be purified from the mistakes due to the carelessness of the copyists, and freed, as far as may be done, from glosses and omissions . . . which are wont to make their way gradually into writings handed down through the centuries."

One of the problems paramount for

the Roman Catholic exegete was to decide what attitude he should adopt toward the Latin Vulgate translation of the Bible. The Council of Trent in the sixteenth century had called this translation "authentic," but this decision caused doubts on what was to be done concerning some manifestly erroneous translations or copyists' errors in the Vulgate. Pius XII gives the answer when he writes that the Vulgate Bible is free from error in matters of faith or morals," and therefore it is "juridically" authentic and may safely be used as an official document of the Church. However, this authenticity is not "critical"; it does not mean that the Vulgate translation cannot be corrected by recourse to other manuscripts, other translations, or the original languages themselves.

Throughout, the encyclical adds, the exegete should seek the literal meaning of the Bible, using every tool of his art to discern this. The spiritual or applied meanings of the Bible may indeed continue to be drawn as developments from the Scripture, but these are not to be claimed to rest in the original as such, nor are they at any time to be speculative.

Of all the prime contributions of the encyclical, the greatest is its canonization, as it were, of the method of searching for literary traditions in order to determine as closely as possible precisely what the inspired writers meant to say and thereby to know the ultimate meaning of what God wished to give man in the inspired message, of which God is the principal author. With a perspicacity that can hardly be praised to excess, Pope Pius points out that the literal meaning of a Biblical passage cannot be determined by comparison with the meaning of words in our own time. In order for words to be interpreted according to the meanings they had in ancient cultures, contextural study is not enough. The very ways of thought of the past must be learned. The commentator on the Bible has no right to determine these ancient meanings *a priori;* he can and must obtain them only after carefully examining the ancient literature of the East. The various literary devices which were used to express truth in the past appeared not merely in poetic descriptions but also in special conceptions of history which run counter to the Western mind. The correct understanding of Biblical inspiration outlaws no mode of human expression whatsoever, provided only that the way of speaking does not contradict the holiness and truth of God. Thus, certain ways of exposition, certain Semitic idioms, certain approximations, certain hyperboles, certain repeated paradoxes can all recur in the Bible, and they should be interpreted accordingly. Pius XII notes that when the Bible is reproached with error, the so-called error on closer examination turns out to be merely a customary mode of expression sanctioned by ancient usage.

The encyclical humbly recognizes that application of these methods and even the adoption of enlightened attitudes toward new research will not remove all problems from Biblical study. Some solutions will be slow in coming; some may never be found. Scripture scholars who work toward these goals should be protected by the Church from unjustified interference in their studies.

Pius then emphasizes that there are relatively few texts in the Bible whose sense has been defined by the Church (theologians estimate this number at a dozen at the maximum). Limitations of doctrine regarding faith and morals do not, therefore, mean that questions have been closed in the discussion of the Bible. The exegete will be free in his studies, using his Catholic faith according to the "analogy of faith" (referred to earlier in the encyclical) so that no interpretation given by him will run counter to the norms of faith and morality, even while the interpretations themselves remain free from prohibition or imposition by the Church.

The encyclical ends by proposing norms for the use of Scripture in teaching the faithful (according to the norms emphasizing the literal sense) and for the teaching of future priests in the seminaries, and it includes a final exhortation for reverence for the Bible and for the full cultivation of its benefits as the word of God.

F.L.F.

THE MYSTICAL BODY OF CHRIST

Author: Pope Pius XII (Eugenio Pacelli, 1876-1958)
Type of work: Dogmatic theology
First published: 1943

Principal Ideas Advanced

The Mystical Body of Christ has more than analogous existence; it is real.
The Mystical Body of Christ is the Church.
Christ is the Head of the Mystical Body, and those to whom the pope addresses the encyclical are its members, as are all the faithful.
Each member of the Mystical Body receives life and light from the Head of the Body, and sustaining help from all other members.
Various members perform different functions in the Mystical Body, each contributing in his way to its health and vigor.

Pope Pius XII was an "intellectual" pope who guided the adaptation of the Church to contemporary conditions by spelling out doctrines that were neglected and sometimes almost forgotten items in the Church's deposit of faith. One of the most important of these doctrines was that of the Mystical Body of Christ. *Mystici corporis Christi* uses the authority both of tradition and Scripture to analyze this doctrine and to stress its importance theologically and socially. Saint Paul is the principal Biblical source.

The Holy Father saw a double need for bringing the doctrine of the Mystical Body to the attention of all Catholics. Modern individualism had infected the thinking of most of the faithful about their relationship to God, and various private practices tended to replace congregational worship. More immediately, World War II divided nation against nation, and the pope wanted to remind Catholics that they bore a real, though mystical relationship to Catholics against whom they were fighting, as well as to those on their own side.

The encyclical is divided into a brief introduction, three principal parts dealing with the doctrine of the Mystical Body and a short conclusion. The first principal part is entitled "Church, Mystical Body of Christ." This doctrine, the Holy Father reminds us, is ultimately a "mystery . . . enveloped in a darkness, rising out of the mental limitations of those who seek to grasp it." But this does not preclude study to develop our limited knowledge of this profound truth. "But We know, too," Pope Pius XII continues, "that well-directed and earnest study of this doctrine and the clash of diverse opinions and their discussion, provided love of truth and due submission to the Church to be the arbiter, will open rich and bright vistas, whose light will help to progress in kindred sacred sciences."

The Mystical Body consists of all members of the Church, sinners as well as saints, who are united in Christ. "Though many," Saint Paul wrote, "we are one body in Christ." No body is formed by a chance grouping of its members, for each organ fulfills a definite function. So it is with the Mystical Body, as Saint Paul explains: "As in one body we have many members but all the members have not the same office; so we being many, are one Body in Christ, and everyone a member one of another." The Mystical Body is nourished and strengthened by the sacraments, especially the Sacrament of the Altar which nourishes the faithful spiritually at the same table and unites them with one another and their Divine Head in Holy Communion.

Christ is the Founder, the Head, the Support and Savior of this Mystical Body. By His preaching Christ began to build the Mystical Body, and on the Cross He completed His work. He manifested and proclaimed it when he sent the Holy Spirit in visible form on His disciples at Pentecost. Christ is the Head of the Mystical Body because of His singular pre-eminence. Thus, He rules and governs the Church, His Body, and He does this not merely in an invisible and extraordinary way, but in a visible and ordinary way through His Vicar, Saint Peter, and his successors.

There are additional reasons why Christ should be called Head of the Mystical Body. First, He took our nature so that His brothers in the flesh might share in His divine nature. He became the Son of Man that we might become sons of God. Second, all the supernatural gifts that the Church receives come from Him. Third, He is the Light of the Church, enlightening every member of the Body to know by faith, and He is the source of all holiness in the Mystical Body: "He selects, He determines, He distributes every single grace to every single person 'according to the measure of the giving of Christ.' Hence it follows that from our Lord as from a fountain-head 'the whole body compacted and fitly joined by which every joint supplieth, according to the operation in the measure of every part, maketh increase of the body unto the edifying of itself in charity.' "

Christ is also the Savior of the Mystical Body. He saved it by His blood on the Cross, and what He began on the Cross "He does not cease to continue always and uninterruptedly."

The second principal part of *Mystici corporis Christi* explores "The Union of the Faithful with Christ." Christ and His Mystical Body form but one mystical person, whose members must be unified because they all work together toward a single end, the sanctification of the members of the Body for the glory of God and His divine Son. The members of the Body are united juridically under Peter and his successors, who were commissioned by Christ to govern His Church as His visible representatives. Members of the Mystical Body are also linked closely together and to God in faith, hope, and charity. "One Lord, one Faith," says Saint Paul; "Whosoever shall confess that Jesus is the Son of God, God abideth in him and he in God."

This bond of faith uniting us to God also unites us closely to one another. "If the same spirit of faith breathes in all," Pope Pius XII concludes, "we all are living the same life 'in the faith of the Son of God, Who loved us and delivered Himself for us.'" Christians are also joined more closely by their united yearning for the Heavenly Kingdom where they can rest in Christ.

No less important is charity as a bond among Christians united with Christ. "Charity, then, more than any other virtue binds us closely to Christ." Charity must also bind us to one another, the pope writes, quoting Saint Paul's warning: "If any man say: I love God, and hateth his brother, he is a liar. For he that loveth not his brother whom he seeth, how can he love God Whom he seeth not? And this commandment we have from God, that he who loveth God also love his brother."

This union of members of the Mystical Body with Christ and with one another reaches its climax in the Eucharistic Sacrifice. The pope writes: "The Sacrament of the Eucharist is itself a striking image of the Church's unity, if we consider how in the bread to be consecrated many grains go to form one substance; and in it the very Author of supernatural grace is given to us, so that through Him we may receive the Spirit of charity, in which we are bidden to live now not our life but the life of Christ, and in all the members of His social Body to love the Redeemer Himself."

The third part of *Mystici corporis Christi* is a "Pastoral Exhortation" to the bishops of the world. Here Pope Pius XII urges them to be on guard against certain erroneous concepts of the Mystical Body. It is necessary to remember that Saint Paul used metaphorical language in teaching this doctrine, but he was careful to distinguish between Christ's physical body and His Mystical Body: "He brings Christ and His Mystical Body into a marvelously intimate union, it is true; but he distinguishes one from the other as Bridegroom and Bride." Another error is believing that membership in the Mystical Body makes good works, private prayers, and frequent confession unnecessary.

The Holy Father concludes this encyclical by exhorting the faithful to love the Church as Christ loves it, to pray for the Church as Christ prayed for it, and to offer their sufferings to "Him Who will one day reward them abundantly." Writing in 1943, the pope sorrowfully observed: "There passes before Our eyes, alas, an almost endless throng of unfortunates for whom We mourn and weep; sick, poor, mutilated, widows, orphans. . . . Let them remember that their sufferings are not in vain, but will be to their great gain and that of the Church, if for this purpose they but take courage and bear them with patience."

Mystici corporis Christi is generally regarded as one of the most important documents in modern Church history. It gathered together doctrinal speculation on the social nature of the Church and individual Christians, winnowed out erroneous concepts, and made official the repudiation of an individualistic religion without condemning private devotions. Thus it prepared the way and encouraged the liturgical revival which culminated twenty years later in Vatican Council II. It also gave added doctrinal incentive for works of justice and charity based upon the potential membership of every member of the human race in the Mystical Body of Christ.

T.P.N.

THE HEART OF MAN

Author: Gerald Vann, O.P. (1906-)
Type of work: Christian humanism
First published: 1944

Principal Ideas Advanced

Exalting reason, science, individualism, and utility at the expense of intuition, religion, community, and art, modern Western man has created a world in which things and persons are treated not as ends in themselves but as means to such selfish ends as pleasure, power, and profit, a world in which morality is based on the doctrine of the ends justifying the means, and a world in which man's heart yearns hopelessly for the reality which only wholeness of personality can bring.

In order to find the integrity of personality for which his heart yearns and thereby to begin the establishment of integrity in the world at large, modern man must be reborn in religion; the Ego now at the center of his personality must die and be replaced by God.

The Heart of Man by Gerald Vann, O.P., is a criticism from a religious point of view of many of the aspects of life in the modern Western world. Science and reason, says Father Vann, have enabled modern man to control his material environment to an extent unprecedented in human history. However, in giving modern man this power, science and reason have robbed him of humility; they have instilled in him a self-conscious, selfish individualism which forces him to look at things and persons not as ends in themselves, not as objects of reverence and worship, but as instruments existing to serve his own selfish ends, as possessions.

Viewing all created things as his potential possessions, man becomes a grasper and plunderer, and nowhere is the degradation of his "grasping, utilizing attitude more terrible," says Father Vann, "than in the relationship between human beings." Even that highest and essentially most sacred of human relationships, love between man and woman, sexual love, is degraded to a matter of one party or both using the other merely as a means of pleasure. Thus, sexual love becomes, Father Vann contends, "simply a biological function or a physical plaything," and thus it no longer functions to enrich and enlarge the personality by destroying the prison of ego; rather, it reinforces the walls of the ego. A good example of this kind of degraded relationship, says Father Vann, is to be found in the affairs of Casanova: "Nothing could be more inaccurate than to speak of Casanova as one of the world's great lovers," maintains Vann, for Casanova "never touched reality at all, never emerged from the narrow, brittle shell of his own little ego." Unlike Casanova, the truly great lover, rather than *utilizing* the body of the loved one, *reverences* that body; for the great lover, contends Father Vann, realizes that the act of sexual love is essentially a religious experience as is suggested in the liturgy of marriage which says, "With my body I worship." Uniting in body, the true lovers become one in personality and in God; theirs is not an act of selfish, individual conquest, but a mutual act of self-surrender, an act in which true wholeness, true personality is born in the death of self.

Besides degrading the relationship between lovers, the individualistic, "grasping, utilizing attitude," says Father Vann, also degrades other forms of human relationships in the modern world. Noteworthy among these relationships is that obtaining between the employer and his workers. It is the general case in this self-seeking, power-mad, grasping modern world, contends Father Vann, that the employers, typically industrial magnates, look upon their workers not as persons to be treated as ends in themselves, but as "hands," as means to profit and to power. Not only have these industrialists ignored their obligation to see that their workers are insured a decent material existence, but also by turning work into mere commercial exploitation they have robbed the workers of the spiritual satisfaction of working at truly creative tasks. "What a sub-human slavery it is when vast industrial organizations are owned and controlled by a few," says Vann, "and the masses are reduced to giving their lives to labor which is uncreative. . . ."

Creative work is as necessary for the wholeness and personal integrity of the individual and thus for the wholeness and integrity of society as love itself, and the industrial giants who deprive the vast majority of men of creative work by regarding work as merely a means to profit and not as an end in itself, not as a form of activity necessary to man's spiritual fulfillment, not as an art, commit a very great sin against mankind. Instead of using their vast power and industrial machinery to create a world of meaningful work for mankind, the giants, says Vann, have used their machinery to make of work for the vast majority of mankind nothing but soul-destroying drudgery, drudgery which is evil, says Father Vann, "not because it is hard, but because it is uncreative."

Robbed by commercial enterprise of

his birthright, creative work, denied the necessary outlet for his instinctual, creative energies, the energies that seek to master and to mould the world through love, constantly frustrated by his inability to find that form of activity which will vitally relate him to the world outside, man, according to the author, forgets "how to see" and "how to love." His frustrated instinct to create expresses itself finally, says Vann, in "an explosion," in crimes of cruelty and violence . . . in economic unrest and piracy and competition . . . in the political horrors of nationalism, hatred and war."

Lying behind the commercial enterprise which exploits man and nature is the same lack of reverence for things and persons which lies behind those who exploit human love; and without this reverence, without the spirit of worship for created things, contends Father Vann, the world and the world's people will remain torn asunder, bereft of spiritual and personal wholeness and integrity. The heart of man, which is the heart of the world, cries out for that spirit of reverence, that sense of worship which will make it whole; it cries out for the rebirth necessary for a new order; it cries out for a restoration of individual integrity, of family integrity, and of world integrity.

Restoring to the world the sense of worship, of reverence for created things, of love and charity which will make the world whole, says Father Vann, is a process which must begin with the individual; he must recognize his own sundered human nature and through self-sacrifice restore that nature to integrity. What has happened to the individual's human nature in the modern world, says Father Vann, is analogous to what happened to the nature of our first parents when they committed original sin and were driven from Eden. Through pride, through the desire for liberation and a sense of individuality, our first parents replaced God's will with their own wills; modern man, driven by the same desire for freedom and individual realization, has replaced God at the center of his personality with Ego. Thus, the true center of personality has been removed, the hierarchy of values broken down, and each element of the personality has attempted to function autonomously with the result being disintegration and anarchy.

Thus, man's task of rebirth and restoration, man's attempt to return the world to wholeness, must start with man's restoring himself to integrity by reversing the process of the Fall; he must replace the Ego now at the center of his personality with God, contends Father Vann. Acting out the old paradoxes of Christianity, man must die to himself in order to be reborn again; he must strip himself naked in order to be clothed radiantly; he must become again as a child in order to become truly a man; he must humble himself in order to be exalted.

Humility means accepting God as master and sovereign, which means that man must stop regarding all things as his creatures; he must recognize his utter contingency; he must see the limitation of reason, recognizing that knowledge *about* things, reasonable, scientific knowledge, has blinded him to knowledge *of* things, intuitional, religious, and artistic knowledge. And in these realizations he will see the shallowness of his Utilitarianism. He will see, maintains Father Vann, that when "we start turning things into mere means to our pleasure or profit, we finish by turning means into ends." A consequence of this is that we make of "science a leader instead of a servant, and so condemn ourselves to chaos or at best to living exclusively on the surface of life."

That man must worship God in all of God's created things if man is to find wholeness in himself and if he is to restore wholeness and integrity to the world at large, is a lesson, Father Vann reminds us, continually taught by the liturgy of the Church. Utilizing the symbols and rhythms of human and natural life, man's psychic rhythms and the rhythms of the tides and seasons, for example, the Church dramatizes in the Mass the reality of sacrifice and the need of man for rebirth and restoration in Christ, emphasizing always that man is not only a unique child of God with individual rights but also a member of Christ's Body and family, with obligations and duties.

The sacraments of Baptism and Penance remind man that he must continually be reborn in Christ, that his selfish ego must die in order to enable his real self, his personality, to be born; and that greatest of sacraments, the Eucharist, continually reminds man that sacrifice through charity, Christ's charity, the highest expression of love, is the only true way to personality, to the union of man with himself, with his fellow man, and with God. It is this dramatic sense of Oneness in Divine sacrifice that equips man for his vocation of recreating the world.

Prepared by the liturgy and by the sacraments to accept the world as a family in Christ, the Christian working to restore the world recognizes that any plan to restore the world not based on the image of the world as a family of worshipers, a family working through love for the perfection and salvation of each of its members, a family recognizing the rights of each of its members but at the same time asking that each of its members accept the sacrifices necessary to insure the good life of all the family, is doomed to failure. "You cannot live for the common good of the nations," says Father Vann, "unless you see the nations as a single family and will to treat them as a single family; and for that you must have the vision of the oneness of the world, the oneness of the world in God."

Rejecting modernism and urging a return of man to a reverence for the liturgical character of existence and for the mystery of human history and destiny, *The Heart of Man,* like other of Father Vann's works, such as *Morals Maketh Man* (1937), and *Eve and the Gryphon* (1946), has proved itself an important part of that body of modern liturgical writing which includes such important books as Romano Guardini's *The Spirit of the Liturgy* (1918), Dietrich von Hildebrand's *Liturgy and Personality* (1933), and Louis Bouyer's *Liturgical Piety* (1957).

J.P.D.

HOMO VIATOR

Author: Gabriel Marcel (1889-)
Type of work: Personalist ethics
First published: 1945

Principal Ideas Advanced

Modern man must live an anguished life in a world crippled by war and made sterile by the rise of technology, a world in which all values have collapsed.

By becoming aware of his position as a wanderer, a pilgrim, on a journey towards a transcendent level, man can succeed in achieving some sort of stability on this earth.

To achieve this realization, he must adopt an attitude of fidelity to the forces that would save him, and he must abandon the attitude of rejection and pride advocated by the atheistic Existentialists.

By so doing, man may resolve the principal problems of modern society: the loss of God, the cleavage between persons, and the despair concerning the possibility of life after death.

Gabriel Marcel, though often grouped with the existentialist philosophers because of his concentration on such themes as the meaning of the person, freedom, and death, presents, in many ways, a unique outlook on life, which differs profoundly from that of the other leading existentialists. Nowhere in his writings is his originality more evident than in the collection of essays written during the Second World War, under the title *Homo viator* (*Man, the Wanderer*). Like his fellow Frenchmen, Albert Camus (1913-1960) and Jean-Paul Sartre, Marcel is concerned with the difficulties facing man in a world which seems to offer nothing but reasons for despair; but, unlike these men, he sees a meaning which transcends the apparent futility of contemporary life. Camus and Sartre regard man as being essentially selfish, as isolated, and as cast into an absurd universe which yields him nothing but frustration. Marcel, on the other hand, extends into our own times the tradition of philosophers like Socrates, Saint Augustine, Saint Thomas Aquinas, and Pascal, in that Marcel views the human person as the culmination of the universe, as the recipient of an infinite Gift, and as a person invested with the ability of choosing freely a life of immortal love. Although he shares with his contemporaries a dim outlook on the depersonalizing forces at work in the world, unlike them he sees behind all this, with a Chesterton-like optimism, the call of the Creator to the persons He has made to transcend their situation by accepting the gifts He has put at their disposal.

Although Marcel treats a variety of topics in his book, they are all orchestrated about the single theme of "creative fidelity." The "nuptial bond" uniting man with other persons, with himself, and with the material world has been severed by two world wars and fragmented by technology. To solve the crises posed by this radical separation of man from being, a spirit of fidelity to the creative forces operative in the world must be regained, a spirit which Marcel attempts to awaken in his readers. From such a commitment arises a liberating hope which will loosen man's spirit, now confined by the dullness of despair. Fidelity means recognizing the sacredness of being, whether it be found in another person, in the act of sexual intercourse, or in life itself. Fidelity is gratitude for the gift of life, for the order that surrounds us, an order considered not as an oppressive imposition of an impersonal force, but as an invitation. This fidelity is creative insofar as it renews both the person who practices it and its recipient, making both "at long last previous to the spirit which animates the inwardly consecrated soul."

Marcel develops his theme of fidelity under three aspects. First, fidelity consists in the free acceptance in love of other persons; second, consequent upon this experience of love is the discovery of oneself; finally, in these experiences, one is gradually led to the experience of transcendence, of an order beyond the temporal, which necessarily involves the Creator of the interpersonal order.

Basic to all of his analyses is the relationship among persons, the attitude one adopts towards others, which results in the transition from self as "ego" to self as "person." The ego is the enclosed individual, motivated by his own selfish desires and fears, oblivious to the people around him. The person, on the other hand, is the man who has accepted full responsibility for his acts in relation to other men. Freedom, the ever-recurring theme of existentialism, is manifested primarily in the acceptance of another person as an autonomous subject.

The rise of science and technology has caused in man a feeling of separation from the world of nature, which Marcel likens to man's moving from the country, where he was close to the earth, to the city, which surrounds him with buildings and machines. This feeling of estrangement from the world has contributed to the loneliness and anxiety experienced so commonly in contemporary society. Sartre and Camus offer, as the response to this feeling, the spirit of absurdity, which consists in recognizing that in answer to our desire for truth, the world offers nothing but meaninglessness; to our desire for love, hatred and duplicity; to our desire for immortality, death. Marcel, however, proposes another answer. He argues that if man, in a spirit of fidelity, opens himself to a genuine experience of the world, he will encounter overpowering reasons for hope instead of despair, reasons not in the sense of abstract concepts, but in the sense of experiential evidence for transcendence, a permanent order of being.

It is the complex of relationships found in marriage, however, that provides the prime example for a study of all the other relationships binding man to being, for the relation between man and wife is the "archetypal us." In marriage we find the most profound realization of the love that can exist among human beings. In the attitude towards the procreative act is found fidelity to life and to the Ultimate Source of life; in the fidelity of a father towards his son is found a superior instance of artistic creation and commitment. The union between man and life is like the nuptial bond; in severing this union, man finds himself divorced from those forces which had previously meant his nourishment.

Attributing many of the difficulties facing the modern family to the mass movements towards urbanization, Marcel sees a deeper significance in this phenomenon for all man. Because he no longer lives close to the land, man has lost all sense of his affinity to nature and life. This divorce of man and nature has weakened those two virtues which contribute most to the success of the marriage bond: fidelity and hope. The fidelity required in marriage manifests itself in that characteristic which Marcel calls "availability." The available person is the one who is open to receive the influence of other persons and of the world; he is like the good host who is genuinely concerned with his guests. Applied to the father of a family, availability means putting oneself at the disposal of those life-forces which are at work in the universe, instead of using them for one's own selfish ends.

Marriage today, however, is considered primarily as a legal pact. Divorce, in this context, becomes inevitable, since a legal contract can be broken by the mutual consent of both parties. But to consider marriage in this way, Marcel declares, is to destroy the very essence of this interpersonal bond, which, since it is based on the commitment of one person to another, partakes of the immortality of love. Moreover, the birth of a child puts an indelible seal on this bond, since the child gains rights over its parents which cannot be set aside. Without the fidelity of husband and wife, the very existence of the child is endangered, for the procreative act is really but a possibility for good, which is realized only when the child that results from this act is treated as a subject, as a person, and not as a thing. In this sense, being a husband and father is like being an artist: "A family is founded, it is erected like a monument whose hewn stone is neither the satisfaction of an instinct, nor the indulgence of a caprice." Fatherhood, then, is truly a vocation, since this activity involves the total personality. Within this vocation, the crucial test is the father's manifestation of fidelity in the procreative act, which results in his assuming responsibility for his child, not in a legalistic sense, but in the sense of permanent commitment to the good of this being in whose creation he has shared. The essence of fatherhood, therefore, consists in that act by which the father places himself at the disposal of the sacred creative forces which would operate through him. Marcel calls this act the creative vow.

Using these analyses of our fidelity towards other persons as the basis of his discussion, Marcel addresses himself to the crucial problems of immortality and value. Love is a demand for a permanent order of existence, and is, at the same time, the most striking evidence for the reality of that order: "To love a being . . . is to say you, you in particular, will never die.", Value has meaning only in this permanent order among persons, for no act can ultimately be called good or evil if there is no lasting worth to the person: ". . . if death is the ultimate reality, value is annihilated in mere scandal, reality is pierced to the heart."

As these interpersonal bonds gain in intensity, there is an increasing awareness of man's orientation towards the suprapersonal, towards the Transcendent. While love, on the one hand, is a pledge of immortality, it leads, on the other, to a discovery that love cannot constitute a closed system. This experience attains its greatest awareness in the bond uniting husband and wife. The sacredness of the nuptial bond can have no meaning apart from an affirmation of an order which transcends the human. Man's experience of permanence in the fidelity involved in marriage would be impossible without a Transcendent Being to guarantee the validity of immortality. Sartre argues that since there is no God, there can be neither meaning nor value in life. Marcel, reversing the argument, argues from our experience of genuine meaning and value, particularly in true love, to the existence of the guarantee of this experience.

It is in the creative vow of the husband and father, though, that we find the clearest evidence for the existence of that Person who transcends the order of human persons. The very nature of the vow expresses man's commitment to an unseen, though indirectly affirmed Being: "I beg you to reveal yourself to me, to make your presence real for me, so that it will be possible for me to consecrate myself with a full understanding—since in my present state I can only see you through the clouds of uncertainty which encircle me." The man who truly recognizes what it means to be a father, realizes that he is but an instrument of a higher Being in his work of artistic creation. Again, the notion of availability appears. Contrary to Sartre's position, Marcel emphasizes the fact that the true man is not the isolated, absolutely free creator, but rather he who puts himself at the disposal of the only Being capable of true creation. It is this act of authentic receptivity which constitutes human as opposed to divine creativity; it is the recognition that a man's child no more belongs to him than a man belongs to himself. In the last analysis, true fatherhood is not a simple duty or function, but a complex fidelity to God and to other persons in the highest degree, resulting in an extension of that order of persons which shall endure forever in union with the Source of this order.

But, Marcel points out, to attain this insight into the nature of the relationship of human to divine creativity is no easy task in this world rent asunder by the horrors of war and the depersonalizing results of technology. Man needs a witness to recall him to an experience of transcendence, a witness which Marcel finds in the German poet, Rainer Maria Rilke (1875-1926). The poetry of Rilke expresses a profound reverence for "souls and things," recalling man to a realization of the sacred. He saw the spiritual, "not as cut off but as being involved in things themselves by the ever closer pact which the poet makes with them. . . ." Raised in an age of science, men are fascinated by things in a way which prohibits their seeing the real significance of these things. We analyze, we dissect, but we never penetrate. It is precisely this lack of insight into the real meaning of things which is the principal cause of the severing of the nuptial bond between man and life.

Even devoted Christians have participated in the desacralization of things. Reacting against the inherent evils of materialism, Christians often emphasize supernatural forces to a point where the sacred forces within things themselves are neglected. Rilke was able to achieve his extraordinary insight into the spiritual because he realized that creativity involves receptivity, fidelity, and availability. For the Christian, as well as for the atheist,

Rilke's experience of reality, expressed in his personal correspondence as well as in his poetry, represents an invitation to a deeper penetration into the mystery of the world, which will reveal a call to rise above ourselves without becoming fixed in any particular state. Death, for Rilke as well as Marcel, is not something final, but an event which leads to a suprapersonal existence, a moment in the development of something which as yet escapes our gaze.

D.H.J.

THE STATE IN CATHOLIC THOUGHT

Author: Heinrich A. Rommen (1897-)
Type of work: Catholic political philosophy
First published: 1945

Principal Ideas Advanced

Although Catholic theology is the context in which the political philosophy of the Catholic Church is developed, there is a proper philosophy of the state based upon natural reason and rational premises.

The nature of man, his intrinsic sociality, and his ultimate destiny are unchangeable; the temporal origin of the state, its structure, and function may vary in form in order to serve the general welfare.

Rational principles indicate the direction which must be taken to solve at any given time in history the fundamental problems that inevitably arise when two perfect societies, state and Church, meet in the concrete context of the individual person who is a member of both societies.

An adequate understanding of the Catholic view of the state can be acquired, Heinrich Rommen argues in his influential work, *The State in Catholic Thought,* only if one first of all comes to understand the context of the historical and spiritual evolution of Western civilization. To define a "Catholic philosophy" of the state would be inadequate at best without the theological construct in which a "Catholic philosophy" is to be found and delineated. The political philosophy of the Greeks and the civic wisdom and juristic prudence of the Romans preceded Christianity and influenced her formulation of the meaning of the state.

With the development of the Catholic Church as the great power structure in Western civilization, Greek and Roman political philosophy became a fundamental part of the formulation of European political thought. Christianity is thus the heir to all the intellectual wealth that Greece and Rome created. But the Christian view transcends its influences, Rommen claims. It is true that the early Fathers of Church history taught Christianity in virtue of their own intellectual frames of reference, be they Greek or Roman or both, but cardinal and essential to their philosophical view was the ever-present theological view of life. For the Fathers, and indeed for Christianity itself, all history is the history of man's salvation. Man is in a context of Fall and Redemption by an Incarnate God: Jesus of Nazareth. Thus, Rommen argues, Christianity proceeds in the world of ideas and events while insisting that the Church is not essentially an effect of the world's ideas and events. The Church has never considered herself a mere ideological superstructure over the growing and withering socio-political forms of nations that at one time or another dominated Europe. Rommen concedes that at given times the Catholic Church has apparently been identified with one or another of the leading nations and has adopted secular philosophies, political forms, and cultures, but an examination of history shows that no matter how deep this identification seems, the Church has maintained a unique identity; consequently, even when nations collapse, the Church survives. The epochal changes, then, affected the temporal adaptations of the Catholic Church, but not its substance. Hence, Rommen argues, absolutism, democratic egalitarianism, the tyranny of totalitarianism, and anticlerical liberalism have each had their day, but the Church has lived with them, through them, and has survived in spite of them.

According to Rommen, it is the theological view of the world that begets a "Catholic political philosophy." The Fathers of the primitive Christian community took the Gospels as their material and reason as their tool and began to build a theology which incorporated the legacy of Greece and Rome. The great theologians of the Middle Ages continued the work as they developed their systems of Scholasticism. When medieval society began to wane and finally disintegrated, the new problems initiated by changing political, social, and economic life were considered in the light of earlier unchanging principles established and accepted in Christian tradition. The approach to new eras in political evolution was diverse in its Christian unity. Historical actuality determined how thoroughly the Church would consider a particular political-philosophical problem.

From the time of the feudal lords to that of capitalist property, writes Rommen, there has been a diversity of approach in philosophical attitudes toward the state. Because the Catholic Church has sometimes been injured because of political involvement, the Church has been in general conservative and wary of political action. Nevertheless, in spite of the diversity of thought and in spite of historical pressures, political philosophy in the Catholic Church has held fast to certain basic concepts: the conception of man's nature and destiny, the conception of the Christian man, the conception of God, and the conception of the natural law. According to Rommen, these Catholic concepts provide the fundamental structure of socio-political life; by these concepts institutions are judged and their right or wrong functioning is evaluated.

Bearing in mind these concepts, writes Rommen, one may turn to the specific and properly philosophical foundations for a Catholic political philosophy. The immediate question then becomes: What is the subject matter of any political philosophy? The answer is that political philosophy is concerned with the essence and nature of the state, the political community, its end, its scope, its properties. To speak of the "essence" or the "nature" of the state is to imply a metaphysics.

From a Catholic point of view, political philosophy, aside from strictly theological implications, must necessarily become political ethics. Political philosophy always involves what the concrete state should be. Its end is a moral objective good that is independent of arbitrary will. It is an objective value against which we measure observed facts.

Consequently, Rommen maintains, political philosophy from a Catholic point of view issues into moral philosophy and both rest upon a metaphysical basis. Thus is born the basic disagreement between the Church philosophy and any modern political philosophy which maintains that political philosophy has nothing to do with moral ends.

According to Rommen, the relationship between individual freedom and political power, and indeed any political theorizing, inevitably involves premises predicated on the nature of man. Prior to positivism and technical science, theorists concerned themselves with the doctrine of the natural status of man. For the Sophists and Stoics, and for Hobbes, Rousseau, and Paine, the philosophy of man determined in good part their political philosophical conclusions. Christian political philosophy in like manner drew specific conclusions and made assertions from a premise of Fall and Redemption which involved the nature of man. In this context, for example, the political philosophy of Saint Thomas Aquinas, of Joseph Marie De Maistre, who was a leading opponent of eighteenth century rationalism and Gallicanism, and of Juan Francisco Donoso Cortés who opposed philosophical liberalism, must be understood. Rousseau's free contract and immediate democracy flows from the optimistic premise that man in his natural state is an autonomous, free, fully self-sufficient individual. Hobbes defines man as a lawless being whose fear of violent death begets a contractual order of law. Evil then becomes the dynamic for the origin of the state. In opposition to such views, Saint Thomas Aquinas posits, as a natural inclination of men, the drive to love other men, to draw together out of love.

Throughout the history of developing and opposing theories, throughout ideological and economic revolution, the Catholic point of view has remained in essence the same: man is a rational being, an independent, self-conscious person. Man is social by nature, and it is in this nature, in its philosophical sense, that the origin and *raison d'etre* of the state is found. Political status, on a Catholic teleological premise, is a necessity for the fulfillment of man. The state is not supernatural although it is divinely established. Further, the state, originating in man's nature, is more than the result of blind physical law. There must always be some form of consent by men to form a state. There is an ordered relation from God to man to state; to obey legitimate political authority is the will of God found in his natural order. Thus, in Catholic political philosophy the legal basis of the state, according to Rommen's account, is found in a "social contract." The strictly biological theory of the origin of the state is rejected and equally the strictly rational theory of the state is rejected. Neither *bios* (life) nor *logos* (reason) alone produces the state. Rather, it is the interaction of both *bios* and *logos* that produces the state, for man himself is essentially a composite of *bios* and *logos*. Ideally, the state individually is established by a contract that involves a transfer from pre-political state to political state which demands free action and human initiative.

Moreover, Rommen points out, the question of political authority, like other aspects of Catholic political thought, has been elaborated and expanded over the years. The foundations of Catholic thought remain the same, though various political and intellectual environments have stimulated outstanding Catholic philosophers to form selective principles pertinent to the kind of problems demanding consideration at a given time. Fathers of the primitive church, emphatically pastoral, vigorously opposed the tyranny of pagan emperors, while at the same time the Fathers defended the legitimate rights of pagan political power.

In the Middle Ages, Rommen claims, the great problem became the relation between temporal and spiritual power, expressed classically as the "doctrine of the two swords." Theorists vexed by the problem, ranged in opinion from Pope Gregory VII and Aegidius Romanus, who in his *De potestate ecclesiastica* defended papal rights, temporal and spiritual, and Nicholas of Cusa, who outlined reforms for the Church and the Empire in his *De concordantia catholica,* to Henry IV, who issued the Edict of Nantes (1598) granting freedom of religion to all, and to William of Ockham who with his contemporary, Marsilius of Padua, was a proponent of the absolute authority of the state and an opponent of papal temporal power. The Reformation and Counter-Reformation raised new problems for Catholic theorists. The "cujus regio, ejus religio" axiom found support in every political-religious camp. Freedom of conscience became an obscure principle in practice. In the sixteenth century it was the great doctors, Francisco Suarez (1548-1617), a philosophical jurist who argued against the divine right of kings; Robert Bellarmine, and Juan de Mariana (1536-1624), the latter being of the opinion in his *De rege et regis institutione* (1599) that it is lawful to put despots to death under certain circumstances, who developed more fully the concepts of the state and Church as perfect societies.

Rommen maintains that modern revolutions and the disintegration of absolutism along with the rise of individualism demanded again a new evaluation on the part of Catholic political thinkers. Historically and environmentally influenced, they reasserted the essential principles and emphasized development of ideas. Ideas concerning the "immortality of the state," the intervention of government in the social struggles of the labor market, and the duty to enact social legislation were their contribution. History testifies to changes in forms of government, and history has produced through its philosophers new theories of government and authoritative form. The translation theory, namely, the theory that constituent power rests by natural law with the people, found approval in the political thought of such Catholic leaders as Pope Leo XIII. The Catholic view that morality should condition social change allowed even a supposedly undemocratic leader, Pope Pius IX, to laud the American Constitution. Such a view makes understandable the statement of Cardinal Satolli, Apostolic Delegate to the United States: "The Magna Chartas of mankind are the Gospel of the Lord and the Constitution of the United States . . ."; this statement appeared at a time when the French hierarchy resisted Leo XIII's policy of reconciliation of French Catholicism with the Third Republic.

The modern "secularized" state, the product of eighteenth and nineteenth century revolutions, emerged built upon the rights of man and of the citizen. Popular sovereignty was the cardinal principle, Rommen explains. No political principle or economic system is in itself opposed to the doctrines of Catholic political theory, but an exclusively materialistic interpretation of the state, as in the secularized states, encounters inevitable opposition from the Catholic philosopher. Catholic political theorists allow and even promote the "neutral" state, a free Church in a free state, but they oppose the adoption of a principle of indifferentism as a basis of tolerance. According to Catholic thinkers, the validity and consequences of divine and natural law cannot be ignored. The state is indeed a perfect society with its independent final end, but it is not an absolute authority everywhere and without any limitation. The Catholic Church similarly asserts that it is itself a perfect society, with its own proper and distinct end. Catholic political theory asserts, as a consequence, rights proper to the Church. Rommen's analysis shows that conflict, philosophical as well as practical, arises when both perfect societies, civil and ecclesiastical, exercise their rights in a concrete context involving individual subjects.

Rommen maintains that solution to the conflict between Church and state is sought by Catholic political theorists in two basic ways, either by co-operation between or separation of the two societies. Co-operation as a working principle is preferred when it is applicable and the instrument of co-operation is ordinarily the concordat. By way of concordat the individual person's life as a citizen and as a faithful member of the Church is protected in the sphere of mixed matters where the rights of both institutions are involved; as, for example, in matrimonial legislation. A compromise in the exercise of rights, but not the abrogation of those native rights is the principal concern of negotiation terminating in the concordat.

In general, according to Rommen, the concordat is considered by a number of Catholic political philosophers, including Rommen, to be the better solution. As a solution, it is viewed as most useful in political situations that obtain where custom and tradition have maintained strong vestiges of an earlier union between Church and states, as, for example, in Italy. Nor is the concordat as a principle of co-operation considered inadequate in political situations where Catholic majorities do not obtain, as, for example, in Germany.

However, co-operation as an operative principle does not always offer adequate solution in terms of general welfare. Hence, contemporary Catholic political theorists have been led to consider more thoroughly the principle of separation of Church and state. Their solution is not yet fully developed, but it does show that the Catholic Church is actively concerned about the problem.

The principle of separation, in the

Catholic view, follows certain general lines, Rommen argues in conclusion. Separation of Church and state in its most acceptable form is found in the United States. While the Catholic Church holds no privileged position in that society, there is no legal or governmental hostility. The state constitutionally supports no particular religious persuasion, and the exercise of religious freedom has practical benefit for all citizens, while militant anti-religious influences are avoided. The Catholic point of view admits but one, true Church as a divinely instituted perfect society to lead men to their ultimate destiny in the supernatural order; the Church asserts itself as a perfect society. In a concrete context, however, peace and progress for the benefit of all men are better served by a neutral state which scrupulously avoids giving privileged status to any religious or anti-religious body. Thus, Rommen asserts, without any pretense of a Catholic canonization of philosophical indifference, the Catholic view can recognize and accept the practical policy of an equitable separation of Church and state.

J.M.C.

THE CHARACTER OF MAN

Author: Emmanuel Mounier (1905-1950)
Type of work: Psychology
First published: 1946

Principal Ideas Advanced

Personality includes the unique, nondetermined area of the self which is outside the limits of scientific investigation, the proper subject of which is characterology.

The individual stakes out a claim upon reality by the act of existence itself, which is his character, and he establishes this claim by defining a future for himself in terms of choices at specific, successive moments in time.

Identity is not a static concept but a dynamic progress in the reconciliation of opposites through man's generous embracing of reality and his inner reflection upon it.

Emmanuel Mounier's *The Character of Man* (*Traité du caractère*), deals with the interaction of the person and the blend of supernatural and natural reality confronting him as he labors to form and perfect his individuality. Observation of this relationship can only roughly identify the mysterious inward wellspring of the self. Mounier claims that we study types or behavioral ruts in well-worn human roads, never the unique individual. These types are found not in their pure state but in blends, and to varying degrees. Character itself, as an object of scientific observation and categorization, is the gauge of real personality's defeat: "We are typical in so far as we have failed to become fully personal." It is the primary task of the characterologist to discover in what ways character transcends the level of the merely mechanical, thereby achieving the level of the personal, which is also the dimension of spiritual liberty; the characterologist does this by establishing the areas common to the psychic inheritance of humanity as a whole. He must do this not in terms of the self's disease but of its "generating theme." For Mounier, this theme is the impress of self upon all reality and of all reality upon the self.

According to Mounier, our basic physical constitution tends either toward the emotional or the stolid, but beyond these two lie many complicated and interworking factors that we may call "the vital response," which is not on the conscious, volitional level. These factors range from the insufficiency of psychic energy in a body overcome with strain to the periodic, rhythmic waves of strength, flexibility, efficiency, and their opposites. Each psychic movement tends with mysterious ambivalence to stimulate the production of an opposite drive. A successful confrontation of reality usually depends upon the achievement of harmony, or a maintenance of tension, between extremes that we call "calm."

Whatever the human type, says Mounier, the person is bound to establish himself in his own space and time (to be conceived of as internal or psychic as well as external or material), and he finds himself and his individual fulfillment through a gradual working out of this embracing and savoring of reality. The spiritually whole personality is aware of a breadth of space and freedom within which he thinks and moves unconstrictedly as he constructs his future; the opposite is true of the mentally ill. Space must be seized and molded by the personality; it is not merely presented for the asking. Our future, writes Mounier, is a living and dynamic force, dominating our existence in time and giving order and significance to the least of our actions. These actions reflect varying degrees of confidence in the future or in reality itself; they range from reflexes which are of only slight effect or duration to a patient waiting upon the results of long-term planning and execution. One must identify oneself with the "intention of the future" and, ultimately, with the will of God. One lives in the present as in an eternity already begun and not merely promised after the sterilities of a present which is itself tedious and profitless. The spiritually healthy personality infuses that present with the recollected past and the rich, mysterious promises of the future. Mounier calls the acceptance of the realities of life and time "generosity," a quality which makes one willing to seek "the adventure of greater being through the sacrifice of having."

Reality can be grasped, says Mounier, only by the struggle which necessarily results from a confrontation of the self with the resistance of the world outside. There are extremes of reaction to this struggle; one man will throw himself into association with the outside; another will withdraw entirely into himself. In such extremes, writes Mounier, "the extravert loses touch with himself, the introvert with the world." We are lured not only by the demon of self but also by the demon of things. Thus, our spirituality must encompass the whole personality in harmonious communion with both self and the world (not in the one-sided, out-worn rejection of either) if it is to be appropriate to the needs of our age.

It is in action, specifically in work, Mounier claims, that our personalities confront reality and are expanded by the resulting interaction with it. The dream becomes the real, the vague becomes the concrete, and the individual character is given form and substance. We confront objective reality successfully to the extent that we strive to impress ourselves upon it: "Our whole behavior is capable of two different fundamental dispositions, according to whether it is directed by a constant of egocentricity or by an objective attitude which puts the self at the service of the world." The egocentric man is rigid, preserving his subjective world at all costs; the generous man is sensitive and responsive to all the nuances of reality, affirming its value and deepening his own values through his contact with it. This dynamic and flexible man is never "adjusted" in any utopian sense to a planned society; he maintains the diversity and adventure of his future and mankind's future. We must not allow reality to mechanize or regiment us, says Mounier; yet we must also not reject reality. The conflict inherent in these contraries is the essential human condition.

According to the author, with every action the personality reveals itself in its entirety and its unity, both in the oneness of faith and works and in that of reflection and execution. Truly constructive activity is opposed to mere fidgeting; it is indicative of subordinating real, long-term interests to short-term or illusory ones. It is a sign of a soul at peace with social and personal reality. Inactivity promotes egoism, a reliance on "verbal formula" rather than on the deed. Meaningless, obsessive behavior (another form of inactivity) is merely a caricature of genuine action with its accompanying satisfaction over changes wrought and plans carried out. Real action cannot be separated from reflection; it is a form of choice and a mysterious exercise of the function of the whole person. The consciousness must be broad and objective enough to embrace many aspects of external reality at once, allowing room for flexibility, decisiveness, and judgment in the formulation of an action. Decision itself is the creative sign of action, its very soul. It must not be dogmatic or blind, but rather influenced by breadth of consciousness, a "profound universality," and sensitivity to the many conflicting factors that must be harmonized and satisfied. Its secret wellspring is the generous acceptance of risk, which in itself is the initial affirmation of being and the condition of growth. Loving reality as he does, the man who is truly strong rejoices in the sacrifice of the merely possible for the achievable. He finds choice, or sacrifice, broadening rather than personally restricting. It is the decision which most reveals will, and not the effort which may follow upon it and which is subject to many vagaries of chance or constitution. The leader is pre-eminently the man of decision, who fills up in his own sufficiency the weaknesses and apathy of others, and who is ready to risk *for* them in a quasi-sacrificial manner.

Throughout life, the individual must balance his opposing drives to commune with or depend upon others and to subordinate all reality and all others to himself. The reality to which he must conform himself is largely a social reality, and his success in this endeavor of meeting and knowing other persons is the measure of his own personalization. The nonadjusted may refuse themselves to others or feel threatened by their presence; they use others as objects, indifferently, or they use them as mirrors with no awareness of the unique value of the other. The healthy personality takes in the other person and himself in one simultaneous act of knowing, without restricting the sphere of autonomy that the other must possess in order to maintain his identity.

Ultimately, Mounier writes, the "real object of self-knowledge is the numinous *Self*, a totality of transcending consciousness," through which we avoid the loss of ourselves in the things we contemplate around us ("excessive adaptation"). The true "affirmation of the self" springs from an awareness of the unity and harmony running through the personality on both the conscious and unconscious levels. It is not simply maintenance of one's unique identity, for this is a static concept and the personality is a dynamic tension of complex and opposing elements. The distinction between proper self-love and ego-centricity must always be made; the grandeur of personalization can be lost through its characteristic "sickness of the self." Reality is the prevention or cure for this disease. Through choice among realities, the personality forms itself by the limiting but bracing intake of experience (exteriorization). This is the complement of a simultaneous withdrawal into the self for the purpose of reflection and self-recovery (interiorization). The dramatic interchange between these two forces as they seize and relinquish possession of the field sets the pace for the forward momentum of the personalization process.

The fine line to be walked between inner and outer reality, writes Mounier, is the same one that must be maintained between instinct (with its strong attachment to reality, simplicity, and human warmth), and intelligence (with its self-consciousness, objectivity, and unity). The intelligence adds to the merely animal reflex a flexibility, potential, and individuality which it would otherwise lack. Only when the intelligence avoids the lure of egocentricity without losing itself in things does it remain pure and free. It must allow for synthesis, in which an idea is fused or balanced with its opposite. This synthesis presents a challenge or forward thrust to affirmation, eliminating cant, incompleteness, and narrowness of mind. The thinker must be aware both of his creative initiative and his passivity, and the constant dialectic of the two, which is true "comprehension." This response is "the highest activity of thought, considered as a form of social life." Thought is a power, according to Mounier, which "completes life, confirms our humanity and plunges into reality in order to transfigure it." Every idea must have its incarnation, its "commitment" to reality. Thought has its end in affirmation and not in suspension of judgment, and the affirmation requires both choice and sacrifice. One must be willing to bear the interior crucifixion by the world resulting from the tension between commitment and spiritual detachment, a tension which can never be resolved in the human state as we know it.

The tension of the committed life is falsely resolved by egocentricity, which immobilizes the self by cutting it off from outside influences which would help it change and grow. Egocentricity, says the author, prevents us from understanding our guilt, even from seeing that it is guilt we feel, and thus it is destructive of morality. It falsifies our relationship with others by causing us to reject our responsibility and to project onto them our faults. It causes us to concentrate on our inner state, whether it be sinful or holy, instead of devoting our attentions to the use of the present moment in the service of God and others, and it thus diverts us from a moral life.

Morality itself, Mounier insists, is only the anteroom of spirituality, as character is only the foundation for the divinised, potential personality. Self-mastery through the study and practice of a pure, committed life is the aim of morality. The aim is not perfection or a chimerical absolute, but an incarnation of a will to good in concrete actions. However definitive it may seem, the character of man urges him beyond its limitations to an up-building, an enlargement, which will help him to embrace those virtues possible and appropriate to that character. These virtues will not simply be possessions, but inclinations rich with the tension of opposites united, bearing fruit in new thrusts of personality growth all organically related to the dominant and unique theme of that personality.

Essential to this process, Mounier claims, is our recognition and acceptance of personality in the "other," an acceptance which lets us share in a common life and breaks down the barriers of egocentricity between us. Generosity generates in its turn new abysses of life and knowledge. The risk this entails, the spiritual vertigo it often produces, is the peril of the religious life, and its glory. As the personality becomes fully vitalized and transformed by the mystery of its love for reality, concludes Mounier, the realm of the psychologist of character is transcended and that of the mystical theologian is attained.

B.J.R.

THEOLOGY AND SANITY

Author: Francis Joseph Sheed (1897-)
Type of work: Popular theology
First published: 1946

Principal Ideas Advanced

A religious view of the world is necessary if man is to preserve his basic sanity.
Revealed mysteries challenge the intellect and provoke it to new growth.
The anthropomorphic conception of God leads persons to the errors of regarding God as an equal and treating Him as an extra.
The universe is sustained by God's continuing presence.
The Church presents man with hope, meaning, and law.

Francis Joseph Sheed insists in *Theology and Sanity* that a religious view of the world is necessary for the health of the mind. God is not simply another object to be known; sanctity and sanity are intimately related to each other. The study of God brings knowledge of and gives meaning to the world He created.

In the chapter entitled "An Examination of Intellect," Sheed points out the dangers of imagination in religious thought. While the nonbeliever tends to regard the spiritual as unthinkable and unreal because it cannot be imagined, the imaginative believer often offers fundamentally empty and useless illustrations of revealed mysteries. Nevertheless, through mystery, the intellect is challenged to growth. Mystery involves truth which man cannot fully understand, but there is some hope of knowledge, for if a mystery were a truth no one could understand, God would not reveal it to man. Sheed wisely reminds his readers not to fret about what they cannot understand, but to enjoy the light they receive. It would be wrong, he says, to confine ourselves to the darkness surrounding the light.

Sheed emphasizes the claim that the image of God as a bearded old man persists deep in the subconsciousness of many people who would consciously reject this image as ridiculous. Such persons are not conscious of the continuing influence of the anthropomorphic image, just as the average reader may not realize that his idea of a character in a novel is derived in part from drawings seen long ago in an illustrated edition of the text. To influences of this image of God Sheed traces "two of the principal modern tendencies about God, the tendency to treat Him as an equal, and the tendency to treat Him as an extra." Sheed is bluntly critical of the widespread idea that God is an extra and especially that religion is of only private concern, without social impact.

The author considers proofs for the existence of God to be of value not only for nonbelievers but also for believers, not because they prove God exists but because they show *what* He is. The proof from contingency is selected for this purpose and is well presented. Then follow the usual considerations of the divine nature and attributes. Since God causes all other beings, Sheed argues, He must be personal; He must know and love. Sheed clarifies the description of God as a simple, infinite, in all things, unchangeable, eternal, living, identical with His knowledge and love.

Five chapters are devoted to the Trinity: the meaning of person and nature, the distinction of the divine Persons, the procession of the Son from the Father and of the Holy Spirit from the Father and the Son, the mission of the Son and that of the Holy Spirit.

The author then considers creation, and he shows his ingenuity in drawing analogies when he tells of the creature's need of the Creator for conservation or preservation of being. A table made of wood, says Sheed, remains when the one who made it leaves, for he did not make the wood. Only the nothingness of which the universe is made would remain if God were to leave it. Again, a mirror reflects an image only as long as it receives it: "So of the nothingness in which God mirrors himself: we may figure it as receptive or passive—carrying receptivity, passivity to the ultimate power. Thus the image is sustained by my continuing presence: the universe is sustained by God's continuing presence. Take me away and the image ceases. Take God away and the universe ceases."

Sheed's ability to confine his work to the essentials required by its nature is especially apparent in Chapter 12, "Angels, Matter, Men." Although the next two chapters, "The Testing of Angels and Men" and "The Fall of Man," keep close to revealed data, they reveal a mind that not only has accepted revelation but has also reflected on it. This is evident in Sheed's explanation of original sin and of the role of the Devil in the world today. Remembering that this book was published at the end of World War II, comments like the following become memorable: "It is hard to look upon this world without coming to a sense that evil is not simply chaotic, that there is a drive and a direction in it which suggests a living intelligence coordinating what would otherwise be only scattered and unrelated plunges of the human will—though the uncoercible will of man sets the Devil problems too."

In "Between the Fall and the Redemption," Sheed briefly surveys pagan and Jewish preparations for Christ. Christ is shown not only as revealing God to man, but also as revealing man to man. In his chapter on "The Redeeming Sacrifice," Sheed strikes a contemporary note when he presents the Resurrection and Ascension as belonging organically to the sacrifice of the Cross: "By the miracle of the Resurrection, God at once shows His acceptance of the Priest as a true priest of a true sacrifice *and* perfects the Victim offered to Him, so that whereas it was offered mortal and corruptible it has gained immortality and incorruptibility. By the Ascension God accepts the offered Victim by actually taking it to Himself."

A chapter on the Redemption and man's need to receive it in himself introduces the Church, the Kingdom of God, established by Christ to apply the fruits of the Redemption to the whole world until the end of time. The hierarchical constitution of the Church is clearly set forth and also the inner life of grace and the sacramental system, both from the aspect of Christ living in the Church and from the aspect of the Christian living in Christ.

In considering the problem "Life after Death," the author's sober discretion about the pains of purgatory is noteworthy, as are his consoling remarks about souls in Heaven as being closer to us ". . . because they are more profoundly in Christ in whom we also are." The second part of the book concludes with a discussion of the last things.

The third and last part of the book is entitled "Oneself," and it includes seven of the thirty-two chapters. The first two chapters in this last part are "Habituation to Reality" and "Habituation to Man." By reason of their interpretation and concrete application of general truths, they seem similar to the first two chapters of the book. The first compares the theologian's knowledge of the world to that of the novelist, the poet, and the natural scientist. The second dwells on the extraordinariness of man as both spirit and matter, and as both individual and social. It shows how the Church provides for these different aspects of man.

Next we are shown the insufficiency

of man without God, the frustration of his action, mind, and will. In contrast to this is the Church, presenting men with hope, meaning, and law. But man, however, does not always recognize this: "These two things—preoccupation with the defects of Catholics, impatience that the Church holds secondary what others hold primary—stand between men and the realization that the Church is their true home."

Grace, the virtues, and the gifts of the Holy Spirit are discussed briefly. Little more than a page is devoted to hope and less than two pages are given to charity; together they receive less space than faith, "the root of the supernatural life." Sheed seems to have placed temperance and fortitude in the will rather than in the sense appetites.

In "The Landscape of Reality" Sheed reflects on the complexity of man as composed of matter as well as of spirit, the Church's concern with the supernatural in man, the obligation of the moral law, and the problem of suffering.

The last chapter, "Idyll and Fact," interprets man's mediocrity as the imperfect response to grace. It ends, as the first chapter began, with a reminder of the relation of sanity to sanctity.

The outstanding merit of this book is its combination of solid Catholic teaching with a newness and freshness of expression. As to content and order, the author is obviously indebted in a special way to Saint Thomas Aquinas. *Theology and Sanity* is the product of clear thinking and reflection on personal experience. Again and again throughout the book one is impressed by the author's presentation of thoroughly traditional Catholic teaching in an original way. The examples are not stereotyped. The style is fluent and lively, sometimes reminiscent of Chesterton. All in all, this is one of the better popular works on theology.

THE MIND AND HEART OF LOVE

Author: Martin Cyril D'Arcy, S.J. (1888-   )
Type of work: Philosophy of Christian love
First published: 1947

Principal Ideas Advanced

Through comparison and contrast of various concepts of love formulated by men such as Plato, Aristotle, Rousselot, de Rougemont, Saints Thomas and Augustine, Nygren, Guthrie, Freud, and Jung, one can arrive at a Christian concept of love which reconciles the coexistence of Eros with Agape.

The Christian concept of love combines both Eros and Agape, excluding neither, but granting that one may predominate over the other in their diverse human forms.

The study of the nature of love is of value and significance, since it is love, finally, which gives dignity to humankind, enabling man to fulfill his nature as a creature made by and for love.

Father D'Arcy begins *The Mind and Heart of Love* with a definition of terms: Eros will represent passionate, assertive, self-centered love, and Agape will represent the spiritual complement of the former, that love which is based on surrender, sacrifice, and charity. The author further likens these terms to the heraldic symbols of the lion, symbol of virile masculine possessiveness, and the unicorn, Christian symbol of gentle feminine surrender. The basic premise of the work is that man reaches the height of his human dignity when fulfilling his human nature through the "give and take" law of love which governs his relationships both with other men and, finally, with God Himself. By surrendering oneself to the love of another, one gives his own love and at the same time takes the love proffered by the beloved, be it the mutual love of friend for friend or lover for lover. On the purely natural level, there is little distinction between human and animal "love," since gratification of a physical nature is the desired end of the giving and taking, but with the introduction of Agape "each self must grow in the taking and giving and each is a sacred life which must be respected. A new cycle begins; the two loves are present and are sublimated if the lower passion is lifted up, as it should be, to the ends of spirit."

In order to understand the exigencies of courtly and passionate love, the first forms under examination by Father D'Arcy, some knowledge of the philosophies which influenced the thought of the Middle Ages is necessary. The author refers at length to a volume entitled *Form and Color* by March Phillips in which Phillips compares the Greek preoccupation with reason or form in art with the Eastern school of emotion or color. While D'Arcy asserts that form and color, reason and emotion, are in opposition to each other, he claims that the two can never be entirely separate; one can and probably will dominate a culture, a society, a person, but the influence of the lesser element will also be felt. Phillips's distinction of form and color can be correlated with D'Arcy's distinction between the workings of the two loves, active (*form:* masculine, possessive), and passive (*color:* feminine, responsive).

It is easy for us to understand self-love, D'Arcy writes, for our human desires are ever before us. But in addition to the form of love which refers all things to self, there is another form which draws us out of ourselves to other things or persons. Again we witness the combination of active and passive love, the understanding of which will provide "an answer to the nature of love and the kind of being we are ourselves."

Western civilization was deeply influenced by the fusion of Greek philosophy with Eastern mysticism which eventually resulted in the cult of Gnosticism, the belief that any form of physical fulfillment in love was "unspiritual" and therefore to be despised. The features of courtly love then emerged, the belief in the nobility of suffering unrequited love, the dark death-wish for annihilation from the bonds of this world in order that union with the beloved might take place the more freely in the world of the spirit. Courtly love differs from the Christian love in that the former tries to outdo Christianity by falling back upon "essence" and refusing to accept the word of Christ, the Son of God, who

Himself gave reconciliation to the infinite and the finite through the Word made flesh—thereby irrevocably granting dignity to that which is human.

The place of Eros in Christian theology is defined largely in terms of the good desired. To the pagan, the end is pleasure or happiness (egocentric); to the Christian the end is God (theocentric). This is not to say that all who seek pleasure or happiness are pagans, for these ends may be sought *relatively*, as means to an End (God), rather than as final ends in themselves. Saint Augustine explains the differences in terms of *caritas* (the pursuit of the possession of God as man's final end) and *cupiditas* (the pursuit of creatures as man's final end). Man may love creatures in proper proportion; that is, insofar as they are reflected "goods" of the love of the Final Good. *Caritas*, then, is a grace proffered by God to man, whereby man through free co-operation with this grace can be elevated beyond his natural finite capacities to enjoy equal friendship with the Son of God.

To say that the self must be annihilated as a condition for perfect love is to propose the impossible, since self-concern is an intrinsic part of the nature of man; but to say that the self must be altered, surrendered, and reformed in the image of the beloved is closer to the truth. Egocentric love takes place when man loves himself, or possibly even God, but for man's own sake. Theocentric love causes man to love himself and God for God's sake, and ecstatic love such as that of the saints and mystics defies reason and loves all things for God's sake alone.

Philia, or the love of friends each for the other, is the involvement of man in the well-being of a fellow man. Explained in terms of "I-It" and "I-Thou" relationships, briefly, egocentric love exists when the "I" loves a thing or a person as an entity to be possessed, an "It," but the "I" cannot relate impersonally or selfishly to a "Thou," for though "we may sink our personality in things or exploit them to our own selfish ends, . . . we cannot do that once we address another person by calling him 'Thou.' There is at once set up a new circulation, a new sharing, which others have described by the name of friendship or *Philia*. And in this new relation the persons do not love their personality at the expense of each other. To say so would be to miss the very heart of the relationship and to drop back into an inferior experience, which is that of things." In his pursuit of completeness as a human being, man's reason does not offer violent opposition to his will; rather, it works to discipline and order that in him which is unruly. Though the intellect leads the way, it is for Agape to provide fulfillment.

Selfhood is the property of humankind. By it man "knows himself morally, and not physically, subject to an absolute, a subjection which is first discerned in the duty of keeping his word, saying what is true and choosing what is right. It is on these grounds he claims to be regarded as a moral person with rights and duties, a self in the full and proper sense of the word." In every self there is a union of Eros and Agape, which are complementary in their interaction. According to Christian philosophy, the self achieves a balance through faith, or "an act of the intellect commanded by the will" leading to spiritual experience. There are present in nature both positive and negative, active and passive, forces or tensions. To distinguish these forces as present in man from those present in animals, we give the name of *animus* to that which in man represents reason (the dominant force) and *anima* to that which represents the will, or that sacrificial force which is affected by the *animus,* and tends toward the spiritual—in short, all the workings of the unconscious and the irrational. In the Christian view, so long as harmony is maintained in the inter-action of these two, man is acting within his human dignity and not on a purely instinctive animal level. *Animus* and *anima* impose rhythm, order, and flexibility upon the human person in conjunction with the special gift of grace from God. When the *animus* separates from *anima,* it becomes sterile, just as *anima* become impotent when it loses sight of God as its final end.

D'Arcy contends that love, when directed toward another person as object, sympathetically evokes a higher value within the object. The lover loves the best in the person; the meeting of the ideal and the actual takes place, so that the lover seems to say "I love the beauty which I find in you, and I would not seek to alter or change you."

Sacrifice has always been a natural outgrowth of man's desire to give concrete manifestation of his love. In both pagan and Christian cultures the universality of sacrifice prevails. In the pagan ritual one finds the raw desire to worship, placate, and unite; in the Christian ritual the motivating desires are the same, but the end differs. The unknown god of the pagan becomes the Creator of the Christian. Because of the Incarnation, man can be united with God through the sacrifice of God the Son to God the Father.

The problem of the nature of love within the philosophical structure of essence (Eros) and existence (Agape) can find solution in the manner proposed by Hunter Guthrie. Briefly, there is disquiet or restlessness (*Angst*) within the nature of man which presses him on to the full realization of himself. The movement of each man towards the possibility of his own perfect being is termed "essence." The movement of "existence," on the other hand, is toward something real. The love arising from these two elements of a single being arises from a desire for knowledge and truth. It is in the act of love that both will and intellect are at the peak of their mutual relationship, and the ideals of the essential self and the existential self are achieved both by being possessed (by God) and by possessing (the Beatific Vision). The Good is that outside ourselves which pertains to existence; the truth is within our essence, in the beholding and possessing of the good. The more perfect our love, the more completely is its object known and possessed.

Personality is a factor which reinforces the personal individuality of man, D'Arcy writes. A person (or personality), according to the definition of Boethius, is the individual substance of a rational nature. Again, the commensurate existence of the two loves held together by the "I" of a person fashions a being's personality. Love, in the power of a creature endowed with reason and will, can elevate that creature to the highest ideal of human and spiritual levels. The presence of both Eros and Agape within man alternately guides him and directs him from self-regarding love to love beyond and outside himself. Man gives and receives, but ultimately the most satisfying object of human love is the Author of love, God Himself; for, even at best, in all purely human intercourse, "We share but in part, and are left lonely."

J.S.

HUMAN DESTINY

Author: Pierre Lecomte du Noüy (1883-1947)
Type of work: Philosophical anthropology
First published: 1947

Principal Ideas Advanced

Man is the apex and culmination of the whole evolutionary process in nature; with unswerving purpose, according to the laws of evolution, nature has worked through countless intermediary experiments toward the production of her masterpiece—man.

The master-plan of evolution is purposive, goal-seeking, "telefinalistic"; unless such a finality is admitted, the entire evolutionary process becomes irrational.

Finality is shown in two ways: (1) through the immanent finality in nature itself, in its ceaseless striving toward the birth of man; and (2) in the transcendent ordering of the whole process by God.

The process of evolution, after the advent of man, enters into its final and crowning stage; in and through man, evolution becomes a spiritual phenomenon, manifested by the progressive and upward movement of the human race from its animal origins toward spiritual values.

Human Destiny, by Pierre Lecomte du Noüy, is a milestone in scientific-philosophical writing. Dr. du Noüy, who was awarded numerous prizes and citations for his work in biophysics, brought to his work on human destiny sound philosophical and scientific training and a deep-rooted religious sensitivity. He was singularly qualified to write such a work, which attempts to synthesize the findings of science and the rational demands of philosophy.

The book is divided into three principal parts: (1) a preparatory discussion on scientific method, including a penetrating analysis of certain key presuppositions of physical science; (2) a relatively nontechnical summary of the findings of paleontology and biology regarding the theory of evolution; and (3) an analysis of man as the ultimate product of material evolution, with several prognostications concerning man's "spiritualization" and continuance of the evolutionary process.

Dr. du Noüy begins *Human Destiny* by stating that the book is intended as a scientifically sound but nontechnical study for intelligent readers. It is not aimed primarily at the scholarly community, but rather at laymen who desire to grasp the key insights and meaning of the prodigious research of the last century. The work is not, however, an oversimplification, nor does the author attempt to evade the many controversies which still engage scientists probing ever deeper into the history and mechanisms of life.

Bearing in mind the requirements of his audience, du Noüy takes great pains to explain what he considers to be the primary concept of modern science; namely, statistical probability. By explanations and examples, du Noüy demonstrates that physical and chemical laws are not rigid *a priori* mechanisms built into nature, but rather mathematical expressions which correspond to the phenomena on our *scale of observation.*

For example, the author points out that there are significant differences between phenomena on the subatomic level and phenomena on the atomic-molecular level. Taking into consideration all of the known physical laws which govern the particles of energy and matter on the subatomic scale of observation, there is no apparent explanation for the qualitative "leaps" which occur when the scale of observation is expanded to the molecular level. In a word, there is no apparent explanation in atomic physics for the qualitative differences between sodium metal, chlorine gas, and common table salt, which the former two produce in combination.

The point of these initial distinctions is to show that the qualitative phenomenon of life is entirely inexplicable on the basis of the statistical laws of chance which reign in the inorganic world. For the inorganic elements of a simple protein molecule to have come together according to the laws of chance is a statistical improbability which borders on impossibility. Given even one such unlikely alignment, a thousand more would be necessary to have produced one truly living organism.

From the very beginning, asserts du Noüy, there has been an extramaterial principle operative in nature. The supposition of a purposive cause is the only solution to the dilemma of evolution. If one considers the evolutional process very carefully, there can be little doubt of a functional finalism. But, this purposiveness is unexplainable unless we posit some extrinsic will which orders this process. To deny that there is such a will casts the pall of irrationality over the whole history of living matter.

Evolution, explains du Noüy, is much like a giant tree. There are many parallel developments (branches), but only one central line (trunk). The branches are nature's trial-and-error attempts to move ahead toward the goal. They terminate and stagnate because, for one reason or another, they cannot lead on toward the goal. Thus, evolution is a tremendous complexus of evolving strains, each a crucible for the designs of nature. The great reptiles, for example, though at one time veritable rulers of the earth, perished because they were not in the real mainstream, pressing ever onward to man.

The one true central strain in evolution eventually culminated in man, and at this point, evolution took on a new aspect. In man, nature made a great leap to intelligence and free will. Whereas all prior evolutive processes were determined extrinsically (the mechanisms of instinct, adaptation, natural selection), in man a new era began, for by his own conscious effort he carries on the evolutional process. This fact, declares Dr. du Noüy, casts into relief the criterion of the evolutionary process and progress—*freedom.*

All of the major plateaus in the history of life are marked by an increasing freedom. Animals were liberated from many of the strictures of plant life; warm-blooded animals gained a great measure of freedom from the requirements of environment; mammals with their superior mode of propagation were substantially liberated in comparison to the egg-layers. Finally, in man, where conscience finally emerges, evolution provides its masterpiece in an animal having the fullest freedom; that is, the ability to determine its own destiny.

This, then, is our human destiny, says Dr. du Noüy: to gradually elevate the human race above its animal heritage, and to liberate it from the bonds of matter. The true dignity of man consists in his being able to opt for this sublime destiny. Individually and collectively man can supplant his instincts and animal mechanisms with spiritual and moral values. This sublimation of human life is accomplished, according to du Noüy, through the instrumentation of a new evolutional mechanism—*tradition.*

By means of the power of articulate speech, man is able to transmit to his progeny the deposit of culture. Thus, within several centuries, man can alter his own behavior more than his ancestral life forms were altered by the evolutional mechanisms in whole epochs of time. Civilization, rather than being isolated cultures, is a continuous and growing common fund of moral and spiritual values. Man is the more civilized the more he is able to pursue the things of the spirit and to subjugate his rebellious animal nature.

Dr. du Noüy is not espousing a Platonic conception of man as an entombed spirit. Nor is he derogating the instincts and mechanisms of man's animal nature. Man, in the conception of Pierre Lecomte du Noüy, is a substantial unity, with both material and spiritual aspects. The point of the author's insistence upon the elevation of man above his nature is not that man completely denigrate his body, but rather, that he liberate himself from his passionate nature, his psychological heritage.

Human Destiny, then, is at once a historical conspectus, a tracing of the lineage of man through the ages, and a prophecy of his future. Dr. du Noüy masterfully blends a wealth of scientific knowledge and a profound respect and reverence for the human spirit. This book stands as a monument in man's quest to understand both the world and himself.

J.P.W.

MEDIATOR DEI

Author: Pope Pius XII (Eugenio Pacelli, 1876-1958)
Type of work: Sacramental theology
First published: 1947

Principal Ideas Advanced

The public worship of the Church is the central act of piety.

It is the duty of Christian people to participate in the public worship of the Church.

The link between worship and the concept of the Mystical Body of Christ is close.

Major dangers in the liturgical movement are two: excesses designed for their novelty, and apathy that rejects any change.

Mediator Dei is an encyclical that is singular in many respects. Primarily, it is unique because it is the first encyclical letter which deals entirely with the liturgy, or worship of the Church. The encyclical, in which Pope Pius XII early took note of the rising interest in liturgical studies and reform which had been evident since the beginning of the twentieth century, gave the liturgical movement a decisive impetus. Scholars of the papacy of Pius XII have listed this as one of the four or five major contributions made by him to the development of modern trends of theological thought in the Catholic Church.

Particularly notable of the teachings of this scholarly pope were his two 1943 encyclicals, *Mystici corporis Christi* (*The Mystical Body of Christ*, and *Divino afflante Spiritu* (*On Biblical Studies*), and then the 1947 letter, *Mediator Dei* (*On the Sacred Liturgy*). The three became recognized as a trio of works which liberated modern scholarship regarding the Bible and worship, especially in the light of mankind united as a body under the headship of Christ.

Even more substantial is the connection seen between the work on the Mystical Body of Christ and this one on the liturgy. It is no exaggeration to say that every basic principle and idea in Pius' *Mediator Dei* is explained in the context of the Mystical Body. In fact, the essential definition of the liturgy advanced by the pope was based squarely on the doctrine of the Mystical Body: "The public worship which our Redeemer as Head of the Church renders to the Father, as well as the worship which the community of the faithful renders to its Founder, and through Him to the Heavenly Father, the worship rendered by the Mystical Body of Christ in the entirety of its Head and members." Pius XII later said, in fact, that his encyclical on the Mystical Body was continued logically by the encyclical on the liturgy.

Containing much that is positive, the encyclical was colored by fears of excesses in liturgical reform which had been noted in some European countries. Nevertheless, the letter became a welcome preamble for changes instituted by Pius and the Second Vatican Council. In 1955, Pope Pius issued his famed reform of the Holy Week rites, and in 1958, there was issued an instruction on music and liturgy. Both of these, along with *Mediator Dei*, became stepping stones to the eventual *Constitution on the Sacred Liturgy*, decreed by Pope Paul VI and the bishops of the world at the close of the second session of Vatican II. Interestingly enough, however, the *Consitution on the Sacred Liturgy* made no direct mention of *Mediator Dei*, but instead it looked primarily to the Scripture for its teaching authority.

Pope Pius, beginning his encyclical on the liturgy, takes note of the visible priesthood of ordained ministers which continue in the Church. These ministers carry on the liturgy of the Church in all places and in all generations. The pope then sets out the duty of the Christian people to participate in the liturgical actions, according to their own stations. He warns of the twofold dangers of excesses or apathy. Extremes in revising the liturgy are to be avoided, he states, but he also offers no comfort for those who would seek refuge in the status quo; "Let not the apathetic and the tepid think themselves approved by us," he wrote. Probing, then, the nature, origin, and development of the liturgy, Pope Pius XII recalls the individual's duty and the duty of all mankind to give honor to God. The Church safeguards and teaches this duty, as it has throughout the centuries.

There are two kinds of worship, the pope writes: external and internal, and both have efficacy. External worship expresses through the senses, in actions and words, the prayer of the community. "But the principal element of divine worship is the internal element, for it is necessary always to live in Christ, to give oneself wholly to Him so that in Him, with Him and through Him there is given to the Heavenly Father that glory which is His due," the pope adds. Liturgy includes, explains the pontiff, the seven sacraments and the songs of divine praise, the reading of the law, as in the Epistles, the reading of Christ's life, as in the Gospel, and the homily or instruction given by the minister. The efficacy of the liturgy, in the case of the Eucharistic Sacrifice (the Mass), and the sacraments, arises first and foremost from the act itself (*ex opere operato*). Secondarily the efficacy is gained from the action of the spotless and united Church (*ex opere operantis Ecclesiae*).

Pius then goes on to defend personal piety, saying that it is not at odds with "Christian piety that ought to be centered in the mystery of the Mystical Body of Christ." The only qualification put on personal piety is stated by Pius as follows: "If the private interior devotions of individuals were to neglect the sublime Sacrifice of the Altar and the Sacraments and were to withdraw itself from the salvation-giving influence which flows from the Head into the members, then, without doubt, it would be a sterile thing and something to be reproved."

This leads the pope to state that the hierarchical Church is the proper regulator of the liturgy, and that the organization and form of the liturgy depends upon the authority of the Church. The liturgy, he states, does not determine or constitute the Catholic faith in an absolute sense or by any power of its own. In the development of the liturgy, both human and divine elements come into play. Finally, in discussion of development, the pope reasserts that the Holy See is the proper arbiter in the approval and introduction of new rites or reforms. It is in this section too that he defends the Latin language as a "clear and beautiful sign of unity and the efficacious remedy against any corruptions of true doctrine."

(Later developments, primarily in the actions of the Vatican Council II, leave changes of liturgical rites within the norms of the *Constitution on Sacred Liturgy* to regional or national bodies of bishops and also provide that the local groups of bishops may determine to what extent Latin would give way to vernacular languages. Such decisions, for example, were made by the American hierarchy on April 2, 1964, and their decrees were submitted to Rome only for *review*.)

In the third major portion of the encyclical, Pope Pius discusses the Eucharistic worship particularly, in terms of the nature and the efficacy of the Sacrifice as a true sacrifice renewed, with Christ Himself as the chief priest and the same victim as at the Sacrifice of Calvary. The ends of the Sacrifice are, according to Pius, praise, thanksgiving, propitiation, and impetration: these all lead to the infinite value of the Eucharistic Sacrifice. As to the role of the faithful, the pope makes it clear that the faithful are not co-celebrants with the priest, and he therefore defends the private celebration of the Mass by a priest even when no one else is present, though this is not as desirable as a public celebration.

Developing this portion, *Mediator Dei's* author stresses how those who worship participate in the Mass, how they should offer themselves as victims, how they may learn the majesty of sacrifice, and how they may be reassured of the dignity conferred on them by their Baptism. Urging the faithful to take part in the Mass, in dialogue Masses and High Masses, by studied use of popular missals which will allow them to follow the actions and words closely, the pope also defends less sophisticated participation because of age, or education, or culture. It is here, too, that he recommends the establishment of diocesan commissions for liturgy.

As to Holy Communion, Pius again teaches the sublime aspects of Holy Communion as a climax to the Eucharistic Sacrifice; at the same time he denies that reception is absolutely necessary for the people, though he urges a spiritual communion that would unite the faithful if the actual Sacrament is not partaken. In this, too, reverent thanksgiving following the Eucharistic Sacrifice is recommended by the pope. Adoration and veneration of the Holy Eucharist, as the consecrated Body and Blood of Christ, are praised in this section of the encyclical.

The Divine Office and the liturgical year are the subjects of the third section of the work. In this, the Divine Office is praised highly because it is the prayer of the Church through the hours of the day and the days of the year. Priests and religious have obligations to read or pray the Office in common, and the pope suggests that lay people also could benefit from this exercise. As to the liturgical cycle, the pope discusses the merits of changing the seasons of prayer through the Church's liturgical books, and he briefly sets out the main idea of each of the year's themes. The teaching power of the feasts of the saints and of the Blessed Virgin Mary also are recommended as enlightening and sanctifying for the faithful.

Lifting *Mediator Dei* into the practical realm, Pope Pius suggests some practical attitudes to be adopted by pastors and bishops as he opens the concluding portion of the encyclical. First, he makes clear, nothing in his commendation of the liturgical movement could be taken to exclude non-liturgical devotions and practices, including the rosary. He also cites spiritual exercises, such as closed retreats, as a benefit to the people. Two particular months of the year, May dedicated to Mary, and June to the Sacred Heart of Jesus, should be maintained for these devotions in order to inspire piety among the faithful.

In a section devoted to the spirit of the liturgy, Pius looks at the fine arts in relation to the liturgy. Music, art, and architecture are described as having a place in the liturgy, and the bishops to whom the encyclical is addressed are asked to be vigilant in protecting the lively use of the arts in churches. Gregorian chant, "which the Roman Church considers as its very own," should be preserved and parts originally designed for the people's use should be restored to them. Nevertheless, the pope denies that modern music must be excluded from Catholic worship, especially as modern music might assist in elevating the minds of the people to prayer. In fact, Pope Pius urges, congregational religious singing should be promoted. In the other fine arts, the same would be true, and new forms and styles may be used if they avoid "excessive realism on the one hand and exaggerated 'symbolism' on the other." He cautions against distortions in new styles of art, however.

This section also carries the pope's instruction that seminaries should impart liturgical training to candidates for the priesthood. Acolytes, or altar boys, should be well-trained in their duties, not only in order that they can assist in the proper performance of the liturgy but also in order that they might be inspired to adopt the priestly life.

Nearing his conclusion, Pope Pius states a phrase which is well known in most liturgical documents, that the liturgy is a source of the Christian life: "The sublime Sacrifice of the Altar is the primary action of divine worship; therefore it is necessary that it should be also the source, and as it were, the center of Christian piety." He warns pastors of flocks not to stop developing the liturgy until the people come to the Eucharistic Banquet in great numbers. This, he states, "is the sacrament of piety, the sign of unity, and the bond of charity."

Following a last exhortation against allowing the liturgical movement to fall into error, especially those of mysticism, quietism, humanism, or archaeologism, *Mediator Dei* makes one final appeal to the liturgy as related to the Mystical Body of Christ: "See to it that everywhere the churches and the altars are crowded by the faithful, in order that, as living members joined to the divine Head, they may be refreshed by the Sacraments and together with Him and through Him they may celebrate the sublime Sacrifice and give due praises to the eternal Father."

D.Q.

GROWTH OR DECLINE?: THE CHURCH TODAY

Author: Emmanuel Cardinal Suhard (1874-1949)
Type of work: Pastoral letter
First published: 1947

Principal Ideas Advanced

To provide the modern world, which is facing a crisis of unity, with the spiritual synthesis necessary for the realization of that unity and to preserve the dignity of the individual, the Catholic Church must evaluate her position as Christ's representative on earth.

Catholics must remember the theandric (divine and human) nature of the Church before deciding upon a plan of action to fulfill Christ's Mystical Body by including all men in His Redemption.

Because each Christian, in possessing a theandric nature, reflects the Church, in order to guarantee the successful application of divine doctrine, his participation in the Church's mission must be unworldly and unchanging in matters of this doctrine, and, at the same time, deeply involved in worldly matters.

It is unique that a pastoral letter written to a particular diocese, in this case the diocese of Paris, should become an internationally significant document. Cardinal Suhard's letter, *Growth or Decline?: The Church Today,* came at a time of such world crisis that his analysis of the situation in his diocese became a statement of the contemporary mission of the universal Church. It gave impetus to a modern apostolic movement which must be guided by the emergence of the laity in the Church and, as a result of the redistribution of the Christian population, by the changing complexion of missionary activity. The letter is a call to Christians for immediate action to fulfill the mission of the Church, which is to propagate the Mystical Body of Christ.

Cardinal Suhard sees the world in an adolescent stage between national cultures, which have broken up through two world wars, and a common culture of a technical, scientific character. The world, in other words, is facing a crisis of unity, and the convulsive quality of modern life, explains Suhard, results from the lack of a spiritual unity in a world tending toward physical unity. The world is in need of a spiritual synthesis, and Suhard sees the Church challenged to supply this synthesis. He cites examples from history to prove that the Church has never been unequal to such a challenge. As civilization has changed, the complexion of the Church has changed, from Jewish to Gentile, from Roman to Barbarian, and it is now in the process of becoming non-European.

Many Christians concerned with the Church's role in the modern world are divided into two camps, which Suhard terms traditionalist and progressivist, or, at times, integralist and modernist. Both sides tend to distort the theandric (divine and human) nature of the Church, the former group to discount the human aspect and the latter the divine. Suhard stresses the necessity of Catholics' coming to a single decision regarding the Church's plan of action in realizing her role. This single decision must be arrived at through synthesis rather than compromise, a synthesis which resides in the theandric nature of the Church as revealed through a study of her theology and history.

The Church, being Christ on earth, possesses His nature, which is both human and divine. Although Christ is God, He assumed a human body and dwelt among men. His Church, therefore, has a divine life and a divine message and, in order to show them forth, it must be visible on earth as a human society. The two natures of the Church cannot be divided. They are essential to her single mission, which is to apply Christ's Redemption to an increasing number of men, to apply, in effect, divine grace to human nature. Because growth of the Church is inseparable from her progress, it is impossible that she remain changeless enough to satisfy the traditionalists. The doctrine she teaches, however, *is*, despite the progressivists, changeless, although it must be expressed in various ways in order to be applied to different men in different ages. Suhard, while examining this theandric nature, explains corruption in the Church, which he attributes, together with the persecutions she has suffered, to the desecration of her divine nature through the failure of her human nature. "During her pilgrimage on earth," he writes, "the Church is *in via*—on the road to the heavenly Jerusalem. And this road is often the road of the Cross. It is a hard road which is not covered without bruises and scars. Her human face, like that of her Master, is often bathed in sweat and blood. Like the Holy Face, too, it is sometimes covered with dirt." It is the divine nature of the Church that is inextricable from faith. Faith is not required for belief in the Church as a human society, as it was not required for contemporaries of Christ to believe in Him as a man. But faith is necessary to believe that the Church is divine, as it was for Christ's contemporaries to believe that He was God.

Any plan of action discounting either one of the natures of the Church would defeat the end of the Church, which is the Second Coming; that is, the eschatological triumph of Christ. Any plan of action discounting her human nature would frustrate the propagation of the Mystical Body of Christ, in other words, would prevent Christ from being fulfilled on earth, and would lead to a tactical Christianity, a Christianity opposed to rather than applied to the world. The world would, therefore, evolve uninfluenced by Christian principles, and the synthesis necessary to solve the modern dilemma would never be achieved. Any plan of action discounting her divine nature, while it would guarantee the Church a position in world developments, would ruin Christian doctrine, eternal divine truth, by contaminating its integrity with the continually fluctuating philosophies of the world. The Church, if it had been controlled by men who discounted her divine nature, would never have survived as a religious force through a history of propagation from Palestine to America and the Far East.

Because Suhard's letter is addressed to Frenchmen, the problems of France are given particular attention. He notes that Frenchmen are falling away from the Church in ever-increasing numbers, and he sees the action of an anti-Christian elite as the cause of such irreligion. This godless elite is negative in its approach to experience, and it is more in opposition to old forms than it is in favor of any system of values. There has grown up a Christian elite, however, to counteract this anti-Christian elite, and the result has been a realization that de-Christianization is not a peculiarly French problem but a global one. The old Christian countries have now become mission territories, and the mission of the Church to fulfill Christ's Body on earth, to apply Christ's Redemption to an increasing number, to provide the spiritual synthesis for a world facing the crisis of unity, will be defeated unless Christian action is organized to oppose effectively, with its positive approach to experience, the negative approach of the pagan elite. Because the Church, as a result of the world's becoming unified, is in the international position to caution the whole world against wars and immorality, she can, with the help of an active elite, truly realize her universality.

Suhard, who was instrumental in the growth of apostolic movements in France, emphasizes the need for Catholic action. Through Catholic action the two natures of the Church will combine in practice as well as theory, for each active Christian or apostle will become the messenger of eternal and transcendent truth and, at the same time, partake in the world. "Messenger of the supernatural, he will not fear to be 'scandal' and 'foolishness in the eyes of men'; citizen of the earth, he 'will render to Caesar the things that are Caesar's' and give himself loyally to the tasks here below." Only through Catholic action can the world be prepared for the Church to fulfill her mission, for, although it is not the role of the Church to interfere in worldly struggles outside her sphere of faith and morals, it *is* the role of the individual Christian, whose rights as a citizen of the world are equal to those of the non-Christian, to partake in such matters and to create worldly situations conducive to the fulfillment of the Church's mission. Whether the humanism of the scientific, technological age will be the humanism of the Cross, in which the perfectibility of man is dependent upon the redemptive suffering and death of Christ, will depend upon Catholic action.

The effectiveness of Catholic action resides in an educated laity, educated not only in religious matters but in worldly ones. "Do not be afraid therefore," Suhard reminds Catholics, "to be less Christian by being more men." Catholic action, to be effective, must disappear, must be absorbed in the world community, in pursuits like science, literature, and politics. Catholics should aim to be the best in such pursuits, should prove that they are just as desirous of truth and just as open as other men in the pursuit of it. Suhard, for example, reminds extremely conservative Catholics that the writings of Saint Thomas Aquinas are not the end of the pursuit of truth. If Thomas himself, he observes, had not been open to truth he would have failed to advance Catholic thought as much as he did. The writings of Thomas Aquinas should serve as a guide rather than as the end in the advancement of knowledge. For such advancement to be effective, however, it must be achieved within the framework of lay-clerical harmony. The lay apostolate must be not only *in* the Church but *of* the

Church, for if not strongly bound to the hierarchy, its members go astray and their efforts are compromised. To be an effective force in the modern world, the Church must not be dominated either by laicism or by clericalism but must be transformed into a single-minded apostolate. According to Suhard, "The profound transformation indispensable to the Christianization of the world, will be accomplished by entrusting to the laity more and more responsibilities and by associating it ever more closely with the efforts of the hierarchy."

For the modern world to be humanized and the mission of the Church accomplished, the value of the individual must not be undermined. The evil of socialism and progressivism resides in the sacrifice of individual liberty to anonymous power, while their appeal lies in the nobility of their dedication to ease the crisis of unity. But the organized apostolate must preserve the liberty of the individual, for it is essential to the Christian concept of humanity; if the modern world is to be given a soul, the individual must be respected. Suhard stresses personal sanctity as the preserver of individuality in an organized apostolate. The apostle must begin the conversion of the world with himself. His first duty is sanctity. "The apostle," writes Suhard, "whether lay or clerical, should place in the forefront of the values of his existence, prayer, silent recollection, mental prayer and all that nourishes it; retreats, recollections and the sacramental life." These practices make up the prime action of the apostle rather than a reprieve from action. The Apostolate must seek transcendent means, grace from God, to be effective in a reform basically virtuous, basically dedicated to having all men share in Christ's Redemption. The development of an interior life has even a more practical application in conversion. Suhard maintains that the Christian can never hope to entice modern man away from his mysticisms with an easily won faith. Only a draught of the Gospels undiluted, only a mystical sharing in the life of Christ, which must be within the experience of inspired apostles, can entice modern man and fulfill the Mystical Body of Christ.

Suhard's *Growth or Decline?* is an evaluation of the position of the Catholic Church in the modern world and an outline of the course of action necessary for her survival.

J.J.M.

ESSAY ON HUMAN LOVE

Author: Jean Guitton (1901-)
Type of work: Philosophical anthropology
First published: 1948

Principal Ideas Advanced

Human love has been one of the most constant and fundamental themes of Western philosophical speculation; nevertheless, the notion of love has never been adequately explored or used as a key to the solution of certain basic problems of philosophical anthropology.

The theory of man has been made to center about the notion of reason, with consequent imbalances especially for the Christian view of man.

The basic form of the problem of human love is the tension between spirit and flesh.

The simplest solution, philosophically, has seemed the negation of flesh and the exaltation of spirit, but contemporary thought perceives the futility of this procedure and seeks to view flesh and spirit in relation to each other and to the whole of life.

The entire problem culminates from the human point of view in the problem of the signification of sex; the basic need of philosophical anthropology is for an integral theory of sexuality and its meaning.

By taking up anew the philosophical theme of human love, Jean Guitton places himself in the direct historical current of one of the most profound and persistent concerns of Western speculation. From the *Symposium* of Plato and before, Western thought has been prolific of reflections on human love, but enormous difficulties have presented themselves which have made it heretofore impossible to fix the basic principle which might enable philosophy to deal unambiguously with the central notion of love. Guitton's treatment is related directly to this situation, because his purpose is to remove the ambiguity by formulating the principle in whose light the phenomenon of human love can be understood in its integrity with human life.

Guitton first discusses the problem of the language of love. Many idioms have been developed, he notes, in the course of Western man's efforts to comprehend this passion. While this multiplicity of idioms has complicated discourse about love, it is impossible, from the philosophical point of view, to eliminate any particular idiom, for each casts its own special light on the common object of concern. A central concern of the philosophical theory of love is, consequently, to comprehend these idioms and the reason for their multiplicity.

Guitton distinguishes and characterizes four idioms: *the poetic, the ascetic, the erotic,* and *the biological.* The salient characteristic of the *poetic* language of love is that it associates love intimately with *beauty*. Under the influence of this association love is detached from the ordinary and the familiar, from the biological and social plane, and is reorientated toward the remote, the ideal, the unfamiliar, the unreal. Thus, the woman of poetic love is never this woman present here before one, but an "innominata," at once abstract and magnified. This movement, when continued, brings one to a form of ecstasy which differs but little, if at all, from the rapture of the mystics. The poetic language takes the form of ritual, liturgy, and incantation. Even so, a quality of insincerity tends to enter into this language, since it seeks to translate all forms of love into this remote, ritualized, and abstracted form, leaving no room for the real claims of concrete experience.

The *ascetical* language of love tends to associate love not with beauty but with moral distinctions between right and wrong, just and unjust; it strives to bring love under the category of *ought*. In this it is very different from the poetic language of love which frequently lays the greatest emphasis precisely upon the impossibility of bringing love under any form of constraint or necessity, affirming it to be of its essence free and impossible to refrain or compel. Associating love with duty and justice, the casuists who most frequently employ the ascetical language of love stretch love on the rack of their distinctions. They speak, for example, of the *jus in corpus,* a concept which would shake the poetic language of love, so woven of the figures of freedom, to its foundation. It is found that the ascetical language of love, again unlike the poetical, has strong practical and social orientations. It seems to be a language which society finds itself compelled to compose in order to control the elemental power of love and to canalize it into manageable patterns. This manner of treating love is necessary, from certain points of view, but it is filled with perils. The erotic language of love has as its basis the alienation, which always threatens, between *spirit* and *intelligence*. Spirit implies mystery and thrives upon it; it sees being always in depth. The intelligence, on the contrary, seeks to dissolve the mystery which clings about all that *is* and precisely about its own being and existing.

When intelligence addresses love, it develops the *erotic* language. This language, always seeing love in its external aspects and extrinsic relations, plays upon the surface of love. In form, erotic language tends to range from the gross language of pornography to the subtleties of *salon* wit; but in every case it has this note: love is reduced to an object among objects and is always treated superficially and extraneously, as a phenomenon completely open and apparent, innocent of any mystery.

The *biological* language, finally, has assumed great importance in our day. It dominates medicine, psychiatry, even psychology. Moreover, it has passed into the language of the *wisdom* of love; that is to say, the key to the secrets of human love are thought to be found in its biological aspects, as when it is asserted that the key to marriage lies in a satisfactory sexual relation. The biological language of love is dominant because in human experience it seems impossible or even deceptive to separate love from sex, from the physical. This inseparability may be interpreted in a number of ways, and these modes of interpretation are reflected in the various forms of the biological idiom of love.

The first manner of interpretating the inseparability of love and the physical may be called reductive; it tends to insist that all explanation of love is to be found in the biological. To this is added, at times, a sociological and psychological dimension, but always with strong biological bases. The method in this case tends to be clinical. The danger of this method, according to Guitton, is that the objective student of love is blinded to the subjective structure of this phenomenon. Thus, when comparisons are instituted, under the biological aspect, between human love and love in other animals, there enters the danger of losing sight of the fact that while the clinical aspects may be similar or even identical, these phenomena transpire in an entirely different context in the human person and in the animal. As a consequence, the biological language of love, which ought to enter intimately into all discourse on human love, because man is essentially spirit and flesh, offers itself as a parody of that integral language which love demands; seeming to say all, biological language says nothing. The biological language of love frequently takes either of two forms, the descriptive and the pathological; and this latter receives a further sophistication when it is suggested that the most direct avenue to love itself may be by way of its deviations.

After treating in this manner the various idioms of love Guitton indicates the overall plan of his book. The three parts of the book, he tells us, correspond to three points of view, three methods which are at once both old and new. The first portion is based on the history of ideas; here the various representations which man has formed of love under the varying influences of religon, poetry, philosophy, and science are reviewed. From the perusal of this portion the reader may draw, above all, the sense of the mystery of love which springs from the fact that sex contains within itself the germ of spirit. The second portion concerns the analysis of that which passes in the human consciousness throughout its career; the effort here is to follow the metamorphoses of love through duration, conceiving it after the manner of an essence which has a career in time. In the third part, the entire level of the inquiry is raised: the inquiry is now directed to the signification of sexuality, both animal and human, to confront it with the demands of reason, to justify it if necessary, and to try to divine the possible hopes of our species and to ask even whether the conditions and hence the nature of love may alter.

Turning to the first portion of his work, Guitton, in the context of the history of ideas, affirms that three great themes have in history sought to express the faces of love: the Platonic theme (the theme of Diotema), the Solomon theme, and the Tristan theme. These three themes correspond to three civilizations: the Greek, the Judaic, and the modern respectively; still, all have one feature in common: they treat love under the mode of exaltation; they subscribe to the common principle that *excess* is the *normal* mode of love.

While the episode of Hector and Andromache in Homer assures us that the Greeks were sensitive to the meaning of married love, this theme is not central to their most important thought, Guitton claims. When Plato, the master of Greek thought, speaks of love, he is not speaking of married love; he is referring rather to the life of the spirit and the means of reaching the highest moments of consciousness. His interest is not so much in love as in the vibrations which love produces in the soul, in the help it offers for the aspirations of the spirit. In Plato there is a close relation between the theory of knowledge and the doctrine on love. His distinction between the "idea" or "essence" and its singularities and concrete appearance is the clue to his distinction between the two aspects of the loved object. The object present is not all; within it and beyond it appears the Idea of beauty which we love in all objects and for the sake of which we love all objects. Hence, it is never possible to love any immediate concrete present thing or person; love is only of the essence, which is impersonal and transcendent. This dualism reappears when Plato comes to consider the biological and social bases or antecedents of love. In the *Banquet* he notes that love moves on two axes, one horizontal, the other vertical and in depth. Along the first it follows the desire to engender bodies for society; on the other axis, it moves toward the pure, essential, and eternal and is concerned to engender only the pure presences of the Ideas. The influence of the Platonic theme of love is impossible to estimate; above all, its power is evident in the fact that it is always the form the doctrine of love takes when it is concerned to emphasize the spiritual aspect of love; that is, love as the path to and indeed the very form of the life of the spirit.

The Biblical or Judaic theme of love may best be illustrated, Guitton believes, by the *Song of Songs*. Under the figure of the young maiden torn between the solications of a king and the protestations of the shepherd, this composition opposes the two loves, one of which, despite its splendor, is but the appearance and falsification of love. The idea of the poem is to exalt the love which is beyond price. Solomon represents the single-minded will to possession, the aggressive desire, which though cloaked in courtesy, yet seeks only to take possession of the object, treating it as an object of commerce, seeking to purchase it at the price of luxuries, the promise of a crown. This is not love, says Guitton, but passion. By contrast, the shepherd represents the love which is born of mutual self-giving and consent. The roots of such love are in God. In this case, nothing is purchased, nothing possessed; hence, there is no fear of any loss. This is a love which grows stronger by its very afflictions, for it is conscious of the freedom of its origin, the liberty of spirit in which it is born.

Under the rubric of the "Tristan theme" Guitton, following the example of Dennis de Rougemont, treats of that passionate love which develops outside of marriage, "romantic" love, as it is called. To the essence of this conception of love belongs the vision of woman as the instrument of fatality, the chosen instrument and vehicle of fate. The Greeks developed the notion of fate, but it was not associated in their thought with love. In the Tristan myth or theme there is as yet no thought of sin. This modern Adam and Eve dwell in an Eden from which they cannot be expelled. They are beyond repentance because they have no sense of sin. Their only sense is that of being fated in love. This fate causes all and justifies all; it is the only principle to which appeal can be made. The moral essence of this romantic love is the duality of fidelities. Isolde is transfixed by this duality. But, still, love cannot be construed in terms of morality alone, as though love were a category of obligation and could be made the object of an option. The state of soul of the lover can be judged only when it is realized that this is a fated love. Fate intervenes in the dialectic of morals to impose an entirely fresh and different criterion for the judgment of the lover and the loved. Nevertheless, romantic love does not terminate in a *justification* of the lover and the beloved; such love does not raise one law above another, one category of obligation above another, but leaves the whole issue, from the moral point of view, in obscurity and ambiguity. The power of fate is not a higher moral law; it is a lawless force, before which obligations are rendered nugatory. The romantic dilemma is insoluble; to demand that it be solved on the basis of the moral imbalances which it seems to imply is to show that one has failed to grasp its very essence. But the fatal love has one power which the love according to the law, matrimony, does not seem to have: it places the afflicted, lover and beloved alike, directly and immediately in relation to eternity. Fate pierces them both with eternity, and it is this element of eternity which places their love beyond all judgments and endows it with a supernal mystery.

Exaltation is the mark of these three themes of love, says Guitton. But in our culture there has existed another and perhaps an even stronger context for all thought and experience of love. That is the context of conflict, involving sin, guilt, tension, and loss. Love is conflict and the source of conflict; the purest expression of this view of love is the conflict which Saint Paul has signalized between spirit and flesh. Love is the name of the war between these; and the problem of love is that of determining the nature of this conflict. Is it an external conflict, as some have suggested, between man and society; or is it a conflict which is of the very essence of man, so that he cannot be delivered from it so long as he endures as human? In the first case, a reorganization of society should suffice to reduce the conflict, as Rousseau dreamed; in the second, only the annihilation of one of the factors, either of flesh or of spirit, will insure the peace which man seeks. But to consider the conflict as external, Guitton claims, is to be deluded: so to think is merely to project an intensely internal conflict onto an imaginary external plane. Some would explain this conflict by prohibition, as do the disciples of Freud and of André Gide; others, like Nietzsche, have placed the blame for this conflict on false ideals, such as the ideals of Christianity, which destroy the equilibrium of nature. But others, among whom Jesus must be placed, have seen this conflict between flesh and spirit as the natural crucible wherein the spirit of man is forged. The conflict springs from no external source, but is constitutive of man; the constitutive character of the conflict is not static but dynamic and indicates a line of development which can culminate in the total integrity of the human subject. Neither element, neither spirit nor flesh, is to be annihilated, for each is to be tested and purified in the other: the flesh in the spirit, whereby the powers of the flesh are sublimated and enabled to carry a meaning quite beyond any they could sustain in themselves; the spirit in the flesh, by which the spirit is made concrete and even humbled but in any case endowed with a quality of immediate existence which it would otherwise lack. There is no escape from this conflict for man; there is only victory or defeat, according to the conditions of the conflict and combat.

The analytic aspect of Guitton's treatment of love comes to its focus in the chapter which he devotes to the "forms of love as oblation." The notion of "oblation" in the context of the theory of love has its roots in the contrast between "possession" and "donation" as the basic alternative forms of love. In the former, love becomes an aggressive extension of the self and carries with it the serious possibility of frustration. This is especially true when the object loved possessively is not a thing but a person. Possession of another person is a literal impossibility, because the personality by its very nature involves inalienable freedom and self-authenticity. Thus, love for another person can be fulfilled only by self-donation, not by any act of possession. Consequently, tragedy seems built into the very movement of the self toward love as possession. Equally true, however, is it that the person who loves is not fulfilled by possessing. Even were it possible to possess another human person, this possession would prove futile, since it is not in this way that the self is fulfilled. The self is fulfilled only by an act of self-giving. The wisdom which leads to this conclusion is the same wisdom which counsels the consideration of the forms of donation, of oblation, as the true forms of fulfilling love.

The two supreme forms of oblation are virginity and matrimony, for each is a pure act of self-giving and hence is orientated toward love in its purest sense. In each form, says Guitton, we have a special synthesis of spirit and flesh, a unification of these tensive opposites which creates a cosmos of value. Yet in each form taken separately there is an element of imbalance. In virginity the negativity toward the fulfillment of the flesh creates this imbalance; in matrimony, it is the cares of the world and the proximate impulse of sensuality which work to this end. Consequently, a synthesis between these forms of oblative love seems necessary. That is to say, it is necessary that the positive element of each be in some form discovered in the other. Guitton cites Coventry Patmore on this point, with relation to the chastity of married love; for the poet asserts that the fulfillment of the flesh in marriage is itself virginity in the most complete sense of the term. For virginity is not sterility but the intactness of the operation of love, complete conformity to its meaning and purpose; and this is surely achieved in married love when the self-donation of the partners is sincere and complete. In like manner, the fulfillment of marriage, that is, fecundity in the values of the spirit, is found to abide at the heart of virginity when it is practiced as a positive virtue and not merely as a mode of sterility. For the flesh of the virgin is not sterile when it is fulfilled in the values of the spirit which must surely be recognized as the ultimate destiny of the flesh. The two forms of oblative love are not therefore truly two in a disjunctive but in a complementary sense; they are the two forms in which the basic nature of love through donation can be realized.

By his own indication, the full culmination of Guitton's essay is reached when he passes from the analytic and descriptive phase to that phase in which he inquires into the meaning and value of love. This he does in the chapter entitled "The Meaning of Sex." Without doubt, this must be considered one of the richest treatments of this problem to be found in any literature. The conclusions Guitton reaches on this theme cannot fail to recall the position assumed by certain thinkers of the Renaissance, especially Pico della Mirandola in his discourse "On the Dignity of Man," for the principle on which they rely proves to be identical. This principle is the status of man in being and existence as a "privileged intermediary" in which all values both above and below reach their synthesis and realization through their mutual mediation. Man is a privileged intermediary in creation. He has his roots in the most material naturalness and, at the same time, is moved by the strongest aspirations to the highest, to the divine. He is truly a *resumen* and a mirror of the whole of being in its unity and diversity, for all the zones of being coincide in him. Through his consciousness he mediates all these zones; through the spiritual movements of his life he sublimates the inferior in order to give his movements being in a higher range of community; at the same time, through the material movements of his being man gives to the spiritual values a concrete seat in existence and prevents their escape into that "realm of the idea" where they remain, intact but sterile. Man's state of privileged intermediary is in turn fulfilled and realized most completely in his power to love. Through love all abstract dualisms are closed up and here the integrity of being is reëstablished. For there is no love without the full range of the zones of being which are reflected in man; and there is no love save when these zones are related in a true system of values. But, concludes Guitton, this is precisely what transpires in human love by its dual movement; namely, the movement to sublimate the movements of the flesh by making them vehicles of spiritual values, ultimately of that charity which is fulfilled surpassingly in the creation of the human person, and the movement to incarnate all spiritual values in the flesh, whereby they become effective covers within the world of existence.

A.R.C.

THE SEVEN STOREY MOUNTAIN

Author: Thomas Merton (1915-)
Type of work: Autobiography of a Catholic convert
First published: 1948

Principal Ideas Advanced

Thomas Merton's early antipathy to Catholicism was first overcome by the reading of William Blake's poetry; a trip to Rome reinforced the inception of his faith.

The study and appreciation of Catholic writers strengthened Merton's growing understanding of the Catholic faith; the letters of Cardinal Newman to Gerard Manley Hopkins brought his indecision to an end: he embraced Catholicism.

After finding life as a Franciscan priest unsatisfactory because it did not demand of him sufficient sacrifice, Merton became a Trappist monk at the monastery in Gethsemani, Kentucky; there he found spiritual freedom and joy.

Shortly after Thomas Merton's birth in France, his family came to the United States and settled in Long Island in 1916. His parents were apathetic concerning religion, but from his grandfather the young Merton contracted a hatred and suspicion of Catholics that was to last for many years. How deeply ingrained that antipathy was is shown by an incident that took place as late as 1937. Merton writes of seeing displayed in a bookstore window a copy of Étienne Gilson's *Spirit of Mediaeval Philosophy*: "I bought it . . . . together with one other book that I have completely forgotten, and on my way home in the Long Island train, I unwrapped the package to gloat over my acquisitions. It was only then that I saw on the first page of *The Spirit of Mediaeval Philosophy,* the small print which said: 'Nihil Obstat . . . Imprimatur.'

"The feeling of disgust and deception struck me like a knife in the pit of the stomach. I felt as if I had been cheated. They should have warned me that it was a Catholic book."

At the insistence of his father, a peripatetic artist, young Merton, at the age of ten, was sent to school first in France and then in England. What he describes as the diabolical spirit of cruelty and viciousness of the children at the lycée made his first weeks at the school a veritable nightmare. Gradually, however, he adjusted to the situation, associating with youngsters whose ideals and ambitions were more or less like his own. Here, during one of the most impressionable periods of life, Merton's religious training was negligible—as was that of the other children at the school, even those who were nominally Catholics. He was elated by his father's decision to send him to England for further schooling. "Liberty! liberty! liberty!" was young Merton's chant.

Much more enjoyable and beneficial were his years at Oakham, an English preparatory school with a competent instructional staff and a congenial atmosphere. It was during his preparatory school period in England that he witnessed the protracted suffering of his father, who was afflicted with a fatal tumor of the brain. The anguish that the son suffered was aggravated by the lack of any spiritual foundation that would help to soften such a blow, for, unaware of the Christian interpretation of human suffering, Merton saw it only as something pointless, inexplicable. His reaction was typical of that of many intelligent but spiritually unenlightened individuals of today: "What could I make of so much suffering? There was no way for me, or for anyone else in the family, to get anything out of it. It was a raw wound for which there was no adequate relief. You had to take it like an animal. We were in the condition of most of the world, the condition of men without faith, in the presence of war, disease, pain, starvation, suffering, plague, bombardment, death. You just had to take it, like a dumb animal."

Paradoxically, it was the reading of William Blake's poetry that awakened the first faint stirrings of faith in his soul. Blake he credits with leading him, in a roundabout way, ultimately to the Faith. Aware of the difficulties and obscurities of Blake's work, and of the remnants of heretical mystical systems which pervade it, Merton does not, of course, recommend the study of Blake to all minds as a perfect way to faith and to the Almighty. Thinking of his own experience and acknowledging the salutary effects that the poet had on him, the future Father M. Louis rates William Blake as a holy man with a sincere love of God. This inception of faith was reinforced in Merton by a trip to Rome. The glimmerings of faith, the temporary religious fervor, however, soon disappeared.

Following a year at Cambridge, the only real fruit of which was his study of Dante, Merton returned to New York. He matriculated at Columbia, was attracted for a few months to communism, and wrote regularly for the undergraduate publications. To Professor Mark Van Doren he acknowledges a special debt of gratitude. Van Doren's sincerity, honesty, and objectivity helped prepare Merton's mind to receive the seed of Scholastic philosophy.

Merton's close friends at Columbia were with one exception non-Catholics. Some of them, like his Jewish friends Robert Lax and Robert Gerdy, were later to become Catholics. It was the providential choice of the subject "Nature and Art in William Blake" for his Master's thesis that helped direct Thomas Merton's faltering, uncertain steps toward a sane conception of virtue and to the Roman Catholic Church. Although he had been in and out of a thousand Catholic cathedrals and churches, it was not until 1938 that he attended Mass for the first time. His reading became more and more Catholic, and he found Crashaw, Waugh, and Hopkins especially inspiring. The indecision and vacillation which had characterized him for months gradually came to an end as he read the soul-searching letters written to Cardinal Newman by Gerard Manly Hopkins on the brink of his conversion. Hopkins's waverings and perplexities seemed very much like his own. Coupled with Merton's final decision to embrace Catholicism was an obscure aspiration of becoming a priest. It was his baptism that was to be the first step at the foot of the Seven Storey Mountain, an ascent steeper than he was then able to imagine.

With the marked tendency of judging himself most severely, Thomas Merton dwells on the misapprehensions of his first steps as a follower of Christ—his failure to realize the importance of being a daily Communicant, his assumption that six weeks of instructions equipped him to be a Catholic, his hesitancy about asking his spiritual adviser questions that rose in his mind. At the time, for instance, Our Lady was to him little more than a beautiful myth. Here the note of regret is especially poignant in the light of his later realization of Our Lady as the world's Mediatrix.

Dan Walsh, a part-time teacher of Scholastic Philosophy at Columbia, not only encouraged Merton in the belief that the priesthood might be his vocation but also tried to direct him towards the Trappists at Gethsemani. Ironically, Walsh's exposition of that order's religious life did not at all appeal to Merton. The Franciscans were to be his choice, but a choice destined to be unsatisfactory because of the conditions under which it was made. Here then, was another step in the arduous journey up the Seven Storey Mountain—a spiritual self-scrutiny, convincing Merton that in view of the way in which he had become satiated with the pleasures offered by the world, not enough sacrifice would be entailed in becoming a Franciscan.

Given a teaching position at the Franciscan College of St. Bonaventure in New York, Merton soon began to feel that at last he was leading a life that was worth while. The academic atmosphere, the opportunity to teach courses in literature and to do some writing on his own, but especially the fact that he was working in and living in a place dedicated to God, produced an initial spiritual serenity. However, he began to realize as the weeks passed that he had not yet found his true vocation. He then made a fateful decision —to attend during the Easter vacation a retreat at the Gethsemani Trappist Monastery in Kentucky. The poetic prose employed in the autobiography at this point, as Merton describes the religious exercises of the Trappists, is that of one now ecstatically aware of the Real Presence and moved by an all-consuming love for the Queen of Angels.

Back once again at St. Bonaventure, Merton felt more and more drawn to the Trappist life. After much soul searching he applied for admission to Gethsemani. On being accepted as a postulant, he realized that at last real freedom had come to him.

Graphically, enthusiastically, Thomas Merton describes the monastery from within—the religious exercises, the food, the facets of human nature reflected in diverse types of monks. He minimizes the elements of sacrifice and self-abnegation which are the core of the Trappist rule. It is the voice of the cheerful ascetic that the reader hears. There is, however, no mistaking the inestimable gratitude he has for the grace of God, which led him Home.

J.E.F.

THE MEANING OF MAN

Author: Jean Mouroux (1901-)
Type of work: Theology of man
First published: 1948

Principal Ideas Advanced

Man is a creature destined to live in both the temporal world and the eternal world of divine realities.

The body is the soul's means of action; hence, the body was made to assist man's communion with God.

The human person is a being who is both spirit and body, both closed and open, both existent and unfulfilled; the paradoxical reality which is man has been redeemed through Christ crucified.

Man, realizing his present state, his dependence on Christ and His grace, is thereby enabled to appreciate his purpose in life and become truly a man, truly a Christian, truly a Res Sacra.

The Meaning of Man by Jean Mouroux is a penetrating analysis of the nature of man. Mouroux has written the work in the form of a reflection; that is, he has described the human situation in all its aspects. The book is not an attempt to present a technical study of man. Rather, it is an account of man's nature and human situation based on Scripture, philosophy, and literature. As such, then, the book is simply, in Mouroux's term, a "witness" to the Christian truth.

At the beginning of the first chapter Mouroux states, "Man is a creature destined to live in two worlds. He is surrounded first by the realities of this world, he lives among things and plants and animals and in the society of other persons like himself, and is active among them in thought and work and love. On the other hand he is called to live with divine realities. Christ is present in the world and in the depths of his soul to introduce him to the society of the Divine Persons and to achieve his consummation in God. Thus he has simultaneously to breathe an eternal and a temporal air."

Mouroux shows himself to be extremely aware of the human situation. He knows that man is immersed in the world, in the temporal realm. He realizes that a Christian finds himself engaged in carnal activity, and that this activity is not without meaning and purpose. In his present state man is in constant contact with the temporal: he is surrounded by the wonders and beauties of nature, by the magnificence and grandeur of the universe, by the community of his brothers. All of these realities should carry him to the Creator of these realities; they should bear him to final union with God. But man finds difficulty in life. He is capable of misusing the temporal order, thereby perverting his purpose in life. Because of original sin man finds himself in a desperate situation. Man's nature can refuse to serve the right order of the universe, and the grandeur of man's nobility can be lost.

The order in man's life can be restored, however, Mouroux claims. In the Redemption the Christian finds the answer to his situation. Mouroux writes: "The significance of everything here below is determined by its relation to Christ, for *all things were created by him and in him*. . . . The human body—mystery of greatness and misery—finds its last explanation and its total consummation in Christ. The body was created in such wise that the Word of God might lay hold of it and assume it; and because the Word was made flesh the body's condition was thenceforth changed. It is redeemed. It awaits its glorification."

In Christ, says Mouroux, the Christian man finds the answer to the riddle of "the mystery of greatness and misery." Through Christ and His Church man can re-establish the order that was destroyed by original sin. He can start to live again as *true* man.

Having introduced the distinction between the temporal world and the world of divine realities, Mouroux argues that the temporal world contains both material and spiritual aspects, for the activities of man in the temporal realm are the activities of a body animated by spirit and engaged in sense apprehension. The soul is more than the organizing activity of the person, however; it is also that which transcends body; it is spirit, engaged in the realm of immanent activity. Finally, the soul in its living relations with God is active religiously; thus, the soul is *anima, spiritus,* and *mens.* The first two activities of the soul realize the temporal world, says Mouroux; the third is concerned with the eternal.

Corresponding to the three activities of the soul are three kinds of values: the material, the human, and the spiritual. Mouroux's book is an exploration of these three kinds of values and an attempt to show how they are rooted in Christian thought.

Mouroux stresses the point that man must recognize the importance of the temporal world. The world is a product of and also a mirror of God. Therefore, man must strive to use the temporal as God intended and thereby offer creation back to the Creator, and, in the same action, come back to God himself.

In the second section of *The Meaning of Man* Mouroux discusses carnal values. In an admirable fashion he illustrates how man must use his whole body; that is, the body as animated by a soul. The soul and body are a unit which must take into account all the factors of each component of the unit. That is, neither the soul nor the body must have priority to the exclusion of the other. The soul needs the body and its functions in order to express itself, for the body is the soul's means of action. The body, while aiding the soul, depends on this animating power for its very life and orientation, for its very nobility. Thus, the body and soul make up a complete unit and within this unit the body rises to noble heights, for it becomes the vehicle of the soul and the means by which man comes to communion with God.

Mouroux does not leave his presentation of the body and its values on a noble level without considering the difficulties that man experiences by reason of his body. *The Meaning of Man* explains well the two forces of good and evil that are operative in man. Man experiences difficulty in this life because his body does not always co-operate fully with his higher faculties. The body is in misery in a true sense and wars against the soul. How can man resolve this duality he experiences within himself?

Jean Mouroux thus has drawn out the problem that confronts the life of every man, the problem that can detroy meaning in man's life or establish meaning in every moment and situation of man's existence. The basic solution is the Redemptive Act of Christ. In a fuller sense it is the life of Christ in His Church, the Redemption and its fruits continued in the life of every member of Christ's Mystical Body.

Mouroux spends the remaining section of the book on spiritual values. Chapter Six, "The Human Person," presents an extremely philosophical treatment of person. It is perhaps the most difficult chapter in the book because of the careful and minute penetration of the author. It is here Mouroux analyzes the meaning of an embodied spirit, of the soul in the body, of the powers of man, and of man's relation to God.

The following chapters, "Spiritual Liberty," and "Christian Liberty," are further analyses of man's nature. Mouroux gives careful attention to the faculty of the intellect and the faculty of the will, explaining them in their essential meaning and then proceeding to discuss the role of grace in regard to these faculties. It is within this framework that the unity, the orientation, the liberty, and the nobility of man become explicit. Within this framework of grace perfecting nature man finds his true meaning. Man discovers himself as capable of love, not only of human love, but also of a love uniting himself to God in a most intimate manner. When man understands his nature in this light, he is then capable of putting meaning into his life. He becomes a holy thing, a *res sacra,* when he stands in his proper relation to God.

Mouroux not only draws wisely from Scripture and the works of the Fathers, but also makes an excellent literary effort of his own. It is this effort on the part of the author, an effort expressive of an intense Christian dedication, that produces a high degree of harmony in the work. In speaking of God's calling all things into existence, for example, Mouroux writes: "For God calls all things to existence, to life, to activity; not from without, but from within; not by uttering a word, but by forming beings, endowing them with a structure and orientation. He calls to the torrent as it breaks from the foot of the glacier to bound uproariously over the rocks and cry aloud its joy as it leaps and flashes in the sun. He calls to the rose to bloom in its crimson robe, and to throw around its beauty this veil of perfume that delights the gods. He calls to the birds to spread their wings to the wind, to soar and sing, each with a note of its own, from the humble chirping of the sparrow to the pure and liquid plaint of the nightingale. Every creature answers the call. They yield to the vital impulse that sweeps them along, they give free way to their own abounding energies, and, in this happy obedience, the thing they seek is their own fulfillment and their own perfection; which for water is to flow, for the rose to bloom, for the bird to utter its song. More deeply still, it is an image of God they seek in this fruition of their being, it is God Himself whom they seek and find without knowing it."

N.P.K.

THE WORLD OF SILENCE

Author: Max Picard (1888-)
Type of work: Phenomenological meditation
First published: 1948

Principal Ideas Advanced

Silence is the firstborn of the basic phenomena which include love, loyalty, and death.

Silence is not merely negative, the absence of speech, for it is an autonomous phenomenon which carries us back to the very origin of things.

The word has supremacy over silence, but when it is divorced from silence, as it generally is today, language becomes meaningless verbal noise.

Max Picard writes out of his own experience in his small but exquisite work, *The World of Silence.* Born of Jewish-Swiss parents in Baden, this convert to Roman Catholicism has lived by a quiet Swiss lake near the

Italian border. *Die Welt des Schweigens* appeared when he was sixty years of age. The mature language, beautiful even in translation, reflects the peace and vigor of his mind and of the mountain valleys in which he has lived.

The book is a series of brief meditations arranged into five sets. *The World of Silence* opens with three reflections on the essential being of silence. There then follow seven reflecions on the relations between silence and speech.

The middle of the work, the third set, comprises sixteen reflections on the meaning of silence in relation to the ego, knowledge, things, history, myth, images, love, the human face, animals, time, childhood and old age, the peasant, men and things, nature, poetry, and the plastic arts. These latter elements are like miniatures set off from each other by walls of silence. Still it is the same basic phenomenon of silence which pervades each consideration and directs it. As the reader meets this phenomenon in one guise or another, as knowledge or myth; in one place or another, as in the human face or in nature; and in one form or another, as poetry or as art, he is helped to see with the eyes of the author the pure being of silence.

Developing a theme already explored in an earlier book, *The Flight from God* (1934), the author goes on in the fourth set to examine in five reflections the status of language today. In the blare of the noise of contemporary speech Picard looks for the ruins of silence, even as Europeans in the roar of guns and bombs picked over the rubble of their civilization. The book ends with two reflections on the relation of silence to hope and to faith.

Picard initially considers the structure of silence. Silence is not just *nothing;* it is not simply that which arises between words or what is left over at the end of them. It has its own presence and, although it is invisible, its own ways of appearing. Silence is proper to the essential being of man, but so is language. Far from despising language, Max Picard sets out to restore it to its original health by revealing the world of silence over which the word should reign and in relation to which it should sound. When that world is hidden or muted, as it is today, language loses its meaning.

Utility and productivity are most highly prized today, Picard claims, whereas silence is regarded as utterly useless. The charge is that silence cannot be turned to profit; it simply *is;* it only exists. In its pure being, however, silence "points to a state where only being is valid: the state of the Divine." Silence keeps the mark of the Divine alive in things. It transcends things and men, for it is without beginning and end, and it contains all things. That is why, Picard writes, silence leads back to origins.

In the moment before he speaks man finds himself suspended at the edge of two worlds, the world of silence and the world of language. It is as though he hesitates and is about to give the unspoken word back to the Creator, but instead he creates words freely out of the silence and establishes himself as man. In the language of Goethe we can sense this proud but gentle victory of the word over silence, and in the language of Pascal each sentence is as fresh and original as the first sentence ever uttered.

Yet the victory is no more absolute than man himself, writes Picard. Man holds his life between the silence before his birth and the silence after his death. From the first silence language takes its innocence, artlessness, and original character; from the second, its impermanence, fragility, and imperfection in representing things.

Silence is more than that which is before and after language, Picard claims. Silence is like a safety-net into which words can drop; it pervades language and is its ever-present listener, for language not only originates out of silence but is cast back into it.

When silence is not the reverse ground of language, words become hard and blatant; they hurry along, tumbling out of other words, jostling and bumping into one another. Indeed, says Picard, modern speech is too often a harsh automatic noise which skims desperately above the surface of silence like a self-declared orphan who refuses to recognize its parent. When language is conscious of its true nature, silence is a blanket of oblivion woven into the words by love, in order that words once expressed can be forgotten and forgiven. In today's speech words are not forgotten in silence; they simply disappear in the general hubbub.

Ancient languages are quite different in their structure, Picard notes. In ancient languages each word arises out of the silence as a shaft or pillar, and each is marked carefully off from the other, surrounded by its silence. There is no scurrying from one word to another. Ancient languages should be taught to the young, Picard suggests, for they are impractical and can thereby free the young from an exclusive attachment to the world of utility. Moreover, ancient languages can point their students towards the realm of silence, to the perfect union of silence and the word in God. Indeed, Picard writes, "languages seem to be like so many expeditions to find the absolute word." Thus, the variety of languages should be preserved, for each one is a limited phenomenon and cannot be expanded indefinitely without obliterating it. The greatest danger to the English language, says Picard, is its universal expansion. Even dialects should be preserved, if only because a speaker weaned on one of them is less able to take the literary language for granted as something ready-made. For such a speaker, language is more likely to demand a deliberate creative act in which the speaker is aware that each word is a creation out of silence. Silence is the medium which is poised between the truth of the human word, that transcends even man who speaks it, and the Incarnate Word, which "was on the way to man from the beginning of time" and before whose creative act the silence quaked and fell asunder.

As Picard sees it, silence is that place in things wherein being harbors a richness that exceeds the words which name them. So, too, in men: a host of unrealized possibilities in a person strengthen and deepen those that are realized. Moreover, irreconcilable qualities in a person are softened and accommodated to each other in silence, and personal development occurs not only in discussion but primordially in silence. True solitude, however, is not an overly anxious, self-conscious inward isolation. An openness to being dwells in silence, and so does love, which is a conspiracy of silence. Picard remarks, in his characteristic poetic-mystical style, that "there is more silence than language in love."

Human history, too, according to Picard, has its silence as well as its sound; contrary to Hegel, the quiet happenings of history are "vindicated" as surely as are the loud facts. Children and the aged are especially close to the primary phenomena of life and death. The old give their words back to the silence from which they took them; and children, like "little hills of silence," remind us of the beginnings of speech.

There is a profound silence in nature, Picard writes. Behind the days and seasons of the year time flows quietly, and the days come not so much from each other as out of the silence. In spring the flowers burst forth so suddenly that they seem to be sounds which, coming out of silence, are turned into color. The animals press through the human world of words "like a caravan of silence." With vigorous phrases which lift his discourse above any obvious level Picard traces the signs of silence in the flight and song of birds, in forest and lake, in mountain and echo. These are the rim of silence, he claims. Natural silence is also delicately traced in unlikelier vessels, such as the noonday brightness, the fury of fire, the storm of wind, and the roar of sea. Nature is a great repository of silence.

Without the human word and its silence, however, says Picard, the natural images of silence are heavy, for they point to a time before man and his word. If man were only a thing of nature he would remain sunk in that wordless silence, but his spirit "redeems the silence that is only nature and links it with that silence from which the word came and in which there is a mark of the silence of God." Man's soul is the storehouse of images which stand in silence but are on the way to speech. Primitive language is haunted by a twin dread, that of having been driven out of silence by the word, and that of again falling back into it through loss of the word. In the fairy tale the relation of word and silence is not fixed; anything can happen, and all things can speak. The languages of proverbs, poetry, and tragedy reveal the origin of the word in silence and show that man is connected with things not only through silence but also and preeminently through the word. In Greek art, too, the figure shines with radiant silence from which the word seems about to break out. Egyptian statues, Chinese paintings, medieval cathedrals —each has a different relation to silence. The most adequate balance between man and things is found in some form of the word which transfigures things in the awareness of the silence proper both to the word and to things.

Today, however, according to the author, empty verbal ghosts sound forth and with their own unreality challenge the reality of man. True words raise protective borderlines between things, whereas noise seeps through them. Noise has become so general that not only words but man himself disappears, and there remains only Noise, independent, autonomous, transcendent. In such a ceaseless barrage mass media can make statements but they cannot express truth, for truth requires a meeting of persons. What once were elemental personal experiences have become a part of the general noise of the radio and other "communication" media. War, for example, is reduced to a reported event, a news item, whereas it used to be suffered as a reality, in grieved and terrified silence. The radio blares and no one listens. It teaches man not to listen. In all this there is the utmost scorn for language, Picard insists. Moreover, the reports come so fast, and they raise so many questions, that a man cannot begin to answer them. There is left in him neither response nor responsibility.

It is as though the noise were the outgrowth of a plan to exterminate every last fragment of silence. The noise produced by our cities is like a kind of industrial fallout, and city-dwellers take the noise that is within them out into the countryside and spread it around the things of nature. If silence remains anywhere it is with the sick, in the catacombs of our society. Even the dead are not untouched, for we can be related to the dead in thankfulness or in grief only in silence: "Nothing has changed the nature of man so much as the loss of silence."

Nevertheless, Max Picard tries to hope amid the ruins of silence. He suggests that the spirit of silence is sleeping in order to recover new strength, and that the noise is only a wall which serves to shelter silence until it awakens refreshed. Picard turns, too, to the mysteries of faith, and especially to the Incarnation of the Word and the love of God. These are separated from man by a layer of silence, and man can respond to them only in silence. In that silence of God, so different from man's silence, word and silence are one. In prayer the human word is poured into silence and meets there the higher silence of God. These then remain: "the quietness of dawn, the furtive fall of night," and the prayerful word. Out of these, Picard concludes with confidence, we can seek to create the silence into which God comes.

K.L.S.

LEISURE, THE BASIS OF CULTURE

Author: Josef Pieper (1904-)
Type of work: Philosophy of culture
First published: 1948

Principal Ideas Advanced

Leisure must have a vital connection with cultus, or worship of the divine; cultus is the prime source of human freedom.

Culture refers to goods freely sought, to the realm of values or goods to be sought in themselves; these goods are gifts conferred upon man by God, and they make up a world beyond the immediate needs and desires of men.

The philosopher has the freedom to marvel at the mystery of Being precisely because he has the leisure to contemplate.

The values at stake here, such as those of philosophy, are not necessary to man's biological survival, but they are indispensable to the complete unfolding of the human person.

In *Leisure, the Basis of Culture,* Josef Pieper declares that without leisure, culture is impossible. On the other hand, Pieper asserts, leisure must enjoy a living relation to *cultus,* or the worship of the divine. The soul of leisure lies in celebration wherein the three elements of leisure, namely, effortlessness, calm, and relaxation, find a common unity. But if celebration is the central meaning of leisure, then leisure can be made possible and justifiable only upon the same basis as the celebration of a feast; that is to say, on the basis of divine worship. There are no feasts without gods. Feasts get their vitality from the fact that they are the celebration of worship of a deity.

Leisure, as found, for example, in the Biblical day of rest, is reserved for worship of the divine. In divine worship a certain space of time is set aside from working hours and is not used for practical pursuits. Every seventh day so set aside from servile effort is a kind of a reserved time, a feast, just as a temple is a place reserved for worship and thus is not to be used for practical gain.

Certainly, contends Pieper, a feast does not celebrate the principle of work. Therefore, Labor Day, to cite a particular case, is no feast in the true sense. Labor Day is a pseudo feast, an outgrowth of the world of work and the deified "worker." This world of work is rich in material goods but poor in spirit, for, on a purely utilitarian basis, the superabundance of cultural values, of goods in themselves, is impossible.

On the other hand, the author claims, divine worship creates real wealth and superabundance in the midst of dire material want, because sacrifice is the living heart of worship. Sacrifice means an offering *freely* given, a true gift, not a *means* to some result plotted in advance. Consequently, the sacrifice of the *cultus* creates a spiritual wealth which is not tied to practical needs or desires. This kind of dedication to the gifts of spirit marks the meaning of a holiday or feast in the true sense.

Pieper is plain in his declaration that if leisure is separated from the cult of the divine, it becomes impossible, leisure then becomes mere laziness, just as work severed from the praise of the divine becomes inhuman toil. Leisure detached from a sense of the divine presence in things resembles sloth in the metaphysical and theological sense of the medieval thinkers; it is but bored and lazy trifling. So also work, if it be cut off from genuine feast days, becomes inhuman, brutish toil without hope. If, as the author suggests, we appeal to antiquity, we see that the leisurely work of Plato's academy was rooted in *cultus,* since the academy was a religious association. Here culture lived on religion through divine worship.

Cultus refers to the sphere of values or goods-in-themselves to which we ought to respond. These values are never means, and thus they are completely outside the sphere of the merely practical. We must bear in mind, Pieper cautions, that a genuine *cultus* arises by divine ordinance; it is not purely the result of human *fiat.* Cultural values are conferred on man by God's free will, and they never can be demanded or in any way dominated and controlled by man's will.

In leisure man is raised above the world of means and ends, and he is turned toward the enjoyment of the superabundance of God's freely given gifts. This raising of man is best accomplished by Christian worship, Pieper maintains. Christian worship draws man out of the narrow world of work and puts him into the center of all creation. Then man is truly free, at leisure, and thus he is best able to join in the sacramental feast with God.

Leisure, in its four essential elements named by the author, enables man to enjoy culture, for leisure is, in the first place, a form of silence which allows reality to enter the receptive soul. Secondly, leisure is a form of happiness that accompanies man's recognition and acceptance of both the mysteriousness of the universe and his own incapacity ever to understand fully this mystery. Furthermore, leisure is a form of confidence manifested in a free and easy way. Man allows himself to contemplate with joy the values which are messages of the divine presence in all things. Finally, leisure is a fruit of man's oneness with all things and, thus, with himself.

At this juncture there arises the question of the nature of man as a spirit capable of enjoying culture through leisure. In the tradition of Thomistic Aristotelianism, Pieper affirms a real unchanging human essence. This essence or nature of man tells us what kind of a world is his. By his interiority or inwardness man has the capacity to establish relations to the "outer," to the world. Only a being, such as man, who has an inner world can have an outer world as well. Indeed, man has an infinite range of relations, so that the more his inner life is deepened in its integration, the more harmonious his relations with the outer world become. By contrast, a plant, for example, has just a few relations, and consequently its environment is quite impoverished compared to that of man.

Pieper observes that man grasps his world most characteristically through knowledge, which is an act of spirit. Spirit has the capacity to relate itself to *all* reality, to the totality of being. Therefore, spirit is the highest form of inwardness. As such it can relate itself to all reality and yet it has as well an infinite capacity of living in itself in self-reliant independence. Assuredly, the latter is traditionally regarded as the decisive element in personality.

The more man acknowledges essential values, says Pieper, the more he enriches personality. Culture refers to the world of values which speak to us as gifts of God's loving superabundance. These values in their innermost essence, which man is able to perceive spiritually, are such that man sees that he *ought* to respond to them in a free, loving way. He can make this response only if he enjoys leisure, that space in time cleared for a worshipful response to eternal values.

But since man most perfectly realizes his nature as a spirit in a body, it is necessary, notes the author, that he be involved in the world of the practical, attending to his biological needs and desires. Man is, in a word, amphibious: he dwells in two environments which are in reality one. Both these surroundings make their legitimate claims on him, but the one, the sphere of culture, of values, is incomparably higher than the other, the world of the merely utilitarian.

The sphere of mere workaday pursuits is inferior to the realm of cultural values which leisure enables us to enjoy. Yet the world of the "worker" is presently taking shape with dynamic force. This is the force of a total utilitarianism which wants to make universal the dominion of useful purpose, of practicality. Pieper warns that the force of this movement makes it impossible to be stopped by those defenders of culture who seek to win the day with such inadequate weapons as "art for art's sake" or any kind of anthropocentric humanism.

The sheer momentum of the drift toward total work may well achieve the result that *all* men will become "workers," members of the proletariat. But what the author hopes for is the abolition of the proletariat. The proletarian is a man fettered to the process of work; that is, the process dominated by mere means and ends considerations. This man is a mere functionary; his total reality consists in his functional role in the economic machinery of public life. In this connection, we are reminded by the author that there is but one institution in the world which forbids useful work on certain days; namely, the Church. The Church sets aside days for public feasts. Thus, the Church, through public action such as this, puts itself on the side of those who seek to make the sphere of leisure available to *all* men, thus deproletarianizing them.

Pieper points out in the course of the two essays which make up his book that these reflections are meant to make men think about the problem posed concerning leisure. His intention is neither to give advice nor to draw up a plan of action. Pieper is convinced that he must make men see that the result desired is not to be achieved by means of action, for which one hopes, but by a reawakening of the feeling for worship.

In his second essay, Pieper turns his attention to philosophy, which he holds to be the most valuable fruit of leisure. Philosophy is pre-eminently a good in itself, he claims; the philosophical act concerns itself with pure *theoria,* with marveling at the mystery of being. The philosopher is free to wonder in this way because he has the leisure to contemplate. To philosophize means to step beyond the sectional, truncated environment of the world of the practical into a position vis-à-vis the universal, the totality of being. The work of philosophy is, as Aquinas said of contemplation, not something human, but superhuman. The philosophical quest is an essentially spiritual quest, since it seeks to know the causes of all things, to know God and the world.

The philosopher searches for his vision of truth by reflecting in a disciplined way on the concrete things which all men daily experience. The philosopher seeks to know the ultimate natures, the universal essences of all things. Thus, he draws away from and questions the values popularly, and perhaps unreasonably, assigned to things. The beginning of philosophy is marveling, and this takes place in a state of detachment from the immediate needs and aims of everyday life. Pure *theoria,* which is a unique relation to being, takes place only in a state of wonder which is undisturbed by will. Wonder moves and shakes us; perhaps at first we are moved to doubt, but if it is true wonder, we move through doubt to hope.

In the traditional sense, however, the innermost meaning of wonder is to be found in a deepened sense of the inexhaustible mystery of being. Thus, the questions raised by philosophy can never be fully answered. Philosophy, unlike the natural sciences, remains always seeking its fuller truth.

The wisdom sought by philosophy, Pieper avers, is sought for its own sake, not for the use to which it can be put. This wisdom is fathomless, and thus the "wondering" which sets man on the road of philosophy puts him on a road which never ends. It is a road which one travels in the spirit of hope, the hope that he will be able to go ever farther into inexhaustible truth. The spiritual nature of the quest for the wisdom of God makes philosophy the central human task. To philosophize means to live the completely human life. As such, this life is truly the life of leisure.

The good for its own sake, of which philosophy is one of the greatest examples, is not necessary to human survival on the biological level, but it is indispensable to the most complete unfolding of the person. This good, Pieper concludes, can be pursued only in leisure, in the festive companionship with the gods, as Plato remarks. In such leisurely comradeship alone does man attain true and complete culture.

J.B.L.

COMMUNISM AND THE CONSCIENCE OF THE WEST

Author: Fulton J. Sheen (1895-)
Type of work: Social philosophy
First published: 1948

Principal Ideas Advanced

The philosophy of communism is on the conscience of the Western world.

The primary problem of communism revolves around the nature of man; thus, it is philosophical and religious rather than an economic or political problem.

Liberalism, now in a state of decline, prepared the ground for communism.

Communism represents an active *barbarism outside Western civilization which has made inroads because of the* passive *barbarism within, which manifested itself in the general demoralization of society.*

The basic issue today is whether man shall exist for the state, or the state for man.

During World War II, when the Soviet Union was our ally against Nazi Germany, Americans naturally tended to interpret communism as generously as possible and to see it as an essentially democratic system with communal instead of individual ownership of productive property. It is against this attitude that Bishop Sheen addresses himself in *Communism and the Conscience of the West.* He sees communism as an absolute, a secular religion based on an erroneous view of man and a denial of any transcendent God.

In a preliminary chapter the author traces the breakdown of nineteenth century liberalism and shows how this breakdown left a vacuum in Western man's ethico-religious thought. Loss of faith in a laissez-faire economy resulted in a reaction toward a totalitarian economy. Optimistic trust in the natural goodness of man gave way to despair about human nature. Trust in individual human reason gave way to "state reason which is Fascism, or class reason which is Communism."

The individual liberties that constitute historical liberalism are secure only in a religious society that gives ethical foundation to those liberties. Thus, liberalism can do no more than mark a transitional era between a Christian society and one that is definitely anti-Christian. Men in the Western world stand at the end of a nonreligious era and at the threshold of a conflict between two religions or absolutes: "The conflict of the future is between the absolute who is the God-man, and the absolute which is the man-God; the God Who became man, and the man who makes himself God; brothers in Christ and comrades in Antichrist."

Bishop Sheen analyzes the philosophy of communism in terms of Marx's combining the dialectic of Hegel with the materialism of Feuerbach to produce dialectical materialism. The method of producing wealth is the basic force in history, for from it flow class antagonisms and the resultant superstructure of political, social, educational, religious, and aesthetic life. Class warfare will continue in the dialectical pattern until workers and owners of productive property are the same. Communism also has its own theory of ethics, according to the author, since ethics "are the product in the last analysis of the economic stage which society has reached at that particular epoch." Whatever promotes the victory of the proletariat in the class struggle is good; whatever obstructs it is evil. "There is not a single Russian idea in the whole philosophy of communism," Bishop Sheen concludes. "It is bourgeois, Western, materialistic and capitalistic in its origin. It was a creature of its age and could never have arisen in the thirteenth or even the eighteenth century, because the influence of Christianity was still too strong in the world."

The Catholic Church has consistently opposed communism, not because communism is anti-capitalistic but because its solutions to the ills of capitalism are themselves inherently wrong. The encyclical *Divini Redemptoris* contains the best brief statement on why the Church condemns communism; the grounds stressed in this encyclical are religious, moral, and philosophical. Some of the basic defects of communism are the following: (1) It is an opiate of the people in that it deadens and paralyzes the human intellect, replacing it with the Party line; (2) it is antidemocratic and antihuman, because it denies the value of the individual man; (3) it is not sufficiently revolutionary, as Christ was revolutionary, for it seeks only to change surface economic institutions rather than effect the basic moral reform of man himself; (4) communism destroys one's love of country and all other proper loyalties; (5) communism perverts the true doctrine of liberty and seeks to enslave all men under a specious doctrine of dialetical materialism.

Communism should not be opposed

with name-calling and hatred, nor should it be opposed on merely economic grounds, Bishop Sheen contends. Men in the Western world are called on to oppose it (1) by making democracy work though the choice of good statesmen, (2) by making "capitalists out of workers by a wide diffusion of private property," (3) by having morality govern labor-capital relations, (4) by sound education not only in the errors of communism, but also in the "great truths of human nature, history and religion," and (5) by presenting frustrated people who might embrace communism with positive ways of achieving social justice.

The theme of this work is succinctly stated in these words: "The situation resolves itself down to this. Modern Christians have truth but no zeal; materialists have zeal but no truth; they have the heat but no light; we have the light but no heat; they have the passion but no ideals; we have the ideals but no passion." Bishop Sheen urges that Christians adopt the zeal, the heat, and the passion of the Communists. Then victory will certainly rest with Christians in the great struggle of our time.

T.P.N.

TRANSFORMATION IN CHRIST

Author: Dietrich von Hildebrand (1889-)
Type of work: Spiritual counsel
First published: 1948

Principal Ideas Advanced

Man in "statu viae" everywhere reveals a deep, natural yearning to transcend the purely terrestrial and achieve a conversion of heart: in the Old Testament he is repeatedly seen searching for a powerful person to help him change; in the New Testament this search ends in Christ, who not only redeems man but offers him a new life.

Contrition is the basis of metanoia; so are man's self-knowledge and his true consciousness, which enables him to make objective contact with values and live a realistic and moral life.

Acquiring virtues such as simplicity, patience, meekness, humility, and confidence in God, man deepens in his response to values, witnesses in his life to the spirit of the Beatitudes and comes, through the surrender of self, to the encounter with God in contemplation.

Transformation in Christ, viewed by such contemporary theologians as Thomas Merton and Romano Guardini as a spiritual classic of rare and acute insight, is a work that gathers the philosophical speculation and profound sympathy for art and literature that have always characterized the writing of Dietrich von Hildebrand and brings these resources to the task of describing the experience of man in his conversion to Christ. In his long career as writer and teacher, von Hildebrand has published several studies which have been religious in range, among them *In Defence of Purity* and *Liturgy and Personality*. Primarily a philosopher, von Hildebrand, a student of Edmund Husserl, the German phenomenologist, became a convert to Roman Catholicism at the age of twenty-four. At Göttingen where he studied and at the University of Munich where later he taught for sixteen years, von Hildebrand established his reputation as a Christian phenomenologist. Well known in Europe, his writings were introduced to American readers when the Rockefeller Foundation brought von Hildebrand from Switzerland, where he had fled to escape Nazi persecutors, to the United States. In the years since then, von Hildebrand has had a distinguished career as teacher and writer, publishing philosophical studies which reveal his abiding interest in such basic philosophical truths as ". . . the objectivity and autonomy of being, the incompatibility of being and nonbeing, the objective validity of values, the existence of personal beings, the freedom of human decision, the fact that every value demands a positive response on the part of the person, the fact that the higher value should be preferred to the lower, and so forth." Von Hildebrand, then, is in the tradition of Plato, Saint Augustine, and such modern thinkers as Cardinal Newman, Søren Kierkegaard (1813-1855), and Gabriel Marcel, all philosophers whose speculative inquiries have had profound religious dimensions. So it is that the existential orientation of von Hildebrand's world view makes him sensitively aware of and able to convey expressively the terror which death has for the man who lives in a subjective universe without God. Indeed his style and method are not at all alien to those of the psychologist and the novelist. Consequently, this work often has the urgency and sense of life that characterize these forms. Not infrequent are his allusions to personalities such as Goethe and Wagner, and the characters of Shakespeare and Dostoevski, in illustrating spiritual and mental states.

Von Hildebrand begins his description of the transformation in Christ by stressing man's terrestrial condition of pilgrimage and search. Man's yearning to transcend his limitations and find personal fulfillment is a natural one, essentially different from any restless worship of change. Von Hildebrand everywhere stresses the person as an incarnation of a divine thought. Change is necessary because "What we generally feel to be our individual nature is far remote from the inward word by which God has called us. By our own force alone we cannot even truly discern that word." The perfection of the person, then, is realized only in the discovery by him of his own individuality as it exists in Christ. Starting out in the search for the genuine self, a search which is at the same time the search for Christ, man struggles to realize in himself the disposition and attitudes which ready him for the ultimate meeting with Christ. Von Hildebrand stresses the fact that system has no realistic place in the analysis of the transformation: virtues reciprocally strengthen each other and it becomes impossible to say, for example, that self-knowledge precedes contrition in the sanctification of the soul. What can be said is that contrition is a basis for creative change in the soul. Von Hildebrand makes real and subtle distinctions between complex emotional reactions and genuinely spiritual compunction. He gives width to the theology of the sacraments, too, by his tendency always to see them in the context of the entire Christian experience.

Von Hildebrand asserts that man learns about the self in a confrontation of the self with God. "Who art Thou," man prays with Saint Augustine, "and who am I?" Like Newman and Martin Buber, von Hildebrand describes man at this stage as aware of two luminous beings, the I and the Thou. This confrontation is most realistically engaged in the circumstances of the liturgy. As Thomas Merton, too, has said in writing of this subject in *No Man Is An Island* and elsewhere, man's advance in sanctity depends on the clarity with which he sees himself, his weaknesses, and the saving grace of God. (Merton would, however, disagree somewhat with von Hildebrand: in Merton's view, psychoanalysis may indeed play a serious part in purifying man's prayer and self-knowledge, whereas von Hildebrand sees it, as he several times says in this work, as an agency whereby objective reality loses, for the experiencing subject, its real resonance.) Here and elsewhere through *Transformation in Christ,* von Hildebrand considers the question, so basic to philosophy, of man's encounter with extra-mental reality; he gives the question its genuine urgency by stressing its bearing on all of man's experience, its most profound ramifications lying in the encounter of man with God. In these and several other themes, this book concerns itself with philosophical topics which are closely related to most of the serious art forms and speculative studies of this century.

Simplicity, patience, meekness, mercy, and humility, the latter ". . . mother and head of all human virtues", are others of the virtues which von Hildebrand describes in this book. While the central presentation of these virtues is the traditional Christian one, it is illuminated by the experience and perception of the writer: analyzing, for example, the relationship between pride and concupiscence, von Hildebrand reveals the ego's perverse insistence on sensual proof of its eminence. Von Hildebrand insists everywhere on stressing the bearing which moral themes have on experiences, and he attempts to persuade the reader of the truth of these themes by verifying them in vivid life experiences. Sometimes he alludes to lives of saints; frequently he returns to Scripture to substantiate his analyses.

Although the book succeeds in circumventing the mechanistic in its approach, there is a logos revealed in its unfolding. So, for instance, it becomes apparent that the early part of the book, concerned as it is with man's spiritual rebirth and struggle toward a deeper supernatural life, does describe the person's ascetical effort. His growth in grace and beatitude, hungering and thirsting after justice, sorrowing and patient, does describe a purgative way; and the surrender of self and contemplation of Christ, a unitive one. Von Hildebrand, however, avoids plotting this pilgrimage in chronological stages, so that even in the early days of his search, "Once he is touched by the *lumen Christi* man will see the world with new eyes. A new light falls on everything, disclosing the secret ties of all reality to the divine essence."

Here and elsewhere in the book, von Hildebrand writes with the enthusiasm and style of the artist. Among the most persuasive pages in the book are those in the chapter called "Recollection and Contemplation" in which he writes lyrically about the "loving absorption in God." *Transformation in Christ* is a devotional study which succeeds in fusing with fervor Dietrich von Hildebrand's insights into the mysteries of man's life with God.

W.A.M.

THE MASS OF THE ROMAN RITE

Author: Josef Andreas Jungmann, S.J. (1889-1962)
Type of work: Liturgics
First published: 1949

Principal Ideas Advanced

The rite of the Roman Mass has undergone, during its history, numerous modifications varying the structure and ceremonies which surround the essential reenactment of the Last Supper.

These changes often reflected, and themselves modified, attitudes of contemporary popular piety and of theology.

The individual ceremonies of the Mass are of varying antiquity, and the individual history and development of each are here presented in detail.

Until relatively recent times, the professional liturgist was regarded in the Church as a sort of second-class citizen a "fringe element." Some Catholics felt suspicious of and resentful toward him, regarding him as an innovator, upsetting the long-established, familiar forms of worship. Others were smilingly indulgent, regarding him as a well-meaning but rather ineffectual student of archaeological curiosities, not very much in contact with real life.

True, the last century did feel some effects from the liturgical giants of the Benedictine Order, such as Dom Marmion and Dom Guéranger, but their influence was predominantly confined to monasteries and to certain elements of the clergy.

Recent years, however, have seen a notable increase in the growth and influence of the liturgical movement, in the United States as well as in Europe. The realization that the Christian life is essentially one of worship and that it is primarily in the official acts of worship of the Church that the Catholic nourishes and expresses this life has led to an increasing concern for the liturgy in the minds of Church scholars and pastors. How intimately were Catholics living this life of worship? How aware were they of it? To what extent had secondary, peripheral ceremonies, such as novenas and various private devotions, overshadowed or displaced in the minds of the faithful the fundamental sacred actions of the Mass and of the sacraments?

In response to these and other questions, a vast liturgical movement began, almost simultaneously, in many places. Liturgical publications and conferences multiplied, and were nourished by an ever-growing group of serious scholars and educators, intent upon making the Church's life of worship meaningful to twentieth century man. The liturgical movement was no longer confined to isolated monasteries, though in many cases these monasteries remained centers of influence in the development of chant, liturgical art, and scholarship. The European monasteries of Solesmes, Beuron, and Maria-Laach were outstanding, and they had their counterparts in America, as, for instance, at Collegeville in Minnesota. Many groups of teaching nuns in the United States were also eager to participate in the movement. Finally, the Jesuits, who traditionally had been considered men of action and scholarship, but hardly men of liturgy, began to make a significant contribution. This present work by Father Jungmann, S.J., is an outstanding example of their contribution and of the quality of the contemporary liturgical movement as a whole.

For most Catholics the liturgical movement was something of which they were only vaguely aware until very recent years, when they began to notice small changes being introduced into the ceremonies of the Mass and discovered that the liturgy of Holy Week had been profoundly revised. Many of the changes were associated with Pope John XXIII, though most of them had been prepared for or instituted under Pope Pius XII. The Ecumenical Council has further focused attention upon the liturgy and has authorized far-reaching changes in it. The average Catholic is likely to find himself somewhat ill-at-ease, confused, and even annoyed at some of these changes. He may even think of them as heretical innovations or perversions of Catholic worship "as he has known it." The point is that Catholic worship "as he has know it" is not the only form that Catholic worship has ever had, and a reading of the first part of Father Jungmann's book, *The Mass of the Roman Rite,* provides convincing evidence for this claim.

In the years prior to World War II, Father Josef Andreas Jungmann was a member of the Jesuit Theological Faculty in Innsbruck, Austria. He was charged with the instruction of young seminarians in the liturgy of the Mass, a task which he cherished. Then, in 1939 Hitler annexed Austria and closed the Jesuit College in Innsbruck. As a result, Jungmann found his teaching activities brought to an end. There still remained for him, however, the opportunity of serving God and the Church through quiet literary work, and this he resolved to pursue. With the collaboration of his superiors, he withdrew to Hainstetten, a tiny village on the Danube between Linz and Vienna, and there he passed the war years quietly but perseveringly working on this masterpiece, originally titled *Missarum solemnia.* As he was completing the final pages of the book in May of 1945, American troops arrived in the vicinity. The book first appeared in English translation in a two-volume edition of over one thousand pages in 1951 and 1955. The present edition of a single volume is a revision and abridgement of that work.

In Part One of his book Father Jungmann traces the form of the Mass through the centuries, starting with the Jewish Paschal liturgy of the Last Supper. The Apostles, for many reasons, dropped this original setting in carrying out Our Lord's command to "Do this for a commemoration of me."

There are indications, despite a paucity of evidence concerning the early liturgy, that the celebration in the early Church was associated with a common meal. This meal retained the pre-Christian, Jewish prayers of thanksgiving (eucharistia), introduced by an invitation from the host to the guests. This invitation seems to have fused, even at this early period, into the double exclamation, "*Sursum corda*" and "*Gratias agamus Domino Deo nostro,*" which we find, along with their corresponding answers, practically unaltered in all succeeding liturgical traditions (as in the Preface of today's Roman rite). The consecration of the bread, which originally was probably separated from that of the wine, seems to have been drawn together with it, and was placed directly after the narrative of the original institution of the sacrament.

Jungmann describes the changes of this period as follows: "Since, on the one hand, the prayer of thanks was thus enriched and rounded out and settled in form, and on the other, the growing communities became too large for these domestic table-gatherings, the supper-character of the Christian assembly could and did fall out, and the eucharistic celebration stood out as the proper form of divine worship. The tables disappeared from the room, except for the one at which the presiding official pronounced the eucharist over the bread and wine. The room was broadened into a large hall capable of holding the whole congregation. Only in isolated instances was the connection with a meal continued into the following centuries."

Another important innovation was the transfer of the celebration to the morning hours and to Sunday: "It was both the Jewish and hellenistic practice to hold the meal . . . at an evening hour, but once the meal disappeared there was nothing to hinder the choice of another time of the day for the celebration. Since Sunday, as the day of the Resurrection, was very early promoted as the day for the celebration, and attention was thus focused on the remembrance of the story of Redemption and especially of its glorious outcome, the next step was easy, namely, to transfer all to the morning hours, since it was in the morning before sunrise that Christ had risen from the dead. The earliest Easter celebration known to us was an evening celebration but it followed the time-schedule mentioned and its climax was not reached till early in the morning at cockcrow. Sunday service, too, would fit nicely into this scheme, for if one began to see in the sunrise a picture of Christ rising from the dead, one would lay considerable store in the notion of greeting Christ himself with the rising of the sun. And besides, as long as Christianity was not publicly acknowledged, the circumstances of the laborer's life would have urged the choosing of an hour outside the usual time of work."

Jungmann points out further details of Apostolic survival in modern liturgy: "If we thus see forming in this early period the large outlines of the later Mass-liturgy, there still remains the task of pointing out a great many details of a later and even present-day practice, in which, within the Mass celebration, a primitive and apostolic liturgy survives, a liturgy adapted by the Apostles from the usage of the synagogue. At the beginning came the greeting with *Dominus vobiscum* or a similar formula, the answer to which was the genuinely Hebraic *Et cum spiritu tuo.* The close of the prayer referred in some way to God's boundless dominion which lasts *in saecula saeculorum.* The stipulated answer of the people remained, in fact, untranslated: Amen. Thus with particular reference to the prayer of thanks, the general scheme remained unaltered, no matter how the contents changed."

A second stream of adaptation from the primitive Judeo-Christian community appears in the service of Biblical readings of the fore-Mass. The emergent Christian Church still retained a tie with the Temple, along with its own eucharistic gatherings. This tie entailed above all attendance at the synagogue for the Sabbath service, which was primarily a reading of the Scriptures. Only after the break with the synagogue, the result of the persecution of the year 44, did the hour of worship devoted to reading take on a distinctively Christian shape and gradually combine with the eucharistic celebration as the fore-Mass.

Saint Justin Martyr, who wrote his *First Apology* in Rome about 150, has preserved for us the earliest full account of a Christian Mass celebration. The description is valid immediately only for Rome, but since Justin traveled throughout the Christian world from East to West, its features were undoubtedly true, in the main, for the whole Christian world. The elements which stand out are: the readings and instruction based upon the memoirs of the Apostles and the prophets, the prayers of thanksgiving, responded to by "Amen" from the whole congregation, and the central consecration and distribution of the Eucharist to the faithful. We also find at this early date, along with the heavy accent on thanksgiving, definite expressions, though less frequent and less developed, of the sacrificial aspects of this central act of worship.

By the third century there was still no fixed formulary for the Mass-liturgy, but only a fixed framework which the celebrant filled out with his own words. There was still a great deal of elasticity and flexibility.

With the coming of the fourth century, however, an important differentiation occurred. In the organization of the Church, especially in the East, there gradually grew up, over and above the individual communities with their individual bishops, certain preponderant centers, especially Antioch and Alexandria. From these centers and their provincial synods, there radiated special legislation that in time gave a particular stamp to the Church life of those affected. Thus, too, divergent liturgies gradually acquired their fixed form.

Jungmann gives a concrete example of how such developments and embellishments occurred in the case of the liturgy of Saint Basil. This Basilian liturgy reveals a new trend which, as it grew, became a characteristic trait of all oriental liturgies. This trend was a growing consciousness of sin and a mounting reverence in the presence of the great mystery, a trend which, as

Jungmann says, increased "to almost gloomy proportions."

Two results followed from this new emphasis, especially in the Orient. One was a decline in the frequency of communion out of excessive reverence. The other was the increasing splendor of the vestments and ceremonies.

Up to this point we have been speaking of liturgies expressed in Greek. There were also liturgies in Aramaic (Syriac), Arabic, Ethiopic, Old Slavonic, and Armenian. Jungmann mentions all of these briefly, but they are not his principal concern.

A Latin Christianity makes its first appearance in North Africa, about the close of the second century, at a time when, in Rome itself, Greek was still the standard liturgical language. Paradoxically enough, although we possess valuable early descriptions, by Justin and others, of the Greek period of the Roman Mass, the early history of the Latin Mass in Rome and in the West in general is dim and uncertain until the sixth century. The liturgies of the West seem to have undergone a development similar to those in the East, whose variety we have already noted. There was one important difference, however: in the West, Latin, which was the sole language of cultured persons during this period, was retained as the only language of the liturgy.

The Mass-liturgies of the West are broadly divisible into two families, the Roman-African and the Gallic. No complete text of the African Mass has come down to us, but it seems to have coincided closely with the Roman. The Gallic liturgies had four main subdivisions: the Gallican, the Celtic, the Old Spanish (also called Mozarabic), and the Milanese or Ambrosian. The last two are still celebrated today, though in small, restricted areas. The Gallican liturgy itself did not last long. In France, the lack of any regulating center and the resulting multiplicity of forms brought on a growing distaste for this particular liturgy, so that by the eighth century the Roman rite was being substituted for it. The Roman rite also spread to the British Isles and to Spain.

The period from the third to the sixth century marks the change-over from Greek to Latin in the Roman Church. It probably was a long, gradual process, with many intermediate forms, but we know almost nothing of the details. Jungmann regards as certain, however, that "the core of our Mass canon, from the *Ouam oblationem* on, including the sacrificial prayer after the consecration, was already in existence by the end of the fourth century." Jungmann further concludes that the framework of the Roman Mass must have been essentially determined by the turn of the fifth century, at least as regards the public utterance of prescribed prayers by the priest.

The fifth century was one of great calamity for the city of Rome, as was the following century, with its Gothic threat and its Lombard invasion. Yet it was in this very period that Roman worship unfolded into ever-increasing splendor. This fact was closely linked with the extraordinary esteem which the Church and the papacy acquired in the Eternal City during these years. The papacy had become the one and only pride and glory of the Roman population. As the pope assumed more and more the support, defense, and administration of the afflicted city, the papal church service became the prime expression of civic life. Jungmann describes a papal stational Mass of this period in all its magnificent completeness and detail.

This Roman Mass was imported into Franco-German territory during the Carolingian era. There it acted upon and was acted upon by the native liturgies. This long and intricate interaction lasted over several centuries.

Out of this shaping and shifting of liturgical forms in the Carolingian territories, a new Mass rite of the Romano-Frankish type was produced. It was both rich in content and sharp in structure, and it soon won widespread acceptance. And here, in Jungmann's words, we come to one of the curiosities of Church history: "Thus we come to that episode which proved to be of such incalculable importance for the entire subsequent history of the Roman liturgy. About the middle of the tenth century the Roman liturgy began to return in force from Franco-German lands to Italy and to Rome, but it is a liturgy which meanwhile had undergone radical changes and a great development. This importation entailed supplanting the local form of the Roman liturgy by its Gallicized version, even at the very center of Christendom."

Throughout the Middle Ages, however, a wide divergence of customs prevailed. One finds a phrase of Saint Gregory the Great cited over and over again: ". . . as long as the Church preserves one faith, there is nothing inconsistent about a divergence of customs."

It was the monasteries which first introduced a more rigid discipline, especially the Benedictines and the Carthusians. The itinerant orders also exerted a strong influence, in particular the Franciscans, who, after first following the liturgical customs of the various localities they visited, finally adopted for themselves the "Missal according to the Rite of the Roman Curia." This type of missal was carried all over the world by the wandering mendicant Friars, and soon became the predominant type of Mass book in Christendom.

Medieval theology and popular reactions led to still further changes, with a new emphasis on the adoration of the Blessed Sacrament. This period also saw the appearance of numerous exaggerations and bizarre magical beliefs regarding the fruits of the Mass, several of which Father Jungmann cites.

Fortunately, the sixteenth century saw the liturgical reforms of the Council of Trent and of Pope Pius V, as well as the establishment of the Congregation of Rites by Pope Sixtus V.

Jungmann also traces the liturgy of the Mass through the exuberance of the Baroque period and the efforts at a return to "noble simplicity" during the Enlightenment. He describes the Baroque period as compared with the late Middle Ages, as follows: "The great abuses have all disappeared. But still the Mass remains a service in which only the priest and his assistants have an active role. The faithful follow the divine action only from a distance."

The activities of nineteenth century liturgists, like Dom Prosper Guéranger, were not free from opposition and controversy, but Jungmann sums up their effect as follows: "It led to a knowledge of the ways and means to bridge, at least in some scant manner, the thousand-year-old cleft between the Mass-liturgy and the people. . . ."

Pope Pius X's efforts at promoting frequent communion certainly encouraged the individual Catholic toward a closer participation in the sacrifice of the Mass, and the whole general trend of the twentieth century liturgical movement has been toward the laity's more intimate sharing in the sacred action. It is this spirit which motivates all the efforts toward common song and prayer, toward use of the vernacular, and toward actual modification of the ceremonies, as in the Holy Week liturgy.

Such is the fascinating story of the evolution of the Roman Mass, although we have been able to give it here only in its barest outlines. It is a story which will provide many interesting surprises for the average Catholic. The spontaneous assumption of most of us is that the Mass has always been as we have known it since we were children. A more accurate acquaintance with its history should make us more open to and less upset by possible changes.

In the second part of Father Jungmann's monumental work he discusses the nature and forms of the Mass, and in the third and fourth parts he discusses in detail the individual ceremonies of the Mass. "In detail" here means in the detail which we habitually associate with the Germanic temperament. Each separate prayer and action is traced in its historical origins and development, from the putting on of the sacred vestments to the priest's departure from the altar. The treatment extends over 365 pages.

This last part of the book is obviously of interest primarily to the expert or the specialist, but its exhaustive detail makes the book ideal as a library reference book or as a gift to a priest or religious.

E.L.B.

SEEDS OF CONTEMPLATION

Author: Thomas Merton (1915-)
Type of work: Spiritual reflections
First published: 1949

Principal Ideas Advanced

The fullness of the Christian life comes in contemplation.

The saint, by detachment from things, and solitude, finds that all creatures are holy and that he is one with all men in the Mystical Body of Christ.

To attain union with God we need God's grace but spiritual gifts can constitute a new and subtler temptation.

We are enslaved by material goods when we regard them as ends rather than means; somewhat similarly, if a man takes pride in what God works in his soul, love of God becomes self-love and is aborted.

Charity relates one to God as the supreme and common good of all men.

Thomas Merton says of *Seeds of Contemplation* that it is the kind of book that almost writes itself in a monastery. Nevertheless, few such books are published and few that are as effective as his. If a genre for this book be sought it would be that which includes Pascal's *Pensées* and Thomas à Kempis's *Imitation of Christ.* The *Seeds of Contemplation* is a devotional work, a collection of thoughts on spiritual development, a work written *ad seipsum* and then published in the hope that its thoughts would find receptive hearts. Who is a receptive reader of *Seeds of Contemplation?* Not the scholar, surely, nor the dilettante who would seek in it aesthetic enjoyment. This is not to say that one interested in developing a doctrine of the spiritual life would not find much in this work, and surely one who approached it aesthetically would be pleased by the style, by the arrangement of the series of meditations which constitutes not so much an argument as a melodic line. Such readers would get something from *Seeds of Contemplation,* but they are not the readers the book seeks. "For this is the kind of book that achieves an effect that is not and cannot be controlled by any human author," Merton writes; "If you can bring yourself, somehow, to read it in communion with the God in Whose Presence it was written, it will interest you and you will probably draw some fruit from it, more by His grace than by the author's efforts. But if you cannot read it under these conditions, no doubt the book will be at least a novelty." These words remind one of Søren Kierkegaard's descriptions of his work as aiming at an effect intended to be edifying, an effect, consequently, over which he as human author had little or no control. Merton's *Seeds of Contemplation* presupposes the Gospels, the Rule of Saint Benedict, and the Catholic tradition of asceticism. It attempts to speak to those who want to reach the fulfillment of the Christian life, a fulfillment Merton identifies with contemplation.

There is a triad which functions in *Seeds of Contemplation,* three terms whose proper relationship is sought: man, God, and creatures. Each term becomes paradoxical when viewed in the Christian perspective. Man is the house of a soul called to a supernatural life, to union with God, and this is not a destiny which simply awaits man in the afterlife. It is a goal men must seek and to a degree reach in the present life. This destiny of his soul makes man problematic because he is body and soul. Is the body to be contemned, distrusted, hated? Can God be loved by bypassing his creatures or must man relate himself to God through creatures? The seeming detour is for men the only direct route. Creatures present themselves as the means but also as possible impediments to an ascent to God. What is the proper attitude toward our human nature in its entirety? What is the proper attitude toward material creatures? What is the proper relation to God? These questions may be said to present the themes of this little book, and its message emerges as a call to a difficult balance of these three initially ambivalent terms.

The world around us functions sacramentally, says Merton. Each event, each creature, is at once itself and a reminder of God and our vocation to union with Him. God addresses us through the created world, and we must make ourselves free to listen to Him there. Paradoxically, these very creatures can enslave us and make us deaf to their further message; our lives may come to be defined by the pursuit of pleasure, wealth, or success. This slavery to things consists in overlooking their place in the created universe. We are not emancipated by despising creatures. Everything that is, is holy. According to the author "The saint knows that the world and everything made by God is good, while those who are not saints either think that created things are unholy, or else they don't bother about the question one way or another because they are only interested in themselves." Each creature praises God, and when creatures are seen in this perspective they do not enslave us but fulfill their true role.

Creatures less than man are good simply by being, writes Merton, but man must become what he is called to be. He must discover what he is supposed to be, and this calls for withdrawal, solitude, meditation. Yet one fruit of this withdrawal is or should be the realization that one's perfection cannot be considered atomically, in separation from other men and other creatures. We are members of one body, of Christ, and perfection of the self is gained in forgetfulness of self. Perfection is not solitary, idiosyncratic, centripetal; the self is a focal point of love which must radiate outward to other men and which draws what light and heat it has from a source that is not the self. Merton emphasizes this central and paradoxical truth of Christian perfection. It is by losing our life that we gain life. Enlightened self-interest is disinterest in self, for the object of Christian love is not one that can be mine exclusively. The man who loves God must love Him as the good of all men, and any love of God which does not want Him to be shared by all men is not love of God but self-love.

According to Merton, the soul must go through a purgation if it is to become capable of this love, and this is not a task we can perform by ourselves; we must depend on God's help to love God. It is difficult and painful to turn from creatures as final objects of desire although, once more, this turning away from creatures is but another way to turn toward them. Philosophers have shown that evildoing cannot be constitutive of happiness for men; concern with creatures as ultimate objects of quest leads to despair. But what we need is not the abstract argument but the realization that this is so. Sin is no delight. Christianity does not take the joy out of life; it is the path to true joy, but a path which leads through intermediate pain when God teaches us not to be bound by creatures but to see them as opportunities of ordering ourselves to their source.

Seeds of Contemplation strikes warning notes that are sounded in the writings of mystics and which cause worldly souls to tremble. At the outset the move we are asked to make seems simple; there is a hurdle we have to cross and beyond it all is serenity and peace. We would like to think that there is some spiritual technique which, if properly learned, could put us in possession, once and for all, of Christian perfection. Break the shackles that bind us to creatures wrongly viewed, overcome sensuality and achieve a realization of the pre-eminence of spiritual goods, and the combat is over. But Merton and the mystics warn us that this is not so. Spiritual goods themselves, being created participations, can constitute a new and subtler danger.

Mystics tell us of wonderful experiences and extraordinary gifts which God chooses to bestow on them, and it is easy for us to think that they are an elect to whom further temptation is practically impossible. Yet the soul, the mystics say, must pass through many stages. He must run the risk of taking pride in his achievements as if they were gifts deserved rather than quite gratuitous. *Corruptio optimi pessima.* The thought that one who has received spiritual gifts of an unimaginable order may plummet to a depth worse than his original condition of worldliness is a vertiginous one. Fear and trembling are concomitants and, it appears, constant companions on the path of love. We find this repellent; we experience what spiritual writers call *acedia,* a distaste for spiritual things. But to live is to run the risk of failure and the more intense our life the greater the possible failure. The clue such writers as Merton offer is an ever-increasing absorption in God, an achieved indifference even to the perfection acquired, the virtues won. Every good gift is granted by the Father of Lights and there must be a continuing transcendence of the created toward the Creator even when the creature in question is a perfection of the soul. Virtues and gifts are not the objects of the quest; they are means toward union with God.

R.M.

PEACE OF SOUL

Author: Fulton J. Sheen (1895-)
Type of work: Apologetics
First published: 1949

Principal Ideas Advanced

Although in earlier times the mind advanced to God from a consideration of the external world, the condition of modern man makes it advisable to find the need for God in an examination of man himself.

Psychiatry and psychoanalysis are too often considered as panaceas which will enable man to find true peace; insofar as these techniques call into question moral responsibility and guilt they represent an impediment to the realization of man's true nature.

There is a restlessness of the human heart which can be replaced by true peace only when man turns in conversion to God and is elevated to the supernatural life.

In *Peace of Soul* the then Monsignor, now Bishop, Fulton J. Sheen attempts an apologetics which, like any effective communication, addresses its readers as they are and not as they might be. There was a time, and Bishop Sheen suggests it was far from being a worse time, when men could be made receptive for conversion by drawing their attention to the physical world whose order and intricacy invite the mind to ascend to God the Creator. For a number of reasons modern man is cut off from this easy access to the world around him. Technology's control over natural forces has given nature the aspect of menace rather than sacrament and vestige of God. Moreover, modern man has come to view himself as a layered thing with the secret springs of his conscious choices buried in a subconscious with inexorable laws of its own. Bishop Sheen proposes to take man, divided man, frustrated man, as the starting point of a discussion which will lead to God.

The three marks of modern man are self-estrangement, isolation from fellow men, and estrangement from God. Bishop Sheen finds analogues for each of these notes in New Testament incidents of possessed people and suggests that the plight of modern man is not wholly new. The anxiety and psychic depression modern man feels is that any man of any time must feel if he ceases to war against the Devil, the flesh, and the world: "Pride, lust, avarice; the devil, the flesh and the world; the pride of life, the concupiscence of the flesh and the concupiscence of the eyes—these constitute the new unholy trinity by which man is wooed away from the Holy Trinity and from the discovery of the goal of life." Love of self and love of person and love of property are not in themselves evil; it is only their abuse which turns men from God to frustration and anxiety. The choice for man is not between a mindlessness or God, or a joyful selfish acquisitiveness or God. It is rather a question of God or despair, anguish, and frustration. The polar answer of the Church to the unholy trinity are the religious vows of obedience, chastity, and poverty. But every man must learn to control his desires, transfer his concern from his body to his soul, and increase his trust in God. According to the author, "Peace of soul comes to those who have the right kind of anxiety about attaining perfect happiness, which is God. A soul has anxiety because its final and eternal state is not yet decided; it is still and always at the crossroads of life. This fundamental anxiety cannot be cured by a surrender to passions and instincts; the basic cause of our anxiety is a restlessness within time which comes because we are made for eternity." The restlessness of the human heart will cease only when we rest in God.

There is a real conflict within man which is not a consequence of personal sins but of original sin. Man must rectify this disorder in himself but he cannot do it without God's help. It is easy to want to be saved and, Bishop Sheen writes, we want to be saved, but not from our sins; we want to be saved, but not at too great a cost; we want to be saved in our own way, not God's. But the greatest impediment to salvation is the denial of guilt, the attempt to trace our apparent faults to the faults of others. When guilt is not denied, it can be salutary, but denial of guilt, the suppression of the sense of responsibility, brings on morbidity and mental illness: "*Nice* people must see themselves as nasty people before they can find peace."

It will be appreciated that Bishop Sheen is proceeding on a parallel with certain psychological theories and offering an alternative to them. In a very real sense *Peace of Soul* is an attack on materialist psychologies and psychoanalytic theories, although there is no total reduction of mental illness to spiritual disorder. Thus, Bishop Sheen discusses the examination of conscience and confession and compares them with psychoanalysis: "Our particular concern here, as usual, is not with either psychiatry or psychoanalytic method, both of which are valid in their spheres. We limit the discussion solely to that single psychoanalytic group who assert these things: Man is an animal; there is no personal responsibility and therefore no guilt; the psychoanalytic method is a substitute for confession." The chapter on confession as over against analysis is one of the best in the book. The confession of sins to the priest is done out of need to avow the wrongs one has committed, with a view to receiving pardon. In psychoanalysis there is a revelation of certain unconscious attitudes; in confession there is the avowal of conscious guilt. One does not seek pardon in analysis, nor does it ask much of our pride. The admission of sin is always accompanied by shame. In confession one is measuring himself against a moral standard that is given, and the recitation can be brief and abstract. In much analysis no standard is assumed, and the narration becomes interminable and detailed. In confession the telling of sins is to a representative of the moral order; the analyst represents the emotional order by way of the process of transference. Finally, in confession forgiveness can be had, grace to change one's life.

Peace of Soul begins by suggesting that nowadays the approach to God is best made by accepting modern man's introspective concern with a shattered self. This self is the target of psychiatry and psychoanalysis and Bishop Sheen wants first to separate true mental illness from sin. He exhibits an animus against efforts to reduce human personality to a number of blind forces which, beneath the level of consciousness, produce the deeds we call our own as well as the reasons we think prompt our acts. In short, he sees some psychiatry and some psychoanalysis as constituting an assault on moral responsibility such that the concept of sin is lost and with it the possibility of remorse and conversion. It is this that leads to a confrontation of the confessional and the analyst's couch. The central point Bishop Sheen wants to make is that without a realization of sin, of responsibility, or guilt, the sinner forecloses the hope of conversion. *Peace of Soul* reaches its climax with discussions of the psychology, the theology, and the effects of conversion.

By the psychology of conversion, Bishop Sheen means the antecedents of conversion, and he cites two: a sense of conflict or crisis, and a strong desire to be united with God. The kind of crisis meant is that in which one becomes aware of his own helplessness and dependence on a higher cause. The crisis may be moral, spiritual, or physical, and it sets up a tension in which the soul feels pursued by God and may then come to long for God: "Conversion does not automatically follow on this longing; unless the desire for God is stronger than old habits and passions, the crisis of desire can end in frustration, the grace of conversion can pass." Peace of soul comes within reach with Baptism and the elevation to the supernatural life, the life of grace. The effects of conversion are the recentering of one's life, the acquisition of a new set of values and a definite change in the conduct of one's life.

Peace of Soul occupies a territory between exhortation and argument, persuasion and doctrine. In treating of psychology, psychiatry, and psychoanalysis, Bishop Sheen is to a great degree content to accept the popular interpretation of them and use that interpretation as a take-off point to remind the intelligent and receptive reader that there is no peace of mind which can replace the peace of soul which is possible only when man sees himself as a creature called to a supernatural destiny. The weaknesses of *Peace of Soul,* its simplifications, may be its greatest strengths as an effort in persuasion. The author is less concerned to remove misconceptions of psychoanalysis than he is to address the further misconception that for man there can be any true peace apart from God.

R.M.

ENTHUSIASM

Author: Ronald Knox (1888-1957)
Type of work: Philosophy of religion
First published: 1950

Principal Ideas Advanced

There is a tendency which runs through the history of Christianity which may be called "enthusiasm" and which consists of the revolt of the charismatic against the institutional.

The enthusiast is an ultrasupernaturalist who rejects the traditional doctrine of grace and thereby becomes a paradoxical mixture of rigorist and antinomian.

Anti-intellectualism is also a mark of enthusiasm, and the enthusiast is as a rule deaf to theology.

Christianity is largely a matter of balance, and the enthusiast upsets the balance by emphasizing and exaggerating some one aspect of Christian belief, with the result that the whole is distorted.

Monsignor Ronald A. Knox tells us that he devoted thirty years to the writing of *Enthusiasm* and that in his career as author, a career which includes such monumental contributions as a translation of the Bible as well as some not inconsiderable detective fiction, this book was always for him *the* book, the one he wanted most to write and to the writing of which he devoted what time he could find among his many other duties over the years. The title, *Enthusiasm,* is immediately informative to scholars but may seem a trifle playful to the uninstructed; Knox would have liked to have been wanting enough in sensibility to have entitled his work *Ultrasupernaturalism.* Knox wanted to supply the word "enthusiasm" with a definition at once informative and supple enough to designate a drift, a possibility, a tendency which has been present since New Testament times, despite the fact that it seems to have been most evident during the seventeenth and eighteenth centuries.

What does Monsignor Knox mean by *enthusiasm?* He is out to deal with a phenomenon he describes as an elusive tendency. It is perhaps not unfair to say that Knox intended to speak of Superchristians. The enthusiast Knox is concerned with in his book is the Christian who becomes chary of organized, institutional Christianity, of sacraments and ritual, of anything which threatens to stifle a spontaneous religiosity. Knox writes: "You have a clique, an elite, of Christian men and (more importantly) women, who are trying to live a less worldly life than their neighbors; to be more attentive to the guidance (directly felt, they would tell you) of the Holy Spirit. More and more, by a kind of fatality, you see them draw apart from their co-religionists, a hive ready to swarm. There is provocation on both sides; on the one part, cheap jokes at the expense of over-godliness, acts of stupid repression by unsympathetic authorities; on the other, contempt of the half-Christian, ominous references to old wine and new bottles, to the kernel and the husk. Then, while you hold your breath and turn away your eyes in fear, the break comes; condemnation or secession, what difference does it make? A fresh name has been added to the list of Christianities."

Knox sees in the history of Christianity a series of such protests of the charismatic against the institutional, with the charismatic itself becoming institutional and providing a springboard for another charismatic outbreak. This occurs not so much at the center as on the border of Christianity and it is not confined to the Catholic Church, since the phenomenon has been at least equally evident among Protestants. The theory that enthusiasm is a recurrent phenomenon in Church history may strike one as a rather sweeping theory, springing from the *a priori,* but given the way in which this book came to be written, it seems safe to assume that the wider theory was a consequence of Knox's careful research and not of the almost indiscernible thread he initially set out to follow. We can imagine that what caught his interest first was not the "fugal melody which runs through the centuries" but the historical phenomenon, not yet seen as the vehicle of a historical theory, whereby some Christians become suspicious of a religion which is commodious enough to include all kinds, saints and sinners, ascetics and those who, in one of the felicitous phrases with which the book abounds, wish only to qualify and not to excel. The enthusiast is pained by the watering down of the Gospel message, the extenuations and accommodations he finds rampant. Away with the world, then, they cry—away with marriage, away with ritual and hierarchy! The painful result is that other Christians who find "enthusiasm" guilty of exaggeration rather than falsehood find themselves aligned with real enemies of religion in their censures of the enthusiast.

A paradoxical feature of enthusiasm, as Knox views it, is the way in which an extreme rigorism often goes hand in hand with antinomianism, so that a given cult may at once condemn marriage and practise licentiousness. This paradoxical conclusion follows from a rejection of the traditional notion of the supernatural which sees the supernatural as built on nature, elevating nature to the life of grace. Thus, for example, conjugal love is elevated in the sacrament of Matrimony. For the enthusiast, or at least for many representatives of the tendency, the body has no part in the spiritual life; marriage is to be set aside, although sexual immorality is not regarded as bad because it fails to touch the essence of the religious commitment, which is spiritual. Another manifestation of this same attitude is anti-intellectualism, which Knox finds to be a mark of enthusiasm. The natural intellect, like the body, becomes an object of suspicion, and the enthusiast is not open to the suggestion that the intellect enables man to find a link between the world and the God of belief. Religious experience takes place in an arena into which the mind cannot meaningfully intrude. Politically, the enthusiast shows a penchant for theocracy and, despairing of establishing this on the wider scene, is prone to withdraw and form special communities where all citizens are members of the sect and where righteousness can reign.

Having attempted a definition by way of character sketch of the enthusiast, Knox goes on to tell the history of enthusiasm. His first discussion takes for its point of departure Saint Paul's first epistle to the Corinthians. Knox finds in Paul's letter to the Church at Corinth a concern for an incipient enthusiasm. Knox sees in the practices at Corinth signs of factionalism, antinomianism, rigorism, and greediness over the Gift of the Spirit. In short, the seeds of enthusiasm were present in Corinth.

In succeeding chapters, Knox discusses Montanism, Donatism, and medieval heresies. In the main part of the book, he deals with such topics as the Anabaptists and the Reformation, Quakerism, Jansenism, Quietism, Malaval, Petrucci and Molinos; Fenelon and Madame Guyon; the French Prophets, the Convulsionaries of Saint-Medard, Moravianism, and, in the longest treatment in the book, John Wesley.

It will be appreciated that it would be pointless to try to résumé a work of such broad canvas where detail must bear the burden. Fortunately, Monsignor Knox concludes his book with a chapter on the philosophy of enthusiasm and, with a reminder that this comes after the lengthy and nuanced discussions mentioned above, we can profitably consider how the author summarizes the phenomenon whose historian he is.

Knox advances the theory that at the source of enthusiasm is the revolt of Platonism against Aristotelianism. He writes: "Your Platonist, satisfied that he has formed his notion of God without the aid of syllogisms or analogies, will divorce reason from religion; it is a faculty concerned with the life of the senses, and nothing assures us that it can penetrate upwards; he is loth to theologize." For the enthusiast, prayer will seek to be void of images, mental or otherwise, and interior worship is the thing. Enthusiasm reveals itself in two kinds of spirituality, evangelical and mystical, the one too generous to ask for salvation, the other too humble to ask for anything else. "More generally characteristic of ultrasupernaturalism is a distrust of human thought-processes," Knox continues; "In matters of abstract theology, the discipline of the intellect is replaced by a blind act of faith. In matters of practical deliberation, some sentiment of inner conviction, or some external 'sign' indicative of the Divine will, claims priority over all considerations of common prudence."

Enthusiasm is a work of erudition which is never stuffy, a work of appraisal which is always informed and never harsh, a delight to read. Knox stresses that Christianity is a matter of balances, and basically he finds that what he calls enthusiasm consists of an imbalance resulting for an exaggerated emphasis on one facet of Christianity.

R.M.

THE END OF TIME

Author: Josef Pieper (1904-)
Type of work: Philosophy of history
First published: 1950

Principal Ideas Advanced

Ages of uncertainty lead one to ponder the meaning of history, as well as one's own position vis-à-vis the world.

It is impossible to philosophize about history without returning to revealed truth.

The presupposition of both the philosophy and theology of history is faith; that is, receptive acceptance of the revealed word concerning history.

Every view of history is determined by some sort of conception of its beginning and end.

The end of history can be known only darkly through prophecy.

Josef Pieper is one of Germany's outstanding Thomist philosophers. His earlier publications closely followed the thought of Saint Thomas Aquinas, but participation in World War II and the uncertainty of life immediately after it led Pieper to explore a branch of philosophy to which the Angelic Doctor gave scant attention: philosophy of history.

In order to keep philosophy a self-contained subject, one school of philosophers accepts as data only what can be demonstrably known by natural reason. Pieper argues against them that one can use theological data, known not by natural reason but by revelation, as long as he thinks *philosophically* rather than *theologically* about such data. Without such data received on faith, he argues, a philosophy of history is impossible.

A philosophy of history must be concerned with historical knowledge by inquiring into the meaning of historical events. But this is not enough. A philosophy of history must also be concerned with the beginning and the end of history, neither of which man has witnessed. Our limited knowledge of the beginning and the end of history comes only from what God has revealed to us about them. Therefore, Pieper concludes, "a philosophizing which refuses to be methodologically open toward theology and to reach an understanding with it, is quite simply unphilosophical."

A philosophy of history cannot ignore salvation and disaster, "this core of history which is accessible only to the believer." If it does ignore the mystery of salvation and disaster, a philosophy of history becomes only a study of culture. Again, a philosophy of history deals with man made in the image of God but afflicted by the results of original sin; the concept of man is based not on natural reason but on revelation.

The future, as well as the past, must be encompassed by a philosophy of history. But the future cannot be known by statistics or calculation, for the essence of history is freedom, decision, uniqueness, unrepeatability, and unpredictable capacity for variation; the future can be known only by prophecy. Such knowledge, however, must always remain opaque until the prophecy has been realized. Nevertheless, enough has been revealed about the end of history to enable the philosopher to "observe historical events and formations from the vantage point of the End," and thus to know more profoundly the meaning of history.

Pieper puts forward the Scholastic argument that there can be no end of historical creatures in the sense of annihilation, for only the Creator can turn creatures back into nothingness, and this, we are assured by faith, He will not do. The author speaks of "an End after which there will no longer be time or history." This involves the transposition of the temporal into the untemporal, which "can be conceived only as affected by a direct intervention of the Creator."

The author centers his attention on Kant and Fichte in his discussion of the "Progress view of history." This view is analyzed as a secularization of the traditional Christian view of history. It makes the goal or end of history a perfect society to be realized in the future, sometime *within* history. This optimistic progress view of history has given way to an extreme pessimism, which is equally far from the Christian view of the end of history.

We know from revelation, Pieper claims, that the end of history will be catastrophic. In traditional Christian thought, indeed, the end-period of history is known as the Dominion of Antichrist. Pieper devotes the last chapter of this work to a meditation on the Antichrist, relying primarily on the Apocalypse but drawing from many later writers in the Christian tradition.

The Antichrist is not to be thought of as a purely spiritual being. He will be a historically powerful figure, even though we know he is "fundamentally already defeated." He will be a world ruler, and the possibility of the Gospel's being preached to all nations will have been realized. The Antichrist will be a Jew, and the Jews will be the first to receive him. He will appeal to men because of his sham sanctity. He will be lord of the world, and the enemy of the world will be the Church, which will undergo terrible persecutions directed against all men of good will. But in the end Antichrist will be defeated and the goal of history will be realized.

T.P.N.

THE MYSTERY OF BEING

Author: Gabriel Marcel (1889-   )
Type of work: Religious metaphysics
First published: Volume I, 1950; Volume II, 1951

PRINCIPAL IDEAS ADVANCED

In the broken world of today, man must regather all his resources by the exercise of a kind of reflection whereby he becomes aware of his true being and its possibilities.

By exercising this reflection, man will discover that he participates in a community of persons and, as an incarnate being, in the material world.

This experience of participation will lead him to an awareness of a fullness of being, an awareness which is the clearest evidence for the existence of a transcendent Person, who guarantees the bonds uniting man to being.

When this transcendent Person (God) is thus viewed in relation to the order of persons, the meaning of such traditional religious concepts as prayer, sin, humility, faith, hope, and charity can be more adequately expressed.

The two volumes entitled *The Mystery of Being* contain the series of lectures given by Gabriel Marcel as the Gifford Lecturer at Aberdeen University in 1949 and 1950. Of all the books published by Marcel, this work most closely approaches a systematic development of his concrete philosophy, since his other philosophical writings are either collections of separate essays and lectures, or journals of his philosophical inquiries. In this work, moreover, are found the concepts which have affected a large number of contemporary philosophers and theologians, particularly within the Catholic intellectual world.

Volume I, subtitled "Reflection and Mystery," which deals with the meaning of man as being in the world, develops the general approaches to the mystery of the human person which will be applied to more specific problems in Volume II, subtitled "Faith and Reality." The major theme of this second volume is the meaning of man in his relationship to an order which transcends his being in the world; namely, to the order of love, faith, grace, and freedom. The entire work is, in Marcel's word, "a search for, or an investigation into, the essence of spiritual reality."

To understand the significance of what, from a superficial reading, might appear rambling and unphilosophical, one must first grasp the method used by Marcel in pursuing these inquiries. His philosophy of the concrete is not aimed at the articulation of a logically connected system of concepts which would exhaust the meaning of the realities being investigated. Like Socrates, Marcel's main concern is to entice his readers to confront themselves and their experience; his philosophy "is essentially of the nature of a kind of appeal to the listener or the reader, of a kind of call upon his inner resources. In other words, such a philosophy could never be completely embodied into a kind of dogmatic exposition of which the listener or reader would merely have to grasp the content." To engage with Marcel in his philosophical method is like setting out on a journey towards a goal only vaguely anticipated; it is like engaging in conversation with a friend when both parties are attempting, in a spirit of truth, to arrive at the meaning of their lives.

The journey upon which Marcel invites his readers to embark proceeds by way of what he calls "secondary reflection" as opposed to "primary reflection." Primary reflection, our normal way of thinking, is directed at an analysis of objects, at a conceptual representation of things. It is the method of the empirical sciences. Primary reflection may be employed in relation to man himself when he is considered as an object, as, for example, when he is described in terms of his job, his family, his temperament, his abilities, and so forth, or when the empirical sciences analyze the structure of his body, the types of reactions he experiences, or the patterns of his social interaction. But there is another sort of knowledge which is directed not at objects but at the self as subject and at other persons as objects. This secondary reflection transcends the objective, analytical modes of thought which are incapable of confronting the most crucial questions about human life. It is a "recuperative" mode of thought inasmuch as it restores man's consciousness of himself as a unified self beyond all the fragmentary "objective" categories imposed upon him; it is "a kind of inward regrouping of one's resources, or a kind of ingatheredness. . . ."

One who rises to the level of secondary reflection is led to the discovery of certain essential aspects of his personal reality. Among these is the "exigence of transcendence," a complex dynamism in man which takes him out of himself. At a basic level, it is revealed as the immediate relation of man to other persons and to objects in the world. On this level, the exigence is similar to what Edmund Husserl (1859-1938), the German phenomenologist, called "intentionality," that characteristic whereby man participates in the other as other. On a higher level, this exigence is man's radical dissatisfaction with any state of achievement in his being, his desire always to go beyond himself. From one aspect, this desire is the "spirit of truth," the drive towards authenticity, which conflicts with other inherent desires and prejudices. Further, it is what Marcel calls the "ontological exigence," the drive towards fullness, conceived not as static perfection, but as a goal always beyond man's earthly reach. Still further, it is like hope, since it is the drive which sustains man, the wayfarer, in spite of the manifold sources of pessimism and despair. And finally, the exigence of transcendence is the desire for nothing less than a personal encounter with God himself.

Continuing to use secondary reflection, one discovers a relationship to one's body different from that relationship revealed by primary reflection, which treats the body as an object, as something that I "have." Secondary reflection reveals that I *am* my body; that which I call *my* body is an integral part of my person. It is this analysis which rejects any idea of the person as being veiled by the body. The other person is known by his gestures, his smile, his words; one need not deduce that behind the gesture, the smile, the word, there exists another person. *My* body, precisely because it is *mine,* and not an object I possess, is the medium whereby I am inserted into the world, whereby I participate in matter, even though I am also in the order of spirit. This participation occurs by way of "feeling," as man opens himself to the world in a spirit of "creative receptivity."

Pursuing his search into the meaning of man by way of secondary reflection, Marcel reaches his central insight that man cannot discover the meaning of his own life outside the bond which unites him to other persons and, ultimately, to the transcendent Person. Until man opens himself to other persons in the attitude Marcel calls "availability," he cannot discover the real meaning of his own experience; he cannot even exercise the recuperative power inherent in secondary reflection. Because "we can understand ourselves by starting from the other, or from others, and only by starting from them. . . ," Marcel contends that the basic metaphysical datum is "We are," as opposed to the "I think" upon which René Descartes constructed his system. Only within this context of intersubjectivity can one attain the fullness of experience which is a prerequisite for the development of any philosophy. It is from this standpoint of intersubjectivity that Marcel approaches all his philosophical themes. His notion of being, for example, is derived from the experience of the interpersonal bond: *"I concern myself with being only in so far as I have a more or less distinct consciousness of the underlying unity which ties me to other beings of whose reality I already have a preliminary notion."* The more one opens himself to the influence of others, the richer becomes his consciousness of existing. The experience of being is an experience of fullness, and of the sort of fullness which is derived from a reciprocal love, without which man would not even question being, for love is the recognition of the other, not as a conceptual object, but in its concrete totality.

Marcel reaches the most profound application of his metaphysics of intersubjectivity when he addresses himself to those themes wherein philosophical research dovetails into religious belief. His reflections on faith, for example, conclude that this central act of religion is not the adherence to a set of abstract propositions; it is, rather, the commitment to a Person, involving all the consequences which such a commitment normally entails. Faith is not, as Friedrich Nietzsche and Jean-Paul Sartre would claim, a dehumanizing act. It is, for the true believer, a "personalizing act," in the words of Jean Mouroux, following the inspiration of Marcel. It is like the commitment of a mother to her son, of husband to wife. When faith is considered as the opening of oneself to God, conceived not as an Aristotelian Prime Mover but as a Supreme Person, the objections of atheists against the cogency of theism fall. The order existing among persons achieves its ultimate guarantee and stability from God as the creator of the personal bond. Moreover, one's belief in God is no more susceptible to disproof than is the love of a mother for her child. Such commitments lie beyond the scope of abstraction.

Just as the act of faith is intelligible only in the light of intersubjectivity, so too are the various elements constituting one's union with the suprapersonal order. Prayer, even when performed in solitude, is an act whereby one unites himself to the community of believers. Its certainty, moreover, lies not in the superficial assurance that this or that particular favor will be granted, but, rather, in the utter confidence that the Person to whom one prays hears him and loves him. From a negative aspect, prayer is the rejection of the temptation to remain shut in on oneself in pride or despair; positively, it is "a receptive disposition towards everything which can detach me from myself and from my tendency to blind myself to my own failings. . . ." Sin consists in yielding to this temptation to become closed in on oneself, to take oneself as the center.

This application of secondary reflection, which is sustained throughout the two volumes of *The Mystery of Being,* leads beyond itself, for the themes of the search are what Marcel calls "mysteries," as contrasted to "problems." A problem exists in the order of objects to be analyzed; a mystery, on the other hand, involves the questioner himself, and cannot be submitted to objective analysis. While a problem admits of clear-cut answers, a mystery can only be circumscribed insofar as pathways towards increasing light can be indicated. Thus, at the end of the two volumes, the reader is left with the lifelong task of confronting the mysteries of himself, of other persons, of freedom, faith, sin, death, immortality, truth, and God.

D.H.J.

ANXIETY AND THE CHRISTIAN

Author: Hans Urs von Balthasar (1905-)
Type of work: Philosophical theology
First published: 1951

Principal Ideas Advanced

Anxiety is a necessary component of Christian living.

Scripture and tradition define the nature of anxiety, and as true anxiety it is that of the Cross.

Indifference to Christ is similar to the indifference of intellect and will to Being, and in this tension lies the essence of anxiety.

Hans Urs von Balthasar believes that the modern world gave the first real impulse to a contemporary psychosis of eternal return, thereby making a place at the heart of ontology and religion for genuine anxiety. Kierkegaard led the attack; Schelling, Hegel, and others offered stimulation. Yet since Kierkegaard could not decide in favor of dogma, his study of anxiety—meant to be wholly Christian—says little about God and Christ. Thus, the half century between Kierkegaard and Freud and the thirty years between

Freud and Heidegger saw the "existence anxiety" of modern man so develop that this kind of anxiety alone became a subject for analysis.

Balthasar points out that the absence of a true theology of anxiety becomes more apparent every day. Only the literary people have had something meaningful to say—Léon Bloy, Georges Bernanos, and Paul Claudel in France, and Gertrud von Le Fort in Germany. So Balthasar decides to take up the challenge, not only to lead Kierkegaard's thought more in the direction of dogmatic theology, but also to confront the overall problem of anxiety as it faces the modern Church.

Revelation provides important data for understanding modern anxiety. Scripture concerns itself with it. But save for a small discussion of servile as opposed to filial fear in the tractates on grace and the sacraments, tradition has said very little explicitly. Balthasar examines the problem of anxiety in terms of the Word of God, then in terms of its confrontation with the Christian life. Finally, he attempts to penetrate deeper into the very nature or essence of anxiety.

The Word of God knows no anxiety. Scripture approaches this area with the same power with which it approaches every characteristic of man as man. Scripture is no more ashamed of anxiety than it is of suffering and death, for Scripture provides man with the means of conquering these dark powers. The Church views anxiety as a universal and neutral foundation of human living; anxiety is the common theme under which the reality of day and the unreality of dream can be subsumed. Since such an ordering has to be done, there must be anxiety.

Nowhere is the anxiety of the evil man theologically described more exactly than in the seventeenth chapter of the Book of Wisdom. This is a description of total anxiety. In the desire to be forgotten by God, the self lies excluded from the light of Providence. Thus, the self flees Providence and is cut off and exiled from destiny. And this is the darkness of the underworld which God will not tolerate.

Balthasar says that the good man knows no such anxiety. This is forbidden. "Fear not!" (Isaias 41:10) Even the blackness of night holds no fears for the good of man. To dwell in the land of the promise of grace is connected with a specific lack of anxiety. Rather, the anxiety of a good man stems from his relation to God. God shows Himself in the Old Law so near and so naked that man is confounded and scarcely understands this blinding love. God is a consuming fire and a jealous God, who demands absolute and total decision for Himself. The thousand threats of punishment in the Law and the Prophets are so terrifying that the man who experiences his precarious situation wonders whether the experience is itself the beginning of the realization of these threats.

A good image is given in the anxiety of Job, the author suggests. Job expresses a tension between the consciousness of his guilt and the divine accusation. On the one hand, Job struggles between the different advice of his friends and his accusers, both of whom influence his sense of guilt; and on the other hand, he senses the dialectic in himself between God's pronouncement of his guilt and his own awareness of innocence. Job stands naked with anxiety before God. No man can live in such immediate contact with God.

In the New Testament Apocalypse the anxiety of the evil man appears multiplied a thousandfold; the darkness of the Old Testament Sheol has become the black eternity of Hell. The anxiety of the good man is also increased, for it reflects the anxiety of the Savior, and this is absolute anxiety.

Balthasar is of the opinion that this early anxiety is a prefigurement of the anxiety of the Christian life. But the Cross remains the ultimate victory over anxiety; human anxiety belongs to the principalities and powers over which Christ on the cross triumphed. All enemies have been definitively conquered, including the ultimate enemy, death. To the extent that the Christian lives the life of truth, he is no longer capable of fear. Anxiety is taken away and a trusting love is put in its place. Thus, anxiety is forbidden to the Christian. Only the man who does not let himself become infected with the neurotic anxiety of modern times has the hope of being able to exercise a Christian influence on his age. All grace is the grace of the Cross. The Cross, however, means anxiety, but it removes all forms of sin anxiety (which means all kinds of false anxiety), and thus it allows one to share in the real anxiety of Christ. Grace radically transforms basic anxiety. The basis of the anxiety of the Cross is nothing other than the love of God, which assumes the totality of the anxiety of the world to conquer it by means of suffering. It is a love which is the opposite of the experience of the sinner. The darkness of faith, hope, and love in the pursuit of perfection is the opposite of that darkness which is sin.

Balthasar summarizes three laws of Christian anxiety. The first law is that Christianity can and will free man from the anxiety of sin, if man accepts the Redemption and its conditions. In place of anxiety man is given a way to God through faith, hope, and love. Since these come from the Cross, they can include in themselves a new form of propitiatory anxiety springing from the solidarity of Catholic life.

This law opens the way to a specifically Christian anxiety, the anxiety of being recognized or discovered, of being unmasked. It is the anxiety of the lukewarm Christian. To some extent this form will remain as long as the event of the Redemption remains eschatological for men. There can be no static relationship between sin anxiety and the anxiety of the Cross. The law of exclusion which governs the situation determines the process from the one form of anxiety to the other. Luther failed to recognize this movement, because his concept of the redemption remained too much under the influence of the Old Law. It is significant that for Kierkegaard's Lutheranism, his basic anxiety is not (as was the case with Calvin) that of man standing before the judgment seat of predestination, but that of man confronted with the abyss of his own spirit. Thus, Kierkegaard is a hyphen between Luther and Heidegger.

The second law of Balthasar reads: to the extent that we are sinners, the redemptive act of the Cross does not simply remove sin anxiety. Rather, to the extent that man makes the truth of the Cross live within him, he frees himself from it. Christ begins His own death anew in every man who lies in the anxiety of death. We want what He wants, says Bernanos, but we do not know what we want. We do not know ourselves, and only in death do we realize fully what we are. It is there that Christ waits for us. This thought is also found profoundly expressed in Gertrud von Le Fort's novel *Song at the Scaffold* (1931) and in Claudel's *The Hostage* (1910).

The third law of Hans Urs von Balthasar is that God gives no one of the faithful a share in the anxiety of the Cross of His Son to whom he has not previously given the total power of Christian mission and joy and the light of faith, hope, and love, and from whom he has not already removed the anxiety of sin.

After discussing at length the sources of Christian anxiety, Balthasar takes up its nature and tries to ground its essence. Ever since Plato, philosophy has pointed up as a basic act *admiratio,* in which reason becomes visible out of the everyday of being. Heidegger was not needed to show this relation to anxiety. The relation between *admiratio* and awe is a platonic one. Saint Thomas Aquinas says that *admiratio* is the beginning of philosophy, while anxiety constitutes a hindrance to genuine philosophical thought. But Hegel, Kierkegaard, and Heidegger have made anxiety into a fundamental act of philosophy and so of *spirit* as such. The basic datum is that of death. Even Aristotle stressed this in pointing out how everyone knows he must die, but because death is not imminent, no one bothers about it.

Philosophy views the total threat to substance as being death. It has described anxiety in view of this threat as anxiety conditioned by the proximateness or remoteness of death. The threat to substance brought about by natural anxiety can never concern the creature as a whole, however. The soul's consciousness of its immortality is so strong that anxiety never places this in question. Closed sensate being has no place for anxiety, for it lacks a note of futurity.

The position of anxiety in spirit is seen in the mutual relation of transcendence and contingency. In every act of knowledge the spirit must leave the starting point of a being in order to arrive at Being by means of reversion to a being. Being is not conceptual. Rather, it is that by which spirit must be comprehended in order to be able to comprehend any existent.

The anxiety element in the structure of knowing lies in the fact that knowing takes place between two limits: Being and a being. It is the problem of the analogy of being, the problem of knowing the singular as this singular and the realization of a universal idea in a singular being. Thus, a being is not an occasion for anxiety but becomes this in its relation to Being.

Hans Urs von Balthasar says that a young man first experiences the terrible disappointment of this world in the sphere of inquiring spirit. The transcendence that appears at first as something delightful and inviting only leads the way back into the actually existing individual grasped in the phantasm, and this individual as such cannot bear the weight of the absolute. This is a tragic experience, which becomes even clearer if spirit is viewed as will and not as intellect. Being as such cannot be an object of choice, but openness to this Being is necessary if one is to be able to exercise choice regarding any individual being.

Kierkegaard said that the deep mystery of innocence is that it is at the same time anxiety. Balthasar seems to believe that in this statement Kierkegaard failed to describe enough, for the Dane did not picture the process as an organic whole. It is not the emptiness of nothingness in the face of its own internal dimensions before which spirit knows anxiety, but the emptiness of the concrete experience of actual distance from God. Anxiety is immanent to spirit on the very basis of the limitlessness of spirit. Yet it has also a transcendental presupposition: distance from God.

This is genuine Christian anxiety, Balthasar insists firmly, because it has its original pattern in Christ. A man achieves full faith and true indifference only when he has abandoned the anxiety of sin. And even if this abandonment were subjectively death, objectively it would exist as greater happiness, as a true share in enduring Trinitarian ecstasy.

In the supernatural order any indifference to Christ is analogous to the indifference of intellect and will to Being, says the author. An actuation comes from God in two moments: abstraction and return to the phantasm, a being stripped of everything but God and the return into the world. Anxiety is experienced before this mission to give witness in the world occurs. Anxiety is not in the force of being sent and it is not in the act of being commissioned. Whoever experiences anxiety before the leap of faith will even use all the covers of false anxiety to avoid the leap. Yet ecclesiastical Christianity is not a "religion of anxiety." It takes courage to be a Christian in the Church, and this courage is not the opposite of anxiety. The anxiety of Christian witness is the anxiety of the Cross, for the Church is the extention of the salvational will of God into time; and this, says Balthasar, is the shadow of the Cross on history.

L.W.R.

MAN AND THE STATE

Author: Jacques Maritain (1882-)
Type of work: Political philosophy
First published: 1951

Principal Ideas Advanced

The body politic is the whole of which the state is but the instrumental agency; the body politic is not sovereign, nor are the people sovereign, but they have a natural right to full autonomy or self-government.

Political society seeks to obtain justice and freedom for its members by means which must be moral, but not so hypermoral as to involve a pharisaical refusal to participate in the realities of politics.

The precepts of natural law and the rights of persons are rooted in a common human nature, and man's knowledge of this law is a connatural knowledge which has only gradually been acquired.

The principles of natural law may be immutable, but they attain their realization according to varying conditions in different societies.

There should be a commitment to a democratic charter; this democratic faith will serve as the practical basis of society and be promoted by an educational system which allows freedom of expression for political heretics and prophetic shock-minorities.

The Church is an autonomous society within the body politic; while the state co-operates with the churches within the community, they are all in a position of equality in view of freedom of conscience; the state indirectly serves the Church by attaining the conditions of civil peace and security wherein it can work, and the Church indirectly serves the state by helping form the consciences of the citizens.

To avoid international anarchy a world government is required, but this government is to preserve and respect national heritages and cultures.

In presenting the Walgreen lectures at the University of Chicago in 1949 Maritain crystallized the reflections on political philosophy he had been making for some thirty years. Known as a thinker who has sought to make principles of his master, Saint Thomas Aquinas, viable in the twentieth century, Maritain has had a special interest in political and moral philosophy which he has expressed in a series of significant works, such as *The Things That Are Not Caesar's* (1927), *Freedom in the Modern World* (1936), *Scholasticism and Politics* (1940), *The Rights of Man and Natural Law* (1943), *Christianity and Democracy* (1944), *The Person and the Common Good* (1947), and his classic analysis of modern social culture, *True Humanism* (1938). The views scattered throughout these works which have been so influential on the leaders of the Christian Democratic Parties of the immediate postwar era are represented and analyzed in *Man and the State.*

Maritain first presents his understanding of a number of key political terms: a *community* is a work of nature and relates to the biological; a *society* is a work of reason and expresses man's social nature; the *nation* is a community which has become conscious of its ethnic origins, aware of its past; whereas the *body politic* pertains to the whole of society of which the *state* is but the topmost part. The *state* is the instrument of the political society by which that society strives to organize itself for its common welfare, the attainment of social justice for its members. The people who compose the *body politic,* while not sovereign, have a natural right to full autonomy which they express in their self-government.

Maritain pays special attention to the concept of sovereignty in his second chapter, wherein he notes that the concept is "intrinsically wrong." The concept originally had to do with the possession of unlimited absolute power. Through Jean Bodin (1530-1596) the term came into political usage in the sixteenth century, when the king was regarded as the image of God in his role of ruler. In the course of time Thomas Hobbes (1588-1679) made use of this notion in referring to the person to whom everyone consents to be subject in order to attain civil peace. Jean Jacques Rousseau (1712-1778) transferred this idea of absolute power to the body politic as expressing the "General Will"; since some leader is needed to personify the expression of this will, Rousseau's philosophy prepared the way for the attempt to justify the dictatorships of the twentieth century with their absolute dictators. Today the concept of national sovereignty stands in the way of more effective world government. Thus, Maritian believes that the concept of sovereignty has had a great detrimental effect on political thought and should be discarded. Whatever was positive about the idea, namely, that the people should have the autonomy of self-government, can be expressed in other ways; "The two concepts of Sovereignty and Absolutism have been forged together on the same anvil. They must be scrapped together."

The political philosopher is confronted with the basic problem of the means of attaining the common good. Since the end is good, the means must be good too. It is a blunder, says Maritain, to think that evil means will serve to attain a good end. This blunder was classically expressed by Niccolò Machiavelli (1469-1527) in *The Prince,* which is a technical rationalization of politics. The apparent success of some Machiavellian leaders is merely the illusion of *immediate success.* It fails in the longer run, for, writes Maritain, "I say that justice works through its own causality toward welfare and success in the future, as a healthy sap works toward the perfect fruit, and Machiavellianism works through its own causality for ruin and bankruptcy, as poison in the sap works for the illness and death of the tree."

However, Maritain warns of the danger of a hypermoralism which might cause someone to withdraw from the realities of political life for fear of soiling his hands. Maritain writes, "This is pharisaical purism: it is not the doctrine of the purification of the means." Maritain makes clear that while the precepts of morality do not change, the way they will apply will vary in different contexts. In some contexts where the moral order is little organized and conditions are primitive, we may have to do what appears to be taking the law into our own hands, as when a man kills someone in self-defense, or a person kills in a resistance movement while liberating his country. "Moralists are unhappy people," says Maritain; "When they insist on the immutability of moral principles, they are reproached for imposing unlivable requirements on us. When they explain the way in which those immutable principles are to be put into force, taking into account the diversity of concrete situations, they are reproached for making morality relative. In both cases, however, they are only upholding the claims of reason to direct life."

Maritain contrasts the situation in a democratic state, where the people supervise or control the state, with the situation in a totalitarian state, where personal values and norms are not considered. The program for the people should be the work of the people, with the initiative for various political measures having its starting point in the consciousness of the smallest local communities. Referring to the spiritual means Mahatma Gandhi (1869-1948) used in the struggle for Indian independence, Maritain stresses the courage involved in enduring. This fortitude he considers the chief means of "spiritual warfare" and a most powerful means of bringing about social change.

Through his many writings in the field of ethics and aesthetics Maritain has sought to explain knowledge by way of affective connaturality. This kind of knowledge is to be contrasted with the explicit, conceptual, rational knowledge of a scientific demonstration. It is, rather, a knowledge which ends up with true conclusions, or judgments, but these have been arrived at by way of intuition or closeness. Knowledge by connaturality is a knowing by loving. It is the knowledge of fortitude a brave man has; the knowledge of justice a just person possesses. Such connatural knowledge of humanity is the knowledge a good poet or playwright possesses and which he expresses in the words of his characters rather than in the statements of a psychological textbook. Such is man's knowledge of natural law as rooted in his conscience. It is a knowledge which consists in the ability to arrive at right judgments about things to be done in a way which is true but not that of scientific reasoning. Such is our knowledge of natural law as it is present in the moral conscience of mankind; and thus men who are committed to very different philosophical ideologies can still, in virtue of listening to what they are and to what they need, agree on a list of human rights and obligations. Maritain writes: "Thus there is a sort of vegetative development and growth, so to speak, of moral knowledge and moral feeling, which is in itself independent of the philosophical systems, although in a secondary way the latter in turn enter into reciprocal action with this spontaneous process. As a result these various systems, while disputing about the 'why,' prescribe in their practical conclusions rules of behavior which appear on the whole as almost the same for any given period and culture."

There are many misunderstandings of the natural law, says Maritain. This is partly due to the fact that there have been many natural law systems, or, better, there has existed in the minds of various thinkers so many caricatures of natural law. Some have misconceived natural law to be the pattern of a written code existing in some sort of platonic heaven, an ideal which in a moral crisis need only be consulted in order to resolve problems. But Maritain first affirms a common human nature which has an end or objective, and he then claims that to act morally is simply to act in a way which is consonant with that nature: "This means that there is, by the very virtue of human nature, an order or a disposition which human reason can discover and according to which the human will must act in order to attune itself to the essential and necessary ends of the human being. The unwritten law, or natural law, is nothing more than that."

What all men know naturally and infallibly is the preamble and principle of natural law: do good and avoid evil. But what is good and what is evil is more difficult to determine. The regulations of natural law are not the deductions from a principle, as are so many theorems of geometry; rather, we are guided by the inclinations of our nature to know in an often obscure way what we are or are not to do in a particular context. There has been in the human race a progressive growth in our understanding of what is moral or immoral. Via this connatural knowledge we have become aware of the respect due a human person, so that gradually, for example, we have become sensitive to the immorality of slavery, and we are ready to honor the rights of each and every person in his integrity and freedom. In our positive laws we seek to realize the principles and precepts of natural law. We seek in the varying modalities and changing conditions of social living to render incarnate the principles of natural law. In our times such a fundamental precept as respect for the persons right to self-government finds its expression in laws affirming universal suffrage. In the same way we are experiencing a growing appreciation of the right "of everyone to share in the educational and cultural heritage of civilized life." Further, our most urgent problems concern the rights of the family and the rights of the worker. Maritain specifies a number of these rights: "The right of the worker to be considered socially as an adult, and to have, some way or other, a share and active participation in the responsibilities of economic life.— The right of economic groups [unions and working communities] and other social groups to freedom and autonomy. . . . The right to relief, unemployment insurance, sick benefits, and social security." Our knowledge of these rights has grown with our progressive insight into the implications of the needs of human nature. In theoretical conflicts over the basis and roots of these rights Maritain sides with those who support a personalistic type of society over against a liberal-individualistic or collectivistic approach.

The theme of *personalism* is repeated in the chapter on the democratic charter. Maritain calls for a personalist democracy of the pluralistic type. That is, he sees the need of a political society which would foster many free associations or subcommunities within the body politic. These would promote greater freedom in their serving as a barrier against totalitarianism. Maritain believes that men of various theoretical outlooks can nevertheless agree upon a set of practical principles which can serve as a charter for democratic society. A body politic has the right and duty to promote among its citizens this secular creed which is the basis for national communion and civil peace: a code which includes a statement of the rights and liberties of the human person, social rights and liberties, family rights and duties, and the rights and duties of groups within the state. Maritain recognizes that there will be political heretics who will not subscribe to a democratic charter; illegal activity must be restrained, but speaking and writing are a different matter. Reflecting on the troubles with police methods and censorship in the past, Maritain argues that the state is not equipped to deal with matters of intelligence and, he says, "each time the State disregards that basic truth, which depends on its own nature, intelligence is victimized." Programs of education conducted by various groups will better serve society than the repression by the state of freedom of expression.

Maritain affirms that authority has its source in the Author of nature but is derived from the will or consensus of the people. The people have a basic right to govern themselves, a right they possess inherently and permanently. Maritain says that whatever a particular political *regime* may be, democratic philosophy is the only true political philosophy. The ruler is the vicar of the people, possessed of authority to rule, but deriving that authority ultimately from God, but through the people who designate him ruler. He is accountable to the people and should be supervised and controlled by the people. The first axiom in a democracy is to trust and respect the people, even while awakening them to the implications of their human dignity.

Maritain pays particular attention to what he calls prophetic shock-minorities within the body politic. These inspired people serve to prepare the way for the great changes that take place to reform society or advance its progress. Such men as the leaders of the Italian Risorgimento or of the liberation movement of Ireland emancipate us and sometimes in a violent way force the people to be free.

In treating the problem of Church and state Maritain says he is speaking as a Catholic philosopher; that is, he is speaking philosophically of a reality which he is regarding from the privileged viewpoint of faith. Starting with the person, Maritain notes his membership in the body politic in virtue of his citizenship and yet his relationship to something supratemporal in virtue of the commitment of his faith. Thus, he has an end which transcends the common good of political society. For unbelievers the Church is a certain institutionalized structure, but for believers it is "the body of Christ supernaturally made up of the human race." The difficulties relating to Church and state historically have arisen from the tensions which dual membership has brought. Maritain in analyzing the relation insists first of all on the freedom of the Church to pursue its mission of preaching the word of God. Second, he notes a superiority of the Church, the spiritual, over the body politic or the state, and next he affirms the need for co-operation between Church and state. However, he reminds us, we no longer live in the Middle Ages, a *sacral* age in which political society had not yet attained its maturity. We live in a secular age wherein each society has its autonomy: political power is not the secular arm of the spiritual power; all members of the body politic are equal; there is no justification for privileges to one group over another. Today we better appreciate the dignity of the person and his freedom of conscience regarding his religious beliefs. Any Church will have its influence in the body politic, but this influence will be in the realm of the hearts and consciences of men.

Maritain hopes that the state will respect the principle of pluralism, and that in the work of co-operation between the state and the churches there will be a recognition, for example, of religious communities which have been formed according to the right of association. The state in promoting the common good will be providing the conditions of civil peace and security whereby religious sects can flourish. Thus, there will be a matter of equality of citizens accorded to all religious groups (except those that profess something immoral such as suicide) and the numerical predominance within the body politic of the members of any Church would not then endanger in any way the rights and liberties of members of other religious groups. There is no room in Maritain's philosophy for a religious intolerance which would make "all non-Christians and non-orthodox second-rate citizens."

In the final chapter, "the Problem of World Government," Maritain again argues against the emphasis on national sovereignty which impedes a greater tendency toward international unity. The present state of affairs is anarchy; the day will have to come when particular states will have surrendered their full independence. The World State which eventually will emerge will be a perfect society having the powers to legislate, execute, and juridically evaluate law, but Maritain realizes that it is utterly impossible to realize such a state now. The World State would, of course, respect the principles of pluralism and thus there would be national structures within it "with their own political structures and lives, their own national and cultural heritages, their own multifarious institutions and communities," all vitalized by a will for a worldwide living together. This is far off, says Maritain; but, he argues, we must work as we can to bring about progress in that direction.

D.J.F.

ASCENT TO TRUTH

Author: Thomas Merton (1915-)
Type of work: Mystical theology
First published: 1951

Principal Ideas Advanced

We must know the truth, we must love the truth we know, and we must act according to the measure of our love.

This basic pattern of human development is realized in a high degree in the contemplative life.

Saint John of the Cross and other great mystics instruct us on the role of intelligence in mysticism.

Thomas Merton published his *Ascent to Truth* two years after *Seeds of Contemplation.* The earlier book was a series of meditations that presupposed, rather than developed, a systematic doctrine of the spiritual life; the meditations were the thoughts of one obviously engaged in the ascent. *Ascent to Truth* is quite another sort of book. In it Merton attempts to present to the interested reader a modern presentation of the spiritual teaching of the sixteenth century Spanish Carmelite, Saint John of the Cross. Given its subject matter and given the author's earnest belief that contemplation has peculiar relevance to the Atomic Age, there is nothing aloof or disengaged in this more systematic work. Merton is addressing our hearts as well as our heads but, and this is one of the themes of the book, it is finally only through the head that the human heart can be reached. The prologue sets the tone of the book.

Beginning with a treatment of the role of mysticism in man's life, Merton argues that the problems of the age, global problems, must finally be settled in the souls of individuals. Man is made for God, and true peace can be found only by turning to God. But such devotion to God is impossible without an interior life. To be in the service of God is to live His life, the life of grace. We dispose ourselves to the reception of grace by the exercise of the theological virtues of faith, hope, and charity. This puts great demands on our intelligence and will, and the activity of these faculties is obstructed by exterior influences, by passions, which turn us from our supernatural goal. Recollection, meditation, prayer, study, and mortification, together with some degree of solitude and retirement, are required. It is a mistake to think that zealous activity can be substituted for this necessity; there is truly a heresy of good works which is only a kind of distraction.

The pattern of our development can be simply stated: "We must know the truth, and we must love the truth we know, and we must act according to the measure of our love." The elements of the pattern are three and are further described by the statement that we must adapt ourselves to objective reality, a task calling for the exercize of man's highest faculties, intelligence and will. Finally, this grasp of reality must be expressed in acts which exhibit harmony with the true order of things. Contemplation is simply a higher way of executing this pattern of human development. The Truth to be known is not some abstraction, a set of true propositions; the Truth is the living God, who is not really known unless He is also loved. Such a knowledge of God cannot be said to have been acquired if it does not affect our lives.

Merton describes his objective as follows: "My chief preoccupation in this work has been not to describe or account for the highest levels of mystical experience, but only to settle certain fundamental questions which refer more properly to the ascetical preparation for graces of mystical prayer. The chief of these questions concerns the relations of the intellect and will in contemplation."

Merton sees a danger of false mysticism abroad which would downgrade the role of intelligence in the contemplative life. The points he wants to make are the following. Contemplative life demands detachment from the senses but is not a rejection of sense experience. It rises above the level of reasoning, but reason plays an essential role in the interior asceticism necessary to travel safely the path of mysticism. Mystical prayer is always essentially intelligent, even though it rises above the natural operation of the intelligence. The will plays an integral part, because without life there can be no contemplation. God is the principal cause of contemplation; it is His free gift and can never be merited in any strict sense by any activity of ours. Finally, mystical contemplation comes to us through Christ, since contemplation is the fullness of the Christian life.

The first part of *Ascent to Truth* deals with dark knowledge. Our lives are lives of distraction, says Merton, because we permit our desires to weave a web of false goods which obscure the mind. These desires aim at creatures, but it is not the creatures which account for illusion but our wrong estimation of them. The dark night of the senses consists in overcoming the desire for created goods as ends in themselves. Merton quotes

Saint John of the Cross, who gives a list of paradoxes: in order to have pleasure in everything, desire to have pleasure in nothing; in order to arrive at possessing everything, desire to possess nothing. It is not pleasure, possessions, or knowledge which mislead us, but the inordinate, passionate desire for them. Saint John of the Cross considers all this to be merely a gloss on the First Commandment, and Merton will insist that the simple demands of the great spiritual writers, demands which strike terror in our worldly hearts, are little more than repetitions of the basic demands of the Christian life. The hardest sayings of the mystical writer often turn out to be little more than paraphrases of Scriptural injunctions. What they present is, fundamentally, the structure of Christianity that is obscured by our worldliness and accommodations with the City of Man: "In other words, the *nada* of Saint John of the Cross is simply a drastically literal application of the Gospel. 'If any of you can renounce not all that he possesses, he cannot be my disciple.' (Luke 14:33)."

The contemplative life of the Catholic is not one which can be indifferent to theology and the teaching of the Church. Mystical knowledge is not opposed to theological knowledge, although, as Merton argues, its need is felt in the crisis that follows on theological knowledge. In speculative theology our knowledge of God is both affirmative and negative; to know that God exists is at the same time to know that one cannot comprehend the existence of God. The complement of the theologian's abstract knowledge is the contemplative's experiential knowledge of God. Merton has no patience for a mystical contempt for theology, for he takes such contempt to be a symptom of spiritual pride. Quietism and rationalism are equally pitfalls for the spiritual life.

Part Two of *Ascent to Truth* is devoted to a discussion of reason and mysticism in the ideas of Saint John of the Cross. This section includes chapters on faith and reason, reason in the life of contemplation, and intelligence in the prayer of quiet. Throughout, Merton is engaged in the subtle and complex task of showing that contemplation is not antirational, that it is essentially an activity of intelligence informed by charity.

The final part of the book deals with doctrine and experience, and here Merton develops the notion that contemplation involves a supraconceptual knowledge of the presence of God. The consummation of the contemplative life is love, and love unites us directly with its object: "It must be quite evident that love is the end and perfection of all contemplation, since contemplation is not an end in itself. Contemplation is not sanctity. The full maturity of the Christian life, to which contemplation is only one of many means—though perhaps it is the most effective means—consists essentially in the perfect love of God and of other men."

The writings of Thomas Merton, perhaps particularly *Ascent to Truth,* have made us conscious that something remarkable has been happening in the Church in America. In an age such as ours when so much of our civilization and culture contrives to draw us outward and alienate us from our true selves, when it is easy, though nonetheless dull, to ring the changes on the superficiality of our lives, it gives us pause to know that far from our cities, distant from but not unconcerned with our desperate activity, there are men and women who may, in the designs of Providence, be writing the real history of our times. Thomas Merton's books make it difficult to be unaware of them or of their significance for us.

R.M.

PHILOSOPHY OF DEMOCRATIC GOVERNMENT

Author: Yves René Marie Simon (1903-1961)
Type of work: Political philosophy
First published: 1951

Principal Ideas Advanced

Civil government is demanded by the very nature of man since there are functions of authority which would be required even in a society of mature persons of understanding and good will in which the substitutional functions of authority based upon deficiencies would be unnecessary.

Democratic government is not correctly interpreted as involving only the illusion of authority, which would be to deny in it the very essence of government and to reduce it to masked anarchy.

Authority in a democracy is characterized, not by any lack of genuineness, but by the fact that the people retain the right to participate in their government by way of giving their advice and consent through communications and periodic elections.

Democracy implies a dynamic tendency toward ever-increasing equality of opportunities for all to develop their talents and to share in the good things of life.

When Thomas Paine argued that government is necessary only because of the wickedness of men, his concern was to show why the power of the state should be limited. The same position has been taken in this century, not only by those who would severely restrict government, but also, strangely, by the proponents of the communist and fascist forms of totalitarianism. Yves Simon opens his discussion in *Philosophy of Democratic Government* with an analysis of this "deficiency theory," as he calls it, and raises the question of whether it is philosophically sound.

The question is one concerning the functions of authority. There is an obvious function of authority in view of the deficiencies, natural and abnormal, temporary and permanent, of some of the persons in most social units. In the family, for example, parents have authority over their children so long as they are not sufficiently mature to make sound decisions concerning their own welfare. The purpose of this paternal authority is to guard the well-being of the children and to bring about their development to the point at which they no longer require this function of authority as a substitute for their own lack of capability to regulate their lives. Justice, then, requires that in the natural course of things such paternal authority be self-liquidating as the deficiencies upon which it is based disappear.

If this *substitutional* function of authority, based as it is upon deficiencies in the governed, were its only function, in civil society or in the family, then continued government would be justified only as long as such deficiencies remained to be eradicated. It becomes important therefore to discover whether authority performs any function consequent upon the very nature of man, and, accordingly, essential to the very existence of human society.

Simon brings this issue into focus by asking whether authority would be required in a human society consisting entirely of mature, enlightened, and virtuous persons. Now it is evident that even such an ideal society would require some method of guaranteeing united action to prevent its disintegration. But when several possible courses of action are open to choice, unity can be assured only by means of authority. Moreover, since continuing explicit concern for the common good of the social body cannot be expected of all its individual members, some person must be entrusted with this responsibility and given this requisite authority. Thus, authority is shown to be indispensable for every genuine human society, in as much as it has essential functions which it alone can perform.

The common opinion that authority is incompatible with democratic freedom is due to the failure to distinguish these essential functions from the merely substitutional functions of authority. Simon goes on to bring out the true character of democratic government by means of an extended discussion of universal suffrage, freedom of expression, and popular participation in government. He shows that while every type of genuinely political government provides the governed with some institutionally organized means of resisting misuse of authority, democratic regimes are unique in their manner of accomplishing this. For in a democracy the people retain control over their governing personnel through the procedure of periodic elections and by their own active interest in civil affairs.

Universal suffrage, while not necessarily bound up with democracy, has gradually gained recognition as a basic tenet of the democratic theory of government. Simon analyzes the presuppositions behind universal suffrage in order to distinguish the real from the mythical. The most compelling argument in favor of the practice, in his view, is simply that it is safer to entrust the selection of governing personnel to the great mass of men who are unavoidably more in touch with the basic realities of human life than are the elite with their somewhat dehumanized attitude toward life and its problems, and their tendencies toward rationalism and excessive experimentation.

Simon also calls attention to the great respect for freedom of expression and the general affinity for liberal attitudes which are characteristic of a democracy. The elective system demands free discussion and responsible use of methods of persuasion. It is particularly important in a democracy that propaganda, so intensive as to become a kind of psychic coercion, not be allowed to take the place of the genuinely persuasive appeal to the people as free men. There is also the need, for institutions external to government, such as a free press, churches, independent labor unions, professional societies, and private schools, especially in order to hold in check any tendencies in democratic societies toward state absolutism.

Simon is led by all these considerations to conclude that authority in its essential functions is in no sense in conflict with democratic freedom, but is required if the common good is to be achieved in freedom. The essential functions of authority will continue to be required and perhaps even to increase. So far as the substitutional functions of authority are concerned, the progress of society toward greater freedom does require, however, that as many tasks as possible be handled by individuals and by the smaller units of society so that this particular role of authority may diminish.

Simon next considers the question raised by Jean Jacques Rousseau and others as to the genuineness of authority as the moral right of some men to make laws and decisions which other men must obey. Can one man bind the conscience of another? Or are all instances of such authority only illusory? A nineteenth century French writer, Paul-Louis Courier, introduced the term "coach-driver theory" which Simon uses to designate the view that it is really the *governed* who make governmental decisions through the mere instrumentality of their chosen representatives. The people thus do what they have decided to do and are not really subject to anyone, but only seem to be so, as do the passengers in a coach who only appear to be subject to the coachdriver's decision as to where they shall be taken and by what route. Authority is, according to this view, a mere illusion. Genuine government does not really exist; there is only anarchy under the appearance of government.

If authority has essential and indispensable functions to perform in a political society, as has already been shown, the "coach-driver theory" is obviously erroneous. What is more, if seriously held, it is destructive of all genuine political society. It is, in effect, only a mistaken device for refusing to acknowledge the moral force of law and of legitimate governmental decision, though, without question, it is capable of giving a plausible account of a number of democratic practices. If a significant number of the people subscribe to this view of government, men may still act in accord with laws and commands of which they approve, and they will even obey other laws when they fear that they cannot escape the sanctions joined to them, but the character of political life will nonetheless be corrupted.

To acknowledge that those who govern do have genuine authority is to raise the question as to how they acquire it. Historically, there were those writers who held that all rulers receive their authority directly from God, though some of them conceded that the ruler is actually *designated* by the people. This has come to be known as the "divine right theory." Gradually another theory was formulated, according to which the people hold authority immediately from God and *transmit* it to their rulers with the provision that they may withdraw it for grave reasons. Simon shows the essential correctness of this "transmission theory," which was worked out, in full agreement with the notions of Saint Thomas

Aquinas, by such well-known Scholastic theologians as Thomas de Vio Cajetan, O.P., Robert Bellarmine, S.J., and Francisco Suarez, S.J. While both the divine right and transmission theories are in accord with the Scriptural statement that "all authority is from God," the transmission theory is also consistent with the Aristotelian doctrine that authority has its basis in the very nature of man.

The transmission theory, though compatible with democracy in a way in which the divine right theory obviously is not, does not of itself imply a democratic form of government. In a democracy the transmission of authority is always incomplete, since the people retain some control over their rulers and some means of participating in their government. Even in a democracy, however, the people do genuinely transmit to governing personnel the authority to pass laws and make governmental decisions, and the people retain only the right to be consulted, to offer advice, and to approve or disapprove governmental actions through elective procedures. It is because of these provisions that democratic government can be said to be "by the consent of the governed."

Simon devotes one chapter of this book to a thorough analysis of the notion of human equality. The American Declaration of Independence, he points out, fortunately proposes a doctrine of equality based on the notion of a universal human nature, which is logically inconsistent with the prevailing nominalistic views of the times. From the doctrine that all men are equally men, and only from this, it follows that all are entitled equally to protection before the law. It also follows that there should be a progressive extension of equality of opportunities for full human development and for full participation in the good things of human life. There is an essential incompatibility between democracy and all forms of exploitation of some men by others, and thus there is an egalitarian tendency in every democratically governed society.

Simon finally comes to consider the disturbing question of whether democratic government can flourish in a modern technological society. Although the rural mode of life is found to be more favorable in many respects to democracy, technology also has some advantages in this respect. One of its great contributions is the labor union, which Simon sees as having brought a new autonomy to the ordinary workers.

The methods of positive science and technology which have greatly enhanced the power at the disposal of some men have also, however, aggravated the continuing problem of assuring that this power be used righteously. While technical knowledge continues to grow with steadily increasing speed, and its products all tend eventually to be used, there is no assurance of a corresponding growth in the knowledge pertaining to their right use. Simon calls the reader's attention to the fact that what is required to solve this problem is not some other type of scientific knowledge, but the virtue of prudence; and this is not to be secured except by steady practice of all the virtues. Greater stress on humanistic knowledge, ethics in particular, would, of course, be desirable, but Simon warns that there is never a guarantee that knowledge of what ought to be done will not be ignored at a time of crisis. The balance will always be precarious, and further advances in techniques affording greater power can but increase the danger.

Some measures can be taken in a democratic society, however, to lessen the danger. Widespread distribution of technical power can be advantageous, as can the direction of interest and energies toward those types of technical achievements which will lend themselves more readily to good use. World peace makes less likely the frantic development of more destructive techniques. At best, however, it can only be expected that wrong use of techniques will continue to increase along with their right use. This means that we must look forward to continuing growth of both good and evil so long as man lives.

What is of particular importance in a democratically governed society, Simon urges, is that the freedom of men be safeguarded from the destructive effects of those currently developing techniques which can be brought to bear upon man's appetitive inclinations to motivate him sub-rationally, and thus affect his ability to make free decisions. Whatever the difficulties for democracy in a highly technological society, however, Simon makes it increasingly clear that democracy is the form of government best suited to cope with these difficulties.

M.F.G.

TRAITÉ DU LIBRE ARBITRE

Author: Yves René Marie Simon (1903-1961)
Type of work: Philosophical psychology
First published: 1951

Principal Ideas Advanced

The scientist's acceptance of determinism is due to his image of the free act as an exception to the principle of the uniformity of nature, an event without a cause.

The experience of free choice is certain but confused; consequently, the testimony from our consciousness of choosing cannot count as a distinct argument for freedom.

The intellect and will co-operate to make choices self-determined and essentially unpredictable.

Freedom of choice properly consists in the active indifference of the practical judgment in the face of any particular good.

The rise of determinism in modern philosophy is closely linked to the success of seventeenth century mechanics in predicting the behavior of moving bodies. The view of classical physics has been that the future position of a moving particle is determined by its present status and the causes presently acting on it. It has seemed to the determinist that to deny that our choices are determined in a way analogous to that which affects the behavior of a particle would be to subvert the principle of causality. Yves Simon is concerned to show in his treatise on free choice that much thinking about this problem has been prejudiced by philosophers who confuse freedom of choice with the freedom from causes. Such philosophers fear what he calls "images of disorder."

Simon writes: "The proposition that disorder, or a tendency to bring about disorder, pertains to the essence of freedom is often expressed or understood in the treatment of moral, political and pedagogical issues; it also appears very often in the less impassionate discussions of the physicists and philosophers of nature. Most scientists hold that freedom, if tolerated anywhere, would jeopardize the orderliness of the scientific universe. Aversion to disorder is the real motive of their faith in unqualified determinism. Indeed according to the dictates of our imagination a free act is an event without a cause, an exception to the law of causality and to the principle of uniformity in natural occurrences. Such a thing cannot exist."

Simon takes the trouble to show the parts of man's personality wherein he is not free. He investigates the difference between free choice and voluntary, that is, unrestrained, activity. We speak of doing something in a voluntary way if there is no coercion of our acting. As far as our feelings go, there is little freedom. Our emotions are stimulated by the things around us, and our responses in the form of reflexes, drives, tendencies, inclinations, and dispositions, belonging, as they do, to a mixed realm of biological reaction and appetite, are spontaneous. We control them and they are formed by our reason, but there is an element of unfreedom about them. The discovery of the sublimation of our sexual drives serves to indicate the mixed character of so much of what we do. There are parts of our activity which we control but over whose origins we have no control. The fact, however, that we direct these drives into areas of artistic and intellectual production is an indication of the autonomy of the will.

Simon, following Saint Thomas Aquinas on this point, studies the determination of the will in its drive to seek the good as such. From his experience of the good things which surround him, man comes to have an understanding, albeit vague, of universal goodness, goodness without limitation or qualification. He calls it happiness in that he feels that attainment of this goal will end his restlessness and quiet his fears. Men go through series of goods as if seeking some infinity, for each particular attractive thing is considered to be desirable as a means towards happiness. There is no freedom in the search for the good; men are necessarily committed to this quest: "In a very proper sense every action of every agent is related to the last end of all things; yet acting for the sake of an end is the privilege of rational agents inasmuch as the knowledge of the notion of finality pertains only to rational agents." The necessity of seeking the good as such, far from curbing or delimiting freedom, is the foundation for it since men are free to be actively indifferent only in the face of particular goods.

The ordinary nonphilosopher who affirms that he is free, if questioned as to the basis of his judgment, would reply in terms of his consciousness of being free. It is true, says Simon, we have a sense of making up our minds, of deliberating, of weighing alternatives before we come to a decision. But, "if freedom were evident as a matter of conscious experience, it would not be denied by anyone; the fact that philosophers are as divided on freedom as on any other subject shows that the problem is not settled by sheer experience. In the discussion of the whole issue keep in mind that the very notion of the settlement of a problem by conscious experience is confused and suspicious." This is not to say, however, that the data of consciousness are worthless. Such data do count for something, for we gain insights into freedom by reflecting on situations in which we are not free, as when we are coerced, over against situations that provide us with a sense of mastery and spontaneity. Thus, Simon maintains, the phrase which defenders of free choice use, namely, "freedom of self-determination," takes on special meaning.

Noting that the will is uniquely determined to seek the good as such, one might ask: "What, then, is the meaning of free will?" The answer would be that not free will, but free choice is what is required in the search for the good. Essential to free choice is the freedom of practical judgment: "Unless judgment is free, the will exercises its operations in a uniquely determined way, as fire burns and the liver secretes bile. The problem is to designate the conditions under which a judgment escapes the necessity of unique determination."

In the analysis of the making of a *liberum arbitrium* there is a constant tendency, says Simon, to suggest a misleading image by speaking of the intellect and will as if they were two separate substances engaged in a dialogue with each other. They may be engaged in a kind of dialogue as each exercises its special causality on the other power, but they are in fact simply distinct powers of one and the same person who judges with his intellect and loves by his will. By a kind of shortcut in speaking and writing philosophers have come to talk of the intellect as doing this, and of the will as doing that. This shortcut is permissible, the author grants, once care has been taken to introduce the required qualifications.

Reflecting on the way our mind works, Simon suggests, we note that our judgments in some few cases are completely determined by the evidence confronting us. That is, in the face of some fundamental principle, such as the principle of noncontradiction, the man understanding the meaning of the words used to enunciate the principle has no option other than to give his assent to the principle. In a similar way, our intellect closes upon the conclusion of a valid syllogism once it is seen that the conclusion issues necessarily from the premises. However, Simon cautions, only a small proportion of our judgments are axioms or conclusions of reasoning processes. A good many judgments are evaluations or decisions about courses of action. In some of these situations the evidence is sufficiently clear to free us from the hesitancy that fear of erring promotes. Under such circumstances, we choose without much deliberation. But in other situations we are more conscious of the limitations involved in the somewhat desirable course of action we are considering, and we turn over in our mind the pros and cons of one alternative or another. Simon writes: "By reason of its being a living relation to the comprehensive good, the will invalidates the claim of any particular good to bring about a determinate judgment of desirability. At the instant when the attraction of a thing good in some respect inclines the mind to utter the proposition: this is good for me, the infinite ambition of the will reverses the perspective. The thing which is good only in a certain respect discloses uncongenial aspects, and the proposition 'this is not good for me' fights with its contradictory for the assent of the mind."

In this activity of interaction, the role of the intellect as the formal cause of choice is to propose particular goods or possible courses of action. The role of the will is to accept or reject these tentatively stated judgments. That is, the will functioning as an efficient cause can move the intellect to think again or to give its assent to the tentative proposal. This is the process of deliberation. Simon, following Aquinas, would focus the moment of free choice in the will's ability to let itself go or hold itself back in the act of deciding. All this is in virtue of the will's determination to the good as such.

"Under the determining impulse of the will, itself determined by its natural object," writes Simon, "the intellect has turned about the partially desirable and partially detestable thing. . . . The indifference of the practical judgment does not originate in any indetermination of intellect or will; it originates in the natural superdetermination of the rational appetite."

This superdetermination of the will to the good as such is the root of the will's active indifference with respect to particular goods. Simon develops through a series of examples the significant contrast that exists between a passive indifference and an active indifference, between an indifference which results from a lack and deficiency and one which results from an abundance. Here the will's freedom is described as "not only an active indifference: it is a dominating indifference." This description recalls the images of disorder with which Simon introduced his analysis of freedom, but now it can be better understood how freedom is not an abdication of causality or a chance event, but a special kind of causality, the causality of self-determination.

Wherever there is self-determination there is a cause for the choice which issues from deliberation, but insofar as the will determines its own direction, men are free. There is nothing of irrationality or lawlessness in this, Simon insists; this view of man's freedom is an affirmation of a person's mastery over himself in a way that is unique in the physical world yet quite fitting to it in view of man's status as the image of God.

D.J.F.

SAINT FRANCIS XAVIER

Author: James Brodrick, S.J. (1891-)
Type of work: Hagiography
First published: 1952

Principal Ideas Advanced

Francis Xavier was a man much like the rest of us, with his own particular limitations and shortcomings.

In other respects, he was extraordinary: in his personality, in the graces he received from God, and in the use he made of his graces.

This distinctive combination of nature and grace enabled Francis to become the greatest missionary of modern times, as he traveled around the world spreading the Word of God.

Hagiography, or sacred biography, has manifested a variety of styles during the history of the Church. In the Middle Ages a stereotyped standard life of a saint was produced into which the name of almost any saint could be inserted. Such a life almost invariably included some prodigy connected with the saint's birth, a prophecy of future sanctity, accounts of assorted miracles, difficulties endured in the form of painful illness or persecution, and finally, a foretelling of the date of death. Within this framework, especially during and after the Renaissance, the saint took on many of the characteristics of the classical hero. Everything about him was extraordinary; he was a sort of spiritual giant.

Such uncritical attitudes often led the hagiographer, consciously or otherwise, to select or "filter" his data. Where pious data was lacking, it could easily be inferred. Where no such data existed at all, its absence was more often than not passed over in silence. One notable exception was the case in which a previously sinful or irreligious life preceded a conversion and later became a spur toward even greater efforts at sanctity. However, even such events as these were generally passed over quickly, and, after the conversion, even relatively minor human failings and limitations were scarcely admissible. "After all," the hagiographer might have asked himself, "what good would it do the pious reader to know about these things? He would profit much more from a recital of heroically virtuous acts." It seems to have escaped such writers that an honest account of the saint's shortcomings and limitations might have brought him much closer to us and enabled him to exercise much more influence on our lives, for the saint would then appear not so much as a distant Olympian hero, but as a brother and friend, who has experienced all our miseries, and who, by his generous co-operation with God's grace, has been able to give to his life that unique and admirable quality which we call sanctity.

Fortunately, in recent years, there has arisen a new breed of hagiographers, who have taken as their task the creation of an accurate, three-dimensional portrait of the saint, with all his strengths and weaknesses, his excellences and limitations. It is perhaps significant that many of these writers are professional historians rather than spiritual directors. Foremost among this group of sacred biographers is Father James Brodrick of the Society of Jesus. Father Brodrick has devoted his talents as historian and biographer mostly to recording the lives of his own brother Jesuits, but when one considers the prominent role which this band of men has played in the life of the Church since the Reformation and the fact that it includes such giants as Ignatius Loyola, Robert Bellarmine and Peter Canisius, one cannot help but agree that this concentration of his attention is well merited.

Francis Xavier, another of Brodrick's Jesuit brothers, died in 1552, and Brodrick was asked in 1952 to write this biography to commemorate the four hundredth anniversary of his death. In this task Brodrick was greatly aided by the work of Father George Schurhammer, another Jesuit scholar, who had devoted more than thirty years to the study of Xavier's life. Brodrick acknowledges this debt in his preface and recognizes Schurhammer's "unremitting and sacrificial labor dedicated to the task of finding the real Xavier under the pyramid of pious accretion built upon his humble bones by the mistaken reverence of biographers and editors throughout four centuries."

Admittedly the biographer has in Xavier's life a subject which lends itself easily to the epic and heroic mode. He was a missionary second in importance only to Saint Paul in the effectiveness of his labors for the extension of the Church. The mere recital of his travels and hardships staggers the imagination.

Xavier came from the minor nobility of the Kingdom of Navarre, in Northern Spain. His Basque family was proud and jealous of its rights. Brodrick describes their relations to their feudal lords as being in the spirit of the vassals of Aragon, whose oath of allegiance to their feudal lord began: "We, who are as good as you, swear to you, who are no better than we. . . ."

Francis was the youngest of five children. Little is known of his boyhood, but "One perfectly safe deduction is that he was bred in the atmosphere of austere Catholic piety."

In 1520, during a revolt of the Navarrese supported by the French against the Emperor Charles V of Spain, Francis' two older brothers fought on the side of the French at the siege of Pamplona. In this same siege another Basque, Ignatius of Loyola, was wounded defending the citadel, an incident that was to have a greater influence on the fortunes of Francis Xavier than any other event of his adventurous life.

The war ended disastrously for the French, and the Xavier brothers returned home to find the eighteen-year-old Francis now a tonsured cleric of the diocese of Pamplona. The gesture committed him to nothing, and it exempted him from whatever military service the emperor might impose.

In 1525 the ambitious Francis left home for the University of Paris, ". . . to an assignation . . . arranged by the providence of God, from which he would have fled in as much dismay as Jonah did to Tarshish, had he had the slightest inkling of it." We have no evidence that he ever saw Xavier castle or his family again. So far as we know he never wrote to his mother, nor do we have any evidence of grief at her death four years later. As Brodrick says, "Even by Basque standards, which are notoriously high, he had a phenomenal capacity for saying nothing."

Francis spent eleven years in Paris (1525-1536), but for the greater part of it, ". . . his history remains almost as much a blank as it was in Navarre." Brodrick's professional attitude toward many of the earlier biographies is well illustrated in a footnote as he begins his chapter on Francis' life in Paris: "The letters given in such older biographies as those of Bouhours . . . or Coleridge. . . , are translations of Latin versions made early by Jesuits who, in all good faith, evidently thought that the best way to honour St. Francis was to put his hurried, repetitive, and often ungrammatical sentences into fine, expansive, Ciceronian prose. Francis, who cared nothing for style and hadn't any, would have been astonished at the magnificent flowing robes wherein they dressed him."

In Paris Francis enrolled in the college of Sainte-Barbe, whose austere regime included rising at 4 A.M., with unbroken prayers and lessons before breakfast at 10 A.M. Study hours were excessive and food was meager. As a student Francis did not distinguish himself: "He had a gift at this time for evading the more onerous requirements of university life and seems to have found his mind's delight anywhere but in books."

In spite of his thin resources, Francis, in order to assert his nobility in the eyes of the world, engaged another student as a valet. This move and other extravagances brought remonstrances from his relatives at home. Apart from a perennial difficulty in making ends meet, Brodrick concludes that Francis must have enjoyed the Parisian life or he would not have stayed there so long. He took particular delight in sports and excelled as a high-jumper. His participation in student life included also clandestine nights on the town. However, according to his own later testimony, more out of fear than out of virtue he avoided the sexual excesses of his comrades.

At Sainte-Barbe he shared a room with a Savoyard of an extraordinarily sweet disposition by the name of Pierre Favre (1506-1546) later to be, with Francis, one of the first members of the Society of Jesus, and its first priest. In 1528, ". . . all of a sudden destiny climbed the stairs of Sainte-Barbe in a shape as strange and unrecognizable as it ever has taken." This destiny was the entrance into Francis' life of Ignatius Loyola, whose presence at the siege of Pamplona we have noted previously. Ignatius had been gravely wounded by a cannon ball, which had crushed one of his legs. The crude and clumsy surgery of his day forced upon him a long and painful convalescence. His spiritual reading and reflection convinced Ignatius that he needed further learning if he was to serve God more effectively, and thus he undertook studies at the famous universities of Alcalà and Salamanca in Spain, and then, finally, in Paris.

Ignatius, with his ascetic ways, was a mystery to many of his fellow students and he was soon the subject of heated controversy. Some were his devoted admirers; others questioned even his orthodoxy. Francis definitely did not like Ignatius and did not want to have anything to do with him; he could hardly have been very happy to see Ignatius assigned to share the same room with him and Pierre Favre.

Even though Favre was soon won over completely to the new arrival with the bright, friendly eyes, Francis resisted Ignatius' every approach for over two years. One bit of hagiographic legend pertaining to this period is handled by Brodrick as follows: "There is a story repeated in all the biographies of Francis from the first printed to the very latest, that Ignatius broke down his resistance by constantly dinning into his ear the text: 'What shall it profit a man if he gain the whole world and lose his own soul?' Such a frontal method of attack is quite uncharacteristic of the great spiritual strategist to whom it is attributed, and not a shred of real evidence exists that he employed it at all."

For several months during 1533 Favre was absent, and Ignatius and Francis had the room to themselves. Nothing whatever is known of the process by which Ignatius finally won Francis over, but when Favre returned in 1534, he found Francis as resolute as himself in his adherence to Ignatius.

Later that same year Ignatius, Francis, and Pierre, together with four other students at the University of Paris who had been won over to Ignatius' ideal of a life dedicated to God's service, pronounced vows of poverty and chastity, and of making a pilgrimage to Jerusalem. The ceremony took place in a tiny, private chapel on Montmartre. This small group was the embryo which would eventually grow into the Society of Jesus.

In the event that they should be unable to obtain passage to Palestine because of a threatened war between Venice and the Turks, the tiny band was resolved to go to Rome and offer themselves to the pope as men prepared to preach the Gospel anywhere in the world at his discretion. It was several years before the group, now grown to nine, would finally abandon the Palestinian project. Meanwhile they traveled about Italy, living upon alms and offering their services for work in hospitals for incurables. On June 24, 1537, Ignatius, Francis Xavier, and the others of their group who were not yet priests were ordained in Venice.

These were years of great privation and labor. Xavier was full of zeal and not always prudent in moderating his work and the rigors of his life. At one point he and one of his companions fell ill and had to be taken to the hospital themselves. There, because of crowding, they were forced to share the same bed, a circumstance which set the stage for the following contest of brotherly charity. Xavier was burning with fever, while his companion was shivering with a chill. Each one, however, tried to minister to the other's comfort rather than to his own. We are thus presented with a picture, both amusing and touching, of the feverish Xavier trying to keep the covers on, while his shivering companion, is trying to throw them off.

The companions traveled about the cities of Northern Italy in groups of two or three preaching the Word of God in Spanish-accented, ungrammatical Italian to all who would give them a hearing. It must have been a strange, even comical, sight, but many who came to laugh were soon hushed, touched by the fire, the love, and the obvious sincerity of the little band.

Though they were still without the least intention of founding a new religious order, they felt that they should choose some name for themselves, so as to be able to answer questions about their affiliation. After much prayer and discussion they finally decided to call themselves the Company of Jesus.

In 1538, after it had become abundantly clear that passage to Palestine would be impossible, the companions journeyed to Rome. The life of Ignatius Loyola had been a very agitated one since his conversion. In those days of religious upheaval, anyone with new or strange ideas was suspect, and Ignatius had been imprisoned more than once by the Inquisition on charges of heresy. Each time, however, he had succeeded in having himself acquitted. Old charges were now renewed against him and his companions, and it was several months before they were able to obtain the requisite testimonials of orthodoxy of doctrine and probity of morals from all the places in which they had labored. The outcome, however, was their complete justification in the eyes of the pope.

The winter of 1538-1539 was a more severe one than Rome had ever known. Up to a tenth of the population died of sheer cold and starvation. In these circumstances the companions, seeing Christ in their neighbors, and already accustomed to begging, set out through the city to obtain straw for beds, wood for fires, and bread for empty stomachs. They then scoured the streets of the city to bring in the freezing homeless. By some miracle of planning they were able to crowd up to four hundred unfortunates into a ramshackle but roomy house.

According to Brodrick's account, this example of charity and devotion made a great impression on the Roman populace, nor did it escape the eyes of the pope. "Why are you so anxious to go to Jerusalem?" he asked. "Is not Italy a good and true Jerusalem, if you desire to bear fruit in the Church of God?" This question seems to have been the immediate cause of the companions' beginning to deliberate seriously as to whether or not they should organize themselves into a more closely knit body. Their deliberations were long and weighty, accompanied by prayer, study, and much argument. They agreed unanimously that they would remain a corporate unity, even though the pope might choose to disperse them throughout the world, and they saw that the best means of preserving their unity in these circumstances, as well as of fulfilling God's will in all things, would be in vowing obedience to one of their number. Thus was born the idea of the Society of Jesus.

In August, 1539, Ignatius reduced the conclusions of their arguments and discussions to five chapters and submitted them to the pope. These chapters contained several ideas considered revolutionary at the time, as, for instance, that the superior general should be elected for life and that the Divine Office should be recited in private rather than in choir, so that the members would be free to devote themselves more completely to the works of charity which they desired to undertake. There was also a special. explicit, fourth vow (besides poverty, chastity, and obedience) of obedience to the pope, binding them to undertake promptly and with alacrity whatever missions or tasks he might choose to assign to them, no matter how distant or dangerous.

Though the pope himself was favorable to the project and began dispersing the companions on apostolic missions throughout Italy and even as far as Ireland, as if the fourth vow were already in effect, there was much opposition within the Roman Curia to the proposed Society, and the matter was not finally settled for more than a year. By then Francis Xavier was halfway around the world.

The good fame of the companions had been spreading. It had even reached Portugal, where King John III was constantly seeking good priests who would bring the knowledge of Christ's salvation to the peoples of his far-flung empire and at the same time keep his own lusty Portuguese soldiers in the paths of righteousness. This latter aim, says Brodrick, was "a task even more difficult than the other." The king had made overtures through his ambassador in Rome to secure the services of these fervent priests for his dominions. The companions were happy to oblige him, but because several of them were absent on missions, they could offer him only two men, Father Simon Rodriguez and Father Nicolaus Bobadilla. It was no secret that Francis Xavier's thoughts and desires turned toward the East. He had frequently expressed himself to that effect, but his chances must now have seemed slim indeed. He was being employed by Ignatius as a secretary, to assist him with his growing correspondence.

Then affairs took an unexpected turn, Brodrick writes. Father Bobadilla, one of the two fathers designated for the mission, became gravely ill. The Portuguese ambassador was leaving Rome for Lisbon on March 15 and expected the new missionaries to be with him. But it was not until March 14 that Ignatius finally called Francis, a man who had truly become the other half of his soul, explained the situation to him briefly, and then concluded, "This is your enterprise." "Such," says Brodrick, "was the unemotional scene, a truly Basque picture, etched in the heart's blood of two fast friends who were to part forever on the morrow."

Francis' recorded reply, "Héme, aqui", echoes the scriptural readiness of Abraham and of the prophet Isaias; "Ecce adsum: Here I am." After this historic acceptance, so significant for the future of the Church in the East, Brodrick adds that Francis, "there and then set to work patching some old pairs of trousers and nondescript soutane."

Thus began the extraordinary journeyings of Francis Xavier, which were to carry him out of Lisbon and around the southern tip of Africa, up the eastern coast of Africa and on to Goa in Portuguese India; then down the Fishery Coast to Ceylon and east through Malaya and Indonesia, and finally northward to Japan. In his search for souls Francis Xavier far outstripped the traders and the empire builders.

Shortly after he left Rome on his way overland to Lisbon, Xavier wrote to Ignatius from Bologna: "As I think that it is only through the medium of letters we shall see one another again in this life—in the next it will be face to face with many embraces—it remains for us during the little time left here below to secure these mutual glimpses by frequently writing."

It is these letters, one over ten thousand words long, which have enabled historians to trace Xavier's footsteps during the rest of his life, and Father Brodrick performs the task with accuracy, sympathy, and humor. The hardships Francis encountered are innumerable. He was named Jesuit superior for all the East, which meant that, besides all the difficulties accompanying his missionary travels, he had the additional burden of attempting to supervise the activities of his sometimes recalcitrant Jesuit brethren based in Goa.

His efforts to spread the Word of God among the pagans carried him into the midst of humble pearl-fishers, blood-thirsty, warring Maharajahs, treacherous pirates and sea captains, subtly disputing Buddhist monks, and Japanese warlords.

Francis's letters reveal to us a man on fire with the desire to bring the message of Christ's Redemption to the pagan world. They also reveal a man who can feel tenderness toward his brethren and is not afraid of acknowledging it, especially in regard to Ignatius, whose letters he read and answered on his knees and whose signature he wore in a packet around his neck. In one of his last letters to Ignatius, we read: "Among many other holy words and consolations of your letter I read the concluding ones, 'Entirely yours, without power or possibility of ever forgetting you, Ignatio.' I read them with tears, and with tears now write them, remembering the past and the great love which you always bore towards me and still bear, while at the same time calling to mind the many trials and perils of Japan from which God delivered me through the intercession of your holy prayers."

His letters also show him to have been an incurable optimist, overly trustful of others. Often the information he was given was incorrect, but this did not seem to bother him in the least or slow him down. His unbounded confidence in Divine Providence was such that lesser lights would probably consider it exaggerated or naïve. Yet it was this confidence which carried him halfway around the world, to India, Indonesia, Japan, and even to the gates of the Celestial Empire of China. There he died, burned out at the age of forty-six and delirious with fever, as he waited in vain on a tiny island off the China coast for a Chinese merchant vessel to take him to the mainland for new hardships and spiritual conquests.

Father Brodrick adds a chapter concerning the extraordinary veneration paid to Saint Francis after his death, but we shall end with his paragraph of commentary following the description of Francis's death: "It was a poor and humble death, not unperplexed, such as befitted a poor and humble man who had no notion whatever that the world would want to remember him. He had brought thousands of others the comforts of the Church in their last moments, but he died himself without anointing or Viaticum. When they packed his frail, exhausted body in lime and put it in the unconsecrated Chinese earth, there was no one to read over it the Church's last farewell to her children. Had he ever been so far untrue to his character as to give a thought to his obsequies, he would surely have been well content that his bones should remain there, as it were, keeping watch until the end of the world, if indeed, he would not have prayed to God with all his heart to be allowed the last privilege of the lowly, an unknown and forgotten grave."

E.L.B.

THE LORD OF HISTORY

Author: Jean Daniélou, S.J. (1905-)
Type of work: Philosophy of history
First published: 1953

Principal Ideas Advanced

The Christian attitude toward history is determined by a series of divine events, each marking a new stage in the actualization of God's design for the world.

For the Christian, history is progressive, with a beginning he can look back upon and a conclusion he can look forward to.

The dynamism of the Christian view of history depends upon the fact of the Incarnation, the entrance of God into time.

Mankind as a whole, as the human family, was saved through Christ, but now this salvation must be extended to individuals all over the world.

In *The Lord of History,* Jean Daniélou distinguishes the Christian view of history from all other interpretations, insisting upon its radical uniqueness. For the Greeks divinity rested in the eternal order of Ideas which the temporal world imitates in its cyclical movement. This separation of the infinite and the finite is typical of archaic systems of thought all over the world. The primitive mind understands the world in dualistic terms, as the interaction of irreconcilable polarities out of which grows a perpetual cyclical movement. Early Christian thinkers such as Origen and Eusebius reflected this ancient system of thought when they viewed Christ as one who had come to reinstate a former condition of existence. Perfection for the Greeks and for early man in general was viewed as something that always stays the same.

According to Daniélou, the Christian view of history is radically different from the attitudes that preceded it, for it understands God to be at work in time through the sacramental life of the Church, building the Kingdom of God and perfecting men for Christ's Second Coming. Saint Augustine was one of the first Christian thinkers to perceive the difference between the Christian view of history and earlier systems of thought. For him, sacred history is that which has "positive beginnings" but no end. Other Church Fathers, among them Saint Gregory of

Nyssa, also felt that it was necessary to establish a specifically Christian view of history.

Since the Incarnation the inner workings of history have centered around the spreading of the Gospel, so that all men may have the chance to believe and thus extend His Kingdom. This work, writes Daniélou, is carried on through the "unfailing efficacy" of the sacraments. What is now going on in the world "is something invisible, yet supremely real, the building up in charity of that mystical body of Christ that shall be revealed in the last day." The extension of God's kingdom is not to be thought of as purely geographical. Our knowledge of God progresses as the Church advances in time, through her saints and thinkers. The temporal world is not evil, according to Daniélou: "Civilization is not devils' work: society and culture belong to creation. They are part of the work of God's hands." God has given man a great privilege, that of co-operating with Him in the perfection of the world. "The new heavens and the new earth shall be our own universe, just as the labours of men have contrived to shape it, only transfigured: so true it is that the history of civilization, no less than the history of the natural creation, belongs within sacred history in the largest sense."

The recognition of the progressive nature of Christianity should prevent men from identifying it with a specific social order. Daniélou writes: "The Christianity of the *bourgeois* has had its day, and Christian people are well aware of the fact: only, what is passing is not Christianity itself, but the particular embodiment of Christianity in a given social organization." The emergence of new social patterns does not mean that the old patterns were not useful in their day, but only that they no longer meet the demands of the present. It is idolatry to treat social systems or classes as if they were absolute realities. History progresses through the successive breakdown of societies that commit the sin of idolatry by thinking of themselves as absolutes. During these periods of social destruction the Church renews itself through a casting off of forms that are not integral to its growth. The resurgent nations of the modern world present a particularly difficult problem for the growth of Christianity because the first reaction of the native convert, writes Daniélou, is to abandon his "traditional aesthetic and intellectual categories along with the paganism they enshrined: he takes his Catholicism as he finds it, from the West." However, in order to thrive in these new nations, the Church must become incarnate in the aesthetic and intellectual categories of the particular culture involved. Pagan culture must not be destroyed, but instead, ways must be found to provide for its flowing naturally into Christianity. Ideally, each culture should have its own variety of Christian civilization while yet remaining within the unifying framework of the Church.

Daniélou claims that the Church in the modern world is no longer identified with a specific society or culture. It has been liberated from an idolatrous identification with "Western culture" and the way has now been prepared for it to become truly universal. Christians in the twentieth century exist as an army of missionaries and martyrs in a world culture that is largely secular. Under these circumstances there is no longer any need for the contemplative to leave the world, because his faith will not be compromised by life in the world as Christians will have to live it, in the immediate future and for some time to come. According to Father Montuclard, the primary challenge facing the Christian in the twentieth century is to revitalize technological society from within by transforming the hearts of men through prayer and sacrifice.

Communism is not simply brutal materialism, Daniélou states; it is an exalted humanism, a religion, a cult of man. Communism, however, does not take into account what happens in the human heart, and since man's real enslavement is spiritual and not economic, it is impossible for communism to liberate man. The cult of technical progress confines man in the contemplation of his own creative power. The religion of progress and the salvation of man through man is the real sin of the contemporary world. Nevertheless, there is a common ground upon which the Christian can agree with the communist. The Christian can share the latter's belief in the capacity of mankind to transform itself.

Communism is partly responsible for the idolatrous enshrinement of science as the only valid means for apprehending reality. The author writes: "Science enlarges the dimensions of the cage in which the mind of man is imprisoned, but all the science in the world will not get him out of it. But in the intuitive perception of symbolism, the mind reaches out from material reality to grasp another reality beyond: this is an enlargement of the spirit." According to Daniélou, there is an objective reality in religious symbolism which is rooted in the nature of things. It is directed toward discovering analogies between the visible and the invisible, the finite and the infinite. Symbolism is "a genuine mode of apprehension of the things of God." Christian symbolism has a uniquely theological character. To the extent that it is grounded in the hierophancies of the physical universe Christian symbolism is natural and accessible to all mankind. However, writes Daniélou, throughout history symbolism has not ceased to grow with "successive accretions of historical significance." The symbolism of the Bible and of the Church as it progresses in time is known as *typology*. The Passover is, from this point of view, a type of the Passion, and the Passover meal of unleavened bread is a type of Holy Communion. Typology is the study of correspondences between the Old and the New Testaments. However, in so far as correspondences continue to evolve in the life of the Church, they may be included in the study of typology.

Daniélou concludes *The Lord of History* with a discussion of the virtues Christians should possess if they are to be true apostles of the Word. Courage is a primary characteristic of the Christian, and Saint Paul is the archetypal possessor of Christian courage. He calls the Christian to warfare against human opponents, material difficulties and the spirits of darkness. Poverty is the condition of spiritual fruitfulness. The Christian, however, should not renounce the world in order to gain the consolations of peaceful solitude. This life is a continual warfare to establish the Kingdom of God, and no man can call himself a Christian if he retreats from the battle. The true apostle must have complete sincerity and integrity. Sincerity rules out mixed motives. It is manifested in purity of intention and unaffected love. Sincerity means trying to make the outer man like the inner man. Christian zeal is the attitude of those who will not compromise in giving God the worship that is due him. Zeal is suffering and indignation because men do not keep faith with God. Zeal is strength to defend God against those who do not honor Him, but since it comes from pure love it has all love's instinctive tact. Christian hope is compounded of humility and trust. It is based on what the Christian knows has already been won for mankind and for each soul through Christ. It is the specifically Christian virtue of life in the temporal world, based on the knowledge that we have come from God and are returning to Him. Finally, writes Daniélou, the distinguishing mark of the Christian is that he has faith in God and believes that no matter what the external circumstances may be, everything is possible with God.

D.M.R.

THE CHRIST OF FAITH

Author: Karl Adam (1876-)
Type of work: Dogmatic theology
First published: 1954

Principal Ideas Advanced

The doctrine concerning Christ lies at the heart of all Catholic dogma.

We receive the belief in Jesus from the living tradition of the Church, not from philosophical or textual criticism.

In all the history of religion there is no analogy to be found to the unique position which Christ occupies in Christianity, in which the personality of the founder rather than His doctrine constitutes the entire content of the religion.

At the very center of all Catholic belief is the Church's doctrine concerning Christ. It is only through and in Him that the awesome mystery of the Trinity is revealed to us. He is obviously at the center of the doctrine of the Redemption; closely connected with the doctrine of the Redemption is the doctrine on original and actual sin, from which we are redeemed. The Church's doctrine on grace, moreover, seeks to explain the transformation of our lives which Christ's redemption of us has brought about. Further, the doctrines on the Church and on the sacraments are concerned essentially with the various channels through which the fruits of the Redemption are brought to us.

The doctrine on Christ, then, is at the very core of the Catholic faith, and a Catholic's appreciation of this totality of belief will be in relation to how well he has penetrated this mystery of Christ and has made it an integral and operative part of his life.

It is precisely in this area that Karl Adam's book, *The Christ of Faith,* can be of great service. Adam, who is widely regarded as one of the most brilliant theologians of the twentieth century, is well equipped to write on the subject chosen. He was born in Bavaria and studied at the seminary at Regensburg and at the University of Munich. In 1900 he was ordained to the priesthood, and in 1904 he obtained his doctorate at Munich. He devoted himself to parish work for a few years and then turned to theological writings. In 1915 he became a professor at the University of Munich. In 1917 he assumed the chair of moral theology at the University of Strasbourg and in 1919 the chair of dogmatic theology at the University of Tübingen. This last is remarkable in that it is one of the few European universities which has fully constituted faculties in both Catholic and Protestant theology. The advent of the Nazis to power in 1933 brought Adam into sharp conflict with the regime because of his outspoken criticism of their efforts to establish a new "German" religion. This conflict reached such a pitch of intensity that Adam's house was riddled with bullets.

Adam has always been intensely interested in the question of Christian unity, and he was deeply involved in the question long before it obtained the popularity and respectability which resulted from the attitudes and acts of Pope John XXIII and Pope Paul VI. For years he collaborated with the movement known as *One and Holy,* which was a reasoned appeal for the return of all Christian faiths to the Mother Church. In these efforts he won the good will and respect of non-Catholics because of his extensive learning and obvious good will. There is a heavy concentration in his writings upon Christ and upon the Mystical Body, a doctrine which he feels can solve the world's problems if it is applied fully and unreservedly.

One of the most frequent, though often unconscious, errors which the educated Catholic easily falls into in his efforts to obtain an increased understanding of his faith is the assumption that he will eventually arrive at a moment when he will be able to "prove" his faith in Christ; that is, that he will somehow or other be able to do away with any element of risk or doubt, will, in other words, have his faith as though it were the conclusion of an airtight syllogism. What this assumption overlooks, however, is that such a conclusion would not really consist in a better understanding of one's faith but in the destruction of faith, in its replacement by a purely rationalistic attitude.

Karl Adam, in *The Christ of Faith,* confronts a wish for an airtight formula with the fact that faith in Christ, that faith which is the very center of all Christian doctrine, is *given to us only by our Mother, the Church.* It is from faith in Christ that the Church herself arose, and it is from her, not from philosophical or textual criticism, that faith comes to us. She is the living tradition of this faith in Christ's divinity, a faith handed down from the Apostles and sealed with their martyrdom. She knows this *through herself,* out of her own self-awareness.

This realization of the inestimable importance of the Church is central in Adam's work. Without this living Church, he insists, the New Testament would be a mere literary composition. Through her, however, we touch the living faith of the Apostles. "Whom do you say that I am?" Christ had asked them. That was and still is the all-important question. Adam writes: "In all the history of religion, there is *no* analogy to be found to this relationship between the Church and Christ. Why? Because it is only in Christianity that the personality of the founder constitutes the entire content of the religion. The Christian is the man who has made Christ his own, who is animated by the spirit of Christ. All other religions that have demonstrably been founded by an historical personality do not regard their founder as the content, the object of their faith, but simply as its mediator."

The tidings of Christ's identity provide the true content of our religion, Adam claims: "Subsequent centuries have attempted to fathom this mystery in all its depth and all its breadth, and bring it to consciousness. In doing so, they took over certain ideas and concepts from elsewhere—from Judaism, from Greek and Hellenistic philosophy. Afterwards they applied regular Scholastic concepts borrowed from Plato and Plotinus and later from Aristotle too. All these borrowings were only using the resources of the age to make still clearer what was inscribed direct and living in all hearts, the image of the Lord. . . . It was always one and the same Christ, proclaimed with ever-new tongues, and with ever-growing penetration and clarity."

The unique relationship of Christ to the Church is the source of our assurance of nondistortion in the image she presents to us. She alone knew Him. She alone can show Him to us as He is: "This overwhelming fact, that Christianity never was anything but the tidings of Christ, that Christ was and is the object of contemplation and thought across many hundreds of years, assures us that the image of Jesus cherished by the congregation of the faithful can never be distorted, that it is the true, original image of Christ, and that therefore we must go to the living Church and not to the critics ouside the faith, if we are searching for the true Christ."

Adam's remark is of extreme importance, especially in the light of the growing interest in and study of the Scriptures by well-educated Catholics. The Christian whose "faith" is based upon Scriptural criticism and not upon the living testimony of the Church possesses "a miserable kind of Christianity, living in constant anxiety as to whether today or the next day criticism would pronounce its death penalty."

Such an overestimation of Biblical criticism is based upon two false assumptions. First, it supposes that Christianity is nothing but Bible Christianity, that it has its origin solely in the Bible, a danger that threatens Protestants much more than it does Catholics. The fact is, of course, that the living faith of the Church antedated *any* Christian literature. Thus, the New Testament did not produce the faith; instead, the faith produced these writings. Indeed, it would even be possible to have a Christianity without the Bible. The second false assumption is that the Church's Christology is a fixed, finished, inflexible, and fossilized thing, given once and for all. The sole source of the doctrine, then, and its exclusive standard for acceptance would be the historical evidence for it. Such an attitude approaches Christianity as a mummy or as a corpse to be dissected rather than as the living thing it is. Thus, some critical scholars fall back upon methods which simply express their own philosophical *a priori* assumptions, such as the impossibility of miracles or any other supernatural events. Once such a method has been adopted as a starting point for examining the faith, it is obvious that only subjective conclusions will be reached. Adam writes: "Because the critic will not use the support offered by the objective spirit of living Christianity, self-perpetuating in the community of faith and love, he has to give free play to his own critical intellect and personal intuition. Instead of the objective spirit of the living Church, transcending every individual and culture, he falls back upon *his own subjective intellect*. And since no human intellect is utterly independent, but is open to manifold outside influences, particularly to social and philosophical trends, systems of thought arise in whose aspect one can tell at a glance whether they have been fathered by Hegel or Marx, Schleiermacher or Nietzsche, Heidegger or Sartre. At one moment Christ parades in the Rationalist's toga, as Goodman Enlightenment. The next, he sobs and sighs like Goethe's Werther. Now he is the stern moralist, firmly upholding the categorical imperative; and now he wears the Jacobin's stocking cap. Or perhaps he is the lonely dreamer, going through the world misunderstood, and dying misunderstood. One thing is certain: 'It was not only each epoch,' remarks A. Schweitzer, 'that found its reflection in Jesus; each individual created him in accordance with his own character.'"

Adam clearly indicates how the individual Christian's act of faith is something completely personal and how the fact that he is in a position to make this act of faith, that is, that he should be objectively and subjectively directed toward the mystery, is based on the testimony of the Church alone.

Adam also discusses the relative roles of intellect and will in the act of faith. Both faculties are involved, for faith is an act of the intellect under the command of the will. Psychologically, belief in Christ is an experience of good, wrought by God, rather than an experience of certainty. As Adam explains that belief, "In its depths it is irrational, incomprehensible, or rather, beyond all conceiving; but nevertheless it is also rational to the extent that the intellect can at least make the good it has experienced credible. . . . If the intellect were capable of making this experience absolutely certain . . . our belief in Christ would be the object of rational cognition alone, and only the clever and knowledgeable would be summoned to the faith. Faith would no longer be a moral act, a leap of the heart and the shaken conscience up to the living God; . . . it would no longer be a mystical, supernatural event . . . but a simple act of intellectual understanding like any other, like examining the structure of an insect's wings."

Turning then to the Church's Christology, Adam presents a concise history of the Christological heresies of the early centuries of Christianity. We sometimes think of our own age as an age of "isms," but what an array of them we find in the early life of the Church: Monarchianism, Arianism, Subordinationism, Docetism, Apollinarianism, Nestorianism, Monophysitism, Monotheletism, Monenergism, and Adoptionism. He gives us a thumbnail sketch of each successive heresy and a short summary of the Church's reaction in each case. The role of the Ecclesiastical Office has been purely defensive; namely, to preserve the tradition in its purest form. On many points disputed among theologians the Office has taken no positive stand, but the Church's one constant device has been to test each new attempt at explanation against its own living faith. If the two agreed, the explanation was allowed to stand; if not, it was condemned and rejected as a misinterpretation and a distortion of the true image of Christ, "that dogmatic image of Christ which alone has permanence in history and alone has made history."

At this point the author presents us with the image of Christ in non-Catholic theology. At first Protestant theology took over the traditional, Catholic image of the Christ of faith, but since the age of "the Enlightenment" it has become the victim of a gradual tendency toward rationalistic thinking. The question "Was Christ the Son of God?" was no longer asked. Instead the problem was to explain how this paradoxical faith could have arisen in Christian communities. This, of course, is a radical question, next to which all the Christological disputes of the early centuries seem tame and relatively harmless.

The various "schools" of Protestant Biblical criticism are presented in turn: the mythological school, based on Hegelian ideas and represented by David Friedrich Strauss; the liberal, anti-Hegelian school of Bruno Bauer, Nietzsche, and others; the eschatological school of Schweitzer and Rudolf Bultmann, seeking for the "original" sources in the Scriptures, below the secondary and tertiary strata; and, most recently and most significantly, the dialectical school of Karl Barth and Emil Brunner, reaffirming the divinity in Christianity, its uniqueness and absoluteness in the face of all humanized versions of the liberals.

This last-mentioned school marks a return to the traditional image of Christ, in opposition to the efforts of Bultmann, for whom the essence of the Christian faith lies in man's realization, as he apprehends the teaching of Christ, of his own complete surrender to the world of the senses; by accepting the message of Christ's death and resurrection, man succeeds in conquering the world and *redeeming himself*: "In spite of Bultmann's protestations to the contrary, his doctrine has abandoned Christ's teaching, which is centered precisely on the supernatural events of his life. Revelation becomes a mere philosophy of religion, which has its roots in Kierkegaard and in Heidegger's Existentialism."

Such disputes are primarily the concern of the Protestants; they touch the Catholic Church only indirectly. She cannot, however, ignore them completely. What she opposes to this critical scholarship is her own consciousness of faith. Were she to oppose it solely with the means of scholarship and not with the power of her faith, she would be sacrificing the very thing that characterizes her, the consciousness of being the living self-perpetuation of Christ's teaching. "The Church has no need to prove Christ," Adam insists; "She herself in all her being and becoming is the unfolded faith in Christ the Lord, the ever-living Christ."

"When we probe the sources of revelation," then, "we are tracing only the reflection which the living image of Christ in the believing Church has brought forth in canonical and post-canonical literature." Adam thus prepares us to follow him in his use of the "dogmatic" method. What chiefly characterizes this method is that it does not draw its evidence about Christ from secular source material but from the living faith of the Church, that faith which has expressed itself in both the Bible and tradition. This dogmatic method is combined where necessary with the apologetic method, which uses purely natural means of perception in order to meet opponents on their own historical ground and prove that our faith in Christ is compatible with reason.

In discussing the Gospels, Adam indicates in great detail the evidence of Jesus' consciousness of being the Messiah and son of God in the strict, metaphysical sense. Adam also abstracts evidence of Jesus' true humanity.

From this point Adam goes back still further in the literary sources, through the Acts of the Apostles, to the belief of the early Christian community. This detailed investigation is of great importance, especially in view of the frequently repeated but seldom examined statement, found in so many summary histories of Christianity or texts of comparative religion, to the effect that Christ's divinity was a Hellenistic invention of Saint Paul.

Through several chapters Adam traces in still greater detail Christ's consciousness of His Messianic mission. He also closely examines the enigmatic title "Son of Man," as well as "Son of God." Then in succeeding chapters he analyzes the interpretation of Christ's self-consciousness by Saint Paul, Saint John, the early Church Fathers, the Scholastics, and Post-Tridentine theology.

The author next discusses that unique union of two natures, the human and the divine, in one person, which is technically called "the hypostatic union." The most important result of this union, apart from its being the foundation for the Redemption itself, is that Christ the man becomes a worthy object of our adoration. Adam even inserts a short exposition of this dogma in relation to devotion to the Sacred Heart. Two effects of this union, namely, the ethical and intellectual perfection of Christ's humanity, are discussed in two additional chapters.

Up to this point Adam has been concerned primarily with the *person* of Christ. In a second, much shorter, section, Adam turns to the *work* of Christ; that is, to our redemption from sin and error through His sacrificial death. The closing chapter treats of the reign of the victorious, risen Redeemer, in the Church, His Mystical Body, and in His eternal glorification.

As the reader can easily see, this work of Karl Adam on Christ leaves practically no aspect of Christology unexamined. There are undoubtedly particular sections and developments which are of interest primarily to the professional theologian. On the other hand, the more basic, fundamental points are ones with which every educated Catholic should be familiar. The opening chapter, on the source of our belief in Christ, is a masterpiece in itself. In addition, the book serves as a handy, ever-present source or reference, to which one may refer for any desired clarification of the Church's doctrine on Christ, as well as for its justification.

E.L.B.

JESUS AND HIS TIMES

Author: Henri Daniel-Rops (1901-)
Type of work: Life of Christ
First published: 1954

Principal Ideas Advanced

The difficulties encountered in attempting a life of Jesus Christ include the fact that it stretches between two mysteries, the Incarnation and the Redemption, both in defiance of logic and demanding an act of faith for acceptance, and the fact that historical records of Christ's life are not really sufficient to fill in anything approaching a complete portrait.

The enigma of Christ's nature is reflected in the basic conflict between the human and divine aspects of Christian teaching and provides the biographer with the central conflict in the character of Christ which makes Him acceptable on our level of reality.

Background material, which includes socio-political conditions in the Roman Empire, especially in the Near East, the peculiar situation of the Jews in their occupied country, the topography of and archaeological finds in Palestine, the examination of available records and their evolution into the Christian canon, cannot be overestimated in determining the historical significance and value of Christ's message.

Because the life of Christ is set definitely in historical time and not—as are traditions concerning some of the Greek gods—in a remote legendary period, many of the people appearing in the narrative concerning Jesus appear in other historical documents. The stumbling block, comments Henri Daniel-Rops in *Jesus and His Times,* is that truly important contemporaries of Christ failed to recognize His existence. There is no record of Him, for example, in the archives of the Roman administration, although there is mention of the early Christian sect. The Roman historian Tacitus (c.55-c.120) mentions Christ in relation to a disturbance in Rome blamed on the early Christians. His record dates to about the year 116 and drew from, among other sources, the writings of Pliny the Elder (23-79), who was on the staff of Titus (c.40-81) in his war against the Jews in the year 70. Among the Jewish historians who are important in establishing the existence of Christ on a secular historical basis is Flavius Josephus (37-c.96), author of

Hebrew Antiquities, who fails to treat Christ directly—although he does describe in detail John the Baptist and the Apostle James—except for one very controversial passage which seems to imply his own acceptance of Christian doctrine, but which many critics refuse to recognize as originally his, charging that it does not fit into his other work or reflect the rather vain, self-satisfied portrait he has left us of himself.

For the fullest knowledge of Christ, then, we are thrown back upon the Gospels, which contain the earliest Christian doctrine and which were part of an established unwritten tradition of rabbinical teaching. The message of Jesus was promulgated through a system of rhetorical devices designed to facilitate learning and retention, such as the use of regular cadences in strophe or anti-strophe, as reflected in the Beatitudes and maledictions in the Sermon on the Mount. It is undoubtedly safe to say that not all of the sayings of Christ have found their way into the Scriptures, and many truths concerning Jesus probably exist in the so-called Apocryphal texts.

The fundamental role of the early Christian communities was to stabilize and confine the Christian canon to the testimony of Matthew, Mark, Luke, and John. Two of the Gospels, Matthew and John, are directly preserved from the errors of legend by the position of the authors as Apostles who communicated first hand information. The other two Gospels, those of Mark and Luke, have the authority of Peter and Paul respectively. Daniel-Rops offers as proof of their historicity the unity of message in the four Gospels and the further unity of narrative and chronology in the Synoptic Gospels, Matthew, Mark, and Luke, all of which were set down around the year 80. Even among these, however, there are differences in emphasis. Saint Matthew's Gospel, written for the Jews, possesses a particularly Jewish quality and seems to concentrate upon the words of Christ. Saint Mark's, written for the Romans, emphasizes, because he traveled with Peter, the role of Peter among the Apostles and stresses the actions rather than words of Christ. Luke was the interpreter of Paul, whose knowledge colors his account. Luke was the best storyteller of the Evangelists and seemed to stress the human aspect of Christ. Saint John's Gospel was written between 96 and 104 and is more metaphysical and mystical than the others. It gains from this later date of writing because John spent sixty years in meditating on the life and teachings of his Master and thus could draw more out of them. Because the Gospels were not set down for biographical but for instructional purposes, the portrait of Christ, however incomplete, that does emerge from them, the Acts of the Apostles, and the Epistles of Saint Paul, is surprising in its scope.

Daniel-Rops considers Palestine itself as the fifth Gospel, for the fact is that the life of Christ was set among villages and mountains which still exist for the historian's study today. The detailed geographical information of the Gospels does not serve merely as local color for Christ's life, but also as confirmation of the authenticity of the Gospels. The manners and customs of the Jewish society in which Jesus grew up, lived, and taught are even more interesting than the geographical background. For information in this regard the biographer draws heavily upon the collection of rabbinical writings in the *Talmud,* a somewhat heterogeneous miscellany of texts, history, and commentaries. Although the *Talmud*, because whatever it offers about Jesus is hostile, insulting, and malevolent, is of little help in supplying any direct historical information concerning Him, it does contain reliable evidence about the concrete realities of the world in which Jesus worked, together with accounts of the methods of rabbinical teaching which He used.

The international situation of the time, that is, the situation of the Roman Empire and that peculiar to the Jewish nation, at once illuminates the contents of Christian teaching, provides reasons for its rapid spread throughout the Empire, and contributes to an evaluation of Christianity as a natural outgrowth of a sterile Judaism. The times were ripe for the coming of Christ. The Jewish community, a unique mixture of religion and politics, was beset by intrigues lessened only by a common disdain for the Roman oppressors. Judea was such an unsettled state that it was governed directly by the Emperor through a procurator, one of whom was Pontius Pilate (reigned 26-c.36), rather than through the petty Bedouin monarchs, in whose number was Herod Antipas (ruler of Galilee, 4-39), who figured in the trial of Christ. The Jewish religion seemed a worship of the Law rather than of God. The prime religious concern seemed to be symbolized by the continual hairsplitting of the scribes, who busied themselves with ". . . codifying, commentating, teaching and refining with that combination of stubbornness and subtlety in which the Jewish character excels." The grand Sanhedrin, a kind of senate or council of a religious-political nature made up of priests and scribes and various elders of the people, was divided into two factions, which reflected the two schools of thought that divided public opinion, the Pharisees and the Sadducees. The latter group, which Daniel-Rops compares to the French *bien pensants*, were people of comfortable position not inclined to spiritual or political patriotism and whose passivity, in all matters barring creature comforts, motivated, to a large extent, the excesses of the Pharisees, who, while safeguarding the integrity of the Jewish spiritual inheritance, became fossilized in the exaltation of their pride and the meticulous cult of the letter of ritual observance. It was, naturally enough, the Pharisees who received with the greatest hostility the teaching of Jesus, which undermined the letter of the law in favor of the spirit of the law.

According to Daniel-Rops, the general failure of the Jews to accept Christ as their Messiah resided in this conflict, and in the political prostration of the Jewish nation and its expectancy of a national rather than a spiritual Redeemer. Jesus incurred Jewish wrath not only by undermining the legal hairsplitting by which Jews distinguished themselves from Gentiles but also by including non-Jews in the Jewish legacy, which he proposed to re-form on a universal rather than national level. When Jesus spoke of the destruction of Jerusalem and of the Temple, He implied the end of national preference in the eyes of God.

The very reasons which caused Christ's failure among the Jews caused His success outside of Israel, the author claims. In stressing the spirit of the Law, which led to an inner rather than exterior religion, Jesus dignified the individual and appealed to the masses of an empire plagued by skepticism and the breakdown of moral standards. Christ's teaching was also attractive in its conception of God as a kind Father, rather than as the terrible Law-giver of the Mosaic tradition. Daniel-Rops illustrates this difference by comparing the conception of God in the "Our Father" to "Hear O Israel," the customary Jewish daily prayer. There were physical as well as spiritual reasons for the rapid spread of Christianity in the Roman Empire. Among these were the Roman peace, the international use of Latin, the roads built by Augustus (63 B.C.-A.D. 14) and, ironically enough, the Jewish dispersion, which had made monotheism and the Old Testament, upon which Christianity was built, known throughout the Empire.

As far as his treatment of the character of Jesus is concerned, Daniel-Rops, like other writers on the subject, includes much material that is already familiar to practically everyone living or educated in Western civilization. The author's most interesting sections on Christ Himself, although he fails to develop them sufficiently, concern the conflict between His human and divine natures, a conflict brought out in the beginning of Christ's ministry when He was tempted in the desert by the Devil. While some theologians believe this confrontation to have been a vision, it symbolizes a real inner struggle which constantly recurred in Christ until His death on the cross. Christ's rejection of the Devil amounted to a rejection of those things—material wealth, power, immunity from death—which would have satisfied His human nature but frustrated the redemptive purpose of His divine nature. This conflict of natures is most dramatically evident in Gethsemane when the humanity of the youthful Christ quaked and revolted at the thought of death. The human struggle in this instance caused a bloody sweat, intensified by a distraught awareness of that death to which He aspired. The mortal combat of the Agony in the Garden was, perhaps, Christ's most difficult moment, the moment during which the conflict between His natures was most acute. On a far more tender, if less powerful, plane is the conflict Jesus experienced when He beheld the tomb of Lazarus. Even though He knew He would raise Lazarus from the dead, the grief of Martha and Mary and the sight of the tomb of His friend caused Jesus to weep. Daniel-Rops, while stressing the extent to which Jesus was moved by this incident, fails to connect it to Jesus' statement (included less than twenty pages earlier) to an aspiring disciple who asks for a delay to bury his dead father, that he should leave the dead to bury the dead and go out immediately to proclaim God's kingdom. The author comments: "Those whom Christ calls must renounce everything, even the most natural affections, for the law of love which Jesus preached has something terrible in it, and cannot be falsified into sentimental insipidity." If the teaching of Jesus can be interpreted so callously, there seems to be in it something alien to the humanity He included in His dual nature. Whether or not the teaching reflects the conflict in Christ, it is this conflict which puts Him on our level of reality.

Besides the author's failure to pursue the human-divine enigma of the Incarnate Christ, a failure which, to some degree, is inevitable, there are other shortcomings in this weighty and significant work. The background touches the foreground in fewer instances than one would wish, and the text is marred in various places by a devotional moralizing that does not befit the overall scholarly tone. An example of this occurs in the treatment of the betrayal of Judas. Daniel-Rops falters in the following manner after attempting to discover a motivation for the betrayal: "Perhaps we can even elucidate from his remorse a possible motive for the betrayal; perhaps he did not desire his Master to be condemned but only thought to teach him a lesson. It is not only the riddle of Judas but of so many other men; what if all of us, like him, were made to suffer for our treachery in full!"

At the beginning of his chapter "Son of Man, Son of God," the author poses a question which, despite his feelings to the contrary, can only be answered in the negative. In reference to the portrait of Christ that appears in the Gospels, he asks: "Haven't they done as well what a master novelist tries to do?" The answer is definitely no, and this is not to be disparaging to either the Gospels or Daniel-Rops' *Jesus and His Times.* Neither his book nor the Gospels is well made in the sense of masterful fiction, but then, their primary purpose is not to be well made but to show forth the life and teachings of our Lord Jesus Christ.

J.J.M.

THE MANNER IS ORDINARY

Author: John LaFarge, S.J. (1880-1963)
Type of work: Autobiography
First published: 1954

Principal Ideas Advanced

While attending Harvard in the late 1890's, John LaFarge, son of the famous American painter and member of one of America's most historically prominent families, decided to join the priesthood.

Ordained a Jesuit, he served for fifteen years among the Negroes and whites in the rural parishes of southern Maryland; during those years he became a champion of the cause of interracial justice.

Appointed to the staff of America *in 1927, Father LaFarge, both as associate editor (1927-1942) and as editor-in-chief (1942-1952), devoted twenty-five years to championing the causes of social and interracial justice and to opposing totalitarianism in all its forms.*

The Manner Is Ordinary is the autobiography of John La Farge, S.J. Born in fashionable Newport, Rhode Island, raised among the wealthy and the distinguished—the Vanderbilts, Van Alens, and Stuyvesant Fishes were among his neighbors; Henry and William James, and Theodore Roosevelt were intimate friends of his father—young John LaFarge feared, when he left for Harvard, that he was too fastidious for the priesthood. Not too many years later, however, as an ordained priest successfully working among the prison and hospital inmates at Blackwells Island (now Welfare Island in New York) and among the impoverished Negroes in the rural parishes of southern Maryland, he knew that his fears had been unjustified.

Although he never regretted attending Harvard and "carrying through" (on the advice of Theodore Roosevelt) with four years of Greek and Latin, LaFarge disliked the atmosphere of religious indifference at the university, and its dull Germanic approach to the classics. One of the few faculty members interested in religion, says LaFarge, was George Santayana, and even he was "hostile to the Catholic faith. . . ." As for the classics, the approach of W. W. Goodwin, then considered Harvard's outstanding Greek scholar, was typical: he was interested in moods and tenses, not in the spirit of Greek thought, nor in what the Greeks had to say. One of LaFarge's chief regrets after graduation was that he had not spent more time following the courses of English professors like Barrett Wendell and Lyman Kittredge. He had studied with Charles Copeland, the famous teacher of English composition, and he felt that the English Department was "one place in the university where you could find good teaching" rather than "mere academic lecturing in the German style."

Graduating in the class of 1901, (the first Harvard graduating class of the twentieth century), LaFarge sailed for Europe and Seminarian studies at Innsbruck. While at Innsbruck (where he was ordained to the priesthood on July 26, 1905) Father LaFarge first came into contact with the great European Catholic social movement and met its important figures, men like Wilhelm von Ketteler and Baron von Hugel; and he had an audience with Leo XIII, author of the great encyclical, *Rerum novarum* (*On the Condition of the Workingman*). It was also at Innsbruck that he experienced, in the group known as the Pan-Germans, the fierce, pagan nationalism that ultimately culminated in Nazism, an ideology Father LaFarge was to fight for many years as an editor of *America.*

Having been ordained and having celebrated his first Mass, Father LaFarge entered his Jesuit novitiate in Poughkeepsie, New York, where he remained as a teacher and chaplain's assistant before moving to Woodstock, Maryland, in 1908 for further philosophical studies.

The death of his father in 1910 so upset the young priest that his superiors thought it wise for him to discontinue for a while the intellectual speculative career he was pursuing and to embark upon some practical work which would cause less mental strain. He was subsequently sent to serve a temporary appointment as assistant to the chaplain in the hospitals and penal institutions on Blackwells Island, where he developed his already strong sympathy for the poor and the defeated. "Innsbruck and Woodstock were schools of knowledge," he says, "but Blackwells Island was a school of life and death."

After eight months at Blackwells, Father LaFarge was assigned as assistant pastor to the Church of St. Alloysius in Leonardtown, Maryland. Establishing catechetical centers for white and colored in the rural, outlying areas of Leonardtown, he began to wonder if the social doctrine of the Church, the doctrine he had heard so much about in Europe, could possibly be used to combat the race prejudice and injustice that existed in the world in which he was then living.

Realizing that justice for the Negro depended on the Negro's being accepted as a person in his own right, not merely as a person subject to other persons' rights, nor merely as a servant, Father LaFarge helped to establish in Leonardtown The Cardinal Gibbons Institute, a secondary school devoted to encouraging and teaching the Negro to become economically independent, and thereby to begin to gain, through his own efforts, the respect that was his due as a child of God. Though the Institute finally closed its doors because of financial stress, it accomplished many of its goals. It demonstrated to the Negro himself and to the public at large that given initial support, the Negro could stand on his own two feet; it awakened the dormant consciences of many Catholics who had previously ignored the inconsistency of their profession of Christianity and their bigoted attitude toward the Negro; and, finally, it laid the groundwork for the Catholic interracial movement in the United States.

On July 22, 1926, Father LaFarge sadly took leave of his parish work in southern Maryland in order to join the staff of *America,* the important Jesuit weekly, as an assistant editor. In the pages of this journal, however, he continued his championing of the cause of the Negro, particularly the rural, Southern Negro, and he was active in helping to found the Catholic Rural Life Movement, dedicated to bettering conditions for both white and Negro farmers.

Early in his career as a Catholic journalist, Father LaFarge also championed the causes of economic justice for the workingman and of international world peace, using as his bases the Catholic teachings that no nation can enjoy unlimited and absolute sovereignty, and that, in the social order, no person can rightly claim absolute possession of material goods. Adopting as his patron, Saint Vincent de Paul—the great father of modern organized charity—Father LaFarge answered those who maintained that the priest's business was to deal with spiritual things and to stay out of politics and social reforms, by never flagging in his journalistic efforts to create a better moral, social, economic, and political order.

Long an enemy of totalitarianism, whether of the left or of the right, Father LaFarge, attending the Eucharistic Congress in 1938, saw in Europe first hand evidence of the horrors of totalitarianism of the right—Hitler's nazism. It was on this trip to Europe that LaFarge met Archbishop (later Cardinal) Stepinac and heard this courageous man speak out with abhorrence of the racist, nationalistic mentality of the Nazis.

While in Rome in 1938, LaFarge was received by the Holy Father, Pius XI, who told him that in the pope's opinion, LaFarge's book *Interracial Justice* was the best work on the subject. Father LaFarge also met with the Superior General of the Society of Jesus, who praised *America* and urged its associate editor to see that the magazine remained one that always told its readers not only what had happened but why it had happened.

Back at his editorial desk in 1938, Father LaFarge championed the cause of the Liturgical Movement, a movement dedicated to, among other ends, replacing the spurious, mawkish devotional art in many, if not most, American Catholic churches, with genuine, living art; he also made enemies of some of his previous liberal friends by attacking Soviet communism as well as German nazism.

Appointed editor in 1942, LaFarge continued to champion the controversial and the unpopular. He insisted to his conservative readers that God has a place in the marketplace, and he made plain to his liberal readers that he could not support racial or labor movements which were underwritten by the Communists. He also risked offending the more pious among his readers by refusing to condemn works of literature simply because they depicted "the whole of man's conduct, including his sinful conduct."

During his years as editor, he watched the Catholic interracial councils and their magazine, the *Interracial Review*, both of which he had helped to establish, grow in strength and popularity and play an important role in gaining social justice for the Negro.

Because of his active support of the Negro cause, Father LaFarge, the only white man invited to do so, spoke at the 1942 March on Washington Rally, the biggest Negro demonstration in the country's history up to that time. It was a demonstration, Father LaFarge contends, that was largely responsible for President Franklin D. Roosevelt's Executive Order 8802, on fair employment practices.

Traveling in Europe after World War II, in 1947, Father LaFarge was received by Pope Pius XII and received congratulations for the work of the Catholic interracial councils in the United States. Heartening to Father LaFarge during his travels was his observation of the attempt being made in France by churchmen such as Cardinal Suhard to bring the Church closer to the workingman. Valiant efforts like those made by Suhard's worker priests, who, except for fulfilling the essential liturgical function of the priesthood, worked during the day as ordinary factory hands, as well as the efforts of groups like the Young Christian Workers in Belgium, were helping to offset some of the religious apathy and anti-clericalism which had for so long plagued the French and other European nations.

Stepping down from his post as editor-in-chief to reassume the post of associate editor, Father LaFarge was honored in 1952 at a dinner commemorating his twenty-five years as a staff writer for *America*. Attending the dinner were people of all faiths, and this fact reminded LaFarge of yet another of his rather controversial attitudes—his insistence on bringing the Catholic out of the ghetto, of the necessity of co-operating with other men of good will, no matter what their religious convictions, in order to advance the common good. Much is gained, contends Father LaFarge, by conferences between people of unlike minds. Scientists, for example, would today be less liable to embark on amateur philosophizing if philosophers would "descend from the clouds and explain to them something of philosophy's proper province and function." And by the same token philosophers and theologians "would learn humility by studying the meticulous procedure observed by genuine scientists and their skill in handling unproved hypotheses."

All Christians, Father LaFarge says in a summary near the close of his autobiography, have the vocation of working for "a world reign of love, justice, and law"; but to bring about such a world the Christian must bear witness to two great truths: "Nothing will convert the world short of a gospel of limitless love; . . . nothing short of a gospel of scrupulous faithfulness to the rights of the humblest person and to our pledges with man and God."

For the thousands who have read it and who will read it, *The Manner Is Ordinary* is and will continue to be an important study in the meaning of the Christian vocation, particularly the vocation of Christian journalism.

J.P.D.

LITURGICAL PIETY

Author: Louis Bouyer (1913-)
Type of work: Liturgical study
First published: 1955

Principal Ideas Advanced

The liturgy is that system of prayers and rites traditionally canonized by the Church as her own prayer and worship; it is not merely the public and official worship of the Church.

The sacraments are not seven independent channels of grace but are all referred to the Eucharist; so, too, the various seasons of the liturgical year should be seen in terms of the sacraments.

The Divine Office is the perfect prayer of the Church, the continuous celebration of the Mystery which is at the heart of the liturgy.

Father Louis Bouyer wrote *Liturgical Piety* against the background of several generations of the liturgical movement. Thus, both recent and traditional views of the liturgy of the Church are reflected in his definition of liturgy: that system of prayers and rites traditionally canonized by the Church as her own prayer and worship.

One of the greatest misconceptions concerning the true nature of the liturgy would have it that the liturgy consists of the external and official worship of Church; that is, that the liturgy is impersonal and ceremonial and not in fact or in intention the vehicle of personal devotion on the part of the faithful. The external view of liturgical rites was and is widespread and it is the single greatest impediment to the realization of the role the liturgy is meant to play in the salvation and sanctification of the members of the Church. According to Father Bouyer, "The liturgy in its unity and in its perfection is to be seen as the meeting of God's people called together in convocation by God's Word through the apostolic ministry, in order that the people consciously united together, may hear God's word itself in Christ, may adhere to that Word by means of the prayer and praise amid which the Word is proclaimed, and so seal by the Eucharistic sacrifice the Covenant which is accomplished by that same Word." Bouyer finds that there are four irreducible elements in the Christian liturgy to which must be added not another element but the deeper reality which permeates the elements and thus the whole; namely, the Mystery. The elements are communion, sacrifice, eucharist or thanksgiving, and memorial. This explanation of the meaning of the liturgy indicates the absolutely central role that the Sacrifice of the Mass will play in the whole liturgy.

In order for the centrality of the Mass to be appreciated, says the author, we have to recapture the proper notion of the order among the sacraments. The Mystery is located in the Mass; it is not thereby excluded from the other sacraments since they cannot be rightly understood apart from the Mass: "As we have said already, the hierarchy cannot be separated, even in the abstract, from the Eucharist, for the Eucharist is the product of the apostolic ministry through which the Church itself is constituted." In speaking of the Sacrament of Orders, Father Bouyer shows its intimate connection with the Sacrifice of the Mass and the way in which the hierarchy relates to ordination. He then goes on to show that Baptism, Confirmation, and Penance function as steps in the initiation into the Mystery the liturgy celebrates. The seven sacraments should not be considered as seven independent channels of grace. In the ancient Church, Baptism and Confirmation had no meaning except as prerequisites to the Eucharist. Penance had as its principal function to remove those impediments of sin which temporally exclude one from communion in the Mystery.

Matrimony is seen in a proper light in this perspective and, because of the current concern with the subject, it seems well to quote Father Bouyer at some length here. In marriage the sexual love of man and woman is blessed; "But this love is blessed in reference to its primary end: the procreation of children. And we can say that it is through the blessing of this primary purpose that sexual love itself is blessed. A man and woman are to be blessed in their nuptial union because they are concurring not only in the multiplication of the sons of Adam, but also in preparing new members for the Mystical Body and so working for its completion." The love which is definitive of Christian marriage is not a selfish love, the love of want and demand; it must be the same sacrificial love which is operative in the liturgical mystery, the divine love which seeks not to serve itself but rather to give life and to give it abundantly. This view of marriage enables men to free themselves from the corrosive effects of secularistic discussions. The primary end of marriage has been questioned and some would describe the end of marriage as the mutual development of the persons involved.

But such a view appears to turn marriage into a kind of sexual therapy. Father Bouyer's description is surely a description of a Christian sacrament: "Thus, their mutual love will not be merely the association of two egotisms, but rather the true image of the love of Christ and the Church, and, through this, an image of the Mystery itself."

Having shown that all the sacraments have their meaning with reference to the Sacrifice of the Mass, Father Bouyer moves on to a discussion of the liturgical year. The liturgical year "is the great and permanent proclamation by the Church of the Word with which she has been entrusted. In the celebration of the liturgical year, therefore, the Mystery is proclaimed, communicated and participated in." The cycle of seasons in the year of the Church must be interpreted as the way of assimilation in our own lives of the pattern Christ has given us.

In his argument showing the manner in which the seven sacraments radiate from the central rite, Father Bouyer has shown most effectively that this public worship of the Church, far from being in contrast to the way each soul must go, is precisely the way Christ has shown. The liturgical life of the Church is the very pattern of the spiritual life. Father Bouyer sharpens this point in discussing the cycle of the liturgical year, observing that there is something odd about the Catholic who carries on private devotions which are out of season from the point of view of the liturgical year. For example, a man whose meditation at Easter time would be on the Holy Trinity would not show a proper appreciation of the import of the liturgy. Liturgical piety is the common activity of the whole Mystical Body of Christ, involving the spiritual life of each member of the Church. Father Bouyer regards it as odd that the liturgy should be regarded as a threat or distraction to one's personal spiritual development. If the "external" worship of the liturgy does not have its counterpart in the internal spiritual development of the faithful, then public worship will soon lose its meaning.

Father Bouyer's emphasis on the personal spiritual import of the liturgy gives a concrete remedy to the weakness pointed out by most spiritual writers; namely, the tendency to regard the search for perfection as private. Spiritual writers are as one in stressing that the love of God must be outgoing in the sense that God is loved not as a private good but as a common good communicable to many. The liturgy is precisely the worship of Christ's Church, and by identifying himself with it, the individual will see that his search for perfection is inevitably bound up with the community of Christians. The imitation of Christ is something which is achieved by way of the seven sacraments; thus, Father Bouyer discusses the various seasons of the liturgical year in their relation to the sacraments. Finally, the Divine Office, properly understood, is seen to be *the* prayer of the Church: "For it would truly be, in its most essential parts, the prayer of the most fervent and responsible members praying for the whole. Thus all Christian prayer would once again flow out from the Eucharistic celebration and flow back again to it, being in the full meaning of the term *perennis laus Mysterii,* the continual praise of the Mystery."

Father Bouyer's argument that the liturgical prayer of the Church is intended to be the means of spiritual perfection of the faithful and not merely public and external is developed against the background of both recent and older liturgical history. This serves to give the book a depth and scope which make it a useful introduction to liturgical studies.

R.M.

THE PHENOMENON OF MAN

Author: Pierre Teilhard de Chardin, S.J. (1881-1955)
Type of work: Christian evolutionary theory
First published: 1955

Principal Ideas Advanced

The world is a system *because of the* plurality *of matter, a* totum *because of the* unity *of matter, and a* quantum *because of the* energy *of matter.*

Each particular element of energy contains a tangential *energy, which relates the element to others of the same order, and a* radical *energy, which moves the element forward toward greater complexity and centricity.*

All things possess a "Without," which the physicist studies, and a "Within," a consciousness or spontaneity which is coextensive with the "Without."

An evolving material complexity is coextensive with an evolving spiritual, or conscious, "centreity," or perfection.

Love, as an attraction to union, is the basic energy of evolutionary development; mankind converges upon the Omega Point, the Incarnate Christ.

French Jesuit, world-renowned anthropologist and paleontologist, philosopher, theologian, mystic, and poet, Pierre Teilhard de Chardin wrote hundreds of articles and two outstanding books, *The Divine Milieu,* completed in 1927, and *The Phenomenon of Man,* composed from 1938 to 1940 while Teilhard was in China. (A short appendix on the role of evil in evolution was added in 1948.)

The importance of *The Phenomenon of Man* and the other writings of Teilhard arises from many factors, but chief among these are the topical nature of the subject, the approach Teilhard takes, and the "scandal" of Teilhard himself. Certainly, in the twentieth century, evolution is taken for granted by all scientists, though they may still debate about its mechanisms. At the same time, evolution has invaded many fields besides biology, including that of Christian theology, where Cardinal Newman's concept of the development of dogma is now generally accepted. As to his approach, Teilhard regarded his task as that of reflecting scientifically on the whole phenomenon of man; he did not succumb to the lure of metaphysics, nor did he satisfy himself with a safe account of some partial aspect of the phenomenon of man. Consequently, as a result of the care with which he built and tested his evolutionary theory, his ideas have a rigor which satisfies the scientific mind and a relevance which appeals to those of religious conviction. Furthermore, his style is more appealing to the non-Catholic and the nonbeliever than is that of the more traditional scholastic writer. Inevitably, this untraditional approach and style have provoked much criticism and even misinterpretation by scholastically trained minds. The "scandal" of Teilhard himself, the fact that there are many persons who are wary of his works, arises from the circumstance that he was not only a Catholic who accepted evolution but also a priest and a Jesuit who openly urged its acceptance by all; he spoke not as an obscure philosopher but as a world-renowned scientist personally committed to the scientific enterprise of proving evolution and personally involved in such major discoveries as that of *Pithecanthropus pekinensis* (Peking Man) and *Eoanthropus dawsoni* (Piltdown Man).

On the advice of a superior, Teilhard made arrangements to leave his unpublished works to Mlle. Jeanne Mortier, his secretary, an arrangement that was canonically approved and within the bounds of the rule of the Society of Jesus. Very shortly after his death in 1955, a distinguished committee of scholars and scientists united to sponsor the publication of all his works. The breadth of this committee indicates the breadth of Teilhard's influence even at a time when most of his writings were still unpublished. The committee included ranking scholars and scientists such as the Abbé Henri Breuil, Maurice Jean de Broglie, Camille Arambourg, Dr. Alberto Blanc, Dr. Johannes Hurzeler, Sir Julian Huxley, Professor G.H.R. Von Koenigswald, Louis Leprince-Ringuet, Professor Hallam L. Movius, Jean Piveteau, Sir Arnold Toynbee, President Sedar-Senghor of the Senegal, and André Malraux.

In the eight years following the publication of *The Phenomenon of Man* in the original French, it sold 120,000 copies in France. Since then the work has been translated into English, German, Dutch, Danish, Norwegian, Finnish, Swedish, Spanish, Italian, Portuguese, Japanese, Polish, Russian. Some two thousand articles and fifty books have been written in response to its author's interpretation of evolution. The reception of the work by non-Catholics and even by nonbelievers has been outstanding. The Catholic world, however, continues to be divided and cautious in its approach to Teilhard's work; to some extent this attitude results from the action of the Holy Office of the Vatican, which banned Teilhard's works from Catholic bookstores in 1957 and then, in 1962, issued a formal "warning," a *monitum*, concerning his books.

An understanding of the methodological approach used in *The Phenomenon of Man* is essential to a proper understanding of the work. The title itself suggests that the book is a study of phenomena, of things as they appear; hence, it is a scientific work and not a metaphysical account of ultimate causes or the essence of things. Teilhard termed his work a "hyperphysics." Although Teilhard's reflections are akin to physics as practiced by the Greek philosophers, *The Phenomenon of Man* cannot be classified as a purely scientific work in the limited sense in which "science" means the experimental and observational study of natural phenomena. Nevertheless, the work is grounded on experimental investigations and phenomenological analysis; it is speculative in the respectable sense in which the work of the theoretical scientist is necessarily speculative. The author does not undertake to resolve metaphysical problems concerning original sin, supernatural grace, moral evil, and the origin of the human soul, but he does attempt to devise a description of natural phenomena which will make sense out of otherwise unrelated features of evolutionary developments. *The Phenomenon of Man* offers an interpretation of the facts of evolution which will allow an extrapolation or projection into the future.

In defense of his approach, Teilhard points out that in bowing to Cartesian dualism modern science has almost completely ignored the "Within" of the world it claims to explain. Science has studied the physical and chemical aspects of our universe, but it has neglected the most important element, that of consciousness, by treating the world as an epiphenomenon, an accidental occurrence which cannot meaningfully be studied. Teilhard seeks to analyze evolutionary phenomena and find "an experimental law of recurrence which would express their successive appearance in time." The law of recurrence is based on two assumptions: "The first is the primacy accorded to the psychic and to thought in the stuff of the universe, and the second is the 'biological' value attributed to the social fact around us."

"Since the stuff of the universe has an inner aspect at one point of itself," Teilhard writes, "there is necessarily a *double aspect to its structure,* that is to say in every region of space and time . . . : *co-extensive with their Without, there is a Within to things.*" The "Within," namely, "consciousness," taken to include every type of psychism from the most primitive awareness to reflective human thought, is thus contrasted to the "Without," the physical, measurable aspect of things.

Cognate with this distinction between a Within and Without of things are the distinctions Teilhard makes in energy. "We shall assume that, *essentially,* all energy is psychic in nature, but add that in each particular element this fundamental energy is divided into two distinct components": a *tangential energy,* which is measurable by physicists, and a *radial energy,* which cannot be measured. Tangential energy is the energy with which chemistry and physics are concerned. Radial energy, however, is the force behind all forms of psychism; it is the energy of love, an attraction toward union or synthesis which lifts a monad to a higher level of existence while preserving its integrity and individuality in a "differentiated union." Thus, radial energy is the energy which makes evolution possible, while tangential energy is the energy which preserves what evolution has achieved.

In the primeval stuff of the universe, atomicity pervades both the Within and the Without of things. Yet radial energy, that "internal propensity to unite, even at a prodigiously rudimentary level, indeed in the molecule itself," is able to pull sub-atomic particles, such as electrons, protons, and anti-particles, into a differentiated union to form atoms. The same energy synthesizes atoms into molecules and then into mega-molecules, the large carbon chains so essential to life. Here we notice the first traces of a phenomenon necessary to the evolutionary process; namely, complexity. Complexity differs from an aggregation in that it is an organized and limited grouping of elements united to form something higher and richer than any mere collection of individual components could achieve.

The threshold from pre-life to life is crossed only once; this step is the first of three critical stages in evolution. After the appearance of life, complexity is complemented by increasing consciousness. Growth in complexity among animals involves growth in psychic awareness or consciousness, and the central nervous system is the prime mark of psychic development. Complexity and consciousness are thus two aspects of the same phenomenon.

In the animal world phenomena occur which prepare and prefigure the evolution of man: mating, the formation of the family, tribal instincts. Awareness of the surrounding world also deepens. Up to this point, on the general plane, evolution is divergent. On each individual plane, the subatomic, atomic, molecular, cellular, and animal, three subphases have been repeated: an initial *divergence,* exploring all the possibilities for expansion and new species; then *convergence,* to consolidate what has been gained and to prepare for the next stage; and, finally, *emergence* into a new and higher level of existence. As the irrational primate stems converged, a new critical threshold was reached, and man emerged.

Since he is dealing with phenomena, Teilhard does not consider the origin of the human soul, although he does mark this as an area for philosophical and theological investigation.

At first, according to Teilhard, mankind followed a subphase of divergence: races and subraces appeared; man spread across the face of the earth. Then, in the Neolithic Age, there was a shift from divergence to convergence both for evolution in general and for man. Family groups were replaced by tribal groups, which in turn were replaced by urban and national unions. Human convergence through national groups continued up to the 1900's when even wider unions, continental and intercontinental, began to lift man above petty nationalisms.

Thus, on the natural level mankind converges and consciousness increases. But a convergent mankind requires a focal point. Extrapolating from the lower stages of evolution, Teilhard isolates the characteristics of a scientific focal point for man's convergence. In order to realize a differentiated union which will preserve what has already been achieved, namely, man's personality, spirituality, and individuality, while lifting him to a higher level of union, the new center of focus must be *personal* since mankind cannot unite around an impersonal point. To attract spiritual beings, the focal point must be *spiritual,* and to attract men, who have an indestructible will to live, the point must be *eternal.* The focal point must function within man; it must be *immanent.* At the same time, it must be supra-personal and extra-personal; therefore, it must be *transcendent.* The only element which fits all these requirements is a personal, eternal, spiritual, immanent, transcendent *love.* Teilhard gives this scientific focus the name "Omega Point," with obvious reference to Christ, the Alpha and Omega of the Apocalypse.

In the appendix or epilogue Teilhard speaks of the Christian phenomenon, summing up from the phenomenological viewpoint the traits of Christianity, which show it as the emerging phylum of evolution, in a process of Christogenesis which, at this critical threshold of mankind, is about to supplant the process of neogenesis, the evolution of mind. Thus, the Mystical Body of Christ is seen as the culmination of evolution, and the present human crises are understandable as birth pangs which indicate the emergence of a new union.

When the essence of Teilhard's thought is studied carefully and without the distractions of his necessary neologisms, it is clear that this thought is strictly traditional and Pauline in scope and expression; there is nothing really new or novel about it. Certainly, other scholars, such as Henri Bergson (1859-1941), Pierre Lecomte du Noüy (1883-1947), and Jan Christian Smuts (1870-1950), have expressed the same ideas from a Christian and even Catholic viewpoint, though not in as detailed or well-developed a form. Sir Julian Huxley and other nonbelievers have expressed the same vision from their naturalistic vantage point, though without the Christian solution which Teilhard gave the evolutionary process. Perhaps, the real "scandal" of Teilhard and *The Phenomenon of Man* lies in his attempt to achieve, in an evolutionary account, a solidly knit synthesis of the biological and spiritual worlds, two worlds which, despite the teachings of Christ, Paul, and many others in the Christian tradition, have continued to be regarded by Platonic-Cartesian dualism as isolated from each other.

SCIENCE, RELIGION AND CHRISTIANITY

Author: Hans Urs von Balthasar (1905-)
Type of work: Theology
First published: 1956

Principal Ideas Advanced

The cosmological age, in which man saw himself as part of an essentially sacred cosmos, has been superseded by the anthropological age, in which man has transcended nature and no longer defines himself in terms of it.

A person's encounter with another person is the prototype of all knowledge, and to experience that encounter fully one must be unconditionally open in an attitude of surrender and love.

The Incarnation should be understood as revealing God both as He can be known and as incomprehensible mystery; one then realizes man's need for both a revealed, fraternal faith and a solitary, undefined experiential encounter with God.

The essence of the love which is Christ's and the Church's is a dynamic mission or search for love among its enemies and not a static or final exclusiveness.

The theme basic to Hans Urs von Balthasar's *Science, Religion and Christianity* is the necessity of balancing the ideas of God's immanence and transcendence. This must be done in such a way that man will not try to move into a new dimension of power, maturity, and spiritual quest without first acknowledging and reforging his bonds with nature and society. The cosmos can no longer be looked upon as divine, nor can man's highest act of worship be to "reproduce the divine order of the cosmos in the small circle of his private and social household." By extending his view of prehistory and thereby seeing the manner in which he has risen out of nature and come to dominate it, man establishes his transcendence of the natural process which produced him. Science has ended the era of magic and pantheism and has effectively discouraged the growth of natural religion. The only way in which man can look with a validly religious attitude upon the cosmos is by becoming aware of a duty to God to act wisely and with compassionate restraint in his newly-assumed dominion over creation. We can neither obey nor surrender ourselves to nature, though we may regard it with love as "our foundation and source." Man, and not nature, is both "concrete and universal" and it is by virtue of his knowledge of himself that he knows the created universe.

The intellectual history of mankind has reflected the slow revolution from the cosmologically-oriented past to the anthropologically-oriented present, Balthasar claims. The magician, operating among men sheltered within nature, was long ago succeeded by the philosopher, by whom the ideas of reason and objective order altered man's beliefs about his relation to the cosmos. Romanticism, coming at the end of the intellect-dominated philosophical period, tried to effect a synthesis of nature, myth, and mana with spirit, art, and law. It was possible for the medieval and the romantic mystics to experience the loss of the individual self, for they saw man as essentially ordered, sheltered, and mirrored by the universe itself. Modern Western man has rejected the idea of a self lost in the cosmos for a self which masters it. In so doing, he has completed the breach with Eastern mysticism. He has also rejected the system of the Scholastics, which would have man weakened and blinded to the extent that he is dominated by matter. Natural religions are no longer being created; indeed, the modern form of natural religion is irreligion. For the modern religious thinker, matter and the struggles inherent in material creation can be viewed "as a condition of the spirit through which it can find itself," and not as a fall into evil from which the soul can only be saved by withdrawal and escape.

Our own time, the author suggests, is marked by the decline of cosmological studies in favor of investigations into symbols, language, archetypes and primitive human history. "Man is the goal of the upward movement, he sees nature coming towards himself. . . ," Balthasar writes; "he is the result and the quintessence of all this becoming which he bears in himself." The old effort to distort modern insights by applying determinism to every phase of life has now been discredited in favor of a more flexible approach, bringing to bear the whole of human life and experience upon every scientific problem. In an era of pluralism, individualism, and mastery over nature, both anthropology and theology should address themselves, Balthasar writes, to "the real, living human being, and explore that ever-growing and ever more fully defined freedom which constitutes man's basic humanity." Man shares responsibility with the Creator, who "respects" his freedom and acknowledges his responsibility. It is now possible to see man as the head or epitome of nature, just as Christ is Head of the Church and is mystically identified with the whole.

Only in the twentieth century is modern man perceived as a whole, not as a "materialistic or evolutionary phantom." Only such a whole man can be held responsible for a vital and voluntary adherence to the communal aspect of human life. Pure individualism must be transcended, since it does not accurately represent reality: "The individual is loved only in view of the whole [God] in which he shares in different degrees and stages."

Every act of knowledge, on whatever level, writes Balthasar, reflects that highest form of human knowledge marked by the *encounter* with another person, an encounter that confirms the objective reality of one's own self and thought. This form of knowledge is marked by an unconditional openness, a sharing of being which makes a man vulnerable to impression and to change. Such an attitude is the universally human approach to both love and knowledge and for each it is essentially the same. From the new awareness of human encounter as a basis and measure for knowledge and action, there come two extremes of philosophic thought: the Marxian idea of the collective which obliterates the individual, and the existentialist dedication to progress and truth through individuals in isolation from one another. It is necessary to achieve a balance uniting collective responsibility with what the author calls the "free consent of persons."

Balthasar argues that a distinctive contribution of the modern era is the concern of man for man. It is as if man discovered that he could no longer depend on finding God in nature or in the landscape of his own soul, and thus he turned to other men for life and meaning. Men are universally aware of their own solitude and homelessness within the cosmos. They reach out to other men, hoping for the consolations of a dialogue, whether in terms of Eros (profane love) or Agape (sacred love). The "flight of the individual," as taught by Søren Kierkegaard, and the "nausea" Jean Paul Sartre feels for all those outside himself are receding into history and it is now generally apparent that "a responsibility of the individual without community is no longer possible."

The role of the Church in such a period is to end its exclusiveness and dispense the sacrament of its charity throughout the world, loving Christ as much in the stranger or enemy as in the brother. One does not need to recognize Christ in the suffering nor need they recognize Him in you to have Him truly and wholly present when you give yourself in charity to the world. Balthasar writes: "The Cosmos becomes sacred through the holiness of the Church, and the Church has not so much to make propaganda in the world, but above all to pray and to remain in charity." While the Church in the West has always kept as its image of the Passion the suffering Christ on the cross, anchored in this world, the

Eastern Church has dwelled on the descent into Hell. The West can learn from this emphasis that Christ may be imitated in His search for other valid loves outside Himself in darkness, where He does not refuse His presence or His providence.

No matter how wretched and in need of love a man may be, says Balthasar, we do him an injustice to let our love go no higher than his person. If we have ceased worshiping our own humanity and merely worship the humanity of another man, we have gained little in our appreciation of transcendence. When one free person encounters another in love, the freedom and autonomy of both can be preserved only by reference to a higher Person. Each must see the other in and through the Person from whom they derive their dignity and worth and in whom they must ultimately find their meaning and fulfillment: "The created person who is loved is grasped in his true reality only in relation to God." When the human ego is held as an absolute, experience has demonstrated that it can be destructive and all-devouring in relation to other egos. If we search for a transcendental object for our love, writes Balthasar, we must not turn to the immanent, but to the incomprehensible, the invisible, to the Personality which can be grasped only in solitude and mystery.

Balthasar contends that God cannot be apprehended as simply another object of knowledge, nor can one automatically rule out the relevance to man of all religion unverifiable by reason. The universal tradition of the mystics affirms that God must dominate the soul as man dominates nature and as the greater always dominates the lesser. The experience is marked not by the houris that wishful human imagination might suggest, but by awareness of divinity as a dark night, as a desert, as a coming to the terrifying abyss of one's own dependency. Ultimately in mysticism, Balthasar writes, "the vision wants to pass into non-vision, into letting-be, into pure adoration without any definite affirmation." This total obedience of the understanding to love and to the actual experience of divine being leads to an abandonment of the striving after specific visions or enlightening concepts; one seeks instead a vital encounter of the whole man with God. The experience is the Christian's most eloquent avenue to the soul of modern man, who lives out his exile in silence and solitude, without the consolations of faith or the awareness of God's presence that might render his desolation joyful.

The difficulty of approaching modern man with Christianity is largely due to his very solitude and to the caution and integrity which he has learned are his only protections against disillusionment. An institutional religion of any kind seems restrictive and unnecessarily bound to the old dead cosmological era. Yet modern man is aware of the claim upon him of the bonds of charity and of his solidarity with the rest of mankind. The perversion of man's freedom is seen in the work of such modern figures as André Gide and Thomas Mann, who portray life as a "disease of being" and spirit as a disease of life. To these authors human nobility or genius is itself a descent into the hell of total decay, of total indifference to the good and evil that man has outgrown. Their insight into Hell reflects that of the novelist Georges Bernanos (1888-1948) and the mystic Saint Catherine of Genoa

(1447-1510), who saw Hell as a condition and experience and not as a place. Bernanos and Saint Catherine saw "the surface of time as transparent, revealing final, eternal decisions and states. Only a thin veil need be drawn back to show heaven and hell as present." One cannot limit man's dynamic spiritual development with mere concepts, as the existentialists and Marxists would like to do; man's spirit cannot be limited except with reference to the possibilities of God Himself, which is to say that man need not consider himself limited at all. Behold man, then, Balthasar urges, not in the mirror of nature, but in his original, God.

B.J.R.

THE DISCOVERY OF GOD

Author: Henri de Lubac, S.J. (1896-)
Type of work: Theology
First published: 1956

Principal Ideas Advanced

The idea of God is the most difficult idea to communicate to others.

The ways to discover God are as many and as varied as His own myriad perfections.

God is a limit-situation and a mystery, who compels our bowing before His incomprehensibility.

A positive theology is less revealing than a negative theology, although both are necessary if we wish to know about God.

In *The Discovery of God,* Father Henri de Lubac provides the reader with a rich source of material for philosophical and theological reflections. The work is not so much a treatise on natural theology as it is a collection of personal insights which the author wishes to share with the reader.

Father Lubac, a Professor of Theology at Lyons, has gone through a rather stormy career, largely because of pressures exerted by conservatives within the Church. However, the past decade has seen a change in the attitude of many within the Church and Lubac's thought has flowered accordingly. In this, as in his many other writings, he draws heavily on traditional sources such as Saint Augustine, Saint Hilary, and Saint Thomas Aquinas, but the influence of the moderns and contemporaries is clearly seen as well. The apparent absurdity and paradox of such conjunctions as God and the presence of evil, God and the created world, and God's goodness and Hell are freely admitted by Lubac, for, he says, we must realize that God is a mystery and a limit-situation. We must concede that we know God only insofar as He reveals Himself to us. In these as well as in other ideas, the views of Søren Kierkegaard (1813-1855), Karl Jaspers, and Karl Barth have strongly and unmistakably colored Lubac's thinking.

The Jesuit Professor is a strong critic of the rationalistic view of God as characterized by Benedictus de Spinoza (1632-1677) and of the anthropomorphic philosophies of God found throughout history. Lubac cautions the philosopher not to give in to the seductions of his intellectual pride. Philosophy, he points out, is a search for intelligibility, and the philosopher remains restless and unsatisfied until he discovers that intelligibility. Because of his quest for complete intelligibility, the philosopher may be prone to ignore a confrontation with mystery, which represents a limit to his endeavor. Accordingly, he may be tempted to *invent* and to superimpose an intelligibility to satisfy the demands of his philosophy.

In the event that the philosopher falls prey to this siren of his own philosophical ego, he runs the risk of portraying God anthropomorphically. The roots of such a portrayal stem from an attempt to see the world as explaining God, instead of God as explaining the world. Essentially, it is a case of "making God in our image" instead of seeing that "we are made in God's image." Lubac advocates that the philosopher be humble enough to admit the limitations of profane knowledge when it focuses upon the mystery of God.

We must be aware of the value which a negative theology can render in our attempt to encounter God philosophically. This approach should not be construed as a negativism, for it does provide us with knowledge rather than with a negation of it. Father Lubac reminds us, then, of the need for simplicity in the attempt to know God, but he warns that the quest should not be viewed in a simplistic manner.

There is a certain sense, Lubac continues, in which it might be said that God is first in all that we know. This is not ontologism as expounded by Vincenzo Gioberti (1801-1852), but a simple recognition that God is an "all." Echoing Saint Thomas Aquinas, we can say that all men know God, but not all know that it is God whom they know. To know being is to know implicitly the source and fount of being; to seek the good is to seek the Supreme Good. If I see my friend in the distance, writes Lubac, but am unable to recognize him as my friend, it is still permissible to claim that it is my friend whom I see. Similarly with respect to God, in knowing the world, I know God; in knowing His effects, I recognize Him, albeit not formally.

One must, of course, account for the fact that many claim not to be able to discover God. It is suggested by Father Lubac that perhaps this inability is due to the fact that it is *their* universe which they examine, and not the universe of *God*. Many scientists and logical positivists fail to appreciate that they have "interfered with" God's universe and have "constructed" a universe to suit the demands of their own intelligibility.

Indeed, says Father Lubac, we must account for the fact that mankind has always entertained the notion of God. All attempts fall short if we explain this wholly in terms of superstition or in terms of a psychological projection of the spirit or in a hundred other ways. After all, one does not try to banish that which is nonexistent; one does not attempt to fight an opponent that is not there. Without succumbing to innatism, the author points out that, in the last analysis, only God can account for the notion of God that men have had throughout the ages. Yet this notion of God, implicitly present in all men, should not be confused with a clear concept of Cartesian (René Descartes, 1596-1665) origin. No concept can ever capture God. Instead, what is meant by the notion of God is the imprint of God on all His works, especially on His work that is man. A denial of God forces a philosopher who is consistent to proclaim either a subsequent denial of the world or the world's absolute absurdity. To some extent, this latter is the position of Jean-Paul Sartre; to claim that "Without God, everything would be possible!" is itself an absurdity. Without God, nothing would be possible and no meaning or intelligibility would be possessed by anything. It is the atheist who is in need of psychoanalysis, not the believer.

The history of philosophy has revealed many "proofs" for the existence of God. In examining these, Father Lubac, like other philosophers, accepts some and rejects others. Yet even in accepting the philosophical demonstrations of Saint Thomas Aquinas (as well as similar intellectual proofs), Lubac makes a number of interesting points, all too seldom conceded by others. He asks, for example, whether a proof of itself has ever really convinced a nonbeliever, or whether a believer has ever been disturbed by an argument against the existence of God. In both cases he answers no.

If a proof is to be convincing, there must first be a predisposition to believe on the part of the one to whom the proof is offered. This is no criticism of the proof, but a psychological fact that any impartial observer can discover for himself. A "will to believe" plays an important part in all such matters, and to ignore it is to close one's eyes to a situation otherwise patent. Despite the intellectual objectivity of such proofs, they often fail to take into account the subjective grounds for certitude and a state of conviction on the part of the hearer. From this subjective point of view, a proof is similar to a missile, in that an anti-missile missile normally follows close upon the development of the former.

Even when seen and accepted, Father Lubac adds, intellectual proofs are but skeletons which need the embellishments only a body can give. If we look upon the proofs as establishing God as a principle or as a term of things, we really have not said much about God, for He is everything else as well. This error is similar to Henri Bergson's (1859-1941) critique of those who define motion in terms of "from which" and "to which": they have captured everything in the definition except motion itself.

Lubac warns us that we must get away from the idea that God is simply one being among many or that He is merely the first in a series. All such notions bear an element of falsity which should be explicitly recognized. Such views pretend that it is we who measure God; they fail to recognize the fact, known to Augustine, that it is God who is the Measurer of all.

The Discovery of God stresses the centralness of God to all things without committing itself to the pantheistic view which praises immanence at the expense of transcendence. In fact, Lubac argues, it is God's very transcendence which permits His immanence to things.

Personalistic throughout, Lubac continually reminds us that "Apologetics is to testimony what the sermon is to the example." In partial accord with the Jewish theologian Martin Buber, Lubac insists that we view God as a Thou and not as a He.

Lubac's recurrent theme in *The Discovery of God* is the problematic nature of the divine, and he argues that our dual requirement is to seek the intelligibility of God and yet to bow before the inexhaustibility of meaning. He best expresses this duality when he writes, "God of the intelligence and God of the consciousness—God of supernatural revelation and God of reason—God of nature and God of history—God of being and God of value—God of reflection and God of prayer—God of the philosopher and God of the mystic—God of the soul and God of the universe—God of social tradition and God of solitary meditation . . . so many opposites and one unity!"

G.F.K.

THE TWO-EDGED SWORD

Author: John L. McKenzie, S.J. (1910-)
Type of work: Scriptural studies
First published: 1956

Principal Ideas Advanced

God spoke to the Hebrews in a mysterious but thoroughly external and objective fashion, convincing some of them that although "wholly other" He was jealously concerned with the Hebrew nation and, in the course of time, with each individual member of their nation and, ultimately, with all men of all nations.

God dealt with the Hebrew nation as though it were a single individual undergoing a spiritual odyssey eventuating in tragedy which, if it were not for the element of hope in the power of God for good, would terminate the story once and for all.

Despite the total collapse and dissipation of the Hebrew state with which its religion was identified, faith in the power and the will of God for good kept Israel from being led into despair and nourished in it a more intense hope for a greater kingdom to be realized under His guidance.

In the initial chapter, "The Sacred Books," of *The Two-edged Sword,* Father John L. McKenzie is critical of Biblical scientists who ". . . have made the Old Testament a battleground, a proving ground, but not the ground from which one ascends to God." He intends to bypass all apologetic and dogmatic uses that have been rightly or wrongly applied. He assures the reader that the Old Testament is a library of religious literature;

"The religion of the Old Testament is the relationship between the Hebrew people and their God, as they experienced it and as they described it." The author also deals with the difficult teaching of the Church concerning divine inspiration, and does so as honestly and as simply as he can without entering into the complicated distinctions required for a full understanding of instrumental causality. If God is not the author of the Scriptures then they are not *sacred* literature but *profane* manuscripts of relative value. But, McKenzie claims, "The Bible is a sacred book; it comes from God, and it brings God to us."

The definite mark of the supernatural pervades all the pages and themes of Hebrew literature. With no apologies, McKenzie concludes his second chapter, "God Speaks to Man," with the statement: "We cannot escape, in the Old Testament, the pervading conviction that God intrudes Himself into the minds of men in an extraordinary but thoroughly objective manner, and that men, possessed of this awareness, become His spokesmen. They remain men, and they sometimes remain men who are petty; but Hebrew faith in the Lord God is meaningless apart from this fundamental belief, that they knew Him at all only because He spoke to them." God revealed Himself to these men of old not in the abstract, but in the only way they could begin to understand. He used their psychological patterns of thought and performed deeds which meant life or death for the entire "covenanted" people.

Modern study has brought to light a fairly good knowledge of the Hebrew contemporaries. As a result, the early chapters of Genesis should be viewed as woven with anti-Canaanite fibers as much as with the unique Hebrew way of writing religious history. In the chapters on origins, both cosmic and human, the author suggests various myths concerning creation which doubtless influenced the Hebrew creation account. Of particular interest to scholars will be the interpretation of the Fall of man in terms of a polemic against the divinization of sex in the ancient world. The key to his interpretation, by which he believes Genesis is placed in its own cultural, religious, ideological background, is the symbolic sexual character of the serpent.

In treating national origins, Israel's patriarchal ancestors, the Exodus, the covenant of Sinai, its peculiar cult and the name of God, the author establishes the core of historical Judaism. The development of Israel as a nation is dealt with in terms of kingship and prophecy. The psychological analysis of the role of prophet, appearing earlier in the work, must be recalled to appreciate the chapters on Israel's national welfare and its relations with neighboring nations: "We could infer for ourselves, even if we did not have the introspection of Jeremiah to inform us, that the word of the Lord was a dreadful psychological burden, mentally and emotionally fatiguing. . . ." And the reason for such an awful burden is given: "The prophet . . . is closer to the Lord than he is to any man." Time and again the principle that the king lies under the will of the Lord and that the prophet is the accredited spokesman for the divine will was a difficult lesson for Israel to learn.

Nonetheless the Hebrew God was a God who instilled hope and not despair. Judaism can be understood only in terms of its hope for the future: "In the Hebrew faith, events tended not to a circle, but to a term: a term which God wills and intends, and to which He directs everything." Both the cyclic and the progressive evolutionary theories of history are challenged by the Hebrew God who becomes personally involved in human affairs. While judgment can be passed on the Hebrew nation by human theories of history, the constant revival and growth of faith and hope in the minds and hearts of the Hebrews when, politically speaking, they had nothing left, becomes a point of embarrassment to the theorists. Long ago the Hebrew God identified Himself with David's kingdom, so much so that David's reign lived on as an ideal to be realized by a still greater act of God who alone can "finally provide that good overcomes evil."

In the chapters devoted to the "wisdom" literature of the Hebrews the author begins to develop the internal, personal response of the individual Hebrew to God. As long as the Hebrew state survived, the external forms of religion were secure and, the Hebrews thought, sufficient before God. But when God removed even the tiny kingdom of Judah the individual Hebrew had to learn how to live "the good life" by his own direction. The men who knew the practical art of right living, that of avoiding conflict while providing security, were called wise men. They were to be imitated, and their sayings passed on to future generations.

But "easy going wisdom" could not answer the profound questions proffered in Judah's blackest hour when exile in a foreign land was a hard, cruel fact. Despair of all *human* ability brought the Hebrew sages to a new dimension of trust in God. The problem of evil, the obvious prosperity of the wicked, led wise men to reëxamine their faith in "the power and will of God for good." In some way the divine will requires a universal reckoning, rewarding and punishing all men according to their actions. "Cosmic justice" also demands some type of resurrection of the body after death. The Hebrew became convinced that God made all things, even the human being, good.

Perhaps it was time for Israel to pray anew, to review the events of God's deeds among men; to contrast the times of good and the times of evil, the times of praise and the times of curse, the times of thanksgiving and the times of ingratitude. Such utterances and many others are found in the Hebrew book of prayer known as the Psalms. McKenzie does not evade the modern objections to the imprecatory psalms. He sees in them the idea that even though there can be no sympathy with evil of any sort, evil can still serve the cause of the justice of the God of the Hebrews.

In his final chapters the author returns to the basic theme of the Old Testament: the God of the Hebrews. The mystery of this "wholly other," this intruder who affects men and history, who is also so completely compassionate, is heightened by the question: Do the Biblical descriptions of divine condescension in the Old Testament rise to the level of love? The reply is that the word and the figure are found in the Old Testament, but the idea of love remains unfinished. Still, ". . . the Old Testament tends to the point where the 'fascination' overcomes the awe, where perfect love expels fear." Was this the preparation given before

God sent His Son, Jesus? Was Jesus, then, the fulfillment of the Old Law? Why did the Jews reject Him? What did the early Church think about the Old Testament? Is the Old Testament a Christian book? How does Jesus appear in the Old Testament? These are some of the questions raised in the final chapter entitled "The Old and New." Basically the author affirms that Jesus is God's response to the Hebrew belief in the power and the will of God for good: "For the life of Jesus and of the Church which is His Body is the fulfillment of the Old Testament, and the Old Testament is inseparably included in the New."

This work is a splendid example of what Biblical scholars can do if they concentrate upon *what* they have unearthed rather than upon *how* they have discovered their findings. The author's scholarship shines through brilliantly while the implements of his trade are kept in the background. On the very first page of the preface he states: "The book is addressed to the general public: to anyone who thinks himself interested enough in the Old Testament to read a book about it which is not too deep or too heavy or too advanced or too big." Popular acclaim attests the fulfillment of this promise. While McKenzie writes primarily for Catholics and acknowledges that his interpretations are colored by his personal convictions, his themes, which run the gamut of the Old Testament, are guided by important Biblical facts he considers obscure to the American reading public. The author's particular genius resides in anticipating the psychological barriers that exist between the modern American reader and the ancient Hebrew writer. With the introduction of every new theme the reader is forewarned in a witty though sober manner what the Hebrew author does not say nor could say to his most recent reader. "The men whom He used could tell a story, but they could not write a history . . . if God wished to write a history, He would have to choose other instruments. . . ." By obviating difficulties encountered by the modern reader of the Bible the author displays a rare mastery of Biblical science. Readers will find his literary style as gentle and as fierce, as high and as deep as the nuances of the Biblical themes he elucidates.

ACT AND BEING

Author: Michele Federico Sciacca (1908-)
Type of work: Philosophy of man
First published: 1956

Principal Ideas Advanced

The essence of being is being as present to and constitutive of the spiritual subject.

Existence and being are attributes of person; the real is the other-than-person in relation to person.

In the love of the other person as person the moral form of being is revealed.

Michele Federico Sciacca, historian of philosophy, philosopher in his own right, and professor of theoretical philosophy at the University of Genoa, Italy, was born at Giarre (Catania), Italy, on July 12, 1908. When he graduated from college in 1926, his philosophical orientation, through Kant and Fichte, was toward transcendental idealism, with reservations, however, as to its capacity to solve the problem of the person, which from the very beginning appears to have been the center of Sciacca's theoretical interest. He pursued the study of philosophy at the University of Catania, where Gino Ferretti provided him with the first incentive to read the philosophy of Giovanni Gentile (1875-1944), and at the University of Naples, where the actual spiritual encounter with Gentile, regarded by the young Sciacca as "Fichte made explicit through Hegel" and therefore as the fulfillment of idealism, occurred.

Sciacca earned the degree of doctor of philosophy in 1930, with a dissertation on *The Philosophy of Thomas Reid,* directed by Antonio Aliotta and since published. The period 1931-1936 marks the realization of an ambitious program of studies of the classical philosophers from the Greeks to Hegel, as well as the deepening of his philosophical investigations, which led him, as a result of a first revision of actualism, to a position of critical spiritualism. Of this period are his *Studies On Ancient Philosophy* and *Studies On Medieval and Modern Philosophy,* both published in 1935, and *Outline of a Critical Spiritualism* (1936) which was forecast in a long article and revealing document of Sciacca's disillusion with immanentism as *the* solution of the problem of the person, "The Crisis of Idealism" (*Ricerche filosofiche,* 1934).

The *Outline* was Sciacca's first systematic attempt to answer the question which led him to abandon immanentism: Where is the consistency of the person, if it cannot be the foundation of itself, and if God does not exist? The *Outline* is a serious examination of the case for transcendence within idealism. This exigency for transcendence, awaiting a philosophical answer, dominated Sciacca's activity in the two following years 1937-1938. The highlights of this period are his studies of Plato, which resulted in *The Dialectic of the Ideas in the "Parmenides" and in the "Sophist"* and *The Metaphysics of Plato, The Cosmological Problem,* both published in 1938, and his first encounter with the work of Antonio Rosmini-Serbati (1797-1855), brought about coincidentally by his collaboration with Gentile on an editorial venture, which resulted in Sciacca's edition of Rosmini's *Principles of Moral Science* and *Comparative and Critical History of the Systems Around the Principle of Morals,* and in an anti-Kantian interpretation of Rosmini, opposite to that of Gentile, in *The Moral Philosophy of Antonio Rosmini* and *Theory and Practice of Will,* both of 1938.

Sciacca's discovery of Rosmini had a decisive influence on his own philosophical development as well as on Rosminian historiography, which discarded the Kantian interpretation of Spaventa and Gentile. In the period 1939-1948 Sciacca's critical spiritualism developed into Christian spiritualism, characterized as the "denunciation of the insufficiency of philosophy to fully resolve the problem of itself to itself, and the essential problem of man in his singularity: hence the conclusion that a philosophy aware of itself can be but a Christian philosophy," and that every authentic philosophy is at least intentionally Christian. To this period belong various theoretical writings collected in *Problems of Philosophy* (1941), *The Moral Problem* (1942), various studies on Maurice Blondel now collected in *Dialogue with Maurice Blondel* (1962), *My Christian Spiritualism* (1944), *Letters from the Countryside* (1945), *The Church and Modern Civilization* (1948). The best synthesis of the author's thought in this period shall be found in *The Problem of God and Religion in Contemporary Philosophy* (1944) and the monograph on *Pascal* (1944).

Christian spiritualism governs Sciacca's interpretation of Italian philosophy from the Middle Ages to the present in *Italian Philosophy* (1941), *The Twentieth Century* (1941), *Italian Philosophy in the Age of Risorgimento* (1948), and of contemporary philosophy both European and American in *Philosophy Today* (1945). Christian spiritualism ushers its author into "objective idealism" or the "philosophy of integrality," marked by the theoretical conquest of "objective inwardness," of the person as synthesis of finite subjectivity and universal being, present to, and constitutive of, spirit (Idea). The transition is marked by *Philosophy and Metaphysics* (1950) where, in the enthusiasm of discovery, some points were overstated and then corrected by the author in the second edition of the work (1962). The theoretical articulation of the philosophy of integrality to date consists of *Objective Inwardness* (1951), *Man the Unbalanced* (1956), *Act and Being* (1956), and *Death and Immortality* (1959).

The great task of the contemporary philosopher, sensitive to the new exigency born of the Cartesian *cogito* and alive to the classical tradition of Plato and Saint Augustine, is the restoration of the problem of being. The point of such task is not an option for idealism or realism, the denial of either or the combination of both. It is, rather, the exploration of the possibility of a distinction, despite the indivisible unity of being and thought. The ontological problem should be placed beyond the subject-object opposition, which is based on a dialectic of exclusion and finally of reduction, in the well-intentioned but ill-conceived attempt to safeguard the authenticity of subjectivity (idealism) or of objectivity (realism). The subect-object opposition is ontologically illusory, claims Sciacca, since subject and object together make up that original synthetic act that is the person. The dialectic by which one understands the person is, then, one of inclusion-distinction, not of exclusion or of reduction. The problem of being is resolved by going to living thought. *Act and Being* constitutes the outline of an ontology directed by these considerations.

Sciacca uses the term "Idea" to designate the primary object of mind. The Idea is given to the person, the spiritual subject, in the person's act of grasping that which is presented to it. The person, says Sciacca, is the synthesis of "pure subjectivity," the spiritual existent, and "pure objectivity," the Idea.

Thus, Sciacca claims, the essence of any being is to be present to mind, to be intuited by the act of the spiritual subject, the person. Man's being is constituted by his action as mind, as that which unifies the Idea and the existent. Man is always actuating himself in the act of grasping Idea; his being is never complete.

Necessarily united to the human subject, the Idea constitutes man in a threefold dialectical relation: (1) to the creative act, which gives him existence, (2) to the Idea, which gives him intelligence, and (3) to the Absolute Being, who, as ultimate end, gives him fulfillment.

Sciacca maintains throughout his work that existence is not reducible to, or identical with, reality. Existence precedes reality and every real, which is from it and is real only in relation to it. The real is that which does not exist to itself and therefore exists for the subject (the person) who perceives it. The person as the ontological synthesis of the ideal, the existential, and the real, forms of the one and identical essence of being. The ontology of created being is the ontology of the person, because only the person synthesizes in itself all the created forms of being.

Empirically, says Sciacca, every existent is situated in an environment which determines him and sets him face to face with other existents and with things. More profoundly, however, the subject's impenetrability may be taken as the subject's position of himself as unique in his ontological secret, in the defense of his singularity. In defending his exclusiveness and concrete inwardness, the existent does not close himself within his secret, but expands himself in the gift of his inwardness to the inwardness of the other. The gift of one's freedom is to recognize, respect, and potentiate the freedom of the other, in order to repropose the active secret of one's existence in a further unveiling-concealing, in a further restatement of one's own autonomy, without suspicion or exclusion, in relation to the autonomy of the other. This secret, impenetrable and always penetrated and never exhausted, is the secret of being. The infinity of this tendency, inward and expansive, of the subject is unaccountable on the sole principle of subjectivity. Man is implication of true infinity, singularity always in act and never actuated, because of the infinity of the Idea that constitutes him as subject and essentiates his every existential act.

According to Sciacca, only the existent is *being-principle,* because he is existence-to-oneself (sentiment). The real is not principle: it is the term of the existent, the perceived that is other than the perceiving subject. The existent, insofar as he perceives (exists to) himself, is both the perceiving principle and the perceived term of the same perceiving principle.

There is no existence to oneself without mind, or mind without existence to oneself. But there is no mind without Idea and no Idea without mind. Man, then, is act of being as (a) Idea, (b) existent or principle of subjectivity, and (c) the act of being of every real. In the order of nature, accordingly, man alone is *complete* subject. Unrepeatably itself, it is active, supreme, incommunicable principle of sensation, intellection, and action.

Only the person *exists,* Sciacca writes. The real exists insofar as it belongs to the person, and in the measure in which the person actualizes it; that is, senses, knows, and wills it. It also follows that a person does not belong to another person, but each is existent for the other existent, in a "bond" rather than a relationship. The interpersonal bond is therefore twofold and simultaneous: one person contains the other, which is its content, and is the content of the other, which contains it.

Only the person is properly *being,* Sciacca claims further. Nothing is more *solid* and consistent than man's existence. Being implies unity. Man alone has an indivisible center: the person. Unity is interior to itself. Only man is such in a universe which he uses and binds to himself, without being used and bound by it, and opens to infinite dimensions. Initiative is proper to being. Only man is initiator, since initiative implies an autonomous will and an efficacious freedom. Permanence, resistance to destruction, immortal subsistence, belong to being essentially. Only man dies and does not perish. Yet, man is concrete implication of solidity and *frailty.* He, who is unity, is fragmented, as if a centrifugal force pulled him away from that indivisible center that he is as person. Inwardly, he is spread out on all things. He has a fundamental destination, alone essential, yet manifold ends draw him to contrasting and delusive aspirations. Immortal, he seems to shipwreck into nothingness at every moment. The "solid" existent is an "unstable" being, who must always conquer and develop his being in order to deserve the name of being.

Autonomous and free subject, man may anchor his existence to either solidity or frailty. By choosing the latter, the plane of pure existentiality, he falsifies the true principle of existence that is actuation of the essence which it implies and in which it is implied. Existence is self-actuation as value and expression of values. The plane of the purely existential, on the other hand, is the plane of the temporary (not of the temporal), of the everyday (that does not make history), of the superficial. It consists in fragments of existence without a unifying and quickening center. Our moments of existence are valuable only insofar as they gather, converge, and unify themselves in value, of which they are partial expressions. Existence, accordingly, is existing in the essential; it is positive actuation of values. Existence is denied as value by both the purely existential and the abstract essential. The level of the abstract essential, as contemplation of the essence in its formal perfection, turns existence into pure contingency. In its instant it denies time. In its formal perfection it denies the vigor of being.

Thus, writes Sciacca, the world cannot "exist" without the existent. The existent, on the other hand, can "live" only in the world. The world, accordingly, is necessary to, and the condition of, the vitality of the body but not of the existence of man, which is the very principle of subjectivity and, as "this" existent, is indestructible. Life, indeed, is value and incarnation of all vital and cosmic, finite and temporal values. On the other hand, life, unlike existence, is not infinite and immortal. Furthermore, the ontological value of the world does not consist in its being reducible to man, but in its being the other than man in relation to man.

The real exists and has value, according to Sciacca, only in the actuality of the act of the existent, who, in turn, cannot actuate his act or construct himself in value without the real that offers itself to his discovery and actuation. The infinity of the real is thus the infinity of the spirit, and the levels of the real are the levels of the existent. At the merely empirical level, for instance, things are things and even man is a thing. At the vital level they are instruments or tools, of a purely economic value. At the esthetic level they are signs of beauty. At the moral level they are good, and at the philosophical level, true.

Otherness, by virtue of the ontological constitutive (Idea), is threefold, says Sciacca. The creature is other than God. The real (nature) is the other-than-man. Another man other-man. Now, diverse modes of otherness demand diverse moral attitudes, since morality is recognition (love) of the other in the order of beings.

Things, the other-than-man, are necessary to one's vitality, writes Sciacca, to one's own actuality and activity at the level of temporal and cosmic values. Man, the other-man, is necessary to oneself at the level of existence, just as the self is necessary to him. Reciprocity is essential to consciousness; that is, to personal existence. The closing of the consciousness of the other is one's own sterility. The fundamental beginning of reciprocity of consciousness is the recognition (love) of each other's liberty. The denial of the other's liberty or autonomous singularity, the denial of the other as person, involves the denial of one's own existence as person. One's free choice of the other as free, as act of recognition of the other in the order of being, is both content and manifestation of being in its moral form.

Consequently, Sciacca maintains, moral being is synonymous with "being as loved." The principle who loves is the subjective being who, by loving his whole being, loves the Idea that is his objective constituent. As loved by the subject, the Idea, principle of objectivity, is *moral being*. Love joins subjective being (the existent) and objective being (the Idea). But existent and Idea form an original unity. Therefore, when the existent, in the light of the Idea, loves his own being, he reflexively actuates the bond between his existential-real and his essential-objective being (Idea). This is his natural self-love and the beginning of his whole voluntary activity. The recognition (love) of his being is his essential moral condition and the foundation of every further recognition or love for every other person and for every real.

Since the moral act is act of *love* for the other in the order of being (*known* by the mind), the moral act is an integral act, that is, sensitive-intellectual-voluntary; and its term is an integral object, that is, existence-essence. In the moral act knowledge is love, no longer formal and abstract knowing; and love is intelligence, not blind passion or animal desire. Love includes and implies the rational act, but completes and surpasses it in a new synthesis. Existence—without loss of essence, to be sure—is essential to the act of moral intelligence, while it eludes the concept (hence reason, and ethical reason).

The intelligence of love (moral intelligence) has no measure other than itself; that is, the order of being as loved, present to the subject in its infinity.

The rational act proceeds by exclusion, Sciacca claims. It seeks the truth in the "just middle" with which it identifies moral perfection and the "virtuosity" of being. The intelligence of love proceeds by inclusion. It advances (as existence in its unreduced concreteness) by alternative affirmation of contraries, in a synthesis which always tends to the extreme morality of being.

Moral being is "violent" because it is the synthesis of a boundless vital and spiritual thirst for self-giving (the subject), and of a value without limit (Idea) which the subject can never fully actuate and express.

Only persons are loved, then, Sciacca concludes. Things are loved only in relation to the person. But then the "thing" is no longer "thing." It is part of the unity that is man, a moment of his existentiality, itself existentiality of the value which man has impressed on it by his "work." Thus, in order to love things one must make them possessions of the person. In order to love persons, on the contrary, one must make them an all-before-which-I-am-nothing. He who loves demands nothing in return because he has nothing to demand, since he promotes himself only to the degree to which he can give himself, his having and his being, to the other person.

Love is goodness unto the end, not merely virtue, Sciacca insists. But exactly because it is so, love is intransigent, pitiless. To him who loves it dictates the harsh law of love, which is the annihilation of oneself for the actuation of the norm, of the order of being. True love destroys to the last element: this is its sublime humanity. Because only then, when it has done its work, thoroughly, love has become living flame, our "nothing" explodes with being, our ashes are afire, and our dust builds as indestructible cement. Love such as this is the witness which the norm of moral being demands in the name of Being, who is Love.

A. R. C.

THE SEAT OF WISDOM

Author: Louis Bouyer (1913-)
Type of work: Marian theology
First published: 1957

Principal Ideas Advanced

In Mary one is able to see all that grace was able to make of a human being who, although not divine, became the Mother of God.

Wisdom, the most sublime form of action, is in God but is also related to the world.

Wisdom is the divine essence; it is to some extent realized in all who are saved, but it was completely realized on the plane of history in Mary, who is the Seat of Wisdom.

Father Louis Bouyer, converted to Catholicism in 1939, Professor of Theology at the Institut Catholique in Paris, presents in *The Seat of Wisdom,* as the subtitle indicates, "An essay on the place of the Virgin Mary in Christian theology." Father Bouyer's Marian theology is no superficial exercise; it is a profound and Scripturally oriented study, giving evidence of both a great love and a great intellect.

Father Bouyer maintains, in his introduction, that a Christianity which does not do homage to our Lady is "a mutilated Christianity," and he adds, "Once refuse to admit the uniqueness of his Mother and the Christ you think you have kept is but a disfigured Christ; no longer do God and man come together in him." Christ, says Bouyer, "was not, strictly speaking, *a* man, a human person, but God made man"; Mary, on the other hand, was "no more than human," but as the Mother of God, she was "all that grace was able to make of a creature, of human nature, while still leaving it in its order as a created being." The author's conclusion, which is reached only after many pages of faithful inquiry and reflection, is that Mary was *a* person, indeed, but *the* person in history in whom the divine Wisdom found its throne, its seat. Father Bouyer's essay may be considered to be a serious theologian's attempt to clarify and justify that claim.

The French Oratorian begins by arguing that although the number of passages in Scripture relating to Mary are not great in number, a Marian theology may nevertheless be built upon them, this by the device of realizing the implications of three great Scriptural themes: (1) Mary stands in relation to Christ as a second Eve to a second Adam, (2) the people of God constitute the Spouse of the Lord, (3) the divine Wisdom seeks personal embodiment.

The detailed defense of the claim that these three themes may be found in Scripture and that both Scripturally and historically they are related will be of interest primarily to the professional theologian and student of theology. But a full appreciation of Bouyer's central thesis depends upon an understanding of the themes themselves, and although such understanding is certainly facilitated and deepened by an examination of the Scriptural texts cited, close attention to Father Bouyer's conclusions will enable the general reader to comprehend the theses.

Perhaps the most illuminating statement concerning the relation of Eve to Adam, a statement which foreshadows the theme of the book itself, the theological theme which unifies and elevates beyond literal meaning the three Scriptural themes, is the statement that "Eve in regard to Adam, the woman in regard to man, appears to be a kind of extension of her companion, and, at the same time . . . the being in and by whom the world, which is foreign to man, takes on a recognisable and engaging aspect."

There is a second aspect to the Eve-Adam relation, a paradoxical aspect, which consists in the fact that the union "appears both as the blessing and the curse of the human race." Both the Old and the New Testament, says Bouyer, testify to the opposition within the relation; it was both a blessing and a curse.

The relation between Eve and Adam is mirrored in the second Scriptural theme, which is concerned with the relation between the Spouse of the Lord, the people or city of God, and God Himself. "In Israel," writes Father Bouyer, "the image of husband and wife is applied to God's relations with his people to signify the love which two lives, two personal beings, show forth themselves in giving themselves to one another." The paradoxical aspect is present in this second theme, just as it was in the first: the spouse is unworthy of her husband; at the same time, she is the unique Beloved.

The Wisdom-theme is not so easily grasped, but primarily because the idea which unifies the first two themes is now brought one level of abstraction higher. The figure of Eve is personal and vivid; the image of the people as the city of God is of a somewhat more general nature, although one is to understand that each person is an integral part of the whole; but when one speaks of Wisdom, meaning by the term not so much the divine order which is embodied but the embodiment of it, one comes to the level at which a distinction must be made between the spirit or form and that which is inspired or formed. The author refers to the identification in the fourth book of Esdras of the "pre-existing Jerusalem with the divine Wisdom," and he adds: ". . . in fact, the ultimate form in which Wisdom is revealed to Israel is that of a supernatural architect who brings into being the universe conceived in the mind of God." In this image Wisdom is the architect, and the universe is the embodiment of the form. But the idea which Bouyer appears to be working toward is the idea that Wisdom manifests itself personally in such a manner that the embodiment of Wisdom may itself be referred to as Wisdom or, even better, as the "seat" of Wisdom. Clarification of this point is facilitated if one moves from Bouyer's explication of the Scriptural theme to his conclusion, in which the Scriptural themes are illuminated and given new relevance through coming together in the image of Mary, our Lady, Spouse of the Lord, and the "Seat of Wisdom."

In his concluding chapter, "Wisdom and the Assumption," Father Bouyer argues that Mary's final realization "at the end of time" as Virgin and Spouse is "prefigured . . . in an antecedent realisation, in the middle of time, as Virgin Mother. It is strictly in this aspect that Mary is, not the final or complete realisation of Wisdom, but its supreme realisation on the plane of history. Mary is truly the Seat of Wisdom, of the uncreated Wisdom shown forth as a creature in her Son . . . ; she is, thereby, the source, within history, of the eschatological Wisdom, created in time to espouse in time its eternal realisation in the Son who is the Word."

This explanation, or summary of ideas developed earlier, is critical. The emphasis to be noted, in attempting to understand Mary's relation to Wisdom, a relation which corresponds, although in various ways, to Eve's relation to Adam, the people's relation to God, the Church's relation to God, the universe's relation to Wisdom, is the emphasis on Mary's status as the realization *in history* of the divine Wisdom. Through her the Word was born *into the world;* through her, after His death, the Spouse of Christ, the Church, was born. Since Mary is the one person in time who made possible the entry into history of the eternal Wisdom and Word, she is the expression of divine Motherhood. Mary is the Seat of Wisdom, then, not only in the sense that the Son is the eternal realization, as the Word, of the divine Wisdom—God's plan for history —but also in the sense that she herself realized all the graces that the Church, "whose collective personality is realised only in individual persons," will ultimately realize.

The Church, then, is finally to be the realization *in history* of God's divine plan, His Wisdom; but Mary, the Mother of God, is the only human being (except for Christ, who was "God made man . . . not, strictly speaking, *a* man") who has already realized, in time, God's Wisdom. She is the source, in time, of the entry of the eternal Wisdom into the world; but she was also, once and for all in time, herself the realization of what, only at the end of its history, would be realized again in the Church. Thus, Father Bouyer writes, the Assumption of Mary, her reunion in body and soul with the risen Son, "is the pledge of the glory Christ will give to his Spouse [the Church], as he has already given it to his Mother [Mary]."

The Seat of Wisdom is a fascinating application of Scriptural themes to the problems of Marian theology. Father Bouyer explores the implications of his thesis in considering the significance of marriage, virginity, motherhood, the Immaculate Conception of Mary, the Incarnation, the Redemption, and the Holy Ghost. An understanding of his discussions depends upon keeping in mind the distinction between a realization *in time* and an *eternal* realization, and also the distinctions between He who acts (God), His divine plan (Wisdom), the eternal embodiment of Wisdom (the Word), the divine embodiment of Wisdom in time (the Son), the personal embodiment of Wisdom in *a* person (Mary), the Mother of Wisdom in time (Mary), and the personal but collective embodiment of Wisdom (the Church).

The Seat of Wisdom is both a theological exercise and an expression of faith. The ideas it expresses do much to bring together the various themes concerning Mary which pervade Scripture and direct the Church in its development.

THE MEETING OF LOVE AND KNOWLEDGE

Author: Martin Cyril D'Arcy, S.J. (1888-)
Type of work: Comparative study of religions
First published: 1957

Principal Ideas Advanced

Many have argued for a perennial philosophy which unites Eastern and Western religion in a highest common factor.

Despite verbal and even deeper similarities, Christianity is fundamentally different from Eastern religions because it aims not at the suppression of the person but at his perfection in a personal relation to a personal God which binds men together in charity.

In *The Meeting of Love and Knowledge,* Father Martin D'Arcy attempts an assessment of the view that there is a perennial philosophy which unites East and West. He has in mind the effort of such writers as Aldous Huxley who seek to show that in the mysticism of the East and West we come upon a common aspiration having a common object; we come upon a highest common factor which enables us to bridge the gap between two cultures which appear on the surface to be quite unlike. Father D'Arcy has the greatest respect for the intention of such authors, and he finds much merit in their work; but in this book he wants to show that their central project has not and cannot meet with success.

The Meeting of Love and Knowledge begins with a discussion of Homo sapiens, moving from the zoölogical meaning of the phrase to a reminder of the ancient ideal of man as a seeker after wisdom. From the very outset the complementarity and contrast of Oriental and Occidental civilizations are present, and Father D'Arcy suggests that in the West the sense of respect for men who devote their lives to seeing life whole has too long been absent, lost in our ever-waxing concentration on the practical, the immediately useful. We have a good deal to learn from the East, D'Arcy declares, if we are to correct this imbalance, but it must also be seen that we have lost the sense of the great philosophical sources of the Western tradition. The Greeks defined philosophy as the quest for wisdom; even Descartes wanted a First Philosophy, a science which would know all things in their first causes. But in our own day philosophy has become a much narrower and less ambitious enterprise, and the narrowing has often come about by calling into question the bulk of human life, by regarding as meaningless those statements which concern themselves with what, for most men, are the most important things. Perhaps too much has been expected of philosophy, but today, more than ever, philosophy must appear inadequate to man.

If philosophy is a quest for wisdom, says D'Arcy, not all wise men have been philosophers, nor have philosophers always been wise. The wisdom that is in question in the concept of perennial philosophy is that which is found in the great religious teachers of mankind. Many authors employ the term "perennial philosophy" to cover the common tenets of religious teaching, Eastern and Western, a highest common factor where the differences fall away and a basic identity of doctrine can be discerned. Perusal of selected passages from these various teachers does indeed show an undeniable similarity of language.

The perennial philosophy, then, is a religious philosophy, and Father D'Arcy suggests that it contains a number of divisions: theological, contemplative, and mystical. Perennial philosophy values experience which is utterly beyond thought, though the mystic may attempt to employ thought and language to describe his experience. According to D'Arcy, "This is the wisdom which Coomaraswamy and Aldous Huxley pronounce to the unitive force in East and West. . . . It is a wisdom which must be sought with the whole heart and mind, and a long novitiate is required before it can be attained. In this pursuit the moral virtues provide the essential prerequisites; for action and knowledge help each other out, and the self must strip away its illusions, its possessiveness and selfishness."

Father D'Arcy finds that such efforts to find the same thing in Eastern and Western religious thinkers overlook basic differences in the very experience which is definitive. There is a great contrast between the impersonal character of the one and the intensely personal character of the other: "In other words, there is this difference between the Christian and the Hindu or Buddhist conception of self-denial, that the former aims to keep the person, the latter to dissolve it." Verbal similarities may mask this difference, but the difference is there and it is basic. The Easterner tends to think of man as comprising two sides, body and divinity, and techniques are devised to free man of the body so that his divine spark can be consumed in the divine fire. That is, the self is overcome and lost; there is no distinction between man and God. This is not the Christian view. So, too, efforts to find sameness in the Buddhist *maitri* and Christian charity must fail. For the Buddhist, this love is merely a phase; for the Christian, charity is the fulfilment. In terms of such differences, Father D'Arcy would range Christianity, Judaism, and Islam on one side, as pointing to a personal God, and, on the other, Hinduism, Buddhism, and Gnostic beliefs.

In attempting to compare Eastern and Western mysticism further, Father D'Arcy introduces a distinction between two kinds of love, a centripetal and a centrifugal love, the one possessive, the other donative. The distinction is reminiscent of the distinction between the love of concupiscence and the love of friendship, as well as of the Thomistic doctrine on the different "movements" of intellect and will. Father D'Arcy writes: "Fully humanized, the possessive impulse shows itself in self-respect, independence, growth of personality and especially in the pursuit of knowledge, where the godlike reason introduces form, order and organization into its world without and within. The self-giving impulse on its part shows itself in communal acts, fellow-feeling, labor without reward and self-sacrificing love." Father D'Arcy wants to see valid mystical experience as not wholly the one or the other of these basic impulses, since what we are dealing with can be called indifferently understanding love or loving understanding. In terms of this distinction, he comes to speak of three forms of mystical experience: nature mysticism, solitary mysticism, and Christian mysticism: "The first is indicated probably in the psychologist's language of the return to the womb, for instance in the Magna Mater worship. The second is a mode of stripping of self so as to procure an experience which is ineffable and felt to be identification with what is supreme and perfect. The third is the Christian, based on knowledge and love, which moves in the circuit of persons and personal love."

The perennial philosophy's rejection of the Incarnation as anything more than a passing moment of religiosity and the denial that the religious experience is not the overcoming of the human person but a personal relation between man and God which involves one with all other human persons and restores the world as well—these are Father D'Arcy's main reasons for objecting to what he calls the gnostic tendency of the perennial philosophy champions. He finds it attractive in its way, of course. The notion that all formulas and creeds are ultimately unimportant and the promise of a complete transcendence of self which ends in an ineffable bliss have their appeal. But such a conception of religion cannot be put forward as essentially the same thing as Christianity. For Christianity, man is a person, body and soul. Matter is real and things are good; the body is good. The perfection of the Christian life is not one which is gained by ceasing to be the person one is. We are called to personal perfection; our person is brought into relation with a personal God and, through this bond of charity, with all other persons. Most fundamental from the theological point of view is the consideration that the attainment of perfection is not for the Christian something of which man is naturally capable. He must be elevated to the supernatural life, come under the sway of grace, become the locus of a life which surpasses any human capacity. No technique, no natural *ascesis* can bring us to a sharing in the divine life or, in any essential sense, make us such that God cannot deny that grace. The new gnosis, by calling man divine, really a part of God, may seem to elevate him. However, as Father D'Arcy shows, the real effect is to deny that man is a self and to assert that his ultimate perfection consists in literally ceasing to be. True wisdom consists in a meeting of love and knowledge, and the love that will give true direction to the knowledge is Christian charity, just as the knowledge that guides our love is Christian revelation.

R.M.

INSIGHT

Author: Bernard J. F. Lonergan, S.J. (1903-)
Type of work: Epistemology; foundations of Christian metaphysics
First published: 1957

Principal Ideas Advanced

A thorough understanding of the process of human knowing will unify the diverse fields which have been generated by that process; namely, mathematics, the behavioral sciences, the empirical sciences, and all the areas of concrete or common-sense knowledge.

The unification of the fields of knowledge will result in a philosophy grounded upon the invariant structures of the human knower, in which all judgments can be reduced to their cognitional origins and thereby become methodically verified.

Following immediately from this analysis of the general structure of knowing is an insight into the corresponding structure of the known, which will yield a verifiable metaphysics.

The study of insight will also reveal the nature of error and a method whereby error may systematically be eliminated from philosophy and metaphysics.

After publishing a series of purely exegetical articles in *Theological Studies* from 1941 to 1949, concerning the cognitional theories and notions of being found in Aristotle and Saint Thomas, Bernard Lonergan developed his own synthesis, *Insight,* which attempts in our times the task undertaken by Saint Thomas's philosophical works in the thirteenth century. Aristotle and Saint Thomas achieved historical significance by turning the tide of currents which would in their day sweep philosophy onto the rocks of skepticism. Lonergan considers that we are living in an age, very similar to that faced by Saint Thomas, in which the whole philosophical tradition stands in need of radical revision. Just as philosophy was about to be swallowed up by theology in the thirteenth century, so today it is about to be engulfed by empirical science. Unless it can be clearly shown that philosophy can add significantly to our knowledge of reality in ways which are distinct both from empirical science and from theology, philosophy will continue to be increasingly devaluated by the leading intellectuals of our age. But without a genuine philosophy there is no knowledge of the real and of being as such, and one is left in relativism and skepticism. Moreover, without the supple and detailed cognitional theory which is a major task of philosophy, it is impossible to secure any synthesis of the principles of reason and faith with the pronouncements of scientific reason.

Insight is written on three levels. At its most fundamental level it is concerned with a study of human understanding as it manifests itself in the insights of men of science, mathematics, and common sense. It is, secondarily, a working out of the philosophical implications of this prior study. Finally, it is "a campaign against the flight from understanding," an analysis of the many ways in which the complex structure of man's knowing can become involved in error.

Fundamental to the whole synthesis is the act of understanding: "Thoroughly understand what it is to understand, and not only will you understand the broad lines of all there is to be understood but also you will possess a fixed base, an invariant pattern, opening upon all further developments of understanding." According to Lonergan, insight into insight is the key to a treasure of intellectual wealth which will solve some of the most crucial problems facing contemporary philosophers.

First of all, insight into insight yields the possibility of developing a criterion for truth. If in our own consciousness we can discover the process whereby we arrive at an indubitably certain judgment, we can then discern the normative pattern for all true judgments. Lonergan, accordingly, leads his readers through the labyrinthine paths of scientific procedures, mathematical insights, and common-sense judgments up to the point where they attain an insight into the truth of the concrete affirmation that they are knowers who are conscious empirically, intellectually, and rationally. "The crucial issue is an experimental issue," he writes, "and the experiment will be performed not publicly but privately. It will consist in one's own rational self-consciousness clearly and distinctly taking possession of itself as rational self-consciousness. Up to that decisive achievement, all leads. From it, all follows."

Insight into insight yields, moreover, the possibility of a philosophy which Lonergan equates with interiority or the conscious subject's "personal appropriation of the concrete, dynamic structure immanent and recurrently operative in his own cognitional activities." Since the time of René Descartes (1596-1650), the trends in philosophy have shifted from a study of objects to a methodical reflection upon the knowing subject in an attempt to salvage the hopeless disarray of the various schools of philosophy. Edmund Husserl (1859-1938), the German philosopher and principal founder of the phenomenological movement, wrote that the dilemma facing philosophers in our own century has become even worse than it was in Descartes' day. With the meteoric rise of the empirical sciences, particularly the behavioral ones, there has been an increasing fragmentation of knowledge, resulting in a society built upon a multitude of irreducible criteria for truth and as many conflicting theories about reality. Because of the progressive specialization in all the departments of knowledge, there seems little hope of unification within the fields of knowledge themselves. As a solution for this problem, Husserl calls for a return to the subject as the single source of all fields of knowledge. It is precisely this task which occupies the major portion of Lonergan's attention in *Insight*.

Lonergan first proposes an analysis of the type of insight found in mathematics, since it is here that the nature of the act of understanding is seen most clearly. He then proceeds to the methods of empirical science which reveal the dynamic context in which insight occurs. It is in the scientific method that are found all the elements of cognitional process: (1) the empirical stage, (2) the level of theory, and (3) the verification of theory which leads to higher viewpoints because of man's desire for theories which comprehend more data. Finally, Lonergan analyzes the insights of men of common sense in which are evident the many factors that can disturb this dynamic pattern and render its conclusions erroneous. This phenomenology of the knowing subject, therefore, leads to the conclusion that there are three distinct components in our cognitional activity: an empirical component, an intellectual component in which we grasp some meaning in the data of experience, and a rational component in which we reflect upon the validity of the meaning we have understood in the second component. Because of that radically human characteristic which Lonergan calls the pure desire to know, the human mind spontaneously moves from experience through understanding to judgment.

At a second level, *Insight* is an examination of the philosophic implications of understanding. After yielding a philosophy which deals with the invariant structures in the knower, insight into insight leads to a metaphysics which unfolds the corresponding structure in the known. Being, the subject of metaphysics, is defined in relation to the most profound dynamism in human knowing as the object of the pure desire to know. But just as this desire progresses through an empirical and theoretical stage to the final noetic component of judgment, so too the objects of judgment are composed of one component corresponding to experience, a second corresponding to understanding, and a third corresponding to judgment. It is from this isomorphism between knowing and being, therefore, that Lonergan argues to the general structure of being in terms of potency, form, and act.

At a third level, *Insight* is "a campaign against the flight from understanding." Insight into the nature of understanding is an insight into the principle sources of error. There exists on the level of experience myriad conflicting feelings, desires, and habits which block the unfolding of the pure desire to know. There is the bias, for example, resulting simply from our bodily makeup, which causes us spontaneously to recognize as real only the "already out there now." There is, moreover, the bias which springs from our spontaneous egoism, causing us to reject insights which might inconvenience us. Besides the bias of the individual, there is also group bias, a collective egoism which refuses to accept insights which might destroy the values of the group. Common to all men is the general bias which disdains theoretical understanding because of its alleged impracticality and removal from everyday living. In place of building society on the firm ground of judgments resulting from insights into the nature of reality, men operate on the level of the "practical" without examining the theoretical errors in their presuppositions, thus aiding the progressive decline of civilizations increasingly based on error.

To the degree that one allows these various drives to interfere with his primordial desire for truth, just so far will he fall into error. Lonergan's purpose is to assist the reader to become aware of these conflicting desires, for "the point here, as elsewhere, is appropriation; the point is to discover, to identify, to become familiar with the activities of one's own intelligence; the point is to become able to discriminate with ease and from personal conviction between one's purely intellectual activities and the manifold of other, 'existential' concerns that invade and mix and blend with the operations of intellect to render it ambivalent and its pronouncements ambiguous."

The philosophy which can be developed from this combination of an insight into the structures of human knowing with an understanding of those factors which hinder the unfolding of these structures possesses three characteristics. First, it will be methodical insofar as it can reduce the statements of philosophers to their origins in cognitional activity, deciding whether that activity is or is not aberrant by appealing to the insights and methods of mathematicians, scientists, and men of common sense. Secondly, it will be a critical philosophy because of its ability to discriminate between the products of the detached and disinterested desire to know and the products of the various other desires of man. Finally, it will be comprehensive, embracing in a single view every statement in every philosophy. This comprehensiveness is not that of a closed system. It results, rather, from the fact that every statement made by every philosopher is either a product of the pure desire to know developing untrammeled through experience, understanding, and judgment, or a result of a conflct of other "existential" concerns with this normative objectivity.

Although *Insight* deals in profound speculation and comprehensive theory, its aim nevertheless is ultimately practical. Lonergan envisages a study of insight as the basis for the possibility of reconstructing the social order.

Without an insight into both insight and error, one cannot distinguish between progress and decline on the cosmic level, nor between moral good and evil on the personal level. Moreover, a study of understanding is fundamental in working out the most crucial problem of man's anxiety-ridden life; namely, the question of the existence of God. On the basis of his phenomenology of the knower and his metaphysics of the known, Lonergan carefully demonstrates the evidence for a Transcendent Cause of intelligibility in the world.

But of itself the study set forth in *Insight* leads its readers to a profound sense of personal inadequacy. The more man exercises the self-reflection required by the method of *Insight*, the more he becomes aware of his radical weakness, his ill-will, and his immersion in bias: "The self-appropriation of one's own intellectual and rational self-consciousness begins as cognitional theory, expands into a metaphysics and an ethics, mounts to a conception and affirmation of God, only to be confronted with a problem of evil that demands the transformation of self-reliant intelligence into an *intellectus quaerens fidem.*" Only the phenomenology of the existential self, the self under the influence of original sin and divine grace, can yield the most comprehensive solutions to the problems posed by the polymorphic consciousness of man. It is this further study which Lonergan hopes will be for speculative theology what *Insight* has been for the *philosophia perennis*.

D. H. J.

ON THE THEOLOGY OF DEATH

Author: Karl Rahner, S.J. (1904-)
Type of work: Speculative theology
First published: 1957

Principal Ideas Advanced

Christianity changes completely man's relationship to death.

From a negation death is transformed into an affirmation, a fulfillment, a movement toward infinite and eternal being.

However, while this belief in the transformation of death has been the constant faith and affirmation of the Church and the faithful from the beginning, speculative thought, seeking the fuller understanding of this affirmation, has not been sufficiently elaborated.

Father Karl Rahner opens his essay *On the Theology of Death* (included in his *Zeitschrift für Katholische Theologie*) with an important distinction between *theology* and *faith*. Faith is the assent, the "yea," of the whole man to the message of God which is received as the "Word of God" from the mouth of the Church. Theology, on the other hand, is the effort conducted with conscious method, to secure a reflective understanding of what has been heard and accepted as the "Word of God." Within theology, moreover, a number of different efforts or purposes can be distinguished. The theologian may direct his efforts to stating as clearly as possible whatever is contained formally and explicitly in the teaching of the Church and the Bible, or he can undertake theological research in a speculative vein, without the protection against error of Church or Bible, in order to add something to our understanding of what has been heard in Revelation. In the latter effort, theological research begins with the doctrine of the Church, compares the single statements or propositions of this doctrine with one another, confronts them with other kinds of knowledge, and elaborates more fully the concepts they involve. Whatever the purposes and method of theology, however, it is clear that while faith and theology converge, indeed are basically inseparable and cannot be kept apart, still they are not the same and are not to be confused. The present essay is an essay in theology in the second of the two senses distinguished, that is, speculative theology; it begins with the teaching of the Church on death and then proceeds not merely to state this doctrine clearly but also to elaborate the concepts implied in it and to bring them into relation with other forms of knowledge.

Beginning with the immediate substance of the Church's doctrine on death, that which is warranted by her teaching authority, Rahner remarks that there are some differences among these propositions which impart a natural order of treatment and hence a basic form to his essay. Some of the propositions of Christian doctrine on death are valid for any human dying. Others qualify death in such a way that they cannot apply to every case of human dying, for example, the "death of the sinner," which is the expression and consequence of human guilt. Finally, it speaks of a dying with Christ, when death no longer has the character of a penalty for sin. On the basis of such distinctions among the kinds of propositions contained in the Church doctrine, a certain order of treatment indicates itself. This order is not systematic, but nevertheless has a distinctly organic and interrelated character.

Rahner selects as the first theme for his meditations on death, the following: *Death is an event which strikes man in his totality*. This must first be understood in the light of the fact that man is a union of *nature* and *person;* this is what is meant by the term "totality." By "nature" Rahner seeks to convey the idea that man has, antecedently to his own personal and free decision and independently of it, a specific kind of existence with definite laws proper to it and, consequently, a necessary mode of development; by "person" the author suggests that this same being, man, disposes freely of himself and is in the last analysis what he makes himself by his free decision. Thus, to say that death strikes man in his totality means that it has for him both a natural and a personal character. The doctrine of the Church expresses both of these dimensions of man's death: the natural, by the doctrine that death is the *separation of body and soul;* the personal, by saying that death is the *definitive end of our pilgrimage*. Both of these aspects of death are universal; they apply to every case of human dying. Therefore, the treatment of them follows the natural order: the universality of death; death as separation of body and soul; death as consummation of human personal development.

The universality of death is an absolute proposition of faith, according to Rahner. This proposition is something very different from the universality of the empirical induction that all men die. This latter proposition presents death simply as an obscure biological puzzle. Nor is death absolutely universal, for its relationship to the future is simply hypothetical. The universality implied in the teaching of faith is absolute because it has direct relation to the whole unthinkable future; because it is based not on any biological necessity but on something proper to man as a spiritual being, death remains completely independent of the outcome of biological discussions.

The Catholic teaching concerning the universality of death, when we abstract from the reasons assigned for that universality, describes death, in the first instance, from the outside as it were, indicating simply its range of impact. A step forward toward the essence of death, though still extrinsic, is made in the description of death as the separation of body and soul. Though not Biblical, this description must be considered a classical theological description of death, a description which states essential features of death. The description refers to the incontestable fact that in death the relationship between body and soul is altered; the soul is no longer the principle holding the body together as a distinct reality governed by its own immanent laws. Moreover, the term "separation" implies in some way the continued existence of the separated elements. Nevertheless, from the theological point of view, this statement of separation remains but a description and by no means an adequate definition of death. For, says Rahner, while it may serve for the biological aspect of the death of man, such a description is entirely silent on the human character of a man's death. It is the *man* who dies; death happens to him as a *whole*. Death affects the soul as well as the body, for in death the soul achieves a certain finality. But of all this the doctrine of death as separation of body and soul says nothing.

A third proposition of faith, according to Rahner's account, views death less existentially and more formally while directing attention to man more as a *person* than as a *nature*. This doctrine states that with death man's *pilgrimage* comes to a definite end. Death brings man, as a moral-spiritual person, a kind of finality and consummation which renders his decision for or against God, reached during the time of his bodily life, final and unalterable. This doctrine of the faith imposes a radical seriousness upon man toward this life. It is a "once and never again" affair which cannot be repeated and within which a decision is made which determines the state of the human principle once and forever. Life is suspended between a real beginning and a true end. Life begins through creation and it ends in such a way that the decision freely worked out in time will in the end become something unchangeable. There is, thus, no eternal return of all things, but a history given once and for all. At the natural level this historical time of human life is uni-directional between the inception of the individual and biological death, through which he achieves his final constitution. The physical world shares this historical character, for the death of the persons in the world slowly brings the world to its consummation in a process parallel to the process of the individual human being between birth and death. Finally, this history belongs to the moral-spiritual principle or person, for through a decision made in his time-life each man establishes the meaning of his eternal existence.

A fourth statement on death, as Rahner sees it, advances the investigation both forward and inward toward a definitive understanding of death in its essence. Death, claims Rahner, is the consequence of sin; our death is the death of Adam, the death of a sinner. This proposition, the author insists, is essential to faith. Death, as it is now universally suffered and encountered by men, is causally related to sin, above all to the sin committed by the head and progenitor of the human race in his quality as head. Man, according to the testimony of the Bible, was created with the possibility of immunity to sin; in the actual order, he dies because he has lost original justice. Man's death is evidence that man has fallen from union with God.

The statement that death is the consequence of the Fall of the first man implies that before his sin the first man was not subject to death. This does not mean that he would have lived on endlessly, had he not sinned; it means, rather, that man certainly would have experienced an end of his life, but in another manner, one in which, maintaining his bodily integrity, he would have carried this life to a perfect fulfillment by an inward movement. He would have experienced a death which instead of being a negation would have been a supreme act of self-affirmation.

What this consideration of the freedom of Adam from death places in relief is not immediately and inevitably the proposition that death is the consequence of sin, but the proposition that death is basically a natural event; hence, from its natural essence death is ambivalent; that is, it can be an event either of salvation or of damnation. The repression of one or the other of these aspects or possibilities of death would end up in a naturalistic or spiritualistic aberration, involving either the debasement of human death to the level of the animal or the pretension that the personality of man, in spite of the fact that he is also a natural being, is not affected by death at all. This ambivalence of death, says Rahner, is its darkness—not the empirical darkness of the individual merely, in which he feels the indeterminateness of his end even as he experiences his end, but the essential darkness of death, the fact that in its essence death has the dual possibility of salvation or damnation. Since death *is* this darkness, the final interpretation of this situation can come not from man but only from God. Death, because of its darkness, is addressed in the right way when it is performed by man as an act in which he surrenders himself fully and with unconditional openness to the disposal of the incomprehensible decision of God. By contrast, it might be said that mortal sin consists precisely in the desire to die autonomously; that is, apart from or even against this decision of God.

But, Rahner argues, although death

is wholly open only to God, there is an aspect of death in its darkness which reveals more concretely the meaning of death as the consequence of sin. For man experiences death as loss. This could not be the case if his death were merely natural. Thus, we are forced to return to the point of departure in the death of Adam and the kind of end his life would have had in that sinless state: the end as affirmation and fulfillment. In that condition death would never have been experienced as loss, but only as fulfillment. Therefore, the fact that man experiences death as loss demands that this death so experienced be referred not to man's natural state but to the Adamic state. With reference to that state, says Rahner, the loss which man experiences in death must be traced to the break in Adam of the relation between his life and its fulfillment by means of the primordial relationship to God through grace. Therefore, the proposition that death is the consequence of sin is not an abstract juridical one, but a concrete and ontological one. It might be said that death is not so much the *consequence* of sin, as its *expression;* that is, its actuality in realized and concrete form. Death is the expression and the visible mark, the actuality, of man's separation from God.

These considerations provide a natural bridge to the most impressive and positive doctrine of Rahner's essay, his doctrine of death in and with Christ as the Christian answer to the entire question of death and, above all, to the problem of death's darkness.

Rahner first considers the death of Christ itself. The first thing which must be said concerning that death is that Christ, as incarnate God, died the death of man, in the proper sense of death, the death of the human race as it had fallen in Adam. It has been established, Rahner claims, that death exhibits several dimensions: it is at once action and suffering, a surrender of the finite bodily constitution and a revelation of the all-cosmic relationship of spirit, the end of the biological life-career and the consummation of the personal life from within. The question may then be asked: On which of these dimensions does the redemptive power of God's death depend? Or does it depend on no one dimension, but on that death as an integral act of the God-man?

At this point Rahner takes issue with the "satisfaction" theory of the redemptive act of Christ, as developed in medieval theology. Needless to say, his position is not a forthright rejection of this theory. On the contrary, Rahner considers the "positive content" of this theory as true. According to medieval theory, the moral acts of Christ, in consequence of the infinite dignity of His divine Person, are of infinite value, in spite of the fact that these acts in themselves, as emanating from a human and existentially free nature, are finite. Since the gravity of an offense is measured by the dignity of the person offended and not by that of the offender, the sin of the free creature is an infinite sin, as being directed against the infinite majesty of God. For this offense no satisfaction could be worked out by a mere creature since the moral value of the satisfaction is measured by the status of the one who offers it and not by that of the one offended. Only Christ, says Rahner, could offer a satisfaction of the moral order equal to the magnitude of the offense and the moral work upon which the restitution of grace to man by God depends is Christ's embracing of death. This is so by the free prescription of God, though any other moral act of Christ might have sufficed to the same end. The core of this theory, Rahner feels, is indeed justified by the fact that the Bible sees the redeeming act of Christ's obedience in His free embrace of death. It remains a question, however, in his view, whether this concept of satisfaction can fully or even adequately express the full reality of Christ's redemptive death. For it is obvious that the Bible sees His death as something more than an act resulting from a free divine decision equal to every other act, and having no specific character to make it the precise act through which redemption was wrought; it is clear that the Bible considers Christ's act as redemptive precisely because it was death which Christ chose. As a consequence, writes Rahner, it must be concluded that despite its core of truth the satisfaction theory leaves open the question as to why we were redeemed by Christ's death and by His death alone. The positive content of the theory may be used as a stepping stone but it is necessary to go beyond it.

The theory which goes beyond the justification theory and fulfills it where it is lacking may be called the *ontological* theory. By the Incarnation Christ assumed human existence, the flesh of sin, in a situation in which that existence could reach its consummation only by passing through death in all its darkness. He not only offered a satisfaction for sin, but He also enacted death as the expression, the manifestation, and the revelation of sin in the world. He did all this in absolute liberty as the act and the revelation of that divine grace which rendered divine the life of His humanity and which, by reason of His own divine Person, belonged to Him of natural necessity. Through His death, death becomes something absolutely different from what it would be in a man who did not possess in his own right the life of grace. Moreover, it is precisely in its darkness that the death of Christ becomes the expression of His living obedience, the free offering of His entire created nature to God. Death, therefore, which had previously been the expression of sin, becomes, without its darkness being lifted, the contradiction of sin, the manifestation of the "yea" to the will of the Father while sin is the essence of the "nay." Therefore, says Rahner, it is correct to say that Christ's obedience is our redemption because it is death, and His death effects our redemption because it is obedience. Through Christ's death, His spiritual reality, which He possessed from the beginning, enacted in His life, and consummated in His death, becomes open to the whole world and is inserted in this world as a permanent determination of its real-ontological character and status.

A question yet remains to be answered, Rahner suggests: How is it that the death of Christ, which was, after all, the death of but one person, finds its effects in all men? The force of the ontological interpretation of the death of Christ lies in its capacity to give a satisfactory, or at least more nearly satisfactory, reply to this all-important question. For, as was noted above in the general philosophical anthropological theory of death, it is only in death that man enters into an open, unrestricted relationship to the world as a whole; that is, to the real-ontological order. But the death of Christ, as the ontological theory makes clear, has its primary effect properly and precisely here, in that it effects a change in this order, imparting to it by Christ's death His own spiritual reality. Hence, says Rahner, it is the entire ontological order, which is transformed by the death of Christ and in which the death of man finds its ultimate meaning, that meditates between the death of Christ and the death of every man. For as man's death releases him to the larger integration with being, and as that entire range of the real has known the transforming power of Christ's death, the character of the latter becomes integral to the former. The world as sanctified by the death of Christ mediates that death to every man.

Hence is born the supreme concept of Rahner's theology of death: that of the dying of the Christian as a dying in Christ, a dying with Christ. In the first place, this dying with Christ is no mere transitive event; it is the structure of the Christian's life. According to the New Testament, our assumption of Christ's death begins in principle with Baptism and faith, while the process of dying with Christ and winning the new life which that dying offers penetrates our life here on earth. If we do not wish to dissolve our dying with Christ during this earthly life into an ethical-idealistic conception and thus lose contact with the real notion of death, we must recognize that according to the New Testament the real death, just as it is the end of human life and has the natural characteristics of that life, is also the death of the just man in Christ. In that moment and that event, the man is assimilated to the death of the Lord. But this cannot rightly be considered to be a single terminal event, Rahner claims; it is the supreme consummation of the whole life of the man, a consummation which gathers up the whole of his human life in one fulfillment. These considerations make it possible to understand just what the Christian, in death, does through the grace of Christ. He experiences his life falling into the emptiness and the enervation of death, as death is an absence from God, into the bitterness of guilt, while still he believes in the mercy of God, hopes still for life in God, and loves this God so far removed from him. Faith, hope, and charity, then, are not poor emotions accompanying the brutal reality of death, inefficaciously persisting side by side with its hard reality. They are, rather, because transformed by grace, the true reality, transforming death. The trinity of faith, hope, and charity says Rahner, makes death itself the highest act of believing, hoping, loving, the very death which seems to be the darkness, the despair, the ultimate coldness itself. These three fundamental powers of Christian existence, entering into death, transform it into an act of obedience and of complete abandonment. In so far as these fundamental acts become constituents of death as an act of man, death itself is changed, Rahner concludes triumphantly; death, which can be the beginning of eternal death, may also be transformed through Christ.

A.R.C.

THE DIVINE MILIEU

Author: Pierre Teilhard de Chardin, S.J. (1881-1955)
Type of work: Spiritual autobiography; Christian philosophy of evolution
First published: 1957 (written in 1927)

Principal Ideas Advanced

The modern world is a world in evolution; hence, the static concepts of the spiritual life must be rethought and the classical teachings of Christ must be reinterpreted.

The active way of life is not inferior to the contemplative life; activity can be adoration, not simply by intention but by the fact that it is essential in the uniting of the whole universe in the Mystical Body of Christ.

The man who dedicates his life to research or worldly activity renounces the shelter of the cloister, accepts the vicissitudes of the unpredictable world of business, and becomes, when animated by the proper spirit, the Grand Detaché, *to an even greater extent than does the contemplative.*

Matter contains a spiritual power which emanates from Christ, who redeemed the whole of creation and awaits its consummation in the Parousia.

The whole of creation and its evolution can be summed up in a single Consecration and Communion in which the Sacred Species are not just the human individuals, but every particle of matter and energy.

Written in the wilderness of the Gobi desert, Somaliland, and the Ordos in 1927, *The Divine Milieu* was not published until 1957. Despite the fact that the work had been examined and approved by several theologians and had even received an *imprimatur* in 1928 from Louvain, the Holy Office deemed its publication inadvisable at that time. When Teilhard died, the manuscript passed into the hands of the scientific committee headed by his secretary, Mlle. Mortier, and was finally published. (See the article concerning *The Phenomenon of Man*). The date of its original composition is very important since the book offers an illuminating theory of the Mystical Body long before Emil Mersch and the enyclical of Pope Pius XII, *Mystici Corporis Christi,* began to explore this vast field of Christian doctrine.

The Divine Milieu is an account of the spiritual aspect of Teilhard's synthesis of evolutionary science and Christian theology. It can stand alone, but is properly understood only when seen against the backdrop of the *Phenomenon* and the evolving universe. It is a devastating refutation of "angelism" and subterranean Manicheanism, that pernicious and persistent heresy which considers matter and the world, if not basically evil, then at least as something very dangerous to the Christian life. The book is also a searching exposition of the purpose and true meaning of Christian intellectual and scientific activity.

The audience for whom Teilhard writes is not the ordinary convinced Catholic, but the "waverers, both inside and outside" the Church, those who, misunderstanding the true Christian doctrine of the relationship between matter and spirit, see in the other-world emphasis of Catholicism a real hindrance to scientific research and devotion to "wordly" pursuits.

The pages of *The Divine Milieu* "do not pretend to offer a complete treatise on ascetical theology—they only offer a simple *description* of a *psychological* evolution observed *over a specific interval* . . . a possible series of inward perspectives gradually revealed to the mind in the course of a humble yet 'illuminating' spiritual ascent. . . ." They comprise, then, a type of spiritual autobiography, the reflections of a priest-scientist, the story of his search for a viable solution to the conflict between the Jansenistic Catholicism of his school years and his ardent passion for the world of nature and science.

Basic in the work is a threefold passion: for scientific research, for the pursuit of all knowledge, sacred or profane, and for spiritual (and physical) union with God above this passing world.

Part One, "The Divinisation of our Activities," asks how Catholics can sanctify their daily actions. The Manichean-Jansenistic-Puritan-Platonic interpretation of Christian spiritual life sums up perfection in the one word "detachment," detachment from the world and all that is material: "The world about us is vanity and ashes." To this common interpretation of Christianity, a modern man may react either by tossing aside all interests in this world and its development and concentrating on Heaven alone, or by dismissing the Gospel as "impractical and unreal and devoting himself entirely to life in this world, or, finally, by attempting an uneasy and irrational compromise, never giving himself whole-heartedly either to the spiritual or to the profane. All three, claims Teilhard, are distortions of Christianity. Even the attempt to sanctify our worldly activities by a "pure intention" falls short of a real solution for "it infuses a precious soul into all our actions; but *it does not confer the hope of resurrection upon their bodies.*"

The true solution lies in a realization that, basic in all Christian teaching, is the fact that *"all endeavor cooperates to complete the world* 'in Christo Jesu.'" We must recognize, writes Teilhard, "that our spiritual being is continually nourished by the countless energies of the tangible world." It is true that God wants the salvation of our souls, but these souls are inseparable in their birth and growth from the entire universe, no matter how our philosophy may mentally separate the creation of the soul from the conception of the body. Beneath our striving as individuals to reach the realm of the spiritual, the whole universe slowly matures and grows organically to form the New Earth, the New Jerusalem, the Mystical (or better, Cosmic) Body of Christ. This change is the essential teaching of Paul in his letter to the Romans (Chapter 8). "In fact, through the unceasing operation of the Incarnation, the divine so thoroughly permeates all our creaturely energies that, in order to encounter and embrace it, we could not find a more appropriate milieu [for spiritual growth] than that of our action." Material cares and "profane" research, devotion to intellectual pursuits, are not unworthy of the spiritual man nor are they burdens and hindrances to perfection.

To realize how what has been considered "profane" activity is really an essential expression of Christian spiritual life, writes Teilhard, we must recall that, by its very nature, work implies detachment. A man who gives himself to a life of activity faithfully and without reserve must overcome inertia. He must detach himself from comfort and the sheltered life, and the more intellectual his labor, the greater the sacrifice required. Work is a birth and always implies birth pangs. In the real Christian scholar, above everyone else, "detachment through action should produce its maximum effectiveness." The Christian scholar must move *through* the finite and partial glimpses of Truth which he discovers in his research; he must detach himself from the lesser expression of truth and move on, by research, to the more accurate and clearer expression of truth until he reaches God, the Author of all knowledge.

Part Two deals with the recognition of our passivities. Passivities, according to Teilhard, are viewed in contrast with our life of action; they are whatever things we must undergo or suffer. In every life there is a world of forces, our circumstances, our environment, our friends, all the external manifestations of God's grace, which work on us and influence us to grow. These forces are the "passivities of growth," friendly and favorable. But there are also the passivities of diminishment, those forces that harm and hinder us. Though in the text we find no explicit or lengthy discussion of sin (moral evil), Teilhard here calls attention to a vital element in the divine milieu. A footnote refers to sin as a "positive gesture of disunion." Such a concept of sin leans heavily on the explanation of evolution found in *The Phenomenon of Man*. If evolution is a history of differentiated unions, then anything which hinders the union on any particular level goes against nature and God's plan. Hence, egotism and self-centeredness of any sort are sinful since they hinder our union with our fellow man. Certainly, violations of charity, that supreme form of radial energy spoken of in the *Phenomenon,* hinder our union with the Omega Point (Christ) and with our fellow man. Love is the binding force in the differentiated union of men around the Omega Point, so that lack of charity is the greatest of sins. This is a teaching in consonance with the most traditional and basic tenents of Christ's teachings.

Passivities of diminishment can be internal: ". . . natural failings, physical defects, intellectual or moral limitations, as a result of which the field of our activities, of our enjoyment, of our vision, has been ruthlessly limited since birth." And there is *time*: "Time, which postpones possession, time which tears us away from enjoyment, time which condemns us all to death—what a formidable passivity is the passage of time. . . ." External passivities come in many forms: upsets, shocks, stumbling stones in our path, disappointments, injuries from others.

A true interpretation of Christian resignation is as necessary today as is a true picture of detachment, Teilhard claims: "To struggle against evil, and to reduce to a minimum even the ordinary physical evil which threatens us, is unquestionably the first act of our Father who is in heaven. . . ." As Christians, writes Teilhard, our first duty is to avoid evil as best we can no matter what its form. Only when we cannot reduce it or can no longer avoid it can we resign ourselves to an "apparent failure"—only apparent, because these "failures" can divert us into more fruitful fields, or lead us into a more spiritual and detached life. Even with those passivities which we do not understand and which we trust will, through God's providence, mold and reform us in Christ, true Christian detachment must satisfy two conditions: "It must enable us to go beyond everything there is in the world and yet at the same time compel us to press forward (with conviction and passion) the development of this same world."

A central point in developing his thesis must be quoted in full to be appreciated: "Why separate and contrast the two natural phases of a single effort? Your essential duty and desire is to be united with God. But in order to be united, you must first of all *be*—be yourself as completely as possible. And so you must develop yourself and take possession of the world *in order to be*. Once this has been accomplished, then is the time to think about renunciation; then is the time to accept diminishment for the sake of *being in another*."

Teilhard's disagreement with Jansenistic-Manichean spirituality is nowhere more clearly evident than in his discussion of the spiritual power of matter. He claims that Christians have often give in to the temptation, so easily met, of contrasting the body and soul, the flesh and spirit, as though one were good and the other evil. Because of the divine milieu which pervades all the universe, all matter is *holy matter*. Hence, the events of our daily lives are not obstacles but created things which, like the steps of Jacob's ladder, are footholds, stages of growth, elements to be taken into ourselves and made part of our being so that in the transfiguration of death the whole universe can become one with Christ. "In other words, the soul can only rejoin God after having traversed *a specific path* through matter. . . ."

Teilhard then discusses his concept of the differentiated union centered on the Omega Point (Christ) to show its differences from pantheism. The difference between pantheism and Teilhard's view of the final state of the universe and mankind in union with God is summarized in the fact that, while pantheistic unions destroy personalities and individualities in the fusion of the *All*, Christian evolution ends in a union with God that preserves our personalities and perfects our individuality by destroying all egocentrisms.

Teilhard then surveys the most important mysteries of Christianity according to early Christian thought. His treatment is in contrast to the most recent emphasis on the passion and death of Christ, for early Christianity stressed the Incarnation especially in relation to the Epiphany and the Eucharist. Teilhard's fascination with these three mysteries leads him to regard them as phases of the same process. God is incarnate in matter. Through the waters of baptism all matter is lifted above itself, just as Christ rises from the waters of the Jordan in His "showing forth," the epiphany. Thus, all matter is effectively united with Christ in the Eucharist. When the priest utters the words of consecration, his words fall directly on the bread and wine, but they also go beyond these limited realities. According to Catholic doctrine, there is *only one Mass and only one Communion,* for Christ died but once. Hence, the words of consecration penetrate every region and element of the universe. "Christ reveals Himself in each reality around us, and shines like an ultimate determinant, like a centre. . . . As our humanity assimilates the material world, and as the Host assimilates our humanity, the eucharistic transformation goes beyond and completes the transubstantiation of the bread on the altar. Step by step it irresistably invades the universe. . . . In a secondary and generalized sense, but in a true sense, the sacramental Species are formed by the totality of the world, and the duration of the creation is the time needed for its consecration."

From the very beginning of evolution and in the vast multitude of individuals, both human and subhuman, generated by that evolution, only a single operation is occurring: the building of the Cosmic Body of Christ in which all things are united with God, in which all matter and all energies are centered on the Omega Point.

The importance of *The Divine Milieu* lies in its message for modern Christianity. Some critics maintain that the work is "the maximum of seduction coinciding with the maximum of error," for they believe that Teilhard confuses the natural and supernatural orders, ignores sin and the gratuitous nature of divine grace, and misinterpretes the Mystical Body of Christ. Other theologians, men of considerable stature in theological circles, maintain that *The Divine Milieu* is perhaps the finest work on the spiritual life to appear in the past one hundred years. These latter critics maintain that Teilhard's spirituality is strictly traditional and Pauline, though set in modern context and phraseology.

CHRISTIAN HUMANISM

Author: Louis Bouyer (1913-)
Type of work: Christian humanism
First published: 1958

Principal Ideas Advanced

God the Creator is also the Redeemer; through Christ the paradox of Creation and the Cross is resolved.

Christ is the incarnation of God's love for man; unaided, man could not join God, so God joined man.

The Christian achieves complete liberty when the Spirit of God governs him.

To be human to the height of one's powers, one must follow Christ; through Him apparent opposites are reconciled: dependence and freedom; intellect and faith; tradition and renewal; action and contemplation; self-development and asceticism.

Christian humanism is the answer of the man of faith to those humanists who believe that man is self-sufficient, that he can, without recourse to God, rise to the height of his powers. Humanism in general stresses the development of the human faculties; Christian humanism emphasizes man's dependence, for the realization of his potentialities, on the Grace of God.

Father Louis Bouyer's *Christian Humanism* is a clear and appealing statement of the thesis that the paradoxes that plague the humanist who attempts to do without the Faith, the paradoxes that lead to the excesses of modernism, can be resolved only if one properly appreciates God's relations to man. Christianity is the religion of the Cross: man, like Christ, is called upon to suffer and to renounce the world. But Christianity is also a religion of the Creation: God created man a free creature. How is the opposition between redemption and creation to be reconciled, and what are the implications of that reconciliation for man in his effort to realize his human nature? Father Bouyer, a priest of the French Oratory, addresses himself to that central question.

In the preface to *Christian Humanism,* Bouyer argues that the truth does not reside either in the latest intellectual fashion, as the modernist supposes, or in an inflexible veneration of past positions. Orthodox Christianity demands thought, inquiry, respect for facts, and a willingness to see deeper than those who accept extreme solutions.

Father Bouyer maintains that all religions tend to idolatry; man has a quite natural tendency, since he is limited in experience, to cast God into man's own image. The fact is that man does not know God, and when God reveals Himself to man, He reveals himself as inaccessible. Nevertheless, God loves man, and because He does, it is possible for man to be reconciled with God and to know Him. Man is made in God's image, and hence it is a mistake to suppose that the anthropomorphic conception of God is accurate; nevertheless, out of His love for man, God came down to man's level, walked with him and talked to him, as to Moses, face to face. This confusion in man's mind between God the inaccessible and God the friend of man is initially a paradox and a mystery; only an understanding of God, an understanding which faith makes possible, can reconcile these apparent opposites.

In a pair of incisive sentences, Father Bouyer expresses the crux of the matter: "God did not will to become man so that man might henceforth think he has the right to deify himself. He became man in order to renew in man the image of God." God is inaccessible unless that renewal occurs; it is through God's action that that renewal is made possible.

Thus it is, writes Father Bouyer, that Christ is the incarnation of God's love for man. God is inaccessible to unaided man, because man has no power or knowledge whereby he can, without God's help, know the Divine; but Christ came to man that man might know God and be renewed. The new man emerges from the old man, and the life of man is seen to be the life in Christ.

Christianity joins with Judaism in declaring that God created the world and made man His partner in the great adventure of reaping the goods of the earth. But, says Father Bouyer, Christianity is also the religion of the Cross. The Cross of Christ is the "key to the meaning of human history"; it is a mystery how this is so unless one comes to understand that Christ's death was not intended to save man from suffering and from death but, rather, to demonstrate to man the necessity of suffering and death. What Christ demanded of men, He demands still: poverty, renunciation of one's family, the bearing of the cross. The problem for modern man, as it was for men in other ages, is the problem of reconciling the generous, creative God with the God of the Cross, the God who demands sacrifice and suffering.

Father Bouyer recognizes the modern tendency to argue for a division of vocations. Let the ascetics, in their negative way, make possible the positive creative life of those who marry, live in the world, and exercise their creative powers in the manufacturing of useful products; let the renunciation of some balance the self-development of others.

But, says Father Bouyer, there is one law of life for man, and it is not to be found by dividing the vocations of men or by accepting the idea that it is through evolution that the paradox of Creation and the Cross is to be resolved. According to Bouyer, the evolutionary view, as represented by Father Teilhard de Chardin, fails to account for two significant discontinuities: the discontinuity of sin and the discontinuity of resurrection. It was sin which took man from the universe of creation to the universe of suffering, of the cross; it was the Resurrection, the way of the Cross, which makes man's radical return to God possible.

The remainder of Bouyer's essay is a careful attempt to show the possibility of resolving the paradoxes which arise whenever man begins to think about his relations to the Divine. Man is dependent upon the Creator; nevertheless, man is free. Man's intellect is his highest faculty; yet it seems to conflict with the Faith; there is a continuing struggle between science and faith. There is also the conflict between those who regard the tradition of the Church as embodying all the truths which a man of faith has to know, and those who argue that faith has to remain at the forefront of moving thought, continually renewing itself, as faith, through the discoveries which man makes. This conflict assumes another form in the argument between those who insist that man be active and those who insist that he be contemplative. Finally, there is the tension of opposites between the view that man's task is to develop himself in the various activities of everyday life and the view that man is to deny himself and limit himself through ascetic discipline.

Bouyer rejects the temptation to take one of each pair of opposites at the expense of the other; the resolution of paradox is not to be achieved by choosing dependence over freedom, say, or faith over science. At the same time, says Father Bouyer, nothing is achieved by maintaining that the opposites are not really opposites; no understanding is achieved by the easy claim that, since what is death to the body is life to the spirit, death and life are one.

Some men have argued, the author reports, that if Christianity is to base itself on a theology of the Cross, one must face the consequence that the Creator has lost interest in His creation. Such a view is intolerable to Father Bouyer. Christ's Cross and Resurrection testify to God's continuing concern with His creation; the Cross restores to creation the promise which it originally had. "Apart from the Cross," writes Father Bouyer, "the creation is doomed to failure, and only by the Cross can it be saved, recovered, and brought to its true end." God's redemptive activity is His answer to the sin which has sullied His creation; creation and redemption are not one, but they are parts of God's single plan.

Father Bouyer maintains that suffering and death did not come into the world with the Cross; they preceded it, and the Cross is God's answer to sin and the effects of sin. For an individual to accept the Cross is for him to acknowledge freely that self-absorption and sin have led to man's desperate condition; only if man freely depends on God is he able to escape from the suffering which his misuse of freedom entails.

Thus, writes Father Bouyer, there is no conflict between being a Christian and being a man. The paradoxes of life are answered when a man commits himself freely to God; the old man becomes the new man. It is sin, for which man is responsible, which creates the apparently irreconcilable conflicts between creation and redemption, dependence and freedom, intellect and faith, tradition and renewal, action and contemplation, self-development and ascetism. Once a man accepts the Cross he finds that he has acknowledged the corrosive and degenerating effect of his own self-absorption and reliance on the material world; a creative advance then becomes possible. Man lives and becomes human when he delivers himself to God, who, through His love, has created man and given him the cross to bear, together with the promise of a new life.

CONTEMPORARY EUROPEAN THOUGHT AND CHRISTIAN FAITH

Author: Albert Dondeyne (1901-)
Type of work: Existential philosophy of Christian faith
First published: 1958

Principal Ideas Advanced

Existential phenomenology is one of the great contributions given to philosophy by contemporary thinkers.

This philosophical method should be seen as complementary, rather than as opposed to traditional philosophical currents of thought.

Certain defects found within existential phenomenology can be corrected by the balanced view of a living Thomism.

Christian faith which is pre-eminently existential must engage in a dialogue with the world in all of the world's concreteness and historicity, in order that the maximal relevance of Christianity be felt.

In his *Contemporary European Thought and Christian Faith,* the Louvainian scholar Albert Dondeyne grapples with the confrontation of Christianity and the dominant movement in current European philosophy: existential phenomenology. He presents the views of a Christian philosopher in dialogue with the world today. Although Marxism and logical positivism (with the latter's emphasis on linguistic analysis) also constitute strong currents of philosophical endeavor, Professor Dondeyne declines to treat them as principals in this volume, for their ideas are so extensive as to demand separate treatment.

Many different philosophers may be placed in the camp of existential phenomenology. Its devotees can be found in atheistic and in Christian circles. Rather than treat sketchily of each, Dondeyne chooses one man as representative of the movement and method, and the author then discusses the ideas in detail. That man is Maurice Merleau-Ponty (1908-1961), whose work *The Phenomenology of Perception* stands as the classic expression of existential phenomenology.

The main divisions of Dondeyne's book comprise discussions or dialogues with current phenomenology, with revitalized Thomism, and with the problem of the relevance of Christian faith in the world of today. Meticulously fair in his appraisal of the strengths and shortcomings of all three, Dondeyne attempts to bring each to bear upon the other, thereby enabling the reader to gather a whole picture of man in the world.

To some extent, according to the author, phenomenology is not new. It is something all philosophers have been striving toward for many centuries. Nevertheless, it was Edmund Husserl (1859-1938) who formulated its methodology explicitly. The legacy left by his genius has borne rich fruit in contemporary times. Such men as Martin Heidegger, Karl Jaspers, Jean-Paul Sartre, and Merleau-Ponty have perfected the technique, and in applying it to the existential world they have enriched immeasurably our insights concerning it. Existential phenomenology does not attempt to define the objects of human consciousness, for it claims that to do so would be to engage in an abstraction which is too closely allied to a system of static and unchanging essences. On the contrary, existential phenomenology attempts to describe that which is given to consciousness; the philosopher endeavors to let the object reveal and disclose itself in all its contingent, historical, concrete, and existential dimensions. The method bears in mind that human intelligibility is just that; namely, *human*. It recognizes, therefore, that the intelligibility of the world is always seen from the point of view of man in his historical and cultural milieu and under his biological limitations. Its strengths, however, can easily become its shortcomings. When carried to extremes, phenomenology reduces metaphysics to a philosophical anthropology and philosophy to a psychologism. In seeing the intelligiblity of human knowledge as relative to man, existential phenomenology runs the risk of falling into pure relativism and subjectivism. In appraising the phenomena encountered by consciousness, it is open to idealistic tendencies. Indeed, no less a philosopher than Husserl succumbed to this seduction.

When properly understood, however, existential phenomenology can add new wealth and new dimensions to classical philosophy, especially to the perennial philosophy of Saint Thomas Aquinas. Yet Thomism itself can return the favor and serve as a corrective to abuses so often attendant upon phenomenological investigations. To accomplish this, Thomism must be a living Thomism of the spirit, rather than a dead one of the letter. As Father Dondeyne points out, "The mission of Thomism is less to create new things or to open up new fields than to carry out the work of synthesis."

In order to synthesize the new, Thomism must understand the new on its own terms. This requires that Thomism enter into living dialogue with the contemporary world and that it speak the language of the contemporary world. It does not imply that Thomism abandon its fundamentals, for the basic claims of Thomism are contributions which can restore a sense of balance and significance to certain strains of current philosophy. Of particular value to contemporary philosophy is Thomism's concrete hold on the existential and its theory of knowledge.

Thomism is at a peculiar advantage in doing this corrective work of synthesis, for it existed prior to the dualism of intellectualism (rationalism) and empiricism introduced by René Descartes (1596-1650). Thomism, unlike the post-Cartesian philosophies, can proceed from a sense of wholeness or unity. Since the time of Descartes the error of mutual exclusivism can be leveled at empiricism and rationalism. Observes Dondeyne, "On the one hand, empiricism makes knowledge a private affair, thus excluding the universality we need in our direct experience; on the other hand, intellectualism emphasizes universality so much that there is no room left for different approaches or for the concrete richness of history." Through the employment of existential phenomenology, it is possible to travel the *via media,* which is always the path toward truth.

Existential phenomenology accepts as its basic tenet the principle that the human condition is to be in the world. Since we are in the world and not above it, a wholly impartial view of being cannot be attained by man. The error of intellectualism as rationalism has been that it attempts the kind of view of things which is proper to God alone.

On the other hand, a radical empiricism reduces man to the status of a mere thing among things; such a view never grasps man in his subjectivity.

There is a principle of the irrational in the foreground of contemporary thought. It is clearly seen in the existential appeal to paradox and absurdity. This irrational is largely a protest of the human spirit against excessive intellectualism as typified by Benedictus de Spinoza (1632-1677) and Gottfried Leibniz (1646-1716). Contemporary Thomism, if it is to be relevant to contemporary man, must forego certain rationalistic tendencies found more in its expositors than in its own doctrines. Even Étienne Gilson has remarked on the Cartesian elements found in Scholasticism, particularly until 1850. To avoid such tendencies, Dondeyne suggests that Thomism abandon the method of logical deductionism based upon a few abstract principles with which no one would really argue. Who would deny, asks Dondeyne, the validity of the principle of identity or of noncontradiction? What is important in logical principles is their manifestation in the concrete empirical order of things. The difficulties previously experienced by Thomism in coming to grips with the contemporary scene represents more a crisis than a failure of neo-Thomism, and it is one which Dondeyne thinks can be met successfully.

The Christian in the world sees contemporary thought beset by metaphysical pluralism and by a sometimes rather blind faith in the ability of science to provide all the answers man seeks. Science merely observes when what is needed is compenetration; thus, in contemporary thought there is an unfortunate juxtaposition of the secular and the religious. Where there should be unity, there appears only opposition. Hence, the problem of faith and reason is facing man once again. Despite a similar confrontation in the Middle Ages and its successful resolution by Saint Thomas Aquinas, the rift between the two is not identically the same. The opposition is no longer between philosophy and religion, but between philosophical-religious thought and the positive sciences. In the Middle Ages, reason was on the defensive. Today religion occupies that position. This is due to a number of factors, among which are the presence of the emerging laity and the great advances being made in profane knowledge. Religious knowledge and interpretations have not always kept apace.

It is legitimate to ask, then, whether Christianity stifles the sense of the historicity of man. The answer is in the negative, for, properly understood, Christianity can lay pre-eminent claim to knowing history through being existential; Christianity must never lose this vision of the historical any more than it can lose its vision of the eternal. It will lose them, however, if it supplies platitudes instead of answers. It will lose them if it fails to rethink its great truths and place them in the perspective of the empirical world. What is needed is a restoration of values, solidly grounded yet flexible enough to meet the challenges of a changing world. What is needed is a re-examination of a sense of life, of truth, and of death.

G.F.K.

THE HUMANITY OF CHRIST

Author: Romano Guardini (1885-)
Type of work: Christology
First published: 1958

Principal Ideas Advanced

The psychological study of the Person of Christ yields fruitful insights into both His divinity and His humanity; however, the profoundest conclusion of all to be derived from any such study is that, in the end, He remains a figure of infinite mystery.

In *The Humanity of Christ, Contributions to a Psychology of Jesus,* Father Romano Guardini attempts to study the figure of Jesus Christ from a psychological standpoint to appreciate better Christ the Man as both the Creator and the executor of His own creation. As the Son of Man, Christ was able to realize human nature more completely than any other man. Through Christ, humanity took on an awareness of its own dignity, not as a mere step in the evolutionary progression from animal matter, but as a being fashioned in the distinct image of his God.

The early Christians fought to establish irrevocably the fact that Christ was more than mere man, that indeed He was both human and divine; the second phase of Christology embraced the mystery of the Incarnation, which resulted in the dogma of the two distinct natures of the Second Person of the Blessed Trinity. In an attempt to give Christ a concrete place in human history, the concept of Him as Man often overshadowed His Godly nature. Through a psychological study of the personality of Christ some deeper appreciation of the perfect degree to which human existence found its fulfillment in Him can be reached.

In Chapter One, "The Setting and the Life," Father Guardini sets down the historical situation awaiting the birth of Christ. Only a small band of religious persons remained firmly within the ancient tradition, but among them were persons like the parents of John the Baptist and others who were close to Jesus in His lifetime. Jesus' early life was characterized by utter simplicity. It was the common people who first responded the most enthusiastically to Him; it was the men and women of humble spirit He chose for His apostles, disciples, and closest friends.

Father Guardini writes: "Jesus' manner must have been very simple, his attitude so natural that people hardly noticed it. His actions proceeded quietly from the needs of the situation. There was nothing incredible about them. His words, too, had this unobtrusive quality about them. If we compare them with the words of an Isaiah, or a Paul, they strike us as being extremely moderate and brief. Compared with the sayings of a Buddha, they seem brief to the point of bluntness, and almost commonplace."

Jesus closely observed the Law in matters of custom and ritual, but He also looked upon the Law as something over which He had power, as indeed He did. Because of His great sense of calmness and serenity, He gave men about him the feeling of being in the presence of One with incredibly mysterious power and personal magnetism. He compares with figures like Socrates, Achilles, Aeneas, and even Buddha in this way, but He is distinctly apart from them in the most fundamental fact that none of them claimed to be the *Word Itself*, which, of course, Christ not only claimed to be, but was.

In Chapter Two, "Actions, Characteristics, Attitudes," Father Guardini explores the thought process of Jesus. Again, simplicity is the keynote. Christ speaks simply and realistically about the profoundest truths. His parables and teachings embraced that imagery which was topical and easily understood by the men of His day, and yet the very fact that He chose so often to speak in parables shows a strain of subtlety which satisfied the intellectuals. Christ's volition and actions were not subject to comparison with those of any other human being since His Kingdom—the power to which

He was at the same time subject and allied—was the Kingdom of God, not of this world, and therefore His will and action in this life on earth was directed toward the accomplishment here of what already *was* in Heaven.

Christ was perfectly at ease with material things, neither despising nor prizing them. He had, rather, what might be termed an appreciation for them as part of the entire creative scheme. All men were approached by Him with an open heart, but He was at the same time reserved, even among those closest to Him. Because of His serenity in most circumstances, Jesus often emerges as a cold and emotionless figure, but hundreds of instances prove this false. His was a personality of warmth, compassion, and experiences fully felt.

The Christian concepts of life and death come, of course, from Jesus who knew life to be a mere preamble to life after death. The proof of His beliefs through His own resurrection make spiritual indestructibility a reality.

In "The Problem of the Structure of Personality," Father Guardini investigates the various structures which have a bearing on the growth of a personality and their relation to the personality of Jesus. Patterns of growth, temperament, and behavior when applied to the figure of Jesus Christ show him to be unique among men, for, as has been pointed out previously, all things which would seem unnatural to any other man, were natural, or actually supernatural to Jesus, for such was His nature and His mission.

Father Guardini emphasizes the unique character of Christ and explains how an evaluation of His humanity requires its own set of standards.

In his fifth and final chapter, "The Utter Otherness of Jesus," Father Guardini demonstrates through numerous Scriptural passages the elements in the personality of Christ which set Him so apart from any other man before or since His time. Love was the fundamental moving force in all that Jesus did, for it was out of love that He took human form, and through the complete surrender and sacrifice required of love He gave up that human life.

Through a study of the psychology of Christ, one eventually is made more aware of His very special role as God-Man, Creator and created, Son of God and at the same time Son of Man. When Christ was born, concludes Father Guardini, "he performed an act of creation; not in the sense that there had been nothing and now something had come into being; but in the sense that an existent being *was,* was drawn into God's existence, and emerged as something new . . . a centre was born which the Son of God drew into his own being. It is there now—the starting-point of new life."

J.S.

AMERICAN CATHOLIC DILEMMA

Author: Thomas O'Dea (1915-)
Type of work: Sociology of Catholicism
First published: 1958

Principal Ideas Advanced

To create an American Catholic intellectual tradition, intellectuality, with its risk of heresy, must be accepted; only then can the vibrancy of the Faith be restored and the conformity based on custom and convention alone be uprooted.

The Church, as a society, has responsibilities on both the spiritual and human levels; however, the natural subordination of the intellectual aspect to the spiritual has been perverted to the complete disparagement of the intellectual.

The reasons for this lie not in the impossibility of reconciliation of faith and reason, but in the latent culture patterns of American Catholicism.

These latent patterns create a sociological atmosphere which stifles the growth of a mature intellectual tradition.

In his *American Catholic Dilemma,* Thomas F. O'Dea subjects the problem of the lack of an American Catholic intellectual elite to sociological analysis. That Catholicism does fall short in this area has been amply demonstrated in numerous articles and surveys, but most effectively in Monsignor John Tracy Ellis' *American Catholics and the Intellectual Life,* in which the author concludes that the American Catholic contribution in the intellectual sphere is noteworthy only for its sparseness. This troubling deficiency not only implies a neglect of Catholicism's responsibility to present its dogma in a challenging, vibrant form to the society of which it is so significant a part, but it also creates a sense of incomplete assimilation in the American Catholic. To the extent that he has adapted to the materialistic strand of American culture he is a member; to the degree that he has not adapted intellectually, he is an alien, quite possibly imbued with a strong feeling of inferiority.

The causes of alienation, at the risk of oversimplification, can be reduced to the external, that is, the pressures exerted by society upon the incoming group, and to the internal, that is, the resistance of the incoming group to undertaking the task of accommodating its existing cultural traits to the new society. These cultural traits comprise manifest and latent cultural patterns, and assimilation problems can be encountered on both levels. Adaptation will most easily occur in areas of cultural unimportance to the incoming group, while tension will appear in those areas to which the incoming group holds strongly, consciously or subconsciously.

According to O'Dea, Catholic isolation within the United States stems from external forces exerted by the American society and, much more importantly, from patterns within the sociological framework of Catholicism itself. The vital necessity for the immigrant Catholics to unite with other Americans in a common cultural life and thereby achieve a complete assimilation was well realized by liberal Catholic leaders of the pre-World War I era. An excellent example of this farsighted attitude is found in Charles J. Bonaparte, a Catholic layman and a recipient of the Laetare Medal, whose opposition to parochial schools was based on this premise. Further examples can be found in the positions of such outstanding Catholic clerics as Cardinal James Gibbons, Archbishop John Ireland, Bishop John Spalding, and Father Isaac Hecker, among others. The assimilation process was expedited by World War I. The crisis of war forged a national solidarity in which all Americans co-operated to achieve a lasting peace. This increased social interaction prompted by war, the shared experiences and memories of the war, all served to make the Catholic more American.

Assimilation, however, ground to a halt in the post-war decade. The shock of war, the growth of governmental control, European instability and the accompanying fear of greater entanglement in European affairs, the intense fear of radicalism, and severe economic disruption which included job competition between returned war veterans and immigrants, fostered an intense fear of the loss of traditional American values and culminated in a violently nativistic movement. Determined to root out elements deemed adverse to historical American ideals, the nativists measured everyone against their definition of American: white, Anglo-Saxon, and Protestant. The enforcement of this narrow standard, which in actuality is the exercise of an external force upon an incoming group, shattered all America into minorities based on religion, race, or nationality, each one isolated within the American society and each one resolved to demonstrate its loyalty to the United States by an exaggerated patriotism. The expression of this patriotism was usually an imitation of a custom thought to be truly American but made suitable to the minority group. It is no accident that from this era can be dated such phenomena as the Catholic Boy Scouts, the Catholic Daughters of America, and the Catholic Mother of the Year.

Catholicism was suspect on two counts: its primary loyalty to "a foreign sovereign" and its heavy immigrant composition. That most of these immigrants had emigrated from countries where the dreaded radicalism was most virulent further weakened the Church's position.

O'Dea points out that the nativistic onslaught also produced an internal upheaval within Catholicism. A heightened sense of defensiveness, combined with the low educational level of the immigrant, engendered a feeling of inadequacy in the laity and prompted a spontaneous acceptance of the clergy's emergence as the natural leaders and defenders of the group. Because the attack was on the basis of religion, the reply came from the specialists in that area, the religious. What becomes predominant in American Catholicism at this time is a culture pattern in which the clergy assumes a "status-conditioned perspective" and in which a life in the world is subordinated to a life of the spirit.

There is no doubt, O'Dea writes, that the experiences of the 1920's have left their impact on American Catholicism. Indeed, Catholics today still attribute their sense of alienation to immigration, low economic status, and the minority experience. However, external conditions have drastically changed in the almost half century that has elapsed. Catholics have, during these years, undergone the fusing effects of a Second World War, the growth of binding nationwide communication media, and a closer attachment with fellow-Americans through suburban living conditions. Accordingly, O'Dea argues that it is "rather late in the day" to ascribe current Catholic defects wholly to these causes.

While not denying the effect of external forces, O'Dea uncovers a more satisfying explanation of the lack of a Catholic intellectual elite by examining the manifest and latent culture patterns within Catholic society itself. Once traditional patterns have been exposed and are understood by reference to environment at a particular time, the reasons for tension and inability to adapt become more evident.

That the manifest content of Catholic culture, that is, the totality of religious dogmas in Catholicism, is not inimical to intellectual activity is inherent, O'Dea writes, in the Catholic conviction "that truth is one and indivisible, and that reason and revelation cannot at their most profound levels be in contradiction with each other." The acceptance of dogma is based on supernatural faith, O'Dea concedes, "but in the act of faith, the intellect is not superseded by grace but supported by it; the intelligibility of the doctrine depends upon the intellectual hold which the believer has on it." There exists, therefore, a hierarchy of ends which gives to reason a supporting role, but faith and reason cannot be mutually antagonistic. The Church's past hesitations in accepting new theories and scientific advances emanated from the human level and were founded in the natural conservatism of all institutions or in an overemphasis on faith to the derogation of reason. In all such conflicts, O'Dea claims, the Church inevitably restored reason to its rightful position.

What is posited on the human level, however, by the very fact of conflict, is a latent culture pattern in which there is an "abiding temptation" to warp the relationship between the spiritual and the intellectual by repudiating the latter. The medieval clergy's monopoly of higher education strengthened this tendency by an emphasis on final end in learning with little attention to the nonreligious in an agricultural society. With generations in which to become established, this latent culture pattern prevented an accommodation to the lay urban society which sprang from the Commercial Revolution. The Church's adamant opposition to the spread of secularism resulted in her rejection by the newly formed middle class. Within the Church itself the traditional distrust of reason intensified, and Catholic thought entered "the modern world on the defensive, . . . suspecting evil of much that was new, healthy and great with promise for the future."

If this sociological analysis is applied to the turbulent post-World War I decade, O'Dea suggests, it becomes most apparent that the importance of the experience of the 1920's for American Catholicism lies not in its utilization as a snug external rationalization of a Catholic lack, but in its recreation of a set of conditions which permitted the emergence of a traditional Catholic latent culture pattern in America. According to the author, "One of the consequences is that there has been produced and maintained in the American Catholic mind a cleavage between the sacred and secular spheres." The idea of vocation is nonexistent in the secular sphere. "Learning, the arts, literature—these fields offer little attraction in terms of Christian vocation. . . ," writes O'Dea; "This naturally intensifies the tendency to see the clergy as thinkers, while the laity devote themselves to worldly tasks which they try to keep as morally innocuous as circumstances permit." The layman looks to the priest for intellectual leadership; the priest, in turn, considers the layman a member of a "spiritual proletariat" whose prime function is to "obey the rules." The atmosphere is a choking one for an intellectual elite.

The emergence of this latent culture pattern has also had deleterious effects on Catholic education and the maturation process of young Catholics. The great emphasis on Catholic education has not produced a Catholic intelligentsia proportionate to the effort exerted. Professor O'Dea's disturbing explanation of this peculiar phenomenon is that it derives from the training of the religious and the socio-economic background from which the Catholic teaching element, religious and lay, is drawn.

Catholics generally are in a lower-middle- or in a lower-class category in American society, and teachers drawn from this social milieu will have an undesirable ingrained attitude on education. According to O'Dea, ". . . lower-middle-class groups do not recognize the importance of intellectual things and are quite likely to see the Catholic subordination of the intellectual values as an 'official' disparagement of those values." If this basic concept is supplemented by a training of the religious largely dominated by a latent culture pattern of derogation of reason and a stressing of final end, Catholic schools will see "their roles in terms of moral formation alone, to the exclusion of proper emphasis upon intellectual development." The distinction between education, or moral understanding, and instruction, or secular knowledge, is perpetuated with a strong tendency for the former to become a "wise" conformity to traditional patterns through memory work. "Obviously," argues O'Dea, "if the intellectual supports are removed from Catholic life, the institutional structures of the Church must fall back on custom and convention."

Maturation demands the subjective experiencing of crises. American Catholic culture, contends O'Dea, tends to evade these subjective crises of maturing and thereby restricts the Catholic adult's Christian outlook to one controlled by the ideas of childhood. O'Dea contends that because of "the failure to develop institutionalized culture patterns to enable Catholic youth to meet the crises of growth openly and with beneficial consequences, immaturity in the cultural and intellectual sense is one of the striking characteristics of American Catholicism as a whole."

In this stultifying climate the intellectual is a source of danger. Although his function as a preserver of tradition is acceptable, his prime duty as a critic and purifier of that tradition creates the fear which generates anti-intellectualism. Confined by the latent culture pattern the Catholic notion of the intellectual is that he is, at worst, a destroyer; at best, the intellectual "symbolizes . . . the facing of crises and the challenges of uncertainty," a symbolization which is an affront to the Catholic culture-inculcated proneness to evade.

Of "great, over-riding importance," O'Dea claims, is the presence on the latent level of formalism, authoritarianism, clericalism, moralism, and defensiveness, all cultural obstacles to a Catholic intellectual elite. The solution to the American Catholic dilemma is to restore the vital balance between faith and reason by a willingness to admit deficiencies and by increased attempts for a better understanding of their causes. Professor O' Dea's book is an edifying contribution not merely as a presentation of the problems, but especially as a framework for future research. In its heuristic quality lies its great value.

E.S.F.

GOD IN MODERN PHILOSOPHY

Author: James D. Collins (1917-)
Type of work: Theological critique
First published: 1959

Principal Ideas Advanced

Underlying the diversity of modern philosophical positions concerning God there is a continuity on the problem level stressing the following three points: (1) the importance of one's starting point in any inference to God, (2) the possibilities and difficulties involved in trying to use a knowledge of God as the deductive principle from which one can draw a knowledge of man and his world, and (3) the relationship between one's conception of God and one's views of the value, dignity, and reality of man and the natural order.

Those positions directed toward proving that man cannot philosophically demonstrate the existence of God or that there is a necessary opposition between the reality of God and the reality of the finite order are valid with respect to certain positions, but are not valid against with respect to all philosophical demonstrations and conceptions of God.

Without achieving a direct insight into the very nature and being of God, man in this life can demonstrate the truth of the proposition that God exists by means of a causal a posteriori *inference grounded in a reflection on the existential character and composition of the beings of his sensible experience, including man himself.*

James Collins's *God in Modern Philosophy* is a book of major significance both as an attempt to grasp the general character and leading ideas of the modern philosophical dialogue concerning God and as an exposition and defense of a realistic theism. It is a masterful combination of historical scholarship and philosophical penetration. In order to determine the major types of philosophical approaches taken toward God in the modern period, Collins conducts a historical induction which begins with an exposition and evaluation of the position of the humanist Cardinal Nicholas of Cusa and which moves through more than thirty philosophers to such contemporary thinkers as the American naturalist John Dewey (1859-1952) and the French existentialist Jean-Paul Sartre. In the course of his exposition and evaluation of other philosophical positions, Collins presents and defends the basic principles of his realistic theism, which he places in the traditions of Saint Augustine, Saint Thomas Aquinas, and John Henry Cardinal Newman.

A concern with such questions as the starting point for a demonstration of God's existence, the nature of this demonstration, and the place of experience in such a demonstration is found, with varying degrees of emphasis, in most of the modern approaches to God. These problems play an especially central role in the rationalistic, empiricist, and Kantian treatments of God. Although later positions do not ignore these problems, these three positions set the tone for these later treatments and provide material for consideration by later philosophers.

Although they were not in total agreement on all issues, the classical seventeenth century rationalists, René Descartes (1596-1650), Benedict Spinoza (1632-1677), and Gottfried Wilhelm Leibniz (1646-1716) agreed that the challenge of skepticism to the possibility of a philosophy of God could be met by showing that human reason in total independence from sense experience could discover those principles upon which it could not only prove the existence of God but also base a complete philosophical system comprehending man and his nature.

After having established the existence of God to their satisfaction on the basis of an analysis of the concept of God which was found not in sense experience but in human reason alone, the seventeenth century rationalists tried to use this knowledge of God as a deductive principle from which they could derive the character and existence of the natural world. Collins describes this procedure as the functionalistic approach to God.

The British empiricists, especially John Locke (1632-1704) and David Hume (1711-1776), rather successfully criticized the rationalistic position. The empiricists maintained that an examination of the scope and limits of human knowledge shows that man's existential knowledge, which includes his knowledge of God, must ultimately be grounded in human sense experience if it is to have any validity.

The German philosopher Immanuel Kant (1724-1804) stands at the crossroads of modern philosophy with respect to discussions concerning God, just as he does with respect to other major philosophical issues. He brought the leading tendencies of rationalism and expiricism to fruition in his own distinctive philosophical system, and, in doing so, he provided later thinkers with material which they used to construct their own philosophical systems. Concentrating his investigations on three points, Kant concluded that man could not demonstrate the existence of God on a speculative level. First, he considered those cognitive conditions which grounded the mathematics and physics of his own day. Second, he described the character of metaphysical knowledge and its way of handling the problem of God, as he found these in the writings of the rationalist Christian Wolff (1679-1754) and of others in the Wolffian tradition. He concluded that this metaphysical knowledge and its application to the problem of God failed to conform to the conditions for valid speculative knowledge which he had discovered in his examination of physics and mathematics. Finally, Kant undertook a more specific examination of those proofs for the existence of God that were then current and tried to show that they were invalid.

Collins maintains that if one is to profit from the history of the problem of God, he must deal with the positions of rationalism, empiricism, and Kantianism jointly in order to keep the extremes in sight in the attempt to develop a valid philosophy of God. Although the empiricists and Kant, in their distinctive ways, presented valid criticism of rationalism, their own positions suffered from an excessively narrow conception of human experience which prevented them from recognizing that man is in direct and intimate cognitive contact with the existing things of his sensible world in the judgments which he makes concerning things immediately present to him. Man grasps in these judgments the beings of his experience as possessing acts of existence which are proper to them and which are not reducible to the conditions of being perceived. Moreover, in using these judgments, man is able to grasp real objects in their own existential intelligibilities, and he does not always impose forms drawn from the human mind on experiential *data,* as Kant was led to believe from his examination of man's cognitive procedure in Newtonian classical physics. Collins holds that Kant erroneously equated the kind of knowledge to be found in Newtonian physics with the whole range of human speculative knowledge.

The fact that Kant limited all speculative knowledge and experience to the knowledge and experience employed in Newtonian physics, together with the fact that he equated metaphysics with rationalistic metaphysics, severely limits the valid scope of his criticisms. They are valid only against those empiricist attempts to prove the existence of God from the *data* of Newtonian physics and those proofs grounded in a rationalistic metaphysics. However, the validity of the Kantian critique does not extend to a realistic theism which grounds itself in the existential character and causal implications of the beings of human experience, as these are grasped in man's existential judgments.

After Kant, the question of the relationship between one's conception of God and one's view of the value of man and of his natural world was brought to the center of the modern dialogue concerning God through the writings of the German idealists, especially those of Georg Wilhelm Friedrich Hegel (1770-1831). Hegel presented the problem in terms of the following alternatives: either accept a view of God as a being who is totally unrelated to the finite world, in which case the Kantian critique is justified, or accept Hegel's dialectical monism in which finite beings are seen as limited modal parts in the total life of the absolute spirit.

Although Hegel himself maintained a distinction between his conception of a theistic God and his own absolute spirit, with the theistic God being at best a metaphorical and inadequate expression of the philosophical absolute, later philosophers did not always retain this distinction, thus saddling the theistic conception with difficulties proper to the Hegelian conception of absolute spirit. This observation is especially true of the atheistic positions taken by such men as the German theologian and philosopher Ludwig Feuerbach (1804-1872), the founder of present-day communism Karl Marx (1818-1883), and those in the American naturalist tradition of John Dewey. Despite their sharp disagreements on other matters, these men agreed in maintaining that the only way to defend the reality and value of man and of the natural world was to make them absolutes in order to exclude the reality of any being above man and nature who would detract from the reality and value of man and his world.

Collins maintains that much of the strength of modern atheism lies in its protest against the devaluation of man by Hegel's absolute. However, this strength does not extend to a realistic theism which is based not on a denial of the proper reality of the finite order, but on a grasp of this reality. Within a theistic context there is no opposition established between God and man, but rather the richness of the divine existence is seen in God's communication to man of an act of existence proper to him. There is no need to make man an absolute in order to safeguard his being and value. Since the theist holds that man possesses a being proper to himself and is not reduced to a mere "mode" of the absolute's life, he acknowledges that man possesses a value and dignity both in the human temporal order and in his relationship to God.

Such men as the French thinker Blaise Pascal (1623-1662), the Danish existentialist Søren Kierkegaard (1813-1855), and John Henry Cardinal Newman do not belong to the main stream of modern philosophical thought. However, each in his own way has contributed to this stream by calling the philosopher's attention to the fact that the relationship between God and man is not wholly confined to the philosophical universe of discourse. Concerned with finding a middle way between the extremes of rationalism and of atheism, Pascal developed the theme of the "hidden God," pointing out, on the one hand, that the divine presence in the world is not such as to permit man to use the concept of God as a deductive principle upon which to construct a philosophical sytsem, and, on the other hand, that God is not so far removed from man's world as to justify an atheistic position.

Kierkegaard saw his main task as being one of criticizing the unwarranted confusion between the Christian God and the Hegelian absolute, a confusion which he correctly recognized as being destructive of both the divine and human personalities. His emphasis on the mystery of faith and on the central role of will and imagination in man's relationship to God is grounded not in a hostility to finite reason, but in his opposition to the reduction of God to Hegel's absolute.

Newman stressed the fact that the problem of proving God's existence must not be regarded as being exclusively a matter of pure logic. Man does not assent to God in the same way that he might assent to the solution of a mathematical problem. A truly human assent to God is a complex psychological affair involving the whole human person. Newman maintained that the evidence for such an assent is to be found in an examination of the moral dimensions of human existence.

Collins tries to show that a realistic theism can incorporate the valid insights of Pascal, Kierkegaard, and

Newman into its own philosophical approach to God. Recognizing that the philosopher's knowledge of God is achieved only indirectly through a knowledge of the existential character of the finite beings of human experience, the realistic theist makes no claim to a direct and exhaustive insight into the divine nature. A causal analysis of the beings in human experience can bring man to see the truth of the proposition that God or a purely actual being exists. Hence, what is directly seen at the conclusion of the theist's argument is the truth of a proposition concerning the existence and nature itself. Since God is known in this indirect and inferential way, the very knowledge of God which the realistic theist possesses forces him to acknowledge the "hidden God," the God that can never be completely grasped by the human knower.

Moreover, the theist's causal inference from the limited beings of his experience to the infinite and transcendent Being upon whom they are causally dependent allows for the true personal reality of both God and man which Kierkegaard wanted to preserve. This inference proceeds from a recognition of the fact that finite beings possess an existence which is, at one and the same time, proper to themselves and dependent on a being who, as the ultimate cause of existence, must be Existence in its pure actuality. This movement from finite beings as effects to God as the transcendent and infinite cause of being allows for both the difference and relationship that must exist between creatures and God, if there is to be any truly personal communication between them.

The fact that realistic theism is grounded in a causal inference from the being of finite things, including man, to the being of God does not mean that we must simply ignore the question of the relationship between man as a moral being and God. Collins maintains that the inclusion of man who is a free and morally responsible agent in the theist's experiential starting point always leaves open the possibility and need for a further exploration of the relationship between man and God which would show the moral relevance of the theist's metaphysical demonstration. Having first established the existence of God as an infinite and transcendent cause, realistic theism must then face the task of trying to show the relevance of its findings to man's moral life and to his personal relationships with God.

Collins's dialogue with modern philosophers has succeeded not only in clarifying the positions which these men have taken with respect to the problem of God, but also in presenting the program of a realistic theism's approach to God. He has spelled out the main lines of this program and has shown its relevance to modern discussions concerning God. However, a program for action or for thought is not the action itself or the thought itself. Collins has left the actual working out of this program for other times and for other men. In the meantime, he has provided us with a book that cannot be ignored by anyone interested in the question of man's philosophical dealings with God.

V.C.P.

AMERICAN CATHOLIC CROSSROADS

Author: Walter J. Ong, S.J. (1912-)
Type of work: Theology of the Church and the world
First published: 1959

Principal Ideas Advanced

The contemporary Catholic intellectual has the obligation to seek for truth by means of the Church and the world, and to study the interrelationships of the two.

The City of God and the City of Man have been reconciled in the Incarnation.

In his preface to *American Catholic Crossroads, Religious-Secular Encounters in the Modern World,* Father Walter J. Ong, S.J., describes the city of the modern Christian as one composed of a combination of Saint Augustine's City of God and City of Man. The City of God should be man's main concern, but because man has a human nature as well, he is also a citizen of, and subject to the threats of, the City of Man. That the two are reconciled in the Incarnation is man's hope and salvation.

Father Ong applauds the fact that within recent times the American Catholic has recognized that a knowledge and awareness of history is essential to the growth not only of his intellect but of his spirituality as well. The development of a sense of history is commensurate with the degree of development of human society itself. As mankind develops to the point where history becomes of deep concern, nature itself takes on a more vital dimension and the place of Christianity and the Catholic church in the cosmic plan becomes more clearly defined. Father Ong writes, "As human nature becomes more and more reflexively aware of itself and of its historical place in a historical cosmos, which through history has arrived at the point where the study of history becomes not merely a possibility but indeed the passion of thinking man, the Church herself becomes more aware of herself in relation to mankind."

The Incarnation was the instrument for the channeling of grace to the material universe, thereby endowing it with irrefutable worth even to those philosophies which take a more negative view of the material cosmos. As the modern Christian lives in a rapidly-changing world which constantly forces him to make new assessments and evaluations, he becomes more aware that these assessments must be made in the light of a faith which does not change as the times change, and that all hope of communion between the material world and Heaven is centered in the Divine Mediator who united the two, Jesus Christ. For today's Christian to participate fully in his own modern world, says Father Ong, he must understand the sweep of history—its "psychological, social, intellectual, and cosmic, as well as religious and political reaches"—for this, ultimately, is the distinctive concern of the modern mind.

Religious pluralism is validly studied only in the light of the total development of the earth and the cosmos, states Father Ong. Saint Paul is probably the most stupendous model for Christian unity and the spreading of the Good News of the Gospel. Through preaching and writing Paul spread the teachings of Christianity to vast sectors of the world—past the narrow limits of geographical divisions and frontiers whenever possible. Medieval society, according to Father Ong, left something to be desired in its methods and concern with the spreading of the Faith. Medieval man too easily accepted the boundaries and divisions set down by mere limitations of communication and appeared to be unconcerned with his own place and function in a complex world. Today, in an age of communication (or "dialogue"), geographical boundaries, while not being annihilated, are assuredly not the problem they were before television, radar, and jet planes. Man is now able to take a stand and share his ideas with almost any other person in the world. Because of this development, both Church and state share the responsibility for the personal development of individuals as men: the Church for man's spiritual side, the state for his physical and material side. According to Father Ong, ". . . finally, dialogue must be between persons who are fully persons by being committed, by having taken a stand in the world of persons. Otherwise it will degenerate into the mere talk of a television commercial. In the tension between personal commitment and a love, not for humanity but for all individual men, the promise of a free society will best be realized."

Father Isaac Hecker, a convert to Catholicism and founder of the Missionary Society of Saint Paul the Apostle (known as Paulists) did much through his organization, his writings, and remarks, to resolve some of the early misunderstandings between European and "American" cultures at a time when the Catholic Church in America was fighting for a place in the lives of its people whose own backgrounds were still largely European in orientation. Father Ong writes: "Father Hecker's international outlook is a lesson for American Catholics today —and all the more because it was so immediately and urgently a genuine product of the American scene. The vocation of the Paulist, or of any Catholic today, is not to be exclusive, not to be provincial, parochial, but to be open, conciliatory, unifying, vis-à-vis the entirety of the human race. Our aim is to win all men without exception to Christ."

There need be no fear of or division between secular knowledge and revealed religion, says the author. The two are complementary, and the one should properly enhance the other. Revealed truths are no less true when set in the modern age. The theory of evolution, for example, is not incompatible with the miracle of Creation. When the Christian recognizes that all mysteries of faith or the universe are the handiwork of God, the order of matter takes on a fuller form. "Thus," Ong writes, "the Church, with her theologians, must keep in touch with the whole universe-in-history, with its sciences and arts especially, in order to preach the Gospel to the whole world ["Catholic" means literally "through-the-whole"], to be present with Christ everywhere at the present front of history along which we ourselves live and which we are called on, under grace, to impregnate with Christ."

The Catholic Church has taken on herself the obligation to "help men to know." The teachers in her schools, especially in her colleges and universities, are therefore obliged to take an active part in furthering their own knowledge through research and publication. Since she promises men the truth, her educators are obliged to seek it out and share it with those of her children entrusted to their tutelage. The Catholic educator who is not abreast of his field and a participator and contributor toward its development falls short of his dedication.

Father Ong reiterates again and again that it is because of the Incarnation that the Church has a permanent relationship with the world. As Christ had a dual nature, so the Church has both a natural and a supernatural function. On the supernatural level, her duties are clearly defined; on the natural level, there is and always will be controversy in terms of boundaries and development. This is the risk the Catholic living in the world today undertakes, but, as Father Ong reassuringly points out, "Living with a certain amount of risk is for the Catholic devoted to the intellectual life, secular or sacred, his own particular share in the cross of Christ."

J.S.

DEATH AND IMMORTALITY

Author: Michele Federico Sciacca (1908-)
Type of work: Metaphysics
First published: 1959

Principal Ideas Advanced

Death and immortality are incapable of philosophical clarification if man is considered to be a totally natural and temporal being.

The recovery of the philosophical authenticity of death and immortality is made possible by a metaphysical reinterpretation of the human person as spiritual.

At the level of spirit, death is no longer an empirical fact but an act of spirit: meaningful, valuable, and philosophically relevant.

The immortality of the human spirit can be definitely established only on the basis of man's objective constitutent: being as Idea.

Death and Immortality is the fourth volume of Michele Federico Sciacca's presentation of his "philosophy of integrality" (the other three being *Objective Inwardness,* 1951; *Man the Unbalanced,* 1956; and *Act and Being,* 1956). *Death and Immortality* is divided into an introduction and three parts: "Death," "Immortality," and "Suicide." The first and second parts, with which this account is concerned, constitute the core of the work.

Sciacca begins his account by arguing that man is essentially a product of nature, a being in dialectical relationship with external causes. But there is in nature a rigorous psychophysical parallelism: the soul is the *idea* of the body; it perceives intuitively its eternal essence; it rejoices when exterior causes enhance its power and is saddened when they diminish it. Since causes are infinite and the body is finite, the latter's effort to achieve permanence is futile. Man's fear of death arises from his failure to anchor himself to his eternal essence, rather than to the modifications and hazards of temporal existence.

Is it *my* being, however, Sciacca asks, that enjoys permanent existence in the unity of divine Substance? If not, both death and my fear of death are meaningless. On the other hand, if my being is autonomous, it cannot be reduced to its eternal elements or be reabsorbed in the divine Substance. Spinoza speaks of singular souls, which are not immortal but "eternal." If there are such souls, life and death do not add or subtract anything from them, hence do not concern them. The problems of the death and immortality of the personal spirit, says Sciacca, are ultimately suppressed by relegating death to the class of nonphilosophical problems and by admitting the eternity of souls, essentially identical to the divine Substance. In order to demonstrate that man is eternal, one must begin with the assertion that man as person is merely appearance, that he does not exist. On this basis, death and immortality clearly need no philosophical reason. Death is a purely empirical fact, irrelevant to man's spiritual essence.

For the romantic, writes Sciacca, there is life and death, nothing more. Being is identified with Nature, divine and omnipotent (naturalism and mystic pantheism). In the real and the human, even the least significant exemplar, the romantic seeks to capture the ideal and the divine, to actuate the infinite. His necessary failure, because the infinite is always greater and truer than every reality, makes him retreat before life and reject it as the evil shadow which hides the purity of the divine. In the termination of life the romantic does not see the condition of a new existence, but the very meaning and goal of life and existence. By loss of hope and lack of a further hope, the positive absolute—existence proper to immortality—is replaced by the negative absolute—death as nothingness of life. The search for the "beautiful death" is the romantic's last effort to evade the finite that has proven to be unconquerably finite.

Love and death are two sentiments which the romantic rarely succeeds in separating, Sciacca maintains. The romantic seeks with his whole soul to eternalize the sublime instant of love in the passing moment, knowing that the moment will pass. He subtracts love from the flow of life, then, by eternalizing it in death itself. In the final analysis, the romantic seeks an eternal felicity realizable within the order of nature and time. His search would not be doomed to failure if man were only body, hence capable of fulfillment in the natural and historical order. If death, on the other hand, is followed by the nothing of existence, the very themes of romanticism—irony, sorrow, boredom, and death—lose that human truth which the themes successfully capture.

According to Schopenhauer, Sciacca

continues, will is blind and irrational vital force. It is the inner being of every individuality and of the whole, both organic and human. As "thing in itself" the will to life is not subject to space, time, and causality. The form of life is the present: the past and the future exist only in concept. The present, therefore, shall never be lacking to will and to life, phenomenon of will. It follows that the fear of death arises from the mistaken identification of the everlasting present of will (as species) with man's own individuality which, as temporal phenomenon, is subject to a temporal ending or death.

Consciousness introduces a new category, the category of singularity, in the species man. The individual man is *this* subject conscious of *being* this man, *not* the species. He cannot "feel himself" live endlessly; therefore, even if he "feels" that the species lives on endlessly, he posits the problem of the end of his life, and the problem of his existence in terms of such end.

According to Hegel's philosophy of the Absolute, as Sciacca sees it, there in no spirit outside history. Thus, Hegel radically historicizes man and all values, and he makes man seek his salvation within the boundaries of nature and time. This wordly salvation consists in mediating nature by thought and in transforming it by action into the world of culture, which is the world of the State. Such a philosophy, like that of the romantics, is inadequate and self-defeating.

Sciacca argues that vital anguish and existential anguish before death are realized at two distinct levels of experience. In fact, the conquest of the former—the pain and repugnance experienced with regard to physical death—leaves existential anguish intact; namely, the fear and horror of the nothingness into which one's whole being might fall. Vital fear can be conquered by appropriate psychological means, says Sciacca, but this fundamental existential fear can be cured only by the proof of immortality, a proof made possible through philosophical discourse.

As human experience, and not merely as the empirical fact of the death of an organism, death has value, says Sciacca; hence, it poses the problem of its meaning, which involves the problem of the meaning of existence itself. Science, constitutionally empirical and methodologically bound by the principle of verification, is unable to pose such problems, which philosophy poses and resolves. In the proposition "I am dead" (scientifically absurd on the basis of verification, yet philosophically meaningful—"I think myself dead" and pose the problem of the meaning of my death), does the positive "I am" resolve itself entirely in the negative "dead"? The problem of immortality is intrinsic to the question to such a degree that, were the philosopher to prescind from, or deny, the immortality of spirit, death could no longer be posed as a philosophical problem. In fact, if the "I am" is entirely negated as being in the fact of the death of the body, the meaning of dying is resolved in the fact of dying. The problem of death, accordingly, would prove to be a seemingly philosophical, but properly a scientific, problem.

Sciacca finds particularly significant "The death of the other." The death of the other is also my experience of death, he writes—an experience in which I, who suffer it without dying it, grasp the ontological meaning of death, but only when the other is my "thou" or my "neighbor." At this level, my first reaction at the death of the other is one of unbelief and of rebellion. He was my "thou" without whom the "I" that I was in relation to him, by right should no longer be. But I live. It is therefore impossible that the other be dead, and it is inconceivable that I may still live without him. This initial moment is clarified and deepened in the moment of my acceptance of the other's death. My sorrow for his loss is also consciousness that the end of his life is the beginning of a new mode of existence of his essentially identical self; that life is not the essence of the person, but the necessary mode of his being in the world. Hence, the urgency to re-establish our communion. I confirm my choice of the other, my immutable fidelity, my act of love. Taken from me at the level of appearance, and restored to me at the level of existence, the other reveals himself the "irreplaceable" term of my act of love which, as act of spirit, is absolute. The temporal dimension of love, in fact, is the inward time of consciousness (spirit), the intensive "today" of experience and freedom where the yesterdays and the tomorrows are actual and living syntheses in the act of the subject. Love, thus, actuates a freedom which is the constant and ever-renewed choice of its very choice; that is, the absolute positivity of freedom itself. Hence the incredulity that the bond, strong of the actuality of spirit, be broken; that the present, temporal dimension of spirit and of love as spiritual act be shattered in an empirical yesterday without tomorrow. By accepting his death and the continuity of my life for him as if nothing had changed, says Sciacca, I implicitly assert his immortality and mine. My experience of the death of the other, as experience of communion, unveils its ontological significance: existence resists destruction in virtue of its very structure and of being, which founds the exigencies of love.

Sciacca maintains that immortality places itself at the level of value; perpetuity, on the contrary, at the level of time. Time can have value only in relation to the total fulfillment of spirit, which is realized only outside the order of nature and history. Man, in fact, is an original synthesis of subjectivity (fundamental bodily, intellectual, and volitional existence) and objectivity (universal being present to, and constitutive of, spirit; the Idea). As such, man is the infinite capacity to feel, think, and will, a capacity which cannot be fulfilled by the finite contents which specify it in the order of nature. If man were not to die, the fulfillment of his ends would be impossible and he would be an absurd being. Temporal perpetuity is therefore absurd. Death and immortality, Sciacca concludes, are demanded by man's being as spirit.

Death manifests itself as both negation and affirmation, defeat and victory, Sciacca claims. He argues that death is the recapitulation of all that constitutes limit in man, of his frailty and insufficiency: it concludes and seals it in the definitive ending of man's temporal life. On the other hand, if the project of spirit, begun and actuated in earthly life, is to reach fulfillment, earthly life must be reduced to nothing, and thus to a state of unprojectibility in time. Yet its very temporal unprojectibility makes the fulfillment of the project possible. This dialectical implication touches man's ontological foundation: death demonstrates that man cannot achieve self-fulfillment in time; yet in virtue of this radical demonstration, death places spirit in the only possible condition to hope for such fulfillment.

Only man dies, says Sciacca, because man alone has consciousness of dying. Other living things perish and corrupt. Memory is act of consciousness (spirit) in which the past is present to consciousness. Accordingly, the past is implied and transcended in remembering. Neither the entire past nor the act in which it is present, however, can exhaust consciousness, whose full actuality is not a temporal event. Death is an act of consciousness, then, the final act which is the total presence as well as the fulfillment of one's past (as memory). As the past is transcended by consciousness, so is death. In its objectivity (Idea), in fact, spirit transcends all acts of life and temporal life as such, Sciacca insists. But death is an act of the life of spirit. Spirit, then, transcends also that act of its life which is death itself.

It is by reason of the presence of spirit, says Sciacca, that the physical fact of the corruption of the organism becomes the spiritual act of dying. It follows that spirit is ulterior to, and inclusive of, death, or there is no death and no spirit at all, since both body and spirit (reduced implicitly to an activity of matter) would perish, and not die. As an act of consciousness (spirit), death is existential act; that is, the knowledge that the animal dies. Death is not the consciousness that also spirit, which is taking cognizance of the death of its body, dies.

According to Sciacca, the problem of immortality poses itself in the following terms: why does every thinking being judge (possess the inward and objective truth) himself immortal precisely as consciousness (spirit), not as physical life, vital instinct, species (body)? An answer can be formulated, Sciacca concludes, only on the basis of man's ontological structure.

"Man is a spiritual animal," a body which incarnates a spirit. Spirit is the thinking of an *ego,* who in this act intuits being in its infinity (Idea) and simultaneously himself, as self-consciousness. There is no abstract thought, but the "I think": thought is always thought of a subject. The first act of thought, accordingly, is to perceive oneself existing as thinking being—"I *am* as thinking" (self-consciousness). To exist, says Sciacca, therefore involves the fundamental experience of being, an experience which is possible only because of the presence of being. If being itself were not present to thought, there would be no thinking, and the existent would not know that he is. Being, then, is the inner object of thought, and thought (spirit) is the inner experience of being or "objective inwardness." Man is not only spirit, however, but also animal sentiment (existence), the synthesis of spirit and body perceived as mine. Man apprehends *his* body with his spirit by an act which transcends the pure animal sentiment which is incapable of self-apprehension. Since the "essence" of body is contained, as its determination, in the intellective act, spirit exceeds body; hence, it cannot be identified with the animal sentiment nor be one of its determinations.

Of the traditional arguments for the immortality of spirit—psychological, moral, and metaphysical—the metaphysical argument is clearly the foundation, Sciacca claims. In fact, either the personal spirit is immortal because of his ontological structure, or personal immortality may be a matter of belief, desire, exigency, but not of rational necessity.

The body can perish, says Sciacca, because the complete actuation of its ends is realizable in the order of nature. There is perfect correspondence between the ends of animal life and the possibility to fulfill them in the course of the vital cycle. While the term of corporeal nature is its vitality, however, the term of spirit is being as Idea, whose infinity is not actualizable in the (finite) order of nature and time. The temporal cycle is essentially inadequate to the development and fulfillment of spirit. It is contradictory, therefore, that spirit should die.

Being as Idea contains and unifies all contraries in its infinity and is, therefore, simple. It cannot be annihilated, accordingly, by the natural forces extrinsic to it or because of its intrinsic nature. But being as Idea is the term which constitutes spirit as such; and, thus, spirit is the objective element of the original synthesis that is man. Consequently, the indestructibility of the Idea is also the indestructibility of spirit. Spirit, whose term is simple, is immortal. The immortal spirit, furthermore, is personal and substantial.

Man is unique singularity, irreducible to the species, by virtue of his spirit, Sciacca writes. Although spirit is irreducible and prior to its own acts, the acts whereby man actuates the infinite potentialities of his essence, which in turn is existentialized in them, are inseparable from spirit. Each act is the finite, subjective, expression of the essence of spirit (universal being as Idea). It is the personal manner in which the essence of spirit actuates itself, as uniquely singular as the original synthesis which makes it possible. What is immortal, accordingly, is the *personal* spirit.

The fundamental intuition of being infinitely transcends every act of sensation, intellection, and volition, whose content is always finite. This applies also to the perception of the body to which spirit is essentially united. The fundamental intuition of the Idea, accordingly, is the first (ontological) act with respect to which every other act is ulterior. It is principle, therefore, and, as principle, substance. The immortal and personal spirit, then, is substance, Sciacca concludes.

Not only do spiritual acts transcend organic life, says Sciacca, but also the values which they express are not relative to it. It is of the essence of truth to be thought, not to be relative to the life of the body. Now, spirit is essentially constituted by the essence of being or first truth, whose fundamental intuition is not relative to its union with the body, nor dependent from it. Death is the substantial disunion of spirit from its own body. Spirit, then, ceases to perceive its own and every other body, but not to intuit being. As fundamental intuitive-volitional sentiment, spirit preserves its personal substantiality, which is *this* substantiality of *this* person. With death, therefore, Sciacca concludes, not only does the essence of person preserve its identity, but also the person wholly experiences his transcendence with regard to the organism and its destruction. The person, as person, proves himself immortal.

A.R.C.

THE HOLLOW UNIVERSE

Author: Charles De Koninck (1906-)
Type of work: Critique of scientific philosophy
First published: 1960

Principal Ideas Advanced

The conclusions of certain exponents of the scientific outlook (for example, Ludwig Wittgenstein, Bertrand Russell, and Hermann Weyl) leave men nothing to wonder at except the "hollowness" or emptiness of human knowledge and of its subjects.

These conclusions are a consequence of taking mathematical physics as the model of a science, of regarding its method as the only way of investigating nature, and of dismissing as nonsensical whatever problems are not soluble scientifically.

Traditional philosophy sets in proper perspective the achievements of science but, more important, its limitations; it shows that the problems which puzzled Plato and Aristotle are not meaningless; that the solutions they and their successors have advanced constitute an invaluable contribution to knowledge.

In *The Hollow Universe* Charles De Koninck faces the "nihilistic and disturbing" consequences of the "bundle-of-events-and-computer-philosophy." He acknowledges the scientific achievements of Bertrand Russell and the other proponents of this position and disclaims any intention of disputing their views in toto. What De Koninck attacks specifically is the assumption that the teachings of this new philosophy are final and that it is the only valid way of approaching reality. His stand is that the traditional philosophy (by which he means that of Plato, Aristotle, and the latter's prominent followers, especially Saint Thomas Aquinas) enables one to understand the tentative and limited scope of the scientific outlook. The author asserts that if traditional philosophy does not succeed in restoring perspective and that if the perennial problems with which it is concerned continue to be dismissed as merely verbal, man, nature, and knowledge will lose significance.

The modern notions of mathematics, physics, and biology are examined in three sections to which an epilogue, "Reckoning with the Computers," is appended. In his discussion of mathematics De Koninck contrasts its ancient prominence as the very model of demonstrative science with the reputation accorded it today. The more recent view is summarized in a quotation from Johann Goethe: "Mathematics has the completely false reputation of yielding infallible conclusions. Its infallibility is nothing but identity. Two times two is not four, but it is just two times two, and that is what we call four for short. But four is nothing new at all. And thus it goes on and on in its conclusions, except that in the higher formulas the identity fades out of sight."

The changed attitude is attributed by De Koninck to the abandonment of the traditional view that mathematics treats of definable natures whose properties are demonstrated through their definitions. The older philosophy distinguished between mathematical science and the art of calculation. De Koninck claims that the modern mathematician concerns himself exclusively with the latter. In calculating, each number is treated as an empty symbol rather than as a definable entity. The irrelevance of considering the nature of a number is manifest from the fact that machines are more capable calculators than men.

The author does not deny that the modern philosophy of mathematics is accurate taken as a study on the art of calculation. He will concede the empty, mechanical character of this mathematics if mathematics and calculation are regarded as one and the same. No special dignity can belong to a discipline which does nothing but replace one set of symbols totally devoid of content with another set identical with the first. But the author does not accept this identification. He insists that the older concept of mathematics as a demonstrative science is still valid today.

Hegel's remarks on the role of mathematics in education are cited to confirm the author's evaluation of modern mathematics. Hegel, also, speaks of the empty unit, the absence of thought, and the dulling mechanical operation of calculating. After noting the perfection with which machines compute, Hegel declares, "If this one circumstance were known about the nature of calculation, we would see what it means to believe that calculation should be the chief instrument for educating the mind, and realize that we are trying to perfect the mind by converting it into a machine." The traditional philosophy, however, assures us that no such consequence need be feared since the emptiness of calculation is not found in what is genuinely mathematical science.

The realm of mathematical physics next comes up for consideration. De Koninck points out that the manner of defining proper to the physicist makes symbolic constructions of motions, length, time, and other physical phenomena; the physicist uses symbols which differ from those of mathematics only by reason of their having a reference to experience. What time is, for example, does not interest the physicist since time cannot be set down in his symbols. Measurements of time, on the other hand, are easily symbolized. In physics, then, the nature of time is irrelevant; only its measurements are important. This is the "hollowness" of physics, the ignoring of qualities not reducible to symbols in order to concentrate on quantitative aspects which can be symbolized.

The author does not contest the usefulness of such a reduction; he merely wishes to point out that we must not lose sight of the fact that it *is* a reduction. He agrees that, from the physicist's viewpoint, man is a swarm of particles or bundle of occurrences, but De Koninck questions the assumption that this point of view is the only legitimate one. It seems to him that, however necessary and valuable questions answerable by measurement may be, there remain further significant problems concerning the natures and other nonquantitative properties of the objects measured.

The modern view of biology considered in *The Hollow Universe* is defined by the following theses: (1) the distinction between living and nonliving is untenable, these terms being meaningless; (2) the place to begin biological investigation is with that which is least complex, with amoebas, for example, rather than with men; and (3) purpose has no role to play in biological explanations. De Koninck shows how these beliefs have come to be held and states his reasons for rejecting them. The first thesis he regards as a consequence of the second. When the biologist examines what is simple, a spore, for example, quiescence and death are so very similar that distinguishing between them may be impossible. But, De Koninck asks, why look to things in which life is so obscure? If one wishes to verify the meaning of the term "life," he ought to go first to those organisms in which life is easily recognized, organisms such as men and horses. "As we first try to pin down and reflect upon the meaning of the term 'life,' why should we be requested to ignore the life already so familiar to us, and to signify which we normally use this term?" From the fact that the biologist cannot tell a living spore from a dead one, he should not infer that "life" has no meaning when he says, "It is good to be alive."

The notion that science must begin with what is simple and most basic the author identifies as a remnant of Cartesianism. Physicists, he believes, have come to regard as untenable Descartes' assumption that what man knows first and best is most basic in the things themselves. In physics later experimenters have discovered the extraordinary complexity of what earlier workers regarded as simple. This lesson has not been learned by the biologists. De Koninck finds it hard to understand why the biologist has not profited by the experience of his fellow scientists. He wonders how those who claim that biological phenomena are easily understood in terms of what is basic in physics and chemistry can ignore what the modern physicist has learned. The latter well appreciates the fact that what is most basic in things is not easily comprehended, that it is reached only after long and difficult inquiry.

The rejection of purpose as relevant in biological explanations De Koninck attacks by analyzing the notion of an organ, one of the important concepts in biology. He argues that the term "organ," as referring to a man's hand or an elephant's trunk, for example, retains the literal sense of "tool," and that a tool presupposes purpose. De Koninck admits that the purposes of various organs become obscure as the investigator moves from man to the lower orders of living things, but he suggests that it would be ridiculous to exclude purpose simply because it is not translatable into symbols.

The question of why biologists dismiss purpose is treated in some detail.

De Koninck finds one explanation in the fact that the method of mathematics and of those sciences which use mathematics necessarily excludes purpose and the good. If man's knowledge of things is invariably mathematical, then the concept of "purpose" is useless not only in biology but also in every other field. But De Koninck insists that science is not coextensive with the mathematical sciences.

The exclusion of purpose or final cause is regarded by the author as having a catastrophic consequence. Since it is final cause "which establishes an intelligible connection between the other causes in nature. . . to banish finality completely will be to imply that nature is basically unintelligible. The scientific account of things will consequently be obliged to shut out all reference to reason as explanatory of anything." How this exclusion of purpose places a crippling restriction on scientific explanations is illustrated by the Aristotelian analogy of a house. It is as if in explaining the structure of a house one could only say "that the wall of a house necessarily comes to be because what is heavy is naturally carried downwards and what is light to the top, wherefore the stones and foundations take the lowest place, with earth above because it is lighter, and wood at the top of all as being the lightest."

The epilogue presents a theological judgment of the scientific philosophy criticized in the earlier sections. De Koninck critically examines the thesis that computing machines "think," and he attempts to understand why scientists will consider theological criticisms of their ideas but not philosophical criticisms. Are there not, he asks, properly philosophical objections to which a computer admirer, one who believes that computers think, must reply?

His explanation of the tolerance of theological objections is that scientific philosophy has silenced traditional philosophy but has not silenced theology. The latter alone remains to propose difficulties. Traditional philosophy has been judged incompetent to discuss scientific problems because philosophy does not measure up to the new standards of exactness. "The new conceptions of scientific rigor are such that no acceptable account of what we already know and understand seems possible." Theology, however, is not so easily silenced, for it derives certain of its principles from divine revelation. It stands ready, then, to judge the scientific philosophy.

What light does theology throw on this matter? De Koninck finds in the sacred writings a number of texts which he feels help in understanding "that bundle of dust and that mechanical calculator which man has made of man." The passages which he cites refer to Lucifer's rejection of God's dominion and to the perversion involved in the rebel angel's revolt. This perversity, as explained by Saint Thomas Aquinas, consists in man's turning away from what is unitary and primary to direct his activity toward what is manifold and scattered. Both revolt from unity and reduction to what is multitudinous seem to De Koninck to be prominent features of the scientific outlook. The rejection of God is easily accomplished in the new philosophy which by its undermining of any standard of truth can deliver man from truths he finds burdensome or disturbing. The turning away from unity and toward multiplicity is best seen in the mere "bundle of occurrences" which Bertrand Russell makes of man.

This last thinker is at the center of the reflections concluding *The Hollow Universe.* Here the author argues that Russell's horror over the prospect of nuclear annihilation is hardly consistent with his philosophical tenets. From the scientific point of view the destruction of a man or of all men is on the same plane as is any other physical transformation; for example, the gradual decay of radium. De Koninck suggests that, despite scientific philosophy, the traditional view of man and of the universe lies at the bottom of Russell's concern for the race's survival, even though he explicitly rejects that traditional view.

R.J.G.

THE PHILOSOPHER AND THEOLOGY

Author: Étienne Gilson (1884-)
Type of work: Intellectual autobiography
First published: 1960

Principal Ideas Advanced

In France early in the century Catholic intellectuals had no useful conception of theology, and theologians were out of touch with contemporary thought.

The Christian philosopher works in the light of his Christian faith.

A rebirth of Christian thought along the lines of the Thomistic conception of theology could prepare the way for the fruitful absorption of such philosophies as that of Bergson into Christian philosophy.

Étienne Gilson, member of the French Academy, historian of medieval thought, wrote *The Philosopher and Theology* at the age of seventy-five. It is not a history of contemporary Catholic thought, he tells us, and we may describe it as an intellectual autobiography written in terms of the problem that has occupied Gilson most deeply. "The subject of this book is the long adventure of a young Frenchman brought up in the Catholic faith who was indebted to the Church for his entire education and to the University of Paris for his philosophical training, who found himself confronted by Clio with the task of discovering the precise nature of theology, and who, after devoting many years to the discussion of this problem, found the answer too late to put it to use." Gilson does not propose to trace here the vagaries of his research into the nature of theology. The book is a collection of essays which form thematically a single essay, rambling yet always to the point, the central point having to do with the status of the Christian as an intellectual.

Gilson begins at the beginning by describing his Catholic boyhood. From an early age the simple verities of the catechism, the profound assertions of the Creed, were part of his thinking. He indulges in an interesting aside, comparing the older catechism with some of the newer ones and makes some telling points against some recent catechisms. The young Catholic should be taught that the belief in God's existence is founded on revelation. Gilson is impatient with the newer approach which would turn each catechetical lesson into an exercise in natural theology, as if the Catholic believes that God exists because it is possible for the metaphysician to prove it.

After attending the Petit Séminaire Notre-Dame-des-Champs, Gilson went to the Sorbonne. The contrast he draws between the two places is significant. Gilson can only speculate as to what it would have been like to take philosophy under Catholic auspices, since his early training was secular, but he discusses some of the manuals in use at the time. The summary rejections of such philosophers as Kant, Hume, Descartes, the dessicated presentation of doctrine, and the rejection of metaphysics made it clear that such handbooks would not prepare one for easy communication with contemporary philosophy. On the other hand, Catholics who devoted themselves to philosophy were remarkably innocent of theology, of the limits of philosophizing, and of the purpose of theological speculation. Gilson contends that it was the failure of Catholic philosophers to distinguish theology from philosophy which led to the Modernist controversy.

Gilson found himself moving toward a personal discovery of the theology of Saint Thomas when he wrote his thesis, *La Liberté chez Descartes et la théologie,* which was published in 1913. This was his first encounter with Saint Thomas Aquinas and other Scholastic theologians. His study of Descartes led Gilson to the remarkable conclusion that, contrary to the widespread view that philosophy had abruptly recommenced with Descartes after slumbering throughout the Middle Ages, the metaphysics of Descartes consisted largely of conclusions plucked from Scholasticism but without the supporting arguments. What had been taken to be propositions in need of proof for the Scholastics became for Descartes self-evident truths, clear and distinct. Even more interesting, Gilson discovered that the philosophy from whose conclusions Descartes borrowed had its natural habitat in theological works. If this was so, the contemporary prejudice concerning the incompatibility of theology and philosophy no longer seemed beyond dispute. Gilson went on to devote himself to the study of medieval philosophy, a philosophy devised by theologians in their theological works.

Gilson's great work on the system of Aquinas, now called in the translation of the fifth edition, *The Christian Philosophy of Saint Thomas Aquinas,* was written in 1919. After that, Gilson went on, in 1924, to write a book on the philosophy of Saint Bonaventure. The debate these books set off prepared the stage for the lengthy discussion throughout the thirties on the nature of Christian Philosophy. Father Pierre Mandonnet assured Gilson that Bonaventure had no philosophy, only a theology, and that the only medieval who had both a philosophy and a theology was Thomas Aquinas. Father Gabriel Théry maintained that neither Aquinas nor Bonaventure were philosophers and that what we call their philosophies are simply doctrines taken from their theologies and arranged by us and designated as philosophy.

Having, in this autobiographical fashion, set the stage for the presentation of his own views on the nature of Christian philosophy, Gilson chooses to come at the matter somewhat indirectly by way of a discussion of the philosophy of Henri Bergson. The admiration Gilson has for Bergson is fairly boundless, and it is clearly painful to him to recall that the work of Bergson was the occasion for much confused debate among Catholics. Gilson describes the Catholics who defended Bergson and the compatibility of his views with those of the Church as having been woefully ignorant of theology. Those who inveighed against Bergson, on the other hand, did so in terms of the mechanical phrases of manual doctrine and there was never anything like a meeting of minds. It is Gilson's view that Bergson represented for the Church an opportunity not unlike that presented in the thirteenth century by the philosophy of Aristotle. Gilson dwells on the parallel between Bergson and Aristotle, particularly their common desire to anchor all metaphysical statements in the science of their times. This great opportunity was lost, and in trying to understand why it was, Gilson goes back to the thirteenth century to see how the Church profited from the doctrine of Aristotle. The answer Gilson finds is that it was thanks to theologians that that earlier philosophical treasure was preserved and exploited. From this follows the melancholy conclusion that nowadays theologians have lost the sense of their discipline. It is not their task simply to pass or reject what philosophers say. Gilson asks us to consider what Thomas Aquinas would have written if, instead of thinking constructively, he had set out to list the points of disagreement between Aristotle and Catholic orthodoxy. The theologian must be able to philosophize as well as any philosopher, but as a Christian his motivation is different; he does whatever he does in the light of his faith. As Gilson puts it, in theology everything depends on faith, but not everything is deduced from the truths of faith. The theologian who philosophizes: that is Gilson's picture of the medieval Scholastic, and it is the pattern of the Christian philosophy he commends.

Christian philosophy is the philosophical actiivty of the Catholic for whom the Christian faith is always present. The Faith is the central fact of the Christian philosopher's life, and at no time can he pretend that what he is doing is uninfluenced by faith. *Philosophandum in fide:* that is Gilson's view of Christian philosophy. One philosophizes in the Faith and for the Faith, employing reason in the service of the truth God has revealed.

In this book as elsewhere it is difficult to grasp the distinction Gilson would make between theology and philosophy but, apart from the difficulties of that question, this charming book speaks movingly of the motives which should animate the Catholic intellectual. In whatever field, the Catholic intellectual should be responsive to the voice of the Church. Gilson's chapters on Thomism as the official philosophy of the Church are judicious and persuasive.

Étienne Gilson is famous for many things. The special mark of this book is that it was written in the fullness of age, with that maturity of which longevity is a necessary though not a sufficient condition. Out of his seasoned wisdom, Gilson warns the Catholic against the hurried judgment that philosophical novelty is the only hope of the Church in the contemporary world. Novelties come and go, and each one is thought to be the Church's one hope for relevance in the modern world. Gilson sketches a tragic picture of a priest who allied himself with such a new movement in philosophy and, having come to feel that his own philosophical concern for the welfare of the Church surpassed that of the Church Herself, left the ranks. Gilson draws from the sad plight of this ardent if misguided apostle the lesson that patience, docility, and trust in the Church are required if one is to be an effective Christian philosopher. Gilson himself is striking proof that wholehearted commitment to the faith and ready responsiveness to the magisterium is a stimulant and not a depressant to profound intellectual labor.

R.M.

NATIONALISM: A RELIGION

Author: Carlton J. H. Hayes (1882-)
Type of work: Intellectual history
First published: 1960

Principal Ideas Advanced

Patriotism is natural and instinctive; nationalism is artificially cultivated.

Extreme nationalism is a supreme loyalty which becomes a religion or a substitute religion.

Extreme nationalism was born in revolutionary France, where it became the most important ideology of the nineteenth and twentieth centuries.

Nationalism was a prime cause of World War I and World War II, of imperialism and international hatreds.

Born in the Western world, nationalism is a dominant factor in the emerging nations of Asia and Africa.

The term "nationalism" is used in two general ways. One group of historians employs the term loosely to include all shades of patriotism and national sentiment. Another group uses it to mean a perversion of patriotism, a subordination of all other loyalties to a blind loyalty to one's own nation and a contempt for or hatred of all other nations. Carlton J. H. Hayes has been the intellectual leader of this second school ever since World War I suggested to him the importance of this topic.

As professor of history at Columbia University, Hayes directed scores of dissertations on various aspects of nationalism, and he meanwhile wrote several books and many articles on the subject. The results of this lifetime of scholarship on nationalism are compressed into *Nationalism: A Religion*. As always, Hayes presents his findings in graceful literary style based on sound scholarship but unfettered by the paraphernalia or the inhibitions of the craft.

Nationalism, Hayes writes, results from an application of patriotism exclusively to the consciousness of nationality. Patriotism is a loyalty normally associated with small groups and local areas, but when the persons involved comprise a national group patriotism can become nationalism. Language and common traditions are the strongest bases of nationality. A national language sets a people apart from others, sharpens their differences, gives them their own peculiar literature, and even promotes their thinking alike. Common traditions, common sufferings and victories, common heroes and martyrs also weld a nation into a conscious community of nationality.

The religious sense "is so ingrained in man that normally he must give expression to it in one way or another," says Hayes. Through the ages man has given expression to his religious sense in Christianity, Islam, Hinduism, Buddhism, and the other great religions. But in modern times millions of people have transferred this religious sense to communism and, even more, to nationalism.

After confining the initial chapters to definition and description, Professor Hayes devotes the body of his work to the historical development of nationalism. He analyzes tribalism as a form of primitive nationalism, and he shows how it was submerged by the advent of trans-tribal empires, religions, languages, and economic groups. The roots of modern nationalism are to be found in later medieval times, particularly in England. Four developments played a large part in resuscitating large-scale national sentiment: "(1) the rise of vernacular literatures and relative decline of Latin, attended by waning of cosmopolitanism among intellectuals and waxing of national cultures; (2) the emergence of the monarchical national state, as a political institution stronger and more efficient than feudal or city state, or surviving relic of the Roman Empire; (3) transformation of guild or manorial local economy into a national-state economy, with resultant national regulation of commerce, industry, and agriculture; (4) disruption of Catholic Christendom and establishment of national churches."

Modern nationalism became a secular religion for the first time in revolutionary France. *La patrie* was accorded religious worship, the French armies fought with crusading zeal, and men were asked to be martyrs for the cause. Typical of this religious zeal was the proposal of the poet Marie-Joseph de Chénier in 1793: "Wrest the sons of the Republic from the yoke of theocracy which still weighs upon them. . . . Devoid of prejudices and worthy to represent the French nation, you will know how to found, on the debris of the dethroned superstitions, the only universal religion which has neither sects nor mysteries, of which the only dogma is equality, of which our lawmakers are the preachers, of which the magistrates are the pontiffs, and in which the human family burns its incense only at the altar of *la patrie*—common mother and divinity."

This intense nationalism was spread throughout Europe by the French armies and embraced by romantics and the middle class everywhere. It was suppressed by the Congress of Vienna in 1815, but it smouldered under the surface throughout the early nineteenth century. It played an important part in evoking the revolutions of 1830 and 1848 and in bringing into being such new national states as Italy, Germany, and Rumania. The advance of literacy and democracy after the mid-century extended the nationalist appeal to all classes.

The period from 1874 to 1914 can be called one of "nationalist imperialism and intolerance." Nationalist competition was a leading factor in the imperialist race, as national European countries were dividing up Africa and Asia, increasing their hatred for one another and their contempt for "backward nations" abroad. Meanwhile, nationalism created intolerance against ethnic minorities, especially Jews, and created tensions against and within the supranational religions.

Nationalism was not only a prime cause of World War I, says Hayes, but it was also an active agent in increasing hatred during the war, and it helped prevent a reasonable peace settlement in 1919. The Peace of Paris was a triumph for national aspirations, insofar as they could be realized, with the creation of a Poland, a Lithuania, a Turkey, and other such national states cut out of the Hapsburg, Ottoman, and Russian empires. But nationalist aspirations were still not satisfied, because pockets of ethnic groups were to be found in almost every European country. Even more dangerous, the nationalist feeling of the defeated countries, especially Germany and Italy, was wounded, and this factor played a part in bringing to power nationalistic dictators.

Nationalism reached its peak of intensity in Europe between the two World Wars. Both in theory and practice it was most aggressively expressed in Facist Italy and Nazi Germany. These aggressively nationalistic movements led to World War II, during which nationalism reached its bitterest extreme. After the second World War nationalism began to recede in Europe, but in the meantime it became the chief moving force in the emerging countries of Asia and Africa.

In a concluding chapter Hayes offers some "reflections on the religion of nationalism." Here he concludes that nationalism, like any religion, calls into play the will, the intellect, the imagination, and the emotions. The nation "is primarily spiritual, even otherworldly, and its driving force is its collective *faith,* a faith in its mission and destiny, a faith in things unseen, a faith that would move mountains." Modern nationalism has its liturgical forms, its holy days, its temples, all tied in with the worship of the nation. It has in modern times developed its own mythology, intolerance of dissent, and expectation of sacrifice on the part of its adherents. Although the fire of nationalism has burned low in the Western world in recent decades, the author concludes, now it "runs like a forest fire over all Asia and Africa."

T.P.N.

MORAL PHILOSOPHY

Author: Jacques Maritain (1882-)
Type of work: Historical survey of ethical systems
First published: 1960

PRINCIPAL IDEAS ADVANCED

Thomistic philosophy, in seeking the foundations for a new moral philosophy, has laid bare both defects and valuable insights in ethical systems of the past.

Negatively considered, the discovery period of ethics terminated in a contest between faith and reason, the illusion period in the immolation of man to an Absolute, and the reorientation period in a crisis over man's concrete, existential situation.

The elements of positive value for the new moral philosophy consisted in the following foundational-insights: the social and economic substructures influencing the social behavior of man; the internal unconscious forces which combine with man's animal nature to color his personal decisions; lastly, man's unique human condition which tempts him to accept or reject his moral situation without adverting to the supernatural situation available in divine grace.

Jacques Maritain's *Moral Philosophy* is the fruit of a lifetime contemplation on the role of Thomistic philosophy in understanding the nature of man and the tangled threads of his moral behavior. In this work Maritain demonstrates anew his ability to detect valuable insights within an opposing system and to incorporate those truths within his Thomistic framework. His object, an adequate statement of the foundations required for a modern day ethics, is a brilliant challenge to those philosophers who formulate their ethics without frankly facing the many pressures that bear upon the decision-making individual.

Maritain begins his historical survey of ethics by maintaining that it was the question-hurling Socrates of Athens (c. 470-399 B.C.) who first outlined an ethics. Despising hypocrites and Sophists, Socrates sought to answer one great question: What is the best possible life? He did not believe that one could find the good life in the antics of the Sophists, those wandering teachers who encouraged a disregard for tradition and a cynicism concerning truth. Nor did the outlook of the pleasure-seeking hedonists seem any better. Losing themselves in the quest for sensual pleasures, these men bartered away the adventures of the intellectual life in exchange for an animal existence.

The years of meditation brought conviction to the mind of Socrates. The good life and the life of virtue were one and the same. Man's search for happiness was fulfilled only by the daily practice of virtue.

Thus it came about, says Maritain, that Socrates, though unnecessarily identifying knowledge with virtue, initiated the study of ethics as man's way of living the good life.

Plato (427-347 B.C.), while agreeing with his master that ethics was man's quest for the good life, argued that happiness consists in more than the daily practice of virtue. For the happiness which man attains, Plato believed, is not merely a daily occurrence but an eternal one; it is the incomparable existence of the immortal soul liberated by the death of the body.

Aristotle (384-322 B.C.), the master philosopher among the Greeks, was in accord with Socrates and Plato in arguing that happiness was the goal of the good life. In addition, Aristotle reasoned that happiness comes to man through three great avenues: contemplation, virtue, and wisdom. As Aristotle explained, the good man contemplates God and in so doing acquires wisdom. Further, as an intellectual-*animal,* man enjoys sensible pleasures in moderation. Hence it is that the good man's life is a threefold combination of contemplation, virtue, and pleasure.

Despite the influence of Stoicism, Maritain reports, the revealed truths of Christianity shook the pillars of Grecian virtues by surpassing them with the theological virtues; Christianity emphasized the ideas of the immortality of the whole man, not merely of the human soul, and the eternal intuitive contemplation of God rather than a mere earthly dreaming of Him. Even though Christianity was external to philosophy, it caused a revolution within it, Maritain claims. One immediate consequence was that ethics became a mixture of Grecian reasoning and Christian revelation, an interpenetration of moral philosophy and moral theology. Ethics was to retain this duality of character until the coming of the German philosopher Immanuel Kant.

Immanuel Kant (1724-1804) attempted, through "a Copernican revolution of philosophy," to set up an ethics independent of self-interest and objective norms, a moral philosophy in which the agent was the autonomous source of all moral codes. A selfless devotion to duty was the keynote characteristic of the Kantian conception of morality, in which the man of good will was considered to be not the charitable man but the man devoted to duty. There was, in consequence, a desecularizing of Christian ideals to the level of duty or law. As Maritain observes, in such a philosophy "respect for the law . . . has taken the place of the love of God. . . ." Similarly, the interior autonomy of the human will was allowed to usurp the external goodness of man's ultimate End. By this strange twist of reasoning the infinite attributes of an unlimited will were attributed to finite creatures.

Kant's vigorous reversal of moral philosophy sent Christian ideals once again back to the level of secular beliefs from which Christianity had raised moral philosophy by introducing a theological ethics.

Maritain writes that in the period which followed Kantianism, ethics regarded man, not as a creature destined for happiness, but as a victim to be sacrificed. Man became an offering placed before such deities as the Absolute Spirit of Hegel, the Communist State of Marx, and the Humanitarian Religion of Comte.

In Germany, for instance, writes Maritain, the master rationalist Georg Hegel (1770-1831) taught a doctrine of Absolute Spirit in which a "God-in-motion" strives to realize itself through a dialectical process. By a triadic movement from thesis to antithesis, to synthesis, Hegelian reality evolved to ever greater perfection. When it was objected that such an explanation was unreal, Hegel pointed to the Biblical parable (John 12:24): "Except a corn of wheat fall to the ground and die, it abideth alone: but if it die it bringeth forth much fruit." The dialectic of the seed, Hegel indicated, was representative of all reality; a simple identity posits its opposite, then negates that opposition to achieve a higher synthesis. This synthesis, in turn, becomes a positive thesis tending toward another antithesis and still higher synthesis until it culminates ultimately in the triumph of Absolute Spirit.

What has happened to man and his quest for happiness in this triplex evolution? Unfortunately, says Maritain, man has been dropped by the wayside, becoming a passing moment in the Hegelian view of the triadic development of Absolute Spirit. Where ethics had once been man's vision of eternal happiness, Hegel conjured instead the phantasm of man being devoured in the dialectic appetite of the Absolute.

Karl Marx (1818-1883), who fashioned a materialistic view of the universe, fused it with Hegel's dialectic. Employing the triadic movement of Hegel but discarding the latter's tenets, Marx believed that history is a materialistic dialectic in which the means of production shape the nature of human society. All forms of human life, Marx said, are subordinated to the ultimate principle of production. Human behavior is dictated by the science of economics.

The Marxian dialectic, Maritain declares, manifests itself in a code of human conduct, emphasizing individual discipline, the virtues of the worker, and the whole-hearted gift of oneself to the cause. However, the specific regulations of Communist ethics are continually changing as human conditions themselves change. In this ethical relativism, the Communist worker becomes a mere means, an instrumentality, smothered in the movement of the state toward its own fulfillment. As with Hegelian philosophy, the Marxian man is immolated in the victory of the Marxist State.

Auguste Comte (1798-1857) required an even more curious sacrifice from man, in that man is required to worship an abstraction of himself. The founder of modern positivism, Comte advocated the doctrine of the "Positive State." Mankind advances, Comte explained, by moving through three progressively better states. Initially a citizen of the "Theological State," in which man imagines that spiritual entities control his world, he evolves to a second or "Metaphysical State." In the Metaphysical State man attempts to explain natural phenomena by inventing metaphysical beings and abstract causes. Finally, however, the intelligent citizen will progress to the Positive State in which all truth is tested by empirical verification, and all superstition is banished.

Rejecting the ideals of Christianity and its false Christian God so as to worship at the altar of humanity, the ethics of positivism adored the new saints; namely, the great explorers, the scientists, and political leaders of the world.

The new ethical code would reflect the constantly changing historical conditions of the world so that ethics themselves would be continually shifting. Man could never make a moral judgment which would be eternally true, for all values would themselves be subject to the ever-changing social conditions.

According to Maritain, modern ethics entered a crucial period of reorientation through the personal impetus of Søren Kierkegaard (1813-1855). Kierkegaard was one of the first of the existentialists to protest against the fictions of philosophy. Man should not spend his life in the empty pursuit of abstractions when his eternal destiny is at stake, the Danish philosopher argued; man would do better to solve the problems of his own concrete situation. These problems are man's fundamental weakness of spirit, his anguish of soul, and his existential insecurity.

Man may be saved, said Kierkegaard, by viewing reality as a period of trial in which he succeeds or fails to establish a personal commitment to the God-in-time, Christ Himself. Preceded by fear and trembling, this great decision can be wrought only by a "leap" of the soul. This is a radical free act whereby man severs connections with his former mode of life so as to exist as a true Christian in the existential sphere of faith.

The Kierkegaardian insistence on man's personal responsibility reoriented ethics in the direction of Christian faith. Unfortunately, Kierkegaard won this victory at a terrible price, for his doctrine that the leap of the soul was primarily an act not of reason but of faith vitiated the power of human reason. Thus, while he rebuilt ethics, it was an ethics which functioned as a means of salvation rather than as one based on the validity of human reason. Kierkegaard was inadvertently opening the door to irrationalism. It was not long in coming.

With the French existentialist Jean-Paul Sartre irrationalism has found its voice. Postulating an outright atheism, Sartre repudiates all rational explanations of human nature. The plight of man, in Sartre's eyres, is that of a pitiful consciousness doomed to an existence of frustration. Man is a thing which seeks to overcome its own condition but is, in fact, free only to annihilate itself. For man, in seeking to escape his own condition, is striving to shed that which makes him human. To be successful he must defeat himself by ceasing to be human. It is this inherent futility which, Sartre contends, reveals the true nature of man: man is a useless passion in a meaningless world.

Since the Sartrean world has no objective values, says Maritain, there exists no external framework upon which man may base an ethics. Thus, Sartre's creature must invent his own values, and once again ethical norms degenerate into a morass of relativism.

The retreat into irrationalism was repeated in the American philosophy of John Dewey (1859-1952) with his emphasis on an "experimental" approach to reality. Forswearing all dogmatic codes and theistic claims, Dewey subscribed to a completely naturalistic ethics. Regulated by the sciences of phenomena, all ethical judgments would be subject to empirical verification. Through this guidance the intelligent citizen, himself the highest type of evolutionary product, would strive for a further evolutionary flowering of "social progress."

Henri-Louis Bergson (1859-1941) agreed that reality was a flux. He insisted, however, that this vital evolution was crowned with a transcendent and eternal realm of being. The moral philosophy required to guide man must itself spring intuitively from vital forces which structure man's world. One of these forces is social pressure, by which even a primitive society imposes its codes upon the individual. Geared only to its own survival, society subjects its citizenry to the "anthill morality" of rigid order, and the result is a closed morality.

Aspiration is the other moral force, according to Bergson; through it man heeds the call to a higher life in the realm of spirit and saintliness. Though it does not contradict the closed morality of social regulations, this open morality transcends those limitations to participate in the world of liberty and love.

Though Bergson derogated the role of intellect, says Maritain, and blurred the distinction between cardinal and theological virtues, Bergson urged that charity, brought to fruition in *open morality,* is ultimately a personal state of creative love.

Maritain contends that the ethical systems he has examined reveal insights which can serve as foundation-stones in constructing a new moral philosophy.

For example, the idea of the animal origin of man and the Freudian idea of the human unconscious are both of genuine value. While the moral philosopher should avoid any simplistic acceptance of either, he must not fail to recognize the influential presence of these ideas in man's personal decisions.

Marx's notion of economic determinism and Comte's social determinism should both be granted status as factors in man's moral behavior, Maritain suggests, though care should be exercised that neither is allowed to negate man's clear-cut powers of reason and choice.

In conclusion, Maritain argues that the existentialists have correctly stressed man's concrete situation, the unhappiness and insecurity which man experiences in daily existence. The prudent moral philosopher, Maritain believes, will not direct man toward a simple acceptance or simple rejection of this condition. Rather, he will instruct him in the reality of divine aid. Consciously participating in divine grace, man is transfigured with new meaning even while retaining his humanity.

The contemporary philosopher is thus able to view man as subject to this manifold of internal and external forces, and as dominating them by human liberty strengthened with grace. Upon these foundation-stones, says Maritain, moral philosophy can erect an ethics designed according to man's eternal destiny.

H.D.

WE HOLD THESE TRUTHS

Author: John Courtney Murray, S.J. (1904-)
Type of work: Social and political philosophy
First published: 1960

PRINCIPAL IDEAS ADVANCED

Catholics are right in morally committing themselves to the religion clauses of the Constitution when these are interpreted not as articles of faith but as articles making for peace in a pluralist society.

The Freedom of the Church is a principle which tends effectively to inhibit the tendency of democratic power to grow to totalitarian proportions.

The problems we face as a result of our religious pluralism, problems such as that of the religious school and that of the legitimacy of censorship, can be solved only if there is willingness to recognize that ideals cannot be legislated and that much patient civil argument to lay bare the roots of disagreement is necessary.

We Hold These Truths is a volume of essays and occasional papers written during the decade preceding its publication in 1960. Its unity derives from the fact that all the essays are in one way or another concerned with "the truths we [Americans and Catholics] hold"—the public philosophy of America, the public consensus, the American "Proposition" to which we, as American citizens, are dedicated. Father Murray's "Catholic Reflections on the American Proposition" (the book's subtitle) leads him to ask: Are there truths we hold? Which are they? Why do we hold them? On what basis do we hold them? Are we right in holding them?

It is important to answer these questions because our awareness of our identity as a people and of our role in the world, says Father Murray, rests on the body of substantive truths we hold as a people. It is particularly important for Catholics to answer these questions because given the belief that "the principles of Catholic faith and morality stand superior to and in control of the whole of civil life," one needs to know to what extent, if any, being a good Catholic is likely to be inconsistent with being a good American.

It is important to argue about these truths, Murray claims, for otherwise they may be forgotten. When civil argument about the American consensus no longer takes place, when it dies from lack of interest or "subsides into the angry mutterings of polemic, or rises to the shrillness of hysteria, or trails off into positivistic triviality, or gets lost in a morass of semantics, you may be sure that the barbarian is at the gates of the City." Engaging in civil dialogue is especially difficult in the United States because American society is religiously pluralist: Protestant, Catholic, Jewish, and secularist, and issues of truth are complicated by issues of religious power and prestige, of religious passion and war. Religious pluralism, with its pluralism of historical and intellectual backgrounds, results in a number of incommensurable universes of discourse; thus, it becomes exceedingly difficult even to be sure that two people who are saying different things (or at least using different terms in discussing some issue) are disagreeing, and it is often difficult to drive confusion away long enough even to reach disagreement. Murray's own expectations are "modest and minimal. . . . We could limit the warfare, and we could enlarge the dialogue. We could lay down our arms (at least the more barbarous kind of arms!), and we could take up argument."

Father Murray has for many years been known as a leading Catholic spokesman on Church-state relations, and he is justly eminent for his vigorous rejection of the view that a system of legal separation of Church and state may be justified only on the level of expediency (*in hypothesi,* when Catholics are in a minority they expect as much freedom as anyone else) and not on the level of principle (*in thesi,* under ideal conditions, when Catholics are in a majority, the propagation of error is not to be tolerated). In his "Civil Unity and Religious Integrity" Murray most explicitly deals with what he sees as the American pattern of Church-state relations set forth in the Constitution, and most explicitly in the First Amendment: "Congress shall make no law respecting an establishment of religion or prohibiting the free exercise thereof. . . ." Catholics ought to be morally committed to the religion clauses of the Constitution which ensure religious freedom and the separation of Church and state, the author writes. But this commitment should be to these clauses as "articles of peace" and not as the "articles of faith" which they tend to be for the secularist and for the Protestant who believes that religious liberty is one of the rights conferred by God on man, the guaranteeing of which becomes a matter of religious obligation.

It is lamentable that American society is religiously pluralist, writes Murray, for religious pluralism entails the holding of false beliefs. Yet our American experience is that the Catholic Church has been left free to fulfill her spiritual mission, and that even though it has received no special favor, neither has it suffered persecution, and history tells us that privilege often proved in the end to be as damaging to the Church as persecution. A new era began in 1783 when the Vatican asked the Continental Congress for permission to establish a bishopric in the United States and was told that, since the matter was purely spiritual, Congress had no jurisdiction; for the first time in centuries the Catholic Church was free to work as it saw fit, without special privilege to be sure, but also without requiring the consent of governing personnel. It has, further, been our American experience that political stability is not necessarily dependent on the possession of but one religious faith, that political unity can be strengthened by the exclusion of religious differences from the area of concern proper to government, and that even the maintenance of the distinction between Church and state in an exaggerated form has benefited religion. In 1884 the bishops at the Third Plenary Council of Baltimore declared: "We consider the establishment of our country's independence, the shaping of its liberties and laws, as a work of special Providence, its framers 'building better than they knew,' the Almighty's hand guiding them." The denial to government of any competence in the field of religion can thus be shown to be a guarantee of freedom of religion (and also an effective check upon the tendency of government to attract all power into its hands.)

In another article explicitly devoted to Church-state relations, namely, "Are There Two or One?" Father Murray argues that the great political contribution of Christianity was its destruction of the "classical" view of society as a homogeneous structure whose head possessed the fullness of both political and religious power. The Gelasian doctrine, "*Two there are,* august Emperor, by which this world is ruled on title of original and sovereign right—the consecrated authority of the priesthood and the royal power" (Pope Gelasius I, 494), revolutionized the politico-social structure of the West, and the "freedom of the Church" was introduced as the mediating principle between the people and public power. Acceptance of the Church as spiritual authority and as made up of Christian people having access to a teaching independent of the state's validation broke down the totalitarian monism of secular power. (Of course, with the fall of the Roman Empire, ecclesiastical leaders temporarily exercised political power: "In 800 A.D., Leo III had a right to crown Charlemagne as Emperor of the Romans; but this was because it was 800 A.D. If there were a Christendom tomorrow—a Christian world-government in a society whose every member was baptized—the Pope, for all the fulness of his apostolic authority, would not have the slightest shadow of a right to 'crown' so much as a third-class postmaster.") Today a substitute has been found for the "freedom of the Church," namely, free democratic political institutions: "*One there is* by which this world is ruled—the power in the people, expressing itself in the preference of a majority; and beyond or beside or above this power there is no other." The life of man is once again organized in but one society, not in two. There is no power which can neutralize the totalitarian monism inherent in the contemporary idolatry of democratic process and power. But, Murray wants to know, when the sole interpreter of moral imperatives to the political order is the free conscience of the individual, can the moral foundations of society be sufficiently stabilized, "apart from all reference to a visibly constituted spiritual and moral authority," by nothing more than the fortunate coincidence of individual private judgments?

In "Creeds at War Intelligibly," Murray asks: What is the competence, and what is the function of the university with regard to the social problem of religious pluralism? He answers that the university is failing its students if it does not find itself taking religion seriously by making a contribution to the genuine understanding of the epistemology of religious truth, of the nature of religious faith, and to the understanding of the various systems of belief both as systems and in relation to other areas of human knowledge. A university is an institution whose function it is to bring all the resources of human intelligence to bear on the problems that confront the mind of man, and only the skeptic or agnostic could be satisfied with the university's present image of itself as being "above" the religious wars that rage beneath the surface of modern life. The student who comes to the university, the Protestant, the Catholic, or the Jew, should reasonably be able to expect to grow in all the branches of knowledge, including the dimension of religious knowledge. And just as he can expect to be taught secular subjects by those who can make the best case for them, so also ought he reasonably to be able to expect to be taught about Judaism, or Catholicism, or Protestantism by one qualified to make the best case at the highest possible intellectual level.

As an example of the sort of problem endemic to a religiously pluralist (divided) society, Father Murray points, in "Is It Justice?", to the Religious School Question: a large section of the community, the Catholic population, claim that they are being treated unjustly with regard to the distribution of tax funds for the support of the school system. He sees a striking analogy between the doctrine of "separate but equal" facilities for Negroes and the present denial of financial aid to religious schools: racial discrimination was always wrong and could never have been defended on moral grounds, but could once have been excused on "sociological" grounds as necessary in the circumstances (in view of the blindness of the public conscience, the inferior cultural status of the Negro at the time, and other factors); so also the segregation of the religious school from public aid could not ever have been defended on moral grounds, involving as it does a violation of distributive justice, but could in the past have been defended on the sociological ground that it was in accord with the nineteenth century concept of the separation of Church and state in education and that it was a necessary concession to quite common prejudice. But in neither of these two cases is the "sociological defense" of traditional mores any longer admissible; in neither case is the nineteenth century version of pluralism, racial or religious, anything more than an anomaly. Father Murray is not sure what the solution to the School Question is or will prove to be. but at least many more people today see a problem, and seeing the problem is of course a necessary condition of finding a solution.

Another issue that tends to exacerbate religious tensions, the issue of censorship, is dealt with in "Should There Be A Law?" Murray suggests that the following four rules be embodied in the public consensus: that each minority group be recognized to have the right to censor for its own members, that no minority be recognized to have the right to demand coercive government censorship of materials judged harmful only by the special standards used by that group, that any minority group be recognized to have a right to use persuasion and peaceful argument to change public morality in any direction it considers desirable, and that no minority group have the right to use force, violence, or coercion to impose its views on other groups. (It is interesting to note that ten lines from this chapter have been cited in a minority opinion of the United States Supreme Court in defense of the position that there should be no prior restraint on a man's use of his freedom of expression.)

Included also in this volume are essays in Murray's best urbane manner on Communist imperialism (in which a hard-line, "brinkmanship" policy is recommended), on modern warfare (aggressive war, war to redress injuries or just grievances, is no longer legitimate; only defensive war can possibly be legitimate, and then on condition that it be "limited war") and on natural law. "Catholic participation in the American consensus has been full and free, unreserved and unembarassed," concludes Father Murray, "because the contents of this consensus—the ethical and political principles drawn from the tradition of natural law—approve themselves to the Catholic intelligence and conscience."

R.L.C.

COME, LET US WORSHIP

Author: Godfrey L. Diekmann, O.S.B. (1908-)
Type of work: Sacramental theology
First published: 1961

Principal Ideas Advanced

Liturgy, or the Church's worship, does not exist for its own sake but to assist people to become holy, to conform to Christ.

The liturgical movement, while presenting new ideas to the faithful, is not faddish.

Combining the Word of Scriptures and the sacraments, the liturgy is both a prime source of Christian life and also the sublime goal of Christian life.

In the history of the Catholic liturgical movement in the United States, few names stand out as prominently as that of the Reverend Godfrey Diekmann, O.S.B., editor of *Worship* magazine. Father Godfrey's work has been on three levels: as an original thinker of the liturgical movement in an effort to bring the force of Apostolic ideas to worship as the central action of Christian life; as a catalyst, through his magazine, for the various thrusts of liturgical reform; and as a popularizer, to translate the new thought of the movement to priests and people so they may experience worship in its truest sense.

The single public showcase of the liturgical movement in the United States has been the annual Liturgical Week, held each summer since 1940. Beginning as a seminar for a few progressive clerics, Liturgical Week has consistently grown over the years so that now thousands of persons take part. The influence of the gatherings has spread throughout the nation's dioceses, and the importance of this movement in North America has been acknowledged as a chief source of fermentation for liturgical reform in the Roman Catholic Church. This reform gained its Magna Charta in the *Constitution on the Sacred Liturgy,* decreed at the second session of the Second Vatican Council on December 4, 1963, and promulgated by Pope Paul VI.

What is proposed in the *Constitution on the Sacred Liturgy,* as the standard of worship for the entire Catholic Church, is described by Father Godfrey's *Come, Let Us Worship.* The book is a collection of thirteen addresses delivered by the author at Liturgical Weeks as far back as 1940. The importance of the teachings expressed in those addresses was to be confirmed twenty-three years later when the bishops of the world embodied them in their decree of the Sacred Liturgy.

In the organization of the separate addresses, Father Godfrey builds from the basic point that liturgy, or worship, in the Christian Church is the actual involvement of the People of God proclaiming the mystery of Christ. Following the Council of Trent, public worship in the Roman rite of the Catholic Church became stagnant, resisting any new development. The Latin liturgy became a rubrical affair that seemed in practice more for the benefit of the clergy than of the faithful. As a result, the gap between the people in the Church and those entrusted to the celebration of liturgy was widened over the three and a half centuries of post-Tridentine times.

Come, Let Us Worship looks at this reaction to the Protestant Reformation and sees the Church becoming more defensive concerning otherwise sound theological postures. In becoming more hardened to change, more faithful to the *status quo* in liturgy, the Church lost touch with the idea of the Mystical Body of Christ, the idea that the laity who made up the faithful were, in a real sense, the Church. Father Godfrey shows that "the doctrine of the Mystical Body became obscured in the five centuries that intervened between the era of the Fathers (ending with Gregory the Great, about A.D. 600) and the beginnings of scholasticism." Obscuring this doctrine led to a confusion of the faithful concerning such matters as the role of the laity in respect to the Eucharist, the place of the sacraments, and the relations in general of the laity and the Church.

In the concentration on the awesome fact of the divinity of Christ, teachings in the Church often lost the concept of the humanity of Christ. Failing to recognize Christ Incarnate helped to bring on the clericalism of the Catholic Mass, which became, in the eyes of the people it should have been serving, a Holy of Holies, to which the ordained priest alone should have access.

"To put it bluntly," Father Godfrey writes, "the laity were in practice excluded from the actual sharing in the heart of the Sacrifice, as soon as Christ's divinity was over-extolled at the expense of His high-priestly humanity." The author then traces the effect of this exclusion, brought about by the use of the dead language Latin and the silent whisperings of the celebrant, on the life of the people attending the services. Gradually there was lost a sense of the glad awareness of membership in the Body of Christ. Mass-goers were confronted with Christ as God who was offended by their sins, instead, as Father Godfrey explains, "of as our Elder Brother who bore our sins and united us into God's own family."

The basic sense of the liturgical movement, then, was to remove these defensive and divisive aspects of the Church's worship and to restore the liturgy, the Mass, the sacraments, the sacramentals, to the people for their benefit.

Treating, in another chapter based on a 1957 Liturgical Week address, an understanding of the sacraments, Father Godfrey seeks again to wipe away false notions that have arisen in the minds of the clergy and people. Before Saint Thomas Aquinas the great emphasis on sacraments was on them as signs. Following the great Doctor of the Church the emphasis became one-sided in the direction of causality. The imbalance since the time of Saint Thomas leads to an "impoverished view of the Sacraments and their role in the spiritual life—a view which is being rectified only in our own day and which has necessitated a liturgical movement or, as it is perhaps better named, a sacramental apostolate."

It is in this sense that *Come, Let Us Worship* and the work of the sacramental apostolate is directed. For it is pointed out by the author that in the early centuries of the Church there was only a single means by which the Christians were instructed in their faith.

That single means was the liturgy. In the actual sacraments, in the mystery of the Eucharistic sacrifice of the Mass, in the homilies and sermons, the early Christians heard the "good news" of God and made their single encounter with Him.

The full sacramental life, then, leads to a fuller and more mature Christian life and outlook, contends the author. The Church does not have the sacraments merely to dispense them; rather the Church is constituted by the sacraments, lives by them, and grows by them. Sacraments are not so much received by the faithful as they are activities of Christ, continuing as His Church, by which he lifts His people up to Himself into a redeemed community. Sacraments, points out the author, consecrate both space and time.

In the days that the liturgical movement was a fringe group working within the Church to save the Church from herself, such leaders as Father Godfrey and other leading sacramental theologians were continually on the defensive. In each instance they had to prove their thesis, not only to make their point to seek the liturgical renewal, but to demonstrate their own loyalty. This fact is evident in almost every work by Diekmann, as well as in the accounts of others, such as Yves Congar, Louis Bouyer, and J. A. Jungmann.

Godfrey Diekmann here again stresses that liturgists want what the Church wants, even though it has not always been fully recognized by the authorities of the Church; namely, that the liturgy, after seven centuries of relative neglect as a teaching organ, be again fully included in the normal teaching activity of the parish school and church. From 1903, when in a *moto proprio,* Pope Saint Pius X called the meetings of the faithful a "most important and indispensable source, which is the active participation in the most sacred mysteries and in the public and solemn prayer of the Church," the idea recurs throughout the liturgical reform that liturgy is a source of the Christian life. Pius XI said, "The liturgy is the most important organ of the ordinary magisterium [teaching power] of the Church." Again and again, the declarations of each successive pope and the successive steps in liturgical reform recalled the liturgy as a source of Christian life, and the *Constitution on the Sacred Liturgy* re-emphasizes the point. Thus, liturgists, who sought changes, continually defended the changes they espoused as ways to worship God properly and fully and to be infused in His divine life.

After first explaining the need for reform, and after setting down the basis of sacramental theology that gives purpose to the liturgical movement, the author proceeds to each of the sacraments themselves, beginning with Baptism as an initiation into Christian life and worship. Again, this *Christ*-ening Sacrament is lifted above a mere washing away of sins: "Baptism, therefore, has not merely the effect of cleansing us from sin, and of giving us the grace of adoption, but is first of all a plunging of our entire being into Christ. His redemptive death and resurrection become ours, and it is because we are baptized, that is plunged into His death (as St. Paul tells us) that we die to sin; and it is because we are baptized into His resurrection that His glorious life becomes ours."

It is important to follow the account step by step, because Father Godfrey lays groundwork for the full and active role of all people in the Church liturgy. In explanation of the sacrament of Baptism as a rebirth into Christ, Father Godfrey shows how the works of a Baptism are renewed in the Christian's life at each Mass and in the other sacraments as well. In his explanation of the whole of the Church's liturgy, he relates each act, each sacrament, the colors of vestments, the feasts, the calendar, into a full picture of living the life in Christ. And in each sense, the didactic purposes of the liturgy is recalled in order to demonstrate what these can mean to Christians.

Through an account of the general form of the Church liturgy and the specific ways by which the liturgy is translated, and through reviewing the life and example of the Blessed Virgin Mary, Mother of Christ, the indwelling of the life of Christ is spelled out by Father Godfrey. Final portions of *Come, Let Us Worship* deal with the practical ordering of liturgical reform through dispensation and changes in the Church law, through the work and powers of the bishops of each place, and through education. In this last chapter, "The Liturgy and Education," which was the only part of the book not originally cast as a Liturgical Week address, Father Godfrey investigates the sense of community contained in *ekklesia* (or Church.) It is also in this practical discussion that he considers the plural "churches" as used by the Apostle Paul, for example, in speaking of the "Church of God at Corinth," the "Church at Cenchrae," the "Church of the Thessalonians," as well as the "Churches of the saints" and "all the Churches everywhere."

In this frame of reference, major conclusions are drawn by the liturgical theologian that the parish is a community of the chosen people whose true citizenship is in Heaven, that these Christians living together in communities of churches, or parishes, have some distinctive characteristics that bind them together, and that much depends on the personal responsibility and the Christian maturity of each individual. The teaching spirit of the liturgy is bound to each of these ideas, in this explanation of the development of liturgical reform.

As Archbishop Edward D. Howard of Portland, Oregon, states in the foreward, "The liturgy is the Church's official school of holiness."

D.Q.

MATER ET MAGISTRA

Author: Pope John XXIII (Angelo Giuseppe Roncalli, 1881-1963)
Type of work: Christian social ethics
First published: 1961

Principal Ideas Advanced

The Church, Mother and Teacher of nations, continues to be concerned about social and economic problems.

The encyclical letter Rerum novarum *of Leo XIII states that work is not a commodity and that labor agreements should be governed by justice and charity; workers have the right to enter into associations.*

The encyclical letter Quadragesimo anno *of Pius XI reaffirms the right to private property, and it maintains that economic affairs be organized in accordance with the common good.*

The present letter teaches that a balance should be maintained between individual freedom and the ordering activity of the state, and it declares that individual men are the foundation, cause, and end of all social institutions.

Unfriendly critics outside the Church sometimes charge that the Church lives in isolation from the practical concerns of human beings. But those inside the Church know that the spirit of the Church is divine and that the Church was founded by Jesus Christ to serve, as Pope John XXIII writes at the beginning of his encyclical letter *Mater et Magistra,* as "Mother and Teacher of nations, so that all who in the course of centuries come to her loving embrace, may find salvation as well as the fullness of a more excellent life." The pope then goes on to remind his readers that "the teaching of Christ joins . . . earth with heaven, in that it embraces the whole man. . . ." Thus, as the encyclical points out, economic and social problems fall within the scope of the Church's concern. Pope John cites, as evidence of the Church's effort to apply Christian principles of justice and charity to problems having to do with workers' conditions, the encyclical letter *Rerum novarum,* issued in 1891 by Pope Leo XIII, and also *Quadragesimo anno,* issued by Pope Pius XI on May 15, 1931, forty years after *Rerum novarum. Mater et Magistra* undertakes to provide a review of these earlier Encyclicals and to propose new steps for dealing with social problems which have arisen since the earlier letters were issued.

Pope John describes *Rerum novarum* as "the most notable evidence of . . . social teaching and action, which the Church has set forth through the centuries," and he adds that "the norms and recommendations contained therein were so momentous that their memory will never fall into oblivion." The pope reminds his readers that when *Rerum novarum* was issued, it was generally believed that no connection existed between economic and moral laws and that natural forces governed all economic matters; labor unions were sometimes forbidden or merely tolerated; those who were economically strong acquired great riches, while the masses of workers "labored in very acute need." In his letter, according to Pope John's summary, Pope Leo XIII stated that work "is an expression of the human person" which "can by no means be regarded as a mere commodity." Thus, wages should be determined by laws of justice and equity. Furthermore, private property is a natural right, and since it is the business of the state to secure the common good in the temporal order, the state should safeguard the rights of workers, improve their living conditions, and oversee labor agreements.

On the fortieth anniversary of *Rerum novarum* Pius XI reaffirmed the principles advanced by Pope Leo XIII, and in the encyclical letter *Quadra-*

gesimo anno ("forty years after") he urged that workers and management join in partnership agreements and profit sharing. He argued that concern for the individuals involved in industry demands that working conditions within industry be improved. Pius XI rejected both communism and socialism as attempts to order society, maintaining that their interest is solely in the temporal welfare of men and that they encourage the restriction of liberty and overlook the "true concept of social authority." Pope John writes that *Quadragesimo anno* makes two basic points: (1) justice and charity must govern all economic undertakings, and (2) a juridical order within countries and among nations must insure that economic activity is in accordance with the common good.

The third important expression of the Church's teaching on social matters was Pope Pius XII's radio broadcast on the feast of Pentecost, June 1, 1941. The pontiff claimed for the Church the competence to judge a given social system in its relation to material goods, labor, and the family. He declared that since every man has the right to the use of material goods, the right to own property should not interfere with the flow of material goods. He further maintained that the regulation of labor relations is the primary responsibility of the individual men involved, but that the state must act to secure the common good whenever the parties concerned do not fulfill their functions. Finally, Pius XII stressed the importance of the private ownership of material goods, which are means to advancing the welfare of the family, and he argued that the right to migrate follows from the right of ownership.

After calling attention to advances in science, technology, and economics and to new social trends, Pope John undertakes an examination of the principles set forth in the earlier declarations and an application of those principles to current problems.

In explaining and developing the former teachings of the Church, Pope John XXIII discusses the place of private initiative and state intervention in economic life. The principle is advanced that a grave evil results when a larger or higher group assumes the functions that a lesser or smaller group can perform. The Encyclical states that our time is marked by the multiplication of social relationships, rendering individuals ever more interdependent. This increase of "socialization" restricts the opportunity for free action by individuals. Thus, it is ever more important that standards of justice and equity prevail in determining what constitutes an appropriate wage.

According to the encyclical, within a country the growth of the economy must be accompanied by a social development so that all citizens, both in labor and in management, may benefit equitably from an increase of national wealth. The conditions under which men work must give them an opportunity to assume responsibility and perfect themselves by their labor. Persons occupied in labor, whether in small businesses, on farms, or in arts and crafts, must be protected and fostered; work agreements in big industry must be modified by partnership arrangements; and the state should make special provision for co-operative associations to protect small enterprises. Private property must both safeguard the rights of the human person and contribute to the good of society, and the rich must share their abundance with the poor so as to convert property into spiritual possessions.

In the body of the encyclical Pope John XXIII sets forth the new aspects of the social question. He provides some norms which justice requires be used in handling the interrelated productive sectors of agriculture, industry, and service. There must be a balanced development of the economic system by these sectors. Today agriculture is in a state of depression regarding both labor productivity and the level of living of farm populations. Thus, it is absolutely necessary that public authorities take action in matters of farm taxes, credit, insurance, essential public services, and price protection. The lines of this action are briefly laid out in the encyclical. Yet it is principally the persons involved, namely, the farmers themselves, who must effect their own economic improvement by appropriate organizations: professional associations and mutual-aid societies. The pontiff praises the rural way of life which seems to have within it everything that makes for man's dignity, development, and perfection.

On the subject of aid to underdeveloped areas within a country, efforts must be made to provide essential public services in accord with the general level of living. These measures for advancement affect the general welfare and must be undertaken by the civil authority. The principle to be followed is that a balanced progress must be made in all sectors of the economy, agriculture, industry, and service, and in all areas of the nation.

One of the pressing questions of our day concerns the relationship between economically advanced and economically underdeveloped countries. Enlightened self-interest, as well as the sense of brotherhood under God, requires that developed nations share responsibility in lending help to nations in the process of development. Strongest of all are the requirements of justice between nations differing in economic development. In the pontiff's own words: "We all share responsibility for the fact that populations are undernourished." Justice and humanity require that the richer countries come to the aid of those in need with both emergency assistance and with long-range co-operation for their scientific, technical, and financial development. The encyclical points out that past errors can be avoided by insuring that improved social conditions accompany economic progress. The aid given by the richer nations must be disinterested in the sense that donor nations should respect the individuality of other countries and not seek to dominate them. While economic aid fosters progress in science, technology, and economic life, it must be kept in mind that temporal progress is not the highest good, but only an instrument for the pursuit of the spiritual values upon which true civilization depends.

Recently the question of "population explosion" has occupied much attention. Statistics seem to indicate that in a matter of decades the population increase will exceed the increase in means of subsistence. But, the pope suggests, the proposal to limit procreation by every possible means has a fatal allure. The truth of the problem is that on a global scale the number of births cannot be seen to outstrip the available resources, either at present or in the immediate future. Nature, which God has provided with almost inexhaustible productive capacity, and man's ingenuity, can combine to meet eventualities. The pontiff points out that past and present advances in science and technology leave little room for pessimism concerning the future. In the case of limited unbalances between population and the necessities of life, as in the underdeveloped nations, progress can be accomplished only by international co-operation. Human life, the family, and marriage are sacred, and means of limiting life which destroy their dignity are unlawful. The pontiff notes with sadness two conflicting trends: on the one hand, the fear of a population explosion and a scarcity of goods; on the other, a fear of a horrible nuclear death as a result of the discoveries of science. The individual person needs prudence and a sense of responsibility on entering marriage. An adequate preparation, including spiritual information, is urged.

Because of advances in science and technology the countries of the world have become more interdependent, the pope notes. It is now necessary that many important human problems be solved by international co-operation. Yet because of distrust among nations of differing philosophies and of accompanying failure to acknowledge the moral order, much energy and great resources are wasted on projects of destruction.

In the final part of the encyclical Pope John XXIII discusses the reconstruction of social relationships which is necessary because of advances in science and technology. According to the pontiff, there will never be peace or justice in the world until men realize their individual dignity. Separated from God by ideas of progress in technology and economic life, man becomes monstrous to himself and others. In the pontiff's own words: "No folly seems more characteristic of our time than the desire to establish a firm and meaningful temporal order, but without God, its necessary foundation." But since, as the Church teaches, "individual men are necessarily the foundation, cause, and end of all social institutions," the application of Christian social principles depends upon the work and effort of lay apostles who must first train themselves by daily practice of these principles. To carry out this noble task laymen must be qualified in their own professions and trained in the social teachings and norms of the Church. Pope John XXIII calls for a renewed dedication to the work of transforming the world; he urges that all men be motivated again by Christian charity and a strong sense of brotherhood in the Mystical Body of Christ.

J.C.R.

THE COUNCIL, REFORM AND REUNION

Author: Hans Küng (1928-)
Type of work: Ecclesiology
First published: 1961

Principal Ideas Advanced

As a result of the convocation of the Second Vatican Council by Pope John XXIII, a whole new atmosphere has appeared in the Church which makes an extensive and universal reform, renewal, or updating of the Catholic Church from within both possible and essential.

Because of the very strong human element in the constitution of the Church, composed as it is of sinful men, and because every culture and age has made its own unique contribution to it both good and bad, the Church is permanently in need of reformation in the image of Christ.

Rooted in a deep appreciation of the lessons of the past, Catholics themselves in the Church and in collaboration with those of other faiths must labor for this reformation.

The Second Vatican Council can be either a great fulfillment or a great disappointment in advancing the cause of Christian reunion and the ecumenical movement, depending on how Catholics meet the challenge of reformation in particular areas of modern Catholic life and structure.

Before the publication of *Konzil und Wiedervereinigung* in April, 1961, Father Hans Küng was known only among the professional theologians, where his monumental work on Karl Barth had earned him a high reputation and a position on the Catholic theological faculty of the University of Tübingen. When his more popularly written book on the Council appeared in German and almost immediately in translations around the world, his name and thought became a rallying point for the opponents of the Tridentine, "nonhistorical," legalistic school of theologians who have been dominant in the Church for 400 years. Forbidden or refused permission to speak at the Catholic University of America and in several American dioceses during a tour of this country in 1962, his reputation soared. Shortly after, his book was banned by chancery officials from the bookdealers' shelves in Rome during the first session of the Council. As a result, his book, whose English title is *The Council, Reform and Reunion* has been one of the most widely circulated (even among non-Romans) and most influential of all books published on the Council.

On June 29, 1959, John XXIII announced his intention to hold an ecumenical council as part of a threefold formula for the reunion of the Christian world under one shepherd—the other two parts being the reform of canon law and a diocesan synod in Rome aimed at practical reforms. The Council, ultimately aimed at encouraging Christian reunion, has two purposes, according to Küng's view; namely, an increase in Christian faith with a true renewal of morality among Christian people, and the adaption of ecclesiastical discipline to the needs and conditions of our time. Such a task will be a "gentle invitation" to reunion. This proposed renewal of Catholic faith is to be a true reform within the Church: "Reformation is not a Protestant preserve." There is a strong Biblical foundation for such a Catholic reformation as Küng urges.

The main focus of this book is then broached as "the permanent necessity of renewal in the Church." As root for this exigency, Küng offers a study of just what, or better who, is the Church. Concentrating on the human element, though not denying the divine constitution of the Church as Christ, Küng views the Church as the "People of God," the congregation of the faithful, or simply, the assembly, emphasizing the dual structure or nature of the Church. "Until the end of time the Church will remain at once a divine mystery and a human structure; one single mystery of light and shadow," he writes. This mysterious complementing of a vocation from Christ the Founder and the response of sinful mankind is the foundation for the perennial need for reform. Tracing briefly the history of the Church as one of many human societies, Küng points out the contributions both good and bad made by various cultures over the ages, Jewish, Greek, Roman, and Germanic. Because of these influences the Church has gradually narrowed into a European-American affair having little impact on the Negro, Oriental, and Polynesian cultures and people. Sinfulness of its individual human members and a "lack of any openness among the Church's leaders, at every level, towards new problems and insights, new forms and values; their narrowness, their procrastination," are the strongest arguments for our present need of reform in the Church. Reform is needed, the author claims, because the Church has become a victim of its own cultural and ideological isolation, its other-world attitudes and preoccupations.

The framework for Catholic renewal is outlined by Küng as involving four phases. "We can suffer": "It would be an equally odd sort of Christian who felt no guilt in himself for the failures and sins of the Church, who was not painfully aware that he is constantly revealing himself as an unreformed member of the Church to be reformed." We must suffer along with non-Roman Christians over all our faults, both Catholic and Protestant, as well as over the fact of schism. "We can pray," which in the concrete means praying not against each other in a sectarian spirit but for each other that God's will and not ours will be accomplished. "We can criticize," for "Criticism, indeed loud criticism, can be a duty." But Christian criticism, Küng emphasizes, must be based on love and therefore restrained, constructive, cooperative and committed to the Church. "We can act" through a personal reformation of our own lives and of the Church as a whole. Here the principles of Yves Congar call for "reform without schism," in which a priority is given to charity and pastoral considerations, remaining a member of the whole community, to having patience and yet avoiding delays, and finally to carrying out a real renewal based on sources and tradition without introducing innovations by way of merely mechanical adaptions. "Sentire in Ecclesia" is properly emphasized over the less accurate but much more commonly parroted "sentire cum Ecclesia." Hence, blind obedience is denounced as a distortion of virtue, and "loyal disobedience" is shown in certain cases to be valid and necessary.

The fourth section of this book deals with efforts at renewal in the Church. Here Küng traces the efforts at renewal and universalization seen in the contest between Peter and Paul over the "Jewish question," in the dynamism found by the early missionaries in the liturgy with its free form, in the foundation of new religious orders to meet new demands, in the translations of Scripture to meet the newly emerging vernaculars, in the practical questions dealt with by the first eight Councils, in the difficulties of the Fourth Lateran Council and the whole series of ineffectual Councils before and during the Renaissance. Then the Protestant conflict; on the Church's side "what was sadly lacking was clear-sightedness (it was not realized that abuses were to a great extent rooted in false structural accretions), self-critical humility, the moral energy and effective will to improve, interest in religious matters, and any effort to live according to the example of Christ. . . . Luther, on his side, for a variety of personal and psychological as well as theological, religious and historical reasons, was incapable of grasping the true form of Catholicism behind its deformity." In discussing Luther and the Protestant Reform, Küng shows that Luther's demands, at that time, were thought to be incompatible with Catholic principles, although many of the demands were truly Catholic, and also that "much of what he rejected as essential to the Catholic Church was in fact thoroughly uncatholic." Beyond this, Luther "took certain perfectly Catholic principles and in some cases formulated them so as to give the maximum risk of misunderstanding, disunity and sheer contradiction, and in others asserted them with a one-sided stress which was not only polemical but actually heretical."

Further lessons for true Christian renewal are then sought in a discussion of the Council of Trent and the defensive attitude (restoration rather than renewal) to which it gave rise under varying circumstances from 1555 down to the present.

The foundation for Christian reunion does not lie in passive appeals for a return to the unity of the Church, nor in individual conversions or simple "moral reform," but rather in putting into practice a basic Catholic principle which Catholics have often ignored and which the modern Protestants have rejected, *ecclesia reformanda.* The Protestants today, because they now style themselves as members of the "reformed Church," must recognize, as the Catholics have in the Second Vatican Council, their need for continual reformation. On the Catholic side, paralleling a new Protestant reformation, there are several positive steps that can be taken to meet the original demands of the Reformers: an appreciation of the *religious* motives underlying their work, a growing regard for Sacred Scriptures, the development of our liturgy into a liturgy truly of the people, and an understanding of the universal priesthood of the faithful in both theory and practice. Several other important steps are mentioned but not developed in detail: an increased adaptation of the Church to the demands of various national cultures (a trend away from Romanism and Europeanism), purification of the papacy from politics, the reform of the Curia, simplification of canon law, a growing understanding of tolerance and the role of individual conscience, suspension of clerical celibacy in certain cases to aid reunion, and interiorization of Christian devotional life.

A reform in Catholic Doctrine, seemingly in contradiction to what has been said thus far about Catholic practice, would appear impossible, for it would imply a deformation in the Christian revelation. Such deformations are possible, certainly, in the selection or misinterpretations of doctrines found in a heresy, but this deformation does not remain within the Church. And yet, while we cannot admit a reformation of the Christian revelation or dogma, it is possible and even necessary to have true reformations in Catholic theology: "What the Catholic Church does recognize in her dogma is the giving of new forms or more developed forms to a doctrine which has not in every respect achieved its complete form." Two factors must be recognized here: the historical development of doctrines and their explanations conditioned by many concrete circumstances, and the polemics of dogma, a factor which emphasizes the fact that most dogmas have been defined against the background of a controversy and, therefore, that these definitions to be seen in the true perspective must be viewed in the full context of revelation and tradition. Doctrine, like the Church, has an unchangeable divine element (revelation) and a changeable human element (the explanation in a particular age and milieu). Here the theologians may delay reunion by their mental blocks, emotional bias, and prejudice, by identifying dogma with the opinion of a particular school, or by making excessive demands for theological agreement and uniformity.

Another obstacle which must be faced in any true reform of the Church is that of possible distortions in popular piety, in the cult of the saints or Marian devotions. It is a very involved question, and Küng limits himself to some remarks on sinning by way of defect as well as by excess in the veneration of Mary and the saints.

But the chief obstacle to reunion, which must be tackled by the Council, is in the two different concepts of the Church (an evangelical community as opposed to a legalistic structure) and in the concrete organizational structure of the Church which results from this theoretical position. The primacy of Peter and of the pope, the continuity and validity of Apostolic succession, the priestly office, and the role of the laity all must be studied carefully. Guided by the example of John XXIII as a father rather than a supreme ruler, the Protestants must come to see the evangelical nature of the papacy and its continuity from Peter despite all the failures recorded by history.

The final section of this book deals with a critique of what we can expect from the Council in general, what topics might profitably come up for discussion and the trend or line these discussions might take, and lastly the impact the Council can have on reunion. The Council will either fulfill a great hope or end as a great disappointment. Reasons both for and against an optimistic outlook are discussed in detail: the objection that public opinion in the Church is insufficiently prepared either for the Council or for reunion; that even were our people prepared for reunion, the theologians would hinder it; that the unwieldy size of a Council today will render it ineffective; that the "Latin" or Italian mentality of most of the bishops is an insurmountable obstacle; and, finally, that while some Catholics may be interested in the Council and reform, the majority is not interested enough to make that spirit effective. Even accepting these problems in their worst light,

Küng maintains that the main question is "whether we Christians have set up too many hindrances to the spread of the Gospel and done too little that is positive. . . . Are our rectifications going to be too limited, our reforms too superficial, all our actions ultimately ineffectual?"

Concentrating on a few essentials, Küng feels the Council should avoid theological definitions and examine some fundamental problems. He feels the episcopal office must be re-examined and an increase of self-government allowed on all levels, implementing the principle of solidarity. Papal authority and infallibility must be seen in the light of a collegial as well as a hierarchical structure. Unity must be sought but not uniformity; hence, laws must be minimal and decentralization maximum. In discussing this in practical application, Küng explores the accomplishments of the German bishops in producing the "German catachism" and the leadership national or regional bishops can play in reforming the Mass and Breviary. Short but important mention is made of such matters as the necessity for dispensations from clerical celibacy, reforms in marriage laws, and the censorship of books where a warning might achieve more than an indexing. Special emphasis is laid on the necessity for the bishop to continue the process of decentralization begun by the concept of "collegiality" and subsidiarity.

R.T.F.

JOSEPH: THE MAN CLOSEST TO JESUS

Author: Francis L. Filas, S.J. (1915-)
Type of work: Josephology
First published: 1962

Principal Ideas Advanced

A Josephology has risen slowly, sporadically, but steadily within the Church, and scholarship has now reached the point where we understand this great saint more truly than ever before.

The marriage of Joseph to Mary was a genuine marriage, despite the fact that it was never consummated.

Joseph can be truly termed the father of Christ; however, this should be understood in the moral order rather than in the natural order.

In *Joseph: The Man Closest to Jesus,* Father Francis L. Filas has combined his four previous books on Joseph and has given them the unity of a single volume. The work brings up to date all previous scholarship on the husband of Mary and the (moral) father of Christ. It can be considered a complement to a Mariology, rather than an infringement on it, for its primary accomplishment is the recovery of Saint Joseph from obscurity.

The Jesuit theologian painstakingly sifts through the vast literature which has accumulated on this saint, dividing the topics in order to cover each in a comprehensive manner. The author begins by treating the various sources which have supplied us with the meager factual data concerning Saint Joseph. In bringing together and in evaluating this material, Filas creates a general picture of Joseph the man. Joseph's ancestry, trade, and the question of his age are all treated at length. Next covered are the perplexing problems surrounding Joseph's marriage. The many conflicting accounts of this event are discussed in detail. The possible claim to genuine fatherhood for Saint Joseph is then appraised and his saintly character is examined. This discussion is followed by a well-documented history of the devotion to Saint Joseph in both the Eastern and Western rites of the Church. Also presented in this volume of nearly 700 pages are the various indulgenced Saint Joseph prayers.

Throughout this work, the author documents his case as carefully as a lawyer presents his brief before the court. One is left with the impression which Saint Francis de Sales had; namely, that next to Mary, Saint Joseph was the most perfect human person.

The universal esteem now accorded Saint Joseph throughout the Church did not always prevail. Indeed, many conservatives once felt that Joseph should be minimized in order that Mary be extolled more greatly, but Mary has gained her indisputable place and there is no longer any need to avoid emphasizing Joseph. (It is interesting to note that not until the present decade was Saint Joseph's name even listed in the Mass, despite the presence there of the names of a number of minor saints.)

Although the Middle Ages might be said to have initiated the Joseph movement, it was mainly in the latter part of the nineteenth century that the star of Saint Joseph rose rapidly. It was prompted in the main by the popes, beginning with the reign of Pius IX (1792-1878).

If a date can be assigned, December 8, 1870, must be regarded as the one which marks the beginning of full recognition being given to the place of Saint Joseph. It was on that day that Pius IX declared Joseph "Patron of the Universal Church." Other popes have increasingly stressed the accelerating Josephology movement. Leo XIII (1810-1903) emphasized devotion to the Holy Family and explicitly indicated that the sources of Joseph's greatness lay in his dual role as virginal husband to Mary and as virginal father to Jesus. Benedict XV (1854-1922) declared Joseph the "Patron of Workingmen," and Pius XII (1876-1958) instituted the feast of "St. Joseph the Worker." John XXIII (1881-1963) ordered the saint's name to be placed in the Canon of the Mass. (The personal efforts of Father Filas contributed to this last recognition in no small measure.)

Throughout the history of the Church, many pious though fictional legends have been propagated by well-intentioned devotees of this great saint. The Jesuit theologian clears the air of all such myths, carefully analyzing and weighing the evidence, proving once again that truth is more compelling, meaningful, beautiful, and inspiring than fantasy.

The Gospels tell us relatively little

about St. Joseph. Filas summarizes the remarks they contain: " (a) Joseph the carpenter is the husband of Mary, who is the virgin mother of Jesus; (b) Joseph is publicly thought to be the natural father of Jesus; (c) Joseph exercises the office and holds the rights of father of Jesus; (d) Joseph is explicitly singled out as a just man—a biblical expression that indicates he was adorned with virtue." However, a careful examination of the given data reveals many conclusions implicitly contained therein. It is in this latter capacity that Filas shows us a theologian at work, digging away at the material, disclosing, compiling, and evaluating the diverse views of various scholars.

Numerous apocrypha such as the *Protoevangel of James* (c. 130), the *Gospel of Thomas* (c. 200) and the *History of Joseph the Carpenter* (c. 350-500) tell us considerably more about this saint than do the Gospel doctrines. Unfortunately, the apocrypha are largely responsible for the numerous fictional stories which have persisted over the years. This makes it difficult to separate fact from fiction. Often these latter writings picture Joseph as an old man when betrothed to Mary. Yet, the author points out, Joseph was only about sixteen years old at the time of his betrothal. Some portray Joseph as a widower and the father of other children by a previous marriage. Again, this theory does not agree with the evidence, and Filas traces the error to its faulty textual foundations.

In general, the Byzantine Church tended to value the apocryphal writings more highly than did the Western Church. It is understandable, then, that greater exaggerations and more numerous inaccuracies would be claimed in respect to Joseph by the former Church than by the latter. Although the Eastern Rite Church has often honored Joseph (even earlier and more consistently than has the Western Rite Church), Father Filas writes that in the Eastern Rite Church Joseph "received liturgical honors only by reason of his service to Jesus and Mary, never independently."

It has always proved difficult to walk the thin line between exaggerated claims and overly cautious views on Joseph. Each position has certain arguments in its favor. Those representing the conservative view of Joseph's greatness can point to the several facts which apparently support their case. One such fact is that the Bible tells us almost nothing about Joseph in any explicit way. Another fact is that for the first thousand years of the Church, there was no real movement detected for a Joseph theology. Many theologians even denied that a genuine marriage ever existed between Joseph and Mary, basing their opinion of the view that the marriage was never consummated. On the other hand, some went so far as to hold the marriage was actually consummated after the Virgin Birth.

Yet the facts are such that the Church has never denied devotion to Joseph, even though it has not always held him in the esteem of our present day.

Those who exaggerated Joseph's position sometimes went so far as to claim for him an immaculate conception, no less than that enjoyed by the Blessed Virgin Mary. In a work which has been placed on the Index, one devotee even asserted that Joseph was the divine father of Christ, in the proper sense of the term "father."

Father Filas gives the reader a sense of perspective by placing truth in the middle of both extremes. It would be rash to presume that Joseph was immaculately conceived, for the entire weight of tradition is against it. Nonetheless, in the author's view, it appears probable that Joseph never sinned. Such a sinless life would have had to be conferred by a special privilege of God, however.

Although we do not know the date of Joseph's death, it is Father Filas's opinion that Joseph died shortly before Christ's own death on the cross and that with the Resurrection of Christ, Joseph himself was assumed into Heaven, body and soul.

In our churches today we notice that most statues or pictures of Saint Joseph portray him with a lily. The symbolism of this lily is traced by Father Filas to the reported miracle of a flower or a dove coming forth out of Joseph's rod, when he was chosen to be Mary's husband. The author rejects claims for the authenticity of the miracle, showing that this symbolism goes back even further to the Biblical passage which speaks of the "flowering of the rod of Jesse." The passage refers to a prediction for the good things to come from such a lineage. Hence, it is important in assessing Joseph on the basis of Scripture, Father Filas writes, that we understand the mentality and the mode of writing employed by the writers of Revelation. A proper understanding will obviate many of the errors which have been propagated unwittingly by over-zealous literal-minded people.

G.F.K.

THE CHURCH

Author: Giovanni Battista Cardinal Montini (Later Pope Paul VI; born 1897)
Type of work: Ecclesiology
First published: 1962

Principal Ideas Advanced

The Church is ultimately a mystery.

The Church continues Christ's mission of salvation for mankind.

We must distinguish between the Church as a divine institution and the Church as a community of men; the former is perfect, the latter is not.

The Church is a distinct society, perfect, independent, juridically autonomous, free.

An ecumenical council is a reflective act concerning the nature of the Church.

The Church is a compilation of lectures and pastoral letters delivered by Cardinal Montini between 1957 and 1962 on the nature of the Church and the place of ecumenical councils in its life. Part One consists of six chapters on various aspects of ecclesiology, such as "the mission of the Church" and "the papacy and unity in the Church." Part Two consists of four chapters on the place of ecumenical councils in the Church. These lectures and letters are scholarly compositions based principally on Scripture and recent papal documents.

According to Cardinal Montini, the Church is essentially the continuation of Christ in history, the meeting-point in time between God and man. It is the way to the Father, the community through which each one of us receives His gifts of love. For God has willed that we live and love in a holy community rather than worship Him and achieve salvation individually. The essential aspects of the Church are historical, mystical, and hierarchical. It was founded in time and has grown in history; it is a mystery whose Head is still Christ, the God-man who has no successors, only visible representatives; and in this Church "there is a hierarchy commissioned to teach, direct and distribute the sacraments, that is, the means of grace."

It is in the parish that we come in contact with the Church itself, the cardinal writes: "And as the great Church, so the parish must be a community of persons, a family that bears witness to and foreshadows the heavenly community of the blessed." In the parish all must love one another, all must pray together, all must participate actively in the public worship of the parish.

The mission of the Church is the continuation and extension of Christ. This involves a two-fold aspect: "First, we find identity, preservation, consistency, communion of life, loyalty, presence—that is, the Church as it is symbolized by the stability of a rock. Second, we find movement, communication, projection in time and space, expansion, dynamism, eschatological hope—this is the Church as it is symbolized by the moving, living and growing body of Christ."

The Church's mission originated with Christ, who passed to His Church a mandate to preserve the Truth and to teach it to all peoples. "The Church's mission is essentially religious. . . . [It] consists in extending Christ's life throughout the world and in helping mankind to participate in his mysteries, the incarnation and redemption." Laymen, too, have an apostolic vocation, writes the cardinal, for the truth and faith engender a responsibility in those who possess it. Their first task is to offer the world a Christian experience that is "admirable, attractive and agreeable," and to love those whom they intend to evangelize.

Christ suffered and died to redeem all mankind. For the Catholic, then, no one ought to be alienated. The Church adapts itself to the thought, culture, customs, and languages of different ages and peoples, but Cardinal Montini adds that it is "impossible for the Church to deny or minimize the truth in order to accommodate itself to various segments of dissident Christians, for the truth is an inviolable deposit entrusted to the Church to be safeguarded and propagated. . . . Truth is the Church's charity in its highest and most indispensable form." The Church loves the alienated, as Christ loves all mankind, and in its love presents to them the truth.

Unity, says Cardinal Montini, is "the essential and most distinctive mark" of Christ's Church, and the papacy is necessary for achieving unity in the Church. It is easy to see the need of the papacy for visible unity, but even more fundamental is unity in the philosophical and theological sense: "Unity is interchangeable with being." Hence, God, who is infinite being, is eminently One. This profound unity fulfills itself in Christ and tends to its ultimate living reality in the future life. It expresses itself in the Church, the continuation of Christ, and "our belonging to this unity should be our joy, our pride, our strength." As Christ's vicar on earth, the pope sums up in his person the full powers of the whole Church. Thus, the author concludes, "there can be no true religious unity without the Church, and no true Church without the papacy."

Cardinal Montini began his discourse at a mission at Florence on "The Church Our Mother" by asserting that "we must understand the Church anew." In this lengthy discussion he first explained what the Church is not. There are corrupt aspects—persons and abuses—in the Church, but these fail to define the "Church's true and total reality." These human deficiencies are to be deplored, but they pertain to man and not to the Church as such. Nor is the Church an ancient, conservative institution. It lives on the past, but it reaches into the future. It is, indeed, "eternally faithful and eternally youthful." Nor does the Church teach an aprioristic, incomprehensible, indisputable, rigid doctrine, for its dogmas are living truths that continue to unfold through its history.

The Church is a mystery, a truth of faith, writes the cardinal; it "is a mystery because it is a divine thought." It is also visible, human, the *congregatio fidelium*. It is given various names in Scripture: the Mystical Body of Christ, the Kingdom of God, the City of God, the communion of saints, Christ's bride, Christ's Body. It is also referred to as Christ's sheepfold, Peter's boat, God's people, and mother. All these are appropriate names of endearment.

Ecumenical councils play decisive roles in the life of the Church. An ecumenical council is "a solemn assembly of the bishops of the whole world, which the Roman pontiff convenes for the purpose of deliberating together, under his authority and presidency, about religious problems that concern the whole of christendom. The council therefore is the supreme form of the Church's magisterium and government."

A council can be considered a reflective act on the nature of the Church, Cardinal Montini suggests. Councils bring into plain view the Church's social, visible, organized, hierarchical aspect; a council mobilizes the whole Church to its full stature, "its total capacity for prayer, doctrine, government, inner reform, missionary tension, eschatological hope." Councils can be looked on as great poles on which are strung the cable of the Church's history; they are concerned with the ever-present problem of reform, for reform must never end. But it must be remembered that no council accomplishes reforms miraculously; reform depends on the hierarchy and the faithful carrying out decrees formulated by a council. Finally, councils relate themselves and the Church to the world and to those alienated from the Church.

The lectures and pastoral letters comprising this book offer profound speculation on the nature of the Church, "the central question around which revolves not only the study of modern theology but the religious spirit of our generation." Certain ideas and phrases are repeated because these chapters were originally lectures and letters delivered on various occasions, and no attempt has been made to change the original texts.

T.P.N.

BELIEF AND FAITH

Author: Josef Pieper (1904-)
Type of work: Philosophy of Christian faith
First published: 1962

Principal Ideas Advanced

Although belief presupposes knowledge, it must be sharply distinguished from the latter with respect to its grounds for assent.

The assent required of belief must be made freely, whether or not the belief concerns the natural or supernatural.

Belief is always rooted in the testimony of a person, and it is intimately connected with love; it may be defined broadly as "the acceptance of something as true on the testimony of another."

Unlike opinion, belief requires an unreserved commitment to the truth of the object of belief.

Josef Pieper's *Belief and Faith* is a restatement, a clarification, and a further development of Saint Thomas Aquinas's views on the nature of belief, its object, and the intellectual-volitional operations which produce it. In this work, as in many of his other numerous philosophical and theological tracts, the author demonstrates the viability of Thomism by applying the Angelic Doctor's insights on faith to the contemporary scene. Pieper in extremely careful to distinguish faith in its strict usage from its more liberal meaning as employed in everyday language. For instance, Pieper would not accept as faith the presumption by the owner of a lost dog that the dog will return by nightfall.

Once the working definition of faith or belief as the "regarding of something as true on the testimony of someone else" has been established, it makes little difference which actual word is used to express this. In German, the word is *Glaube* (and it appears in the original title of the work, namely, *Über den Glauben*); in Latin, the word is *fides,* and it commonly appears in Saint Thomas's writings.

Pieper, who is a professor at the University of Münster, treats first of the general nature of belief, and he then proceeds to examine its particular manifestations in the natural and supernatural orders. He hurriedly examines the principal ideas on belief as expressed in the writings of the early Church Father Saint Augustine, the German philosopher Immanuel Kant

(1724-1804), the English convert John Henry Newman, the American pragmatist William James (1842-1910), the Danish religious existentialist Søren Kierkegaard (1813-1835), the Jewish theologian Martin Buber, the contemporary philosopher, Karl Jaspers, and a leading Catholic theologian, Karl Rahner.

Despite vast differences among these men on other topics, there is a surprising agreement of some basic points when it comes to examining the positions they hold as to the distinguishing features of faith. For example, all stress the firm and unconditional quality of the assent in belief; all affirm the superiority of will over intellect in matters of belief; and lastly, all acclaim the practical importance of belief in everyday life.

In attempting to assuage the similarities and differences between faith and knowledge, Pieper seizes upon common experience and makes a number of interesting observations. One such insight is that despite the clarity found in an assent based upon knowledge, as contrasted to the opaqueness revealed by an assent based on faith, the latter never reveals any diminished rigor of assent that might differentiate it from the former. Indeed, the reverse is nearly always the case, for between knowledge and ignorance is the middle ground of opinion which commands a half-hearted assent at best. Not so with faith, which brooks no traffic with a middle ground. A half-hearted act of faith is self-contradictory, for belief is always an all-or-nothing affair. Because of this absolute quality of faith one must guard against the concomitant danger of fanaticism.

At this juncture Pieper states that the inquiry must be made as to why one person believes something to which another refuses to give his assent. One can further ask how it is possible for one only to *believe* that which another *knows*. In such a comparison the secondary character of belief is much in evidence. In order to possess faith or belief, Pieper writes, the believer must first acquire some knowledge of the object. It is simply impossible to believe that which we do not know in some way, even though only by weak analogy. For example, unless we can know God in some way, as through His works of nature, we cannot possibly believe in Him. Yet whenever cognition becomes fully enriched and entirely intelligible, faith is dispelled and no longer necessary. In such a situation, the believer has been transformed into a knower. One can know without having faith, then, but one can never believe without knowing in some measure.

Paradoxically, though, Pieper writes, while faith presupposes knowledge, the acquisition of knowledge often requires an act of belief as its complement, for in order to learn, belief in the teacher is a *conditio sine qua non.* Further, belief in oneself is necessary. Belief, then, does not blind us, as has been frequently charged; instead it serves to open up the mind to new possibilities. Faith permits us to be certain of many things which would otherwise escape us because of their inaccessibility. To believe, then, is not to know, and to know is not to believe.

Yet there is still another sense, Pieper continues, in which to believe *is* to know, but to know in a special way. Just as knowing implies a union between the knower and the object known, so belief involves a similar (but not identically the same) union. In fact, it requires a communion between the believer and the knower whose testimony the believer accepts. Once this testimony is accepted, the believer becomes one with the knower and grasps the truth through the medium of the knower.

In discussing the assent which is made in knowing and that which is made in believing, Pieper essentially follows the Thomistic approach. In knowing, we give our intellectual assent to the truth of the object because it is seen or understood by us. Put differently, we assent because we are "forced" to do so, being dominated by the clarity of the object. In such a situation the will exerts little bearing on the assent, for "we see what we see, and we know what we know." But the case is immeasurably different in matters of belief. Here the truth of the object is not sufficiently clear to command the submission of our intellect to it. The object's translucency escapes us. Since the object of faith is opaque at best, our interest is drawn to the good rather than to the true, although these in no sense oppose each other. This opaqueness of the object is due more to the fault of our intellect, however, than to the object itself. It is this fault that renders impossible the intellect's capacity to be proportioned to the object. Only if the latter case prevailed, would the intellect be required to give its assent. In a state of disproportion between intellect and object, the object can never compel us to accept it. If we are to accept it, there is an absolute necessity for what the American psychologist and philosopher William James called a "will to believe."

Speaking analogously, then, faith is an act which involves greater freedom than does knowledge. Yet freedom is not to be confused with a sheer arbitrariness. One might describe faith as an intellectual act, but only insofar as it is moved by the will (rather than by the object) to make the assent. If one speaks of supernatural faith, one would have to add that there must be an inward movement of grace disposing these powers for their respective operations.

In one of the most interesting sections of the book, Pieper raises the question as to whether there is a difference between believing in what a person says and believing in the person. The author indicates his answer by siding with the views of the French Catholic existentialist Gabriel Marcel. Although these views may be rooted in Thomism, they have lacked subsequent development. Still, in principle at least, the answers given by Saint Thomas, Marcel, and Pieper are the same. In order to believe *that* a thing is so, we must believe *in* the one communicating this information. That *one* must always be a person; hence, genuine faith can have reference only to persons revealing something they know. Faith necessarily involves interpersonal relationships. For instance, the student believes *what* the professor says, only if that professor is trustworthy as a person. This is why we can believe what God reveals, for He above all others, exhibits personality and supreme trustworthiness.

Since faith intimately involves intellect, will, and the whole person, writes Pieper, it is only natural that faith should be related to love as well. It is love for the person of the witness that makes faith possible.

Faith, of course, does not eliminate

doubts or uncertainties, but these have no bearing on the commitment that the faithful person makes in his act of belief. This is manifested particularly in the faith which is observed between two lovers, for it is a faith which is virtually unshakable.

Pieper contends in conclusion that a phenomenological analysis reveals a connection between faith, hope, and love. To consider any one of the three in total isolation from the others is to miss an essential aspect of the truth.

G.F.K.

ZEN CATHOLICISM

Author: Dom Aelred Graham, O.S.B. (1907-)
Type of work: Catholic appraisal of Buddhism
First published: 1963

Principal Ideas Advanced

Catholicism needs to become more existential, contemporary, ecumenical, and open-minded.

The insights of the tradition of Zen Buddhism can provide a fount of great wealth for Catholics, for both possess a common spirit of meditation and selflessness.

Catholics must once again seek a total Christian wisdom, making their faith a genuine and living commitment instead of reducing it to an artificial intellectualization.

Dom Aelred Graham's *Zen Catholicism* is one of the most important of the many books this Benedictine monk has written. It is in accord with the ecumenical spirit in that it calls attention to the need for Catholicism to broaden its perspectives in practice, if not in theory. Dom Graham, who alternately gives the impression of being a liberal and a conservative, reveals in this work the necessity for appropriating truth wherever it may be found. *Zen Catholicism* has set an excellent example in this respect, synthesizing as it does insights on the meaning of life given by contemporary philosophers (Ludwig Wittgenstein, 1889-1951), by medieval theologians (Saint Thomas Aquinas and Saint Augustine) and by Oriental pagan thinkers (Gautama Buddha, c. 560- c. 480 B.C.).

This is not to imply that Dom Graham is guilty of pure syncretism or eclecticism; rather does it indicate his quest for a Christian world view. In this respect the book definitely bears the stamp of an Augustinian spirit. Although a definite intellectual, the author decries the aridity of a pure intellectualism. He appeals more to love than to syllogistic knowledge as the principal characteristic and pervading spirit of Christianity. Yet this existential love paradoxically produces a knowledge gained by connaturality.

Graham makes an eloquent plea for

a return to simplicity as the clarion call of a dynamic Catholicism. He cites the dictum of Saint Augustine, "Love God, and do as you please," as one perennially valid guideline for such simplicity. What this means is clearly spelled out. It implies a de-emphasis on legalism in morality, the situation having gotten so out of hand as to mislead people into accepting the two as synonymous. Without taking away from the *magisterium* of the Church, Graham insists that greater stress be laid on personal conscience as a base for moral action.

Coupled with this appeal for a return to simplicity is the call to casualness in the Christian. It is not a casualness of indifference which Graham advocates, but a casualness recommended by the Gospels in bidding us "not to be anxious." Writing from the long tradition of the Benedictines, Graham's work shows particular authenticity here, for his religious order is capable of a perspective which more militant and more newly founded orders do not possess. As an antidote to the intensive seriousness of our age, Graham advises us on the importance of *not* being earnest.

The author ranges freely over a wide variety of topics in this delightful and ecumenical book. Among these are providence, sex, the ego, suffering, spirituality, anti-clericalism, morality, linguistic analysis, and enlightenment. But by far the most important subject treated is Zen Buddhism. Graham argues his case well that an appreciation of Zen should be most natural in Catholic circles, for the word "Zen" means meditation. The term "Buddha" need not alarm Catholics either, for it merely refers to one who is enlightened. There is no reason other than custom why we should not call Christ the Buddha of them all. Since any one seeking enlightenment is in search of "Buddha," he may be termed a minor buddha in his own right.

Graham never permits his enthusiasm for the existential element in Zen Buddhism to blind him to certain of the latter's faults. He roundly condemns the lack of an ethical system in Buddhism, a flaw which can lead its disciples down the path of excessive individualism. He also berates those who seek Buddhism as a pure naturalism to the detriment of a search for values. But it is not only with respect to Buddhism that he dons the role of a critic. He plays the part equally well in his appraisal of certain human shortcomings in the Church. In this, he reminds the reader of the Danish religious thinker Søren Kierkegaard (1813-1855).

Graham severely criticizes that version of Christianity which tends to become institutionalized and ossified. These tendences, against which we must always be on our guard, reduce the Church to an entity of pure externals, never realizing it as a living organism, as the Mystical Body of Christ.

In trying to correct the erroneous impressions many have with respect to Zen Buddhism, Graham labors at great length to point out that Zen is neither pantheistic nor philosophical. Rather, Zen should be seen as a "pure experience," as a freeing of the self for meditation. Hence, to want to debate Zen is already to assume a position which commences from a misunderstanding of it. Although Zen can be described in an infinite number of ways, quite simply one could characterize it as "unself consciousness."

In explaining this interpretation of Zen Buddhism, the author provides convincing evidence that because of certain habits of thinking, perhaps determined in part by occidental language patterns, we find it difficult to grasp reality in its fundamental meaning. Zen (meditation) helps us to transcend this barrier of language-thought patterns by releasing us from preconceptions. Thus, Zen contains both negative and positive features.

Making this more concrete, Graham introduces the logical distinction between seeing oneself as an "I" and as a "me." The "I" constitutes the subject and is the true self. On the other hand, the "me" is the conscious ego and might be termed the "I" viewed inauthentically as object. Thus, the "me" tends to get in the way of grasping reality and the true self, for it interposes itself between the "I" and the world of deepest reality. Existentially, it should be clear that my authenticity is constituted primarily by the fact that I am a subject, rather than an object. In these and other clarifications, the emphasis on personalism over individualism is unmistakable.

In the days of the early Fathers of the Church, the West and the East confronted each other more often and more naturally than is the case today. Thus, in Graham's encounter between East and West, we can expect to see the attitudes revealed by the early patricians, rather than those shown by the nineteenth century apologetes. Graham is not moving backward in his ecumenical effort, for he is addressing the contemporary world in asking for a Church renewal stemming from a common base.

On more than one occasion, Graham uses Zen as a convenient subject from which he can launch into a discussion of problems and tensions existing within contemporary Catholicism. His attitude betrays a Zen paradox, combining, as it does, charity with provocation. He comes to grips with some controversial themes currently being discussed by Church conservatives and liberals. Relative to the conservative's concern that the average Catholic may be scandalized by new interpretations and mature reflective thought within the Church, he writes, "We fear to scandalize the simple people, the ordinary folk; yet is it a less offense to scandalize the educated and thoughtful, who are equally God's children?"

Paving the way for overcoming what is termed a "lifeless, routine, unchallenging presentation of the Faith," Dom Graham probes deeply and, for some, quite painfully. Like Socrates, he gives no easy answers. Rather, he makes the demand that *we* do the thinking, and he insists that responsibility belongs to the person. He excoriates those who have never had one honest thought they can call their own. He is merciless with others who refuse to digest what they have learned. He labels as "man-eating Thomists," those who *uncritically* accept the writings of Saint Thomas, word for word and example for example. It is clear that such a mentality is more at ease debating than in understanding.

Graham urges theologians and philosophers within the Church to employ historical and linguistic criticism in interpreting doctrines and views held by spokesmen in years gone by. Without drawing explicit conclusions himself, he asks that many dicta which have previously been considered sacrosanct, be re-examined in the light of the cultural and intellectual milieu in which they were formulated. He warns us that habits of thought carried on over centuries may not necessarily reflect truth as immutable law. He also hints strongly that rationalistic and legalistic elements have been gnawing steadily at what is natural in natural law.

Graham's forte lies in asking meaningful questions to which convincing answers have not always been given. He suggests that possibly the "anti-feminism" of Saint Paul, the early "Manicheanism" of Saint Augustine, and the "Aristotelian teleology" of Saint Thomas have colored theologians' approaches used in solving problems. The appeal to acceptance of common principles in the solution of a problem at most begs the question, for what is needed is an understanding of the key terms used.

Although the book is a lucid explanation of Zen Buddhism and a probing inquiry into contemporary Catholicism, it makes yet another valuable contribution. The 228 pages of this work are dotted by countless gems of wisdom, each providing a source for rich meditation. Typical of these is the following: "A little of what you fancy does you good. Nature regenerated by grace does not cease to be nature; it still calls for fulfillment rather than frustration; therefore it should be moderately indulged. To deny nature its due is apt to make the individual more, rather than less, egoistic." In another passage, the wisdom of this Benedictine also shows through: "When closely examined, there is a salutary fatalism about the Catholic doctrine of grace and free will, which it is helpful rather than otherwise to keep in mind. The depressing thing would be if we really were, in any ultimate sense, masters of our fate and captains of our soul." Again, "There is more to be said than is often allowed for trusting one's instincts; they can on occasion prove a safer guide to appropriate action than the careful calculations of reason."

Occasionally one detects a tincture of mysticism in Dom Graham's work. He stresses that in many ways God is beyond good and evil, understood by the ethical categories of human experience. He insists that any positive theology be offset by a negative theology which possesses the truth more deeply than the former. Many of his ideas bear a strong affinity with the views of Oriental mystics such as Lao-Tzu (c.604-c.531 B.C.) and also with the views of mystics within the Christian tradition. He quotes Dionysius the Pseudo-Areopagite, Saint Teresa of Avila, and Saint John of the Cross. Nevertheless, the total picture sees Graham upholding the well balanced views of Aquinas.

Three supplementary discussions and a postscript at the back of the book seem somewhat out of place, but no one who reads these would want them omitted. The first discussion is concerned with Yoga. A brief description of it and its importance to Zen Buddhism is given, followed by the relationship of the two to Catholicism.

The second discussion is on monasticism, a topic on which Graham is knowledgeable from experience as well as inquiry. He shows the parallel between monastics in Zen and those within the Church. He singles out the inauthenticity of certain misconceptions of monasticism and highlights its preoccupation with love over austerity.

The third discussion, on Saint

Thomas, is particularly interesting and provocative. Despite, or perhaps because of, a thorough aquaintance with Thomism, Dom Graham writes that "St. Thomas's mind moves at the same level of thought as the metaphysical tradition culminating in Zen Buddism." The Benedictine deomonstrates a remarkable ability to discover and assimilate what is living in a man's thought. He offers sage advice on the teaching of Thomism and distinguishes sharply its spirit from its letter. Here, as throughout the book, one theme predominates: the letter killeth, but the spirit giveth life.

The final section of the book presents a critique of the American philosopher Walter Kaufmann. On this single occasion, Dom Graham is positively scathing in his criticism of Kaufmann's views. The Benedictine spares no effort in taking to task the principal themes of Kaufmann as expressed in the latter's *The Faith of a Heretic* (1961).

Summing up, Graham's book is a combination of scattered themes, somehow all drawn together into a delightfully intelligible whole. The central theme appears to be a reminder of the necessity for taking the riches of every man's thought so that we may be able to practice a more meaningful and dynamic religious life.

G.F.K.

THE MILLENNIUM OF EUROPE

Author: Oscar Halecki (1891-)
Type of work: Philosophy of history
First published: 1963

Principal Ideas Advanced

The most important part of Europe's heritage is the Christian.

Any real progress depends on the observance of divine commandments or moral laws.

One of the tragedies of history is that Western Europe has never been sufficiently interested in Eastern Europe.

From living together for centuries, humanism has become more Christian and Christianity more human than ever before.

Lasting peace is possible only when Christian principles are applied to public life.

Oscar Halecki taught medieval history and wrote extensively on this period for forty years. Since World War II he has turned his attention to the larger sweeps of history, writing such works as *The Limits and Divisions of European History* (1950) and *Borderlands of Western Civilization* (1952). In *The Millennium of Europe* his philosophy of history reaches its completion. This work deals with the last thousand years of European history, but from its study the author draws a number of "laws" which constitute a Christian view of history as it works out God's plan through human agents.

In this work Professor Halecki proposed to re-examine the last millennium of European history in an attempt "to discover the meaning of European history for the Europeans themselves and for mankind as well." His attempt, he writes in the preface, is to provide a "Christian interpretation of history" considering the "development of mankind from the point of view . . . of moral laws or rather divine commandments on whose observance any real progress depends."

"Millennium" can be used in three different senses. First, it can commemorate an event which occurred a thousand years before. Second, it can refer to the intervening thousand years. Third, it can mean a philosophical and symbolic view of the number "1,000," which prompts the human mind to find a solution to the present crisis and direct the beginnings of the next millennium of human history. The author develops all three senses of the word. An introductory section sketches out the first millennium of Christianity. The main body of the work studies the sweep and significance of events in the second millennium, and a three-chapter epilogue analyzes the present as the beginning of the third.

At the beginning of the first millennium of European history the Mediterranean was the center of civilization. At the end of this millennium and the beginning of the next the center of European culture had moved northward. As it encompassed Germanic and Slavic peoples it became more diversified in nationality, speech, and culture. The Roman Empire was replaced by a large number of big and little independent states. By the end of the second millennium of European history the Atlantic has replaced the Mediterranean as the center of European civilization, and America is related to Europe as the New Testament is to the Old.

Throughout his discussion of the millennium of Europe the author insists on the continuity of history, on the past living into the present and into the future. Thus, he argues, it is impossible for America to deny its European past, for this is the heritage which it has adapted to its own environment.

Viewed from the standpoint of Europe's millennium of history, Professor Halecki writes, the eleventh, twelfth and thirteenth centuries are the only ones to which the designation "medieval" can properly be applied. The preceding and succeeding centuries are more properly transitional.

In the main part of this study the author touches on the principal crises in Europe's last thousand years of history: the Reformation, colonial expansion, the defense against the Turks, the constant struggle for freedom from tyranny, industrial and political revolutions, imperialism, and international wars. The most distinctive feature of this survey is the inclusion of and stress on Eastern Europe as an integral part of the story.

The survey of European history from 962 (when Otto was crowned Holy Roman Emperor) and 966 (when the king and people of Poland were converted) to the 1960's takes us to "The Threshold of the Next Millennium" and the pressing task of solving the crisis of civilization. The author points out "interesting analogies" between the end of the tenth and twentieth centuries. There was fear both times that history was about to end cataclysmically, and efforts were made toward integrating the European community. Turning to the present crisis, Professor Halecki insists that it is necessary for Europeans to have more than economic and political integration to be lastingly successful in their drive toward integration. Europeans must also develop their common cultural heritage. Halecki writes: "Such prospects of a progressive unification of Europe, covering all the various spheres of human life, are today unquestionable, stimulating possibilities which, in contrast to equally justified fears, cause Europe's millennium to approach its end not without hopes for a better future."

Requisite conditions of stable European integration are (1) a greater interest of Western Europe in its Eastern counterpart, (2) closer co-operation between the old Europe and the new Europe across the Atlantic, and (3) "the full development of the most important part of Europe's heritage, the Christian." The last chapters spell out the author's thinking on these conditions. He shows how Europe and America have a common heritage to preserve: the love of freedom under God with due respect for each human person. Any Atlantic Community must be built on these ideas, he claims, and it must take the political shape of a federalism that respects local differences while providing organization to achieve common goals.

Such organization of the Atlantic Community, the author holds, must rest on the twin pillars of Christianity and Graeco-Roman humanism. He believes that after long association humanism has become more Christian and Christianity has become more humanistic. The result is a move toward a new Christian humanism on which the hope of the future rests. Christian principles must be applied to public as well as private life in "a new effort to create an international society or community, respecting the traditions and the self-government of all its members and using their heritage for establishing a lasting peace, the only condition being that religion can freely develop." This, the author argues, is not an unrealizable utopia, for there is an evident rebirth and renewal of Christianity today: "It is highly significant that Europe's millennium is ending, not with attempts to create a Christian empire as took place in 962, but with the gathering, in 1962, of an ecumenical council of the Catholic Church."

The Millennium of Europe is a philosophy of history which holds that true progress is not in material and technological advances, valuable as these can be, but rather in conforming social and political institutions to divine law and thus achieving the greatest possible measure of human freedom and peace.

T.P.N.

PACEM IN TERRIS

Author: Pope John XXIII (Angelo Giuseppe Roncalli, 1881-1963)
Type of work: Social thought
First published: 1963

Principal Ideas Advanced

Peace demands order; there must first of all be order among individuals themselves because of human dignity.

There must also be orderly relations between individuals and public authorities, both because the dignity of man demands this kind of order and because the social authority of human communities comes ultimately from God.

Order demands a reciprocity of rights and duties among states.

Because of the advance of science there must be an orderly relationship between sovereign nations.

Peace depends upon an order which is founded on truth, built according to justice, integrated by charity, and put into practice in freedom.

Pope John XXIII addresses the encyclical letter *Pacem in terris* to all men of good will, and he observes that the peace all men seek can be established only if the divine order is sincerely observed.

Optimistic in tone from the first word until the last, the encyclical lays down principles which, if followed, will release man from his shackles of despair and raise him to the highest reaches of his hopes, hopes placed in the eternal destinies that belong to him.

Pope John clearly indicates that he is not merely repeating the social doctrines of his predecessors but is recommending a new course—one based on order. This new social order will be a true second spring, a rejuvenation of the affairs of the human race. And in the spirit of modern existentialism, he boldly confronts the world with modern problems in every field of endeavor: politics, culture, economics, and ecclesiastical affairs.

Nor will these problems be solved, the pope avers, unless they be discussed in an "order founded on truth, built according to justice, vivified and integrated by charity, and put into practice in freedom." Note that in this summation of his encyclical Pope John emphasizes the necessity of freedom.

The pope's discussion begins with some cogent remarks concerning the rights of man. These rights are means by which man can attain his ends; thus, they are inviolable as well as fundamental. Man's basic rights are the rights to life, liberty, and the pursuit of happiness. These rights are based not only on Scripture but also on the natural law. The pope addresses his encyclical to "all men of good will," none excepted. Time and again he makes references to the natural law, natural rights, or the nature of the law. Man's rights do not depend on the state or on the whims of leaders. They depend on the Creator of man and his nature. Thus, in the first part of the letter Pope John lists the fundamental rights that must be afforded every man if a true and lasting peace is to be attained. They are explicitly stated: "The right to life, to bodily integrity, and to the means which are necessary and suitable for the proper development of life"; namely, food, clothing, shelter, and social services. To these subsistent rights, he adds cultural, conjugal, economic, and political rights.

Lest one think too selfishly, Pope John immediately warns that man has many duties corresponding to these rights. Since the pope is writing in an existential situation, he obviously feels that it is not enough for him merely to indicate the problem; he must spell it out, and he does. Men are not merely to acknowledge the concepts of rights and duties, but they are also to face the facts of the world's situation. It is easy to acknowledge that there is starvation in India but mere acknowledgment does not help the starving child in Bombay. Each man owes it to society to admit his personal obligations in this regard.

Man's rights and duties are based on the dignity of the human person and on the Incarnation of the Son of God, who died for each and every man. At this point in the letter the pope sets forth his notion of "freedom" for man. Man is not to be ordered and coerced by fear into following the law. A society based on force alone is inhuman; the good society is based on truth, justice, charity, and freedom. Human society is realized in freedom because freedom is the basic fundamental principle of the political order. Indeed, the deepest cry of human society for the realization of its hopes arises from the specific quality of freedom. In these days, the pope insists, no program can hope to succeed unless it admits the sublime dignity of man, for man is a creature of an infinite God who has granted him the specific dignity of true freedom. Because of this natural dignity, all men are equal. "Hence," the pope contends, "racial discrimination can in no way be justified. . . ."

Pope John also reviews the origin of authority. Society cannot survive without authority, but legitimate authority must be capable of causing a true sense of obligation in man, and only God, ultimately, can cause this sense of obligation to exist. One of the deepest human traits is freedom, the pope writes, and the state has no right to employ nonhuman means for directing man. The state receives its authority from God. Only in this framework of God-given authority will man come to realize that these obligations to God and to the state truly ennoble him. Obedience to the law is true liberty, but it must always be related to God. If this is understood, man will live in true dignity, and the leaders he himself elects will have legitimate authority from the same source as man's own dignity.

One of the blessings of man is that he is social and, consequently, has rights and duties in the social field. One of the duties of each man is to offer his fair share in the attainment of the common good. In return, the state is obligated to govern men and protect their rights according to true standards of justice.

The pope writes that since no one form of government is best, the citizens themselves should choose their own government. Let all citizens share in the government, the pope urges, for in this way government and the people will benefit. A government elected by the people, reinforced with authority from God, and cognizant of the true aspirations of the electorate will preserve the basic dignity of the human race.

In his third section the pope reaffirms "that political communities are reciprocally subjects of rights and duties." Therefore, their relationships should be regulated according to truth, justice, active solidarity, and freedom. Authority in these communities must be truly asserted, for authority is a means to the common good. Truth demands that false notions of race superiority be eliminated not only in the states themselves but also between states. Justice demands that basic rights not be denied or threatened by deceit or force. And while the majorities owe much to the minorities, the pope adds, let not these minorities forget that they, too, are members of larger communities and so they must not overexalt their positions to the detriment of their nation.

If nations would only co-operate in common endeavors, writes Pope John, many evils, such as the industrial dislocation of workers, harsh treatment of political refugees (who never lose their human rights), stockpiling of war materials, and even war itself would disappear. With freedom as the basic principle, men become more than ever convinced that international disputes can be settled by negotiation rather than by thermonuclear war. Reflection on the horrors of nuclear war should lead men more earnestly to seek peaceful solutions of political problems.

Finally, the great problem of world government once more arises. Is it desirable or expedient or necessary to have an institution like the United Nations? The pope argues in the affirmative, saying that through such an organization men can share technological and scientific knowledge to the benefit of the entire human race. Thus, there is more than the distinctive common goods of any one political community; there is a universal common good for all men. In former times the search for the common good could be made through normal diplomatic channels, but in the light of present development a new authority is demanded. Here the principle of subsidiarity applies. Let the smaller nations do what they can; when they reach the impossible, then let the larger members of the world community step in to help. Therefore, the pope concludes, it would seem that because of present circumstances, some sort of a United Nations is required as a dictate of the natural law.

Here the pope explicitly congratulates the United Nations for its work and especially for its "Universal Declaration of Human Rights," which he calls "An act of the highest importance." Even though some reservations about the Declaration might be noted, the dignity of the human person is, nevertheless, explicitly recognized and recorded in this powerful document.

In this pastoral exhortation Pope John XXIII also stresses the importance of living in such a manner in the temporal sphere that a new synthesis is created between the scientific, technical, and professional elements on the one hand, and spiritual values on the other. A former synthesis has been lost or destroyed and will not be resurrected except with the help of a new emphasis on Christian education. However, since virtually all the principles mentioned in the encyclical are based on the natural law, all men of good will can co-operate in restoring the balance among societies. And if there be error in any peoples, then let the error be condemned without denying the personal dignity of the man who errs.

Pope John admits that there will continue to be injustice in the world, but he adds that this fact should not depress those capable of reforming institutions. Most of the important decisions will be made by the governing members of the society involved, and these leaders must be imbued with principles derived from the inalienable dignity of man. If this dignity be looked at in the light of divinely revealed truth, then it will surely be valued more deeply. According to the pope, this dignity has been enhanced by the Incarnation when the Second Person of the Trinity took upon Himself the form of man. Human nature, the pope reminds us, was redeemed by the blood of Christ, who made all men, none excluded because of color or condition, the children and friends of God and heirs of His eternal glory.

Thus, the encyclical makes it plain that Pope John recognized the Church on earth as the Church on the way to sanctification, towards its state of perfection, made up of all men, rich and poor, ruler and subject, saint and sinner.

Social problems have often been thrust upon men at times when they have been unable or unwilling to comprehend them. Pope John envisions a spirit that can inspire both leaders and their educated subjects. He looks for a second spring in the social order, a rejuvenation of the human race. In his letter he shows his concern for the countless people who must live out their lives in the most humble circumstances; who will probably always be looked down upon by more fortunate men; who hesitate to appear in public frequently because they do not have sufficient clothing; who must live day by day on a mere subsistence level with no hope of a brighter future to encourage them; who, through no fault of their own, will be unemployed for days or weeks at a time while their leaders live in luxury and enjoy education, power, and honor. These inequalities must be eradicated from the personal plane and also removed from governmental and international levels if peace and order are to become realities.

One further observation: the encyclical has been interpreted too loosely by some as an invitation to break down the barriers against communism and to engage in dialogue with the Kremlin. This interpretation has been refuted by the "Observatore Romano" as being too selective and out of context. Any sincere Marxist would have to admit that everything the pope stands for here—his emphases on the dignity of man, the privileges and duties of the human person, and the economic rights of the workers—runs diametrically opposed to the doctrines of communism.

Finally, for the layman interested in taking part in the councils of the Church, Pope John issues a direct plea that he be given a greater part in the work of the Church, and the pope indicates that this plea is only the beginning of closer co-operation between priest and layman.

With this encyclical letter the Church has a new call to face present-day problems, a new respect for the present historical situation with its own pattern of constant evolution and adaptation to change. The letter is a reminder to all men that peace will come only when man has the courage to order himself and his world according to the will of God.

J.D.C.

AUTHOR INDEX

ABELARD, PETER
Historia calamitatum, 307
Sic et non, 291
ACTON, JOHN EMERICH EDWARD DALBERG
History of Freedom and Other Essays, The, 739
ADAM, KARL
Christ of Faith, The, 1000
Spirit of Catholicism, The, 778
AELFRIC
Homilies, 272
AELRED, SAINT
Spiritual Friendship, 319
ALACOQUE, MARGARET MARY, SAINT
Autobiography of Saint Margaret Mary Alacoque, The, 615
ALBERT THE GREAT, SAINT
Commentary on Aristotle's *De anima*, 360
Summa de creaturis, 352
ALCUIN
Concerning Rhetoric and Virtue, 261
ALEXANDER OF HALES
Summa universae theologiae, 382
ALPHONSUS MARY DE' LIGUORI, SAINT
Glories of Mary, The, 624
AMBROSE, SAINT
Epistle XXI: To the Most Clement Emperor and Most Blessed Augustus, 127
Hymns of Saint Ambrose, The, 152
On the Christian Faith, 112
On the Duties of the Clergy, 145
Sermo contra Auxentium, 132
ANSELM OF CANTERBURY, SAINT
Cur Deus Homo, 286
Proslogion, 280
ARISTIDES
Apology of Aristides, The, 10
ASSER, JOHN
Life of Alfred, 268
ATHANASIUS, SAINT
Discourses Against the Arians, 94
Incarnation of the Word of God, The, 84
ATHENAGORAS
Plea for the Christians, A, 27
On the Resurrection of the Dead, 30
AUGUSTINE, SAINT
City of God, The, 188
Confessions, The, 165
De magistro, 140
De trinitate, 173
Enarrations on the Psalms, 196
Faith, Hope, and Charity, 184
First Catechetical Instruction, The, 161

BACON, ROGER
Opus majus, 398
BALTHASAR, HANS URS VON
Anxiety and the Christian, 969
Science, Religion and Christianity, 1021
BASIL, SAINT
Against Eunomius, 98
Letters of Saint Basil, The, 110
Treatise on the Holy Spirit, 107
BEDE, SAINT
Ecclesiastical History of the English People, 258
BELLARMINE, ROBERT CARDINAL, SAINT
Political Writings, 564
BELLOC, HILAIRE
Path to Rome, The, 734
Servile State, The, 754
BENEDICT, SAINT
Rule of Saint Benedict, The, 234
BERNARD, SAINT
Letters of Saint Bernard of Clairvaux, The, 332
On the Necessity of Loving God, 311
On the Steps of Humility and Pride, 296
BLONDEL, MAURICE
L'Action, 706
BLOY, LÉON
Woman Who Was Poor, The, 726
BODIN, JEAN
Six Books of the Republic, The, 552
BOETHIUS, ANICIUS MANLIUS SEVERINUS, SAINT
Consolation of Philosophy, The, 229
De trinitate, 223
BONAVENTURE, SAINT
Meditations on the Life of Christ, 455
Mind's Road to God, The, 371
Three Ways, The, 356
BOSSUET, JACQUES BÉNIGNE
Discourse on Universal History, 608
BOUYER, LOUIS
Christian Humanism, 1058
Liturgical Piety, 1014
Seat of Wisdom, The, 1037
BRODRICK, JAMES, S.J.
Origin of the Jesuits, The, 868
Saint Francis Xavier, 990
BROWNSON, ORESTES AUGUSTUS
American Republic, The, 667

CAJETAN, SAINT
Commentary on the *Summa theologiae* of Saint Thomas, 516
CAMUS, JEAN PIERRE
Spirit of Saint Francis of Sales, The, 597
CASSIAN, JOHN
Institutes of the Monastic Life, The, 193
CATHERINE OF GENOA, SAINT
Dialogue Between the Soul and the Body, The, 530
CATHERINE OF SIENA, SAINT
Dialogue of Saint Catherine of Siena, The, 473
CHESTERTON, GILBERT KEITH
Everlasting Man, The, 785
Orthodoxy, 744
St. Francis of Assisi, 781

CLEMENT OF ALEXANDRIA
Stromateis, 44
CLEMENT I, SAINT
Letter of the Church of Rome to the Church of Corinth, The, 4
COLLINS, JAMES D.
God in Modern Philosophy, 1071
CRASHAW, RICHARD
Carmen Deo nostro, 600
CYPRIAN, SAINT
On the Unity of the Catholic Church, 75
CYRIL OF JERUSALEM, SAINT
Catechetical Lectures, The, 90

DANIÉLOU, JEAN, S.J.
Lord of History, The, 997
DANIEL-ROPS, HENRI
Jesus and His Times, 1006
DANTE ALIGHIERI
De monarchia, 438
Divine Comedy, The, 443
D'ARCY, MARTIN CYRIL, S.J.
Meeting of Love and Knowledge, The, 1040
Mind and Heart of Love, The, 909
DAWSON, CHRISTOPHER
Making of Europe, The, 824
Progress and Religion, 798
DE KONINCK, CHARLES
Hollow Universe, The, 1084
DENZINGER, HEINRICH JOSEPH DOMINICUS
Enchiridion symbolorum et definitionum, 658
DIEKMANN, GODFREY L., O.S.B.
Come, Let Us Worship, 1103
DIONYSIUS OF ALEXANDRIA, SAINT
Treatise on the Promises, 78
DIONYSIUS THE PSEUDO-AREOPAGITE
Mystical Theology, The, 218
On the Divine Names, 215
DONDEYNE, ALBERT
Contemporary European Thought and Christian Faith, 1061
DONOSO CORTÉS, JUAN FRANCISCO MARÍA DE LA SALUDAD
Essay on Catholicism, Liberalism, and Socialism, 650
DOWSON, ERNEST CHRISTOPHER
Poems of Ernest Dowson, The, 720
DRYDEN, JOHN
Hind and the Panther, The, 611
DU NOÜY, PIERRE LECOMTE
Human Destiny, 913
DUNS SCOTUS, JOHN
De primo principio, 423
Opus Oxoniense, 427

ECKHART, JOHANN
Treatises and Sermons of Meister Eckhart, The, 451
EINHARD
Life of Charlemagne, The, 265
ERASMUS, DESIDERIUS
Enchiridion militis Christiani, 498
Paraclesis, The, 505
Praise of Folly, The, 501
EUSEBIUS PAMPHILI
Ecclesiastical History, 88

FILAS, FRANCIS L., S.J.
Joseph: The Man Closest to Jesus, 1115

FRANCIS DE SALES, SAINT
Introduction to the Devout Life, An, 568
Love of God, The, 584
FRANCIS OF ASSISI, SAINT
Extant Writings of Saint Francis of Assisi, The, 349

GALILEI, GALILEO
Dialogue Concerning the Two Chief World Systems, 593
Letter to the Grand Duchess Christina, 579
GASQUET, FRANCIS NEIL AIDAN CARDINAL
Parish Life in Mediaeval England, 736
GERARD, JOHN
Autobiography of a Hunted Priest, The, 571
GILSON, ÉTIENNE
Philosopher and Theology, The, 1088
Spirit of Mediaeval Philosophy, The, 816
Unity of Philosophical Experience, The, 845
GRAHAM, DOM AELRED, O.S.B.
Zen Catholicism, 1124
GRATIAN, JOHANNES
Decretum Gratiani, 324
GREGORY NAZIANZEN, SAINT
Five Theological Orations, The, 116
GREGORY OF NYSSA, SAINT
Great Catechism, The, 120
Lord's Prayer, The, 136
GREGORY OF TOURS, SAINT
History of the Franks, 244
GREGORY THAUMATURGUS, SAINT
Oration and Panegyric Addressed to Origen, The, 69
GREGORY THE GREAT, SAINT
Dialogues, 241
Pastoral Care, 237
GUARDINI, ROMANO
Humanity of Christ, The, 1064
Lord, The, 849
GUITTON, JEAN
Essay on Human Love, 923

HALECKI, OSCAR
Millennium of Europe, The, 1128
HAYES, CARLTON J. H.
Nationalism: A Religion, 1091
HEFELE, KARL JOSEPH VON
History of the Councils, 686
HENRY OF BRACTON
Treatise on the Laws and Customs of England, 367
HERMAS
Shepherd, The, 12
HILARY OF POITIERS, SAINT
Treatise on the Mysteries, 103
HILTON, WALTER
Ladder of Perfection, The, 494
HIPPOLYTUS, SAINT
Refutation of All Heresies, 58
HOPKINS, GERARD MANLEY
Poems of Gerard Manley Hopkins, The, 760
HÜGEL, FRIEDRICH JOHN VON, BARON
Mystical Element of Religion, The, 749
HUGH OF ST. VICTOR
Noah's Ark, 304
Treatise Concerning the Pursuit of Learning, 300
HUYSMANS, JORIS-KARL
En Route, 716

IGNATIUS LOYOLA, SAINT
Spiritual Exercises, 534
IGNATIUS OF ANTIOCH, SAINT
Epistles of Saint Ignatius of Antioch, The, 7
INNOCENT III, POPE
De contemptu mundi, 342
De sacro altaris mysterio, 345
IRENAEUS, SAINT
Against the Heresies, 37
Demonstration of Apostolic Teaching, The, 47
ISIDORE OF SEVILLE, SAINT
Etymologies, The, 248

JEROME, SAINT
De viris illustribus, 148
Letters of Saint Jerome, The, 180
JOHN CHRYSOSTOM, SAINT
Discourse on the Priesthood, 123
Homilies of Saint John Chrysostom, The, 154
JOHN CLIMACUS, SAINT
Ladder of Divine Ascent, The, 254
JOHN OF PARIS
De potestate regia et papali, 432
JOHN OF ST. THOMAS
Ars logica, 589
Cursus theologicus, 605
JOHN OF SALISBURY
Policraticus *and* Metalogicon, 335
JOHN OF THE CROSS, SAINT
Ascent of Mount Carmel *and* The Dark Night of the Soul, The, 558
JOHN XXIII, POPE
Mater et magistra, 1106
Pacem in terris, 1131
JOINVILLE, JEAN DE
Life of Saint Louis, The, 435
JÖRGENSEN, JOHANNES
Autobiography of Johannes Jörgensen, The, 801
Saint Francis of Assisi, 756
JOURNET, CHARLES
Church of the Word Incarnate, The, 875
JULIAN OF NORWICH
Revelations of Divine Love, 476
JUNGMANN, JOSEF ANDREAS, S.J.
Good News—Yesterday and Today, The, 843
Mass of the Roman Rite, The, 949
JUSTIN MARTYR, SAINT
First Apology *and* The Second Apology, The, 19

KNOWLES, DOM DAVID, O.S.B.
Monastic Order in England, The, 870
KNOX, RONALD
Enthusiasm, 961
KÜNG, HANS
Council, Reform and Reunion, The, 1110

LACTANTIUS
Divine Institutes, The, 81
LAFARGE, JOHN, S.J.
Manner Is Ordinary, The, 1010
LAMENNAIS, FÉLICITÉ ROBERT DE
Essay on Indifference in Matters of Religion, 632
LANFRANC
Liber de Corpore et Sanguine Domini, 283
LEO THE GREAT, SAINT
Letters and Sermons of Saint Leo the Great, The, 211
Tome, 201

LEO XIII, POPE
Aeterni Patris, 691
Immortale Dei, 695
Rerum novarum, 699
LINGARD, JOHN
History of England, The, 638
LONERGAN, BERNARD J. F., S.J.
Insight, 1043
LUBAC, HENRI DE, S.J.
Catholicism, 856
Discovery of God, The, 1025

MACHIAVELLI, NICCOLÒ
Prince, The, 523
McKENZIE, JOHN L., S.J.
Two-Edged Sword, The, 1028
MAISTRE, JOSEPH MARIE DE
Les soirées de Saint-Pétersbourg, 630
MARCEL, GABRIEL
Homo viator, 893
Mystery of Being, The, 966
MARCION
Martyrdom of Saint Polycarp, The, 16
MARITAIN, JACQUES
Art and Scholasticism, 766
Degrees of Knowledge, 828
Man and the State, 973
Moral Philosophy, 1094
MATTHEW PARIS
Chronica majora, 376
MAXIMUS THE CONFESSOR, SAINT
Ascetic Life, The, 252
MERTON, THOMAS
Ascent to Truth, 979
Seeds of Contemplation, 955
Seven Storey Mountain, The, 930
MEYNELL, ALICE
Poems of Alice Meynell, The, 775
MINUCIUS FELIX
Octavius, 50
MIVART, ST. GEORGE JACKSON
On the Genesis of the Species, 682
MÖHLER, JOHANN ADAM
Symbolism, 640
MONTINI, GIOVANNI BATTISTA CARDINAL (POPE PAUL VI)
Church, The, 1118
MORE, THOMAS, SAINT
Treatise on the Passion, 538
Utopia, 509
MOUNIER, EMMANUEL
Character of Man, The, 902
MOUROUX, JEAN
Meaning of Man, The, 933
MURRAY, JOHN COURTNEY, S.J.
We Hold These Truths, 1098

NEWMAN, JOHN HENRY CARDINAL
Apologia pro vita sua, 661
Essay on the Development of Christian Doctrine, An, 644
Grammar of Assent, A, 678
Idea of a University, The, 653
NICHOLAS OF CUSA
Of Learned Ignorance, 482

O'DEA, THOMAS
American Catholic Dilemma, 1066
ONG, WALTER J., S.J.
American Catholic Crossroads, 1076

ORIGEN
Contra Celsum, 71
On First Principles, 65
OROSIUS, PAULUS
Seven Books of History Against the Pagans, The, 178
OTLOH OF ST. EMMERAM
Book of Proverbs, 276
OTTO OF FREISING
Two Cities, The, 316

PASTOR, LUDWIG VON
History of the Popes from the Close of the Middle Ages, The, 796
PATRICK, SAINT
Writings of Saint Patrick, The, 207
PAUL VI, POPE (See MONTINI)
PÉGUY, CHARLES
Basic Verities, 879
PETER LOMBARD
Book of Sentences, The, 328
PETRARCH
On His Own Ignorance, 469
PICARD, MAX
World of Silence, The, 936
PICO DELLA MIRANDOLA, GIOVANNI
Oration on the Dignity of Man, 487
PIEPER, JOSEF
Belief and Faith, 1121
End of Time, The, 964
Leisure, the Basis of Culture, 940
PIUS XI, POPE
Atheistic Communism, 858
Casti connubii, 808
Christian Education of Youth, The, 804
Mit brennender Sorge, 860
Quadragesimo anno, 812
PIUS XII, POPE
Divino afflante Spiritu, 883
Mediator Dei, 915
Mystical Body of Christ, The, 886
POLYCARP, SAINT
Epistles of Saint Polycarp, The, 16
POMERIUS, JULIANUS
Contemplative Life, The, 220
PROSPER OF AQUITAINE, SAINT
Call of All Nations, The, 204

RAHNER, KARL, S.J.
On the Theology of Death, 1047
RICHARD OF ST. VICTOR
Benjamin minor *and* Benjamin major, 339
ROMMEN, HEINRICH A.
State in Catholic Thought, The, 897
ROPER, WILLIAM
Lyfe of Sir Thomas More, Knighte, The, 543
RUFINUS OF AQUILEIA
Commentary on the Apostles' Creed, A, 169
RUYSBROECK, BLESSED JAN VAN
Spiritual Espousals, The, 461

SCHEEBEN, MATTHIAS JOSEPH
Mysteries of Christianity, The, 672
SCHLEGEL, FRIEDRICH VON
Lectures on the Philosophy of Life, 635
SCIACCA, MICHELE FEDERICO
Act and Being, 1031
Death and Immortality, 1078
SERTILLANGES, ANTONIN GILBERT
Intellectual Life, The, 771
SHEA, JOHN DAWSON GILMARY
History of the Catholic Church in the United States, A, 702
SHEED, FRANCIS JOSEPH
Theology and Sanity, 906
SHEEN, FULTON J.
Communism and the Conscience of the West, 944
God and Intelligence in Modern Philosophy, 788
Peace of Soul, 958
SIMON, YVES RENÉ MARIE
Philosophy of Democratic Government, 982
Traité du Libre Arbitre, 986
STURZO, LUIGI
Church and State, 864
SUAREZ, FRANCISCO, S.J.
Treatise on Laws, 575
SUHARD, EMMANUEL CARDINAL
Growth or Decline?: The Church Today, 920
SULPICIUS SEVERUS
Dialogues of Sulpicius Severus, The, 157
SUSO, BLESSED HENRY, O.P.
Little Book of Eternal Wisdom, The, 458

TASSO, TORQUATO
Jerusalem Delivered, 548
TATIAN
Discourse Against the Greeks, The, 23
TEILHARD DE CHARDIN, PIERRE, S.J.
Divine Milieu, The, 1054
Phenomenon of Man, The, 1017
TERESA OF ÁVILA, SAINT
Interior Castle, The, 561
Way of Perfection, The, 555
TERTULLIAN
Apology of Tertullian, The, 41
Treatises on Marriage, 54
THEOPHILUS, SAINT
Theophilus to Autolycus, 33
THÉRÈSE OF LISIEUX, SAINT
Story of a Soul, The, 729
THOMAS À KEMPIS, SAINT
Imitation of Christ, The, 491
THOMAS AQUINAS, SAINT
De veritate, 379
Hymns of Saint Thomas Aquinas, The, 421
On Being and Essence, 364
On Free Choice, 406
On Kingship, 391
On Spiritual Creatures, 402
On the Power of God, 394
On the Soul, 409
On the Virtues in General, 413
Summa contra Gentiles, 385
Summa theologiae, 416
THOMPSON, FRANCIS
Hound of Heaven and Other Poems, The, 709
TURGOT, ANNE ROBERT JACQUES
Two Discourses on Universal History, 628

UNKNOWN
Cloud of Unknowing, The, 466
Didache, The, 1
Epistle to Diognetus, 62
Little Flowers of Saint Francis, The, 448
UNKNOWN FRANCISCAN MONK
Meditations on the Life of Christ (see also BONAVENTURE, SAINT), 455

VANN, GERALD, O.P.
Heart of Man, The, 889

VERGERIO, PIER PAOLO
On the Education of a Gentleman, 479

VEUILLOT, LOUIS
Life of Our Lord Jesus Christ, The, 665

VICO, GIOVANNI BATTISTA
New Science, The, 618

VINCENT OF LÉRINS, SAINT
Commonitory, A, 198

VIVES, JUAN LUIS
On Education, 519

VON HILDEBRAND, DIETRICH
Liturgy and Personality, 835
Transformation in Christ, 946

VONIER, DOM ANSCAR, O.S.B.
Key to the Doctrine of the Eucharist, A, 793

WAUGH, EVELYN
Edmund Campion, 838